Frommer's®

Scandinavia

24th Edition

by Darwin Porter, Danforth Prince & Roger Norum

Wiley Publishing, Inc

Published by:
WILEY PUBLISHING, INC.
111 River St.
Hoboken, NJ 07030-5774

ISBN 978-0-470-95140-8 (paper); ISBN 978-1-118-09021-3 (ebk); ISBN 978-1-118-09022-0 (ebk); 978-1-118-09023-7 (ebk)

Editor: Alexia Travaglini
Production Editor: Katie Robinson
Cartographer: Roberta Stockwell
Production by Wiley Indianapolis Composition Services

Front Cover Photo: Aurora borealis: Hammerfest, Norway © Per-Andre Hoffmann / LOOK-foto / PhotoLibrary.
Back Cover Photo: Dalarna, Sweden © Berndt-Joel Gunnarsso / Nordic Photos / AGE Fotostock, Inc.

For information on our other products and services or to obtain technical support, please contact our Customer Care Department within the U.S. at 877/762-2974, outside the U.S. at 317/572-3993 or fax 317/572-4002.

Wiley also publishes its books in a variety of electronic formats. Some content that appears in print may not be available in electronic formats.

Manufactured in the United States of America

5 4 3 2 1

CONTENTS

5 INTRODUCING COPENHAGEN 90

6 EXPLORING COPENHAGEN 115

7 EXPLORING THE DANISH COUNTRYSIDE 150

8 THE BEST OF NORWAY 202

9 OSLO 206

10 BERGEN 256

11 EXPLORING THE NORWEGIAN COAST 275

12 THE BEST OF SWEDEN 311

13 INTRODUCING STOCKHOLM 317

14 EXPLORING STOCKHOLM 343

15 GOTHENBURG 373

16 SKÅNE (INCLUDING HELSINGBORG & MALMÖ) 397

17 EXPLORING THE SWEDISH COUNTRYSIDE 435

18 THE BEST OF FINLAND 463

19 HELSINKI 470

20 EXPLORING THE FINNISH COUNTRYSIDE 509

21 FAST FACTS & WEBSITES 540

LIST OF MAPS

HOW TO CONTACT US

In researching this book, we discovered many wonderful places—hotels, restaurants, shops, and more. We're sure you'll find others. Please tell us about them, so we can share the information with your fellow travelers in upcoming editions. If you were disappointed with a recommendation, we'd love to know that, too. Please write to:

Frommer's Scandinavia, 24th Edition
Wiley Publishing, Inc. • 111 River St. • Hoboken, NJ 07030-5774
frommersfeedback@wiley.com

ADVISORY & DISCLAIMER

Travel information can change quickly and unexpectedly, and we strongly advise you to confirm important details locally before traveling, including information on visas, health and safety, traffic and transport, accommodation, shopping and eating out. We also encourage you to stay alert while traveling and to remain aware of your surroundings. Avoid civil disturbances, and keep a close eye on cameras, purses, wallets and other valuables.

While we have endeavored to ensure that the information contained within this guide is accurate and up-to-date at the time of publication, we make no representations or warranties with respect to the accuracy or completeness of the contents of this work and specifically disclaim all warranties, including without limitation warranties of fitness for a particular purpose. We accept no responsibility or liability for any inaccuracy or errors or omissions, or for any inconvenience, loss, damage, costs or expenses of any nature whatsoever incurred or suffered by anyone as a result of any advice or information contained in this guide.

The inclusion of a company, organization or Website in this guide as a service provider and/ or potential source of further information does not mean that we endorse them or the information they provide. Be aware that information provided through some Websites may be unreliable and can change without notice. Neither the publisher or author shall be liable for any damages arising herefrom.

ABOUT THE AUTHORS

Darwin Porter and **Danforth Prince** (chapters 1–7 and 12–21) have produced numerous titles for Frommer's. Porter wrote the first ever Frommer's guide to Scandinavia, and has been covering the destination ever since. He is also the coauthor of *Frommer's Norway, Frommer's Denmark,* and *Frommer's Sweden*. Prince, formerly of the Paris bureau of *The New York Times,* has been a frequent traveler and researcher to Scandinavia since 1980. His byline has appeared on four different guides to the Scandinavian countries, including Finland.

Born in New York City and raised in Westchester County, **Roger Norum** (chapters 1, 8–11, and 21 [www.rogernorum.com]) has studied literature and taught creative writing in Norway. He writes and photographs features on travel and food for a number of European magazines, including *Departures, Wanderlust,* and *Olive*. In 2010, he was awarded the silver prize for Travel Writer of the Year by the British Guild of Travel Writers. Roger currently divides his time between Oxford, England, and Kathmandu, Nepal, where he is finishing up research for his doctoral degree in social anthropology.

FROMMER'S STAR RATINGS, ICONS & ABBREVIATIONS

Every hotel, restaurant, and attraction listing in this guide has been ranked for quality, value, service, amenities, and special features using a **star-rating system.** In country, state, and regional guides, we also rate towns and regions to help you narrow down your choices and budget your time accordingly. Hotels and restaurants are rated on a scale of zero (recommended) to three stars (exceptional). Attractions, shopping, nightlife, towns, and regions are rated according to the following scale: zero stars (recommended), one star (highly recommended), two stars (very highly recommended), and three stars (must-see).

In addition to the star-rating system, we also use **seven feature icons** that point you to the great deals, in-the-know advice, and unique experiences that separate travelers from tourists. Throughout the book, look for:

special finds—those places only insiders know about

fun facts—details that make travelers more informed and their trips more fun

kids—best bets for kids and advice for the whole family

special moments—those experiences that memories are made of

overrated—places or experiences not worth your time or money

insider tips—great ways to save time and money

great values—where to get the best deals

The following abbreviations are used for credit cards:

AE	American Express	DISC	Discover	V	Visa
DC	Diners Club	MC	MasterCard		

TRAVEL RESOURCES AT FROMMERS.COM

Frommer's travel resources don't end with this guide. Frommer's website, **www.frommers.com**, has travel information on more than 4,000 destinations. We update features regularly, giving you access to the most current trip-planning information and the best airfare, lodging, and car-rental bargains. You can also listen to podcasts, connect with other Frommers.com members through our active-reader forums, share your travel photos, read blogs from guidebook editors and fellow travelers, and much more.

SCANDINAVIA IN DEPTH

1

SCANDINAVIA TODAY

Denmark

The smallest of the Scandinavian countries (about half the size of Maine), its total landmass equals about 41,400 sq. km (16,000 sq. miles), most of which is on the peninsula of Jutland, which borders Germany. The major islands are Zealand, Funen, and Bornholm. Denmark has adequate space for its population of 5.5 million people, but its population density is much greater than that of the other Scandinavian countries.

No country in the European Union has less poverty or a fairer distribution of wealth than Denmark. Denmark boasts one of the world's highest standards of living plus a comprehensive social welfare system, funded through extremely high taxes. Danes enjoy 7½-hour workdays, cradle-to-grave security, state-funded hospitals and schools, and a month-long vacation every year. A progressive, modern, and liberal state, it was one of the first countries to recognize same-sex marriages.

Denmark is an avid producer and consumer of art and culture. Some 12,000 books a year are published in Denmark. There are 42 newspapers, and the theater and film industries are thriving in spite of cutbacks in government funding.

Norway

This long, narrow country stretches some 1,770km (1,097 miles) north to south, but rarely more than 96km (60 miles) east to west. Norway is a land of raw nature. It occupies the western and extreme northern portion of the Scandinavia peninsula, bordering Finland, Sweden, and Russia. In the west, its 21,342km (13,232 miles) of coastline confront the often-turbulent North Atlantic Ocean.

When you factor in the arctic desolation of the north, Norway averages about 20 people per square mile. Most of the four million inhabitants are concentrated in the swag-bellied south, where the weather is less severe. Even so, the population of Oslo, the capital, is less than half a million. Aside from Oslo, there are no really big cities; the populations of Bergen and Trondheim are 210,000 and 135,000, respectively.

Norway continues to top the list of the international prosperity index, which ranks 110 nations according to their economic fundamentals as well as the wellbeing of their citizens. (Denmark, Finland, and Sweden have made the top 10, too.) Although many people have emigrated from Norway—about one million to America alone—immigration into Norway from other countries has been limited. The largest minority group is the Sami, who live in the far north; they have broad powers of self-government, including their own parliament. About 3.2% of the population originally came from Great Britain, Denmark, and Sweden.

Most business is conducted in English. Norway has two official languages, Riksmal and Landsmal, both of Danish origin. The Sami, the indigenous people of the north, have their own language.

Sweden

Sweden is one of the most paradoxical nations on Earth. An essentially conservative country, it is nonetheless a leader in social welfare, prison reform, and equal opportunity for women.

Despite trouble maintaining its once-bustling economy, Sweden has long enjoyed some of the highest wages and the best standard of living in Europe.

With a population density of only 48 people per square mile, there's ample space for all of Sweden's nine million residents. About 85% of Sweden's citizens live in the southern half of the country. The north is populated by the two chief minority groups: the Sami and Finnish-speaking northeasterners.

Once home to an ethnically homogenous society, Sweden has experienced a vast wave of immigration in the past several years. Today more than 10% of Sweden's residents are immigrants or the children of immigrants. Much of this influx is from other Scandinavian countries. Because of Sweden's strong stance on human rights, it also has become a major destination for refugees from Africa and the Middle East.

Finland

Covering an area of 335,000 sq. km (130,000 sq. miles) and home to five million people, Finland has a relatively low population density—about 38 people per square mile. More than one-third of its territory lies above the Arctic Circle, home to one of its large minority groups—the Sami. Helsinki, the capital, has a population of about half a million.

Finland's welfare system is among the best in the world. Universal healthcare is offered, supplemented by extensive preventive health education. Maternal health is stressed through free medical care and a maternity package consisting of either money for the infant's basic needs or the actual products, such as clothes, diapers, bottles, and bibs (only 15% of families choose the cash). Families with children under 17 also receive allowances from the state. Children get free medical and dental care through the age of 19.

Finland's literacy rate is nearly 100%. This has been achieved through an emphasis on bilingualism (Finnish and Swedish) as well as free schooling. Because of the obscurity of the Finnish language, Finns have had to master other languages, primarily English, French, and German. Finland is arguably the best-educated nation in Europe.

The Finns are generally a homogenous group, having one of the most genetically pure gene pools in the world. Most Finns live in the southern region, many in the Helsinki area. Finland's two principal minority groups—the Sami in the north and the Roma (gypsies) in the south—constitute less than 1% of the entire population.

LOOKING BACK AT SCANDINAVIA

Denmark

Two famous kings emerged from Denmark during the 10th century, Gorm the Old (883–940) and his son, Harald Bluetooth (935–85). Their reigns resulted in the unification of Denmark with power centralized at Jelling in Jutland. Harald, through the hard work of a core of Christian missionaries trained in Frankish territories to the south (especially in Hamburg), also introduced Christianity, which eventually became the country's predominant religion.

Harald eventually extended Danish influence as far as neighboring Norway. The links he established between Denmark and Norway weren't severed, at least politically, until the 1800s. Harald's son, Sweyn I, succeeded in conquering England in 1013, more than 50 years before the Norman invasion in 1066.

Under Sweyn's son, Canute II (994–1035), England, Denmark, and part of Sweden came under the rule of one crown. After Canute's death, however, the Danish kingdom was reduced to only Denmark. Canute's nephew, Sweyn II, ruled the Danish kingdom, and upon his death his five sons governed Denmark successfully. In 1104, the foundation was laid for a Danish national church.

THE BALTIC: A DANISH "LAKE"

The few remaining links between Denmark and the Frankish Holy Roman Empire were severed under Archbishop Eskil (1100–82) and King Valdemar I (1131–82). During a celebration at Ringsted in 1190, the Danish church and state were united, partly because of the influence of Archbishop Absalon (1128–1201), a soldier and statesman who is honored today as the patron saint of Copenhagen.

In 1169, Denmark began what would evolve into a long series of conquests that increased its sphere of influence within city-states along the Baltic, including the ports of Estonia (which was conquered by the Danes in 1219), Latvia, eastern Germany, Poland, Sweden, and Russia. Part of Denmark's military and mercantile success derived from the general weakness of the German states to the south; part of it was because of a population explosion within Denmark.

Valdemar II (1170–1241) strengthened Denmark's control over the Baltic and came close to transforming it into a Danish lake. Grateful for their help, he ennobled many of his illegitimate sons and empowered many of his military cohorts with aristocratic titles and rewarded them with land.

The result was a weakening of the monarchy in favor of an increasingly voracious group of nobles, whose private agendas conflicted with those of the king. Civil wars ensued, and three of the four successive kings were killed in battle.

Between 1332 and 1340, Denmark had no king and was ruled by an uneasy coalition of nobles. Valdemar IV Atterdag (1320–75) retained his grip on the Danish throne only by signing the peace treaty of Stralsund in 1370 with the towns of the Hanseatic League.

A UNITED SCANDINAVIA

Valdemar IV died in 1375, leaving Denmark without a male heir. Finally, Olaf (1375–87), the infant son of Valdemar's daughter Margrethe through her marriage with King Haakon VI Magnusson (1339–80) of Norway, came to the throne.

During Olaf's infancy, Margrethe ruled the country as regent. When both her husband, Haakon, and 17-year-old Olaf died, she was acknowledged as queen of Norway and Denmark. A patroness of the arts and a savvy administrator of the national treasury, she was eventually granted wide political leeway in Sweden.

Although the three nations had already been combined under the stewardship of Margrethe, they were merged into a united Scandinavia in 1397. Margrethe arranged for her nephew, Eric of Pomerania (1382–1459), to be crowned king of all three countries as Eric VII.

Margrethe's designated heir, Eric VII, was childless. He was dethroned in 1439 and replaced by his nephew Christopher of Bavaria. His reign lasted only about 9 years, after which Sweden pressed for autonomy. It elected Karl Knutson (Charles VIII) as its Stockholm-based king in 1471. Denmark and the relatively weak Norway shared King Christian I (1426–81).

THE 16TH CENTURY

Christian II (1481–1559) ascended the throne in 1513. He went so far as to turn over control of the kingdom's finances to his mistress's mother, Sigbrit Villoms, the frugal and canny widow of a Dutch burgher. Many Renaissance-style reforms were activated under Christian II's reign, without which Denmark might have erupted into full-fledged revolution.

Christian II recaptured Sweden in 1520 but was defeated by the Swedish warrior-king Gustavus Vasa a year later. Christian was deposed in 1522, whereupon he fled to the Netherlands. In the spring of 1532, he returned to Denmark, where he was incarcerated until his death, first in Sønderborg Castle and then in Kalundborg castle.

His successor, Frederik I (1471–1533), signed a charter granting the nobility many privileges. Under his regime, the Franciscans, an order of Roman Catholic monks, were expelled from their conspicuously wealthy houses of worship, and Lutheran ministers were granted the freedom to roam throughout Denmark preaching. Upon Frederik's death, the Reformation took earnest hold within Denmark. In the process, vast Catholic-owned estates were forfeited to the Danish crown.

The Danish Lutheran Church was founded in 1536 during the reign of Christian III (1534–59). Before the end of the 1570s, Protestantism was firmly entrenched within Denmark. Disciples of Martin Luther were brought in to organize the new Reformed Church of Denmark.

WARS WITH SWEDEN

Much of the 17th century in Denmark was consumed with an ongoing series of wars with its archenemy, Sweden. Despite that, the reign of the Danish King Christian IV (1577–1648) was one of relative prosperity. The Danes worked hard, investing time and money in the development of their "overseas territory," Norway.

Tensions between Denmark and Sweden also intensified during this period. Sweden invaded Jutland and quickly defeated the Danes. By the Treaty of Christianople, Denmark was forced to cede to Sweden many of its former possessions, including scattered communities in Norway and the Baltic island of Gotland.

Danish king Frederik III (1609–70) tried to regain the lost territories when Sweden went to war with Poland, but Charles X defeated him. Frederik gave Sweden additional territory, including the island of Bornholm. Charles X attacked Denmark in an attempt to take control of the whole country, but this time Denmark won, regaining its lost territories. Sweden ended the war after the death of Charles X in 1660.

The Skåne War (1675–79) was an ill-advised military campaign started by the Danish king Christian V (1646–99). Its outcome included Denmark's loss of Skåne, a valuable territory in southern Sweden.

Frederik IV (1671–1730), Christian V's successor, resumed the war with Sweden in 1699. Named the Great Northern War, it raged, more or less inconclusively, from 1699 to 1730. Southern Sweden was not recovered.

THE 19TH CENTURY & THE NAPOLEONIC WARS

Despite the sweeping changes in the map of Europe engendered by Napoleon's military campaigns, Denmark strongly defended its right to remain neutral. In 1801, fearing that Denmark's formidable navy might be persuaded to cooperate with the French, England destroyed part of the Danish fleet in a battle at sea.

In 1807, as the threat of Napoleon's conquest of Europe became more of a reality, England ordered the Danes to transfer their navy to British rule within 8 days or be bombarded. When the Danes refused, English warships opened fire on Copenhagen, heralding the end of Danish neutrality.

Because of England's embargoes on Denmark and the destruction of many Danish ships, Denmark lost control over its overseas colony of Norway, and trade came to an almost complete standstill. At a treaty that was signed at Kiel the same year, Denmark was forced to yield Norway to Sweden and Heligoland to England. Without a navy and crippled by huge debts and a loss of much of its prestige, Denmark sank into poverty.

WORLD WAR I & ECONOMIC CHAOS

When World War I broke out, Denmark found itself on a razor's edge and struggled to remain neutral, but its position astride the shipping lanes favored by both England and Germany made this especially perilous.

Eventually, through cooperation and joint commitments with Sweden and Norway, Denmark managed to retain its fragile hold on wartime neutrality, but at a high price in terms of unemployment, higher taxes, and endless neuroses and self-doubts.

Partly in reaction to the traumas of their untenable situation, the Danes signed a new constitution on June 5, 1915, establishing a two-chamber parliament and granting equal voting rights to men and women.

THE COMING OF HITLER & NAZI OCCUPATION

When World War II broke out in 1939, Denmark declared its neutrality. Denmark's ties with Iceland were severed, and the United States and Great Britain occupied Greenland and the Faroe Islands, respectively.

Despite the nonaggression pact, Nazi forces invaded and occupied Denmark in 1940. In 1943, Hitler sent General Hermann von Hanneken to impose martial law on Denmark. Danish resistance continued against the German occupying forces, often in the form of sabotage of German-controlled industries and military installations.

In February 1945, as the defeat of Germany appeared imminent, thousands of refugees from Germany poured across the border, seeking safety in Denmark. When Germany surrendered in 1945, British troops occupied most of Denmark.

POSTWAR DENMARK

After 1945, the Liberal Party under Knud Kristensen assumed control of Denmark. In 1947, Kristensen resigned. The Social Democratic Party, which had ruled under Frederik IX, then governed the country. The economy remained sluggish until 1948.

In 1949, Denmark joined NATO. In 1953, the Scandinavian Council was formed, composed of Denmark, Norway, Sweden, and Iceland; the council lasted until 1961. Also in 1953, Denmark adopted a new constitution, providing for a single-chamber parliament.

In 1972, Denmark became the sole Nordic member of the EEC. That same year, Queen Margrethe, born in 1940 (the year of the Nazi invasion), became queen of Denmark upon the death of her father, Frederik IX.

Norway

Norway has been inhabited since the end of the Ice Age. The earliest Scandinavian settlers hunted reindeer and other game in these northern lands. Some 5,000 to 6,000 years ago, the inhabitants turned to agriculture, especially around the Oslofjord. Artifacts show that in the Roman era, Norway had associations with areas to the south.

THE AGE OF THE VIKINGS

Prehistory ended during the Viking era, roughly A.D. 800 to 1050. Much of what is known about this era wasn't written down, but has been conveyed through sagas passed by word of mouth or revealed by archaeological finds. Some scholars consider the looting of the Lindisfarne monastery in northern England in 793 the beginning of the "age of the Vikings."

"The Vikings are coming!" became a dreadful cry along the coasts of Europe. From Norway, the Vikings branched out to settle in the Orkney and Shetland Islands (now part of Scotland). They also settled in the Scottish Hebrides and on the Isle of Man. Viking settlements were established on Greenland and Iceland, which had previously been uninhabited.

The road to the unification of Norway was rough. In 872 Harald Fairhair, after winning a battle near Stavanger, conquered many of the provinces, but other battles for unification took decades. Harald was followed by his son, Eric I—"Bloody Axe," to his enemies. Eric began his reign by assassinating two of his eight brothers and later killed five other brothers. His one surviving brother, Haakon, succeeded him as king in 954. Haakon tried unsuccessfully to convert Norway to Christianity. After he died in the Battle of Fitjar (960), Harald II Graafell, one of Eric's sons, became king of Norway. Cruel and oppressive, he died in battle in 970.

Haakon, son of Sigurd of Lade, became the next king of Norway. He resisted Danish attacks and ruled for about 25 years, but died in a peasant riot in 995. After the Battle of Swold in 1000, Norway was divided between Denmark and the Jarl of Lade.

Olaf II Haraldsson was a Viking until 1015, when he became king of Norway. Although oppressive and often cruel, he continued to spread Christianity. Canute of Denmark invaded Norway in 1028, sending Olaf fleeing to England. Canute's son, Sweyn, ruled Norway from 1028 to 1035. Sweyn was forced out when Olaf II was proclaimed a saint and his son, Magnus I, was made king. Magnus was also king of Denmark, a position he lost when Canute's nephew led a revolt against him and he was killed. Olaf's sainthood firmly established Christianity in Norway.

Harald Sigurdsson (known as Harald III) ruled Norway from 1046 until his death in 1066. His death marks the end of the Viking age.

THE MIDDLE AGES

Wars with Denmark continued, and civil wars raged from 1130 to 1227. Norwegian towns and the church continued to grow. Under Haakon V in the 13th century, Oslo became the capital of Norway. The Black Death reached Norway in 1350 and wiped out much of the population.

From 1362 to 1364, Norway and Sweden had a joint monarch, Haakon VI (1340–80), son of the Swedish king, Magnus Eriksson. Haakon married Margrethe, daughter of the Danish king Valdemar Atterdag. Their son, Olaf, was chosen to be the Danish king upon Valdemar's death in 1375. He inherited the throne of Norway after his father died in 1380, bringing Norway into a union with Denmark, which lasted until 1814.

UNION WITH DENMARK

When Olaf died at the age of 17, Margrethe became regent of Norway, Denmark, and Sweden. She ruled through her nephew, Eric of Pomerania, who had become king of Norway in 1389. He was recognized as a joint ruler at Kalmar. Margrethe was actually the power behind the throne until her death, in 1412. Eric of Pomerania tried to rule the three countries, but Sweden and Norway rebelled. Eric fled in 1439 and Christopher III of Bavaria became the ruler, imposing Danish rule.

During the Napoleonic Wars (1807–14), famine was widespread. In 1814 Frederik VI of Denmark surrendered to Napoleon's opponents and handed Norway over to Sweden. That officially ended 434 years of Danish rule over Norway.

SECESSION FROM SWEDEN

On May 17, 1814, an assembly adopted a constitution and chose Christian Frederik as the Norwegian king. May 17 is celebrated as Norwegian National Day. The Swedes objected and launched a military campaign, eventually subduing Norway. The Swedes accepted the Norwegian constitution, but only within a union of the two kingdoms. Christian Frederik fled.

In August 1905, the Storting decided to dissolve the union with Sweden. Sweden agreed to let Norway rule itself. In October 1905, Norway held an election, and the son of Denmark's king was proclaimed king of Norway. He chose the name Haakon VII.

AN INDEPENDENT NORWAY

Free at last, Norway enjoyed peace and prosperity until the beginning of World War II. Even though the economy was satisfactory, thousands of Norwegians emigrated to the United States around the turn of the 20th century. In 1914 Norway joined Sweden and Denmark in declaring a policy of neutrality. Despite the declaration, around 2,000 Norwegian seamen lost their lives in the war because of submarine attacks and underwater mines.

In 1920 Norway joined the League of Nations, ending its policy of isolation. At the outbreak of World War II, Norway again declared its neutrality. Nonetheless, the Nazis attacked on April 9, 1940, and Norway fell after a 2-month struggle. The government and the royal family fled into exile in England, taking 1,000 ships of the Norwegian merchant fleet. In spite of the resistance movement, Nazis occupied Norway until the end of the war in 1945. Vidkun Quisling, the Norwegian minister of defense in the 1930s, served the Nazis as leader of the puppet government.

Quisling was executed following the Nazi retreat from Norway. On June 7, 1945, the government-in-exile returned from Britain. The retreating Nazis had followed a scorched-earth policy in Finnmark, destroying almost everything of value. In the late 1940s, Norway began to rebuild its shattered economy.

After an abortive attempt to form a Nordic defense alliance, Norway and Denmark joined NATO in 1949. By the 1960s, oil prospecting in the North Sea yielded rich finds, which led to a profound restructuring of Norwegian trade and industry. In 1972 Norway voted not to enter the Common Market, following a bitter political dispute.

Norway had a non-Socialist government from 1981 to 1986. In 1986 Labor Party leader Gro Harlem Brundtland headed a minority government as Norway's first female prime minister. She introduced seven women into her 18-member cabinet. Soon, however, tumbling oil prices and subsequent unemployment led to a recession. The Labor government lost the 1989 elections. A center-right coalition assumed control of government. In November 1990, Brundtland returned to office as prime minister, this time with nine women in her 19-member cabinet. In 1991 Olav V died and was succeeded by his son, Harald V.

Today the Norwegian government faces many of the same problems that confront other nations: violent crime, drugs, immigration control, unemployment, acid rain, and pollution. Concern about acid rain and pollution, much of which comes from Great Britain, was so great that riots erupted when Margaret Thatcher visited in 1987.

Although some Conservatives objected, Norway applied for membership in the European Union (E.U.) in 1993. In November 1994, Norwegians rejected a nonbinding referendum on E.U. membership. But that does not mean the country has no economic links with the rest of Europe. In 1994 Norway reinforced its commitments to membership in the EEAA (European Economic Area Agreement), an association initiated in 1992 to ensure its access to the E.U.'s single market.

Today Norway continues pushing forward with major engineering projects. The country is connecting its sparsely inhabited outcroppings and linking its interior fjord-side villages in an effort to stem the flow of people to larger towns and villages.

In 2005 the world's largest single-arched bridge was opened between Sweden and Norway and inaugurated by King Harald V of Norway and King Carl XVI Gustaf of Sweden. The Svinesund Bridge spans a fjord south of Oslo, stretching for 2,300 feet. The occasion also marked Norway's celebration of 100 years of independence from Sweden.

Norway in 2008 became the third-biggest exporter of oil in the world after Saudi Arabia and Russia. Its future looks good as an oil-producing nation.

Sweden

THE VIKINGS

Although documented by little other than legend, the Viking age (roughly A.D. 700–1000) is the Swedish epoch that has most captured the attention of the world. Before this period, Sweden had been relatively isolated, although travelers from the south brought some artifacts from different civilizations.

The base of Viking power at the time was the coastal regions around and to the north of what today is Stockholm. Either as plunderers, merchants, or slave traders, Swedish Vikings maintained contact with both Russia and Constantinople, and with parts of western Europe. Swedish Vikings joined their brother Vikings in Norway and Denmark in pillaging, trading with, or conquering parts of Ireland and the British Isles.

CHRISTIANITY & THE MIDDLE AGES

With the aid of missions sent from Britain and northern Germany, Christianity gradually made headway, having been introduced in 829 by St. Anskar, a Frankish missionary. It did not become widespread, however, until the 11th century. In 1008 Olaf Skottkonung, the ruler of a powerful kingdom in northern Sweden, converted to Christianity, but later in the century, the religion experienced hardships, with civil wars and a pagan reaction against the converting missionaries.

Ruling from 1130 to 1156, King Sverker united the lands of Svear and Gotar, which later became the heart of modern Sweden. A strong centralized government developed under this king.

Christianity finally became almost universally accepted under Eric IX, who ruled until 1160. He led a crusade to Finland and later became the patron saint of Sweden. By 1164, his son, Charles VII, had founded the first archbishopric at Uppsala. The increasing influence of this new religion led to the death of the Viking slave trade, and many Vikings turned to agriculture as the basis of their economy.

Sweden's ties with the Hanseatic ports of Germany grew stronger, and trade with other Baltic ports flourished at the city of Visby on the island of Gotland. Sweden traded in copper, pelts, iron, and butter, among other products.

Sweden's greatest medieval statesman was Birger Jarl, who ruled from 1248 to 1266; during his reign, he abolished serfdom and founded Stockholm. When his son, Magnus Laduläs, became king in 1275, he granted extensive power to the Catholic Church and founded a hereditary aristocracy.

AN INTRA-NORDIC UNION

Magnus VII of Norway (1316–74) was only 3 years old when he was elected to the Swedish throne, but his election signaled a recognition of the benefits of increased cooperation within the Nordic world. During his reign, there emerged distinct social classes, including the aristocracy, the Catholic clergy (which owned more than 20% of the land), peasant farmers and laborers, and a commercial class of landowners, foresters, mine owners, and merchants.

In 1350, the Black Death arrived in Sweden, decimating the population.

In 1389, the Swedish aristocracy, fearing the growing power of the Germans within the Hanseatic League, negotiated for an intra-Nordic union with Denmark and the remaining medieval fiefdoms in Norway and Finland. Despite the ideals of the union, it collapsed after about 40 years because of a revolt by merchants, miners, and peasants.

Queen Margrethe's heir (her nephew, Eric of Pomerania; 1382–1459) became the crowned head of three countries (Norway, Denmark, and Sweden). He spent most of his reign fighting with the Hanseatic League. Deposed in 1439, he was replaced by Christopher of Bavaria, whose early death in 1448 led to a major conflict and the eventual dissolution of the Kalmar Union. The Danish king, Christian II, invaded Stockholm in 1520, and established an unpopular reign; there was much civil disobedience until the emergence of the Vasa dynasty, which expelled the Danes.

THE VASA DYNASTY

In May 1520, a Swedish nobleman, Gustavus Vasa, returned from captivity in Denmark and immediately began to plan for the military expulsion of the Danes from Sweden. In 1523 he captured Stockholm from its Danish rulers, won official recognition for Swedish independence, and was elected king of Sweden.

In a power struggle with the Catholic Church, he confiscated most Church-held lands (vastly increasing the power of the state overnight) and established Lutheranism as the national religion.

The next 50 years were marked by Danish plots to regain control of Sweden and Swedish plots to conquer Poland, Estonia, and the Baltic trade routes leading to Russia. A dynastic link to the royal families of Poland led to the ascension of Sigismund (son of the Swedish king Johan III) in Warsaw. When his father died, Sigismund became king of both Sweden and Poland simultaneously. His Catholicism, however, was opposed by Sweden, which expelled him in 1598. He was followed by Karl (Charles) IX (1566–1632), who led Sweden into a dangerous and expensive series of wars with Denmark, Russia, and its former ally, Poland.

By 1611, as Sweden was fighting simply to survive, Gustavus II Adolphus (1594–1632) ascended the throne. After organizing an army composed mainly of farmers and field hands (financed by money from the Falun copper mines), he secured Sweden's safety and with his armies penetrated as far south as Bavaria. He died fighting against the Hapsburg emperor's Catholic army near the city of Lützen in 1632.

When he died, his heir and only child, Christina (1626–89), was 6 years old. During her childhood, power was held by the respected Swedish statesman Axel Oxenstierna, who continued the Thirty Years' War in Germany for another 16 years. It finally concluded with the Treaty of Westphalia in 1648. Christina, who did not want to pursue war and had converted to Catholicism (against the advice of her counselors), abdicated the throne in 1654 in favor of her cousin, Charles X Gustav (1622–60). After his rise to power, Charles X expelled the Danes from many of Sweden's southern provinces, establishing the Swedish borders along the approximate lines of today.

Under Frederick I (1676–1751), Sweden regained some of its former prestige. He formed an alliance with England, Prussia, and France against Russia. Although he initiated many reforms, encouraged the arts, and transformed the architectural landscape of Stockholm, Gustavus III (1746–92) revived the absolute power of the monarchy, perhaps as a reaction against the changes effected by the French Revolution. He was assassinated by a group of fanatical noblemen while attending a ball at the opera.

THE 19TH CENTURY

The next king was Gustavus IV (1778–1837). Because he hated Napoleon, Gustavus IV led Sweden into the Third Coalition against France (1805–07). For his efforts, he lost Stralsund and Swedish Pomerania; in the wars against Russia and Denmark, Sweden lost Finland in 1808. The next year, following an uprising, Gustavus IV was overthrown and died in exile.

Napoleon arranged for his aide, Jean Bernadotte (1763–1844), to become heir to the Swedish throne. Bernadotte won a war with Denmark, forcing that country to cede Norway to Sweden (1814). Upon the death of Charles, Bernadotte became king of Sweden and Norway, ruling as Charles XIV. During his reign, Sweden adopted a policy of neutrality, and the royal line that he established is still on the throne today.

The Industrial Revolution of the 19th century changed the face of Sweden. The Social Democratic Party was launched in 1889, leading to a universal suffrage movement. All males acquired the right to vote in 1909.

THE 20TH CENTURY

Norway declared its independence in 1905 and Sweden accepted the secession. Sweden adhered to a policy of neutrality during World War I, although many Swedes were sympathetic to the German cause. Many Swedish volunteers enlisted in the White Army during the Russian Revolution of 1917.

In 1921, women gained the right to vote. The Social Democratic Party continued to grow in power, and after 1932 a welfare state was instituted.

Although Sweden offered weapons and volunteers to Finland during its Winter War against the Soviet Union in 1939, it declared its neutrality during World War II. Throughout the war, Sweden accepted many impoverished and homeless refugees. The rescue attempts of Hungarian Jews led by Swedish businessman and diplomat Raoul Wallenberg have been recounted in books and films.

Sweden joined the United Nations in 1946 but refused to join NATO in 1949. Rather more disturbing was Sweden's decision to return to the Soviet Union many German and Baltic refugees who had opposed Russia during the war. They were presumably killed on Stalin's orders.

Dag Hammarskjöld, as secretary-general of the United Nations in 1953, did much to help Sweden regain the international respect that it had lost because of its wartime policies. In 1961, toward the end of his second 5-year term, he died in a plane crash.

In 1995, Sweden, along with Finland and Austria, was granted full membership in the European Union, thereby providing a context for much-needed economic growth.

POSTMILLENNIUM

The government presently spends 46% of the gross national product on welfare, more than any other industrialized country. The income taxes required to support this public outlay take 59% of the pay of people. Employers pay up to 41% of employee remuneration into social security and pension plans. The former Communist Party now is called the Left Party, and it has steadily been growing in approval with voters.

Finland

As the Ice Age receded throughout Scandinavia, widely scattered Stone Age settlements emerged among the lakes and forests of what is now Finland. The tribes that established these communities were probably nomadic Sami of Mongolian origin, although the mists of time have greatly obscured the exact nature of the communities.

With the arrival of new tribes of Finno-Ugric origin (starting in the 1st c. A.D.) and other unrelated Germanic tribes from the southern edge of the Gulf of Finland, the original Sami retreated farther and farther north. The arrival of the Vikings, mentioned in written records beginning about A.D. 800, led to the establishment of cultural and trade routes as far east as Constantinople. Early in their recorded history, inhabitants of the region now known as Finland had many contacts with the Russian empire as well as the kingdoms of Estonia and Latvia. They also established trade links with the shores of the southern Baltic—the area that's now Poland and part of Germany.

SWEDISH INTRUSIONS

In A.D. 1155, Eric IX, assisted by the English-born bishop of Uppsala, St. Henry, launched a crusade for the political and religious conversion of the Finnish tribes. Their major opposition was from the Novgorodians (a powerful Russian kingdom) in eastern Finland (Karelia), who were seizing land and spreading the Russian Orthodox faith from the east. A famous battle occurred in 1240 at the River Neva, when Alexander Nevski, a noted hero of Russian literature, defeated Sweden. Later, a treaty between Sweden and the Novgorodians in 1323 divided Finland's easternmost province of Karelia between Novgorod and Sweden. Eastern Finland, from that moment on, became part of the Russian-Byzantine world; that region would not be reunited with the rest of Finland again except for a brief period early in the 20th century.

Meanwhile, with the largest portion of Finland under Swedish rule, most of the population enjoyed considerable autonomy and mercantile prosperity. The Swedish language became dominant. Under Sweden's king, Gustavus Vasa, Helsinki became one of the Swedish Empire's most important trading bases in the Baltic. Lutheranism was introduced into Finland by Michael Agricola (1506–57) who, because of his translation of the New Testament into Finnish and his compilation of a Finnish grammar, is called "the father of Finnish literature."

Sweden's King Johan III (1537–92) granted Finland the status of Grand Duchy in 1581. Unfortunately, Finland became a battleground in the continuing wars among

Russia, Sweden, Denmark, and Poland. New boundaries were established in 1671, when Russia was forced to yield certain lands in Karelia.

Finland entered the Thirty Years' War on Sweden's side, to which it was subjugated, its own language and culture suppressed in favor of Sweden's. The great famine of 1676 killed one-third of the population.

During the reign of Sweden's King Charles XII (1682–1718), Russia invaded and occupied Finland from 1713 to 1721. At the end of the war Sweden still ruled Finland, although some eastern territories, including southern Karelia, passed back to Russia. Russia gained new territories in another Swedish-Russian war, which raged from 1741 to 1743.

In 1808, at the peak of the Napoleonic Wars, Russia finally seized all of Finland. Under Tsar Alexander I (1777–1825), Finland was granted the status of Grand Duchy, and throughout the 19th century it enjoyed broad autonomy, developing a democratic system without interference from St. Petersburg.

LIFE UNDER THE RUSSIANS

Turku was the capital of Finland until 1821 when the tsar moved it to Helsinki. In 1878, under Tsar Alexander II (1818–81), Finland gained its own independent conscript army, and the Finnish language became the official language, replacing Swedish.

Although Tsar Alexander III (1845–94) tried to follow a liberal policy toward Finland, most of his advisers were opposed, preferring to keep Finland as a buffer zone between the Russian capital (then St. Petersburg) and the rest of Europe. Alexander's conservative and reactionary son, Nicholas II (1868–1918), revoked Finnish autonomy in 1899 and began an intensive campaign of Russification. Russian became the official language in 1900, and the following year the separate Finnish army was abolished. Mass arrests followed. In 1905 Finland called a national strike to protest these conditions, forcing Nicholas II to ease some of his edicts. In 1906 Finland was permitted to have a unicameral parliament (the Diet) composed of 200 elected deputies, but it had little real power.

At the outbreak of World War I, Russia totally dominated Finland, and Finnish autonomy became just a memory. Finland lost its status as a Grand Duchy and became just a dominion of its more powerful neighbor to the east.

AN INDEPENDENT FINLAND

Finland was saved by the outbreak of the Russian Revolution and the collapse of tsarist rule. The Russian provisional government restored Finnish autonomy on March 20, 1917. Nevertheless, the Finns called a general strike, seeking total independence. A civil war followed, in which the leftist, pro-Russian Red Guard, supporting Russian troops in Finland, was opposed by the conservative-nationalist civil guard, the Whites.

On November 15, 1917, a proclamation placed control of the country's affairs in the hands of a Finnish government, and on December 6, President Svinhufvrud (1861–1944) declared the independence of Finland. Russia recognized Finnish independence on January 5, 1918.

Baron Carl Gustaf Emil von Mannerheim (1867–1951) assumed control of the Whites with the intention of driving Russia out of Finland. With the help of a German expeditionary force, he managed to win the civil war, which ended on May 16, 1918.

On December 12, 1918, Mannerheim was named regent of Finland, and a constitution was adopted in June 1919, making Finland a republic. The new document called for the election of a president every 6 years. In his position, Mannerheim wielded executive power, as did K. J. Stahlberg (1865–1952), the first president.

Russia and Finland signed a peace treaty at Tartu in October 1920. Russia got East Karelia. Finland joined the League of Nations on December 16, 1920, and the following year the League ruled that Finland was entitled to the Åland Islands.

The 1920s saw continuing struggles between the government and Finnish communists. In 1923 the Communist Party was outlawed, but it returned under the title of the Democratic League. During the 1930s, many social and economic reforms were carried out.

WARS WITH RUSSIA

A Soviet-Finnish nonaggression pact was signed on January 12, 1932, but Russia continued to make demands on Finland, including the annexation of the Hanko peninsula for use as a Soviet naval base. When Finland refused, Russian troops invaded on November 30, 1939.

The Winter War of 1939 to 1940 was one of the harshest ever in Finland, but the Finns, greatly outnumbered, resisted with bravery and courage. In March 1940 they accepted Russian terms, ceding territories in the north, the province of Viipuri, and the naval base at Hanko. The inhabitants of those districts left their homeland and moved within Finland's new borders.

Resentment against Russia led to a treaty with Germany. Hitler's request for transit rights across Finland was granted. Finland tried to remain neutral when the Nazis invaded Russia on June 22, 1941, but Russia bombed towns in southern Finland and Mannerheim launched the Russo-Finnish Continuation War. Territories that had been lost to Russia were retaken. But in 1944 Russia launched a large-scale attack, forcing Finland to ask for peace. Russia retook the territory it had ceded to Finland and imposed severe war reparations. The situation was complicated since German troops stationed in northern Finland refused to withdraw. Therefore, Finland had to launch a war against the Nazis in Lapland in 1945.

Mannerheim became president in 1944 but was obliged to step down in 1946 because of ill health. In Paris in 1947 Finland and Russia signed an armistice.

MODERN FINLAND

J. K. Paasikivi assumed the presidency in 1946, and concluded a mutual assistance treaty with the Soviet Union in 1948. In 1955 Finland joined the United Nations.

In 1956 Urho Kekkonen became president of Finland; he continued in office during the long Cold War era, resigning in 1982 because of ill health. During his 25 years in office, Kekkonen successfully pursued a precarious policy of neutrality, earning a reputation for skillful diplomacy. At the end of his tenure, he saw the decline of the Communist Party in Finland. In 1975 he hosted the Conference on Security and Cooperation in Europe, where he received the heads of state and the heads of government of 35 countries who signed the Helsinki Agreement on international human rights.

Upon Kekkonen's resignation in 1982, Mauno Koivisto was elected president. Nearing the end of the long Cold War, Koivisto was reelected to a second 6-year term in 1988. The country celebrated its 75th year of independence in 1992. After 12 years in office, the two-term Finnish president, Koivisto, stepped down in 1994. In his place, Martti Ahtisaari was elected president. In 1995 Finland joined the European Union.

While Sweden and Denmark have chosen to remain outside the Economic and Monetary Union, Finland continues to support a European single currency (Norway and Iceland aren't members of the E.U.).

RECOMMENDED BOOKS

Denmark

HISTORY & PHILOSOPHY *A Kierkegaard Anthology,* edited by Robert Bretall, explores the work of the Copenhagen-born philosopher who developed an almost pathological sense of involvement in theology. A representative selection of some of his more significant works is included.

Of Danish Ways, written by two Danish-Americans, Ingeborg S. MacHiffic and Margaret A. Nielsen, is a delightful account of this land and its people. It has a little bit of everything: history, social consciousness, customs, food, handicrafts, art, music, and theater.

BIOGRAPHY & LITERATURE *Andersen's Fairy Tales,* by H. C. Andersen, and *The Complete Hans Christian Andersen Fairy Tales* include all his most important works, such as *The Little Mermaid, The Tinderbox,* and *The Princess and the Pea.*

Out of Africa, Letters from Africa, and *Seven Gothic Tales* are all by Karen Blixen (who wrote under the name Isak Dinesen), one of the major authors of the 20th century, who gained renewed fame with the release of the 1985 movie *Out of Africa,* with Meryl Streep and Robert Redford. *Isak Dinesen,* by Judith Thurman, chronicles Blixen's amazing life from an unhappy childhood in Denmark to marriage to Baron Blixen to immigration to Kenya to her passionate love affair with Denys Finch Hatton.

Norway

MODERN LITERATURE The best female novelist to emerge between the two world wars was Sigrid Undset (1882–1949). She was awarded the Nobel Prize in Literature in 1928. Today she is mainly praised for her three-volume masterpiece *Kristin Lavransdatter,* which tells of love and religion in medieval Norway. She was a Christian writer, and her values were not political. With the coming of the Nazis, her books were banned and she fled Norway.

Among contemporaries, the bestselling author today is Norwegian fantasy writer Margit Sandemo, whose novel *Spellbound* has been translated into English. Some 40 million copies of her novels are in print. Two other popular writers today are Dag Solstad (1941–), who has a great ability to describe modern consciousness, and Herbjørg Wassmo (1942–), who enjoys international acclaim for her novels such as *Dina's Book* (1989), which was made into a film in 2002 with French actor Gérard Depardieu.

Finally, *The Norwegians,* by Arthur Spencer, is the best book on the market today for understanding the Norwegian people and their advanced society.

TRAVEL LITERATURE Norwegian travel writing has been linked to voyages of discovery. Both Fridtjof Nansen (1861–1930) and Roald Amundsen (1872–1928) published detailed travel accounts. Nansen's books, such as *The First Crossing of Greenland* (1890), are still widely read, as are the works of Amundsen, including *The South Pole* (1912).

The Kon-Tiki Expedition, by Thor Heyerdahl, details the saga of a modern-day Viking, who set out on a balsa raft with five comrades and sailed 6,920km (4,290 miles) in 1947—all the way from Peru to Polynesia. *Kon-Tiki Man: An Illustrated*

Biography of Heyerdahl, by Thor himself, highlights his attempt to document his idea that Polynesia was settled by people migrating west from South America.

Sweden

BIOGRAPHY *Sweden in North America (1638–1988),* by Sten Carlsson, follows the lives of some of the 2% of the North American population that has some sort of Swedish background—from Greta Garbo to Charles Lindbergh.

Alfred Nobel and the Nobel Prizes, by Nils K. Ståhle, traces the life of the 19th-century Swedish industrialist and creator of the coveted awards that bear his name.

Garbo: Her Story, by Antoni Gronowicz, is a controversial, unauthorized memoir based on a long and intimate friendship; it goes beyond the fabulous face, with many candid details of this most reluctant of movie legends.

PIPPI LONGSTOCKING TALES The world was saddened to learn of the death in 2002 of Astrid Lindgren, the Swedish writer of the Pippi Longstocking tales, who died at the age of 94 at her home in Stockholm. One of the world's most widely translated authors, Lindgren horrified parents but captivated millions of children around the globe with her whimsical, rollicking stories about a carrot-haired *enfant terrible.* In 1999 she was voted the most popular Swede of the century, having produced more than 70 books for young people. The best known is *Pippi Longstocking,* first published in 1945.

Finland

FICTION *The Unknown Soldier,* by Väinö Linna, presented on both stage and screen, is a masterpiece that depicts soldiers in the Winter War with Russia. Most portraits of that period portrayed Finnish soldiers as larger than life—"heroes in white"—but this was a more realistic "warts and all" depiction.

FOLKLORE *Kalevala* is the greatest cultural masterpiece of the Finnish folkloric repertoire. It was gathered by Lönnrot, a regional doctor, and it is the embodiment of the oral traditions of ancient Finland and has been translated into many languages, including English.

EATING & DRINKING IN SCANDINAVIA

Denmark

Danish food is the best in Scandinavia—in fact, it's among the best in Europe.

The favorite dish at midday is the ubiquitous *smørrebrød* (open-faced sandwiches)—a national institution. Literally, this means "bread and butter," but the Danes stack this sandwich as if it were the Leaning Tower of Pisa.

Smørrebrød is often served as an hors d'oeuvre. The most popular, most tempting, and usually most expensive of these delicacies is prepared with tiny Danish shrimp, on which a lemon slice and caviar often perch, perhaps even with fresh dill.

For dinner, the Danes tend to keep farmers' hours: 6:30pm is common, although restaurants remain open much later. Many main-course dishes are familiar to North Americans, but they're prepared with a distinct flourish in Denmark—for example, *lever med løg* (liver and fried onion), *bøf* (beef, in a thousand different ways), *lammesteg* (roast lamb), or that old reliable staple, *flæskesteg med rødkål* (roast pork with red cabbage).

Danish chefs are noted for their fresh fish dishes. The tiny Danish shrimp, *rejer,* are splendid; herring and kippers are also greeted with much enthusiasm. Top-notch fish dishes include *rodspætte* (plaice), *laks* (salmon), *makrel* (mackerel), and *kogt torsk* (boiled cod).

Danish cheese may be consumed at any meal and then eaten again on a late-night *smørrebrød* at Tivoli. Danish bleu is already familiar to most people. For something softer and milder, try havarti.

Danish specialties that are worth sampling include *frikadeller,* the Danish meatballs (prepared in various ways); a Danish omelet with a rasher of bacon covered with chopped chives and served in a skillet; and Danish hamburger patties topped with fried onions and coated with a rich brown gravy.

As for drinks, Carlsberg and Tuborg beer are Denmark's national beverages. A bottle of Pilsener costs about half the price of a stronger export beer with the fancy label. Value-conscious Danes rely on the low-priced *fadøl* (draft beer); visitors on a modest budget might want to do the same.

Akvavit (schnapps) comes from the city of Aalborg in northern Jutland. The Danes usually drink it at mealtime, followed by a beer chaser. Made from a distilling process using potatoes, it should be served only icy cold.

For those with a daintier taste, Cherry Heering is a delightful liqueur that can be consumed anytime except with meals.

Norway

In major towns and cities, lunch is generally served from 1 to 3pm. The *middag,* the main meal of the day, is generally eaten between 4:30 and 6pm. Many restaurants serve this popular *middag* from 1 to 8pm. In late-closing restaurants, it's possible to dine much later, until around midnight in Oslo. Long after *middag* time a Norwegian family will have *aftens,* a *smørbrød* supper that will see them through the night.

Norwegians are proud—and rightly so—of many of their tempting specialties, ranging from boiled cod (considered a delicacy) to reindeer steak smothered in brown gravy and accompanied by tart little lingonberries, which resemble wild cranberries.

Norway relies on fish, both freshwater and saltwater, for much of its food supply. Try the aforementioned boiled cod, *always* served with boiled potatoes. In early summer, *kokt laks* (boiled salmon) is a highly rated delicacy. *Kreps* (crayfish) is another big production (as it is in Finland), and *ørret* (mountain trout) is a guaranteed treat. A recommendation for top-notch fare: *fiske-gratin* (fish soufflé).

Norwegians love their fatty smoked eel *(roket al),* although many foreigners have a tendency to whip by this one on the *smörgåsbord* (smorgasbord) table. The national appetizer is brine-cured herring with raw onions.

You may want to try reindeer steak or *faar-i-kaal,* the national dish, a heavily peppered cabbage-and-mutton stew served with boiled potatoes. A fisher's or a farmer's favorite is *lapskus* (hash, to us), prepared with whatever's left over in the kitchen. *Kjøttkaker,* the Norwegian hamburger—often pork patties—is served with sautéed onions, gravy, and boiled potatoes.

Rumgraut is a sour-cream porridge covered with melted butter, brown sugar, and cinnamon. If they're in season, try the amber-colored *muiter* (cloudberries). An additional treat is a pancake accompanied by lingonberries.

Incidentally, smorgasbord and *smørbrød* are very popular in Norway, although customarily, smorgasbord in Norway is only a prelude to the main meal.

The Norwegians, like the Danes, are essentially beer drinkers. *Pils,* a light lager, is fairly low in alcohol content, but the *lagerøl* is so low in alcoholic content (less than 2.5%) that it's a substitute for water only. The stronger Norwegian beer is called Export and is available at higher prices. Two other types of beer are Brigg and Zero.

The other national drink is *akevitt* (sometimes written as *aquavit* or *schnapps*), the "water of life." Norwegians gulp down beer as a chaser.

Sweden

The fame of the *smörgåsbord* (smorgasbord) is justly deserved. Using a vast array of dishes—everything from Baltic herring to smoked reindeer—the smorgasbord (never served in the evening) can be eaten either as hors d'oeuvres or as a meal in itself.

One cardinal rule of the smorgasbord: Don't mix fish and meat dishes. It is customary to begin with *sill* (herring), prepared in many ways. Herring usually is followed by other treats from the sea (jellied eel, smoked fish, and raw pickled salmon); then diners proceed to the cold meat dishes, such as baked ham or liver paste, which are accompanied by vegetable salads. Hot dishes, often Swedish meatballs, come next and are backed up by cheese and crackers, and sometimes a fresh fruit salad.

In lieu of the 40-dish smorgasbord, some restaurants have taken to serving a plate of *assietter* (hors d'oeuvres). It's best to go early, when dishes are fresh.

The average times for meals in Sweden are generally from 8 to 11am for the standard continental breakfast, noon to 2:30pm for lunch, and as early as 5:30pm for dinner to around 8 or 8:30pm (many restaurants in Stockholm are open to midnight).

Generally, Swedish chefs tend to be far more expert with **fish dishes** (freshwater pike and salmon are star choices) than with meat courses. The Swedes go stark raving mad at the sight of *kraftor* (crayfish), in season from mid-August to mid-September. This succulent, dill-flavored delicacy is eaten with the fingers, and much of the fun is the elaborate ritual surrounding its consumption.

A platter of thin **pancakes,** served with lingonberries (like cranberries), is the traditional Thursday-night dinner in Sweden. It often is preceded by yellow split-pea soup seasoned with pork.

The state monopoly, Systembolaget, controls the sale of alcoholic beverages. Licensed restaurants may sell alcohol after noon only (1pm on Sun).

Schnapps or aquavit, served icy cold, is a superb Swedish drink, often used to accompany smorgasbord. The run-of-the-mill Swedish **beer** (Pilsener) has only a small amount of alcohol. All restaurants serve *lättol* (light beer) and *folköl,* a somewhat stronger brew. Swedish vodka, or ***brännvin,*** is made from corn and potatoes and flavored with different spices. All *brännvin* is served ice-cold in schnapps glasses.

Finland

In Finland, full-fledged restaurants are called *ravintola.* Inexpensive lunches are available at places called *kahvila* and *baari.* A *baari* serves light food and perhaps a mild beer, although coffee is more common. All well-known alcoholic beverages are available throughout Finland in fully licensed restaurants and bars.

Potatoes, meat, fish, milk, butter, and rye bread are the mainstays of the Finnish diet. Soups are popular, especially pea soup and rich meat soups.

Every Finn looks forward to the crayfish season between July 20 and September. After devouring half a dozen, they down a glass of schnapps. Called *rapu,* the crayfish is usually boiled in salted water and seasoned with dill.

The icy-cold waters of Finland produce very fine fish, some of which are unknown elsewhere in the world. A cousin to the salmon, the 2-inch-long *muikku fritti* is found in Finland's inland waters. Its roe is a delicacy. The most common fish is *silakka* (Baltic herring), which is consumed in vast quantities. Rarely larger than sardines, the herring is not only pickled, but fried or grilled. Sometimes it's baked between layers of potatoes with milk, cheese, and egg. The fish is usually spiced with dill.

Finland's version of the Swedish *smörgåsbord* is called *voileipäpöytä* (which means "bread and butter table"). Expect not only bread and butter, but an array of dishes, including many varieties of fish (for example, pickled salt herring and fresh salted salmon) and several cold meat dishes, including smoked reindeer.

Along with elk, bear, and reindeer tongue, Finns like the sharp taste of *puolukka,* a lingonberry. The Arctic cloudberry is a rare delicacy.

Some Finnish hors d'oeuvres are especially good, particularly *vorschmack.* Herring is ground very fine, then blended with garlic, onions, and lamb; the mixture is then cooked in butter over a low flame for a long time, often several hours. One of the best-known regional specialties is Savonian *Kalakukko,* a mixture of Finnish whitefish and pork baked in rye dough.

The national beverage of Finland is milk (sometimes curdled), which is safe to drink (as is water) throughout the country. Two famous Finnish liqueurs should be tasted: *lakka,* made from the saffron-colored wild cloudberry, and *mesimarja,* made from the arctic brambleberry. Many Finns are heavy drinkers (schnapps is their favorite for an all-around tipple).

PLANNING YOUR TRIP TO SCANDINAVIA

2

WHEN TO GO

Denmark

Denmark's climate is mild for a Scandinavian country. Summer temperatures average between 61°F and 77°F (16°C–25°C). Winter temperatures seldom go below 30°F (–1°C), thanks to the warming waters of the Gulf Stream. From the weather perspective, mid-April to November is a good time to visit.

Denmark's Average Daytime Temperatures

	JAN	FEB	MAR	APR	MAY	JUNE	JULY	AUG	SEPT	OCT	NOV	DEC
°F	32	32	35	44	53	60	64	63	57	49	42	37
°C	0	0	2	7	12	16	18	17	14	9	6	3

Denmark Calendar of Events

Note: Dates below apply at press time. Check with websites or local tourist boards for exact dates.

MAY

Carnival in Copenhagen. A great citywide event. There's also a children's carnival. For information, call ✆ **45-29-404-557** or go to www.copenhagencarnival.dk. Mid-May.

Ballet and Opera Festival, Copenhagen. Classical and modern dance and two operatic masterpieces are presented at the Old Stage of the Royal Theater in Copenhagen. For tickets, contact the Royal Theater, PO Box 2185, DK-1017 Copenhagen (✆ **45-33-69-69-81;** www.kglteater.dk). Mid-May to June.

Aalborg Carnival. This is one of the country's great spring events. The streets fill with people in colorful costumes. Thousands take part in the celebration, which honors the victory of spring over winter. For information, call ✆ **45-99-31-75-00** or visit www.visitaalborg.com. Late May.

JUNE

Viking Festival, Frederikssund, 8 miles southwest of Hillerød. For 2 weeks every summer, "bearded Vikings" present old Nordic sagas in an open-air setting. After each performance, a traditional Viking meal is served. Call ✆ **47-31-06-85** or visit www.vikingespil.dk for more information. Late June to early July.

Sankt Hans Aften ("St. John's Eve")**,** nationwide. The midsummer solstice is celebrated throughout Denmark. It is the longest day of the year. Festivities throughout the nation begin at around 10pm with bonfires and celebrations. June 23.

JULY

Roskilde Festival. Europe's biggest rock festival has been going strong for 30 years, now bringing about 90,000 revelers each year to the central Zealand town. Besides major rock concerts, which often draw big names, scheduled activities include theater and film presentations. For more information, call ✆ **46-36-66-13** or see www.roskilde-festival.dk. Early July.

Copenhagen Jazz Festival. International jazz musicians play in the streets, squares, and theaters. Pick up a copy of *Copenhagen This Week* to find the venues. For information, call ✆ **33-93-20-13,** or go to www.jazzfestival.dk. Early July.

July 4th, Rebild. Rebild National Park, near Aalborg, is one of the few places outside the United States to honor American Independence Day. For more information, contact the Aalborg Tourist Bureau, Østerågade 8, DK-9000 Aalborg (✆ **99-31-75-00;** www.visitaalborg.com). July 4th.

Funen Festival. This annual musical extravaganza draws big, international headliners. The festival's music is often hard-core rock, but gentler, classical melodies are presented as well. It takes place in the city of Odense, on the island of Funen. For more information, call the Odense tourist bureau (✆ **66-12-75-20;** www.visitodense.com). Early July.

AUGUST

Fall Ballet Festival (Copenhagen). The internationally acclaimed Royal Danish Ballet returns home to perform at the Old Stage of the Royal Theater just before the tourist season ends. For tickets, contact the Royal Theater, PO Box 2185, DK-1017 Copenhagen (✆ **33-69-69-69;** www.kglteater.dk). Mid-August to September.

Århus Festival Week. A wide range of cultural activities—including opera, jazz, classical and folk music, ballet, and theater—is presented. It's the largest cultural festival in Scandinavia. Sporting activities and street parties abound as well. For more information, contact ✆ **87-30-83-00** and visit www.aarhusfestival.dk. Late August to early September.

Norway

In the summer, the average temperature in Norway ranges from 53°F to 69°F (12°C–21°C), but can reach into the 80s (about 27°C). In January it hovers around 27°F (–3°C), ideal weather for winter sports.

The Gulf Stream warms the west coast, where winters tend to be temperate. Rainfall, however, is often heavy here. Above the Arctic Circle, the sun shines night and day from mid-May until late July. For about 2 months every winter, the North Cape is plunged into darkness.

May to mid-June is when the scenery in Norway is at its most spectacular, with fruit trees in blossom, snow in the mountains, and meltwater swelling the waterfalls. Low-season rates apply during this period.

Late June to early August is the high season in Norway, when the weather is warmest and the schools are on holiday. All the man-made tourist attractions are open, and public transport services are more frequent.

Mid-August to October is a time when accommodations are at mid- or low-season rates. September is good berry- and mushroom-picking weather. The glorious colors of autumn are at their best in October.

Norway's **summers** are unpredictable. The Gulf Stream keeps the western fjord area and the coast up into the arctic north much warmer than you might expect. The west coast receives the most rain, but the area farther east is drier. The sea temperature can reach 64°F (18°C) or higher on the south coast, where swimming is a popular pastime.

The warmest weather occurs on the eastern side of the southern mountains, including the south coast between Mandal and Oslo. Even in the north, summer temperatures are pleasantly warm; however, the weather can be wet and changeable.

Land of the Midnight Sun

In these locations, you can see the whole disk of the sun all night on the given dates:

Place	From	To
Nordkapp	May 13	July 29
Hammerfest	May 16	July 26
Vardo	May 17	July 25
Tromsø	May 20	July 22
Harstad	May 24	July 18
Svolvær	May 28	July 14
Bodø	June 3	July 8

In **winter** much of Norway is transformed into a snow-clad paradise from November to April. The best way to enjoy it is on skis. Active types can go tobogganing, skating, ice fishing, ice climbing, dog sledding, and more.

Norway's Average Daytime Temperatures (°F/°C)

	JAN	FEB	MAR	APR	MAY	JUNE	JULY	AUG	SEPT	OCT	NOV	DEC
OSLO												
Temp. (°F)	25	26	32	41	51	60	64	61	53	42	33	27
Temp. (°C)	–4	3	0	5	11	16	18	16	12	6	-1	-3
BERGEN/STAVANGER												
Temp. (°F)	35	35	38	41	40	55	59	58	54	47	42	38
Temp. (°C)	2	2	4	5	4	13	15	14	12	8	6	3
TRONDHEIM												
Temp. (°F)	27	27	31	38	47	53	58	57	50	42	35	31
Temp. (°C)	-3	-3	-1	3	8	12	14	14	10	6	2	-1

THE MIDNIGHT SUN In the summer, the sun never fully sets in northern Norway, and even in the south, the sun may set around 11pm and rise at 3am. Keep in mind that although the sun shines at midnight, it's not as strong as at midday. Always bring a warm jacket or sweater.

Norway Calendar of Events

Dates are approximate. Check with the local tourist office before making plans to attend a specific event.

JANUARY

Northern Lights Festival, Tromsø. Classical and contemporary music performances by musicians from Norway and abroad. Visit www.nordlysfestivalen.no for details. Late January.

FEBRUARY

Kristiansund Opera Festival. Featuring Kristiansund Opera's productions of opera and ballet, plus art exhibitions, concerts, and other events. Visit www.oik.no for details. Early February.

MARCH

Holmenkollen Ski Festival, Oslo. One of Europe's largest ski festivals, with World Cup Nordic skiing and biathlons, international ski-jumping competitions, and Norway's largest cross-country race for amateurs. Held at Holmenkollen Ski Jump on the outskirts of Oslo. To participate, attend, or request more information, contact Skiforeningen, Kongeveien 5, Holmenkollen, N-0787 Oslo 3 (✆ **22-92-32-00;** www.skiforeningen.no). Early March.

Narvik Winter Festival. Sports events, carnivals, concerts, and opera performances highlight this festival dedicated to those who built the railway across northern Norway and Sweden. Visit www.vinterfestuka.no for details or call ✆ **76-95-03-50.** Second week of March to mid-April.

Birkebeiner Race, Rena to Lillehammer. This historic international ski race, with thousands of participants, crosses the mountains between Rena and Lillehammer, site of the 1994 Olympics. It's a 53km (33-mile) cross-country trek. For details, call ✆ **41-77-29-00** or go to www.birkebeiner.no. Mid-March.

APRIL

Voss Jazz Festival. Three days of jazz and folk music performances by European and American artists. Visit www.vossajazz.no or call ✆ **56-52-99-11** for details. First week of April.

MAY

Bergen International Festival (Bergen Festspill). A world-class music event, featuring artists from Norway and around the world. This is one of the largest annual musical events in Scandinavia. Held at various venues in Bergen. For information, contact the Bergen International Festival, Slottsgaten 1, 4055, Dregen N-5835 Bergen (✆ **55-21-06-30;** www.festspillene.no). Late May to early June.

JUNE

Faerder Sailing Race. Some 1,000 sailboats participate in this race, which ends in Borre, by the Oslofjord. Call ✆ **23-27-56-00** or go to www.kns.no for details. Mid-June.

North Cape March. This trek from Honningsvåg to the North Cape is one of the world's toughest. The round-trip march is 68km (42 miles) long. Details at www.northkapp.no. Mid-June.

Emigration Festival, Stavanger. A festive commemoration of Norwegian immigration to North America, with exhibitions, concerts, theater, and folklore. For details call ✆ **51-53-88-60.** Mid-June.

Midnight Sun Marathon, Tromsø. This marathon in northern Norway starts at midnight and draws eager runners from over 30 countries. For details, visit ✆ **77-67-33-63** or go to www.msm.no. Mid-June.

Midsommernatt (Midsummer's Night), nationwide. Celebrations and bonfires explode all over Norway in honor of the midnight sun. June 23.

Emigration Festival, Kvinesdal. Commemorates the Norwegian emigration to the United States. Late June to early July.

JULY

Kongsberg International Jazz Festival. International artists participate in one of the most important jazz festivals in Scandinavia, with open-air concerts. Call ✆ **32-73-31-66** or visit www.kongsberg-jazzfestival.no for details. Early July.

Exxon Mobil Bislett Games, Oslo. International athletic competitions are staged in Oslo, with professional participants from all over the world. For details, call ✆ **22-59-17-59** or visit www.diamondleague-oslo.com. Early to mid-July.

Molde International Jazz Festival. The "City of Roses" is the site of Norway's oldest jazz festival. It attracts international stars from both sides of the Atlantic every year and is held at venues in Molde for 6 days. For details, contact the Molde Jazz Festival, PO Box 415, N-6401 Molde (✆ **71-20-31-50;** www.moldejazz.no). Mid-July.

Norway Cup International Youth Soccer Tournament, Oslo. The world's largest youth soccer tournament attracts 1,000 teams from around the world to Oslo. Call ✆ **22-28-90-57** or visit www.norwaycup.no. Late July to early August.

AUGUST

Telemark International Folk Music Festival, Bø. An international festival of folk music and folk dance takes place in the home of many famous fiddlers, dancers, and singers. Call ✆ **33-95-19-19** or go to www.telemarkfestivalen.no. Early August.

Peer Gynt Festival, Vinstra. Art exhibitions, evenings of music and song, parades in national costumes, and other events honor Ibsen's fictional character. Call ✆ **95-90-07-70** or visit www.peergynt.no for details. Early August.

Oslo Jazz Festival. This annual festival features music from the earliest years of jazz (1920–25), as well as classical concerts, opera, and ballet. For details, call the Oslo Tourist Bureau at ✆ **22-42-91-20** or go to www.oslojazz.no. Second week of August.

Chamber Music Festival, Oslo. Norwegian and foreign musicians perform at Oslo's Akershus Castle and Fortress, which dates from A.D. 1300. Call ✆ **23-10-07-30** or visit www.oslokammermusikkfestival.no for details. Mid-August.

SEPTEMBER

Oslo Marathon. This annual event draws some of Norway's best long-distance runners. Visit www.oslomarathon.com for details. Mid-September. Call ✆ **22-69-31-20-21** or visit www.marathonguide.com.

DECEMBER

Nobel Peace Prize Ceremony, Oslo. A major event on the Oslo calendar, attracting world attention. Held at Oslo City Hall on December 10. Attendance is by invitation only. For information, contact the Nobel Institute, Henrik Ibsen Gate 51, N-0255 Oslo 2 (✆ **22-12-93-00;** http://nobelprize.org).

Sweden

Sweden's climate is hard to classify because temperatures, influenced by the Gulf Stream, vary considerably from the fields of Skåne to the wilderness of Lapland (the upper 10th of Sweden lies north of the Arctic Circle).

The country as a whole has many sunny days in summer. July is the warmest month, with temperatures in Stockholm and Gothenburg averaging 64°F (18°C). February is the coldest, when temperatures in Stockholm average around 26°F (–3°C).

During summer, the northern parts of the country—from Halsingland to northern Lapland—may have the warmest weather and the bluest skies.

SUMMER The ideal time to visit Sweden is from June to August. All its cafes and most attractions, including open-air museums, are open and thousands flock north to enjoy the midnight sun. Summer also is the most expensive time to fly to Sweden, as this is peak season. To compensate, hotels sometimes grant summer discounts.

FALL & SPRING September and May through June—when spring comes to the Swedish countryside and wildflowers burst into bloom—are almost prettier than the Swedish summers.

WINTER Scandinavia's off-season is about November 1 to March 21. You'll need to keep bundled up heavily through April. Cultural activities, including opera, dance, ballet, and theater, abound. Skiers also go to Sweden in winter, but it is pitch dark in the north of Sweden, and the slopes are artificially lit.

Of course, one of the most eerie and fascinating things you can experience in Sweden in the winter is to see the shimmering northern lights.

Sweden's Average Daytime Temperatures (°F/°C)

	JAN	FEB	MAR	APR	MAY	JUNE	JULY	AUG	SEPT	OCT	NOV	DEC
Stockholm	27/-3	26/-3	31/-1	40/4	50/10	59/15	64/18	62/17	54/12	45/7	37/3	32/0
Karesuando	6/-14	5/-15	12/-11	23/-5	39/4	54/12	59/15	51/11	44/7	31/-1	9/-13	5/-15
Karlstad	33/1	30/-1	28/-2	37/3	53/12	63/17	62/17	59/15	54/12	41/5	29/-2	26/-3
Lund	38/3	36/2	34/1	43/6	57/14	63/17	64/18	61/16	57/14	47/8	37/3	37/3

Sweden Calendar of Events

The dates given here may in some cases be only approximations. Check with the tourist office if you plan to attend a specific event. For information on Walpurgis night and midsummer celebrations, call the local tourist offices in the town where you plan to stay. (See individual chapters for phone numbers.)

JANUARY

Kiruna Snow Festival, Kiruna. The biggest snow festival in Europe takes place in this far northern city under the northern lights, featuring dog sledding and reindeer racing. Call the Kiruna Lapland Tourist Bureau for more information at ✆ **0980/188-80,** or go to www.snofestivalen.se. January 27 to February 1.

Gothenburg Film Festival, Gothenburg. Entering its fourth decade, this festival attracts film buffs from all over Europe, showing 400 movies often months before their official release. For more information, call the Gothenburg Film Festival at ✆ **031-339-30-00,** or go to www.giff.se. January 23 to February 2.

APRIL

Walpurgis Night, nationwide. Celebrations with bonfires, songs, and speeches welcome the advent of spring. These are especially lively celebrations among university students at Uppsala, Lund, Stockholm, Gothenburg, and Umeå. Contact the local tourist board for info. April 30.

MAY

Drottningholm Court Theater. Some 30 opera and ballet performances, from baroque to early romantic, are presented in the unique 1766 Drottningholm Court Theater in Drottningholm, with original decorative paintings and stage mechanisms. Call ✆ **08/660-82-25** (www.dtm.se) for tickets. Call ✆ **08/556-931-02** for information. Late May to late September.

JUNE

Midsummer, nationwide. Swedes celebrate Midsummer Eve all over the country. Maypole dances to the sound of the fiddle and accordion are the typical festive events of the day. Dalarna observes the most traditional celebrations. Check www.sweden.se. Mid-June.

JULY

Around Gotland Race, Sandhamn. The biggest and most exciting open-water Scandinavian sailing race starts and finishes at Sandhamn in the Stockholm archipelago. About 450 boats, mainly from Nordic countries, take part. Call ✆ **08/571-530-68** in Stockholm for information, or visit www.gotlandrunt.se. Two days in mid-July.

Rättviksdansen (International Festival of Folk Dance and Music), Rättvik. Every other year for some 20 years, around 1,000 folk dancers and musicians from all over the world have gathered to participate in this folkloric tradition. Check http://goscandinavia.about.com. Last week in July.

Stockholm Jazz Festival, Stockholm. This is a big summer event occurring on the grounds and inside the Modern Art Museum on the island of Skeppsholmen. An outdoor band shell is erected, and members of the audience sit on the lawn to hear top jazz artists from Europe and America. Tickets cost 350SEK to 450SEK per person. For more information, search www.stockholmjazz.com. Last week in July for 7 days.

Gay Pride, Tantolunden at Liljeholmsbron, Stockholm. A 1-week event, the largest Gay Pride Festival in the Nordic countries features workshops, concerts, theater, and attractions. There's even a local parade where Vikings go gay and/or in drag. For more information, call Stockholm Pride at ✆ **08/33-59-55;** www.stockholmpride.org. July 31 to August 6 (dates can vary).

AUGUST

Medieval Week, Gotland. Numerous events are held throughout the island of Gotland—including medieval tours, concerts, plays, festivities, and shows. For more information, contact the Office of Medieval Week, Hästgatan 4, S-621 56 Visby (✆ **0498/29-10-70**). Early August.

Minnesota Day, Utvandra Hus, Växjoü (Småland). Swedish-American relations are celebrated at the House of Emigrants with speeches, music, singing, and dancing; the climax is the election of the Swedish-American of the year. Call ✆ **0470/201-20** for information. Second Sunday in August.

DECEMBER

Nobel Day, Stockholm. The king, members of the royal family, and invited guests attend the Nobel Prize ceremony for literature, physics, chemistry, medicine, physiology, and economics. Attendance is by invitation only. The ceremony is held at the concert hall and followed by a banquet at City Hall. Visit http://nobelprize.org for info. December 10.

Lucia, the Festival of Lights, nationwide. To celebrate the shortest day and longest night of the year, young girls called "Lucias" dress in white gowns and headdresses, holding lighted candles. They are accompanied by "star boys"—young men in white with wizard hats, each holding a wand with a golden star. One of the "Lucias" is crowned queen. In olden days, Lucia was known as "Little Christmas." December 13.

Actual planned events change from year to year and vary from community to community. The best place for tourists to observe this event is at the open-air museum at Skansen in Stockholm.

Finland

Spring arrives in May, and the summers are short. A standing joke is that in Helsinki, summer lasts from Tuesday through Thursday. July is the warmest month, with temperatures averaging around 59°F (15°C). The coldest months are January and February, when the Finnish climate has been compared to that of New England. Snow arrives in southern Finland in December, in northern Finland in October. In Lapland, snow generally lasts until late April.

Finland's Average Daytime Temperatures

	JAN	FEB	MAR	APR	MAY	JUNE	JULY	AUG	SEPT	OCT	NOV	DEC
HELSINKI												
°F	26	27	33	44	57	66	69	66	57	48	39	31
°C	-3	-3	1	7	14	19	21	19	14	9	4	-1
TAMPERE												
°F	24	24	32	44	57	66	72	68	58	45	36	29
°C	-4	-4	0	7	14	19	22	20	14	7	2	-2
JYVÄSKYLÄ												
°F	20	22	32	42	58	67	69	65	54	43	32	24
°C	-7	-6	0	6	14	37	21	18	12	6	0	-4
IVALO												
°F	17	17	26	27	47	60	67	62	50	37	28	21
°C	-8	-8	-3	-3	8	16	37	17	10	3	-2	-6

THE MIDNIGHT SUN The following places and dates are the best for seeing the midnight sun in Finland: **Utsjoki,** from May 17 to July 28; **Ivalo,** from May 23 to July 22; **Sodankylä,** from May 30 to July 5; on the **Arctic Circle** and **Rovaniemi,** from June 6 to July 7; **Kuusamo,** from June 13 to July 1; and **Kemi,** from June 19 to June 25. Helsinki has almost 20 hours of daylight during the summer months.

Finland Calendar of Events

The dates given in this calendar can vary from year to year. Check with the Scandinavian Tourist Board for the exact dates and contact information (see "Visitor Information," in chapter 21).

FEBRUARY

Finlandia Ski Race-Ski Marathon, Hameenlinna-Lahti. With almost 80km (50 miles) of cross-country skiing, this mass event is part of the Euroloppet and Worldloppet competitions. For more information, call ✆ **81-83-68-13** or visit www.finlandiahiihto.fi. Late February.

MARCH

Oulu Tar Ski Race, Oulu. This cross-country ski race has taken place each year, without interruption, since it was first established more than a century ago. Following a course that stretches more than 76km (47 miles)—and with hundreds of participants—it's the oldest long-distance cross-country ski race in the world. For more information, call ✆ **08-558-558-00,** or go to www.oulu.ouka.fi. Early to mid-March.

APRIL

Walpurgis Eve Celebration. After a long, cold winter, most Helsinki residents turn out to celebrate the arrival of spring. Celebrations are held at Market Square, followed by May Day parades and other activities the next morning. Check www.istc.org. April 30.

MAY

May Day. Parades and other celebrations herald the arrival of spring. For information, search www.finnguide.fi. May 1.

Women's 10km. This is a 10km (6-mile) foot race for women. For more detailed information on this event, contact any office of the Scandinavian Tourist Board (✆ **212/885-9700** in the U.S., or 09/310-1691; www.hel.fi). Late May.

JUNE

Kuopio Dance Festival. This international dance event has a different theme every year, such as dances in Japan, the Middle East, and North Africa. For more information, call ✆ **358/017-182-584** or visit www.kuopiodancefestival.fi. Mid- to late June.

Midnight Sun Film Festival, Sodankylä. The world's northernmost film festival features nostalgic releases from the great film masters—mainly European—but also new names in the film world. For more information, call ✆ **81/66-14-522** or visit www.msfilmfestival.fi. Dates vary.

JULY

Savonlinna Opera Festival. One of Europe's best-known music festivals, this is part of a cultural tradition established in 1912. Dozens of performances are held in the island fortress of Olavinlinna Castle in July. Internationally renowned artists perform a variety of works, including at least one Finnish opera. For details and complete information, contact the Savonlinna Opera Festival, Olavinkatu 27, FIN-57130 Savonlinna (✆ **015/47-67-50;** www.operafestival.fi). Early July to early August.

Kaustinen Folk Music Festival. This is the biggest international folk festival in Scandinavia. For more information, contact the Folk Arts Centre (✆ **06/888-6444;** www.kaustinen.fi). Dates vary.

AUGUST

Turku Music Festival. A wide range of music is presented from the Renaissance and the baroque periods (played on the original instruments) to modern, light music (✆ **02/262-0814;** www.tmj.fi). Second week of August.

Helsinki City Marathon. This event attracts both Finnish and foreign runners of varying abilities. Information can be found at ✆ **02/262-0814** or www.tmj.fi. Mid-August.

Helsinki Festival. A major Scandinavian musical event, the Helsinki Festival presents orchestral concerts by outstanding soloists and ensembles; chamber music and recitals; exhibitions; ballet, theater, and opera performances; and jazz, pop, and rock concerts. For complete information about the program, contact the Helsinki Festival, Lasipalatsi Mannerheimintie 22–24 FIN-00100 Helsinki (✆ **09/612-651-00;** www.helsinginjutlaviikot.fi). Mid-August to early September.

OCTOBER

Baltic Herring Market. Since the 1700s, there has been an annual herring market along the quays of Helsinki's Market Square in early October. Prizes and blue ribbons go to the tastiest herring. Fishers continue the centuries-old tradition of bringing their catch into the city and selling it from their boats. Call ✆ **09/173-331** for information. First week in October.

ENTRY REQUIREMENTS

What You Can Bring Home from Scandinavia

U.S. Citizens: For specifics on what you can bring back and the corresponding fees, download the invaluable free pamphlet *Know Before You Go* online at **www.cbp.gov**. (Click on "Travel," and then click on "Know Before You Go," under the "Travel Smart" heading. Or contact the **U.S. Customs & Border Protection (CBP),** 1300 Pennsylvania Ave., NW, Washington, DC 20229 (✆ **877/287-8667** or 202/354-1000) and request the pamphlet.

Canadian Citizens: For a clear summary of Canadian rules, write for the booklet *I Declare,* issued by the **Canada Border Services Agency** (✆ **800/622-6232** in Canada, or 204/983-3500; www.cbsa-asfc.gc.ca).

U.K. Citizens: For information, contact **HM Revenue & Customs** at ✆ **02920/501-261** (from outside the U.K., 020/8929-0152), or consult their website at www.hmrc.gov.uk.

Australian Citizens: A helpful brochure available from Australian consulates or Customs offices is *Know Before You Go.* For more information, call the **Australian Customs Service** at ✆ **1300/363-263,** or log on to www.customs.gov.au.

New Zealand Citizens: Most questions are answered in a free pamphlet available at New Zealand consulates and Customs offices: *New Zealand Customs Guide for Travellers, Notice no. 4.* For more information, contact **New Zealand Customs,** The Customhouse, 17–21 Whitmore St., PO Box 2218, Wellington (✆ **04/473-6099** or 0800/428-786; www.customs.govt.nz).

Denmark

U.S., Canadian, U.K., Irish, Australian, and New Zealand citizens with a **valid passport** don't need a visa to enter Denmark if they don't expect to stay more than 90 days and don't expect to work there. If after entering Denmark you want to stay more than 90 days, you can apply for a permit for an extra 90 days at your home country's consulate. If your passport is lost or stolen, head to your consulate for a replacement.

WHAT YOU CAN BRING INTO DENMARK

Foreign visitors can bring along most items for personal use duty-free, including fishing tackle, a pair of skis, two tennis rackets, a baby carriage, two hand cameras with 10 rolls of film, and 400 cigarettes or a quantity of cigars or pipe tobacco not exceeding 500 grams (1 lb.). There are strict limits on importing alcoholic beverages. However, for alcohol bought tax-paid, limits are much more liberal than in other countries of the European Union.

Norway

Citizens of the United States, Canada, Ireland, Australia, New Zealand, and the U.K. need a valid **passport** to enter Norway. You need to apply for a visa only if you want to stay more than 3 months.

A British Visitor's Passport is also valid for holidays and some business trips of less than 3 months. The passport can also include your spouse, and it's valid for 1 year. Apply in person at a main post office in the British Isles, and the passport will be issued that day.

WHAT YOU CAN BRING INTO NORWAY

With certain food exceptions, personal effects intended for your own use can be brought into Norway. If you plan to take them with you when you leave, you can bring in cameras, binoculars, radios, portable TVs, and the like, as well as fishing and camping equipment. Visitors of all nationalities can bring in 200 cigarettes, or 250 grams of tobacco and 200 sheets of cigarette paper, or 50 cigars; and 1 liter of spirits or 1 liter of wine. Upon leaving, you can take with you up to NOK25,000 ($5,000/£2,500) in cash.

Sweden

U.S., Canadian, U.K., Irish, Australian, and New Zealand citizens with a **valid passport** don't need a visa to enter Sweden if they don't expect to stay more than 90 days and don't expect to work there. If after entering Sweden you want to stay more than 90 days, you can apply for a permit for an extra 90 days, which as a rule is granted immediately. Go to the nearest police headquarters or to your home country's consulate. If your passport is lost or stolen, head to your consulate as soon as possible.

WHAT YOU CAN BRING INTO SWEDEN

Foreign visitors can bring along most items for personal use duty-free, including fishing tackle, a pair of skis, two tennis rackets, a baby carriage, two hand-held cameras with 10 rolls of film, and 400 cigarettes or a quantity of cigars or pipe tobacco not exceeding 500 grams. Strict limits exist on importing alcoholic beverages. For alcohol bought tax-paid, limits are much more liberal than in other countries of the European Union.

Finland

American, Canadian, Australian, and New Zealand citizens need only a valid **passport** to enter Finland. Members of E.U. countries (except Greece), Liechtenstein, San Marino, and Switzerland are allowed entry with a valid **identity card** issued by those countries. You need to apply for a visa only if you want to stay more than 3 months. For U.K. subjects, a **visitor's passport** is also valid for a holiday or even for some business trips of less than 3 months. The passport can include both a husband and wife, and it's valid for 1 year. You can apply in person at a main post office in the British Isles, and the passport will be issued that same day.

WHAT YOU CAN BRING INTO FINLAND

All personal effects, including cameras and a reasonable amount of film (or other items intended for your own use) can be brought in duty-free. You can bring in 200 cigarettes or 250 grams of other manufactured tobacco. You can also bring in 15 liters of beer, 2 liters of wine, and 1 liter of spirits *or* 2 liters of beer and 2 liters of wine. You must be over the age of 18 to bring in beer or wine and over 20 to bring in other alcohol. There are no restrictions on the amount of euros that can be taken in or out of the country.

GETTING THERE & GETTING AROUND

Getting to Scandinavia

BY PLANE

Flying in winter—Scandinavia's off-season—is cheapest; summer is the most expensive. In any season, midweek fares (Mon–Thurs) are the lowest.

SAS (Scandinavian Airlines Systems; ✆ **800/221-2350** in the U.S., or 0870/6072-7727 in the U.K.; www.flysas.com) has more nonstop flights to Scandinavia from more North American cities than any other airline, and it has more flights to and from Denmark and within Scandinavia than any other airline in the world. From Seattle and Chicago, SAS offers nonstop flights to Copenhagen daily in midsummer and almost every day in winter; from Newark, New Jersey, there are daily flights year-round to Copenhagen.

Nonstop flights to Copenhagen from the greater New York area take about 7½ hours; from Chicago, around 8½ hours; from Seattle, 9½ hours.

FROM NORTH AMERICA All transatlantic flights from North America to Norway land at Oslo's Fornebu airport. **SAS** (✆ **800/221-2350** in the U.S.; www.flysas.com) flies nonstop daily from Newark to Oslo. The trip takes about 7½ hours. Most other SAS flights from North America go through Copenhagen. Flying time from Chicago is 11 hours; from Seattle, it's 12 hours, not including the layover in Copenhagen. From New York, **Continental** (✆ **800/525-0280;** www.continental.com) flies 4 days a week in the summer (Thurs–Sun) to Oslo direct. In winter there are New York–to-Oslo flights on Saturday, Sunday, and Thursday.

Sweden-bound travelers from the U.S. East Coast usually choose **SAS** (✆ **800/221-2350** in the U.S.; www.flysas.com). Another major competitor is **American Airlines** (✆ **800/433-7300** in the U.S.; www.aa.com), which offers daily flights to Stockholm from Chicago, and excellent connections through Chicago from American's vast North American network. Travelers from Seattle usually fly SAS to Copenhagen, then connect to one of the airline's frequent shuttle flights into Stockholm.

Other airlines fly to gateway European cities and then connect to other flights into Stockholm. **British Airways** (✆ **800/AIRWAYS** [247-9297] in the U.S. and Canada; www.britishairways.com), for example, flies from 24 North American cities to London/Heathrow, and then connects with onward flights to Stockholm. **Delta** (✆ **800/225-2525** in the U.S.; www.delta.com) also flies at frequent intervals to London, from which ongoing flights to Stockholm are available on either SAS or British Airways. Finally, **Icelandair** (✆ **800/223-5500** in the U.S.; www.icelandair.com) has proved to be an excellent choice for travel to Stockholm, thanks to connections through its home port of Reykjavik.

People traveling **from Britain** can fly **SAS** (✆ **0870/6072-77-27** in the U.K.; www.flysas.com) from London's Heathrow to Stockholm on any of five daily nonstop flights. Flying time is about 2½ hours each way. Likewise, SAS flies daily to Stockholm from Manchester, making a brief stop in Copenhagen en route. Flight time from Manchester to Stockholm is about 3½ hours each way.

With more flights to Helsinki from more parts of the world (including Europe, Asia, and North America) than any other airline, **Finnair** (✆ **800/950-5000** in the U.S.; www.finnair.com) is the only airline flying nonstop from North America to Finland (an 8-hr. trip). From New York, Finnair flies to Helsinki every day. The airline also maintains twice-weekly nonstop service to Helsinki throughout the year from Miami.

Finnair (✆ **0870/241-4411** in London; www.finnair.com) also offers more frequent service to Helsinki from several airports in Britain; there are three or four daily nonstop flights from either Heathrow or Stansted airport, and one or two daily flights from Manchester. Flight time from London to Helsinki is 2 hours, 50 minutes; from Manchester, it's 3 hours, 40 minutes.

Several other airlines fly from all parts of the world to gateway European cities and then connect to Helsinki. Foremost among these is **British Airways** (**BA;** ✆ **800/AIRWAYS** [247-9297] in the U.S., or 0870/850-9850 in the U.K.; www.britishairways.com), which offers hundreds of daily flights into the U.K. from all over the world. From London's Heathrow, BA offers one or two daily nonstop flights to Helsinki, depending on the day of the week.

FROM THE U.K. **British Airways** (✆ **800/AIRWAYS** [247-9297], or 0844/493-0787 in the U.K.; www.britishairways.com) offers convenient connections through Heathrow and Gatwick to Copenhagen. The price structure (and discounted prices on hotel packages) sometimes makes a stopover in Britain less expensive than you might have thought. **SAS** offers five daily nonstop flights to Copenhagen from Heathrow (1¾ hr.), two daily nonstops from Glasgow (2 hr.), and three daily nonstops from Manchester (2 hr., 20 min.). Other European airlines with connections through their home countries to Copenhagen include **Icelandair** (✆ **800/223-5500** in the U.S., or 0870/787-4020 in the U.K.; www.icelandair.com); **KLM** (✆ **800/225-2525** in the U.S., or 0870/507-4074 in the U.K.; www.klm.com); and **Lufthansa** (✆ **800/645-3880** in the U.S., or 0870/8377-747 in the U.K.; www.lufthansa.com). Be aware, however, that unless you make all your flight arrangements in North America before you go, you might find some of these flights prohibitively expensive.

For Norway-bound passengers from the U.K., **British Airways** (✆ **0844/493-0787** in the U.K.) operates at least four daily nonstops to Oslo from London. **SAS** (✆ **0870/6072-7727** in the U.K.) runs four daily flights from Heathrow to Oslo. Flying time from London to Oslo on any airline is around 2 hours.

BY TRAIN

Rail Passes for North American Travelers

EURAILPASS The Eurailpass permits unlimited first-class rail travel in any country in western Europe except the British Isles (good in Ireland). It is strongly recommended that you purchase passes before you leave home as not all passes are available in Europe; also, passes purchased in Europe will cost about 20% more. Numerous options are available for travel in France. Passes are available for purchase online (www.eurail.com) and at various offices/agents around the world. Travel agents and railway agents in such cities as New York, Montreal, and Los Angeles sell Eurailpasses. You can purchase them at the North American offices of CIT Travel Service, the French National Railroads, the German Federal Railroads, and the Swiss Federal Railways. See "Where to Buy Rail Passes," below.

The **Eurail Global Pass** allows you unlimited travel in 20 Eurail-affiliated countries. You can travel on any of the days within the validity period, which is available for 15 days, 21 days, 1 month, 2 months, 3 months, and some other possibilities as well. Prices for first-class adult travel are 529€ for 15 days, 683€ for 21 days, 841€

for 1 month, 1,188€ for 2 months, and 1,464€ for 3 months. Children 4 to 11 pay half fare; those 3 and under travel for free.

A **Eurail Global Pass Saver,** also valid for first-class travel in 20 countries, offers a special deal for two or more people traveling together. This pass costs 450€ for 15 days, 581€ for 21 days, 715€ for 1 month, 1,010€ for 2 months, and 1,245€ for 3 months (per person).

A **Eurail Global Youth Pass** for those 12 to 25 allows second-class travel in 18 countries. This pass costs 345€ for 15 days, 445€ for 21 days, 547€ for 1 month, 772€ for 2 months, and 952€ for 3 months.

The **Eurail Select Pass** offers unlimited travel on the national rail networks of any three, four, or five bordering countries out of the 22 Eurail nations linked by train or ship. Tickets allow for 5, 6, 8, 10, or 15 days of rail travel within any 2-month period. A sample fare: For 5 days in 2 months you pay 334€ for three countries. **Eurail Select Pass Youth** for travelers 25 and under allow second-class travel within the same guidelines as Eurail Select Pass, with fees starting at 218€. **Eurail Select Pass Saver** offers discounts for two or more people traveling together, first-class travel within the same guidelines as Eurail Select Pass, with fees starting at 284€ per person.

WHERE TO BUY RAIL PASSES Travel agents in all towns and railway agents in major North American cities sell all these tickets, but the biggest supplier is **Rail Europe** (✆ **877/272-RAIL** [272-7245]; www.raileurope.com), which can also give you informational brochures.

Many different rail passes are available in the United Kingdom for travel in Britain and continental Europe. Stop in at the **International Rail Centre,** Victoria Station, London SWIV 1JY (✆ **0870/5848-848** in the U.K.). Some of the most popular passes, including Inter-Rail and Euro Youth, are offered only to travelers under 26 years of age; these allow unlimited second-class travel through most European countries.

SCANRAIL PASS If your visit to Europe will be primarily in Scandinavia, the ScanRail pass may be better and cheaper than the Eurailpass. This pass allows its owner a designated number of days of free rail travel within a larger time block. (Presumably, this allows for days devoted to sightseeing scattered among days of rail transfers btw. cities or sites of interest.) You can choose a total of any 5 days of unlimited rail travel during a 15-day period, 10 days of rail travel within a 1-month period, or 1 month of unlimited rail travel. The pass, which is valid on all lines of the state railways of Denmark, Finland, Norway, and Sweden, offers discounts or free travel on some (but not all) of the region's ferry lines as well. The pass can be purchased only in North America. It's available from any office of **Rail Europe** (✆ **800/848-7245**) or **ScanAm World Tours,** 108 N. Main St., Cranbury, NJ 08512 (✆ **800/545-2204;** www.scandinaviantravel.com). You must call or use the reservation request form on their website to obtain pricing information.

Rail Passes for British Travelers

If you plan to do a lot of exploring, you may prefer one of the three rail passes designed for unlimited train travel within a designated region during a predetermined number of days. These passes are sold in Britain and several other European countries.

An **InterRail Pass** is available to passengers of any nationality, with some restrictions—they must be under age 26 and able to prove residency in a European or North African country (Morocco, Algeria, and Tunisia) for at least 6 months before buying the pass. It allows unlimited travel through Europe, except Albania and the republics of the former Soviet Union. Prices are complicated and vary depending on the countries you want to include. For pricing purposes, Europe is divided into eight zones; the cost depends on the number of zones you include. For ages 25 and under, the most expensive option (599€) allows 1 month of unlimited travel in all eight zones and is known to the staff as a "global." The least expensive option (249€) allows 5 days of travel within 10 days.

Passengers age 26 and older can buy an **InterRail 26-Plus Pass.** The cost varies from 249€ to 599€ for 16 days to 599€ to 899€ for 1 month. Passengers must meet the same residency requirements that apply to the InterRail Pass (described above).

For information on buying individual rail tickets or any of the just-mentioned passes, contact **National Rail Inquiries,** Victoria Station, London (✆ **0845/748-4950**). Tickets and passes also are available at any of the larger railway stations, as well as selected travel agencies throughout Britain and the rest of Europe.

Getting to Denmark

BY CAR

You can easily drive to Denmark from Germany. Many people drive to Jutland from Hamburg, Bremerhaven, and Lübeck. A bridge links Jutland and the central island of Funen. In 1998 a bridge opened that goes across the Great Belt from Funen to the island of Zealand, site of the city of Copenhagen. The bridge lies near Nyborg, Denmark. Once in West Zealand, you'll still have to drive east across the island to Copenhagen.

Car-ferry service to Denmark from the United Kingdom generally leaves passengers at Esbjerg, where they must cross from Jutland to Copenhagen. From Germany, it's possible to take a car ferry from Travemünde, northeast of Lübeck, which will deposit you at Gedser, Denmark. From here, connect with the E-55, an express highway north to Copenhagen.

BY TRAIN

If you're in Europe, it's easy to get to Denmark by train. Copenhagen is the main rail hub between Scandinavia and the rest of Europe. For example, the London-Copenhagen train—through Ostende, Belgium, or Hook, Holland—leaves four times daily and takes 22 hours. About 10 daily express trains run from Hamburg to Copenhagen (5½ hr.). There are also intercity trains on the Merkur route from Karlsruhe, Germany, making calls at Cologne, Hamburg, and Copenhagen. The Berlin-Ostbahnhof-Copenhagen train (8½ hr.) connects with eastern European trains. Two daily express trains make this run.

Thousands of trains run from Britain to the Continent, and at least some of them go directly across or under the Channel, through France or Belgium and Germany into Denmark. For example, a train leaves London's Victoria Station daily at 9am and arrives in Copenhagen the next day at 8:25am. Another train leaves London's Victoria Station at 8:45pm and arrives in Copenhagen the next day at 8:20pm. Both go through Dover-Ostende, or with a connection at Brussels. Once you're in Copenhagen, you can make rail connections to Norway, Finland, and Sweden. Because of the time and distances involved, many passengers rent a couchette (sleeping berth), which costs around £20 per person. Designed like padded benches stacked bunk style, they're usually clustered six to a compartment.

If you plan to travel extensively on European and/or British railroads, it would be worthwhile for you to get a copy of the latest edition of the Thomas Cook *European Rail Timetable*. It's available online at www.thomascookpublishing.com.

EURAIL DENMARK PASS For those who plan to travel only in Denmark, a series of cost-cutting passes are offered. The major one is the **Eurail Denmark Pass,** offering both first- and second-class unlimited travel on Denmark's national rail network. For travel any 3 or 7 days within a 1-month period, the 3-day pass costs $99 to $179 for adults (first and second class), or $50 to $75 for children ages 4 to 11. The 7-day pass goes for $155 to $279 for adults or $75 to $140 for children.

Two or more passengers traveling together can take advantage of the **Eurail Denmark Saverpass,** offering unlimited travel in first and second class. On this deal, you get 3 days of travel in 1 month for $99 to $155 for adults or $50 to $75 for children 4 to 11. For 7 days in 1 month, the cost ranges from $155 to $239 for adults or $75 to $120 for children.

A better deal for passengers 25 and under is the **Eurail Denmark Youthpass,** costing $89 for 3 days in 1 month or $139 for 7 days.

BY SHIP & FERRY

It's easy to travel by water from several ports to Denmark. Liners carrying cars and passengers operate from England, Germany, Poland, Norway, and Sweden. Check with your travel agent about these cruises.

FROM ENGLAND **DFDS Seaways** (✆ **45/33-42-30-10;** www.dfdsseaways.com) runs vessels year-round between Harwich, England, and Esbjerg in West Jutland. The crossing takes 16 to 20 hours. The same line also sails from Newcastle upon Tyne to Esbjerg, but only in the summer, as part of a 22-hour passage. Overnight cabins and space for cars are available on both routes.

FROM NORWAY & SWEDEN **Hurtigruten** (✆ **866/552-0371;** www.hurtigruten.us) operates vessels from Oslo to Hirtshals in North Jutland.

Stena Line runs popular sea links from Oslo to Frederikshavn, North Jutland (11½ hr.), and from Gothenburg, Sweden, to Frederikshavn (3 hr.). For information, schedules, and fares, contact **Stena Line UK, Ltd.** (✆ **08447/70-70-70;** www.stenaline.co.uk). For 24-hour updates on sailing, call ✆ **08705/755-755.**

Getting to Norway

BY CAR

If you're driving from the Continent, you must go through Sweden. From **Copenhagen,** take the E-47/55 express highway north to Helsingør and catch the car ferry to Helsingborg, Sweden. From there, the E-6 runs to Oslo. From **Stockholm,** drive across Sweden on E-18 to Oslo.

BY TRAIN

Copenhagen is the main rail hub for service between Scandinavia and the rest of Europe. There are three daily trains from Copenhagen to Oslo. All connect with the Danish ferries operating to Norway through either Helsingør or Hirtshals.

Most rail traffic from Sweden into Norway follows the main corridors between Stockholm and Oslo and between Gothenburg and Oslo.

If you plan to travel a great deal on Norwegian railroads, it's worth securing a copy of the Thomas Cook *European Rail Timetable.* It's available online at www.thomascookpublishing.com.

Thousands of trains run from Britain to the Continent, and at least some of them go directly across or under the Channel, through France or Belgium and Germany into Denmark, where connections can be made to Norway. For example, a train leaves

London's Victoria Station daily at 9am and arrives in Copenhagen the next day at 8:25am. Another train leaves London's Victoria Station at 8:45pm and arrives in Copenhagen the next day at 8:20pm. Both go through Dover-Ostende, or with a connection at Brussels. Once you're in Copenhagen, you can make rail connections to Oslo. Because of the time and distances involved, many passengers rent a couchette (sleeping berth). Designed like padded benches stacked bunk style, they're usually clustered six to a compartment.

BY SHIP & FERRY

FROM DENMARK The trip from Frederikshavn at the northern port of Jutland in Denmark to Oslo takes 11 hours. Call **Stena Line** (© **96-20-02-00;** www.stenaline.com) for general reservations.

FROM SWEDEN From Strømstad, Sweden, in the summer the daily crossing to Sandefjord, Norway, takes 2½ hours. Bookings can be made through **Color Line,** Tollbugata 5, N-3210 Sandefjord (© **47-22-94-42-00;** www.colorline.com).

FROM ENGLAND **SeaEurope Holidays,** 6801 Lake Worth Rd., Ste. 107, Lake Worth, FL 33467 (© **800/533-3755;** www.seaeurope.com), is a U.S.-based company that will arrange a variety of seagoing options for you, all before you land in mainland Europe. For example, if you'd like arrangements made for you to sail from Newcastle in England to Bergen in Norway, these trips can be arranged.

Getting to Sweden

BY CAR

FROM GERMANY You can drive to the northern German port of Travemünde and catch the 7½-hour ferry (www.directferries.co.uk) to the Swedish port of Trelleborg, a short drive south of Malmö. This route saves many hours by avoiding transit through Denmark. If you want to visit Denmark before Sweden, you can take the 3-hour car ferry from Travemünde to Gedser in southern Denmark. From Gedser, the E-64 and the E-4 express highways head north to Copenhagen. After a visit here, you can take the Øresund Bridge from Copenhagen to Malmö.

FROM NORWAY From Oslo, E-18 goes east through Karlstad all the way to Stockholm. This is a long but scenic drive.

BY TRAIN

Copenhagen is the main rail hub between the other Scandinavian countries and the rest of Europe. Seven daily trains run between Copenhagen and Stockholm, six between Copenhagen and Gothenburg. All connect with the Danish ferries that operate to Sweden via Helsingør or Frederikshavn.

At least three trains a day depart from Oslo to Stockholm (travel time: about 6½ hr.). One of the trains leaves Oslo around 11pm. Three trains run from Oslo to Gothenburg daily (travel time: about 4 hr.).

BY SHIP & FERRY

FROM DENMARK Ferries ply the waters for the brief run from Helsingør, a short drive north of Copenhagen, and Helsingborg, Sweden, just across the narrow channel that separates the countries. The 25-minute trip on a conventional ferry (not a catamaran) runs at 10- to 40-minute intervals, 24 hours a day. Operated by **Scandlines** (© **33/15-15-15** in Copenhagen; www.scandlines.dk), it's one of the most popular ferry routes in Europe. Round-trip passage costs $118 for a car with up to nine passengers; the ticket is valid for up to 12 months.

FROM ENGLAND Two English ports, Harwich (year-round) and Newcastle upon Tyne (summer only), offer ferry service to Sweden. Harwich to Gothenburg takes 23 to 25 hours, Newcastle to Gothenburg 27 hours. Boats on both routes offer overnight accommodations and the option of transporting cars. Prices are lower for passengers who book in advance through the company's U.S. agent. For details, call **Sea Europe Holidays,** 6801 Lake Worth Rd., Ste. 107, Lake Worth, FL 33467 (✆ **800/533-3755** in the U.S.; www.seaeurope.com).

FROM GERMANY **Stena Line Ferries** (✆ **031/85-80-00;** www.stenaline.com) sails daily from Kiel to Gothenburg. The trip takes 14 hours and costs from 139€ to 404€ for a one-way passage.

Getting to Finland

BY CAR

FROM WESTERN SCANDINAVIA The quickest routes to Finland are the E-3 or E-4 to Stockholm, and the year-round 14- to 16-hour ferry from there to Helsinki.

FROM GERMANY From Travemünde there's a year-round high-speed car ferry that takes 22 hours to reach Helsinki.

FROM DENMARK Take the car ferry from Helsingør to Helsingborg in Sweden or the Øresund Bridge from Copenhagen to Malmö, and then drive to Stockholm and catch the car ferry to Helsinki or Turku.

BY TRAIN

A rail and ferryboat link between London and Helsinki goes via Ostende (Belgium), Cologne, Hamburg, and Stockholm. If you've taken the ferry from Stockholm and are arriving at Turku, on the west coast of Finland, you can catch one of the seven daily trains (including the high-speed Pendolino) that take you across southern Finland to Helsinki. The trip takes 2¼ hours. Rail connections are also possible from London to Hook of Holland (the Netherlands), Bremen, Hamburg, and Stockholm. However, each of these itineraries takes about 50 hours, plus a 2-hour stopover in Stockholm. It's possible to reserve sleepers and couchettes, but do so as far in advance as possible. Helsinki is also linked by rail to the major cities of Finland.

BY BUS

Although there are international bus links to Finland, this is the least convenient mode of transportation. One of the most popular is a bus connection from Stockholm—it includes a sea crossing to Turku, with continuing land service to Helsinki.

It's also possible to take coaches from Gothenburg going cross-country to Stockholm and to the ferry dock beyond, with land travel resuming after Turku on the same bus all the way to Helsinki.

For information about international bus connections and reservations, contact **Oy Matkahuolto Ab,** Simonkatu 3, FIN-00101 Helsinki (✆ **09/682-701;** www.matkahuolto.fi).

BY SHIP & FERRY

FROM SWEDEN Frequent ferries run between Sweden and Finland, especially between Stockholm and Helsinki. Service is on either the Viking or Silja Line. Each company also operates a twice-daily service from Stockholm to Turku on Finland's west coast.

FROM GERMANY The Silja Line also maintains regular passenger service from June 5 to September 15 between Travemünde (Germany) and Helsinki. You can get

By Package, the Easiest Way to Go

For travelers who feel more comfortable if everything is prearranged—hotels, transportation, sightseeing excursions, luggage handling, tips, taxes, and even meals—a package tour is the obvious choice, and it may even help save money. A reliable tour operator is Scantours, Inc., 3439 Wade St., Los Angeles, CA 90006 (✆ 800/223-7226 or 310/636-4656; www.scantours.com).

information about the **Silja Line** at Mannerheimintie 2, FIN-00101 Helsinki (✆ **8600/15-700;** www.tallinksilja.com). Information on the **Viking Line** is available at Mannerheimintie 14, FIN-00101 Helsinki (✆ **09/123-51;** www.vikingline.fi).

Getting Around Scandinavia

The best way to get around Scandinavia is by private car on the excellent road network. In lieu of that, nearly all major towns are serviced by trains, except certain offshore islands, which can be reached only by ferryboat. If you're traveling extensively in Europe, special European passes are also available.

BY PLANE

SAS'S "VISIT SCANDINAVIA" FARE The vast distances encourage air travel between Scandinavia's far-flung points. One of the most worthwhile promotions is SAS's **Visit Scandinavia Pass.** Available only to travelers who fly SAS across the Atlantic, it includes up to six coupons, each of which is valid for any SAS flight within or between Denmark, Norway, and Sweden. Each coupon costs $60, $80, and $100, depending on the route. The pass is especially valuable if you plan to travel to the far northern frontiers of Sweden or Norway; in that case, the savings over the price of a regular economy-class ticket can be substantial. For information on buying the pass, call **SAS** (✆ **800/221-2350;** www.flysas.com).

Getting Around Denmark

BY PLANE

For those in a hurry, **SAS** (✆ **32-32-00-00** in Denmark) operates daily service between Copenhagen and points on Jutland's mainland. From Copenhagen it takes about 40 minutes to fly to Aalborg, 35 minutes to Århus, and 30 minutes to Odense.

Fares to other Danish cities are sometimes included in a transatlantic ticket at no extra charge, as long as the additional cities are specified when the ticket is written.

BY TRAIN

Flat, low-lying Denmark, with its hundreds of bridges and absence of mountains, has a large network of railway lines that connect virtually every hamlet with the largest city, Copenhagen. For **information, schedules, and fares** anywhere in Denmark, call ✆ **70-13-14-15.** Waiting times for a live person on this telephone line range from long to very long. Alternatively, you can check the Danish National Railways website, **www.dsb.dk**, for schedules and prices, and to reserve seats.

A word you're likely to see and hear frequently is *Lyntog* (Express Trains), which are the fastest trains presently operational in Denmark. Be warned in advance that the most crowded times on Danish trains are Fridays, Sundays, and national holidays, so plan your reservations accordingly.

On any train in Denmark, children between the ages of 4 and 15 are charged half-price if they're accompanied by an adult, and up to two children 3 and under can travel free with an adult on any train in Denmark. Seniors 65 or older receive a discount of 20% for travel on Fridays, Sundays, and holidays, and a discount of 45% every other day of the week. No identification is needed when you buy your ticket, but the conductor who checks your ticket might ask for proof of age.

The Danish government offers dozens of discounts on the country's rail networks—depending on the type of traveler, days or hours traveled, and destination. Because discounts change often, it's best to ask for a discount based on your age and the number of days (or hours) you intend to travel.

BY BUS

By far the best way to visit rural Denmark is by car, but if you want or need to travel by bus, be aware that you'll probably get your bus at the railway station. (In much of Scandinavia, buses take passengers to destinations not served by the train; therefore, the bus route often originates at the railway station.) The arrival of trains and departure of buses are usually closely timed.

For seniors 65 and over, round-trip bus tickets are sometimes offered at one-way prices (excluding Sat, Sun, and peak travel periods around Christmas and Easter). Most discounts are granted only to seniors who are traveling beyond the city limits of their point of origin.

BY CAR

RENTALS Avis, Budget, and Hertz offer well-serviced, well-maintained fleets of cars. You may have to reserve and pay for your rental car in advance (usually 2 weeks, but occasionally as little as 48 hr.) to get the lowest rates. Unfortunately, if your trip is canceled or your arrival date changes, you might have to fill out a lot of forms for a refund. All three companies may charge slightly higher rates to clients who reserve less than 48 hours in advance and pay at pickup. The highest rates are charged to walk-in customers who arrange their rentals after they arrive in Denmark. ***Note:*** If at all possible you should reserve a car before you leave North America.

The Danish government imposes a whopping **25% tax on all car rentals.** Agencies that encourage prepaid rates almost never collect this tax in advance—instead, it's imposed as part of a separate transaction when you pick up the car. Furthermore, any car retrieved at a Danish airport is subject to a one-time supplemental tax of 255DKK, so you might prefer to pick up your car at a downtown location. Membership in certain travel clubs or organizations (such as AAA or AARP) might qualify you for a modest discount.

Avis (✆ **800/331-1212** in the U.S. and Canada; www.avis.com) maintains four offices in Copenhagen: two at the arrivals hall of the airport, one at Landgreven 10 (✆ **70-24-77-64**), and another at Kampmannsgade 1 (✆ **70-24-77-07**).

Budget (✆ **800/527-0700** in the U.S.; ✆ **800/472-3325** in Canada; www.budget.com) has two rental locations in Copenhagen. The larger branch is at the Copenhagen airport (✆ **35-53-39-00**), and the other office is at Vesterfarimagsgade 7 (✆ **33-55-70-00**).

Hertz (✆ **800/654-3001** in the U.S. and Canada; www.hertz.com) has two offices in Copenhagen, one at the airport (✆ **33-17-90-20**) and the other at Ved Vesterport 3 (✆ **33-17-90-20**).

Also consider using a small company. **Kemwel** (✆ **800/678-0678** in the U.S.; www.kemwel.com) is the North American representative for Van Wijk and Hertz in

Denmark. It may be able to offer attractive rental prices to North Americans who pay in full at least 10 days before their departure. Seniors and members of AAA get a 5% discount.

DRIVING RULES A valid driver's license from your home country is required. If you are in your own car, you need a certificate of registration and national plates. This is especially important for the people of Britain, who often drive to Denmark. Each rental agency should provide you with a triangular hazard warning sign. It's Danish law that you have this signal. Seat belts are required in both the front and the rear of the vehicle, and you must drive with low beams on at all times, even in the bright sunlight. Talking on a cellphone is illegal. Be on the lookout for bicycle riders, who have the right of way if they are heading straight and an auto is making a turn.

GASOLINE (PETROL) Stations are plentiful throughout the land, and prices—subject to almost daily fluctuations—are extremely high. Most stations take credit cards and are self-service. In general, stations open daily at 6 or 7 in the morning, usually shutting down at 9pm (later in more congested areas).

Getting Around Norway

BY PLANE

Norway has excellent domestic air service. In addition to SAS, an independent airway, **Wideroe Flyveselskap,** provides quick and convenient ways to get around a large country with many hard-to-reach areas. For more information, call ✆ **47-75-11-11-11** or visit www.wideroe.no.

In a partnership with SAS, **Braathens** (✆ **47-915-05400;** www.sas.no) carries more passengers on domestic routes than any other airline in Norway. It has regularly scheduled flights inside Norway, linking all major Norwegian cities as well as more remote places not covered by other airlines. It also offers frequent flights along the coast, from Oslo to Tromsø and to Longyearbyen on the island of Spitsbergen.

BY TRAIN

Norway's network of electric and diesel-electric trains runs as far as Bodø, 100km (62 miles) north of the Arctic Circle. (Beyond that, visitors must take a coastal steamer, plane, or bus to Tromsø and the North Cape.) Upgraded express trains (the fastest in the country) crisscross the mountainous terrain between Oslo, Stavanger, Bergen, and Trondheim. For information and reservations, log on to the Norwegian State Railways (NSB) (✆ **81-50-08-88**) at www.nsb.no.

The most popular and most scenic run covers the 483km (299 miles) between Oslo and Bergen. Visitors with limited time often choose this route for its fabled mountains, gorges, white-water rivers, and fjords. The trains make frequent stops for passengers to enjoy breathtaking views.

Second-class travel on Norwegian trains is recommended. In fact, second class in Norway is as good as or superior to first-class travel anywhere else in Europe, with reclining seats and lots of unexpected comforts. Of course, first-class train travel in Norway is better, though not necessarily *that* much better, than second class. For those who want the added comforts and can afford it, first class is the way to go.

The one-way fare from Oslo to Bergen is NOK775, plus a mandatory seat reservation of NOK40. Another popular run, from Oslo to Trondheim, costs NOK852 one-way in second class.

One of the country's obviously scenic trips, from Bergen to Bodø, is not possible by train because of the terrain. Trains to Bodø leave from Oslo. Express trains are called *Expresstog,* and you have to read the fine print of a railway schedule to figure out whether an Expresstog is much faster than a conventional train.

On express and other major trains, you must reserve seats at the train's starting station. Sleepers are priced according to the number of berths in each compartment. Children 4 to 15 years of age and seniors are granted reduced fares.

There are special compartments for persons with disabilities on most medium- and long-distance trains. People in wheelchairs and others with physical disabilities, and their companions, may use the compartments. Some long-distance trains offer special playrooms ("Kiddie-Wagons") for children, complete with toys, games, and books.

EURAIL NORWAY PASS A restricted rail pass applicable only to the state railway lines, the Eurail Norway Pass is available for 3 to 8 days of unlimited second-class rail travel in 1 month. It's suitable for anyone who wants to cover the long distances that separate Norwegian cities. The pass is available in North America through **Rail Europe** (© **800/848-7245;** www.raileurope.com). For 3 days of travel in 1 month, the cost is $263; for 4 days, $285; for 5 days, $315; for 6 days, $358; for 8 days, $399. Children 4 to 15 years of age pay half the adult fare, and those 3 and under ride free. Discount passes are available for youth 16 to 25 (Norway Youth Pass) and for travelers over 60 (Norway Senior Pass).

MINIPRIS TICKETS NSB's regional trains offer unlimited travel for NOK199 to NOK299. The offer is valid for a limited number of seats. You can purchase the ticket by logging on to www.nsb.no. Tickets are often sold out, so make reservations as soon as possible. At this price, tickets are not refundable and a change of reservation is not possible. A supplement of NOK75 will grant you access to the NSB Komfort Class section.

BY BUS

Where the train or coastal steamer stops, passengers can usually continue on a scenic bus ride. Norway's bus system is excellent, linking remote villages along the fjords. Numerous all-inclusive motorcoach tours, often combined with steamer travel, leave from Bergen and Oslo in the summer. The train ends in Bodø; from there you can get a bus to Fauske (63km/39 miles east). From Fauske, the Polar Express bus spans the entire distance along the Arctic Highway, through Finnmark (Lapland) to Kirkenes near the Russian border and back. The segment from Alta to Kirkenes is open only from June to October, but there's year-round service from Fauske to Alta. Passengers are guaranteed hotel accommodations along the way.

Buses have air-conditioning, toilets, adjustable seats, reading lights, and a telephone. Reservations are not accepted on most buses, and payment is made to the driver onboard. Fares depend on the distance traveled. Children 3 and under travel free, and children 4 to 16 and seniors pay half-price. For the Oslo-Sweden-Hammerfest Express 2000, a 30-hour trip, reservations must be made in advance.

For more information about bus travel in Norway, contact **Norway Buss Ekspress AS,** Karl Johans Gate (© **81-54-44-44;** www.nor-way.no), in Oslo, or **Passage Tours of Scandinavia** (© **800/548-5960** in the U.S.).

BY CAR & FERRY

Dazzling scenery awaits you at nearly every turn if you drive through Norway. Some roads are less than perfect (dirt or gravel is frequent), but all are passable (you'll even be able to drive to the North Cape). Most mountain roads are open by May 1; the so-called motoring season lasts from mid-May to the end of September. In western

Norway, hairpin curves are common, but if you're willing to settle for doing less than 240km (149 miles) a day, you needn't worry. The easiest and most convenient touring territory is in and around Oslo and south to Stavanger.

Bringing a car into Norway is relatively uncomplicated. If you own the car you're driving, you must present your national driver's license, car registration, and proof that the car is insured. (This proof usually takes the form of a document known as a Green Card, which Customs agents will refer to specifically.) If you've rented a car in another country and want to drive it into Norway, be sure to verify at the time of rental that the registration and insurance documents are in order—they probably will be. Regardless of whether you own or rent the car you're about to drive into Norway, don't assume that your private North American insurance policy will automatically apply. Chances are good that it will, but in the event of an accident, you may have to cope with a burdensome amount of paperwork.

If you're driving through any of Norway's coastal areas, you'll probably have to traverse one or many of the country's famous fjords. Although more and more bridges are being built, Norway's network of privately run ferries is essential for transporting cars across hundreds of fjords and estuaries. Motorists should ask the tourist bureau for the free map *Norway by Car* and a timetable outlining the country's dozens of car-ferry services. The cost for cars and passengers is low.

RENTALS Avis, Budget, and Hertz offer well-serviced, well-maintained fleets of rental cars in Norway. Prices and terms tend to be more favorable for those who reserve vehicles from home before their departure and who present evidence of membership in such organizations as AA (Automobile Association), AAA (American Automobile Association), or AARP.

The prices quoted here include the 23% government tax. The major U.S.-based car rental firms are represented in Norway, including **Budget** (© **800/527-0700** in the U.S. and Canada; www.budget.com); **Hertz** (© **800/654-3001** in the U.S.; www.hertz.com); and **Avis** (© **800/331-1212** in the U.S.; www.avis.com). Despite pressure from the telephone sales representative, it pays to ask questions and shop around before you commit to a prepaid reservation. Each company maintains an office at the Oslo airport, in the center of Oslo, and at airports and city centers elsewhere around the country.

Note: Remember that prices and the relative merits of each company can and will change during the lifetime of this edition, depending on promotions and other factors.

Kemwel (© **877/820-0668;** www.kemwel.com) monitors the availability of rental cars in markets across Europe, including Norway. Originally established in 1908 and now operating in close conjunction with its affiliated company, **Auto Europe** (© **888/223-5555;** www.autoeurope.com), it offers convenient and prepaid access to thousands of cars, from a variety of reputable car-rental outfits throughout Europe; sometimes you'll find more favorable rates than those you might have gotten by contacting those companies directly.

DRIVING RULES Driving is on the right, and the law requires that you keep your headlights on at all times. Every passenger, including infants, must wear seat belts. Children 5 and under must ride in the back. A driver must yield to cars approaching from the right. On most major highways, the maximum speed limit is 90 kmph (55 mph). On secondary routes, the speed limit ranges from 70 kmph (43 mph) to 80 kmph (50 mph). Do not drink and drive. Norway has perhaps the strictest laws in Europe about drinking and driving, and there are roadside checks. Speeding is also severely punished, and most highways are monitored by radar and cameras.

Winter Motoring in Norway

If you're going to drive in Norway in winter, you must be prepared for the conditions. Most of the main roads are kept open by snowplows year-round, but the road surface will often be hard-packed snow and ice. Journey times will be much longer than in summer, 50km (31 miles) per hour is a typical average, and in bad weather there can be long delays over mountain passes. Most Norwegians use winter tires with metal studs, which come with all rental cars. Temperatures as low as 25°F (–4°C) are common. A good ice scraper and snow brush are essential, as is a diesel engine.

GASOLINE (PETROL) There are plenty of gas stations in Norway, and unleaded gasoline *(blyfri bensin)* and diesel fuel are sold from self-service pumps. Those pumps are labeled *kort* and are open day and night. Most of them accept regular bank credit cards or else oil company credit cards. In the countryside of Norway, hours gas stations operate vary widely.

BY CRUISE SHIP

Norway's fjords and mountain vistas are among the most spectacular panoramas in the world. Many ship owners and cruise lines offer excursions along the Norwegian coast.

One of the most prominent lines is **Cunard** (✆ **800/7CUNARD** [728-6273] in the U.S. and Canada; www.cunard.com; or ✆ 0845-071-0300; www.cunard.co.uk in the U.K.).

Seven-day cruises are offered on the new Cunard flagship, *Queen Mary* 2. This vessel re-creates the grandeur of those old queen liners, *Queen Mary* and *Queen Elizabeth,* but on a larger, more modern scale. The 150,000-ton ship carries a total of 2,620 passengers.

Departing from Southampton, England, the ship calls at Oslo and Bergen and cruises the North Sea. En route it also stops at the most frequently visited fjords, including the Eidfjord. Prices for the 6-day cruise include round-trip airfare to London on British Airways from 79 gateway cities throughout the world.

In its tour of Baltic capitals, **Norwegian Cruise Line** (✆ **866/234-7350;** ncl.com) stops at Helsinki, Stockholm, and Copenhagen, but, ironically, doesn't go as far as Norway itself.

Getting Around Sweden

BY PLANE

For transatlantic flights coming from North America, Stockholm is Sweden's major gateway for Scandinavia's best-known airline, **SAS** (Scandinavian Airlines System). For flights arriving from other parts of Europe, the airport at Gothenburg supplements Stockholm's airport by funneling traffic into the Swedish heartland. In the mid-1990s, SAS acquired **LIN Airlines (Linjeflyg);** thus, it now has access to small and medium-size airports throughout Sweden, including such remote but scenic outposts as Kiruna in Swedish Lapland. Among the larger Swedish cities serviced by SAS are Malmö, capital of Sweden's château country; Karlstad, center of the verdant and folklore-rich district of Värmland; and Kalmar, a good base for exploring the glassworks district.

During the summer, SAS offers a number of promotional "minifares," which enable one to travel round-trip between two destinations for just slightly more than the price of a conventional one-way ticket on the same route. Children 11 and under travel free during the summer, and up to two children 12 to 17 can travel with a parent at significantly reduced rates. Airfares tend to be most reduced during July, with promotions almost as attractive during most of June and August. A minimum 3-night stopover at the destination is required for these minifares, and it must include a Friday or a Saturday night. When buying your tickets, always ask the airline or travel agency about special promotions and corresponding restrictions.

Those 25 and under can take advantage of SAS's special **standby fares,** and seniors 66 and over can apply for additional discounts, depending on the destination.

BY TRAIN

The Swedish word for train is *tåg,* and the national system is the Statens Järnvägar, the Swedish State Railways.

Swedish trains follow tight schedules. Trains leave Malmö, Helsingborg, and Gothenburg for Stockholm every hour throughout the day, Monday through Friday. Trains depart every hour, or every other hour, to and from most big Swedish towns. On *expresståg* runs, seats must be reserved.

Children 11 and under travel free when accompanied by an adult, and those up to age 18 are eligible for discounts.

BY BUS

Rail lines cover only some of Sweden's vast distances. Where the train tracks end, buses usually serve as the link to remote villages. Buses usually are equipped with toilets, adjustable seats, reading lights, and a telephone. Fares depend on the distance traveled; for example, the one-way fare for the 525km (326-mile) trip from Stockholm to Göteborg is 330SEK to 340SEK. **Swebus** (✆ **0771/218-218;** www.swebus.se), the country's largest bus company, provides information at the bus or railway stations in most cities. For travelers who don't buy a special rail pass (such as Eurail or ScanRail), bus travel can sometimes be cheaper than traveling the same distances by rail. It's a lot less convenient, however—except in the far north, where there isn't any alternative.

EURAIL SWEDEN PASS If you're traveling just in Sweden, this pass allows you unlimited travel on the national rail system of Sweden from 3 to 8 days in 1 month. You have a choice of first- or second-class travel, with discounts for youths and seniors. Prices are as follows: first class for adults $329 to $499; second class for adults $255 to $385; youth $189 to $289.

BY FERRY

Considering that Sweden has some 100,000 lakes and one of the world's longest coastlines, ferries play a surprisingly small part in its transportation network.

After the car-ferry crossings from northern Germany and Denmark, the most popular route is from the mainland to the island of Gotland, in the Baltic. Service is available from Oskarshamn and Nynäshamn (call ✆ **0771/22-33-00,** Destination Gotland, for more information). The famous "white boats" of the Waxholm Steamship Company (✆ **08/679-58-30;** www.waxholmsbolaget.se) also serve many destinations in the Stockholm archipelago.

BY CAR

Sweden maintains an excellent network of roads and highways, particularly in the southern provinces and in the central lake district. Major highways in the far north are kept clear of snow by heavy equipment that's in place virtually year-round. If you rent a car at any bona fide rental agency, you'll be given the appropriate legal documents, including proof of adequate insurance (in the form of a Green Card) as specified by your car-rental agreement. Current driver's licenses from Canada, the United Kingdom, New Zealand, Australia, and the United States are acceptable in Sweden.

RENTALS The major U.S.-based car-rental firms are represented throughout Sweden, both at airports and in urban centers. The companies' rates are aggressively competitive, although promotional sales will favor one company over the others from time to time. Prior to your departure from North America, it will be advantageous to phone around to find the lowest available rates. Membership in AAA or another auto club may enable you to get a moderate discount. Be aware that you may avoid a supplemental airport tax by picking up your car at a central location rather than at the airport.

Avis (✆ **800/331-1212;** www.avis.com) offers a wide variety of cars and has offices in all major cities in Sweden.

Hertz (✆ **800/654-3131;** www.hertz.com) has offices located in all major cities, as well as major airports.

One auto supplier that might not automatically come to mind is **Kemwel** (✆ **800/678-0678;** www.kemwel.com), a broker that accumulates into one database the availability of rental cars in markets across Europe, including Sweden. Originally established in 1908, and now operating in close conjunction with its sister company, **Auto Europe** (✆ **800/223-5555;** www.autoeurope.com), it offers convenient and prepaid access to thousands of cars from a variety of reputable car-rental outfits throughout Europe, sometimes at rates a bit more favorable than those you might have gotten if you had gone through the hassle of contacting those companies directly. Car rentals are prereserved and prepaid, in dollars, prior to your departure for Europe, thereby avoiding the confusion about unfavorable currency conversions and government tax add-ons that you might have discovered after your return home. You're given the option at the time of your booking whether you want to include collision damage and other forms of insurance. Most car rentals can be picked up either at the airport or in the downtown offices of cities throughout Sweden, and there's usually no penalty for one-way rentals.

DRIVING RULES It's been a long time since Swedish drivers drove on the left. Today they must drive on the right and use seat belts, and even passengers in the rear must strap in. Drivers are required to have on their low-beam headlights during the day even if the sun is shining. Signs indicate five basic speed limits depending on the area in which you're driving. These range from 30 kmph (19 mph) to 110 kmph (68 mph) on long stretches of major state highways that carry an "E" in their route numbers.

GASOLINE (PETROL) Prices, subject to change almost daily, never go down. They are, in effect, among the highest in the world. Gasoline stations are self-service. Know which pump you're using: those marked SEDEL take bills of 20 or 100 *kronor,* those marked KASSA are paid for at the on-site cashier, and those labeled KONTO are for motorists paying with a credit card. Lead-free gasoline is available at nearly all gas stations in Sweden.

Getting Around Finland

BY PLANE

Finnair (✆ **800/950-5000** in the U.S.; www.finnair.com), along with its domestic subsidiaries, Karair and Finnaviation, offers reasonably priced air transportation to virtually every settlement of any size in Finland, including some that are not accessible by any other means. Its routes cover the length and breadth of the country with at least 100 flights a day.

If you plan to travel extensively throughout Scandinavia or into the Baltic countries, then consider the **Finnair Nordic Air Pass.** It is available only from May 1 to September 30, and you must have a transatlantic plane ticket to be eligible. Call **Finnair** (© **800/950-5000**) for more information.

BY TRAIN

Finland has its own **Finnrailpass** for use on the country's elaborate network of railroads. It's a flexipass, entitling the holder to unlimited travel for any 3, 5, or 10 days within a 1-month period on all passenger trains of the VR Ltd. Finnish Railways. Prices are as follows: 195€ for 3 days within 1 month in first class or 131€ in second class; 260€ for 5 days within 1 month in first class or 175€ in second class; and 353€ for 10 days within 1 month in first class or 237€ in second class. Children pay 50% of the adult fare. Travelers over 65 and children 6 to 16 are charged half the full fare (it may be necessary to show proof of age); children 5 and under ride free.

Second-class trains in Finland are comparable to first-class trains in many other countries. The Finnrailpass should be purchased before you enter Finland; sometimes it's available at border stations at the frontier.

Because Finnish trains tend to be crowded, you should reserve a seat in advance—in fact, seat reservations are obligatory on all express trains marked "IC" or "EP" on the timetable.

For more information, contact **VR Ltd. Finnish Railways,** PO Box 488, Vilhonkatu 13, FIN-00101 Helsinki (© **09/2319-2902;** www.vr.fi). In the United States, contact **Rail Europe** (© **800/848-7245** or 800/4-EURAIL [438-7245]; www.raileurope.com).

BY BUS

Finland has an extensive bus network operated by private companies. Information on bus travel is available at the **Helsinki Bus Station,** Kamppi terminal and Simonkentta. For more information you can call © **358/200-4000** or else go to www.expressbus.fi. If you call, you'll be charged 1.65€ for an operator's fee. Tickets can be purchased on board or at the bus station. Ask about a Coach Holiday Ticket, allowing travel up to 1,000km (621 miles) during any 2-week period.

BY TAXI IN FINNISH CITIES

Service on most forms of public transportation ends around midnight throughout Finland, forcing night owls to drive themselves or to rely on the battalions of *taksi* (taxis) that line up at taxi stands in every Finnish town. In Helsinki, taxi stands are strategically situated throughout the downtown area, and it's usually less expensive to wait in line at a stand until one arrives. If you decide to call a taxi, they can be found under *taksiasemat* in the local directory. ***Note:*** You have to pay the charges that accumulate on the meter from the moment the driver first receives the call, not from when he or she picks you up.

BY CAR

Because of the far-flung scattering of Finland's attractions and the relative infrequency of its trains and long-distance buses, touring the country by car is the best way to savor its sights and charms, especially during the summer months. Bear in mind that driving conditions can be very bad during the long winter months. Snow tires are compulsory in winter. All car-rental companies supply winter tires during the appropriate seasons as part of their standard equipment.

Visitors bringing a motor vehicle into Finland must have a driver's license and a clearly visible sign attached to the vehicle showing its nation of origin. This rule is enforced at the border. Your home driver's license will be honored; an international driver's license is not required.

RENTALS **Avis** (✆ **800/331-1212** in the U.S. and Canada; www.avis.com), **Budget** (✆ **800/527-0700** in the U.S. and Canada; www.budget.com), and **Hertz** (✆ **800/654-3001** in the U.S. and Canada; www.hertz.com) are represented in Finland. Each company maintains 22 to 24 locations in Finland, usually in town centers or at airports, and sometimes in surprisingly obscure settings. For those who want to begin and end your tour of Finland in different cities, a drop-off within Finland can be arranged for a modest surcharge. A drop-off outside Finland, however—if allowed at all—is much more expensive.

Kemwel (✆ **800/678-0678;** www.kemwel.com) is an auto-rental broker that accumulates into one database the availability of rental cars in markets across Europe, including Finland. Originally established in 1908, and now operating in close conjunction with its sister company, **Auto Europe** (✆ **800/223-5555;** www.autoeurope.com), it offers convenient and prepaid access to thousands of cars, from a variety of reputable car-rental outfits throughout Europe.

DRIVING RULES Finns drive on the right side of the road, as in the U.S. and Europe. Speed limits are strictly enforced. It's illegal to drive a motor vehicle under the influence of alcohol (blood alcohol may not exceed 0.5%), and the penalties for doing so are severe. Be careful to watch for elk and reindeer crossing signs.

GASOLINE (PETROL) Prices are extremely high and subject to daily changes. Most stations take credit cards and are self-service at the pump. Stations are plentiful in the more congested south. However, if driving in the wilderness of the north, tank up before heading out for a long stretch.

FLY & DRIVE Government taxes, insurance coverage, and the high cost of gasoline (petrol) can make the use of a rented vehicle in Finland more expensive than you might have assumed. One way to reduce these costs is to arrange for your fly-drive trip through **Finnair** (✆ **800/950-5000**). When you book your flight, the airline may be able to arrange a lower car-rental price through Budget, Hertz, or Avis than you could have gotten on your own.

BY FERRY & LAKE STEAMER

Finland's nearly 188,000 lakes form Europe's largest inland waterway. Although railroads and highways now link most Finnish towns and villages, the romantic old steamers (and their modern counterparts) give both Finns and visitors a relaxing way to enjoy the inland archipelago areas of Finland in summer.

The excursion trips of most vessels last from just a couple of hours to a full day. In some cases you can travel from one lakeside town to another. There are even a couple of car ferries that cross some of the biggest lakes, significantly reducing the time required to drive around the lake. Unlike highway ferries, which are few in number today but can be used at no charge, the car ferries charge a fare for both cars and passengers. Information on all lake traffic schedules and fares is available from local tourist offices.

STAYING HEALTHY

Scandinavia is viewed as a safe destination, although problems, of course, can and do occur anywhere. You don't need to get shots, most foodstuff is safe, and the water in cities and towns is potable. If you're concerned, order bottled water. It is easy to get a prescription filled in towns and cities, and nearly all places throughout Scandinavia contain hospitals with English-speaking doctors and well-trained medical staffs.

General Availability of Healthcare

If a medical emergency arises, your hotel staff can usually put you in touch with a reliable doctor. If not, contact the American Embassy or a consulate; each one maintains a list of English-speaking doctors. Medical and hospital services aren't free, so be sure that you have appropriate insurance coverage before you travel.

Contact the **International Association for Medical Assistance to Travelers** (**IAMAT; © 716/754-4883** in the U.S., 416/652-0137 in Canada; www.iamat.org) for tips on travel and for lists of local, English-speaking doctors. The United States **Centers for Disease Control and Prevention** (**© 800/232-4636** or 404/498-1515; www.cdc.gov) provides up-to-date information on health hazards by region or country and offers tips on food safety. **Travel Health Online** (www.tripprep.com), sponsored by a consortium of travel medicine practitioners, may also offer helpful advice on traveling abroad. You can find listings of reliable medical clinics overseas at the **International Society of Travel Medicine** (www.istm.org).

MONEY & COSTS

ATMS Plus, Cirrus, and other networks connecting automated teller machines operate throughout Scandinavia. The easiest and best way to get cash away from home is from an ATM (automated teller machine). The **Cirrus** (**© 800/424-7787;** www.mastercard.com) and **PLUS** (**© 800/843-7587;** www.visa.com) networks span the globe; look at the back of your bank card to see which network you're on. Keep in mind that many banks impose a fee when a card is used at another bank's ATM, and that fee can be up to $5 or more for international transactions. On top of this, the bank from which you withdraw cash will likely charge its own fee.

> **Bank Fees for Credit Cards**
>
> **For all restaurants in Denmark, there is an assessed bank fee from 3% to 7% on credit cards if the card is not a Danish card.**

Denmark

Although Denmark is a member of the European Union, the Danes rejected the euro as their form of currency. They continue to use the ***krone*** (crown), which breaks down into 100 ***øre.*** The plural is ***kroner.*** The international monetary designation for the Danish *kroner* is DKK.

FOR AMERICAN READERS At this writing, $1 = approximately 5.50DKK. Stated differently, 1DKK = approximately 18¢.

FOR BRITISH READERS At this writing, £1 equaled approximately 8.80DKK, or stated differently, 1DKK = approximately 11p.

FOR CANADIAN READERS At press time, C$1 equaled approximately 5.40DKK. Stated differently, 1DKK = approximately 19¢.

REGARDING THE EURO At the time of this writing, 1DKK = .13€. Stated differently, 1€ equaled approximately 7.50DKK.

Norway

The Norwegian currency is the ***krone*** (plural: ***kroner***), written as NOK. There are 100 ***øre*** in 1 *krone*. Banknotes are issued in denominations of 50, 100, 200, 500, and 1,000 *kroner.* Coins are issued in denominations of 50 *øre,* 1 *krone,* and 5, 10, and 20 *kroner.*

THE NORWEGIAN KRONE

At press time for this edition, faced with some of the greatest fiscal instability since before World War II, U.S. and Norwegian currency experts held widely varying opinions about the 2-year outlook for the interrelated values of the *krone,* the dollar, the pound, and the euro.

FOR AMERICAN READERS At the time of this writing, $1 = approximately NOK6. Stated differently, NOK1 = approximately 16¢.

FOR BRITISH READERS At this writing, £1 = approximately NOK9.60, or NOK1 = approximately 10p.

FOR CANADIAN READERS At press time, C$1 equaled approximately NOK5.65. Stated differently, NOK1 = approximately 17¢.

REGARDING THE EURO At the time of this writing, 1€ = NOK8, or, stated differently, NOK1 = .12€.

Sweden

Sweden's basic unit of currency is the ***krona*** (or **SEK**). Note that the Swedes spell the plural *kronor* with an *o* instead of an *e* as in the *kroner* of Denmark and Norway. One *krona* is divided into 100 ***oüre.*** Banknotes are issued in denominations of 20, 50, 100, 500, 1,000, and 10,000 *kronor*. Silver coins are issued in denominations of 50 *oüre* and 1SEK and 5SEK.

FOR AMERICAN READERS At the time of this writing, $1 = approximately 6.95SEK. Stated differently, 1SEK = approximately 14¢.

FOR BRITISH READERS At this writing, £1 = approximately 11SEK, or 1SEK = approximately 9p.

FOR CANADIAN READERS At press time, C$1 equaled approximately 6.50SEK. Stated differently, 1SEK = approximately 15¢.

REGARDING THE EURO At the time of this writing, 1€ = 9.30SEK, or, stated differently, 1SEK = .10€.

Finland

The **euro,** the new single European currency, became the official currency of Finland and 11 other participating countries on January 1, 1999 and went into general circulation in 2002.

FOR AMERICAN READERS At the time of this writing, $1 was worth approximately .73€. Inversely stated, 1€ was worth approximately $1.36.

FOR BRITISH READERS At press time, £1 equaled approximately $1.60, and approximately 1.18€.

FOR CANADIAN READERS At press time, C$1 equaled approximately $1 and approximately .73€.

SAFETY

Scandinavia has a relatively low crime rate with rare, but increasing, instances of violent crime. Most crimes involve the theft of personal property from cars or residences or in public areas. Pickpockets and purse snatchers often work in pairs or groups, with one distracting the victim while another grabs valuables. Often they operate in or near the major rail stations. Hotel breakfast rooms and lobbies attract professional, well-dressed thieves who blend in with guests and target purses and briefcases left unguarded by unsuspecting tourists and business travelers. Valuables should not be left unguarded in parked vehicles.

SPECIALIZED TRAVEL RESOURCES

GLBT Travelers

DENMARK

In general, Denmark is one of the most gay-friendly countries in Europe and was one of the first to embrace same-sex marriages. Antidiscrimination laws have been in effect since 1987. Most Danes are exceptionally friendly and tolerant of lifestyles of any sexual preference.

The **Danish National Association for Gays and Lesbians** (**Landsforeningen for Bøsser og Lesbiske,** abbreviated as LBL) maintains its headquarters at Teglgaardstræde 13, 1007 Copenhagen (✆ **33-13-19-48;** www.lbl.dk), with branches in at least four of the larger cities of Denmark.

NORWAY

As one of the most sophisticated countries on the planet, it naturally follows that Norway is also one of the most gay friendly. Most Norwegians are tolerant of the lifestyles of others, including their sexual preference. Obviously, an urban center such as Oslo will accommodate a more openly gay life than in rural areas.

In Norway gays and lesbians have the same legal status as heterosexuals, with the exception of adoption rights. Legislation passed in 1981 protects gays and lesbians from discrimination. In 1993 a law was passed recognizing the "partnerships" of homosexual couples—in essence, a recognition of same-sex marriages. The age of consent for both men and women in Norway is 16 years of age.

SWEDEN

Stockholm is the gay capital of Scandinavia, and even gay marriage is now legal in this enlightened, sophisticated country. The age of consent is almost uniformly the same as for heterosexuals, usually 15 or 16.

The **Federation for Gay and Lesbian Rights (RFSL),** Sveavägen 57 (PO Box 350), S-10126 Stockholm (✆ **08/501-62-900;** www.rfsl.se), open Monday through Friday from 9am to 5pm, operates a **Gay Switchboard** (✆ **08/501-62-970**), staffed with volunteers daily from 8am to 11pm.

FINLAND

SETA ry, Hietalahdenkatu 2B, FIN-00180 Helsinki (✆ **09/681-2580;** www.seta.fi), is a good source of information about gay life in the capital and Finland as a whole. The office is open Monday to Thursday 10am to 3pm.

Travelers with Disabilities

NORWAY

Norway has been in the vanguard of providing services for people with disabilities. In general, trains, airlines, ferries, department stores, and malls are accessible. For information about wheelchair access, ferry and air travel, parking, and other matters, contact the appropriate tourist board (see "Visitor Information," p. 549). The **Norwegian Association of the Disabled,** Schweigaardsgt 12, 9217 Grønland, 0185 Oslo (✆ **24-10-24-00;** www.nhf.no), also provides useful information.

DENMARK

In general, Denmark's trains, airlines, ferries, department stores, and malls are accessible. For information about wheelchair access, ferry and air travel, parking, and other matters, contact the **Danish Tourist Board** (see chapter 21, "Fast Facts & Websites").

Useful information for people with disabilities is provided by *De Samvirkende Invalideorganisationer* (**Danish Disability Council,** abbreviated in Denmark as DSI), Bredgade 25, 1260 Copenhagen, Denmark (✆ **33-11-10-44;** www.dch.dk). Established in 1934, it organizes 29 smaller organizations, each involved with issues of concern to travelers with disabilities, into one coherent grouping that represents the estimated 300,000 persons with disabilities living in Denmark today.

SWEDEN

About two million people in Sweden have a disability; as a result, Sweden is especially conscious of their needs. In general, trains, airlines, ferries, and department stores and malls are wheelchair accessible. Always call ahead to check on accessibility in hotels, restaurants, and sights you want to visit.

For information on youth hostels with special rooms for those with disabilities, contact **Svenska Turistföreningen,** PO Box 25, S-10120 Stockholm (✆ **08/463-21-00;** www.stfturist.se).

FINLAND

Finland has been in the vanguard of providing services for people with disabilities. In general, trains, airlines, ferries, department stores, and malls are accessible. For information about wheelchair access, ferry and air travel, parking, and other matters, contact the Scandinavian Tourist Board (see "Visitor Information," p. 542).

In Finland, you may obtain general information from **Rullaten ry,** Hile Meckelborg, Pajutie 7, FIN-02770 Espoo, Finland (✆ **09/805-73-93;** www.rullaten.fi).

Senior Travelers

Mention the fact that you're a senior when you first make your travel reservations. All major airlines and many Scandinavian hotels offer discounts for seniors. Often people 68 and over are entitled to 50% off the price of first- and second-class train tickets. Ask for the discount at the ticket office.

INTRAV (✆ **800/680-2858;** www.tourvacationstogo.com) is a high-end tour operator that caters to the mature, discerning traveler, not specifically seniors, with trips around the world that include guided safaris, polar expeditions, private jet adventures, small boat cruises down jungle rivers, and trips to the Norwegian fjords.

Family Travelers

Scandinavians like kids but don't offer a lot of special amenities for them. For example, a kiddies' menu in a restaurant is a rarity. You can, however, order a half portion, and most waiters will oblige.

At attractions—even if it isn't specifically posted—inquire if a kids' discount is available. European Union citizens 17 and under are admitted free to all state-run museums.

Recommended family travel Internet sites include **Family Travel Forum** (www.familytravelforum.com); **Family Travel Network** (www.familytravelnetwork.com); **Traveling Internationally with Your Kids** (www.travelwithyourkids.com); and **Family Travel Files** (www.thefamilytravelfiles.com).

Single Travelers

Travel Buddies Singles Travel Club (© **800/998-9099;** www.travelbuddiesworldwide.com), based in Canada, runs intimate, single-friendly group trips and will match you with a roommate free of charge. **TravelChums** (© **212/787-2621;** www.travelchums.com) is an Internet-only travel-companion matching service with elements of an online personals-type site, hosted by the respected New York–based Shaw Guides travel service.

Many reputable tour companies offer singles-only trips. **Singles Travel International** (© **877/765-6874;** www.singlestravelintl.com) offers singles-only trips to places like Scandinavia. **Backroads** (© **800/462-2848;** www.backroads.com) offers more than 160 active-travel trips to 30 destinations worldwide, including Denmark.

Responsible Tourism

Responsible tourism is conscientious travel. It means being careful with the environments you explore, and respecting the communities you visit. Sweden, Norway, and Finland contain one of the last great wildernesses in Europe. Two overlapping components of sustainable travel are ecotourism and ethical tourism.

DENMARK

Denmark's capital, Copenhagen, is among the most bicycle-friendly in the world, with 32% of this eco-centric city's commuters traveling on two wheels. Only 30% drive, the rest walking or taking a train or bus.

Denmark is one of the most eco-conscious countries in the world, with wind energy supplying 20% of its needs, perhaps 35% by 2015.

The little country has its own eco-certification for green hotels, the **Green Key,** founded in 1994. Some 70% to 80% of the country's hotels and restaurants have been certified as green.

Denmark also has a long tradition of producing organic and environmentally friendly food—and to a certain extent also biodynamic food. Its cities and larger towns also offer organic places to eat.

For more information about green travel in Denmark, check out **www.eco-info.dk**.

NORWAY

Rivaled only by Sweden, Norway has the most pristine land in Europe. If you don't have time to explore it all, make it the west coast, fabled for its fjords and beautiful scenery. This part of the world contains some of the country's most famous natural attractions, with vast wild and unspoiled nature.

You can go for spectacular glacier walks, take hiking trails, go on kayak trips and bold river-rafting expeditions. There is skiing in Norway in both summer and winter.

For **Norway Green Tours,** check **www.norwaygreentours.com;** booking is directly online (there is no phone number).

SWEDEN

Visit Sweden (www.visitsweden.se) is an organization promoting Sweden abroad, but also branding the country a "green" destination. The staff is projecting an overall environmentally friendly profile with hotels trying to cut down on carbon emissions and the provision of an overall green infrastructure.

Train travel has gradually been taking share from air travel within Sweden, as visitors become more environmentally conscious. High-speed trains make train travel a viable alternative to air travel, which causes far more pollution. Air travel used to be, by far, the quickest way to travel domestically in Sweden, but security measures have increased the overall travel time, and the gap between train and air travel in terms of overall time is decreasing.

FINLAND

Green Tourism of Finland (www.greentourism.fi) provides Finnish nature tourism with sustainable development. The umbrella organization brings together companies in the tourist industry to promote an eco-friendly country, containing some of the greatest wilderness left in Europe.

GTF awards accommodations, restaurants, and transport services that comply with an eco-friendly environment. Finland, along with the other Scandinavian countries, is the most eco-conscious nation on the planet. For more information you can write **Green Tourism of Finland,** Anttilantie 7, 82380 Tolosenmäki unla Finland.

SPECIAL-INTEREST TRIPS & ESCORTED TOURS

The oldest travel agency in Britain, **Cox & Kings,** Gordon House 10, Greencoat Place, London SW1P 1PH (**✆ 020/7873-5000;** www.coxandkings.co.uk), was established in 1758. Today the company specializes in unusual, if pricey, holidays. Its offerings in Scandinavia include cruises through the spectacular fjords and waterways, bus and rail tours through sites of historic and aesthetic interest, and visits to the region's best-known handicraft centers, Viking burial sites, and historic churches.

To cycle through the splendors of Scandinavia, you can join Britain's oldest and largest association of bicycle riders, the **Cyclists' Touring Club,** CTC Parklands, Railton Road Guildford, Surrey GU2 9JX (www.ctc.org.uk). Founded in 1878, it charges £37 a year for adult membership, which includes information, maps, a subscription to a newsletter packed with practical information and morale boosters, plus recommended cycling routes through virtually every country in Europe.

Denmark

BUS TOURS **ScanAm World Tours** (**✆ 800/545-2204;** www.scandinaviantravel.com) offers a tour through the "Heart of Fairy Tale Denmark." You can choose a 5-day, 4-night trip through Hans Christian Andersen country, including a visit to Odense (his birthplace) and an excursion to Legoland. Tours begin at $710 per person.

SELF-DRIVE TOURS Several companies offer self-drive tours, which usually include accommodations, rental cars, and customized itineraries. **Scantours Inc.** (✆ **800/223-7226;** www.scantours.net) features the 5-day "Taste of Danish Castles & Manor Houses" tour, which is available year-round. Prices begin at $360 per person. The company also sponsors a tour of Danish inns. The 4-day self-drive tour includes accommodations, breakfast, car rental, and an itinerary. The typical price for an inn is $182 per night in a double room, and the trip builds from there.

BICYCLE TOURS An excellent way to explore the flat, rolling Danish countryside is on a bicycle. Numerous organizations (including Scantours Inc. and ScanAm Tours) sponsor bike tours through various regions of the country. You can choose one that covers the castles, beaches, and fjords of northern Denmark; the southern Funen islands; the beaches and marshland of western Jutland; or the lake country in eastern Jutland. **Blue Marble Travel** (✆ **201/465-2567;** www.bluemarble.org) offers 7-day excursions to Hans Christian Andersen country and several small islands in the Baltic for $2,150 per person. **Dansk Cyklist Forbund,** Rømersgade 7, DK-1362 Copenhagen (✆ **33-32-31-21;** www.dcf.dk), can provide the latest information on cycling tours in Denmark.

ADVENTURE TRAVEL OPERATORS In North America, a few companies offer adventure trips to Denmark. **Crossing Latitudes,** 420 W. Koch St., Bozeman, MT 59715 (✆ **406/585-5356;** www.crossinglatitudes.com), offers sea kayaking and backpacking expeditions throughout the region; and **Blue Marble Travel** (✆ **201/465-2567;** www.bluemarble.org), features reasonably priced biking and hiking trips in Denmark.

Norway

One of the best tour operators to Norway is **ScanAm World Tours** (✆ **800/545-2204;** www.scandinaviantravel.com). Its best and most highly sought-after itinerary is its **Norway in a Nutshell Fjord Tours.** These tours, which cost $208 to $619 per person from May to September, take 2 days and 1 night. They include a tour of the famous Flåm Mountain Railroad and a 2-hour cruise on the Aurland Fjord and the Naeroy Fjord. Tours are operated from Oslo to Bergen or vice versa. The company also operates many other tours, the most useful being the 8-day, 7-night tour of Oslo and Bergen, plus the fjord country, for those wanting to cover just the highlights of Norway. Prices include only land and begin at $2,032 per person.

Grand Circle Travel (✆ **800/959-0405;** www.gct.com) offers 17-day tours of the Norwegian fjords and Lapland, with carefully chosen hotels and big Norwegian breakfasts. Highlights of this tour are Bergen, Trondheim, the Lofoten Islands, and Geirangerfjord.

Sweden

One good source of package deals is the airlines themselves. Most major airlines offer air/land packages, including **American Airlines Vacations** (✆ 800/321-2121; www.aavacations.com), **Delta Vacations** (✆ 800/8000-1504; www.deltavacations.com), **Continental Airlines Vacations** (✆ 800/829-7777; www.covacations.com), and **United Vacations** (✆ 888/854-3899; www.unitedvacations.com). Several big **online travel agencies**—Expedia, Travelocity, Orbitz, Site59, and Lastminute.com—also do a brisk business in packages.

ScanAm World Tours (✆ **800/545-2204;** www.scandinaviantravel.com) offers some of the country's best tours, taking you on Göta Canal cruises or else along the lakes, on the waterways, and into the folkloric district of Dalarna. Minimum tours are for 2 nights, including hotels, costing from $436 per person. From here, tours range upward to 5 nights, including hotels, costing from $963 per person.

"Gotland Island and the City of Roses" is a cruise on the Gotland Line from Stockholm to Nynäshamn or from Oskarshamn to Visby, including 2 nights at the Visby Hotel or Hotel Solhem. The 3-day tour is available May through September.

Scantours (✆ **800/223-7226;** www.scantours.com) offers the most widely diverse tours of Sweden, ranging from Göta Canal cruises to a combined Stockholm and Helsinki jaunt, lasting 5 days and 4 nights.

Finland

The best tours of Finland are offered by **Finnair** (✆ **800/950-5000** in the U.S.; www.finnair.com), including its most popular, the **Midnight Sun Flight** (Helsinki-Rovaniemi-Helsinki). Any Finnair office around the world can provide information about tours for exploring Finland.

If you'd like to see as much as possible of Finland's highlights in the shortest possible time, consider one of the **Friendly Finland Tours,** lasting 3 to 6 days. This tour is operated by the **Finland Travel Bureau,** Kaivokatu 10A, PB 319, FIN-00101 Helsinki (✆ **806/0097-000;** www.smt.fi). Bookings can be made through any travel agent.

There's no better way to discover the natural beauty of Finland's lake region than by cruising its waters. **Five Stars of Scandinavia** (✆ **800/722-4126;** fax 360/923-048290; www.5stars-scandinavia.com) conducts the best tours of Finland's Lake District. From June to August, one of their most popular tours is a 2-night/3-day tour of the Saimaa Lakeland, highlighted by a visit to the town of Savonlinna. Except for international airfares, prices begin at $1,290 per person, based on double occupancy, with a single supplement of $550.

Finnsov Tours Oy Ltd., Eerikinkatu 3 (✆ **09/436-69-60;** http://finnsov.fi), in Helsinki offers the most comprehensive tours of both the countryside of Finland and St. Petersburg and Moscow. Discuss your needs with the staff at Finnsov—musical festivals, an overnight in a glass igloo, a journey to see the aurora borealis (northern lights). The company's tours above the Arctic Circle are especially recommended, including action-packed adventures to Rovaniemi, capital of Lapland.

For a complete list of tour programs contact the **Finnish Tourist Board** (✆ **212/885-9700;** fax 212/885-9710; www.visitfinland.com).

THE ACTIVE VACATION PLANNER

Denmark

BEACHES With some 8,000km (5,000 miles) of coastline, Denmark has many long strips of sandy beaches. In many cases, dunes protect the beaches from sea winds. Most of these beaches are relatively unspoiled, and the Danes like to keep them that way (any polluted beaches are clearly marked). Many Danes like to go nude at the beach. Nudist beaches aren't clearly identified; often you'll see bathers with and without clothing using the same beach. The best beach resorts are those on the north coast of Zealand and the southern tip of the island of Bornholm. Beaches on the east coast of Jutland are also good, often attracting Germans from the south. Funen also has a number of good beaches, especially in the south.

BIKING A nation of bikers, the Danes have organized their roads to suit this national sport. Bikers can pedal along a network of biking routes and paths protected from heavy traffic. The Danish landscape is made for this type of vacation. Most tourist offices publish biking-tour suggestions for their own district; it's a great way to see the sights and get in shape at the same time. The **Dansk Cyklist Forbund (Danish Cycling Federation)**, Rømersgade 5, DK-1362 Copenhagen (© **33-32-31-21;** www.dcf.dk), publishes excellent guides covering the whole country. They can also provide information about a number of prepackaged biking vacations that are available.

FISHING Since no place in Denmark is more than 56km (35 miles) from the sea, fishing is a major pastime. Denmark also has well-stocked rivers and lakes, including fjord waters around the Limfjord. Anglers between the ages of 18 and 67 must obtain a fishing permit from the Danish Directorate of Fisheries for 30DKK for 1 day and 90DKK for 1 week; these are available at any post office. Jutland is known for its good trout fishing; salmon is also available, but it is found more readily in Norway. Anglers who fish from the beach can catch eel, mackerel, turbot, sea trout, plaice, and flounder. For more information about fishing in Denmark, contact **Sportsfiskerforbund,** Worsåesgade 1, DK-7100 Vejle (© **75-82-06-99;** www.sportsfiskeren.dk).

GOLF Denmark's undulating landscape is ideal for the construction of golf courses. Prospective golfers should bring with them a valid golf club membership card from home. For information on the best courses near where you're staying, contact local tourist offices.

HANG GLIDING & PARAGLIDING Although Denmark is a relatively flat country, good possibilities for paragliding do exist. The **Danish Union of Windgliders** provides information about suitable locations. As a rule, the union has arranged with local landowners that a slope or some other suitable place may be used. Since equipment cannot be rented in Denmark, clients must bring their own. More information is available from **Dansk Drageflyver Union** (© **46-14-15-09;** www.dansk drageflyverunion.dk).

SAILING Denmark has about 600 harbors, both large and small, including the island of Bornholm. Those who like to sail have many opportunities to do so, especially in the open waters of the Baltic or in the more sheltered waters of the South Funen Sea between Lolland/Falster and Zealand. The Limfjord in North Jutland is also ideal for sailing. Many sailing boats are available for rent, as are cruisers. For information, contact the tourist offices.

WALKING About 20 pamphlets describing walks of short or long duration in Danish forests are printed in English and are available from local tourist offices.

Norway

BIKING, HIKING & MORE For the serious cyclist, there are two great routes in Norway: the North Sea Cycleway and the Old Navvy Road. Each of them is only partially paved. The coastal route is much easier, whereas the Old Navvy Road runs across open mountains, passing through pastures and meadows en route down to the nearest fjord. Pick up detailed maps of routes and how to reach them in tourist offices throughout Norway.

Since the Old Navvy Road follows the Bergen-Oslo train tracks for most of the way, the usual starting point is Haugastøl, known for its herring and jazz.

The North Sea Cycleway stretches for 296km (184 miles) and is mostly rural, with woodland, moors, and crags, passing many a meadow. It runs through such ports as Flekkefjord and Egersund, passing such larger towns as Sandnes and Stavanger.

The Old Navvy Road, called Rallarvegen in Norwegian, was built from 1895 to 1902, starting in the tree-lined east and climbing into the open mountains, with panoramic views of snow-covered slopes; high-altitude, incredibly blue lakes; and the Hardangerjøkulen glacier. The most dramatic point along the route is from Vatnahalsen, where the road descends the 21 hairpin bends of Myrdalskleiva, continuing down the Flamsdal Valley to Flåm. The road has been a cycle track since the 1970s.

Bike rentals abound in Norway. Inquire at your hotel or the local tourist office. The Norwegian Mountain Touring Association (see below) provides inexpensive lodging for those on overnight bike trips. For suggestions on tours, maps, and brochures, contact **Den Rustne Eike,** Vestbaneplassen 2, N-0458 Oslo (**© 98-63-19-69;** www.denrustneeike.no). They can arrange guided tours in the Oslo area and elsewhere in Norway. Tours last from 3 hours to 14 days.

In July and August, 7-day bike trips run through the Lofoten Islands. They offer moderately rolling terrain, dramatic scenery, traditional *rorbuer* (fishing cottage) lodging, and hearty regional cuisine. Prices begin at NOK17,000. Tours are offered by **Backroads** (**© 800/GO-ACTIVE** [462-2848]; www.backroads.com).

To cycle through the splendors of Norway, you can join Britain's oldest (1878) and largest association of bicycle riders, the **Cyclists' Touring Club,** CTC Parklands, Railton Road, Guildford, Surrey GU2 9JX (**© 0844/736-8450;** www.ctc.org.uk). Adult membership costs £37, which includes information, maps, a subscription to a newsletter packed with practical information and morale boosters, plus recommended cycling routes through virtually every country in Europe. The organization's knowledge of scenic routes is especially comprehensive. Membership can be arranged over the phone with a credit card.

One of the best bets for mountain biking is the Setesdal region, with its many small roads and forest trails. **Setesdal Rafting Centre** (**© 37-93-11-77;** www.trollmountain.no), 7km (4¼ miles) north from Evje on the main road (Rte. 9), is an expert in the area, offering both guided trips and bikes for rent with helmets from mid-April to late October.

The Øyer mountains are also excellent for cycling, and the scenery is splendid. For more information, including suggested cycle tours in the Øyer mountains, consult the **Øyer Tourist Office** (**© 61-27-70-00**), and rent bikes from **Hafjellsporten Sports** (**© 61-27-76-11;** www.sporten-hafjell.no).

Norway has more than two dozen 18-hole golf courses, and the **Norwegian Golf Federation** (**© 67-15-46-00;** www.ecs.net) can provide information on all of these. Many golf clubs are open to foreign guests. Greens fees tend to be moderate. Our two favorite clubs are the 18-hole **Oslo Golf Klubb,** at Bogstad, Oslo (**© 22-51-05-60;** www.oslogk.no), and the 18-hole **Meland Golf Club,** Meland/Frekhaug (**© 56-17-46-00;** www.melandgolf.no), 36km (22 miles) north of Bergen.

Norway's mountains and wilderness are among the most spectacular in the world. The **Norwegian Mountain Touring Association,** Storgata 7, N-0101 Oslo (**© 40-00-18-70;** www.turistforeningen.no), maintains affiliations with all the hiking associations of Norway and provides maps and advice. The association offers guided hikes that last from 5 to 8 days. They cost from NOK4,500 to NOK9,200, including meals and lodging. Local associations mark the routes and operate a network of cabins for hikers to share.

Blue Marble Travel (**© 201/465-2567;** www.bluemarble.org), features reasonably priced biking and hiking trips in Norway. **European Walking Tours,** 1401 Regency Dr. E., Savoy, IL 61874 (**© 800/231-8448** or 217/398-0058; www.walkingtours.com), sponsors walking tours for the mature traveler in Norway. The operator, Jacqueline Tofté, is a native of the Swiss Alps and has charted routes across meadows, through remote valleys, and over mountain passes or alongside serene lakes. The tours include searches for wildflowers, birds, and mountain animals, with lessons in local architecture, traditions, and history thrown in as well.

> **23 Hours of Daylight**
>
> **The Norwegian summer has magnificent long, sunny days. Temperatures often reach 86°F (30°C). Daylight on the longest days can last 23 hours, warming the lakes and fjords for all watersports.**

Throughout Norway you'll find riding schools with horses for rent. Many country hotels in Norway also keep a few horses for the use of guests. Many organizations offer horseback tours of Norway's wilderness, enabling visitors to see some of the more spectacular scenery. Tours can range from a few hours to a full week. Luggage is transported by car. One tour organizer is **Borton Overseas,** 5412 Lyndale Ave. S., Minneapolis, MN 55419 (✆ **800/843-0602** or 612/882-4640; www.bortonoverseas.com).

Our favorite place to go mountain riding is offered by **Voss Fjellhest** outside the resort of Voss (✆ **90-75-48-40;** www.vossfjellhest.no). In Panoramic fjord and mountain scenery, you'll be taken on day or weekend rides, where everything is arranged for you, including accommodations and meals.

CANOEING, KAYAKING & RAFTING Canoeing and kayaking, two increasingly popular sports, allow visitors to reach places that are otherwise almost inaccessible. Both activities should provide you with a unique opportunity to observe Norway's animals and birds without frightening them with the sound of an engine.

Some of our best experiences out on a canoe have been with the **Setesdal Rafting Center** (✆ **37-93-11-77;** www.trollaktiv.no), 7km (4¼ miles) north from Evje on the main road, Route 9. The region of Setesdal, known for its mountains, rivers, and varied wildlife, contains a stunning stretch of the River Otra—ideal for canoeing—extending from the rafting center south to the village of Evje. En route you'll pass several osprey nests and beaver lodges. The center is also the best place in southern Norway for white-water rafting from mid-April to late October. From late June until September, water temperatures can reach 68°F (20°C), which makes the River Otra the warmest in Norway. Both half-day and full-day trips can be arranged. **Crossing Latitudes,** 420 W. Koch St., Bozeman, MT 59715 (✆ **406/585-5356;** www.crossinglatitudes.com), is another source for sea-kayaking and backpacking expeditions.

If you'd like to go rafting on the Sjoa River, billed as "the wildest in Norway," you can obtain full information from the **Vågå Tourist office,** Vågavegen 37, N-2680 in Vågå (✆ **61-21-29-90;** www.visitjotunheimen.no), which also provides information about horseback riding, mountain or glacier climbing, mountain biking, and canoeing.

The rivers around Voss resort, in Norway's fjord country, have some of the finest river rafting. **Voss Rafting Center** (✆ **56-51-05-25;** www.vossrafting.no) offers rafting and other watersports such as river-boarding and canyoning. Overnight stays in the wild along with meals can be arranged.

FISHING With a quarter of Norway's coastline at your disposal, nearly 14,000km (8,680 miles), you obviously have plenty of opportunities for sea fishing.

Norway has long been famous for its salmon and trout fishing, with more than 100 salmon rivers flowing into its fjords. The best months for salmon are June, July, and sometimes August. Sea-trout fishing takes place from June to September and is best in August. The brown-trout season varies with altitude.

Fishing in the ocean is free. To fish in lakes, rivers, or streams, anyone over 16 must have a fishing license. The cost of a license to fish begins at around NOK266. National fishing licenses can be purchased at local post offices. For more information, contact the **Bergen Angling Association,** Fosswinckelsgate 37, M-5004 Bergen (✆ **55-34-18-08;** www.bergensportsfiskere.no).

A U.S.-based company that can arrange fishing (as well as hunting) excursions anywhere within Norway and the rest of Scandinavia is **Five Stars of Scandinavia,** 13104 Thomas Rd., KPN, Gig Harbor, WA 98329 (✆ **800/722-4126;** www.5stars-of-scandinavia.com). For a truly unusual fishing experience, consider renting one of their old-fashioned fishermen's cottages in the isolated Lofoten Islands. The rustic-looking, fully renovated cottages each lie adjacent to the sea and evoke 19th-century isolation. Five Stars will rent you a cottage for as short a period as 1 night, but we recommend a minimum stay of 3 nights to appreciate this offbeat adventure.

The River Gudbrandsdalslågen, running through a beautiful valley and Hafjell Hunderfossen, is one of the best fishing rivers of Europe, set against a backdrop of the Øyer mountains, with its many fishing lakes and rivers. The main types of fish caught are burbot, trout, char, and grayling. Many lakes in the mountains have rowboats for free use, and permits are easily obtainable at gas stations, grocery stores, hotels, or inns. For more information, contact the **Øyer Tourist Office** at ✆ **61-27-70-00.**

SAILING Norway's long coast can be a challenge to any yachting enthusiast. The most tranquil havens are along the southern coast. To arrange rafting trips or boat trips, along with boat rentals and evening parasailing, contact **SeaAction** (✆ **33-33-69-93;** www.seaaction.com).

SKIING Norway is the birthplace of skiing, predating the sport in Switzerland or Austria. It boasts 30,000km (18,600 miles) of marked ski trails.

From November until the end of May, both cross-country and downhill skiing are available, but don't expect the brilliant sun of the Alps. The days get long just before Easter, when skiing is best. Lights illuminate many of the tracks for winter skiers, which proves especially helpful in January and February.

From December to April, daylight is limited, but it's still possible to have a full day's skiing if you start early. The bigger resorts have at least one floodlit downhill slope, and many towns and villages have a floodlit cross-country track *(lysløype)*. The days lengthen rapidly in January and February. Mid-February is the most popular period, and accommodations prices are higher then. Early March offers a combination of good skiing conditions and low prices. Easter time is popular with Norwegians, and hotel prices are very high then. Beginning Easter Monday, low-season rates apply again. Skiing in the higher elevations is possible until May, and you can even ski all summer in a few places. For information about summer skiing, get in touch with **Stryn Sommerskisenter** (✆ **57-89-10-10;** www.strynefjellet.com). The largest mainland glacier in Europe is at Jostedalsbreen, near Stryn.

Snowboard and skiing facilities in the country are excellent overall. The winter season is longer than in southern Europe. The bigger resorts in Norway have plenty to interest beginners and intermediate skiers for a week or more, and there are many black-diamond runs for the more experienced. Families can find free lift passes and helmets for kids 6 and under, plus plenty of nursery slopes and day-care centers. Lift passes are relatively inexpensive, rental equipment is often cheaper than in other ski countries, queues are usually short, and the slopes are uncrowded.

The Cradle of Skiing

A 4,000-year-old rock carving from Nordland shows that Norwegians were already using skis then. Telemark county is regarded as the "cradle of skiing" because Sondre Nordheim from Morgedal created an interest for the sport there in the 1870s and 1880s. He devised a binding that made it possible to turn and jump without losing the skis, and also designed a ski with inwardly curved edges—the Telemark ski—that became the prototype of all subsequent skis.

Norway is best known for its cross-country skiing, which is superb at ski resorts everywhere. An endless network of marked trails *(skiløyper)* crosses rolling hills, forests, frozen lakes, and mountains. Numerous small ski centers offer inexpensive ski rentals and tuition. All the downhill resorts also have extensive trail networks.

Norwegian ski resorts are known for their informality, which is evident in the schools and the atmosphere. The emphasis is on simple pleasures, not the sophistication often found at alpine resorts. (Incidentally, the word *ski* is an Old Norse word, as is *slalom.*)

Geilo and **Hemsedal** are the best-known downhill resorts for keen downhill skiers. Geilo has the most extensive lift system, but Hemsedal has steeper runs and more spectacular scenery. There is also good cross-country skiing near both resorts. The huge mountain area of **Golsfjellet,** between Hemsedal, Gol, and Valdres, is excellent for experienced cross-country skiers. The main railway between Oslo and Bergen serves Geilo directly and Hemsedal via a bus connection from Gol (3–4 hr.).

Geilo is our favorite ski resort in Norway because you can step off a train and onto a ski lift. Voss, its rival, has more folklore and better architecture. A lot of Geilo consists of large structures that evoke army barracks. But in winter the white snow is all forgiving, and you will have arrived at an alpine paradise. The best slope at Geilo is the Skiheiser, with 24km (15 miles) of some of the best skiing this side of the Swiss Alps. With 18 lifts and 33 ski runs, Geilo is competitive with any resort in Norway.

Trysil in eastern Norway is less famous than Geilo and Hemsedal, but it also offers good downhill skiing and a particularly fine choice of self-catering chalets and apartments with skiable access to the lifts. Trysil is easy to reach by a direct express bus service from Oslo airport (3 hr.). Of course, Trysil is more of a backwater and doesn't possess the après-ski life of more established resorts such as Voss and Geilo.

The **Valdres** area between Hemsedal and Lillehammer is famous for its scenery of rolling forested hills with high mountains in the distance. The Aurdal ski center has the unbeatable combination of superb cross-country terrain and good downhill facilities. A good base for both is one of the excellent chalets at the top of the downhill slopes. Direct bus service connects Valdres to central Oslo (3 hr.).

The owners of ski resorts in Voss, Geilo, and Lillehammer aren't going to fall over dead out of fear that Valdres is going to take over all their business (it hasn't happened so far). But many world-class skiers are increasingly frequenting this resort to avoid the crowds and to enjoy slopes at a more leisurely pace.

Lillehammer has been well known since the Winter Olympics in 1994, and the competitive facilities are world-class. The main downhill slopes are at **Hafjell,** 15km (9¼ miles) north of Lillehammer. The cross-country skiing through the gentle hills, scattered forests, and lakes of the Sjusjøen area is endless and particularly good for beginners. Lillehammer itself is more cosmopolitan than the other ski towns and has a wide range of shops and places to eat and drink.

We love Geilo's small-scale winter charm, but no other resort in Norway can compete with all the multifarious offerings of Lillehammer. Facilities here are more wide ranging and better organized than in Voss or Geilo. Lillehammer might lack charm, but it more than makes up for that with experienced instructors in its ski schools, good lifts and smooth alpine slopes, and sheer vastness. (It has 402km/249 miles of prepared, illuminated cross-country tracks.)

North of Lillehammer is the Gudbrandsdal Valley, surrounded by extensive cross-country areas linked by two long-distance trails: "Troll løype" to the east and "Peer Gynt løype" to the west. Skiers of all abilities enjoy this area, and downhillers find several good ski centers. This region, including **Gålå** and **Fefor,** is especially well served by mountain hotels.

For those traveling with their own car, the **Telemark** area is easily accessible from Haugesund or Kristiansand (3–5 hr.). **Gaustablikk,** near the town of Rjukan, is the best all-around center, with several lifts and downhill runs of all standards, plus many kilometers of cross-country trails to suit all abilities. Although the skiing is good here, it lacks much in après-ski life, restaurants, and hotels.

Voss is well known and easily reached from Bergen in about 90 minutes by car or train, but the location near the west coast suffers from unreliable weather, particularly early and late in the season. It is well worth considering for a short break, though, or if you want to combine skiing with a winter visit to the fjord area.

Even though it's trying hard, Voss still has a long way to go before it overtakes either Geilo or Lillehammer. Nonetheless, it offers ski lifts, chairlifts, and an aerial cableway that can carry skiers up to 788m (2,585 ft.). We are especially fond of Mjølfjell, reached by going up the Raundalen Valley. This area offers some of the best cross-country skiing in Norway. Voss also emphasizes Norwegian folklore more than either Geilo or Lillehammer.

WHALE- & BIRD-WATCHING Some of Europe's noteworthy bird sanctuaries are on islands off the Norwegian coast or on the mainland. Rocky and isolated, the sanctuaries offer ideal nesting places for millions of seabirds that vastly outnumber the local human population during certain seasons. Foremost among the sanctuaries are the **Lofoten Islands**—particularly two of the outermost islands, Vaerøy and Røst—and the island of Runde. An almost .5km (¼-mile) bridge (one of the longest in Norway) connects **Runde** to the coastline, a 2½-hour drive from Ålesund. Runde's year-round human population is about 150, and the colonies of puffins, cormorants, razor-billed auks, guillemots, gulls, and eider ducks number in the millions. Another noteworthy bird sanctuary is at **Fokstumyra,** a national park near Dombås.

The isolated island of **Lovund** is a 2-hour ferry ride from the town of Sandnesjøen, south of Bodø. Lovund ("the island of puffins") has a human population of fewer than 270 and a bird population in the hundreds of thousands. You can visit Lovund and the other famous Norwegian bird-watching sites on your own, or sign up for one of the organized tours sponsored by **Borton Overseas,** 5412 Lyndale Ave. S., Minneapolis, MN 55419 (✆ **800/843-0602** or 612/882-4640; www.bortonoverseas.com).

Brochures and pamphlets are available from the tourist board **Destination Lofoten** (✆ **76-09-12-65;** www.lofoten-info.net).

In Norway you can catch a glimpse of 20m (66-ft.), 40,000-kilogram (88,185-lb.) sperm whales, the largest toothed whales in the world. You can also see killer whales, harbor porpoises, minke whales, and white-beaked dolphins. Whale researchers conduct 6-hour whale-watching tours in the Arctic Ocean.

Whale-watching in the Lofoten Islands can be arranged by **Borton Overseas,** 5412 Lyndale Ave. S., Minneapolis, MN 55419 (✆ **800/843-0602** or 612/882-4640; www.bortonoverseas.com).

Sweden

ADVENTURE TOURS For overall adventure travel, including skiing, hiking, and biking, the best bet is **Borton Overseas,** 5412 Lyndale Ave. S., Minneapolis, MN 55419 (✆ **800/843-0602** or 612/822-4640; www.bortonoverseas.com), which offers sea kayaking and backpacking expeditions in Sweden. Tours should be arranged before you go.

BIKING Much of Sweden is flat, which makes it ideal for cycling tours. Bicycles can be rented all over the country, and country hotels sometimes make them available free of charge. For more detailed information, contact the **Swedish Cycle Promotion Organisation,** Tulegatan 53, SE-11353 Stockholm (✆ **46-19-21-15-32;** www.balticseacycling.com).

FISHING In Stockholm, within view of the king's palace, you can cast a line for what are some of the finest salmon in the world. Ever since Queen Christina issued a decree in 1636, Swedes have had the right to fish in waters adjoining the palace. Throughout the country, fishing is an everyday affair; it's estimated that one of every three Swedes is an angler.

If you'd like to fish elsewhere in Sweden, you'll need a license; the cost varies from region to region. Local tourist offices in any district can give you information about this. Pike, pikeperch, eel, and perch are found in the heartland and the southern parts of the country.

GOLFING With about 400 rarely crowded courses, Sweden may have more golf enthusiasts than any other country in Europe after Scotland. Visitors are often granted local membership cards, and greens fees vary, depending on the club. Many golfers fly from Stockholm to Boden in the far north in the summer months to play by the light of the midnight sun at the **Björkliden Arctic Golf Course,** which opened in 1989 some 240km (149 miles) north of the Arctic Circle. It's not only the world's northernmost golf course, but it's one of the most panoramic, set against a backdrop of snow-capped peaks, green valleys, and crystal lakes. The narrow fairways and small greens of this 9-hole, par-36 course offer multiple challenges. For details, contact the **Björkliden Arctic Golf Club,** Kvarnbacksvägen 28, Bromma S-16874 (✆ **08/564-888-30;** www.bjorklidensgolfklubb.se).

For general information on courses in Sweden, check with the **Svenska Golffoürbundet** (✆ **08/622-15-00**).

HIKING Sarek, in the far north, is one of Europe's last real wilderness areas; Swedes come here to hike in the mountains, pick mushrooms, gather berries, and fish.

Providing temporary accommodations in the area, the **Svenska Turistfoürening,** Stureplan 4C, PO Box 25, SE-10120 Stockholm (✆ **08/463-21-00;** www.svenska turistforeningen.se), operates mountain huts with 10 to 30 beds. They know the northern part of Sweden very well, and can advise you about marked tracks, rowboats, the best excursions, the problems you're likely to encounter, communications, and transportation. They also sell trail and mountain maps.

HORSEBACK RIDING There are numerous opportunities for overnight horseback pack trips in such wilderness areas as the forests of Värmland or Norrbotten, where reindeer, musk oxen, and other creatures roam. The most popular overnight horseback trips start just north of the city of Karlstad in Värmland. Covered-wagon trips with overnight stopovers also exist. A typical horseback trip begins in the lakeside village of Torsby and follows a forested trail up a mountain. An average of 4 hours a day is spent on the horse, with meals cooked over an open fire.

In northern Sweden, two popular starting points are Funäsdalen, close to the Norwegian border, and Ammarnäs, not far from the Arctic Circle and the midnight sun. These trips begin in June. Local tourist offices can provide further information.

Sweden also has many riding stables and riding schools. Ask about them at local tourist offices. One of the most popular excursions is a pony trek through the region surrounding Sweden's highest mountain, Kebnekaise.

If you prefer to make your horseback riding arrangements before you depart the United States, perhaps as part of an organized bus, rail, or self-drive tour, **Passage Tours of Scandinavia,** 235 Commercial Blvd., Fort Lauderdale, FL 33308, can custom-design a suitable tour for you, usually configured with visits to Sweden's cultural, architectural, or historical highlights en route. You can also explore the offerings of **World Horse Riding** (**✆ 46-46-14-52-25;** http://worldhorseriding.com). For trail riding in the southern parts of Sweden, check out the offerings of **Krulliga Hästen,** Ellanda Planen SE-36032 Gemla (**✆ 0470/707-808;** www.krulligahasten.se).

KAYAKING Stockholm's fabled archipelago is wonderful for kayaking. There are no tides or dangerous currents, so even visitors with little or no experience in kayaking feel safe. Kayak tours are organized to follow the best wind and weather conditions between the inhabited skerries and larger islands. The best outfitter for kayak adventures throughout Sweden is **Crossing Latitudes** (**✆ 800/572-8747** in the U.S. or 46-70-670-1153 in Sweden).

RAFTING White-water rafting and river rafting are the two major forms of this sport. For white-water rafting you go in a fast river boat, the trip made all the more exciting by a series of rapids. Throughout the country there are both short trips and those lasting a week or so.

River rafting is much tamer since you go gently down a slow-moving river in Sweden's heartland. For information about the best river rafting in Sweden, contact **Kukkolaforsen-Turist & Konferens,** Kukkolaforsen 184, Haparanda Norrbottens SE-95393 läns (**✆ 922/310-00**). If you want to try log-rafting, we recommend a lazy trip down the Klarälven River, winding through beautiful and unspoiled valleys between high mountains, with sandy beaches where you can swim. There's excellent fishing for pike and grayling. You travel through northern Värmland at a speed of 2kmph (1¼ mph) from the mouth of the Vingängssjön Lake in the north to Edebäck in the south, a distance of 109km (68 miles) in 6 days. Overnight accommodations are arranged either on the moored raft or ashore. Each raft can accommodate between two and five people, and the trips are available from May to August. Contact **Branäs Sport,** Klara Strand 66, S-68063 Likenäs (**✆ 0564/352-00**).

SAILING & CANOEING Canoes and sailing boats can be rented all over the country; you can obtain information about this from the local tourist office. Often hotels situated near watersports areas have canoes for rent. Canoe tours can be arranged by **Nature Travels ltd.,** 26 Andover Green, Bovington, Wareham, BH20 6LN in England (**✆ 01929/463774;** www.naturetravels.co.uk).

Finland

ADVENTURE TOURS Summer and winter are both great periods for a holiday in Finland. Apart from the midnight sun and the northern lights, Finland has much to offer the adventurer. For information about adventure vacation packages in Lapland, we recommend **Lapland Winter Wonderland Holidays** at **© 0845/092-0363.** It might be more convenient to contact one of the U.S. tour operators: **Nordique Tours** (**© 800/995-7997;** www.picassotours.com) and **Scantours** (**© 800/223-7226;** www.scantours.co.uk).

BICYCLING In Finland, you can either rent a bike and cycle on your own, or join one of dozens of cycling tours. One 6-day/5-night tour in the Åland Islands, for example, takes you along an excellent road network, past low hills and shimmering water. For bookings, contact **Ålandsresor,** Torggatan 2, PO Box 62, FIN-22101 Mariehamn (**© 018/28-040;** www.alandsresor.fi). Some hotels, holiday villages, camping sites—even tourist information offices—rent bicycles. More information is available from the **Cycling Union of Finland,** Radiokatu 20, FIN-00093 Helsinki (**© 09/278-65-75;** http://uec-federation.eu).

CANOEING The **Finnish Canoe Federation,** Olympiastadion, Eteläakaarre, FIN-00250 Helsinki (**© 09/49-49-65;** www.kanoottiliitto.fi), arranges guided canoe tours along the country's most scenic waterscapes. One- and two-seat kayaks or canoes are available for rent, and charts of the coastal waters are provided.

FISHING Finland has more than 6,000 professional fishers and about 1.5 million people fishing for recreation. Visitors in both summer and winter can make arrangements for fishing, with lure and fly permitted.

In Finland most fishing waters are privately owned; cities and private companies also own fishing waters. The National Board of Forestry administers state fishing waters, mainly in northern and eastern Finland.

Visitors must buy a general fishing license to fish recreationally in Finland (a separate license is needed for the Åland Islands). You can get a general fishing license from post offices; it costs 6€ per person and is valid for 1 week; a year's license costs 27€. More information is available from the **Federation of Finnish Fisheries Association,** Köydenpunojankatu 7B, FIN-00180 Helsinki (**© 09/684-45-90;** www.ahven.net).

GOLFING There are 98 golf courses in Finland and 66,000 members of the **Finnish Golf Union,** Radiokatu 20, FIN-00240 Helsinki (**© 8158/2244;** www.ecs.net), the organization that keeps tabs on the locations and attributes of every golf course in Finland. The best courses are in Helsinki and include Tali Manor, 6.5km (4 miles) from the center, and the Espoo Golf Course. Information about golf courses and their pars, entry requirements, and greens fees is available from the Finnish Golf Union. The **Travel Experience Oy** (**© 09/622-9810;** www.travel-experience.net) offers golf tour packages to Finland, including golf tournaments under the midnight sun.

HIKING Finland is an ideal country for hiking. The northern wilderness boasts the highest fells (rolling and barren hills), clear streams, and lots of open country. Eastern Finland's forested hills and vast woodlands conceal many lakes and deep gullies. Western Finland's low, cultivated plain is cut by fertile river valleys leading to the Gulf of Bothnia. Central Finland is known for its thousands of lakes and rolling woodlands, and the south of Finland, though densely populated, has many forests suitable for hiking. Hiking maps and a special brochure on hiking are available from the Scandinavian Tourist Board abroad.

SKIING Skiing conditions in Finland are among the best in the world. The season is long and the trails are good. The best skiing season in northern Finland is March through April, when there may be up to 16 hours of sunshine daily. But the early winter—*kaamos,* the season when the sun doesn't appear at all—has its own attractions for visitors who want to experience something different.

Finland is about 1,125km (700 miles) long, with distinct differences at each end. The south consists of gently rolling hills, with elevations averaging up to .9m (3 ft.), but the farther north you go, the more deeply forested and mountainous the country becomes. The highest hills are in Lapland.

The slopes of Finnish ski resorts are maintained in excellent condition. Skiing instruction—both cross-country and downhill—is available at most resorts, and equipment can be rented on the spot.

Long-distance ski races are becoming increasingly popular, and the long trails, ranging from 40 to 90km (25–55 miles), attract more and more participants from all over the world every year. As many as 15,000 skiers take part in the biggest event—the Finlandia Ski Race. A fair number of resorts organize guided ski treks. They last a few days, and overnight accommodations are arranged along the trail in farmhouses or, in Lapland, in wilderness huts or shelters.

STAYING CONNECTED

Cellphones

For many, **renting** a phone is a good idea. (Even worldphone owners will have to rent new phones if they're traveling to non-GSM regions.) While you can rent a phone from any number of overseas sites, including kiosks at airports and at car-rental agencies, we suggest renting the phone before you leave home. North Americans can rent one before leaving home from **InTouch USA** (✆ **800/872-7626** or 703/222-7161; www.intouchglobal.com) or **RoadPost** (✆ **888/290-1616** or 905/272-5665; www.roadpost.com).

Internet & E-Mail

WITH YOUR OWN COMPUTER

More and more hotels, cafes, and retailers are signing on as Wi-Fi "hot spots." To locate international hot spots that provide **free wireless networks,** go to **www.jiwire.com**.

Wherever you go, bring a **connection kit** of the right power and phone adapters, a spare phone cord, and a spare Ethernet network cable—or find out whether your hotel supplies them to guests.

WITHOUT YOUR OWN COMPUTER

To find cybercafes check **www.cybercaptive.com** and **www.cybercafe.com**. Cybercafes are found in all large cities, especially Copenhagen, Oslo, and Stockholm. But they do not tend to cluster in any particular neighborhoods because of competition.

TIPS ON ACCOMMODATIONS

Accommodations in Scandinavia range from the most basic, perhaps lacking private bathrooms, to the most deluxe. Outside of the big cities, you are likely to encounter first class in the top category instead of luxe accommodations. The one thing you'll not find is a truly cheap hotel. Even the most inexpensive hotels might be considered a bit pricey in some parts of the world. To compensate, many hotels, especially chain members, offer discounted rates on weekends when hotels lose their most reliable client—the commercial traveler. The most prevalent chain hotel in Scandinavia is **Best Western** (✆ **800/937-8376;** www.bestwestern.com).

Alternative Accommodations

HOME STAYS **Friendship Force,** 34 Peachtree St. NW, Ste. 900, Atlanta, GA 30303 (✆ **404/522-9490;** www.thefriendshipforce.org), is a nonprofit organization that encourages friendship among people worldwide. Dozens of branch offices throughout North America arrange visits, usually once a year. Because of group bookings, the airfare to the host country is usually less than the cost of individual APEX tickets. Each participant spends 2 weeks in the host country, the first as a guest in the home of a family and the second traveling in the host country.

Servas, 1125 16th St., Ste. 201, Arcata, CA 95521 (✆ **707/825-1714;** www.usservas.org), is an international nonprofit, nongovernmental, interfaith network of travelers and hosts whose goal is to help promote world peace, goodwill, and understanding. Servas hosts offer travelers hospitality for 2 days. Travelers pay an $85 annual fee and a $25 list deposit after being approved.

HOME EXCHANGES One of the most exciting breakthroughs in modern tourism is the home exchange. Sometimes the family automobile is even included. Of course, you must be comfortable with the idea of having strangers in your home, and you must be content to spend your vacation in one place. One potential problem, though, is that you may not get a home in the area you request.

Intervac USA, 30 Corte San Fernando, Tiburon, CA 94920 (✆ **800/756-HOME** [4663]; www.intervacusa.com), is part of the largest worldwide exchange network. It contains over 10,000 homes in over 36 countries. Members contact each other directly. The cost is $85 plus postage, which includes the purchase of three of the company's catalogs, plus the inclusion of your own listing in whichever catalog you select. If you want to publish a photograph of your home, there is an additional charge of $15. Fees begin at $90, going up to $150.

The **Invented City** (✆ **415/902-4064;** www.invented-city.com) publishes home-exchange listings three times a year. For the $50 membership fee, you can list your home with your own written descriptive summary.

Home Link, 2937 NW 9 St., Fort Lauderdale, FL 33311 (✆ **800/638-3841** or 954/566-2687; www.homelink.org), will send you five directories a year for $130.

SUGGESTED SCANDINAVIA ITINERARIES

3

THE REGIONS IN BRIEF

Denmark

ZEALAND Home to Denmark's capital, **Copenhagen,** the island of Zealand draws more visitors than any other region. The largest island in Denmark, Zealand is also the wealthiest and most densely populated. Other cities include **Roskilde,** about 30km (19 miles) west of Copenhagen, which is home to a landmark cathedral (burial place of many kings) and a collection of Viking vessels discovered in a fjord. In the medieval town of **Køge,** witches were burned in the Middle Ages. One of the most popular attractions on the island is **Helsingør** (Elsinore in English), about 40km (25 miles) north of Copenhagen, where visitors flock to see "Hamlet's Castle." Off the southeast corner of the island is the island of **Møn,** home to Møns Klint, an expanse of white cliffs that rises sharply out of the Baltic.

JUTLAND The peninsula of Jutland links the mostly island nation of Denmark with Germany. It is the only part of Denmark on the European continent. Jutland has miles of coastline, with some of northern Europe's finest sandy beaches. Giant dunes and moors abound on the west coast, whereas the interior has rolling pastures and beech forests. Jutland's more interesting towns and villages include **Jelling,** heralded as the birthplace of Denmark and the ancient seat of the Danish kings. The Viking port of **Ribe** is the oldest town in Denmark. It's known throughout the world as the preferred nesting ground for numerous endangered storks. The resort of **Fanø,** with its giant dunes, heather-covered moors, and forests, is an excellent place to bird-watch or view Denmark's varied wildlife. The university city of **Århus** is Jutland's capital and second only to Copenhagen in size. **Aalborg,** founded by Vikings more than 1,000 years ago, is a thriving commercial center in northern Jutland.

FUNEN With an area of 2,980 sq. km (1,150 sq. miles), Funen is Denmark's second-largest island. Called the "garden of Denmark," Funen is known to the world as the birthplace of Hans Christian Andersen. Orchards, stately manors, and castles dot its rolling countryside. **Odense,** Andersen's birthplace, is a mecca for fairy-tale writers and fans from around the world. Nearby is Egeskov Castle, resting on oak columns in the middle of a small lake. Funen has a number of bustling ports, including **Nyborg** in the east and **Svendborg** at the southern end of the island. **Ærøskøbing** is a medieval market town that's a showplace of Scandinavian heritage.

BORNHOLM In the Baltic Sea, southeast of Zealand and close to Sweden, is the island of Bornholm. Prehistoric monuments and runic stones pepper the countryside, and numerous fishing villages dot the shoreline. On the northern coast, near **Hammerhus,** the Bornholm Animal and Nature Park is home to many native species as well as some that have been introduced from other parts of Scandinavia. Some of Europe's largest castle ruins dot this region of the island. The town of **Rønne** is the site of Denmark's oldest regional theater; it stages numerous concerts and shows year-round. The island of **Christiansø,** off the coast of Bornholm, was the site of Denmark's penal colony, where criminals spent their lives in slavery.

Norway

WESTERN NORWAY Western Norway is fabled for its fjords, saltwater arms of the sea that stretch inland. Many date from the end of the last ice age. The longest fjord in western Norway is the Sognefjord, north of Bergen, which penetrates 177km (110 miles) inland. The capital of the fjord district is **Bergen,** the largest city on the west coast. **Lofthus,** a collection of farms extending along the slopes of Sørfjorden, offers panoramic views of the fjord and the **Folgefonn Glacier.** Hiking is the primary activity in this region. The area north of the **Hardangerfjord** is a haven for hikers. Here you'll find Hardangervidda National Park, on Europe's largest high-mountain plateau, home to Norway's largest herd of wild reindeer. The town of **Voss** is surrounded by glaciers, fjords, rivers, and lakes.

CENTRAL NORWAY Fjords are also common in central Norway; the two largest are the Trondheimsfjord and Narnsfjord. It's not unusual for roads to pass waterfalls that cascade straight down into fjords. Many thick forests and snowcapped peaks fill central Norway. The town of **Geilo,** halfway between Bergen and Oslo, is one of Norway's most popular ski resorts. It boasts more than 129km (80 miles) of cross-country trails. **Trondheim,** central Norway's largest city, is home to Nidaros Domen, the 11th-century cathedral that was once the burial place for kings. **Røros** is a well-preserved 18th-century mining town. The medieval city of **Molde,** Norway's capital during World War II, plays host to one of Europe's largest jazz festivals. **Geiranger,** site of the Seven Sisters waterfall, is one of Norway's most popular resorts.

EASTERN NORWAY On the border with Sweden, eastern Norway is characterized by clear blue lakes, rolling hills, and green valleys. Campers and hikers enjoy the great forests of the Hedmark region, site of Norway's longest river, the Glomma (Gløma), which runs about 580km (360 miles). The area has many ski resorts, notably **Lillehammer,** site of the 1994 Winter Olympics. Norway's most visited destination is the capital, **Oslo,** which rises from the shores of the Oslofjord. The city of **Fredrikstad,** at the mouth of the Glomma, was once the marketplace for goods entering the country. Its 17th-century Kongsten Fort was designed to defend Norway from Sweden. **Tønsberg,** Norway's oldest town, dates to the 9th century. This area is also the site of the **Peer Gynt Road,** of Ibsen fame, and the mountainous region is home to numerous ski resorts.

SOUTHERN NORWAY Southern Norway is sometimes referred to as "the Riviera" because of its unspoiled and uncrowded—but chilly—beaches. **Stavanger,** the oil capital of Norway, is the largest southern city and is also quite popular. There's much to explore in this Telemark region, which is filled with lakes and canals popular for summer canoeing and boating. **Skien,** birthplace of the playwright Henrik Ibsen (1828–1906), is primarily an industrial town. The southern part of **Kristiansand**

links Norway with continental Europe. Close by is 10km (6¼-mile) **Hamresanden Beach,** one of the longest uninterrupted beaches in Europe. More fjords lie along the western half of the district, notably the Lysefjord, Sandefjord, and Vindefjord.

NORTHERN NORWAY The "Land of the Midnight Sun" is a region of craggy cliffs that descend to the sea and of deep, fertile valleys along the deserted moors. It has islands with few, if any, inhabitants, where life has remained relatively unchanged for generations. The capital of the Nordland region is **Bodø,** which lies just north of the Arctic Circle; it's a base for fishing trips and visits to the wild Glomfjord. Norway's second-largest glacier, **Svartisen,** is also in the area, as is the city of **Narvik,** a major arctic port and the gateway to the **Lofoten Islands.** The islands, which have many fishing villages, are one of the most beautiful areas of Norway.

TROMS Troms is the name of the province, and Tromsø, from which polar explorations are launched, is its capital. Troms contains one of Norway's most impressive mountain ranges, the Lyngs Alps, which attract winter skiers and summer hikers. Alta, site of the Altafjord, is reputed to have the best salmon-fishing waters in the world.

FINNMARK At the top of Norway is the Finnmark region, home of the Sami. Settlements here include **Kautokeino** (the Sami town) and **Hammerfest,** the world's northernmost town. Most tourists come to Finnmark to see the **North Cape,** Europe's northernmost point and an ideal midnight-sun viewing spot. **Vardø** is the only Norwegian mainland town in the Arctic climate zone. In the 17th century, Vardø was the site of more than 80 witch burnings. The town of **Kirkenes** lies 274km (170 miles) north of the Arctic Circle, close to the Russian border.

Sweden

GÖTALAND This is the most populated part of Sweden and includes eight provinces—Östergötland, Småland (the "Kingdom of Crystal"), Västergoütland, Skåne, Dalsland, Bohuslän, Halland, and Blekinge—plus the islands of Oüland and Gotland. The Goüta Canal cuts through this district. **Gothenburg** is the most important port in the west, and **Stockholm,** the capital, is the chief port in the east. Aside from Stockholm, **Skåne,** the château district, is the most heavily visited area, with its dunes, moors, and pasturelands. Many seaside resorts line the west and east coasts.

SVEALAND The central region encompasses the folkloric province of **Dalarna** (**Dalecarlia** in English) and **Värmland** (immortalized in the novels of Selma Lagerloüf). These districts are the ones most frequented by visitors. Other provinces include Våstmanland, Uppland, Soüdermanland, and Nårke. Ancient Svealand often is called the cultural heart of Sweden. Some 20,000 islands are along its eastern coast.

NORRLAND Northern Sweden makes up Norrland, which lies above the 61st parallel and includes about 50% of the landmass. It's inhabited by only about 15% of the population, including Sami and Finns. Norrland consists of 24 provinces, of which **Lapland** is the most popular with tourists. It's a land of thick forests, fast-flowing rivers, and towering mountains. Lapland, the home of the Sami reindeer herds, consists of tundra. **Kiruna** with its iron-ore deposits is one of Norrland's most important cities.

Finland

HELSINKI & THE SOUTHERN COAST More than 25% of Finland's people live in **Helsinki,** the capital of the country and the center of entertainment and culture; it's also a crossroads between western and eastern Europe. The eastern and central areas of the south are characterized by fertile farmland, crisscrossed by many rivers. The western land in the south has many shallow lakes and ridges. **Porvoo,** 48km (30 miles) northeast of Helsinki, was founded by the Swedes in 1346. It was the site of the first Finnish Diet, when the country became a Grand Duchy. **Kotka** is home to the Langinkoski Imperial Fishing Lodge, used by Czar Alexander III.

TURKU & THE ÅLAND ISLANDS The city of **Turku,** Finland's oldest city and former capital, is on the west coast. Its location on the Gulf of Bothnia, combined with a mild climate (its port remains ice-free year-round), have made this city an important center for trade and commerce. **Naantali,** 19km (12 miles) northwest of Turku, is one of the finest examples of a medieval Finnish town. At the entrance to the Gulf of Bothnia, only 120km (75 miles) from Stockholm, are the **Åland Islands** (about 6,500 in total). Only about 80 of the islands are inhabited, and all of their residents speak Swedish. The only significant town in the Ålands is **Mariehamn,** a fishing and tourist community founded in 1861.

THE LAKE REGION Central Finland is an important tourist area, with many resorts along the shores of the lakes. In this region you'll find **Tampere,** Finland's second-largest city, nestled on an isthmus between two lakes. **Lahti** is on the shores of Lake Vesijärvi, the gateway to Finland's most scenic lake systems. The resort of **Lappeenranta,** founded in 1649 just 16km (10 miles) from the Russian border, has been one of Finland's most popular spa resorts. Here you'll find Linnoitus, a fortress that was used by the Swedes and the Russians to stave off hostile attacks along this contested border. **Imatra,** in the southeast near the Russian border, is as close to St. Petersburg as it is to Helsinki. Outside town is the Imatra Rapids, one of Europe's most powerful waterfalls. The most visited town in the Lake Region is **Savonlinna,** with its 15th-century castle, Olavinlinna. This spa town was a favorite resort of Russian tsars.

FINNISH LAPLAND Lapland makes up more than one-third of Finland. This is the Land of the Midnight Sun, reindeer, and the Sami, with their traditional garb. Lapland is largely forested and untamed; bears and wolves still rule the land. Fishing and logging are the mainstays of the economy. Eight kilometers (5 miles) south of the Arctic Circle, the capital city, **Rovaniemi,** is a modern new town, rebuilt after the Nazis destroyed it during their retreat from Finland. The port of **Kemi,** which is at the mouth of the Kemikoji River, is the transit point for the many thousands of logs that are felled in Lapland. The village of **Tankavaara** is a major destination for those hunting for gold. The Sami village of **Inari,** on the shores of Lake Inari, is a thriving community that depends on reindeer farming and tourism. Not far from here is Finland's largest ski resort, **Saariselk.** Lapland is also home to Finland's largest national park, **Lemmenjoki,** and countless panoramic waterfalls and swift rivers.

DENMARK IN 1 WEEK

After a visit of 2 or 3 days to **Copenhagen,** Denmark's capital, you can set out to explore more of the island of Zealand on which Copenhagen sits. The highlights of North Zealand, both of which can be visited in a day, include the **Louisiana Museum of Modern Art** and **Kronborg Slot,** popularly called "Hamlet's Castle."

After an overnight, you can continue on to the cathedral city of **Roskilde** for another night before crossing the bridge onto the neighboring island of **Funen,** where you can spend 2 nights in its capital, **Odense,** birthplace of Hans Christian Andersen. Later you can head south for a night in the port city of **Svendborg** before a car ferry to the island of Ærø, the most beautiful in the Danish archipelago.

Denmark/Denmark & Sweden

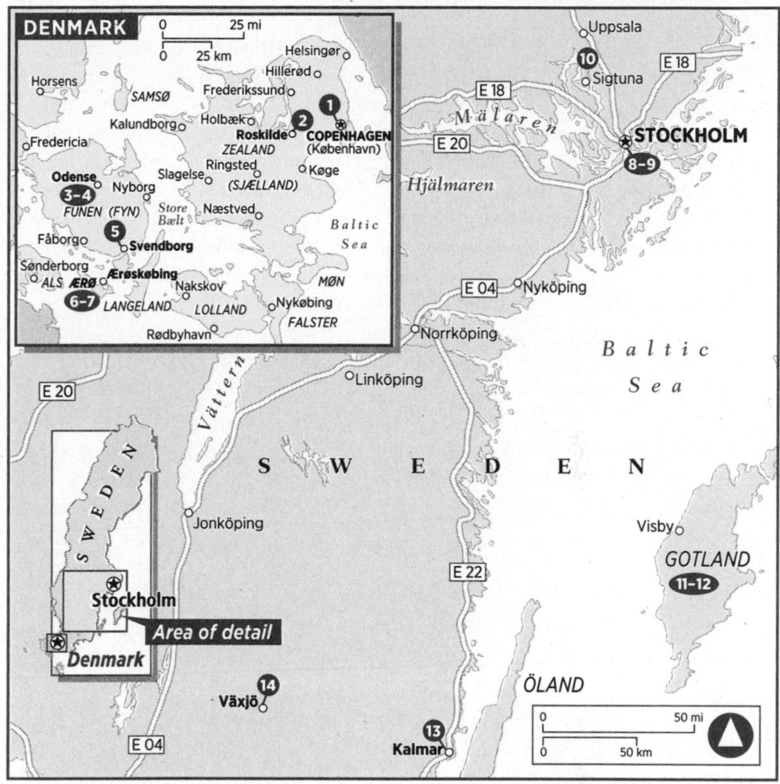

Day 1: Louisiana Museum ★★★ & Helsingør ★

On **Day 1** of our driving tour, after wrapping up your visit to Copenhagen and renting a car, head north in the morning to the town of Humlebaek, 32km (20 miles) north of Copenhagen, for a morning visit to the **Louisiana Museum of Modern Art** (p. 127), which opens at 10am. This is one of the greatest art museums of Scandinavia, and you'll want to give it at least 1½ hours.

From Copenhagen, follow coastal road 152, known as Strandvej. The scenic drive takes about 45 minutes. After a visit, continue north from Humlebaek into Helsingør, a distance of 14km (8½ miles), following the same Strandvej route. Once in Helsingør, you can check into a hotel for the night, but if you don't want to change hotels so often, you can use Copenhagen as your base and return there for the night.

There are many attractions in Helsingør, but the one magnet for most visitors is **Kronborg Slot** (p. 129), fabled as "Hamlet's Castle." Allow at least 1½ hours for an afternoon visit here after lunch in Helsingør.

Day 2: The Cathedral City of Roskilde ★★

On the morning of **Day 2,** leave Helsingør (or Copenhagen if you spent the night there) for a drive west to Roskilde. The distance is 32km (20 miles) west of Copenhagen, or 72km (45 miles) southwest of Helsingør. From Copenhagen, head west on the E-21 express highway; from Helsingør, follow Route 6 southwest.

If you're on Route 6 from Helsingør, you can stop off for a morning visit to **Hillerød,** a distance of 25km (15 miles) southwest of Helsingør, or 35km (22 miles) north of Copenhagen. This town possesses one of the great treasures of Denmark, the **Frederiksborg Castle** (p. 127), which has been called the Danish Versailles. Surrounded by a moat, it's the most beautiful royal residence in Denmark and the setting for the Museum of National History, with one of Denmark's greatest collections of historical paintings. Allow at least 1½ hours for a visit.

From Hillerød, continue along Route 6 southwest into Roskilde, where you can check into a hotel for the night. In the afternoon, visit the **Roskilde Domkirke** (p. 130) and try to take a 90-minute tour boat of the **Roskilde Fjord** (p. 141). If you can't schedule a visit to the fjord, then call on the **Lejre Research Center** (p. 131), which in spite of its dull name is actually a reconstructed Iron Age village.

Days 3 & 4: Odense ★★ & H. C. Andersen

On the morning of **Day 3,** leave Zealand altogether and drive west to the neighboring island of Funen, whose capital is **Odense,** lying 134km (83 miles) to the west of Roskilde. From Roskilde, take Route 14 southwest to the express highway E-20, continuing west to the port of Korsør, where you cross the Great Belt Bridge into Funen, entering the island through its gateway city of Nyborg. Once on land in Funen, continue west along E-20 until you see the cutoff arteries leading north into the center of Odense. Once here, book into a hotel for a 2-night stay.

After lunch you can take in some of the major sights of the city, including **H. C. Andersen's Childhood Home** (p. 155). If it's summer, you might even hook up with a 2-hour walking tour, taking in all the highlights. Check with the tourist office.

On the morning of **Day 4,** visit **Funen Village ★★** (p. 155), an open-air regional museum depicting life in Denmark in the 1700s and 1800s. In a busy afternoon you can visit **Egeskov Castle ★★★** (p. 156), one of the grandest in Denmark, as well as **Ladbyskibet** (p. 157), 19km (12 miles) northeast of Odense, to see the ruins of a 10th-century Viking ship.

Day 5: Svendborg ★: Favorite Port for Yachties

On the morning of **Day 5,** check out of your hotel in Odense and drive 43km (27 miles) south to the port city of Svendborg, following Route 9. Once in Svendborg, check into a hotel for the night and set out to see the rather minor sights in town, including **Anne Hvides Gård** (p. 160), **Skt. Jørgens Kirke** (p. 160), and **Skt. Nicolai Kirke** (p. 160). After lunch you can explore nearby islands, each linked to Svendborg by a bridge. These include the horseshoe-shaped **Thurø,** called the Garden of Denmark, and **Tåsinge** (p. 161), where you can visit several attractions such as the church tower at **Bregninge Kirke**

(p. 165) for its panoramic views. After a call on the 17th-century **Valdemars Slot ★★** (p. 162), you can spend the rest of the afternoon just exploring at random. Since the island is so small, it's almost impossible to get lost. Return to Svendborg for the night.

Days 6 & 7: Ærø ★★: Denmark's Most Beautiful Island

On the morning of **Day 6,** leave Svendborg by driving to the port, where you can board a car ferry heading for the island of **Ærø,** 29km (18 miles) across the water south of Svendborg. Check into a hotel in the picture-postcard capital of Ærøskøbing for 2 nights, and set out to explore the island.

Start by walking the cobblestone streets of this most enchanting of Danish villages. The main attraction of the town is Ærøskøbing itself, although there are specific sights of minor interest, including the **Ærø Museum** (p. 165) and an 18th-century church, **Ærøskøbing** (p. 165). Dine in an old *kro* (inn), and later walk down by the water to watch the yachts and other boats bobbing in the harbor at night.

On the morning of **Day 7,** set out on a leisurely motor tour of Ærøskøbing. We'd head east to the "second city" on **Marstal,** really just a little port town. After a 2-hour visit here you can take the southern road all the way to the little port **Søby** in the northwest. From Søby, you can drive southeast back to Ærøskøbing for the night.

The following morning you can take the ferryboat back to Svendborg, where you can drive north once again toward Odense, linking with the E-20 to carry you east across the Great Belt Bridge to Zealand and back to Copenhagen, where you can make air or rail connections to your next destination.

DENMARK & SWEDEN IN 2 WEEKS

After a 1-week tour of Denmark (see above), many visitors extend their Scandinavian trip for another week with a tour of Sweden. Rather than driving between Copenhagen and Stockholm, we suggest taking a shuttle flight. After a 2- or 3-day visit based in the Swedish capital, you can rent another car for a final look at Sweden during week 2, exploring some of the southern tier of the country. You can see the highlights of **Stockholm** in just 2 days, and take a 1-day trip to visit two ancient cities—**Sigtuna** and **Uppsala,** the latter the site of one of Scandinavia's greatest universities. The itinerary also calls for 2 days on the island of **Gotland,** highlighted by the medieval walled city of **Visby.** Back on the mainland, you'll have 2 days left to see the old port of **Kalmar** and its famous castle and to go shopping in the **glassworks district** of Sweden.

Days 8 & 9: Stockholm ★★★: Gateway to Sweden

You've spent the first 7 days exploring Denmark, so on **Day 8,** arrive in **Stockholm** as early as you can so you will have more time for sightseeing. After checking into a hotel for 2 or 3 nights, set out to explore the capital of Sweden.

Take our 2-hour walking tour of **Gamla Stan** (**Old Town;** coverage begins on p. 353). After lunch in an Old Town tavern, head for the **Royal Palace ★★** (p. 343).

In the afternoon, explore Scandinavia's top attraction, the 17th-century man-of-war, the ***Royal Vasa*** ★★★ (p. 349), pulled from the bottom of the sea. For a night of fun, go to **Skansen** on Djurgården (p. 349), which is an open-air museum with a vast array of attractions. It stays open until 10pm in summer.

On the morning of **Day 9,** set out to see all the highlights you missed on Day 8. The two greatest attractions that remain are both outside the city. If you work out the transportation details, you can see the first sight, **Drottningholm Palace and Theater** ★★★ (p. 350), in the late morning and the second attraction, **Millesgården** ★★★ (p. 351), by the end of the afternoon. For your final evening in Stockholm, head to **Gröna Lunds Tivoli** ★ (p. 369), an amusement park for family fun. It's not as great as the original Tivoli in Copenhagen, but visitors still enjoy it.

Day 10: Sigtuna ★ & Uppsala ★★★

On the morning of **Day 10,** you can still use Stockholm as your base, returning that evening, or else you can check out and stay in Uppsala.

Head northwest of Stockholm for 48km (30 miles) to visit the ancient town of **Sigtuna** on a north arm of Lake Mälaren. This is Sweden's oldest town, founded at the beginning of the 11th century. To reach it, drive north on the express highway, E-4, until you reach the turnoff leading west into the center of Sigtuna. Spend 2 hours wandering its old streets before returning to the E-4 for the final lap to **Uppsala,** 68km (42 miles) northwest of Stockholm.

Have lunch in this old university city. In the afternoon, visit **Uppsala Domkyrka,** the largest cathedral in Scandinavia; the **Linnaeus Garden and Museum,** founded by the world's most famous botanist; and end the day at **Gamla Uppsala** to see what remains of Old Uppsala, founded 15 centuries ago as the capital of the Svea kingdom.

Days 11 & 12: Gotland ★★ & Visby ★★★

On the morning of **Day 11,** leave Stockholm, or Uppsala as the case may be, and drive 219km (136 miles) south of Stockholm to catch the car ferry at Nynäshamn for the 3-hour journey to the island of Gotland.

After disembarking, visit the medieval walled city of **Visby** for a 2-night stopover. Spend the afternoon exploring its medieval streets (coverage begins on p. 446).

On the morning of **Day 12,** set out to discover the island on your own wheels, having armed yourself with a detailed map from the tourist office. Return to Visby by nightfall.

Day 13: Kalmar ★: The Key to Sweden

On the morning of **Day 13,** check out of your hotel in Visby, driving to the embarkation point for the Swedish mainland. Take a ferry that goes from Visby to the eastern coast port of Oskarshamn. Once here, follow **E-66** south to the port of **Kalmar,** 409km (254 miles) from Stockholm. You can arrive in Kalmar in time for a late lunch.

In the afternoon, visit **Kalmar Slott,** a castle founded in the 12th century and once called the key to Sweden because of its strategic position. In the fading afternoon, wander Kalmar's warren of cobblestone streets and market squares, most of them a holdover from the 17th century. Check into a hotel in Kalmar for the night.

Day 14: Växjö & the Kingdom of Crystal ★★★

On the morning of **Day 14,** your final day in Sweden, leave Kalmar in the morning and drive 110km (68 miles) to **Växjö,** the capital of the so-called Kingdom of Crystal, or the glassworks district. From Kalmar, head west on Route 25.

Once in Växjö, check into a hotel for the night. If your ancestors came from this district, you'll want to visit the **House of Emigrants.** If not, you can spend the rest of the day visiting the glass factories, the best of which are **Boda Glasbruk, Orrefors Glasbruk,** and **Kosta Glasbruk.** Feel free to skip one or two of these if you become "glassed out."

After an overnight at Växjö, you can head back north to Stockholm the following morning for transportation links to your next destination.

DENMARK FOR FAMILIES IN 1 WEEK

Denmark offers many attractions that kids enjoy, none more notable than Tivoli Gardens in Copenhagen. Our suggestion is to explore **Copenhagen** for 2 days, spend Day 3 visiting "Hamlet's Castle" in the north, and then head to the island of Funen, centering at its capital, **Odense,** birthplace of famed writer Hans Christian Andersen. Finally, we go to Jutland, which is Denmark's mainland link to the continent (via Germany). Here we visit its two major attractions, **Århus** and **Aalborg,** both containing Tivoli-like amusement parks of their own, plus numerous other attractions.

Days 1 & 2: Arrival in Copenhagen ★★★

Before renting a car to explore the countryside, you can take in the glories of Copenhagen itself, the most kid-friendly of all Scandinavian capitals. After you've checked into a hotel for 2 nights, take one of the bus and boat tours to get oriented. See "Organized Tours" (p. 141). Follow this up with a guided tour of **Amalienborg Palace ★★** (p. 118), where Queen Margrethe II lives with her royal family. After lunch, descend on **Tivoli Gardens ★★★** (p. 118), where you can wander for hours and grab dinner.

On the morning of **Day 2,** visit ***Den Lille Havfrue*** **★** (p. 119), *The Little Mermaid,* the most photographed statue in Scandinavia. After that, explore **Ny Carlsberg Glyptotek ★★★** (p. 115), one of the greatest art museums in Europe. If your child is older, he or she will enjoy the art here, which includes a prehistoric sculpture of a hippopotamus. In the afternoon, visit **Frilandsmuseet ★★★** (p. 126), an open-air museum and reconstructed village that evokes life in the 19th century, lying at Lyngby on the fringe of Copenhagen.

When you return to Copenhagen, you can do as many families do and pay a final visit to **Tivoli Gardens,** or else you can visit another amusement park, **Bakken** (p. 133), on the northern fringe of the city. If you like merry-go-rounds and roller coasters, Bakken is even more fun than the carefully manicured Tivoli.

Day 3: Helsingør ★ & Roskilde ★★

On the morning of **Day 3,** check out of your hotel and drive 40km (25 miles) north of Copenhagen, taking the E-4 express highway. Once at Helsingør you can pay a morning visit to the Dutch-Renaissance-style **Kronborg Castle,** legendary home of Shakespeare's fictional Hamlet.

Denmark for Families in 1 Week

After a visit of 1½ hours, you can head for our final destination of the day—the cathedral city of **Roskilde,** 72km (45 miles) southwest. It's reached by following Route 6 all the way. Check into a hotel in Roskilde for the day, and set about to explore this ancient city. Call first at the **Roskilde Domkirke** (p. 130). Kids delight in seeing the 16th-century clock, where a tiny sculpted St. George on horseback marks the hour by charging a dragon. Afterward, drive 20km (12 miles) north of Roskilde to see the **Viking Ship Museum** (p. 130), displaying the remains of five wrecked Viking-era ships. Return to Roskilde for the night.

Days 4 & 5: H. C. Andersen's Odense ★★

On the morning of **Day 4,** drive west from Roskilde for 134km (83 miles) until you reach Odense. To do so, you have to cross the Great Belt Bridge into Nyborg, lying west on the Funen side. From Nyborg, E-20 will carry you to Odense, where you can check into a hotel for 2 nights. In Odense, follow the same family-friendly itinerary as outlined in Days 3 and 4 under "Denmark in 1 Week," earlier.

Days 6 & 7: Denmark's Beautiful Island of Ærø ★★★

Leave Odense on the morning of **Day 6,** driving south to Svendborg, a distance of 43km (27 miles), following Route 9. Once at Svendborg, take a car ferry over to the island of Ærø, 29km (18 miles) from Svendborg. Once here, check into a hotel in the tiny island's capital, **Ærøskøbing,** for 2 nights and set about to explore this Lilliputian town with a driving tour of the island to follow on Day 7.

Use the same family-friendly itinerary as outlined under Days 6 and 7 under "Denmark in 1 Week," earlier.

After a visit to Ærø, you can return to Copenhagen the following day, using a bridge and a ferry boat. Copenhagen is a distance of 176km (110 miles) to the east of Ærø.

SWEDEN FOR FAMILIES IN 1 WEEK

Our suggestion is to limit **Stockholm** to 2 days, **Gothenburg** to 1 day, and combine a visit to **Malmö,** Sweden's third-largest city, and the university city of **Lund** on your seventh and final day. The entire family can enjoy a drive across Sweden, bypassing the **Göta Canal** and spending the night in the ancient town of **Mariestad.**

Days 1 & 2: Stockholm ★★★: Family Fun in the Capital

On the morning of **Day 1,** set out to explore **Stockholm** by taking our walking tour of **Gamla Stan** (**Old Town;** p. 353). Have lunch in the Old Town and follow with a visit to the **Kungliga Slottet** ★★ (p. 343), the royal palace. Kids also enjoy seeing the **Changing of the Royal Guard** ★ (p. 346), but that can be difficult to schedule. The palace is such a vast complex that children always find lots of attractions here to interest them. After a stroll through, head for the **Vasamuseet** ★★★ (***Royal Vasa;*** p. 349), the 17th-century man-of-war that sank on its maiden voyage. Spend your first night in Stockholm at **Gröna Lunds Tivoli** ★ (p. 369), a vast amusement park that will be the highlight of the Swedish capital for many kids.

On the morning of **Day 2,** set out to see many of the highlights of **Stockholm** you didn't have time for on Day 1. Begin the day by taking in the vast compound of **Skansen** ★★★ (p. 349), Sweden's greatest open-air museum. This vast parkland has old workshops and some 150 antique buildings. Expect to spend the entire morning here. To cap your afternoon, the whole family will enjoy one of the **canal cruises** offered by Stockholm Sightseeing (p. 360). No doubt your kids will demand to be taken back to **Gröna Lunds Tivoli** ★ (p. 369) for their final night in Stockholm.

Day 3: Mariestad ★ & the Göta Canal ★★★

The **Göta Canal** is the most scenic water route in Sweden, linking Stockholm in the east with the second-largest city of Gothenburg in the west. In all, it's a journey of 560km (347 miles), which can be comfortably broken up into 2 days of driving. Leave Stockholm on the morning of **Day 3,** taking the E-3 expressway west all the way to the town of **Mariestad.** In the first day you'll need to cover 318km (197 miles). Mariestad is the best center for taking cruises on

Sweden for Families in 1 Week

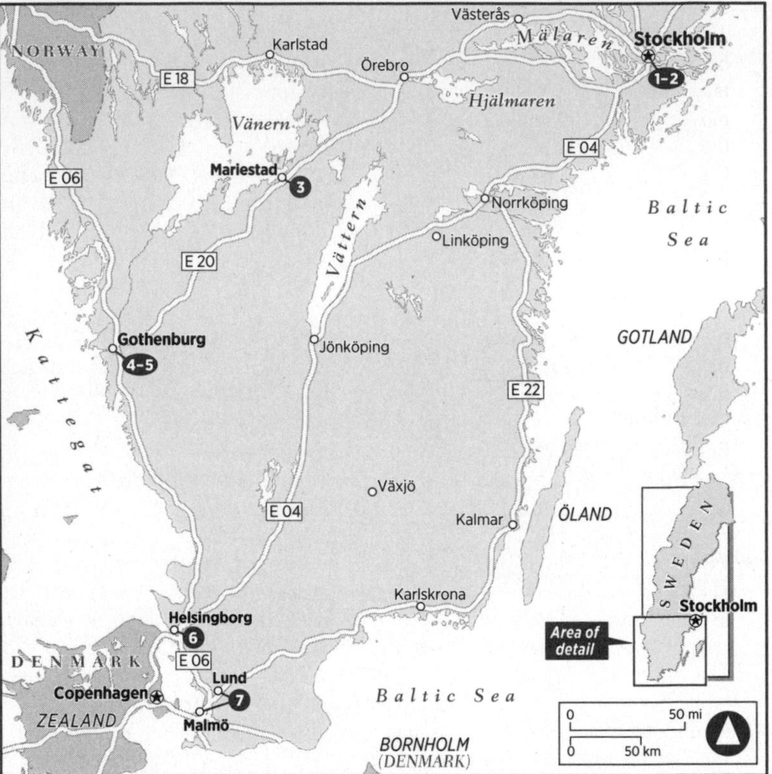

Lake Vänern, which, with its 20,000 small islands and islets, is the world's largest freshwater archipelago. Try to get as early a start in Stockholm as you can so you'll arrive in Mariestad in time to take one of the cruises. Check with the tourist office as soon as you arrive in Mariestad to see what's available.

Days 4 & 5: Arrival in Gothenburg ★★★

On the morning of **Day 4,** leave Mariestad and continue in a southwest direction 180km (112 miles) along E-3 to the capital of the west coast of Sweden, the maritime city of **Gothenburg.** Some kids we've encountered traveling in Sweden with their families have told us they like Gothenburg more than Stockholm.

On your first day, take the classic **Paddan boat ride ★★** (p. 389), traveling through the moat and canal out to the harbor and the giant dockland. Return for a stroll along the **Avenyn,** the main street of Gothenburg and the scene of an active street life.

As the afternoon fades, head for **Liseberg Park ★★** (p. 386), the largest amusement park in Scandinavia. You can spend the evening here, as it's open until 10 or 11pm in summer. Dozens of restaurants, including fast-food joints, await you. Return to your hotel where you will need a 2-night booking to take in the highlights of Gothenburg.

On the morning of **Day 5,** get up early to visit the **fish auction** at the harbor, beginning at 7am (p. 386). After seeing **Feskekörka** (p. 386), the "fish church," take tram 6 to the **Guldhedens Vattentorn** (p. 385), a water tower, for the most panoramic view of Gothenburg. Later, go to the **Götaplatsen** (p. 386) in the center of Gothenburg to gaze upon the **Poseidon Fountain,** sculptured by Carl Milles, Sweden's greatest sculptor. This is a great place for a family photo.

Later in the afternoon, explore **Botaniska Trädgården ★★** (p. 388), with its array of natural amusements. In the late afternoon or early evening, nearly all families return to **Liseberg Park ★★** (p. 386) for another night of fun.

Day 6: Helsingborg: Gateway to Denmark

On the morning of **Day 6,** leave Gothenburg and drive south for 230km (143 miles) to **Helsingborg** at the narrowest point of the Öresund, a body of water that separates Sweden and Denmark. At this point the two countries are only 5km (3 miles) apart, and Denmark lies a 25-minute ferry ride from Helsingborg. From Gothenburg, drive south on the E-6 to reach Helsingborg.

After checking into a hotel for the night, set about to explore the attractions of Helsingborg, including the **Fredriksdal Open-Air Museum and Botanical Garden** (p. 403), and the **Sofiero Slott** (p. 404), a former royal residence 5km (3 miles) north of Helsingborg.

In the midafternoon you can cross over on the ferry to **Helsingør** in Denmark to visit the so-called Hamlet's Castle. Return to Helsingborg for the night.

Day 7: Lund ★★ & Malmö ★★

On the morning of **Day 7,** your final day in Sweden, leave Helsingborg in the morning and drive along E-6 in the direction of **Malmö.** At the junction with Route 66, make a detour north to the university and cathedral city of **Lund.** Lund is 56km (35 miles) from Helsingborg.

At Lund, entice your child to accompany you to the **Domkyrkan ★★★** (p. 423), or Cathedral of Lund. The 14th-century astronomical clock here is sure to enchant with its Middle Ages–style tournament complete with clashing knights and the blare of trumpets. Before the morning fades, you can also visit the **Kulturen ★★** (p. 424), an open-air museum of old houses, complete with a kid-pleasing carriage museum. After lunch in Lund, head on to Malmö for the night, where you can check into a hotel. Malmö lies only 18km (11 miles) south of Lund; take Route 66.

With the time remaining in the afternoon, you can visit **Malmöhus Slott ★★** (p. 411), the old Malmö castle that has so many museums and galleries that everyone will find something of interest here. After dinner, reward your kids with a visit to **Folkets Park** (People's Park), Amiralsgatan 35 (© **040/709-90**), a compound filled with Tivoli-like amusements, including a playhouse just for kids.

The following morning it will be just a short drive over Öresund Bridge and into **Copenhagen,** where transportation arrangements can be made to most parts of the world.

FINLAND IN 1 WEEK

After your whirlwind tour of Denmark, Norway, and Sweden, there remains the more remote country of Finland in the far east, hovering over Russia. You can either fly or sail to Helsinki, the capital of Finland, from Stockholm, or other points.

After a 2-day visit to Helsinki, with side trips, you can rent a car to see the two other major destinations in the country, the cities of Tampere and historic Turku. If time remains, you can use Turku as an embarkation point for the Åland Islands for a 2-day visit.

Days 1 & 2: Helsinki ★★★: Gateway to Finland

Arrive in Helsinki in the morning if you can so you'll have more time for sightseeing and visiting the main attractions, some of which are in the environs. Check into a hotel for 2 nights.

Before the morning fades, visit the **Ateneum Art Museum ★★** part of the **Finnish National Gallery** (p. 490), spending at least 2 hours here.

After lunch, you can spend the rest of the afternoon exploring the **Seurasaari Open-Air Museum ★★★** (p. 493) with the biggest collection of historic buildings in the country, including the 18th-century Suomenlinna Fortress. You can take a ferryboat from Market Square to reach this mini-archipelago in the Baltic.

Back in town, and if it's a summer night, you can head for the **Linnanmäki Amusement Park** 3km (2 miles) north of Helsinki. This is a fun fair for all ages, with splashing fountains, rides, restaurants, cafes, and theaters.

On the morning of the second day, you can pick up your prearranged rental car and explore some of the sights in the heavily forested Finnish countryside.

Heading out of town, drive 39km (24 miles) along E-79 north to Järvenpää where a signpost points to **Ainola ★★** (p. 493). This log-constructed building was the former home of Jean Sibelius, Finland's greatest composer, who lived here for more than half a century. Both Jean and Aino, his wife, are buried on the property.

Return to Helsinki by lunchtime, and plan a second excursion in the afternoon to the historic town of **Porvoo ★★** 48km (30 miles) northeast of Helsinki. Instead of driving, we'd recommend a summer trip aboard one of two boats that sail to Porvoo from Market Square in Helsinki. For complete details, see p. 495.

Once at Porvoo, you can visit its late-13th-century cathedral and the studio of Albert Edelfelt, one of Finland's most famous painters. Return to Helsinki for the night.

Day 3: Tampere ★

Leave Helsinki in the morning and head north along the expressway, E-79, following the signs to **Hämeenlinna,** a distance of 98km (61 miles). Consider a luncheon stopover in Hämeenlinna: Finland's oldest inland town, founded in 1639, was the birthplace of Jean Sibelius. You can explore the old castle on the shores of Lake Vanajavesi.

After Hämeenlinna, continue northwest along E-79 into **Tampere,** 172km (107 miles) from Helsinki. Check into a hotel for the night in Finland's second-largest city.

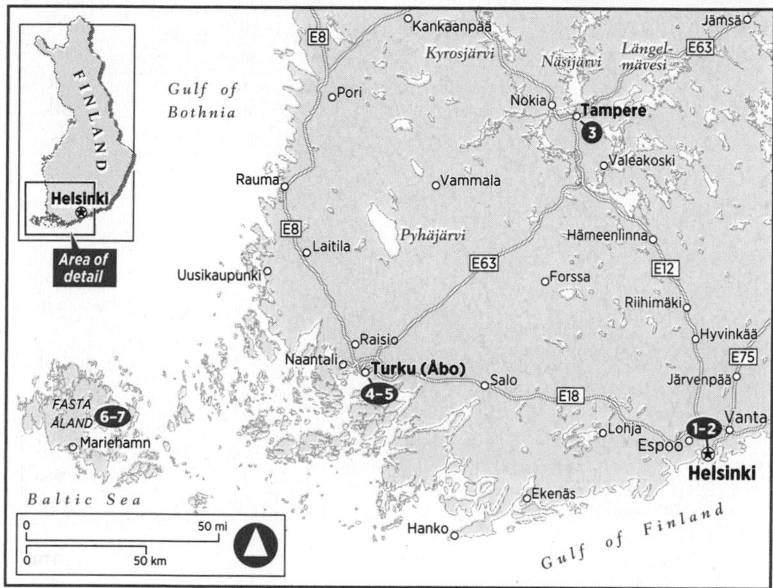

The city is built on a narrow isthmus between two lakes. **Tampere Art Museum** and **Tuomiokirkko ★★★**, its cathedral, are easy to explore. See p. 531 for details. If it's summer, attend a night performance at the **Pyynikki Summer Theater ★★★** (p. 531).

Days 4 & 5: Turku ★★★

In the morning of **Day 4,** leave Tampere and follow E-80 155km (96 miles) southeast to the historic seaport of **Turku,** the oldest city in Finland and its former capital. Check into a hotel for 2 nights and set out to explore the major sights, including the twin museums of **Aboa Vetus ★★** and **Ars Nova ★** (p. 510); **Taidemuseo ★★** (p. 512), the second major art museum in Finland, and **Tuomiokirkko ★★★** (p. 512), the mother of the Lutheran Church of the country, dating from the 13th century.

On the morning of **Day 5,** while still based in Turku, take a summer boat ride aboard the SS *Ukkopekka* (p. 516) to the town of Naantali, famous for its **Old Town ★★★**. Spend a day here, wandering and exploring, perhaps visiting **Kultaranta ★★★**, the stunning summer residence of the president of Finland (p. 517).

Secure the makings of a picnic and enjoy it on the grounds of **Moominworld** (p. 517), with a beach and several other attractions. Return to Turku for the night.

Days 6 & 7: Åland Islands ★★

On **Day 6,** you can leave the port of Turku and take a seagoing ferry to **Mariehamn,** the capital of the Ålands, an archipelago lying off the west coast of

Finland between Stockholm and Turku (p. 520). The archipelago consists of 6,500 islands, islets, and skerries.

After arriving in Mariehamn, the only real town, check into a hotel for 2 nights. In the afternoon you can visit the **Ålands Museum ★** and the **Museum Ship *Pommern* ★**.

On **Day 7,** explore the other islands, which are connected by a series of bridges, causeways, and ferry services.

After a final night in Mariehamn, return to Helsinki for your ongoing transportation.

WESTERN FJORD COUNTRY IN 1 WEEK

This driving tour of the fjords of western Norway, one of the world's greatest tourist attractions, is far more scenic than the environs of Oslo. Of course, one of the grandest parts of it may be seen by boat—not by car—traversing the most scenic of the fjords such as Sognefjord.

If all the fjords were laid out in a straight line, they would measure 21,347km (13,264 miles), the distance between the north and south poles. Throw in Europe's largest glacier, little fjordside farming villages, and jagged snowcapped peaks, and you've got beauty galore. The Ice Age did a good job in carving out this wonderland of nature.

Day 1: Ålesund ★★: Top of the Fjord Country

Spread over three islands and opening onto two bright blue fjords, **Ålesund** is a good launch pad for a driving tour of the fjord country, lying 1,186km (737 miles) northwest of Oslo. Because it is such a long distance from Oslo, it's best to fly here and rent a car before setting out. There are no rail lines to Ålesund.

Before heading out from Ålesund, you can explore the rebuilt Art Nouveau town, including its most important attraction, the **Sunnmøre Museum,** one of the fjord country's best open-air museums.

Day 2: Åndalsnes & Romsdalsfjord ★

Leave Ålesund on the morning of Day 2, driving east to the resort of **Åndalsnes,** a distance of 127km (79 miles), following A69. When here check into a hotel for the night. At Åndalsnes, try to hook up with a summer excursion, especially one involving a hike thought the **Romsdalen Alps** enveloping Åndalsnes. The summit of **Nesaksla Mountain** towers over Åndalsnes at 715m (2,345 ft.). You can ask about boat trips on **Romsdalsfjord,** one of the most beautiful in western Norway.

Day 3: The Trollstigvein ★ to Geirangerfjord

On the morning of Day 3, leave Åndalsnes and head south on one of the great motor drives in Norway, the **Trollstigvein.** This 20-hour drive along Route 63 takes you to the fjord resort of **Geiranger,** a distance of 85km (53 miles). At one point the highway climbs 620m (2,034 ft). When it opened in 1952 (and even today), the **Ørnevein,** or Eagle's Road, section was a marvel of engineering. Nearly one dozen hairpin turns await you, opening onto panoramic views over **Geirangerfjord.**

Western Fjord Country in 1 Week

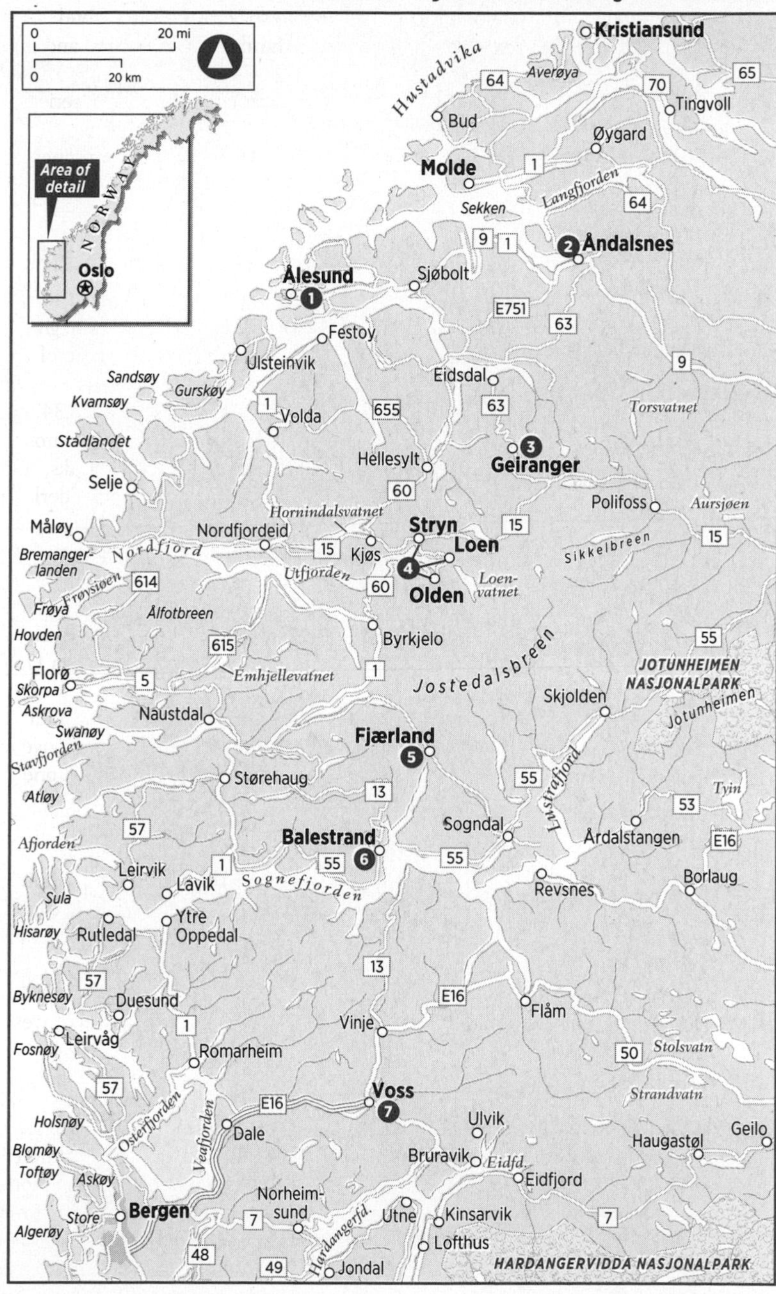

At the resort of **Geiranger,** explore the area in the afternoon after checking into a hotel for the night. Its waterfalls, such as the **Seven Sisters,** are among the most dramatic in the world. If it's summer, and you arrive late, there's also an evening tour of the Geirangerfjord.

Day 4: A Trio of Resorts: Stryn, Loen & Olden

On the morning of Day 4, leave Geiranger and take the ferry across the Geirangerfjord to Hellesylt, a scenic hour's boat ride away. At Hellesylt, follow the signs south to **Stryn,** a distance of 50km (30 miles), traveling along Route 60. You can check into a hotel for the night at Stryn, Loen, or Olden because the cluster of resorts are close together.

Each of these resorts is a base for exploring one of the natural wonders of Norway, the ice plateau of **Jostedalsbreen National Park,** lying between Sognefjord and Nordfjord. The glacier is the largest in Europe, and you must have a qualified guide to tour it.

Day 5: Fjaerland ★★

On the morning of Day 5, head 60km (37 miles) to the south to **Fjaerland,** where you can check into a hotel for the night. When at Fjaerland, spend the afternoon touring **Bøyaøyri Estuary,** a protected nature reserve north of the village, and visit the exhibits at the **Norwegian Glacier Museum.**

Day 6: Balestrand ★★ & the Sognefjord ★★★

On the morning of Day 6, leave Fjaerland and journey by car ferry to **Balestrand,** a scenic boat ride taking only 45 minutes. Check into a hotel for the night before setting out to explore one of the world's deepest and most beautiful fjords, the famous **Sognefjord.** This fjord stretches for 205km (127 miles), and a scenic boat ride on it will consume your afternoon.

Day 7: Voss: ★ Summer Fun in a Winter Playground

On Day 7, it's just a 90km (56 mile) drive south to **Voss,** where you can check into a hotel for the night. Route 13 links Balestrand to Voss, but the section between Vangsnes and Balestrand is by car ferry. A wide range of activities await you in Voss. It's also a good "escape" point back to either Bergen or Oslo; which can be your transportation hubs for leaving Norway.

THE BEST OF DENMARK

Denmark presents visitors with an embarrassment of riches—everything from exciting Copenhagen and historic castles to unusual offshore islands and quaint villages. To help you decide how best to spend your time, we've compiled a list of our favorite experiences and discoveries. In the following pages, you'll find the kind of candid advice we'd give our close friends.

4

THE best TRAVEL EXPERIENCES

- **A Day (and Night) at Tivoli Gardens:** These 150-year-old pleasure gardens are worth the airfare to Copenhagen all by themselves. They offer a little bit of everything: open-air dancing, restaurants, theaters, concert halls, an amusement park . . . and, oh yes, gardens as well. From the first bloom of spring until the autumn leaves start to fall, they're devoted to lighthearted fun. The gardens are worth a visit any time but are especially pleasant at twilight, when the lights begin to glint among the trees. See chapter 6.
- **A Week Down on the Farm:** The best way to see the heart of Denmark and meet the Danes is to spend a week on one of their farms. Nearly 400 farms around the country take in paying guests. Stick a pin anywhere on a map of Denmark away from the cities and seacoast, and you'll find a thatched and timbered farm, or perhaps a more modern homestead. Almost anyplace makes a good base from which to explore the rest of the country on day trips. Although there's no official agency to arrange such holidays, many visitors seeking this kind of offbeat accommodation often surf the Internet for farms that advertise their willingness to receive guests. Another way to hook up is to decide what part of Denmark you'd like to visit and then contact the nearest tourist office for a list of farms willing to accept paying guests.
- **On the Trail of the Vikings:** Renowned for 3 centuries of fantastic exploits, the Vikings explored Greenland to the north, North America to the west, and the Caspian Sea to the south and east from roughly A.D. 750 to 1050. Their legacy lives on in Denmark. Relive the age at the **Nationalmuseet** in Copenhagen, which displays burial grounds of the Viking period, along with the largest and richest hoards of treasure, including relics from the "Silver Age." Even Viking costumes are

exhibited. See p. 122. At Roskilde, explore the **Viking Ship Museum,** containing five vessels found in a fjord nearby, the largest of which was built in Ireland around 1060 and manned by 60 to 100 warriors. See p. 130. If you're in Ribe, check out the **Ribe VikingeCenter** (p. 179), which re-creates a Viking village, right down to the falconry demonstration that is always a crowd pleaser. See chapters 6 and 7.

- **In the Footsteps of Hans Christian Andersen:** To some visitors, this storyteller is the very symbol of Denmark. The fairy tale lives on in Odense, on the island of Funen, where Andersen was born the son of a shoemaker in 1805. His childhood home, a small half-timbered house on Munkemøllestræde, where he lived from 1807 to 1817, has been turned into a museum. You can also visit the H. C. Andersens Hus, where much of his memorabilia is stored (including his walking stick and top hat), and take a few moments to listen to his tales on tape. But mostly you can wander the cobblestone streets that he knew so well, marveling at the life of this man—and his works—that, in the words of his obituary, struck "chords that reverberated in every human heart," as they still do today. See p. 156.

THE best SCENIC TOWNS & VILLAGES

- **Ærøskøbing:** This little village on the country's most charming island (Ærø) is storybook Denmark. A 13th-century market town, Ærøskøbing is a Lilliputian souvenir of the past, complete with little gingerbread houses. You expect Hansel and Gretel to arrive at any moment. See "Across the Water to Ærø" in chapter 7.
- **Odense:** The birthplace of Hans Christian Andersen is visited by thousands of the storyteller's fans every year. Denmark's third-largest city still has a medieval core, and you can walk its cobblestone streets and admire its half-timbered houses, including the H. C. Andersens Hus. Other than its associations with the writer, Odense is a worthwhile destination in its own right, filled with attractions (including St. Canute's Cathedral). On the outskirts you can explore everything from the 1554 Renaissance castle, Egeskov, to a 10th-century Viking ship at Ladby. See "Odense: Birthplace of Hans Christian Andersen" in chapter 7.
- **Ribe:** On the island of Jutland, this is the best-preserved medieval town in Denmark—known for its narrow cobblestone lanes and crooked, half-timbered houses. An important trading center during the Viking era, it's known today as the town where the endangered stork—the subject of European myth and legend—nests every April. The National Trust protects the medieval center. From April to mid-September a night watchman circles Ribe, spinning tales of the town's legendary days and singing traditional songs. See "Ribe" in chapter 7.
- **Ebeltoft:** On Jutland, this well-preserved town of half-timbered buildings is the capital of the Mols hill country. It's a town of sloping row houses, crooked streets, and local handicraft shops. The town hall looks as if it had been erected for kindergarten children; in Ebeltoft you can also visit the 1860 frigate *Jylland,* the oldest man-of-war in Denmark. See "Ebeltoft" in chapter 7.

THE best ACTIVE VACATIONS

- **Biking:** A nation of bikers, Denmark has organized the roads to suit the national sport. A network of bike routes and paths is protected from heavy traffic, and much of the terrain is flat. Bicycling vacations are available as inclusive tours that cover bike rental, ferry tickets, and accommodations en route. Some deluxe tours transport your luggage from one hotel to the next. For more information, contact the **Danish Cycling Federation,** Rømersgade 5, DK-1362 Copenhagen (✆ **33-32-31-21;** www.dcf.dk).

- **Camping:** With about 550 officially sanctioned campgrounds, Denmark has one of the highest numbers, per capita, of campgrounds of any nation in the world, and living in a tent or a pop-up trailer in the great outdoors is something of a national obsession. There are plenty of campsites near the city limits of Copenhagen, and many more are around the country in areas of scenic or historic interest, some near the sea. The official website of the **Danish Camping Federation** is www.campingraadet.dk. For information about the nation's campsites, visit the website, call, or write at Campingrådet, Mosedalsvej 15, DK-2500 Valby (✆ **39-27-88-44**). Other sources of information about camping are available at www.visitdenmark.com (the official website of the Danish Tourist Board), or an equivalent site, www.dk-camp.dk, which lists more than 300 campsites that are privately owned. You can obtain a free *DK Camping Danmark* catalog at all DK-CAMPing grounds, tourist offices, and many service stations.
- **Fishing:** For centuries, much of Denmark relied on the sea and whatever the country's fishermen could pull out of it for its diet. Since then, no *smørrebrød* buffet has been complete without a selection of shrimp, herring, and salmon. The preparation of plaice, cod, eel, perch, and trout are culinary art forms. The seas off Funen, especially within the Great Belt, have yielded countless tons of seafood, and that tradition has encouraged anglers and sport enthusiasts to test their luck in the rich waters of the Baltic. Many outfitters can introduce you to the mysteries of fresh- and saltwater fishing.
- **Golf:** There are about 130 golf courses scattered across the flat, sandy, and sometimes windy landscapes of Denmark, many of them landscaped around the sand dunes, ponds, forests, and rocky outcroppings for which the country is well known. Most of the clubs welcome visitors, although in some cases you might be asked to present a membership card from your club at home. Local tourism offices are usually well versed in steering golfers to worthwhile courses, but for some insight into what's available, visit www.golfonline.dk.
- **Horseback Riding:** Riding schools throughout Denmark rent horses, and local tourist offices can hook you up with a stable if one is available in their area. Our favorite place for riding is **Krogbækgaard,** Læso, DK-9940 (✆ **98-49-15-05;** www.rideferie.dk). It is on Langeland, a long and narrow tidal barrier off the southern coast of Funen. The stable houses 120 Islandic ponies, a sturdy breed that survives well in the harsh climate and scrub-covered landscape of this wind-swept island.

THE best FESTIVALS & SPECIAL EVENTS

- **July 4th Festival** (Rebild, near Aalborg): This is one of the few places outside the United States that celebrates U.S. independence. Each year Danes and Danish Americans gather for picnic lunches, outdoor entertainment, and speeches. See chapter 2 and chapter 7.
- **Aalborg Carnival:** Celebrated in late May, this is one of the country's great spring events. Happy revelers in colorful costumes fill the streets. Almost 10,000 people take part in the celebration, honoring the victory of spring over winter. See chapter 7.

- **Copenhagen Jazz Festival:** One of the finest jazz festivals in Europe takes place in July. During this festival, you can find some of the best musicians in the world jamming here in the Danish capital. Indoor and outdoor concerts—many of them free—are presented. See chapter 2.
- **Viking Festival** (Frederikssund): During this annual festival (mid-June to early July), bearded Vikings revive Nordic sagas in an open-air theater. After each performance, there's a traditional Viking banquet. See chapter 2.

THE best CASTLES & PALACES

- **Christiansborg Palace** (Copenhagen): The queen receives official guests here in the Royal Reception Chamber, where you must don slippers to protect the floors. The complex also holds the Parliament House and the Supreme Court. From 1441 until the fire of 1795, this was the official residence of Denmark's monarchy. You can tour the richly decorated rooms, including the Throne Room and banqueting hall. Below you can see the well-preserved ruins of the 1167 castle of Bishop Absalon, founder of Copenhagen. See p. 122.
- **Rosenborg Castle** (Copenhagen): Founded by Christian IV in the 17th century, this red-brick Renaissance castle remained a royal residence until the early 19th century, when the building was converted into a museum. It still houses the crown jewels, and its collection of costumes and royal memorabilia is unequaled in Denmark. See p. 120.
- **Kronborg Slot** (Helsingør): Shakespeare never saw this castle, and Hamlet (if he existed at all) lived centuries before it was ever built. But Shakespeare did set his immortal play here. Intriguing secret passages and casemates fill its cannon-studded bastions, and it often serves as the backdrop for modern productions of *Hamlet.* The brooding statue of Holger Danske sleeps in the dungeon, but, according to legend, this Viking chief will rise again to defend Denmark if the country is endangered. See p. 129.
- **Frederiksborg Castle** (Hillerød): Known as the Danish Versailles, this moated *slot* (castle) is the most elaborate in Scandinavia. It was built in the Dutch Renaissance style of red brick with a copper roof, and its oldest parts date from 1560. Much of the castle was constructed under the direction of the master builder, Christian IV, from 1600 to 1620. Fire ravaged the castle in 1859, and the structure had to be completely restored. It is now a major national history museum. See p. 127.
- **Egeskov Castle** (Kværndrup): On the island of Funen, this 1554 Renaissance "water castle" is amid splendid gardens. The most romantic example of Denmark's fortified manors, the castle was built in the middle of a moat, surrounded by a park. The best-preserved Renaissance castle of its type in Europe, it has many attractions on its grounds, including airplane and vintage automobile museums. See p. 156.

THE best OFFBEAT EXPERIENCES

- **Cycling Around Ærø:** Regardless of how busy our schedule, we always like to devote at least 1 sunny day on what we view as the greatest cycling trip in Denmark: a slow, scenic ride around the island of Ærø, off the coast of Funen. The island, relatively flat, its countryside dotted with windmills, evokes the fields of

Holland, but is unique unto itself. Country roads will take you across fertile fields and into villages of cobbled streets and half-timbered houses. You'll think Hans Christian Andersen planned the island just for you. This is small-town Denmark at its best. Yes, you'll even pass a whistling postman in red jacket and gold-and-black cap looking like an extra in a 1940s film. See p. 163.

- **Journeying Back to the 1960s:** The counterculture of the 1960s lives on in Christiania, a Copenhagen community at the corner of Prinsessegade and Badsmandsstræde on Christianshavn. Founded in 1972, this anarchists' commune occupies former army barracks; its current residents preach a gospel of drugs and peace. Christiania's residents have even organized their own government and passed laws, for example, to legalize drugs. They're not complete anarchists, however, since they venture into the city at least once a month to pick up their social welfare checks. Today you can wander about their community, which is complete with a theater, cafes, grocery stores, and even a local radio station. See chapter 5 under "Christianshavn."
- **Exploring Erotica:** In 1968, Denmark was the first country ever to "liberate" pornography, and today, the **Erotica Museum,** at Købmagergade 24 (© **33-12-03-11**) in Copenhagen, is devoted to the subject. Learn about the sex lives of such famous figures as Nietzsche, Freud, and even Duke Ellington. Founded by a photographer of nudes, the museum has exhibits ranging from the tame to the tempestuous.
- **Calling on Artists & Craftspeople:** West Jutland has many open workshops where you can see craftspeople in action; you can meet the potter, the glassblower, the painter, the textile designer, and even the candlestick maker. Local tourist offices can tell you which studios are open to receive guests in such centers as Tønder, Ribe, and Ærø.

THE best BUYS

- **Danish Design:** It's worth making a shopping trip to Denmark. The simple but elegant style that became fashionable in the 1950s has made a comeback. Danish modern chairs, glassware, and even buildings have returned. Collectors celebrate "old masters" such as Arne Jacobsen, Hans Wegner, and Poul Kjærholm, whose designs from the 1940s and 1950s are sold in antiques stores. Wegner, noted for his sculptured teak chairs, for example, is now viewed as the grand old man of Danish design. Younger designers have followed in the old masters' footsteps, producing carefully crafted items for the home—everything from chairs and desks to table settings and silverware. For the best display of Danish design today, walk along the pedestrian-only Strøget, the major shopping street of Copenhagen. The best single showcase for modern Danish design may be **Illums Bolighus,** Amagertorv 10 (© **33-14-19-41;** www.illumsbolighus.dk).
- **Crystal & Porcelain:** Holmegaard crystal and Royal Copenhagen porcelain are household names, known for their beauty and craftsmanship. These items cost less in Denmark than in the United States, although signed art glass is costly everywhere. To avoid high prices, you can shop for seconds, which are discounted by 20% to 50% (sometimes the imperfection can be detected only by an expert). The best center for these collectors' items in Copenhagen is **Royal Copenhagen Porcelain,** Amagertorv 6 (© **33-13-71-81;** www.royalcopenhagen.com).

- **Silver:** Danish designers have made a name for themselves in this field. Even with taxes and shipping charges, you can still save about 50% when purchasing silver in Denmark as compared with in the United States. If you're willing to consider "used" silver, you can get some remarkable discounts. The big name in international silver—and you can buy it at the source—is **Georg Jensen,** Amagertorv 6, Copenhagen (© **33-11-40-80;** www.georgjensen.com).

THE best HOTELS

- **Hotel d'Angleterre** (Copenhagen; www.remmen.dk; © **33-12-00-95**): Some critics rate this as the finest hotel in Denmark. As it drifted toward mediocrity a few years back, a massive investment was made to save it. Now the hotel is better than ever—housing a swimming pool and a nightclub. Behind its Georgian facade, much of the ambience is in the traditional English mode. Service is among the finest in Copenhagen. See p. 198.
- **Falsled Kro** (Falsled; www.falsledkro.dk; © **62-68-11-11**): Not only does this house Funen Island's finest accommodations, but it's the quintessential Danish inn, with origins dating from the 1400s. This Relais & Châteaux property has elegant furnishings as well as a top-quality restaurant, rivaling the best in Copenhagen. See p. 163.
- **Hotel Hesselet** (Nyborg; www.hesselet.dk; © **65-31-30-29**): This stylish modern hotel on Funen Island occupies a woodland setting in a beech forest. The spacious rooms are artfully decorated, often with traditional furnishings. A library, Oriental rugs, and an open fireplace add graceful touches to the public areas. Many Copenhagen residents come here for a retreat, patronizing the hotel's gourmet restaurant at night. See p. 153.
- **Hotel Dagmar** (Ribe; www.hoteldagmar.dk; © **75-42-00-33**): Jutland's most glamorous hotel was converted from a private home in 1850, although the building itself dates back to 1581. This half-timbered hotel encapsulates the charm of the 16th century, with such adornments as carved chairs, sloping wood floors, and stained-glass windows. Many bedrooms are furnished with antique canopy beds. A fine restaurant, serving both Danish and international dishes, completes the picture. See p. 180.
- **Phoenix Copenhagen** (Copenhagen; www.phoenixcopenhagen.com; © **33-95-95-00**): The Danish Communist Party used to have its headquarters here, but the "Reds" of the Cold War era wouldn't recognize this pocket of posh today. It reeks of capitalistic excess and splendor, from its dazzling public rooms with French antiques to its rooms with dainty Louis XVI styling. See p. 99.

THE best RESTAURANTS

- **Era Ora** (Copenhagen; © **32-54-06-93;** www.era-ora.dk): This 20-year-old restaurant has the best Italian food in Denmark and is the domain of two Tuscan-born partners who have delighted some of the most discerning palates in Copenhagen. Denmark's superb array of fresh seafood, among other produce, is given a decidedly Mediterranean twist at this citadel of refined cuisine. See p. 106.
- **Falsled Kro** (Falsled; © **62-68-11-11;** www.falsledkro.dk): Even if you don't stay here, consider stopping for a meal. A favorite among well-heeled Europeans, this restaurant produces stellar French-inspired cuisine and often uses seasonal produce

from its own gardens. The succulent salmon is smoked on the premises in one of the outbuildings, and the owners breed quail locally. Such care and attention to detail make this one of Denmark's top restaurants. See p. 163.

- **Godt** (Copenhagen; ✆ **33-15-21-22;** www.restaurant-godt.dk): Even the queen of Denmark dines at this superb restaurant, celebrated locally for its international cuisine. The best and freshest of produce and various ingredients at the market are fashioned into the most pleasing and quintessential of international dishes. See p. 107.
- **Den Gamle Kro** (Odense; ✆ **66-12-14-33;** www.dengamlekro.eu): Hans Christian Andersen used to patronize this inn established in 1683. It's still going strong, feeding its top-notch Danish and French cuisine to locals and visitors alike. Its fixed-price menus are market fresh and skillfully prepared. See p. 158.
- **The Paul** (Copenhagen; ✆ **33-75-07-75;** www.thepaul.dk): Winning a coveted Michelin star, this is the best restaurant among the deluxe dining rooms of famous Tivoli Gardens. Drawing gourmet diners with its carefully crafted international menu, it offers an inspired cuisine among beautiful gardens. There is a daring and innovation here that you won't find in any other Tivoli restaurant. See p. 105.

5 INTRODUCING COPENHAGEN

From its humble beginnings, Copenhagen has become the largest city in Scandinavia, home to 1.8 million people, and seat of one of the oldest kingdoms in the world. After all these decades, Copenhagen remains the "fun" capital of Scandinavia—and also the most affordable.

Many Copenhageners still bike to work along the city's canals. We still join the locals who follow their noses to the cafes where the smell of freshly baked bread lures us in for a morning Danish and a cup of freshly brewed coffee. Along the way, we still pass that little old shopkeeper out soaping down his glass windows.

Copenhagen, the capital of Denmark, got its name from the word *køben-havn,* which means "merchants' harbor." It grew in size and importance because of its position on the Øresund, the sound between Denmark and Sweden.

Copenhagen is a city with much charm, as reflected in its canals, narrow streets, and old houses. Its most famous resident was Hans Christian Andersen, whose memory lives on. Another of Copenhagen's world-renowned inhabitants was Søren Kierkegaard, the "father of existentialism."

ESSENTIALS

Visitor Information

The **Copenhagen Tourist Information Center,** Vesterbrogade 4A (**© 70-22-24-42;** www.visitcopenhagen.dk), adjacent to the main entrance of Tivoli, dispenses information. It's open in July and August Monday to Saturday 9am to 8pm, Sunday 10am to 6pm; September Monday to Saturday 9am to 6pm; October to April Monday to Friday 9am to 4pm, Saturday 9am to 2pm; May and June Monday to Saturday 9am to 6pm, Sunday 10am to 2pm.

Neighborhoods in Brief

Tivoli Gardens Steeped in nostalgia, these amusement gardens were built in 1843 on the site of former fortifications in the heart of Copenhagen, on the south side of Rådhuspladsen. Some 160,000 flowers and 110,000 electric lights set the tone, and a collection of restaurants, dance halls, theaters, beer gardens, and lakes attract many thousands of visitors every year.

Strøget This pedestrians-only urban walkway stretches between Rådhuspladsen and Kongens Nytorv, two of the city's most visible and busiest plazas. En route along its trajectory are two spectacular, although smaller, squares, Gammeltorv and Nytorv, "old" and "new" squares. The word "Strøget" usually doesn't appear on any maps. Instead, Strøget encompasses five interconnected streets: Frederiksberggade, Nygade, Villelskaftet, Amagertorv, and Østergade.

Nyhavn/Kongens Nytorv Originally conceived in the 1670s by the Danish king as a shelter from the storms of the North and Baltic seas, and as a means of hauling building supplies into central Copenhagen, Nyhavn (New Harbor) today is the site of a denser concentration of restaurants than any other neighborhood in Copenhagen. Moored beside its granite embankments you'll see old or even antique fishing boats, some of which remain in place to preserve the sense of old-fashioned nostalgia. For many generations, Nyhavn was the haunt of sailors looking for tattoos, cheap drinks, and other diversions. Nowadays it's one of the most obviously gentrified sections of the city, with outdoor terraces, which are mobbed during warm-weather months with chattering, sometimes hard-drinking Danes on holiday. At the top or western terminus of the Nyhavn canal is the five-sided Kongens Nytorv (King's New Market), site of the deluxe Hotel d'Angleterre and the Royal Theater.

Indre By This is the Old Town, the heart of Copenhagen. Once filled with monasteries, it's a maze of streets, alleyways, and squares. The neighborhood around Gammeltorv and Nørregade, sometimes called the Latin Quarter, contains many buildings linked with the university. The **Vor Frue Kirke** (cathedral of Copenhagen) and **Rundetårn** (Round Tower) are here.

Slotsholmen This island, site of Christiansborg Palace, was where Bishop Absalon built Copenhagen's first fortress in 1167. Today it's the seat of the Danish parliament and home of Thorvaldsen's Museum. Bridges link Slotsholmen to Indre By. You can also visit the Royal Library (site of a recent hypermodern new wing described later in this guidebook as the Black Diamond), the Theater Museum, and the Royal Stables. The 17th-century Børsen (stock exchange) is also here.

Christianshavn Set on the opposite side of Copenhagen's harbor from the rest of the city, this was the "new town" ordered by master builder King Christian IV in the early 1500s. The town was originally constructed in the Dutch Renaissance style to house workers in the shipbuilding industry. Visitors come today mainly to see the Danish Film Museum on Store Søndervoldstræde and **Vors Frelsers Kirke,** on the corner of Prinsessegade and Skt. Annæ Gade. Sightseers can climb the spire of the old church for a panoramic view. Within the Christianshavn district is the offbeat community of **Christiania.** In 1971, many young and homeless people moved in, without the city's permission, proclaiming Christiania a "free city" (that is, partially exempt from the rules and regulations of the Danish government) within the orbit of Greater Copenhagen. It has been a freewheeling and controversial place ever since. Once filled with barracks for soldiers, Christiania is within walking distance of Vor Frelsers Kirke at Christianshavn. You can enter the area on Prinsessegade. The craft shops and restaurants here are fairly cheap because the residents refuse to pay Denmark's crippling 25% sales tax.

Vesterbro Once a slum loaded with junkies and prostitutes, Vesterbro would be comparable to the East Village in New York City. Its main street, **Istedgade,** runs west from the Central Railway Station. Don't come here for monuments or museums, but for hip cafes, bars, music, and ethnic restaurants. No longer a slum, Vesterbro's sense of newfound hip centers on the cafes and bars around the Halmtorvet, Vesterbro's main square. Expect gentrification but also cultural diversity such as Turkish-Kurdish gift shops, food markets loaded with fruit you might not immediately recognize, barbers from Istanbul, and, from time to time, a sex shop like those that proliferated here during the 1970s and 1980s.

Nørrebro Adjacent to Vesterbro (see above), Nørrebro takes the immigrant overflow and is also rich in artisan shops and ethnic restaurants, especially Turkish and Pakistani. This area has been a blue-collar neighborhood since the middle of the 19th century. The original Danish settlers have long since departed, replaced by immigrants who are not always greeted with a friendly reception in Copenhagen. The area also abounds with trend-conscious artists, students, and musicians who can't afford the high rents elsewhere. Numerous secondhand clothing stores—especially around Sankt Hans Torv—give Nørrebro the flavor of a Middle Eastern bazaar. Antiques shops (believe us, many of the furnishings and objets d'art aren't authentic) also fill the area. Most of these "antiques" stores lie along Ravnsborgade. The district is also home to a historic cemetery, Assistens Kirkegård, burial ground of both Hans Christian Andersen and Søren Kierkegaard, just to the west of Nørrebrogade. If you're looking for the two densest concentrations of the nightlife for which the district has become famous, head for either **Sankt Hans Torv** or Blågårdsgade.

Frederiksberg Heading west of the inner city along Vesterbrogade, you will reach the residential and business district of Frederiksberg. It grew up around **Frederiksberg Palace,** constructed in the Italianate style with an ocher facade. A park, Frederiksberg Have, surrounds the palace. To the west of the palace is the **Zoologisk Have,** one of the largest zoos in Europe.

Dragør Dragør is a fishing village south of the city that dates from the 16th century. Along with Tivoli, this seems to be everybody's favorite leisure spot. It's especially recommended for those who want to absorb the aura of an 18th-century Danish village but only have time to see the Copenhagen area. Walk its cobblestone streets and enjoy its 65 old red-roofed houses, designated as national landmarks.

GETTING THERE & GETTING AROUND

Arriving

BY PLANE You arrive at **Kastrup Airport** (✆ **32-31-32-31;** www.cph.dk), 12km (7½ miles) from the center of Copenhagen. air-rail trains link the airport with the Central Railway Station in the center of Copenhagen. The ride takes 13 minutes, and costs 35DKK. Directly under the airport's arrivals and departures halls, the air rail terminal is just an escalator ride from the gates. From the airport to the city center, you can also take bus no. 5A to the Central Station in Copenhagen; the fare is 35DKK. Another choice is to take the metro (line M2) from the airport to Central Station. It takes 35 minutes and costs 35DKK. A taxi to the city center costs between 190DKK and 250DKK.

BY TRAIN Trains arrive at the **Hovedbanegården** (**Central Railroad Station;** ✆ **70-13-14-15** for rail information), in the center of Copenhagen, near Tivoli Gardens and the Rådhuspladsen. The station operates a luggage-checking service, but room bookings are available only at the tourist office (see "Visitor Information," above).

From the Central Railroad Station, you can connect with the **S-tog,** a local train; trains depart from platforms in the terminal itself. The information desk is near tracks 5 and 6.

BY BUS Buses from Zealand and elsewhere pull into the Central Railroad Station. For bus information, call ✆ **36-13-14-15** daily 7am to 9:30pm.

BY CAR If you're driving from Germany, a car ferry will take you from Travemünde to Gedser in southern Denmark. From Gedser, get on E-55 north, an express highway that will deliver you to the southern outskirts of Copenhagen. If you're coming from Sweden via the Øresund Bridge, it will deposit you on the city's eastern outskirts, close to Kastrup Airport. From here, it's a short drive into the center.

Getting Around Town

BY PUBLIC TRANSPORTATION

A joint zone fare system includes Copenhagen transport buses; state railway, metro, and S-tog trains in Copenhagen and North Zealand; plus some private railway routes within a 40km (25-mile) radius of the capital, enabling you to transfer from train to bus and vice versa with the same ticket.

BASIC FARES A *grundbillet* (basic ticket) for both buses and trains costs 23DKK. Up to two children age 13 and under ride for half fare when accompanied by an adult. For 125DKK you can purchase a ticket allowing 24-hour bus and train travel through nearly half of Zealand; it's half-price for children 13 to 15, and free for children 12 and under.

DISCOUNT PASSES The **Copenhagen Card** (www.copenhagencard.dk) entitles you to free and unlimited travel by bus and rail throughout the metropolitan area (including North Zealand), 25% to 50% discounts on crossings to and from Sweden, and free admission to many sights and museums. The card is available for 1 or 3 days and costs 224DKK and 459DKK, respectively. Up to two children age 9 and under are allowed to go free with each adult card. Otherwise, children ages 10 to 15 pay 115DKK and 225DKK for 1 or 3 days. Buy the card at tourist offices, the airport, train stations, and most hotels. For more information, contact the Copenhagen Tourist Information Center (see the previous section, "Essentials") or click on www.cphcard.com.

Eurailpasses (which must be purchased before you leave home; p. 30) can be used on local trains in Copenhagen.

BY BUS Copenhagen's well-maintained buses are the least expensive method of getting around, and most buses leave from Rådhuspladsen in the heart of the city. A basic ticket allows 1 hour of travel and unlimited transfers within the zone where you started your trip. For information, call © **36-13-14-15.**

BY METRO Operating 24 hours, the metro links the western and eastern sections of Copenhagen to the center. Copenhagen has two metro lines. Through the city center and west to Frederiksberg, M1 and M2 share a common line. To the southeast, the system serves Amager, with the 13.7km (8½-mile) M1 running through the neighborhood of Ørestad, and the 14.2km (9-mile) M2 serving the eastern neighborhoods and Kastrup Airport. The metro has 22 stations, of which 9 are underground. Nørreport is the transfer station to the **S-tog** system, the commuter rail link to the suburbs. Metro trains run every 2 minutes during rush hours and every 15 minutes at night. Fares are integrated into the existing zonal systems (see "Basic Fares," above).

BY S-TOG The S-tog connects the heart of Copenhagen, most notably the Central Station, with the city's suburbs. Use of the tickets is the same as on buses (see "Basic Fares," above). You can transfer from a bus line to an S-tog train on the same ticket. Eurailpass holders generally ride free. For more information, call © **70-13-14-15.**

BY CAR

Because of the widespread availability of traffic-free walkways in Copenhagen, and its many parks, gardens, and canalside promenades, the Danish capital is well suited to pedestrian promenades. It's best to park your car in any of the dozens of city parking lots, then retrieve it when you're ready to explore the suburbs or countryside. Many parking lots are open 24 hours, but a few close between 1 and 7am; some close on Saturday afternoon and on Sunday when traffic is generally lighter. The cost ranges from 10DKK to 29DKK per hour. Two centrally located parking lots are **Industriens Hus,** H. C. Andersens Blvd. 18 (✆ **33-91-21-75**), open Monday to Friday 7am to midnight, Saturday 9am to 1am, Sunday 9am to midnight; and **Q-Park,** Israels Plads 1 (✆ **70-25-72-12;** www.q-park.dk), open daily from 6am to midnight for entry. (You can exit from this facility any time, 24 hr. daily.) For more information about parking in Copenhagen, call ✆ **47-70-80-80-90.**

BY TAXI

Watch for the FRI (free) sign or green light to hail a taxi, and be sure the taxis are metered. **Taxa 4x35** (✆ **35-35-35-35;** www.taxa.dk) operates the largest fleet of cabs. Tips are included in the meter price. The meter begins at 24DKK when hailed on the street and 37DKK when you book over the phone. Cabs cost an additional 12DKK per kilometer on weekdays between 7am and 4pm; 13DKK between 4pm and 7am and all day Saturday and Sunday; and 16DKK Friday and Saturday between 11pm and 7am and on all national holidays.

BY BICYCLE

To reduce pollution from cars (among other reasons), many Copenhageners ride bicycles. In her younger days, even the queen of Denmark could be seen cycling around. You can rent a bike at **Københavns Cyklebors,** Gothersgade 157 (✆ **33-14-07-17;** www.cykelboersen.dk). Depending on the bike, daily rates range from 75DKK to 150DKK, with deposits from 300DKK to 500DKK. Hours are Monday to Friday 9am to 5:30pm and Saturday 10am to 1:30pm.

[FastFACTS] COPENHAGEN

American Express Amex is represented throughout Denmark by **Nyman & Schultz,** Nørregade 7A (✆ **33-13-11-81;** bus: 34 or 35), with a branch in Terminal 3 of the Kastrup Airport. Fulfilling all the functions of American Express except for foreign exchange services, the main office is open Monday to Thursday 8:30am to 4:30pm, and Friday 8:30am to 4pm. The airport office remains open until 8:30pm Monday to Friday. On weekends, and overnight on weekdays, a recorded message, in English, will deliver the phone number of a 24-hour Amex service in Stockholm. This is useful for anyone who has lost a card or traveler's checks.

Business Hours Most **banks** are open Monday to Friday 10am to 4pm (to 6pm Thurs). **Stores** are generally open Monday to Thursday 9am to 6pm, Friday 9am to 7 or 8pm, and Saturday 9am to 2pm; most are closed Sunday. **Offices** are open Monday to Friday 9 or 10am to 4 or 5pm.

Currency Exchange Banks give better rates than currency kiosks. The main branch of Den Danske Bank (the Danish Bank), Holmens Kanal 2–12 (✆ **33-44-00-00;** www.danskebank.dk), is open Monday to Friday from 10am to 4pm (to 5:30pm Thurs). When banks are closed, you can exchange money at **Forex** (✆ **33-11-22-20**) in the Central Railroad Station, daily 8am to 9pm, or at the **Change Group,** Østergade 61 (✆ **33-93-04-55;** bus: 9 or 10), Monday to Friday 8:30am to 8:30pm, and Sunday 10am to 6pm.

Emergencies Dial ✆ **112** to report a fire or to call the police or an ambulance. State your phone number and address. Emergency calls from public telephones are free (no coins needed).

Hospitals In cases of illness or accident, even foreigners are entitled to free medical treatment in Denmark. One of the most centrally located hospitals is **Rigshospitalet,** Blegdamsvej 9 (✆ **35-45-35-45;** bus: 6A).

Pharmacies An *apotek* (pharmacy) open 24 hours a day is **Steno Apotek,** Vesterbrogade 6C (✆ **33-14-82-66;** bus: 29), opposite the Central Railroad Station.

Police In an emergency, dial ✆ **112.** For other matters, go to the police station at Halmtorvet 20 (✆ **33-25-14-48**).

Post Office For information about the Copenhagen post office, phone ✆ **80-20-70-30.** The main post office, where your *poste restante* (general delivery) letters can be picked up, is located at Hovebanegården in the Central Station. It's open Monday to Friday 11am to 6pm and Saturday 10am to 1pm.

Safety Compared with other European capital cities, Copenhagen is relatively safe. However, since the early 1990s, with the increase of homelessness and unemployment, crime has risen. Guard your wallet, purse, and other valuables as you would when traveling in any big city.

Toilets Free public toilets are at Rådhuspladsen (Town Hall Square), at the Central Railroad Station, and at all terminals. Look for the signs TOILETTER, WC, DAMER (women), or HERRER (men).

Transit Information Day or night, phone ✆ **70-13-14-15** for bus, metro, and S-tog information.

WHERE TO STAY

High season in Denmark is May to September, which pretty much coincides with the schedule at Tivoli Gardens. Once Tivoli closes for the winter, lots of rooms become available.

Several moderately priced hotels in Copenhagen are known as **mission hotels;** they were originally founded by a temperance society, but now about half of them are fully licensed to serve alcohol. They tend to cater to middle-class families.

RESERVATIONS SERVICE At Vesterbrogade 4A, across from Tivoli's main entrance, the Tourist Information Center maintains a useful hotel-booking service, **Værelsænvisningen** (✆ **70-22-24-42**). In person, the charge, whether you book into a private home, a hostel, or a luxury hotel, is 100DKK per person. This fee is waived when booking by telephone or Internet. You'll also be given a city map and bus directions. This particular office doesn't accept advance reservations; it can arrange private accommodations if the hotels in your price range are already full. The office is open April 19 to September 30, daily 9am to 9pm, and October to April 18, Monday to Friday 9am to 5pm and Saturday 9am to 2pm.

Nyhavn & Kongens Nytorv

VERY EXPENSIVE

Clarion Collection Hotel Neptun ★ Founded in 1854, the hotel was meant to be the gathering place for the bohemian and literati set. These days, commercial clients, a scattering of tourists, and even tour groups dominate the client list, but the main lounge still evokes an upper-crust living room in an English country house, with its traditional furnishings and even a chess table. Many of the modern bedrooms open onto two covered interior courtyards, adding a little glamour to the joint. Another feature of the hotel is an outdoor terrace on the sixth floor where you can order drinks in the summer.

Where to Stay & Dine in Copenhagen

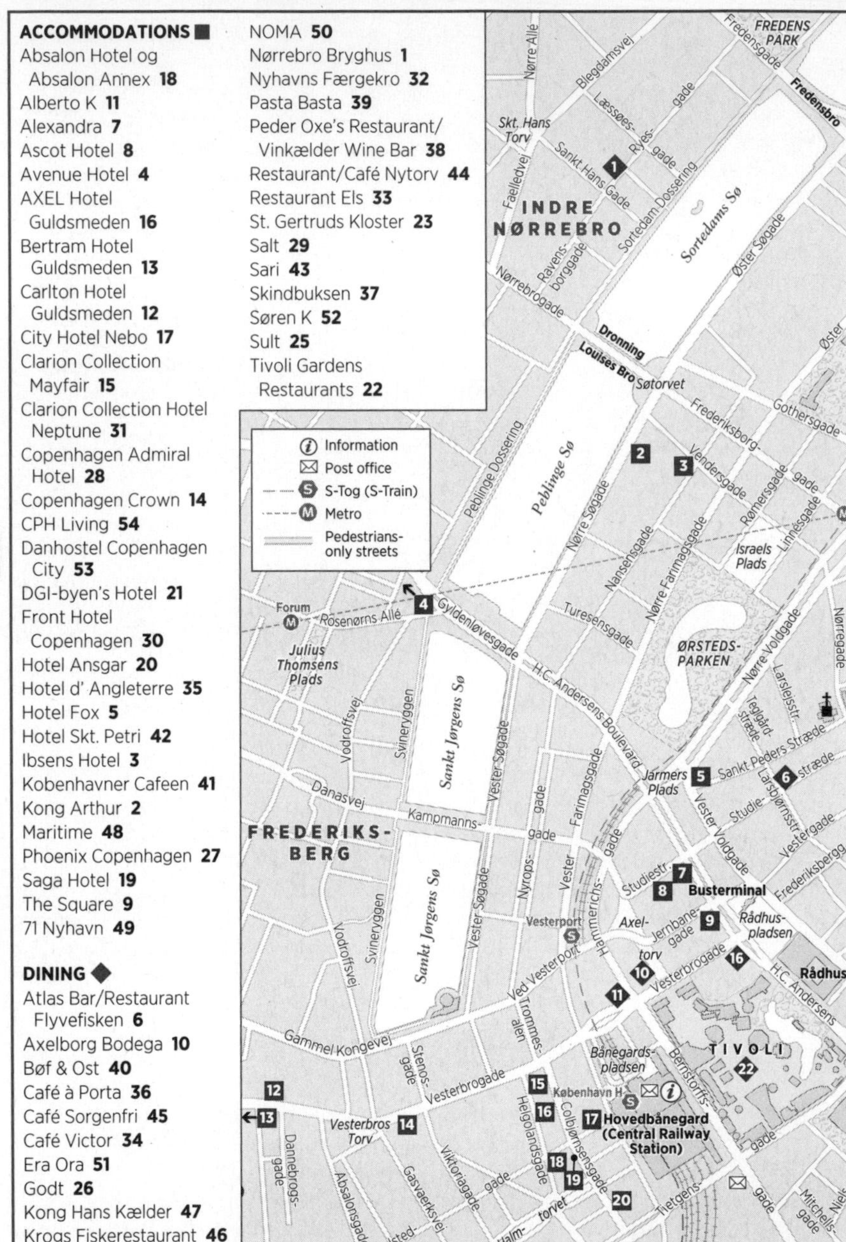

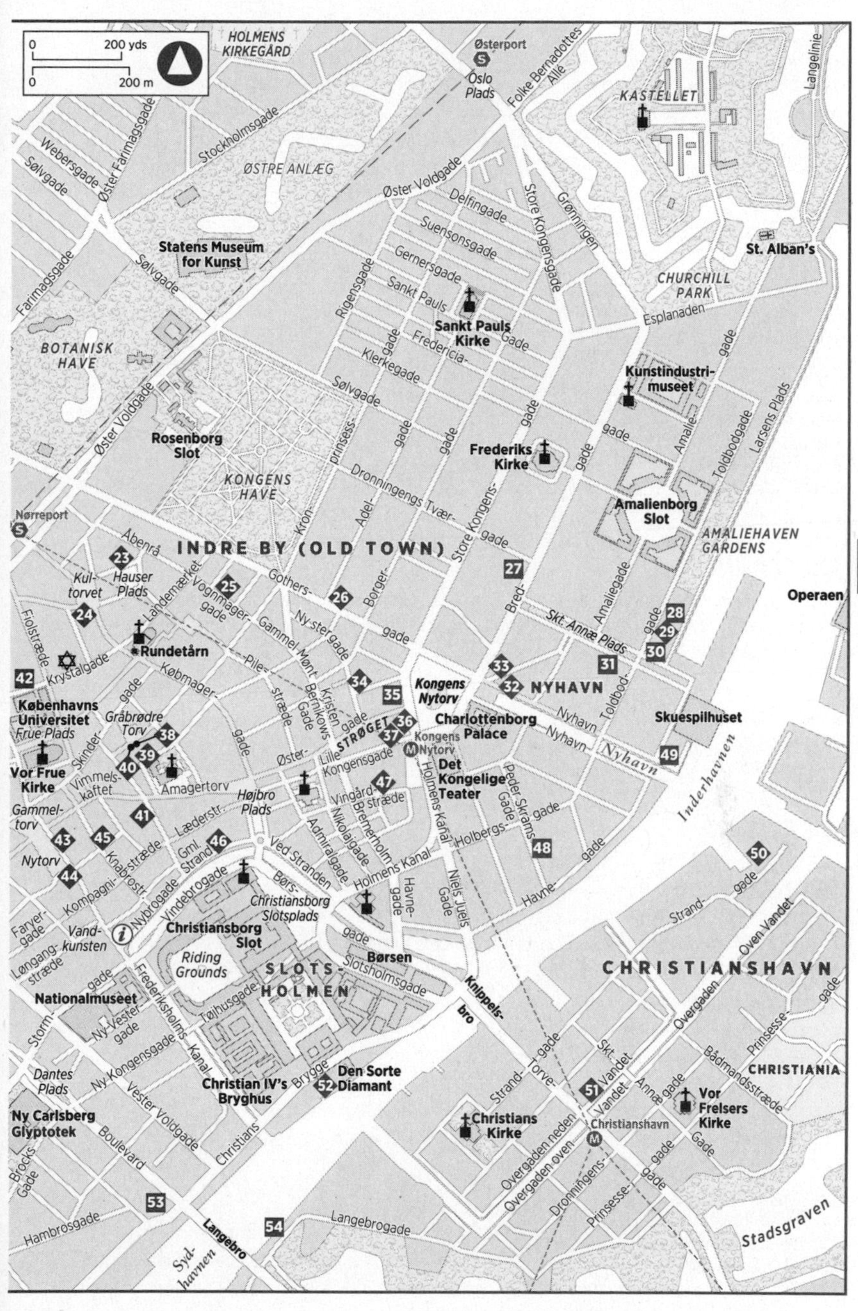

0 200 yds
0 200 m
HOLMENS KIRKEGÅRD
Østerport
Oslo Plads
Folke Bernadottes Alle
KASTELLET
Langelinie
Webersgade
Sølvgade
Øster Farimagsgade
Stockholmsgade
ØSTRE ANLÆG
Øster Voldgade
Delfingade
Suensonsgade
Store Kongensgade
Grønningen
Statens Museum for Kunst
Sølvgade
Gernersgade
Sankt Pauls
Rigensgade
St. Alban's
CHURCHILL PARK
Farimagsgade
Sankt Pauls Kirke
Esplanaden
BOTANISK HAVE
Fredericia-gade
Klerkegade
Kunstindustri-museet
Øster Voldgade
Sølvgade
Amalie-gade
Toldbodgade
Larsens Plads
Rosenborg Slot
prinsess
Frederiks Kirke
KONGENS HAVE
Dronningens Tvær-gade
Amalienborg Slot
Nørreport
Adel-
Store Kongens-
AMALIEHAVEN GARDENS
Åbenrå
INDRE BY (OLD TOWN)
Kron-
27
23
Hauser Plads
Kul-torvet
25
Gothers-
26
Borger-
Bred-
Operaen
Landemærket
Vognmager-gade
Skt. Annæ Plads
Amaliegade
28
29
30
24
Gammel Mønt
Ny-stergade
gade
Fiolstræde
Rundetårn
31
Krystalgade
42
Pile-
33
32
NYHAVN
Købmager-
34
Kongens Nytorv
35
Københavns Universitet
Gråbrødre Torv
Frue Plads
Bernikows Gade
Kristen
STRØGET
36
Charlottenborg Palace
Nyhavn
Toldbod-
Skuespilhuset
38
37
Kongens Nytorv
Skinder-
39
Lille Kongensgade
Øster-
Det Kongelige Teater
Nyhavn
49
Vor Frue Kirke
40
Vimmels-kaftet
Amagertorv
47
Vingård-stræde
Inderhavnen
Gammel-torv
Højbro Plads
Peder Skrams Gade
41
Læderstr.
Nikolajgade
Bremerholm
Holmens Kanal
43
45
Gml. Strand
46
Admiralgade
Holbergs-gade
48
Nytorv
Knabrostr.
Ved Stranden
50
44
Kompagni-stræde
Vindebrogade
Nybrogade
Børs-gade
Holmens Kanal
Havne-gade
Niels Juels Gade
Havne-gade
Christiansborg Slotsplads
Farver-gade
Vand-kunsten
Christiansborg Slot
Strand-gade
Oven Vandet
Løngang-stræde
Riding Grounds
SLOTS-HOLMEN
Børsen
Slotsholmsgade
CHRISTIANSHAVN
Nationalmuseet
Frederiksholms Kanal
Tøjhusgade
Knippels-bro
Overgaden
Ny Vester-gade
Storm-
Prinsesse-gade
Dantes Plads
Ny Kongensgade
Brygge
Den Sorte Diamant
52
Torve-gade
Skt. Annæ gade
51
Vandet
Bådmandsstræde
CHRISTIANIA
Christian IV's Bryghus
Vor Frelsers Kirke
Ny Carlsberg Glyptotek
Vester Voldgade
Strand-
Christians Kirke
Christianshavn
Overgaden neden
Overgaden oven
Boulevard
Christians
Dronningens-
Prinsesse-
Brocks Gade
53
Langebrogade
54
Stadsgraven
Hambrosgade
Langebro
Sydhavnen

Skt. Annæ Plads 18–20, DK-1250 København. www.clarionhotel.com. ✆ **877/424-6423** or 33-96-20-00. Fax 33-96-20-66. 133 units. 1,030DKK–2,880DKK double; from 2,680DKK suite. Rates include buffet breakfast. AE, DC, MC, V. Parking 280DKK. Bus: 11 or 29. **Amenities:** Restaurant; bar; babysitting; bikes; room service. *In room:* A/C, TV, hair dryer, minibar, Wi-Fi (free).

Front Hotel Copenhagen ★ From the outside, this boxy-looking building might remind you of the rash of angular modern construction that blossomed throughout central Europe during the Cold War. On the inside, it's one of the hottest and most appealing hotels in town, enjoying a link with the nearby Hotel d'Angleterre, and a location close to the very central Nyhavn Canal. Throughout, the decor is minimalist and somewhat self-consciously linked to the spartan-looking heyday of Denmark's modern design movement. Bedrooms benefit from very large windows, high-quality Danish modern furniture, lots of sunlight, and panoramic views. Bedrooms contain furniture, some of it upholstered with black leather, that evoke the best in postmillennium design.

Skt. Annæ Plads 21, PO Box 9076, DK-1022 København. www.scandichotels.com. ✆ **33-13-34-00.** Fax 33-11-77-07. 132 units. 1,190DKK–3,490DKK double. AE, DC, MC, V. Parking 300DKK. Metro: Kongens Nytorv. **Amenities:** Restaurant; bar; airport transfers (490DKK); exercise room; sauna. *In room:* A/C, TV, DVD (in some), CD player (in some), minibar, Wi-Fi (free).

Hotel d'Angleterre ★★★ ☺ With 250 years of history, the d'Angleterre is one of the oldest deluxe bastions in the world, although it's kept abreast of the times with modern comforts. The seven-story property at the top of Nyhavn is a member of the Leading Hotels of the World. It was built as a private club for English merchants before its transformation into a hotel in 1805. Hans Christian Andersen was among the first celebrity guests. The midsize-to-spacious bedrooms are beautifully furnished in a medley of styles. We prefer the Empire and Louis XVI rooms, though you may opt for the conservatively modern.

Kongens Nytorv 34, DK-1050 København. www.remmen.dk. ✆ **33-12-00-95.** Fax 33-12-11-18. 123 units. 1,930DKK–4,230DKK double; from 5,630DKK suite. AE, DC, MC, V. Parking 400DKK. Metro: Kongens Nytorv. **Amenities:** Restaurant; bar; babysitting; bikes; concierge; exercise room; indoor heated pool; room service; spa. *In room:* A/C, TV, hair dryer, minibar, Wi-Fi (free).

EXPENSIVE

Copenhagen Admiral Hotel This former grain warehouse was turned into a hotel in 1988, and is the most serious rival of 71 Nyhavn, which has a slight edge. Since it is only 2 blocks from the Nyhavn Canal, many rooms with French balconies open onto harbor views. Huge timber ceiling beams and roof supports evoke the warehouse; otherwise, the hotel is completely modern, carrying a four-star rating from the government. No two of the midsize rooms here are identical, but each comes with rustic wooden beams and tasteful Danish furniture from classic designers. All the furniture is custom made of solid teak.

Toldbodgade 24–28, DK-1253 København. www.admiralhotel.dk. ✆ **33-74-14-14.** Fax 33-74-14-16. 366 units. 1,275DKK–1,870DKK double; 1,925DKK–2,890DKK suite. AE, MC, V. Parking 135DKK. Bus: 11, 25, or 29. **Amenities:** Restaurant; bar; airport transfers (708DKK); bikes; room service; sauna. *In room:* TV, hair dryer, minibar, Wi-Fi (95DKK per day).

Hotel Skt. Petri ★★★ For the world's fashionistas and interior designers, this is a mandatory stopover. Since the 1930s the site of this hotel was the much-loved department store, Dalle Valle. Today, in a reincarnation, it's become one of the grandest hotels in Copenhagen. Modern Danish design, as interpreted by interior designer Per Arnoldi, is showcased here. Rooms are individually done in a minimalist yet elegant style, with bright, cheerful colors and such touches as Mondrian-inspired headboards. Opt for a double with terrace on the fifth or sixth floors. The ceilings in most rooms are a bit low, but the lobby rises three floors, embracing an atrium garden.

Krystalgade 22, DK-1172 København. www.hotelsktpetri.com. ✆ **33-45-91-00.** Fax 33-45-91-10. 268 units. 2,295DKK–2,695DKK double; from 2,895DKK suite. AE, DC, MC, V. Parking 380DKK. S-tog: Nørreport. **Amenities:** Restaurant; bar; exercise room; room service. *In room:* A/C, TV, hair dryer, minibar.

71 Nyhavn ★★ Few people dream of sleeping in a warehouse until they check in here. Back in 1804 this building on the corner between the harbor and Nyhavn Canal housed everything from bales of cotton from America to live chickens from the Danish countryside. Today the massively restored red-brick structure, converted into a hotel in 1971, is one of the most successful examples of recycling in the Danish capital. We like to wake up in the morning here, pulling back the draperies for a view of the old ships anchored at Nyhavn. If there's a downside, it's the smallness of most of the bedrooms, though each has crisscrossing timbers, soft leather furniture, and dark wood accents.

Nyhavn 71, DK-1051 København. www.71nyhavnhotel.com. ✆ **33-43-62-00.** Fax 33-43-62-01. 150 units. 975DKK–2,050DKK double; 1,925DKK–4,170DKK suite. AE, DC, MC, V. Parking 195DKK. S-tog: Kongensnytorv. **Amenities:** Restaurant; bar; babysitting; room service. *In room:* A/C, TV, hair dryer, minibar, Wi-Fi (free).

MODERATE

Maritime This hotel on a tranquil street near the waterfront has some expensive neighbors, such as the d'Angleterre, but it keeps its prices more affordable. For its location alone, near Nyhavn Canal, it's a recommendable choice. We used to be put off by a certain rigid staff attitude, although on our last visit we found the staff far more helpful and cooperative. The hotel has benefited from some refurbishing and updating, while keeping to its maritime theme. Even though the building itself is a century old—maybe older—all the well-furnished, midsize bedrooms are up-to-date, both comfortably and tastefully furnished.

Peder Skrams Gade 19, DK-1054 København. www.hotel-maritime.dk. ✆ **33-13-48-82.** Fax 33-15-03-45. 64 units. 700DKK–1,990DKK double. Rates include buffet breakfast. MC, V. S-tog: Kongensnytorv. **Amenities:** Restaurant; bar; bikes. *In room:* TV, hair dryer, Wi-Fi (free).

Phoenix Copenhagen ★★ Though it falls a bit short of its goal, this government-rated four-star hotel poses a serious challenge to the discreet grandeur of the d'Angleterre. It saw the light of day in the 1680s when it was constructed to accommodate the aristocratic courtiers of Amalienborg Palace. Tons of white and colored marble were imported to create a modern version of the Louis XVI style. Beautiful wool carpeting and chandeliers add glamour to the standard guest rooms, but many are a bit too small for our tastes. If you're willing to pay more, opt for one of the business-class rooms or perhaps a suite.

Bredgade 37, DK-1260 København. www.phoenixcopenhagen.com. ✆ **33-95-95-00.** Fax 33-33-98-33. 213 units. 1,125DKK–2,695DKK double; 2,225DKK–7,695DKK suite. AE, DC, MC, V. Parking 225DKK. Bus: 1A, 11, 15, or 25. **Amenities:** Restaurant; bar; babysitting; bikes; room service. *In room:* A/C, TV, hair dryer, minibar, Wi-Fi (free).

Near Rådhuspladsen (Town Hall)

EXPENSIVE

Alexandra ★ ☺ Some of its overnight guests have called this longtime favorite the most authentic Danish hotel in Copenhagen. It may be a bit threadbare in places, but much of its furniture was designed by such Danish modern masters as Arne Jacobsen and Ole Wanscher, with lighting by Paul Henningsen. Bedrooms are comfortable and well maintained, with a striking Danish design. The staff will add an extra bed for families traveling together.

H. C. Andersens Blvd. 8, DK-1553 København. www.hotel-alexandra.dk. ✆ **33-74-44-44.** Fax 33-74-44-88. 61 units. 1,745–2,545DKK double; extra bed 395DKK. Rates include buffet breakfast. AE, DC, MC, V. Parking 135DKK. Bus: 2A, 5A, 6A, 10, or 11. **Amenities:** Restaurant; bar; bikes; room service; Wi-Fi (free, in lobby). *In room:* TV, hair dryer.

Ascot Hotel ★ This is one of the best small hotels in Copenhagen, despite the perception that it's in need of some sprucing up. On a side street about a 2-minute walk from Town Hall Square, the inn of personality and charm was built in 1902 (on 492 wooden pilings rescued from a medieval fortification that had previously stood on the site). In 1994, the hotel annexed an adjacent building designed in the 19th century as a bathhouse; its black-marble columns and interior bas-reliefs are historically notable. Martin Nyrop, who designed the landmark Town Hall, also was the architect for the bathhouse.

Studiestræde 61, DK-1554 København. www.ascot-hotel.dk. ✆ **33-12-60-00.** Fax 33-14-60-40. 175 units. 1,490DKK–1,590DKK double; 2,950DKK suite. AE, DC, MC, V. Parking 150DKK. Bus: 5A, 6A, or 10. **Amenities:** Restaurant; bar; exercise room; room service; spa. *In room:* TV, hair dryer, Wi-Fi (free).

Bertram Hotel Guldsmeden ★ This is the more elegant twin of the also-recommended Carlton Hotel Guldsmeden. Both are within about 270m (900 ft.) of one another, on a wide and busy boulevard that runs into the rear of Copenhagen's Central Railway station, within about a 10-minute walk. Rising six stories, the hotel originated in 2006, after a 19th-century town house was restored. Rooms overlook the courtyard, the noisy Vesterbrogade, or the quieter neighborhood in back. Furniture in the bedrooms was imported from Indonesia, and includes four-poster beds.

Vesterbrogade 107, 1620 København. www.hotelguldsmeden.dk. ✆ **33-25-04-05.** Fax 33-25-04-02. 47 units. 1,080DKK–2,195DKK double. Rates include buffet breakfast. AE, DC, MC, V. Parking 150DKK. Bus: 6A. **Amenities:** Restaurant; bar; babysitting; bikes; room service. *In room:* TV, hair dryer, minibar, Wi-Fi (20DKK per day).

Carlton Hotel Guldsmeden ★ In a much-renovated 19th-century town house in the heart of the rapidly gentrifying Vesterbro neighborhood, within a 15-minute walk west from Tivoli and the Central Railway Station, this is a government-rated three-star hotel offering good value and occasional doses of genuine charm. The structure might be old, but the bedrooms are contemporary-looking and up-to-date, ranging from small to midsize. Each is handsomely decorated in a vaguely French colonial style with high ceilings, wood paneling, and four-poster beds imported from Indonesia. The best rooms contain such luxuries as fireplaces, balconies with summer furniture, and claw-foot bathtubs instead of showers.

Vesterbrogade 66, DK-1620 København. www.hotelguldsmeden.dk. ✆ **33-22-15-00.** Fax 33-22-15-55. 64 units. 895DKK–995DKK double; from 1,095DKK junior suite. AE, DC, MC, V. Parking 95DKK. Bus: 6A. **Amenities:** Bar; bikes; room service. *In room:* TV, hair dryer, minibar, Wi-Fi (20DKK per day).

DGI-byen's Hotel ★ There's no hotel like this one in all Copenhagen. Right behind the Central Station and convenient to most public transportation, this government-rated three-star hotel attracts sports lovers to its precincts, which contain a bowling alley, a gigantic swim center, a spa, a climbing wall, a shooting range, and, oh yes, a hotel. (The "DGI" within its name translates as "Danish Gymnastics Association.") This is a dynamic, flexible so-called multicenter attracting schoolchildren, sports clubs, company executives, and regular visitors. Bedrooms, midsize to large, reflect the presuppositions and tenets of Danish modern design. Interiors are simple yet tasteful and comfortable with dark wood furnishings and blond wood floors. Swimming is free to hotel guests within the public indoor pool.

Tietgensgade 65, DK-1704 København. www.dgi-byen.dk. ✆ **33-29-80-50.** Fax 33-29-80-59. 104 units. 1,895DKK–1,995DKK double. Rates include buffet breakfast. AE, DC, MC, V. Parking 140DKK. **Amenities:** Restaurant; bar; babysitting; exercise room; 5 indoor heated pools; spa; Wi-Fi (free, in lobby). *In room:* TV, hair dryer.

The Square ★★ In the bull's eye center of Copenhagen, the elegant Square overlooks Town Hall Square. Tight, minimalist lines characterize this exquisitely designed hotel that is close to the Strøget shopping street, Tivoli, and Central Station. Most bedrooms open onto a spectacular view of the city, and are filled with stylish modern furnishings in a simple, tasteful format. The reception room is integrated with the lobby bar, which contains specially designed furnishings punctuated by Arne Jacobsen's famous circular chair, "the Egg."

Rådhuspladsen 14, DK-1550 København. www.thesquarecopenhagen.com. ✆ **33-38-12-00.** Fax 33-38-12-01. 267 units. 1,085DKK–1,590DKK double; 1,540DKK–2,265DKK suite. AE, DC, MC, V. Parking 200DKK. Bus: 2A, 5A, 6A, or 10. **Amenities:** Bikes; room service; Wi-Fi (free, in lobby). *In room:* A/C, TV, hair dryer, minibar.

MODERATE

Hotel Fox ★ ☺ At Hotel Fox, one of Copenhagen's most unusual and trend-conscious hotels, each room is a highly idiosyncratic work of art, ranging from tongue-in-cheek enclaves of camp to rigorously streamlined case studies for postindustrial minimalism. Choices, among many others, include a boxing-themed room, one filled with taurine (bull-inspired) souvenirs, one with syrupy reminders of Heidi, and one devoted to an all-American theme, complete with supersize beds.

Jarmers Plads 3, DK-1551 København. www.hotelfox.dk. ✆ **33-13-30-00.** Fax 33-14-30-33. 61 units. 930DKK–1,390DKK double. AE, DC, MC, V. Parking 240DKK nearby. Bus: 5A, 6A, 14, or 81N. **Amenities:** Restaurant; bar; bikes. *In room:* TV, hair dryer, Wi-Fi (free).

Kong Arthur ★ ☺ Most guests checking in here think this hotel was named after England's legendary King Arthur. Actually, the Arthur in its name comes from Arthur Frommer, one of the early owners of this hotel and the founding father of the Frommer's guides. Right by the Copenhagen lakes and close to Rosenborg Palace, Kong Arthur is a government-rated four-star hotel just a 15-minute walk from Tivoli Gardens. Charm, high-quality comfort, and a welcoming atmosphere greet you today, but back in 1882, things were a bit more rawboned here.

Nørre Søgade 11, DK-1370 København. www.kongarthur.dk. ✆ **33-11-12-12.** Fax 33-32-61-30. 155 units. 1,320DKK–1,940DKK double; from 2,030DKK suite. AE, DC, MC, V. Parking 150DKK. S-tog: Nørreport. **Amenities:** Restaurant; bar; babysitting; bikes; exercise room; Jacuzzi; room service; sauna; Wi-Fi (free, in lobby). *In room:* TV, hair dryer, minibar.

INEXPENSIVE

City Hotel Nebo The neighborhood that surrounds this hotel, alas, is still the heart of Copenhagen's (dwindling) red-light district, but families have been checking in and out of it for generations. Its ownership is a Christian foundation with an express philosophy of affordability. Backpackers often rent the low-economy rooms that share the adequate hallway facilities. For more money you can rent small but tastefully decorated doubles, or even one of the family rooms that each sleep up to four guests.

Istedgade 6, DK-1650 København. www.nebo.dk. ✆ **33-21-12-17.** Fax 33-23-47-74. 84 units, 45 with bathroom. 650DKK–699DKK double without bathroom, 850DKK–899DKK double with bathroom; 750DKK–1,200DKK family room for 3, 990DKK–1,300DKK family room for 4. Rates include buffet breakfast. AE, DC, MC, V. Parking 90DKK. Bus: 5A, 6A, 10, or 66. **Amenities:** Bikes. *In room:* TV.

Copenhagen Crown In business for more than a century, this welcoming hotel lies only a short walk from Tivoli Gardens and the main train station. You enter through a tranquil, beautiful courtyard, evoking Copenhagen of long ago. The traffic-clogged Vesterbrogade is a short distance away but this is a well-maintained, safe, quiet haven. The midsize bedrooms are classically and tastefully decorated, some of them opening onto Vesterbrogade.

Vesterbrogade 41, DK-1620 København. www.copenhagencrown.dk. ✆ **33-21-21-66.** Fax 33-21-00-66. 80 units. 809DKK–1,050DKK double. Rates include buffet breakfast. AE, DC, MC, V. Bus: 6A or 26. Parking nearby 140DKK. **Amenities:** Restaurant; bar; bikes. *In room:* TV, hair dryer, minibar, Wi-Fi (50DKK per day).

On Helgolandsgade & Colbjørnsensgade

In the 1970s this area behind the railroad station was one of the major pornography districts of Europe, but subsequent hotel renovations, much-publicized civic efforts, and the gradual decline of the porno shops have led to a continuing gentrification. With the original 19th-century facades mostly still intact, and often gracefully restored, the district is safer than you might think and offers some of the best hotel values in town.

EXPENSIVE

AXEL Hotel Guldsmeden ★★ In the Vesterbro district, behind Tivoli and the Central Station, this luxurious choice is the latest member of the Guldsmeden family. It seemingly has everything, including a spa, private penthouse suites, an organic restaurant, teak four-poster beds, small balconies, and all the latest technology. Bedrooms blend a traditional Balinese style with original paintings, Persian rugs on wooden floors, and attractive comfortable bedrooms.

Helgolandsgade 11, DK-1653 København. www.hotelguldsmeden.com. ✆ **33-31-32-66.** Fax 33-31-69-70. 129 units. 1,015DKK–1,255DKK double; 3,995DKK suite. AE, DC, MC, V. Bus: 1A, 10, 26, or 66. Parking nearby 220DKK. **Amenities:** Restaurant; bar; bikes; room service; sauna. *In room:* TV/DVD, hair dryer, minibar, Wi-Fi (20DKK per day).

MODERATE

Clarion Collection Mayfair ★ The hotel chain known for offering havens of charm and comfort has moved in on the long-established Mayfair 2 blocks west of the Central Station to give it a new zest for life. Rated three stars by the government, the hotel isn't as well known as it should be, but has enjoyed refurbishing and redecorating, making it a choice address in Copenhagen. In some of its furnishings and decor, it evokes a well-heeled private home in England. Bedrooms come in a wide range of sizes, but each is tastefully furnished and comfortable, with full marble bathrooms. The best accommodations here have small sitting areas.

Helgolandsgade 3, DK-1653 København. www.choicehotels.no. ✆ **877/424-6423** in the U.S., or 70-12-17-00. Fax 33-23-96-86. 105 units. 1,240DKK–1,990DKK double; from 1,795DKK suite. AE, DC, MC, V. Bus: 5A, 10, or 29. **Amenities:** Bar; babysitting; bikes. *In room:* TV/DVD, fax, hair dryer, minibar, Wi-Fi (free).

INEXPENSIVE

Absalon Hotel og Absalon Annex ★ This family-run lodging, one of the best-managed hotels in the neighborhood, consists of four town houses that were joined into one building and became a hotel in 1938. It has a spacious blue-and-white breakfast room, and an attentive staff directed by third-generation owners. The guest rooms are simple and modern, and come in various sizes ranging from cramped to spacious; those on the fifth floor have the most character. These rooms get the most light and are elegantly furnished in a modified Louis XIV style or in a classical English style, with marble bathrooms with tubs. Overflow guests are housed in one of the rather functional rooms in the Absalon Annex.

Helgolandsgade 15, DK-1653 København. http://absalonhotel.dk. ✆ **33-24-22-11.** Fax 33-24-34-11. 262 units. 995DKK–1,495DKK double; 1,295DKK–1,890DKK suite. Rates include continental breakfast. AE, DC, MC, V. Bus: 2A, 6A, 10, or 40. Parking nearby 140DKK. **Amenities:** Wi-Fi (100DKK per day, in lobby). *In room:* TV, hair dryer (in some).

Hotel Ansgar Just when we were about to drop this tired old workhorse from the guide, it burst into bloom again, with renovated and modernized bedrooms. Decorating magazines may not be too impressed but you get tasteful rooms that are comfortable but plain in Danish modern—no clutter here. Although its prices have risen, the hotel is still a good value and has been ever since it opened in 1885 in a five-story structure. Think of the rooms as cozy instead of small—it's better that way. Two dozen large rooms can accommodate up to six (that's a bit crowded) and are suitable for Brady Bunch–style families. The bedrooms contain well-kept bathrooms with Danish modern shower units (no great compliment).

Colbjørnsensgade 29, DK-1652 København. www.ansgar-hotel.dk. ✆ **33-21-21-96.** Fax 33-21-61-91. 81 units. 750DKK–1,200DKK double; extra bed 200DKK. Rates include buffet breakfast. AE, DC, MC, V. Parking nearby 250DKK. Bus: 5A, 10, or 29. **Amenities:** Bikes; room service. *In room:* TV, Wi-Fi (free).

Saga Hotel In 1947 two developers purchased two late-19th-century apartment buildings that had survived the Nazi occupation and set out to gut them and turn them into hotels. The Saga is rather like it was when it was created, although it has kept up with the times with improvements such as Internet access. The five-story building still has no elevator and some of its rooms are still without a private bathroom. As such, it attracts groups of international visitors in summer and Danish students and convention groups in winter. The rooms are small to midsize, each furnished in Danish modern, and most are equipped with a private bathroom with tub/shower combo.

Colbjørnsensgade 18–20, DK-1652 København. www.sagahotel.dk. ✆ **33-24-49-44.** Fax 33-24-60-33. 79 units, 31 with bathroom. 480DKK–750DKK double without bathroom; 600DKK–950DKK double with bathroom. AE, DC, MC, V. Bus: 10. *In room:* TV, Wi-Fi (free).

At Nansensgade

Ibsens Hotel ★ ☺ The Brøchner-Mortensen family succeeds in combining an old-fashioned nostalgia with all the modern amenities today's traveler demands. A government-rated three-star hotel in the Nansensgade area, right by the lakes, it is convenient for trips to both Rosenborg Palace and Tivoli Gardens. In an area filled with cafes and trendy restaurants, the hotel first opened its doors in 1906, surviving wars, occupation, and changing tastes, and somehow keeping abreast of it all. The guest rooms are comfortably and tastefully furnished, each well maintained. A bonus is free access to the Helle Thorup Spa next door.

Vendersgade 23, DK-1363 København. www.ibsenshotel.dk. ✆ **33-13-19-13.** Fax 33-13-19-16. 118 units. 990DKK–1,580DKK double; 1,690DKK–1,820DKK suite. AE, DC, MC, V. Bus: 5A. Parking 150DKK. **Amenities:** 2 restaurants; bar; babysitting; bikes. *In room:* TV, Wi-Fi (free).

The Southern Harborfront

Much of Copenhagen is expanding westward onto the harborfront of Copenhagen. City planners for this new district have insisted that pedestrians be granted unrestricted access to the harborfront promenade, allowing them to stroll from *Den Lille Havfruen (Little Mermaid)* near the northern entrance to the harbor to as far south as the Copenhagen Island Hotel and the immediately adjacent Tyske Shopping Plaza. En route, across the harbor, are hypermodern structures of international renown, among them the new Opera House.

CPH Living ★ In the harbor of Copenhagen, Scandinavia's only floating hotel is furnished with the best of a Scandinavian design that is definitely nautical, with steel and hardwood decking throughout. With a dozen rooms, this houseboat is 90m (300 ft.) north of Havnebadet. Bedrooms are midsize, and all accommodations are equipped with floor-to-ceiling windows, original artwork, and heated floors. Bathrooms are a special feature on upper-floor rooms; you can enjoy the pulsating harbor life while taking your shower.

570 Langebrogade Kaj, DK-1411 København. www.cphliving.com. ✆ **61-60-85-46.** 12 units. 1,000DKK–1,495DKK double. Rates include buffet breakfast. AE, MC, V. S-tog: Dybbølsbro. *In room:* TV, Wi-Fi (free).

Danhostel Copenhagen City This addition to the country's roster of youth hostels opened in 2005 in a white-sided high-rise venue; it's only a 15-minute walk from Tivoli and the Central Railroad Station. Rising 16 floors, this mother of all youth hostels has room for more than 1,000 occupants at a time, making it the largest in Europe. Each of the accommodations contains between 4 and 12 beds; a bathroom with toilet, sink, and shower; and virtually no other amenities. Other than breakfast, no meals are served. To stay in this hostel you have to hold a valid international hostel card (160DKK for 12 months) or purchase a guest card (35DKK per night). Both can be purchased on arrival at reception.

H. C. Andersens Blvd. 50, DK-1553 København. www.danhostel.dk/copenhagencity. ✆ **33-11-85-85.** Fax 33-11-85-88. 1,020 beds. 520DKK–1,170DKK double. Rental of bed linen 60DKK extra. Breakfast 74DKK extra per person. AE, DC, MC, V. Closed Dec 22–Jan 3. Bus: 5A. **Amenities:** Bikes; concierge; Internet (29DKK, in lobby). *In room:* No phone.

Frederiksberg

EXPENSIVE

Avenue Hotel ★★ ☺ Cozy, inviting, and of immense appeal, the Avenue is in a historic building designed by architect Emil Blichfeldt, known mostly for having designed the main entrance to Tivoli Gardens. The site was formerly a poorhouse, lunatic asylum, and forced labor camp for "drunks, beggars, and vagabonds." Today the Avenue is filled with grace notes such as a lounge with a sandstone fireplace and comfortable sofas, a secluded courtyard patio in summer, and even a kiddie sandpit with toys. Bedrooms have been completely restored, with the latest conveniences added. None of the rooms is the exact same size or shape, although each has a high ceiling and, in most cases, small bay windows and French doors. Many accommodations are large enough for families. The hotel is only a 5-minute ride from the Central Station.

Åboulevard 29, DK-1960 Frederiksberg. www.avenuehotel.dk. ✆ **35-37-31-11.** 68 units. 1,195DKK–1,495DKK double; 1,695DKK family unit. Rates include breakfast buffet. AE, DC, MC, V. Bus: 12, 66, or 69. **Amenities:** Room service. *In room:* TV, fridge, minibar, Wi-Fi (free).

Ørestad

MODERATE

Crowne Plaza Hotel One of Copenhagen's newest and largest hotels is part of the massive sprawl known as Copenhagen Towers, both an office and hotel complex geared to be energy efficient. The unique building complex has sprouted up in Ørestad City, with the largest integrated solar power cells in Denmark as well as a groundwater cooling system. Energy consumption has been reduced by 90%. The centerpiece of the development is the sleek 25-story hotel, a major transportation hub for the airport, the motorway, and the metro. Bedrooms are midsize and decorated with stylish Scandinavian furniture. Each unit overlooks the skyline of Copenhagen and the Øresund region. Numerous regional trains zip you into the heart of the city. Ørestads Blvd. 114–118, DK-23 2300 København. www.cpcopenhagen.dk. ✆ **88-77-66-55.** Fax 88-77-66-11. 366 units. 995DKK double; 1,295DKK family unit; from 1,495DKK suite. AE, DC, MC, V. Parking 150DKK. **Amenities:** 2 restaurants; free airport shuttle; exercise room; room service. *In room:* A/C, TV/DVD, hair dryer, minibar, Wi-Fi (free).

WHERE TO DINE

It's been estimated that Copenhagen has more than 2,000 cafes, snack bars, and restaurants, and a higher number of Michelin-starred restaurants than any other city in Europe. Of those, 12 restaurants had at least one Michelin star, each within a rectangular area measuring 2km (1¼ mile) on each side. The most convenient restaurants are either in Tivoli Gardens or around Rådhuspladsen (Town Hall Square), around the Central Railroad Station, or in Nyhavn. Others are in the shopping district, on streets off of Strøget. Reservations are not usually important, but, when in doubt, it's best to call in advance. Nearly everyone who answers the phone at restaurants speaks English.

Tivoli Gardens

Prices at the restaurants in Tivoli are about 30% higher than elsewhere. To compensate, skip dessert and buy something less expensive (perhaps ice cream or pastry) later at one of the many stands in the park. Take bus no. 2A, 5A, 11, or 15 to reach the park and any of the following restaurants.

Note: Most of these restaurants are open only from May to mid-September.

VERY EXPENSIVE

The Paul ★★★ INTERNATIONAL Come here for superb food, a sense of international and hip whimsy, and a creative and upbeat sense of fun. Winning a coveted Michelin star, the first for a restaurant in Tivoli Gardens, this is one of the three or four most sought-after culinary landmarks in town. It's found in the Glassalen, a greenhouse-style building once used as a concert hall. The mastermind behind this sophisticated venue is British-born chef Paul Cunningham, who brings fresh spectacular ideas to his cuisine. The first time we visited, we asked Paul to serve us what Bill Clinton had tasted on his visit. What arrived was hardly Bubba food but a divine free-range chicken from the island of Bornholm served with a confit of veal sweetbreads. We also tasted a perfect butter-roasted Dover sole with corn, capers, and chanterelles. The rhubarb-and-vanilla terrine for dessert brought an enchantment to the already enchanted setting of Tivoli.

Tivoli. ✆ **33-75-07-75.** www.thepaul.dk. Reservations recommended. 3-course lunch menu 425DKK; 7-course dinner with wine 895DKK. AE, DC, MC, V. Tues–Sat noon–2:30pm and 6–8:30pm. Closed Oct–Mar.

EXPENSIVE

Divan II ★★ DANISH/FRENCH Though not the rival of Paul, this landmark restaurant, established in 1843 in a garden setting, is one of the finest in Tivoli. Expect flowered garden terraces, splashing fountains, and an interior decor inspired by a lattice-ringed greenhouse. The service is uniformly impeccable, and the cuisine is among the most sophisticated in Copenhagen. Try the breast of free-range cockerel from Bornholm; it's braised in white wine and served with morels and fresh shallots. Roasted rack of Danish veal with new peas and morels, or *tournedos* Rossini, are always appealing. An ongoing staple is the "Madame Waleska," steamed filets of sole that are elaborately presented with truffles and a lobster-studded Mornay sauce. Strawberries Romanoff finishes off the meal delightfully.

Tivoli. ✆ **33-75-07-50.** www.divan2.dk. Reservations recommended. Main courses 130DKK–270DKK; fixed-price menus 265DKK–410DKK. AE, DC, MC, V. Daily noon–4pm and 5–9:30pm. It's closed whenever Tivoli is closed.

MODERATE

Færgekroen DANISH If you like honest, straightforward fare, without a lot of trimmings, and don't like to spend Tivoli prices, a mug of cold beer is waiting for you here. In a cluster of trees at the edge of the lake, this restaurant resembles a pink half-timbered Danish cottage. In warm weather, try to sit on the outside dining terrace. The menu offers drinks, snacks, and full meals. The latter might include an array of omelets, beef with horseradish, fried plaice with melted butter, pork chops with red cabbage, curried chicken, and fried meatballs. The food, prepared according to old recipes, is like what you might get down on a Danish farm. A pianist provides singalong music from Tuesday to Saturday starting at 8pm. The owners of this place recently invested in their own on-site microbrewery, which produces two kinds of beer, both of which taste wonderful.

Tivoli. ✆ **33-75-06-80.** www.faergekroen.com. Main courses 175DKK–225DKK. AE, DC, MC, V. Daily 11am–midnight (hot food until 9:45pm). Closed mid-Sept to mid-Apr.

Nyhavn & Kongens Nytorv

VERY EXPENSIVE

Era Ora ★★★ ITALIAN This is on virtually everyone's list as the very best Italian restaurant in Denmark and is one of the best restaurants in Copenhagen. Established in 1983 by Tuscan-born partners Edelvita Santos and Elvio Milleri, it offers an antique-looking dining room, with additional seating for parties of up to 12 in the wine cellar. The cuisine is based on Tuscan and Umbrian models, with sophisticated variations inspired by Denmark's superb array of fresh seafood and produce. Traditional favorites include a platter of 10 types of antipasti, arguably the best version of these Italian hors d'oeuvres in the country. The chefs' homemade pastas with the town's most savory Italian sauces are freshly made each day. In autumn the rack of venison is justifiably praised by food critics, and the veal dishes are the best we've sampled in Copenhagen.

Overgaden Neden Vandet 33B. ✆ **32-54-06-93.** www.era-ora.dk. Reservations required. Fixed-price dinner menus 880DKK; fixed-price lunch 325DKK–495DKK. AE, DC, MC, V. Mon–Sat noon–3pm and 7pm–1am. Bus: 2A or 66. Metro: Christianshavn.

Godt ★★★ INTERNATIONAL Its cuisine is as haute as ever, but Godt's reputation has been eclipsed by trendier and more newsworthy restaurants just as good. Nonetheless, it still remains a favorite of ours. A consistent small-scale choice that's known to everyone in the neighborhood, including the queen, this very formal restaurant offers two floors of minimalist and modern decor and never exceeds more than 20 diners at a time. Food is prepared fresh every day, based on what's best at the market. Certain dishes appear frequently on the menu—perhaps the sautéed Norwegian redfish with a purée of celery and watercress sauce that is an example of the chef's prowess. Using handpicked ingredients, the chef turns out a perfectly roasted rack of hare with fresh cranberries and roasted chanterelles. Desserts are excellent, especially the fresh figs marinated with black currant liqueur, wrapped in phyllo pastry and served with a coulis of pears and a velvety chocolate mousse.

Gothersgade 38. ✆ **33-15-21-22.** www.restaurant-godt.dk. Reservations required. Fixed-price menus 495DKK–660DKK. AE, MC, V. Tues–Sat 6pm–midnight. Closed July and Dec 23–Jan 3. Bus: 11.

Kong Hans Kælder ★★★ FRENCH/DANISH/ASIAN This vaulted Gothic cellar, once owned by King Hans (1455–1513), not only is in the oldest building in Copenhagen, but also is the site of the best restaurant. Five centuries ago the site of the restaurant was a vineyard, a tradition still honored by the name of the street—Vingårdsstræde. Grapes were an ingredient in many of the dishes of the time. Hans Christian Andersen once lived upstairs, writing *Love in the Nicola Tower.*

Chef Thomas Rode Andersen has turned the cellar into a Relais Gourmands, and he is mainly inspired by the classic traditions of French gastronomy, though he feels free to draw upon the cuisines and raw materials of other countries. In autumn fresh partridge and pigeon arrive from the fields, the same place where the mushrooms are gathered. He even smokes his own salmon on-site for 36 hours in an antique oven. Freshly caught fish and shellfish come from harbors nearby. The menu is inventive, sublime, and full of flavor, with market-fresh ingredients decisively seasoned.

Vingårdsstræde 6. ✆ **33-11-68-68.** www.konghans.dk. Reservations required. Main courses 450DKK–850DKK; fixed-price menu 1,100DKK. AE, DC, DISC, MC, V. Mon–Sat 6pm–midnight. Closed July 20–Aug 10 and Dec 23–26. Bus: 1A, 11, or 15.

NOMA ★★★ NORDIC This is the best restaurant in the world, or so said a panel of the world's most venerated food critics and gourmands in 2010. With a certain testosterone-driven enthusiasm, the chef here celebrates the cuisine of the cold North Atlantic. In fact, the name of the restaurant is short for *nordatlantiskl mad,* or North Atlantic food. During its relatively short life, this showcase of Nordic cuisine has received greater amounts of favorable press than any other restaurant in Denmark. Being housed in an antique, stone-sided warehouse in Christianshavn creates an almost religious duty to import ultrafresh fish and shellfish three times a week from Greenland, Iceland, and the Faroe Islands. Chef Rene Redzepi poaches, grills, pickles, smokes, or salts fish according to old Nordic traditions. Come here for crayfish, lobster, halibut in a foamy wasabi-flavored cream sauce, and practically any other creature that thrives in the cold waters of Nordic Europe.

Strandgade 93. ✆ **32-96-32-97.** www.noma.dk. Reservations recommended. Fixed-price menus 1,095DKK–1,395DKK. AE, DC, MC, V. Tues–Sat noon–1:30pm and 6–10pm. Bus: 2A, 40, or 66.

EXPENSIVE

Restaurant Els DANISH/FRENCH This former coffeehouse is one of the most upscale restaurants in Nyhavn. Meticulously preserved since 1854, it's lined with murals that feature maidens in diaphanous dresses cavorting in a mythical garden. Hans Christian Andersen was a regular here, and just before our arrival, novelist John Irving dropped in for lunch with a Danish journalist. Each day there's a different fixed-price menu, as well as a la carte offerings. Most dishes are well prepared, including pepper-pickled salmon served with fresh herbs and watercress; grilled calves' liver with onion marmalade, tomatoes, and thyme; and saddle of lamb with a compote of plums and red onions. The restaurant's name, incidentally, is the nickname of the founder's wife, Elsa.

Store Strandstræde 3 (off Kongens Nytorv). ✆ **33-14-13-41.** www.restaurant-els.dk. Reservations recommended. Main courses 175DKK–245DKK; sandwiches (lunch only) 95DKK–135DKK; fixed-price 3-course dinner 285DKK; fixed-price 4-course dinner 448DKK; fixed-price 4-course dinner 1,298DKK with wine. AE, DC, MC, V. Daily 11am–midnight. Closed July. Metro: Kongens Nytorv.

Salt ★★★ INTERNATIONAL Two centuries earlier the British fleet leveled the harborfront here, but now the British have returned—this time to design one of the most gorgeous waterside restaurants in the city. In the Copenhagen Admiral Hotel, Salt, with its seasonally adjusted menus, was the creation of British designer Sir Terence Conran. The chefs take superb and market-fresh ingredients to the limits of their innate possibilities. Some of their most sublime concoctions are braised oxtail with sweetbreads, blackberries, and schnapps of wild berries; braised pork shank with truffle oil and almonds; and saddle of rabbit poached in Calvados with stewed apples. Their desserts are worthy of awards, especially their chocolate layer cake with nutmeg ice cream, cloudberries from the Arctic, and burnt almonds.

In the Copenhagen Admiral Hotel, Toldbogade 24–28. ✆ **33-74-14-44.** www.saltrestaurant.dk. Reservations required. Main courses 185DKK–295DKK; fixed-price 2-course menu 315DKK; fixed-price 3-course menu 375DKK; fixed-price 4-course menu 445DKK. AE, DC, MC, V. Daily 11am–4pm and 5–10pm. Bus: 11, 25, or 29.

MODERATE

Café à Porta ★ DANISH/ENGLISH Hans Christian Andersen used to come here for takeout, but he'd have to peddle a lot of fairy tales to be able to afford it today. Copenhagen's version of a high-ceilinged, congenially battered grand cafe is directly on Copenhagen's most central square, close to the posh dining terrace of Hotel d'Angleterre. It's a comforting and generously proportioned lineup of rooms from the Belle Epoque, with some add-on layers of decor from the *La Dolce Vita* era of the '50s. Established nearly 200 years ago by a Portuguese merchant, Señor à Porta, the restaurant has old-fashioned accents including zinc-topped bars, and marble and wood parquet floors. Menu items range from the straightforward and simple, such as freshly made, crisp salads, to well-stuffed sandwiches. As the day goes on, more complicated dishes are served, including grilled lobster and a tender, plate-size Wiener schnitzel. That all these same dishes were being served at the turn of the 20th century doesn't bother the chefs, who prepare old favorites such as flank steak with french fries or a *tournedos* Rossini like Hemingway ate at the liberation of Paris in 1944.

Kongens Nytorv 17. ✆ **33-11-05-00.** www.cafeaporta.dk. Salads and sandwiches 85DKK–145DKK; main courses 185DKK–275DKK; fixed-price dinner menus 265DKK–995DKK. AE, DC, MC, V. Mon–Fri 8am–4pm and 5–10pm; Sat 11am–4pm and 5:30–10pm. Metro: Kongens Nytorv.

Café Victor DANISH/FRENCH Since 1981 this cafe/restaurant has been a Copenhagen tradition, and its cappuccino machine is hard at work all day long. Hip and artsy, this is a Danish version of a bustling French bistro, replete with zinc bar tops, a staff clad in black and white, and row upon row of expensive whiskeys and cognacs lined up behind the bar. At lunchtime, menu items include meal-size servings that focus on, among others, club sandwiches; a platter piled high with five different kinds of herring; smoked eel with scrambled eggs and chive; steamed paupiette of fish; terrine of foie gras; and filet of pork with cream sauce. At dinner, look for Victor's "Crazy" Caesar salad; mussels in white wine; seared tuna with fennel, spinach, and lime-flavored salsa; grilled rib-eye steak; and asparagus-studded risotto.

Ny Østergade 8. ✆ **33-13-36-13.** www.cafevictor.dk. Reservations recommended. Lunch platters, salads, and sandwiches 49DKK–185DKK; dinner main courses 195DKK–265DKK. AE, DC, MC, V. Mon–Wed 8am–1am; Thurs–Sat 8am–2am; Sun 11am–11pm. Bus: 11.

INEXPENSIVE

Nyhavns Færgekro ★ DANISH/FRENCH The "Nyhavn Ferry Inn" near the harbor has a long tradition and many loyal fans, of which we include ourselves. The house is old, dating from the final years of the 18th century. From the popular summer terrace, diners enjoy not only their food but also a view of the surrounding 18th-century houses and the canal. Inside, the decor is unusual, with a spiral stairway from an antique tram and lights that serve as call buttons when you want service from the staff. A daily homemade buffet has 10 types of herring in different styles and sauces, including fried, *rollmops* (rolled or curled herring), and smoked. You can also order *smørrebrød*—everything from smoked eel with scrambled eggs to chicken salad with bacon. A true Dane, in the tradition of Nyhavn, orders a schnapps or *akvavit* at lunch. Denmark has a tradition of making spicy *akvavit* from the herbs and plants of the land. Dinners here are relatively limited, usually configured as a fixed-price menu, with main courses including a choice of either grilled salmon or grilled entrecôte—nothing particularly imaginative but perfectly adequate and well prepared.

Nyhavn 5. ✆ **33-15-15-88.** www.nyhavnsfaergekro.dk. Reservations required. Lunch herring buffet 119DKK; fixed-price dinner 225DKK. DC, MC, V. Daily 10am–4pm and 5–11:30pm. Closed Jan 1 and Dec 24–25. Metro: Kongens Nytorv.

Restaurant/Café Nytorv ☺ DANISH In a building at the most distant end of the most elegant square in central Copenhagen is this cozy, low-ceilinged place that, like so many others in the area, used to shelter drunks, sailors, and prostitutes. Very little has changed since the early 1960s in terms of decor, which is reminiscent of 19th-century Copenhagen, and don't come here expecting cutting-edge cuisine either, as it hasn't changed since the '20s. But prices are relatively affordable for this part of town; *smørrebrød* are suitably thick; and the *Københavner platte,* a platter piled high with Danish herring, cheese, and *frikadeller* (meatballs), is suitably filling. Menu items include Danish pork sausage with potatoes, beef sirloin with béarnaise, *frikadeller* with potatoes, *biksemal* (Danish hash), and Madagascar-style pepper steak. The kids' menu is hard to turn down for diners of any age.

Nytorv 15. ✆ **33-11-77-06.** www.nytorv.dk. Reservations recommended. Sandwiches 69DKK–99DKK; main courses 129DKK–199DKK; fixed-price lunch menu 249DKK; fixed-price dinner menu 595DKK. AE, DC, MC, V. Daily 9am–11pm. Bus: 14.

Skindbuksen DANISH This local favorite is more Danish than the queen, and probably a lot more fun. Although it's in an expensive neighborhood, it's an affordable down-home type of place. This atmospheric landmark has long drawn in the neighborhood beer drinkers. Many locals, often old sailors, swear by its *skipperlabskovs,* the Danish version of a meat-and-potato hash that has sustained many a mariner over the years, and this popular dish is often sold out at noon. A good variety of *smørrebrød* is always a luncheon favorite, but other dishes include homemade soups, pâtés, fresh shrimp, and a very popular and tender beef served with béarnaise sauce. Live piano music is a fixture Monday to Saturday from 8pm to 12:30am.

Lille Kongensgade 4 (off Kongens Nytorv). ✆ **33-12-90-37.** www.skindbuksen.dk. Reservations recommended. Main courses 109DKK–189DKK. MC, V. Sun–Thurs 10am–midnight; Fri–Sat 10am–2am. Metro: Kongens Nytorv.

Near Rådhuspladsen & Tivoli

VERY EXPENSIVE

Alberto K ★ DANISH/ITALIAN Named for the innovative hotelier and international gourmet Alberto Kappenberger, this restaurant is the most successful in wedding Danish raw materials with the culinary techniques of the new Italian kitchen. From the homemade durum bread freshly baked that morning to the just-caught lobster, the chefs here place a great emphasis on freshness. Most fusion dishes are successful, including Danish rabbit with Umbrian truffle oil, or Danish lump fish with fresh rosemary grown in the Tuscan countryside. Pigeon and woodland mushrooms are served with polenta, pumpkin, chestnuts, and wood sorrel, or North Sea cod and oysters arrive with tiny spheres of fresh apple, each drizzled in Prosecco. The restaurant is on the 20th floor of the Radisson Blu Hotel and has gorgeous views.

In the Radisson Blu Royal Hotel, Hammerichsgade 1. ✆ **33-42-61-61.** www.radissonblu.com/royalhotelcopenhagen. Fixed-price menus 625DKK–775DKK. AE, DC, MC, V. Mon–Sat 6–10pm. Bus: 14 or 16.

EXPENSIVE

Sult ★ DANISH/FRENCH If you were turned on by the novel *Sult* (meaning "Hunger"), by Norwegian author Knut Hamsun, you might want to try out the restaurant whose moniker pays homage to the book. This fashionable, trendy eatery is inside the Danish Film Institute's center and is both a cultural and a gourmet experience. The setting is like a modern museum with wood floors, towering windows, and lofty ceilings. Chef Fredrik Ohlsson has traveled the Continent for his culinary inspiration, although he specializes in French cuisine. Using market-fresh ingredients, he often elevates his food to the sublime. Just describing the rather simple dishes does not suggest their artfulness in seasonings and natural flavors. The fixed-price menus are tasty, and the wine list is impressive but rather high priced.

Vognmagergade 8B. ✆ **33-74-34-17.** www.sult.dk. Reservations recommended. Main courses 105DKK–250DKK; fixed-price 12-course menu 400DKK. AE, DC, MC, V. Tues–Sat noon–10pm; Sun 10am–10pm. S-tog: Nørreport.

MODERATE

Atlas Bar/Restaurant Flyvefisken DANISH/THAI/INTERNATIONAL This joint has always been a darling of local hipsters, and you may want to join them for a slice of Copenhagen life often not seen by the casual visitor. The cuisine at these two restaurants (prepared in the same kitchen) includes lots of vegetarian food inspired by the fare of Thailand, Mexico, and India, with a Danish overview toward tidiness and coziness. On the street level, the cramped, cozy Atlas Bar serves a busy lunchtime crowd, but slackens off a bit at night, when the wood-sheathed Flyvefisken (Flying Fish) opens for dinner upstairs. Upstairs, expect a bit more emphasis on Thai cuisine and its fiery flavors, including lemon grass, curries, and several spicy fish soups native to Bangkok. Although the authenticity of the Thai cuisine has lost a bit of its zest in the long jump from Thailand, it's still a change of pace from typical Danish fare. Expect crowds here, especially at lunch.

Lars Bjørnstræde 18. ✆ **33-14-95-15.** www.atlasbar.dk. Reservations recommended. Lunch main courses 60DKK–185DKK; dinner main courses 120DKK–210DKK. AE, DC, MC, V. Atlas Bar Mon–Sat noon–10pm. Restaurant Flyvefisken Mon–Sat 5:30–10pm. Bus: 11.

Søren K ★ INTERNATIONAL/FRENCH Named after Denmark's most celebrated philosopher, this is an artfully minimalist dining room that's on the ground floor of the Black Diamond (the ultramodern, intensely angular addition to the Royal Library). It has the kind of monochromatic gray and peach–toned decor you might find in Milan, and glassy, big-windowed views that stretch out over the nearby canal. Menu items change frequently, but the chef never cooks with butter, cream, or high-cholesterol cheese, making a meal here a low-cholesterol as well as a savory experience. In a land known for its "butter-and-egg men," this type of cooking is heresy. Some Danes boycott it but foreign visitors, especially those watching their waistlines, flock here for a superb meal of dishes such as a velvety foie gras, a carpaccio of veal, and a truly superb oyster soup. Attention to detail and a proud professionalism distinguish such main dishes as veal chops served with lobster sauce and a half-lobster or else roasted venison with nuts and seasonal berries with a marinade of green tomatoes.

On the ground floor of the Royal Library's Black Diamond Wing, Søren Kierkegaards Plads 1. ✆ **33-47-49-49.** www.soerenk.dk. Reservations recommended. Lunch main courses 85DKK–215DKK; dinner main courses 175DKK–235DKK; 2-course fixed-price dinner 285DKK; 5-course fixed-price dinner 490DKK. AE, DC, MC, V. Mon–Sat 11am–midnight. Bus: 66 or 902.

INEXPENSIVE

Axelborg Bodega DANISH Since 1912 down-home cooking Danish style has been served in this cafe across from Benneweis Circus and near Scala and Tivoli. In fair weather you can sit out enjoying a brisk Copenhagen evening and people-watching. Most regulars here opt for the *dagens ret* (daily special), which is the equivalent of the old blue-plate special served at diners throughout America in the 1940s. Typical Danish dishes are featured on those specials, invariably *frikadeller* and the inevitable pork chops, which was the favorite dish of the Nazi occupation forces in the early '40s. A wide selection of *smørrebrød* is also available, costing 57DKK to 89DKK each. Although the atmosphere is somewhat impersonal, this is a local favorite; diners enjoy the recipes from grandma's attic.

Axeltorv 1. ✆ **33-11-06-38.** www.axelborgbodega.dk. Reservations recommended. Main courses 109DKK–179DKK. DC, MC, V. Restaurant daily 11am–9pm. Bar daily 11am–2am. Bus: 11.

Café Sorgenfri SANDWICHES The English translation for this place means "without sorrows." Should you have any sorrows, you can drown them in your beer here in this cafe sheltered in a house from 1796. The draft beer flows freely throughout the day in the cafe's antique interior. Don't come here expecting fine dining, or even a menu with any particular variety. With its subdued lighting and fresh flowers, this place has thrived for 150 years selling beer, schnapps, and a medley of *smørrebrød* that appeals to virtually everyone's sense of workaday thrift and frugality. With only about 50 seats, the joint is likely to be crowded around lunch hour, with somewhat more space during the midafternoon. Everything inside smacks of old-time Denmark, from the potted shrubs that adorn the facade to the well-oiled paneling that has witnessed many generations of Copenhageners selecting and enjoying sandwiches, two to four of which might compose a reasonable lunch. You'll find it in the all-pedestrian shopping zone, in the commercial heart of town.

Brolæggerstræde 8. ✆ **33-11-58-80.** www.cafesorgenfri.dk. *Smørrebrød* 49DKK–159DKK. AE, DC, MC, V. Mon–Sat 11am–11pm; Sun noon–6pm. Bus: 14.

Kobenhavner Cafeen DANISH Danes go here for their comfort-food fix, and we like to join them. One of the smallest (about 45 seats) restaurants in this pedestrian-only zone, the Kobenhavner works hard to convey a sense of old-time Denmark. An inn has been on this site since the 12th century, but the current structure dates from the 19th. The setting is cozy, and you can enjoy authentically old-fashioned dishes just like Danish grandmothers make. Expect a roster of open-faced sandwiches at both lunch and dinner; *frikadeller;* grilled filets of plaice with butter sauce and fresh asparagus; roasted pork with braised red cabbage; and *biksemal,* a type of seafood hash that was served several times a week in many Danish homes throughout World War II. One of the most appealing items, a specialty of the house, is the *Kobenhavner platte,* which features several preparations of herring, marinated salmon, shrimp, meatballs, fresh vegetables, and fresh-baked, roughly textured bread with butter.

Badstuestæde 10. ✆ **33-32-80-81.** Reservations recommended. *Smørrebrød* 69DKK–128DKK; main courses 130DKK–199DKK. AE, DC, MC, V. Daily 11:30am–10pm. Bus: 5 or 6.

Sari DANISH For some reason this eatery seems to attract a lot of foreign visitors, especially English hipsters. Its good food, and a location across the square from City Hall also guarantees a large number of lawyers and their clients. This is a bustling and old-fashioned emporium of Danish cuisine. The setting is a half-cellar room illuminated with high lace-draped windows that shine light down on wooden tables and 50 years of memorabilia. Menu items at lunch might include *frikadeller,* heaping platters of herring, Danish cheeses, smoked meats and fish, salads, and a worthy assortment of *smørrebrød.* The dinner menu is more ambitious, calling for a harder effort on the part of the kitchen staff, who turn out pickled salmon and several fine cuts of beef—our favorite choices—served with either a béarnaise or pepper sauce. Also look for the catch of the day, prepared in virtually any way you like. The food is typically Danish and well prepared, and you get no culinary surprises; but then, you are rarely disappointed.

Nytorv 5. ✆ **33-14-84-55.** www.cafesari.dk. Reservations recommended. Main courses 159DKK–179DKK. AE, DC, MC, V. Daily 11am–midnight. Bus: 14.

Near Rosenborg Slot

VERY EXPENSIVE

St. Gertruds Kloster ★★★ INTERNATIONAL Surely this is how the medieval kings of Denmark must have dined, with Hamlet pondering his famous question in the background. The most romantic restaurant in Denmark, it's a great place to pop the question. Since the labyrinth of 14th-century underground vaults is without electricity, the 1,500 flickering candles, open grill, iron sconces, and rough-hewn furniture create an elegant ambience. The chefs display talent and integrity, and every flavor is fully focused, each dish balanced to perfection. Try the fresh, homemade foie gras with black truffles, lobster served in a turbot bouillon, venison (year-round) with green asparagus and truffle sauce, or a fish and shellfish terrine studded with chunks of lobster and salmon. These dishes range from the merely good to the sublime.

Hauser Plads 32. ✆ **33-14-66-30.** www.sgk.as. Reservations required. Main courses 178DKK–295DKK; fixed-price menu 380DKK–498DKK. AE, DC, MC, V. Mon–Sat 5–11pm. Closed Dec 24–26 and Jan 1. Metro: Nørreport.

At Gråbrødretorv

Gråbrødretorv (Grey Friars Square), in the heart of Copenhagen's medieval core, is named after the monks who used to wander through its premises in medieval times. Now viewed as charming and hip, the area is a late-night destination that's not unlike what you'd find in Paris's Latin Quarter. The setting is low-key, unpretentious, and representative of the brown-brick architecture typical of historic Copenhagen.

MODERATE

Bøf & Ost DANISH/FRENCH   Even if the food weren't good, we'd come here on a summer evening to people-watch at a cafe-style table overlooking Grey Friars Square. This neighborhood favorite created a bit of a buzz when it first opened in a 1728 building constructed over cellars from a medieval monastery. But that buzz has long died down as fickle foodies have found newer places other than "Beef & Cheese" to pamper their stomachs. Even though abandoned by media in search of something new, the lobster soup still wins us over, and we often follow with some of the best beef tenderloin steaks in town. After all, Bøf & Ost has to live up to its namesake. The cheese in its name is justified when a platter with six different selections of the best cheese in the country arrives for you to devour with crusty fresh-baked bread.

Gråbrødretorv 13. ✆ **33-11-99-11.** www.boef-ost.dk. Reservations required. Main courses 159DKK-275DKK; fixed-price lunch menu 198DKK. DC, MC, V. Daily 11:30am-1am. Closed Jan 1. Bus: 14.

Pasta Basta ITALIAN   This affordable restaurant's buffet loaded with cold antipasti and salads is one of the best deals in town. With more than nine selections on the enormous buffet, it's known as the "Pasta Basta Table" (*basta* means roughly "that's enough food" in Italian). The restaurant itself is decorated in the style of ancient Pompeii, and is on a historic cobblestone street off the main shopping boulevard, Strøget. Its fans and devotees praise it for its policy of staying open late and for the chefs' preparation of 15 different homemade pasta dishes. Our favorite is saffron-flavored fettuccine in a white-wine sauce with grilled salmon strips and a garnish of salmon caviar. Other menu choices include carpaccio served with olive oil and basil, a platter with three kinds of Danish caviar (whitefish, speckled trout, and vendace), thin-sliced salmon with a cream-based sauce of salmon roe, and Danish suckling lamb with fried spring onions and tarragon.

Valkendorfsgade 22. ✆ **33-11-21-31.** www.pastabasta.dk. Reservations recommended. Main courses 98DKK-198DKK; 2-course fixed-price menu 225DKK. DC, MC, V. Daily 11:30am-2am. Bus: 11.

Peder Oxe's Restaurant/Vinkælder Wine Bar ★ DANISH   The setting alone has a certain romance, since in the Middle Ages it was the site of a monastery for gray-robed friars who were forbidden to own any possessions and were forced to beg for a living. Today, the restaurant hand-selects only the finest raw materials for its classic dishes. The cooks serve only beef from free-range cattle, along with freshly caught fish and shellfish. Game from the Danish countryside appears on the menu in autumn, and Danish lamb, among the best in Europe, is a standard feature. Other dishes include a tantalizing lobster soup, tiny Danish bay shrimp, open-faced sandwiches, and Danish hamburgers. The chefs cook the best fried herring in all of Copenhagen here, and here's their secret: They coat filleted fish with Dijon mustard, grated fresh horseradish, and caviar before rolling them in rye flour and pan-frying them in Danish country butter.

Gråbrødretorv 11. ✆ **33-11-00-77.** www.pederoxe.dk. Reservations recommended. Main courses 135DKK-225DKK; fixed-price lunch menu 138DKK. DC, MC, V. Daily 11:30am-1am. Bus: 11.

Near Christiansborg

VERY EXPENSIVE

Krogs Fiskerestaurant ★★★ SEAFOOD   Orson Welles claimed that this restaurant, one of the oldest in Copenhagen, dating from 1910, was the only place north of the Riviera that knew how to make a bouillabaisse. Only a short walk from Christiansborg Castle, the restaurant stands in a historic district of 19th-century houses, and its building dates from 1789 when it opened as a fish shop. The canalside plaza where fishermen moored their boats is now the site of the restaurant's outdoor terrace. The chefs strike a studied balance between modernized traditional dishes and updated haute cuisine classics, including a divine plaice meunière with lemon, parsley, and brown butter. The Dover sole is prepared tableside, and the shellfish selection, served hot or cold, is without equal in Copenhagen. This is a most engaging restaurant, especially among the over-50 set; before the waiter arrives with the bill, make sure you've taken your heart medication.

Gammel Strand 38. ✆ **33-15-89-15.** www.krogs.dk. Reservations required. Main courses 350DKK-450DKK; fixed-price 7-course menu 785DKK. AE, DC, MC, V. Mon–Sat 6–11pm. Bus: 1A, 2A, or 11.

In Nørrebro

Nørrebro Bryghus ★ DANISH This is the best and most appealing restaurant in the Nørrebro district, a big-time, big-city brewery/restaurant that dwarfs almost every other restaurant in the neighborhood. Occupying two floors of what was originally built in 1857 as a metal foundry, it brews between 10,000 and 20,000 liters (2,640–5,280 gal.) of beer per month, as many as 10 different kinds. In addition, many of the dishes served here are braised, fried, or stewed in beer. And if you're interested in how the fruit of the hops is actually concocted, you can sign up for any of the free brewery tours conducted here every Monday to Thursday from 5 to 6pm (Danish-language versions) and from 6 to 7pm (English-language versions). Menu items change with the season and with whatever beer happens to have been brewed within the previous week or so. Examples include crisp-fried whitefish served with roasted and glazed fennel in Pacific Pale Ale in a coriander *beurre blanc* and tarragon sauce. One of the genuinely sought-after facets of this place involves reserving the "brewmaster's table" for a specially composed seven-course meal, each course liberally soused with a different beer, with a minimum of eight diners needed for the full-fledged experience.

Ryesgade 3. ✆ **35-30-05-30.** http://noerrebrobryghus.dk. Reservations not necessary, except for brewmaster's table. Fixed-price menus 150DKK-430DKK; special 7-course menu 1,400DKK. AE, DC, MC, V. Restaurant Sun-Wed 11:30am-3pm and 5:30-10pm; Thurs-Sat 11:30am-3pm and 5:30-10:30pm. Bar Sun-Wed 11:30am-3pm and 5:30pm-midnight; Thurs-Sat 11:30am-3pm and 5:30pm-2am. Bus: 3A.

EXPLORING COPENHAGEN

6

Around-the-clock summer fun is offered in the Danish capital, everything from a free-love-and-drug commune to beer breweries, baroque palaces, and art-filled museums. On a summer evening, no man-made attraction is greater than Tivoli pleasure gardens. Several annual summer festivals take place here, and live bands perform in parks to keep Copenhagen rocking when the sun shines.

There is talk of a renaissance in Copenhagen, as much of the city, with its copper-domed landmarks, is cutting edge. Seedy old buildings are being restored—many turned into boutique hotels, and at trendy restaurants, young Danes are reinventing the cuisine of their ancestors.

Museums are more user-friendly, and even the queen is appearing on the streets in scarlet red. The culture and charm of old Copenhagen is still here, but in a word the city has become "cool," spurred in part by the young and the changes brought by newly arriving immigrants.

The summer sun may not set until 11pm, but in winter expect cold, cloudy, dark, rainy weather. "We brood like Hamlet then," said a local. "But winter or summer, we're super friendly and welcoming . . . and in English too."

IN & AROUND TIVOLI GARDENS

Ny Carlsberg Glyptotek ★★★ The Glyptotek, behind Tivoli, is one of the great art museums of Europe. Founded by the 19th-century art collector Carl Jacobsen, Mr. Carlsberg himself, the museum includes modern art and antiquities. The modern section has French and Danish art, mainly from the 19th century. Sculpture, including works by Rodin, is on the ground floor, and works of the Impressionists and related artists, including van Gogh's ***Landscape from St. Rémy*** ★, are on the upper floors. The **Etruscan collection ★★★**—sarcophagi, a winged lion, bronzes, and pottery—is a favorite of ours and the best such collection outside Italy. In 1996 the Ny Glyptotek added a French masters' wing, which can be reached only through the Conservatory. You'll find an extensive collection of French masterpieces, including works by Manet, Monet, Degas, and Renoir, as well as an impressive collection of French sculpture, including 31 Rodins. The display features Cézanne's famous

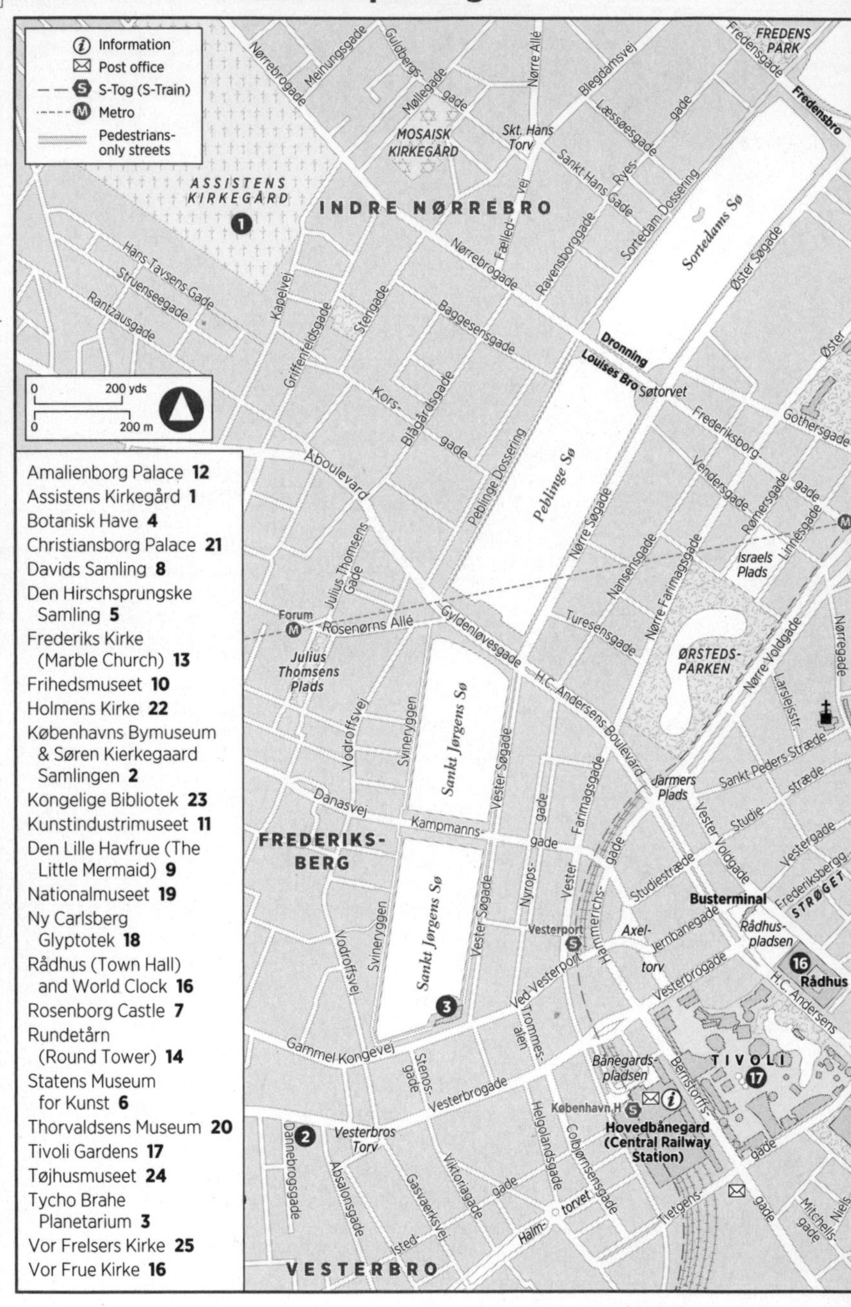

Information
Post office
S-Tog (S-Train)
Metro
Pedestrians-only streets
0 200 yds
0 200 m
Amalienborg Palace 12
Assistens Kirkegård 1
Botanisk Have 4
Christiansborg Palace 21
Davids Samling 8
Den Hirschsprungske Samling 5
Frederiks Kirke (Marble Church) 13
Frihedsmuseet 10
Holmens Kirke 22
Københavns Bymuseum & Søren Kierkegaard Samlingen 2
Kongelige Bibliotek 23
Kunstindustrimuseet 11
Den Lille Havfrue (The Little Mermaid) 9
Nationalmuseet 19
Ny Carlsberg Glyptotek 18
Rådhus (Town Hall) and World Clock 16
Rosenborg Castle 7
Rundetårn (Round Tower) 14
Statens Museum for Kunst 6
Thorvaldsens Museum 20
Tivoli Gardens 17
Tøjhusmuseet 24
Tycho Brahe Planetarium 3
Vor Frelsers Kirke 25
Vor Frue Kirke 16
ASSISTENS KIRKEGÅRD
MOSAISK KIRKEGÅRD
INDRE NØRREBRO
FREDENS PARK
FREDERIKSBERG
VESTERBRO
TIVOLI
ØRSTEDS-PARKEN
Sortedams Sø
Peblinge Sø
Sankt Jørgens Sø
Nørrebrogade
Meinungsgade
Guldbergsgade
Møllegade
Nørre Allé
Blegdamsvej
Fredensgade
Fredensbro
Skt. Hans Torv
Læssøesgade
Sankt Hans Gade
Ryesgade
Sortedam Dossering
Fælledvej
Ravnsborggade
Øster Søgade
Hans Tavsens Gade
Struenseegade
Rantzausgade
Kapelvej
Griffenfeldsgade
Stengade
Baggesensgade
Dronning Louises Bro
Søtorvet
Korsgade
Blågårdsgade
Peblinge Dossering
Frederiksborggade
Gothersgade
Åboulevard
Vendersgade
Rømersgade
Nørre Søgade
Linnésgade
Israels Plads
Julius Thomsens Gade
Nansensgade
Nørre Farimagsgade
Forum
Rosenørns Allé
Julius Thomsens Plads
Gyldenløvesgade
Turesensgade
H.C. Andersens Boulevard
Nørre Voldgade
Nørregade
Larsleisstr.
Vodroffsvej
Svineryggen
Vester Søgade
Farimagsgade
Sankt Peders Stræde
Jarmers Plads
Studiestræde
Danasvej
Kampmannsgade
Vester Voldgade
Vestergade
Nyropsgade
Vester Farimagsgade
Frederiksberggade
STRØGET
Busterminal
Hammerichsgade
Vesterport
Axeltorv
Jernbanegade
Rådhuspladsen
Rådhus
Ved Vesterport
Vesterbrogade
H.C. Andersens
Trommesalen
Gammel Kongevej
Stenosgade
Bånegardspladsen
Bernstorffsgade
København H
Hovedbånegard (Central Railway Station)
Helgolandsgade
Colbjørnsensgade
Vesterbros Torv
Dannebrogsgade
Absalonsgade
Gasværksvej
Viktoriagade
Halmtorvet
Istedgade
Tietgensgade
Mitchellsgade
Niels

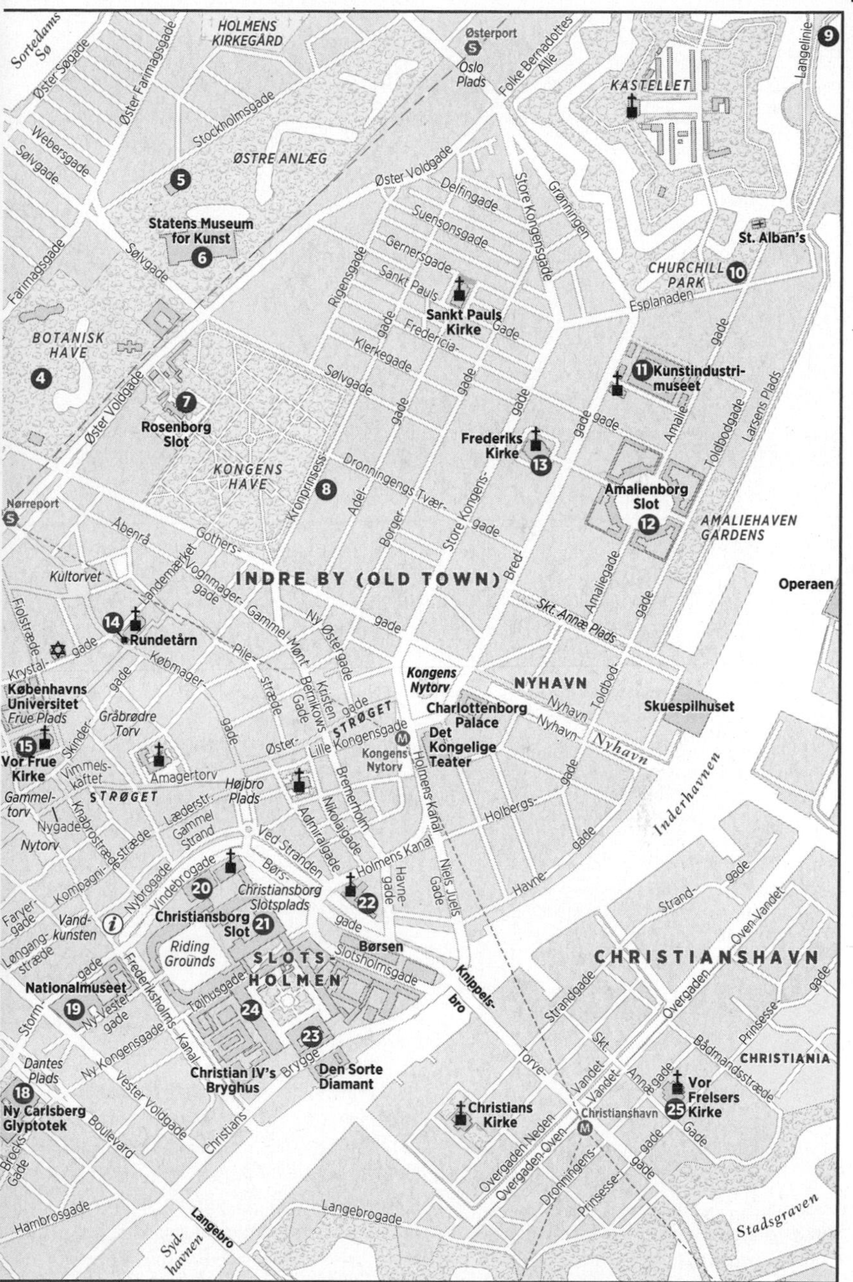
HOLMENS KIRKEGÅRD
ØSTRE ANLÆG
Statens Museum for Kunst
BOTANISK HAVE
Rosenborg Slot
KONGENS HAVE
KASTELLET
St. Alban's
CHURCHILL PARK
Sankt Pauls Kirke
Kunstindustri-museet
Frederiks Kirke
Amalienborg Slot
AMALIEHAVEN GARDENS
Operaen
INDRE BY (OLD TOWN)
NYHAVN
Skuespilhuset
Rundetårn
Københavns Universitet
Vor Frue Kirke
Charlottenborg Palace
Det Kongelige Teater
Kongens Nytorv
STRØGET
Inderhavnen
Christiansborg Slot
Riding Grounds
SLOTSHOLMEN
Børsen
Nationalmuseet
Christian IV's Bryghus
Den Sorte Diamant
CHRISTIANSHAVN
CHRISTIANIA
Christians Kirke
Vor Frelsers Kirke
Ny Carlsberg Glyptotek
Stadsgraven
Langebro
Knippelsbro
Nørreport
Østerport
Christianshavn

Portrait of the Artist **★★**, as well as about **35 paintings ★★** by former Copenhagen resident Paul Gauguin.

Dantes Plads 7. ✆ **33-41-81-41.** www.glyptoteket.dk. Admission 60DKK adults, free for children 17 and under, free for everyone Sun. Tues–Sun 11am–5pm. Bus: 1A, 2A, 15, or 33. See map p. 116.

Rådhus (Town Hall) and Verdensur (World Clock) This towering monument, the City Hall of Copenhagen, is said to have been inspired by the main tower at the Piazza del Campo in Siena. Statues of Hans Christian Andersen and Niels Bohr (the Nobel Prize–winning physicist) are worth a look. Jens Olsen's **World Clock** is open for viewing Monday to Friday 10am to 4pm and Saturday at 1pm. Frederik IX set the clock on December 15, 1955. The clockwork is so exact that it's accurate to within half a second every 300 years. Climb the tower for an impressive view, but it's 300 steps with no elevator.

Rådhuspladsen. ✆ **33-66-25-82.** Admission to Rådhus 30DKK adults, 5DKK children 5–12, free for children 4 and under. Guided tour of Rådhus 30DKK Mon–Fri 3pm, Sat 10 and 11am. Guided tour of tower Oct–May Mon–Sat noon; June–Sept Mon–Fri 10am, noon, and 2pm, Sat noon. Bus: 6A or 26. See map p. 116.

Tivoli Gardens ★★★ Created in 1843, Tivoli Gardens is in an 8-hectare (20-acre) garden that is the virtual symbol of Denmark. Tivoli is filled with schmaltz but somehow with its glitz, glamour, and gaiety it manages to win over hardened cynics. Children prefer it during the day but adults tend to like it better at night, when it is aglow with tiny lights. It features thousands of flowers, a merry-go-round of tiny Viking ships, games of chance and skill (pinball arcades, slot machines, shooting galleries), a Ferris wheel of hot-air balloons and cabin seats, and "the Demon," the biggest roller coaster in Denmark. There's also a playground for children.

An Arabian-style fantasy palace, with towers and arches, houses more than two dozen expensive restaurants, from a lakeside inn to a beer garden. Take a walk around the edge of the tiny lake with its ducks, swans, and boats.

A parade of the red-uniformed Tivoli Boys Guard takes place on weekends at 3:50 and 5:50pm, and their regimental band gives concerts on Saturday at 3:50pm on the open-air stage. The oldest building at Tivoli, the Chinese-style Pantomime Theater with its peacock curtain, offers pantomimes in the evening.

For nighttime happenings in Tivoli, see "Copenhagen After Dark," p. 145.

Vesterbrogade 3. ✆ **33-15-10-01.** www.tivoli.dk. Admission 95DKK adults, 50DKK children 3–11; combination ticket including admission and all rides 205DKK adults, 170DKK children 3–11. Closed mid-Sept to mid-Apr. Bus: 2A, 5A, 11, or 15. See map p. 116.

AMALIENBORG PALACE & ENVIRONS

Amalienborg Palace ★★ These four 18th-century French-style rococo mansions—opening onto one of the most attractive squares in Europe—have been the home of the Danish royal family since 1794, when Christiansborg burned. Visitors flock to see the changing of the guard at noon when the royal family is in residence. The official and private rooms in Amalienborg, reconstructed to reflect the period 1863 to 1947, all belonged to members of the royal family, the Glücksborgs, who ascended the throne in 1863. The king's large study is decorated in lavish neo-Renaissance style. Many treasures are exhibited in the museum rooms today: works of art from the imperial workshops and from jewelers such as Fabergé, as well as souvenirs, embroideries, and handicrafts made by the grandchildren. Also open to the public are the studies of Frederik VIII and Christian X. The final period room in the museum is the study of Christian X (1870–1947), the grandfather of current queen Margrethe II, who was king from 1912 to 1947. Along with the period rooms, a costume gallery and a jewelry room are open to the public.

Christian VIII's Palace. ✆ **33-12-21-86.** www.rosenborgslot.dk. Admission 70DKK adults, 45DKK students, free for children 17 and under. May–Oct Tues–Sun 10am–4pm; Nov–Apr Tues–Sun 11am–4pm. Metro: Kongens Nytorv. See map p. 116.

Davids Samling ★ This museum houses the Nordic world's greatest collection of art from the **World of Islam ★★★**, dating from the 7th to the 19th century and looted from such distant points as Spain and West India. The collection includes an astonishing array of pottery, weaponry, glassware, silverware, texts, and textiles, among other exhibits. Christian Ludvig David, a lawyer in the Danish High Court with wide-ranging tastes, died in 1960, leaving his carefully chosen treasure-trove to the city. The museum also includes floors devoted to European fine and applied art from the 18th to the 20th century.

Kronprinsessegade 30. ✆ **33-73-49-49.** www.davidmus.dk. Free admission. Tues and Fri–Sun 1–5pm; Wed–Thurs 10am–5pm. Bus: 6A or 26. See map p. 116.

Den Lille Havfrue (The Little Mermaid) ★ The statue *everybody* wants to see in Copenhagen is Edvard Eriksen's slightly smaller than life-size bronze of *Den Lille Havfrue,* inspired by Andersen's famous fairy tale *The Little Mermaid.* The 1.2m (4-ft.) bronze mermaid was unveiled in 1913, and the statue has become an important symbol to Copenhageners. Tragedy struck in 1964 when she was decapitated. The culprits at that time were never discovered, and the head was never recovered. In the early 1900s some unknown party cut off her arm. The original mold exists so it's possible to recast the bronze and weld back missing body parts. On January 6, 1998, vandals again severed her head. The head turned up at a TV station, delivered by a masked figure. Welders put her head back on, making the seam invisible.

Because of the attacks, the statue, seen by about one million visitors a year, may actually be moved out of the reach of both vandals and tourists to a safer, more secure place. In 2006 another Little Mermaid sculpture was unveiled, a "genetically modified sister," 400m (1,312 ft.) from the original. The new bronze is by Bjørn Nørgaard, a professor at the Royal Danish Academy of Fine Arts. Like the original, Nørgaard's mermaid also sits on a rock, but her features are twisted and her limbs exaggeratedly long and skeletal. Nørgaard created the sculpture for the Danish Pavilion at Expo 2002, the world's fair held in Hanover, Germany.

Langelinie on the harbor. Free admission. Bus: 1A, 6A, or 15. See map p. 116.

Frihedsmuseet (Museum of Danish Resistance, 1940–45) ★ As World War II buffs, we always pay at least one visit here on every trip to Copenhagen. In 1942 Hitler sent King Christian X a birthday greeting. The response was terse. In retaliation, Hitler sent Werner Best, one of the architects of the Gestapo, to rule Denmark. Hitler used Denmark mainly as a larder to feed his Nazi armies during the war. The Danes resisted at every turn, including safely spiriting away 7,000 Danish Jews to neutral Sweden. This museum also reveals the tools of espionage and sabotage that the Danes used to throw off the Nazi yoke in World War II. The museum highlights the workings of the outlaw press, the wireless communications equipment, and illegal films; relics of torture and concentration camps; British propaganda leaflets dropped in the country; satirical caricatures of Hitler; information about Danish Jews, and, conversely, about Danish Nazis; and material on paralyzing nationwide strikes. In all, this moment in history is graphically and dramatically preserved.

Churchillparken. ✆ **33-47-39-21.** www.frihedsmuseet.dk. Free admission. May–Sept Tues–Sun 10am–5pm; Oct–Apr Tues–Sun 10am–3pm. Bus: 1A, 15, or 25. See map p. 116.

Kunstindustrimuseet (Museum of Decorative and Applied Art) ★ With more than 300,000 decorative objects on view, this is the finest design museum in Scandinavia. The rococo building itself is one of the historic landmarks of Copenhagen, containing four wings surrounding a garden. It was part of the Royal Frederik Hospital, built from 1752 to 1757 during the reign of King Frederik V. Pride of place is given to furniture, tapestries, other textiles, pottery, porcelain, glass, and silver, and there are many exhibits focusing on the innovative role of Danish modern design—mostly furniture and fabrics—since the 1930s. There are also rare collections of Chinese and Japanese art and handicrafts. The library contains around 65,000 books and periodicals. The gardens surrounding the museum are open during museum hours. In summer theatrical performances are staged here for both adults and children, and the museum restaurant offers alfresco cafe-style tables when the weather is fair. With its manicured grounds and beautiful old linden trees, as well as strategically placed sculptures, these gardens are one of the most charming of the outdoor spaces of Copenhagen.

Bredgade 68. ✆ **33-18-56-56.** www.kunstindustrimuseet.dk. Admission to museum 60DKK adults, free for children 17 and under. Free admission to library. Museum Tues–Sun 11am–5pm. Library Tues–Sat 11am–5pm. S-tog: Østerport. Bus: 1A or 15. See map p. 116.

Orlogsmuseet (Royal Naval Museum) Do you ever lie awake at night wondering what happened to the propeller from the German U-boat that sank the *Lusitania?* Look no further: It's here at this former naval hospital in Søkvasthuset, opening onto the Christianshavn Kanal. More than 300 model ships, many based on designs that date from as early as 1500, are also on view, and some of them were designed and constructed by naval engineers, serving as prototypes for the construction of actual ships that ventured into the cold, dark waters of the North Sea. The models are wide ranging—some are fully "dressed," with working sails, whereas others are cross-sectional with their frames outlined. A vast array of other naval artifacts includes an intriguing collection of figureheads, some of which are artworks themselves. For us, nothing is as glamorous or splendid as the ornate state barge from 1780.

Overgaden Oven Vandet 58. ✆ **33-11-60-37.** www.orlogsmuseet.dk. Admission 40DKK adults, free for children 17 and under. Tues–Sun noon–4pm. Bus: 2A, 40, or 350S.

ROSENBORG CASTLE & BOTANICAL GARDENS

Botanisk Have (Botanical Gardens) ★ Cacti, orchids, and palm trees always draw us to the most splendid 10 hectares (25 acres) in all of Denmark. Planted from 1871 to 1874—and still around to thrill us to this day—these botanical gardens are on a lake that was once part of the city's defensive moat around Rosenborg Slot, which fronts the gardens. In fact, after a visit to Rosenborg, we always like to come here to wind down after devouring so many royal treasures. Greenhouses grow both tropical and subtropical plants, none finer than the **Palm House ★★**, which appears even more exotic this far north. Retreat here on a rainy day and imagine you're in the Tropics. An alpine garden also contains mountain plants from all over the world.

Gothersgade 128. ✆ **35-32-22-22.** www.botanic-garden.ku.dk. Free admission. May–Sept daily 8:30am–6pm; Oct–Apr Tues–Sun 8:30am–4pm. Closed Dec 24. S-tog: Nørreport. Bus: 5A, 6A, 11, 42, or 43. See map p. 116.

Den Hirschsprungske Samling (Hirschsprung Collection) ★ The setting for the museum is romantic, as it's beautifully situated in the green parklands of Østre Anlæg on the old ramparts of Copenhagen. Heinrich Hirschsprung (1836–1908), a tobacco manufacturer, bequeathed his treasures to the Danish state, which housed them in a neoclassical building constructed in 1911 in back of the Fine Arts Museum. Never has the "dancing light and sparkling waters" of the Danish seashore and countryside been so evocatively captured as it is in this highly personal collection of art from Denmark's "Golden Age" of painting (1800–50). Just as long as the painters were Danish, Hirschsprung collected their art over a period of 40 years—paintings, drawings, and sculptures, including the Skagen artists, the symbolists, and the *Fynboerne* (Natives of Funen). A great intimacy was created by the museum's decision to exhibit beautiful interiors featuring furniture from the homes and studios of many of the artists.

Stockholmsgade 20. ✆ **35-42-03-36.** www.hirschsprung.dk. Admission 50DKK adults, free for children 17 and under, free to all Wed. Wed–Mon 11am–4pm. Bus: 6A, 14, 40, 42, or 43. See map p. 116.

Rosenborg Slot (Rosenborg Castle) ★★★ This palace is the greatest and purest Renaissance structure in Denmark, since its facade hasn't changed since 1633. It has survived fires and wars, and stands to delight us today. Christian IV conceived of the palace in 1606 but it began with **Kongens Have ★**, the King's Garden, which still surrounds the palace today, and is one of the more delightful places in Copenhagen for a stroll. The king liked the place so much he built a summer pavilion here, which eventually led to the creation of this monumental red-brick *slot* (castle), inspired by the Dutch Renaissance style, and today one of the most beautiful and evocative monuments of Denmark. It houses everything from narwhal-tusked and ivory coronation chairs to Frederik VII's baby shoes—all artifacts from the Danish royal family, who used the elegant building as a storage bin for royal artifacts. Its biggest draws are the dazzling **crown jewels and regalia ★★★** in the basement Treasury, which houses a lavishly decorated coronation saddle from 1596 and other treasures. Try to see the **Knights Hall ★** in Room 21, with its coronation seat, three silver lions, and relics from the 1700s.

Øster Voldgade 4A. ✆ **33-15-32-86.** www.rosenborgslot.dk. Admission 75DKK adults, 45DKK students and seniors, free for children 16 and under. Jan 2–Feb 11, Feb 21–Apr 20, Apr 26–30, and Nov 1–Dec 22 castle Tues–Sun 11am–2pm, treasury Tues–Sun 11am–4pm; Feb 12–20, Apr 21–25, May 1–31, Sept 1–Oct 31, and Dec 27–30 castle and treasury daily 11am–4pm, June 1–Aug 31 daily 10am–5pm. S-Tog and metro: Nørreport. Bus: 6A, 11, 42, 43, 184, or 185. See map p. 116.

Statens Museum for Kunst (Royal Museum of Fine Arts) ★★★ ☺ The largest museum in Denmark houses painting and sculpture from the 13th to the present century, the collection originally acquired by the kings of Denmark. In 1750 Frederik V launched the collection by purchasing vast art from the Continent, especially Flemish and Dutch paintings, but also Italian and German works. Bruegel, Rubens, Rembrandt, and Memling are just some of the artists waiting to dazzle you. Of all these works, we are drawn to a masterpiece by Andrea Mantegna, ***Christ as the Suffering Redeemer*** **★★★**. The so-called Danish Golden Age of painting from the 19th century forms one of the greatest treasures of the museum. Except for Edvard Munch from Norway, most of these Scandinavian artists will not be known to the general public.

Generous donations or long-term loans have beefed up the former royal collection of paintings and sculptures. In 1928 Johannes Rump donated a huge collection of early French modernists. The predictable Braque and Picasso works are here, but there is a stunning collection of **25 paintings by Henri Matisse ★★**. The **Italian school ★★** is also a rich trove of art, with works by Filippino Lippi, Titian, and Tintoretto. The museum also contains one of the world's oldest collections of **European prints and drawings ★★★**, including contributions from Giacometti, Rembrandt, Degas, and Toulouse-Lautrec.

Also on-site is a **Children's Museum** on the ground floor, with hands-on displays. At a workshop held daily from 2 to 4pm, kids can draw, paint, and sculpt.

Sølvgade 48–50. ✆ **33-74-84-94.** www.smk.dk. Free admission. Tues and Thurs–Sun 10am–5pm; Wed 10am–8pm. Bus: 6A, 14, 26, 40, 42, 43, 184, or 185. See map p. 116.

CHRISTIANSBORG PALACE & ENVIRONS

Christiansborg Slot (Christiansborg Castle) ★★★ Over the centuries Christiansborg Castle has led a rough life ever since the founding father of Copenhagen, Bishop Absalon, completed the first castle here in 1167. That one burned down—and so did the next two palaces. Christiansborg Slot was a royal residence beginning in 1416 when Erik of Pomerania moved in. The royals lived here until fleeing to more comfortable quarters at Amalienborg Slott in 1794. Christian VI ordered that the entire castle be torn down in 1732, finding it "an eyesore." But his new place burned down on the night of February 26, 1794. What is left today is a granite-and-copper palace from 1928. It stands on Slotsholmen, a small island in the center of Copenhagen that has been the seat of political power in Denmark for 800 years. It houses the Danish Parliament, the Supreme Court, this prime minister's offices, and the Royal Reception Rooms. A guide will lead you through richly decorated rooms, including the Throne Room, Banqueting Hall, and the Queen's Library. Under the palace, visit the well-preserved ruins of the 1167 castle of Bishop Absalon.

You can also see **Kongelige Stalde & Kareter ★**, Christiansborg Ridebane 12 (✆ **33-40-10-10**), the royal stables and coaches. Elegantly clad in riding breeches and jackets, riders exercise the royal horses. Vehicles include regal coaches and "fairy tale" carriages, along with a display of harnesses in use by the royal family since 1778. This attraction is open October to April Saturday and Sunday 2 to 4pm, May to September Friday to Sunday 2 to 4pm.

Christiansborg Slotsplads. ✆ **33-92-64-92.** www.ses.dk. Guided tour of Royal Reception Rooms 70DKK adults, 35DKK children 7–14. Admission to castle ruins 40DKK adults, 20DKK children 7–14. Stables 20DKK adults, 10DKK ages 7–14. Guided tours of Reception Rooms May–Sept daily 11am, 1pm, and 3pm; Oct–Apr Tues–Sun at 3pm. Ruins May–Sept daily 10am–4pm; Oct–Apr Tues–Sun 10am–4pm. English-language tours of parliament year-round daily 11am, 1pm, and 3pm. Bus: 1A, 2A, 6, 15, or 26. See map p. 116.

Nationalmuseet (National Museum) ★★★ ☺ The nucleus of this museum started out as Frederik II's "Royal Chamber of Curiosities" in 1650. It grew to become the Nordic world's greatest repository of anthropological artifacts. Today, the museum is divided into five different departments, beginning with the Prehistoric Wing on the ground floor, with artifacts from the reindeer stalkers of the Ice Age to the Vikings, with runic stones, helmets, and fragments of battle gear. In a sumptuous once-royal palace, the museum appeals even to kids, who gravitate to the Children's Museum geared to ages 4 to 12. Dating from around 1200 B.C., the world-famous ***Sun Chariot*** ★★★ is an elegant Bronze Age piece of pagan art that was unearthed by a farmer plowing his ground in 1902.

In the Runic Stone Hall, the **Hjortespring Boat** ★★ dates from around 300 B.C. This "war canoe" is the oldest plank-built boat unearthed in the north of Europe. One of the most stunning displays in this hall is the **Golden Age Room** ★★★, with its dazzling display of gold objects, some dating back to 1000 B.C. The Peoples of the World Department is one of the oldest ethnographical collections in the world, with artifacts ranging from Papua New Guinea to Central America. This section also displays artifacts of the Eskimo culture that still flourishes in Greenland, which is under the control of Denmark. The **Royal Collection of Coins and Medals** ★★ is in one of the loveliest rooms (no. 146) in Copenhagen, with views over Christiansborg Slot. The **Collection of Antiquities** ★★★ has been called "the British Museum in miniature." It contains everything from two fragments from the Parthenon, stolen by a Danish naval officer in 1687, to Holy Roman cups depicting Homeric legends.

Ny Vestergade 10. ✆ **33-13-44-11.** www.natmus.dk. Free admission. Tues–Sun 10am–5pm. Closed Dec 24–25 and Dec 31. Bus: 2A or 11. See map p. 116.

Thorvaldsens Museum ★ This is the oldest art gallery in Denmark, having opened on September 18, 1848. This museum on Slotsholmen, next door to Christiansborg, houses the greatest collection of the works of Bertel Thorvaldsen (1770–1844), the biggest name in neoclassical sculpture. He's famous for his most typical, classical, restrained works, taken from mythology: Cupid and Psyche, Adonis, Jason, Hercules, Ganymede, Mercury—all of which are displayed at the museum. The museum also contains Thorvaldsen's personal, and quite extensive, collection—everything from the Egyptian relics of Ptolemy to the contemporary paintings he acquired during his lifetime. After many years of self-imposed exile in Italy, Thorvaldsen returned in triumph to his native Copenhagen, where he died a national figure and was buried here in the courtyard of his own personal museum.

Bertel Thorvaldsens Plads 2. ✆ **33-32-15-32.** www.thorvaldsensmuseum.dk. Admission 20DKK adults, free for children 17 and under, free to all Wed. Tues–Sun 10am–5pm. Closed Jan 1, Dec 24–25, and Dec 31. Bus: 1A, 2A, 15, 26, or 29. See map p. 116.

Tøjhusmuseet (Royal Arsenal Museum) ★ This arsenal museum is the finest of its kind in the world. The long Arsenal Hall on the ground floor is itself an architectural curiosity, the longest arched hall in Europe, with its cross vaults supported by 16 heavy center pillars. Displayed here is an armada of weapons, some 350 historical guns, mortars, and howitzers, with artillery equipment dating from 1500 through the present. The Armory Hall upstairs was once a storehouse for hand weapons, and today has 7,000 of these killers, some dating as far back as 1300. Christian IV's original arsenal building was constructed between 1589 and 1604 with the thickest walls in Copenhagen, measuring 4m (13 ft.). The royal suits of armor are almost works of art unto themselves, but the most beautiful craftsmanship is evident in the ivory-inlaid pistols and muskets.

Tøjhusgade 3. ✆ **33-11-60-37.** www.thm.dk. Admission 30DKK adults, 15DKK students and seniors, free for children 17 and under. Tues–Sun noon–4pm. Closed Jan 1, Dec 23–26, and Dec 31. Bus: 1A, 2A, 11, 14, 15, 26, 29, 40, or 66. See map p. 116.

IN THE OLD TOWN (INDRE BY)

Rundetårn (Round Tower) For the most **panoramic view ★★★** of the city of Copenhagen, climb the spiral ramp (no steps) leading up to the top of this tower, which was built in 1642. The spiral walk to the top is unique in European architecture, measuring 268m (880 ft.) and winding itself seven times around the hollow core of the tower, forming the only link between the individual parts of the building complex. Obviously not wanting to walk, Peter the Great, in Denmark on a state visit, galloped up the ramp on horseback, preceded by his carriage-drawn czarina. Rundetårn is also the oldest functioning observatory in Europe, in use until 1861 by the University of Copenhagen. Now anyone can observe the night sky through the astronomical telescope in the winter months.

Købmagergade 52A. ✆ **33-73-03-73.** www.rundetaarn.dk. Admission 25DKK adults, 5DKK children 5-15. May 21-Sept 20 daily 10am-8pm; Sept 21-May 20 daily 10am-5pm. Mid-Oct to mid-Mar also from 7-10pm. Bus: 11. See map p. 116.

Vor Frue Kirke (Copenhagen Cathedral) For such an important European capital as Copenhagen, the cathedral of the Danish capital is relatively modest. It's lacking in art and treasures because of a fanatical attack by Lutheran zealots who destroyed precious items during the darkest days of the Reformation. The cathedral itself, designed by C. F. Hansen, was the third such building erected here. The original Gothic structure was ravaged by fire in 1728, and the second cathedral damaged by British bombardments in 1807. The church is often used for funerals of the country's greatest men and women—the funeral of Hans Christian Andersen took place here in 1875, and that of Søren Kierkegaard in 1855. We enjoy coming to listen to certain musical events (ask at the tourist office for details) and to see several sculptures by the great Thorvaldsen, including his majestic ***Christ and the Apostles* ★★**.

Nørregade 8. ✆ **33-37-65-40.** www.domkirken.dk. Free admission. Mon-Fri 8am-5pm. Bus: 11 or 14. See map p. 116.

THE CHURCHES OF COPENHAGEN

For information on the Copenhagen Cathedral, see "In the Old Town (Indre By)," above.

Frederiks Kirke (Marble Church) ★ In many ways this landmark church is more richly decorated and impressive than Copenhagen's cathedral, Vor Frue Kirke. Instead of Frederikskirke, Danes often call this building *Marmorkirken* (Marble Church). Just a short walk from Amalienborg Palace, it began unsuccessfully in 1749. The original plan was to use quarries of expensive Norwegian marble. The treasury dried up in 1770, and work came to a halt. It wasn't resumed until late in the 19th century when an industrialist, C. F. Tietgen, put up the money for its completion. This time a cheaper Danish marble was used instead. The original design was for neoclassical revival, but in the end the church was constructed in the Roman baroque style, opening in 1894. Inspired by Michelangelo's dome for St. Peter's in Rome, the Danish church was crowned with a copper dome, measuring 46m (151 ft.) high, making it one of the largest in the world.

Frederiksgade 4. ✆ **33-15-01-44.** Free admission. Dome to church 25DKK adults, 10DKK ages 5-14. Church Mon-Thurs 10am-5pm; Fri-Sun noon-5pm. Dome June 15-Aug 31 daily 1 and 3pm; Sept-June 14 Sat-Sun 1 and 3pm. Bus: 1A, 15, 25, or 26. See map p. 116.

Holmens Kirke This Lutheran church became world famous in 1967 when Queen Margrethe II married Prince Henrik here. Built in 1619, this royal chapel and naval church is across the canal from Slotsholmen, next to the National Bank of Denmark. Although the structure was converted into a church for the Royal Navy in 1619, its nave was built in 1562 as an anchor forge. By 1641 the ever-changing church was renovated to its current, predominantly Dutch Renaissance style. The so-called royal doorway was brought from Roskilde Cathedral in the 19th century. Inside, the extraordinary feature of this church is its ostentatious **baroque altar ★★** of unpainted oak, a carved pulpit by Abel Schrøder the Younger that extends right to the roof. In the burial chamber are the tombs of some of Denmark's most towering naval figures, including Admiral Niels Juel, who successfully fought off a naval attack by Swedes in 1677 in the Battle of Køge Bay. Peder Tordenskjold, who defeated Charles XII of Sweden during the Great Northern War in the early 1700s, is also entombed here.

Holmens Kanal 21. ✆ **33-13-61-78.** www.holmenskirke.dk. Free admission. Mon–Fri 9am–2pm; Sat 9am–noon. Bus: 1A, 15, 26, or 29. See map p. 116.

Vor Frelsers Kirken The architect of the 1752 staircase of the "Church of Our Savior" was Laurids de Thurah. It's said that he constructed the staircase encircling the building the wrong way. Climbing to the top, and belatedly realizing what he'd done, he jumped to his death. A good story, but it's not true. According to more reliable reports, he died poverty-stricken in his sleep in his own bed in 1759. The green-and-gold tower of this Gothic structure is a Copenhagen landmark, dominating the Christianshavn area. Inside, view the splendid baroque altar, richly adorned with a romp of cherubs and other figures. Four hundred vertigo-inducing steps will take you to the top, where you'll see a gilded figure of Christ standing on a globe, and a **panoramic view ★★★** of the city. ***Warning:*** The steps grow narrower as you approach the pinnacle.

Skt. Annægade 29. ✆ **32-54-68-83.** www.vorfrelserskirke.dk. Free admission to church. Admission to tower 25DKK adults, 10DKK children 5–14, free for children 4 and under. Apr–Aug Mon–Sat 11am–4:30pm, Sun noon–4:30pm; Sept–Oct Mon–Sat 11am–3:30pm, Sun noon–3:30pm; Nov–Mar daily 11am–3:30pm. It is possible to visit the tower only Apr–Oct. Metro: Christianshavn. See map p. 116.

OUTSIDE COPENHAGEN

Museums

Arken Museum for Moderne Kunst (Arken Museum of Modern Art) ★ 🎁

This major modern art museum remains the most undiscovered museum in Copenhagen because it's a 15-minute train ride from the center of town in the dreary suburb of Ishøj. Constructed of white concrete and steel, and evoking the hull of a beached ship, it was built in 1996 to celebrate Copenhagen's designation as European City of Culture for that year. Architectural critics were appalled when 25-year-old Søren Robert Lund was selected to design the museum while still a student at the Royal Danish Academy of Fine Arts. In time Lund won over some of his attackers, especially after the building won two awards for its design. Artists who show their works here remain almost universal in their condemnation of Lund, feeling that the frame with its curious "marine architecture" competes with the art exhibited inside. The museum supplements its trove of 300 works of art with temporary exhibitions devoted to, say, the works of Picasso. In addition to gallery space, the museum has a concert hall, sculpture courtyards, and a restaurant.

Ishøj Strandpark, Skovvej 100. ✆ **43-54-02-22.** www.arken.dk. Admission 85DKK adults, 70DKK seniors and students, free for children 17 and under. Tues–Sun 10am–5pm; Wed 10am–9pm. Train: E or A to Ishøj Station, then bus 128.

Frilandsmuseet (Open-Air Museum) ★★★ One of the largest and oldest (1897) open-air museums in the world, this reconstructed village in Lyngby on the fringe of Copenhagen recaptures Denmark's one-time rural character. The "museum" is nearly 36 hectares (89 acres), and includes more than 50 re-created buildings—farmsteads, windmills, and fishermen's cottages. Exhibits include a half-timbered 18th-century farmstead from one of the tiny wind-swept Danish islands, a primitive longhouse from the remote Faroe Islands, thatched fishermen's huts from Jutland, tower windmills, and a potter's workshop from the mid–19th century. Folk dancers in native costume perform, and there are demonstrations of lace making and loom weaving.

Adjacent to the open-air museum is **Brede Værk ★**, an intact industrial plant that gives a complete picture of a former factory community that closed in 1956. Still intact are the cottages of the working-class families and their former eating house, which has been turned into a restaurant. **Brede House ★★** is a neoclassical manor dating from 1795. The owner of the mill, Peter van Hemert, lived here with his family before he went bankrupt in 1805.

The park is about 14km (8⅔ miles) from the Central Railroad Station. There's an old-world restaurant at the entryway to the museum.

Kongevejen 100, Lyngby. ✆ **33-13-44-11.** www.nationalmuseet.dk. Free admission. Mar 27–Oct 24 Tues–Sun 10am–5pm. Closed Oct 25–Mar 26. Bus: 184.

Beaches

Locals and visitors are flocking to a newly created beach, **Amager Beach Park ★**, which opened in 2006, just a 15-minute drive from the center of Copenhagen. The beach lies on the Øresund coastline with a view of Sweden and the Øresund Bridge, which now links Denmark with Sweden. You can swim, sunbathe, scuba dive, race boats, or just admire the ships on the Øresund Sound while having a cup of coffee. Off the existing Amager Beach, a completely new island was created with wide, sandy beaches and bathing jetties. Tons of sand were brought in to create the island beach, which is 4.5km long and 50m (164 ft.) wide. In a newly dug lagoon are paddling beaches for children. From the city center it takes only 7 minutes to go to Amager Beach by Metro. Take the Metro to one of three stations: Øresund, Amager Strand, or Femøren and then walk only 5 minutes to the beach. For more information, check with **www.amager-strand.dk**.

The beach closest to Copenhagen is **Bellevue** (S-tog: Klampenborg), but the water is not recommended for swimming. Klampenborg, the community that's adjacent to Bellevue Beach, can provide distractions in addition to a beach: It's the site of the "White City" or "White Town," a residential community designed in the 1930s by modernist master Arne Jacobsen, and revered by Danes as a prime example of the workability of Danish architecture and design.

If you don't mind traveling farther afield, take a trip (by train or car) to the beaches of North Zealand—**Gilleleje, Hornbæk, Liseleje,** and **Tisvildeleje.** Although these are family beaches, minimal bathing attire is worn.

To reach any of these beaches, take the train to Helsingør, and then continue by bus. Or you can make connections by train to Hillerød and switch to a local train;

check at the railroad station for details. If you drive, you may want to stay for the evening discos at the little beach resort towns dotting the north coast of Zealand.

Humlebæk (Louisiana Museum)

32km (20 miles) N of Copenhagen

GETTING THERE

BY TRAIN Humlebæk is on the Copenhagen-Helsingør train line; there are two trains per hour that leave Copenhagen's main railway station heading toward Humlebæk (trip time: 40 min.). Once you reach Humlebæk, the Louisiana Museum is a 10-minute walk.

BY BUS Take the S-tog train, line A or B, to Lyngby station. From there, take bus no. 388 along the coast road. There's a bus stop at the museum.

BY CAR Follow the Strandvej (coastal road no. 152) from Copenhagen. The scenic drive takes about 45 minutes.

EXPLORING

Louisiana Museum of Modern Art ★★★ ☺ In a spacious old park with a panoramic view across Øresund to Sweden, this is one of the greatest museums of modern art in the Nordic world. The modest collection of Scandinavian art that opened here in 1954 has grown and grown with bequests and donations, and future architects have added more galleries onto the existing 19th-century villa.

The museum opened with works by the COBRA group, the name of artists from the cities of *CO*penhagen, *BR*ussels, and *A*msterdam. These original works are displayed along with some of the finest paintings and sculpture by international artists such as Calder, Dubuffet, Max Ernst, Giacometti, Picasso, and Warhol.

The museum has one of the largest exhibition spaces in Europe, and major exhibitions of contemporary art are staged here. There is also an extensive program of concerts, lectures, films, discussions with authors, and public debates. Children find their own haven here, especially at the **Børnehuset,** or children's house, and the **Søhaven,** or Sea Garden.

Gl. Strandvej 13. ✆ **49-19-07-19.** www.louisiana.dk. Admission 95DKK adults, 85DKK students, free for children 18 and under. Tues–Fri 11am–10pm; Sat–Sun 11am–6pm. Closed Dec 24–25 and Dec 31.

Hillerød

35km (22 miles) NW of Copenhagen

GETTING THERE

The S-tog from Copenhagen arrives every 10 minutes all day (trip time: 40 min.).

BY TRAIN Trains link Hillerød with Helsingør in the east, and there are also rail links with Gilleleje and Tisvildeleje.

BY BUS Hillerød has good bus connections with the major towns of North Zealand: bus no. 305 from Gilleleje; bus nos. 306, 336, and 339 from Hornbæk; and bus nos. 336 and 339 from Fredensborg.

BY CAR From Copenhagen, take Route 16 north.

EXPLORING

Frederiksborg Slot (Frederiksborg Castle) ★★★ Frederiksborg Castle is the most beautiful royal residence in Denmark. Surrounded by a moat, the *slot* (castle) was constructed on three islands in a lake. Like Kronborg, it was built in Dutch Renaissance style (red brick, copper roof, sandstone facade). The oldest parts date from 1560 and the reign of Frederik II. His more extravagant son, Christian IV, erected the main part of the castle from 1600 to 1620. Danish monarchs used it for some 2 centuries. From 1671 to 1840, Danish kings were crowned in Christian IV's chapel, which is still used as a parish church. Since 1693 it has been a chapel for the knights of the Order of the Elephant and of the Grand Cross of Danneborg. Standing in the gallery is an old organ built by Esaias Compenius in 1610. Every Thursday from 1:30 to 2pm, the chapel organist plays for museum visitors.

Since 1878 the castle has housed **Det Nationalhistoriske Museum (the Museum of National History).** Founded by the brewer J. C. Jacobsen as part of the Carlsberg Foundation, it encompasses the Great Hall and the former Audience Chamber of Danish monarchs. The museum contains the best collection of portraits and historical paintings in the country, all the stiff-necked greats and the wannabes. You can explore 70 of its rooms, each with paintings, gilded ceilings, and tapestries covering entire walls. The 20th-century collection on the third floor is a bit livelier, with its chronologically arranged exhibits. There are portraits and paintings here, but somehow the photographs are even more intriguing.

The castle is a 15-minute walk or a short taxi ride from the train station.

In Frederiksborg Slot. ✆ **48-26-04-39.** www.frederiksborgmuseet.dk. Admission 60DKK adults, 15DKK children 6–15, free for children 5 and under. Nov–Mar daily 11am–3pm; Apr–Oct daily 10am–5pm. Bus: 701 from Hillerød Station.

Frederiksborg Castle Garden ★★ For decades these gardens were used by three kings of Denmark, including Frederik IV, Christian VI, and Frederik V. They were designed by Johan Cornelius Krieger in just 5 years, from 1720 to 1725. In a flight of fancy, he got carried away, creating a cascade with water canals and fountains, along with promenades, groves of trees, and even a parterre sporting royal monograms to flatter the egos of his patrons.

Sadly, during the reign of Christian VII (1766–1808), he wasn't in the mood for a baroque romp. The tightwad king, preoccupied with military matters, felt the gardens had grown out of style, and he also complained that they were too expensive for his royal purse to maintain. By 1933, the gardens had decayed. But in recent times, funding was found to re-create the gardens as they were in their baroque heyday. As many as 65,000 box plants and 166 pyramid-shaped yews have been planted in the parterre, while 375 limes and 7,000 hornbeam plants create the avenues and groves. The cascade floor consists of nearly half a kilometer (¼ mile) of dressed granite stones. During the summer, the Frederiksborg Castle Garden forms the venue for several recurring concerts, maypole celebrations, and other cultural events.

Rendelæggerbakken 3. ✆ **48-26-04-39.** Free admission. May–Aug daily 10am–9pm; Sept and Apr daily 10am–7pm; Oct and Mar daily 10am–5pm; Nov–Feb daily 10am–4pm. Bus: 701 from Hillerød Station.

Helsingør (Elsinore): In Search of Hamlet ★

40km (25 miles) N of Copenhagen, 24km (15 miles) NE of Hillerød, 72km (45 miles) NE of Roskilde

GETTING THERE

BY TRAIN There are frequent trains from Copenhagen (trip time: 50 min.).

BY CAR Take E-4 north from Copenhagen.

BY FERRY Ferries ply the waters of the narrow channel separating Helsingør (Denmark) from Helsingborg (Sweden) in less than 25 minutes. They're operated around the clock by **Scandlines** (✆ **33-15-15-15;** www.scandlines.dk), which charges 42DKK ($7.20/£4.20) each way for a pedestrian without a car, and 275DKK ($47/£28) each way for a car with up to nine persons inside. Between 6am and 11pm, departures are every 20 minutes; 11pm to 6am, departures are timed at intervals of 40 to 80 minutes. The process is simple and straightforward: You simply drive your car onboard and wait in your car. Border formalities during the crossing between Denmark and Sweden are perfunctory, but carry a passport.

EXPLORING

Kronborg Slot ★★★ There is no evidence that Shakespeare ever saw this sandstone-and-copper Dutch Renaissance–style castle, full of intriguing secret passages, but he made it famous in *Hamlet*. The castle, on a peninsula jutting out into Øresund, was restored in 1629 by Christian IV after it had been gutted by fire. Other events in its history include looting, bombardment, occupation by Swedes, and use as a barracks (1785–1922). The entire castle is surrounded by a deep moat—but no dragon. You approach the castle via a wooden bridge and by going through Mørkeport, a gate from the 16th century. The octagonal tower is the Trumpeters Tower, one of the landmarks of town. This will lead you to the main courtyard of Kronborg.

Note: Instead of entering the castle at once, you can walk around the moat to the waterfront, where you can view a spectacular vista of the Swedish coast. At the platform—backed by massive bronze guns—Hamlet is said to have seen the ghost of his father, shrouded in pea-soup fog.

The starkly furnished Great Hall is the largest in northern Europe. Originally 40 tapestries portraying 111 Danish kings were hung around this room on special occasions. They were commissioned by Frederik II and produced around 1585. Only seven remain at Kronborg; the rest have disappeared except for seven in the Nationalmuseet in Copenhagen. The church, with its original oak furnishings and the royal chambers, is worth exploring. The bleak and austere atmosphere adds to the drama. Holger Danske, a mythological hero who is believed to assist Denmark whenever the country is threatened, is said to live in the basement. That "hero" didn't emerge when Nazi storm troopers invaded Denmark on Hitler's orders, but the legend, like the legend of Hamlet, still persists. Also on the premises is the **Danish Maritime Museum** (✆ **49-21-06-85**), which explores the history of Danish shipping. Unless you're really nautical, you might skip this if you're rushed for time. However, that would mean you'd miss seeing the world's oldest surviving ship's biscuit, dating from 1852. There is also an impressive collection of model ships and other sailors' memorabilia. More intriguing are relics of Denmark's colonial past in the West Indies (Caribbean), West Africa, Greenland, and even India.

Guided tours are given every half-hour October to April. In summer you can walk around on your own. In 2000, Kronborg was added to UNESCO's World Heritage List.

Kronborg 2C. ✆ **49-21-30-78.** www.kronborgcastle.com. Admission 65DKK adults, 25DKK children 6–14, free for children 5 and under. Joint ticket for the tower and the Danish Maritime Museum 90DKK adults, 25DKK children 6–14. May–Sept daily 10:30am–5pm; Apr and Oct Tues–Sun 11am–4pm; Nov–Mar Tues–Sun 11am–3pm. Closed Dec 25.

Roskilde ★★

32km (20 miles) W of Copenhagen

GETTING THERE

BY TRAIN Trains leave three times an hour from Copenhagen's Central Railroad Station on the 35-minute trip to Roskilde.

BY BUS Buses depart from Roskilde several times daily from Copenhagen's Central Railroad Station.

BY CAR Take the E-21 express highway west from Copenhagen.

EXPLORING

Roskilde Domkirke ★★★ There's no church in Copenhagen, or anywhere else in Denmark for that matter, to rival this towering edifice. This cathedral made Roskilde the spiritual capital of Denmark and northern Europe. Today it rises out of a modest townscape like a mirage—a cathedral several times too big for the town surrounding it. Construction started in 1170 when Absalon was bishop of Roskilde. Work continued into the 13th century, and the building's original Romanesque features gave way to an early Gothic facade. The twin towers weren't built until the 14th century.

The Domkirke is the final abode of 38 Danish monarchs whose tombs are here, ranging from the modest to the eccentric. Not surprisingly, Christian IV, the builder king who was instrumental in the construction of nearly all of Copenhagen's famous towers and castles, is interred in a grandiose chapel here with a massive sculpture of himself in combat, a bronze likeness by the Danish sculptor Bertel Thorvaldsen. In humble contrast is a newer addition, from 1972, of the simple brick chapel of King Frederik IX, which stands outside the church. This chapel is octagonal in shape and decorated with hand-painted tiles designed by the architects Johannes and Inger Exner and Vilhelm Wohlert. Other notable tombs include the white marble sarcophagus of Queen Margrethe I.

In King Christian I's Chapel, which dates from the 15th century, there is a column marked with the heights of several kings. The tallest monarch was Christian I, at 2.1m (6 ft. 9 in.). This, no doubt, was an exaggeration, as his skeleton measures only 1.9m (6 ft. 2 in.). A large, bright cupola graces the late-18th- and early-19th-century chapel of King Frederik V. Note also the Gothic choir stalls, each richly and intricately carved with details from both the Old and New Testaments.

The gilded winged altar in the choir was made in Antwerp in the 1500s and was originally intended for Frederiksborg Castle. Pictures on the wings of the altar depict scenes from the life of Jesus, ranging from the Nativity to the Crucifixion. Following the fire, the renowned artist Anna Thommesen created a new altar cloth.

For us, the most charming aspect of the cathedral is its early-16th-century clock poised on the interior south wall above the entrance. A tiny St. George on horseback marks the hour by charging a dragon. The beast howls, echoing through the cavernous church, causing Peter Doever, "the Deafener," to sound the hour. A terrified Kirsten Kiemer, "the Chimer," shakes in fright but pulls herself together to strike the quarters.

Insider's tip: Free concerts on the cathedral's pipe organ, which dates from the 1500s, are often held at 8pm on Thursdays in summer. Check with the tourist office.

Domkirkestræde 10. ✆ **46-35-16-24.** www.roskildedomkirke.dk. Admission 25DKK adults, 15DKK children 10–15, free for children 9 and under. Apr–Sept Mon–Sat 9am–5pm, Sun 12:30–5pm; Oct–Mar Tues–Sat 10am–4pm, Sun 12:30–4pm. Bus: 358, 607, or 852.

Vikingeskibshallen (Viking Ship Museum) ★★ If the cathedral weren't reason enough to visit Roskilde, the Viking ships displayed here certainly are. These types of ships sailed to England, to Hamburg on the German coast, and—dare we speculate?—even to the east coast of North America. Displayed here are five vessels found in Roskilde Fjord and painstakingly pieced together from countless fragments of wreckage. It's presumed that the craft were deliberately sunk about 20km (12 miles) north of Roskilde at the narrowest section of the fjord to protect the settlement from a sea attack. The discovery was relatively unpublicized until 1957, when the Danish National Museum carried out a series of underwater excavations.

A merchant cargo ship used by the Vikings, a small ferry or fishing boat, and a Danish Viking warship similar to the ones portrayed in the Bayeux Tapestry are also displayed, and a longship—a Viking man-of-war that terrorized European coasts—was also discovered. Copies of Viking jewelry may be purchased in the museum gift shop, and there's also a cafeteria.

To understand the attraction better, watch the short film, *The Ships of the Vikings,* about the excavation and preservation of the ships and the building and navigation of *Roar Ege,* a Viking ship replica.

In 1997 the Viking Ship Museum opened a museum harbor for its collection of Nordic vessels, including *Roar Ege,* plus another Viking ship replica, *Helge Ask.* The museum's restored sloop, *Ruth,* is also moored here. And workshops where you can try your hand at old maritime crafts, such as rope- and sail-making, woodworking, and other activities, are located opposite the Boat Yard.

Vindebader 12. ✆ **46-30-02-00.** www.vikingeskibsmuseet.dk. Admission May–Sept 100DKK adults; Oct–Apr 70DKK adults; free for children 16 and under. Daily 10am–5pm. Bus: 216 or 607.

Ledreborg Park Og Slot ★ One of the last remaining aristocratic families of Denmark, the Holstein-Ledreborgs, still live in this castle and are willing to share their treasures with you in fair weather. A baroque manor house and French/English–style park 7km (4⅓ miles) southwest of Roskilde and 43km (27 miles) west of Copenhagen, Ledreborg is one of the best-preserved monuments in Denmark. Built by Johan Ludwig Holstein, a minister to Christian IV, the Holstein-Ledreborg family has owned this 33-room house with a landscaped garden and 88-hectare (217-acre) park for eight generations. Between 1741 and 1757 it was turned from a farmhouse into a baroque manor. Inside are a collection of 17th- and 18th-century antiques and a gallery of Danish paintings. It's approached by a 6km (3¾-mile) alley of lime trees, some 2 centuries old. Near the manor is a grave dating from the late Stone Age, approximately 3000 B.C.

Ledreborg Allé 2, Lejre. ✆ **46-48-00-38.** www.ledreborgslot.dk. Admission 25DKK. May–Sept daily 11am-4pm. Closed Oct–Apr. From Copenhagen's Central Railroad Station, take the direct train to Lejre, which leaves hourly and takes 35 min.; from Lejre station, take the 3-min. bus 233 to the castle and park. From Roskilde, there are frequent buses to Lejre, followed by the short bus ride to the castle and park.

Lejre Research Center ★ ☺ Imagine being able to wander back into a village reconstructed from the Iron Age. Not only that, but getting to see workers, wearing the costumes of the era, going about their daily chores. You're even invited to take part in these activities. Such a thing is possible if you head here and have some 2 hours to spare. Eight kilometers (5 miles) west of Roskilde, this archaeological research center, Lejre Research Center, is the site of a reconstructed Iron Age community on 10 hectares (25 acres) of woodland. The main feature is clay-walled and thatch houses built with tools just as they were some 2,000 years ago. Staffers re-create the physical working conditions as they thatch Iron Age huts, work fields with *ards* (oxen-pulled plows), weave, and make pottery by an open fire. They also sail in dugout canoes, grind corn with a stone, and bake in direct fire. Visitors can take part in these activities. Jutland black pottery is produced here, and handicrafts and books are for sale at the gift shop. There are tables where you can enjoy a picnic lunch.

Slagealléen 2, Lejre. ✆ **46-48-08-78.** www.lejre-center.dk. Admission 95DKK adults, 60DKK children 3-11. Tues-Fri 10am-4pm; Sat-Sun 11am-5pm. Closed mid-Sept to Apr. Take the train from Copenhagen to Lejre, then bus 233 to the center. From Roskilde, there are frequent buses to Lejre; then take bus 233.

LITERARY LANDMARKS

Fans of **Hans Christian Andersen** may want to seek out the various addresses where he lived in Copenhagen, including Nyhavn 18, Nyhavn 20, and Nyhavn 67. He also lived for a time at Vingårdsstræde 6.

Assistens Kirkegård (Assistens Cemetery) ★ Dating from 1711, the largest burial ground in Copenhagen is now a lively public park where families come for picnics and aspirant rock bands perform before a live, captive audience. It also contains the graves of the two towering literary figures of Denmark, Hans Christian Andersen and Søren Kierkegaard—as well as many other famous Danes including Carlsberg patriarch Christen Jacobsen.

Kapelvej 4. ✆ **35-37-19-17.** www.assistens.dk. Free admission. Jan-Feb 8am-4pm; Mar-Apr and Sept-Oct 8am-6pm; May-Aug 8am-8pm; Nov-Dec 8am-8pm. Bus: 3A, 12, 66, or 69. See map p. 116.

Københavns Bymuseet & Søren Kierkegaard Samlingen We come here not so much to see the city museum exhibits, but to learn more about one of Denmark's most enigmatic authors, Søren Kierkegaard. The life of the "Father of Existentialism" is illustrated by personal belongings, drawings, letters, books, and old photographs. Born in Copenhagen on May 3, 1813, he collapsed on the street and died in his beloved city at the age of 42. His most famous work was created in 1843 when he wrote his philosophical novel, *Enten/Eller (Either/Or)*.

If you hang around, you can check out some of the city museum collections, including exhibits devoted to immigration. The section on old shop fronts evoking Copenhagen of yesterday is intriguing if you'd like to see the city the way it was.

Vesterbrogade 59. ✆ **33-21-07-72.** www.kbhbymuseum.dk. Admission 20DKK adults, free for children 17 and under, free to all Fri. Daily 10am-5pm. Bus: 6A, 26, or 83N. See map p. 116.

Kongelige Bibliotek (Royal Library) ★ With its high-ceilinged reading rooms, the Danish Royal Library, dating from the 1600s, is the largest and most impressive in the Norse countries. The library owns original manuscripts by such Danish writers as H. C. Andersen and Karen Blixen (Isak Dinesen). The Black Diamond is a gargantuan and sharply angular granite annex that extends the venerable antique structure out and over the waterfront traffic artery, expanding it in a dazzling (and dizzying) study in architectural contrasts. If you have the time, don't suffer from any kind of vertigo, and aren't stopped by a security guard, consider taking the elevator to the highest floor of the echoing interior spaces of the Black Diamond. From the catwalks and walkways of the top floor, the sense of height, the interplay of sunlight and shadows, and the perspectives can be both terrifying and awe-inspiring. Along with space for 200,000 books, the Black Diamond features a bookshop, an upscale restaurant called Søren K (p. 111), six reading rooms, a courtyard for exhibitions, and a 600-seat concert hall. After viewing the interiors of both sections of the library, you can wander through its formal gardens, past the fishpond and statue of philosopher Søren Kierkegaard.

Søren Kierkegaards Plads 1. ✆ **33-47-47-47.** www.kb.dk. Free admission. Mon-Fri 10am-5pm. Bus: 66 or 902. See map p. 116.

ESPECIALLY FOR KIDS

Copenhagen is a wonderful place for children, and many so-called adult attractions also appeal to kids. **Tivoli** is an obvious choice, as is the statue of ***Den Lille Havfrue (The Little Mermaid)*** at Langelinie. Try to see the changing of the Queen's Royal Life Guard at **Amalienborg Palace,** including the entire parade to and from the royal residence. Kids also enjoy **Frilandsmuseet,** the open-air museum. (For details on these sights, see listings earlier in this chapter.) Other attractions great for kids include the following:

Bakken Amusement Park This is Tivoli on a bad hair day but a lot of fun if you don't like your amusement parks too manicured. On the northern edge of Copenhagen, about 12km (7½ miles) from the city center, this park is a local favorite, featuring roller coasters, dancing, a tunnel of love, and a merry-go-round. Open-air restaurants are plentiful, as are snack bars and ice-cream booths. Some individual attractions charge a separate admission fee—proceeds support this unspoiled natural preserve. The performers in the cabaret show at **Bakkens Hvile** ★★ rival the Rockettes at New York City's Radio City Music Hall and remain the most popular revue in Denmark. There are no cars in the park—only bicycles and horse-drawn carriages.

Dyrehavevej 62, Klampenborg. ✆ **39-63-35-44.** www.bakken.dk. Admission to all rides 210DKK for adults and children. Summer daily noon-midnight. Closed mid-Sept to late Mar. S-tog: Klampenborg (about 20 min. from Central Railroad Station); then walk through the Deer Park or take a horse-drawn cab.

Danmarks Akvarium (Denmark Aquarium) Opened in 1939, a year before the Nazi invasion of Denmark, this aquarium is worth a look only if you happen to be visiting the grounds of the royal residence, **Charlottenlund Slot** (the palace is not open), in Hellerup, a coastal suburb of Copenhagen. It was enlarged in 1974, but still features only 90 or so tanks of the usual marine "suspects"—sharks, turtles, piranhas, and both the fish that can survive in the North Sea and those from more tropical waters.

Strandvejen, in Charlottenlund Fort Park, Charlottenlund. ✆ **39-62-32-83.** www.akvarium.dk. Admission 100DKK adults, 55DKK children 3–11, free for children 2 and under. July–Aug daily 10am–6pm; Sept–Oct and Feb–May daily 10am–5pm; Nov–Jan daily 10am–4pm. S-tog: Charlottenlund. Bus: 14 or 166.

Experimentarium (Hands-On Science Center) ★★ In the old mineral-water-bottling hall of Tuborg breweries 5km (3 miles) north of Copenhagen in Hellerup, this most interactive museum in the Nordic world encourages visitors to use all five of their senses as they participate in some 300 interactive exhibitions and demonstrations divided into three themes: "Man," "Nature," and "The Interaction Between Man and Nature." Visitors hear what all the world's languages sound like, make a wind machine blow up to hurricane force, dance in an inverted disco, program a robot, spin in a human-size gyroscope, and more. Exhibitions change frequently and thrill adults too.

Tuborg Havnevej 7, Hellerup. ✆ **39-27-33-33.** www.experimentarium.dk. Admission 148DKK adults, 97DKK children 3–11, free for children 2 and under. Mon and Wed–Fri 9:30am–5pm; Tues 9:30am–9pm; Sat–Sun 11am–5pm. Closed Dec 23–25, Dec 31, and Jan 1. S-tog: Hellerup or Svanemøllen. Bus: 1A, 14, or 21.

Tycho Brahe Planetarium The exhibitions on natural science and astronomy at this planetarium may leave you with a hankering for space travel. The permanent exhibition, "The Active Universe," doesn't quite answer all the questions of the mysteries of space, but it deals with a lot of them. An installation honors the famed Danish astronomer Tycho Brahe (1546–1601). Of course, Brahe got a lot of things wrong—after all, he disagreed with Copernicus and still believed that the Earth stood at the center of the universe. But he did some things right, including mapping the position of more than 1,000 fixed stars—all this with the naked eye since Galileo didn't emerge with his telescope until 1610. IMAX films are shown on a dome-shaped screen, creating the marvel of the night sky, with its planets, galaxies, star clusters, and comets.

Gammel Kongevej 10. ✆ **33-12-12-24.** www.tycho.dk. Admission 130DKK adults, 80DKK children 10–13, free for children 9 and under. Tues–Sun 9:30am–8:30pm; Mon 11:30am–8:30pm. Bus: 14 or 15. See map p. 116.

Zoologisk Have (Copenhagen Zoo) This zoo has come a long way, baby, since 1859 when it opened with stuffed birds, a seal in a bathtub, and a turtle in a bucket. Today at its location in Frederiksberg, west of the center of Copenhagen, it is home to 3,300 animals and 264 species. You get to see everything from the musk oxen and reindeer of the far north to the hungry lions of Kenya. Kids can pet beasts that are "not too wild," but the highlight for the kiddies is an Eiffel-like tower that rises 40m (131 ft.). ***Warning:*** The zoo is mobbed on Sundays in summer.

Roskildevej 32, Frederiksberg. ✆ **72-20-02-00.** www.zoo.dk. Admission 140DKK adults, 80DKK children 3–11, free for children 2 and under. Nov–Feb daily 9am–4pm; Mar Mon–Fri 9am–4pm, Sat–Sun 9am–5pm; Apr–May and Sept Mon–Fri 9am–5pm, Sat–Sun 9am–6pm; June–Aug daily 9am–6pm; Oct daily 9am–5pm. S-tog: Valby. Bus: 6A, 93N, or 832.

COPENHAGEN ON FOOT

WALKING TOUR 1: THE OLD CITY

START: **Rådhuspladsen**

FINISH: **Tivoli Gardens**

TIME: **Allow 1½ hours for this walking tour.**

BEST TIMES: **This tour is perfect for any sunny day, but avoid rush hour, which falls between 7:30 to 9am and 5 to 6:30pm on weekdays.**

---

1 Rådhuspladsen (Town Hall Square)

Pay a visit to the bronze statue of Hans Christian Andersen, the spinner of fairy tales, which stands near a boulevard bearing his name. Also on this square is a statue of two *lur* horn players that has stood here since 1914.

Bypassing the *lur* horn players, walk east along Vester Voldgade onto a narrow street on your left:

2 Lavendelstræde

Many houses along here date from the late 18th century. At Lavendelstræde 1, Mozart's widow (Constanze) lived with her second husband, Georg Nikolaus von Nissen, a Danish diplomat, from 1812 to 1820.

Walking Tour: The Old City

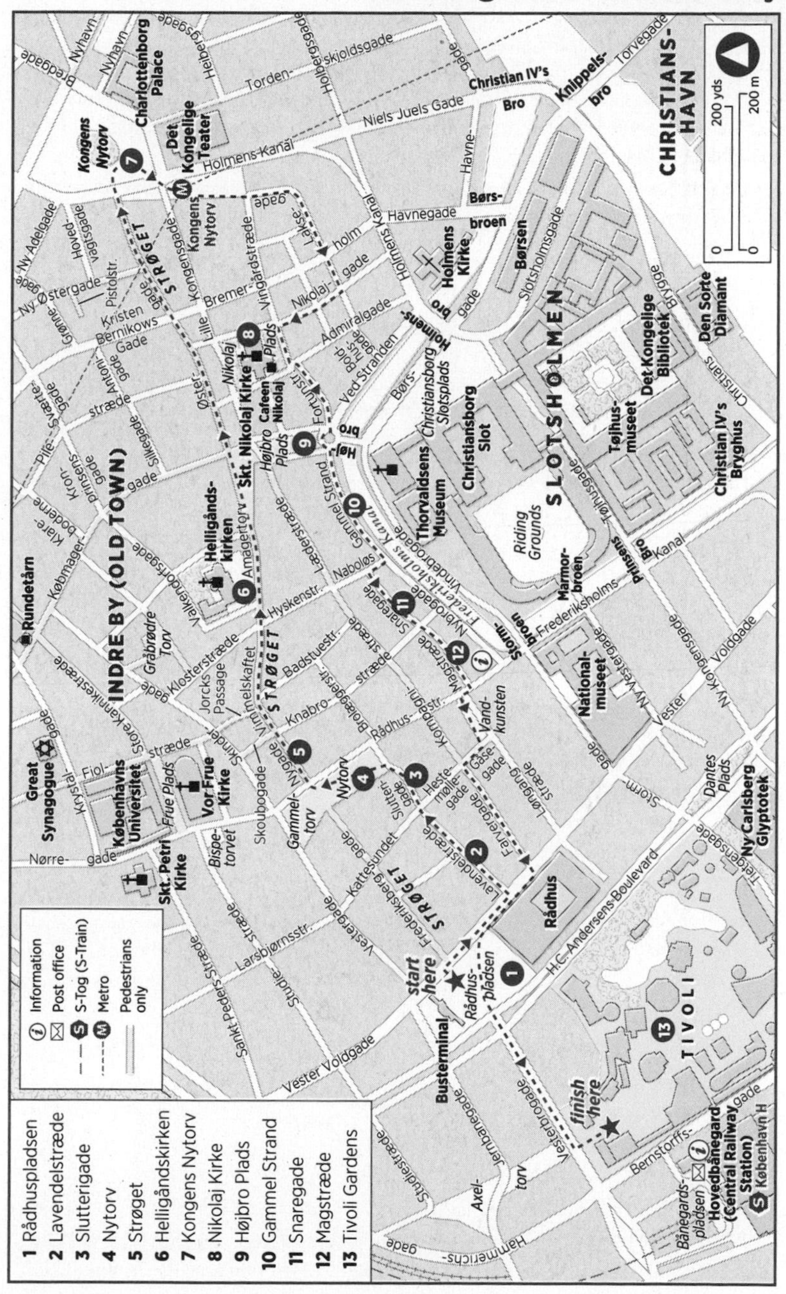

The little street quickly becomes:

3 Slutterigade

Courthouses rise on both sides of this short street, joined by elevated walkways. Built between 1805 and 1815, this was Copenhagen's fourth town hall, now the city's major law courts. The main courthouse entrance is on Nytorv.

Slutterigade will lead to:

4 Nytorv

In this famous square, you can admire fine 19th-century houses. Philosopher Søren Kierkegaard (1813–55) lived in a house adjacent to the courthouse.

Cross Nytorv, and veer slightly west (to your left) until you reach Nygade, part of the:

5 Strøget

At this point, this traffic-free shopping street has a different name. (It actually began at Rådhuspladsen and was called Frederiksberggade.) The major shopping street of Scandinavia, Strøget is a stroller's and a shopper's delight, following a 1.2km (¾-mile) trail through the heart of Copenhagen.

Nygade is one of the five streets that compose Strøget. Head northeast along this street, which becomes winding and narrow Vimmelskaftet, and then turns into Amagertorv. Along Amagertorv, on your left, you'll come across the:

6 Helligåndskirken (Church of the Holy Ghost)

Complete with an abbey, Helligåndskirken is the oldest church in Copenhagen, founded at the beginning of the 15th century. Partially destroyed in 1728, it was reconstructed in 1880 in a neoclassical style. Some of the buildings on this street date from 1616. The sales rooms of the Royal Porcelain Factory are at Amagertorv 6.

Next you'll come to Østergade, the last portion of Strøget. You'll see Illum's department store on your left. Østergade leads to the square:

7 Kongens Nytorv

Surrounding Copenhagen's largest square, with an equestrian statue of Christian IV in the center, are many restored antique buildings. The statue is a bronze replica of a 1688 sculpture.

At Kongens Nytorv, head right until you come to Laksegade. Then go south along this street until you reach the intersection with Nikolajgade. Turn right. This street will lead to the:

8 Nikolaj Church

The building dates from 1530 and was the scene of the thundering sermons of Hans Tausen, a father of the Danish Reformation.

After seeing the church, head left down Fortunstræde to your next stop, a square off Gammel Strand:

9 Højbro Plads

You'll have a good view of Christiansborg Palace and Thorvaldsens Museum on Slotsholmen. On Højbro Plads is an equestrian statue honoring Bishop Absalon, who founded Copenhagen in 1167. Several old buildings line the square.

Continue west along:

10 Gammel Strand

From this waterfront promenade—the name means "old shore"—the former edge of Copenhagen, you'll have a panoramic look across to Christiansborg Palace. A number of antique buildings line this street, and at the end you'll come upon the Ministry of Cultural Affairs, occupying a former government pawnbroking establishment, dating from 1730.

To the right of this building, walk up:

11 Snaregade

This old-fashioned provincial street is one of the most evocative of the old city. Walk until you reach Knabrostræde. Both streets boast structures built just after the great fire of 1795. Where the streets intersect, you'll see the Church of Our Lady.

Make your way back to Snaregade, and turn right to one of Copenhagen's best-preserved streets:

12 Magstræde

Proceed along to Rådhusstræde. Just before you reach Rådhusstræde, notice the two buildings facing that street. These are the oldest structures in the city, dating from the 16th century.

Walk across Vandkunsten, a square at the end of Magstræde, and then turn right down Gasegade, which doesn't go very far before you turn left along Farvergade. At this street's intersection with Vester Voldgade, you'll come to the Vartov Church. Continue west until you reach Rådhuspladsen. Across the square, you'll see:

13 Tivoli Gardens

You'll find the entrance at Vesterbrogade 3. Attracting some 4.5 million visitors every summer, this amusement park has 25 different entertainment choices and attractions, and just as many restaurants and beer gardens.

WALKING TOUR 2: KONGENS NYTORV TO LANGELINIE

START:	**Kongens Nytorv**
FINISH:	***Den Lille Havfrue (The Little Mermaid)* sculpture at the harbor**
TIME:	**Allow 2 hours for this walking tour.**
BEST TIMES:	**This tour is perfect for any sunny day, but avoid rush hour, which falls between 7:30 to 9am and 5 to 6:30pm on weekdays.**

Although the Nyhavn quarter, once a boisterous sailors' town, has quieted down, it's still a charming part of old Copenhagen, with its 1673 canal and 18th-century houses.

1 Kongens Nytorv

The "King's New Market" dates from 1680. It is the location of Magasin, the biggest department store in the capital, plus an equestrian statue of Christian IV.

On the northeast side of the square is:

2 Thott's Mansion

Completed in 1685 for a Danish naval hero and restored in 1760, it now houses the French Embassy. Between Bredgade and Store Strandstræde, a little street angling to the right near Nyhavn, is Kanneworff House, a beautifully preserved private home that dates from 1782. On the west side of the square, at no. 34, is the landmark Hotel d'Angleterre. Also here is an old anchor memorializing the Danish seamen who died in World War II.

On the southeast side of the square is:

3 The Royal Theater

Founded in 1748, the theater presents ballet, opera, and plays. Statues of famous Danish dramatists are out front. The present theater, constructed in 1874, has a neo-Renaissance style.

With your back to the Hotel d'Angleterre, walk toward the water along:

4 Nyhavn

Once filled with maritime businesses and seamen's bars and lodgings, Nyhavn is now "restaurant row." First, walk along its north (left) side. In the summer, cafe tables border the canal, giving it a festive atmosphere. At the port end of the canal, you can see Christianshavn across the harbor.

On the quieter (south) side of the canal, you can see:

5 Charlottenborg Palace

The style of the building, now the Danish Academy of Fine Arts, is pure baroque. The name comes from Queen Charlotte Amalie, who moved there in 1700. Beautiful old homes, antiques shops, and more restaurants line the southern bank. Nyhavn was the home of Hans Christian Andersen at various times. He lived at no. 20, where he wrote his first fairy tales, in 1835, and at no. 67 from 1845 to 1864. He spent the last 2 years of his life at no. 18, where he died in 1875.

Walk back to the harbor end of Nyhavn, and turn left onto Kvæsthusgade, which will take you to:

6 Skt. Annæ Plads

Before the radical transformation of Copenhagen's harborfront, ferries used to depart from piers here for other destinations in Scandinavia, including Oslo. Now, however, the harborfront, and the back of this desirable long and narrow square, is the site of one of the biggest urban transformations in the city's history. The ferryboat terminals have moved to the commercial neighborhood of Nordhavn, and the city seems to be watching what will eventually emerge from this site, just a short walk from Nyhavn and its rows of restaurants.

Walk inland along the *plads,* and turn right onto Amaliegade, which leads under a colonnade into symmetrical majesty of the cobble-covered Amalienborg Plads, site of:

7 Amalienborg Palace

In the square's center is a statue of Frederik V. When the queen is in residence, the changing of the guard takes place here daily at noon. The palace is the official residence of the queen and her French prince, but sections of it are open to visitors. The palace is actually composed of a quartet of nearly identical baroque mansions, each interconnected with galleries or subterranean passages,

Walking Tour: Kongens Nytorv to Langelinie

and each positioned at cardinal points of the same octagon-shaped courtyard. The queen lives in the wing that's adjacent to the neoclassical colonnade.

Between the square and the harbor are the gardens of:

8 Amaliehavn

Among the most beautiful in Copenhagen, these gardens were laid out by Jean Delogne, who made lavish use of Danish granite and French limestone. The bronze pillars around the fountain were the work of Arnaldo Pomodoro, an Italian sculptor. From your waterfront vantage, look across the harbor at the most exciting recently constructed building in town, the **Danish Opera House,** with a soaring rooftop that evokes the reinforced concrete structures of Le Corbusier, and a design that evokes the outspread wings of a dove. It was designed by Henning Larsen, "The House Architect of Copenhagen," with perfect acoustics and "chandeliers that might have been inspired by a show palace in Las Vegas."

After viewing the waterfront gardens, walk away from the water, crossing Amalienborg Plads and emerging onto Frederiksgade. Continue along this street until you reach:

9 Frederiks Kirke

This church is often called the *Marmorkirken,* or "Marble Church." Construction began in 1740, but had to stop in 1770 because of the costs. The church wasn't completed until 1894—using Danish marble instead of more expensive Norwegian marble. The church was modeled on and intended to rival St. Peter's in Rome; indeed, it ended up with one of the largest church domes in Europe. Supported on a dozen towering piers, the dome has a diameter of 32m (105 ft.).

Facing the church, turn right and head north along Bredgade, passing at no. 62 the:

10 Medicinsk Museion (Medical History Museum)

The collection is gruesome, with fetuses, dissected heads, and the like.

Continue along Bredgade, making a right at Churchillparken on Esplanaden where you will find:

11 Café Lumskebugten ☕

Before you approach *The Little Mermaid,* grab a tea and a snack. Dating from 1854, this cozy, old-fashioned cafe serves a cold plate throughout the afternoon, either beef tartare, fish cakes with mustard sauce, marinated salmon, baked cod, or shrimp. Esplanaden 21 (✆ **33-15-60-29**).

Bredgade ends at Esplanaden, which opens onto Churchillparken, a green belt bordering the water. Turn right and walk along Esplanaden until you come to Churchillparken and the:

12 Frihedsmuseet

The Danish Resistance Museum commemorates the struggle against the Nazis from 1940 to 1945.

After leaving the museum, walk toward the water along Langelinie, where signs point the way to:

13 *The Little Mermaid*

Perched on rocks just off the harbor bank, *Den Lille Havfrue,* the most photographed statue in Scandinavia, dates from 1913. The bronze figure, by Edvard Eriksen, was modeled after the figure of prima ballerina Ellen Price. In time, this much-attacked and abused statue became the symbol of Copenhagen.

ORGANIZED TOURS

BUS & BOAT TOURS The boat and bus sightseeing tours in Copenhagen range from get-acquainted jaunts to in-depth excursions. Either of the following tours can be arranged through **Copenhagen Excursions** (✆ **32-54-06-06;** www.cex.dk) or **Vikingbus** (✆ **32-57-26-00;** www.vikingbus.com). **Paaske Bus** (✆ **32-66-00-00;** www.paaskebus.dk) also runs inexpensive bus tours (www.sightseeing.dk). All boat tours leave from Nyhavn.

For orientation, hop on a bus for the 1½-hour **City Tour,** which covers scenic highlights like *The Little Mermaid,* Rosenborg Castle, and Amalienborg Palace. Tours depart from the City Hall Square daily at 9:30am and 11:30am, May 15 to September 30. They cost 140DKK for adults, 70DKK for children 11 and under.

The **City and Harbor Tour** is a 2½-hour trip by launch and bus that departs from Town Hall Square. The boat tours the city's main canals, passing *The Little Mermaid* and the Old Fish Market. It operates May 15 to September 30, daily at 9:30am and 11:30am. It costs 175DKK for adults, 80DKK for children 11 and under.

Shakespeare buffs may be interested in an afternoon excursion to the castles of North Zealand. The 7-hour tour explores the area north of Copenhagen, including Kronborg (Hamlet's castle); briefly visits Fredensborg, the queen's residence; and stops at Frederiksborg Castle and the National Historical Museum. Tours depart from Town Hall Square, running February to April and October to December Wednesday and Sunday at 10:15am; May to September Wednesday, Saturday, and Sunday at 10:15am. The cost is 480DKK for adults, 240DKK for children 11 and under.

GUIDED WALKS THROUGH COPENHAGEN **"History Tours"** (✆ **28-49-44-35;** www.copenhagen-walkingtours.dk) offers historical guided walks in Copenhagen from March to October on Saturday and Sunday at 10am. The walking tours last 1 hour and 30 minutes; the price is 80DKK for adults, 25DKK for children 10 to 15. Free for children 9 and under. Booking is not necessary. Tours leave from Højbro Plads at the equestrian statue of Bishop Absalon.

A VISIT TO COPENHAGEN'S MOST FAMOUS BREWERY Carlsberg is the most famous beer in Denmark and the country's best-known brand internationally. Its old-fashioned brewery was constructed in 1847, and enlarged in 2005 with the addition of a microbrewery devoted to the production of at least four "affiliated" brews marketed under the brand name of "Jacobsen." Jointly, the brewery turns out at least three million bottles of beer a day. From the visitor center you can take a self-guided tour of both sides of the brewery, walking around an observation gallery where signs and videos explain the brewing process. The factory is open for visits May to August Tuesday, Wednesday, and Friday to Sunday 10am to 5pm; Thursday 10am to 7:30pm. From September to April Tuesday to Sunday 10am to 5pm. Adults pay 90DKK (admission includes two beers or two soft drinks). Children 12 to 17 pay 50DKK (admission includes two soft drinks; free admission for children 11 and under). Entrance (and access to the self-guided tours) costs 45DKK per person (no discount for children). The entrance to the brewery is graced with a pair of sculpted elephants, each with armored regalia that includes a swastika—an ancient Hindu symbol for good luck way before Hitler's time. You have the option of buying more drinks at the on-site pub. Take bus no. 26 from Copenhagen Central Station or from the Town Hall Square in Copenhagen to **Carlsberg Brewery,** Gamle Carlsberg Vej 11, Valby (✆ **33-27-12-82;** www.visitcarlsberg.dk).

ACTIVE SPORTS

BICYCLING The absence of hills and the abundance of parks and wide avenues with bicycle lanes make cycling the best way to explore Copenhagen. Bike-rental shops and stands are scattered throughout the city. Two suggestions are **Københavns Cyker,** Reventlowsgade 11 (✆ **33-33-86-13;** www.copenhagen-bikes.dk; bus: 10), and **Dan Wheel,** Colbjørnsensgade 3 (✆ **33-21-22-27;** bus: 6A, 26, or 83N). A deposit of 500DKK is required. Alternatively, **City Bike** is a great way to get around central Copenhagen. Bike racks are located throughout the city center; the service is free and you unlock your bike with a 20DKK deposit. When you return the bike your deposit is returned. Bikes are available from April to November (www.bycyklen.dk).

GOLF Denmark's best-known golf course, and one of its most challenging to golfers around the world, is at the **Rungsted Golf Klub,** Vestre Stationsveg 16, Rungsted (✆ **45-86-34-44;** www.rungstedgolfklub.dk). It's in the heart of Denmark's "Whiskey Trail," a string of homes and mansions known for their allure to retirees, about 21km (13 miles) north of Copenhagen close to the Rungsted Kyst Station. To play, you must present evidence of a 21 handicap on Saturday and Sunday, or 25 on weekdays. If you're an advanced golfer, call for information and to arrange a tee time. Greens fees run 375DKK to 600DKK for a full day's use of the club's 18 holes. With advance notice, you can rent clubs for 300DKK. No carts are allowed on the ecologically fragile course, which is open year-round, except when it is snowing.

SWIMMING In spite of an often bone-chilling climate, swimming is a favorite Danish pastime. The **Frederiksborg Svømmehal,** Helgesvej 29 (✆ **38-14-04-00;** www.frederiksbergsvoemmehal.dk; bus: 2A, 18, 82N, or 831), is open to the public Monday to Friday 7am to 9pm, Saturday 7am to 3pm, Sunday 9am to 3pm. Tickets cost 36DKK. You can also try **Sundby Swimming-pool,** Sundbyvestervej 50 (✆ **32-58-55-68;** bus: 5A, 33, or 872); or **Kildeskovshallen,** Adolphsvej 25, Gentofte (✆ **39-77-44-00;** bus: 95N or 176; www.kildeskovshallen.dk).

THE SHOPPING SCENE

SHOPPING AREAS Copenhagen is in the vanguard of shopping in Europe, and much of the action takes place on **Strøget,** the pedestrian street in the heart of the capital. The jampacked street is lined with stores selling everything from porcelain statues of *Youthful Boldness* and open-faced sandwiches piled high with Greenland shrimp to pizza slices and some of the most elegant porcelain in Europe.

In two nearby walking areas—**Gråbrødretorv** and **Fiolstræde**—you can browse through antiques shops and bookshops.

Bredgade, beginning at Kongens Nytorv, is the antiques district, where prices tend to be very high. **Læderstræde** is another shopping street that specializes in antiques.

BEST BUYS In a country famed for its designers and craftspeople, the best buys are in stainless steel, porcelain, china, glassware, toys, functionally designed furniture, textiles, and jewelry, particularly silver jewelry set with semiprecious stones.

In addition to the centers described below, for excellent buys in Scandinavian merchandise, as well as tax-free goods, we recommend the **shopping center at the airport.** A VAT-refund office is located nearby.

STORE HOURS In general, shopping hours are 9:30am or 10am to 5:30pm Monday to Thursday, to 7pm or 8pm on Friday, and to 2pm on Saturday. Most shops are closed Sunday, except the kiosks and supermarket at the Central Railroad Station. Here you can purchase food until 10pm or midnight. The Central Railroad Station's bakery is open until 9pm, and one kiosk at Rådhuspladsen, which sells papers, film, and souvenirs, is open 24 hours.

Shopping A to Z

AMBER

The Amber Specialist The owners, known to customers as the "Amber Twins," will sell you "the gold of the north." This petrified resin originated in the large coniferous forests that covered Denmark some 35 million years ago. The forest disappeared, but the amber lasted, and is now used to create handsome jewelry. This shop carries a large collection of stunning amber set in 14-karat gold. Frederiksberggade 28. ✆ **33-11-88-03.** www.houseofamber.com. Bus: 28, 29, or 41.

ART GALLERIES & AUCTION HOUSES

Bruun Rasmussen Established shortly after World War II, this is Denmark's leading auction house. July is usually quiet, although the premises remain open for appraisals and purchases. The season begins in August, with an auction of paintings and fine art. Viewing time is allowed before auctions, which are held about once a month. There are also auctions of art, wine, coins, books, and antique weapons. Bredgade 33. ✆ **88-18-11-11.** www.bruun-rasmussen.dk. Bus: 11 or 95N.

Galerie Asbæk This modern-art gallery has a permanent exhibit of the best local artists, along with changing shows by Scandinavian and foreign artists. A bookshop and cafe serving French-inspired Danish food is on the premises. Graphics and posters are for sale. Bredgade 20. ✆ **33-15-40-04.** www.asbaek.dk. Bus: 1A, 11, 15, 25, or 26.

BOOKS

Boghallen This big store at Town Hall Square carries many books in English, as well as a wide selection of travel-related literature, including maps. It stocks books in English on Danish themes, such as the collected works of Hans Christian Andersen. Rådhuspladsen 37. ✆ **33-47-25-60.** www.politikensboghal.dk. Bus: 2A, 5A, 6A, 95N, or 96N.

DANISH DESIGN

Bald & Bang ★ 🎁 This outlet showcases what are perhaps the most sophisticated lamps in Europe. Launched by entrepreneurs Anders Bang and Gitte Bald, it began by selling only one item, the IQlight, a lamp shade from the heyday of disco in the '70s. Designed by Holger Strøm in 1972, the lamp had long become passé until Bald and Bang brought it back in 2000. Some of their latest lamp designs include the futuristic "Fuse." They also reach into Denmark's design past to rediscover golden oldies, including Louis Weisdorf's 1965 "Turbo," made from a dozen pieces of interlocking aluminum. Rømersgade 7. ✆ **33-36-07-76.** www.bald-bang.com. Bus: 40.

DDC Shop ★ 🎁 On the premises of the Danish Design Centre, this store is like a small exhibition of Danish design . . . except every one of the high-quality items are offered for sale. The shop showcases products that evoke some of the best craftsmanship of modern Danish designers today. H. C. Andersens Blvd. 27. ✆ **33-69-33-69.** www.ddc.dk. Bus: 1A, 2A, 12, 15, 33, or 40.

Georg Jensen Damask ★★ This store is not to be confused with the more famous Georg Jensen, the purveyor of the nation's finest silver, but this Jensen family has been turning out the nation's finest home textiles since the 15th century. Most fine households in Denmark contain the firm's high-quality and well-designed table linens and towels. Some major designers such as the legendary Arne Jacobsen are also showcased here; her works include geometrically patterned cloth in anthracite and white. Ny Østergade 19. ✆ **33-12-26-00.** www.damask.dk. Bus: 11.

Jørgen L. Dalgaard ★ This relatively small shop has been hailed as one of Copenhagen's best-kept design secrets. Opened in 1974, it is a showcase for the decorative arts of the 20th century, and its owner is a specialist in Danish stoneware, porcelain, and glass. There is also a wide range of Danish furniture from 1920 to 1980. The big names in Swedish glass, Orrefors and Kosta Boda, are on display, but you can also ogle the work of lesser-known Finnish designers such as Tapio Wirkkala and Timo Sarpaneva. Bredgade 2. ✆ **33-14-09-05.** www.jdalgaard.dk. Bus: 1A, 11, 15, 25, or 26.

Klassik Moderne Møbelkunst ★ In 1990, rosewood and teak Scandinavian furniture was viewed as not only old-fashioned but also in bad taste. All that has changed now, and these furnishings are a regular feature in decorating magazines. This shop specializes in furniture design from 1920 to 1975, and lamps and lighting by Paul Henningsen. It also offers a selection of Danish arts and crafts, including glass, ceramics, and woodworks, from the post–World War II "Golden Age" of Scandinavian design. A wide range of Danish modern art, paintings, and sculpture going back to early modernism is on display. Bredgade 3. ✆ **33-33-90-60.** www.klassik.dk. Bus: 1A, 11, 15, 25, or 26.

Normann Copenhagen Locals flock to this international design firm in a long-deserted old movie house in the Østerbro district to purchase Danish furniture and housewares, including avant-garde ceramics. Jan and Poul are the two "Normanns," though their real surnames are Andersen and Madsen, respectively. Østerbrogade 70. ✆ **35-27-05-40.** www.normann-copenhagen.com. Bus: 3.

Rosendahl ★★ When this company's founder, Erik Rosendahl, invented a cone-shaped wine stopper that would fit all wine bottles, it took Denmark by storm. Today, Rosendahl is one of the country's leading producers of innovative accessories for the table and professional, easy-to-use kitchen utensils for the home. Each object—from clear glass to bone china—exhibits Rosendahl's fine craftsmanship and clear sense of practical design. Bremerholm 1. ✆ **70-27-66-33.** www.rosendahl.dk. Bus: 1A, 3A, 14, 15, or 80N.

DEPARTMENT STORES

Illum ★ One of Denmark's top department stores, Illum is on Strøget. Take time to browse through its vast store of Danish and Scandinavian design. There are a restaurant and a special export cash desk at street level. Østergade 52. ✆ **33-14-40-02.** www.illum.dk. Bus: 11.

Magasin ★★ A classy department store, Magasin is the biggest in Scandinavia. It offers a complete assortment of Danish designer fashion, a large selection of glass and porcelain, and souvenirs. Goods are shipped abroad tax-free. Kongens Nytorv 13. ✆ **33-11-44-33.** www.magasin.dk. Metro: Kongens Nytorv.

GLASSWARE, PORCELAIN & CRYSTAL

Royal Copenhagen Porcelain ★★★ Royal Copenhagen's trademark, three wavy blue lines, has come to symbolize quality. Founded in 1775, the factory was a royal possession for a century before passing into private hands in 1868. Royal Copenhagen's Christmas plates are collectors' items. The factory has turned out a new plate each year since 1908, most of the designs depicting the Danish countryside in winter. There's a huge selection of seconds on the top floor, and unless you're an expert, you probably can't tell the difference. Visitors are welcome at the **factory** at Søndre Fasanvej 9 (✆ **38-14-48-48**), where tours are given Monday to Friday from 9am to 3pm. (Tours, which occur about 15km/9⅓ miles west of Copenhagen, can be arranged, along with transportation, by contacting the Royal Copenhagen store at the phone number listed above.) Purchases cannot be made at the factory.

There are also various porcelain and silver retailers in this same location, as well as the Royal Copenhagen Antiques shop, which specializes in buying and selling antique Georg Jensen, Royal Copenhagen, Bing & Grøndahl porcelain, and Michelson Christmas spoons. In the Royal Scandinavia retail center, Amagertorv 6 (Strøget). ✆ **33-13-71-81.** www.royalcopenhagen.com. Bus: 11 for the retail outlet; 14 for the factory.

HOME FURNISHINGS

Illums Bolighus ★★★ A center for modern Scandinavian and Danish design, this is one of Europe's finest showcases for household furnishings and accessories. It stocks furniture, lamps, rugs, textiles, bedding, glassware, kitchenware, flatware, china, jewelry, and ceramics. The store also sells women's and men's clothes and accessories, and there's even a gift shop. Amagertorv 10 (Strøget). ✆ **33-14-19-41.** www.illumsbolighus.com. Bus: 11.

Lysberg, Hansen & Therp This major interior-decorating center offers fabrics, carpets, and furniture. The model apartments are furnished in impeccable taste. The company manufactures its own furniture in traditional design and imports fabrics, usually from Germany or France. The gift shop has many hard-to-find creations. Bredgade 77. ✆ **33-14-47-87.** www.lysberg.com. Bus: 1A, 15, or 25.

Paustian ★★★ Copenhagen's leading furniture showroom, in the somewhat distant industrial Nordhavn section, will ship anywhere in the world. The finest of Scandinavian design is on display, along with reproductions of the classics. There's a well-recommended adjoining restaurant. Kalkbrænderiløbskaj 2. ✆ **39-16-65-65.** www.paustian.dk. S-tog: Nordhavn.

JEWELRY

Hartmann's Selected Estate Silver & Jewelry ★ 🎁 This shop buys silver and jewelry from old estates and sells it at reduced prices. If you're lucky, you might even find some heirloom Georg Jensen estate silver. Ulrik Hartmann, the store's owner, launched his career as a 10-year-old trading at a local flea market, but went on to greater things. The shop is near Kongens Nytorv. While in the neighborhood, you can walk for hours, exploring the auction rooms, jewelry shops, and art galleries in the vicinity. Bredgade 4. ✆ **33-33-09-63.** www.hartmanns.com. Metro: Kongens Nytorv.

Kære Ven One of the city's oldest diamond dealers, in business for more than 100 years, this outlet advertises itself as offering "prices from another century." That's a gross exaggeration, but you can often find bargains in antique jewelry, even old Georg Jensen silver. An array of rings, earrings, necklaces, and bracelets are sold, along with other items. A few items in the store are sold at 50% off competitive prices, but you have to shop carefully and know what you're buying. Store Kongensgade 30. ✆ **33-11-43-15.** www.kaereven.dk. Bus: 1A, 11, 15, or 25.

SILVER & GIFTS

Georg Jensen ★★★ Georg Jensen is legendary for its silver. For the connoisseur, there's no better address. On display is the largest and best collection of Jensen Holloware in Europe. The store also features gold and silver jewelry in traditional and modern Danish designs. In the Royal Scandinavia retail center, Amagertorv 6 (Strøget). ✆ **33-11-40-80.** www.georgjensen.com. Bus: 11.

COPENHAGEN AFTER DARK

Danes know how to party. A good night means a late night, and on warm weekends, hundreds of rowdy revelers crowd Strøget until sunrise. Merrymaking in Copenhagen is not just for the younger crowd; jazz clubs, traditional beer houses, and wine cellars are routinely packed with people of all ages. Of course, the city has a more highbrow cultural side as well, with excellent theaters, operas, ballets, and one of the best circuses in Europe.

Tivoli Gardens ★★★

In the center of the gardens, the large **open-air stage** books vaudeville acts (tumbling clowns, acrobats, aerialists) who give performances every Friday night at 10pm, and on an arbitrary, oft-changing schedule. Jazz and folkloric groups also perform here during the season. Admission is free.

The 150-year-old outdoor **Pantomime Theater,** with its Chinese stage and peacock curtain, is near Tivoli's Vesterbrogade 3 entrance and presents shows Tuesday to Thursday at 6:15 and 8:15pm; Friday at 7:30 and 9pm; Saturday at 8:15 and 9:30pm; and Sunday at 4:30 and 6:30pm. The repertoire consists of 16 different commedia dell'arte productions featuring the entertaining trio Pierrot, Columbine, and Harlequin—these are authentic pantomimes that have been performed continuously in Copenhagen since 1844. Admission is free.

The modern **Tivolis Koncertsal** (concert hall) is a great place to hear top artists and orchestras, led by equally famous conductors. The concert hall can seat 2,000, and its season—which begins in late April and lasts for more than 5 months—has been called "the most extensive music festival in the world." Performances of everything from symphony to opera are presented Monday to Saturday at 7:30pm, and sometimes at 8pm, depending on the event. Good seats are available at prices ranging from 275DKK to 850DKK when major artists are performing—but most performances are free. You can buy tickets at the main booking office on Vesterbrogade 3 (✆ **33-15-10-12** or 45-70-15-65; www.tivoli.dk) or on the Web by clicking on www.billetnet.dk.

Tivoli Glassalen (✆ **33-15-10-12;** www.tivoli.dk) is in a century-old octagonal gazebo-like building with a glass, gilt-capped canopy. Shows are often comedic/satirical performances in Danish, and these usually don't interest non-Danish audiences. A noteworthy exception to this is the annual Christmas programs, presented in November and December, in English. There are also musical reviews, with a minimum of any spoken language, presented throughout the year. Tickets range from 70DKK to 475DKK.

The Performing Arts

For tickets to most of the musical, cultural, and sports-themed entertainment venues of Denmark, check out **Billetnet,** a local branch of Ticketmaster. You can purchase tickets through www.billetnet.dk, or by calling ✆ **70-15-65-65.**

Discount tickets are sold the day of the performance and may be purchased Monday to Friday noon to 5pm and Saturday noon to 3pm.

Det Kongelige Teater (Royal Theater) Performances by the world-renowned **Royal Danish Ballet ★★★** and **Royal Danish Opera ★★★**, dating from 1748, are major winter cultural events in Copenhagen. Because the arts are state-subsidized in Denmark, ticket prices are comparatively low, and some seats may be available at the box office the day before a performance. The season runs August to June. Kongens Nytorv. ✆ **33-69-69-69.** www.kgl-teater.dk. Tickets 85DKK–895DKK, half-price for seniors 67 and over and people 25 and under. Metro: Kongens Nytorv.

Operaen (Copenhagen Opera House) ★★★ Opened by Queen Margrethe, this 1,700-seat opera house is the luxurious home of the Royal Danish Opera. The opera house is the gift of the A. P. Møller and Chastine McKinney Møller Foundation, which is headed by Mærsk McKinney-Møller, one of the wealthiest men in the country. Designed by Danish architect Henning Larsen, the opera house uses precious stones and metals, including 105,000 sheets of gold leaf, and chandeliers that outsparkle and outshine anything in Las Vegas. In addition to the international artists, the opera house also showcases the works of such Danish composers as Carl Nielsen and Poul Ruders. You can dine at the on-site **Opera Restaurant** before curtain time, with a three-course menu costing 250DKK. The season runs from mid-August until the beginning of June. During that period, tours of the building are offered daily on a frequently changing schedule, which usually requires a phone call as a means of confirming the schedule. Ekvipagemestervej 10. ✆ **33-69-69-33,** box office 33-69-69-69. www.operaen.dk. Tickets standing-room space 75DKK; seats 250DKK–895DKK. Bus: 901, 902, or 903.

The Club & Music Scene

DANCE CLUBS

NASA Its name has changed several times in the past decade, but even so, this is the most posh and prestigious of three nightclubs that occupy three respective floors of the same building. The late-night crowd of 25- to 40-year-olds includes many avid fans of whatever musical innovation has just emerged in London or Los Angeles. Technically, the site is a private club, but polite and presentable newcomers can usually gain access. It's open only Friday and Saturday midnight to 6am. Gothersgade 8F, Bolthensgaard. ✆ **33-93-74-15.** www.nasa.dk. Cover 60DKK for nonmembers. Metro: Kongens Nytorv.

The Rock Thanks to an armada of designers who developed it, and thanks to its self-appointed role as a "Design Disco," its interior is more artfully outfitted than any other in Copenhagen. Expect lots of postmodern gloss, references to the California rave movement, an occasional emphasis on dance music of the 1980s, a small corner outfitted like a cozy beer hall, and a clientele that seems familiar with the music and ambience of some very hip clubs in Europe and the States. It's open Friday and Saturday 11pm till at least 5:30am. Skindergade 45. ✆ **33-91-39-13.** www.the-rock.dk. Cover 60DKK–150DKK. Bus: 14.

Rust Rust sprawls over a single floor in the Nørrebro district where the clientele is international and high-energy. Since 1989 faithful patrons have been flocking to its restaurant, several bars, a dance floor, and a stage where live musicians perform every Thursday night beginning around 9pm. Meals are served Wednesday to Saturday 5:30pm to around midnight, and at least someone will begin to boogie on the dance floor after 9:30pm, as drinks flow. No one under age 21 is admitted but you'll see very few over age 45. Open Wednesday to Saturday 9pm to at least 5am. Guldbergsgade 8. ✆ **35-24-52-00.** www.rust.dk. Cover 60DKK Wed and Fri–Sat; 30DKK Thurs. Bus: 3A or 80N.

Vega In this brick-built circular 19th-century monument in Vesterbrø are two venues devoted to live concerts. Performances begin any time between 8 and 11pm. After the concert, partake of the handful of restaurants and bars inside, some with live music of their own. Most venues require a minimum age of 20, and entrance to the bars and restaurants is free. Enghavevej 40. ✆ **33-26-70-11** or 33-25-70-11. For concert schedules, click on www.vega.dk. Cover 100DKK–180DKK. Bus: 3A or 80N.

COPENHAGEN'S BIGGEST NIGHTCLUB

Cirkusbygningen Wallmans In a former circus building near Town Hall Square, this spectacular Las Vegas–style dinner show is a bit corny and very Scandinavian, but it's wildly popular among both visitors and locals. Some 1,000 guests can be entertained here by 22 artists on nine stages while enjoying a four-course dinner (incidentally, the performers also wait on your table). After the show, the space becomes a gigantic nightclub. Doors open Wednesday to Saturday only, except in November when the club is also open on Tuesday. The bar opens at 6:15pm, and the restaurant opens at 6:45pm. Shows stretch out with breaks from 6:55 to 10:55pm; dancing goes on till around 2am. Jernbanegade 8. ✆ **33-16-37-00.** www.wallmans.com. Cover 745DKK–1,095DKK. Bus: 5A, 6A, 11, 12, or 14.

JAZZ, ROCK & BLUES

Copenhagen JazzHouse ★ The decor is modern and uncomplicated and serves as a consciously simple foil for the music and noise. This club hosts more performances by non-Danish jazz artists than any other jazz bar in town. Shows begin relatively early, at around 8:30pm, and usually finish early, too. Around midnight on Friday and Saturday, the club assumes a dance club vibe (until 5am). It's closed Mondays; check online for showtimes. Niels Hemmingsensgade 10. ✆ **33-15-47-00.** www.jazzhouse.dk. Cover charge 80DKK-300DKK when live music is performed. Bus: 11.

La Fontaine This fun dive hasn't changed much since the 1950s. Small, and cozy to the point of being cramped, it functions mostly as a bar. Live music is performed on Friday and Saturday from 11pm to 3am, and Sundays from 9pm to 1am. The club is open daily 7pm to 5am. There is usually no cover on weeknights. Kompagnistræde 11. ✆ **33-11-60-98.** www.lafontaine.dk. Cover 60DKK Fri–Sat. Bus: 11.

Mojo Blues Bar Mojo is a candlelit drinking spot that offers blues music, 90% of which is performed by Scandinavian groups. This grubby but strangely appealing spot is open daily 8pm to 5am. Løngangstræde 21C. ✆ **33-11-64-53.** www.mojo.dk. Cover 80DKK Fri–Sat. Bus: 14.

The Bar Scene

Café Zirup On a street that's packed with worthy competitors, this cafe and bar is loaded with people who seem fun, charming, and engaged with life and their companions. The venue is youthful and hip. Salads, sandwiches, and platters cost from 79DKK to 200DKK. Open Monday to Thursday 10am to midnight, Friday and Saturday 10am to 2am. Læderstræde 32. ✆ **33-13-50-60.** http://zirup.dk. Bus: 11.

1105 ★★ British maverick mixologist Gromit Eduardsen, in the view of some aficionados, serves the best drinks in town. Drinks here are creative, imaginative, and a rhapsody to the taste buds. Expect unusual combinations such as Tanqueray gin, lime juice, honey, cardamom, and black pepper, or the Señor Hansi: a smooth blend of tequila, agave syrup, lime juice, passion fruit, and wheat beer foam. In the background, a DJ plays Motown, disco, and jazz to a cool crowd mostly in their mid-30s to mid-40s. Open Wednesday, Thursday, and Saturday 8pm to 2am, Friday 4pm to 2am. Kristen Bernikows Gade 4. ✆ **33-93-11-05.** www.1105.dk. Bus: 1A, 250, or 350.

Library Bar ★ Frequently visited by celebrities and royalty, the Library Bar was once rated by the late Malcolm Forbes as one of the top five bars in the world. In a setting of antique books and works of art, you can order everything from a cappuccino to a cocktail. The setting is the lobby level of the landmark Hotel Plaza, commissioned in 1913 by Frederik VIII. The bar was originally designed and built as the hotel's library, with Oregon pine used for the paneling. It's open daily from 4pm to midnight (till 1am on Fri and Sat). In the Hotel Plaza, Bernstorffsgade 4. ✆ **33-14-92-62.** www.profilhotels.com. Bus: B, 6A, or 26.

Nyhavn 17 This is the last of the honky-tonk pubs that used to make up the former sailors' quarter, and even this last bastion has seen a rapid gentrification in recent years. This cafe is a short walk from the patrician Kongens Nytorv. In summer you can sit outside. It's open Sunday to Thursday 10am to 2am and Friday and Saturday to 3am. Nyhavn 17. ✆ **33-12-54-19.** www.nyhavn17.dk. Bus: 1, 6, 27, or 29.

Ruby ★★★ Behind an unmarked door in a 1700s building is arguably the best bar in Copenhagen. The bartenders at Ruby lead the pack in terms of innovation, changing the cocktail menu seasonally with such drinks as "Burnt Fig" (caramelized fig syrup with cognac and cream) or a "Thai'ed Up Martini" (Plymouth gin with Thai basil). In spring you can order a "Primavera" made with white grapefruit juice, Galliano L'autentico herbal liqueur, Campari, and Agrapart & Fils champagne. Hours are Monday to Wednesday 4pm to 1am, Thursday to Saturday 4pm to 2am. Nybrogade 10. ✆ **33-93-12-03.** www.rby.dk. Bus: 1A, 2, 11, 14, or 26.

COPENHAGEN'S BEST WINE BAR

Hvids Vinstue ★★ Built in 1670, this old wine cellar is a dimly lit safe haven for an eclectic crowd, many patrons—including theatergoers, actors, and dancers—drawn from the Royal Theater across the way. In December only, a combination of red wine and cognac is served. It's open Monday to Saturday 10am to 1am, Sunday 10am to 8pm. Open-faced sandwiches are 65DKK to 85DKK, and include a free beer. Kongens Nytorv 19. ✆ **33-15-10-64.** www.hviidsvinstue.dk. Metro: Kongens Nytorv.

Gay & Lesbian Clubs

Centralhjornet Copenhagen's oldest gay bar has been attracting clientele since the early 20th century. Old-fashioned, wood-paneled, and cozy, it's absolutely mobbed with gay and, to a lesser extent, lesbian tourists during the Christmas holidays. It's open every day of the year from noon to midnight. Between October and May, there's a drag show every Thursday night beginning around 10pm. Kattesundet 18. ✆ **33-11-85-49.** www.centralhjornet.dk. Bus: 14.

Cosy Bar It runs a fine line between a crowd that favors leather, and what you'd expect from a working crew of men performing manual labor down by the harborfront. Popular and cruisy, it's open Sunday to Thursday 10pm to 6am, Friday and Saturday 10pm to 8am. Studiestræde 24. ✆ **33-12-74-27.** Bus: 5A, 6A, 11, or 14.

Jailhouse Copenhagen Set amid the densest concentration of gay men's bars in town, this is the bar most quickly cited as an amicable and amenable watering hole for the leather, bear, and S&M communities. Imagine a large, shadowy space with a prominent, beer-soaked bar, battered walls and floors, and iron bars that subdivide the space into a series of simulated jail cells. If you're in the mood for a meal, there's a restaurant upstairs, where crisp white napery contrasts with simulations of cellblocks. The bar is open Sunday to Thursday 3pm to 2am, Friday and Saturday 3pm to 5am, and entrance is free. The restaurant is open only Thursday to Saturday 6 to 11pm, with a fixed-price, three-course meal going for 249DKK. Studiestræde 12. ✆ **33-15-22-55.** www.jailhousecph.dk. Bus: 11 or 14.

The Men's Bar This amicable and fraternal establishment is the only leather bar in town, filled with a mash-up of uniforms, leather, Levi's, and gay-icon memorabilia. Note that if it's a particularly hot day, someone might encourage you to take off your shirt, in exchange for which, if you're a newcomer, the bartender is likely to give you a free glass of schnapps. It's open daily 3pm to 2am. A beer will set you back 26DKK. Teglgaardstræde 3. ✆ **33-12-73-03.** www.mensbar.dk. Bus: 5A, 6A, 14, or 81N.

7

EXPLORING THE DANISH COUNTRYSIDE

Denmark, a relatively flat country with good roads, is easy to explore on your own in several driving tours. Ferries connect Copenhagen and Zealand to Bornholm. A new bridge links Funen and Zealand. Another bridge connects Funen and Jutland, which is linked to the mainland of Europe.

If you have time for only one destination outside Copenhagen, make it **Funen.** It's the most visited island, mainly because of its capital, **Odense,** the birthplace of Hans Christian Andersen and home to some of northern Europe's best-preserved castles.

Denmark's western peninsula, **Jutland** (also called Jylland), is the only part of the country that's connected to the European mainland; its southern border touches Germany.

Bornholm, "the pearl of the Baltic," can be reached only by plane or boat. Inhabited since the Iron Age, the island is quite different from the rest of Denmark. A visit is a good choice if you're looking for something offbeat.

FUNEN

After visiting Copenhagen and "Hamlet's Castle" in North Zealand, nearly all visitors head for **Odense,** the capital of the island of Funen (*Fyn* in Danish), lying to the west of Zealand. While Hans Christian Andersen was born in Odense, and houses and memorabilia associated with him are the big attractions, there is so much more here, including the most fantastic island in Scandinavia, little old "time-warp" Ærø of the southern coast. Hop gardens, Viking runic stones, orchards of fruit trees, busy harbors, market towns, swan ponds, thatch-roof houses, once-fortified castles, and stately manor homes invite exploration by car.

Funen has some 1,125km (700 miles) of coastline, with wide sandy beaches in some parts, and woods and grass that grow all the way to the water's edge in others. Steep cliffs provide sweeping views of the Baltic or the Kattegat.

Although ferryboats have plied the waters between the islands and peninsulas of Denmark since ancient times, recent decades have seen the development of a network of bridges. In 1934 the first plans were developed for a bridge over the span of water known as the **Storebælt (Great Belt),** the 19km (12-mile) silt-bottomed channel that separates Zealand (and Copenhagen) from Funen and the rest of continental Europe. After many delays caused by war, technical difficulties, and lack of funding, and after the submission of 144 designs by engineers from around the world, construction began in 1988 on an intricately calibrated network of bridges and tunnels.

On June 14, 1998, her majesty, Queen Margrethe II, cut the ribbon shortly before driving across the Great Belt Bridge. The project incorporated both railway and road traffic divided between a long underwater tunnel and both low and high bridges. (The rail link has operated since 1997.) Only some aspects of the Channel Tunnel between England and France are on par with the staggering scale of this project.

Nyborg: Gateway to Funen

130km (81 miles) W of Copenhagen, 34km (21 miles) E of Odense

One of the oldest towns in Denmark, founded 7 centuries ago, Nyborg lies at the western terminus of the Storebælt Bridge and is the easternmost town on the island of Funen. Local residents thought the opening of the bridge would boost tourism, but that has happened only marginally. Most motorists, especially tourists, rush through town en route to Odense to pay their respects to the memory of Hans Christian Andersen.

That's a shame, really, because Nyborg deserves at least 2 hours of your time, which will allow you to visit its old Torvet, the market square in the center, the ruins of a medieval castle, and some old cross-timbered houses. Like so many other cities or towns of Denmark, Nyborg was more strategic in the Middle Ages than it is today.

Its location in the middle of the trade route between Zealand in the east and Jutland in the west helped boost its importance. In medieval times, about 1200 to 1413, Nyborg was the capital of Denmark. Medieval buildings and well-preserved ramparts are testaments to that era. Nyborg's town square, the **Torvet,** was created in 1540, when a block of houses was demolished to make room for the royal tournaments of Christian III.

In summer, Denmark's oldest open-air theater, **Nyborg Voldspil,** is the setting for an annual musical or operetta under the leafy beeches on the old castle ramparts. Throughout the summer, classical music concerts (featuring international soloists) are performed in the castle's Great Hall. Inquire at the tourist office (see "Visitor Information," below) for further details.

Dating from the mid-1600s, the Tattoo is an ancient military ceremony with musical accompaniment. This old custom has been revived to honor the corps who played an important role in the Schleswig wars in 1848 and again in 1864. In tribute to the old corps, the present-day Tattoo participants wear a green uniform with its characteristic cap, or *chakot*. The corps marches through the center of town at 9pm each year on June 30, thereafter every Tuesday in July and August.

ESSENTIALS

GETTING THERE You can reach Nyborg by **train or bus** (via ferry). Trains leave Copenhagen every hour, and there's frequent bus service from Copenhagen as well. From Odense, eastbound trains arrive two times an hour.

VISITOR INFORMATION The **Nyborg Turistbureau,** Torvet 9 (✆ **65-31-02-80;** www.visitnyborg.dk), is open July 1 to August 15 Monday to Friday 9am to

5pm, and Saturday 9am to 1pm; August 16 to December 22 and January 2 to June 30 Monday to Friday 9am to 4pm, and Saturday 9:30am to 12:30pm.

GETTING AROUND Bus nos. 1, 3, and 4 serve all in-town destinations listed below.

SEEING THE SIGHTS

Mads Lerches Gård (Nyborg Og Omegns Museet) ★ Of all the places in Funen, this 1601 house, the former home of the town mayor, provides the best insight into what life was like in the 17th century—that is, if you had some money in the bank. The house, painted a reddish pink, is filled with exhibitions on local history, but far more intriguing than that are the antiques-filled period chambers spread over 30 rooms on two floors. There's even a small brewery on-site.

Slotsgade 11. ✆ **65-31-02-07.** www.ostfynsmuseer.dk. Admission 30DKK adults, 25DKK students, free for children 17 and under. Apr–May and Sept–Oct 21 Tues–Sun 10am–3pm; June–Aug Tues–Sun 10am–4pm. Closed Oct 22–Mar. Bus: 1, 3, or 4.

Nyborg Slot (Nyborg Castle) ★ This hardly compares to Windsor Castle in England, but to the Danes it's just as important. Dating from 1170, this is one of the oldest of Denmark's royal castles. Originally it was built to defend the country from the Wends of North Germany. King Erik Glipping signed Denmark's first constitution in this moated castle in 1282, and Nyborg became the seat of the Danish Parliament, the Danehof, until 1413 when Copenhagen took over.

In a regrettable decision, much of the Slot was demolished in 1722 to provide building materials for Odense Castle. Nevertheless, parts of the original ramparts remain. From these bastions, Danes rained down hot tar on their invaders. If you walk these ramparts today, you'll have a **panoramic view ★** of Nyborg and the sea. The terrace in front is still lined with bronze guns facing the town center, and the town gate, **Landporten ★**, can be seen just north of the castle.

Most intriguing is the still remaining **Danehof ★**, the hall where Parliament met. The walls are painted with geometric murals, and there is an extensive collection of armaments such as guns and swords, suits of armor (rather impressive), and old royal paintings (not too impressive). Other rooms open to view include the King's Room, the Knights' Hall, and even the apartment once occupied by the royal kids.

Slotspladen. ✆ **65-31-02-07.** www.ostfynsmuseer.dk. Admission 50DKK adults, 40DKK students, free for children 17 and under. Apr–May and Sept–Oct 21 Tues–Sun 10am–3pm; June–Aug daily 10am–4pm. Closed Oct 22–Mar. Bus: 1, 2, or 3.

Vor Frue Kirke (The Church of Our Lady) This is still a place of worship even though it dates from the Middle Ages. Unfortunately restorers and decorators descended on the church in 1870 and completely changed it, so we're not allowed to see the purity of its original simple architectural details. Even so, it's still a worthy place to wander about for 30 to 45 minutes. We found that the greatest treasure here is a **baroque pulpit ★** in stunning detail.

The Gothic spire of the church is a landmark for miles around, and the interior is split into a trio of aisles and endowed with woodcarvings, carved old epitaphs, candelabra, and model ships. The elegant wrought-iron gate you see was forged in 1649 by Casper Fincke, the court-appointed craftsman to King Christian IV. The most evocative aspect of the church, which we discovered while strolling about Nyborg one night, is that at 9:45pm the Watchman's Bell from 1523 is still rung, a tradition that dates back for centuries. Lying at the end of Kongegade in the town center, Vor Frue Kirke can be entered through its south door. Nearby at Adelgade and Korsbrodregade stands a large stone-built house, **Korsbrodregården,** dating from 1396. This was the

Chapter House of the Order of St. John, its vaulted cellar converted today into a gift shop.

Adelgade. ✆ **65-31-16-08.** Free admission. Daily 9am–6pm.

WHERE TO STAY

Hotel Hesselet ★★★ Such an elegant hotel of high international standard comes as a surprise in this sleepy, provincial town. One of the most stylish hotels in Funen, outclassing most of those in Odense itself, is idyllically set among beech trees, opening onto a view of the Great Belt with its Storebæltsbro suspension bridge. Request a room with a view of this sea spectacle, or else you'll be assigned accommodations opening onto a forest. Inside, the hotel creates a glamorous aura in its public lounges with Asian artifacts and plush Oriental carpets, a large fireplace, sunken living rooms, and a cozy library lined with leather-bound volumes. Bedrooms are sumptuously furnished and spacious, each with tasteful appointments.

Christianslundsvej 119, DK-5800 Nyborg. www.hesselet.dk. ✆ **65-31-30-29.** Fax 65-31-29-58. 59 units. 1,775DKK–2,175DKK double; 2,525DKK–4,495DKK suite. Rates include buffet breakfast. AE, DC, MC, V. Free parking. **Amenities:** Restaurant; bar; babysitting; bikes; children's playground; exercise room; Jacuzzi; indoor heated pool; room service; sauna; 2 outside tennis courts (lit). *In room:* TV, hair dryer, minibar, Wi-Fi (free).

WHERE TO DINE

Central Cafeen ★ DANISH/FRENCH This is one of the finest restaurants along the east coast of Funen, set directly across the street from City Hall in a 1787 house that has contained some kind of restaurant here since 1854. With a sense of local history and a deep-seated pride, it offers four separate, cozy dining rooms. The composition of the set-price menus changes every month to take advantage of seasonal produce. First-rate ingredients are used, often shrimp and lobster. Begin with a bowl of the creamy lobster bisque, going on to the fried plaice with a lobster-and-shrimp sauce. Roasted salmon appears with fresh spinach, and meat-eaters gravitate to the fried pork cutlets in a parsley sauce. The sumptuous desserts are made daily, and there is an impressive but pricey wine list to back up the cuisine.

Nørregade 6. ✆ **65-31-01-83.** Reservations recommended. Main courses 145DKK–210DKK; fixed-price 3-course menu 318DKK. AE, DC, MC, V. Mon–Sat 11am–9:30pm. Bus: 1, 3, or 4.

Odense: Birthplace of Hans Christian Andersen ★★

156km (97 miles) W of Copenhagen, 34km (21 miles) W of Nyborg, 43km (27 miles) NW of Svendborg

Many people make their living off Hans Christian Andersen and all the visitors his memory brings to Odense. But the town never seemed to appreciate the boy until the world discovered his writing. In some respects, Odense treated him the way Salzburg treated Mozart. Actually, the storyteller had a very unhappy childhood in Odense and left as soon as he was old enough to make his way to Copenhagen.

His cobbler father was always out of money and had been forced to marry Hans's ill-tempered, peasant mother when she was 7 months pregnant. The Andersen grandmother was insane and, as noted by Andersen himself, a "pathological liar."

But those unpleasant memories are long gone today, and Odense is proud of its world-famous son, hawking souvenirs and dusting off the writer's memorabilia to each new generation. This ancient town, the third largest in Denmark, has changed greatly since Andersen walked its streets, but its historic core still evokes the fairy-tale town that Andersen knew so well.

Odense is in the heart of Funen and home to more than 185,000 inhabitants. It's one of the oldest cities in the country, with a history stretching back some 1,000 years. The city's name stems from two words—*Odins Vi* (Odin's shrine), suggesting that the god Odin must have been worshiped here in pre-Christian times. Long before Odense became a pilgrimage center for fans of Andersen, it was an ecclesiastical center and site of religious pilgrimage in the Middle Ages.

Odense today is not just a fairy-tale town, but an industrial might in Denmark, its harbor linked by a canal to the Odense Fjord and thus the Great Belt. It's a center of electro-technical, textile, steel, iron, and timber production.

In summer Odense takes on a festive air, with lots of outdoor activities, including music and theater taking place on its squares and in its piazzas. Cafes and pubs are lively day and night.

ESSENTIALS

GETTING THERE You can easily reach Odense by **train or bus** from Copenhagen, as about 12 trains or buses a day leave Copenhagen's Central Railroad Station for Odense (trip time: 3 hr.). **By car,** from Nyborg, head west on E-20 to Allerup and then follow Route 9 north to Odense.

VISITOR INFORMATION **Odense Tourist Bureau** is at Rådhuset, Vestergade 2A (© **66-12-75-20;** www.visitodense.com). It's open mid-June to August, Monday to Friday 9am to 6pm, Saturday and Sunday 10am to 3pm; September to mid-June, Monday to Friday 9:30am to 4:30pm and Saturday 10am to 1pm.

GETTING AROUND Bus no. 2 serves all in-town destinations listed below. A typical fare is 18DKK.

SEEING THE SIGHTS

Less than a kilometer (½ mile) west of the city center is **Bowl'n'Fun,** Grønekøkkenvej (© **70-11-11-55;** www.bowlnfun.dk; bus: 91 or 92), a complex of amusements and diversions that are entirely devoted to popular American culture. It incorporates facilities for indoor go-cart racing, an indoor version of American-style miniature golf, several bowling alleys, and a small-scale collection of rides and games inspired by the theme parks of Florida. Each individual attraction within the park maintains its own hours and entrance policies, but the best way to appreciate this site's activities is to head here anytime daily between noon and 6pm, when for an all-inclusive fee of 170DKK, you'll have unlimited access to all of them.

Carl Nielsen Museet (Carl Nielsen Museum) At the Odense Concert Hall, you can learn about the life and music of Denmark's greatest composer, Carl August Nielsen (1865–1931).

This towering musician developed a unique polytonal and contrapuntal musical form, his operas including *Saul and David* in 1903 and *Maskerade* in 1906. He also composed symphonies, concertos, and choral and chamber music. Nielsen single-handedly "woke up" Danish music after its sleepy decline of decades. In the museum you can listen to some of his greatest works, even a polka he penned as a child before joining the Odense Military Band as a trumpet player at the tender age of 14.

A biographical slide show brings to life the cultural icon, whose six symphonies, several operas, hymns, and popular songs (many of which are patriotic) are still played around the world today.

Nielsen married a famous sculptor, Anne Marie Carl-Nielsen, strangely keeping her husband's first name in her full name. Although hardly as well known as her husband, she created works still on view in Denmark, including her equestrian statue of Christian IX that stands outside the Royal Stables in Copenhagen.

Claus Bergsgade 11. ✆ **65-51-46-01.** http://museum.odense.dk. Free admission. Jan–May and Sept–Dec Mon–Wed 2–5pm; June–Aug Fri–Sun noon–4pm.

Danmarks Jernbanemuseum (Railway Museum) ★ ☺ This is one of the best transportation museums in Scandinavia, appropriately located adjacent to the Odense train station. It's a very active museum and not some dull depot of long-abandoned locomotives, although there are those here too, the best of which is a **royal carriage ★** that once carried his majesty, King Christian IX.

The history of locomotives and carriages, from the first train in Denmark, dating from 1847, until more modern times, is on display, including a "B-Machine," a moving vehicle from 1869. A replica of a 19th-century train depot is on view along with two dozen engines and various saloon cars. Model ferries, buses, model railway tracks, and even Wagons-Lits restaurant cars and ferries are on view. The entire family can go on the minitrains and take a simulated ride in a large diesel locomotive.

Dannebrogsgade 24. ✆ **66-13-66-30.** www.jernbanemuseum.dk. Admission 60DKK adults, 30DKK children 5–13, free for children 4 and under. Daily 10am–4pm.

Funen Village/Den Fynske Landsby ★★ ☺ If Hans Christian Andersen were to come back to life, he'd feel that the world had never changed if he were to land in this village. This is the Danish version of Scotland's mystical "Brigadoon," where some 30 buildings, dating from the 17th to the 19th centuries, keep alive the village milieu of yesterday, with half-timbered houses, flower gardens, a grazing cow (or goat), and a communal pond.

In a scenic setting in the Hunderup Woods, these old buildings include a tollhouse, weaver's shop, windmill, farming homestead, vicarage, village school, brickworks, and the inevitable jail. Each was reassembled on this site and authentically furnished. You can visit workshops to see craftspeople, including a basket maker, spoon cutter, weaver, and the village blacksmith.

As an added treat, plays and folk dances are staged at a Greek-style theater. You can take the bus, but the best way to get here is to take a boat from Munke Mose in Odense down the river to Erik Boghs Sti. After you disembark, it's a 15-minute scenic walk to the museum. A one-way fare is 50DKK for adults or 35DKK for children 10 to 15, free for children 9 and under.

Sejerskovvej 20. ✆ **65-51-46-01.** Admission 60DKK adults, free for children 16 and under. Mid-June to mid-Aug daily 9:30am–7pm; Apr to mid-June and mid-Aug to mid-Oct Tues–Sun 10am–5pm; mid-Oct to Mar Sun 11am–3pm. Bus: 110 or 111.

H. C. Andersens Barndomshjem (H. C. Andersen's Childhood Home) ☺ Visit Andersen's humble childhood abode, where the fairy-tale writer lived from 1807 to 1819. From what is known of Andersen's childhood, his mother was a drunken, superstitious washerwoman, and Andersen was a gawky boy, lumbering and graceless, the victim of his fellow urchins' cruel jabs. However, all is serene at the cottage today; in fact, the little house with its tiny rooms has a certain unpretentious charm, and the "garden still blooms," as in *The Snow Queen*. The museum is only mildly diverting, worth no more than 15 or 20 minutes of your time.

Munkemøllestræde 3. ✆ **65-51-46-01.** http://museum.odense.dk. Admission 25DKK adults, free for children 16 and under. June–Aug daily 10am–4pm; Sept–May daily 11am–3pm.

H. C. Andersens Hus (Hans Christian Andersen House) ★★ ☺ Though not the rival of the Shakespeare properties in Stratford-upon-Avon, the object of most Funen pilgrimages is to the house of the great spinner of fairy tales himself, Hans Christian Andersen. When it opened in 1908, it became one of the first writer museums in the world focusing on the life and work of a single author. In various memorabilia, such as hundreds of documents, manuscripts, and reprints of his books in 100 languages (including Zulu), you learn of the writer's life from his birth as the son of a poor cobbler in Odense, to his hard times in Copenhagen, until his eventual debut upon the world stage.

We even learn about some aspects of his love life, as when he fell for Jenny Lind, "the Swedish Nightingale," who did not return his affection. Letters to such fellow famous writers as Charles Dickens are also on exhibit. The storyteller lives again as you get to see some of his props, such as his famous walking stick, Fred Astaire–like top hat, and battered portmanteau.

Bangs Boder 29. ✆ **65-51-46-01.** http://museum.odense.dk. Admission 60DKK adults, free for children 16 and under. June 28–Aug daily 9am–6pm; Sept–June 27 Tues–Sun 10am–4pm.

NEARBY ATTRACTIONS

Egeskov Slot (Egeskov Castle) ★★★ This moated Renaissance castle is the best preserved of its type in Europe. Plan to spend at least a morning or an afternoon here. Constructed in 1554, it is still privately owned and inhabited by the descendants of Henrik Bille, who purchased the castle in 1784. The location of Denmark's most splendid fortified manor is outside of the town of Kværndrup, 29km (18 miles) south of Odense.

The castle was built on oak pillars in the middle of a moat or small lake, for which thousands of oak trees in the neighboring forests were cut down.

The most dramatic story in the castle's history is about an unfortunate maiden, Rigborg, who was seduced by a young nobleman and bore him a child out of wedlock. Banished to the castle, she was imprisoned by her father in a tower from 1599 to 1604.

Because of the private living quarters, only some of the castle is open to view, including the restored **Great Hall ★★**, which is now a venue for chamber music concerts on 10 summer Sundays beginning in late June and starting at 5pm. The inhabitants of this castle were great hunters, and you can visit a hunting room with some of their most prized trophies, including elephant tusks and the heads of tigers. You can also view precious antiques and classical paintings.

For us the spectacular **gardens ★★★** in the 12-hectare (30-acre) park are even more beautiful than the interior. Laid out in the 1730s, the gardens are among the most dramatic in Denmark. The **Fuchsia Garden ★★★** contains the largest collection of fuchsias in Europe with about 75 different species. The English Garden with its tree-studded green lawns sweeps down to the streams and the castle lake. In summer the rose beds are a delight to behold, the prize flower being the pink "Egeskov Rose." The site also includes a kiosk where you can purchase rose jelly; a museum of antique cars, old airplanes, and horse-drawn carriages; and the world's largest maze, which is made of cut beech hedges and is several centuries old.

Egeskovgade 18, Kværndrup. ✆ **62-27-10-16.** www.egeskov.dk. Admission including castle, park, and maze 195DKK adults, 105DKK children 4–12; park, maze, and museum 150DKK adults, 80DKK children 4–12. Free for children 3 and under. July park and castle daily 10am–7pm; June and Aug park 10am–6pm, castle 10am–5pm; Sept and May park and castle 10am–5pm. Closed Oct–Apr. Train: From Odense or Svendborg every hour. Bus: 920 from Nyborg.

Ladbyskibet Admittedly, the ruins of a 10th-century Viking ship, discovered in 1935, don't compare to those discovered in the Oslofjord and displayed on Oslo's Bygdøy peninsula. But if you're not going on to Oslo, this is your best shot at seeing what one of those ships looked like.

This is the only Viking ship discovered to date in Denmark. Archaeologists are puzzled why more Viking ships haven't been unearthed in Denmark because they were used as coffins for burying chieftains. In this one, the corpse of the pagan chieftain buried was never found, just the bones of nearly a dozen horses and dogs. Other utensils, believed to be of use in Valhalla, were also interred with the corpse. Remains of the ship are displayed in a burial mound along with replicas from the excavation (the originals are in the National Museum of Copenhagen).

Vikingevej 123, Ladby. ✆ **65-32-16-67.** www.kertemindemuseer.dk. Admission 50DKK adults, free for children 17 and under. Mar–May and Sept–Oct Tues–Sun 10am–4pm; June–Aug daily 10am–5pm; Nov–Feb Tues–Sun noon–4pm. Bus: 482 from Kerteminde. 19km (12 miles) northeast of Odense.

WHERE TO STAY

Clarion Hotel Plaza ★★★ This is Odense's classiest address, with far more personality, atmosphere, and glamour than its closest rival, the also-recommended Radisson Blu (see below). One of Funen's most alluring hostelries, the Plaza is less than half a kilometer (¼ mile) outside of the town center, and only a 5-minute walk from the train station. A stately place to stay, it fronts the city's finest and leafiest park, Kongens Have.

After you check in and inspect the formal lounges, an old-fashioned early-20th-century elevator takes you to the midsize-to-spacious bedrooms, many of which evoke life in an English country home, opening onto scenic views. The rooms are handsomely decorated, often with antique reproductions.

Østre Stationsvej 24, DK-5000 Odense. www.hotel-plaza.dk. ✆ **877/424-6423** in the U.S., or 66-11-77-45. Fax 66-14-41-45. 68 units. July–Aug 950DKK double, 1,940DKK suite; Sept–June 1,245DKK-1,345DKK double, 1,945DKK suite. Rates include buffet breakfast. AE, DC, MC, V. Free parking. Bus: 31, 33, 35, or 36. **Amenities:** Restaurant; bar; exercise room; room service. *In room:* TV, hair dryer, minibar, Wi-Fi (free).

Hotel Ansgar ☺ When this hotel opened in 1902 it attracted clean-living, nondrinking Christians. Today, those associations are gone, and there's even a bar on-site. Just a 5-minute walk from the train depot, behind a brick-and-stone facade, the hotel has been considerably renovated, with the installation of modern furniture and double-glazed windows to cut down on the traffic noise. As befits the style of the hotel's era, the rooms range from small to spacious, each comfortably furnished with Italian pieces and well-kept bathrooms with tub/shower combos. The staff does much in summer to attract the family trade, even giving kids a coupon for free ice cream.

Østre Stationsvej 32, DK-5000 Odense. www.hotel-ansgar.dk. ✆ **66-11-96-93.** Fax 66-11-96-75. 64 units. June–Aug 700DKK–900DKK double; Sept–May 1,145DKK double. Rates include buffet breakfast. AE, DC, MC, V. Free parking. Bus: 32. **Amenities:** Restaurant; bar; children's playground. *In room:* TV, hair dryer, minibar, Wi-Fi (free).

Radisson Blu H. C. Andersen Hotel ★★ It may lack the nostalgic charm of the Plaza, but commercial travelers find this first-class hotel more convenient and livelier, with a roster of facilities that includes a casino. In summer, fans of Andersen from abroad fill its 1960s Nordic-style bedrooms, since it's near a former Hans Christian Andersen residence in the heart of the city. This red-brick hotel, one of the finest on the island of Funen, welcomes you into a plant-filled lobby and a glass-roofed reception area, where you encounter the most efficient staff in Odense.

The tasteful, conservatively decorated, and comfortably appointed bedrooms come in a variety of sizes—some large, others, especially the singles, a bit cramped, with the most tranquil rooms opening onto the interior.

Claus Bergs Gade 7, DK-5000 Odense. www.radissonblu.com/hotel-odense. ✆ **800/333-3333** in the U.S., or 66-14-78-00. Fax 66-14-78-90. 145 units. 1,195DKK–1,895DKK double. Rates include buffet breakfast. AE, DC, MC, V. Bus: 4 or 5. **Amenities:** Restaurant; bar; exercise room; room service; sauna. *In room:* TV, hair dryer, minibar, Wi-Fi (free).

WHERE TO DINE

Den Gamle Kro ★ DANISH/FRENCH For all we know, Hans Christian Andersen used to drop into this place—after all, it's been serving food and drink to the locals since 1683. A 5-minute walk from the city center, it is unusual architecturally in that it was constructed within the courtyards of several antique buildings, but has been modernized with its timeworn stone capped by a sliding glass roof.

A cellar-level bar is lined with antique masonry, and the street-level restaurant rests under centuries-old beams. The food has remained consistently good over the years, and we've dropped in for lunch for some of the best *smørrebrød* selections in town, including shrimp and dill stacked on top of freshly baked bread.

If you return for dinner, you'll find some of the best fixed-price meals in town. There's nothing you're served here that you haven't tasted before, including beef tenderloin flavored with herbs or herb-sprinkled trout sautéed in butter, but the ingredients are market fresh and skillfully prepared by the kitchen staff, which also creates yummy, freshly made desserts.

Overgade 23. ✆ **66-12-14-33.** www.dengamlekro.eu. Reservations recommended. Main courses 189DKK–338DKK; fixed-price meals 298DKK–418DKK. AE, DC, MC, V. Daily 11am–10:30pm (Sun to 9:30pm). Bus: 2.

First Hotel Grand Restaurant & Bar ★ DANISH/FRENCH Some of the best set menus in town are served at this sophisticated brasserie attached to a hotel. Chefs prepare dishes with a fine precision and a sensitivity to natural ingredients. The hotel bar has become a popular rendezvous, evoking a luxurious salon in warm, intimate colors with a private library.

On one of the set menus you might begin with an innovative soup that includes sautéed pumpkin and pumpkinseeds, with bacon adding an extra layer of flavor. Or you might order a foie gras terrine with beetroot. Other main courses designed to intrigue are the fresh catch of the day, often served with olives, fresh tarragon, and a tangy vinaigrette sauce. But the house special is a tender entrecôte of veal with herb butter and an *aioli* sauce. The location is 200m (656 ft.) from the train station.

Jernbanegade 18. ✆ **66-11-71-71.** Reservations recommended. Fixed-price menus 220DKK–250DKK. AE, DC, MC, V. Mon–Sat noon–2pm and 5:30–10pm.

Under Lindetraeet ★ DANISH/INTERNATIONAL This inn, located across the street from the H. C. Andersen Museum, has been a landmark and a local favorite since the 1960s, and it is the most popular restaurant in town. It's one of the finest restaurants in town, with a menu based on fresh, first-class ingredients. Skillfully prepared dishes include tender Danish lamb, filet of plaice with butter sauce, *escalope* of veal in sherry sauce, fried herring with new potatoes, and an upscale version of *skipperlabskovs,* the famed sailors' hash. The atmosphere is Old World, and in summer, meals and light refreshments are served outside under linden trees.

Ramsherred 2. ✆ **66-12-92-86.** www.underlindetraet.dk. Reservations required. Main courses 95DKK–245DKK; fixed-price menus 330DKK–700DKK. AE, DC, MC, V. Tues–Sat 6–9:30pm. Closed July 4–24. Bus: 2.

SHOPPING

Inspiration Zinch ★, Vestergade 82–84 (✆ **66-12-96-93**), offers the widest selection of Danish design and handicrafts on the island of Funen. All the big names are here, everything from Royal Copenhagen to Georg Jensen, but you will also come across younger and more modern designers. In the heart of the Old Town, opposite Hans Christian Andersen's house, you'll find a display of Danish crafts and Christmas decorations in a typical atmosphere of Old Funen at **Klods Hans,** Hans Jensens Stæde 34 (✆ **66-11-09-40**). Another outlet is **Smykker,** Klaregade 3 (✆ **66-12-06-96**), which offers museum copies of Bronze Age, Iron Age, and Viking jewelry—all made in gold, sterling silver, and bronze in the outlet's own workshop. **College Art,** Grandts Passage 38 (✆ **66-11-35-45;** www.collageart.dk), has assembled a unique collection of posters, lithographs, silk-screens, original art, and cards. Finally, if none of the above shops has what you want, head for **Rosengårdcentret** at Munkerisvej and Ørbækvej (✆ **66-15-91-18;** www.rosengaardcentret.dk). It's Denmark's biggest shopping center, with nearly 110 stores all under one roof.

Svendborg

43km (27 miles) S of Odense, 147km (91 miles) W of Copenhagen

Svendborg is the second-biggest town in Funen (with 42,000 residents), it's a major commercial and tourist hub for South Funen, and it has none of the fairy-tale overlay that Odense hypes. It's a sailors' town and has had a long history as a maritime center. Until 1915, it was the home port for a big fleet of sailing ships because of its position on the beautiful Svendborg Sound, which provides convenient access to Baltic ports.

Although shipbuilding is a ghost of itself, there are a couple of shipyards that still construct wood-hulled ships and are around to repair visiting yachts plying the waters off the coast of South Funen.

Frankly, we'd spend only a night here, as the islands of Ærø and Tåsinge (see below) are more alluring. But if you give Svendborg a day, you'll find much to do.

Svendborg is a lively modern town, with museums, constantly changing art exhibits, and sports. It has swimming pools, beaches, and a yachting school. Its best beach, **Christiansminde,** is one of several in Funen flying the blue flag indicating nonpolluted waters.

Svendborg is also a market town, and on Sunday morning, you can visit the cobblestone central plaza where flowers and fish are sold. Wander through the many winding streets where brick and half-timbered buildings still stand. On **Ragergade** you'll see the old homes of early seafarers. **Møllergade,** a pedestrian street, is one of the oldest streets in town, with about 100 different shops.

Literary buffs know that the German writer Bertolt Brecht lived at Skovsbo Strand, west of Svendborg, from 1933 to 1939, but he left at the outbreak of World War II. During this period he wrote *Mother Courage and Her Children,* which is still performed around the world.

ESSENTIALS

GETTING THERE You can take a **train** from Copenhagen to Odense, where you can get a connecting train to Svendborg, with frequent service throughout the day. From our last stopover in Odense, **drive** south on Route 9, following the signs into Svendborg.

VISITOR INFORMATION Contact the **Svendborg Tourist Office,** Centrumpladsen 4 (✆ **62-23-57-00;** www.visitsydfyn.dk), open June 20 to August 21, Monday to Friday 9:30am to 6pm and Saturday 9:30am to 2pm; January 2 to June 19 and August 22 to December 22, Monday to Friday 9:30am to 5pm, and Saturday 9:30am to 12:30pm; closed December 23 to January 1.

GETTING AROUND **Bus no. 800** serves all in-town destinations listed below. **Bike rentals** for hotel guests, at 80DKK per day, can be obtained at the Hotel Svendborg, Centrumpladsen 1 (✆ **62-21-17-00;** bus: 800 or 931). Biking routes and maps are available at the tourist office.

SEEING THE SIGHTS

Anne Hvides Gård This cross-timbered house in the center of the Torvet, the old market square, is the oldest secular house in Svendborg, dating from 1558 and operated today as a branch of the County Museum. This is one of those "let's raid the attic to see what we can find" type of museums. Its most dramatic features are the recreations of interiors from the 18th and 19th centuries, and there are plenty of silver objects, glassware, copper and brass utensils, and the inevitable faience. Temporary cultural exhibitions are also presented here.

Fruestræde 3. ✆ **62-21-34-57.** www.svendborgmuseum.dk. Admission 25DKK adults, free for children 17 and under. July–Oct Tues–Sun 11am–3pm; off-season by arrangement with the main office.

Skt. Jørgens Kirke (St. George's Church) Only the Church of Skt. Nicolai (see below) exceeds the beauty of this one, whose origins go back to the 12th century when it was originally a chapel for lepers who were forced to live outside the town in an attempt to control spread of the disease. The church itself was named for that fearless knight St. George, patron of lepers. The core of the church is a Gothic longhouse with a three-sided chancel from the late 13th century. During restoration of the church in 1961, an archaeological dig of the floor disclosed traces of a wooden building believed to be a predecessor of the present house of worship.

Strandvej 97. ✆ **62-21-40-20.** www.sctjoergens.dk. Free admission. Tues–Wed 10am–1pm; Thurs 10am–1pm and 4–6pm; Fri 10am–noon.

Skt. Nicolai Kirke (St. Nicholas's Church) Svendborg's oldest church is among a cluster of antique houses off Kyseborgstræde, in the vicinity of Gerrits Plads just south of the market square. Built before 1200 in the Romanesque style and last restored in 1892, its red-brick walls and white vaulting complement the fine altarpiece by Joachim Skovgaard in 1894. The magnificent **stained-glass windows** ★ were designed by Kræsten Iversen during Denmark's darkest days in recent history, the Nazi occupation that lasted from 1940 to 1945. Nearby you can admire a statue by Kai Nielsen (1882–1924), a native son who went on to greater glory and became a famous sculptor.

Kirkestræde 3. ✆ **62-21-28-54.** www.sct-nicolai-kirke.dk. Free admission. May–Aug daily 10am–3pm; Sept–Apr daily 10am–noon.

Viebæltegård You might not want to spend more than 30 minutes in this museum; but if the day is sunny, we like to come here to enjoy a picnic lunch in the museum garden. The headquarters for the County Museum is housed in a former poorhouse/workhouse from 1872, the only one of its kind still existing in Denmark. The complex of "social welfare" buildings has been converted into museums of history, displaying artifacts from ancient times to the Middle Ages, including finds from fields around Svendborg and South Funen in general. More intriguing is to visit the crafts workshops on-site, watching goldsmiths, potters, and printers at work, and there's also an on-site museum shop that has some wonderful crafts for sale.

Grubbemøllevej 13 (near Dronningemæn). ✆ **62-21-02-61.** www.svendborgmuseum.dk. Admission 40DKK adults, free for children 17 and under when accompanied by an adult. Summer Tues–Sun 10am–4pm; winter Tues–Sun 1–4pm.

WHERE TO STAY

Hotel Ærø Extensive renovations have once again turned Svendborg's oldest hotel into an acceptable choice for overnighting. The bedrooms are decorated in a romantic English style, evocative of the 19th century. Even if you don't stay here, consider it for a dinner, as it serves what is arguably the most authentic Danish cuisine in town, including those Ping-Pong-size meatballs known as *frikadeller,* a large platter containing plaice with hollandaise, and many meat dishes, as well as several *smørrebrød* selections.

Brogade 1, DK-5700 Ærøfaergen. www.hotel-aeroe.dk. ✆ **62-21-07-60.** Fax 63-20-30-51. 33 units. 995DKK double; 1,300DKK suite. Extra bed 250DKK. Rates include buffet breakfast. DC, MC, V. **Amenities:** Restaurant; bar; bikes; room service. *In room:* TV.

Hotel Svendborg ★ Built in the 1950s, not a great decade for architecture, this hotel nonetheless is stylish inside and offers the best accommodations in Svendborg, the rooms spread across four floors above the commercial core of town. It's never been our favorite, as we prefer more evocative or romantic addresses, but during the 2 nights we spent here we were exceedingly comfortable and found the English staff helpful and informative about the area. Guest rooms range from small to spacious, and each is furnished in a tasteful Scandinavian modern design with excellent bathrooms. The eight apartments, each with kitchen, can be rented to one to four guests.

Centrumpladsen 1, DK-5700 Svendborg. www.hotel-svendborg.dk. ✆ **62-21-17-00.** Fax 62-21-90-12. 133 units, 8 apts. 945DKK–1,395DKK double; 1,995DKK suite; 1,650DKK apt for 2; 2,200DKK apt for 4. Rates include buffet breakfast. AE, DC, MC, V. Free parking. Bus: 800 or 931. **Amenities:** Restaurant; bar; room service. *In room:* TV, hair dryer, minibar, Wi-Fi (free).

WHERE TO DINE

Svendborgsund DANISH/FRENCH Many Danes, often sailors and visiting yachters, come here to grab drinks in the separate bar area; but the food in the restaurant is good and wholesome, and the cooks following recipes familiar to their grandmothers. In summer, the terrace is a magnet, and you can eat and drink alfresco, taking in a picture-postcard view of all the ferryboats, trawlers, and pleasure yachts in the harbor. Built of white-painted stone in the 1830s, this waterfront restaurant is the oldest in town. The food is for the meat-potatoes-and-onion crowd—in fact, that is the most popular dish to order here, called *biksemad* in Danish. The chef specializes in fresh fish, and does so exceedingly well, but he also provides a few dishes for the carnivore, notably some tasty pork chops or tender Danish lamb. Svendborgsund is about a 5-minute walk south of the center of town.

Havnepladsen 5A. ✆ **62-21-07-19.** www.restaurantsvendborgsund.dk. Reservations recommended. Main courses 148DKK–228DKK; lunch *smørrebrød* 55DKK–125DKK. MC, V. Daily 11am–10pm.

Nearby Attractions on Tåsinge

Ærø is the major tourist attraction of Funen, outside Odense, but the lesser known island of Tåsinge is for lovers, the most romantic hideaway in all of Denmark. Although sleepy, it is still the largest island in the South Funen archipelago, and it's been connected to Funen by the Svendborg Sound Bridge since 1966. The location is only 3km (2 miles) south of Svendborg via the bridge, but a distance of 43km (27 miles) south of Odense.

Route 90, which is the main road, crisscrosses the island, but we'll let you in on a secret. When you see a signpost marked Tåsinge, take it to the northeastern sector of the island. Once here, you'll find the "skipper town" of **Troense ★★**, one of the best preserved and most idyllic villages in all of Denmark. Many half-timbered houses still stand on **Badstuen** and **Gronnegade ★**, the latter declared by many makers of landscape calendars as "the prettiest street in Denmark." While exploring Troense, you can dart in for a quick look at the town's maritime museum, **Sofartssamlingerne I Troense,** Strandgade 1 (✆ **62-22-52-32**), and then visit nearby **Valdemars Slot** (see below).

The island was the setting for a famous tragic love story depicted in the 1967 film *Elvira Madigan.* After checking out of a hotel in Svendborg, Danish artist Elvira Madigan and her lover, Sixten Sparre, a Swedish lieutenant, crossed by ferry to Tåsinge, where together they committed suicide. The Romeo and Juliet of Denmark were buried in the Landet Kirkegård, Elvira Madigansvej, at Landet, in the middle of Tåsinge, where many brides, even today, throw their wedding bouquets on their graves.

The island is best explored by car—follow Route 9 and drive over the causeway—or you could take local bus no. 200, 211, or 212. You can also take the vintage steamer MS *Helge* (✆ **62-23-30-85** for information; www.mshelge.dk), which departs several times daily from the harbor at Svendborg. The steamer operates from May 13 to September 12. A one-way ticket costs 60DKK; a round-trip, 120DKK. Tickets are sold onboard.

SEEING THE SIGHTS

Valdemars Slot ★★ ☺ Although not quite as stellar an attraction as Egeskov (p. 156), this palace is our second favorite on Funen, and it looms large in history, having been given to naval hero Niels Juel for his third victory over the Swedes in 1678. The castle was built between 1639 and 1644 by Christian IV for his son, Valdemar, in a romantic style, and it is still occupied today by a charming, handsome couple, Caroline and Rory Fleming, who welcome guests (some groups) to stay overnight.

You can eat here after enjoying one of four museums, including a big-game trophy room, a toy museum, and a yachting museum. Children take special delight in the toy museum, whose collection covers the past 125 years. Along with several thousand toys, there are books, comics, and model cars. By far the most intriguing are the room interiors themselves, filled with artifacts and antiques. Guests today treat the property better than the Swedish soldiers who once occupied it, sending the copper roof back home to Sweden to make bullets and stabling their horses in the church.

Valdemars Castle Church, in the south wing, was consecrated in 1687 and has been used for worship ever since. Two stories high, it's overarched by three star vaults and illuminated by Gothic windows.

Slotsalléen 100, Troense. ✆ **62-22-61-06.** www.valdemarsslot.dk. Admission 80DKK adults, 40DKK children 4–12, free for children 3 and under. Apr–June and Aug daily 10am–5pm; July daily 10am–6pm; Sept Tues–Sun 10am–5pm; Oct 1–19 Sat–Sun 10am–5pm. Take the MS *Helge* from Svendborg Harbor. By car, from Troense, follow Slotsalléen to the castle.

WHERE TO DINE

Restaurant Slotskælderen DANISH/FRENCH In a wing of the main attraction of Tåsinge, Valdemars Slot, you can dine either like royalty or else more democratically at a bistro. Inside the thick stone walls of one of the region's most foreboding castles, this restaurant is divided into an unpretentious Danish bistro and an upscale French restaurant. The bistro serves such down-home dishes as schnitzels, *lobscouse* (hash), and roulades of beef with Danish beer and *akvavit.* The views over the tidal flats and sea are better from the restaurant, but most visitors prefer the informality and lower prices of the bistro. For more elegant dining, with formal place settings, you can enjoy haute cuisine like that served in the best of Paris's luxe restaurants, feasting on venison in the autumn, a delicate foie gras, a velvety lobster bisque, and only the choicest cuts of tender beef.

In Valdemars Slot, Slotsalléen 100, Troense. © **62-22-59-00.** www.valdemarsslot.dk. Main courses 80DKK–168DKK. MC, V. Thurs–Sun 11:30am–5pm. Closed Nov–Mar.

Nearby at Millinge

Falsled Kro ★★★ The epitome of a Danish roadside inn, this former 15th-century smugglers' inn has been converted into a premier Relais & Châteaux, the finest hotel in Funen, west of Faaborg on Route 329, just 40km (24 miles) from Odense and 42km (25 miles) from Svendborg. Perhaps our most delightful memory of a stay here is when the owner allowed mushroom gatherers with their baskets to come onto the property and pick wild mushrooms, including cèpes, horns of plenty, chanterelles—some with an apricot aroma—and field mushrooms tasting of aniseed. The most delectable of all morels are available as early as April.

The *kro* (inn) offers tradition and quality in its colony of beautifully furnished thatched buildings clustered around a cobblestone courtyard with a fountain. The spacious rooms are often furnished with antiques, and some of the units are in converted outbuildings or cottages across the road. Regardless of your room assignment, expect the comfort to be equal.

Assensvej 513, Falsled, DK-5642 Millinge. www.falsledkro.dk. © **62-68-11-11.** Fax 62-68-11-62. 20 units. 1,775DKK–2,975DKK double; 3,175DKK suite. AE, DC, MC, V. Bus: 935. **Amenities:** Restaurant; bar; babysitting; bikes; room service; Wi-Fi (free, in lobby). *In room:* TV, hair dryer, minibar.

Across the Water to Ærø ★★★

29km (18 miles) S of Svendborg, 74km (46 miles) S of Odense, 177km (110 miles) SW of Copenhagen

If this small Danish island, off the southern coast of Funen, didn't exist, Hans Christian Andersen would have invented it. Its capital, Ærøskøbing, is a Lilliputian souvenir of the past and is awash in a rainbow of colors.

Many of Denmark's offshore islands are dull and flat with red-brick market towns best passed through hurriedly. But Ærø is a place at which you'll want to linger, wandering its sleepy one-lane roads, walking the cobblestone streets of its hamlets, or merely spending a day at the beach. The best sands are along the northern and eastern coastlines, and chances are, even in July, you'll end up with a strip of sand all to yourself.

The place is small so it's easy to get around—30km (8 miles) long and 8km (5 miles) at its widest point. The number of wind-swept "souls" is also small, no more than 7,000 hearty islanders, with less than a thousand in the capital of Ærøskøbing.

There are only three towns that could even be called that. If time is fleeting, explore only **Ærøskøbing,** the best-preserved town of 18th-century Denmark. The largest town is the ancient seaport of **Marstal,** where mariners once set out to conquer the Seven Seas. Though its maritime glory is a distant memory, there's still a bustling marina and a shipyard that makes wooden vessels as they did in Viking days. Yachts sail into **Søby,** the third town with a still active shipyard and a sizable fishing fleet.

Small fishing harbors, wheat fields, storybook hamlets of half-timbered houses, a dilapidated church or two from the Middle Ages, beer gardens, old windmills, and yacht-filled marinas make Ærø the kind of island you search for—but rarely find—in all of Scandinavia. Sure, Ærø is all cliché charm, but a cliché wouldn't be that unless it existed once upon a time.

ESSENTIALS

GETTING THERE The only way to reach Ærø is by **ferry;** car ferries depart Svendborg six times daily (trip time: 1 hr.). For a schedule, contact the tourist office or the ferry office at the harbor in Svendborg. Bookings are made through **Ærøfærgerne** in Ærøskøbing (✆ **62-21-09-80;** www.aeroe-ferry.com). An average car can be transported for 392DKK round-trip, a passenger paying 179DKK round-trip.

GETTING AROUND It's best to take a car on the ferry since there's limited **bus service** on Ærø (✆ **62-53-10-10** in Ærøskøbing for bus information). The tourist office (see below) provides bus schedules, which change seasonally. Tickets are 70DKK for the day and can be bought on the bus.

If you'd like to take a bus tour of the island, call **Jesper "Bus" Jensen** (✆ **62-58-13-13**). His bus holds 12 to 14 passengers, costing 500DKK for a 3-hour minimum.

VISITOR INFORMATION The **Ærøskøbing Turistbureau,** Ærøskøbing Havn 4 (✆ **62-52-13-00**), is open June 15 through August, Monday to Friday 10am to 3:30pm, Saturday 10am to 3pm; September to June 14, Monday to Friday 9am to 4pm.

CYCLING AROUND THE ISLAND

Ærø is one of the best islands in Denmark for cycling because of its low-lying terrain and scenic paths. Local tourist offices provide maps outlining routes for 30DKK, and you can use these maps for bike rides but also for walks. Numbers 90, 91, and 92 mark cycle trails around the coast. Bike rentals cost 70DKK a day, and rentals in Ærøskøbing are available at **Nørremark Cykelforretning,** Møllevejen 77 (✆ **62-53-14-77**); and at **Søby Cykelforretning,** Langebro 4A (✆ **65-58-14-60**). Another place to rent a bike is **Pilebækkens Cykler,** Pilebækken 11 (✆ **62-52-11-10**).

The road continues west to Tranderup, where you can visit **Tranderup Kirke,** a Romanesque building with Gothic vaulting. Inside, the large carved figure depicting Mary and the infant Jesus dates from around the 14th century and is one of the oldest ecclesiastical pieces on the island. The triptych is from around 1510, and the large mural over the chancel arch reveals the date of its execution in 1518. Originally, the spires of Tranderup resembled those of Bregninge (see below), but they were rebuilt in a neoclassical style in 1832; the largest bell was cast in 1566 and is still in use.

After a visit, follow the signs west to the village of **Vodrup,** which was founded in the 13th century and is mentioned for the first time in 1537 as "Wuderup." The village disappeared in the 17th century when the land became part of Vodrup Estate. When the estate was dissolved, the village came back.

The cliffs at Vodrup, **Vodrup Klint ★★**, have an unusual geology: Large blocks of land have slipped down and resemble huge steps. The soil lies on top of a layer of gray clay, which can be seen at the base of the cliffs by the beach. The layer of clay is full of snail and cockle shells, left here by the sea. Water seeping down through the earth is stopped by the clay. When the clay absorbs enough water, it becomes so "movable" that it acts as a sliding plane for the layers above. The last great landslide here occurred in 1834.

Vodrup Klint is one of the most southerly points in Denmark, attracting creatures such as lizards and many species of plants—the carline thistle grows on these cliffs, blooming from July to September. An unusual characteristic of the cliffs is a proliferation of springs, where water bubbles out by the foot of the slopes. When the cattle need water, farmers need only push a pipe into the cliff face and let the water collect in a pool.

Fyn County has bought the cliffs, roughly 35 hectares (86 acres), and set them aside for public use. Animals are allowed to graze the fields in the summer months, and you can walk on all areas of the land. Cycle trail 91 runs right past Vodrup Klint, so it's often a stopover for bikers.

The route continues west to Bregninge and **Bregninge Kirke,** a 13th-century building with grandiose vaults that were added during the late 15th century. Its impressive spire shows the influence of east Schleswig (Germany) building traditions and is roofed with oak tiles. The murals inside date from around 1510—one, for example, depicts the Passion of Christ, another, the life of John the Baptist. The magnificent **triptych** ★ dates from shortly before the Reformation and was made by the German sculptor Claus Berg. The crucifix in the nave is from the latter Middle Ages, and the 1612 pulpit was executed in the Renaissance style.

After visiting the southern part of Ærø, you can continue northwest into Søby.

EXPLORING THE ISLAND

The neat little village of **Ærøskøbing** ★★ was a 13th-century market town that came to be known as a skippers' town in the 17th century. Called "a Lilliputian souvenir of the past," few Scandinavian towns have retained their heritage as much as Ærøskøbing. In the heyday of the windjammer, nearly 100 commercial sailing ships made this their home port.

The ferry from Fåborg docks at **Søby,** in the northwest part of the island. Before you rush to Ærøskøbing, visit a mellow manorial property, **Søbygård.** Now in ruins, this manor house in the center of Søby is complete with a moat and dank dungeons.

Marstal, a thriving little port on the east coast of Ærø, has had a reputation in sailors' circles since the days of the tall ships. The harbor, protected by a granite jetty, is still busy. It has a shipyard that produces steel and wooden vessels, an engine factory, a ferry terminal, and one of Denmark's biggest yacht basins. The street names attest to Marstal's seafaring background—Skonnertvej, Barkvej, and Galeasevej (Schooner, Bark, and Ketch roads); Danish naval heroes such as Rasmus Minor and Christen Hansen; and Seven Ferry Lanes.

Visit the **seamen's church,** with the spire and illuminated clock, in the town center. Inside are ship models and an altarpiece that depicts Christ stilling the tempest at sea.

Twice a day, a mail boat takes a limited number of passengers on a 45-minute trip to tiny **Birkholm Island** for swimming and exploration. There are no cars on Birkholm. Reservations on the mail boat can be made at the Marstal Tourist Office.

SEEING THE SIGHTS

Ærø Museum This is the best local museum, found at the corner of Nørregade and Brogade. In the old days it was inhabited by the bailiff, but today you'll find a rich exhibit of the island's past. The collection includes antiques and paintings from the mid-1800s.

Brogade 35 (at the corner of Nørregade). ✆ **62-52-29-50.** www.arremus.dk. Admission 30DKK. Oct 18–Apr 18 daily 11am–3pm; Apr 19–Oct 17 Mon–Fri 10am–4pm, Sat–Sun 11am–3pm.

Ærøskøbing Kirke This church was built between 1756 and 1758 as a replacement for a rather dilapidated church from the Middle Ages. In its present state, the

13th-century font and the pulpit stem from the original structure, and were donated by Duke Philip of Lyksborg in 1634, the year he bought Gråsten County on the island of Ærø. The altarpiece is a copy of Eckersberg's picture, which hangs in Vor Frue Kirke in Svendborg. The colors selected for the interior of the church, along with the floral motifs, were the creation of Elinar V. Jensen in connection with an extensive restoration project carried out in 1950.

Søndergade 43. ✆ **62-52-11-72.** Free admission. Daily 8am–5pm.

Flaske-Peters Samling This museum commemorates the seafaring life documented by Peter Jacobsen's ships in bottles. Upon his death in 1960 at the age of 84, this former cook, nicknamed "Bottle Peter," had crafted more than 1,600 bottled ships and some 150 model sailing vessels built to scale, earning him the reputation in Ærøskøbing of "the ancient mariner." The museum also has Ærø clocks, furniture, china, and carved works by sculptor H. C. Petersen.

Smedegade 22. ✆ **62-52-29-51.** www.arremus.dk. Admission 30DKK adults, free 17 and under. Summer daily 10am–5pm; off-season Tues–Fri 1–3pm, Sat 10am–noon.

WHERE TO STAY

In Ærøskøbing

Hotel Ærøhus ★ Cozy intimacy and nostalgia are combined at this classic Danish inn, with many traditional features from its past, such as copper kettles hanging from the ceiling and warm lamps glowing, but it has modern amenities as well. We like to hang out here on a summer evening at the barbecue grill that glows long after everyone has been fed. An old-fashioned lounge, a typical Danish courtyard, and a luxuriant garden are part of the allures of this place.

The midsize-to-spacious bedrooms are traditionally furnished in a vaguely French boudoir style for the most part. Offering live music on most summer weekends, the inn lies a 3-minute walk from the harbor.

Vestergade 38, DK-5970 Ærøskøbing. www.aeroehus.dk. ✆ **62-52-10-03.** Fax 63-52-31-68. 30 units, 18 with bathroom. 800DKK double without bathroom; 1,250DKK double with bathroom. Rates include buffet breakfast. MC, V. Free parking. **Amenities:** Restaurant; bar; bikes. *In room:* TV, hair dryer.

Pension Vestergade 44 ★ One of the most historically appealing buildings of Ærøskøbing is in the center of the village, 180m (591 ft.) from the ferryboat piers, within an antique (ca. 1784) half-timbered structure that the Danish historical authority considers almost sacrosanct. This allegiance to maintaining the building in its pristine original condition has restricted its owner, English-born Susanna Greve, from adding private bathrooms to its venerable interior. This enormous apricot-colored building was built by a local sea captain for his two daughters, and it's divided into two almost exactly equal halves. Only half of the house is occupied by this B&B. Within Susanna's half, you'll find scads of Danish and English antiques. The inn maintains five bathrooms, each opening onto corridors and public areas, for six accommodations, more than most other B&Bs in Denmark, so most visitors find the bathroom situation acceptable.

Vestergade 44, DK-5970 Ærøskøbing. www.pension-vestergade44.dk. ✆ **62-52-22-98.** 6 rooms, none with private bathroom. 780DKK–980DKK double. Rates include continental breakfast. No credit cards. *In room:* No phone, Wi-Fi (free).

In Marstal

Hotel Ærø Strand ★ Surrounded by sea grass and sweeping vistas of the water, this first-class hotel is the largest and most up-to-date on the island, even though it opened back in 1989. It is a 5-minute walk from the center and less than half a kilometer (¼ mile) from the beach. The hotel is about the only place on Ærø that could be called a holiday resort, offering midsize-to-spacious bedrooms, each decorated in Danish modern set against pastel-colored walls, and each containing a sleek tiled bathroom. The suites are twice the size of the regular rooms and worth the extra money if you can afford it.

Egehovedvej 4, DK-5960 Marstal. www.hotel-aeroestrand.dk. ✆ **62-53-33-20.** Fax 62-53-31-50. 100 units. 945DKK–1,790DKK double; 2,390DKK suite. Rates include buffet breakfast. DC, MC, V. Free parking. Closed Dec 20–Jan 2. Bus: 790 to Marstal. **Amenities:** Restaurant; bar; bikes; Jacuzzi; indoor heated pool; sauna; outdoor tennis court; Wi-Fi (free, in lobby). *In room:* TV.

BORNHOLM ★★

153km (95 miles) E of Copenhagen

Surrounded by the Baltic Sea, in the important shipping lanes that connect St. Petersburg with Copenhagen and the Atlantic, Bornholm is only 37km (23 miles) off the coast of Sweden, and about 153km (95 miles) east of Copenhagen and the rest of Denmark. Prized as a strategic Baltic military and trading outpost since the early Middle Ages (but sadly the site of many bloody territorial disputes among the Danes, Germans, and Swedes), Bornholm is home to 45,000 year-round residents. An additional 450,000 visitors arrive during the balmy months of summer. Besides tourism, which is growing rapidly, the economy relies on trade, fishing, herring processing, agriculture, and the manufacture of ceramics, which, thanks to the island's deep veins of clay, has been a major industry since the 1700s.

Covering a terrain of granite and sandstone is a thin but rich layer of topsoil; the island's rock-studded surface is made up of forests and moors. The unusual topography and surprisingly temperate autumn climate—a function of the waters of the Baltic—promotes the verdant growth of plants: figs, mulberries, and enough lavish conifers to create the third-largest forest in Denmark (right in the center of the island). In addition, one of Denmark's largest waterfalls, Døndalen, is in the north of Bornholm in a rift valley and is best viewed from spring through fall.

Bornholmers' villages are still idyllic, evocative of the old way of life in their well-kept homesteads, as are fishing hamlets with their characteristic smokehouse chimneys, often used for smoking herring. Most hurried visitors bypass this Baltic island where Danish families who can't afford a Mediterranean holiday go to romp on the sandy beaches in summer. We like to skip the overcrowded summers altogether and visit either in the late spring or early fall, when Bornholm appears at its most dramatic seasonal change. The best beaches of Bornholm lie in the southwestern section of the island, between the towns of Balka and the main beach town of Dueodde.

Because of its location at the crossroads of warring nations, Bornholm has had a turbulent history, even as recently as 1945. Strongholds and fortified churches protected local inhabitants when the island was a virtual plaything in the power struggle between royal and religious forces. It was plundered by pirate fleets, noblemen, and the Hanseatic towns of Pomerania. It didn't experience peace until after it revolted against Swedish conquerors at the end of Denmark's war with Sweden in 1658. A group of liberators shot the island's Swedish Lord, and the Bornholmers handed their land over to the king of Denmark.

The liberation of Bornholm—unlike the rest of Denmark—was slow to come in 1945. Even when the Nazis had surrendered, the local German commandant on

Bornholm refused to give up the island to the Allies. In response, the Soviets rained bombs down on Rønne and Nexø (the two main towns), and then invaded the island and occupied it for several months before returning it to the crown of Denmark. During the long Cold War, Bornholm became one of NATO's key surveillance bases.

The island's cuisine is obviously influenced by the surrounding sea. Baltic herring, cod, and salmon are the traditional dishes. One of the most popular local dishes is called *Sun over Gudhjem,* a specialty of smoked herring topped with a raw egg yolk in an onion ring. It's served with coarse salt and chives, or, most often, radishes. In autumn, the small Bornholm herring are caught and used for a variety of spiced and pickled dishes. Another local dish is salt-fried herring served on dark rye bread with beetroot and hot mustard.

Essentials

GETTING THERE

BY FERRY There are no ferries from Copenhagen to Bornholm. You can get a night ferry from Køge (45km/28 miles south of Copenhagen) to Bornholm. Run by Bornholmstraffiken (✆ **56-95-18-66;** www.bornholmstrafikken.dk), these ferries depart year-round from the pier at Baltic Kaj. Passage costs 263DKK per person each way (fare includes the cost of a private cabin). The fare for transporting a car, up to five passengers, is 1,512DKK each way. Ferries depart year-round from Køge at 11:30pm, with scheduled arrival the following morning at 6am.

Bornholmstraffiken (✆ **56-95-18-66;** www.bornholmstraffiken.dk), operates 2½-hour ferries from Ystad on the southern coast of Sweden, with up to four departures daily. A car with a maximum of five passengers costs 1,038DKK each way. You can also travel from Sassnitz-Mukran (Rügen) in north Germany for a 3½-hour crossing to Bornholm, arriving at Rønne. From Germany, one-way passage for a car with a maximum of five passengers is 783DKK. Each of these ferries has a restaurant or bistro featuring a buffet with Danish and Bornholm specialties.

BY PLANE **Cimber Sterling** (✆ **70-10-12-18;** www.cimber.com) has about nine flights a day from Copenhagen to Bornholm's airport, 5.5km (3½ miles) south of Rønne. Depending on restrictions, round-trip fares range from 567DKK to 2,500DKK.

GETTING AROUND

BY CAR The best place on the island for car rentals is **Europcar,** Nodre Kystvej 1 in Rønne (✆ **877/940-6900** in the U.S., or 56-95-43-00). Its least expensive rentals begin at 3,440DKK per week, including unlimited mileage and insurance coverage, as well as the government tax. In addition, **Avis** is at Dampskibskajen 3–5, in Rønne (✆ **800/230-4898** in the U.S., or 56-95-48-99).

BY BICYCLE During sunny weather, biking around the island is almost as popular as driving. If you want to do as the Danes do, rent a bike; the prices are pretty much the same throughout the island—about 70DKK a day. A suggested bike-rental company in Rønne is **Bornholms Cykleudleijning,** Nordre Kystvej 5 (✆ **56-95-13-59;** www.bornholms-cykeludlejning.dk). Open from May 1 to September 15 daily 8am to 6pm. It is closed the rest of the year.

VISITOR INFORMATION

The tourist office, the **Bornholm Welcome Center,** Nordre Kystvej 3, Rønne (✆ **56-95-95-00;** www.bornholm.info), is open June to August daily 10am to 5:30pm; April, May, September, and October Monday to Friday 9am to 4pm, Saturday 10am to 1pm; November to March Monday to Friday 9am to 4pm.

Exploring the Island

Even if you have a car available, you might want to take a bike tour. Ask at any tourist office for a map of the island's more than 190km (120 miles) of bicycle trails and divide this tour into several days, hitting the highlights mentioned below at your own pace.

The tour begins at Rønne, but you could join in at almost any point; basically, the route goes counterclockwise around the island's periphery. Be aware that Bornholm's highways do not have route numbers; even though some maps show the main east-west artery as Route 38, local residents call it "the road to Nexø."

RØNNE

Your arrival point is Rønne, the capital of the island, but there are far more rewarding targets away from the main town, which lies on the western coast facing the island of Zealand and is the site of the major harbor and airport.

But, once here, you'll find Rønne has a certain charm as you walk its historic Gamle Stan, or Old Town, with its cobblestone streets flanked by cross-timbered houses, many of them brightly painted in colors such as yellow and orange.

The best streets for seeing Bornholm as it used to be are **Laksegade** and **Storegade,** plus the triangular sector lying between **Store Torv** and **Lille Torv.** You'll find even more charm in many of the island's smaller towns or hamlets.

Because of Soviet aerial attacks in 1945, most of Rønne was left in shambles, so what you see today is essentially a modern town with a population of some 15,000. The parents of today's inhabitants rebuilt Rønne wisely in the postwar years, opting for an old-fashioned architectural look, which makes most of the houses look older than they actually are.

If you arrive by ferry, you'll notice **St. Nicolai Church,** dedicated to the patron saint of seafarers, on Harbour Hill, towering over the small South Boat Harbor just below. It wasn't until the 18th century that locals moved ahead with plans for a large trading harbor here, and even today the harbor is expanding to service ferries and the many cruise ships that call at Rønne in increasing numbers.

Should you experience a rare hot day in Denmark, you'll find that vast stretches of sand lie both south and north of Rønne. These beaches are popular with Danish families, many from Copenhagen, in summer.

Seeing the Sights

Bornholms Museum (Museum of Bornholm) ★ To open this museum, islanders raided their attics for any curiosities that might be of interest to the general public and came up with a number of objects, ranging from antique toys from the 19th century to gold objects discovered by farmers who were plowing their fields. Installed in what used to be the major hospital on the island, the museum traces the history of Bornholm's unique position in the Baltic through displays on archaeology, folkloric costumes, ethnology, and seafaring and agrarian traditions. Several rooms are outfitted with 19th-century antique furniture, island-made silverware, and accessories. Of special interest is the collection of Bornholm-made clocks, copied from a shipment of English clocks that was salvaged from a Dutch shipwreck in the late 1700s. Since Bornholm is known for its ceramics and glassware, it's no surprise that there are nearly 5,000 pieces of glassware and handcrafted ceramics.

Skt. Mortensgade 29. ✆ **56-95-07-35.** www.bornholmsmuseum.dk. Admission 50DKK, free for children 17 and under. Mid-May to mid-Oct Mon–Sat 10am–5pm; mid-Oct to mid-May Mon–Sat 1–4pm.

Forsvarsmuseet (Armed Forces Museum) Today this museum attracts World War II buffs, but originally the citadel was built in 1650 for defensive purposes in the southern part of town. With its massive round tower, this old castle is like an armed fortress, with guns, blades, weapons, war maps, and models of fortification. There are even military uniforms of the men who fought each other, plus a rare collection of antique armaments. By far the most intriguing exhibitions depict the Nazi occupation of the island from 1940 to 1945.

Arsenalvej 8. ✆ **56-95-65-83.** www.bornholmsmuseer.dk. Admission 50DKK adults, 30DKK children 4-16, free for children 3 and under. June–Oct Tues–Sun 10am–4pm.

Hjorth's Fabrik (Bornholm Ceramic Museum) ★ Bornholm has long been famed for its beautiful ceramics, and this working ceramics museum showcases the craft better than any other place on the island. In 1858, a small-scale factory, Hjorth's Ceramics, was established to make pottery from the island's rich deposits of clay, surviving until 1993. In 1995, this museum was established in the company's original factory. Inside, you'll find an intriguing hybrid between an art gallery and an industrial museum. You'll see the island's best examples of the dark-brown, yellow, and gray pottery that was produced in abundance beginning in the 1700s; samples of the dishes and bowls made by the Hjorth company over the years; and some of the work of Bornholm's modern-day potters. Throughout the year several ceramic artists maintain studios inside, casting, spinning, or glazing pots in full view of visitors. The museum shop sells modern-day replicas of Hjorth ceramics, and many exhibits trace the production process from start to finish.

Krystalgade 5. ✆ **56-95-01-60.** www.bornholmsmuseer.dk. Admission 50DKK adults, free ages 17 and under. May–Oct Mon–Sat 10am–5pm; Nov–Apr Mon–Fri 1-5pm, Sat 10am–1pm.

Where to Stay

Hotel Griffen ★ ☺ This hotel is the largest on Bornholm, and though it falls a few notches below the Radisson Hotel Fredensborg (see below), it's one of the most inviting. When you check in here, the helpful staff will likely offer to help you rent a bike (the island trail starts right in front of the hotel) and pack a picnic lunch for the trip. Though it was constructed in the dull architectural era of the 1970s, the hotel's buildings have a certain style, designed to evoke 18th-century hip-roofed manor houses. Two of the four buildings contain the bedrooms, which are separated from the dining, drinking, and convention facilities in the other structures. The small-to-midsize bedrooms are furnished in a modern but minimalist style, each comfortable and tasteful.

Ndr. Kystvej 34, DK-3700 Rønne. www.hotelgriffen.dk. ✆ **56-90-42-44.** Fax 56-90-42-45. 140 units. 790DKK–1,245DKK double; from 1,550DKK suite. Rates include buffet breakfast. AE, DC, MC, V. **Amenities:** Restaurant; bar; bikes; Jacuzzi; indoor heated pool; room service; sauna; Wi-Fi (free, in lobby). *In room:* TV, hair dryer.

Radisson Hotel Fredensborg ★★ ☺ There are hotels on Bornholm with more atmosphere and charm, but this chain hotel is clearly the market leader for international luxury. However, what passes for luxe living on Bornholm wouldn't make the grade in Copenhagen. One of the few hotels on island to remain open all year, Fredensborg lies in a wooded, tranquil location adjacent to a beach and less than a kilometer (about ½ mile) south of Rønne harbor. Its Danish modern style from the 1960s wouldn't win architectural awards, but its midsize-to-spacious bedrooms are the island's best appointed, each comfortable and tasteful with a private balcony or terrace overlooking the Baltic.

Strandvejen 116, DK-3700 Rønne. www.bornholmhotels.dk. ✆ **800/333-3333** in the U.S., or 56-90-44-44. Fax 56-90-44-43. 72 units. 1,275DKK–1,475DKK double; 1,550DKK–1,750DKK suite. Rates include buffet breakfast. AE, DC, MC, V. **Amenities:** Restaurant; bar; babysitting; room service; sauna; outdoor tennis court (lit). *In room:* TV, hair dryer, minibar, Wi-Fi (free).

Where to Dine

Di 5 Stâuerna ★★ DANISH/FRENCH/INTERNATIONAL This is the best and most upscale restaurant on island, with a clientele that tends to select it for celebratory meals and family gatherings. Its name translates as "the five rooms," each of which is outfitted in a Danish country style. There's always a platter of the fish of the day, which is usually fried in butter and served with new potatoes—a style that Bornholmers have enjoyed since their childhood. Other more elaborate options include Hereford beefsteak prepared *cordon bleu*–style, with salted cured ham and Emmenthaler cheese; *tournedos* of beef flambéed in Calvados and served with apples and onions; and our favorite: Bornholm lamb served with a sauce concocted from rosemary, olive oil, and tarragon.

In the Radisson Hotel Fredensborg, Strandvejen 116. ✆ **56-90-44-44.** www.bornholmhotels.dk. Reservations recommended. Main courses 220DKK–265DKK; 4-course fixed-price menu 405DKK. AE, DC, MC, V. Daily 11am–9:30pm.

Rådhuskroen ★ 🎁 DANISH This is the most visible and, in its own way, most charming restaurant in Rønne, although it doesn't use the pricey ingredients or employ the expensive chefs hired by the previously recommended Di 5 Stâuerna. It's in the cellar of the Town Hall, a 140-year-old building with a long history of feeding island residents—and feeding them well. Wall sconces cast romantic shadows over a collection of antique furniture and accessories, and a well-trained service staff serves fresh and well-prepared dishes such as filet of salmon in a "summer sauce" of fresh tomatoes, chives, and herbs, and two sizes of tender and well-prepared beefsteak.

Nørregade 2. ✆ **56-95-00-69.** www.hansens-beufhus.dk. Reservations recommended on weekends. Main courses 168DKK–330DKK. AE, DC, MC, V. Mon–Sat noon–3pm and 5–9pm.

FROM RØNNE TO NEXØ

From Rønne, drive east along the island's modern highway, A-38, following the signs toward Nexø. Stop in **Nylars** (about 5km/3 miles from Rønne), a town that's known as the site of the best-preserved of Bornholm's four round churches. The **Nylarskirke** (✆ **56-97-20-13;** www.nylarskirke.dk), built around 1250 and rising prominently from the center of a community with no more than about 50 buildings, contains frescoes that depict the Creation and the expulsion of Adam and Eve from the Garden of Eden. The cylindrical nave has three floors, the uppermost of which was a watchman's tower in the Middle Ages. You can also view two fragments of a runic stone. From Rønne, you can take bus no. 6 if you don't have a car; the bike path from Rønne to Åkirkeby also passes by the church. Admission is free. Open May to October 20, Monday to Friday 9am to 5pm.

Continue driving another 5km (3 miles) east until you reach **Åkirkeby,** the only inland settlement of any size and Bornholm's oldest (the town charter dates from 1346). The little town was important in medieval times when islanders had to move inland to avoid attacks from enemies at sea.

Åkirkeby is also home to the island's oldest and largest church, **Åkirke,** Torvet (✆ **56-97-41-03**), originally built around 1250. This church isn't as eccentric as some of the others. It's a sandstone-fronted monument built with defense in mind, as you'll note from the small windows. Inside, a Romanesque baptismal font is incised with runic inscriptions believed to be carved by the master craftsman Sigraf on the island of Gotland. Other runic inscriptions appear on the cloverleaf-shaped arches. The church is open daily 10am to 4pm, charging 10DKK for visitors.

Åkirkeby is a good point to cut inland if you wish to see some of Bornholm's woodlands, among the densest in Denmark, with forests filled with oak, hemlock, fir, spruce, and beech trees. The tourist office in Rønne (see "Visitor Information," above) will give you a map outlining the best of the trails that cut through Bornholm's largest forest, **Almindingen,** in the center of the island. It can be reached by following a marked road north from Åkirkeby. The forest is also the location of the island's highest point, **Rytterknægten,** a 160m (525-ft.) hill with a lookout tower, Kongemindet, with a staircase you can climb for a panoramic view of the dense woodlands.

You can also pick up information at a minor, rarely used tourist office that's much less visible than the island's main office in Rønne. It's the **Sydbornholms Turistbureau,** Torvet 30 (© **56-97-37-20**), at Åkirkeby. The opening hours of the tourist office are mid-May to mid-August Monday to Friday 9am to 5pm, Saturday 9am to 1pm; from mid-August to mid-May Monday to Friday 10am to 12:30pm and 1:30 to 4pm.

A minor museum for devoted automobile fans is the **Bornholms Automobilmuseum,** Grammegardsvej 1 (© **56-97-45-95;** www.bornholmsautomobilmuseum.dk), displaying vintage cars and motorcycles, plus some farm equipment and tractors that highlight the 20th century's advances in agrarian science. Antique cars and tractors derive from such manufacturers as Delahaye, Opel, Ford, Adler, Singer, Jaguar, and Fiat. It's open May to October, Monday to Saturday 10am to 5pm. The rest of the year it's closed, and admission costs 50DKK per person.

From Åkirkeby, cut southeast for 4.5km (2¾ miles), following the signs to **Pedersker,** a hamlet with only three shops (which close down during the cold-weather months). Six kilometers (4 miles) later you'll reach **Dueodde,** the name of both a raffish beachfront community and the entire region around the southernmost tip of the island. The village of Dueodde marks the southern edge of a stretch of coastline that is the finest beach on the island. The oceanfront bounty—and the best beaches on the island—stretch northward and eastward to the town of **Balka,** 5km (3 miles) beyond, encompassing stretches of white sand whose grains are so fine that they were used for generations to fill hourglasses. The towns are little more than backdrops for seasonal kiosks and a scattering of holiday homes for mainland Danes and Swedes. Most of the landscape is a virtual wilderness of pine and spruce trees, salt-tolerant shrubs, and sand dunes, some of which rise more than 12m (39 ft.) above the nearby sea.

The focal point of this southeastern coastline is the **Dueodde Fyr (Dueodde Lighthouse),** the tallest lighthouse on the island, built in 1962 to warn ships away from the extreme southern tip of the island. Weather permitting, you can climb to its top during daylight hours May to October for a fee of 5DKK, which you pay directly to the lighthouse keeper. For information, call the tourist office in Dueodde (© **56-49-70-79**).

From Dueodde, continue along the coast in a northeasterly direction, passing through the unpretentious fishing hamlets of **Snogebæk** and **Balka.** Immediately north of Balka the road will deliver you north to Nexø, the second major town of the island after Rønne, opening onto the eastern coast facing Sweden.

Where to Stay & Dine

Hotel Balka Strand This is the only hotel along Bornholm's beach-fringed eastern coast that remains open year-round, so it stays busy even in midwinter, usually with conferences. Originally built in the 1970s and doubled in size in 1992, the hotel's exterior could easily fit into any number of towns in America's heartland. There's nothing particularly Bornholmian about it; rather it's imbued with a more international aura. The building is laid out in a one-story format about 150m (490 ft.) from one of the island's best bathing beaches adjoining a protected nature preserve ideal for walks or hikes. The neatly kept midsize bedrooms are comfortably and tastefully furnished in Danish modern.

Boulevarden 9, DK-3730 Nexø. www.hotelbalkastrand.dk. ✆ **56-49-49-49.** Fax 56-49-49-48. 95 units, half with kitchenettes. 895DKK–1,495DKK double. Rates include buffet breakfast. MC, V. From Nexø, drive 2.5km (1½ miles) south along the coastal road, following the signs to Balka and Dueodde. **Amenities:** Restaurant; bar; bikes; children's playground; outdoor heated pool; room service; sauna. *In room:* TV, hair dryer, Wi-Fi (free).

FROM NEXØ TO GUDHJEM

Nexø, with a year-round population of 3,900, is the island's largest fishing port. It's home to excellent replicas of the privately owned 17th- and 18th-century buildings that were considered architectural highlights of the island before World War II. In May 1945, several days after the rest of Denmark had been liberated from the Nazis, the Russians bombed Nexø heavily for 2 days. It had been a final holdout of Nazi soldiers during the closing days of the war. (Bornholm was also the last area of Denmark to get rid of its Soviet "liberators," who didn't completely evacuate until 1946.)

One of the town's more eccentric monuments is the **Nexø Museum,** Havnen (✆ **56-49-25-56;** www.nexoemuseum.dk), open daily May to October 10am to 4pm. For an entrance fee of 40DKK, you'll see displays of fishing-related equipment that has sustained the local economy, and memorabilia of the Danish author Martin Andersen (1869–1954)—better known as Martin Andersen Nexø, a pen name he adopted in honor of his native village. His novel *Pelle the Conqueror,* set in Bornholm and later made into an Oscar-winning film, revealed how Danish landowners in the early 20th century exploited Swedish newcomers to the island. Admittedly, this is hardly a subject that interests most people, and you may want to pass it by in favor of outdoor fun, which is what Bornholm is all about.

Continue 5.5km (3½ miles) north along the coastal road, following the signs to **Svaneke.** Denmark's easternmost settlement has fewer than 1,200 year-round residents. It bears some resemblance to eastern regions of the Baltic with which it has traded, and it has many 17th- and 18th-century cottages along cobblestone streets leading to the harbor. Many writers, sculptors, and painters buy homes in Svaneke, an idyllic retreat from the urban life of Copenhagen. Svaneke is the most photogenic town on Bornholm; in 1975 it won the European Gold Medal for town preservation.

From Svaneke, leave the Baltic coastline and head inland through the northern outskirts of the third-largest forest in Denmark, the **Almindingen.** Dotted with creeks and ponds, and covered mostly with hardy conifers, it's known for its wildflowers—especially lilies of the valley—and well-designated hiking trails. Then, head for **Østermarie,** a village of about 40 relatively nondescript buildings. Three kilometers (2 miles) northwest of Østermarie is the more culturally significant **Østerlars,** home to the largest of the island's distinctive round churches, the **Østerlarskirke,** Gudhjemsveg 28 (✆ **56-49-82-64;** www.oesterlarskirke.dk; bus: 1 from Gudhjem). It's open early April to mid-October, Monday to Saturday 9am to 5pm, charging 10DKK to enter. The Vikings originally built it around 1150, using rocks, boulders, and stone slabs. The church was dedicated to St. Laurence and later enlarged with chunky-looking buttresses; it was intended to serve in part as a fortress against raids by Baltic pirates. Inside are several wall paintings that date from around 1350, depicting scenes from the life of Jesus.

From Østerlars, drive 3.2km (2 miles) north, following the signs to **Gudhjem (God's Home),** a steeply inclined town that traded with the Hanseatic League during the Middle Ages. Most of its population died of the plague in 1653 and 1654, but the town was repopulated some years later by Danish guerrilla fighters and sympathizers following territorial wars with Sweden. You'll find a town with many fig and mulberry trees and steep slopes that give it a vaguely Mediterranean flavor.

Seeing the Sights in Gudhjem

Especially charming are Gudhjem's 18th-century half-timbered houses and the 19th-century smokehouses, known for their distinctive techniques of preserving herring with alderwood smoke. Its harbor, blasted out of the rocky shoreline in the 1850s, is the focal point for the town's 1,200 permanent residents.

Gudhjem Museum Frankly, we find the temporary art exhibits and the outdoor sculptures more intriguing than the permanent collection of locomotives and other rail-related memorabilia housed here. Its exhibits depict the now-defunct rail line that once crisscrossed the island.

Stationsvej 1. ✆ **56-48-54-62.** www.bornholmsmuseer.dk. Admission 25DKK adults, 10DKK children. Mid-May to mid-Sept Mon–Sat 10am–5pm; Sun 2–5pm. Closed mid-Sept to mid-May.

Landsbrugs Museum (Bornholm Agricultural Museum) Inside a timbered, thatch-roof farmhouse originally built in 1796, you're taken in the world of Bornholm farmers, a sort of Ma and Pa Kettle exhibition with pigs, goats, cows, and barnyard fowl similar to those that were bred on the island a century ago. The farmhouse and its surrounding garden is a journey back in time. You can see the brightly colored interior of the house as it was in the 19th century, complete with farm implements. Among the Danish woolen sweaters and wooden spoons made locally and sold on-site is the best homemade mustard we've ever tasted in Denmark.

Melstedvej 25 (1km/⅔ mile south of Gudhjem). ✆ **56-48-55-98.** Admission 50DKK adults, free 16 and under. Mid-May to June and mid-Sept to mid-Oct Mon, Thurs, and Sun 10am–5pm; July–Aug daily 10am–5pm.

CONTINUING ON TO ALLINGE & SANDVIG

To get to Allinge (15km/9 miles) from Gudhjem, proceed west along the coastal road, enjoying dramatic vistas over granite cliffs and sometimes savage seascapes. The entire coastline is known as **Helligdoms Klipperne (Cliffs of Sanctuary),** for the survivors of the many ships that foundered along this granite coastline over the centuries.

Midway along the route you'll see the island's newest museum, the **Bornholms Kunstmuseet (Art Museum of Bornholm),** Helligdommen (✆ **56-48-43-86;** www.bornholms-kunstmuseum.dk), which opened in 1993 and contains the largest collection of works by Bornholm artists. It's open June to August daily 10am to 5pm; April, May, September, and October, Tuesday to Sunday 10am to 5pm; November to March, Tuesday and Friday 1 to 5pm, Saturday and Sunday 10am to 5pm. Admission is 70DKK adults, free for children ages 18 and under. From the rocky bluff where the museum sits, you can see the isolated island of **Christiansø,** about 11km (7 miles) offshore, home to about 120 year-round residents, most of whom make their living from the sea.

Continue driving northwest until you reach the twin communities of **Allinge** and **Sandvig.** Allinge's architecture is noticeably older than that of Sandvig. The 200- and

300-year-old half-timbered houses were built for the purveyors of the herring trade, and the smokehouses preserved the fish for later consumption or for export abroad. The newer town of Sandvig, to the northwest, flourished around the turn of the 20th century, when many ferries connected it with Sweden, and became a stylish beach resort. The woods that surround the twin communities are known as the **Trolleskoe (Forest of Trolls),** home to wart-covered and phenomenally ugly magical creatures that delight in brewing trouble, mischief, and the endless fog that sweeps over this end of the island.

From Allinge, detour inland (southward) for about 4km (2½ miles) to reach **Olsker,** site of the **Olskirke (Round Church of Ols),** Lindesgordsvej (✆ **56-48-05-29**). Built in the 1100s with a conical roof and thick walls, it's the smallest of the island's round churches. It was painstakingly restored in the early 1950s. Dedicated to St. Olav (Olav the Holy, king of Norway, who died in 1031), it looks something like a fortress, an image the original architects wanted very much to convey. From June to September and October 17 to October 18, it's open Monday to Saturday 2 to 5pm; April, May, and October 1 to October 16, it's open Monday to Friday 10am to 1pm. It's closed the rest of the year. Entrance costs 10DKK.

Now double back to Allinge and head north toward Sandvig, a distance of about a kilometer (less than a mile). You'll soon see **Madsebakke,** a well-signposted open-air site that contains the largest collection of Bronze Age rock carvings in Denmark. There's no building, enclosed area, or even curator. Simply follow the signs beside the main highway. The carvings include 11 depictions of high-prowed sailing ships of unknown origin. The carvings were made in a smooth, glacier-scoured piece of bedrock close to the side of the road.

From here, proceed just over a mile to the island's northernmost tip, **Hammeren,** for views that—depending on the weather—may extend all the way to Sweden. Here you'll see the island's oldest lighthouse, **Hammerfyr** (1871).

Where to Stay in Sandvig

Strandhotellet ★★ 🎁 Though it was originally built as a house of stables in 1896, it was converted a decade later into the largest and most stylish hotel in Bornholm. That glory is long gone, but the venerable old hotel is a worthy detour for diners who drive from other parts of the island, and the three floors of spartan accommodations, with exposed birchwood and (in most cases) sea views, offer well-maintained bathrooms.

Strandpromenaden 7, DK-3770 Sandvig. www.strandhotellet.dk. ✆ **56-48-03-14.** Fax 56-48-02-09. 49 units. 750DKK–1,195DKK double. Rates include buffet breakfast. AE, DC, MC, V. **Amenities:** Restaurant; bar; children's playground; sauna; Wi-Fi (free in lobby). *In room:* TV.

Where to Dine in Sandvig

Strandhotellet Restaurant DANISH/SEAFOOD Today's hotel dining room, attracting both residents and visitors to the island, grew out of a 1930s dance hall and supper club that once flourished here. The chefs have to import a lot of their produce, but use whatever is fresh at the local markets. The smoked filet of wild salmon with a savory tomato tapenade got us off to a fine start and was followed by a platter of various fish, the actual dish varying depending on the catch of the day. The meat lovers will enjoy the beef medallions with a ragout of fresh vegetables.

Strandpromenaden 7, Sandvig. ✆ **56-48-03-14.** Main courses 165DKK–180DKK. AE, DC, MC, V. Daily 5:30–9:30pm.

FROM ALLINGE & SANDVIG BACK TO RØNNE

For your final adventure, turn south, following the signs pointing to Rønne. After less than a kilometer (½ mile) you'll see the rocky crags of a semiruined fortress that Bornholmers believe is the most historically significant building on the island—the **Hammershus Fortress ★**, begun in 1255 by the archbishop of Lund (Sweden). He planned this massive fortress to reinforce his control of the island. Since then, however, the island has passed from Swedish to German to Danish hands several times; it was a strategic powerhouse controlling what was then a vitally important sea lane. The decisive moment came in 1658, when the Danish national hero Jens Kofoed murdered the Swedish governor and sailed to Denmark to present the castle (and the rest of the island) to the Danish king.

Regrettably, the fortress's dilapidated condition was caused by later architects, who used it as a rock quarry to supply the stone used to construct some of the buildings and streets (including Hovedvagten) of Rønne, as well as several of the structures on Christiansø, the tiny island 11km (6¾ miles) northeast of Bornholm. The systematic destruction of the fortress ended in 1822, when it was "redefined" as a Danish national treasure. Much of the work that restored the fortress to the eerily jagged condition you'll see today was completed in 1967. Hammershus escaped the fate of the second-most-powerful fortress on the island, Lilleborg. Set deep in Bornholm's forests, Lilleborg was gradually stripped of its stones for other buildings after its medieval defenses became obsolete.

Some 4km (2½ miles) south of Hammershus—still on the coastal road heading back to Rønne—is a geological oddity called **Jons Kapel (Jon's Chapel);** it can be seen by anyone who'd like to take a short hike (less than 1km/⅔ mile) from the highway. The rocky bluff has a panoramic view over the island's western coast, where, according to ancient legend, an agile but reclusive hermit, Brother Jon, preached to the seagulls and crashing surf below. To get here, follow the signs from the highway.

To get back to Rønne, continue southward another 13km (8 miles), passing through the hamlet of **Hasle** en route.

JUTLAND

Dramatically different from the rest of Denmark, Jutland ("Jylland" in Danish) is a peninsula of heather-covered moors, fjords, farmland, lakes, and sand dunes. Besides its major tourist centers—Ribe in the south, Århus and Aalborg (Ålborg) in the north—it has countless old inns and undiscovered towns.

Jutland borders the North Sea, the Skagerrak, and the Kattegat. It extends 400km (250 miles) from the northern tip, Skagen, to the German border in the south. The North Sea washes up on many kilometers of sandy beaches, making this a popular vacation spot.

The meadows are filled with rich bird life and winding rivers; nature walks are a popular pastime. The heart of Jutland is mainly beech forest and lake country, sprinkled with modest-size towns and light industry. Steep hills surround the deep fjords of the east coast. Gabled houses in the marshlands of southern Jutland add to the peninsula's charm. Two of the most popular vacation islands are Rømø and Fanø, off the southwest coast. Here, many traditional homes of fishermen and ship captains have been preserved.

Our driving tour of Jutland begins at Ribe. If you're arriving in east Jutland from Copenhagen, take Route 32 west. From mainland Europe, take Route 11 from Tønder. Esbjerg is connected to Ribe by Route 24, which joins Route 11 south.

Ribe ★★

32km (20 miles) S of Esbjerg, 300km (186 miles) W of Copenhagen

This is one of Denmark's oldest towns, and if you have to miss all the other cities of Jutland, spend a night here, where local residents ask, "Will the storks return on April 1?" Every year some wood storks—now an endangered species—fly to Ribe to build their huge nests on top of the red-roofed, medieval, half-timbered, and crooked houses, which flank the narrow cobblestone lanes.

One of New York's most legendary citizens, Jacob A. Riis, was born in Ribe. When "the town's prettiest girl" broke his heart, he headed for New York in 1870. Once here, he was shocked by the city's inhumane slums, which he wrote about in his first book in 1890, *How the Other Half Lives*. A friend of Theodore Roosevelt, Riis was offered the job of mayor of the city, but turned it down to pursue his efforts to get a million people off the streets and into decent housing. For such work, he became known as "the most beneficial citizen of New York." In time, he returned to Ribe where "the prettiest girl" said yes this time. His former residence lies at the corner of Skolegade and Grydergade, a plaque marking his former abode.

As a former port, Ribe was an important trading center during the Viking era (around A.D. 900) and became an Episcopal seat in 948, when one of the first Christian churches in Denmark was established here. It was also the royal residence of the ruling Valdemars around 1200.

In medieval days, sea-trade routes to England, Germany, Friesland, the Mediterranean, and other ports linked Ribe, but then its waters receded. Today it's surrounded by marshes, much like a landlocked Moby Dick. On a charming note, the town watchman still makes his rounds—armed with his lantern and trusty staff—since the ancient custom was revived in 1936.

ESSENTIALS

GETTING THERE There's hourly **train service** from Copenhagen (via Bramming). The schedule is available at the tourist office. **By car,** from Kolding, head west across Jutland on the E-20 motorway, but cut southwest when you reach Route 32, which will carry you into Ribe.

VISITOR INFORMATION The **Ribe Turistbureau,** Torvet 3 (✆ **75-42-15-00;** www.ribetourist.dk), is open June and September Monday to Friday 9am to 5pm, Saturday 10am to 2pm; July and August Monday to Friday 9am to 6pm, Saturday 10am to 5pm (from mid-July to mid-Aug it's also open on Sun 10am–2pm); October through May Monday to Friday 10am to 4:30pm, Saturday 10am to 2pm.

GETTING AROUND If you'd like to bike your way around the area, you can **rent bikes** for 75DKK at **Ribe Vandrerhjem (Youth Hostel),** Skt. Pedersgade 16 (✆ **75-42-06-20;** www.danhostel-ribe.dk).

SEEING THE SIGHTS

The historic core of Ribe is **Gamle Stan ★★★**, the gem of all Old Towns on the peninsula of Jutland. Beginning at the **Torvet ★★★** or old market square, you can fan out in all directions, covering most of the major streets or lanes of interest in about 2 hours. The well-preserved medieval center surrounds the cathedral, the Ribe Domkirke (see below).

The tourist office sells a copy of a guided walking tour of Ribe for 10DKK. Our favorite hotel (Dagmar) and our favorite restaurant (Weis Stue) open onto the main square.

From Torvet many streets radiate out—take **Skolegade,** for example, opening onto the west side of the Domkirke. A plaque marks the spot where Riis spent his final decade at **Hans Tausen's House,** which dates from the early 17th century. At the corner of Sønderportsgade and Stenbrogade stands **Det Gamle Rådhus** (see below), the oldest existing town hall in Denmark.

A memorial tablet at the corner of Sønderportsgade and Bispegade marks the spot where on November 9, 1641, Maren Spliid was burned at the stake, the last victim of Denmark's witch hunts.

To the east of Torvet lies **Skt. Catharine Kirke** (p. 179), the only remaining church built before the Reformation.

Arm yourself with a tourist-office map and discover other streets that evoke the Middle Ages, of which **Fiskergade** is one of the most evocative, with its narrow alleys that lead to the riverfront.

Det Gamle Rådhus (Town Hall Museum) Originally built in 1496, the Town Hall Museum today houses some rather unimpressive artifacts and archives from Ribe's illustrious past. These include a gruesome 16th-century executioner's axe, ceremonial swords, the town's money chest, antique tradesmen's signs, and a depiction of the "iron hand," still a symbol of police authority. ***Note:*** Look for storks building a nest on top of this, Denmark's oldest existing town hall.

Von Støckends Plads. ✆ **76168810.** www.detgamleraadhusiribe.dk. Admission 15DKK adults, free children 17 and under. June–Aug daily 1–3pm; May and Sept Mon–Fri 1–3pm. Closed Oct–Apr.

Ribe Domkirke ★★ Denmark's earliest wooden church, built around A.D. 860, once stood on this spot. In 1150 it was rebuilt in the Romanesque style, opening onto the main square of town, but over the years has been remodeled and altered considerably. The **south portal ★** remains a rare example of Danish Romanesque sculpture, and is known for its carved tympanum depicting the *Descent of Christ from the Cross*. Most of the *kirke* was built of a soft porous rock (tufa) found near the German city of Cologne and shipped north along the Rhine River. Before the Dom was completed, 100 years would go by. Several Gothic features such as arches were later added, but the overall look is still Rhineland Romanesque. The wide nave is flanked by aisles on both sides, and the church is surmounted by a dome. The interior holds treasures from many eras, including mosaics, stained glass, and frescoes in the eastern apse by the artist Carl-Henning Pedersen, who created them in the 1980s. Older treasures include an organ designed by Jens Olufsen in the 1600s plus an elaborate altar from 1597 by the renowned sculptor Kens Jens Asmussen.

The Devil, or so it is said, used to enter the Domkirke through the **"Cat's Head Door" ★★**. At the south portal of the transept, it was once the principal entryway into the church. The triangular pediment depicts Valdemar II and his queen, Dagmar, positioned at the feet of Mary and her infant son. Daily at noon and 3pm the cathedral bell still tolls in mourning of Dagmar's death during childbirth.

For the most **panoramic view ★★** of Ribe and the surrounding marshes, climb the 248 steps to the cathedral tower left over from 1333. A watchman once stood here on the lookout for floods, which frequently inundated Ribe.

Torvet (town center) off Sønderportsgade. ✆ **75-42-06-19.** www.ribe-domkirke.dk. Admission 10DKK adults, 5DKK children 3–14. Daily May–Sept 10am–5pm; Apr and Oct 11am–4pm; Nov–Mar 11am–3pm.

Ribe Kunstmuseet (Ribe Art Museum) Of minor interest, this museum with its more than 600 paintings and sculpture is dedicated to art from various epochs in Danish history, from around 1750 to 1940, which marked the beginning of the Nazi occupation. The museum is housed in a stately villa in a garden on the Ribe River, the former residence of a factory owner built from 1860 to 1864 based on drawings made by the royal surveyor L. A. Winstrup.

Skt. Nicolai Gade 10. ✆ **75-42-03-62.** www.ribe-kunstmuseum.dk. Admission 40DKK adults, free for children 17 and under. July–Aug daily 11am–5pm; Sept–Dec and Feb 12–June Tues–Sun 11am–4pm. Closed Jan–Feb 11.

Ribe VikingeCenter ★ Two kilometers (1¾ miles) south of the town center is this complex, where locals reconstruct all things Viking: the buildings, costumes, utensils, tools, and equipment—even the food. The smell of baking bread will lure you to open fires where it is baked by women dressed in early medieval costumes. Such crafts as pottery making and leather work are demonstrated, but it's the falconry demonstrations that really enthrall visitors. Horses, cows, sheep, hens, and geese run about as in olden days. The centerpiece of the re-created town is a "great house" revealing an early Danish manor reserved for the town's most powerful baron. Other buildings from around 1050 can also be explored.

Lustrupvej 4. ✆ **75-41-16-11.** www.ribevikingecenter.dk. Admission 80DKK adults, 40DKK children 3–14, free for children 2 and under. May–June and Sept Mon–Fri 10am–3:30pm; July–Aug daily 11am–5pm. Guided tours in English are offered May–June and Sept daily at 10:10am; July–Aug daily at 11:10am. Tours cost 250DKK for 30 min. or 500DKK for 1 hr.

Skt. Catharine Kirke ★ The Spanish Black Friars (Dominicans) came to Ribe in 1228 and began constructing a church and chapter house (the east wing of a monastery). Parts of the original edifice can still be seen, especially the southern wall. The present church, near Dagmarsgade, with nave and aisles, dates from 1400 to 1450, the tower from 1617. Only the monks' stalls and the Romanesque font remain from the Middle Ages, with the delicately carved pulpit dating from 1591, the ornate altarpiece from 1650. The brothers were kicked out in 1536 at the time of the Reformation, and in time the complex became both an asylum for the mentally ill and, later, a wartime field hospital. You can walk through the cloisters and see ship models and religious paintings hanging in the southern aisle. Tombstones of Ribe citizens from the Reformation and later can be seen along the outer walls of the church.

Skt. Catharine's Plads. ✆ **75-42-05-34.** Free admission to church; cloisters 10DKK adults, 5DKK children 13 and under. May–Sept daily 10am–noon and 2–5pm; Oct–Apr daily 10am–noon and 2–4pm. Closed during church services.

A Side Trip to Rømø ★

Rømø, the largest Danish island in the North Sea, is about 9km (5½ miles) long and 6.5km (4 miles) wide. It has a certain appeal because of its wild, wind-swept appearance. In the summer it attracts lots of tourists (especially Germans), possibly because of the nude sunbathing. In the off-season it's one of the sleepiest places in Europe, making it great for rest and relaxation.

To reach Rømø, take the 9.5km (6-mile) stone causeway from mainland Jutland. Or take a bus south from Ribe to Skaerbaek, and then bus no. 185 across the tidal flats.

WHERE TO STAY

Den Gamle Arrest ★★ No other hotel on Jutland's peninsula has done a better job of spinning its old life into something new. This previous town jail is now a charming hotel, made from the same bricks as the town's more prestigious addresses. Located on the main town square, the hotel's former life is evident in a few of the cramped "jail cells" and the brick wall on the grounds that bears the prisoners' inscriptions. However, the ground floor boasts a bridal suite with four-poster bed and a garden with roses, fountains, and stone sculptures.

Torvet 11, DK-6760 Ribe. www.dengamlearrest.dk. ✆ **75-42-37-00.** Fax 75-42-37-22. 12 units, 2 with bathroom. 640DKK–690DKK double without bathroom; 840DKK–1,040DKK double with bathroom. Rates include buffet breakfast. No credit cards. **Amenities:** Restaurant; bar. *In room:* TV (in some), no phone.

Hotel Dagmar ★★★ The most famous hotel in Denmark outside Copenhagen is also the oldest in the country, dating from 1581. Converted from a private home in 1850, it's also the most glamorous hotel in South Jutland, taking its name from the medieval Danish queen. The bedrooms have been carefully restored, respecting the hotel's age while adding modern conveniences. Most of the units, as befits a building of this vintage, have low ceilings, sloping floors, and windows with deep sills. Textiles are in autumnal colors, and the walls are decorated with original paintings. Each bedroom is also individually decorated and comes in various shapes and sizes.

Torvet 1, DK-6760 Ribe. www.hoteldagmar.dk. ✆ **75-42-00-33.** Fax 75-42-36-52. 50 units. 1,195DKK–1,645DKK double. Rates include buffet breakfast. AE, DC, MC, V. **Amenities:** 3 restaurants; bar; room service. *In room:* TV, hair dryer, minibar.

Hotel Fru Mathies For those who like to travel the B&B route, this is one of the best—and most affordable—choices in town. Set behind a bright yellow stucco facade, a very short walk from the city's pedestrian zone, this hotel was named after its present guardian and supervisor, Fru (Mrs.) Inga Mathies. There's a shared TV/living room on the premises, and the small bedrooms are simple but cozy affairs, each with a bathroom equipped with a tub/shower combo and modest numbers of old-fashioned accessories.

Saltgade 15, DK-67660 Ribe. www.frumathies.dk. ✆ **75-42-34-20.** Fax 75-41-02-44. 6 units. 700DKK double. Rates include buffet breakfast. AE, DC, MC, V. **Amenities:** Bar. *In room:* TV, minibar, no phone.

WHERE TO DINE

Restaurant Backhaus DANISH This place has served as a restaurant or an inn for as long as anyone in Ribe can remember. Today, steaming platters of all-Danish food arrive in generous portions at reasonable prices. Menu specialties include a Danish platter containing artfully arranged presentations of herring, cheeses, and vegetables that taste wonderful with the establishment's earthy, rough-textured bread. Tomato soup with sour cream comes with a surprising but refreshing dab of horseradish. The chef tells us that the most frequently ordered dish is tender pork schnitzels with boiled potatoes and braised red cabbage. However, we found that the sautéed strips of beef tenderloin with fried onions hit the spot on a cold, windy, rainy day. Dessert might be a hazelnut pie with vanilla ice cream.

On the premises are seven simple rooms, stripped-down but comfortable hideaways that are well maintained. With breakfast included, doubles cost 550DKK. With the exception of about a week every year at Christmas, the hotel is open year-round.

Grydergade 12. ✆ **75-42-11-01.** www.backhaus-ribe.dk. Reservations recommended. Main courses 105DKK–190DKK. MC, V. Daily 10am–10pm. Closed 1 week around Christmas.

Restaurant Dagmar ★★ DANISH/INTERNATIONAL Honoring a beloved medieval queen, this restaurant opposite the cathedral is a major address and stopover for those making the gastronomic tour of Denmark. Its four dining rooms are a 19th-century "dream" of ornate furnishings and objets d'art, a tribute to the heyday of the Belle Epoque era. The chefs showcase a varied cuisine that is refreshingly authentic and based on the best of market-fresh ingredients. Care, craftsmanship, and a concern for your palate go into every dish served by the best waitstaff in town. We usually opt for one of the two fresh North Sea fish dishes of the day, but we also like the scallops topped with a sweet-potato crisp, and in autumn we go for the sautéed stuffed quail with mushrooms accompanied by a *beurre blanc* sauce. The chefs shine brighter with their regional cuisine, but they also borrow freely from international larders, serving tender veal tenderloin with one of the tastiest shallot mousses we've ever sampled and a delectable port-wine sauce.

In the Hotel Dagmar. ✆ **75-42-00-33.** www.hoteldagmar.dk. Reservations required. Main courses 198DKK–265DKK. Fixed-price dinner menus: 2 courses at 225DKK, 3 courses at 285DKK, 4 courses at 335DKK, 5 courses at 385DKK, 6 courses at 435DKK, 7 courses at 485DKK; fixed-price lunch menu at 225DKK. AE, DC, MC, V. Daily noon–10pm.

Restaurant Saelhunden ★ DANISH/INTERNATIONAL One of the most evocative and cheerful restaurants in Ribe occupies a venerable but cozy brick building with a history dating from 1634. Set beside the river that flows through the city, the restaurant has flourished since 1969 and has a staff that, like the menu, comes from throughout Europe. The cuisine is based on fresh ingredients and, for the most part, sticks to tried-and-true favorites beloved by the Danish palate, including smoked salmon or platters of meatballs. The dish that most locals seem to order is the fried filets of plaice with boiled potatoes. Other items include at least three kinds of steaks that feature T-bone, French-style entrecôte, and something known as "English steak." A local delicacy is smoked and fried dab, a flat fish not unlike flounder that flourishes in the local estuaries. No one will mind if you come here just for a beer or a simple snack. In summertime, it mirrors a beer garden in Hamburg with an outdoor terrace.

Skibbroen 13. ✆ **75-42-09-46.** www.saelhunden.dk. Reservations recommended. Main courses 115DKK–229DKK. MC, V. Daily noon–9pm. Beer served till 11pm.

Weis Stue ★ DANISH For old-fashioned dining in a mellow atmosphere, there is no better place in Ribe than this small, charming, brick-and-timber inn on the market square near the cathedral and the Hotel Dagmar, which owns it. The food in this ground-floor restaurant is plentiful and well prepared, based on the best from field, air, and stream. We like the marinated herring with raw onions and the always divine little shrimp they served with mayonnaise. For something more substantial, we feast on smoked Greenland halibut with scrambled eggs, a local favorite, as is the liver paste with mushrooms. For more standard dishes, you can order a very good filet of beef flavored with onions. We end with a selection of Danish cheese.

The inn also has eight upstairs guest rooms that are cozy but don't have private bathrooms. A double costs 495DKK, including breakfast.

Torvet 2. ✆ **75-42-07-00.** www.weis-stue.dk. Reservations recommended. Main courses 175DKK–245DKK; 2-course fixed-price menu 239DKK. AE, DC, MC, V. Daily 11am–10pm.

Fanø ★★

47km (29 miles) NW of Ribe, 283km (176 miles) W of Copenhagen

Off the coast of South Jutland, Fanø, at least in our view, is the most beautiful of all North Sea islands—and we've sailed to all of them. It is the one place in Denmark which we most prefer for some R & R. Come here to enjoy the outdoors and nature, ducking into the man-made attractions only if it's a rainy day.

Consisting of a landmass of some 54 sq. km (21 sq. miles), with a population of 3,500, Fanø is known for its white sandy beaches, which have made it a popular summer resort. Set against a backdrop of dunes heath, the best beaches are in the northwest, mostly in and around the hamlets of Rindby Strand and Fanø Bad.

Nordby, where the ferry arrives, is a logical starting point for exploring the island. Here you'll find heather-covered moors, wind-swept sand dunes, fir trees, wild deer, and bird sanctuaries. From Ribe, Fanø makes for a great day's excursion (or longer if there's time).

Sønderho, on the southern tip, and only 14km (8½ miles) from Nordby, with its memorial to sailors drowned at sea, is our favorite spot—somewhat desolate, but that's its charm.

It was a Dutchman who launched Denmark's first bathing resort at Nordby in 1851. It consisted of a raft on which some bathing huts had been set up. The bathers entered the huts, undressed, put on different clothes, pulled down an awning to the water's surface, and bathed under the awning. How modest of them.

Until 1741 Fanø belonged to the king, who, when he ran short of money, sold the island at an auction. The islanders themselves purchased it, and the king then granted permission for residents to build ships, which led to its prosperity. From 1741 to 1900, some 1,000 sailing vessels were constructed here, with the islanders often manning them as well. Inhabitants built many beautiful houses on Fanø with moneys earned, and some of these charming, thatched homes still stand today. There are some in the northern settlement of Nordby, but more gems are found in the south at Sønderho.

Although Nordby and Sønderho are the principal settlements, beach lovers head for the seaside resort of **Fanø Bad,** which is also a popular camping area. From Fanø Bad the beach stretches almost 4km (2½ miles) to the north. Bathing here is absolutely safe as a sandy bottom slopes gently into the North Sea, and there are no ocean holes or dangerous currents.

Fanø adheres to old island traditions more than any other island in Denmark, with the exception of Ærø. As late as the 1960s, some of the senior women on Fanø still wore the "Fanø costume," which originally consisted of five skirts, but today's costumes are likely to have only three. When the skirt was to be pleated, it was wet, laced up, and sent to the baker, who steamed it in a warm oven. Today you'll see it only at special events and festivals.

ESSENTIALS

GETTING THERE **By car** from Ribe, head north on Route 11 to Route 24. Follow Route 24 northwest to the city of Esbjerg, where you can board a **ferry** operated by **Fanøtrafikken** (✆ **70-23-15-15;** www.fanoetrafikken.dk for information and schedules). May to October, ferries depart Esbjerg every 20 minutes during the day (trip time: 12 min.). In winter, service is curtailed, with departures during the day every 45 minutes. A round-trip ticket costs 40DKK adults or 20DKK children 5 to 15, and one average-size car, along with five passengers, is carried for 385DKK to 425DKK round-trip.

GETTING AROUND Local **buses** meet passengers at the ferry dock, crisscrossing the island about every 40 minutes, with vastly curtailed service in winter. The bus will take you to the communities of Nordby in the north and Sønderho in the south, with stops at Rindby Strand and Fanø Bad. For bus information call the tourist office (✆ **70-26-42-00**). Many visitors like to explore Fanø by **bike,** and rentals cost from

75DKK per day, at **Unika Cykler,** Mellemgaden 12 (✆ **75-16-24-60;** www.unikacykler.dk).

VISITOR INFORMATION The **Fanø Turistbureau,** Færgevej 1, Nordby (✆ **70-26-42-00;** www.visitfanoe.dk), is open November to March Monday to Friday 10am to 5pm; April to June, September and October Monday to Friday 10am to 5pm, and Saturday 10am to 2pm; July and August Monday to Friday 9am to 5pm, Saturday and Sunday 10am to 4pm.

WHERE TO STAY & DINE

Hotel Fanø Badeland ☺ This hotel takes no chances with the likely possibility that fog or rain might ruin the swimming. Although it sits on Fanø's western edge, close to one of the best beaches on the island, it has the added benefit of a glass-enclosed complex of indoor pools. 3.2 kilometers (2 miles) south of the hamlet of Nordby, the hotel was built amidst wind-swept scrubland. The midsize rooms are urban-looking, minimalist, and angular. Each has either one or two bedrooms outfitted with simple, durable furniture and no-nonsense accessories.

Strandvejen 52–56, DK-6720 Fanø. ✆ **75-16-60-00.** Fax 75-16-60-11. www.fanoebadeland.dk. 126 units, each with kitchenette. 964DKK–1,325DKK 1-bedroom unit for up to 4 occupants; 1,062DKK–1,564DKK 2-bedroom unit for up to 6 occupants. MC, V. Bus: 631. **Amenities:** Restaurant; bar; children's playground; exercise room; indoor heated pool; room service; sauna; indoor tennis court. *In room:* TV.

Sønderho Kro ★★★ Dating from 1722, one of Denmark's oldest and most charming inns is run by hosts Niels and Birgt Steen Sørensen. A Relais & Châteaux lodging, the thatch-roof inn in the heart of the village of Sønderho is the best we've ever encountered in South Jutland. Each of the bedrooms is individually decorated, and windows open onto views over a nearby dike, the marshlands, and the North Sea. Lace curtains, lovely tapestries, and four-poster beds add to the old-fashioned allure. The inn is 13km (8 miles) south of the Nordby ferry dock, where a bus carries non-motorists the final distance into Sønderho.

Kropladsen 11, Sønderho, DK-6720 Fanø. ✆ **75-16-40-09.** Fax 75-16-43-85. www.sonderhokro.dk. 13 units. 1,250DKK–2,050DKK double. Rates include continental breakfast. AE, DC, MC, V. Free parking. **Amenities:** Restaurant; room service. *In room:* TV, hair dryer.

Århus ★

160km (99 miles) NE of Fanø, 175km (109 miles) W of Copenhagen

It's "the world's smallest city," but happens to be the second-largest city in Denmark and the capital of Jutland. Because Copenhagen is so far to the east, Århus has also been called "the capital of the West." A large student population makes for a vast cultural life, which reaches its peak in late summer when visitors flock here for an arts festival.

There is a lot to see and do here, and rather than spend time in man-made attractions we like to visit the city's bars, the best in Jutland, and its sidewalk cafes. There are sandy beaches nearby and a number of museums, but the best way to experience Århus life is by walking its cobblestone streets and having a picnic at one of the city parks.

The city's current economic growth is based on communications, the food industry, electronics, textiles, iron and steel, and Danish design, as well as the harbor, which is now the second most important in Denmark, rivaled only by Copenhagen.

Originally Århus was a Viking settlement, founded as early as the 10th century; its original name, Aros, meaning estuary, comes from its position at the mouth of a river,

The Århus Card

The Århus Card includes free admission to 20 museums and attractions, free parking in the center of Århus, and unlimited travel by public transportation. A 2-day pass costs 149DKK for adults and 69DKK for children 3 to 12. The Århus Pass is sold at the tourist office, many hotels, camping grounds, and kiosks throughout the city.

Århus Å. The town experienced rapid growth, and by 948 it had its own bishop. An Episcopal church was built here in 1060, and a cathedral was started at the dawn of the 13th century. This prosperity came to a temporary end in the late Middle Ages, when the town was devastated by the bubonic plague. The Reformation of 1536 also slowed the growth of Århus. But the coming of the railway in the 19th century renewed prosperity, which continues to this day. Try to plan at least a full day and night here—or two if you can spare the time.

ESSENTIALS

Getting There

BY PLANE **Århus airport** is in Tirstrup, 43km (27 miles) northeast of the city. **SAS** (✆ **800/221-2350** in North America, or 32-32-14-50 in Århus; www.aar.dk) operates 5 flights a day from Copenhagen, Monday to Friday, and about six on Saturday and Sunday. **Ryanair** (✆ **00353/12-48-08-56;** www.ryanair.com) has one flight per day between Arhus and London Stansted. An airport bus runs between the train depot at Århus and the airport, meeting all major flights. The cost of a one-way ticket is 95DKK.

BY TRAIN About 25 trains a day travel between Århus and Copenhagen (trip time: 3 hr.). Some 20 trains a day connect Aalborg with Århus (1 hr., 40 min.). From Frederikshavn, the North Jutland port and ferry-arrival point from Norway, some 20 trains a day run to Århus (3 hr.).

BY BUS Six buses daily make the run to Århus from Copenhagen (3 hr.).

BY CAR From the east, cross Funen on the E-20 express highway, heading north at the junction with the E-45. From the north German border, drive all the way along the E-45. From Frederikshavn and Aalborg in the north, head south along the E-45.

Getting Around

A regular bus ticket, valid for one ride, can be purchased on the rear platform of all city buses for 19DKK.

Visitor Information

The tourist office, **Tourist Århus,** Banegårdspladsen 20 (✆ **87-31-50-10;** www.visitaarhus.com), is open June 28 to September 5 Monday to Friday 10am to 5:30pm, and Saturday 10am to 3pm; September 6 to June 27 Monday to Friday 10am to 5pm.

SEEING THE SIGHTS

For the best introduction to Århus, head for the town hall's tourist office, where a 2-hour **sightseeing tour** leaves Monday to Friday at 2pm July 1 to August 31, costing 125SEK per person.

In addition to the major museums listed below, you can also visit two museums on the grounds of Århus University, Nordre Ringgade. They include **Steno Museet,** C.

F. Møllers Allé (✆ **89-42-39-75;** www.stenomuseet.dk.; bus: 2, 3, or 4), which displays exhibits documenting natural science and medicine. You'll see beautiful 19th-century astronomical telescopes, a 1920s surgical room, and some of the first computers made in Denmark in the 1950s. Posters, models, and do-it-yourself experiments, including tests of Galileo's demonstrations of gravity and of electromagnetism, are also on display. In addition, you can walk through an herbal garden with some 250 historical medicinal herbs. There is also a Planetarium, with daily shows Tuesday to Sunday at 11am, 1pm, and 2pm, and Wednesday also at 8pm. Admission to the museum costs 45DKK for adults and free for ages 17 and under. Admission to the planetarium is 45DKK for adults, 30DKK for ages 18 and under. The museum is open Tuesday to Friday 9am to 4pm, Saturday and Sunday 11am to 4pm.

Also at the university is a **Naturhistorisk Museum,** Wilhelm Meyers Allé 210, Universitetsparken (✆ **86-12-97-77;** www.naturhistoriskmuseum.dk; bus: 2 or 3), filled with mounted animals from all over the world, some of which are displayed in engaging dioramas. The collection of Danish animals, especially birds, is unique within Denmark. Skeletons, minerals, and a display devoted to the evolution of life are some of the other exhibits. It's open daily 10am to 4pm (to 5pm July–Aug). It's closed on Mondays November to March. Admission is 50DKK adults, and free for those 17 and under.

Århus Domkirke (Cathedral of St. Clemens) ★ As European city cathedrals go, the Domkirke at Århus is low on the totem pole. When it was built in 1201 in the Romanesque style, it probably had greater style. But in the 1400s, after a fire, it was rebuilt in the Gothic style, with a soaring 96m (315-ft.) whitewashed nave (the longest in Denmark), practically as deep as its spire is tall. The interior is relatively plain, except for one of the few pre-Reformation survivors, a grand **tripartite altarpiece ★★**. Behind the altar is a painted glass window, the creation of Emanuel Vigeland, brother of the more celebrated Gustav Vigeland of Norway. Chalk frescoes from medieval times depict scenes from the Bible in lavender and black, among other colors. Our favorite is a depiction of St. George slaying a dragon to save a princess in distress. Also depicted is the namesake of the church, St. Clement, who drowned with an anchor around his neck, making him the patron saint of sailors. Before you leave, climb the tower for a **panoramic view ★★** over Århus and its surrounding area. (After the cathedral, we suggest a visit to the nearby medievalesque **arcade** at Vestergade 3, with half-timbered buildings, a rock garden, an aviary, and antique interiors.)

Bispetorvet. ✆ **86-20-54-00.** www.aarhusdomkirke.dk. Free admission. May–Sept Mon–Sat 9:30am–4pm; Oct–Apr Mon–Sat 10am–3pm. Bus: 3 or 56.

Den Gamle By ★★★ ☺ Outside of Copenhagen, Denmark's only government-rated three-star museum re-creates a Danish market town as it appeared in the olden days. More than 75 historic buildings, many of them half-timbered, were uprooted from various locations throughout the country and placed here to illustrate Danish life from the 16th to the 19th centuries in a re-created botanical garden. The open-air museum differs from similar attractions near Copenhagen and Odense in that the Århus museum focuses more on rural life. Visitors walk through the authentic-looking workshops of bookbinders, carpenters, hatters, and other craftspeople. There is also a pharmacy, a school, and an old-fashioned post office. A popular attraction is the Burgomaster's House, a wealthy merchant's antiques-stuffed, half-timbered home, built at the end of the 16th century. Be sure to see the textile collection and the Old Elsinore Theater, erected in the early 19th century. The museum also houses a collection of china, clocks, delftware, and silverware. Summer music programs are staged, and there's a restaurant, tea garden, bakery, and beer cellar. Many activities and programs are designed especially for kids.

Viborgvej 2. ✆ **86-12-31-88.** www.dengamleby.dk. Admission 50DKK-125DKK adults, free for children 17 and under. Sept-Oct and Apr-May daily 10am-5pm; June-Aug daily 9am-6pm; Nov-Dec and Feb-Mar daily 10am-4pm; Jan daily 11am-3pm. Bus: 3, 14, or 25.

Rådhuset (Town Hall) Just before the outbreak of World War II, Arne Jacobsen, one of Denmark's greatest designers, drew up the plans for this Town Hall. Built between 1936 and 1941 to commemorate the 500th anniversary of the Århus charter, it's been the subject of controversy ever since. The outer skeleton of the building evokes scaffolding that was abandoned, although the interior has light, open spaces, and plenty of glass. It can be seen only on a guided tour. An elevator (and 346 steps) runs to the top of the 59m (194-ft.) tower, where a carillon occasionally rings. ***Note:*** The guided tour at 11am includes the tower. The elevator and stairs are open three times a day: 11am, noon, and 2pm.

Rådhuspladsen. ✆ **87-31-50-10.** Temporarily closed for renovations; check its status at the time of your visit. Bus: 3, 4, 5, or 14.

THE MANOR HOUSES OF EAST JUTLAND

Clausholm ★★ Seventeenth-century Clausholm is a splendid baroque palace, one of the earliest in Denmark. It was commissioned by Frederik IV's chancellor, whose adolescent daughter, Anna Sophie, eloped with the king. When Frederik died, his son by his first marriage banished the queen to Clausholm, where she lived with her court until her death in 1743.

The rooms are basically unaltered, but few of the original furnishings remain. The salons and ballroom feature elaborate stucco ceilings and decorated panels, and an excellent collection of Danish rococo and Empire furnishings has replaced the original pieces. The Queen's Chapel, where Anna Sophie and her court worshiped, is unchanged and contains the oldest organ in Denmark. In 1976, the Italian baroque gardens were reopened, complete with a symmetrically designed fountain system.

Clausholm is about 13km (8 miles) southeast of Randers and 31km (19 miles) north of Århus.

Voldum, Hadsten. ✆ **86-49-16-55.** www.clausholm.dk. Admission (including guided tour) 80DKK adults, free for children 13 and under. Castle July only daily 11am-4pm; park May-Sept only daily 11am-5pm. Bus: 231 from Randers.

The Museums at Gammel Estrup ★ One of the most elegant Renaissance manors in Central Jutland lies 39km (24 miles) northeast of Århus. Today this compound of buildings is the site of the **Jutland Manor House Museum,** complete with a great Hall, a chapel, and richly decorated stucco ceilings, and the **Danish Agricultural Museum,** which celebrates the role of Danish farming over the past thousand years. The entire compound dates from the 14th century, but the structures you see were extensively rebuilt and remodeled in the early 1600s. Expect a glimpse into medieval fortifications, baronial furnishings, the changing nature of tools and machines used during Danish plantings and harvests, and an enormous sense of pride in Denmark and its traditions.

Jyllands Herregårdsmuseum, Randersvej 2, Auning. ✆ **86-48-34-44.** www.gl-estrup.dk. Admission 85DKK adults, free for children 17 and under. Agricultural Museum Jan-Mar and Nov-Dec Tues-Thurs 10am-3pm; Fri-Sun 10am-4pm; Apr-June and Sept-Oct daily 10am-5pm; July-Aug daily 10am-6pm. Manor House Museum Apr-June and Sept-Oct daily noon-4:30pm; July-Aug daily noon-4:30pm. Bus: 119. From Randers, take Rte. 16 east to Auning.

Rosenholm Slot ★ One of Jutland's stateliest Renaissance manors was built in 1559 on a small island in the middle of a lake. Stone lions guard the bridge that leads to the castle where the Rosenkrantz family has lived for more than 4 centuries. The four-winged castle is encircled by 14 hectares (35 acres) of landscaped parkland. We find Rosenholm far more impressive than the queen's more modest digs at Marselisbourg. The Great Hall is graced with a portrait of King Frederik V, and most of the other salons and galleries are furnished and decorated in a Moorish-inspired Spanish style—or else with rococo adornments (a bit much at times). The Winter Room is walled with leather, and French and Flemish tapestries, some 3 centuries old, adorn the Tower Room and the Corner Room. The location is 21km (13 miles) north of Århus and 1km (⅔ mile) north of the village of Hornslet.

Hornslet. ✆ **86-99-40-10.** www.rosenholmslot.dk. Admission 75DKK, free for children 5 and under. June 1–19 Sat–Sun 11am–4pm; June 20–Aug 31 daily 11am–4pm. Closed Sept–May. Bus: 119 or 121 from Århus.

WHERE TO STAY

Low-cost accommodations in this lively university city are limited. Those on a modest budget should check with the tourist office in the Rådhuset (✆ **87-31-50-10**) for bookings in **private homes.**

Depending on the day of the week or the time of the year you check in, rooms in many of the hotels labeled inexpensive aren't inexpensive at all, but more moderate in price.

Hotel La Tour ☺ If you're not too demanding, this is quite a good choice, especially for families on a holiday. Since its construction in 1956 and its rebuilding in 1986, this hotel has followed a conscious policy of downgrading (yes, downgrading) its accommodations and facilities from a once lofty status to a middle-brow formula. The result is a hotel that's far from being the best in town—viewed, we imagine, as a great success by the management. The hotel, in an unimaginative two-story building, is 3.5km (2¼ miles) north of Århus center. It offers well-maintained, simple bedrooms.

Randersvej 139, DK-8200 Århus. www.latour.dk. ✆ **86-16-78-88.** Fax 86-16-79-95. 101 units. 785DKK-875DKK double; 1,175DKK suite. Rates include buffet breakfast. AE, DC, MC, V. Bus: 2, 3, or 11. Free parking. Closed Dec 21–Jan 2. **Amenities:** Restaurant; bar; children's playground; room service. *In room:* TV, hair dryer, minibar, Wi-Fi (95DKK per day).

Hotel Royal ★★★ If you're looking for the best modern facilities, check into the Radisson Blu (see below). But for traditional extravagance and royal luxury, this has the most glamorous accommodations in town, attracting celebs such as Madonna and Sting. The gilt date on its neobaroque facade commemorates the hotel's establishment in 1838. There have been numerous additions and upgrades since. The Royal stands close to the city's symbol, its cathedral. A vintage elevator takes you to the guest rooms, many of them quite spacious.

Stove Torv 4, DK-8000 Århus. www.hotelroyal.dk. ✆ **86-12-00-11.** Fax 86-76-04-04. 69 units. 1,850DKK double; 2,150DKK–2,550DKK suite. Rates include buffet breakfast. AE, DC, MC, V. Bus: 26, 56, or 58. **Amenities:** Restaurant; bar; babysitting; room service; sauna. *In room:* TV, minibar, Wi-Fi (free).

Radisson Blu Scandinavia Hotel Århus ★★★ This is one of the most modern and dynamic hotels in Denmark, and a place that municipal authorities show off to visiting dignitaries. It was built in 1995 above the largest convention facilities in Jutland and is the most popular convention hotel in the region. Of course, for that reason, we like it less. However, should you arrive when a convention isn't taking place, the hotel can be a honey. Bedrooms occupy floors 4 to 11 of a glass-and-stone-sheathed tower that's visible from around the city. Each room has a tasteful decor that's different from its immediate neighbor, incorporating Scandinavian, English, Japanese, or Chinese themes.

Margrethepladsen 1, DK-8000 Århus C. ✆ **800/333-3333** in the U.S., or 86-12-86-65. Fax 86-12-86-75. www.radissonsas.com. 234 units. 1,151DKK–1,835DKK double; from 2,500DKK suite. Rates include buffet breakfast. AE, DC, MC, V. Bus: 1, 2, 6, or 16. Parking 90DKK. **Amenities:** Restaurant; bar; babysitting; exercise room; room service; sauna. *In room:* TV, hair dryer, minibar, Wi-Fi (free).

Villa Provence ★ Living up to its name, this small hotel brings a touch of sunny Provence to a tranquil square in Århus. A designer hotel built in the style of Southern France, Villa Provence offers well-designed bedrooms and suites, each individually furnished. Decorated with 1940s French movie posters, the units have traditional quilts on wrought-iron beds that sit on wide-planked oak floors. The mood is set in the stylish lounge, where you can order an aperitif. Another oasis is the courtyard in the rear, with its tall lime trees and cobblestones.

Fredens Torv 12, DK-8000 Århus. ✆ **86-18-24-00.** Fax 86-18-24-03. www.villaprovence.dk. 41 units. 1,195DKK–2,200DKK double; 2,200DKK–2,800DKK suite. Rates include buffet breakfast. AE, DC, MC, V. Parking 110DKK. **Amenities:** Room service. *In room:* TV, hair dryer, Wi-Fi (free).

WHERE TO DINE

Ferdinand Brasserie ★★★ DANISH/FRENCH In the most exclusive hotel in Århus, this delightful restaurant is imbued with a romantic atmosphere and serves quality food prepared with the best and freshest of ingredients. Tables sit on beautiful hardwood floors, and are elegantly set. Inventiveness goes hand in hand with solid technique, and the kitchen also takes full advantage of the region's riches, with seafood predominating. Some of the best starters include a seafood terrine or else poached hake with watercress and a hollandaise sauce. For a main course, you might enjoy the fried mullet with cabbage, shrimp, and potatoes, or else the beef tenderloin with sautéed foie gras and a truffle sauce. Look for fresh asparagus in late spring, the finest of game dishes in the autumn, and the freshest catch of the day.

Åboulevarden 28. ✆ **87-32-14-44.** Reservations required. Main courses 175DKK–295DKK. DC, MC, V. Mon–Sat noon–3pm and 6–10pm.

Restaurant Margueritten ★ DANISH/FRENCH/ITALIAN One of the town's better restaurants was carved out of what used to be stables for horses. This is a cozy place for lunch and an ideal venue for a romantic dinner. Old Danish stripped furniture and beamed ceilings enhance the ambience, and in summer a beautiful little garden in the rear is open. This menu is modern and always uses the freshest regional produce. Chefs offer such dishes as guinea fowl with a stuffing of tiger shrimp; the distinctive flavor comes from the marinade of yogurt and tandoori spices. Some of the best dishes we found on the menu included filet of wild pork with a balsamic chocolate sauce, medallion of beef in a cognac sauce with mixed vegetables, and a tangy breast of duck with a raspberry sauce and fresh plums that have been marinated in port. The English-speaking waitstaff is polite and helpful.

Guldsmedgade 20. ✆ **86-19-60-33.** Reservations required. 1-course fixed-price menu 190DKK–220DKK; 2-course menu 260DKK; 3-course menu 280DKK; lunch main courses 68DKK–145DKK. DC, MC. Mon–Sat 11:30am–11pm.

Restaurant Skovmøllen ★ DANISH/INTERNATIONAL Since it was constructed of straw, wood, and stone more than 300 years ago, this building has functioned as a farmhouse, a gristmill, and a simple cafe. It's beside the Giber River, 10km

(6/4 miles) south of Århus, close to the Moesgård Museum. Beneath a beamed ceiling and frequent reminders of old-time Denmark, you can order typically Danish platters at lunchtime, and straightforward, not particularly esoteric dishes that are just a bit more cosmopolitan at night. Lunches might include meatballs, *smørrebrød* (open-faced sandwiches), herring platters, or roasted pork with onions and braised cabbage. The more elaborate dinners feature shrimp cocktails, steak with french fries, stuffed filets of plaice with new potatoes, and salmon chops with garlic butter sauce. The place is always dependable, the cookery always reliable, but its main allure is as a charming, country-flavored getaway from the city.

Skovmøllenvej 51. ✆ **86-27-12-14.** www.skovmollen.dk. Reservations recommended. Fixed-price menus 245DKK for 2 courses, 285DKK for 3 courses, 310DKK for 4 courses. MC, V. June–Aug Tues–Sun noon–6pm; Sept–May Fri–Sun noon–5pm. From downtown Århus take bus no. 6.

Teater Bodega DANISH Originally established at a different address in 1907, Teater Bodega moved across the street from both the Århus Dramatic Theater and the Århus Cathedral in 1951. It offers an amusing dining ambience for local actors and theatergoers, its walls covered with illustrations of theater costumes and other thespian memorabilia. The food is solid and flavorful in the Danish country style. Various kinds of Danish hash, including *biksemad,* are served along with regular or large portions of Danish roast beef. Although the beef dishes are good, a waiter assured us that most locals go for a platter of the freshly caught plaice or flounder.

Skolegade 7. ✆ **86-12-19-17.** www.teaterbodega.dk. Reservations recommended. Main courses 125DKK–248DKK; lunch *smørrebrød* 58DKK–138DKK. Fixed-price menus 198DKK–298DKK. DC, MC, V. Mon–Sat 11am–11:30pm. Bus: 6.

SHOPPING

Århus is the biggest shopping venue in Jutland, with some 400 specialty stores, each of them tightly clustered within an area of about 1.3 sq. km (½ sq. mile). The centerpiece of this district is the Strøget, whose terminus is the Store Torv, dominated by the Århus Domkirke. You might try a large-scale department store first. One of the best is **Salling,** Søndergade 27 (✆ **86-12-18-00;** www.salling.dk), with some 30 specialty boutiques, all under one roof. A wide range of articles for the whole family is sold here, including body-care items, clothing, gifts, toys, music, and sports equipment. **Magasin du Nord,** Immervad 2–8 (✆ **86-12-33-00;** www.magasin.dk), is the largest department store in Scandinavia, in business for more than 125 years. The staff will assist foreign visitors with tax-free purchases.

"The greatest silversmith the world has ever seen" is the praise often used to describe **Georg Jensen,** Søndergade 1 (✆ **86-12-01-00;** www.georgjensen.com). A tradition since 1866, Georg Jensen is known for style and quality, producing unique silver and gold jewelry, elegant clocks and watches, and stainless steel cutlery, among other items. A leading goldsmith, **Hingelberg,** Store Torv 3 (✆ **86-13-13-00;** www.hingelberg.dk), is the licensed Cartier outlet, and offers a wide selection of top-quality designer jewelry.

Galleri Bo Bendixen, Store Torv 14 (✆ **86-12-67-50;** www.bobendixen.dk), offers the brilliantly colored designs of Bo Bendixen, the famous Danish graphic artist. The shop also sells a wide range of gifts and garments for children and adults.

In an attractive old house in the heart of the city, **Bülow Duus Glassblowers,** Studsgade 14 (✆ **86-12-72-86;** www.bulow-duus.dk), is a working glass-blowing shop that is open to the public. Drinking glasses, candlesticks, bowls, and other items are for sale. For traditional Danish pottery, head for **Gavlhuset,** Møllestien 53 (✆ **86-13-06-32;** www.lissa.dk).

If you haven't found what you're looking for after all that, head for **Inspiration Buus,** Ryesgade 2 (✆ **86-12-67-00;** www.inspiration.dk), which sells top-quality gifts, kitchenware, tableware, and toiletry articles, much of it of Danish design.

Silkeborg

44km (27 miles) W of Århus, 280km (174 miles) W of Copenhagen

In the heart of the Danish lake district, this town of 35,000 opens onto the waters of Lake Longsø, where we like to go for a stroll at night to see the largest color fountain in Scandinavia. If you don't like the lake (highly unlikely), there's always the Gudenå River, the longest in Denmark. The Danes themselves come here to go canoeing, hiking through the surrounding hills, or boating on the lake. Silkeborg has some notable attractions, but its natural beauty is just as appealing.

In 1845, Michael Drewsen, whose statue is seen in the heart of town on the Torvet main square, built a paper mill on the east side of the river, and in time other industries sprouted up, leading to great prosperity for the town. Unlike some little towns of Denmark, with their narrow cobblestone streets, Silkeborg is spaciously laid out. A progressive town, it is scenic, historic yet modern, with a vast shopping district of 200 specialty stores, the largest marketplace in Central Jutland, a multiplex cinema, dozens of restaurants, and a convention center.

ESSENTIALS

GETTING THERE From Århus, follow Route 15 west to Silkeborg. If you aren't driving, there's frequent train service from Copenhagen via Fredericia.

GETTING AROUND Numerous **bus routes** service the city; all local buses depart from the stop on Fredensgade. There's no number to call for information. Tickets cost 19DKK per individual ride.

VISITOR INFORMATION The **Silkeborg Turistbureau** is at Åhavevej 2A (✆ **86-82-19-11;** www.silkeborg.com). It's open June 15 to August, Monday to Friday 9:30am to 5:30pm, Saturday and Sunday 10am to 2pm; September, October, and April to June 14, Monday to Friday 9:30am to 4pm, Saturday 10am to 1pm; November to March, Monday to Friday 10am to 3pm.

SEEING THE SIGHTS

Although we can never resist the charms of "The Tollund Man" (see below), the greatest adventure for us is to sail aboard the world's last coal-fired paddle steamer, the ***Hjejlen*** ★★★, which has been sailing since 1861. It follows the route of the Gudenå River, going along a waterway of 161km (100 miles) through Jutland's wonderful lake district. **Himmelbjerget,** or "Sky Mountain," is the major attraction along the route. Departures are daily from Silkeborg harbor at 10am and again at 2pm from mid-June to mid-August, with a round-trip costing 115DKK for adults or half-price for children 4 to 11 (3 and under free). For schedules and more information, call **Hjejlen Co., Ltd.,** Silkeborg (✆ **86-82-07-66;** www.hjejlen.com).

AQUA Ferskvands Akvarium og Museum ★ ☺ North Europe's largest freshwater aquarium is called "the inside-out aquarium" since the circular building is submerged in the waters of the lake. Through the large seascape windows, you can look into the lake and watch both fish and water plants. In a beautiful park at AQUA, you can observe bird life with plenty of beavers around to amuse you. One section boasts AQUA's largest indoor aquarium with its "dancing eels," along with zander, sturgeon, crayfish, and the freshwater turbot. In another section of the park, children can actually touch the big sturgeon, carp, flounder, or other fish. Bring food for a picnic in the park or pay a visit to the AQUA Café for lunch.

Vejsøvej 55. ✆ **89-21-21-89.** www.ferskvandscentret.dk. Admission 105DKK adults, 55DKK children 3–12. July–Aug daily 10am–6pm; off-season Mon–Fri 10am–4pm, Sat–Sun 10am–5pm.

Silkeborg Kunstmuseum (Silkeborg Museum of Art) ★★ This is one of the great provincial art museums of Scandinavia. In one of the most beautiful areas of Silkeborg, in old parkland bordering the banks of the Gudenå River, Asger Jorn, a leading figure in 20th-century European art, donated his impressive collection of 5,000 paintings by 150 artists. Jorn himself was a virtual Renaissance man when it came to art, excelling in painting, sculpture, ceramics, tapestries, drawings, and graphics. The museum is also richly imbued with an important collection of **Danish art ★** from the 20th century. The privately owned gallery supplements its permanent collection with changing exhibitions of paintings and sculpture.

Gudenåvej 9. ✆ **86-82-53-88.** www.silkeborgkunstmuseum.dk. Admission 70DKK adults, free for children 17 and under. Apr–Oct Tues–Sun 10am–5pm; Nov–Mar Tues–Fri noon–4pm, Sat–Sun 10am–5pm. Bus: 10.

Silkeborg Museum One of the world's greatest human treasures from antiquity is the world-famous and much-photographed **Tollund Man ★★★**. Discovered in a peat bog in 1950, he is the most perfectly preserved human being to have survived the ages. When he lived during the Iron Age (roughly 500 B.C.–A.D. 500), the great city of Athens was in decline, the second Punic War was being fought, and the finishing touches were being put on the Great Wall of China. When his body was discovered, locals called the police, thinking it was a recent murder. You can even see the wrinkles in his forehead. His head capped by fur, the Tollund Man was strangled by a plaited leather string, probably as part of a ritual sacrifice for a successful peat harvest. He was also a vegetarian, as scientists have determined.

Sleeping near the Tollund Man for centuries is the **Elling Woman ★★**, whose body was discovered in 1938 about 60m (200 ft.) from where the Tollund Man was later discovered. Wrapped in a sheepskin cape, she had been hanged with a leather thong, the V-shaped furrow still to be seen around her neck today. Scientists estimate that she was about 25 years old when she died in 210 B.C., probably the result of another ritual sacrifice.

After seeing these rather gruesome sights, you can admire the setting of the museum in a manor house by the Gudenå River, directly east of the Torvet or market square. The building itself dates back to 1767 and is the oldest structure in Silkeborg.

The museum also displays exhibits devoted to regional history and local handicrafts, including an antique glass collection, the renowned **Sorring ceramics ★**. The museum carries a special exhibition of a clog maker's workshop, a collection of stone implements, antique jewelry, and artifacts from the ruins of Silkeborg Castle.

Hovedgaardsvej 7. ✆ **86-82-14-99.** www.silkeborgmuseum.dk. Admission 50DKK, free for children 18 and under. May to mid-Oct daily 10am–5pm; mid-Oct to Apr Sat–Sun noon–4pm. Bus: 10.

WHERE TO STAY

The Silkeborg Turistbureau (see above) can book you into nearby **private homes.**

Hotel Dania ★ If you crave modernity and facilities, check into the Radisson Blu (see below). But if you want tradition, your best choice is the town's oldest hotel, dating from 1848. Much improved over the years, it's been modernized without losing its charm. The bedrooms either overlook the lake or the Torvet, the main town square.

Antiques fill the corridors and reception lounge, but the midsize-to-spacious guest rooms have been decorated in Danish modern, each unit containing a neatly kept bathroom with tub/shower combo. Outdoor dining on the square is popular in the summer, and the **Underhuset** restaurant serves typical Danish food along with Scandinavian and French dishes. The hotel's dining room measures as one of the longest restaurants in Denmark.

Torvet 5, DK-8600 Silkeborg. www.hoteldania.dk. © **86-82-01-11.** Fax 86-80-20-04. 49 units. 995DKK–1,599DKK double; 1,599DKK–2,704DKK suite. Rates include buffet breakfast. AE, DC, MC, V. Parking 35DKK. Bus: 3. **Amenities:** Restaurant; bar; babysitting; room service. *In room:* TV, hair dryer, minibar.

Radisson Blu Hotel ★★★ This 150-year-old former paper factory is now the most modern hotel in the area. The location is not quite as central as the Dania, but the Radisson is right by the harbor, a short walk from attractions, shops, and restaurants. The chain hotel is also a favorite venue in Silkeborg for conferences, as the town's convention center, Jyst Musik & Teaterhus, is nearby. The hotel offers the finest and most modern doubles and suites in Greater Silkeborg, successfully combining Danish modern with traditional styling.

Papirfabrikken 12, DK-8600 Silkeborg. www.radissonblu.com. © **88-82-22-22.** Fax 88-82-22-23. 100 units. 1,365DKK–1,645DKK double; 2,045DKK–2,500DKK suite. Rates include buffet breakfast. AE, DC, MC, V. Free parking. **Amenities:** Restaurant; bar; room service; sauna; Wi-Fi (free, in lobby). *In room:* A/C, TV, fridge, hair dryer, minibar.

WHERE TO DINE

Piaf ★ MEDITERRANEAN The most exotic and deliberately counterculture restaurant in town occupies a solid, 80-year-old brick building in the historic core. It was named after the uncanny resemblance of its owner, Anni Danielsen (who's known for her fondness for black dresses), to the late French chanteuse Edith Piaf. Artwork is offset with brick walls, potted plants, poster-image testimonials to the late Gallic sparrow, and deliberately mismatched tables, plates, ashtrays, and accessories. Lunch platters tend to be light, airy, and flavorful; dinners, more substantial with excellently chosen ingredients—always fresh—deftly handled by a skilled kitchen staff. Both are inspired by the tenets of Spanish, Greek, Provençal, and Italian cuisine. Look for heaping platters of paella, roasted lamb with rosemary, carpaccio, and sliced veal, with bowls of bouillabaisse. What's the only item you're likely not to find on the menu? Pork, since it reminds most of the clients of the cuisine served in Denmark during their childhood, and which is consequently something avoided within this consciously exotic setting.

Nygade 31. © **86-81-12-55.** www.restaurant-piaf.dk. Reservations recommended. Fixed-price menus 385DKK–675DKK. DC, MC, V. Tues–Sat 6–10:30pm.

Ebeltoft ★

97km (60 miles) E of Silkeborg, 53km (33 miles) NE of Århus, 336km (209 miles) W of Copenhagen

Wandering the cobblestone streets of Ebeltoft is like going back to a town 200 years ago. This town of half-timbered houses had a long slumber of about 2 centuries, when it economically stagnated. When it woke up in the 1960s, it found its old buildings and streets had become a tourist attraction. So instead of tearing down buildings, locals restored them with their increased prosperity.

Ebeltoft, "apple orchard" in Danish, is the capital of the Mols hill country, an area of great scenic beauty in Central Jutland. Allow at least 3 hours to wander its streets—in some cases, hidden-away lanes—and to explore its old inns. Sometimes a ruddy-faced fisherman will consent to have his picture taken, assuring you that he is still following the same profession as his grandfather.

Ebeltoft's Viking-age wooden "dragon boats" have given way to expensive yachts in the harbor. Life at Ebeltoft developed around this beautiful harbor and its scenic bay, Ebeltoft Vig.

In the Middle Ages, Ebeltoft was a thriving port, enjoying trade with Germany, Sweden, and, of course, Copenhagen. However, after a dispute in 1659, the Swedish army invaded, sacking the port and setting fire to the merchant fleet. Ebeltoft never really recovered from this almost fatal blow until it became a tourist destination in the 1960s. Ironically, it was Swedish tourists who first discovered the antique charms of Ebeltoft, with its timber-framed buildings topped with red-tile roofs.

ESSENTIALS

GETTING THERE There's no direct **train service** to Ebeltoft. From Copenhagen, take the train (via Fredericia) to Århus; at Århus Central Station, board bus no. 123 for Ebeltoft. **By car,** head east on Route 15 from Silkeborg through Århus and continue around the coast, then follow Route 21 south to Ebeltoft.

GETTING AROUND **Bikes** can be rented at **L&P Cykler,** Nørre Allé 5 (✆ **86-34-47-77**), open Monday to Friday 8am to 5:30pm, Saturday 8am to noon. Rental fees are around 70DKK to 95DKK per day.

VISITOR INFORMATION Contact the **Ebeltoft Turistbureau,** Strandvejen 2 (✆ **86-34-14-00;** www.ebeltoftby.dk), open June 15 to August Monday to Saturday 10am to 6pm and Sunday 11am to 4pm; and September to June 14 Monday to Friday 9am to 4pm and Saturday 10am to 1pm.

SEEING THE SIGHTS

Det Gamle Rådhus (The Old Town Hall) This is the smallest town hall in Denmark. It looks like something erected just for kindergarten children to play in—a 1789 building, blackened half-timbering, a red-brick with timbered facade, and a bell tower. Its museum houses an ethnographic collection from Thailand and artifacts from the town's history. It's in the town center north of Strandvejen.

Torvet. ✆ **86-34-55-99.** www.ebeltoftmuseum.dk. Admission 20DKK, free for children 17 and under. May–June daily 10am–3pm; July–Aug 20 daily 11am–5pm; Aug 21–Sept daily 11am–3pm; Oct–Mar Sat–Sun 11am–3pm.

Fregatten Jylland ★ Moored at the harbor, the *Jylland* is the oldest man-of-war in Denmark (1860) and the world's longest wooden ship at 71m (233 ft.). The vessel is an impressive monument to Ebeltoft's maritime heyday, and the restoration of the three-masted ship was financed by Mærsk McKinney Møller, a local shipping tycoon. Stand on the bridge and gun deck, imagining the harbor 2 centuries ago, and, down below, check out the captain's room and the galley with several miniature sea-battle scenarios on display.

Strandvejen 4. ✆ **86-34-10-99.** www.fregatten-jylland.dk. Admission 105DKK adults, 45DKK children 4–12, free for children 3 and under. Jan 2–Mar 21 and Oct 25–Dec 30 daily 10am–4pm; Mar 22–June 13 and Aug 23–Oct 24 daily 10am–5pm; June 14–Aug 22 daily 10am–7pm.

WHERE TO STAY & DINE

Hotel Ebeltoft Strand ★ ☺ This hotel is the best choice in the town center, although summer visitors will find the swanky Molskroen (see below) along the coast more inviting. Constructed in 1978, the comfortable, well-furnished guest rooms often have a private balcony or terrace, overlooking Ebeltoft Bay or the Mol hills. Each of the units, painted in pastel-like Nordic colors, comes with a well-kept bathroom with tub/shower combo. Family rooms can be composed by joining another room, with an extra bed for kids (under the age of 18). In winter, guests retreat to a cozy lounge with a fireplace, but in summer the terrace with a view of the water is preferred.

Nordre Strandvej 3, DK-8400 Ebeltoft. www.ebeltoftstrand.dk. © **86-34-33-00.** Fax 86-34-46-36. 72 units. 1,245DKK double. Rates include buffet breakfast. AE, DC, MC, V. Free parking. Bus: 123 from Århus. **Amenities:** Restaurant; bar; children's playground; indoor heated pool; room service. *In room:* TV, hair dryer, minibar, Wi-Fi (free).

Molskroen ★ Perched northwest of Ebeltoft on the coast, this half-timbered structure began life in 1923 as a private manor, but has been expanded and altered over the years. Many rooms have terraces overlooking Mols hills, and a fine white sandy beach is only 100m (328 ft.) away. The medium-size guest rooms are now sleek, functional, and comfortable. Ten of the bedrooms are found in the annex, a red-brick building with a tiled roof. Accommodations here are every bit as good as in the main building. Nine of these annex accommodations are individually furnished junior suites set on two floors, with four beds in each room, making them suitable for families.

Hovegaden 16, Femmøller Strand, DK-8400 Ebeltoft. www.molskroen.dk. © **86-36-22-00.** Fax 86-36-23-00. 18 units. 1,580DKK–1,880DKK double; 2,400DKK–3,500DKK suite. Rates include buffet breakfast. AE, DC, V. Free parking. Closed Dec 24–Jan 8. Bus: 123 from Århus. **Amenities:** Restaurant; bar; babysitting; room service. *In room:* TV, fax, hair dryer, minibar, Wi-Fi (free).

Aalborg ★

132km (82 miles) NW of Ebeltoft, 383km (238 miles) W of Copenhagen

We won't pretend that Aalborg is our favorite city in Jutland (Århus is), but you can have a great time if you explore the attractions, especially some of those in the environs.

The largest city in northern Jutland, Aalborg (Ålborg) opens onto the Limfjord and is known worldwide for its aquavit. Although essentially a shipping town and commercial center, Aalborg makes a good base for sightseers, with its many hotels and attractions, more than 300 restaurants, and diverse nightlife.

History is a living reality in Aalborg. The city was founded 1,000 years ago when the Viking fleets assembled in these parts before setting off on their predatory expeditions. The city's historic atmosphere has been preserved in its old streets and alleys. Near the Church of Our Lady are many beautifully restored and reconstructed houses, some of which date from the 16th century.

Denmark's largest forest, **Rold,** where robber bandits once roamed, is just outside town. **Rebild National Park** is the site of the annual American Fourth of July celebration.

Not far from Aalborg, on the west coast of northern Jutland, some of the finest beaches in northern Europe stretch from Slettestrand to Skagen. The beach resort towns of **Blokhus** and **Løkken** are especially popular with Danes, Germans, and Swedes.

ESSENTIALS

GETTING THERE You can **fly** from Copenhagen to Aalborg; the **airport** (© **98-17-11-44;** www.aal.dk) is 6.5km (4 miles) from the city center.

There is frequent **train service** from Copenhagen by way of Fredericia to Århus; there you can connect with a train to Aalborg, a 90-minute ride.

Aalborg's **bus station** is the transportation center for North Jutland and is served from all directions. For all bus information in North Jutland, call **Nordjyllands Trafikselskab** (✆ **99-34-11-11;** www.nordjyllandstrafikselskab.dk).

From Ebeltoft **by car,** follow Route 21 north until you reach the junction with Route 16. Drive west on Route 16 until you come to E-45, which runs north to Aalborg.

GETTING AROUND For bus information, call ✆ **99-34-11-11.** Most buses depart from Østerågade and Nytorv in the city center. A typical fare costs 18DKK, although you can buy a 10-trip tourist pass for 130DKK to ride on all the city buses. Information about bus routes is available from the ***Aalborg Guide,*** which is distributed free by the tourist office.

VISITOR INFORMATION The **Aalborg Tourist Bureau** is at Østerågade 8 (✆ **99-31-75-00;** www.visitaalborg.com). It's open June and August, Monday to Friday 9am to 5:30pm, Saturday 10am to 1pm; September to May, Monday to Friday 9am to 4:30pm, Saturday 10am to 1pm. In July it is open Monday to Friday 9am to 5:30pm, Saturday 10am to 4pm.

SPECIAL EVENTS The **Aalborg Carnival ★★**, scheduled each year from May 22 to May 28, is one of the major events of spring in Jutland. Streets are filled with festive figures in colorful costumes strutting in a parade. Up to 100,000 people participate in this annual event, marking the victory of spring over winter's darkness. The whole city seems to explode in joy. There's also the **Aalborg Jazz and Blues Festival** August 13 to August 19. Jazz fills the whole city at dozens of clubs, although most activity centers on C. W. Obels Plads. Every year on the Fourth of July, Danes and Danish Americans meet to celebrate America's **Independence Day** in the lovely hills of Rebild.

SEEING THE SIGHTS

Aalborg Marinemuseum ☺ This enthralling museum gives you a hands-on experience with the interior of a submarine, *Springeren,* which is primed and ready for action. The 23m (75-ft.) sub was one of the last to be designed and built in Denmark. Also on-site is the torpedo boat *Søbjørnen,* the world's fastest. You can see the inspection ship, *Ingolf,* that was on active duty in the bone-chilling waters around Greenland until 1990. Other exhibits depict life at sea, the port of Aalborg, and activities at the Aalborg shipyard. At the Cafe Ubåden (Cafe Submarine), you can order food and drink. There's also a playground on-site.

Vester Fjordvej 81. ✆ **98-11-78-03.** www.aalborgmarinemuseum.dk. Admission 80DKK adults, 40DKK children 6–14, free for children 5 and under. May–Sept daily 10am–5pm; off-season daily 10am–4pm. Bus: 12 or 13.

Aalborg Tårnet (Aalborg Tower) Whenever we visit a city or town, and if there is a lookout point, we always head there first for a panoramic overview. In Aalborg, that perfect view (that is, if it's a clear day) is seen from this tower, rising 105m (344 ft.) into the air. Reached by stairs or elevator, its view takes in everything from the smokestacks to the beautiful Limfjord. Weather permitting, you can see the North Sea and even Rold Forest in the south. The tower itself is no beauty—rather ugly in fact—but it does have its rewards, including its location on a hill in back of the Nordjyllands Kunstmuseum and at the border of Mølleparken, the best woodland for walking or hiking in the area.

Søndre Skovvej, at Skovbakken. ✆ **98-77-05-11.** www.aalborgtaarnet.dk. Admission 30DKK adults, 20DKK children 3–11, free for children 2 and under. Apr–June daily 11am–5pm; July–Aug 8 daily 10am–5pm; Aug 9–Sept 26 and Oct 14–22 daily 11am–5pm. Closed Oct–Mar, except for 1 week in Oct. Bus: 11, 14, or 16.

Aalborg Zoologiske Have (Aalborg Zoo) ★★ ☺ We've seen bigger and better zoos in our lives, but this remains one of our favorites because of its success in the breeding of near-extinct animals such as the Siberian tiger. More than 1,300 animals are on parade here, including crocs, zebras, tigers, giraffes, polar bears, and orangutans. Apes and beasts of prey are kept under minimal supervision. They live in such simulated conditions as an African savannah or a rainforest from South America. Kids can romp around a large playground like the resident monkeys. Other adventures include a riverbank for crocs, a pampa for anteaters, or a forest full of bears.

Mølleparkvej 63. ✆ **96-31-29-29.** www.aalborg-zoo.dk. Admission 140DKK adults, 85DKK children 3–11, free for children 2 and under. Nov to mid-Feb daily 9am–3pm; mid-Feb to Mar 27 daily 9am–4pm; Mar 28–Apr 29 and Oct daily 9am–5pm; Apr–June and Aug 9–31 daily 9am–7pm; July–Aug 8 daily 9am–8pm. Last ticket is sold 1 hr. before closing. Bus: 11. 4km (2½ miles) south of Aalborg.

Budolfi Domkirke (Cathedral of St. Budolf) Even if you don't visit this church, you'll hear its carillon make beautiful music daily every hour from 9am to 10pm. This elaborately decorated and whitewashed cathedral is dedicated to the patron saint of sailors. The baroque spire of the church is Aalborg's major landmark. The church you see today is the result of 800 years of rebuilding and expansion. On the south wall is a fresco depicting St. Catherine of Alexandria and some grotesque little centaurs. Look for the altarpiece from 1689 and the pulpit from 1692—both carved by Lauritz Jensen. The marble font from 1727 was a gift to the church. Note too the gallery in the north aisle with its illustrations of the Ten Commandments. A similar gallery in the south aisle illustrates the suffering of Christ and bears the names of a number of prominent Aalborg citizens from around the mid–17th century. A series of cocks crow the hour from four matching clock faces on the church's tower.

Algade. ✆ **98-12-46-70.** www.aalborgdomkirke.dk. Free admission. June–Aug Mon–Fri 9am–3pm, Sat 9am–noon; Sept–May Mon–Fri 9am–3pm, Sat 9am–noon. Bus: 3, 5, 10, or 11.

Helligåndsklostret (Monastery of the Holy Ghost) Once when we were doing a magazine article on the Danish resistance movement during the Nazi occupation from 1940 to 1945, our trail led us to this site, often called the "Aalborg Kloster." Here we learned that it was the secret headquarters of the "Churchill Club," which was the first Resistance group established in Denmark to fight the Nazi menace. This vine-covered monastery is the oldest social-welfare institution in Denmark, as well as the oldest building in Aalborg. Built near the heart of town in 1431 and designed with step-shaped gables, it contains a well-preserved rectory, a series of vaulted storage cellars—some of which occasionally functioned as prisons—a whitewashed collection of cloisters, and a chapter house whose walls in some areas are decorated with 16th-century frescoes. The complex can be visited only as part of a guided tour.

C. W. Obels Plads. ✆ **98-12-02-05.** www.aalborgkloster.dk. Guided tour 40DKK adults, 10DKK children 3–12. Guided tour late June to mid-Aug Mon–Fri 1:30pm. Bus: 1.

Jens Bangs Stenhus (Jens Bang's Stone House) ★ This is the finest example of Renaissance domestic architecture in the north of Europe. This glittering six-floor mansion, built in 1624, once belonged to a wealthy merchant, Jens Bang. Bang deliberately made his house rich with ornamentation and ostentation as a challenge to the other good citizens of the town. It was rumored that he revenged himself on his many enemies by caricaturing them in the grotesque carvings on the facade of the house. In spite of his wealth, he was never made a member of the town council, and to this day his image is depicted on the south facade sticking his tongue out at the Town Hall. The historic wine cellar, Duus Vinkjælder, is the meeting place of the Guild of Christian IV. On the ground floor is an old apothecary shop. The mansion itself is still privately owned and is not open to the public.

Østerågade 9. Bus: 3, 5, 10, or 11.

Nordjyllands Kunstmuseet (Museum of Modern and Contemporary Art) ★ ☺ This building is a prime example of modern Scandinavian architecture. Built from 1968 to 1972, it was designed by Elissa and Alvar Aalto and Jean-Jacques Baruël as a showplace for 20th-century Danish and international art. The nucleus of the collection dates from 1850 but it's been added to over the years with many purchases and bequests. The Carlsberg Foundation, those beer barons, have donated some of the most notable works, including William Scharff's *Nocturne Series* and J. F. Willumsen's *War Invalids*. The greatest treasure-trove of art came from two dental technologists, Anna and Kresten Krestensen, who amassed a notable collection of Danish and international art from 1920 to 1950. In later years, as funds became available, the museum purchased works by great international artists including Fernand Léger, Max Ernst, and Wassily Kandinsky. Many events are staged for children, including picture hunts, family tours, and children's museum exhibits.

Kong Christians Allé 50. ✆ **99-82-41-00.** www.nordjyllandskunstmuseum.dk. Admission 60DKK adults, free for children 17 and under. Free admission in Dec. Daily Tues–Sun 10am–5pm (Feb–Apr and Sept–Nov Tues to 9pm). Closed Dec 24, 25, 31, and Jan 1. Bus: 15.

WHERE TO STAY

Chagall Ever since the 1950s, this hotel has been an affordable choice in pricey Aalborg. In honor of its namesake, most of the bedrooms have reproductions of Marc Chagall's paintings. The midsize bedrooms are designed in sophisticated Danish modern. On-site is a cafe-style lounge in the lobby where breakfast is served. As a grace note, the hotel offers an inner courtyard where you can sit out in summer, enjoying the far-too-few nights of warm weather.

Vesterbro 36–38, Postboks 1856, DK-9000 Aalborg. www.hotel-chagall.dk. ✆ **98-12-69-33.** Fax 98-13-13-44. 89 units. 880DKK–1,100DKK double. Rates include buffet breakfast. AE, DC, MC, V. Parking 85DKK. **Amenities:** Exercise room; Jacuzzi; sauna. *In room:* TV, hair dryer, minibar, Wi-Fi (free).

Helnan Phønix Hotel ★★★ In the town's most sumptuous mansion is the oldest, largest, most historic, and most prestigious hotel in Aalborg, close to the bus station. It originated in 1783 on the main street of town as the private home of the Danish brigadier general assigned to protect Aalborg from assault by foreign powers. In 1853, it was converted into a hotel. Today, it appears deceptively small from Aalborg's main street, and very imposing if you see its modern wings from the back. Bedrooms are tastefully and elegantly appointed with dark wood furnishings. Some of the rooms have exposed ceiling beams.

Vesterbro 77, DK-9000 Aalborg. www.helnan.dk. ✆ **98-12-00-11.** Fax 98-10-10-20. 210 units. 995DKK–1,195DKK double; 2,600DKK suite. Rates include buffet breakfast. AE, DC, MC, V. Parking 60DKK. **Amenities:** Restaurant; bar; exercise room; Jacuzzi; room service; sauna. *In room:* TV, hair dryer, minibar, Wi-Fi (free).

Park Hotel ★ This hotel has been putting up wayfarers who arrive at the rail terminus opposite the building since 1917. One of the oldest hotels in the city, the Park (not to be confused with Park Inn Chagall) became so popular that a modern block of tasteful, comfortable rooms was added when an extension was tacked on in 1990. The original architectural details of the main building remain relatively intact in spite of modernization. Today the hotel enjoys a well-deserved reputation for its coziness and comfort, with personal service as a hallmark.

J. F. Kennedys Plads 41, DK-9100 Aalborg. www.park-hotel-aalborg.dk. ✆ **98-12-31-33.** Fax 98-13-31-66. 81 units. 1,070DKK–1,185DKK double; 1,515DKK suite. Rates include buffet breakfast. AE, DC, MC, V. **Amenities:** Restaurant; bar; room service. *In room:* TV, hair dryer, Wi-Fi (free).

WHERE TO DINE

Jomfru Anegade is the most famous restaurant-filled street in Jutland. If you can't find good food here, you didn't try. It's got something for most palates and pocketbooks.

Kniv og Gaffel ★★ FRENCH/DANISH This is a romantic choice for dining, housed in the oldest preserved citizen's house, dating from 1552, in Aalborg. The street takes its name from Maren Turis, a woman who lived here in the 16th century and was accused of witchcraft, tried, but found not guilty. Today, you'll experience only lots of atmosphere, and wonderful food served by candlelight. Its old oak tables fill up every night, and the wooden floors are buckled and slanted with age. The house specialty is thick steaks, the best in Aalborg, although you can order an array of other dishes as well, each prepared with first-rate market-fresh ingredients. On our most recent rounds, we enjoyed fresh Norwegian salmon baked with mushrooms and served with a béarnaise sauce. The chicken breast platter is delectably cooked here with homemade basil and tomato sauce and served with a garden salad and baked potato.

Maren Turis Gade 10. ✆ **98-16-69-72.** Reservations recommended. Main courses 80DKK–195DKK. DC, MC, V. Mon–Sat noon–midnight. Bus: 1, 3, or 5.

Mortens Kro ★★★ 🎁 FRENCH/DANISH This artful restaurant is the domain of Morten Nielsen, the most gifted chef in Aalborg. Consequently, it is the best place to dine in the city. The chef wanted a "New York look but with Parisian ambience," the latter evoked by the champagne bar. This top-rate restaurant exhibits a lot of flair, obeys well-rehearsed rules of cooking technique, and blends classic French cuisine beautifully with Danish flavors. Passionately fond of his trade, the chef takes great care with his appetizers, as evoked by such choices as a seafood plate with a sauté of mint- and lemon-flavored rice noodles. For a main course, he prepares delicacies such as filet of seawolf marinated with chili and lemon and served with a golden saffron risotto. The fresh lobster is divine—boiled to perfection and served with a lemon-flavored homemade mayonnaise. DJs entertain during the weekends.

Mølleå 2–6, Mølleå Arkaden. ✆ **98-12-48-60.** www.mortenskro.dk. Reservations recommended. Main courses 189DKK–248DKK; fixed-price menus 548DKK–848DKK. DC, MC, V. Mon–Sat 5:30–10pm. Bus: 3, 5, 10, or 11.

Skagen ★

105km (65 miles) NE of Aalborg, 488km (303 miles) W of Copenhagen

Since the 19th century, Skagen (pronounced *Skane*) has been the leading artists' colony of Denmark. As is inevitable in such cases, hordes of tourists followed in the footsteps of the artists to discover the northernmost tip of Jutland on its east coast. A sort of "bony finger" of land points into the North Sea at the second-biggest fishing port in Denmark.

We find the combination today of Nordic sailors—Skagen has been a fishing port for centuries—and a colony of artists an intriguing mix. The early artists were more isolated here, but the coming of the railway in 1890 opened up Skagen to the world with its link to the terminus of Frederikshavn.

We've spent hours here in both September and October wandering the heather-covered moors, the undulating stretches of dunes, and some of the best, but not the warmest, beaches in Europe. We particularly like to stand at the point where the North Sea meets the Baltic, the subject of countless landscape paintings. It's not unknown to have visitors applaud the spectacular sunsets here. By the end of July, the visitors are in retreat, and Skagen happily reverts to the locals again.

ESSENTIALS

GETTING THERE **By car,** take the E-45 northeast to Frederikshavn. From there, head north on Route 40 to Skagen. Several **trains** a day run from Copenhagen to Århus, where you connect with another train to Frederikshavn. From Frederikshavn there are 12 daily trains to Skagen.

VISITOR INFORMATION The **Skagen Turistbureau** is at Vestre Strandvej 10 (**© 98-44-13-77;** www.skagen-tourist.dk). Open January 2 to March 31 and November 1 to December 23 Monday to Friday 10am to 4pm, Saturday 10am to 1pm; April 1 to June 13, and August 30 to October 31 Monday to Friday 9:30 to 4pm, Saturday 9:30am to 2pm; June 14 to June 27 and August 7 to August 29 Monday to Friday 9am to 5pm, Saturday 10am to 2pm; and June 28 to August 6 Monday to Saturday 9am to 6pm, Sunday 10am to 4pm. Check the website for closures, including a few days around Christmas and New Year's, and certain public holidays.

SEEING THE SIGHTS

Since it opened in 1907, **Skagen Havn (Skagen Harbor)** ★ has been one of the major attractions in town. It's seen at its best when the boats come back to land their catches (times vary). For early risers, the fish auction "at the rack of the morning" is a popular attraction. Mid-May to mid-October, the oldest part of the harbor is a haven for the boating crowds centered around one of the marinas. Many yachting people in Jutland use Skagen as their favorite harbor haven.

Gammel Skagen (Old Town) ★ lies 2.5km (1½ miles) from Skagen Havn. Signs point the way. Originally Gammel Skagen was the fishing hamlet—that is, until Skagen Havn opened in 1907. Today, Gammel Skagen is a little resort town with large beach hotels that are mainly timeshares.

An attraction worth exploring is **Rådjerg Mile,** a migrating dune moving at the rate of about 11m (36 ft.) annually. 16km (10 miles) south of town, it can be reached via Kandestederne. This dune was formed on the west coast in the 16th century during the great sand drift that characterized the landscape until the 20th century. The dune continues to move yearly, eastward toward the forest.

Den Tilsandede Kirke This church buried in sand dunes 1.5km (1 mile) south of town is an amusing curiosity. The only part that's visible is the upper two-thirds of the tower. When Hans Christian Andersen visited in 1859, he called the church "the Pompeii of Skagen." The only things hidden under the dunes are the remnants of a wall, the old floor, and perhaps the baptismal font. By 1775, the church had fallen into disrepair and was used by fewer and fewer members. By 1795 it was closed down, and in 1810 it was partly demolished, the stones sold to people in the area as building materials for their private houses. Today red stakes in the ground indicate the placing and extent of the nave and vestry.

Ⓒ **98-44-43-71.** Admission 20DKK adults, 10DKK children 5–12. June–Aug daily 11am–5pm; Sept–May Sat–Sun 11am–5pm.

Nordsøen Oceanarium ★★ The main attraction of this two-story oceanarium in Hirtshals is the giant aquarium itself, with some 4.5 million liters (1.2 million gal.) of seawater. Visitors can gaze upon an 8m-high (26-ft.) column of water, or view the "ocean" through an aquarium window, the thickest in the world.

The large aquarium has been designed to house schools of fish of the North Sea, including herring, mackerel, garfish, and horse mackerel. Among the large creatures, several species of North Sea sharks can be viewed. Each day divers feed the shoal fish and the sharks, and describe life in the aquarium to visitors.

The original museum is devoted to modern Danish sea fishing, detailing man's exploitation of the North Sea—for better or worse. Displays of the daily lives of fishermen, equipment, and vessels are placed alongside exhibits depicting the resources of the North Sea. Seals are common along the coast of Denmark, but you seldom spot them. However, in the on-site seal pool, you can observe the animals at close range—above as well as underwater. Feeding times for the seals are daily at 11am and again at 3pm.

Willemoesvej 2, Hirtshals. Ⓒ **98-94-41-88.** www.nordsoenoceanarium.dk. Admission 145DKK adults, 70DKK children 3–11, free for children 2 and under. July–Aug daily 9am–6pm; Sept–June daily 9am–5pm. From Skagen take Rte. 40 south to the junction with Rte. 597 heading west into Hirtshals, a distance of 50km (31 miles).

Skagen By- & Egnsmuseum This museum, a 15-minute stroll from the train depot, is evocative of a time long gone. The lifesaving station here reminds us of how the seas sometimes violently clash in the depths of winter, as demonstrated by the dramatic photographs of ships and men in distress. The homes of well-to-do fishermen as well as their poorer cousins were moved to this open-air museum to demonstrate how life was lived in Skagen from 1830 to 1880. A maritime museum is filled with nautical memorabilia, and an original Dutch windmill is all that's left of the many that used to dot the landscape.

P. K. Nielsensvej 8-10, Fortidsminderne. Ⓒ **98-44-47-60.** www.skagen-bymus.dk. Admission 35DKK, free for children 17 and under. May–June and Aug–Sept Mon–Fri 11am–4pm, Sat–Sun 11am–4pm; July Mon–Fri 10am–5pm, Sat–Sun 11am–4pm; Mar–Apr and Oct Mon–Fri 10am–4pm; Nov–Feb Mon–Fri 11am–3pm.

Skagens Museum ★★ The glory days of the artists of Skagen school of painting come alive at this impressive museum of their work. The apogee of their art was created from the beginning of the 1870s until the turn of the 20th century. The Skagen artists were inspired by naturalism and open-air painting, their favorite motif being quaint cottages or the fishermen working on local beaches. The artists came to celebrate the North Sea landscapes, everything bathed in that special light that seems to exist in Skagen.

The major artists of this period included Michael Ancher (1849–1909) and his wife, Anna (1859–1935). You'll also see works by another of the school's leading painters, P. S. Krøyer (1851–1909), plus many more—the entire collection consists of 1,800 paintings, sculptures, drawings, and graphic works.

Brøndumsvej 4. Ⓒ **98-44-64-44.** www.skagensmuseum.dk. Admission 80DKK, free for children 17 and under. May–Sept daily 10am–5pm; Apr and Oct Tues–Sun 11am–4pm; Nov–Mar Wed–Fri 1–4pm, Sat 11am–4pm, Sun 11am–3pm.

WHERE TO STAY

Finns Hotel Pension Originally built in 1909 in a style that the owner refers to as "a Norwegian wood house," this old-fashioned Danish homestead is designed like houses that Scandinavian immigrants made popular during the 19th century in American states such as Minnesota. In a residential neighborhood of Skagen, a 10- to 15-minute walk northeast of center and a 3-minute walk from the beach, it's decorated with old furniture and antiques. Many rooms have beamed ceilings and a charming but vaguely claustrophobic allure. Our only warning involves a rigidity on the part of the hardworking managers and staff, who establish very clear-cut rules for new arrivals; they aren't noted for their flexibility, and maintain an aggressive "take it or leave it" approach. If you give advance notice, they'll prepare a two-course evening meal, which is served only to residents, for a price of 275DKK per person. If you agree to this, on pain of severe reproach, don't be late for dinner. Children 14 and under are not accepted.

Østre Strandvej 63, DK-9990 Skagen. www.finnshotelpension.dk. ✆ **98-45-01-55.** Fax 98-45-05-55. 6 units, 3 with bathroom. 850DKK–975DKK double with bathroom; 700DKK double without bathroom. Rates include buffet breakfast. MC, V. Closed Oct–Mar. *In room:* No phone.

Ruth's Hotel ★★★ This is a bastion of both comfort and gastronomy—its restaurant, in fact, is one of the greatest outside Copenhagen. In the sand dunes of Old Skagen, it is by the beach just 4km (2½ miles) from the center of modern Skagen. The bedrooms are superior to anything at Skagen, beautifully furnished and designed, exuding spaciousness and light. Some units have a Jacuzzi. A private balcony or terrace opens onto a view of the sea.

The spa is one of the best in Jutland, complete with solarium, sauna, Turkish baths, therapy pool, and gym. The hotel restaurant, Ruth's Gourmet, is one of the top five in the country outside of Copenhagen, yet we hesitate to recommend it because it requires reservations a month in advance. If you're lucky enough to get a table, you'll be rewarded with Chef Michel Michaud's repertoire of sublime dishes, which embrace the best of fine French cuisine and tradition, with a carefully chosen wine carte. You stand a better chance of dining on the airy, sunlit terrace of the on-site Brasserie; the food here is watched over by Chef Michaud himself.

Hans Ruths Vej 1, Gammel Skagen, DK-9990 Skagen. www.ruths-hotel.dk. ✆ **98-44-11-24.** Fax 98-45-08-75. 53 units. 1,725DKK–2,150DKK double; 2,150DKK–3,850DKK suite. AE, DC, MC, V. **Amenities:** Restaurant; bar; exercise room; heated indoor pool; room service; spa. *In room:* TV, hair dryer, Wi-Fi (free).

WHERE TO DINE

Skagen Fiske Restaurant ★★ SEAFOOD One of the best-known seafood restaurants in Jutland occupies the red-sided, gable-roofed building that was erected directly beside the harbor in 1907. You'll enter a bar on the establishment's street level, where the floor is composed of the actual beachfront—nothing more than sand. One floor above is the nautically decorated dining room. Lunches usually include flavorful platters of fish cakes, Norwegian lobster, peel-your-own-shrimp, three different preparations of herring, or grilled filets of sole with lemon sauce. Dinners are more elaborate, consisting of whatever fish has been hauled in that day by local fishermen, prepared any way you specify, with virtually any sauce that's reasonably available.

Fiskehuskai 13. ✆ **98-44-35-44.** www.skagen-fiskerestaurant.dk. Reservations recommended. Lunch platters 30DKK–55DKK; dinner main courses 195DKK–395DKK. AE, DC, MC, V. Daily 10am–10:30pm. Closed Jan–Feb.

THE BEST OF NORWAY

8

The "Land of the Midnight Sun" offers a truly unique and unforgettable travel experience. Norwegians view their scrub-covered islands, snow-crested peaks, and glacier-born fjords as symbols of a strong wilderness culture. The majestic scenery inspired the symphonies of Grieg, the plays of Ibsen, and the paintings of Munch. The landscape has also shaped the Norwegians' view of themselves as pastoral dwellers in one of the world's most splendid countrysides.

Norway is a land of tradition, exemplified by its rustic stave churches and its folk dances. But Norway is also an extremely modern place. This technologically advanced nation is rich in petroleum and hydroelectric energy. Norwegians enjoy a well-developed national social insurance system that provides pensions, health insurance, unemployment insurance, and rehabilitation assistance.

One of the last great natural frontiers of the world, Norway invites exploration. So that you don't exhaust yourself with difficult decisions on where to go, I've compiled the best deals and once-in-a-lifetime experiences in this chapter. What follows is the best of the best.

THE most unforgettable TRAVEL EXPERIENCES

- **Experiencing "Norway in a Nutshell":** One of Europe's great train rides, this 12-hour excursion is Norway's most exciting. The route encompasses two arms of the Sognefjord, and the section from Myrdal to Flåm—a drop of 600m (1,968 ft.)—takes you past seemingly endless waterfalls. Tours leave from the Bergen train station. If you have limited time but want to see the country's most dramatic scenery, take this spectacular train trip. See "Flåm: Stopover on Europe's Most Scenic Train Ride," in chapter 11.
- **Exploring the Fjord Country:** Stunningly serene and majestic, Norway's fjords are some of the world's most awe-inspiring sights. Bergen can be your gateway; two of the country's most famous fjords, the Hardangerfjord and the Sognefjord, can easily be explored from here. If you have time for only one, my vote goes to the Sognefjord for its sheer, lofty

walls that rise to more than 1,000m (3,280 ft.) along its fantasy landscape of towering cliffs. See p. 256.

- **Seeing the Midnight Sun at the Arctic Circle:** This is one of the major reasons visitors go to Norway. The Arctic Circle marks the boundary of the midnight sun of the arctic summer and the sunless winters of the north. The midnight sun can be seen from the middle of May until the end of July. The Arctic Circle cuts across Norway south of Bodø, from which bus excursions visit the circle. The adventurous few who arrive in the winter miss the midnight sun but are treated to a spectacular display of the aurora borealis, the flaming spectacle of the arctic winter sky. See chapter 11.

THE best HIKE

- **Lofoten Fishing Villages:** The best hikes in Norway don't always have to be up steep mountains. In the remote Lofotens in the north of Norway, while based on the glaciated island of **Moskenesøy,** I like to hike along a seascape of little fishing villages stacked up one after the other like a string of pearls. The mountain peak of Hermannsdalstind, rising to 1,029m (3,375 ft.), offers a scenic backdrop. Begin in the north, at the little fishing village of Hamnøy, and then hike southward to other quaint settlements at Sakrisøy, Reine, Moskenes, Sørvägen, and the curiously named Å. To extend the hike at Sørvägen for another 2 hours, you can hike inland along a signposted rambler's trail to get acquainted with the handsome interior of a Lofoten island. See "The Lofoten Islands," in chapter 11.

THE best DOWNHILL SKIING

- **Voss:** This excellent winter resort has eight chairlifts and an aerial cableway carrying passengers up to a peak of 788m (2,625 ft.). In all, there are 40km (25 miles) of alpine slopes that have been compared favorably to those in western Austria. One ski lift climbs 900m (2,952 ft.) from Traastolen to the top of the mountain of Slettafjell, with a wide and varied choice of downhill runs. See "Voss: A Winter Playground," in chapter 11.

THE most scenic BOAT TRIP

- **Sognefjord:** If you take only one fjord trip in your life, make it the panoramic Sognefjord in western Norway. Excursions depart the harbor at Bergen (p. 256). As you sail along, it's like a fantasy view of Norway, as the deep blue fjord waters are broken by many waterfalls. Sognefjord is the longest fjord in Norway, stretching for a distance of 205km (127 miles) until the mountains of the Jotunheimen National Park. Along the banks of this fjord—best explored in the late spring and summer—are farms, 19th-century villages, and lush landscapes. In springtime, plum, pear, apple, and cherry trees grow profusely.

THE most memorable LANDSCAPE DRIVE

- **Overland Route Oslo/Bergen:** The mountainous drive from Oslo to Bergen is one of the great scenic trips of Europe. You'll venture through mountain passes and even make a ferry crossing here and there. Along the way, you'll pass fjords and snowcapped mountains, along with waterfalls, fjord villages, and an ancient stave church. The most memorable stopover is at the town of Flåm, which is on the Aurlandsfjord, a tip of the Sognefjord, the most scenic fjord in Norway (p. 283). If time allows, I recommend you plan at least 2 days for this memorable tour. See "Flåm: Stopover on Europe's Most Scenic Train Ride," in chapter 11, for specific directions.

THE best WILDLIFE VIEWING

- **The Puffins of Vaerøy:** In the remote Lofoten Islands in the north of Norway is one of Europe's great bird-watching retreats. The thinly populated island is the nesting place for more than 1.5 million seabirds, including sea eagles, auks, guillemots, kittiwakes, cormorants, the arctic tern, petrels, gulls, and other species, which breed from May to August. Many birders come here just to see the famous puffins at the seabird rookeries. See p. 301.

THE best HOTELS, INNS & RESORTS

- **Grand Hotel** (Oslo; www.grand.no; ✆ **23-21-20-00**): This has long been Norway's premier hotel, and is the last of Oslo's classic old-world palaces. Opened in 1874, it's very popular among North American tour groups. Ibsen and Munch were regular visitors. The opulent suites house the Nobel Peace Prize winner every year. See p. 211.
- **First Hotel Grims Grenka** (Oslo; www.grimsgrenka.no; ✆ **23-10-72-00**): Near Akershus Castle, Oslo's only boutique and design hotel is definitely worth its *havsalt* (sea salt). It offers 50 low-key but colorful rooms with large beds on raised platforms, shag carpets, freestanding marble baths, and custom toiletries. A downstairs bar serves organic teas, top-shelf drinks—and caviar. The restaurant is also excellent. See p. 211.
- **Hotel Ullensvang** (Loftus i Hardanger; www.hotel-ullensvang.no; ✆ **53-67-00-00**): My favorite inn within the fjord country, the Ullensvang, from 1846, is on the bank of the Hardangerfjord. It was once the retreat of the composer Edvard Grieg, whose piano is still in a cottage on the grounds. See p. 277.
- **Fretheim Hotel** (Flåm; www.fretheim-hotel.no; ✆ **57-63-63-00**): This hotel dates from 1866, and it's no wonder given the jaw-dropping views overlooking fjord waters. Guest rooms are modern and comfortable, and the restaurant is excellent. See p. 284.
- **Hotel Mundal** (Fjaerland; www.hotelmundal.no; ✆ **57-69-31-01**): On the banks of the Fjaerlandsfjord, this hotel is another waterside stunner. Modern updates and improvements have ensured that it's still a wonderful choice in one of the most scenic parts of the western fjord country. See p. 282.
- **Radisson Blu Hotel Norge** (Bergen; www.radissonblu.com/hotelnorge-bergen; ✆ **800/333-3333** in the U.S., or 55-57-30-00): This grand hotel on Norway's west coast is sleek, modern, and cosmopolitan. It is located on the city's park, and offers every modern amenity you could ever expect from an upscale hotel, including free Wi-Fi. Excellent staff and service. See p. 260.

THE best DINING EXPERIENCES

- **Tjuvholmen Sjømagasin** (Oslo; ✆ **23-89-77-77;** www.sjomagasinet.no): Opened on newly reclaimed land at the Aker Brygge waterfront, this chic seafood restaurant serves outstanding lobster, king crab, and fish in a sprawling dining room with panoramic views of Oslofjord harbor—and of the open kitchen. Pick your catch straight from steel casks, then hand it to the team of chefs. The restaurant is run by Bjørn Tore Furset, a local wunderkind whose empire includes city eateries Havsmak, Ekeberg, and Argent. See p. 221.
- **Hanne På Høyden** (Bergen; ✆ **55-32-34-32;** hannepaahoeyden.wordpress.com): Chef Hanne Frosta runs this outstanding organic, farm-to-plate restaurant, which pays special attention paid to the tender meat and succulent fish dishes. See p. 265.

THE best MUSEUMS

- **Viking Ship Museum** (Oslo): Three stunning burial vessels from the Viking era were excavated on the shores of the Oslofjord and are now displayed in Bygdøy, Oslo's "museum island." The most spectacular is the *Oseberg,* from the 9th century, a 20m (66-ft.) dragon ship with a wealth of ornaments. See p. 229.
- **Edvard Munch Museum** (Oslo): Here you'll find the most significant collection of the work of Edvard Munch (1863–1944), Scandinavia's most noted artist. The museum, his gift to the city, contains a staggering treasure-trove: 1,100 paintings, 4,500 drawings, and about 18,000 prints—including *The Scream,* which was restored after theft and vandalism several years ago. See p. 225.
- **Norwegian Folk Museum** (Oslo): Some 140 original buildings from all over Norway were shipped here and reassembled on 14 hectares (35 acres) at Bygdøy. Although Scandinavia is known for such open-air museums, this one is the best. The buildings range from a rare stave church, constructed around 1200, to one of the oldest wooden buildings still standing in Norway. Old-time Norwegian life is captured here like nowhere else. See p. 228.

THE best OF NORWAY ONLINE

- **Norwegian Tourist Board** (www.visitnorway.com): This is the country's official travel authority, with plenty of tips on attractions and special interests, accommodations, dining, and entertainment, along with maps and notes on the weather.
- **Explore Fjord Norway** (www.fjordnorway.com): This site focuses on one of Scandinavia's most visited attractions, the fjord country of western Norway. It provides information on fjord trips and cruises, with details for the active vacationer on climbing, walking, and cycling, plus information about fjord culture.
- **Official Site of the Oslo Tourist Office** (www.visitoslo.com): The site explores the city in detail, with tips on attractions, restaurants, activities, accommodations, and shopping.

OSLO

Over the years, Oslo, the capital of Norway, has grown from a sprawling country town into a sophisticated metropolis. Fueled by oil money from the "black gold" of the North Sea, Oslo today is permeated with a Nordic joie de vivre in contrast to its staid, dull reputation of times past. Oslo still manages, in spite of its growing numbers, to have more green belts than any other European capital. There are still virgin forests in Oslo and hundreds of hiking trails that lead you to fjords or mountains. No slouch in the cultural department, either, Oslo has some of the greatest museums in all of northern Europe. Its only real shortcoming is that it's one of the most expensive cities in the world.

ORIENTATION

Arriving

BY PLANE

Planes from all over the world fly into **Oslo International Airport** in Gardemoen (✆ **06400** or 91-50-64-00), about 50km (31 miles) east of downtown Oslo, a 45-minute drive from the center. All domestic and international flights coming into Oslo arrive through this much-upgraded airport, including aircraft belonging to SAS, British Airways, Norwegian, and Ryanair. Two smaller airports, **Torp** (✆ **33-42-70-00;** www.torp.no) and **Rygge** (✆ **69-23-00-00;** www.ryg.no), both south of Oslo's city center, serve various discount European airlines.

There's regular bus service from all three airports into downtown Oslo. Bus service for Gardemoen is maintained by **SAS** (✆ **81-50-01-76;** www.flybussen.no), whose buses deliver passengers to the Central Railway Station and to most of the SAS hotels within Oslo. The cost is NOK130 per person. For Rygge, contact **Rygge Expressen** (www.rygge-ekspressen.no); the ticket price is NOK130. For Torp, contact **Torp Expressen** (www.torpekspressen.no); the ticket price is NOK190. There's also a high-speed railway service, **Flytoget** (✆ **81-50-07-77;** www.flytoget.no), between Gardemoen and Oslo's main railway station, requiring a transit time of only 19 minutes and departing approximately every 10 minutes, priced at NOK140 per person each way. There are also local trains to both Rygge and Torp airports. If you want to take a taxi, be prepared for a minimum of NOK700 for up to four passengers plus luggage to Gargemoen; both other airports will cost significantly more. If you need a "maxi-taxi," a minivan that's suitable for between 5 and 15 passengers plus luggage, you'll be assessed NOK900.

High-Speed Link from Stockholm

A high-speed train between Stockholm and Oslo takes only 4 hours and 50 minutes between these Scandinavian capitals. Depending on the day, there are two to three trains daily in each direction. This high-speed train now competes directly with air travel.

BY TRAIN

Trains from the Continent, Sweden, and Denmark arrive at **Oslo Sentralstasjon,** Jernbanetorget 1 (✆ **81-50-08-88** for train information), located at the beginning of Karl Johans Gate, in the center of the city. The station is open daily from 4:30am to 1am. From the Central Station, trains leave for Bergen, Stavanger, Trondheim, Bodø, and all other rail links in Norway. You can also take trams to all major parts of Oslo. Lockers and a luggage office are available at the station, where you can exchange money, if needed.

BY CAR

If you're driving from mainland Europe, the fastest way to reach Oslo is to take the car ferry from Frederikshavn, Denmark. From Frederikshavn, car ferries run to several towns near Oslo and to Gothenburg, Sweden. You can also take a car ferry from Copenhagen to several points in western Sweden, or from Helsingør, Denmark, to Helsingborg, Sweden. Hwy. E-6 runs the length of Sweden's western coast from Malmö through Helsingborg and Gothenburg, right up to Oslo. If you're driving from Stockholm to Oslo, take E-3 west to Örebro, where it connects with E-18 to Oslo. Once you near the outskirts of Oslo from any direction, follow the signs into the Sentrum.

BY FERRY

Ferries from Europe arrive at the Oslo port, a 15-minute walk (or a short taxi ride) from the center. From Denmark, Scandinavia's link with the Continent, ferries depart for Oslo from Copenhagen, Hirtshals, and Frederikshavn.

From Strømstad, Sweden, in the summer the daily crossing to Sandefjord, Norway, takes 2½ hours; from Sandefjord, it's an easy drive or train ride north to Oslo.

Visitor Information

Assistance and information for visitors are available at the **Tourist Information Office,** Fridtjof Nansens Plass 5, N-0160 Oslo (www.visitoslo.com). Free maps, brochures, sightseeing tickets, and guide services are available. The office is open June to August daily 9am to 7pm, April to May and September Monday to Saturday 9am to 5pm, and October to March Monday to Friday 9am to 4pm. The information office at the **Oslo Sentralstasjon (Central Station),** Jernbanetorget 1, is open daily from May to September 8am to 8pm and October to April 8am to 6pm. The centralized phone number to call all the tourist offices in Oslo is ✆ **81-53-05-55.**

Neighborhoods in Brief

Oslo is made for walking—in fact, you can walk from the Central Station all the way to the Royal Palace (Slottet) in a straight line. Except for excursions to the museum-loaded Bygdøy peninsula and the Holmenkollen Ski Jump, most attractions can be covered on foot.

Central Oslo Oslo is not neatly divided into separate neighborhoods or districts. It consists mainly of central Oslo, with the Central Station to the east of the city center and the Royal Palace to the west. Karl Johans Gate, the principal street, connects these two points. Central Oslo is the heart of the city—the most crowded and traffic-congested, but also the most convenient place to stay. Those on the most rushed of schedules—the average visitor spends only 2 days in Oslo—will want to book accommodations in the center. It's not a real neighborhood per se, but it's the core of the city, as Piccadilly Circus is to London. Most Oslo hotels and restaurants are here, as are almost 50 museums and galleries—enough to fill plenty of rainy days. The best of the lot include Akershus Castle, the Historical Museum, and the National Gallery.

The streets Drammensveien and Frognerveien lead northwest to Frogner Park (Frognerparken), whose main entrance is on Kirkeveien. This historical area is the site of the Vigeland Sculpture Park, which displays some of Gustav Vigeland's masterpieces.

Old Town The Old Town (or Gamlebyen) is south of the Parliament Building (the Stortinget) and Karl Johans Gate. This section contains some of the city's old-fashioned restaurants, along with the Norwegian Resistance Museum and the Old Town Hall. A stay here is the same as staying in central Oslo (see above). The only difference is that the streets of the Old Town have more old-fashioned Norwegian flavor than the more modern parts of central Oslo.

Aker Brygge One of Oslo's newest neighborhoods, Aker Brygge is an excellent place for dining and diversions, but with few hotels. For sights along the waterfront, it's the best place for long walks to take in the harbor life. It emerged near the mouth of the Oslofjord in the old wharf area formerly used for shipbuilding yards. Fueled by oil wealth, steel-and-glass buildings now rise from what had been a relatively dilapidated section. Some of the best shops, theaters, restaurants, and cultural attractions are located here.

Eastern Oslo The main attractions in eastern Oslo are the Botanisk Hage (Botanical Garden), the Zoological Museum, and the Munch Museum in Tøyen—little more is worth seeing here. Unless you're interested in seeing those sights mentioned, you might skip eastern Oslo. However, thousands of visitors head here just to see the Munch Museum (p. 225).

West End This chic residential area is graced with some of the city's finest hotels and restaurants. It's a more tranquil setting than the center and only 15 minutes away by public transportation. Many visitors who stay here don't mind the short commute and prefer this area to the more traffic-clogged center. However, for walking and sightseeing, central Oslo and its port are more alluring. There is little to see in the West End unless you like walking up and down pleasant residential streets.

Bygdøy Farther west—6km (3¾ miles) by car, but better reached by car ferry—is the Bygdøy peninsula. Here you'll find such attractions as the Norwegian Folk Museum, the Viking ships, the polar ship *Fram,* and the Kon-Tiki Museum. Break up your sightseeing venture with a meal here, but plan to stay elsewhere.

Frogner The suburb of Frogner begins .8km (½ mile) west of Oslo's center and stretches for a mile or so. Unless you specifically have business here, you can probably skip this section of the city.

Grønland District Behind the S-station, the main rail station for Oslo, is the Grønland district, where many Oslovians go for ethnic dining and great nightlife. There is little of sightseeing interest here, though the large immigrant population has given it some real local appeal, with some great budget Indian and Pakistani restaurants. Come here for affordable dining, not for long, leisurely walks. On a hurried visit, you could afford to skip Grønland entirely.

Grünerløkka At last, once-staid Oslo has grown big and diverse enough to have its own trendy, counterculture district. Lying in east Oslo is trendy Grünerløkka, which most of its inhabitants refer to affectionately as

"Løkka." This once-run-down sector of Oslo traditionally was known as the worker's district. Today many professional Oslovians are moving in to restore apartments, and the district is the site of several fashionable cafes and restaurants. If you're young with a roving eye at night, you might want to check out some of the establishments in this area.

Oslofjord Oslo neighborhoods lie along the Oslofjord, which stretches more than 97km (60 miles) north from the Skagerrak to Oslo. Basins dotted with islands fill the fjord. (There are 40 islands in the immediate Oslo archipelago.) Chances are, you won't be staying or dining along the fjord, but might consider a boat trip along the water, as it's a grand attraction on a summer day.

Holmenkollen Nearly all visitors want to see Holmenkollen, a wooded range of hills northwest of the city rising to about 226m (741 ft.). You can reach it in 35 minutes by electric train from the city center. Skiers might want to stay here in winter, lodging at the Holmenkollen Park Hotel Rica (p. 216). Otherwise, visit for the view and perhaps make it a luncheon stopover, then head back to the historic core.

Marka Oslo's forest is a sprawling recreation area with hiking, bicycle riding, skiing, fishing, wild-berry picking, jogging trails, and more. It contains 343 lakes, 500km (310 miles) of ski trails, 623km (386 miles) of trails and roads, 11 sports chalets, and 24 ski jumps and alpine slopes. If you like to go for long walks on summer days, Marka's the spot for you. It's also one of the best places in Greater Oslo for a picnic.

GETTING AROUND

Oslo has an efficient citywide network of buses, trams (streetcars), and subways. Buses and electric trains take passengers to the suburbs; from mid-April to October, ferries to Bygdøy depart from the harbor in front of the Oslo Rådhuset (City Hall).

DISCOUNT PASSES The **Oslo Pass** can help you become acquainted with the city at a fraction of the usual price. It allows free travel on public transportation, free admission to museums and other top sights, discounts on sightseeing buses and boats, a rebate on your car rental, and special treats in restaurants. You can purchase the card at hotels, fine stores, and tourist information offices; from travel agents; and in the branches of Sparebanken Oslo Akershus. Adults pay NOK230 for a 1-day card, NOK340 for 2 days, and NOK430 for 3 days. Children's cards cost NOK100, NOK120, and NOK160.

BY BUS, TRAM & SUBWAY Jernbanetorget is Oslo's major **bus and tram** terminal stop. Most buses and trams passing through the heart of town stop at Wessels Plass, next to the Parliament, or at Stortorvet, the main marketplace. Many also stop at the National Theater or University Square on Karl Johans Gate, as well as stopping through Oslo's suburbs.

The **subway (T-banen)** has four branch lines to the east. The Western Suburban route (including Holmenkollen) has four lines to the residential sections and recreation grounds west and north of the city. Subways and trains leave from near the National Theater on Karl Johans Gate.

For schedule and fare information, call **Trafikanten** (✆ **81-50-01-76;** www.trafikanten.no). The automated machines on board stamp and validate tickets. Drivers sell single-trip tickets for NOK40; children travel for half-fare, though you can save money if you buy these ahead of time at various ticket machines. An eight-coupon Flexi card costs NOK190 and is half-price for children. Maxi cards can be used for unlimited transfers for 1 hour from the time the ticket is stamped.

BY TAXI If you need a taxi, call © **23-23-23-23,** available 24 hours a day. Reserve at least an hour in advance.

Hiring a taxi is very expensive in Oslo. Tariffs start at NOK46 for hailed taxis in the streets or at NOK50 if you summon one in advance. In addition to regular fares, there are pricey surcharges between 5 and 10pm; these increase even further between 10pm and 6am. All taxis have meters. When a cab is available, its roof light goes on. Taxis can be hailed on the street, provided they're more than 91m (298 ft.) from a taxi rank. The most difficult time to hail a taxi is Monday to Friday 8:30 to 10am and 3 to 5pm, and Saturday 8:30 to 10am.

BY CAR Driving is not a practical way to get around Oslo because parking is limited. The efficient public transportation system makes a private car unnecessary. You can reach even the most isolated areas by public transportation.

Among the multistory parking lots in the city center, the best is **Vestre Vika P-hus,** Dronning Mauds Gate (© **81-53-21-32**). The cost of parking a car in a public garage is NOK60 per hour or NOK195 for 24 hours. Illegally parked cars are towed away. For car problems, call the **NAF Alarm Center** (© **22-34-14-00**), available 24 hours a day.

BY FERRY Beginning in mid-April, ferries depart for Bygdøy from Pier 3 in front of the Oslo Rådhuset. For schedules, call **Båtservice** (© **23-35-68-90**). The ferry or bus to Bygdøy is a good choice because parking there is limited. Other ferries leave for various parts of the Oslofjord. Inquire at the **Tourist Information Office,** Fridtjof Nansens Plass 5, N-0160 Oslo (© **24-14-77-00**).

[Fast FACTS] OSLO

American Express American Express Reisebyrå, Maribores Gate 13 (© **22-98-35-00**), is open Monday to Friday 9am to 6pm, Saturday 10am to 4pm.

Area Code The country code for Norway is **47.** If you're calling from outside the country, the city code for Oslo is **2.** Inside Norway, no area or city codes are needed. Telephone numbers have eight digits.

Currency Exchange **Banks** will exchange most foreign currencies or cash traveler's checks. Bring your passport for identification. If banks are closed, try automated machines at the Oslo Sentralstasjon to exchange currency. For foreign currency exchange go to **Forex,** at Oslo Sentralstasjon, Jernbanetorget 1 (© **22-17-60-80**). It's open Monday to Friday 8am to 8pm and Saturday 9am to 5pm.

Drugstores A 24-hour pharmacy is **Jernbanetorvets Apotek,** Jernbanetorget 4A (© **22-41-24-82**).

Embassies & Consulates See "Fast Facts: Norway" in chapter 21.

Emergencies Dial the Oslo **police** at © **112;** to report a **fire,** call © **110;** call an **ambulance** at © **113.**

Newspapers & Magazines English-language newspapers and magazines are sold—at least, in the summer months—at newsstands (kiosks) throughout Oslo. International editions, including the *International Herald Tribune* and *USA Today,* are always available, as are the European editions of *Time* and *Newsweek.*

Police Dial © **112.**

Post Office The **Oslo General Post Office** is at Dronningensgatan 15 (© **23-14-90-00** for information). Enter at the corner of Prinsensgate. It's open Monday to Friday 8am to 5pm and Saturday 9am to 2pm; it's closed Sunday and public holidays. You can arrange for mail to be sent to the main post office in care of general delivery. The address is Poste Restante,

PO Box 1181-Sentrum, Dronningensgatan 15, N-0101 Oslo, Norway. You must show your passport to collect it.

Safety Of the four Scandinavian capitals, Oslo is widely considered the safest. However, it is still a major city, so don't be lulled into a false sense of security. Be careful, and don't carry your wallet visibly exposed or sling your purse over your shoulder.

Taxis See "Getting Around," above.

Toilets Clean public toilets can be found throughout the city center, in parks, and at all bus, rail, and air terminals. For a detailed list, contact the Tourist Information Office.

Weather See the temperature chart in "When to Go," in chapter 2.

WHERE TO STAY

By North American and European standards, hotels in Oslo are very expensive. Oslovian hotels lose most of their business travelers, their main revenue source, during the peak tourist months in midsummer. July is always a month for discounts. Some hotels' discounts begin June 21. Regular pricing usually resumes in mid-August.

The most economy-minded visitors can cut costs by staying at one of the old-fashioned hotels that offer a number of rooms without private bathrooms. Sometimes a room will have a shower but no toilet. Even the rooms without bathrooms usually have a sink with hot and cold running water.

HOTEL RESERVATIONS The worst months for finding a place to stay in Oslo are May, June, September, and October, when many business conferences are held. July and August are better, though that's the peak of the summer tourist invasion.

If you happen to arrive in Oslo without a reservation, head for the **Oslo Tourist Information Office,** Fridtjof Nansens Plass 5 (✆ **81-53-05-55**), which can find you a room in your price category. The minimum stay is 2 days. Don't try to phone—the service is strictly for walk-ins who need a room on the night of their arrival.

Central Oslo

VERY EXPENSIVE

First Hotel Grims Grenka ★ ☺ While this sleek spot once lagged behind its competitor the Millennium, this is now one of the city's most desirable addresses. This elegant boutique hotel, whose lobby has a seven-story glassed-in atrium with Oriental carpets, columns, and a fireplace, has a personalized feel and excellent, professional staff. This is one of the few hotels anywhere where I prefer the regular rooms to the oddly laid-out, curiously spartan suites, where lots of room might be devoted, say, to an interior hallway. Each of the suites is thematically decorated, based on the life of a famous Scandinavian, such as opera and ballet personalities Kirsten Flagstad, Ingrid Bjoner, and Indra Lorentzen. Rooms and suites are accessed via a labyrinthine path of stairs and angled hallways.

Kongensgate 5, N-0153 Oslo. www.grimsgrenka.no. ✆ **23-10-72-00.** 45 units. NOK1,495–NOK2,195 double; from NOK2,495–NOK2,995 suite. Rates include breakfast. AE, DC, MC, V. Parking NOK100–NOK170 per night. T-banen: Stortinget. **Amenities:** Nightclub; fitness room; wellness center; outdoor Jacuzzi on roof terrace; sauna. *In room:* A/C, TV, kitchenette, minibar, Wi-Fi.

Grand Hotel ★★★ ☺ Norway's most famous guests still arrive at the country's premier hotel, and there's a chance you'll catch glimpse of CEOs, Nobel Prize winners, and movie stars. Tradition and style reign supreme here, as they did when the Grand opened its doors in 1874 in a Louis XVI revival–style building imbued with

Where to Stay & Dine in Oslo

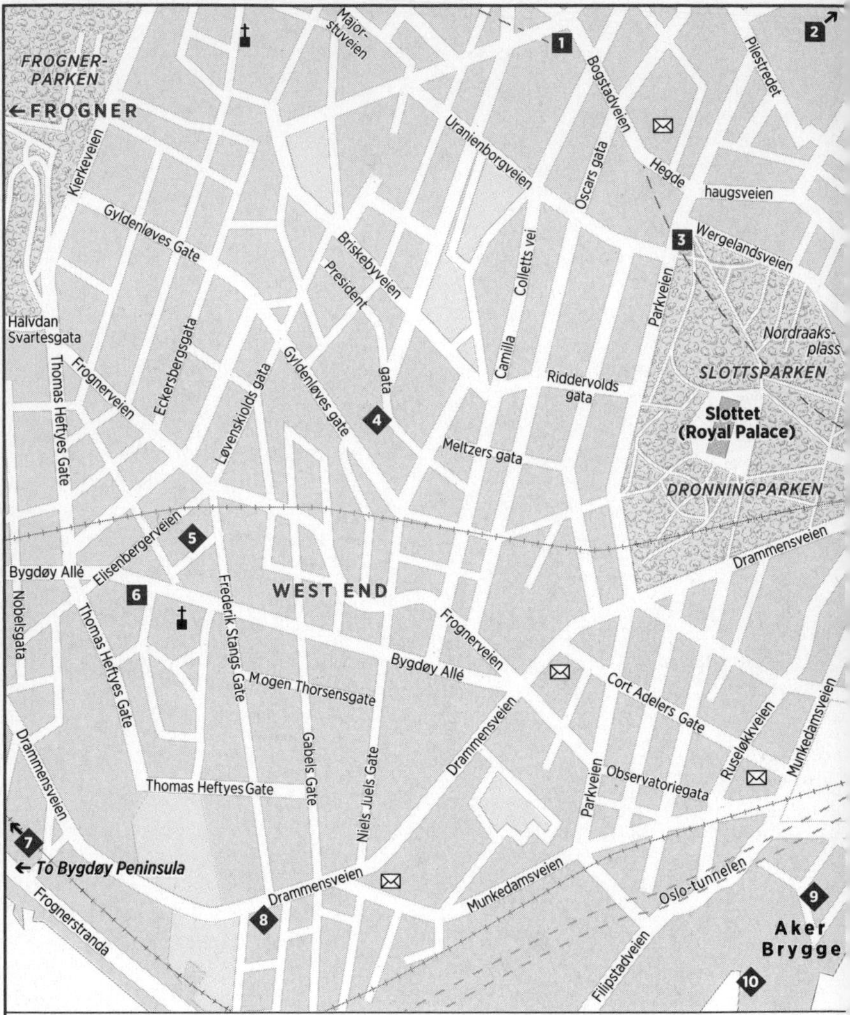

FROGNERPARKEN
FROGNER
WEST END
SLOTTSPARKEN
Slottet (Royal Palace)
DRONNINGPARKEN
Nordraaksplass
Aker Brygge
To Bygdøy Peninsula

ACCOMMODATIONS

Best Western Hotell Bondeheimen **14**
Cochs Pensjonat **3**
First Hotel Grims Grenka **26**
Grand Hotel **17**
Hotel Bastion **28**
Hotel Bristol **15**
Radisson BLU Airport Hotel **2**
Radisson BLU Scandinavia Hotel **11**
Rica Hotel Bygdøy Allé **6**
Thon Hotel Cecil **21**
Thon Hotel Gardermoen **2**
Thon Hotel Gyldenløve **1**

DINING

Brasserie 45 **18**
Bristol Grill **16**
Ekeberg **29**
Engebret Café **27**

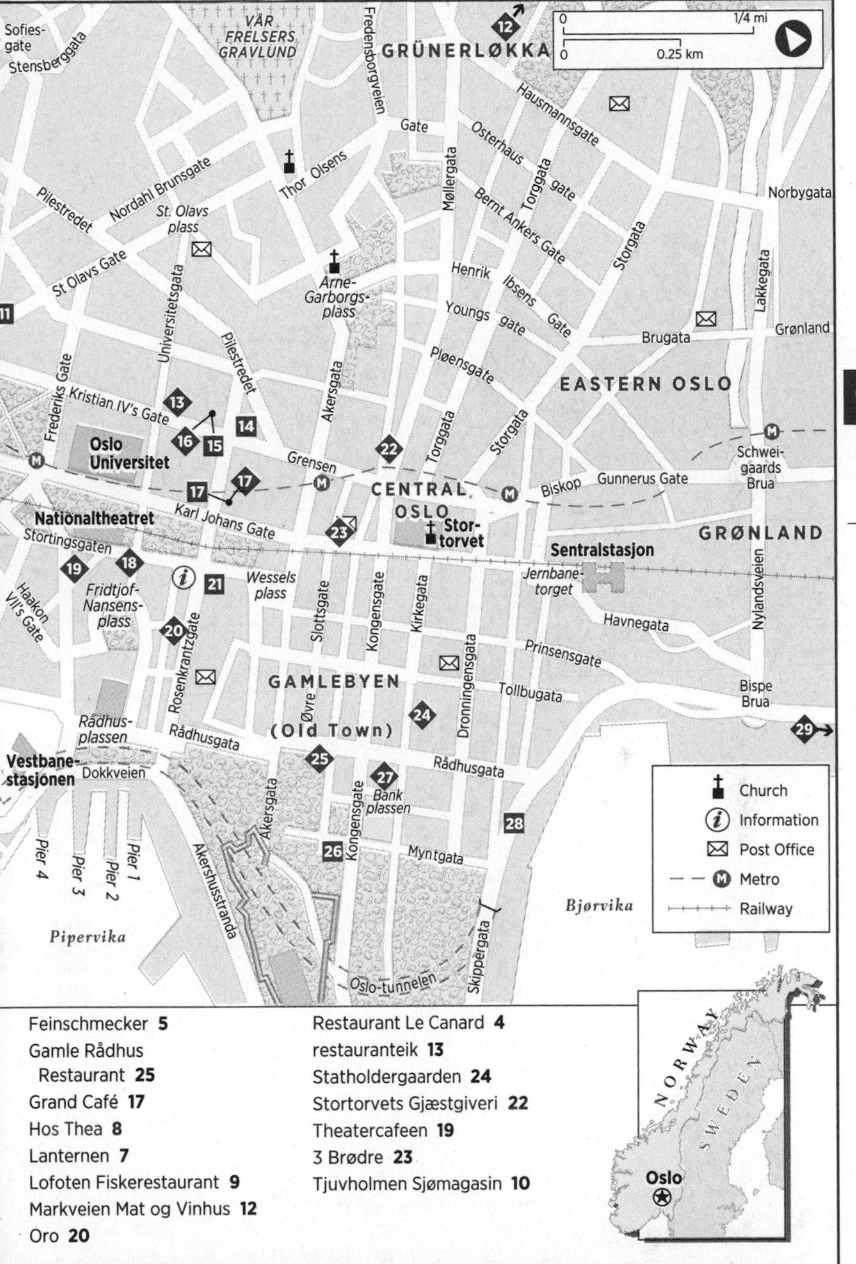

Sofies-gate
Stensberggata
VÅR FRELSERS GRAVLUND
Fredensborgveien
GRÜNERLØKKA
0 1/4 mi
0 0.25 km
Hausmannsgate
Gate
Osterhaus gate
Thor Olsens
Møllergata
Torggata
Bernt Ankers Gate
Norbygata
Nordahl Brunsgate
Pilestredet
St. Olavs plass
St Olavs Gate
Arne-Garborgs-plass
Henrik Ibsens Gate
Storgata
Lakkegata
Youngs gate
Brugata
Grønland
Universitetsgata
Pilestredet
Akersgata
Pløensgate
EASTERN OSLO
Frederiks Gate
Kristian IV's Gate
Oslo Universitet
Torggata
Storgata
Grensen
Schwei-gaards Brua
CENTRAL OSLO
Biskop
Gunnerus Gate
Nationaltheatret
Karl Johans Gate
Stor-torvet
Stortingsgaten
GRØNLAND
Sentralstasjon
Wessels plass
Jernbane-torget
Fridtjof-Nansens-plass
Slottsgate
Kongensgate
Kirkegata
Nylandsveien
Haakon VII's Gate
Rosenkrantzgate
Havnegata
Prinsensgate
Dronningensgata
GAMLEBYEN (Old Town)
Tollbugata
Bispe Brua
Øvre
Rådhus-plassen
Rådhusgata
Rådhusgata
Vestbane-stasjonen
Dokkveien
Akersgata
Bank plassen
Kongensgate
Church
Information
Post Office
Metro
Railway
Myntgata
Pier 4
Pier 3
Pier 2
Pier 1
Akershusstranda
Bjørvika
Skippergata
Pipervika
Oslo-tunnelen
NORWAY
SWEDEN
Oslo
Feinschmecker 5
Gamle Rådhus Restaurant 25
Grand Café 17
Hos Thea 8
Lanternen 7
Lofoten Fiskerestaurant 9
Markveien Mat og Vinhus 12
Oro 20
Restaurant Le Canard 4
restauranteik 13
Statholdergaarden 24
Stortorvets Gjæstgiveri 22
Theatercafeen 19
3 Brødre 23
Tjuvholmen Sjømagasin 10

touches of Art Nouveau. Guest rooms are in the 19th-century core or in one of the tasteful modern additions, such as the eight-story extension that contains larger, brighter doubles. Children enjoy the indoor heated pool, and the reception staff keeps a list of local activities that will amuse kids. The hotel has several restaurants that serve international and Scandinavian food. The Palmen, the Restaurant Julius Fritzner, and the Grand Café (p. 218), the most famous cafe in Oslo, all offer live entertainment.

Karl Johans Gate 31, N-0159 Oslo. www.grand.no. ✆ **800/223-5652** in the U.S., or 23-21-20-00. 292 units. NOK1,495–NOK2,400 double; from NOK9,000–NOK25,000 suite. Rates include buffet breakfast. AE, DC, MC, V. Parking NOK330. T-banen: Stortinget. **Amenities:** 3 restaurants; 2 bars; nightclub; babysitting; fitness center; health club; indoor heated pool; room service; sauna; Wi-Fi; rooms for those w/ limited mobility. *In room:* A/C, TV, minibar, hair dryer.

Hotel Bristol ★★★ ☺ Imbued with character, this 1920s-era hotel competes aggressively and gracefully with two other historic properties, the Grand and the Continental. Of the three, the Bristol consistently emerges as the hippest and the most accessible. Set in the commercial core of Oslo, 1 block north of Karl Johans Gate, the Bristol is warm, rich with tradition, and comfortable. It also isn't as formal as either the Grand or the Continental, attracting the media, arts, and showbiz communities, with a sense of playfulness and fun that's unmatched by either of its rivals. Units are comfortable and dignified, but not as plush or as intensely "decorated" as the rooms in either of its grander competitors. Lavish public areas still evoke the Moorish-inspired Art Deco heyday in which they were built. There's enormous life and energy in this hotel—thanks to active restaurants, such as the Bristol Grill (p. 218), piano bars, and a sense of elegant yet unpretentious conviviality.

Kristian IV's Gate 7, N-0164 Oslo 1. www.bristol.no. ✆ **22-82-60-00.** 252 units. NOK2,650–NOK3,200 double; NOK8,000 suite. Rates include breakfast buffet. AE, DC, MC, V. Parking NOK300. Tram: 10, 11, 17, or 18. **Amenities:** 2 restaurants; 2 bars; nightclub/dance bar; small-scale exercise room and fitness center; room service; spa. *In room:* A/C, TV, hair dryer, minibar.

Thon Hotel Cecil ★ This contemporary hotel enjoys a central location, with many restaurants, sights, and shops within a short walk of the main entrance of the hotel. Dating from 1989, it was constructed on the site of a previous hotel destroyed by fire. As if inspired by a much grander Hyatt, most of its rooms are built to open onto a central atrium. Only four rooms on each of the eight floors overlook the street (the sometimes rowdy—at least, at night—Rosenkrantzgate). The well-maintained rooms are cozy and contain neatly kept bathrooms.

Stortingsgate 8 (entrance on Rosenkrantzgate), N-0130 Oslo. www.thonhotels.no. ✆ **23-31-48-00.** 111 units. NOK1,545–NOK2,295 double; NOK2,145–NOK3,595 suite. AE, DC, MC, V. Parking NOK235. T-banen: Stortinget. **Amenities:** Rooms for those w/limited mobility. *In room:* A/C, TV, hair dryer, minibar, Wi-Fi.

EXPENSIVE

Radisson Blu Scandinavia Hotel ★ As the sun sets over Oslo, it's great to gather with friends at Summit 21, a bar on the 21st floor, for one of the grandest vistas of the city. This black, angular hotel doesn't quite escape the impersonal curse of its 1975 construction, but it tries nobly and succeeds rather well on its interior. With 22 floors, this is Oslo's third-biggest hotel (after the Radisson Blu Plaza Hotel and the Clarion Hotel Royal Christiana), the second-tallest building, and the first hotel that most Oslovians think of when they hear the name "Radisson Hotel." Bedrooms are relatively large, very comfortable, and come in about a dozen different

Hotellvegen, PO Box 163, N-2061 Gardemoen. www.radissonblu.com. ✆ **63-93-30-00.** 503 units. NOK1,595–NOK2,095 double; NOK1,995 junior suite; from NOK3,900 suite. Rates include buffet breakfast. AE, DC, MC, V. Free parking. **Amenities:** 2 restaurants; bar; health club; room service; sauna; rooms for those w/limited mobility. *In room:* A/C, TV, hair dryer, minibar, Wi-Fi.

INEXPENSIVE

Thon Hotel Gardermoen The Thon chain strikes again with the first budget hotel (opened in 2006) at Gardermoen airport. In spite of its smart, stylish decor, it is an affordable choice, with a shuttle running between the hotel and the airport, a distance of 5 minutes away by bus. Spread out over 13 two-story buildings, rooms are comfortably furnished, albeit a bit small. The standard singles feature just one bed, but most rooms are doubles with two single beds.

Balder Allé 22, N-2065 Gardermoen. www.thonhotels.com. ✆ **64-00-45-00.** 260 units. NOK925–NOK1,075 double. AE, DC, MC, V. Free parking. **Amenities:** Restaurant; bar; room service; rooms for those w/limited mobility. *In room:* TV, Wi-Fi.

WHERE TO DINE

You can now dine internationally without leaving the city of Oslo. The influx of immigrants in recent years has led to the growth of Mexican-, Turkish-, Moroccan-, Chinese-, Greek-, and American-style restaurants. Among European cuisines, French and Italian are the most popular. The largest concentration of stylish restaurants is at Aker Brygge, a former shipbuilding yard on the harborfront.

Not all restaurants in Oslo are newcomers. Some have long been associated with artists and writers—the Grand Café, for example, was the stamping ground of Henrik Ibsen and Edvard Munch.

Central Oslo

VERY EXPENSIVE

Oro ★★★ CONTINENTAL/MEDITERRANEAN Is this the best restaurant in Oslo, as some critics maintain? Oro is definitely among the top five choices. This very stylish Michelin star winner is run by chef Mads Larsson, who directs the kitchen of a three-faceted establishment that includes a European gourmet restaurant, Oro Bar & Grill, and a boutique-style deli (Mon–Fri 11:30am–3pm) for enthusiasts who want to haul raw ingredients back home. I recommend the restaurant's fixed-price menus, one of which is a five-course vegetarian option.

Tordenskiolds 6A (entrance on Kjeld Stubs Gate). ✆ **23-01-02-40.** Reservations required. 5-course fixed-price menu NOK545–NOK795. AE, DC, MC, V. Mon–Sat 11am–3pm and 5–10pm. T-banen: Stortinget.

restauranteik ★ INTERNATIONAL In the Clarion Collection Hotel Savoy, one floor above street level, immediately adjacent to Oslo's National Gallery, this is a hip, trendy, expensive, and highly visible restaurant that has attracted such big names as the prime minister of Norway since its opening in 2003. The five on-staff chefs are given free rein to express their creativity in the form of food that's inspired by Thai, Chinese, Japanese, American, Continental, or all-Norwegian culinary motifs. Some dishes that win over palates include pan-fried redfish served with pea purée, orange-braised fennel, a lightly pickled tomato, and shellfish sauce; and the grilled lamb cutlets, served with risotto-style orzo pasta and a concentrated rosemary sauce.

Universitesgata 11. ✆ **22-36-07-10.** Reservations recommended. 5-course fixed-price menu NOK465. AE, DC, MC, V. Tues–Sat 6–11pm (last seating). Closed 1 week at Easter, 1 week at Christmas, and 4 weeks in midsummer. T-banen: Tullenløkka.

EXPENSIVE

Grand Café ★★ NORWEGIAN Over the decades, this 1874 cafe has served as the living and dining room for the elite of Kristiania (an old name for Oslo). The country's greatest artists have dined here with foreign diplomats, kings, and explorers. While not as chic as it once was, I am still loyal to it and view a night here as part of my Norwegian experience. A large mural on one wall depicts Ibsen and Edvard Munch, along with other, less famous, former patrons. The atmosphere and tradition here are sometimes more compelling than the cuisine, but if you like solid, honest flavors, this is the place to eat. The menu relies on Norwegian country traditions (how many places still serve elk stew?).

In the Grand Hotel, Karl Johans Gate 31. ✆ **23-21-20-00.** Reservations recommended. Main courses NOK165–NOK320. AE, DC, MC, V. Mon–Fri 11am–11pm; Sat noon–11pm; Sun 1–10pm. T-banen: Stortinget.

Theatercafeen ★ INTERNATIONAL The *New York Times,* with a great deal of justification, listed this cafe as among the 10 most famous on the planet. If you like to eat and drink in opulence, head here for your grand fix. The last of the grand Viennese cafes in northern Europe, this long-standing favorite was founded a century ago to rival the Grand Café. Each has its devotees, although I like this one better because of its old world schmaltz. Serenaded by piano and a duet of violins, with soft lighting, antique bronzes, cut-glass lighting fixtures, and Art Nouveau mirrors, it's the type of place that encourages lingering. The entire establishment was renovated in 2010, adding a new smaller eatery and bar. Menu items are well prepared and traditional, and are adjusted accordingly to get the best flavors out of each season.

In the Hotel Continental, Stortingsgaten 24. ✆ **22-82-40-50.** Reservations recommended. Main courses NOK235–NOK295; open-faced sandwiches NOK130 at lunch. AE, DC, MC, V. Mon–Sat 11am–11pm; Sun 3–10pm. T-banen: Stortinget.

MODERATE

Bristol Grill ★★ CONTINENTAL This is the premier dining room of the Hotel Bristol (p. 214), one of Oslo's most prestigious hotels. You'll find old-world charm, formal service without a lot of flash or frenzy, and elegant decor that evokes a baronial hunting lodge from the 1920s, when the restaurant was founded. In the '30s, the place evolved into the dining venue you'll see today, with a gentleman's-club allure that eventually welcomed big-name entertainers. You'll pass through a cozy, woodsy-looking piano bar to reach the restaurant. With a culinary focus that has radically improved over the years, the menu continues to be one of the finest in the Norwegian capital as it beautifully adjusts to take advantage of the best ingredients in all four seasons. There's a spectacular version of bouillabaisse, prepared with Nordic (not Mediterranean) fish and seasoned with saffron. One of the chef's most successful specialties is medallions of venison sautéed with vanilla and bacon, served on a bed of mushrooms with a terrine of potatoes.

In the Hotel Bristol, Kristian IV's Gate 7. ✆ **22-82-60-20.** Reservations recommended, especially at night. Main courses NOK220–NOK295; 3-course menu NOK410. AE, DC, MC, V. Daily 5–11pm. Tram: 10, 11, 17, or 18.

INEXPENSIVE

Brasserie 45 ★ ☺ CONTINENTAL After taking in an Ibsen play at the National Theater, this is the perfect nearby restaurant for dinner. Airy and stylish, this second-story bistro overlooks the biggest fountain along downtown Oslo's showplace promenade. It is a family business, and the hard-working owners employ a certain discerning taste to treat you to the best of Mother France's kitchen. In recent years they have added Asian inspiration to their menu: Onion soup and smoked moose, naturally, appear on the menu but the uniformed staff also bears steaming platters of less-traditional cuisine—king prawns in a spicy Thai sauce, anyone? Great kids' menu.

Stortingsgaten 20. ✆ **22-41-34-00.** Reservations recommended. Main courses NOK139–NOK235; fixed-price menu NOK295–NOK335. AE, DC, MC, V. Mon–Thurs 3–11:30pm; Fri–Sat 2pm–midnight; Sun 2–10pm. T-banen: Sentrum.

Old Town (Gamlebyen/Kvadraturen)

VERY EXPENSIVE

Statholdergaarden ★★ NORWEGIAN I know of no grander and more tranquil setting in Oslo for a luxury restaurant than this restored 17th-century house offering a first-floor dining room with original decor. Beautifully laid tables are placed under period stucco ceilings, whose motifs reappear on the china. At this century-old restaurant (set in a building dating from 1640), menu items change frequently, according to what's in season. Some of the best examples of the cuisine here include fried sea bass with *petit pois*–truffle crème, chanterelles and cabbage; and herb-infused filet of lamb served with mushrooms, bean ragout, and chèvre-pecan nut croquette. Other great bets? The grilled scallop and langoustine salad with coriander-marinated mango, and a mustard-glazed filet of lamb served with chanterelles and root vegetable *millefeuille*. Don't confuse this upscale and prestigious site with the less-expensive bistro Statholderens Krostue, which occupies the building's vaulted cellar.

Rådhusgate 11. ✆ **22-41-88-00.** Reservations recommended. Main courses NOK385–NOK395; 4-course fixed-price menu NOK895; 5-course fixed-price menu NOK980; 6-course fixed-price menu NOK1,050. AE, DC, MC, V. Mon–Sat 6pm–midnight. Tram: 11, 15, or 18.

EXPENSIVE

Gamle Rådhus Restaurant ★ NORWEGIAN One of the oldest restaurants in Oslo, Det Gamle Rådhus is in Oslo's former Town Hall (1641). This is strictly for nostalgia buffs, as the restaurant is not at all cutting edge. It's there for those wanting to see Oslo the way it used to be, who won't mind that the fires of innovation died a long time ago. You'll dine within a network of manorial-inspired rooms with dark wooden panels and Flemish, 16th-century-style wooden chairs. In the spacious dining room, a full array of open-faced sandwiches is served on weekdays only. A la carte dinner selections can be made from a varied menu that includes fresh fish, game, and Norwegian specialties. If you want to sample a dish that Ibsen might have enjoyed, check out the house specialty (and acquired taste), *lutefisk*—but hold your nose. This traditional Scandinavian dish is eaten just before Christmas and is made from dried fish that has been soaked in lye and then poached in broth. More to your liking might be smoked salmon (cured right on the premises), a parfait of chicken livers, freshwater pikeperch from nearby streams sautéed in a lime sauce, filet of reindeer with lingonberry sauce, or Norwegian lamb coated with herbs and baked with a glaze.

Nedre Slottsgate 1. ✆ **22-42-01-07.** Reservations recommended. Main courses NOK210–NOK345. AE, DC, MC, V. Mon–Fri 11:30am–3pm and 4–10pm; Sat 1–3pm and 4–10pm. Kroen Bar Mon–Sat 4pm–midnight. Closed last 3 weeks in July. Bus: 27, 29, 30, 41, or 61.

MODERATE

Engebret Café NORWEGIAN A favorite since 1857, this restaurant sits directly north of Akershus Castle in two buildings that have been joined together to form this establishment. It has an old-fashioned atmosphere and good food, served in a former bohemian literati haunt once favored by Henrik Ibsen, Edvard Grieg, and Bjørnstjerne Bjørnson. During lunch, a tempting selection of open-faced sandwiches is available. The evening menu is more elaborate; you might begin with a terrine of game with blackberry port-wine sauce, or Engebret's always reliable fish soup. Main dishes include a truly savory wild boar with whortleberry sauce, Norwegian reindeer, salmon Christiania, or Engebret's big fish pot.

Bankplassen 1. ✆ **22-82-25-25.** Reservations recommended. Main courses NOK235–NOK345; 3-course lunch menu NOK275. AE, DC, MC, V. Mon–Fri 11:30am–11pm. Bus: 27, 29, or 30.

Stortorvets Gjæstgiveri ★ NORWEGIAN Many legends surround this nostalgic dining room. It is the oldest restaurant in Oslo, composed of a trio of wood-framed buildings, the most antique of which dates from the 1700s. The inn's upstairs bedchambers with their wood-burning stoves are virtually unchanged since their original construction, although they're now used as private dining rooms. This restaurant changes radically throughout the day: Expect a cafe near the entrance; an old-fashioned, charming, and usually packed restaurant in back; and outside dining in good weather. Menu items are traditional, well prepared, and flavorful, and include steamed mussels in white wine and garlic, poached salmon in a creamy butter sauce with horseradish, or pan-fried trout served with asparagus in Parma ham, mushrooms, and mussel sauce. A specialty is roast reindeer in a port sauce spiked with wild berries.

Grensen 1. ✆ **23-35-63-60.** Reservations recommended. Small platters and snacks NOK98–NOK145; main courses NOK179–NOK349. AE, DC, MC, V. Cafe and restaurant Mon–Sat 11am–10:30pm. Tram: 12 or 17.

3 Brødre ★ MEXICAN Diners once came here for old-fashioned Norwegian fare, but "Three Brothers" now serves food from south of the border—the U.S. border, that is. In their heyday in the 19th century, the "brothers" (the glove manufacturers who once occupied this building) were said to have kept more fingers from freezing off than any other manufacturer in Norway. The food served now is zesty and well prepared, and you'll get hearty portions at reasonable prices. Get those fajitas you've been hungering for, including one version made with jumbo prawns, or dig into double-cheese enchiladas and burritos. The entire street level houses the bustling bar, while a piano bar is the upstairs attraction. Lighter meals, such as snacks and sandwiches, are available on the outside dining terrace in the summer.

Øvre Slottsgate 13. ✆ **23-10-06-70.** Main courses NOK168–NOK246. AE, DC, MC, V. Mon–Sat 7pm–midnight. Street-level bar Mon–Sat 11pm–2:30am. Piano bar Wed–Sat 5pm–2am. Bus: 27, 29, or 30.

Aker Brygge

EXPENSIVE

Lofoten Fiskerestaurant ★★ SEAFOOD This is the Aker Brygge district's most appealing—and best—seafood restaurant. Opening onto the waterfront, the interior sports nautical accessories that evoke life on an upscale yacht. In good weather, tables are set up on an outdoor terrace lined with flowering plants. Menu items change according to the available catch, with few choices for meat eaters. The fish is served in generous portions, and is always very fresh. Look for culinary inspirations from Italy and France, and an ample use of such Mediterranean flavors as pesto. Old-guard diners don't find their tried-and-true dishes on the menu but are introduced to Norwegian fish enriched with various sauces and accompaniments, including baked halibut with garlic cream. Other temptations include sea bass baked with spices, filet of beef with rosemary jus and pimientos, or baked salmon with horseradish butter.

Stranden 75, Aker Brygge. ✆ **22-83-08-08.** Reservations recommended. Main courses NOK140–NOK265 lunch, NOK185–NOK325 dinner. AE, DC, MC, V. Mon–Sat 11am–11pm; Sun noon–10pm. Bus: 27.

Tjuvholmen Sjømagasin ★★ SEAFOOD Recently opened on a stretch of reclaimed land at the far end of Aker Brygge, this chic, silvery seafood restaurant is run by Bjørn Tore Furset, the local wunderkind restaurateur whose empire includes city eateries Havsmak, Ekeberg, and Argent. His philosophy is all about fresh, locally sourced ingredients. The heralded restaurant seats up to 300 diners—from well-heeled locals to in-the-know tourists—in a sprawling dining room that offers panoramic views of Oslofjord harbor. You can pick your catch right out of the casks that greet you as you walk in, then hand them to the team of chefs manning the open kitchen, and watch them cook your food. Or try a dish from the seafood bar, where things are a bit more informal. The restaurant serves excellent grilled lobster (Norwegian- or American-caught), Varanger king crab, and chargrilled Hordaland trout.

Tjuvholmen Allé 14. ✆ **23-89-77-77.** www.sjomagasin.no. Main courses NOK270–NOK395; 3-course fixed-price menu NOK465, 5-course NOK595. AE, DC, MC, V. Mon–Sat 11am–midnight. Bus: 27.

West End

EXPENSIVE

Feinschmecker ★★ SCANDINAVIAN One of the most prestigious restaurants in Oslo, Feinschmecker will entertain you with the same style and verve it's produced for such guests as King Harald and Queen Sonya. The dining room's antique furniture and small-paned windows evoke old-time style despite the building's modernity. Menu items change frequently, but there are a few favorites that regularly reappear. The quality of materials shines through dishes that are immaculately presented, such as the grilled scallops with crispy potatoes; sautéed ocean crayfish tails with apple cider, wild rice, and sun-dried tomatoes; and rack of Norwegian lamb.

Balchensgate 5. ✆ **22-12-93-80.** Reservations recommended. Main courses NOK325–NOK395; fixed-price 4-course menu NOK745; fixed-price 7-course menu NOK925. AE, DC, MC, V. Mon–Sat 4:30–11pm. Closed 3 weeks in July. Tram: 12 or 19 to Ilesberg.

MODERATE

Hos Thea ★ 🎁 SCANDINAVIAN/SPANISH This century-old building, once a private home, is in a West End neighborhood 3km (1¾ miles) south of Oslo's center. Is it worth the trip? A lot of foreign foodies who had read about this place in European gourmet magazines think so. The stylish, well-managed restaurant also attracts a loyal crowd of people active in the media and the arts. The waitstaff and chefs share duties, so the person who prepares your meal is likely to carry it to your table as well. Depending on the staff's mood and the season, the superbly prepared menu items might include filet of Hardanger mountain trout with herbed crème fraîche or Røros reindeer with traditional cream sauce and Russian peas. The venison, which comes from the north of Norway, is handled delicately and served with a sauce of mixed Nordic summer berries.

Gabelsgate 11 (entrance on Drammensveien). ✆ **22-44-68-74.** Reservations recommended. Main courses NOK245–NOK275; fixed-price 4-course menu NOK465; fixed-price 6-course menu NOK665. AE, DC, MC, V. Daily 4:30–11pm. Tram: 10 or 13.

Bygdøy

EXPENSIVE

Lanternen ★ CONTINENTAL Norwegian yachties and their refined palates adore this charming, welcoming, and sophisticated place set close to the arrivals point for the Bygdøy ferry from the quays near Town Hall. From the windows of its newly renovated woodsy, modern interior, you'll see a thousand odd privately owned sailboats and small yachts bobbing in the nearby marina, giving the entire venue a distinctly nautical appeal. Appetizers and main courses are wisely limited but well chosen and intriguing to the taste buds: Think creamy fish soup or chili-flavored steamed mussels flavored with fresh garlic and white wine. Mains range from poached sole with lobster sauce and shrimp to an herb-marinated filet of lamb. I recommend the baked chicken breast, enlivened with the additions of cured ham and mozzarella, and bound with a Madeira-laced sauce.

Huk Aveny 2. ✆ **22-43-78-38.** Reservations recommended. Main courses NOK165–NOK245. AE, DC, MC, V. Mon–Sat 11:30am–10:30pm; Sun 1–8pm. Closed 1st 2 weeks of Jan. Bus: 30 or the Bygdøy ferry from the quays near Town Hall.

Frogner

VERY EXPENSIVE

Restaurant Le Canard ★ FRENCH/CONTINENTAL This deluxe restaurant is just about a kilometer (½ mile) west of the center in one of Oslo's more fashionable neighborhoods. The classically oriented cooking demonstrates first-class workmanship without being showy. The mansion that contains this prestigious restaurant is almost as intriguing as the cuisine. Religious symbols are scattered throughout the building, which was designed in the 1880s by a noted Jewish architect named Lowzow. (Look for the Star of David in some of the stained-glass windows, and representations of the Lion of Judah here and there.) The always impeccable menu might include scallops in risotto with pumpkin and truffle or grilled wild turbot from Trøndelag in *pied de cochon* and celery root. One enduringly popular dish is a perfectly roasted duck—that is, with most of the fat cooked off—set off to perfection with a blend of mango and olive jus.

President Harbitzgate 4. ✆ **22-54-34-00.** Reservations recommended. Main courses NOK240–NOK395; fixed-price menus NOK695–NOK1,095. AE, DC, MC, V. Mon–Sat 6–11pm. T-banen: Nationaltheatret.

Holmenkollen

EXPENSIVE

De Fem Stuer (Five Small Rooms) ★★ NORWEGIAN/CONTINENTAL Its turn-of-the-20th-century "National Romantic" architecture has firmly established this restaurant as something of a historic monument for the diners who trek, ski, or ride uphill on tram no. 1 from Oslo to reach it. On the lobby level of Holmenkollen Park Hotel Rica (p. 216), the restaurant is in a section that retains its original Viking revival (or "dragon-style") construction. As its name implies, the restaurant contains five separate dining areas, four of them small and cozy to the point of being cramped and intimate, the other being high-ceilinged and stately looking. The menu changes twice a month, but some of the better dishes are the guinea hen with foie gras, the pesto-griddled ocean crayfish with tiny peas, ginger- and chicken-stuffed quail with morels and shiitake mushrooms in a port-wine sauce, and filet of reindeer with parsnips.

In the Holmenkollen Park Hotel Rica Oslo, Kongeveien 26. ✆ **22-92-20-00.** Reservations recommended. Main courses NOK285–NOK350; fixed-price menus NOK565–NOK855. AE, DC, MC, V. Mon–Sat noon–2:30pm and 6–11pm. Tram: 1 (to its terminus).

MODERATE

Holmenkollen Restaurant NORWEGIAN/CONTINENTAL Partially built from logs and local stone, and perched near the summit of a hill outside Oslo, close to the city's world-renowned ski jump, this restaurant evokes a mountain chalet. Originally built in the 1930s, it is a frequent target for bus tours whose participants are hauled up to admire the high-altitude view over Oslo and to get a good meal. Main courses in the self-service restaurant include rib-sticking fare that's substantial and unpretentious, including platters of roast meats or fish, but also salads and pastas. Meals in the upstairs dining room might begin with a Caesar salad with herb-roasted chicken and a Parmesan crust or a chilled gazpacho served with pan-fried shrimp. Take delight in the pan-fried trout with spring-fresh asparagus and a chive sauce, or the roasted filet of veal with baby summer vegetables in a wine sauce. Steamed halibut is another delectable treat, with leeks, fresh dill, and a butter sauce. A great time to come is on Sunday between noon and 4pm for the sprawling lunch buffet (NOK395).

Holmenkollveien 119. ✆ **22-13-92-00.** Reservations recommended. Main courses in restaurant NOK195–NOK295; platters in the self-service restaurant NOK90–NOK280. AE, DC, MC, V. Cafeteria daily 11:30am–4pm. Restaurant Mon–Sat 10:30am–10pm; Sun 10:30am–10pm. Tram: 1.

Grünerløkka

MODERATE

Markveien Mat og Vinhus ★ NORWEGIAN/FRENCH/ITALIAN In the heart of the always trendy Grünerløkka area, this restaurant evokes the Oslovian version of the Left Bank bohemian life. The walls are covered with the art of a local painter, Jo Stang, and the waiters welcome diners—in their terms—as "we would in our own home." This is an excellent choice for dining on well-prepared cuisine. The ambitious menu includes such delights as arctic trout with chanterelles and vermouth sauce and rack of lamb with baked garlic and squash. Many dishes are flavored with a sauce made of fresh herbs. For something more truly Norwegian, try the occasionally appearing reindeer in a green peppercorn sauce, with bacon and Brussels sprouts.

Torvbakkgate 12. ✆ **22-37-22-97.** Reservations recommended. Main courses NOK258–NOK278; fixed-price menus NOK465–NOK735. AE, DC, MC, V. Mon–Sat 5–11pm. Closed July 15–Aug 7. Tram: 12.

Oslofjord

MODERATE

Ekeberg ★ NORWEGIAN/INTERNATIONAL The view from here of the Oslofjord was said to have inspired Edvard Munch in the creation of his masterpiece, *The Scream.* When the all-white building, designed by Oslovian Lars Backer, was completed in 1929, it was said to be one of the foremost functionalist buildings in Europe. By the end of the 1990s, the restaurant was closed and left to decay until its new owners took it over and completely renovated it. Today it is a modern building with the classic features retained from 1929. This complex contains several places to eat, including a bar/lounge, but Ekeberg is clearly the best place for dining. Most foreigners visit just for lunch, enjoying the fish soup, mussels steamed in wine, or the open sandwiches (one made with smoked trout). At night you can dine more festively, enjoying main dishes such as reindeer sirloin with mushrooms, chestnuts, and spinach; or the Hardanger trout with bacon and asparagus.

Kongsveien 15. ✆ **23-24-23-00.** www.ekebergrestauranten.com. Reservations recommended. Lunch main courses NOK130–NOK160; 3-course fixed-price lunch NOK375–NOK475. Dinner main courses NOK150–NOK285; fixed-price dinner NOK230–NOK620. AE, DC, MC, V. Mon–Sat 11am–midnight; Sun noon–10pm. Tram: 18 or 19.

EXPLORING OSLO

Oslo is most often viewed as a summer destination. Because Oslovians are starved for sunlight, everyone takes to the outdoors in summer, and many of them virtually stay up around-the-clock this time of year. If you come in winter, you'll find short days, with darkness descending around 3pm. But Oslovians counter the climate by becoming the candlelit center of the world, and the flickering lights make barhopping a warm, cozy experience. To compensate for those long, dark nights, the nightlife of Oslo becomes even more frenetic in the winter months. From rock clubs to Mozart concerts, after-dark activity in Oslo is more amped up than ever before. The city's cultural events and special art exhibitions also pick up during the winter.

Seasons aside, some travelers would be happy to come to Oslo anytime just for the views of the harborfront city and the Oslofjord. Panoramas are a major attraction, especially the one from Tryvannstårnet, a 117m (384-ft.) observation tower atop 570m (1,870-ft.) Tryvann Hill in the outlying area. Many other attractions are worthy of your time and exploration, too. The beautiful surroundings make these sights even more appealing.

Oslo Attractions

If you've budgeted only a day or two for Oslo, make the most of your time and see only the "platinum" attractions, saving the "gold" and "silver" rated sights for your return visit. I've narrowed the major attractions down to "the Big Six."

Henie-Onstad Kunstsenter (Henie-Onstad Art Center) ★★★ Norway's largest collection of modern art is worth the trip to the museum's beautiful setting beside Oslofjord, 11km (6¾ miles) west of Oslo. It was inaugurated in 1968 to house a gift of some 300 works of art from Sonja Henie, former figure skating champion and movie star, and her husband, shipping tycoon Niels Onstad.

Henie's bequest, beefed up by later additions, virtually spans modern art in the 20th century, from cubism with Braque to surrealism with Ernst. In fact, the collection is so vast that it frequently has to be rotated. I'm always particularly drawn to the CoBrA Group, with works by its founder, Asger Jorn, and by Karel Appel. You can head downstairs to Henie's trophy room to see her three Olympic gold medals—she was the star at the 1936 skating competition—and 10 world championship prizes. Henie garnered 600 trophies and medals, all of which are on display.

Besides the permanent collection, plays, concerts, films, and special exhibits take place. An open-air theater-in-the-round is used in the summer for folklore programs, jazz concerts, and song recitals. A top-notch, partly self-service restaurant, the Piruetten, is also on the premises.

Høkvikodden, Sonja Henlesvie 31. ✆ **67-80-48-80.** www.hok.no. Admission NOK80 adults, NOK30 ages 6–16, free for children 5 and under. Free for all Wed. Tues–Fri 11am–7pm; Sat–Sun 11am–5pm. Bus: 151, 161, 252, or 261.

Munch Museet (Edvard Munch Museum) ★★★ Edvard Munch (1863–1944) was Scandinavia's greatest painter and, in an act of incredible generosity, donated this collection to his beloved Oslo. The treasure-trove is so vast—1,100 paintings, 4,500 drawings, and 18,000 prints—that it can be shown only in rotation. The curators keep a representative sampling of his works on display at all times, so you can trace his development from Impressionism to symbolism.

Love, death, darkness, and anxiety were his overarching themes. The latter was best expressed in his most famous painting, *The Scream,* which is actually a series composed of four versions. This museum's version of the Munch masterpiece is valued at $75 million. Unsurprisingly, its August 2004 theft caused a huge international uproar, especially within art communities. Fans of Munch's *The Scream* and his *Madonna* (also nicked by the robbers) can once again gaze upon these paintings, which were recovered in the summer of 2006. Police were cagey at a news conference about how the paintings were recovered. *The Scream* and *Madonna* were part of the artist's "Frieze of Life" series, focusing on the artist's usual themes: sickness, death, anxiety, and love, many of which the museum's curator probably experienced during the paintings' disappearance.

Especially moving are Munch's early works, such as *At the Coffee Table* (1883), where you can see the preliminary vision that would grow into a future masterpiece. By the 1890s, Munch's paintings had matured into virtual masterpieces. Most fascinating, though, is a series of self-portraits, which explore his mental state at peak moments of his life, such as *The Night Wanderer* (1923) and *Self-Portrait by the Window* (1940).

Tøyengata 53. ✆ **23-49-35-00.** www.munch.museum.no. Admission NOK95 adults, NOK50 children 16–18, free for children 15 and under. Free for all Oct–Mar. June–Aug daily 10am–6pm; Sept–May Tues–Fri 10am–4pm, Sat–Sun 11am–5pm. T-banen: Tøyen. Bus: 60.

Nasjonalgalleriet (National Gallery) ★★★ This museum houses Norway's greatest and largest collection of art. Most visitors flock here to see Edvard Munch's *The Scream,* one of four versions, this one painted in 1893. This painting was stolen in 1994 and, like the version taken from the Munch Museum in 2004 (see above), was subsequently recovered. *The Scream,* which is reproduced in countless posters around the world, still inspires artists today and continues to work its way into popular culture. For example, in a 2006 episode of *The Simpsons,* Bart and his friends steal a copy of *The Scream* in a parody of the real thefts.

Munch has paintings here beyond *The Scream,* a total of 58 of his works, some of them among his most celebrated, including *The Dance of Life, Moonlight,* and *Ashes.* Most of Munch's works on show were painted in the closing years of the 19th century. There are also several self-portraits of Munch—the reason he was called "the handsomest man in Norway."

The leading Norwegian Romantic landscape painter Johan Christian Dahl (1788–1857) is in fine form here, but some find his paintings a little too sentimental. A favorite is Christian Krohg, who painted it like it was, drawing inspiration from sailors to prostitutes. Scandinavian painting in general is also showcased, with one salon containing works from the Golden Age of Danish painting.

Although not extensive compared to some national collections, European painting in general is well displayed, with old masters represented from Van Dyck to Rubens, from El Greco (a remarkable *St. Peter Repentant*) to Cézanne and Matisse. Van Gogh weighs in with a self-portrait, Picasso with his *Guitar.* Look for the works of Gustav

Oslo Attractions

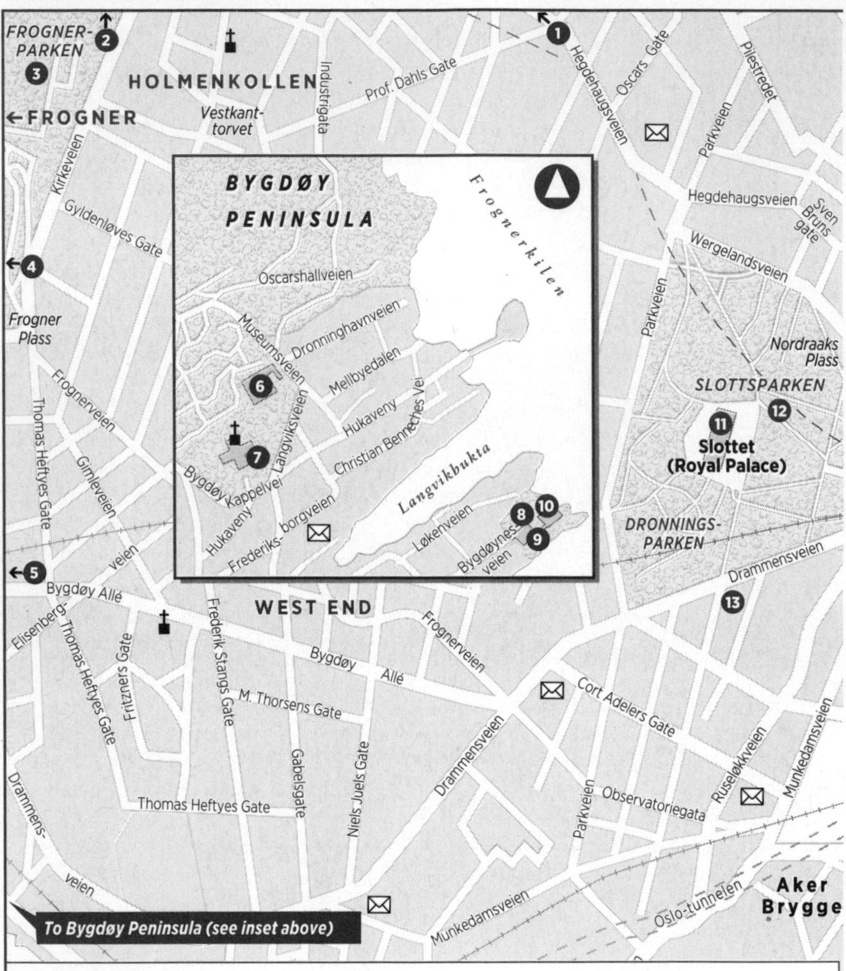

Akershus Slott og Festning **28**
Astrup Fearnley Museum of Modern Art **26**
Aula (Great Hall) **19**
Barnekunst Museum (International Children's Art Museum) **2**
Botanisk Hage og Museum (Botanical Gardens) **14**
Den Norske Opera **16**
Emanuel Vigeland Museum **1**
Forsvarsmuseet (Armed Forces Museum) **29**
Frogner Park **3**
Henie-Onstad Kunstsenter **5**
Historisk Museum (University Museum of Cultural Heritage) **17**
Ibsen Museum **13**
Kunstindustrimuseet (Museum of Decorative Arts & Design) **15**
Munch Museet **14**
Museet for Samtidskunst (Museum of Contemporary Art) **25**
Nasjonalgalleriet (National Gallery) **18**
Nationaltheatret **20**
Nobel Peace Center **23**
Norges Hjemmefrontmuseum (Norwegian Resistance Museum) **27**
Norges Parken Tusenfryd **30**
Oslo Bymuseum (City Museum) **4**
Oslo Domkirke (Oslo Cathedral) **22**
Oslo Konserthus **24**
Oslo Universitet **19**

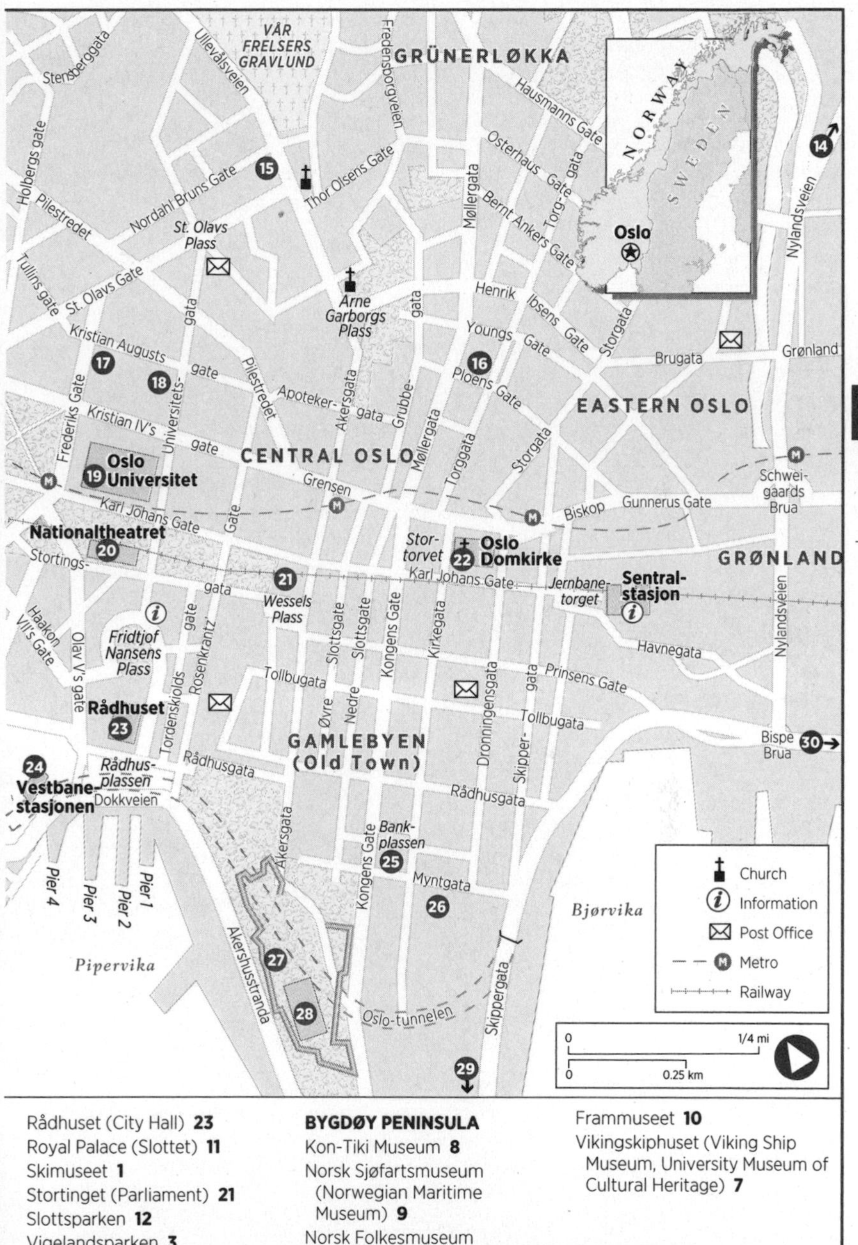

Rådhuset (City Hall) **23**
Royal Palace (Slottet) **11**
Skimuseet **1**
Stortinget (Parliament) **21**
Slottsparken **12**
Vigelandsparken **3**

BYGDØY PENINSULA
Kon-Tiki Museum **8**
Norsk Sjøfartsmuseum (Norwegian Maritime Museum) **9**
Norsk Folkesmuseum (Norwegian Folk Museum) **6**
Frammuseet **10**
Vikingskiphuset (Viking Ship Museum, University Museum of Cultural Heritage) **7**

Vigeland, although you'll get better acquainted with him at Vigelandsparken (see below).

All the art displayed was created before 1945, the year Norwegians freed themselves from the Nazi yoke.

Universitetsgaten 13. ✆ **21-98-20-00.** www.nationalmuseum.no. Free admission. Tues-Wed and Fri 10am-6pm; Thurs 10am-7pm; Sat-Sun 11am-5pm. Tram: 10 or 12.

Norsk Folkemuseum (Norwegian Folk Museum) ★★★ ☺ Take a tour of Norway in just 1 day. From all over the country, museum curators moved 155 buildings from their original site and, with great difficulty, transported and reassembled them on 14 hectares (35 acres) on the Bygdøy peninsula. Among the old buildings is the **Gol Stave Church ★★★**, moved here a century ago. Dating from 1200—still with no windows—it came from the town of Gol, 224km (139 miles) northwest of Oslo. One of the oldest such museums in the world, the Folk Museum contains many buildings from the medieval era, including the Raulandstua, one of the oldest wooden dwellings still standing in Norway. Wander the streets of **Gamblebyen** or **Old Town ★**, a reproduction of an early-20th-century Norwegian town. The rural buildings are grouped together by region of origin, and the urban houses are laid out in the form of an old town.

Eventually, the curators decided to make this open-air folk museum a living, breathing entity. They feature a variety of activities, including horse-and-buggy rides, folk music, dancing by men and women in native dress, traditional arts and crafts, and even "Norwegian evenings," a summer food tasting of regional specialties and folk dancing. Artisans demonstrate age-old crafts such as pottery, weaving, silversmithing, and the making of candles, which you can purchase in their workshops. At the Christmas fair, some 120 old-fashioned stands also sell handmade products.

Inside, the museum's 225,000 exhibits capture every imaginable facet of Norwegian life, past and present. Furniture, household utensils, clothing, woven fabrics, and tapestries are on display, along with fine examples of Norwegian rose-painting and woodcarving. Farming implements and logging gear pay tribute to the development of agriculture and forestry. Also look for the outstanding exhibit on Norway's Sami population.

After the millennium, the museum incorporated the **Bygdo Royal Farm,** with its cultivated fields and grazing lands offering hikes along the trails.

All together, the museum is a living textbook of Norwegian culture that is not to be missed.

Museumsveien 10. ✆ **22-12-37-00.** www.norskfolke.museum.no. Admission NOK100 adults, NOK25 children 16 and under. Jan 2-May 14 and Sept 15-Dec 30 Mon-Fri 11am-3pm, Sat-Sun 11am-4pm; May 15-Sept 14 daily 10am-6pm. Ferry: From Pier 3 facing the Rådhuset (summer only). Bus: 30 from the Nationaltheatret.

Vigelandsparken ★★★ The sculptures of Gustav Vigeland, the most prominent among Norwegian sculptors of the 20th century, are at once some of the most beloved and disdained in Europe. Wherever you stand on them, it's well worth exploring this park, which holds 227 of Vigeland's monumental sculptures, mostly devoted to the theme of mankind's destiny. The artist worked for a total of 4 decades on this 30-hectare (74-acre) park but, sadly, died 1 year before his lifetime achievement could be completed.

The chief treasure here is the **Vigeland Monolith ★★★**, a 16m (52-ft.) sculpture composed of 121 colossal figures, all amazingly carved into one piece of stone.

The monolith is easy to spot, as it rises on top of the highest hill in the park. Summer lovers often visit it at night, as it's floodlit and somehow seems even more dramatic at that time. A set of circular steps envelops the statue. On the steps leading up to the monolith are 36 groups of other figures carved in stone by the great artist. The column itself, with its writhing figures, is said to symbolize the struggle of life and the transcendence of everyday life, which is one of the main themes running through Vigeland's work.

The "best of the rest" of the sculptures are along a paved axis stretching for 1km (½ mile). These sculptures depict Vigeland's interpretation of life beginning at birth and ending in death. The most famous of these statues, which you'll quickly recognize because it is one of the most reproduced pieces of art in Oslo, is ***The Angry Boy (Sinnataggen)*** ★★. Based on a sketch Vigeland made in London in 1901, it shows a kid stomping his feet and scrunching his face in anger.

Frogner Park, Nobelsgate 32. ✆ **23-49-37-00.** Free admission to park; museum NOK50 adults, NOK25 children. Museum free to all Oct–Mar. Park daily 24 hr. Museum June–Aug Tues–Sun 10am–5pm; Sept–May Tues–Sun noon–4pm. Tram: 12.

Vikingskipshuset (Viking Ship Museum, University Museum of Cultural Heritage) ★★★ ☺ A fascinating chapter in Viking history came alive when three Viking funereal ships were discovered in the Oslofjord between 1867 and 1904. All the vessels, each dating from the 9th century, had been buried in a blue clay that preserved them. The ***Oseberg*** ★★, which required 30 oarsmen to move it through the waters, is the most impressive, with its dragon and serpent carvings. Apparently, the ship was the resting place of a noblewoman; though plundered for much of its booty, many of the queen's burial furnishings are on display.

The finest remaining example of a Viking longship, the ***Gokstad*** ★, when unearthed, had also been sacked by ancient grave robbers. Among the few artifacts uncovered were bedposts with animal head ornamentation, fragments of a sledge, and even a gaming board (think early Las Vegas). The largest ship of the lot, the *Gokstad* could accommodate 32 oarsmen and travel at a speed of 12 knots. Built around the same time as the *Gokstad,* the *Tune* is less impressive, though it was the tomb of a powerful chieftain. The badly damaged ship was intentionally not restored so that visitors can see the details of shipbuilding in the Viking era.

Impressions

I am anchored to my work so that I cannot move. If I walk down the street one day a thousand hands from work hold on to me. I am tied to the studio and the road is never long.

—Gustav Vigeland, 1912

For kids, the ships here conjure up the legend and lore of the Viking era that flourished in the Middle Ages. I've seen kids stand in awe looking up at the excavated ships long after their parents have taken in the exhibitions. ***Tip:*** If you go between 11:30am and 1pm, you'll tend to avoid the summer mobs who descend on this building, whose rounded white walls give it the feeling of a burial tomb.

Huk Aveny 35, Bygdøy. ✆ **22-85-19-00.** www.khm.uio.no. Admission NOK60 adults, NOK30 children. Oct–Apr daily 10am–4pm; May–Sept daily 9am–6pm. Ferry: From Pier 3 facing the Rådhuset (summer only). Bus: 30 from the Nationaltheatret.

Other Top Attractions

MUSEUMS

Astrup Fearnley Museum of Modern Art ★ This is one of those special spots art lovers stumble across in their travels, wondering why such a place isn't better known. Actually, this privately funded museum has been around since 1993, when Norway's leading architects and designers constructed the stunningly designed building to showcase both Norwegian and international post–World War II art. Works by '60s icon Yoko Ono can be seen here. The equally controversial British artist Damien Hirst is also on view with his installation of *Mother and Child Divided*. The changing exhibitions are often drawn from the museum's permanent collection, much of which is kept in storage. On my last visit, I feasted on another British blood-and-gore type, Francis Bacon, along with the gentler Lucian Freud and Gerhard Richter. Introduce yourself to some locally known Norwegian artists of great stature, especially Knut Rose, Bjørn Carlsen, and Arne Ekeland. If you prefer your sculptures oversize, wander through the garden, with such works as Niki de St. Phalle's sparrow.

Dronningensgatan 4. ✆ **22-93-60-60.** http://afmuseet.no. Admission NOK60 adults, free for children 18 and under. Wed–Sun noon–5pm. T-banen: Stortinget. Tram: 1, 2, 10, or 12. Bus: 27, 29, 38, 51, or 56.

Emanuel Vigeland Museum ★ I'll let you in on something if you promise not to tell. This museum has been accurately dubbed Oslo's best-kept secret, and sometimes the work of Emanuel Vigeland (1875–1948), the younger brother of Gustav, rivals that of his more celebrated sibling's. The main attraction here—besides the fact that Emanuel was the architect of his own museum—is a barrel-vaulted room covered with frescoes that depict human life from conception to death. Some of the scenes are explicitly erotic, and his works have been simultaneously acclaimed and denounced as "decadent." The most curious of the motifs I discovered is on the short wall by the entrance. Still embraced in copulation, a dead couple yields a mighty pillar of smoke and infants: creation, death, and birth inseparably linked. To further a theme, Emanuel decided to turn the museum into his mausoleum. His ashes were laid to rest in an urn above the entrance.

Grimelundsveien 8. ✆ **22-14-57-88.** www.emanuelvigeland.museum.no. Admission NOK40. Mid-May to mid-Sept Sun noon–5pm; mid-Sept to mid-May Sun noon–4pm. T-banen: No. 1 Frognerseteren to Slemdal station (then a 7-min. walk).

Historisk Museum (University Museum of Cultural Heritage) From the cold arctic wastelands to the hot, sunny islands of Asia, this museum—owned by the University of Oslo—is a vast treasure-trove, containing everything from a carved *stavkirke* (wooden church) to a 1,000-year history of the coins of Norway. Viking artifacts and a display of **gold and silver ★** from the 2nd through the 13th centuries are in the Treasure House. In the medieval hall, keep an eye out for the reddish Ringerike Alstad Stone, which was carved in relief, and the **Dynna Stone ★**, an 11th-century runic stone honoring the handsomest maiden in Hadeland. There's also a rich collection of ecclesiastical art in a series of portals from stave churches.

Frederiksgate 2 (near Karl Johans Gate). ✆ **22-85-99-64.** Free admission. May–Sept Tues–Sun 9am–6pm; Oct–April Tues–Sun 10am–4pm. Closed Dec 24–26, Dec 31, Jan 1, May 1., and May 17. Tram: 11, 17, or 18.

Kunstindustrimuseet (Museum of Decorative Arts and Design) ★ Founded in 1876, this is one of the oldest museums in Norway and among the oldest applied-arts museums in Europe. Since 1876 it has owned the bold, imaginative **Baldishol**

tapestries ★ from the early part of the 12th century. Few Draculas could resist furnishing their home with the antique dragon-style furniture. Royal wardrobe is also on display, including the wedding gown Queen Sonja wore in 1968 (Lady Di had no competition here). The collection of **18th-century Norwegian silver ★**, glass, and faience (a type of glazed pottery) is stunning, and there is also an impressive selection of contemporary furniture and crafts.

Café Solliløkken and the museum shop on the ground floor are in rooms from the 1830s that originally were in a small country house. The cafe offers homemade pastries and light meals, mostly sandwiches and salads, but also some hot Norwegian specialties every day (most often fish).

St. Olavs Gate 1. ✆ **22-03-65-40.** www.nationalmuseum.no. Free admission. Tues-Wed and Fri 11am-5pm; Thurs 11am-7pm; Sat-Sun noon-4pm. T-banen: Stortinget. Bus: 37.

Museet for Samtidskunst (National Museum of Contemporary Art) Opened in 1990, this collection of works acquired by the state after World War II presents an array of international and Norwegian contemporary art. Previously grouped together in the National Gallery, the works have more room to breathe here, in what was once the central bank of Norway. I once saw a painting here of a three-headed woman with 14 breasts, but don't worry—exhibits change frequently.

Bankplassen 4. ✆ **22-86-22-10.** www.nationalmuseum.no. Free admission. Tues-Wed and Fri 11am-5pm; Thurs 10am-7pm; Sat-Sun noon-5pm. Tram: 10 or 12. Bus: 60.

Nobel Peace Center One of Oslo's newest attractions, the ultramodern center presents the history of the founding father of the prize, Alfred Nobel, "the dynamite king," and the biographies and careers of Nobel Peace Prize laureates such as Nelson Mandela. In addition to changing exhibits, a permanent exhibition illustrates the careers of the laureates through film, including recordings of actual Peace Prize ceremonies. If you're lucky, you might catch a glimpse of one of the winners of the Peace Prize who sometimes come to the renovated train station to give lectures.

Radhusplassen. ✆ **48-30-10-00.** www.nobelpeacecenter.org. Admission NOK80 ages 16 and over, NOK55 seniors/students, free 15 and under. June-Sept 15 daily 10am-7pm; off-season Tues-Sun 10am-8pm. Tram: 10 or 12.

Skimuseet (Ski Museum) ★ ☺ Founded in 1923, this is the oldest ski museum in the world—as such, even the royal family of Norway has added their skis to the collection. At Holmenkollen, an elevator takes visitors up the jump tower for a **panoramic view ★★★** of Oslo and the fjord, one of the greatest vistas you are likely to experience in Norway. At the base of the ski jump, the Skimuseet displays a wide range of exhibits, including a 4,000-year-old pictograph from Rødøy in Nordland that documents skiing's lengthy history. The museum also has skis and historical items from various parts of Norway—from the first "modern" skis, dating from about 1870, to a ski dating from around A.D. 600. Artifacts from the Antarctic expeditions of Amundsen are on display, as well as the Scott expeditions into the snowy wastelands. You can even see relics of Fridtjof Nansen's slog across the Greenland icecap. A historical version of Survivorman, he built a boat from his sled and canvas tent to row the final 100km (62 miles) to "the end of the world." The museum will remain closed during most of 2011 due to renovation at the Holmenkollen complex.

Kongeveien 5, Holmenkollen. ✆ **22-92-32-00.** www.holmenkollen.com. Admission (museum and ski jump) NOK90 adults, NOK45 children. May and Sept daily 10am-5pm; June-Aug daily 9am-10pm; Oct-Apr daily 10am-4pm. T-banen: Holmenkollen SST Line 15 from near the Nationaltheatret to Voksenkollen (30-min. ride), then an uphill 15-min. walk.

Stenersen Museum ★ 🎁 Part of the City of Oslo Art Collections, the most avant-garde temporary exhibitions in Oslo are presented here on a regular basis alongside three of the greatest private collections in Norway. Rolf E. Stenersen, a financier, author, and collector (1899–1978), donated some 300 paintings, even watercolors and prints by Edvard Munch, though you can see better Munchs at the National Gallery and his namesake museum. What you get here are the best examples of flourishing interwar Norwegian modernism, including some 300 paintings and 100 drawings from Amaldus Nielsen, "the painter of the south," whose best works were set in southern Norway. Finally, the widow of Ludvig O. Ravensburg donated some 160 works by her artist husband (1871–1958). Known for his burlesque humor, he was a relative of Munch.

Munkedamsveien 15. ✆ **23-49-36-00.** www.stenersen.museum.no. Admission NOK45, NOK25 students and children. Free to all Oct–Mar. Tues and Thurs 11am–7pm; Wed and Fri–Sun 11am–5pm. Tram: 10 or 12. T-banen: Nationaltheatret.

Vigeland Museum ★ This museum is for connoisseurs who didn't get enough of the monumental artist Gustav Vigeland in Vigelandsparken (p. 228). Opposite the southern entrance to Frognerparken, this was the 1920s former home of the great sculptor and also served as his studio. When he died in 1943, his ashes were placed in the tower of the museum. On the ground floor, nine rooms show a wide medley of his sculptures and drawings, while two rooms upstairs display plastic sketches, drawings, and woodcuts. His apartment upstairs is comprised of two sitting rooms, a library, and a bedroom—not exactly monastic, but not luxurious at all. Of a certain historical interest, Vigeland also sculpted two busts of two of the most famous of all Norwegians, Edvard Grieg and Henrik Ibsen. The museum was closed at press time but is due to reopen by spring 2011.

Nobels gate. ✆ **23-49-37-00.** www.vigeland.museum.no. Admission NOK50 adults, NOK25 seniors, students, and children 7–16, free for children 6 and under. Free to all Oct–Mar. June–Aug Tues–Sun 10am–5pm; off-season Tues–Sun noon–4pm. T-banen: Majorstuen.

HISTORIC BUILDINGS

Akershus Slott og Festning (Akershus Castle & Fortress) ★★ ☺ It has withstood fierce battles, drawn-out sieges, and a few fires, and changed shape architecturally since King Hakon V ordered it built in 1299, when Oslo was named capital of Norway. A fortress, or *Festning,* with thick earth-and-stone walls surrounds the castle, with protruding bastions designed to resist artillery bombardment. The moats and reinforced ramparts were added in the mid-1700s. For several centuries it was not only a fortress, but also the abode of the rulers of Norway. Now the government uses it for state occasions. From the well-manicured lawns there are **panoramic views** ★ of Oslo and the Oslofjorden. In summer, concerts, dances, and even theatrical productions are staged here. Forty-minute English-language guided tours are offered Monday to Saturday at 11am and 1 and 3pm, and on Sunday at 1 and 3pm.

Festnings-Plassen. ✆ **23-09-39-17.** Admission NOK65 adults, NOK25 children. Sept–May Sat–Sun noon–5pm; June–Aug Mon–Sat 10am–4pm, Sunday 12:30–5pm. Tram: 10 or 12.

Oslo Domkirke (Oslo Cathedral) ★ Oslo's restored 1697 cathedral at Stortorvet (the marketplace) contains works by 20th-century Norwegian artists, including bronze doors by Dagfin Werenskiold and a 1950 tempera ceiling by Hugo Louis Mohr. The choir features stained-glass windows crafted by Emanuel Vigeland (not to be confused with the sculptor, Gustav), and in the transepts are those by Borgar Hauglid. The **pulpit and altarpiece** ★, carved in the late 17th century with lovely motifs of acanthus leaves, also remain to delight. The five-story-tall organ dates from the 18th century and would challenge even a budding Norwegian Liberace. A bilingual service (in Norwegian and English) is conducted on Wednesday at noon, and an organ recital is presented on summer Saturdays at 1pm. ***Tip:*** For a great panoramic view of Oslo, go to the nightwatchman's room in the steeple, which was added in 1850.

Stortorvet 1. ✆ **23-31-46-00.** www.oslodomkirke.no. Free admission. Daily 10am–4pm. T-banen: Stortinget. Bus: 17.

Rådhuset (City Hall) Inaugurated in 1950, the City Hall, whose architecture combines romanticism, classicism, and functionalism, has been called everything from "aggressively ugly" to the pride of Norway. Aesthetics aside, the whole world looks toward this simple red-brick building with its iconic double towers every December when the Nobel Peace Prize is awarded. Luminaries such as Yasser Arafat (1994); Martin Luther King, Jr. (1964); Nelson Mandela (1993); and Jimmy Carter (2002) have claimed their prizes under this roof. It houses, among other things, a stunning 25×13m (82×43-ft.) wall painted by Henrik Sørensen, and the mural *Life* by Edvard Munch. Tapestries, frescoes, sculpture, and woodcarvings by Dagfin Werenskiold are also on display. Guided tours in English are available, though far from necessary. Be sure to check out the astronomical clock and Dyre Vaa's swan fountain in the courtyard.

Rådhuspladsen. ✆ **23-46-16-00.** Free admission. Daily 9am–6pm. 45-min. guided tours Mon–Fri at 10am, noon, and 2pm. Tram: 10 or 12.

Stortinget (Parliament) This yellow-brick building sounds a grace note amid the urban landscape. The original neo-Romanesque exterior, constructed from 1861 to 1866, has been preserved, and the finest artists decorated the interior, with works depicting scenes from the country's history or daily life. You're shown through on a guided tour and can see where some of the world's most progressive and socially conscious politicians meet. The tours, which last 20 minutes, are open to the public. (There's no need to book ahead, but try to arrive 15 min. before the tours begin.)

Karl Johans Gate 22. ✆ **23-31-35-96.** www.stortinget.no. Free admission. Guided tours in English July 1–Aug 15 Mon–Fri 10 and 11:30am, and 1pm; Sept 15–June 15 Sat 10 and 11:30am, and 1pm. Closed Aug 16–Sept 14 and June 16–30. T-banen: Stortinget. Tram: 13, 15, or 19.

On Bygdøy

South of the city, the peninsula is reached by commuter ferry (summer only) leaving from Pier 3, facing the Rådhuset (Town Hall). Departures during the day are every 40 minutes before 11am and every 20 minutes after 11am, and a one-way fare costs NOK40 (an Oslo Pass also works here). The no. 30 bus from the Nationaltheatret also runs to Bygdøy. The museums lie only a short walk from the bus stops on Bygdøy.

For reviews of Bygdøy's **Vikingskipshuset** (p. 229) and **Norsk Folkemuseum** (p. 228), see "Oslo Attractions," earlier in this chapter.

Kon-Tiki Museum ★ ☺ *Kon-Tiki* is a world-famous balsa-log raft. In 1947, the young Norwegian scientist Thor Heyerdahl and five comrades sailed it from Callao, Peru, to Raroia, Polynesia (6,880km/4,266 miles). It was not Heyderdahl's aim to discover new lands. He wanted to prove that the people of Polynesia originally came from South America. He showed how ancient civilizations could have done so by using a raft such as *Kon-Tiki*. Besides the raft, there are other exhibits from Heyerdahl's subsequent visits to Easter Island. They include casts of stone giants and small originals, a facsimile of the whale shark, and an Easter Island family cave, with a collection of sacred lava figurines hoarded in secret underground passages by the island's inhabitants. The museum also houses the original papyrus *Ra II,* in which Heyerdahl crossed the Atlantic in 1970. Although kids like to be taken here, adults will find it fascinating as well. For those who get really interested, they can read Heyerdahl's account of his adventures in his book, *Kon-Tiki,* published in countless editions around the world (available in the museum shop, of course).

Bygdøynesveien 36. ✆ **23-08-67-67.** www.kon-tiki.no. Admission NOK60 adults, NOK25 children. Apr–May and Sept daily 10am–5pm; June–Aug daily 9:30am–5:30pm; Oct and Mar daily 10:30am–4pm; Nov–Feb 10:30am–3:30pm. Ferry: From Pier 3 facing the Rådhuset (summer only). Bus: 30 from the Nationaltheatret.

Norsk Sjøfartsmuseum (Norwegian Maritime Museum) ★ ☺ Norway is extremely proud of its seafaring past, a glorious tradition that lives on at this museum that chronicles the maritime history and culture of the rugged country, complete with a ship's deck with helm and chart house. One somewhat gruesome section focuses on shipwrecks. Many boats speak of adventure, including the Gibraltar Boat, a fragile craft in which Norwegian sailors fled Morocco to the safety of British Gibraltar in World War II. There's also a three-deck section of the passenger steamer *Sandnaes,* and a carved-out tree trunk is said to be the oldest surviving Norwegian boat. The Boat Hall features a fine collection of original small craft. The fully restored polar vessel *Gjoa,* used by Roald Amundsen in his search for the Northwest Passage, is also on display. The three-masted schooner *Svanen* (Swan) is moored at the museum. Built in Svendborg, Denmark, in 1916, *Svanen* sailed under the Norwegian and Swedish flags. The ship now belongs to the museum and is used as a training vessel for young people.

Bygdøynesveien 37. ✆ **24-11-41-50.** www.norsk-sjofartsmuseum.no. Admission to museum and boat hall NOK60 adults, free for children. Mid-May to Aug daily 10am–6pm; Sept to mid-May Mon–Wed and Fri–Sun 10am–4pm, Thurs 10am–6pm. Ferry: From Pier 3 facing the Rådhuset (summer only). Bus: 30 from the Nationaltheatret.

OSLO ON FOOT: WALKING TOURS

WALKING TOUR 1: HISTORIC OSLO

START:	**Aker Brygge**
FINISH:	**Royal Palace**
TIME:	**2½ hours**
BEST TIME:	**Any day when it's not raining**
WORST TIMES:	**Rush hours (weekdays 7–9am and 5–7pm)**

Start at the harbor to the west of the Rådhuset at:

1 Aker Brygge

This steel-and-glass complex is a rebuilt district of shops and restaurants that was developed from Oslo's old shipbuilding grounds. It has a fine view of Akershus Castle.

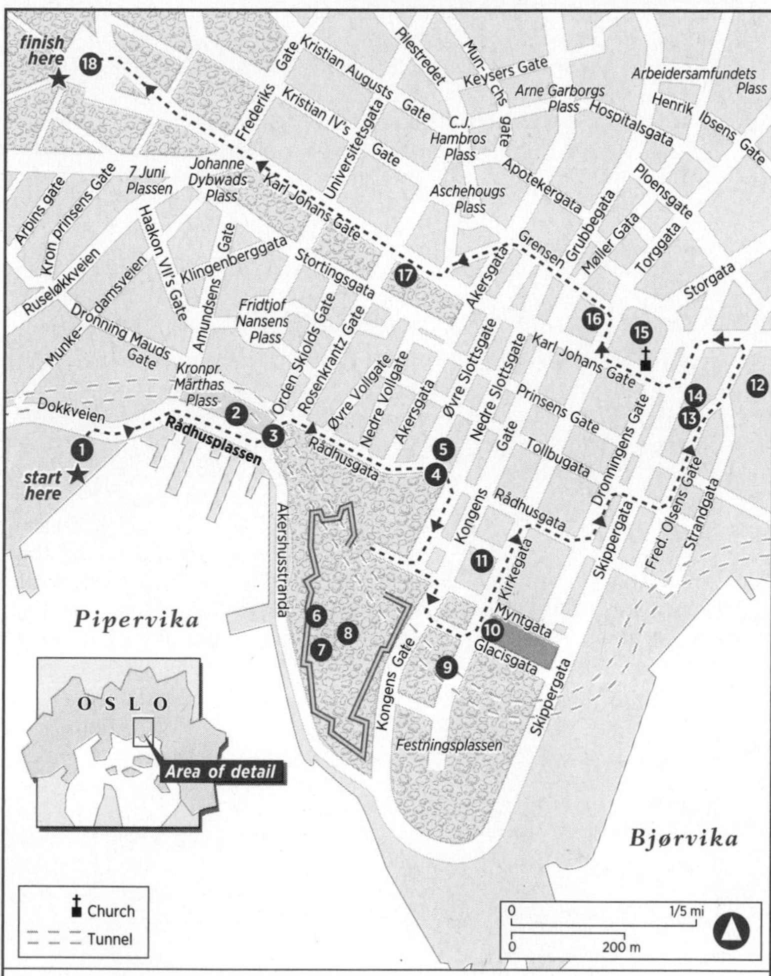

1 Aker Brygge
2 Rådhuset
3 Statue of Franklin D. Roosevelt
4 Christiania Torv
5 Kafé Celsius
6 Norges Hjemmefrontmuseum
7 Akershus Slott og Festning
8 Execution Site
9 National Monument to the German Occupation
10 Grev Wedels Plass
11 Bankplassen
12 Oslo Sentralstasjon
13 Karl Johans Gate
14 Basarhallene
15 Oslo Domkirke
16 Stortorvets Gjaestgiveri
17 Stortinget
18 Slottet

Head east along Rådhuspladsen, looking to your left at the:

2 Rådhuset

The Oslo City Hall, built in 1950, is decorated with artwork by Norwegian artists.

Climb the steps at the east end of the square and a small hill to see the:

3 Statue of Franklin D. Roosevelt

Eleanor Roosevelt flew to Oslo to dedicate this statue.

This area is the heart of the 17th-century Renaissance city. Take Rådhusgata east to the traffic hub of:

4 Christiania Torv

The yellow house on your left, the Young Artists Association, was once the home of a dreaded executioner. His fee depended on the type of execution performed.

5 Kafé Celsius

To the right of the Young Artists Association is Oslo's oldest residential house, Kafé Celsius, Rådhusgata 19 (© **22-42-45-39**). It's a charming arts-oriented cafe that serves tasty food. Sandwich prices start at NOK90. You can also order pasta salads and such dishes as ratatouille or tortellini. On cold days they start up the fireplace. It's open Monday to Saturday 11am to midnight, Sunday 11:30am to 7:30pm.

Continue along Rådhusgata, turning right onto Nedre Slottsgate. Walk to the end of the street. At Myntgata, turn right and pass through a gate. You are now on the greater grounds of Akershus Castle. The first building on the right is the:

6 Norwegian Resistance Museum

The museum has displays on events related to the Nazi occupation of Norway from 1940 to 1945.

Also at the site is:

7 Akershus Castle & Fortress

The structure dates from 1300 but was rebuilt in the 17th century. Take a guided tour and walk the ramparts.

In front of the Norwegian Resistance Museum, pause on the grounds to look at the:

8 Execution Site

Here the Nazis shot prisoners, often Norwegian freedom fighters. There's a memorial to the resistance movement, and you'll have a good view of the harbor in the distance.

Cross the drawbridge to the east, right before Kongensgate, and continue through the castle grounds to the:

9 National Monument to the German Occupation

This commemorates Norway's suffering at the hands of the Nazis.

After seeing the monument, turn left (north) into:

10 Grev Wedels Plass

This is the site of Den Gamle Logen (Freemason's Lodge). Ibsen wrote poems here in 1850. At no. 9 and Dronningensgatan 4 is the Astrup Fearnley Museum of Modern Art, with changing exhibits of Norwegian and international art from the postwar period.

Head north along Kirkegata until you reach:

11 Bankplassen

This former site of the old Bank of Norway is now the Museum of Contemporary Art (Bankplassen 4), with the state collection of international and Norwegian modern art acquired since World War II. This square was once Oslo's social center. Ibsen staged his first play here in 1851 (at a theater that burned down in 1877).

From Bankplassen, turn right onto Revierstredet and left onto Dronningensgatan. At one time the waterfront came up to this point. Go right at the Central Post Office onto Tollbugata. At the intersection with Fred Olsens Gate, turn left and walk to the:

12 Oslo Sentralstasjon

Trains arrive at Oslo's rail hub from the Continent here and depart for all points linked by train in Norway.

Turn left onto the main pedestrian-only street:

13 Karl Johans Gate

The street stretches from the Central Station in the east to the Royal Palace in the west end.

On your right you'll pass the:

14 Basarhallene

Boutiques and shops, hawking everything from food to clothing to crafts, fill this huge complex.

Turn right at Kirkegata, heading for the:

15 Oslo Domkirke

This 17th-century cathedral resides at Stortorvet, Oslo's old marketplace. Like the City Hall, the cathedral is decorated with outstanding works by Norwegian artists.

Stop in at Grensen 1:

16 Stortorvets Gjaestgiveri

Old Oslo atmosphere lives on at this drinking and dining emporium (© **23-35-63-60**) on a busy commercial street. Dating from the 1600s, it is often filled with spirited beer drinkers. A beer costs NOK50. It's open Monday to Saturday from 11am to 11pm, Sunday (from Sept–Apr only) 3pm to 9pm.

From Stortorvet, walk west on Grensen until you reach Lille Grensen. Cut left onto this street, returning to Karl Johans Gate. On your left at Karl Johans Gate 22 will be the:

17 Norwegian Parliament (Stortinget)

Constructed from 1861 to 1866, it's richly decorated with works by contemporary Norwegian artists.

Continue west along Karl Johans Gate, passing many of the monuments covered on "Walking Tour 2: In the Footsteps of Ibsen & Munch" (see below). Eventually you'll reach Drammensveien 1, the:

18 Royal Palace (Slottet)

This is the residence of the king of Norway and his family. Only the park is open to the public.

WALKING TOUR 2: IN THE FOOTSTEPS OF IBSEN & MUNCH

START:	**National Theater**
FINISH:	**National Gallery**
TIME:	**2 hours**
BEST TIME:	**Any day when it's not raining**
WORST TIMES:	**Rush hours (weekdays 7–9am and 5–7pm)**

The tour begins at Stortingsgata 15, just off Karl Johans Gate near the Students' Grove in Oslo's center, site of the:

1 Nationaltheatret (National Theater)

Study your map in front of the Henrik Ibsen statue at the theater, where many of his plays were first performed and are still presented. The Norwegian National Theater (✆ **81-50-08-11**), inaugurated in 1899, is one of the most beautiful in Europe.

Facing the statue of Ibsen, continue up Stortingsgata toward the Royal Palace (Slottet). Cut left at the next intersection and walk along Ruselokkveien. On the right, the **Vika Shopping Terraces,** an unattractive row of modern storefronts tacked onto an elegant 1880 Victorian terrace, used to be among Oslo's grandest apartments. During World War II it was the Nazi headquarters.

Continue along this complex to the end, turning right onto Dronnings Mauds Gate, which quickly becomes Lokkeveien. At the first building on the right, you come to:

2 Ibsen's private apartment

Look for the blue plaque marking the building. The playwright lived here from 1891 to 1895. When his wife complained that she didn't like the address, even though it was one of Oslo's most elegant, they moved. Ibsen wrote two plays while living here.

Turn right onto Arbinsgate, and walk to the end of the street until you reach Drammensveien. At Arbinsgate 1 is the:

3 Ibsen Museum

In the first building on the left, at the corner of Arbinsgate and Drammensveien, you'll see an Omega store, but look for the blue plaque on the building. Ibsen

Walking Tour: In the Footsteps of Ibsen & Munch

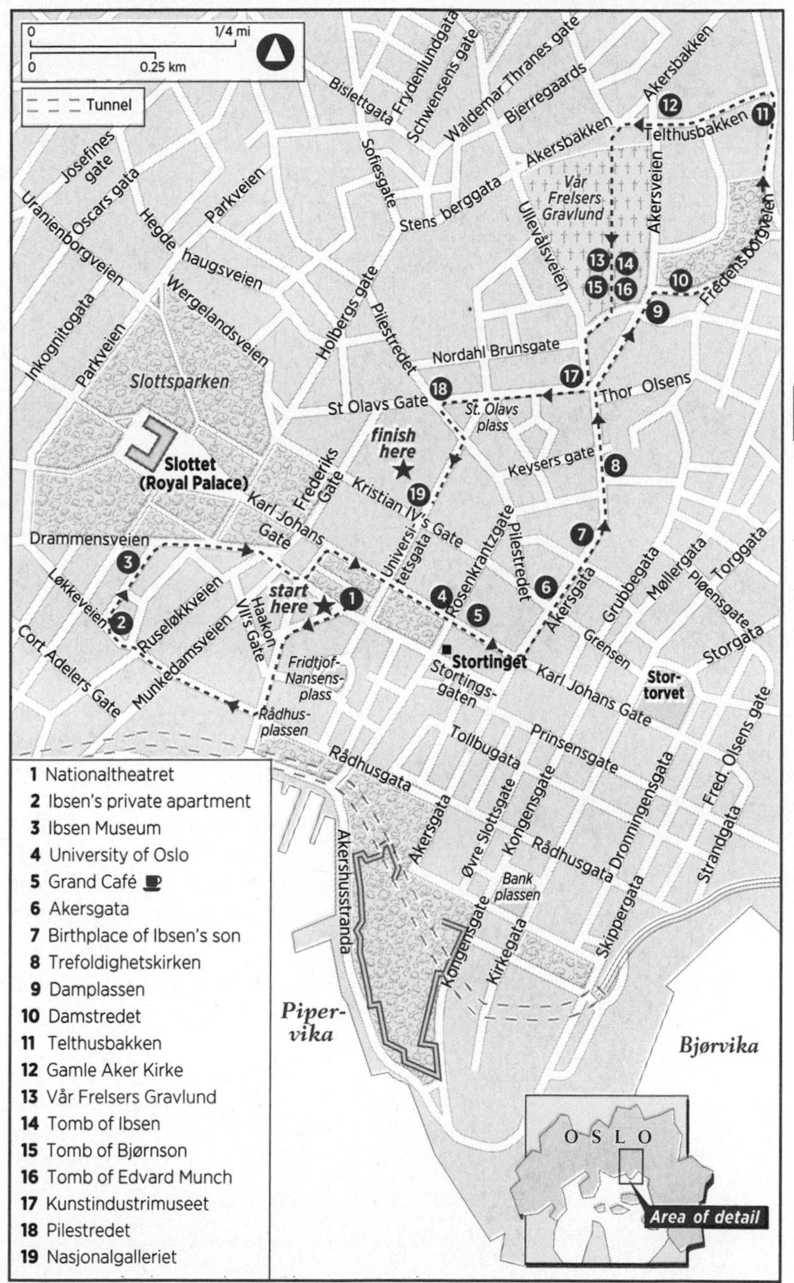

lived here from 1895 until his death in 1906. He often sat in the window, with a light casting a glow over his white hair. People lined up in the street below to look at him. The great Italian actress Eleanora Duse came here to bid him a final adieu, but he was too ill to see her. She stood outside in the snow and blew him kisses.

The king of Norway used to give Ibsen a key to enter the private gardens surrounding the Royal Palace. Today, everybody has that privilege.

Turn right on Drammensveien and continue back to the National Theater. Take Karl Johans Gate, on the left side of the theater, and walk east. On your left at Karl Johans Gate 47, you'll pass the:

4 University of Oslo

Aula, the Great Hall of the university, is decorated with murals by Edvard Munch. The hall is open to the public from June 20 to August 20, daily from 10am to 3pm. For information, call © **22-85-95-55.**

Twice a day Ibsen followed this route to the Grand Café. Admirers often threw rose petals in his path, but he pretended not to see. He was called "the Sphinx" because he wouldn't talk to anybody.

Stop in at:

5 Grand Café

This cafe, Karl Johans Gate 31 (© **23-21-20-00**), was the center of social life for the literati and the artistic elite, including Munch. Today a favorite with many visitors, but also with hundreds of Oslovians who appreciate tradition, it is the single most famous cafe in all of Scandinavia (see "Where to Dine," earlier in this chapter). On the far wall of the cafe, you can see Per Krogh's famous mural, painted in 1928. Ibsen, with a top hat and gray beard, is at the far left, and Munch—called the handsomest man in Norway—is seated at the second window from the right at the far right of the window. The poet and playwright Bjørnstjerne Bjørnson can be spotted on the street outside (second window from the left, wearing a top hat), because he wouldn't deign to come into the cafe. You can order food and drink, a big meal, or a snack here.

Returning to the street, note the **Norwegian Parliament** building (Stortinget) on your right. Proceed left, and turn left onto Lille Grensen. Cross the major boulevard, Grensen, and walk straight to:

6 Akersgata

This street was used for Ibsen's funeral procession. Services were conducted at the Holy Trinity Church on June 1, 1906.

Veer left to see the:

7 Birthplace of Ibsen's son

On your left, at the corner of Teatergata and Akersgata, is the site of the famous Strømberg Theater, which burned down in 1835. It was also a residence, and Ibsen's son was born here in 1859.

Also on Akersgata is:

8 Trefoldighetskirken (Holy Trinity Church)

This church was the site of Ibsen's funeral.

A little farther along Akersgata is St. Olav's Church. Turn on the right side of this imposing house of worship onto Akersveien and go to:

9 Damplassen

This small square—one of the most charming in Oslo—doesn't appear on most maps. Norway's greatest poet, Henrik Wergeland, lived in the pink house on the square from 1839 to 1841.

Take a right at the square and head down:

10 Damstredet

The antique, wooden houses along this typical old Oslo street are mainly occupied by artists.

Damstredet winds downhill to Fredensborgveien. Here, a left turn and a short walk will take you to Maridalsveien, a busy but dull thoroughfare. As you walk north along this street, look, on the west side, for a large unmarked gateway with wide stone steps inside. Climb to the top, follow a little pathway, and go past gardens and flower beds. Pass a set of brick apartment buildings on the left, and proceed to:

11 Telthusbakken

Along this little street, you'll see a whole row of early Oslo wooden houses. Look right in the far distance at the green building where Munch used to live.

Telthusbakken leads to Akersveien. On your left you can see the:

12 Gamle Aker Kirke (Old Aker Church)

Enter at Akersbakken, where Akersveien and Akersbakken intersect. Built in 1100, this is the oldest stone parish church in Scandinavia that's still in use. It stands on a green hill surrounded by an old graveyard and a stone wall.

A short block from the church along Akersbakken (veer left outside the front of the church and go around a corner), you'll come to the north entrance of the city's expansive burial ground:

13 Vår Frelsers Gravlund (Our Savior's Cemetery)

In a section designated the "Ground of Honor" are the graves of famous Norwegians, including Munch, Ibsen, and Bjørnson.

Signs don't point the way, but it's easy to see a tall obelisk. This is the:

14 Tomb of Ibsen

His wife, Susanna, whom he called "the cat," is buried to the playwright's left. She died in 1914. The hammer on the obelisk symbolizes his work *The Miner,* indicating how he "dug deep" into the soul of Norway.

To the right of Ibsen's tomb is the:

15 Tomb of Bjørnson

The literary figure Bjørnstjerne Bjørnson (1832–1910) once raised money to send Ibsen to Italy. Before the birth of their children, Ibsen and Bjørnson agreed that one would have a son and the other a daughter, and that they would marry each other. Miraculously, Ibsen had a son, Bjørnson a daughter, and they did just that. Bjørnson wrote the national anthem, and his tomb is draped in a stone representation of a Norwegian flag.

To the far right of Bjørnson's tomb is the:

16 Tomb of Edvard Munch

Scandinavia's greatest painter has an unadorned tomb. If you're visiting on a snowy day, it will be buried, because the marker is close to the ground. Munch died during the darkest days of the Nazi occupation. His sister turned down a request from the German command to give Munch a state funeral, feeling that it would be inappropriate.

On the west side of the cemetery, you'll come to Ullevålsveien. Turn left on this busy street, and head south toward the center of Oslo. You'll soon see St. Olav's Church, this time on your left. Stay on the right (west) side of the street. At St. Olavs Gate 1, where Ullevålsveien intersects with St. Olavs Gate, is the:

17 Kunstindustrimuseet (Museum of Applied Art)

Even if you don't have time to visit the museum, you may want to go inside to the Café Solliløkken (p. 231).

After visiting the museum, continue along St. Olavs Gate to:

18 Pilestredet

Look to the immediate right at no. 30. A wall plaque on the decaying building commemorates the fact that Munch lived here from 1868 to 1875. In this building he painted, among other masterpieces, *The Sick Child.* He moved here when he was 5, and many of his "memory paintings" were of the interior. When demolition teams started to raze the building in the early 1990s, a counterculture group of activists known as "The Blitz Group" illegally took over the premises to prevent its destruction. On its brick-wall side, his masterpiece *The Scream* was re-created in spray paint. The protesters are still in control of the city-owned building, and they are viewed as squatters on very valuable land. It's suspected that if a more conservative government comes into power, officials will toss out the case, throw out the activists, and demolish the building. For the moment, however, they remain in control.

At Pilestredet, turn left. One block later, turn right onto Universitesgata, heading south toward Karl Johans Gate. You'll pass a number of architecturally interesting buildings and will eventually arrive at Universitesgata 13, the:

19 National Gallery

The state museum has a large collection of Norwegian as well as foreign art. Two rooms are devoted to masterpieces by Munch.

Parks & Gardens

Marka ★★, the thick forest that surrounds Oslo, is just one of the giant pleasure parks in the area. You can also take a tram marked HOLMENKOLLEN from the city center to Oslomarka, a forested area where locals go for summer hikes and for winter skiing. The ride to the stop at Oslomarka takes only 20 minutes, and there are trains every 30 minutes or so, depending on the season. The area is dotted with about two dozen *hytter* (mountain huts) where you can seek refuge from the weather, if needed. **Norske Turistforening,** Youngstorget 1 (✆ **40-00-18-68**), sells maps with the hiking paths and roads of the Oslomarka clearly delineated. It's open Monday to Friday 9am to 4pm. A favorite trail—and you should have this pinpointed on a map—is a signposted walk to **Sognsvannet ★**, which is a beautiful loch (lake) flanked by forested hills and encircled by an easy hiking trail stretching for 4km (2½ miles). In winter, the loch is iced over; but, in summer, those with polar-bear blood can take a dip. Even in summer, swimming here is like taking a bath in ice water. In lieu of swimming, then, you might find the banks of this lake better suited for a picnic.

Slottsparken The park surrounding the Royal Palace (Slottet) is open to the public year-round. The changing of the guard, albeit a weak imitation of the changing of the guard at London's Buckingham Palace, takes place daily at 1:30pm. When the king is in residence, the Royal Guard band plays Monday to Friday during the ceremony. The palace was constructed from 1825 to 1848. Some first-time visitors are surprised at how relatively unguarded it is, without walls or rails. You can walk through the grounds but can't go inside unless you have managed to swing an invitation from the king. The statue at the front of the castle (at the end of Karl Johans Gate) is of Karl XIV Johan himself, who ruled Norway and Sweden. He ordered the construction of this palace but died before it was finished. Allot about 20 minutes.

Drammensveien 1. Free admission. Daily dawn–dusk. T-banen: Nationaltheatret.

Literary Landmarks

Ibsen Museum Now theatergoers from around the world can pay tribute to Ibsen by visiting his former apartment. In 1994, Oslo opened this museum to honor its most famous writer, Ibsen, who lived here from 1895 until his death in 1906. Within walking distance of the Nationaltheatret, the apartment was where Ibsen wrote two of his most famous plays, *John Gabriel Borkman* and *When We Dead Awaken*. The museum curators have tried to re-create the apartment (a longtime exhibit at the Norwegian Folk Museum) as authentically as possible. The study, for example, has Ibsen's original furniture, and the entire apartment is decorated as though Ibsen still lived in it. The attraction has been called "a living museum," and regularly scheduled talks on playwriting and the theater, recitations, and theatrical performances take place here. Allow 25 minutes.

Henrik Ibsens Gate 26. ✆ **22-12-35-50.** www.ibsen.net. Admission NOK85 adults, NOK25 children. Mid-May to mid-Sept daily 11am–6pm; mid-Sept to mid-May Mon–Wed and Fri–Sun 11am–4pm, Thurs 11am–6pm. Guided tours in English at noon, 1, and 2pm. Tram: 13, 15, or 19.

Oslo Bymuseet (City Museum) Housed in the 1790 Frogner Manor at Frogner Park, site of the Vigeland sculptures (see the earlier listing for Vigelandsparken, p. 228), this museum surveys the history of Oslo over the past 1,000 years—the red coats that the city's first policemen wore, the first fire wagon, relics of the great fire of 1624, the exhibits of the Black Death from 1348 to 1350. It also contains mementos of Henrik Ibsen, from the chair and marble-topped table where he sat at the Grand Café to the glasses from which he drank. Frogner Park, with its streams, shade trees, and lawns, is an ideal spot for a picnic. If not that, then go for that delicious ice cream or pastries served at the on-site Café Mathia. It takes about an hour to view the highlights of the museum.

Frognerveien 67. ✆ **23-28-41-70.** www.oslobymuseum.no. Free admission. Tues–Sun 11am–4pm (June–Aug closes at 5pm). Tram: 12.

Organized Tours

NORWAY YACHT CHARTER **Båtservice Sightseeing,** Rådhusbrygge 3, Rådhuspladsen (✆ **23-35-68-90**), offers a 90-minute boat tour. You'll see the harbor and the city, including the ancient fortress of Akershus and the islands in the inner part of the Oslofjord. Cruises depart from Pier 3 in front of the Oslo Rådhuset (City Hall). They run from mid-May to late August daily every half-hour from 9:45am to 3:45pm during the high season, less frequently at the beginning and end of the season. Tickets are NOK170 for adults, NOK85 for children.

If you have more time, take a 2-hour summer cruise through the maze of islands and narrow sounds in the Oslofjord. From May to September, they leave daily at 10:30am and 1, 3:30, and 5:45pm (slightly more often in July and Aug); the cost is NOK240 for adults, NOK120 for children. Refreshments are available onboard.

CITY TOURS **H. M. Kristiansens Automobilbyrå,** Hegdehaugsveien 4 (✆ **23-15-73-00**), has been showing visitors around Oslo for more than a century. Both of their bus tours are offered daily year-round. The 4-hour "Oslo Highlights" tour is offered at 10:15am. It costs NOK320 for adults, NOK160 for children. The 2-hour "Oslo Panorama" tour costs NOK215 for adults, NOK105 for children. It departs at 10:15am. The starting point is in front of the Nationaltheatret. Arrive 15 minutes before departure; tours are conducted in English by trained guides.

Sports & Activities

From spring to fall, the Oslofjord is a center for swimming, sailing, windsurfing, and angling. Daily excursions are arranged by motor launch at the harbor. Suburban forest areas await hikers, bicyclists, and anglers in the summer. In the winter, the area is ideal for cross-country skiing (on marked trails that are illuminated at night), downhill or slalom skiing, tobogganing, skating, and more. Safaris by Land Rover are arranged year-round.

BATHS The most central municipal bath is **Vestkantbadet,** Sommerrogata 1 (✆ **22-56-05-66;** www.vkbspa.no), which offers a Finnish sauna and Roman baths. This municipal bath is near the American Embassy, just a kilometer (½ mile) north from Oslo's center. It's primarily a winter destination and is closed in July. Admission is NOK130. The baths are open Monday to Wednesday 9am to 8:30pm, Thursday to Friday 9am to 7:30pm, and Saturday 9am to 4:30pm (sometimes 8pm). Mondays and Wednesdays are reserved for men; the other days are reserved for women. Prices for massages start at NOK400 for 25 minutes. If you book a massage (✆ **22-44-07-26**), you can use the baths free.

The much larger **Frognerbadet,** Middelthunsgate 28 (✆ **23-27-54-50**), in Frogner Park, is an open-air pool near the Vigeland sculptures. The entrance fee is NOK78 for adults and NOK37 for children. It's open mid-May to early September Monday to Friday 7am to 7:30pm, Saturday and Sunday 10am to 6pm. Take tram no. 2 from the Nationaltheatret.

BEACHES You most likely didn't come to Oslo to go to the beach. Even if you did, you'll find that you often have to swim from a rocky shore. Sun-loving Oslovians, desperate to absorb whatever sun they can get on a summer day, often take to whatever remotely resembles a beach. Their few short weeks of summer last until around mid-August, when snow flurries start appearing in the Oslo sky.

Our favorite beach, and the most easily accessible from the center of Oslo, is **Huk,** on Bygdøy peninsula. To reach Huk, take bus no. 30 A—marked BYGDØY—to its final stop. Should you arrive by boat on Bygdøy, follow the signs along Juk Aveny to the beach. My recommendation is to go over for the day; view the Viking Ship Museum, the Folk Museum, and other attractions in the morning; then head for the beach—preferably with the makings of a picnic—for the early afternoon. In case there are any prudes in your party, be duly warned: Half of the beach (the northwestern side) is reserved for nudists. That same warning should go for all beaches in Norway; many Scandinavians enjoy stripping down for the beach.

Once you get here, don't expect a traditional Hawaiian beach. The beach is mostly grass lawns and some smooth rocks that you can lie on to sun yourself like a lizard. If the beach at Huk is overcrowded, as it's likely to be on a summer day, take a 10-minute walk through the forest a bit north of where the bus stops. This leads to the more secluded beach at **Paradisbukta.**

These beaches are my favorites primarily because of their proximity to the center, not because they rival anywhere in the Mediterranean. But my secret reason to go there is to people-watch. After a day at the beach, you'll soon agree with a common assessment: Norwegians are among the healthiest-looking in the world.

Our second-favorite beach is at **Hovedøya,** on the southwestern shore of the rocky island of Hovedøya. To get here, board boats 92 or 93 leaving from the pier at Oslo called Vippetangen. From late May to mid-August, these boats depart daily from around 6am to midnight. This is the closest island to the mainland, and it's wildly popular in summer, as ideal for a picnic as it is for walks. The island is filled with walking paths, most of which lead to the ruins of a 12th-century Cistercian monastery.

You can also reach a number of beaches on the east side of the fjord by taking bus no. 75 B from Jernbanetorget in East Oslo. Buses leave about every hour on weekends. It's a 12-minute ride to **Ulvøya,** the closest beach to the fjord and one of the best and safest for children. Nudists prefer a section here called **Standskogen.**

FISHING Good fishing is to be found in the Oslofjord and in the lakes that envelop Oslo. An especially popular "fishing hole" is the vast area of Marka (see "Skiing," below). You can rent canoes from **Tomm Murstad** at Tryvannsvn 2 at Holmenkollen (© **22-49-67-07** or 22-13-95-00; www.sjoleir.no) to use for fishing. For information on the nearest place to buy a fishing license, or for more information, contact **Oslomarkas Fiskeadministrasjon** at Sørkeldalen 914, Holmenkollen (© **40-00-67-68;** www.ofa.no).

SKATING Oslo is home to numerous skating rinks. One of the best is the **Narvisen Skating Rink,** Skikersuppa, Karl Johan (© **22-33-30-33**), open daily 11am to 9pm, charging adults NOK55 for skate rentals, children NOK30. The rink is closed from April to November.

SKIING A 15-minute tram or bus ride from central Oslo to Holmenkollen will take you to Oslo's winter wonderland, **Marka,** a 2,579km (1,599-mile) ski-track network. Many ski schools and instructors are available in the winter. You can even take a sleigh ride. Other activities include dogsled rides, snowshoe trekking, and Marka forest safaris. There are 14 slalom slopes to choose from, along with ski jumps in all shapes and sizes, including the famous one at Holmenkollen. For information and updates on ski conditions, you can call Skiforeningen, Kongeveien 5 (© **22-92-32-00**). The tourist office can give you details about the venues for many of these activities.

Outside the City

LILLEHAMMER ★★

170km (105 miles) N of Oslo, 364km (226 miles) S of Trondheim

Hunderfossen Familiepark (Hunderfossen Family Park) ☺ At this kiddie fun park, you'll find a presentation of the most popular Norwegian fairy tales, more than 50 activities for children and adults, and lots of space to roam around. There are a merry-go-round and Ferris wheel, as well as carnival booths, a cafeteria, and a swimming pool. A 12m-tall (39-ft.) troll at the gate welcomes visitors. The park is 12km (7½ miles) north of Lillehammer on E-6.

Fåberg. ✆ **61-27-72-22.** www.hunderfossen.no. Admission 300NOK ($60/£30) adults, 195NOK ($39/£20) seniors, 245NOK ($49/£25) children 3-13, free for children 2 and under. May–Sept daily 10am–6pm. Closed Oct–Apr. Bus: Hunderfossen from Lillehammer.

Maihaugen Open-Air Museum (Sandvig Collections) ★★ Many Norwegian towns have open-air museums featuring old buildings that have been moved and put on display. This is one of the best of them. This museum consists of 180 buildings, from manor houses to the cottage of the poorest yeoman worker, and there are more than 40,000 exhibits. The houses reassembled here and furnished in 17th- to 18th-century style came from all over the Gudbrandsdal (Gudbrands Valley). Of particular interest is the Garmo Stave Church, built in 1200.

Maihaugveien 1. ✆ **61-28-89-00.** www.maihaugen.no. Admission 80NOK-100NOK ($16–$20/£8–£10) adults, 40NOK-50NOK ($8–$10/£4–£5) children 6-16, free for children 5 and under. May 18–Sept daily 10am–5pm; Oct–May 17 (indoor museum only) Tues–Sun 11am–4pm. Bus: 007.

SKIING

Lillehammer has a 94m (308-ft.) slope for professionals and a smaller jump for the less experienced. The lifts take skiers 457m (1,499 ft.) above sea level up the slalom slope, and there are more than 402km (249 miles) of maintained skiing trails.

The **Lillehammer Ski School** offers daily classes, and several cross-country tours are held weekly. For more information, contact the **Lillehammer Tourist Office,** Jernbanetorget 2 (✆ **61-28-98-00;** Mon–Fri 9am–4pm).

Fifteen kilometers (9¼ miles) north of town, **Hafjell Alpine Center** (✆ **61-27-47-06**) was the main venue for Olympic alpine competitions in 1994. It has seven lifts and 20km (12 miles) of alpine slopes. A "ski bus," costing 50NOK ($10/£5) one-way and taking 20 minutes, runs here from the center of Lillehammer about six times per day. Lillehammer is also the starting point for 402km (249 miles) of prepared cross-country tracks, 5.8km (3½ miles) of which are illuminated.

Lillehammer gears up in December for its winter sports season. In addition to the ski center, there's an admission-free **skating rink** where you have to bring your own skates. It's open in the winter Monday to Friday from 11am to 9pm, Sunday 11am to 5pm. In the winter, you'll also discover festivals, folklore nights, and ski races.

In winter, **Nordseter** is the focal point of two slopes for both the beginner and the intermediate-level downhill skier. It also has a vast network of cross-country ski trails. A lift pass, valid for a full day, costs 340NOK ($68/£34) per person, and ski equipment (either downhill or cross country) rents for 305NOK ($61/£31) per day.

SHOPPING

SHOPPING AREAS Oslo is one of the most shopper-friendly cities in Scandinavia, with traffic-free streets set aside for prospective buyers. The heart of this district is the **Stortorvet,** where more than two dozen shops sell everything from handicrafts to enameled silver jewelry. At the marketplace on Strøget, you can stop for a glass of beer at an open-air restaurant in fair weather. Many stores are clustered along **Karl Johans Gate** and the streets branching off it.

BEST BUYS Look for bargains on sportswear, silver and enamelware, traditional handicrafts, pewter, glass by Hadeland Glassverk (founded in 1762), teak furniture, and stainless steel.

SHOPPING HOURS Most stores are open Monday to Friday from 9am to 5pm, Saturday 9am to 3pm. Department stores and shopping malls keep different hours—in general, Monday to Friday 9am to 8pm and Saturday 9am to 6pm. Many shops stay open late on Thursday and on the first Saturday of the month, which is called *super lørdag* (super Saturday). During the holiday season, stores are also open on Sunday.

SHOPPING MALLS

Our favorite place for wandering and shopping in Oslo is **Aker Brygge ★★** (✆ **22-83-26-80**), a former shipbuilding yard that was recycled into a postmodern complex of steel-and-glass buildings. In all, there are nearly 65 shops here, most of them upmarket fashion boutiques. There are also 40 restaurants, along with pubs, movie houses, and theaters. When it's raining, duck into the indoor shopping mall. Even if you don't buy anything, Aker Brygge makes for a great people-watching experience. The location is right on the harborfront across from the Tourist Information Center at Vestbanen.

Paléet ★★, Karl Johans Gate 37–43, is set on Oslo's most central and most opulent shopping street. The weatherproof complex consists of 45 different shops and boutiques, all of them relatively upscale and flooded with light from skylights. You can purchase candles, incense, sweaters, art, housewares, cosmetics—you name it. Thirteen different restaurants, including burger and beer joints and one serving Indian food, refuel weary shoppers. You can also stop to admire a bronze statue of skating great (and former movie star) Sonja Henie.

Oslo City ★, Stenersgate 1, opposite the Central Station, is the biggest shopping center in Norway—loaded with shops and restaurants, though they are not quite as upscale as in the previous two malls. **Galleri Oslo,** at Vaterland, has been called Europe's longest indoor shopping street. Businesses are open daily until midnight, including Sunday. A walkway connects Galleri Oslo to the Central Station.

Shopping A to Z

ANTIQUES

Blomqvist Kunsthandel ★★ Built as an auction house by its original owners in 1870, this place is full of history and style. Its two large rooms have glass ceilings creating tons of natural light. Inside you'll find either one of their six annual auctions or one of their many Norwegian art exhibitions. In 1918, a gallery show released the full collection of an artist by the name of Edvard Munch. His prints and canvasses can still be seen here during temporary exhibitions. While this venue acts as an auction house, items up for bid include antiquities ranging from fine jewelry and paintings to furniture and sculpture. Tordenskiolds 5. ✆ **22-70-87-70.** T-banen: Nationaltheatret.

ARTS & CRAFTS

Kunstnernes Hus ★★ This is the best place to see and to purchase the latest in cutting-edge Norwegian art. This is an artist-run exhibition hall for contemporary art that first opened in 1930 and since that time has been one of the country's major showcases for the presentation of avant-garde national art. On the ground floor are two well-lit galleries and a reception area, and on the floor above are two more sky-lit galleries. Admission is NOK50 for adults and NOK25 for students and ages 7 to 17. Children 6 and under go in free. Hours are Tuesday and Wednesday 11am to 4pm,

Thursday and Friday 11am to 6pm, and Saturday and Sunday noon to 6pm. Wergelandsveien 17. ✆ **22-85-34-10.** T-banen: Sentrum.

Pur Norsk ★★ Since the minds behind cutting-edge design house Norway Says parted ways last summer, the downtown boutique of Pur Norsk is now the best place in the country to get your Nordic design fix. They sell innovative Norwegian-designed housewares and objets d'art including tumblers, wine glasses, kitchenware, and furniture items—little of which you're likely to have encountered before. You can also pick up many Norway Says classics here—they're soon to become collectors' items. Theresesgate 14. ✆ **22-46-40-45.** www.purnorsk.no. T-banen: Stensgata.

BOOKS

Bjorn Ringstrøms Antikvariat ★ One of the largest bookstores in Oslo houses a wide selection of Norwegian and Norwegian-American authors. They are also deeply rooted in books pertaining to Norwegian history and politics. A wide range of collectibles can also be found, ranging from antique books and color plates to records and maps. This century-old structure is directly across the street from the Museum of Applied Art. Sad to report, those days when you could walk in and buy an original edition of Ibsen's plays for NOK50 have gone with the wind. Ullevalsvn 1. ✆ **22-20-78-05.** T-banen: Stortinget.

Tanum Karl Johan ★ This fine bookstore in the center of town is the largest and most comprehensive in Oslo. It offers a vast selection, including many English titles. Karl Johans Gate 37–41. ✆ **22-41-11-00.** T-banen: Stortinget.

DELI

Fenaknoken ★ This place is the most famous deli in Oslo. Quality, not quantity, is their self-described motto, and they do live up to their words. You'll find everything you need to create the perfect outdoor meal. Cured and smoked meats from all over Europe hang on its walls, along with homemade jams and jellies on their shelves, a wide array of sharp and mild cheeses, and, as they claim, the best **smoked salmon ★★★** in the world, although I don't agree with Sean Lennon, who claimed that it is "better than world peace." A specialty of the house is *Fenalnlaar,* cured and seasoned sheep's meat. The only beverage is beer, which is supplied by a local brewery. For your actual picnic, I suggest you take your food to one of the beaches, either **Huk** on the Bygdøy peninsula (p. 244) or **Hovedøya** (p. 245). Tordenskiolds 7. ✆ **22-42-34-57.** T-banen: Nationaltheatret.

DEPARTMENT STORES

GlasMagasinet ★ Claiming that smaller boutiques tend to charge more, locals usually head for this big department store, which specializes in unusual home and kitchen accessories. Since 1739, this has been a leading outlet for knitwear, pewter, traditional rose-painting, and crystal. Today there are more than 20 fashion shops alone, and **Hadeland Glassverk ★★★** is the largest outlet in Norway for glass goods. You can also find a moderately priced coffee shop and a fairly decent restaurant. Stortorvet 9. ✆ **22-42-53-05.** T-banen: Stortinget. Tram: 11 or 17.

Steen & Strøm ★★ The largest department store in Norway, Steen & Strøm specializes in Nordic items, especially for the outdoors. Look for hand-knit sweaters and caps, hand-painted wooden dishes reflecting traditional Norwegian art, and pewter dinner plates made from old molds. There's a souvenir shop on the ground floor. Kongensgate 23. ✆ **22-00-40-00.** T-banen: Stortinget.

FASHION

H&M This large worldwide chain of stores is very well known for selling fashionable goods at reasonable prices. They carry everything from children's apparel to trendy clothing for men and women. Also on the menu are accessories, including a large selection of handbags and belts. Stenersgate 1 (Oslo City Shopping Center). ✆ **23-15-99-00.** T-banen: Jernbanetorget.

Oleana ★ This shop carries the award-winning designs of Solveig Hisdahl. Clothing items are made mainly of wool and silk and include elegant knitwear, skirts, cardigans, and shawls. Other items feature jewelry and silk scarves from some of the top Norwegian designers. Michelle Obama purchased four shift dresses here in 2009. Stortingsgaten 8. ✆ **22-33-31-63.** T-banen: Nationaltheatret.

Ove Harder Finseth ★★ This unique clothing store stars the painstaking and laborious productions of designer Ove Finseth. Each one-of-a-kind dress or gown is full of color (no black or gray), intricately detailed, and wonderfully ornate. The client list is quite impressive. Even the princess of Norway had her wedding gown designed here. Custom-made jewelry, bags, and hats are also sold. Pilius Plass 3. ✆ **22-37-76-20.** T-banen: Girneanetorgen.

Peak Performance ★★ This store is the number-one choice for the outdoorsman who seeks the most stylish performance clothing. There is a tremendous selection of jackets, shirts, accessories—their numerous styles and colors of Gore-Tex and fleece items is a real draw. Bogstadsvn 13. ✆ **22-96-00-91.** T-banen: Majorstuen.

FOLK COSTUMES

Heimen Husflid ★★ This leading purveyor of modern and traditional Norwegian handicrafts and apparel carries antique, reproduction and original regional and national folk costumes, known in Norwegian as *bunads.* More than three dozen different styles of bunads include many different counties of Norway, both north and south. Cozy, hand-knit sweaters in traditional Norwegian patterns are a special item. Pewter and brass goods are first-rate. It's about a block from Karl Johans Gate. Rosenkrantzgate 8. ✆ **23-21-42-00.** T-banen: Stortinget. Tram: 7, 8, or 11.

FURNITURE

Rom for Ide ★★ This is one of those stores that never seems to follow trends but always ends up looking trendy. This furniture outlet, hidden away from the city's shopping streets, specializes in modern yet classic designs. The contemporary and sleek look is the product of Norway's best and brightest new designers. Aside from the furniture, the Norwegian arts and crafts here are also great buys. Jacob Aallsgate 54. ✆ **22-59-81-17.** T-banen: Majorstuen.

JEWELRY, ENAMELWARE, PEWTER & SILVER

Esaias Solberg ★ 🎁 Opened in 1849 and long beloved by Oslovians, this is the largest and oldest venue for antique and secondhand gold and silver in Oslo. Brands of watches sold here include Rolex and Patek Phillipe, as well as countless others. They also sell diamond-studded gold and silver necklaces, brooches, and earrings. Outside of jewelry, they also offer some wonderful antique coffee sets, trays, and goblets. The owner of this place has a simple motto: "Antique jewelry is no more expensive than modern jewelry, and any secondhand jewelry sells at half of what it originally cost." Kirkeresten. ✆ **22-86-24-80.** T-banen: Jernbanetorget.

Heyerdahl ★ Want to outfit yourself like a Viking chieftain or bejewel yourself like an ancient queen? Between the City Hall and Karl Johans Gate, this store offers an intriguing selection of silver and gold Viking jewelry. There are articles in pewter and other materials, including Viking vessels, drinking horns, and cheese slicers. The store also has an array of woodcarvings depicting trolls, as well as one of Oslo's largest collections of gold and silver jewelry. Roald Amundsens Gate 6. ✆ **22-41-59-18.** T-banen: Nationaltheatret.

MUSIC

Los Lobos Straight out of 1950s Hawaii, this independent music store caters to all genres and styles of music outside of the mainstream. Aside from music ranging from blues to techno, you'll find cigarette cases, Hawaiian and bowling shirts, tons of denim, belt buckles, snakeskin boots, and much more. Don't expect to find the Top 40 here; this place is for the more alternative music listener. Thorvald Meyers Gate 30. ✆ **22-38-24-40.** Tram: 11 or 12 (to Olaf Ryes).

Norsk Musikforlag This centrally located store's selection of CDs and records is the best in Oslo. Kirkergata 30. ✆ **23-60-20-10.** T-banen: Stortinget.

SWEATERS

Oslo Sweater Shop Some 5,000 handcrafted sweaters are in stock here, close to the Royal Palace. Try them on before you buy. In theory, at least, you can tell the origin of a Norwegian sweater by its pattern and design, but with the increase in machine-made sweaters and the increased sophistication of Norwegian knitwear, the distinctions are increasingly blurred. Here, as in virtually every other sweater shop in Oslo, only about 10% of the sweaters are handmade—the remainder are high-quality and first-rate but most likely were crafted on an electric knitting machine. Sweaters start at around NOK1,000, rising to several thousands of *kroner.* Other items include necklaces, pewterware, souvenirs, and Norway-inspired trinkets. Next to the Clarion Hotel Royal Christiania, Biskop Gunnerus Gate 3. ✆ **22-42-42-25.** Bus: 30, 31, or 41.

OSLO AFTER DARK

Oslo has a bustling nightlife that thrives past midnight. The city boasts more than 100 night cafes, clubs, and restaurants, several dozen of which stay open until 4am.

Oslo is also a favorite destination of international performing artists in classical, pop, rock, and jazz music. Autumn and winter are the seasons for cabaret, theater, and concerts. There are four cabarets and nine theater stages throughout the city.

For movie lovers, Oslo has a fair amount to offer, as well. The city has one of the most extensive selections in Europe, with 30 screens and 5 large film complexes. Films are shown in their original languages, with subtitles.

The Entertainment Scene

The best way to find out what's happening is to pick up a copy of ***What's On in Oslo,*** detailing concerts and theaters and other useful information. Oslo doesn't have agents who specialize in discount tickets, but it does have an exceptional number of free events. *What's On in Oslo* lists free happenings as well as the latest exhibits at art galleries, which make for good early evening destinations.

The world-famous **Oslo Philharmonic** performs regularly under the leadership of Mariss Janson at the Oslo Konserthus. There are no Oslo performances between June 20 and the middle of August.

If you visit Oslo in the winter season, you might be able to see its thriving opera and ballet company, **Den Norske Opera.** Plays given at the **Nationaltheatret** (where plays by Ibsen are regularly featured) are in Norwegian, so those who know the language should enjoy hearing the original versions of his plays.

The Performing Arts

Den Norske Opera & Ballet ★★★ One of the greatest cultural advancements in Norway occurred in the spring of 2008 when this long-awaited opera house opened. Smack at the Oslo Fjord waterfront, this graceful Italian marble building, which resembles a glacier slipping its way into the fjord, won the 2009 Mies van der Rohe award for contemporary architecture. It's the new home of the finest opera and ballet troupes in Norway. The stunning very modern structure cost $840 million. The horseshoe-shaped main auditorium seats 1,369 listeners. Stage and theater technology are state of the art. Den Norske plans 300 performances a year. The "Song of Norway" never was better. The box office is open Monday to Friday from 10am to 8pm, Saturday from 11am to 6pm. Kirsten Flagstads Plass 1, in Bjørvika. © **21-42-21-00.** www.operaen.no. Tickets NOK180–NOK450 except for galas.

Oslo Konserthus ★★★ Two blocks from the Nationaltheatret, this is the home of the widely acclaimed Oslo Philharmonic. Performances are given autumn to spring, on Thursday and Friday. Guest companies from around the world often appear on other nights. The hall is closed from June 20 until mid-August, except for occasional performances by folkloric groups. The box office is open Monday through Friday 11am to 5pm and Saturday 11am to 2pm. Munkedamsveien 14. © **23-11-31-11.** Tickets NOK200–NOK800. T-banen: Stortinget.

Theater

Nationaltheatret (National Theater) ★★★ This theater at the upper end of the Students' Grove opens in September, so it may be of interest to off-season drama lovers who want to hear original versions of Ibsen and Bjørnson. Avant-garde productions go up at the **Amfiscenen,** in the same building. There are no performances in July and August. Guest companies often perform plays in English. The box office is open Monday through Friday from 9:30am to 6pm and Saturday 11am to 6pm. Johanne Dybwads Plass 1. © **81-50-08-11.** www.nationaltheatret.no. Tickets NOK150–NOK400 adults, NOK85–NOK170 students and seniors. T-banen: Nationaltheatret. Tram: 12, 13, or 19.

Summer Cultural Entertainment

Det Norske Folkloreshowet (Norwegian Evening) performs from July to August at the Norwegian Folk Museum, Museumsveien 10 (© **22-12-37-00** for reservations). The performances are on Tuesday, Wednesday, Friday, and Saturday at 5:30pm. Tickets cost NOK250 for adults, NOK50 for children (T-banen: Stortinget).

The ensemble at the **Norwegian Folk Museum,** on Bygdøy, often presents folk-dance performances at the open-air theater in the summer. See *What's On in Oslo* for details. Most shows are given on Sunday afternoon. Admission to the museum includes admission to the dance performance. Take the ferry from Pier 3 near the Rådhuset.

Special & Free Events

Oslo has many free events, including summer jazz concerts at the Nationaltheatret. In front of the theater, along the Students' Grove, you'll see street entertainers, including singers, clowns, musicians, and jugglers.

Concerts are presented in the chapel of **Akershus Castle & Fortress,** Akershus Command, on Sunday at 2pm. During the summer, promenade music, parades, drill marches, exhibits, and theatrical performances are also presented on the castle grounds.

In August, the **Chamber Music Festival** at Akershus Castle & Fortress presents concerts by Norwegian and foreign musicians.

The **Oslo Jazz Festival,** also in August, includes not only old-time jazz, but also classical concerts, opera, and ballet performances.

Films

American and British films are shown in English with Norwegian subtitles. Tickets are sold for specific performances only, and often for specific seats. Many theaters have showings nightly at 5, 7, and 9pm, but really big films are usually shown only once an evening, generally at 7:30pm.

Because of the city's long winter nights, filmgoing is big business in Oslo. Two of the city's biggest theaters are the **Saga Kino,** Stortingsgata 28 (T-banen: Nationaltheatret; ✆ **82-05-00-01**), and Klingenberg Kino, Olav V's Gate 4 (T-banen: Nationaltheatret; ✆ **82-05-00-01**). Most tickets cost between NOK90 and NOK130 for adults and are half-price for children. During matinees (usually on Mon and Thurs) the cost is reduced to NOK70 for adults and half-price for children.

The Club & Music Scene

DANCE CLUBS & DISCOS

There are standard age requirements to enter clubs and bars in Oslo and throughout Norway. For those taverns or other places holding a liquor license only for beer and wine, a visitor must be 18 years old or older. For establishments serving hard liquor, the minimum age is 20.

Smuget ★ This is the most talked-about nightlife emporium in Oslo, with long lines of the best and brightest, especially on weekends. It's behind the Grand Hotel in a 19th-century building that was once a district post office. There's an active dance floor with disco music and a stage where live bands (sometimes two a night on weekends) perform. The clientele—mostly ages 20 to 30—includes artists, writers, rock stars, and a cross section of the capital's night owls. The complex is open Monday through Saturday nights. A restaurant serves a range of international cuisines from 11am to 3am; live music plays from 10pm to 3am; and there's disco music from 10pm till very late. Half-liters of beer cost NOK45; main courses run NOK135 to NOK249. Rosenkrantzgate 22. ✆ **22-42-52-62.** Cover NOK80–NOK120. T-banen: Stortinget.

Jazz & Rock

Blå ★ This is the leading jazz club in Oslo. Dark and industrial, with lots of wrought iron and mellow lighting, this place books some of the best jazz acts in the world. The crowd is a mix of young and old, dressed in casual but sophisticated attire. The weeknights focus strictly on jazz, with the weekend providing more of a disco atmosphere, recruiting DJs from all over the world to spin the best in techno and house. It's open Friday to Saturday 9pm to 3:30am and weekdays depending on events. Brenneriveien 9C. ✆ **98-25-63-86.** Cover NOK30–NOK110, depending on the act. Tram: 11, 12, or 13.

Café Mono If you're looking for a relatively underfinanced punk-rock nightclub with beer-stained walls and a decor that could withstand, undisturbed, an invasion from a foreign army, this is it. It's a haven for the alternative, boozy, and occasionally alienated youth culture of Oslo. There's recorded music virtually all the time, a changing roster of live bands (many of them from the U.S.) appearing every Sunday to Thursday beginning around 10:30pm, and recorded house and garage-style dance music every Friday and Saturday. Whenever there's live music, the cover varies from NOK10 to NOK80, with better-known groups charging a good deal more; otherwise, it's free. It's open Monday to Saturday 3pm to 3:30am. Pløensgate 4. ✆ **22-41-41-66.** www.cafemono.no. T-banen: Stortinget.

Muddy Waters ★ If you long for blues music, make your way to this club, with its two fully equipped stages. At least one live band plays almost every night, often with big names, both local and international. This is not necessarily a club for moppets, as a slightly older crowd (at least those over 30) flocks here. Beer costs NOK55. Open daily 2pm to 3am. Grensen 13. ✆ **22-40-33-70.** Cover Fri-Sat usually NOK90. T-banen: Sentrum.

Rockefeller/John Dee With a capacity of 1,200 patrons, this concert hall and club is one of the largest establishments of its kind in Oslo. It's one floor above street level in a 1910 building, formerly a public bath. Live concerts feature everything from reggae to rock to jazz. When no concert is scheduled, films are shown on a wide screen. Simple foods, such as pasta and sandwiches, are available in the cafe. Most of the crowd is in the 18-to-40 age bracket. It's usually open Sunday to Thursday from 8pm to 2:30am, and Friday and Saturday from 9pm to 3:30am. Showtime is about an hour after the doors open. Torggata 16. ✆ **22-20-32-32.** Most tickets NOK100–NOK250, though some can be as much as double this price, depending on act. T-banen: Stortinget.

NIGHTCLUBS

Cosmopolite This lively international club plays music from all over the world, from Lapland to Africa. A young crowd in their 20s and early 30s comes here to hear folk music, tango from Argentina, jazz, funk, or whatever. Latin American salsa is often featured, and there's a big dance floor. Open nightly 8pm to 3am. Møllergata 26. ✆ **22-11-33-08.** Cover generally NOK150. T-banen: Jernbanetorget.

The Dubliner ★ This cozy and rustic bar is one of the oldest Irish pubs in Oslo. Housed in a building dating from 1666, the Dubliner holds true to its traditional Irish ancestry once you're inside. The crowd here does vary in age from 20 to 50 but consists mostly of Oslo's Irish and English communities. It offers a typical pub-grub type of menu and plenty of Irish beers on tap. On Friday and Saturday nights, traditional and contemporary Irish music can always be heard. On Tuesday, they hold jam sessions, where local musicians can bring their instruments and play at being rock stars for the night. It's open Sunday and Monday noon to 1am, Tuesday to Thursday noon to 2am, and Friday and Saturday noon to 3am. Rådhusgate 28. ✆ **22-33-70-05.** Cover Fri-Sat NOK80. T-banen: Stortinget.

The Bar Scene

PUBS & BARS

Bar For a late afternoon drink, try this simply named spot. Actually a slight misnomer, it comprises three intimate bars, as well as an Asian-inspired restaurant. It has become Oslo's hippest place for a drink since it opened in late 2009. Gregarious, gorgeous clientele come for both *vorspiel* (a pre-party drink) and *nachspiel* (a late-night after-party). Bygdøy Allé 18. ✆ **40-00-38-34.** Tram: 12.

Bar 1 For a connoisseur of brandy, this small cognac-and-cigar bar is the ultimate. You'll find close to 300 different varieties of cognac, plus a selection of the finest whiskeys. Accompany your libation with one of their wide selection of Cuban and Dominican cigars. As you could imagine, you'll find a subdued yet sophisticated post-40 crowd here. It's open daily 4pm to 3:30am. Holmensgate 3. ✆ **22-83-00-02.** Tram: 22.

Beach Club This place embodies (and is actually modeled after) a classic American diner, adding plenty of Norwegian flair. Its large booths and tables are welcoming—and the burgers are great. There is a bar but not much of a social scene, with mostly businessmen having drinks. Mellow, loungy music plays every night. It's open Tuesday to Friday 11am to midnight, Saturday noon to midnight. Aker Brygge. ✆ **22-83-83-82.** T-banen: Nationaltheatret.

Bibliotekbaren (Library Bar) In a lobby that evokes the Edwardian era, this is a perfect spot for people-watching—that is, middle-aged-people-watching. Sheltered behind racks of leather-bound books, which you can remove and read, you'll feel like you're in a well-furnished private club. There's live piano music at lunchtime, when you can order from a selection of open-faced sandwiches for NOK60 to NOK100. It's open daily from 10am to 11:30pm; alcohol service starts at 1:30pm. In the Bristol Hotel, Kristian IV's Gate 7. ✆ **22-82-60-22.** T-banen: Stortinget.

Fridtjof's Pub This Norwegian pub offers a cozy retreat for a late-night drink. It consists of a ground floor with deep red walls, comfortable sofas, and some tables and chairs. The second floor has much of the same, providing an unobstructed view of the crowd below whose ages range from 20 to 50. Both floors have interesting photos of polar expeditions, mainly because it's named after Fridtjof Nansen, the first Norwegian to successfully explore the north pole. In summer, the party usually moves outside, where you can enjoy views of the harbor and city hall directly across the street. It's open daily noon to 1am. Fridtjof Nansen's Plass 7. ✆ **93-25-22-30.** T-banen: Nationaltheatret.

Oro Bar This glamorous tapas bar, associated with the restaurant Oro, evokes the stylish and hip locales of warmer climates. An intensely fashionable crowd in their 30s and 40s—and in intensely expensive clothing—drops in for meals and people-watching. You can eat or just have a drink. Small sandwich plates start at NOK129. It's open Monday to Saturday 6pm to 2am. Tordenskiolds 6A (entrance on Kjeld Stubs Gate). ✆ **23-01-02-40.** T-banen: Stortinget.

Oslo Mikrobryggeriet This small, English-style pub attracts a mixed, 30-something crowd. Aside from some cognac and whiskey, offerings include six in-house beers, the most popular being "Oslo Pils." With its cozy and warm atmosphere and good music, this brewery is sure to please. It's open daily 3pm to 1am. Bogstadvn 6. ✆ **22-56-97-76.** T-banen: Majotsstuem.

Skybar ★ On the top floor of the Radisson Blu Plaza Hotel, this bar is known as the most vertigo-inducing and panoramic in Oslo. And at 100m (328 ft.) above the ground, it's also northern Europe's highest. In the ultramodern interior, surrounded by a glass ceiling and walls, you'll find Oslo's young, professional elite in their 20s, 30s, and 40s sipping on sophisticated cocktails. The view and people-watching are worth the trip. It's open Monday to Thursday 4pm to 1am, Friday and Saturday 4pm to 1:30am. Sonja Henie Plass 3. ✆ **22-05-80-00.** T-banen: Central Station.

CAFES

Café-Bar Memphis This is a hip, industrial-looking bar with a fondness for such U.S.-derived kitsch as Elvis memorabilia and late, late drunken nights that feature Jack Daniel's and beer. There's a limited roster of menu items (seafood pastas, scrambled eggs with ham or bacon and toast), but most of the clients come to sip well-priced cocktails with friends and colleagues. It's open Monday to Thursday 11am to 1am, and Friday and Saturday 11am to 3am. Thorvald Meyers Gate 63. ✆ **22-04-12-75.** Tram: 11, 12, 13, or 30.

Lorry This busy, suds-drenched cafe was established 120 years ago as a working-class bar. Since then, the surrounding neighborhood (virtually across the street from the park that flanks the Royal Palace) has zoomed upward in prestige and price. Now the cafe's low-slung, wood-sided building is tucked among villas. There's an outdoor terrace for warm-weather dining, but the heart and soul of the place is its Victorian, black-stained interior. Offerings include 130 kinds of beer, 12 of which are on tap. The menu consists of salads, sandwiches, and burgers, as well as larger dishes, priced at NOK98 to NOK189 each, but from around 10:30pm to closing, all everybody seems to do here is drink. It's open Monday to Saturday 11am to 3:30am, and Sunday noon to 1:30am. Parkveien 12. ✆ **22-69-69-04.** Tram: 11.

GAY & LESBIAN BARS

This city of slightly under 600,000 residents has few gay bars. Pick up a copy of *Blick,* available at most newsstands within the central city. Otherwise, call the **Norwegian LGBT Association,** Valkyriegaten 15 A, at ✆ **23-10-39-39** Monday through Friday between 9am and 4pm. Alternatively, explore the website www.visitgayoslo.no.

London Pub This is the most consistent and reliable gay pub in Oslo, with a relatively mature crowd of unpretentious gay men and—to a much lesser extent—women. Set within the cellar of a building a few steps from the prestigious Bristol Hotel, it contains a battered-looking, beer hall–style trio of underground rooms with two bar areas and a pool table. During busy periods, usually late in the week, this place can be fun, convivial, and genuinely welcoming to newcomers from faraway places, though its fairly quiet early in the week. It's open daily from 3pm to 3:30am. The attached disco, **London Club,** is upstairs and is a bit more animated and festive. It's open daily 8pm to 3:30am, and occasionally has a cover charge of NOK40. C. J. Hambros Plass 5 (entrance on Rosenkrantzgate). ✆ **22-70-87-00.** T-banen: Stortinget.

BERGEN

Bergen—one of Europe's most underrated cities—is enveloped by majestic mountains, the world's most spectacular fjords, and one of Europe's largest glaciers. In summer, when most visitors arrive, a youthful energy prevails before the deep freeze of winter settles in. Moreover, the July sun shines all night long—and it's party time, often until morning. But there is plenty of life in the wintertime as well; it just moves in from the streets to the taverns and music clubs. On even the most rushed of itineraries, try to spare at least 2 days for Bergen to experience the natural beauty still preserved here.

10

In western Norway, the landscape takes on an indescribable beauty, with iridescent glaciers; deep fjords that slash into rugged, snowcapped mountains; roaring waterfalls; and secluded valleys that lie at the end of twisting roads. From Bergen, the most beautiful fjords to visit are the **Hardangerfjord** (best at blossom time—May and early June), to the south; the **Sognefjord,** Norway's longest fjord, immediately to the north; and the **Nordfjord,** north of that. A popular excursion on the Nordfjord takes visitors from Loen to Olden along rivers and lakes to the **Brixdal Glacier.**

On the Hardangerfjord, you can stay over at a resort such as **Ulvik** or **Lofthus.** From many vantage points, it's possible to see the **Folgefonn Glacier,** Norway's second-largest ice field. It spans more than 260 sq. km (101 sq. miles). Other stopover suggestions include the summer resorts (and winter ski centers) of Voss and **Geilo.** For resorts in the fjord district, see chapter 11, "Exploring the Norwegian Coast."

Bergen, with its many attractions and excellent transportation, makes the best hub for exploring the fjord district. It's an ancient city that looms large in Viking sagas. Until the 14th century, it was the seat of the medieval kingdom of Norway. The Hanseatic merchants established a major trading post here until the 18th century. Seafaring Bergen has given the world two quintessential Norwegian cultural icons—the composer Edvard Grieg and the playwright Henrik Ibsen.

Bergen has survived many disasters, including several fires and the explosion of a Nazi ship during World War II. It's a city with important traditions in shipping, banking, insurance, and industry; and its university is one of the most respected in the Nordic countries.

ORIENTATION

Arriving

BY PLANE Planes to and from larger cities such as Copenhagen and London land at the **Bergen airport** in Flesland, 19km (12 miles) south of

THE world's (SECOND-) LONGEST TUNNEL

Thanks to a tunnel, you can now drive from Oslo to Bergen without having to take a ferry across water. Opened in 2001, the **Lærdal Tunnel ★★★**, stretching for 25km (15 miles), was the longest in the world until a similar tunnel in Japan opened a few years ago, just eclipsing the Norwegian one by a few kilometers. It is on E-16, the main road between Bergen and Oslo. The entrance to the tunnel begins at a point 296km (184 miles) northwest of Oslo. Costing roughly $1.1 billion, it is said to be the safest road tunnel on the globe.

Along with high-tech monitoring, fire safety, and air treatment, the tunnel features a trio of large turning caverns (in case you change your mind and want to go back), 16 turning points, and nearly 50 emergency lay-bys. Some 400 vehicles per hour can go through the tunnel, the ride taking just 20 minutes.

The area up above gets severe weather in winter, but all is calm in the tube. The high mountain passes at 1,809m (5,934 ft.) are closed in winter. The panoramic, high-mountain road between Aurland and Laerdal, the so-called Snow Road, is open only in summer.

the city. Dozens of direct or nonstop flights go to just about every medium-size city in Norway on such airlines as **SAS** (✆ **91-50-54-00;** www.sas.no).

Frequent **airport bus** service connects the airport to the Radisson Blu Royal Hotel and the city bus station. Departures are every 15 minutes Monday to Friday and every 30 minutes Saturday and Sunday. The one-way fare is NOK90.

BY TRAIN Day and night trains arrive from Oslo and stations en route. For information, call ✆ **81-50-08-88.** Travel time from Oslo to Bergen is roughly 8½ hours. Visit www.nsb.no for information.

BY BUS Express buses travel to Bergen from Oslo, Trondheim, Ålesund, and the Nordfjord area. The trip from Oslo takes 11 hours. Visit www.nor-way.no for information.

BY CAR A toll is charged on all vehicles driven into the city center at all times. A single ticket costs NOK15.

The trip from Oslo to Bergen is a mountain drive filled with dramatic scenery. Because mountains split the country, there's no direct road. The southern route, E-76, goes through mountain passes until the junction with Route 47, then heads north to Kinsarvik and makes the ferry crossing to E-16 leading west to Bergen. The northern route, Hwy. 7, through the resort of Geilo, heads to the junction with Route 47, then south to Kinsarvik. Take the ferry and then go west on E-16.

Visitors with a lot of time may spend 2 or 3 days driving from Oslo to Bergen. Fjords and snowcapped peaks line the way, and you can photograph waterfalls, fjord villages, and ancient stave churches.

To reduce driving time, motorists can use a tunnel—11km (6¾ miles), the longest in northern Europe—that goes between Flåm (see "Flåm: Stopover on Europe's Most Scenic Train Ride," in chapter 11) and Gudvangen. From Gudvangen, follow E-16 southwest to Bergen.

Visitor Information

The **Bergen Tourist Office,** Vågsallmenningen 1 (✆ **55-55-20-00;** www.visitbergen.com), provides information, maps, and brochures about Bergen and the rest of the region. It's open June to August daily 8:30am to 10pm, May and September daily 9am to 8pm, October to April Monday to Saturday 9am to 5pm. Staff can help you find a place to stay, exchange foreign currency, and cash traveler's checks when banks are closed. You can also buy tickets for city sightseeing or for tours of the fjords.

GETTING AROUND

The **Bergen Card** entitles you to free bus transportation and (usually) free museum entrance throughout Bergen, plus discounts on car rentals, parking, and some cultural and leisure activities. It's a great value. Ask for it at the tourist office (see "Visitor Information," above). A 24-hour card costs NOK190 for adults, NOK75 for children 3 to 15. A 48-hour card is NOK250 for adults, and NOK100 for children 3 to 15. Children under 3 travel or enter free.

By Bus

The **Central Bus Station (Bystasjonen),** Strømgaten 8 (✆ **55-55-90-70**), is the terminal for all buses serving the Bergen and Hardanger areas, as well as the airport bus. The station has luggage storage, shops, and a restaurant. City buses are marked with their destination and route number. For **bus information** in the Bergen area, call ✆ **177.** A network of variously colored city buses serves the city center only. For information, call ✆ **55-59-32-00.**

By Taxi

Taxis are readily available at the airport. To request one, call ✆ **55-99-70-10.** A ride from the Bergen airport to the city center costs around NOK340.

By Car

PARKING Visitors can park on most streets in the city center after 11pm. For convenient indoor parking, **Bygarasjen Busstation** (✆ **55-56-88-70**), a large garage near the bus and train stations, is about a 5-minute walk from the city center. It's open 24 hours a day and charges NOK20 per hour. You can park for 24 hours for NOK100.

RENTAL CARS You might want to rent a car to explore the area for a day or two. **Budget** (✆ **800/527-0700** in the U.S.; www.budget.com) maintains offices at the airport (✆ **55-22-75-27**) and downtown at Vestre Strømkaien 5 (✆ **55-32-60-00**). Its least expensive car is NOK661 per day, which includes the 23% government tax, collision-damage waiver, and unlimited mileage. Rates per day are lower for rentals of a week or more.

Hertz (✆ **800/654-3001** in the U.S.; www.hertz.com) has locations at the airport (✆ **55-22-60-75**) and downtown at Nygårdsgaten 89 (✆ **55-96-40-70**). For a 2-day rental, the smallest car, a Volkswagen Polo, costs NOK2,099.

Avis (✆ **800/331-1212** in the U.S.; www.avis.com) has branches at the airport (✆ **55-11-64-30**) and downtown at Lars Hillesgate 20 (✆ **67-25-56-50**). For a 1-day rental, its smallest car, a Fiat 500, costs NOK1,210 with unlimited mileage. The price includes the 23% tax and the optional collision-damage waiver. Of course, rates are subject to change. The lowest rates are almost always offered to those who reserve their cars from their home country before they leave.

By Ferry

You can take the Beffen ferry across the harbor Monday to Friday from 7am to 4:15pm; they don't run on Saturday or Sunday. One-way fares are NOK20 for adults and NOK10 for children. Ferries arrive and depart from either side of the harbor at Dreggekaien and Munkebryggen. For information, call ✆ **56-14-07-02.**

By Coastal Steamer

Bergen is the cruise capital of Norway, home to a flotilla of well-engineered ships (the Hurtigruten) that carry passengers, cars, and vast amounts of freight up and down the coast. At least 10 of the boats begin and end their itineraries in Bergen and make about 30 stops en route before landing 5 to 6 days later at Kirkenes, far north of the Arctic Circle, near the Russian border. You can book a berth on any one of these ships for short- or long-haul transits and do a quick bit of sightseeing while the ship docks in various ports.

The most popular tour is a 12-day unescorted northbound cruise—Oslo-Bergen-Kirkenes-Oslo—visiting 34 ports and starting at US$1,482 (early booking rate) per person, based on double occupancy. It's best to book these cruises through the New York City office of **Hurtigruten** (✆ **866/552-0371;** www.hurtigruten.us). If you're already in Norway, talk to any travel agent. You can make arrangements through Bergen-based **Cruise Spesialisten,** Ulriksdahl 7 (✆ **55-59-68-40**) or with its competitor, **Kystopplevelser,** on Strandkaien 4 (✆ **55-31-59-10**). Both companies distribute brochures and lots of information concerning the stalwart Norwegian cruise ships that make frequent runs up and down the Norwegian coast.

Other routes head south from Bergen to Stavanger and other ports, and tours go to some of the fjords to the south. For information and reservations, contact the Bergen Line, Cruise Spesialisten (see above), or a local operator. The best operator is **Fjord 1** (✆ **55-90-70-70;** www.fjord1.no), which runs fast ferries from Bergen to Sognefjord, the world's longest fjord.

[FastFACTS] BERGEN

Area Code The country code for Norway is **47.** Most land-based telephones within Bergen begin with 55. (Cellphones, however, are not bound by that general rule and might begin with virtually anything.) In Norway, all telephone numbers have eight digits, the first two of which are usually defined as the "area code." It's always necessary to dial all eight digits.

Banking Bergen has dozens of banks. The most visible is **Dnb Norske Bank,** Lars Hilles Gate 30 (✆ **55-21-10-00**). Branches of many of its competitors can be found near the Radisson Blu Hotel Norge, on Nedre Ole Bulls Plass 4.

Business Hours Most **banks** are open Monday to Friday from 9am to 3pm, and Thursday until 6pm. Most **businesses** are open Monday to Friday 9am to 4pm. **Shops** are generally open Monday to Wednesday and Friday 9am to 4:30pm, Thursday 9am to 7pm (sometimes also on Fri until 7pm), Saturday 9am to 3pm.

Currency Exchange You can exchange currency at the Bergen airport. In town you can exchange money at several banks. When the banks are closed, you can exchange money at the tourist office (see "Visitor Information," above).

Drugstores One convenient pharmacy is **Apoteket Nordstjernen,** in Bergen Storsenter shopping mall (✆ **55-21-83-84**). It's open Monday to Saturday 8am to 11pm and Sunday 10am to 11pm.

Embassies & Consulates Most foreign nationals, including citizens of the United States, will have to contact their embassies in Oslo (see "Embassies & Consulates," in "Fast Facts: Norway," chapter 21) if they have a problem. Exceptions to this rule include the **United Kingdom,** which maintains a consulate in Bergen, at Øvre Ole Bulls Plass 1 (✆ **55-36-78-10**); and Canada, which keeps a consular address at PO Box 2439, Solheimsviken 5824, Bergen (✆ **55-29-71-30**).

Emergencies For the **police,** dial ✆ **112;** to report a **fire,** call ✆ **110;** for an **ambulance,** dial ✆ **113.**

Hospitals A medical center, **Accident Clinic (Legevakten),** is open around-the-clock. It's at Vestre Stromkaien 19 (✆ **55-56-87-00**).

Police Call ✆ **112.**

Post Office The main post office is at Småstrandgaten 3 (✆ **55-54-15-00**), 1 block from Torget. It's open Monday to Friday 8am to 5pm (Thurs until 6pm), and Saturday 9am to 2:30pm. If you want to receive your mail in care of general delivery, the address is Poste Restante, N-5002 Bergen. You'll need your passport to pick it up.

Telephone Most locals have mobile phones. As a result there are only a few public phone booths left. Phone cards are available in various denominations at newspaper kiosks and pharmacies. To call abroad, dial ✆ **00;** to call collect, dial ✆ **115.**

WHERE TO STAY

Easily found at Vågsallmenningen 1, the **Bergen Tourist Office** (see "Orientation," earlier in this chapter) books guests into hotels and secures accommodations in private homes. More than 30 families take in guests during the summer. The booking service costs NOK50, and prospective guests also pay a deposit that's deducted from the final bill. Double rooms in **private homes** usually cost from NOK600 to NOK1,000, with no service charge. Breakfast is not served. All of the recommended accommodations come with private bathrooms unless otherwise indicated.

Expensive

Clarion Collection Hotel Havnekontoret ★★★ This is still the most sought-after place to stay in town. Right on the scenic Bryggen harborfront, the hotel was created from the historic house of the Bergen Port Authority. Architects recycled the building into a first-class hotel of grace and charm, respecting the past style, keeping many early-20th-century neoclassiccal and baronic features. Book into one of the tower rooms, as the views over the harbor and the cityscape are spectacular. The six-floor property features rooms with a contemporary, colorful decor, each with a state-of-the-art bathroom. Bedrooms also have all the most up-to-date amenities. The hotel also maintains the best fitness equipment in town, and its buffet restaurant serving breakfast and dinner is even patronized by certain locals looking for a good start to their day.

Slottsgaten 1, N-5835 Norway. www.clarionhotel.com/hotel-bergen-norway-no097. ✆ **55-60-11-00.** 116 units. NOK1,895–NOK2,795 double; NOK2,795–NOK12,180 suite. Rates include buffet breakfast. AE, DC, MC, V. Parking NOK100. Bus: 1, 5, or 9. **Amenities:** Restaurant; bar; fitness room; room service; sauna; rooms for those w/limited mobility. *In room:* TV, hair dryer, minibar, Wi-Fi.

Radisson Blu Hotel Norge ★★★ This Radisson Blu is the traditional prestige hotel and an even better address than the Radisson Blu Royal (below). In the city center, near Torgalmenningen, the Norge has been a Bergen tradition since 1885, and it continues to be a favorite of local celebrities. Rooms feature double-glazed windows, bedside controls, and ample bathrooms with showers and, in some cases, bathtubs big enough for two. The ninth-floor units open onto private balconies overlooking the nearby lush park. The hotel's Ole Bull restaurant serves international food, while Søtt + Salt offers up some of the town's freshest seafood. There's also an on-site piano bar, the American Bar. The Contra Bar, on the street level, near the reception area, is a leading nightlife venue, and the Metro disco is in the cellar, both with separate entrances.

Nedre Ole Bulls Plass 4, N-5807 Bergen. www.radissonblu.com/hotelnorge-bergen. ✆ **800/333-3333** in the U.S., or 55-57-30-00. 347 units. NOK2,195-NOK2,595 double; NOK3,695-6,195 suite. Rates include breakfast. Children 17 and under stay free in parent's room. AE, DC, MC, V. Parking NOK240; reserve with room. Bus: 2, 3, or 4. **Amenities:** 2 restaurants; 2 bars; dance club; babysitting; fitness center; heated indoor pool; room service; sauna; spa; rooms for those w/limited mobility. *In room:* TV, hair dryer, minibar.

Radisson Blu Royal Hotel ★★ Opened in 1982, this hotel was built on the fire-ravaged site of an old warehouse at Bryggen that had stood here since 1702. The hotel offers a choice of standard rooms, business-class rooms, and suites, the latter decorated with locally made arts and crafts, creating one of the coziest ambiences in Bergen. The guest rooms are beautifully maintained, with lithographs and comfortable, upholstered furniture. The hotel has a pub, Madame Felle, named after a lusty matron who ran a sailors' tavern on these premises during the 19th century. The pub's outdoor terrace does a thriving business in summer, and the separate nightclub, Bryggen Piano Bar, is just next door.

Bryggen, N-5835 Bergen. www.radissonblu.com. ✆ **800/333-3333** in the U.S., or 55-54-30-00. 273 units. NOK1,275-NOK2,895 double; NOK4,600 suite. Rates include breakfast. AE, DC, MC, V. Parking NOK200. Bus: 1, 5, or 9. **Amenities:** 2 restaurants; 2 bars; nightclub; babysitting; fitness center; heated indoor pool; room service; sauna; rooms for those w/limited mobility. *In room:* TV, hair dryer, minibar, Wi-Fi.

Moderate

Augustin Hotel ★ 🎁 The clear winner in the moderately priced category is the oldest family-run hotel in Bergen. The Augustin has one of the best locations in Bergen—right in the harborfront shopping district—with front rooms that have harbor views. Constructed in 1909 in the *Jugendstil* or Art Nouveau style, the Augustin rises six floors. In 1995, it more than doubled in size by adding a new wing, with modern rooms (equipped with larger showers and tubs) designed by award-winning Bergen architect Aud Hunskår. Less up-to-date and somewhat less desirable rooms remain in the old section. The hotel is decorated with lots of art, much of which comprises pieces from well-known contemporary Norwegian artists. The Altona tavern, once the haunt of Bergen artists and concertmasters in the 17th century, has been creatively integrated into the hotel. The hotel was built on the Altona's foundation, and its nostalgic memory is evoked in the hotel's wine cellar, which is open to the public. Even if you're not a guest, I'd recommend a visit to the on-site Brasserie No22, with some of the best shellfish and meat grills in town.

C. Sundts Gate 22-24, N-5004 Bergen. www.augustin.no. ✆ **55-30-40-00.** 109 units. NOK1,150-NOK2,050 double. AE, DC, MC, V. Parking NOK100. Bus: 2 or 4. **Amenities:** Restaurant; bar; rooms for those w/limited mobility. *In room:* A/C, TV, hair dryer, minibar.

Clarion Hotel Admiral ★ Just minutes from such attractions as the Bergen Fish Market right on the Bergen harbor, with panoramic views of Bryggen and the old wharf, location alone is this place's major selling point. In 1906, the now-recycled building was one of the largest warehouses in Bergen, with six sprawling floors peppered with massive trusses and beams. It was miraculously transformed into this modern bastion in 1987. Some rooms are small, but others are midsize to spacious, with shiny modern bathrooms. Many rooms lack water views, but the ones that do open onto flower-bedecked balconies. This member of the Clarion chain is not as luxurious and well appointed as the Clarion Collection, above.

C. Sundts Gate 9, N-5004 Bergen. www.choicehotels.no. ✆ **55-23-64-00.** 211 units. Mon–Thurs NOK1,480–NOK2,495 double, NOK3,000 suite; Fri–Sun NOK1,080–NOK1,780 double, NOK1,510–NOK2,550 suite. Rates include buffet breakfast. AE, DC, MC, V. Parking NOK150; reserve with room. Bus: 2, 4, or 11. **Amenities:** 2 restaurants; bar; room service; rooms for those w/limited mobility. *In room:* TV, hair dryer, minibar.

Neptun Hotel ★ The Neptun offers a far livelier ambience and decor than the more run-of-the-mill Clarion (above). It was built in 1952 long before many of its more streamlined and trend-conscious competitors. Its eight-story premises attract lots of business, especially from Norwegians riding the Hurtigruten (coastal steamers), who consider it a worthwhile and solid choice in the upper-middle bracket. Each of the bedrooms has a decorative theme related to its name. For example, rooms named after Ole Bull, Nordahl Grieg, Ludvig Holberg, Salvador Dalí, and Joan Miró have photos or artworks commemorating their namesakes' lives and achievements. The hotel's premier restaurant, Lucullus, is one of Bergen's best; there's also a likable, bustling brasserie named Pascal.

Valkendorfsgate 8, N-5012 Bergen. www.neptunhotell.no. ✆ **55-30-68-00.** 124 units. NOK1,395–NOK2,145 double; NOK4,995 suite. AE, DC, MC, V. Parking NOK180. Bus: 20, 21, or 22. **Amenities:** 2 restaurants; bar; room service. *In room:* A/C, TV, hair dryer, minibar.

Inexpensive

Bergen Travel Hotel ☺ This recently refurbished place is fine for a good night's sleep—but not a lot more—at an affordable price. In the center of Bergen, the five-story building has been a hotel since the 1970s, although it absorbed a building across the street in 2005. Bedrooms come in various sizes, and each has pale colors and contemporary furniture crafted from dark-grained hardwoods. Some of the accommodations used to be small private apartments, so they can generously accommodate four or more people, which makes them a family favorite. Bedrooms have wooden floors and comfortable but simple furnishings, and four of the units come with small kitchens.

Vestre Torgate 20A, N-5015 Bergen. www.hotelbergen.com. ✆ **55-59-90-90.** 61 units. NOK990–NOK1,320 double. Rates include continental breakfast. AE, DC, MC, V. Closed Dec 22–Jan 4. No on-site parking. Bus: 2, 3, or 4. **Amenities:** Pub. *In room:* TV.

Comfort Hotel Holberg ★ Near the Nykirken, a 15-minute walk from Bergen's Fish Market, this seven-story hotel built around 1995 (and refurbished in 2009) commemorates the life of the late-18th-century writer and dramatist Holberg, "the Molière of the North," one of the most famous writers in Danish and Norwegian letters. (The writer was born in a since-demolished house on the site of this hotel's parking garage.) The hotel's lobby is a testimonial to the author's life, with an informative biography, memorabilia, and photographs of stage productions based on his works. Bedrooms are a modernized reinterpretation of the Norwegian "farmhouse" style, with wooden floors, rough-textured half-paneling stained in tones of forest green, and big windows, some of them floor-to-ceiling, that swing open directly onto a view of the quiet residential street below.

Strandgaten 190, Pb 1949 Nordnes, N-5817 Bergen. www.choicehotels.no. ✆ **55-30-42-00.** 149 units. NOK780–NOK2,200 double. Rates include buffet breakfast. AE, DC, MC, V. Parking NOK160. Bus: 1, 5, or 9. **Amenities:** Restaurant; bar. *In room:* TV, hair dryer, minibar, Wi-Fi.

Steens Hotel—Bed & Breakfast ★ Among the more established B&Bs, the Steens is the best Bergen has to offer. This is a stylish 1890 house that has been successfully converted to receive guests. Owned and operated by the same family since 1950, Steens offers great accommodations at reasonable prices. The bedrooms are moderate in size and comfortable, and the bathrooms, though small, are well maintained. The best rooms are in front and open onto a park; each unit comes with a neatly maintained private bathroom equipped with a shower. The thoughtful, personal touches include hot coffee served throughout the day in the public rooms that evoke a historic aura. The B&B is within a short walk of the bus or rail station.

22 Parkveien, N-5007 Bergen. www.steenshotel.no. ✆ **55-30-88-88.** 18 units. NOK1,340 double. Extra bed NOK250. Rates include Norwegian breakfast. AE, MC, V. Free parking. Bus: 1 or 5. **Amenities:** Breakfast room; lounge. *In room:* TV.

On the Outskirts

Solstrand Hotel & Bad ★★★ This is the most prestigious resort in the region around Bergen. Discerning travelers appreciate its isolated location beside the fjord, as well as its history, which dates to 1896. The setting evokes a romantic getaway to the countryside. Bedrooms are cheerfully painted, high-ceilinged affairs, with a sophisticated mixture of antique and modern furniture. The in-house restaurant serves lunch buffets, priced from NOK390 per person, and a la carte at dinner (three courses NOK460). Advance reservations are recommended for meals, which—especially on Sunday afternoons—are a magnet for extended families from the surrounding region. The hotel's many amenities include free use of rowboats and putt-putt motorboats, as well as access to a nearby 9-hole golf course.

N-5200 Os (24km/15 miles south of Bergen). www.solstrand.com. ✆ **56-57-11-00.** 135 units. Mon-Thurs NOK2,480 double; Fri-Sun NOK2,280 double. Rates include buffet breakfast. AE, DC, MC, V. Free parking. Closed Dec 22-Jan 3 and 1 week at Easter. From Bergen, drive south along the E-39, following the signs to Stavanger, turning off at the markers to either Os (the region) or Osøyro (the hamlet that functions as the centerpiece of the Os region). **Amenities:** Restaurant; bar; exercise room; indoor heated pool; saunas; spa; tennis court; watersports program. *In room:* TV, hair dryer, minibar.

WHERE TO DINE

Expensive

Enhjørningen (the Unicorn) ★★ SEAFOOD Part of the charm of this restaurant on the Hanseatic wharf derives from the unlevel floors, the low doorways, and the inconvenient access via narrow staircases to its second-floor dining room. In one of the old wooden buildings of the Bryggen complex, adjacent to the harbor, it boasts a history and a name that were recorded as early as 1304. After several fires and the removal of lots of rotted timbers, the inn has been restored to its 1700s condition. You'll sit in one of several old-fashioned dining rooms set railway style (end to end) and outfitted like an early-19th-century parlor with framed oil paintings, usually landscapes. It's usually mobbed, especially in midsummer. Choices include savory fresh mussels steamed in white wine with cream, curry, and saffron; oven-baked halibut with saffron *beurre blanc* sauce; herb-fried medallions of monkfish with a morel cream sauce; and bacalao (dried cod) served au gratin with a crusty layer of cheese and boiled potatoes. The star offering of the restaurant's small offering of meat dishes is a grilled filet of beef with a pepper-flavored cream sauce. At Christmas, they serve the pungent *lutefisk,* a whitefish that many Norwegians associate with their childhoods.

Bryggen. ✆ **55-32-79-19.** Reservations recommended. Main courses NOK295–NOK330; fixed-price menus NOK530. AE, DC, MC, V. Mon–Sat 4–11pm. Closed 2 weeks at Christmas. Bus: 4, 5, 80, or 90.

Finnegaardsstuene ★★★ NORWEGIAN/FRENCH This is one of the leading gourmet restaurants on the west coast of Norway. The foundations of this popular restaurant were laid around 1400, when Hanseatic League merchants used it as a warehouse. Today some of the woodwork dates from the 1700s, and four small-scale dining rooms create a cozy atmosphere. The chefs have created magic in sleepy Bergen with their well-thought-out menu and carefully prepared dishes. It changes with the season and the inspiration of the chef. Some of the best dishes might include breast of local duck with wild mushrooms, parsley risotto, and burgundy sauce; or halibut filet, with thyme-flavored, semi-dried tomatoes, and saffron fondant potatoes. Another specialty is slow-roasted French pigeon with foie gras.

Rosenkrantzgate 6. ✆ **55-55-03-00.** Reservations recommended. Main courses NOK295–NOK315; fixed-price menu NOK595–NOK825. AE, DC, MC, V. Mon–Sat 6–11pm. Closed 1 week at Easter and Dec 22–Jan 8. Bus: 5 or 21.

To Kokker ★ FRENCH/NORWEGIAN To Kokker ("Two Cooks"—in this case, Norway-born partners Daniel Olsen and Grete Halland) is a favorite with celebrities ranging from Britain's Prince Andrew to a bevy of French starlets. Savvy local foodies increasingly gravitate here for the chef's well-considered juxtaposition of flavors and textures. Menu items include such time-tested favorites as foie gras with the traditional accompaniments; gooseliver terrine with balsamico syrup; filet of venison with chanterelle sauce; and herb-fried monkfish served with mushroom sauce. The 1703 building is adjacent to the oldest piers and wharves in Bergen. The classic dining room, one floor above street level, has a warmly tinted decor of deep red and soft orange, old paintings, and a solidly reliable staff.

Enhjørninggården 3. ✆ **55-30-69-55.** Reservations required. Main courses NOK295–NOK340; 5-course menu NOK675. AE, DC, MC, V. Mon–Sat 5–10pm. Bus: 1, 5, or 9.

Moderate

Bølgen & Moi NORWEGIAN This is a franchise restaurant located in the same building as the Bergen Art Museum. If you're visiting the museum, it makes the ideal choice for lunch, but it's also good and affordable enough to return for an evening visit. Many workers from the neighborhood patronize the local bar for drinks and conversation. On the lunch menu you can begin with the fish soup, following with a burger or pizza, perhaps one of the well-stuffed sandwiches, my favorite being the crayfish, shrimp, and crab. At night the menu grows more elaborate, with such main courses as grilled salmon with salmon caviar or medallions of veal in a morel cream sauce. Braised pork belly might appear with an apple marmalade. Starters include a surprisingly tasty shellfish risotto with scallops, mussels, and pan-fried cod's tongue. Sundays is a lunch buffet only (NOK295).

Rasmus Meyers Alle 9. ✆ **55-59-77-00.** Main courses NOK229–NOK320 dinner; fixed-price menus NOK495–NOK645. AE, DC, MC, V. Tues–Sat 11am–10pm; Sun noon–5pm. Bus: 1, 5, or 9.

Egon NORWEGIAN/INTERNATIONAL The 1876 building that contains this member of a well-respected nationwide restaurant chain is one of the most distinctive, with some of the most elaborate carved masonry, along the quays. True to its origins as the city's *kjøttbasaren* (meat market), the upstairs of the building contains a half-dozen boutique-style butcher shops and fishmongers. During a 20th-century restoration, archaeologists discovered the rotted keel of a 14th-century wooden ship beneath its foundations. Today the building's ground floor contains a restaurant that's either appealing in its coziness and historicity or daunting because of its ever-present mobs. Menu items include grilled poultry and a grilled tenderloin steak, fresh fish, soups, salads, and pastas, all served in generous portions by a staff that often seems more than a bit harassed. Some food items have just a hint of Americanized flair, especially a "party platter" that's piled high with nachos, chicken fingers, and onion rings. There are also a bacon-wrapped tenderloin of beef and Cajun-blackened chicken cutlets.

Vetrlidsalmenning 2. ✆ **55-55-22-22.** Reservations recommended. Main courses NOK165–NOK299. AE, DC, MC, V. Daily 11am–midnight. Bar daily 11am–1am. Bus: 5 or 21.

Hanne På Høyden ★★★ NORWEGIAN Run by Chef of the Year Hanne Frosta, this outstanding organic, farm-to-plate restaurant has become one of the country's most popular. Everything about it screams ecological. At lunch, dishes include the likes of *smørbrød,* soups, and salads. Dinner off the limited menu is heavier fare—though portions are reasonable—and your prettily arranged dish will undoubtedly be whatever ingredients are available according to season, from reindeer to fish or fresh greens. The frenetic decor manages to keep the eye moving from one photo or unusual piece of decorative flair while simultaneously bringing a sense of calm to your meal with its serene colors.

Fosswinckelsgt 18, Bergen 5007. ✆ **55-32-34-32;** hannepaahoeyden.wordpress.com. Reservations recommended. NOK145–NOK320. AE, DC, MC, V. Mon–Sat 11.30am–6:00pm and 4:00pm–10:00pm.

Holbergstuen NORWEGIAN One floor above street level, this restaurant was established in 1927 midway between the harborfront and Ole Bulls Plass. It was named in honor of the 18th-century writer Ludvig Holberg. He divided his time between Bergen and Copenhagen, and both cities ferociously claim him as part of their cultural heritage. The setting is much like a tavern, with beamed ceilings, an open log fire, lots of exposed wood, and a vivid sense of Old Norway. Some of the most intriguing menu items include grilled stockfish with a bacon and a cabbage stew or else grilled salmon with new potatoes. A local favorite is the pan-fried filet of cusk with creamed spinach, root vegetables, rösti potatoes, and orange- and beetroot sauce. This is a longtime favorite; come here for old-fashioned flavors, not trendy experiments.

Torgalmenningen 6. ✆ **55-55-20-55.** Reservations recommended. Main courses NOK239–NOK299. AE, DC, MC, V. Mon–Sat 11am–11pm; Sun 2–10pm. Bus: 1, 5, or 9.

Wesselstuen NORWEGIAN/CONTINENTAL Other and better restaurants have opened to successfully challenge this longtime favorite, but this is one of the city's most beloved and most traditional. Named for the 18th-century Danish/Norwegian humorist Peter Wessel, it has some of its namesake's framed illustrations and all the trappings of an 18th-century wine cellar. It's decorated in old-tavern style with beamed ceilings, and its adjoining pub is a famous meeting place for locals. The chefs can be experimental at times, and the menu has kept up with the times with more modern ingredients and sauces, but they're also soundly grounded in the classics. Some of the more reliable main dishes include baked trout served with cucumber, crème fraîche, and boiled potatoes, and steamed klipfish of cod served with pea stew, bacon, carrot, and boiled potatoes. Two other specialties are filet of pork marinated in chili, and grilled beef ribs with an herb sauce.

Øvre Ole Bulls Plass 8. ✆ **55-55-49-49.** Reservations recommended. Main courses NOK199–NOK289; fixed-price menus NOK435. AE, DC, MC, V. Mon–Sat 11am–11pm; Sun 2pm–midnight. Bus: 2, 3, or 4.

Inexpensive

Kaffistova NORWEGIAN This elegant cafeteria looks more like a full-service restaurant, with its linen tablecloths and upscale cutlery. On the ground floor of Hotel Hordaheimen, this no-nonsense place offers aggressively unpretentious and relatively quick meals. Lunchtime features open-faced sandwiches *(smørbrød)* and simple platters of the day. Dinner offerings are a bit more elaborate, with carved meats, pepper steak, meatballs, and an excellent version of mushroom soup. Especially Norwegian-style meals include *kjøttkaker* (rissoles) and *vossakorv* (potato dumplings with salted meat, mashed Swedish turnips, and traditional sausage), the latter of which is on the menu from Thursday to Sunday.

In the Hotel Hordaheimen, C. Sundts Gate 18. ✆ **55-33-50-00.** Main courses NOK70–NOK140 lunch, NOK145–NOK190 dinner. AE, DC, MC, V. Sun–Fri 11am–7pm. Bus: 21, 22, or 23.

SEEING THE SIGHTS

The Top Attractions

The best way to begin is to take a stroll around **Bryggen ★★★**. This row of Hanseatic timbered houses, rebuilt along the waterfront after a disastrous fire in 1702, is what remains of medieval Bergen. The northern half burned to the ground in 1955. Bryggen has been incorporated into UNESCO's World Heritage List as one of the most significant cultural and historical re-creations of a medieval settlement, skillfully blending with the surroundings of modern Bergen. It's a center for arts and crafts, where painters, weavers, and craftspeople have their workshops, some of which are open to the public.

Akvariet (Bergen Aquarium) ★★ ☺ A 15-minute walk from the city center, this aquarium contains the most extensive collection of marine fauna in Europe, lying on the outmost reaches of the Nordnes district, with a panoramic view of the entrance to the port of Bergen. The exceptional marine life includes seals, penguins, lobsters, piranhas, and a "bearded" cod. Nothing is uglier than the Norwegian catfish, which wins all those most hideous-looking contests. In the outer hall you can get the feel of the fish—dip your hand into the shallow pool of unpolluted water pumped up from a depth of 120m (394 ft.) in the fjord outside. Nine glass tanks, each containing about 236,250 liters (62,500 gal.) of water, flank the hall. Downstairs, a wide range of marine life in 42 small aquariums demonstrates many colorful forms of sea life and illustrates evolutionary development. Kids should enjoy the shark tunnel, and the seal and penguin feeding time, daily at 11am, and 2 and 6pm in the summer, or in the winter daily at noon and 4pm. Every hour you can watch the 3-D film *SOS Planet,* as well as Ivo Caprino's film about the Bergen Aquarium. Not only that, you can attend concerts and folkloric musical performances.

Nordnesbakken 4. ✆ **55-55-71-71.** www.akvariet.com. Admission NOK150 adults, NOK100 children, NOK400 family ticket (slightly cheaper in off-season). May–Aug daily 9am–7pm; Sept–Apr daily 10am–6pm. Bus: 11 from the Fish Market.

Impressions

Reaching Bergen we fail to find it particularly attractive. Everything is fishy. You eat fish and drink fish and smell fish and breathe fish.

—Lilian Leland, *Traveling Alone: A Woman's Journey Round the World,* 1890

Bergen Attractions

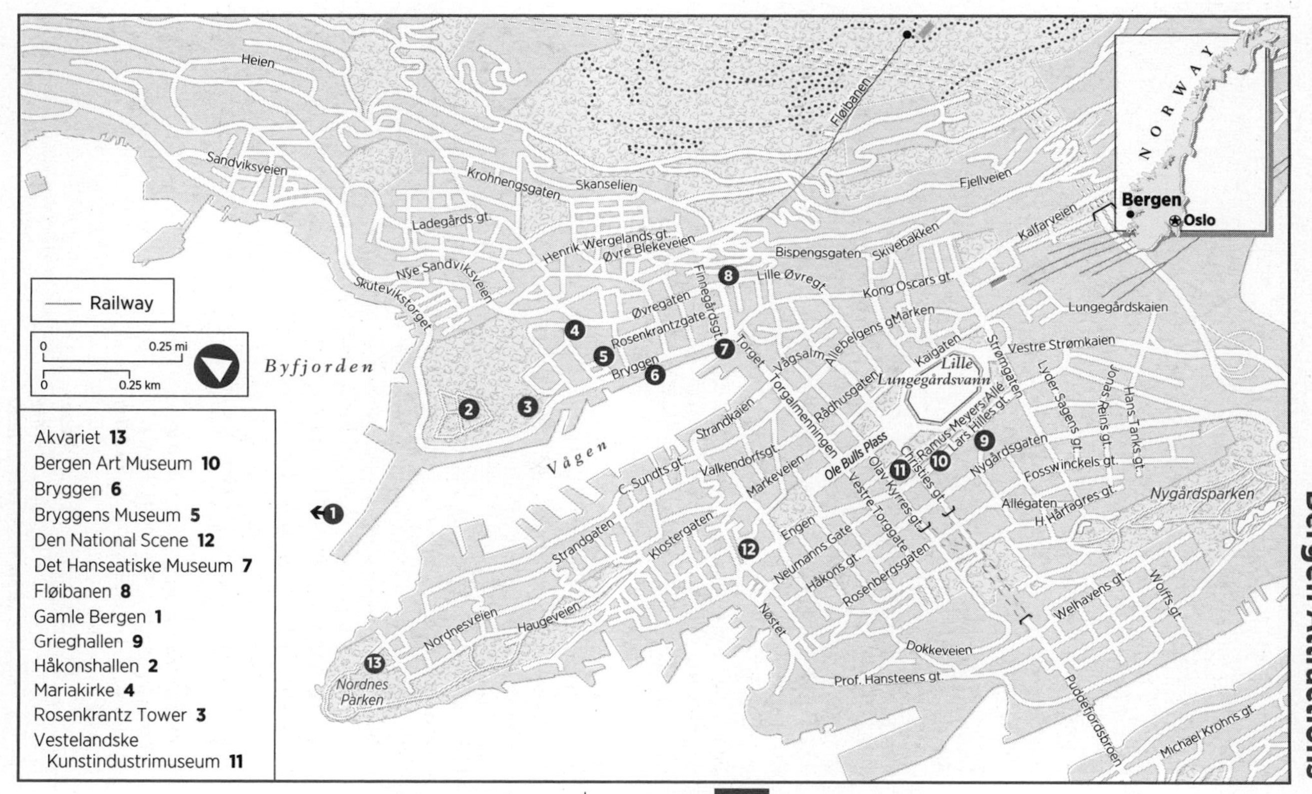

Bergen Art Museum ★★★ This ever-growing and expanding art museum exhibits one of the most impressive collections of paintings in Norway. In the tri-level Lysverk Building overlooking Lille Langegard Lake, the museum's collection consists of more than 9,000 works of art. Bergen Billedgalleri is devoted to both Norwegian and international art extending from the 13th to the 20th centuries. The collection is known for its magnificent **Greek and Russian icons ★** from the 1300s and its **Dutch paintings ★** from the 1700s. Seek out, in particular, *Birch in the Storm,* a famous painting by J. C. Dahl, as well as *Vardøhus Fortress,* by Peder Balke. As for the gallery's **modern art** collection, there is a bit of camp, as in their display of poetry and an exhibition by Yoko Ono, as well as Bjørn Carlsen's mixed-media piece *Mother, I Don't Want to Die in Disneyland.* The photography of Tom Sandberg confirms his reputation as one of Scandinavia's greatest photographers.

The impressive Rasmus Meyer Collection features paintings from the 18th century up to 1915. It's worth the visit here to gaze upon **Edvard Munch's masterpieces ★★**, especially the dark trio *The Woman in Three Stages, Melancholy,* and *Jealousy.* Some of the best paintings of the **Norwegian Romantics** also hang here, including works by J. C. Dahl, Harriet Backer, and Nikolai Astrup, the latter known for depicting dramatic landscapes in western Norway. In addition to the art, note the decorated ceiling and wall painting in the **Blumenthal Room ★** from the 18th century.

The greatest **modern art ★★** in western Norway is found in the Stenersen Collection. Most of the work, by Norwegian and international artists, stems from the 20th century and includes northern Europe's most extensive collection of **Paul Klee's works ★★**. Nearly every modern art master you could think of is here: Picasso, Edvard Munch once again, Joan Miró, Vassily Kandinsky, and Max Ernst, as well as many lesser-known artists.

Rasmus Meyers Allé 3–9. ✆ **55-56-80-00.** www.kunstmuseene.no. Combined ticket to all 3 galleries NOK80 adults, NOK50 students, free for children 16 and under. Mid-May to mid-Sept daily 9am–7pm; mid-Sept to mid-May daily 11am–7pm. Bus: 1, 5, or 9.

Bergen Museum ★ This outstanding collection holds everything from Henrik Ibsen mementos and whale skeletons to beautiful Viking age objects and Egyptian mummies, as well as some of the best church and folk art in Norway. Part of the University of Bergen, this two-in-one museum consists of both a Cultural and a Natural History Department. Founded in 1825, the museum formed the basis for launching the university in 1946 after the defeated Nazis had ended their occupation.

Naturhistorisk Samlinger is filled with displays and exhibitions from the Ice Age, including prehistoric fossils. However, visitors come here mainly to see the **whale collection ★** (northern Europe's largest collection) and the exhibits of snakes, Norwegian birds, and crocodiles (displayed in various ways—stuffed, fossilized, preserved in jars). The origins of the creatures in the collection range from Greenland to Africa. You can also visit a plant house and a botanical garden.The Kulturhistorke Samlinger features exhibitions and displays on art history, archaeology, and anthropology. You'll also find the largest collection of **Norwegian church art ★** in the country, a display of delicate Viking jewelry, and exhibits devoted to such North American cultures as the Aleut and Inuit.

Cultural History Dept., Håkon Sheteligs Plass 10; Natural History Dept., Muséplass 3. ✆ **55-58-29-20.** www.uib.no/bergenmuseum. Admission for both museums NOK50 adults, NOK25 seniors, free for children and students. June 1–Aug Tues–Fri 10am–4pm, Sat–Sun 11am–4pm; off-season Tues–Fri 10am–3pm, Sat–Sun 11am–4pm. Bus: 2, 3, or 4.

Bryggens Museum This museum was built on the site of Bergen's earliest settlement. While digging into the 800-year-old foundations of the original building, the architects uncovered a Pandora's box of medieval tools, pottery, runic stones, and even ancient skulls. The items they dug up from 1955 to 1972 served to greatly enhance the museum's eventual collection. The museum also illustrates the daily and cultural life of Bergen in the Middle Ages. Call ahead to find out about its regularly changing exhibits, as well as its folk-music and dance performances.

Dreggsallmenning 3, Bryggen. ✆ **55-58-80-10.** www.bymuseet.no. Admission NOK60 adults, free for children 15 and under. May–Aug daily 10am–5pm; Sept–Apr Mon–Fri 11am–3pm, Sat noon–3pm, Sun noon–4pm. Bus: 20, 21, 22, 23, 50, 70, 71, 80, or 90.

Det Hanseatiske Museum ★ In one of the best-preserved wooden buildings at Bryggen, this museum illustrates Bergen's commercial life on the wharf centuries ago. German merchants, representatives of the Hanseatic League centered in Lübeck, lived in these medieval houses built in long rows up from the harbor. With dried cod, grain, and salt as articles of exchange, fishermen from northern Norway met German merchants during the busy summer season. Life was cold, dark, and grim for the German stockfish tradesmen who lived here in the remote regions of Norway during long, cold winters. Merchants weren't allowed to build fires for fear of setting all the wood-framed buildings along the wharf ablaze. The Black Death eventually swept through the region, destroying their monopoly on the trade. The museum is furnished with authentic articles dating from 1704.

Finnegårdsgaten 1A, Bryggen. ✆ **55-54-46-90.** Admission May–Sept NOK50 adults, Oct–Apr NOK30 adults, free for children 14 and under year-round. June–Aug daily 9am–5pm; Sept–May Tues–Sat 11am–2pm. Bus: 20, 21, 22, 23, or 24.

Domkirken (Bergen Cathedral) For 9 centuries, this has been a place of worship, but it's amazing that the cathedral is here at all—after all, it's been burned down five times. The first stone church was built in the mid–12th century and dedicated to Olav the Holy, patron saint of Norway. By the 13th century, the Dom was in the hands of the Franciscan brothers, but the fires that swept Bergen in 1248 and again in 1270 caused massive damage. Under a grant from King Magnus ("the Law-mender"), the friars reconstructed a beautiful church, which stood here in 1301. Regrettably, the massive Bergen fires of 1463 and 1488 both swept over the church. With the coming of the Lutheran Reformation, the first Lutheran bishop claimed the old Franciscan church and turned it into the cathedral of Norway's oldest diocese. Unfortunately, two more fires destroyed the cathedral in 1623 and 1640. The present building dates from its major restoration in the 1880s, which saw the addition of beautiful stained-glass windows with biblical motifs. All that remains from the 13th century are the Gothic choir stalls and the foundations of the towers. Since the Battle of Bergen in 1665, a cannonball has been embedded in the west wall.

Kong Oscarsgate and Domkirkegate. ✆ **55-59-32-70.** Free admission. Late May to Aug Mon–Sat 11am–5pm, Sun 10am–1pm; off-season Tues–Fri 11am–2pm, Sat 11am–3pm, Sun 10am–2pm. Bus: 1, 5, or 9.

Fisketorget (Fish Market) ★ Always big on social programs, Norway enforced a law at Fisketorget between 1630 and 1911: Rich Bergen citizens living within a 40km (25-mile) range of the market were forbidden to purchase fish there. Only the poor were allowed to buy goods, and for daily house use only. Presumably, rich people could afford to go further afield to dine on a seafood meal. Now that it is open to everyone in Bergen, head to this bustling market at lunchtime for freshly opened oysters and freshly boiled shrimp to eat as you take in views of the waterfront. Some vendors also offer a baguette for your lunch—none better than smoked salmon with some mayonnaise and fresh cucumber. The market is a photographer's delight, with fishermen in their Wellington boots, and weather-beaten fishmongers (often women) in dirty long, white aprons as the catch of the day is hauled in.

Bergen Harbor. Free admission. June–Aug daily 7am–7pm; Sept–May Mon–Sat 7am–4pm. Bus: 1, 5, or 9.

Fløibanen A short walk from the Fish Market is the station where the funicular heads up to Fløien, the most famous of Bergen's seven hills. The nearly 90-year-old funicular was recently upgraded with new cable cars to haul visitors up to the top of the 320m (1,050-ft.) Mount Fløien. Today two modern carriages featuring glass ceilings and panoramic windows shuttle visitors to the top to take in the spectacular vista. Once there, you can take one of several paths that provide easy walks through a lovely wooded terrain with views of lakes and mountains in the distance. In summer, you can order lunch at the restaurant here, which is open daily and also serves as a souvenir shop.

Vetrlidsalm 23A. ✆ **55-33-68-00.** www.floibanen.com. Round-trip NOK70 adults, NOK35 children ages 4–15. Apr–Aug Mon–Fri 7:30am–midnight, Sat 8am–11pm, Sun 9am–11pm; Sept–Mar Mon–Thurs 7:30am–11pm, Fri 7:30am–11:30pm, Sat 8am–11:30pm, Sun 9am–11pm.

Gamlehaugen The king's official Bergen residence was originally occupied in the 19th century by Christian Michelsen, one of the first prime ministers of Norway after it separated from Denmark in 1814. It's open for just a short time each summer, and a visit here will give you a good sense of how the upper class lived at the beginning of the 19th century. The wood-sided villa is about 10km (6¼ miles) south of the city, overlooking the Nordåsvannet estuary. The interior is a happy marriage of the once-fashionable National Romanticism combined with elegant Art Nouveau. Its gardens are open to the public all year. Don't expect the hoopla you might see at Buckingham Palace—the venue is understated, discreet, and (probably for security reasons) aggressively mysterious. The building was under renovation at press time, but is due to reopen in 2011.

Fjøsanger. ✆ **55-92-51-20**; www.gamlehaugen.no. Admission NOK50 adults, NOK25 children 4–15. June–Aug Tues–Sun noon–3pm. Guided tours in English at noon, 1pm, and 2pm. Bus: Fjøsanger-bound bus 60 from the Central Bus Station.

Mount Ulriken ★★ Closed down for a long time for extensive repairs, this cable car reopened in 2009. For the grandest view in western Norway, visit Bergen's highest mountaintop, Ulriken, at 643m (2,109 ft.). The attraction is at Landaas, 5km (3 miles) southeast from the center of Bergen. The Ulriksbanen (✆ **53-64-36-43**), the most famous cable car in western Norway, runs up the mountain. A shuttle bus departs for the Ulriksbanen from the Tourist Information Office in Bergen (p. 257). From the uppermost station of the cable-car station, you can walk for 4 to 5 hours north along a well-trodden track to the top of the Fløibanen funicular railway, with scenic vistas in all directions. This is my favorite walk in the Bergen area.

Landaas. ✆ **55-55-20-00** for the cable car. Return fare NOK145 adults, NOK180 children 4–15. Combined cable car and shuttle bus NOK245 adults, half-price children. Sept–Apr shuttle bus departures every half-hour on the hour 9am–5pm; May–Aug 9am–9pm. Cable car operates several times an hour in summer, daily 9am–9pm; off-season cable car operates 3–4 times an hour, daily 10am–5pm.

Norges Fiskerimuseum (Norwegian Fisheries Museum) This museum is primarily targeted at fishing aficionados, though it does manage to stir up some controversy, as does Norway itself, with its exhibits on whaling and sealing. Norway, along with Japan, has been severely criticized by the environmentally aware community regarding the killing of endangered species such as the whale. The nature and management of fisheries over the past 150 years are presented in detail, as are exhibits on the sea and its vast, though diminishing, resources. The processing of fish, such as the vital cod, is explained along with exportation methods.

Bontelabo 2. ✆ **55-32-27-10.** Admission NOK40 adults, NOK20 students and seniors, free for children 15 and under. May 15–Sept 15 Mon–Fri 9am–4pm, Sat–Sun 10am–4pm; Sept 16–May 14 Mon–Fri 10am–4pm, Sun 11am–4pm. Bus: 1, 5, or 9.

Troldhaugen (Trolls' Hill) ★★★ This can be the most romantic setting in Norway if you arrive just as Edvard Grieg's music is drifting up from a summer concert in the 200-seat Troldsalen, a concert hall on the grounds. This Victorian house, in beautiful rural surroundings, was the summer villa of composer Edvard Grieg and the site where he composed many of his famous works in a setting on Lake Nordås. The house still contains his furniture, paintings, and other mementos. His Steinway grand piano is frequently used at concerts given in the house during the annual Bergen festival, and at Troldhaugen's summer concerts. Grieg and his wife, Nina, a Norwegian soprano, are buried in a cliffside grotto on the estate.

Troldhaugveien 65, Hop. ✆ **55-92-29-92.** Admission NOK60 adults, free for children 15 and under. May–Sept daily 9am–6pm; Oct–Apr 10am–4pm. Bus: 20, 23, 24, or 50. Take the bus south towards Nesttun, then get off at the Hopsbraoen exit. Turn right, then follow well-marked path to Troldhaugen (15-min. walk).

OUTDOOR ACTIVITIES

FISHING In the region around Bergen, anyone can fish in the sea without restrictions. If you plan to fish in fresh water (ponds, streams, and most of the best salmon and trout rivers), you'll need a permit, which you can get from the local tourist office closest to the body of water you intend to fish in. The tourist office in Bergen itself does not sell permits. You'll also need the permission of the owner of the land on either side of the stream. The best fjord fishing, where you can angle for such catches as cod, mackerel, haddock, and coalfish, is offered by **Reisemål Ryfylke** (✆ **51-75-95-10;** www.ryfylke.com).

Information and fishing permits, which cost NOK105 to NOK170, are available from **Bergen Sportsfiskere (Bergen Angling Association),** Damsgaardsveien 106 (✆ **55-34-18-08;** www.bergensportsfiskere.no). It's open Monday to Friday 9am to 3pm.

SWIMMING The **Sentralbadet,** Theatergaten 37 (✆ **55-56-95-70**), has a heated indoor pool. An open-air pool whose season is limited to the fleeting Nordic summer is at **Nordnes Sjøbad,** Nordnes. For hours, check with the Bergen Tourist Office (p. 257). At either pool, adults pay NOK58.

WALKING Only 10 minutes away from town by the funicular, several roads and footpaths lead to **Mount Fløien,** an unspoiled wood and mountain terrace with lakes and rivers. The **Bergen Touring Club,** Tverrgaten 4 (✆ **55-33-58-10**), arranges walking tours farther afield and supplies information on huts and mountain routes all over Norway. It also provides maps and advice on where to hike. The office is open Monday to Friday 10am to 3pm (until 5pm on Thurs).

SHOPPING

The Shopping Scene

SHOPPING AREAS Bargain hunters head to the **Fish Market (Fisketorget) ★★**. Many local handicrafts from the western fjord district, including rugs and handmade tablecloths, are displayed here. This is also one of the few places in Norway where bargaining is welcomed. The market keeps no set hours, but it is best visited between June and August daily, 7am to 7pm, and September to May, Monday to Saturday, 7am to 4pm. Take bus no. 1, 5, or 9.

HOURS Stores are generally open Monday to Friday from 9am to 4:30pm (until 7pm Thurs and sometimes Fri), Saturday 9am to 3pm. Shopping centers outside the city are open Monday to Friday 10am to 8pm and Saturday 9am to 6pm. Some food stores stay open until 8pm Monday to Friday and 6pm on Saturday.

Shopping A to Z

ART GALLERIES

Hordaland Art Center and Café ☺ An artistic focal point of the historic neighborhood that contains it, this is a publicly funded art gallery that puts on as many as 12 different art exhibitions each year. Originally completed in 1742, it served as a school for the children of the local parish for many years. A children's play area is on-site, and a cafe has pastries, sandwiches, and platters on offer. Hours are Tuesday to Sunday noon to 4pm (cafe open Sat–Sun). Klosteret 17, Nordnes. ✆ **55-90-85-90.** A 5-min. walk from Torgallmenningen.

FASHION

Kløverhuset ★★ Next to the Fish Market on the harbor, this four-story shopping center has been Bergen's largest and best fashion store since 1923. Bargains include moderately priced and attractively designed knit sweaters, gloves, and Sami jackets. Hours are Monday to Friday 9am to 8pm; Saturday 9am to 6pm. Strandgaten 13-15. ✆ **55-31-37-90.**

GLASSWARE & CERAMICS

Tilbords Interiør Bergen Storsenter ★★ This outlet has Bergen's best and most extensive collection of glassware, porcelain, and pottery. All the big names are here, including Arabia from Finland and Kosta Boda from Sweden, and even Wedgwood from England. Still, this is a true showcase of Scandinavian design. Much of the merchandise is made by local builders, and the glass, ceramics, and pottery are of the highest quality. You'll want to pull up a big truck to the store. The price tags will help you express restraint, however. Torgallmenningen 8. ✆ **55-96-00-10.**

HANDICRAFTS

Husfliden ★★ Since 1895, Husfliden has been the premier name in Norwegian handicrafts. Top-quality merchandise is sold here, especially hand-woven textiles. The Norwegian sweaters are among the best in town, and there is even a department for national costumes. Many items such as iron bowls and candlesticks are for table settings. Handmade pewter, wooden bowls, hand-woven rugs, and fireplace bellows are other useful items. Well-made, quality wooden toys are also sold here. Vågsallmenningen 3. ✆ **55-54-47-40.**

JEWELRY

Juhls' Silver Gallery ★ Next to the Radisson Blu Royal Hotel, along the harborfront, Juhls' displays the town's most unusual selection of quality jewelry. The designers take for their inspiration the constantly changing weather of the far north and, in their words, provide "a cultural oasis in a desert of snow." Hours are Monday to Friday 9am to 8pm; Saturday 9am to 6pm; Sunday 1am to 7pm. Bryggen. ✆ **55-32-47-40.**

SHOPPING MALL

Galleriet ★ This is the most important shopping complex in the central Bergen area, with 70 stores offering tax-free shopping. Close to the Fish Market, it displays a wide array of merchandise and features summer sales and special exhibitions. It has several fast-food establishments, too. Torgalmenningen 8. ✆ **55-30-05-00.**

SPORTSWEAR

G-Sport Gågaten This store has virtually everything you'd need for every sport available in Norway. Inventory changes radically throughout the seasons, with an emphasis on cycling and hiking in summer and downhill and cross-country skiing in winter. There are special high-energy food supplies (a tablespoon will give you the temporary strength of a gorilla) and high-tech outdoor gear whose high price tags reflect the newest trends in sportswear and rough-weather gear. Hours are Monday to Friday 9am to 5pm; Thursday 9am to 7pm; Sunday 10am to 4pm. Strandgaten 59. ✆ **55-23-22-22.**

BERGEN AFTER DARK

The Performing Arts

Den National Theater ★★ September to June is the season for Norway's oldest theater, founded in the mid–19th century. It stages classical Norwegian and international drama, contemporary plays, and musical drama, as well as visiting opera and ballet productions. Engen 1. ✆ **55-54-97-00.** www.dns.no. Tickets NOK340. Bus: 2, 3, or 4.

Grieghallen ★★★ The modern Grieg Hall, which opened in 1978, is Bergen's monumental showcase for music, drama, and a host of other cultural events. The stage is large enough for an entire grand opera production, and the main foyer comfortably seats 1,500 guests for lunch or dinner. Snack bars provide drinks and light snacks throughout the performances.

The Bergen Philharmonic Orchestra, founded in 1765, performs here from September to June, often on Thursday at 7:30pm and Saturday at 12:30pm. Its repertoire consists of classical and contemporary music, as well as visiting opera productions. International conductors and soloists perform periodically. ***Tip:*** Ticket prices on Thursday tend to be at the lower end of the price scale, and prices on Friday and Saturday tend to be at the upper end. Edvard Griegs Plass 1. ✆ **55-21-61-00.** www.grieghallen.no. Tickets NOK120–NOK470. Closed July–Aug. Bus: 2, 3, or 4.

Summer Cultural Entertainment

Bergen Folklore ★ The Bergen Folklore dancing troupe performs from early June to mid-August on Tuesday at 9pm. The program, which lasts about an hour, consists of traditional folk dances and music from rural Norway. Tickets are on sale at the tourist office (see "Orientation," earlier in this chapter) and at the door. Bryggens Museum, Bryggen. ✆ **97-52-86-30.** Tickets NOK100 adults, free for children. Bus: 1, 5, or 9.

Films

Konsertpaleet, Neumannsgate 3 and **Magnus Barfot,** Magnus Barfotsgt. 12 (✆ **55-56-90-83**), shows all films in their original versions. The earliest performance is at 11am, the latest at 11pm. Tickets usually cost NOK85.

Bars & Clubs

Bryggen Piano Bar ★ This is one of Bergen's more elegant dance clubs, attracting a somewhat conservative crowd in their 40s and 50s. That seems to change a bit on Saturday with the arrival of noisy, fun-seeking 20-somethings who make the place more raucous and animated. Light meals are available, but most people just show up to drink. They also show larger sports matches. Cocktail drink prices begin at around NOK100, though this drops considerably during the regular happy hour. It's open Thursday to Saturday 10pm to 2:30am. In the Radisson Blu Royal Hotel, Bryggen. ✆ **95-10-22-22.** Cover NOK75–NOK100, free to hotel guests. Bus: 1, 5, or 9.

Café Opera Built in the 1880s, this large stone- and timber-built structure was originally conceived as a warehouse; today it functions as both a restaurant and a cafe. After the kitchen closes, it becomes an animated nightclub. It's open Tuesday to Saturday 11am to 2:30am. On Tuesday night, there is an open jam session where musicians can entertain or poets can read. On other nights, DJs spin. The cafe is host to international DJs and bands on most Fridays and Saturdays. The 20s and 30s crowd finds this to be one of the more entertaining joints after dark for drinking, talking, and flirting—but very few of them actually get up and dance. Engen 18. ✆ **55-23-03-15.** No cover. Bus: 2, 3, or 4.

Kontoret (The Office) The most frequented pub in the city center, the Kontoret lies immediately adjacent, through a connecting door, to the Dickens restaurant, where platters of rib-sticking English food cost from NOK149 to NOK169. In the Kontoret, the decor captures the feel of an office from the early 1900s, replete with banged-up manual typewriters and oaken countertops that evoke the green eyeshades and ink-stained printing rituals of an earlier era. The local brew is called Hansa, a half-liter of which costs NOK60. It's open Sunday to Thursday 4pm to 12:30am, Friday and Saturday 4pm to 2am. Kong Olav V Plass 4. ✆ **55-36-31-33.**

Madam Felle Dark, woodsy-looking, and cozy, this is an animated and crowded pub with limited food service and live music that packs the place with 20- and 30-somethings 4 nights a week. On those nights (always Fri–Sat, plus 2 weeknights whose schedule changes frequently), live music plays between 9 and 11pm, with a cover charge that might be free or that might rise to anywhere between NOK80 and NOK280. The pub is named after a strong-willed early-20th-century matriarch who became a noted innkeeper at a spot near here, and who's something of a legend in Bergen. Bryggen. ✆ **55-54-30-58.** Bus: 20, 21, 22, 70, 80, or 90.

Smakverken Café You wouldn't expect such a hip nightclub and pub to be in an art museum, but in the case of this large, high-ceilinged cube of a room on the museum's rear side, that's exactly the case. Patrons in their 20s and 30s are drawn to the danceable music emerging from a DJ station on one side; a bar at another end of the room serves beer and sandwiches, and electronic art in kaleidoscopic color is beamed against yet another. The cafe itself is open daily 11am to 5pm; the nightclub is open Saturdays 10pm to 2:30am. Windows directly overlook the large, octagonal reflecting pool on the museum's back side. Pastas and salads cost from NOK90. In the Bergen Art Museum, Rasmus Meyers Allé 3 and 7. ✆ **92-24-91-04.** Bus: 1, 5, or 9.

EXPLORING THE NORWEGIAN COAST

11

No single place in all of Norway holds the enchantment of the fjord country, the single most intriguing region in all of the Scandinavian countries. It's such a superlative spot that National Geographic rated the Norwegian fjords as "the world's best travel destination." Gouged out by glaciers, studded with deep valleys, and characterized by rolling fells and rugged mountain plateaus, the fjord country is a land of farmlands, blossoming orchards, small villages, cascading waterfalls, and Scandinavia's most complex geography. It's a place to slow down and take your time. Just getting from point to point is a bit of an endeavor—but, oh, those views along the way.

Norwegian fjords are narrow arms of the sea, snaking their way inland. It took roughly 3 million years to form the furrows and fissures that give western Norway its distinctive look. At some points the fjords become so narrow that a boat can hardly pass between the mountainsides. Fjords have been of enormous significance to Norwegians through the ages. They served as lifelines to those who settled in the harsh mountain landscape. Instead of building roads to each house and village, they used the easily accessible and navigable fjords. Thus, inland and coastal regions were linked together as the fjords enabled commodities to be transported to the old trading stations. Imagine how centuries ago people would once row across their local fjord in order to attend church on Sunday mornings.

Bergen is the best departure point for trips to the fjords: To the south lies the famous **Hardangerfjord** and to the north the **Sognefjord,** cutting 178km (110 miles) inland. Voss, about 1½ hours from Bergen, is a famous ski resort that is also well situated between both the Hardangerfjord and the Sognefjord.

We'll start in the towns around the Hardangerfjord—**Lofthus, Kinsarvik, Eidfjord,** and **Ulvik**—make a detour to **Voss,** and then move north to the towns around the Sognefjord, including **Balestrand** and **Flåm.**

GETTING THERE Bergen is the traditional gateway to the fjord country. From Bergen, you have a choice of several options for making your way about the district; the most expensive is by private car. Most of the towns and villages have road connections, although you'll have to take several car ferries to cross the fjords. Boat excursions, many of which leave from Bergen, are the traditional way to see the fjords. In summer, dozens of possibilities for these excursions await you. Contact the tourist office in Bergen for details (see "Orientation," in chapter 10).

Of the towns recommended in this chapter, Voss, both a winter ski center and a summer mountain resort, has the best rail connections with Oslo and Bergen. All of the fjord towns and villages are also connected by buses that make their way through the mountains and along the fjords, boasting vistas in all directions. Of course, travel by bus from place to place can be time-consuming, and often there are only a handful of departures a day (usually no more than five), depending on business, so you'll have to plan your connections in advance.

Details about bus routes in the fjord district are available at the Central Station in Bergen. Also visit www.nsb.no for train schedules and www.nor-way.no for bus schedules.

ULVIK: MISTY PEAKS & FJORDSIDE FARMS ★

149km (92 miles) E of Bergen

Ulvik is a rarity—an unspoiled resort. It lies like a fist at the end of an arm of the Hardangerfjord and is surrounded in the summer by misty peaks and fruit farms. It's the beautiful setting, not an array of attractions, that draws visitors. Ulvik's claim to fame? It's where potatoes first grew in Norway. The village's 1858 church is attractively decorated in the style of the region. It's open June to August daily from 9am to 5pm. Classical concerts, often presented by visiting chamber orchestras from other parts of Europe, are offered in summer inside the church. When a concert is to be presented, notices are posted throughout the town. Other than the enchantment of the hamlet itself, the real reason to stay here is for walking and hiking.

Essentials

GETTING THERE If you're not driving, you can reach Ulvik by train or bus from Bergen or Oslo. From either city, take a train to Voss, where you can catch a bus for the 40km (25-mile), 45-minute ride to Ulvik. Buses run from Voss daily, five times in the summer, three in the winter. In Ulvik the bus stops in front of the Ulvik church in the town center. There's no formal bus station.

VISITOR INFORMATION Contact the **Ulvik Tourist Office,** in the town center (✆ **56-52-62-80;** www.visitulvik.com). It's open June 1 to September 15 Monday to Friday from 9am to 5pm and Sunday 11am to 3pm; September 16 to May 14 Monday to Friday 9am to 2pm. The office can arrange excursions, from trips on fjord steamers to bus tours of the Osa mountains.

Seeing the Sights

A number of do-it-yourself excursions begin at Ulvik; see the tourist office for details. They change seasonally and depend on the weather. Our favorite walk is along the northern tip of the Hardangerfjord, a paradise for hikers. It's home to some 1,000 people and the Continent's largest herd of wild reindeer. Mountain trout attract anglers to the area. I've been through this area in July when the cherries ripen, followed in just 3 weeks or so by the most delicious-tasting plums, pears, and apples. It's a great opportunity for a summer picnic, and you can stop to buy fresh fruit and other foodstuffs at one of the roadside farm kiosks.

The Ulvik area offers some of the best walks in the fjord country. These are part of what is known as the **Kulturlandskapsplan ★** and are divided into four different walks, including the stone-covered grave mounds at Nesheim and Tunheim, the cotter's farm at Ljonakleiv, and a restored country mill in Nordallen in Osa. The tourist office sells a manual, *Heritage Trails of Ulvik,* outlining details on all these walks. The same office will provide information about organized walks on Tuesday and Thursday in summer along forest roads and into the mountains.

Where to Stay & Dine

Hotel Ullensvang ★★★ Dating from 1846, the Ullensvang is right on the bank of the Hardangerfjord. Expanded over the years, the hotel has been run by the same family for four generations. These family members extend a hearty Norwegian welcome to their guests, whom they feed and house most comfortably. Not surpriseingly, it's all about the views and the outdoors here, but service is good and the restaurant is well run with a passable, if pricey, buffet served at dinnertime. ***Note:*** The breakfast buffet can be a bit crowded since everyone wants to get a jumpstart on the day's tours and activities; plan to hop right into the fray and be sure to ask staff to restock if items run out.

N-5787 Loftus i Hardanger. www.hotel-ullensvang.no. ✆ **53-67-00-00.** 172 units. NOK1,880–NOK 2,375 double. Rates include buffet breakfast. MC, V. **Amenities:** Restaurant; babysitting; fitness room; free parking; pool; tennis; Wi-Fi (fee; in public areas). *In room:* TV, A/C, hair dryer, Internet.

Rica Brakanes Hotel ★★★ There's a famous view of the Hardangerfjord and the surrounding forest from this well-recommended hotel. This is one of the most impressive fjord resorts in the area, although it began modestly enough in 1860 when it opened as a five-bedroom inn. Over the years, it grew, but the building came to a terrible end when German warships opened fire on it in April 25, 1940. When money became available in the postwar era, it was reconstructed and reopened in May 1952. With its custom-designed furniture and textiles, and its very stylish interior, it was hailed as Norway's leading fjord hotel. Soon Princess Juliana of the Netherlands checked in, and she later returned when she was elevated to the throne as queen. Today all that remains of the original building is one small dining room. The new parts of the hotel are airy, sunny, and comfortable. The guest rooms are midsize to spacious and well maintained. In the summer, plane rides over the fjords can be arranged, and windsurfing and boat rentals are available.

N-5730 Ulvik. www.brakanes-hotel.no. ✆ **56-52-61-05.** 143 units. NOK1,155–NOK1,850 double. Rates include buffet breakfast. AE, DC, MC, V. **Amenities:** Restaurant; bar; fitness center; indoor heated pool; sauna; 2 tennis courts; rooms for those w/limited mobility. *In room:* TV, minibar, Wi-Fi.

VOSS: A WINTER PLAYGROUND ★

38km (24 miles) W of Ulvik, 101km (63 miles) E of Bergen

On the main road between east and west Norway, there are few better pit stops than Voss. A heavily folkloric site situated between two fjords, Voss is a famous year-round resort and the birthplace of the American football hero Knute Rockne. Even if trolls no longer strike fear in the hearts of farm children, revelers dressed as trolls still appear in costumed folklore programs to spice things up a bit for visitors.

Voss is a natural base for exploring the two largest fjords in Norway, the **Sognefjord** to the north and the **Hardangerfjord** to the south. In and around Voss are glaciers, mountains, fjords, waterfalls, orchards, rivers, and lakes.

Essentials

GETTING THERE From Ulvik, take Hwy. 20 to Route 13; then follow Route 13 northwest to Voss. If you're not driving, there's frequent train service from Bergen (travel time is 1¼ hr.) and Oslo (5½ hr.). There are six daily buses from Bergen (1¾ hr.), though no longer direct buses from Oslo.

VISITOR INFORMATION The **Voss Tourist Information Center** is at Evangervegen on the lakeside opposite the train station (✆ **56-52-08-00;** www.visitvoss.no). It's open June to August Monday to Friday 8am to 7pm, Saturday 9am to 7pm, Sunday noon to 7pm; September to May Monday to Friday 8:30am to 3:30pm. The **VisitVoss Booking Office** (✆ **40-71-77-00**), Vangsgata 20, offers an accommodations booking service and also organizes activities in and around Voss. Opening hours are not decided yet, but it will be similar to that of Voss Tourist Information (the Voss Tourist information will of course also be able to make reservations).

Seeing the Sights

St. Olav's Cross, Skulegata, near the Voss Cinema, is the oldest relic in Voss, believed to have been raised when the townspeople adopted Christianity in 1023.

A ride on the **Hangursbanen cable car** (✆ **47-00-47-00**) will be a memorable part of your visit. It offers panoramic views of Voss and its environs. The mountaintop restaurant serves refreshments and meals. The hardy take the cable car up and then spend the rest of the afternoon strolling down the mountain, which is our personal favorite of all the walks possible in the area (visit the tourist board's website for a great description of the walk). A round-trip ride costs NOK90 for adults, NOK55 for children 7 to 15, and is free for children 6 and under. Entrance to the cable car is on a hillside, a 10-minute walk north of the town center. It's open in summer and winter but closes during the "between season" months: May to mid-June and September to December.

Vangskyrkja Once an ancient pagan temple stood on this site. In 1271, a Gothic-style stone-built church grew up here. This church has suffered, beginning with a 1536 Lutheran Reformation that destroyed much of its original architecture. What remains is a timbered tower, a Renaissance pulpit, a stone altar, and a triptych, along with fine woodcarvings and a painted ceiling. It's a miracle that anything is left after an aerial attack by the invading Nazis destroyed most of Voss—but the church was relatively undamaged. The church lies a 5-minute walk east of the train station.

Vangsgata 3. ✆ **56-52-38-80.** Admission NOK20 adults, free for children 16 and under. Daily 10am–4pm. Closed Sept–May.

Voss Folkemuseum I've seen bigger and better folk museums than this, but if you have an hour or so in Voss, you might check it out. Almost a kilometer (½ mile) north of Voss on a hillside overlooking the town, this museum consists of more than a dozen farmhouses and other buildings dating from the 1500s to around 1870. They were not moved here but were built on this site by two farm families.

Mølster. ✆ **56-51-15-11.** www.vossfolkemuseum.no. Admission NOK50 adults, free for children. May 18–Sept 15 daily 10am–5pm; Sept 16–May 16 Mon–Fri 10am–3pm, Sun noon–4pm.

The Great Outdoors

Voss continually adds to its facilities and is definitely in the race to overtake Geilo and Lillehammer as Norway's most popular winter playground. Its eight chairlifts, various ski lifts, and aerial cableway carry passengers up 788m (2,585 ft.) across two separate ski centers. In all, there are 40km (25 miles) of alpine slopes, plus two marked cross-country trails.

A mere 5km (3 miles) from the town center is Voss Resort, accessible via the Hangursbanen cable car. One ski lift (900m/2,952 ft. long) goes from Traastolen to the top of Slettafjell (with a wide choice of downhill runs), the Bavallen lift is for the slalom slopes, and the downhill runs are at Lonehorgi.

In the summertime, this is Valhalla for fishermen, as there are some 500 lakes and rivers in the greater vicinity of Voss. A local fishing license, costing NOK85, is available at the post office or the tourist office (these can also be booked online at the tourist office's website). You can catch trout and char using just local tackle. Fishing guides can be booked through the tourist office.

Voss also offers the best paragliding in Norway, with flights conducted daily in summer from 11am to 5pm, costing NOK1,500 per person for a tandem flight. The starting point is **Nordic Ventures** (© **56-51-00-17**), in the center of town.

Parasailing and para-bungy are possible at the Vangsvatnet, in front of the Park Hotel Vossevangen. The season is from May to October. Parasailing costs NOK550, para-bungy costs NOK1,800, water-skiing NOK300, and banana boating NOK800. For information, call **Nordic Ventures** (© **56-51-00-17;** www.nordicventures.com).

River sports are big, and there are a number of outfitters, mainly the **Voss Rafting Center** (© **56-51-05-25**), offering not only rafting, but canyoning and river-boarding as well, at prices beginning at NOK770 per person. Their base is at Nedkvitnesvegen 25, roughly 4km (2½ miles) from Voss town in Skulestadmo. There is a pick-up service from Holbergsplass next to Park Hotel Vossevangen. The season is from May 1 to October 1. Other outfitters include **Voss Ski & Surf** (© **56-51-30-43**), featuring river kayaking for both neophytes and more skilled kayakers; and **Nordic Ventures** (© **56-51-00-17;** www.nordicventures.com), offering guided sea kayaking through the Sognefjord, past waterfalls and mountain scenery.

Where to Stay & Dine

Elysèe FRENCH/NORWEGIAN At this, the town's best restaurant, the food is more satisfying than at Fleischers and based on the freshest ingredients available locally. Ever had baked sea scorpion? You can here. But if that frightens you away, try the filet of lamb marinated in honey prepared like cooks did it in the Middle Ages. In season there is always a lusty game dish on the menu, and everything served here is backed up with one of the best wine lists in the area. Nothing satisfies us for a dessert more than the homemade ice cream with fresh berries and a vanilla sauce. The decor of this prestigious restaurant includes *trompe-l'oeil* murals based on a modern interpretation of the Pantheon.

In the Park Hotel Vossevangen, Utträgate. © **56-53-10-00.** Reservations recommended. Main courses NOK245–NOK300; lunch smorgasbord NOK335; fixed-price 3-course dinner NOK425. AE, DC, MC, V. Sun–Thurs 1–10:30pm; Fri–Sat 1–11pm.

Fleischers Hotel ★★★ ☺ In business since the late 1800s, this fjord hotel's peaked, chalet-style roofs and dormers makes it look like something you'd encounter along a lake in Switzerland. Still run by the founding family, the Fleischers, the hotel was modernized and expanded, but much of its original charm remains throughout. The Fleischers can name-drop with the best of them: King Edward of England when he was Prince of Wales in 1885, Emperor Wilhelm II of Germany in 1890 (his private toilet is still displayed in the reception area), and in 1907 the King of Siam. On the lakefront beside the Voss train station, the gracious frame hotel has a modern wing with 30 units and terraces overlooking the lake. In the older part of the hotel, the rooms are old-fashioned and more spacious. The restaurant serves an a la carte menu; main courses cost NOK180 to NOK405. In the summer, a buffet of local fish and Norwegian specialties is served for NOK370. This hotel is very kid friendly, featuring a children's pool with many activities, including a playground and movies.

Evangervegen 13, N-5700 Voss. www.fleischers.no. ✆ **56-52-05-00.** 90 units. NOK1,690 double. Rates include buffet breakfast. AE, DC, MC, V. **Amenities:** Restaurant; bar; lounge; babysitting; children's activities; indoor heated pool; room service; 2 saunas; 1 room for those w/limited mobility. *In room:* TV, hair dryer, minibar.

Park Hotel Vossevangen ★ If Fleischers is a bit stuffy for you, Park Hotel Vossevangen offers a livelier venue and a younger crowd. Originally two separate hotels now joined by a covered passageway, the guest rooms here are attractively furnished and contain well-kept bathrooms, with many offering views onto Lake Vossevangen. The hotel is family owned and houses the best restaurant in town, the Elysèe (see description above) as well as the Café Stationen, the Pentagon Disco, and the Piano Bar. It's in the town center, a few minutes' walk from the train station.

Uttrågate, N-5701 Voss. www.parkvoss.no. ✆ **56-53-10-00.** 131 units. NOK1,550–NOK1,650 double. Rates include buffet breakfast. AE, DC, MC, V. **Amenities:** Restaurant; bar; lounge; babysitting; rooms for those w/limited mobility. *In room:* TV, minibar.

BALESTRAND: CENTER FOR SOGNEFJORD ★★

90km (56 miles) N of Voss, 219km (136 miles) NE of Bergen, 204km (126 miles) SW of Fjaerland

You might well get fjord fever if you stay here at the junction of Vetlefjord, Esefjord, and the Fjaerlandsfjord for too long—that's a lot of fjords to take in. But there's more. Balestrand is on the northern rim of the Sognefjord, Norway's longest and deepest fjord; it measures some 1,308m (4,290 ft.) deep.

When Esias Tegnèr wrote of the snow-covered mountains and the panoramic Sognefjord in the saga of *Fridtjof the Brave,* the book sold widely and inspired a number of artists to visit the area during the mid–19th century.

Soon Hans Gude, Hans Dahl, Johannes Flintoe, and other well-known Scandinavian artists were painting the fjord and mountain landscapes. Their art became so popular that regular visitors were soon flocking to Balestrand to take in the glories of the area for themselves—and so they have continued to this day.

Essentials

GETTING THERE From Voss, continue driving north on Route 13 to Vangsnes and board a car ferry for the short crossing northwest to Balestrand. You can also take a train from Bergen or Oslo to Voss or Flåm, and then make bus and ferry connections north to Balestrand. Bus and ferry schedules are available at the Voss Tourist Office (✆ **56-52-08-00**) and the Flåm Tourist Office (✆ **57-63-21-06**). From Bergen there are daily express boats to Balestrand; the trip takes 3½ hours.

VISITOR INFORMATION The **Tourist Office** (© **57-69-16-17;** www.visitbalestrand.no) is in the town center. From June to August, it's open Monday to Saturday 8am to 6pm and 10am to 5:30pm on Sunday; May and September daily 10am to 1pm and 3pm to 5:30pm; October to April Monday to Saturday 9am to 4pm.

Seeing the Sights

The staff at the tourist office can help you plan a tour of the area and put you in touch with local craftspeople. There you can pick up a list of constantly changing excursions and buy tickets for one of the scheduled 1½-day tours.

If it's a summer day, we suggest a leisurely stroll south along the banks of the fjord. You'll pass many 19th- and early-20th-century homes and gardens along the way. Less than 1km (½ mile) south along the fjord, you'll come to two **Viking age burial mounds.** One mound is topped by a statue of the legendary King Bele.

If your appetite's whetted by all the apple trees dotting the landscape, you'll also find several idyllic spots for a picnic.

Want still more walks? Take the small ferry that leaves Balestrand and crosses Esefjord to the Dragsvik side. At this point, you can walk along an old country road that is now abandoned but was in use during the early part of the 20th century. This is a scenic stroll through "forgotten" Norway that goes along for 8km (5 miles).

Kaiser Wilhelm II, a frequent visitor to Balestrand (he was here when World War I broke out, and was kindly asked by the Norwegian king to peacefully sail out of town on his yacht), presented the district with two statues of Old Norse heroes, King Bele and Fridtjof the Brave. They stand in the center of town. Another sight is the English church of **St. Olav,** a tiny wooden building that dates from 1897. The church is closed to the public, but its construction can be admired from outside.

You can explore the area by setting out in nearly any direction on scenic country lanes with little traffic or a wide choice of marked trails and upland farm tracks. The tourist office (see above) sells a touring map for NOK90. There's good sea fishing, as well as lake and river trout fishing. Fishing tackle, rowboats, and bicycles can all be rented in the area.

Back in Balestrand, near the ferry dock, you can visit the **Sognefjord Aquarium** (© **57-69-13-03;** www.kringsja.no), with its exhibition of saltwater fish. Especially mysterious is the marine life from the world's deepest fjord. The cast of denizens of the deep include Esefjord herring "lip fish," eels, and sharks. The exhibition consists of a number of large and small aquaria, both indoors and out on the jetty. The marine environments have been authentically re-created, including the tidal belt at Munken and the sandy seabed around Staken. A man-made model of Sognefjord shows the currents of the fjord and provides an impression of its depth.

A Boot for the Kaiser

Kaiser Wilhelm II of Germany was on holiday in the village of Balestrand, visiting a friend, when World War I broke out. Norwegian authorities gave the kaiser an ultimatum to leave their territory by 6pm that very day. Not being a man to have his pleasures cut short, Kaiser Wilhelm took his jolly good time drinking his tea and savoring impressions of the surrounding landscape before heading full steam out on the fjord aboard his yacht, minutes before the deadline expired.

There is also an audiovisual presentation. The admission of NOK70 includes an hour of canoeing on the fjord. It's open April to mid-June Monday to Friday 9:30am to 5pm, mid-June to mid-August daily 9:30am to 5pm.

Excursions on the Sognefjord ★★★

The mighty **Sognefjord,** one of the greatest and most impressive—also one of the deepest—fjords in the world, stretches for a total length of 205km (127 miles). It spreads its powerful "fjord fingers" as far as **Jostedalsbreen,** the country's largest glacier, and up to Jotunheimen, Norway's tallest mountain range. The widest and most dramatic part of the fjord stretches from the coast to Balestrand. After Balestrand, the fjord grows much narrower.

If you have a choice, opt for a late spring visit when thousands upon thousands of fruit trees can be seen in full bloom along both banks of the Sognefjord. This region is one of the most beautiful on Earth when the blossoms burst forth at that time. The entire district is ideal for skiing, sailing, mountain hiking, and other outdoor activities.

The best way to see the fjord is to take a boat from Bergen operated by **Fylkesbaatane** (✆ **57-75-70-00;** www.fjord1.no). Balestrand is a stopover on the Bergen-to-Flåm ferry route, with departures from Bergen leaving once a day, taking 5½ hours and costing NOK470 per person.

Where to Stay & Dine

Hotel Mundal ★★★ On the banks of the Fjaerlandsfjord, a scenic branch of the greater Sognefjord, this hotel has been run by the same family since it opened its doors back in 1891. With its peaked roofs, wooden scrollwork, round tower, and cavernous dining room, it is one of Norway's most classic examples of Victorian architecture. Yet the historic architecture doesn't take away from any of the modern conveniences and amenities you'd expect.

Fjaerland, Sogndal 6848. www.hotelmundal.no. ✆ **57-69-31-01**. 34 units. NOK1,600–NOK2,520 double. Rates include breakfast. MC, V. May 1–Sept 30. Open on request Oct–April. **Amenities:** Restaurant; bar; babysitting; free parking. *In room:* TV, free Wi-Fi.

Kviknes Hotel ★★ There was an inn on this site back in 1752, and the present owners, the Kvikne family, who took the inn over in 1877, are still in charge today. The hotel was built in the Swiss style, and its public rooms are now graced with art and antiques. The entire place oozes some serious old-world charm.

Patrons who have enjoyed the family hospitality over the years include movie stars, international artists, royalty, emperors, prime ministers, and even presidents. At its core it's an elaborately detailed building with balconies opening onto the edge of the fjord in many of the rooms. The units in the original structure offer old-fashioned Norwegian style, flowery fabrics, and spacious bathrooms with tub/shower combinations. Those in the annex have more of a bland Nordic style. The hotel offers a large dining room (where there's lunches and an extensive buffet every night) with a beautiful fjord view, several lounges, and a dance club. Sports such as water-skiing, windsurfing, and fjord fishing can be arranged, as can helicopter flights to **Jostedalsbreen,** the largest glacier in continental Europe.

Kviknevegen 8, N-6898 Balestrand. www.kviknes.no. ✆ **57-69-42-00.** 200 units. NOK1,660–NOK2,210 double; NOK2,660 suite. Rates include buffet breakfast. AE, DC, MC, V. Closed Oct–Apr. **Amenities:** Restaurant; bar; babysitting; fitness center; Jacuzzi; room service; sauna; rooms for those w/limited mobility. *In room:* TV, hair dryer.

FLÅM: STOPOVER ON EUROPE'S MOST SCENIC TRAIN RIDE ★

96km (60 miles) SE of Balestrand, 165km (102 miles) E of Bergen, 131km (81 miles) E of Voss

Flåm (pronounced "Flawm") is on the Aurlandsfjord, a tip of the more famous Sognefjord. In the village you can visit the old church (1667), with painted walls done in typical Norwegian country style. But, believe us, the thrill is in the getting there, not in any fantastic attractions once you've arrived.

The best and most exciting way to approach Flåm is aboard the **electric train from Myrdal ★★★**, which connects to trains from Bergen and Oslo. The Flåm Railway is the most thrilling train ride in Scandinavia, and possibly the world. The gradient is 55/1,000 (that is, a gradient of 1 in 18) on almost 80% of the line. The twisting tunnels that spiral in and out of the mountain are manifestations of the most daring and skillful engineering in Norwegian railway history. The electric train follows a 19km (12-mile) route overlooking an 883m (2,896-ft.) drop, stopping occasionally for passengers to photograph spectacular waterfalls. The trip takes 50 minutes. In winter, about four or five trains a day make the run to Flåm. In summer 10 trains a day run beginning at 7:40am and run throughout the day. Tickets must be purchased in advance. The one-way fare from Myrdal to Flåm is NOK240 (www.flaamsbana.no); try to walk or cycle back as it is a beautiful setting.

Essentials

GETTING THERE By **car** from Balestrand, take Route 55 east along the Sognefjord, crossing the fjord by ferry at Dragsvik and by bridge at Sogndal. At Sogndal, drive east along Route 5 to Mannheller, then take the car ferry to Fodnes. From here, continue to Lærdal, from where you can choose between the Aurlandsfjellet, a national scenic mountain road that is open between June and mid-October, or the world's longest road-tunnel (25km/15 miles) with special lighting effects that leads towards Aurland and Flåm.

Bus travel is less convenient. One **bus** a day runs Monday to Saturday between Aurland and Flåm. The trip takes 30 minutes.

From May to September, several **ferries** per day cross the fjord between Aurland and Flåm. The trip takes 30 minutes.

Flåm can also be reached by high-speed **express boats** from Bergen, Balestrand, and Leikanger. The boats carry passengers only. In Bergen, call **Fjord 1** (✆ **55-90-70-70;** www.fjord1.no); the one-way trip costs NOK665.

VISITOR INFORMATION The **tourist office** (✆ **91-35-16-72;** www.alr.no), near the railroad station, will rent bikes for NOK110. It's open May to September daily 8:30am to 8:30pm. Also visit www.visitflam.com for information on bike rentals from the Fretheim Hotel; they rent bicycles for NOK50 per hour or NOK250 per day.

Seeing the Sights

Flåm is an excellent starting point for car or boat excursions to other well-known centers on the **Sognefjord ★★★**, Europe's longest and deepest fjord. Worth exploring are two of the wildest and most beautiful fingers of the Sognefjord: the **Nærøyfjord** and the **Aurlandsfjord.** Ask at the tourist office about a summer-only cruise from Flåm to both fjords. From Flåm by boat, you can disembark in Gudvangen or Aurland and continue by bus. Alternatively, you can return to Flåm by train.

The Nærøyfjord is the wildest and most beautiful arm of the Sognefjord that was named to the UNESCO Heritage List in 2005. Sightseeing boats run between Flåm, Aurland, and Gudvangen daily throughout the year, offering vistas of snow-topped mountains, waterfalls, and idyllic farms splayed about the mountainsides. It's great for spotting seals, eagles, and porpoises. A kayak is another excellent way to experience the fjord.

There are also a number of easy walks in the Flåm district. If time is limited, make that walk along the banks of the **Aurlandsfjord,** leaving the day-trippers and the crass souvenirs in the center of Flåm far behind. The setting along the shoreline supports apple orchards, little hamlets, a fisherman's cottage here and there, and farmland where you can sometimes stop in and buy freshly picked fruit.

A map with detailed information on the city and surrounding walks is available from the tourist office for free.

Where to Stay & Dine

Fretheim Hotel ★★ In the midst of an impressive scene of mountains and waterfalls, this 1866 hotel opens onto a panoramic vista of fjord waters. Long renowned for its hospitality and now equipped with a modern annex, it houses you comfortably in attractive and well-maintained, if a bit basic, bedrooms. A wide range of activities is available from fishing to wine tasting to hiking. Salmon is the chef's specialty in the hotel's first-class restaurant, which focuses on local ingredients, and they serve their own housesmoked meats and sausages.

Flåm 5742; www.fretheim-hotel.no. ✆ **57-63-63-00.** 118 units. NOK995–NOK1,195 double. Rates include buffet breakfast. AE, DC, MC, V. **Amenities:** Restaurant; bar, free parking, pool, room service, Wi-Fi (fee; in public areas). *In room:* Hair dryer, Internet.

Heimly Pension This is the most affordable choice in town, next to Aurlandsfjord, only 400m (1,312 ft.) from the Flåm railway. It is a cozy family-run B&B dating from the 1930s and still carrying the aura of that time. Designed in the style of an A-frame chalet, it offers a ground-floor lounge where international travelers gather. The small to midsize guest rooms are decent enough, though they won't win any design awards. The best views over the fjord are on the two upper floors. A lively pub and a good restaurant serving home-style meals are in an annex across the road.

N-5742 Flåm. www.heimly.no. ✆ **57-63-23-00.** 25 units. NOK995–NOK1,150 double. Rates include buffet breakfast. AE, DC, MC, V. Closed Dec 24–Jan 2. **Amenities:** Restaurant; bar. *In room:* No phone.

GEILO: A WINTER WONDERLAND

130km (81 miles) SE of Flåm, 239km (148 miles) E of Bergen, 245km (152 miles) W of Oslo

Most motorists in summer driving between Oslo and Bergen (or vice versa) have to make a choice—Geilo or Voss? Voss tends to be somewhat more popular due to its folkloric activities, while Geilo is the sure winner in the colder months—not least of all because of its great skiing. A good part of the fun of visiting this town in winter, as it is in any alpine retreat, is to enjoy the lavish après-ski life of drinking and dining. In that regard, Geilo as a resort ranks higher than any other ski area in Norway, even when compared to more famous Lillehammer.

Geilo lies some 798m (2,618 ft.) above sea level in the Hol mountain district. Although it's not strictly in the fjord country, it's included here because it's a "gateway" there en route from Oslo to Bergen. The Geilo area boasts 130km (81 miles) of marked cross-country skiing tracks.

Essentials

GETTING THERE From Flåm, motorists return to Aurland to connect with Route 50, which runs southeast through Steine, Storestølen, Hovet, and Hagafoss. In Hagafoss, connect with Route 7 going southwest into Geilo. If you're dependent on public transportation, forget about the meager long-distance bus service and opt for the train connections via Oslo or Bergen. From Oslo, the fare is NOK459 per person one-way, and the trip takes 3½ hours; from Bergen, it's NOK413 one-way and takes 3 hours. If you book in advance online, you can cut this fare by as much as 50%.

VISITOR INFORMATION The **Turistinformasjonen** office is at Vesleslåttev-eien 13 in the town center (✆ **32-09-59-00**). It's open June to mid-August Monday to Friday 8:30am to 6pm, Saturday and Sunday 9am to 3pm; mid-August to June Monday to Friday 8:30am to 4pm, Saturday 9am to 2pm. The town doesn't employ street addresses, but everything is laid out easily enough to find. Also visit www.visitgeilo.com for information.

Seeing the Sights

The most exciting possibility is to book an organized tour at the tourist office for glacier trekking on **Hardangerjøkulen,** at 1,860m (6,101 ft.). These are available Tuesday, Wednesday, and Friday between July and mid-September, depending on whether the snow has melted on the glacier. The tour takes 10 hours and costs NOK650 per person, including a train ride to and from Finse.

A pair of other tours are offered as well: rafting from NOK350 to NOK800 and a nature and troll safari for NOK400 (NOK250 for children). This latter jaunt is offered Monday, Wednesday, and Friday from late June to mid-August, as well as occasionally during the winter months.

Back in the center of town, but only in July, you can visit **Geilojordet,** a 17th-century farm, which is open daily from 11am to 5pm. Some old houses, 2 or 3 centuries old, have been moved to the site and are open for guided tours. You can see how farmers lived at the time and visit such buildings as a storage house or the cattle barn. Cultural activities are also presented at the time, including folk-music shows. On-site is a cafe serving coffee, cakes, and drinks.

Geilo is both a summer and a winter destination, although its claim to fame is as a skiing resort, the main season lasting from January to March. If you plan on doing a lot of skiing, it's best to purchase the **Vinterlandkoret Ski Pass** at the tourist office. This pass, costing NOK340 per day or NOK1,415 per week, is good for all five ski centers in the area, as well as the network of slopes in such nearby resorts as Ål, Uvdal, and Hemesdal.

Of the five different ski centers, our most preferred is **Geilo Skiheiser** (✆ **32-09-59-20**), with 35km (22 miles) of slopes, many as good as those in the Swiss Alps, plus 220km (137 miles) of cross-country trails along with 20 lifts. Lift tickets cost NOK355 for adults and NOK265 for children.

Where to Stay & Dine

Dr. Holms Hotel ★★★ ☺ This is our preferred stopover when driving across Norway between Oslo and Bergen. One of the most famous resort hotels in Norway, it is also the area's finest place to stay. Here, near the railroad station, you get elegance, comfort, and traditional styling, as the hotel is filled with art and antiques. Dr. J. C. Holms, a specialist in respiratory diseases who established the resort so that patients could breathe fresh mountain air, opened the hotel in 1909. After being occupied by the Nazis from 1940 to 1945, it was freed by the Norwegian Resistance in May 1945. There have been many changes since, including the addition of two wings and a swimming complex. The latest major overhaul took place at the time of the millennium, but since then other smaller improvements have been made to keep the hotel operating in tiptop shape. Original works of art decorate the hotel. Guest rooms, including 11 family rooms, are beautifully furnished in a romantic English style.

N-3580 Geilo. www.drholms.com. ✆ **32-09-57-00.** Fax 32-09-16-20. 126 units. NOK1,490–NOK3,290 double. Rates include buffet breakfast. AE, DC, MC, V. **Amenities:** 2 restaurants; cafe; bar; babysitting; fitness center; 2 Jacuzzis; indoor heated pool; children's pool; room service; sauna; rooms for those w/ limited mobility. *In room:* TV, minibar, Wi-Fi.

Thon Vestlia Resort ★★★ ☺ Check into Dr. Holms Hotel for a time-mellowed atmosphere of tradition, but book into this vastly enlarged and modernized hotel for contemporary comfort, including the best spa between Oslo and Bergen. From a hotel originally built in the 1960s, Helene Hennie, one of Norway's most renowned interior architects, designed and worked on the resort. As part of the complex, there are 34 double and family rooms in small cabins surrounding the main hotel building. Eleven slightly worn-down cabins are in idyllic locations in the birch forest with views over Ustedalsfjord and Geilo itself. The restaurant offers solid Scandinavian and Continental meals. Some of the best cross-country skiing in the area begins at the resort's doorstep. The kid-friendly resort has a playground and the best skiing in Norway for children; there's even a ski lift system suitable for kids and a children's ski club. In summer, guests go hiking, boating, horseback riding, or play golf. The best nighttime entertainment is also provided at the hotel, including live dance music almost every evening year-round except Sunday.

N-3580 Geilo. www.vestlia.no. ✆ **32-08-72-00.** 120 units. NOK1,250–NOK1,750 double, including full board; NOK6,990 penthouse. AE, DC, MC, V. **Amenities:** 3 restaurants; dance bar; babysitting; fitness center; golf course; Jacuzzi; indoor heated pool; sauna; exclusive spa; tennis court; rooms for those w/ limited mobility. *In room:* TV, minibar.

TRONDHEIM TO NARVIK

Trondheim

If you have a day or two to spare after visiting Oslo and Bergen, make it to Trondheim, Norway's third city. We often prefer it during "term time," when 25,000 students bring it to vibrant life, biking around town, drinking in the bars, hanging out in the cafes, and listening to the sounds of jazz, often imported from New Orleans.

If you're heading north from here, take time appreciating the city life before journeying into the northern wilds, which are rarely tamed but for the odd city or large settlement. If you're arriving in Trondheim from the north, you'll view it as a return to civilization and all those pleasures it brings.

Noted for its timbered architecture, Trondheim retains much of its medieval past, notably the Gothic-style Nidaros Cathedral. Pilgrims came from all over Europe to worship at the shrine of Olaf, who was buried in the cathedral and canonized in 1031. The city's fortunes declined during the Reformation. Under the Nazi occupation

Trondheim became the base of German naval forces in northern Norway, with U-boats lurking deep in its fjord.

Today Trondheim is a progressive city with a rich cultural life, as well as a high-technology center for research and education. Its town center is compact and best explored on foot; most of the historic core of Trondheim lies on a small triangular island surrounded by water but linked via bridges.

ESSENTIALS

ARRIVAL BY PLANE Flights to Trondheim land at **Vaernes airport** (✆ **74-84-30-00**), lying 32km (20 miles) east of the city center. Most visitors fly here from either Bergen or Oslo. There are also daily connections to and from Copenhagen. Service is provided by **SAS** (✆ **74-80-41-00;** www.sas.no), **Widerøe** (✆ **81-00-12-00**), and **Norwegian** (✆ **81-52-18-15**).

After you arrive at the airport, you can take an airport bus, **Flybussen** (✆ **73-82-25-00**), costing NOK90 for a one-way trip into the center. The trip takes 40 minutes, ending at the rail depot. From the center of Trondheim, buses leave from Erling Skakkes gate daily from 5am to 9pm. Departures Monday to Friday are every 15 minutes, with curtailed departures on Saturday and Sunday. You can also take a taxi from the airport to the center, costing a minimum of NOK500 for up to three people.

ARRIVAL BY TRAIN Two trains a day arrive from Stockholm (trip time: 12 hr.) and three trains per day arrive from Oslo (trip time: 7 hr.) into **Trondheim Sentralstasjon.** A typical fare—say, from Oslo to Trondheim—costs NOK852 one-way. Trondheim also has links to Bodø if you're heading for the Arctic Circle. This latter trip takes 10 hours, costing around NOK982 one-way. For rail information, call ✆ **81-50-08-88** or visit www.nsb.no.

ARRIVAL BY BUS Buses from various parts of Norway arrive at the **Rutebilstasjon,** or city bus terminal, adjoining Trondheim Sentralstasjon, where the trains pull in. Trondheim lies at the crossroads of bus travel in Norway, as it is a transportation hub between southern Norway, including Oslo and Bergen, and northern Norway, including the city of Bodø. The most frequented bus route is from Oslo, taking 9½ hours and costing NOK860 one-way. The more difficult route from Bergen takes more than 10 hours, costing NOK789 one-way. For information about long-distance buses, contact **Norway Buss Ekspress** (✆ **81-54-44-44;** www.nor-way.no). There are also very inexpensive seats available on the **Lavprisexpressen** (✆ **67-98-04-80**) buses, with tickets for as little as NOK49. However, to get them this cheap you must purchase at least several days in advance.

ARRIVAL BY BOAT The **Hurtigruten coastal steamer** (✆ **81-00-30-30**) stops in Trondheim. In addition, **Fosen Teraffikklag Kystekspressen boats** (✆ **73-89-07-00**) travel between Kristiansund N and Trondheim, taking 3½ hours and costing NOK525. Departures are at Pirterminalen Quay in Trondheim.

ARRIVAL BY CAR From Oslo, motorists can take the express highway E-6 north, going via Lillehammer all the way into Trondheim.

VISITOR INFORMATION Contact the **Trondheim Tourist Office,** Munkegate 19 (✆ **73-80-76-60;** www.trondheim.no), near the marketplace. In peak season—from mid-June to early September—it is open Monday to Friday 8:30am to 6pm, Saturday and Sunday 10am to 6pm; from June 2 to June 22, it's open Monday to Friday 8:30am to 6pm, Saturday and Sunday 10am to 4pm. During other months, hours are Monday to Friday 9am to 4pm, Saturday 10am to 2pm.

GETTING AROUND You can travel all over Trondheim and to outlying areas on city buses operated by **Team Traffikk** (it also goes by the name of AtB), Kongens Gate 34 (✆ **73-87-14-00**). Tickets for **single rides** are sold on buses for NOK30 for adults, NOK15 for children 4 to 16; children 3 and under travel free. If you don't have exact change and offer a banknote that's worth more than the bus fare, you'll receive a credit slip from the driver, which can be redeemed at the TT office or on a later trip. A **day card** for 24 hours of unlimited rides costs NOK70 per person or NOK120 for a family.

For a local **taxi,** TrønderTaxi maintains a special five-digit telephone number (✆ **07373**) that's in service 24 hours a day. The biggest taxi ranks are found at Torvet, the market square, and also at the central rail station. For local bus information serving the Greater Trondheim area, call ✆ **81-53-52-30.**

Trondheim is a city that's known for its allegiance to all things "green" (ecologically speaking). As such, it maintains a fleet of several hundred red-painted bicycles at bike racks scattered around the city. To secure one, head for the tourist office and pay a fee of NOK70, plus a cash or credit card deposit of NOK200, in exchange for which someone will give you a sort of credit card. After you insert it into a slot on the bike rack, it releases the bike, which you're then free to use for up to 5 days without additional charge. When you're through with the bike, bring it back undamaged and your deposit will be returned. The whole system will make you want to write an ode to the joys of visiting a civilized country.

WHERE TO STAY

Many hotels offer special summer prices from mid-June to the end of August. The rest of the year, hotels feature weekend discounts if you stay 2 nights.

Expensive

Britannia Hotel ★★ For old-world tradition, the Britannia can't be beat. This grande dame of Trondheim hotels was built in 1897, with a white-stucco facade, a majestic slate-covered dome, and a tower evocative of the grand Victorian monuments of England. Though it may lack cutting-edge glamour, the hotel features an ornate Palm Garden (p. 290), with its Art Nouveau winter garden, fountain, and piano. The renovated guest rooms have wooden floors, and the most tranquil units front the courtyard but are also the smallest rooms. One unique feature is a series of "Artists' Rooms," decorated with works from nationally famous artists, but for all-out grandeur, try one of the 11 regal suites, half of which are duplexes. If you like boas and gilt-plated "ice," you can check into the Flettfrid Andresen Room (no. 724)—it's the campiest room in Norway.

Dronningens Gate 5, N-7001 Trondheim. www.britannia.no. ✆ **73-80-08-00.** 247 units. Mon–Thurs NOK1,695–NOK2,295 double, Fri–Sun NOK1,295–NOK1,595 double; NOK3,500–NOK6,500 suite. Rates include buffet breakfast. AE, DC, MC, V. Parking NOK225. Bus: 3, 4, 5, or 7. **Amenities:** 3 restaurants; 4 bars; babysitting; fitness center; indoor heated pool; room service; sauna; spa; rooms for those w/limited mobility. *In room:* TV, hair dryer, minibar, Wi-Fi.

Radisson Blu Royal Garden Hotel ★★★ This glittering extravaganza on the see-and-be-seen circuit is Trondheim's largest and best hotel. It lacks the tradition of the Britannia but outdistances the Clarions for pure luxury and amenities. This is the most architecturally dramatic and innovative hotel in Trondheim. Originally built in 1984 to replace a row of waterfront warehouses that had burned down in a fire, it rises abruptly on stilts just above the Nid River. Inside is an intriguing array of angled glass skylights, stone floors, soaring atriums, and plants. Rooms are comfortable and tastefully contemporary. The most elegant of the hotel's restaurants is the Prins Olavs Grill.

Kjøpmannsgata 73, N-7010 Trondheim. www.radissonblu.com. ✆ **73-80-30-00.** 298 units. Sun–Thurs NOK1,595–NOK1,900 double; Fri–Sat NOK1,095–NOK1,495 double; NOK3,000–NOK5,000 suite. Rates include buffet breakfast. AE, DC, MC, V. Parking NOK195. Bus: 1 or 4. **Amenities:** 2 restaurants; bar; health club and exercise center; Jacuzzi; indoor heated pool; room service; sauna. *In room:* TV, hair dryer, minibar, Wi-Fi.

Moderate

Clarion Collection Hotel Bakeriet ★ One of the most atmospheric hotels in Trondheim occupies the premises of what functioned between 1863 and 1963 as the largest bakery in Norway. It calls to mind a museum, thanks to a number of displays that showcase the ovens, cooling racks, and paraphernalia associated with the building during its early days. Kids should eat up these displays, including the elaborate 20th-century bakers' costumes lining the upstairs hallways leading to the large and very comfortable bedrooms. Many of these have carefully finished half-paneling and easy chairs and settees.

Brattørgata 2, N-7010 Trondheim. www.choicehotels.no. ✆ **73-99-10-00.** 109 units. NOK890–NOK2,390 double; year-round NOK2,540 suite. Rates include breakfast and a light evening supper. AE, DC, MC, V. Parking NOK200. Bus: 1 or 4. **Amenities:** Breakfast room and lounge; babysitting; bike rental; fitness room; Turkish bath; sauna; rooms for those w/limited mobility. *In room:* TV, hair dryer, minibar, Wi-Fi.

Inexpensive

Thon Hotel Trondheim This six-story hotel near the market square is a deliberately simple, relatively inexpensive B&B with medium-size guest rooms but offering little flair or frill. Outfitted with sun-kissed color schemes, many of the rooms contain an extra foldaway bed. The beds are comfortable, and the bathrooms, while small, are equipped with tub/shower combinations. Constructed in 1913, the hotel was renovated and expanded in 1990, with additional small-scale renovations conducted ever since.

Kongens Gate 15, N-7013 Trondheim. www.thonhotels.no. ✆ **73-88-47-88.** 115 units. NOK925–NOK1,570 double. AE, DC, MC, V. Parking NOK160. Bus from airport stops here. **Amenities:** Breakfast room; rooms for those w/limited mobility. *In room:* TV, hair dryer, minibar.

WHERE TO DINE

Be sure to try the local specialty, ***vafler med øst*** **(waffle and cheese),** sold at most cafeterias and restaurants. Most restaurants will automatically add around a 15% service charge to your bill. If you like the service, it's customary to leave some extra small change as well.

Expensive

Credo ★★ CONTINENTAL This is Trondheim's trendiest restaurant, and includes an art gallery and jazz bar as well. The contemporary setting features modern furniture and white walls that showcase a changing array of paintings (most of which are for sale) on loan from a nearby art gallery. The seasonal cuisine infuses fresh local meats, vegetables, and produce with cooking techniques inspired by France, Italy, and Spain. Menu items change with the inspiration of the chef but especially tasty is the changing array of game dishes featuring duck, elk, pheasant, venison, and grouse. The cellar boasts nearly 2,000 varieties of wine, including a collection of German Rieslings that is among the most comprehensive in Scandinavia. For more about this place as a jazz bar, see "Trondheim After Dark," below.

Ørjaveita 4. ✆ **73-53-03-88.** www.restaurantcredo.no. Reservations recommended. Fixed-price menus NOK550–NOK660. AE, DC, MC, V. Restaurant Mon–Sat 6–10pm (last order). Bar Mon–Sat 4pm–3am. Closed July and 1 week at Christmas and Easter. Bus: 3, 4, or 5.

Palm Garden ★★★ NORWEGIAN/INTERNATIONAL This is the most elegant restaurant in Trondheim, housed in the first-rate Britannia Hotel (p. 288). Illuminated with a Victorian-era skylight, the place is rife with medieval and Belle Epoque atmosphere, and filled with palms. Lunch is a sandwich-and-salad buffet that attracts many of the town's leading business clients. Dinner is grand and elaborate, with an array of top-quality dishes prepared with the finest of ingredients. Begin, perhaps, with a marinated wild salmon in a fennel bouillon with apple salsa, or else a creamed curry mussel soup (the little ravioli in the soup are stuffed with mussels). For real Norwegian flavor, opt for the "top side of stag," with fresh mushrooms, creamed vegetables, and—just the right touch—red whortleberry chutney.

In the Britannia Hotel, Dronningens Gate 5. ✆ **73-80-08-00.** Reservations recommended. Lunch salads and sandwiches around NOK120; dinner main courses NOK240–NOK310. AE, DC, MC, V. Daily 11:30am–2:30pm and 6–10pm. Bus: 5, 6, 7, or 9.

Moderate

Blåbrygga ★ SEAFOOD This is one of the two most popular seafood restaurants in Trondheim. It's not as chic, cutting edge, and sophisticated as Havfruen, but it serves an intelligent, imaginative cuisine at somewhat better prices. Named after a 1950s-era cargo ship (*Fru Inger,* or "Miss Inger") now moored in Mexico, it's in a glass-sided pavilion that overlooks a fleet of fishing vessels moored beside a canal, a short walk from the railway station. Inside, a navy-blue color scheme, varnished mahogany, and pin lighting work to enhance the nautical decor. I recommend lime-and-chili-marinated scampi served on a salad bed of arugula and fresh tomato as a starter. Drawn from the cold, deep waters of Norway, the braised monkfish is served with fresh veggies, mashed potatoes, and white-wine sauce.

Fosenkaia. ✆ **73-51-60-71.** Reservations recommended. Main courses NOK220–NOK245. AE, DC, MC, V. Sun–Thurs 2–11pm; Fri–Sat 2pm–midnight. Bus: 1 or 4.

Vertshuset Grenaderen ★ 🎁 NORWEGIAN For rustic charm and authentic Nordic meals, this longtime favorite is hard to beat. The setting is a rather upscale rendition of the blacksmith shop this space was over a century ago. Today, amid flickering candles and a collection of 19th-century wood- and metal-working tools, there is a strong air of *olde worlde* Norway. Menu items include some time-tested workhorses such as gin-marinated smoked salmon; cream of fish and shellfish soup; small-scale platters of fish roe; that air-dried standby of *lutefisk,* served with bacon; several kinds of grilled beefsteaks, some accompanied with grilled shrimp; barbecued pork ribs; and a dessert specialty: wild-berry parfait with whiskey sauce. One of the town's best values is the lunchtime buffet, served year-round; in autumn, it focuses on fresh game dishes from the surrounding tundras and forests. A more elaborate version of that same buffet is also served throughout the day on Sunday.

Kongsgårdsgata 1. ✆ **73-51-66-80.** Reservations recommended. Main courses NOK145–NOK310; lunchtime buffet NOK150 (until 4pm); 3-course fixed-price menu NOK198; Sun buffet NOK195. AE, DC, MC, V. Mon–Sat noon–midnight; Sun 1–9pm. Closed Mon Dec–Apr. Bus: 5, 6, 7, or 9.

Inexpensive

Restaurant Egon AMERICAN This is one of the friendliest joints in Trondheim and a good place to meet the city's younger set. It's in the center of town in an early-20th-century stone building that was once a local bank. Within a labyrinth of dark, woodsy-looking pub areas and dining rooms, the restaurant serves the Norwegian equivalent of American-style diner food, including pizzas cooked in an open brick oven. In summer, the venue spills out onto the terrace outside.

Thomas Angellsgate 8 (entrance on Søndregate). ✆ **73-51-79-75.** Pizzas, burgers, salads, and platters NOK155–NOK298. AE, DC, MC, V. Mon–Sat 11am–midnight; Sun noon–11pm. Bus: 1 or 4.

Tavern på Sverresborg ★ NORWEGIAN No restaurant in town offers more authentic Norwegian cuisine than this historic eatery, 4.8km (3 miles) south of the city and immediately adjacent to the Trondelag Folk Museum. Built as a private merchant's house in 1739 and later transformed into a clapboard-sided tavern with wide-plank flooring and antique rustic accessories, it's one of the few wooden buildings of its age in this area. The most desirable and oft-reserved table is directly in front of a fireplace in a side room. There's an emphasis on 18th- and 19th-century recipes, such as *spekemat,* a thinly sliced collection of ham, meat, salami, and smoked mutton, served with flatbread, scrambled eggs, and sour cream. From the "taste of Norway" menu, you can also enjoy homemade fishcakes fried in butter or lightly cured herring with beets, sour cream, and onion rings. Another good dish is marinated chicken breast with a sour cream sauce sprinkled with chervil and parsley.

Sverresborg Allé, at Trøndelag Folk Museum. ✆ **73-87-80-70.** Reservations recommended. Main courses NOK75–NOK335. AE, DC, MC, V. Mon–Fri 4pm–midnight; Sat–Sun 2pm–midnight. Bus: 8.

SEEING THE SIGHTS

Nidaros Domkirke (Cathedral of Trondheim) ★★★ Thousands upon thousands of medieval pilgrims visited this grand cathedral, and it remains an extremely popular stop today. Dating from the 11th century, Nidaros easily dwarfs Oslo Cathedral as the most important, historic, and impressive ecclesiastical building in Scandinavia. It's in the town center, near the Rådhus. The burial place of the medieval Norwegian kings, it was also the site of the coronation of Haakon VII in 1905, an event that marked the beginning of modern Norway.

Construction actually began on the cathedral in 1070, and some of its oldest parts still remain, primarily from the middle of the 1100s. Following the battle of Stiklestad, King Olaf Haraldson was entombed under the high altar. In time, Olaf became Saint Olaf, and his remains were encased in a gem-studded shrine.

The cathedral has weathered several disastrous fires that swept over Trondheim, though it was reconstructed each time in its original Gothic style. (The section around the transept, however, is Romanesque.) During the Reformation, the cathedral was looted of precious relics. By 1585, Nidaros had been reduced to the status of a parish church. Around 1869 major reconstruction work was begun to return the gray sandstone building to its former glory.

The west facade is particularly impressive, with its carved figures of royalty and saints. It's especially appealing after dark, when the facade is floodlit (the lights usually stay on every evening till midnight—it's worth a stroll even if you have to make a detour to do it). The interior is a maze of mammoth pillars and columns with beautifully carved arches that divide the chancel from the nave. The grandest feature is the stunning **rose window ★**. The cathedral's **stained-glass windows ★**, when caught in the proper light, are reason enough to visit. Gustav Vigeland, the famous sculptor, carved the **gargoyles and grotesques ★** for the head tower and northern transept. A small museum inside displays the **crown jewels ★★** of Norway.

Bispegaten 5. ✆ **41-79-80-00.** Admission to cathedral and museum NOK50 adults, NOK25 children. Cathedral and museum May 1–June 10 Mon–Fri 9am–3pm, Sat 9am–2pm, Sun 1–4pm; June 11–Aug 19

Mon-Fri 9am-6pm, Sat 9am-2pm, Sun 1-4pm; Aug 20-Sept 14 Mon-Fri 9am-3pm, Sat 9am-2pm, Sun 1-4pm; Sept 15-Apr 30 Mon-Fri noon-2:30pm, Sat 11:30am-2pm, Sun 1-3pm. Bus: 5, 6, 7, or 9.

Ringve Museum ★★ This is the only Norwegian museum specializing in musical instruments from all over the world. On the Ringve Estate on the Lade Peninsula, the building originated in the 1740s as a prosperous manor house and farmstead. The mansion was the birthplace of Admiral Tordenskiold, the Norwegian sea hero. The museum today consists of two parts—the manor house and a permanent exhibition in the estate's former barn. In the barn you can hear the unique sounds of Norwegian folk music instruments; there's even a hands-on exhibition where you can express your inner folk musician. At specified times, concerts are given on carefully preserved antique instruments, including an impressive collection of spinets, harpsichords, clavichords, pianofortes, and string and wind instruments. Also on the premises is an old *kro* (inn) that serves waffles, light refreshments, and coffee.

Lade Allé 60 (3.3km/2 miles east from the center of town at Ringve Manor). ✆ **73-87-02-80.** www.ringve.no. Admission NOK80 adults, NOK30 children 7-15, NOK60 students, NOK160 families. Mid-Apr to mid-May Mon-Fri and Sun 11am-4pm; mid-May to mid-June daily 11am-3pm; mid-June to Aug 5 daily 11am-5pm; Aug 6-Sept 9 daily 11am-3pm; Sept 10 to mid-Apr Sun 11am-4pm. During hours, multilingual guided tours depart at least once per hour, sometimes more frequently. Bus: 3 or 4.

Sverresborg Trøndelag Folk Museum ★★★ ☺ This is the best folkloric museum in Norway, and it's chock-full of farmhouses, cottages, churches, and town buildings, representing aspects of everyday life in the region over the past 3 centuries. Kids often find this attraction a sort of "Trondheim Disneyworld," but this educational, entertaining space is more real than Mickey Mouse land. 5km (3 miles) west of the center, the complex is composed of 60 historic buildings, all made from wood and stone and all laboriously dismantled and reassembled. Among the compound's most intriguing buildings are Trondheim's first all-brick building and the 200-year-old barns, many with sod roofs, many painted red, and most built of weathered natural wood. There's a cafe on the premises, but if you want a good meal, I recommend that you head next door to the celebrated restaurant **Tavern på Sverresborg** (see "Where to Dine," above), which serves traditional Norwegian dishes. The proudest structure here is Norway's northernmost stave church.

On the grounds of the folk museum, within an antique building hauled in from some other part of the province, is a separate museum, the **Sverresborg Ski Museum.** Entrance to the ski museum is included in the price of admission to the Folk Museum, and hours are the same, too. Tracing the history of skiing in Norway, it contains antique skis dating from the 1600s, some carved in patterns inspired by the Vikings, and some with fur or sealskin cladding, which prevented them from sliding backward during cross-country skiing. The museum is also surrounded by a nature park with animals.

Sverresborg Allé. ✆ **73-89-01-00.** www.sverresborg.no. Admission NOK85 adults, NOK35 children, NOK210 families, free for children 4 and under. June-Aug daily 11am-6pm; Sept-May daily 11am-3pm. Bus: 8.

ORGANIZED TOURS

At the tourist office (p. 287), you can purchase tickets for guided tours of the city, lasting 2 hours and taking in the highlights. Departure is from Torvet or Market Square daily at 11am between May 26 and August 24. Adults pay NOK195, while children 15 and under enter free if they're accompanied by an adult.

The tourist office publicizes a 1½-hour sea tour, going along the canal harbor and up the River Nidelven and out to the fjord. From June 18 to August 13, it leaves Tuesday to Sunday at noon and 2pm, costing NOK140 for adults and NOK55 for ages 3 to 14. From August 14 to September 17 tours are on Wednesday, Friday, and Sunday at 2:30pm.

TRONDHEIM AFTER DARK

If you're here in late July or early August at the time of the week-long **St. Olaf Festival,** Dronningensgt 1B (✆ **73-84-14-50;** www.olavsfestdagene.no), you can enjoy organ concerts, outdoor concerts, and even opera at the Nidaros Cathedral. The internationally acclaimed **Trondheim Symphony Orchestra ★★★**, Olavskvartalet, Kjøpmannsgata 46 (✆ **73-99-40-50**), presents concerts weekly with some of Europe's most outstanding conductors and soloists. Depending on the event and the day of the week, tickets cost from NOK100 to NOK270. Tickets can also be purchased at the main post office in Trondheim.

Bar Credo Upstairs from one of Trondheim's hippest and most charming restaurants (the also-recommended Credo, p. 289), this bar does a flourishing after-dark business in its own right. Come here for a view of the dozens of modern paintings hanging on the walls—the place doubles as an art gallery, and many of the works are for sale. Live music is presented nearly every night from young and ambitious jazz artists deriving from points throughout Norway and the rest of Europe. The space is divided into a trio of silver-toned rooms, with lots of flickering candles, making the scene even more intimate. In fact, the venue is cozy enough that you might make some new friends. The bar has a separate entrance from the restaurant Credo. Open Monday to Saturday 4pm to 3am. Ørjaveita 4. ✆ **73-53-03-88.**

Den Gode Nabo ("The Good Neighbor") Pub ★ This is our favorite pub in Trondheim, occupying the cellar of a 250-year-old warehouse. In a low-ceilinged labyrinth of rough-hewn timbers and planking are a number of banquettes, behind which the bar serves 16 kinds of draft beer. But when the weather is pleasant, everyone heads out to the wooden platform floating on the river Nid, with great views of Trondheim's antique warehouses built on pilings sunk deep into the riverbed. The pub food includes the establishment's best-known dish, the "Good Neighbor" fish plate. Priced at NOK125, it contains heaping portions of vegetables, potatoes, and (usually grilled) fish of the day, accompanied by whatever sauce the chef has dreamed up. You can be a good neighbor at this place every day between 4pm and 1am. Øvre Bakklandet 66. ✆ **40-61-88-09.**

Bodø ★

479km (297 miles) N of Trondheim, 1,430km (887 miles) N of Bergen, 1,305km (809 miles) N of Oslo

This is a great place to spend a day or two—not for the city itself, which is dull architecturally (save for a brand-new cultural center, due to open in 2013), but for the attractions of nature in the wilds that envelop the town. This seaport, the terminus of the Nordland railway, is just north of the Arctic Circle. Visitors arrive here, the capital of Nordland, for a glimpse of the midnight sun, which shines from June 2 to July 10. But don't expect a clear view of it. What those tourist brochures don't tell you is that many nights are either rainy or hazy, cutting down considerably on your enjoyment of the spectacle. From December 15 to December 29, Bodø gets no sunlight at all.

Bodø is Nordland's largest city, with some 47,000 inhabitants living at the northern entrance to Salt Fjord. Although burned to the ground by the retreating Nazis at the end of World War II, the city dates back to 1816, when it was founded by merchants from Trondheim seeking a northern trading post.

Bodø faces an archipelago rich in bird life, and no other town in the world boasts such a large concentration of sea eagles. From Bodø, you can take excursions in many directions to glaciers and bird islands; the most attractive are the Lofoten Islands (p. 298).

ESSENTIALS

GETTING THERE If you're not driving or traveling by coastal steamer, you can reach Bodø from major cities throughout Norway, usually with connections through either Trondheim or Oslo, on **SAS** (✆ **91-50-54-00;** www.sas.no) and **Norwegian** (✆ **81-52-18-15;** www.norwegian.no). The airport is just over a kilometer (½ mile) southwest of the city center and is accessed by regular bus service (ask at the airport desk for the latest schedule); cost is NOK90 each way. It is also possible to hire one of the many taxis waiting at the arrivals gate, with which a trip to the town center costs roughly NOK100. Alternatively, some may choose to simply walk to town, which won't take more than 15 minutes (follow Hernesveien from the airport exit). Bodø is at the end of the Nordland rail line.

Two **trains** a day leave Trondheim for Bodø. The trip takes 9 hours, 40 minutes, and the journey, known as the Nordlandsbanen, is one of Europe's most exhilarating overnight train journeys. Visit www.nsb.no for information.

For **bus** information, contact **SB Nordlandsbuss** in Bodø (✆ **47-88-39-99**), or alternatively, for general travel info in Nordland, call ✆ 177. Fauske is a transportation hub along the E-6 highway to the north and Route 80 west to Bodø. From Fauske there are two buses a day to Bodø. The trip takes an hour and 10 minutes. If you take the train from Stockholm to Narvik (north of Bodø), you can make bus connections to Fauske and Bodø, a total trip of 5 hours. Know in advance that if you're taking public transportation, you are likely to pass through Fauske on your way to and from other parts of Norway's far north. The complete schedule is available at www.177nordland.no.

Motorists can continue north from Mo i Rana, the last stopover, until they come to the junction with Route 80 heading west to Bodø.

VISITOR INFORMATION The **tourist office, Destination Bodø,** is at Sjøgata 3 (✆ **75-54-80-00;** www.visitbodo.com), in the town center. It's open September 1 to May 31 Monday to Friday 9am to 3:30pm; June 1 to August 31 Monday to Friday 9am to 8pm, Saturday 10am to 6pm, Sunday noon to 8pm. The town is relatively flat, and bikes can be hired at Sirilund Handel on Kjerringøy (www.kjerringoy.info).

SEEING THE SIGHTS

Bodø Domkirke As Norwegian cathedrals go, the Bodø Dom ranks low on the totem pole. But when the Nazis bombed their previous church on May 27, 1940, locals were eager to open a major place of worship even if they could find no Michelangelo—or money—to build it. What they came up with is fairly respectable. Completed in 1956, this is the most notable building constructed since those German bombers flew over. It features tufted rugs depicting ecclesiastical themes, wall hangings, and a stained-glass window that captures the northern lights. A memorial outside honors those killed in the war with the inscription NO ONE MENTIONED, NO ONE

FORGOTTEN. There's also an outstanding spire that stands separate from the main building.

Torv Gate 12. ✆ **75-51-95-30.** Free admission. Mid-June to Aug Tues–Fri noon–3pm. Closed Sept–May.

Galleri Bodøgaard 2.5km (1½ miles) from the heart of town, this museum exhibits the largest private ethnographical collection in north Norway. Boats, artifacts of daily life, and tools used in hunting and fishing are just some of the collection items on parade. The site encompasses the Russian prisoner-of-war camp at Bodøgaard.

Skeidalen 2. ✆ **90-72-08-43.** Admission NOK50 adults, free for children. Tues–Fri 9am–3pm; Sat–Sun noon–4pm (hours subject to change—check before coming here).

Nordlandmuseet (Nordland Museum) In the town center, the main building of this museum is one of the oldest structures in Bodø. Here you'll find, among other exhibits, artifacts recalling the saga of local fishermen and artifacts from the Sami culture. There's also a "dry" aquarium, with stuffed fish, along with silver treasure dating from the Viking era. An open-air part of this museum contains more than a dozen historical buildings moved to the site, plus a collection of boats. Part of the exhibit includes *Anna Karoline of Hopen,* the only surviving Nordland cargo vessel.

Prinsengate 116. ✆ **75-50-35-00**. www.saltenmuseum.no**.** Admission NOK35 adults, children NOK10. May–Aug Mon–Fri 9am–4pm, Sat–Sun 11am–4pm; rest of year Mon–Fri 9am–3pm, Sat 11am–3pm.

Norsk Luftfartsmuseum (Norwegian Aviation Museum) ☺ So this is where that infamous U-2 spy plane ended up. In 1960, the ill-fated plane made headlines around the world when it was shot down over the Soviet Union, creating a major diplomatic incident. The spy plane was en route from Peshawar in Pakistan to Bodø. This museum, shaped like an airplane propeller, takes you on its own exciting "fly-over" of Norway's civil and military aviation history. You're allowed to have a close encounter with large and small aircraft such as the Spitfire and JU52. Hands-on demonstrations reveal to you the dynamics of flight. In addition to the exhibition of aircraft, the museum shows a collection of photographs about the largest predators in the Nordic countries, including lynx, bears, wolves, wolverines, and, more surprisingly, humans. The museum was built on the site of a German World War II airfield.

The museum lies 2km (1¼ miles) north of town. Olav V Gata. ✆ **75-50-78-50.** www.luftfart.museum.no. Admission NOK95 adults, NOK40 children 15 and under. Mid-June to mid-Aug Sun–Fri 10am–7pm, Sat 10am–5pm; Sept–May Mon–Fri 10am–4pm, Sat–Sun 11am–5pm. Bus: 23 or marked CITY NORD.

OUTDOOR ACTIVITIES

If you'd like to go horseback riding under the midnight sun, **Bodø Hestecenter,** Soloya Gård (✆ **75-51-41-48**), about 14km (8¾ miles) southwest of Bodø, rents horses. Buses go there Monday to Friday mornings and evenings and on Saturday morning. For more information, ask at the Bodø Tourist Office (see "Visitor Information," above). The cost is NOK120 for a 45-minute ride.

At the tourist office (see above), you can pick up maps detailing the best hiking in the area. The best area is through **Bodømarka (Bodø forest),** with its 35km (22 miles) of marked hiking and cross-country skiing trails. For detailed touring, including overnighting in the forest, contact **Bodø og Omegn Turist-forening,** the **Bodø Trekking Association** (✆ **75-52-14-13**), which operates a dozen cabins in the forest.

Bodø is now home to Norway's most modern indoor water park, the **Nordlansdbadet** (✆ **75-59-15-00** or 40-60-28-41; www.bodospektrum.no), which offers plenty of waterbound activities for kids as well as a dedicated spa and well-being section for adults. In addition to multiple pools—an exercise pool, diving pool, therapy pool, and wave pool, among others—there are several water chutes, fountains, grottoes, Jacuzzis, saunas, and a water mushroom. The park is located just opposite the Norwegian Aviation Museum.

THE MAELSTROM From Bodø, you can take a bus to the mighty maelstrom, the **Saltstraumen Eddy ★**, 33km (20 miles) south of the city. The variation between high- and low-tide levels, which occurs four times per day at varying times throughout the year, pushes immense volumes of water through narrow fjords, creating huge whirlpools known as "kettles." When the eddies and the surrounding land vibrate, they produce an odd yelling sound. Saltstraumen is nearly 3.3km (2 miles) long and only about 167m (548 ft.) wide, with billions of gallons of water pressing through at speeds of about 10 knots; it is the world's strongest maelstrom. Buses from Bodø run five times a day Monday to Saturday, twice on Sunday. The cost is NOK75 for adults round-trip, half-price for children 11 and under. A round-trip taxi excursion costs in excess of NOK600 for two passengers; check with **Bodø Taxi** (✆ **07550;** www.bodotaxi.no) for more information; they also have a daily departure to Saltstraumen to connect with the arrival of the Hurtigruten.

Many locals within this maritime community, as well as the staff at the Bodø Tourist Office, will be alert to the schedule of high and low tides on the day of your arrival. The maelstrom phenomenon occurs four times within any 24-hour period, twice for incoming tides, twice for outgoing tides, with a brief interlude between high and low tides when the waters are almost eerily still.

VISITING A GLACIER One of Norway's major tourist attractions, **Svartisen Glacier ★★★** can be visited south of Bodø. About 161km (100 miles) from Bodø, the glacier can be reached by car, although a boat crossing over the Svartisenfjord is more exciting to us. Tours to the glacier on the Helgeland Express, a combination bus-and-ferry excursion, are offered from Bodø several times in the summer (usually every second Sat July–Aug). The cost is NOK800 for adults, NOK600 for children 15 and under. **Nordland Turselskap** (✆ **90-63-60-86;** www.nordlandturselskap.no) and **Explore Nordland** (✆ **99-23-49-72;** www.explorenordland.no) both arrange tours to Svartisen Glacier; check their websites for more information. The tours leave Bodø at 1pm and return around 8pm on the same day. You can go ashore to examine the Engaglacier and see the nearby visitor center (✆ **75-75-10-00**). The local tourist office can provide more information. Depending on ice conditions, the visitor center may be able to arrange boat transportation across a narrow but icy channel so that you can have a closer look at the ice floe.

WHERE TO STAY

The **Bodø Tourist Office** (see "Visitor Information," above) can help you book a room in a hotel. It also maintains a list of local B&Bs and will book you a room for a fee of NOK30.

Expensive

Radisson Blu Hotel ★★ By far the finest and most expensive hotel in the area, this glistening structure is an inviting waterfront oasis that features panoramic views of the water. The good-size guest rooms are furnished in sleek contemporary style and decorated in a number of motifs, including Japanese, Nordic, Chinese, and British. The Royal is on the main street at the harborfront and offers some of the best drinking and dining facilities in Bodø, including the Sjøsiden Restaurant. Live music and dancing are offered every Saturday night in the Moloen Bar. But, in my view, the greatest place for a drink is the Top 13 Rooftop Bar.

Storgata 2, N-8000 Bodø. www.radissonsas.com. ✆ **800/333-3333** in the U.S., or 75-51-90-00. 190 units. NOK895–NOK1,395 double; NOK1,695–NOK2,195 suite. Rates include buffet breakfast. AE, DC, MC, V. Free parking. **Amenities:** 2 restaurants; 2 bars; lounge; babysitting; fitness center; room service; sauna; rooms for those w/limited mobility. *In room:* TV, hair dryer, minibar, Wi-Fi.

Moderate

Skagen Hotel ★ This discovery offers a lot of charm amid a somewhat bleak landscape. Helpful, well-connected staff make this hotel the best in this part of Norway for arranging memorable adventures, including wilderness camping and adventure weekends in some of the most magnificently varied landscape reachable from Bodø. Other adventures include deep-sea rafting, sea eagle feedings, fishing trips, canoeing, rock climbing, and glacier walks. Bedrooms are of average size, comfortably furnished and individually decorated, often in attractive cherrywood and with unique, large reading chairs. Thoughtful extras here include breakfast served at 6am or coffee and tea always available in the library. Additionally, there is a free buffet served nightly from 7 to 10pm.

Nyholmsgata 11, N-8001 Bodø. www.skagen-hotel.no. ✆ **75-51-91-00.** 72 units. NOK925–NOK1,725. AE, DC, MC, V. Free parking. **Amenities:** Bar; gym; sauna; rooms for those w/limited mobility. *In room:* TV, hair dryer, minibar, Wi-Fi.

WHERE TO DINE

Bjørk NORWEGIAN/INTERNATIONAL This award-winning restaurant is regularly ranked as one of the best in northern Norway. The location is a red-brick building a short walk away from the Radisson Blu hotel (where it used to reside) in the downtown Glashuset shopping mall. Inside are touches of red, blue, and black; a roaring fireplace; a well-trained staff; and a tempting combination of Norwegian and international cuisine. You might begin with a carpaccio of venison, say, or perhaps grilled scallops served with terrine of oxtail, or even fried scampi with a sweet-and-sour "Asian" sauce. Main courses focus on some of the freshest fish in Bodø, including codfish served with shredded beetroot; poached anglerfish in a peanut-based satay sauce; breast of duckling with an herb-based creamy risotto; and stockfish served with tarragon-flavored wine sauce and fresh root vegetables. But they also serve simple, down-home dishes, for example, pizza.

Glashuset Shopping Centre, Storgata 8. ✆ **75-52-52-50.** Reservations recommended. Main courses NOK250–NOK275. AE, DC, MC, V. Daily 10am–10pm.

BODØ AFTER DARK

The largest nightclub in Bodø is the **Rock Café,** Tollbugata 13B (✆ **75-50-46-33**), which can hold up to 550 patrons, most of them usually in their 20s and 30s. Live bands perform twice a month, while DJs spin on other days. It's open Friday and Saturday 9pm to 3am. Somewhat smaller, but occasionally more popular is **G Nattklubb** (✆ **75-56-17-00;** www.utibodo.no), downtown at Sjøgata 14 and open Friday and Saturday 10pm to 3am. There is a live DJ, and it tends to be big among thirty- and forty-somethings.

Somewhat less frenetic is **Nordlænningen,** Stogata 16 (✆ **75-52-06-00;** www.norlænningen.no), a laid-back cellar pub featuring daily live music, such as blues, country, or rock, to a crowd ranging in age from 20 to 50. They also serve pub grub, everything from burgers to omelets. Local artists' paintings dominate the decor. A cover charge is imposed only on Friday and Saturday nights, ranging from NOK70 to

NOK100. It's open Monday to Thursday 1pm to 1:30am, Friday and Saturday 1pm to 2:30am, and Sunday 2pm to 1:30am.

The Lofoten Islands

Svolvær (southernmost point of the Lofoten): 280km (174 miles) N of Bodø, 1,425km (884 miles) NE of Bergen, 1,250km (775 miles) N of Oslo

The island kingdom of Lofoten, one of the most beautiful regions of Norway, is 197km (122 miles) north of the Arctic Circle. Its population of 35,000 is distributed over both large and small islands. Many Norwegian visitors come here to fish, but the area also offers abundant bird life and flora. The midnight sun shines from May 25 to July 7.

Hans Olsen, a local guide, told us, "If you are not already a poet by the time you come here, you will be by the time you leave." He was referring, of course, to the area's beauty, the remoteness of the archipelago, and the mystical arctic light.

The Lofoten Islands stretch from Vågan in the east to Røst and Skomvaer in the southwest. The steep Lofoten mountain peaks—often called the Lofotwall—shelter farmland and deep fjords from the elements.

The major islands are **Austvågøy, Gimsøy, Vestvågøy, Flakstadøy, Moskenesøy, Vaerøy,** and **Røst.** The southernmost part of Norway's largest island, Hinnøy, is also in Lofoten. Vestfjorden separates the major islands from the mainland of Norway.

In winter, the Gulf Stream makes possible the world's largest cod-fishing event. Called **Lofotfisket,** it takes place between January and March, though this has dwindled in importance in recent years. Arctic sea cod spawn beyond Lofoten, especially in the Vestfjord, and huge harvesting operations are carried out between January and April.

The first inhabitants of the Lofoten Islands were nomads who hunted and fished, but excavations show that agriculture existed here at least 4,000 years ago. The Vikings pursued farming, fishing, and trading; examples of Viking housing sites can be seen on Vestbågøya, where more than 1,000 burial mounds have been found.

From the 14th century on, the people of Lofoten had to pay taxes to Bergen. This was the beginning of an economic dominance lasting for 6 centuries—first executed by the German Hanseatic tradesmen and then by their Norwegian heirs.

Harsh treatment of local residents by the Nazis during the World War II was key in forging the famous Norwegian Resistance movement. Allied forces, which landed here to harass the German iron-ore boats sailing from Narvik, withdrew in June 1940. They evacuated as many Lofoten residents as they could to Scotland for the duration of the war.

Today the Lofotens have modern towns with shops, hotels, restaurants, and public transportation.

In addition to hotels, guesthouses, and campsites, the Lofoten Islands offer lodging in old traditional fishing cottages known as *rorbuer.* The larger (often two-story), usually more modern version, is a *sjøhus* (sea house). The traditional *rorbu* was built right on the edge of the water, often on piles, with room for 10 bunks, a kitchen, and an entrance hall used as a work and storage room. Many *rorbuer* today are still simple and unpretentious, but some have electricity, a woodstove, a kitchenette with a sink, and running water. Others have been outfitted with separate bedrooms, private showers, and toilets. The best and most convenient booking agent is **Destination Lofoten** (see "Visitor Information," below).

ESSENTIALS

GETTING THERE On the eastern coast of Austvågøy, **Svolvær** is the largest town on the archipelago's largest island. It lacks the charm of the island's other fishing communities, but nothing tops it as a refueling stop. The port is a bit dull, but its surroundings of craggy backdrops and sheltered bays form a dramatic Lofoten backdrop. From Bodø, drive east on Route 80 to Fauske. Take E-6 north to Ulvsvåg and head southwest on Route 81 toward the town of Skutvik. From Skutvik, take the 1½-hour ferry to Svolvær (2–4 sailings daily). For ferry information and reservations, contact **Torghatten Nord** (✆ **81-00-30-30;** www.torghattennord.no). Passengers without cars pay NOK83 adults, NOK42 children, each way for passage to Svolvær from Skutvik. One-way transport of a car costs NOK286, which includes the driver. In 2007, the Lofast E-10 road was opened, which for the first time in history connected Svolvær to the mainland.

You can fly to Svolvær on **Widerøe,** which has seven flights a day from Bodø. For information, call ✆ **75-11-11-11** for reservations, or visit www.wideroe.no.

You can also travel the Lofotens by using a combination of rail, bus, and ferry. Many visitors take a train to Bodø and then transfer to a bus that crosses from Bodø to Svolvær on a ferry. Most bus departures from Bodø are timed to coincide with the arrival of trains from Oslo, Bergen, and other points. Buses also take passengers from elsewhere in Norway to Ulvsvåg, then on to Skutvik, where you can board a ferry to Svolvær. For information on train-bus-ferry connections, contact **Visit Bodø Office** (✆ **75-54-80-10**).

A coastal steamer, departing from Bodø at 3pm daily, also calls at Stamsund and Svolvær.

VISITOR INFORMATION Contact **Destination Lofoten,** PO Box 210, N-8301 Svolvær (✆ **76-06-98-00;** www.lofoten.info), on the harborfront in a big red building right in the middle of the town square. It's open January 1 to May 16 Monday to Friday 9am to 3:30pm; May 17 to June 6 Monday to Friday 9am to 4pm, Saturday 10am to 2pm; June 7 to June 20 Monday to Friday 9am to 8pm, Saturday 10am to 2pm, Sunday 4 to 8pm; June 21 to August 8 Monday to Friday 9am to 10pm, Saturday 9am to 8pm, Sunday 10am to 8pm; August 9 to August 22 Monday to Friday 9am to 8pm, Saturday 10am to 2pm; August 23 to December 31 Monday to Friday 9am to 3:30pm.

GETTING AROUND At the tourist office at Svolvær, you can pick up a free pamphlet, *Lofoten Info-Guide,* with information about all ferries and buses throughout the archipelago. All inhabited islands are linked by ferry, and buses service the four major islands, including Svolvær. Motorists can drive the E-10 from Svolvær to the outer rim of Lofoten, a distance of 130km (81 miles). One of the **great drives ★★ in the north of Norway,** this route will give you a good overall look at the Lofotens.

My preferred method of getting around the Lofotens is by bike. Cycles can be rented at most of the archipelago's little hotels.

Svolvær

This bustling (well, bustling for the Lofotens, that is) modern port town is on the island of **Austvågøy,** the northernmost in the archipelago. Most of the Lofoten cultural attractions are within an easy reach if you decide to base here. Svolvær attracts the most visitors and has some of the area's best hotels and restaurants. Still, the most adventurous travelers will make use of it as a transit point and place to stock up on supplies before heading out to more remote destinations.

SEEING THE SIGHTS

Lofoten Krigsminnemuseum, Fiskergata 12 (✆ **91-73-03-28;** www.lofoten krigmus.no), is the finest museum in the north devoted to the tragic World War II era. There's a little-known collection of 1940s photographs, some of which document the 1941 commando raid on the islands. Also on display is a collection of military uniforms. Admission is NOK40 for adults and children. It's open only from mid-May to mid-August Monday to Saturday 10am to 10pm, and Sunday noon to 3pm and 6 to 10pm. The rest of the year it's open a few hours each day, though when exactly can vary wildly.

Daredevils are lured to Svolvær in an attempt to conquer the most daring (and dangerous) climb in the Lofotens. They surmount the **Svolværgeita (Svolværur goat),** at 40m (131 ft.). This stone column is perched on a hill behind the port and is known for its two pinnacles, which locals have labeled the horn or horns of a goat. There's a 1.5m (5-ft.) jump between the two "horns"; if you don't make it, you're as good as dead.

One of the most dramatic boat rides in the Lofotens is the short trip into the impossibly narrow **Trollfjord ★★**, stretching for 2km (1¼ miles). This is part of the channel that separates the Lofoten island of Austvågøy from the Vesterålen island of Hinnøya. Coastal steamers can barely navigate this narrow passage without scraping the rock walls on either side. One of the most visited sites in the Lofotens, this fjord cuts its way westward from the Straits of Raftsundet, opening onto an idyllic Lofoten landscape, famed as the subject of many paintings.

Trollfjord is the easternmost island in Lofoten and was the scene of the Battle of the Trollfjord, as related by Johan Bojer in his novel *The Last Viking*. The battle, which took place more than a century ago between fishermen in small vessels and those in larger steamships, was first recorded on canvas by one of its witnesses, the artist Gunnar Berg (1863–93). His painting is on view at the Svolvær Town Hall. Ask at the tourist office (see "Visitor Information," above) about linking up with a boat tour of Trollfjord. Departures are from late April to September, costing NOK350 per adult, NOK150 children.

For the best and most scenic walks in the area, take the ferry ride over to the islet of **Skrova.** Here you can stroll around and leisurely take in the seascapes. Before heading over, pick up the makings of a picnic at one of the shops in Svolvær and prepare to enjoy it in splendid isolation. You can visit Skrova either via the express boats from Svolvær to Bodø/Narvik or the car ferry between Svolvær and Skutvik. The crossing to Skrova takes half an hour and costs roughly NOK80 per person. Additionally, the boat from Skutvik to Svolvær stops at Skrova.

WHERE TO STAY

Anker Brygge ★★ ☺ On a tiny island in the middle of Svolvær harbor and connected with a bridge to the "mainland," this is one of the most atmospheric lodging choices in the area. The quay-side structure dates from 1880, when it was a fish-landing station with its own saltery and barrel factory. In 1996, it was converted into an inn. Guests can stay in individual red-painted cottages that are rustically adorned with timbers but also have all the modern conveniences. Cabins, called *rorbu* cabin suites, can sleep up to six guests, so they're ideal for families. Each *rorbu* cabin is distinctively furnished; you may feel as if you're staying at some remote lodge in the wilds of a far northern frontier post. Two dozen odd *rorbu* suites are on the quay side or along the shore, with views of the harbor and the Lofoten mountains.

Lamholmen, N-8300 Svolvær. www.anker-brygge.no. ✆ **76-06-64-80.** Fax 76-06-64-70. 80 units. NOK1,350 double; NOK2,390 cottages and suites for 2–6 people. Rates include continental breakfast. AE, DC, MC, V. **Amenities:** Restaurant (closed Jan–Feb); bar; sauna. *In room:* TV.

Svinøya Rorbuer ★★ Nothing comes as close to an authentic Lofoten experience as staying in one of these cottages across a bridge on the island of Svinøya, site of Svolvær's first settlement. You'll be welcomed at the reception area, which was once the general store for the community and was the first shop ever to open in Svolvær. Then you'll be shown to one of the red historic restored cabins. The main building is from 1820, some of the cabins are from the 19th century, and others are modern but constructed in the old style. All of these fishermen's cabins are furnished to a high standard. Extra amenities include a well-equipped kitchen. The inn contains the town's best restaurant, the Børson Spiseri (see below).

Gunnar Bergs vei 2, N-8300 Svolvær. www.svinoya.no. ✆ **76-06-99-30.** 30 cabins. NOK1,000–NOK2,970 double. Rates include continental breakfast. AE, DC, MC, V. **Amenities:** Restaurant; bar; Jacuzzi. *In room:* Kitchen (in some), no phone, Wi-Fi.

WHERE TO DINE

Børson Spiseri ★ SEAFOOD The town's best restaurant is housed in the previously recommended Svinøya Rorbuer (see above) across a bridge on the island of Svinøya. I'd come here for the atmosphere alone, but fortunately the food is just as first-rate. The restaurant has been installed in an old quay-side building from 1828, a setting for an "arctic menu" that features some of the freshest fish I've ever consumed in the north. The setting is old-fashioned, with antiques from 2 centuries ago, along with maritime artifacts such as fishing equipment and old boats. The chef dishes out specialties such as deep-fried cod tongue with sour cream, traditional Lofoten dried cod with bacon and potatoes, and filet of salmon fried in butter and accompanied by mussels or else grilled stockfish with a fennel risotto.

Gunnar Bergs vei 2. ✆ **76-06-99-30.** Reservations recommended. Main courses NOK265–NOK309. AE, DC, MC. Daily 5–10pm. Closed Jan and Mon in winter.

Vaerøy

Remote craggy Vaerøy, along with the even more remote island of Røst, is to the far southwest of the Lofoten archipelago and is a bird-watcher's paradise. Vaerøy's **Mount Mostadfjell ★★** is the nesting place for more than 1.5 million seabirds, including sea eagles, auks, puffins, guillemots, kittiwakes, cormorants, arctic terns, eider petrels, gulls, and others that breed from May to August.

Vaerøy's population is only 750 hearty souls who live on an island of Lilliputian fishing villages; white-sand beaches open onto Arctic-chilled waters, towering ridges, and seabird rookeries.

Ferries from Bodø (✆ **76-96-76-00**) arrive here in 4½ hours and cost NOK525 for a one-way passage with car. For passengers without a car, it's NOK147 each way. There is also a ferry link from Moskenes that takes less than 2 hours, costing NOK210 one-way.

If you have the wherewithal, you could also travel quickly and in style from Bodø to Værøy by helicopter (✆ **77-60-83-00;** www.lufttransport.no).

SEEING THE SIGHTS

The hamlet of **Sørland** lies to the east and south of the mountainous area on the island. At Nordland there is a large pebble beach, **Mollbakken,** right by the road from Sørland. Several burial sites from the Stone Age and also the Viking age have been found here.

The mighty bird cliffs of Mount Mostadfjell are on the southwesterly side, facing the ocean. During the summer, trips to these cliffs are organized every day. Contact the tourist office (see above) for more information. If you don't like to join groups, you can explore on your own, as many hiking trails lead to the bigger of the seabird rookeries. One jaunt starts at the end of the route curving along the north of the island 6km (3¾ miles) from Sørland. This is my favorite walk in the remote southern islands because it not only has the best bird-watching in Norway, but it also leads rather eerily over the Isthmus of Eidet to the almost abandoned fishing village of **Mastad,** which opens onto the rugged waters of the eastern shore. At one time, some 150 inhabitants lived here, catching puffins as a source of income, then curing the meat in salt. An unusual puffin dog, called the Mastad, was used to catch the puffins.

Those with a good amount of stamina—and a good set of hamstrings—might venture to make the steep climb from Mastad up to the **Måhornet peak,** at 435m (1,427 ft.). Allow 1 arduous hour each way.

The only man-made attraction at Vaerøy is the Vaerøy **Kirke,** a wooden church with an onion-shaped dome at Nordland. It was taken apart and moved from the village of Kabelvåg and reassembled at Vaerøy in 1799. This is the oldest church in Lofoten. The altarpiece, from around 1400, is a late medieval English alabaster relief, depicting the Annunciation, the three Magi (or wise men), the Resurrection, and the Ascension. The church is usually open to visitors in summer but keeps no regular hours.

WHERE TO STAY & DINE

Gamle Prestegård (Old Vicarage) ★ 🎁 Built in 1898, this used to be the residence of a Lutheran priest. The hotel is run and owned by the charming Hege Sørli, who welcomes guests in style. Her rooms have been modernized and are tastefully and comfortably furnished. Five of the units contain a small bathroom with shower; guests in the other accommodations share the adequate public facilities. Sometimes it's possible to arrange to have dinner here. She doesn't keep a sign out, but it's the house to the left of the church.

N-8063 Vaerøy. www.prestegaarden.no. © **76-09-54-11.** 11 units. NOK690 double with shared bathroom; NOK790 double with private bathroom. Rates include buffet breakfast. No credit cards.

Kornelius Kro Restaurant NORWEGIAN The most popular venue in town is this 110-seat restaurant, installed in a modern building at the Kornelius Kro hotel, which offers a number of sizable red-sided cabins (NOK1,350 double for up to 4 people). It is decorated with antique fish netting and nautical equipment. The lounge bar with its cozy fireplace is enjoyed by both locals and visitors. You can eat dinner by firelight or candlelight. Everything is very informal here, and the place is always open in summer (but only for groups in winter). You might begin with a shrimp cocktail, then move to the Norwegian salmon, cod, or steak with vegetables—as wonderfully hearty a meal as you can get up in these parts.

Sørland. © **76-09-50-10.** Meals NOK179–NOK235. MC, V. Daily 7–9am and 5–10pm.

Narvik

301km (187 miles) NE of Bodø, 1,647km (1,021 miles) NE of Bergen, 1,479km (917 miles) N of Oslo

This ice-free seaport on the Ofotfjord is in Nordland *fylke* (county or province), 403km (250 miles) north of the Arctic Circle. Narvik, founded in 1903 when the Ofoten (not to be confused with "Lofoten") railway line was completed, boasts Europe's most modern shipping harbor for iron ore. It's also the northernmost electrified railway line in the world. It covers a magnificent scenic route, through precipitous mountain terrain and tunnels, over ridges, and across tall stone embankments.

Only 11km (6¾ miles) from Narvik, Straumsnes station is the last permanent habitation you'll encounter as you go east. The last Norwegian station, Bjørnfjell, is well above the timberline and about 3 hours from Kiruna, Sweden, some 140km (87 miles) north of the Arctic Circle. You can catch a train at Kiruna to Stockholm. If you're driving from Kiruna to Narvik, take Route 98 heading northwest to E-6 heading southwest toward Narvik.

Narvik played a focal role in World War II history. On April 9, 1940, 10 Nazi destroyers entered Narvik waters to sink two Norwegian battleships. On April 10, a series of five British destroyers arrived to take the German boats on in combat. The tragic battle at sea resulted in the sinking of two destroyers on each side.

On April 12, the British sent planes to attack German forces. Allied soldiers were successful in reclaiming Narvik by late May. However, the victory was only momentary. In early June, the Nazis came back to decimate Narvik. The port of Narvik became a graveyard not only of many men, but also of ships from Germany, Britain, Norway, France, and the Netherlands. On June 8, 1940, Narvik surrendered to the invading Nazis, who remained in the city until the Allies chased them out on May 8, 1945.

Modern, rebuilt Narvik can be something of an eyesore at times. Still, its setting right amid panoramic forests, majestic fjords, and towering mountains makes it an appealing choice worth a visit. As an added plus, the midnight sun shines here from May 27 to July 19.

ESSENTIALS

GETTING THERE From the Lofoten Islands, catch the car-ferry to Skutvik, operating three times a day. Follow Route 81 northeast to the junction with E-6, and then take E-6 north to Bognes. Cross the Tysfjord by ferry and continue north on E-6 to Narvik.

The train from Stockholm to Narvik (several weekly) takes 19 to 23 hours. From Stockholm to Narvik, the train costs from NOK760 one-way (the prices vary per day). There are also two buses a day from Fauske/Bodø (5 hr.). Check www.sj.se, www.bokatag.se, or www.177.no for information.

VISITOR INFORMATION The **Narvik Tourist Office** is at the railway station at Stasjonsveien 1 (✆ **46-92-24-66;** www.destinationnarvik.com). It's open Monday to Friday 10am to 3pm; June to August, it's also open on Saturday 9am to 2pm.

SEEING THE SIGHTS

To get a good look at Narvik, take the **Gondolbanen cable car** (✆ **76-97-72-82;** www.narvikfjellet.com), whose departure point is located directly behind the Norlandia Narvik Hotel, a 10-minute walk from the town center. The car operates from March to October, and the round-trip fare is NOK100 for adults, NOK80 for children 6 to 15 (free for 5 and under). In just 13 minutes, it takes you to an altitude of

640m (2,099 ft.), at the top of Fagernesfjell. Here you can soak in the impressive panorama of the town and its surroundings or visit the simple restaurant at the tip.

From the peak here, you can "hike till you drop," as one local advised us. Marked trails branch out in several directions, all equally impressive. A downhill mountain bike trail also starts near the cable car's final stop. From mid-February to mid-June and in August and September, the cable operates Monday to Friday from 1 to 9pm and every Saturday and Sunday from 10am to 5pm. From mid-June to the end of July, it operates daily from noon to 1am.

Nordland Røde Kors Krigsminnemuseum (War Museum) Near Torghallen in the town center, this museum re-creates the tragic events of the early 1940s, revisiting the epic struggle of the Narvik campaign of 1940 and the dreaded years of Nazi occupation from 1940 to 1945. Events from Narvik's destruction by the Germans, who occupied it until the end of the World War II, are the focus here. Exhibits detail Germany's battle for Narvik's iron ore and how Nazi forces fought troops from France, Poland, and Norway, and a considerable British flotilla at sea. Experiences of the civilian population and foreign POWs are also highlighted.

Kongensgate. ✆ **76-94-44-26.** www.fred.no. Admission NOK60, NOK35 children. Late Apr to early June Mon–Sat 10am–4pm, Sun noon–4pm; early June to late Aug Mon–Sat 10am–9pm, Sun noon–6pm; late Aug to late Apr Mon–Fri 11am–3pm.

WHERE TO STAY & DINE

Pub und Kro INTERNATIONAL Less expensive and less formal than the Grand Royal's main dining room (see below), this cozy restaurant is one of the most popular venues for dining and drinking in town. The menu offers an array of fresh Norwegian dishes such as reindeer, cod filet, and a great pepper steak sided with fresh vegetables.

In the Quality Hotel Grand Royal, Kongensgate 64. ✆ **76-97-70-77.** Reservations recommended. Main courses NOK199–NOK355. AE, DC, MC, V. Mon–Fri 11am–11pm; Sat noon–11pm; Sun 1–9pm.

Quality Hotel Grand Royal ★ The monolithic exterior can be somewhat off-putting, but the Grand Royal is nevertheless the largest and best-equipped lodging in Narvik. It opens onto the main street in the town center, between the train station and the harbor. Built in the 1920s, it was originally named the Grand Royal because the late King Olav was a frequent visitor and his portraits adorn some of the public rooms. The comfortable, amply sized rooms are tastefully and traditionally furnished, and all but a handful have been renovated and upgraded. The artfully contemporary lobby bar is one of the most alluring cocktail bars in northern Norway. The Royal Blue, the finest restaurant in town, is also here.

Kongensgate 64, N-8501 Narvik. www.choicehotels.no. ✆ **76-97-70-00.** 119 units. NOK756–NOK1,352 double. Rates include buffet breakfast. AE, DC, MC, V. Bus: 14, 15, 16, or 17. **Amenities:** 2 restaurants; 2 bars; babysitting; sauna; rooms for those w/limited mobility. *In room:* TV, hair dryer, minibar, Wi-Fi.

NARVIK AFTER DARK

An animated (and sometimes hard-drinking) bar that attracts lots of good-looking locals from the younger set is **Telegrafen,** Dronningens gata 56 (✆ **76-95-43-00**), Narvik's reigning disco in town, with a good selection of beers and whiskeys. Bands occasionally play, and it's a good spot to come to catch telecasts of sporting events too.

NORTHERN NORWAY: TOWARD THE NORTH CAPE

Hammerfest: World's Northernmost Town

2,314km (1,435 miles) N of Bergen, 144km (89 miles) N of Alta, 2,195km (1,361 miles) N of Oslo

In his travelogue *Neither Here Nor There*, author Bill Bryson found Hammerfest to be an "agreeable enough town in a thank-you-God-for-not-making-me-live-here sort of way." However, locals, for their part, are quick to defend how civilized they are, pointing out that they were the first town in Europe to have electric street lighting while Paris and London were lit by gas.

That Hammerfest is here at all is a sort of miracle. The town was founded because of its natural harbor, a feature of town that is as important today as it was then. A hurricane flattened it in 1856, and one of Norway's worst fires leveled it again in 1890, the year the town got that street lighting. Hitler ordered that "no building be left standing" during the infamous Nazi retreat of 1945. But Hammerfest bounced back and has been attracting visitors from all over the world who use it as a base for exploring the North Cape in summer. Arctic hunters enjoy their last few drinks in cozy bars here before setting off on expeditions into the wilderness. You just might encounter a polar bear wandering the streets as you stroll back to your hotel.

But it will be oil, not tourism, fueling the economy of Hammerfest, at least for the next 30 years. In 2006, the pumps started sucking oil from the offshore oil wells, which are estimated to possess 195 billion cubic meters of the black gold. At present, running for some 145km (90 miles), the world's longest undersea pipeline goes from the mammoth natural gas fields in the Barents Sea to the small island of Melkøya out in the bay off the coast of Hammerfest.

The Hammerfest area stretches from Måsøy, near the North Cape, to Loppa in the south, the wide region including the rugged coasts along the Arctic Sea. The city lies 70° 39' 48" N and achieved its town status on July 7, 1789, making it the oldest town in northern Norway. But is Hammerfest really the world's northernmost town, as often claimed? Other communities exist north of here but locals say that they are villages—not towns.

A **Meridianstøtta,** or meridian column, stands on the Fuglenes peninsula, across from the harbor. The monument commemorates the work of scientists from Norway, Sweden, and Russia who conducted surveys at Hammerfest between 1816 and 1852 to establish a meridian arc between Hammerfest and the Danube River at the Black Sea. This led to an accurate calculation of the size and shape of Earth.

Today Hammerfest is a modern town with an open and unique atmosphere, where the town's square and harbor are natural meeting places.

ESSENTIALS

GETTING THERE If you don't take the coastal steamer, you can drive, although it's a long trek. From Oslo, take E-6 north until you reach the junction with Route 94 west. Hammerfest is at the end of Route 94. During the summer there are three buses a week from Oslo, which take 29 hours. SAS has daily flights from Oslo and Bergen to Alta, where you can catch a bus to Hammerfest (Apr–Sept only). For bus information, call **Veolia Transport** (✆ **78-40-70-00;** www.veolia.no).

VISITOR INFORMATION The **Hammerfest Tourist Office,** Havnegata 3 (**© 78-41-21-85;** www.hammerfest-turist.no), in the town center, is open in summer daily from 9am to 5pm, in winter daily 10am to 2pm. The tourist office also organizes hour-long sightseeing tours departing at 11:30am and costing NOK220.

SEEING THE SIGHTS

This is the world's northernmost town of significant size and a port of call for North Cape coastal steamers. Sami from nearby camps often come into town to shop. Count yourself lucky if they bring their reindeer.

The port is free of ice year-round, and shipping and exporting fish is a major industry. The sun doesn't set from May 12 to August 1, and it doesn't rise from November 21 to January 23.

For the best panoramic view of the town, take a zigzag walk up the 72m (236-ft.) **Salen** "mountain." Atop Salen is a 6m-tall (20-ft.) square tower, with walls built of gray and blue stones. The old tower was torn down during World War II but was restored in 1984. On a clear day, you can see the offshore islands.

There is also a Sami "turf hut" here, **Mikkelgammen,** which can be booked 2 days in advance if you'd like to have a Sami meal here. Guests gather around a campfire for a traditional three-course meal, or *bidos*. You'll get reindeer soup as well as reindeer meat for your main course, followed by arctic cloudberries in whipped cream. The cost of the meal is NOK245 per person. It is followed by a Sami program called *Joik,* which consists of chantlike singing and stories about life in the far north.

Why not take time to do as 230,000 others have and join the **Royal and Ancient Polar Bear Society** (**© 78-41-31-00**) here? Apply in person while you're in Hammerfest. Membership costs a one-time fee of NOK180, and some proceeds are used to protect endangered arctic animals through conservation programs. The society's building is filled with stuffed specimens of arctic animals, and there is a free exhibition. The society is in the same building as the tourist office. There's a small museum devoted to the hunting heyday of Hammerfest, which lasted from 1910 to 1950, when eagles, arctic foxes, and polar bears were trapped by the English, and by German officers during World War II. It's in the basement of the town hall, on Rådhuspladsen. The center is open only June to August Monday to Friday from 6am to 6pm, and during the winter from 9am to 3pm.

Located a 5-minute walk from the harbor, **Hammerfest Kirke (Church),** Kirkegate 33 (**© 78-40-29-20;** www.kirken.hammerfest.no), was consecrated in 1961 and is known for its avant-garde architecture. Unusual for a church, this *kirke* doesn't have an altarpiece. Instead, you get a large and detailed stained-glass window that is quite beautiful. The altarpiece is found in a hall lying to the right of the main sanctuary. Local carver Knit Arnesen carved the friezes, depicting the history of Hammerfest. Note the chapel across from the church. Dating from 1933, it is the only structure in Hammerfest to survive the Nazi scorched earth retreat. Admission is free, and the church is open in summer from Monday to Friday 9am to 3pm.

WHERE TO STAY

Rica Hotel Hammerfest ★ The town's largest hotel has been kept up fairly well, though parts of it can feel a bit grim and foreboding. It's a mite more comfortable than the Thon, although lacks its character. The best appointed and most spacious accommodations in Hammerfest are here in the form of a junior suite here. The largest hotel in town was built in the mid-1970s on steeply sloping land and has been regularly spruced up since then. The standard, midsize guest rooms are decorated with Nordic-inspired pastels, but the look is strictly functional.

Sørøygata 15, N-9600 Hammerfest. www.rica.no. ✆ **78-42-57-00.** 80 units. NOK1,200–NOK1,795 double; NOK1,600–NOK2,295 junior suite. AE, DC, MC, V. **Amenities:** Restaurant; bar; disco; babysitting; fitness center; sauna. *In room:* TV, hair dryer, minibar, Wi-Fi.

Thon Hotel Hammerfest ★ The entire hotel is currently under renovation, but is due to open by early 2011. Thon opens onto views of the harbor, standing right on the Rådhuspladsen (Town Hall Square). Built in 1964, the good-size bedrooms are tastefully and comfortably furnished in modern Scandinavian decor, each with a small bathroom with a shower. Suites open onto views of the harbor. The staff can arrange such adventures as rides in a snowmobile or on horseback, and can advise about fishing in local waters. The on-site trio of bars is livelier than the watering hole at the Rica (above).

Strandgt. 2–4, N-9600 Hammerfest. www.thonhotels.com. ✆ **78-42-96-00.** 50 units. NOK1,745 double; from NOK1,890 minisuite. Rates include buffet breakfast. AE, DC, MC, V. Closed Dec 20–Jan 2. **Amenities:** Restaurant; 3 bars; room service; sauna; rooms for those w/limited mobility. *In room:* TV, hair dryer, minibar, Wi-Fi.

WHERE TO DINE

Hammerfest Mat og Vinhagen ★★ NORTHERN NORWEGIAN A recent change of management has updated this rustic restaurant, which first became famous in the late 1990s when a Trondheim radio station voted it the best restaurant in Norway. It's adjacent to the town's largest pier, overlooking the harbor. Inside, every effort has been made to simulate the wild splendor of northern Norway, with the use of roughly textured wood, stone, and many yards of natural hemp knotted into ropes that form curtains. The kitchen opens to the dining room, adding to the cozy feel.

Many recipes and ingredients are derived from northern Norway, with an emphasis on fish and game. You might try reindeer filet carpaccio, or sun-dried carp filet, served with mustard sauce.

Strandgata 24. ✆ **78-41-37-66.** Reservations recommended. Main courses from NOK245. AE, DC, MC, V. Mon–Thurs 2:30–11pm; Fri 1–11pm; Sat 6–11pm.

HAMMERFEST AFTER DARK

A recently opened club, **Oppe og Nede** (✆ **90-59-29-30;** http://onhammerfest.blogspot.com), also known as ON, has become the hottest place to be seen in town. Also a restaurant serving decent Scandinavian main courses, it is better known for its dance floor and a bar across two separate floors. The upper floor tends to be strictly for twenty-, thirty-, and forty-somethings, while the downstairs bar (weekends only) is usually filled with teenagers. It is open Monday from 10:30am to 3pm, Tuesday from to Thursday 10:30am to 1am, Friday from 10:30am to 3am, Saturday from 11am to 3am, and Sunday 3pm to 10pm. Until the renovation on the Thon Hotel Hammerfest is completed (the hotel has three places for nightlife—Banyean, Hans Highness, and the generic hotel bar), this is your best option in town.

Honningsvåg & the North Cape ★★

130km (81 miles) NE of Hammerfest, 2,444km (1,515 miles) NE of Bergen

You have to journey a long way to see **Nordkapp (North Cape),** the most celebrated attraction in northern Norway. More proximate to the north pole than to Oslo, the mighty rock stands at a latitude of 71° 10' 21" N. The attraction is generally viewed from mid-May to the end of July, when the midnight sun does not drop below the horizon. Before you've come all this way, I'll let you in on a secret. Nordkapp is touted as the northernmost point of continental Europe, although it actually isn't (see our box, "Europe's Real Northernmost Point," below). To the Sami, the North Cape held great religious significance and was a site for sacrifices. The name of North Cape came from the British explorer, Richard Chancellor, who drifted here in 1553 when on the hunt for the Northeast Passage.

Considered the world's northernmost fishing village, the gateway to the North Cape is a completely modern fishing harbor set in a land of forests, fjord waters, and crashing waterfalls, everything bathed in summer by the eerie light of the midnight sun. Only the chapel withstood the village's destruction by Germans in 1944. It's some 80km (50 miles) nearer to the north pole than Hammerfest, on the Alta-Hammerfest bus route.

Honningsvåg is on the southern side of the island of Magerøy, connected to the North Cape by a 35km (22-mile) road.

ESSENTIALS

GETTING THERE If you don't take the coastal steamer (visit www.hurtigruten.com for information), you can reach Honningsvåg by car. From Oslo (a very long trip—about 30 hr. June–Sept), take E-6 north to the junction with Route 95 north. Since an underwater tunnel was opened in 1999, it is now possible to drive all the way out to the Honningsvåg and North Cape without use of a ferry. Both SAS and Norwegian fly from Oslo and Bergen to Alta; SAS and Widerøe fly from Alta onto Honningsvåg. There are also direct, year-round buses from Alta to both Hammerfest and Honningsvåg. For bus information, call **Veolia Transport** (✆ **78-40-70-00**).

VISITOR INFORMATION The **North Cape Tourist Office,** in the Nordkapphuset (✆ **78-47-70-30;** www.nordkapp.no), can give you information on sightseeing boat trips, museums, walks, and deep-sea fishing. The office is open mid-June to mid-August Monday to Friday from 8:30am to 8pm, Saturday noon to 8pm; mid-August to mid-June Monday to Friday 9:30am to 3:30pm.

A SPECIAL EVENT The **North Cape Festival,** held for 1 week in mid-June each year, presents a wide display of local culture. During the festival, participants in the **North Cape March** trek from Honningsvåg to the North Cape and back, a total of around 70km (43 miles).

SEEING THE SIGHTS

Check at the tourist office (see above) about organized tours of the area. In the summer, tours visit the splendid bird colony on the little island of **Gjesvaerstappan ★★**. All sorts of arctic seabirds, including kittiwakes, skuas, razorbills, gannets, puffins, and cormorants, can be seen on the cliffs, along with seals. The details of each tour will vary according to the molting and breeding seasons of the birds, so for further information about tours available at the time of your visit, contact **Birdsafari** (✆ **78-47-57-73;** www.birdsafari.com). You will need to get to Gjesvær village, either by taxi or local bus (see www.veolia-transport.no for bus transport details).

Nordkapphallen The North Cape Hall visitor center has a video presentation and museum exhibits. Downstairs you'll find an excellent video and a cave with a panoramic window facing the Arctic Ocean. On the way to the cave, you'll see several scenes from the history of the North Cape. A monument commemorates the visit of King Oscar (king of Norway and Sweden) to the Cape in 1873, and another exhibit commemorates the arrival of King Chulalongkorn of Siam (now Thailand) who came for a look at the Cape in 1907. There's also a monument marking the terminus of the

"Midnight Sun Road." You might be dismayed at the steep entrance price, but the exhibits and the views from within manage to artfully and effectively evoke the drama of the far north. Call before you visit; even in high season, open hours and days are subject to change without notice, and it's firmly closed between October and March.

Nordkapp. ✆ **78-47-68-60.** www.nordkapp.no. Admission NOK215-NOK235 adults, NOK75-NOK80 children 17 and under, NOK505-NOK550 family. May 1-May 17 daily 11am-3pm; May 18-Aug 17 daily 11am-1am; Aug 18-31 daily 11am-10pm; Sept 1-30 daily 11am-3pm; Oct 1-Apr 30 12:30-4pm (access during these months by convoy only). For bus reservation, contact local Veolia Transport (✆ 78-47-58-44; www.veolia-transport.no) by 3pm the day before travel.

Nordkappmuseet This museum displays the cultural history of the North Cape, including fishery artifacts and an exhibit that details the effects of World War II on the North Cape. The museum lies at the harbor and town center, a 3-minute walk from the coastal steamer and the Rica Hotel Honningsvåg.

In the Nordkapphuset, Fiskeriveien 4. ✆ **78-47-28-33.** www.nordkappmuseet.no. Admission NOK50, NOK20 children 6-16, free for children 5 and under. June 5-Aug 15 Mon-Sat 11am-8pm, Sun noon-7pm; Aug 16-June 4 Mon-Fri noon-4pm.

WHERE TO STAY

Honningsvåg Brygge ★ This hotel in the center of town has plenty of character. The family-run establishment served as a fish factory until the 1970s, when the owners decided to convert it into a hotel. Since then, discerning travelers to the North Cape have been making their way here for quiet nights in contemporary-meets-rustic decor. There is exposed wood everywhere—walls, ceiling, and floors—but the furnishings are modern. Bedrooms are small to midsize, each cozy and comfortably furnished. It also has an excellent, first-rate restaurant serving a number of Arctic Ocean delicacies.

Vagen 1A, N-9751 Honningsvåg. www.hvg-brygge.no. ✆ **78-47-64-64.** 27 units. NOK1,100-NOK1,300 double; NOK1,350-NOK1,800 suite. Children 11 and under stay free in parent's room. Rates include continental breakfast (during summer only). AE, DC, MC, V. **Amenities:** Restaurant; bar; rooms for those w/limited mobility. *In room:* No phone.

Rica Hotel Honningsvåg The North Cape's northernmost hotel is centrally located near the quay. Advance reservations are strongly advised. This five-story, yellow-fronted building features guest rooms that offer views of the harbor and fairly standard furnishings. The rooms and bathrooms are on the small side (each has its own shower), but the beds are comfortable enough. There are two on-site restaurants, the Caroline and the Grillen. The hotel also runs an unpretentious grill and offers disco action on Friday and Saturday nights. The hotel is entirely nonsmoking.

Storgata 4, N-9751 Honningsvåg. www.rica.no. ✆ **78-47-72-20.** 174 units. NOK1,430-NOK1,680 double. Rates include buffet breakfast. AE, DC, MC, V. Closed in winter. **Amenities:** Restaurant; lounge; sauna; rooms for those w/limited mobility. *In room:* TV.

WHERE TO DINE

Corner NORWEGIAN Ever tried arctic pizza? This is the place for it, along with an array of other regional dishes. Many local fishermen as well as international visitors flock here for good, affordable food. The 1960s building and decor don't necessarily appeal to refined tastes, but the chef will feed you well at a reasonable price. There are no appetizers to speak of, but the main courses are generous. Your best bet is the grilled and locally caught salmon, which comes with fresh vegetables and potatoes. You can also order fresh grilled cod or halibut. Meat eaters may find the veal

Europe's Real Northernmost Point

It comes as a surprise to some visitors that the Continent's actual northernmost point is not the North Cape, but Knivskjelodden, which is west of the cape. Europe's northernmost point is at 71° 11′ 08″ N. You can hike the trail, which is not too difficult if you're in good shape. Wear sturdy boots, of course. Figure on about 5 hours there and back. Once here, you'll have a panoramic sweep ★ of the North Cape Plateau. After you've walked the world's northernmost hiking trail, you can sign your name in the hiking association's minute book at Knivskjelodden.

To reach Knivskjelodden, head southwest from the North Cape for 6km (3¾ miles) until you reach a car park. Once at the car park, you still have 3km (2 miles) to go to the northernmost point from the beginning of the Knivskjelodden Track. In all, it's a round-trip of 18km (11 miles) from the North Cape.

schnitzel satisfying. No matter what main course you choose, finish your meal with a slice of apple pie and ice cream. A live band sometimes entertains in the adjoining bar.

Fiskerveien 2A. ✆ **78-47-63-40.** Main courses NOK175–NOK259. AE, DC, MC, V. Summer Mon–Thurs 10am–11:30pm; Fri–Sat 10am–2am; Sun noon–11:30pm. Closed winter.

A Trip to the North Cape

The **Nordkapp (North Cape)** symbolizes the "top of Europe." In prehistoric times, the North Cape Horn was a Sami place of sacrifice. The North Cape's name used to be Knyskanes, but, in 1553, it was renamed "North Cape" by the Lord Richard Chancellor of England, who was searching for a sea passage to China. The road to the North Cape is open to traffic from May 1 to October 20.

The first tour ships arrived in 1879. They anchored in Hornvika Bay, and the visitors had to climb 280m (918 ft.) up to the plateau. After the road from Honningsvåg opened in 1956, the flow of tourists turned into a flood. In summer, buses to the North Cape leave daily from outside the tourist office at Fergeveien 4 at Honningsvåg, stop briefly at the ferry terminal across from the North Cape Hostel, and then continue to the visitor center at the North Cape. The one-way passage from Honningsvåg to the North Cape, a travel time of 45 minutes, is NOK120 adults, NOK80 children 17 and under. For more information, call **Veolia Transport** (✆ **78-47-58-40;** www.veolia-transport.no).

On the road to the Cape is a Sami encampment. It's a bit contrived, but visitors do have an opportunity to go inside one of the tents, and they come away with an idea of how nomadic Sami used to live.

THE BEST OF SWEDEN

12

In the towns and cities of Scandinavia's largest country, you can let yourself be dazzled by the contemporary or wander back to a bygone era. From the castles and palaces in the south to the barren tundra of Lapland, we have combed this vast land of forests, lakes, and glacier-ringed mountains to bring you the best.

THE best TRAVEL EXPERIENCES

- **Soaking Up Local Culture:** Home to a great cultural tradition, Sweden is acclaimed for its symphony orchestras, theater, ballet (including the renowned Swedish Cullberg Ballet), and opera companies. During the long days of summer, open-air concerts are staged all over the country (local tourist offices can provide details). Many concerts, especially those featuring folk dancing and regional music, are free.
- **Seeing the Country from the Water:** Passengers glide through Sweden's scenic heartland, between Stockholm and Gothenburg, on a Göta Canal cruise. The route takes you along three of the country's largest lakes and through 58 carefully calibrated locks. The cruise, available between mid-May and mid-September, offers the best of Sweden in a nutshell. See chapter 17.
- **Exploring the Land of the Midnight Sun:** Above the Arctic Circle, the summer sun never dips below the horizon. You have endless hours to enjoy the beauty of the region and the activities that go with it, from hiking to white-water rafting. After shopping for distinctive wood and silver handicrafts, dine on filet of reindeer served with cloudberries, or climb rocks and glaciers in Sarek National Park. See "Swedish Lapland" in chapter 17.

THE best SCENIC TOWNS & VILLAGES

- **Lund:** This town, 18km (11 miles) northeast of Malmö, rivals Uppsala as a university town. It, too, is ancient—Canute the Great founded it in 1020. Centuries-old buildings, winding passages, and cobblestone streets fill Lund; its ancient cathedral is one of the finest expressions of Romanesque architecture in northern Europe. See chapter 16.

- **Jokkmokk:** Just north of the Arctic Circle, this is the best center for absorbing Sami culture. In early February, the Sami hold their famous "Great Winter Market" here, a tradition that's 4 centuries old. You can visit a museum devoted to Sami culture and then go salmon fishing in the town's central lake. See chapter 17.
- **Rättvik:** This great resort borders Lake Siljan in the heart of Dalarna, a province known for its regional painting, handicrafts, and folk dancing. Timbered houses characterize Dalarna's architecture, and on a summer night you can listen to fiddlers. See chapter 17.
- **Visby:** On the island of Gotland, this was once a great medieval European city and Viking stronghold. For 8 days in August, during Medieval Week, the sleepy Hanseatic town hosts an annual festival featuring fire-eaters, belly dancers, and jousting tournaments. With the ruins of 13th- and 14th-century churches and memories of prosperity, Visby is intriguing in any season. See chapter 17.

THE best ACTIVE VACATIONS

- **Fishing:** Sweden offers some of the world's best fishing in pristine lakes and streams, and you can even fish in downtown Stockholm. Many varieties of fresh and saltwater fish are available in Sweden's waters.
- **Golfing:** Many Swedes are obsessed with golf. Most courses, from the periphery of Stockholm to Björkliden (above the Arctic Circle), are open to the public, and enthusiasts can play under the midnight sun. Halland, south of Gothenburg, is called the Swedish Riviera, and it's the golf capital of the country. Båstad is the most fashionable resort in Halland, and you can play a game of golf here at two prestigious courses: the **Båstad Golf Club** in Boarp (© **0431/783-70;** www.bgk.se) and the **Bjäre Golf Club,** Salomonhög 3086 (© **0431/36-10-53;** www.bjaregolfklubb.se), both right outside the center of Båstad. See chapter 16.
- **Hiking:** The Kungsleden ("King's Trail") might provide the hike of a lifetime. It takes you through the mountains of Lapland, including Kebnekaise, which at 2,090m (6,965 ft.) is the highest mountain in Sweden. This 500km (310-mile) trail cuts through the mountains of Abisko National Park to Riksgränsen on the Norwegian frontier. For more information about this adventure, contact the **Svenska Turistföreningen (Swedish Touring Club),** Stureplan 4C, S-104 62 Stockholm (© **08/463-21-00;** www.stf.nu). The club will also provide information about hiking and outdoor venues in any season in each of Sweden's 25 provinces. See chapter 17.
- **Skiing:** In Lapland, you can enjoy both downhill and cross-country skiing year-round. In Kiruna, serious skiers head for the Kebnekaise mountain station, where there are dog-sledding and other winter sports. South of the city of Gällivare, you arrive at Dundret, or "Thunder Mountain," for some of the finest skiing in the north. The area's best hotel is **Dundret** (© **0970/145-60;** www.dundret.se), and its staff possesses all the expertise needed to link you up with both cross-country skiing and skiing on the downhill slopes. Inaugurated in 1955, its chairlift to the top of the slopes was the first of its kind in Sweden.
- **White-Water Rafting:** White-water enthusiasts gravitate to the northern stretches of the Klarälven River; aficionados of calmer waters move to points near its southern terminus. One of the most respected outfitters for excursions along any length of this historic river is **Vildmark in Värmland,** PO Box 209, SE-68525 Torsby (© **0560/14040;** www.vildmark.se). Established in 1980, it offers canoe excursions along the

northern lengths of the river between April and October, providing canoes, instruction, and all equipment. A 4-day experience covering about 48km downstream (30 miles) costs 2,570SEK per adult; a 7-day jaunt covering twice that distance costs 3,240SEK per person. Less structured trips are offered by a competitor in Värmland, 150km (93 miles) north of Karlstad. Here, you can contact **Branäs Sport,** Branäs Fritidsanläggnin, S-68060 Sysslebäck (✆ **054/132-600;** www.branas.se), an operation that devotes most of its time to the rental of cross-country skis.

THE best FESTIVALS & SPECIAL EVENTS

- **Walpurgis Eve:** One of Europe's great celebrations to welcome spring takes place in Sweden on April 30. Bonfires, songs, festivals, and all sorts of antics herald the demise of winter. The best—and rowdiest—celebrations are at the university cities of Umeå, Lund, Uppsala, Stockholm, and Gothenburg.
- **Stockholm Waterfestival:** In August, much of the city turns out for a weeklong festival along the waterfront. Theoretically, the concept behind the festival is water preservation, but entertainment ranges from concerts to fireworks.
- **Drottningholm Court Theater** (Drottningholm): In May, Sweden's cultural highlight is a series of 30 opera and ballet performances presented at this theater, which dates from 1766. The theater's original stage machinery and settings are still used. Drottningholm Palace (the "Versailles of Sweden") is on an island in Lake Mälaren, about 11km (7 miles) from Stockholm. See chapter 14.
- **Medieval Week** (Gotland): On Gotland, Swedes celebrate the Middle Ages for a week each August. Visby, especially, swarms with people in medieval garb. Many of them—from the blacksmith to the cobbler—tend market stalls as musicians play the hurdy-gurdy or fiddle, and jesters play the fool. A program of 100 medieval events, from tournaments to a nightly king's procession, is scheduled in Visby. See chapter 17.

THE best MUSEUMS

- **Royal Warship *Vasa*** (Stockholm): In the Djurgården, this 17th-century man-of-war—now a museum—is a popular tourist attraction and deservedly so. The *Vasa* is the world's oldest known complete ship. It capsized and sank on its maiden voyage in 1628 before horrified onlookers. The ship was salvaged in 1961 and has been carefully restored; 97% of its 700 original decorative sculptures were retrieved. See chapter 14.
- **Nationalmuseum (National Museum of Art,** Stockholm): One of the oldest museums in the world (2012 is its 220th birthday), the National Museum houses Sweden's treasure-trove of rare paintings and sculpture. From Rembrandt and Rubens to Bellini and van Gogh, a panoply of European art unfolds before your eyes. See chapter 14.
- **Millesgården** (Lidingö, outside Stockholm): Sweden's foremost sculptor, Carl Milles (1875–1955), lived here and created a sculpture garden by the sea. Milles relied heavily on mythological themes in his work, and many of his best-known pieces are displayed in what's now a museum. See chapter 14.

- **Göteborgs Konstmuseum** (Gothenburg): This is the city's leading art museum, a repository of modern painting that's strong on French Impressionism. Modern artists such as Picasso and Edvard Munch are also represented, as are sculptures by Milles. See chapter 15.
- **Åjtte** (Jokkmokk): This is the best repository of artifacts of the Sami people. Integrating nature with culture, the museum depicts how the Sami lived and struggled for survival in a harsh terrain, and shows the houses they lived in and the animals and weapons needed for their livelihood. See chapter 17.

THE best OFFBEAT EXPERIENCES

- **Log-Rafting on the Klarälven River:** You can enjoy a lazy trip down the river, winding through beautiful, unspoiled valleys among high mountains, with sandy beaches where you can occasionally swim. There's excellent fishing for pike and grayling. You travel through northern Värmland at a speed of 2kmph (1¼ mph) from the mouth of the Vingängssjön Lake in the north to Edebäck in the south. It takes 6 days to cover the 110km (68 miles). Overnight accommodations are on the moored raft or ashore. Each raft can accommodate two to five people, and the trips are available from May to August. Participants in the rafting expeditions down the Klarälven River will make their own rafts on the first day of the experience (it can last 1, 2, 3, or 6 days, and incorporate some or all of the river's length). Pine logs are lashed together with rope. Other offerings include beaver- and elk-watching safaris, white-water rafting expeditions, and canoeing. Contact **Vildmark i Farmland,** PO Box 209, 68525 Torsby (✆ **0560/140-40;** www.vildmark.se).
- **Exploring the Orsa "Outback" by Horse & Covered Wagon:** In the province of Dalarna (central Sweden), you can rent a horse and covered wagon (with space for up to five) for a 3- or 5-day trek across the forest and tundra of the Orsa "outback," an almost unpopulated area of wild beauty. For more information, contact **Häst och Vagn Svante Inemyr,** Torsmo 1646, S-79491 Orsa (✆ **0250/55-30-14;** http://itadventure.se/hast.vagn). On-site, they have 18 horses and 60 huskies for dog-sledding tours.
- **Playing Golf by the Light of the Midnight Sun:** In a land where the Sami and reindeer still lead a nomadic life, you can play at the Björkliden Arctic Golf Course, some 240km (150 miles) north of the Arctic Circle (near the hamlet of Björkliden, 97km/60 miles west of Kiruna). The 9-hole course is open between late June and late August only. For information, contact the **Björkliden Arctic Golf Club** at ✆ **0980/641-00;** www.bjorklidensgolfklubb.se. The rest of the year, contact its affiliate, the Stockholm-based **Bromma Golf Course,** Kvarnbacksvägen 28, 16874 Bromma, Stockholm (✆ **08/564-888-40**). See chapter 14.
- **Seeing Lapland on a Safari:** On this tour you can explore the last wilderness of Europe and record your impressions on film. You can see Swedish Lapland up close and become acquainted with the Sami people's rich culture. Highlights include visits to old churches and village settlements (usually along a lake), and seeing reindeer. The outdoors outfitter **Borton Overseas** (✆ **800/843-0602;** www.bortonoverseas.com) offers summer tours of the tundra between May and early September, and winter tours of the snow-covered tundra from January to April. The winter is arguably the most beautiful time to see the tundra.

- **Riding the Rails of the Longest Stretch of Abandoned Railway Track in Europe:** Around 1900, a consortium of logging companies, with the help of the Swedish government, built a railway track running across a 180km (112-mile) stretch of forested wilderness between Dalarna and Värmland, beginning and ending in the hamlets of Perfberg and Venfbro. Trains stopped running along the track in 1967, and today the stretch of rails is part of Sweden's national patrimony. You can ride along these tracks in specially designed foot-pedaled trolleys, in tandem with up to four passengers. Since there's only one track, travel can become inconvenient if you meet up with another trolley headed in the opposite direction. An outfit that's highly experienced in this and many other forms of outdoor activities in the Swedish wilderness, during both summer and winter, is **Dalarnas & Värmlands Äentyrscentrum AB,** Ulfshittan 6, 78196 Borlänge, Sweden (© **0243/25-11-07;** www.dalarnasaventyr.se).

THE best BUYS

- **Glass:** In the deep woods of Småland, Swedish glasswork has helped set the world standard. Glass has been a local tradition since King Gustav Vasa invited Venetian glass blowers to come to Sweden in the 16th century. The first glass was melted here in 1556. The oldest name in Swedish glass, Kosta, was founded in 1742 and is now part of the Orrefors group, the best-known manufacturer. Fifteen major glassworks in Småland, which encompasses Växjö and Kalmar, are open to visitors. Glass is sold at department stores and specialty outlets throughout Sweden.
- **Handicrafts:** Designers create a wide variety of objects in wood, pewter, enamel, tapestry, brass, and even reindeer skins and antlers. Many handicrafts are based on Viking designs, and most objects are in the traditional Sami style. Shoppers eagerly seek wall textiles, leatherwork, hand-woven carpets, and embroidered items. Swedish cutlery and china are valued for their quality and craftsmanship. Stockholm has the widest selection of shops, and Gothenburg and other towns have specialty outlets.
- **Swedish Design:** Good design and craftsmanship are the hallmarks of Swedish housewares—swinging metal CD racks, wooden chickens on rockers, tea wagons, and more. One of the best places to find products of Swedish design is in the constantly changing display at **DesignTorget,** in the Kulturhuset (© **08/644-16-78;** www.designtorget.se) in the center of Stockholm. It's open daily year-round. See chapter 14.

THE best HOTELS

- **Grand Hotel** (S. Blasieholmshamnen 8, Stockholm; www.grandhotel.se; © **08/679-35-00;** p. 323): Opposite the Royal Palace, this is the most prestigious hotel in Sweden. Well-known guests have included celebrities and Nobel Prize winners. It dates from 1874 and is continuously renovated to keep it in excellent condition. The rooms are luxuriously decorated, and the bathrooms are Italian marble with heated floors.
- **Lady Hamilton Hotel** (Storkyrkobrinken 5, Stockholm; www.ladyhamiltonhotel.se; © **08/506-401-00;** p. 329): This is one of Old Town's stellar properties. It's made up of three buildings that have been artfully connected and provide sumptuously furnished accommodations for those who prefer an old-fashioned atmosphere.

- **Victory Hotel** (Lilla Nygatan 5, Stockholm; www.victory-hotel.se; ✆ **08/506-400-00;** p. 330): In the Old Town, this small but stylish hotel was built in 1642. It's famous for the treasure once buried here, part of which can be seen at the Stockholm City Museum. The well-furnished guest rooms typically have exposed beams and pine floors. On a small rooftop terrace, tables are arranged around a fountain.
- **Radisson Blu Scandinavia Hotel** (Södra Hamngatan 59–65, Gothenburg; www.radissonblu.com; ✆ **800/333-3333** in the U.S., or 031/758-50-00; p. 377): Fashioned in marble and glass with bay windows, this hotel, with innovative styling and beautiful architecture, is more than just a typical chain hotel. Balconies overlook a vast atrium with eye-catching elevators and trees. Amenities include everything from a gym and sauna to a well-equipped health club; the gourmet dining room has a bar.
- **Grand Hotel** (Bantorget 1, Lund; www.grandilund.se; ✆ **046/280-61-00;** p. 425): Since 1899 this has been the prestigious address for those visiting this university and cathedral city. Enlarged and much evolved over the years, it is a citadel of comfort, tradition, and charm for those visiting the southern tier of Sweden.

THE best RESTAURANTS

- **Operakällaren** (Operahuset, Karl XII's Torg, Kungsträdgården, Stockholm; ✆ **08/676-58-00;** www.eng.operakallaren.se; p. 332): This historic monument, part of the Royal Opera Complex, dates from 1787. The chef is a culinary adviser to the king and queen. This is the best place to sample Sweden's legendary *smörgåsbord*—a groaning table of delectable dishes with an emphasis on fresh fish. All the northern delicacies, from smoked eel and reindeer to Swedish red caviar and grouse, appear on the menu.
- **Mathias Dahlgren** (Stockholm; ✆ **08/679-35-84;** www.mathiasdahlgren.com; p. 331); In the Grand Hotel, this is one of the great restaurants of Sweden, and its most exclusive. Its namesake chef, for whom the restaurant is named, has been honored as "chef of the year" twice in the postmillennium. From a regional dish to a grand six-course tasting menu, Dahlgren will enthrall your taste buds.
- **Wedholms Fisk** (Nybrokajen 17, Stockholm; ✆ **08/611-78-74;** www.wedholmsfisk.se; p. 334): This classic Swedish restaurant serves some of the capital's finest local food, skillfully prepared with a French touch. Traditional and haute cuisine dishes have been modernized. Each dish seems guaranteed to ignite your enthusiasm, although nothing is showy or ostentatious. The fresh ingredients retain their natural flavor.
- **Sjömagasinet** (Klippans Kulturreservat, Adolph Edelsvärdsgata 5, Klippan, outside Gothenburg; ✆ **031/775-59-20;** www.sjomagasinet.se; p. 381). By far the most interesting restaurant in town, this is one of the finest seafood places on the west coast of Sweden. In a converted warehouse, it serves an array of fresh fish in wonderful concoctions, and the sauces and preparations never diminish the flavor of the seafood. *Pot-au-feu* of fish and shellfish with chive-flavored crème fraîche is worth the trek out of town.

INTRODUCING STOCKHOLM

13

Stockholm is the most regal, elegant, and intriguing city of Scandinavia. It presides over a country the size of California (without the massive population) and believes in high taxes and big government. It is one of the world's most liberal, progressive, and democratic societies, a devotee of such issues as same-sex unions and gender equality.

Because of Sweden's neutrality during World War II, it was saved from aerial bombardment. Much of what you see today is antique, especially the historical heart, Gamla Stan (the Old Town). Yet Sweden is one of the world's leading exponents of functionalism, or *funkis.* Swedish fashion and design in glassware, furnishings, and industrial products remain at the cutting edge.

Stockholm is built on 14 islands in Lake Mälaren, which marks the beginning of an archipelago of 24,000 islands, skerries, and islets stretching all the way to the Baltic Sea. A city of bridges and islands, towers and steeples, cobblestone squares and broad boulevards, Renaissance splendor and steel-and-glass skyscrapers, Stockholm also has access to nature just a short distance away.

Although the city was founded more than 7 centuries ago, it did not become the official capital of Sweden until the mid–17th century. Today, Stockholm reigns over a modern welfare state.

ORIENTATION

Arriving

BY PLANE You'll arrive at **Stockholm Arlanda airport** (**© 08/797-60-00;** www.arlanda.se for information on flights), about 45km (28 miles) north of the city on the E-4 highway. A long, covered walkway connects the international and domestic terminals.

Depending on traffic, the fastest, but not necessarily the cheapest, way to go from the airport to the Central Station within Stockholm is on the **Arlanda Express** train (www.arlandaexpress.com), which takes only 20 minutes and is covered by the Eurailpass. This high-speed line is the finest option for the rail traveler. Trains run every 15 to 20 minutes daily from 5am to midnight. If you don't have a rail pass, the cost of a one-way ticket is 240SEK for adults and 120SEK for seniors and students 8 to 25 (those 7 and under ride free). For more information, call **© 771/720-200.**

A slower (about 40 min.) but cheaper option involves taking a bus from outside the airport terminal building. It will take you to the **City Terminal** (www.flygbussarna.se), on Klarabergsviadukten, for 99SEK.

A taxi (www.flygtaxi.se) to or from the airport is expensive, costing 435SEK to 600SEK or more. (See "Getting Around," below, for the name of a reputable taxi company.)

BY TRAIN Trains arrive at Stockholm's **Centralstationen** (**Central Station; ✆ 07/717-57-575**) on Vasagatan, in the city center where connections can be made to Stockholm's subway, the T-bana. Follow the TUNNELBANA sign, which is sometimes abbreviated to merely the capital letter "T" in blue ink on a white background, enclosed in a blue circle.

Only large towns and cities can be reached by rail from Stockholm's Centralstationen.

BY BUS Buses also arrive at the Centralstationen city terminal, and from here you can catch the T-bana (subway) to your final Stockholm destination. For bus information or reservations, check with the bus system's **ticket offices** at the station (**✆ 08/588-228-28;** www.flygbussarna.se). Offices in the station labeled BUS STOP sell bus tickets. For travel beyond Sweden, call **Euroline** (**✆ 31/10-02-40;** www.eurolines.com).

BY CAR Getting into Stockholm by car is relatively easy because the major national expressway from the south, E-4, joins with the national expressway, E-3, coming in from the west, and leads right into the heart of the city. Stay on the highway until you see the turnoff for Central Stockholm (or Centrum).

Parking in Stockholm is extremely difficult unless your hotel has a garage. Call your hotel in advance and find out what the parking situation is, as most hotels do not offer parking. However, if you're driving into the city, you can often park long enough to unload your luggage; a member of the hotel staff will then direct you to the nearest parking garage.

BY FERRY Large ships, including those of the **Silja Line,** Sveavägen 14 (**✆ 08/22-21-40;** www.tallinksilja.com), and the **Viking Line,** Centralstationen (**✆ 08/452-40-00**), arrive at specially constructed berths jutting seaward from a point near the junction of Södermalm and Gamla Stan. This neighborhood is called Stadsgården, and the avenue that runs along the adjacent waterfront is known as Stadsgårdshamnen. The nearest T-bana stop is Slussen, a 3-minute walk from the Old Town. Holders of a valid Eurailpass can ride the Silja ferries to Helsinki and Turku at a reduced rate.

Other ferries arrive from Gotland (whose capital is Visby), but these boats dock at Nynäshamn, south of Stockholm. Take a Nynäshamn-bound bus from the Central Station in Stockholm or the SL commuter train to reach the ferry terminal at Nynäshamn.

Visitor Information

The **Stockholm Tourist Center,** Vasagatan 14 (**✆ 08/508-285-08**) is across from the Central Station. The office dispenses maps, brochures, and advice for free; tickets to sporting and cultural events, tourist cards, the Stockholm Card, and books are for sale. The staff will also reserve rooms for you, on-site, at hotels and youth hostels. Opening hours are January to April and September 16 to December Monday to Friday 9am to 6pm, Saturday 10am to 5pm, and Sunday 10am to 4pm. Hours May to

September 15 are Monday to Friday 9am to 7pm, Saturday 10am to 5pm, and Sunday 10am to 4pm.

The largest organization of its kind in all of Sweden is the **Kulturhuset,** Sergels Torg 3 (✆ **08/508-315-08;** www.kulturhuset.stockholm.se). It was built in 1974 by the city of Stockholm as a showcase for Swedish and international art and theater. There are no permanent exhibits; instead, the various spaces inside are allocated to a changing array of paintings, sculpture, photographs, and live performance groups. Kulturhuset also serves as the focal point for information about other cultural activities and organizations throughout Sweden and the rest of Europe. Inside are a snack bar, a library (which has newspapers in several languages), a reading room, a collection of recordings, and a somewhat bureaucratic openness to new art forms. Open Tuesday to Friday 11am to 7pm, Saturday and Sunday 11am to 5pm. No admission is charged.

Neighborhoods in Brief

As you'd expect of a city spread across 14 major islands in an archipelago, there are many neighborhoods, but those of concern to the average visitor are in central Stockholm.

We'll begin with the most nostalgic and evocative—and our longtime favorite for sleeping or dining.

Gamla Stan (Old Town) The "cradle" of Stockholm, Gamla Stan is at the entrance to Lake Mälaren on the Baltic. Its oldest city wall dates from the 13th century. The Old Town, along with the excavated wreck of the *Vasa,* is the most popular attraction in Stockholm. The hotels here are in general the most evocative of 18th-century Stockholm, built in romantic architectural styles, and there are many options for drinking and carousing as twilight falls. The downside of this area is that there are few hotels, and they tend to be expensive; there are, however, dozens of restaurants. Gamla Stan's major shopping street is the narrow Västerlånggatan, reserved almost exclusively for pedestrians, but many artisans' galleries, souvenir shops, and antiques stores abound on its small lanes. Its main square, and the heart of the ancient city, is Stortorget.

Norrmalm North of Gamla Stan, what was once a city suburb is now the cultural and commercial heart of modern Stockholm. Chances are your hotel will be in this district, as the area is generously endowed with hotels in all price ranges; it's also the most convenient location, as it encompasses the City Terminal and the Central Station. Hotels here are not the most romantic in town, but they're generally modern, up-to-date, and well run.

The most famous park in Stockholm, Kungsträdgården (King's Garden), is also in Norrmalm. In summer, this park is a major rendezvous point. Norrmalm also embraces the important squares of Sergels Torg and Hötorget, the latter a modern shopping complex. Norrmalm's major pedestrian shopping street is Drottninggatan, which starts at the bridge to the Old Town.

Vasastaden As Norrmalm expanded northward, the new district of Vasastaden was created. It's split by a trio of main arteries: St. Eriksgatan, Sveavägen, and Odengatan. The area around St. Eriksplan is called "the Off-Broadway of Stockholm" because it has so many theaters. Increasingly, this district has attracted fashionable restaurants and bars, and has become a popular residential area for young Stockholmers who work in fields such as journalism, television, and advertising.

Vasastaden is slightly more removed from the scene of the action, but it's still a good bet for hotels. In New York City terms, Norrmalm would be like staying in the Times Square area, whereas Vasastaden would be equivalent to staying on the Upper East Side. Hotels in Vasastaden come in a wide range of price categories.

Kungsholmen Once known as "Grey Friars Farm," Kungsholmen (King's Island), to the west of Gamla Stan, is the site of City Hall. Established by Charles XI in the 17th century as a zone for industry and artisans, the island now has been gentrified. One of its major arteries is Fleminggatan. Along Norrmälarstand, old Baltic cutters tie up to the banks. Stockholm's newspapers have their headquarters at Marieberg on the southwestern tip of the island.

Södermalm South of Gamla Stan, Södermalm (where Greta Garbo was born) is the largest and most populated district of Stockholm. Once synonymous with poverty, this working-class area is becoming more fashionable, especially with artists, writers, and young people. If you don't come here to stay in one of the moderately priced hotels or to dine in one of its restaurants, you might want to take the Katarina elevator, at Södermalmstorg, Slussen, for a good view of Stockholm and its harbor. Admission is 10SEK, free for ages 6 and under.

Östermalm In central Stockholm, east of Birger Jarlsgatan, the main artery, is Östermalm. In the Middle Ages, the royal family used to keep its horses, and even its armies, here. Today it's the site of the Army Museum. There are wide, straight streets, and it is also home to one of the city's biggest parks, Humlegården, dating from the 17th century.

This is another area of Stockholm that's a hotel district. Östermalm doesn't have quite the convenience of Norrmalm and Vasastaden, but it's still not so far removed from the action as to be called inconvenient. In summer, when visitors from all over the world are in town, this is a good place to hunt for a room. Because Norrmalm and Vasastaden are close to the Central Station, hotels in those neighborhoods tend to fill up very quickly.

Djurgården To the east of Gamla Stan is Djurgården (Deer Park), a forested island in a lake that's the summer recreation area of Stockholm. Here you can visit the open-air folk museums of Skansen, the *Vasa* man-of-war, Gröna Lund's Tivoli (Stockholm's own version of Tivoli), the Waldemarsudde estate and gardens of the "painting prince" Eugen, and the Nordic Museum. The fastest way to get here is over the bridge at Strandvägen/Narvavägen.

Skeppsholmen On its own little island, and reached by crossing Skeppsholmsbron, a bridge from the Blasieholmen district, Skeppsholmen is like a world apart from the rest of bustling Stockholm. Although it makes for a pleasant stroll, most people visit it to see the exhibits at the Moderna Museet.

GETTING AROUND

By Public Transportation

You can travel throughout Stockholm county by bus, local train, subway (T-bana), and tram, going from Singö in the north to Nynäshamn in the south. The routes are divided into zones, and one ticket is valid for all types of public transportation in the same zone within 1 hour of the time the ticket is stamped.

REGULAR FARES The basic fare for public transportation (in Stockholm this means subway, tram/streetcar, or bus) requires tickets purchased from the agent in the tollbooth on the subway platform. Tickets can also be purchased from vending machines at most metro and commuter railway stations, as well as in a number of other locations. Each ticket costs 30SEK, and allows travel to points within most of urban Stockholm, all the way to the borders of the inner city. You can transfer (or double back and return to your starting point) within 1 hour of your departure free. For more information, search http://sl.se/English.

SPECIAL DISCOUNT TICKETS Your best transportation bet is to purchase a **tourist season ticket.** A 1-day card, costing 100SEK for adults and 60SEK for ages

7 to 20 and seniors, is valid for 24 hours of unlimited travel by T-bana, bus, and commuter train within Stockholm. It also includes passage on the ferry to Djurgården. Most visitors will prefer the 3-day card for 200SEK for adults and 120SEK for ages 7 to 20 and seniors, valid for 72 hours in both Stockholm and the adjacent county. The 3-day card also is valid for admission to Skansen, Kaknästornet, and Gröna Lund. Kids up to 7 years of age can travel free with an adult. These tickets are available at tourist information offices, in subway stations, and at most news vendors. Call ✆ **08/600-10-00** for more information.

Stockholmskortet (**Stockholm Card;** www.stockholmtown.com) is a personal discount card that allows unlimited travel by bus, subway, and local trains throughout the city and county of Stockholm (except on airport buses). You can take a sightseeing tour with City Sightseeing, where you can get on and off as often as you please. These tours are available daily from mid-June to mid-August. In addition, the card enables you to take a boat trip to the Royal Palace of Drottningholm for half-price. Admission to 80 museums and attractions is also included in the package.

You can purchase the card at several places in the city, including the Tourist Center in Sweden House, Hotell Centralen, the Central Station, the tourist information desk in City Hall (in summer), the Kaknäs TV tower, SL-Center Sergels Torg (subway entrance level), and Pressbyrän newsstands. The cards are stamped with the date and time at the first point of usage. A 24-hour card costs 395SEK for adults and 195SEK for ages 7 to 20 and seniors; a 48-hour card is 525SEK for adults and 225SEK for children and seniors; and a 72-hour card is 625SEK for adults and 245SEK for children and seniors.

BY T-BANA (SUBWAY) Before entering the subway, passengers tell the ticket seller the destination, then purchase tickets. Subway entrances are marked with a blue T on a white background. For information about schedules, routes, and fares, phone ✆ **08/600-10-00.**

BY BUS Where the subway line ends, the bus begins; therefore, if a subway connection doesn't conveniently cover a particular area of Stockholm, a bus will. The two systems have been coordinated to complement each other. Many visitors use a bus to reach Djurgården (although you can walk) because the T-bana doesn't go here.

By Car

If you're driving around the Swedish capital, you'll find several parking garages in the city center as well as on the outskirts. In general, you can park at marked spaces Monday through Friday from 8am to 6pm. Exceptions or rules for specific areas are indicated on signs in the area.

By Taxi

Taxis are expensive—in fact, the most expensive in the world—with the meter starting at 45SEK. The cost is from 375SEK per hour. Those that display an illuminated dome light can be hailed directly on the street, or you can order one by phone. **Taxi Stockholm** (✆ **08/15-00-00;** www.taxistockholm.se) is one of the city's larger, more reputable companies. Unlike other Nordic nations, Sweden has not been successful at regulating its taxi industry. More than any other nation in Scandinavia, in Sweden, it's best to inquire before you get in whether the taxi is metered or—if the driver is proposing a set price—what the price will be.

By Ferry

Ferries from Skeppsbron on Gamla Stan (near the bridge to Södermalm) will take you to Djurgården if you don't want to walk or go by bus. They leave every 20 minutes Monday to Friday 7:40am to midnight, and about every 15 minutes on Saturday to Sunday, 9am to midnight. It costs 40SEK for adults, 25SEK for those 7 to 25 and for seniors, free for children under 7.

By Bicycle

The best place to go cycling is on Djurgården. You can rent bicycles from **Djurgårdsbrons Skepp o Hoj,** Djurgårdsbron (✆ **08/660-57-57**), for about 250SEK per day. It's open May to August daily from 10pm to midnight.

[FastFACTS] STOCKHOLM

Area Code The international country code for Sweden is **46;** the city code for Stockholm is **08** (if you're calling Stockholm from abroad, drop the 0). You do not need to dial 8 within Stockholm; do so only if you're outside the city.

Currency Exchange There's a currency exchange office, **Forex,** at the Central Station (✆ **08/411-67-34;** www.forex.se), open daily from 7am to 9pm. It's fully approved by both the Bank of Sweden and the Swedish tourist authorities, offers some of the best exchange rates in town, and takes some of the lowest commissions for cashing traveler's checks. Several other offices are scattered throughout the city.

Drugstores **C. W. Scheele,** Klarabergsviadukten 64 (✆ **0771/450-450**), remains open 24 hours a day.

Embassies & Consulates See "Fast Facts: Sweden" (p. 547).

Emergencies Call ✆ **112** for the police, ambulance service, or the fire department.

Hospitals Call **Medical Care Information** at ✆ **08/32-01-00** and an English-speaking operator will inform you of the hospital closest to you; operators are available 24 hours daily.

Police Call ✆ **112** in an emergency.

Post Office The main post office is at Centralstationen 10126 (✆ **08/781-20-42**), open Monday to Friday 8am to 6pm, and Saturday 8am to 2pm.

Taxis See "Getting Around," above.

Toilets Public facilities can be found in Central Station, in all subway stations, and in department stores, as well as along some of the major streets, parks, and squares. In an emergency, you can use the toilets in most hotels and restaurants, although generally they're reserved for patrons.

WHERE TO STAY

By the standards of many U.S. or Canadian cities, hotels in Stockholm are very expensive. If these high prices make you want to cancel your trip, read on. Dozens of hotels in Stockholm offer reduced rates on weekends all year, and daily from around mid-June to mid-August. For further information, inquire at a travel agency or the tourist center (see "Orientation," earlier in this chapter). In summer it's best to make reservations in advance, just to be on the safe side.

Most of the moderately priced hotels are in Norrmalm, north of the Old Town, and many of the least expensive lodgings are near the Central Station. There are comparably priced inexpensive accommodations within 10 to 20 minutes of the city, easily reached by subway, streetcar, or bus. We'll suggest a few hotels in the Old Town, but these choices are limited and more expensive.

BOOKING SERVICES **Hotell Centralen,** Vasagatan (✆ **08/508-285-08;** www.stockholmtown.com), on the street level of the Central Station, is the city's official housing bureau; it can arrange accommodations in hotels, pensions (boardinghouses), and youth hostels—but not in private homes. There is no booking fee. It's open Monday to Friday 9am to 6pm, Saturday 9am to 5pm, and Sunday 10am to 4pm.

Norrmalm (Center of Stockholm)

VERY EXPENSIVE

Grand Hotel ★★★ Opposite the Royal Palace, this hotel—a bastion of elite hospitality since 1874—is the finest in Scandinavia. The most recent restoration retained the grand and conservatively modern styling of the lobby, but added 72 additional bedrooms and made major changes to the bar and to the grander of the two hotel restaurants. Despite major alterations at roughly 10-year intervals throughout this hotel's life, its old-world style and sense of luxury have always been maintained. Guest rooms come in all shapes and sizes, all elegantly appointed in any of seven different decorative styles. The priciest rooms overlook the water, and we'd recommend that you go for these first, although they are invariably sought after. The hotel's ballroom is an exact copy of Louis XIV's Hall of Mirrors at Versailles.

Södra Blasieholmshamnen 8, S-103 27 Stockholm. www.grandhotel.se. ✆ **08/679-35-00.** Fax 08/611-86-86. 368 units. 2,635SEK–6,700SEK double; 5,950SEK junior suite; from 10,200SEK suite. AE, DC, MC, V. Parking 495SEK. T-bana: Kungsträdgården. Bus: 62. **Amenities:** 2 restaurants; bar; airport transfers (1,450SEK); concierge; exercise room; indoor heated pool; room service; spa. *In room:* TV/DVD, CD player, hair dryer, minibar, Wi-Fi (free).

Lydmar Hotel ★★★ It took a certain daring for the owner, Per Lydmar, to open this pocket of posh next door to the illustrious Grand Hotel and steal its thunder. Nothing, of course, can compete with the tradition and history of the Grand, but some hotel connoisseurs now hail Lydmar as the best in the city. It's like living in a country house, yet it's in the center of Stockholm. Those who appreciate luxury travel will find a safe haven here, overlooking the Royal Palace and the waterfront. The bedrooms are marvelously spacious, stylish, a bastion of comfort and convenience, and beautifully decorated in a sophisticated, yet at times rustic design. Public spaces are decorated with documentary-type photos. There is also an intimate music venue and a restaurant and lounge patronized by as many locals as visitors.

Södra Blasieholmshamnen 2, S-111 48 Stockholm. www.lydmar.com. ✆ **08/22-31-60.** Fax 08/22-31-70. 46 units. 2,800SEK–3,500SEK double; 5,600SEK suite. AE, DC, MC, V. Bus: 46, 55, 62, or 76. **Amenities:** Restaurant; bar; room service. *In room:* A/C, TV, hair dryer, Wi-Fi (free).

EXPENSIVE

Berns Hotel ★★ This is the hotel of choice for many celebrities visiting Stockholm. That can be either good or bad for the other clients. But when not hosting rock stars, the Berns can actually be rather subdued. During its 19th-century heyday, beginning in 1863, this was the most elegant hotel in Sweden, with an ornate Gilded Age interior that was the setting for many a legendary rendezvous. In 1989, following

Where to Stay & Dine in Stockholm

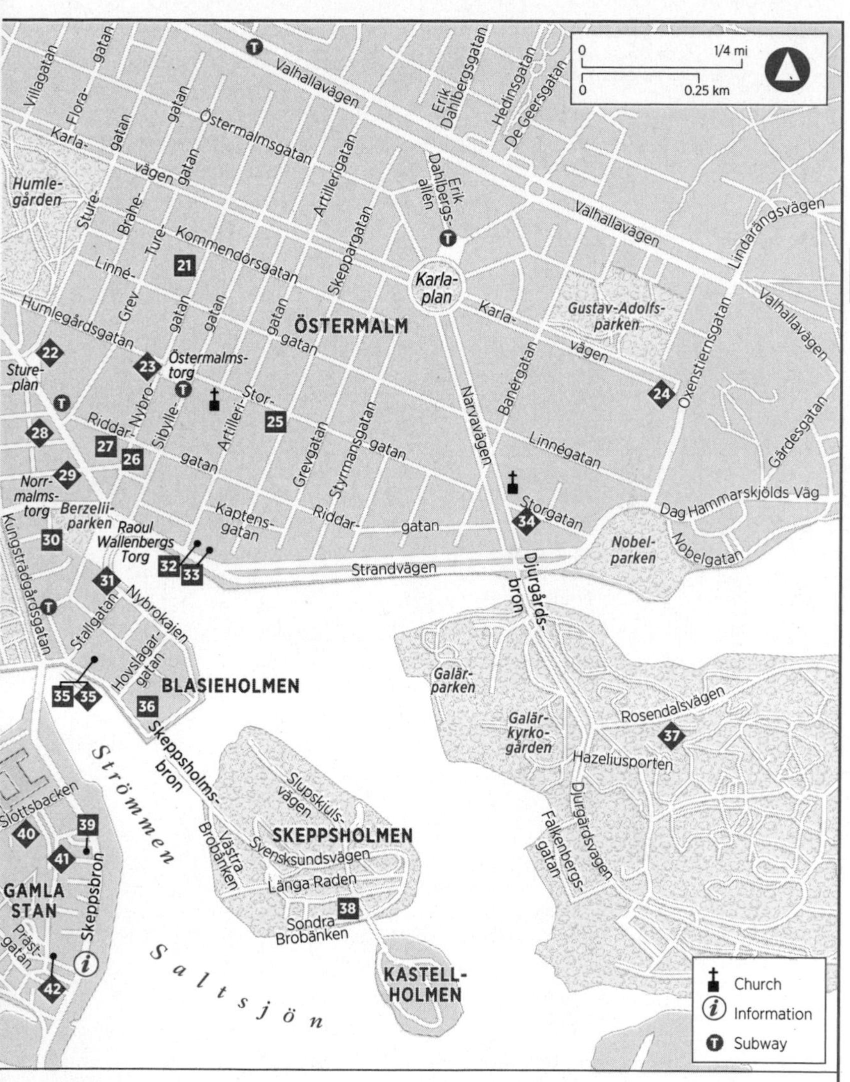

DINING ◆

Aquavit Raw Bar & Grill **8**
Bakfickan **11**
Berns **30**
Clas på Hörnet **2**
Cattelin Restaurant **16**
Divino **3**
Den Gyldene Freden **42**
Djuret **18**
Eriks Bakfica **34**
Fem Små Hus **41**
F12 **12**
Frantzén/Lindeberg **20**
KB Restaurant **29**
Lisa Elmquist **23**
Magnus Ladulås **40**
Mälardrottningen **19**
Mathias Dahlgren **35**
Operakällaren **11**
Prinsens **28**
Restaurangen **7**
Spring **24**
Stadshuskällaren **14**
Stortorgskallären **17**
Sturehof **22**
Tranan **1**
Ulla Winbladh **37**
Vassa Eggen **6**
Veranda **35**
Wedholms Fisk **31**

years of neglect, it was rebuilt in the original style. The guest rooms are soundproof and comfortably isolated from the activity downstairs.

Näckströmsgatan 8, S-111 47 Stockholm. www.berns.se. ✆ **08/566-322-00.** Fax 08/566-322-01. 82 units. 2,650SEK–5,250SEK double; 5,250SEK–10,500SEK suite. Rates include buffet breakfast. AE, DC, MC, V. Parking 465SEK. T-bana: Östermalmstorg. **Amenities:** Restaurant; bar; babysitting; concierge; room service; sauna. *In room:* TV, hair dryer, minibar, Wi-Fi (free).

Hotel Diplomat ★ This hotel is a bit stuffy but that's what its guests prefer. Well-managed, discreet, and solid, the Diplomat is a conservative operation that knows how to handle business clients and corporate conventions. Built in 1911, it retains hints of its original Art Nouveau styling. Public areas are more streamlined. The individually conceived guest rooms are decorated with well-crafted furniture. Many rooms contain bay windows overlooking the harbor; most of the less expensive accommodations face a quiet inner courtyard. Rooms range in size from cramped singles to spacious doubles with sitting areas and high ceilings.

Strandvagen 7C, Östermalm, S-104-40 Stockholm. www.diplomathotel.com. ✆ **08/459-68-00.** Fax 08/459-68-20. 128 units. 1,530SEK–3,295SEK double; 2,695SEK–4,995SEK suite. Rates include buffet breakfast on weekends. AE, DC, MC, V. Parking 495SEK. T-bana: Storeplan. **Amenities:** Restaurant; 2 bars; babysitting; bikes; exercise room; room service. *In room:* TV, hair dryer, minibar, Wi-Fi (free).

Nordic Hotel ★★ There's nothing in Scandinavia quite like this hotel, which was voted "the World's Sexiest Hotel" by *Elle* magazine. On either side of a new square, Vasaplan, the hotel is adjacent to the express rail link with the airport, or the central rail station. You're given a choice of a room of "watery calm" in the 367-room Nordic Sea or "post-minimalist luminescence" in the 175-room Nordic Light.

Nordic Sea turns to the ocean for its inspiration and features a 9,085-liter (2,400-gal.) aquarium and steel walls constructed from ship hulls. The comfortable rooms have a certain elegant simplicity. These accommodations range in size from extra small to extra large. Nordic Light, equally modern, equally angular, and positioned just across the boulevard from its more conservative twin, is the more intriguing of the two hotels. The suggestive light patterns projected onto the bleach-walls of both the bedrooms and the public areas of the Nordic Light re-create the ever-changing patterns of the lights of the north.

Vasaplan 4–7, S-101-37 Stockholm. www.nordichotels.se. ✆ **800/337-4685** in the U.S., or 08/505-630-00. Fax 08/505-630–40. 367 units in Nordic Sea, 175 units in Nordic Light. 1,251SEK–4,000SEK double Nordic Sea; 1,215SEK–4,000SEK double Nordic Light. Rates include buffet breakfast. AE, DC, MC, V. Parking 395SEK. T-bana: Centralen. **Amenities:** Restaurant; 2 bars; exercise room; room service; sauna. *In room:* TV, minibar, Wi-Fi (120SEK per day).

Scandic Sergel Plaza ★★ ☺ This classic hotel was designed in 1984 as living quarters for parliament members who come into Stockholm from the provinces. Of course, today, its rooms are open to all, and it is an especially inviting choice for families. The hotel is at the entrance to Drottninggatan, the main shopping street. The elegant public decor includes 18th-century artwork and antiques. The beautifully decorated guest rooms are done up in a tasteful but traditional modern style, using reproductions. The best rooms are the executive floors with enhanced luxury and services.

Brunkebergstorg 9, S-103 27 Stockholm. www.scandic-hotels.com. ✆ **08/517-263-00.** Fax 08/517-263-11. 403 units. 1,110SEK–2,790SEK double; 3,310SEK–5,000SEK suite. Rates include buffet breakfast. AE, DC, MC, V. Parking 310SEK. T-bana: Centralen. Bus: 47, 52, or 69. **Amenities:** Restaurant; bar; bikes; children's playground; concierge; exercise room; room service; sauna. *In room:* TV/DVD, CD player, hair dryer, minibar, Wi-Fi (free).

Story Hotel ★★ 🎁 A real discovery, this gem of a hotel in a traditional town house can trick you into thinking you live there. Sit back in one of the retro velvet-upholstered armchairs from the 1970s, placed on an Asian carpet, taking in the art on the walls, and you'll feel right at home. All that's missing is a pair of your bedroom slippers. The luxurious bedrooms come in a wide range of shapes, styles, and decor, ranging from the 11-sq.-m (123-sq.-ft.) Super Squeeze to the 35-sq.-m (380-sq.-ft.) Lily Dam Suite, with a separate room with a pullout sofa and two balconies. Throughout a chic decor is combined with modern conveniences, including a self-service check-in. The hotel is around the corner from the Stureplan shopping and nightclub district.

Riddargatan 6, S-114 25 Stockholm. www.storyhotels.com. ✆ **08/545-093-40.** 82 units. 1,790SEK–2,390SEK double; from 3,190SEK suite. Rates include breakfast. AE, DC, MC, V. T-bana: Östermalmstorg. **Amenities:** Restaurant; bar; room service. *In room:* A/C, TV, hair dryer, Wi-Fi (free).

MODERATE

Clarion Hotel Sign ★★ The biggest hotel in Stockholm is a sort of overblown diorama of Swedish sensibility from the sleek lobby decorated with Arne Jacobsen chairs to the black toilet paper in the bathrooms. For convenience of transportation, it's the best located in Stockholm, adjacent to the Central Station and the Arlanda Express. Its combination of architecture and design celebrates Scandinavia. Admittedly, the bedrooms are small, but with a decor from Scandinavia's top furniture designers. Select a room facing the tranquil rear garden or else one with a panoramic view of Stockholm and a green park. The **Aquavit Grill & Raw Bar** is a sister to its famous sibling in Manhattan. On the eighth floor is one of the first spas in Sweden, with a heated outdoor pool and a panoramic view.

Östra Järnvägsgatan 35, S-101 26 Stockholm. www.clarionsign.com. ✆ **08/676-98-00.** Fax 08/676-98-99. 550 units. 1,045SEK–2,800SEK double; 3,150SEK–5,000SEK suite. AE, DC, MC, V. Bus: All buses to Central Station. **Amenities:** Restaurant; bar; outdoor pool; room service; spa. *In room:* A/C, TV, hair dryer, Wi-Fi (free).

Elite Hotel Stockholm Plaza ★ This would not be our first choice for a hotel in Stockholm, and it's a bit pricey for what you get. But it certainly came in handy one night when we flew into Stockholm unexpectedly and nearly all the hotels were full. Built on a triangular lot that might remind some visitors of New York's Flatiron Building, this first-class hotel is a well-run choice in the city center.

Birger Jarlsgatan 29, S-103 95 Stockholm. www.elite.se. ✆ **08/566-220-00.** Fax 08/566-22-020. 143 units. 1,020SEK–2,500SEK double; 2,100SEK–4,800SEK suite. Rates include buffet breakfast. AE, DC, MC, V. Parking 280SEK. T-bana: Hötorget or Östermalmstorg. **Amenities:** Restaurant; bar; room service; sauna. *In room:* TV, hair dryer, minibar (in some),Wi-Fi (free).

Esplanade Hotel ★ This informal hotel, which defines itself as a four-star "hotel garni," where the only meal served is breakfast, is immediately adjacent to the more expensive and more richly accessorized Diplomat. Constructed as part of the same Beaux Arts architectural complex—at the time, a boardinghouse—as the Diplomat in 1910, it was transformed into a hotel in 1954, occupying two floors of a six-story building, the remainder of which are devoted to offices. Many of the rooms are furnished in old-fashioned style. Single rooms are minuscule. Four rooms open onto a view of the water, and the high-ceilinged lounge features a balcony with a view of Djurgården.

Strandvägen 7A, S-114 56 Stockholm. www.hotelesplanade.se. ✆ **08/663-07-40.** Fax 08/662-59-92. 34 units. Mon–Thurs 2,395SEK–2,595SEK double; Fri–Sun 1,795SEK double. Rates include buffet breakfast. AE, DC, MC, V. Parking nearby 290SEK. T-bana: Östermalmstorg. Bus: 47 or 69. **Amenities:** Room service; sauna. *In room:* TV, hair dryer, minibar, Wi-Fi (free).

Sheraton Stockholm Hotel & Towers ★ ☺ We've already gone on record as shying away from impersonal chain hotels, but for many visitors this is one of the best in its category. Sure, it's short on Swedish charm but excellent by other hotel standards, attracting many business travelers and even families, both foreign and domestic. Sheathed with Swedish granite, this eight-story hostelry is within view of Stockholm's City Hall (Rådhuset). The guest rooms are the largest in the city, with one king-size or two double beds with bedside controls and closets with mirrored doors. A family of three or four can fit comfortably into most of them.

Tegelbacken 6, S-101 23 Stockholm. www.sheratonstockholm.com. ✆ **800/325-3535** in the U.S. and Canada, or 08/412-34-00. Fax 08/412-34-09. 465 units. 1,345SEK–3,695SEK double; from 3,445SEK suite. AE, DC, MC, V. Parking 375SEK. T-bana: Centralen. **Amenities:** 2 restaurants; bar; babysitting; concierge; exercise room; indoor heated pool; room service; sauna. *In room:* A/C, TV, hair dryer, minibar (in some), Wi-Fi (100SEK per day).

INEXPENSIVE

Hotell Kom When we first checked into this establishment, it was a youth hostel. Although still owned by the Swedish version of the YWCA and YMCA, the hotel is now vastly improved and upgraded, and that's reflected in its prices. You still get good value and a warm welcome here. Rooms, although small, are tastefully and comfortably furnished in the latest Swedish modern style. The building itself is well maintained and up-to-date, and many of the rooms open onto good views of the cityscape.

Döbelnsgatan 17, S-11140 Stockholm. www.komhotel.se. ✆ **800/780-7234** or 08/412-23-00. Fax 08/412-23-10. 128 units. Mon–Thurs 1,470SEK–2,140SEK double; Fri–Sun 1,110SEK–1,470SEK double. Rates include buffet breakfast. AE, DC, MC, V. Parking 190SEK. T-bana: Rådmansgatan. **Amenities:** Exercise room; sauna. *In room:* TV, hair dryer, minibar, Wi-Fi (free).

Hotell Örnsköld Years ago when we were checking out this hotel, we spotted the great Swedish director, Ingmar Bergman, passing through. Only later did we learn that he wasn't calling on a mistress but was checking prop storage and staff housing, which even today are partial functions of this establishment near the Royal Dramatic Theatre. The five-story building that contains this hotel was built in 1910, and the hotel is on the second floor. High-ceilinged rooms have simple, contemporary furnishings, and more expensive units are big enough to hold extra beds. "Cabins" are tiny, basic rooms at budget-friendly prices.

Nybrogatan 6, S-11434 Stockholm. www.hotelornskold.se. ✆ **08/667-02-85.** Fax 08/667-69-91. 27 units. 1,495SEK–2,195SEK double; 450SEK–550SEK cabin. Rates include continental breakfast. AE, MC, V. T-bana: Östermalmstorg. **Amenities:** Wi-Fi. *In room:* TV, hair dryer, free Internet, minibar.

Hotel Tegnérlunden ★ ☺ Stay here if you want comfort but not a lot of style. Like a London town house hotel, this hidden facility is next to a leafy park, unusual for Stockholm, and its best feature is its airy rooftop breakfast room. The famous playwright August Strindberg used to walk by the door, allegedly working up quotations. In spite of a big expansion, the hotel still retains a personal atmosphere. Many of the tasteful, functionally furnished rooms are suitable for families because of their size.

Tegnerlunden 8, S-113 59 Stockholm. www.hoteltegnerlunden.se. ✆ **08/54-54-55-50.** Fax 08/54-54-55-51. 102 units. 2,490SEK double; 3,090SEK suite. Rates include buffet breakfast. AE, DC, MC, V. Parking 250SEK in nearby garage. Bus: 47, 53, or 69. **Amenities:** Bar; sauna. *In room:* TV, hair dryer, Wi-Fi (free).

Mornington Hotel ★ With more than 200 rooms, this hotel is just too big to live up to its slogan, "a home away from home." But it does try to conjure up that image with its friendly and helpful staff, among the finest we've discovered in chilly Stockholm. There are grace notes such as a library with more than 4,000 volumes and a small rock garden. To play up its image as an English-inspired hotel, they've even added rows of flower boxes to brighten up the concrete exterior. It was built in 1956 and has been renovated several times. Most rooms still have standard decor, and many are quite small.

Nybrogatan 53, S-102 44 Stockholm. www.mornington.se. ✆ **08/507-33-000.** Fax 08/507-33-039. 215 units. 1,365SEK–2,320SEK double. Rates include buffet breakfast. AE, DC, MC, V. Parking 245SEK. T-bana: Östermalmstorg. Bus: 49, 54, or 62. **Amenities:** Restaurant; bar; exercise room; room service; sauna. *In room:* TV/DVD, hair dryer, Wi-Fi (free).

Pärlan "Pearl" (its English name) is in the Östermalm district, immediately east of the center. On a tranquil street, it is near the landmark Östermalmstorg, with its market and theaters. It's also convenient to the ferries taking you through the Stockholm archipelago. Once a girls' school in the early 1950s, the building was later transformed into one of the more charming of the boutique hotels of Stockholm. Pärlan is on the second floor of a restored building from the 1800s. It's furnished in a funky style, a fusion of antiques with other trappings perhaps bought at flea markets.

Skepparegatan 27, S-114 52 Stockholm. www.parlanhotell.com. ✆ **08/663-50-70.** Fax 08/667-71-45. 9 units. 1,150SEK–1,395SEK double. Rates include buffet breakfast. AE, MC, V. T-bana: Storeplan. *In room:* TV, Wi-Fi (free).

In Gamla Stan (Old Town)

EXPENSIVE

First Hotel Reisen ★★ In the 18th century, this hotel facing the water was the most famous coffeehouse in the Old Town, just a few alleys from the Royal Palace. Sea captains, sailors, and tradesmen frequented the place. In 1819 the Merchant Society took it over and turned it into a nautical-style hotel. Today it's a comfortable and stylish hotel, decked out with dark wood, brick walls, and beautiful fabrics, although it doesn't quite match the charm and atmosphere generated by its two competitors nearby, Lady Hamilton and Victory (see below). The three-building structure attractively combines the old and the new; rooms are furnished with a mix of modern and traditional designs.

Skeppsbron 12, S-111 30 Stockholm. www.firsthotels.com/reisen. ✆ **08/22-32-60.** Fax 08/20-15-59. 144 units. 1,350SEK–2,550SEK double; 3,050SEK–5,000SEK suite. Rates include buffet breakfast. AE, DC, MC, V. Parking 425SEK. Bus: 53 or 62. **Amenities:** Restaurant; bar; concierge; exercise room; indoor pool; room service; sauna. *In room:* TV, hair dryer, minibar, Wi-Fi (free).

Lady Hamilton Hotel ★★★ Named after Lord Nelson's beloved mistress, this inn is one of the most atmospheric choices in the Old Town. In 1975, Majlis and Gunnar Bengtsson transformed it into Old Town's most romantic stopover. During restoration they found a well from 1300 where former residents used to fetch water; now a pool, it can be used by guests for a cool dip. Dozens of antiques are scattered among the well-furnished guest rooms, and most rooms have beamed ceilings. The beds (queen-size or double) are of high quality. Top-floor rooms have skylights and memorable views over the Old Town. You'll get a sense of the origins of this hotel when you use the luxurious sauna, which encompasses the stone-rimmed well that formerly supplied the building's water.

Storkyrkobrinken 5, S-111 28 Stockholm. www.ladyhamiltonhotel.se. ✆ **08/506-401-00.** Fax 08/506-40-110. 34 units (some with shower only). 1,990SEK–3,050SEK double. AE, DC, MC, V. Parking 395SEK. T-bana: Gamla Stan. Bus: 48. **Amenities:** Bar; babysitting; room service; sauna. *In room:* TV, hair dryer, minibar, Wi-Fi (120SEK per day).

Victory Hotel ★★ Named after the naval hero Lord Nelson's flagship, this exclusive boutique hotel is also the flagship of the Bengtsson family's private hotel chain in Old Town. Small but stylish, the Victory offers warm, inviting rooms, each named after a prominent sea captain. They sport a pleasing combination of exposed wood, antiques, and 19th-century memorabilia. The hotel rests on the foundations of a 1382 fortified tower. In the 1700s, the building's owners buried a massive silver treasure under the basement floor—you can see it in the Stockholm City Museum. There's a shiny brass elevator, but from the stairs you'll see one of Sweden's largest collections of 18th-century nautical needlepoint, much of it created by sailors during their long voyages.

Lilla Nygatan 5, S-111 28 Stockholm. www.victory-hotel.se. ✆ **08/506-400-00.** Fax 08/506-400-10. 45 units (some with shower only). 1,990SEK–3,658SEK double; 3,390SEK–7,500SEK suite. Rates include buffet breakfast. AE, DC, MC, V. Valet parking 395SEK. T-bana: Gamla Stan. Bus: 53. **Amenities:** Restaurant; bar; babysitting; plunge pool; room service; sauna. *In room:* A/C, TV, hair dryer, minibar, Wi-Fi (120SEK per day).

MODERATE

Mälardrottningen ★ During its heyday, this was the most famous yacht in the world, the subject of gossip columns everywhere, thanks to the complicated friendships that developed among the passengers and, in some cases, the crew. Built in 1924 by millionaire C. K. G. Billings, it was the largest motor yacht in the world (72m/236 ft.). It was later acquired by Barbara Hutton. The below-deck space originally contained only seven suites. The yacht was converted into a hotel in the early 1980s and permanently moored beside a satellite island of Stockholm's Old Town. The cabins are now cramped and somewhat claustrophobic, but being Hollywood buffs, we love to stay here and pay our respect to the stars who sailed aboard the vessel.

Riddarholmen, S-11128 Stockholm. www.malardrottningen.se. ✆ **08/545-187-80.** Fax 08/24-36-76. 61 units. Mon–Thurs 1,100SEK–2,000SEK double; Fri–Sun 950SEK–1,800SEK double. Rates include buffet breakfast. AE, DC, MC, V. Parking 220SEK. T-bana: Gamla Stan. **Amenities:** Restaurant; bar; sauna. *In room:* TV, hair dryer, Wi-Fi (free).

On Skeppsholmen

EXPENSIVE

Hotel Skeppsholmen ★★ In the 18th century it was a military barracks. In the 21st century top designers transformed it into a triumph of Swedish style and design, a minimalist yet supremely comfortable property housed in two long, low buildings. There's still a sense of antiquity here, however, since structural changes were forbidden because of the historic value of the building. The original wooden floors and beautiful large windows remain; otherwise the interior is completely modernized including the bedrooms, with the latest in Swedish design along with Duxiana beds and bathrooms with rain showers. Since the hotel opens onto the waterfront, ask for seaview accommodations. The restaurant combines traditional recipes with a modern twist. If you're visiting the neighboring modern museum, you can stop in for a Swedish *fika*—coffee, lemonade, and a choice of buns, cakes, and cookies.

Gröna gången 1 S-111-86 Stockholm. www.hotelskeppsholmen.com. ✆ **08/407-23-29.** 81 units. 1,546SEK–2,998SEK double; from 6,000SEK suite. AE, DC, MC, V. T-bana: Kungsträdgården. Bus: 65. **Amenities:** Restaurant; bar; room service. *In room:* A/C, TV, hair dryer, Wi-Fi (free).

On Långholmen

INEXPENSIVE

Långholmen Hotel Beginning in 1724, on the little island of Långholmen, this structure was a state penitentiary for women charged with "loose living." The last prisoner was released in 1972 and today it's a restored and reasonably priced hotel, which, in addition to comfortable but small rooms, also houses a museum of Sweden's prison history and a good restaurant. Instead of a prison induction area, you get the hotel's reception area and a 24-hour snack bar. Accommodations were carved from some 200 cells, creating cramped but serviceable rooms equipped with small showers and toilets.

Långholmsmuren 20, S-102-72 Stockholm. www.langholmen.com. ✆ **08/720-85-00.** Fax 08/720-85-75. 102 units. Sun–Thurs 1,840SEK–1,950SEK double; Fri–Sat 1,320SEK double. AE, MC, V. Rates include buffet breakfast. T-bana: Hornstul. Bus: 1 or 62. Free parking with permit. **Amenities:** Restaurant; bar; bikes. *In room:* TV, hair dryer, Wi-Fi (free).

On Södermalm

EXPENSIVE

Hotel Rival ★★★ 🎁 This is the leading hotel, and by far the most intriguing place to stay, on the rapidly gentrifying island of Södermalm. Originally opened in 1937, this hotel-cafe-bakery-cinema received a new lease on life in 2002, via funding by former ABBA member Benny Andersson. The Rival might almost be defined as a sprawling series of nightclubs, bistros, and entertainment lounges, on top of which a network of bedrooms is available for whatever rock star or rock-star wannabe happens to be in residence in Stockholm. Bedrooms are partially wood-sheathed, loaded with the electronic equipment you'd need to play CDs or DVDs. The more animated, close-to-the-action bedrooms open onto the Mariatorget—one of Stockholm's loveliest squares.

Mariatorget 3, S-11891 Stockholm. www.rival.se. ✆ **08/545-789-00.** Fax 08/545-789-24. 99 units. 1,495SEK–3,090SEK double; 3,690SEK–5,790SEK suite. AE, DC, MC, V. Parking (nearby) 395SEK. T-bana: Mariatorget. **Amenities:** 2 restaurants; 3 bars; concierge; exercise room; room service. *In room:* A/C, TV/DVD, CD player, hair dryer, minibar, Wi-Fi (40SEK per hour).

WHERE TO DINE

Split pea soup, sausages, and boiled potatoes are still around, but in the past decade Stockholm has emerged as a citadel of fine dining. Part of this derives from the legendary freshness of Swedish game and produce; part comes from the success of Sweden's culinary team at cooking contests everywhere. Today there are an estimated 1,500 restaurants and bars in Stockholm alone.

Food is expensive in Stockholm, but those on a budget can stick to self-service cafeterias. At all restaurants other than cafeterias, a 12% to 15% service charge is added to the bill to cover service, and the 21% value-added tax also is included in the bill. Wine and beer can be lethal to your final check, so proceed carefully. For a good value, try ordering the *dagens ratt* (daily special), also referred to as *dagens* lunch or *dagens* menu, if available.

Norrmalm (Center of Stockholm)

VERY EXPENSIVE

Mathias Dahlgren ★★★ SWEDISH INTERNATIONAL The chef, for whom this exclusive restaurant is named, was named "chef of the year" in Sweden twice in the postmillennium. In the Matsalen (the Dining Room), meals start with a marble-size ball of bread that was a staple of his childhood. Dahlgren can get humble and regional, as evoked by his pigs' cheek paired with sausage, Jerusalem artichokes, and black trumpet mushrooms. Or he can go grand with more elaborate dishes such as his six-course tasting menu. Matbaren (the Food Bar) has simpler Swedish dishes such as braised ox cheek with a purée of pickled cucumber and sautéed onions.

In the Grand Hotel, Södra Blasieholmshamnen 8. ✆ **08/679-35-84.** www.mathiasdahlgren.com. Reservations required. Main courses Matsalen 325SEK–455SEK; tasting menu 1,500SEK; small plates Matbaren 135SEK–315SEK. AE, DC, MC, V. Matsalen Tues–Sat 7pm–midnight; Matbaren Mon–Fri noon–2pm, Mon–Sat 6pm–midnight. Bus: 62.

Operakällaren ★★★ FRENCH/SWEDISH Opposite the Royal Palace, this is the most famous and unashamedly luxurious restaurant in Sweden. Among its claims to fame, it turned Stockholmers into serious foodies. Its promise of a world-class French-inspired cuisine has lured us back time and time again, although we dread facing the final bill. Its lavishly elegant decor and style are reminiscent of a royal court banquet at the turn of the 20th century. The service and house specialties are impeccable. Many come here for the elaborate fixed-price menus; others prefer the classic Swedish dishes or the modern French ones. A house specialty that's worth the trip is the platter of northern delicacies, with everything from smoked eel to smoked reindeer, along with Swedish red caviar. Salmon and game, including grouse from the northern forests, are prepared in various ways. There's a cigar room too.

Operahuset, Karl XII's Torg, Kungsträdgården. ✆ **08/676-58-00.** www.eng.operakallaren.se. Reservations required. Main courses 320SEK–520SEK; 8-course degustation 1,200SEK or 2,095SEK with wine. AE, DC, MC, V. Tues–Sat 6–10pm. Closed Dec 25–Jan 8 and July 12–Aug 4. T-bana: Kungsträdgården.

EXPENSIVE

Aquavit Raw Bar & Grill ★★ SWEDISH Contemporary elegance and a certain culinary daring combine at this outpost of the famed New York restaurant. In an elegant setting, the chefs use prime regional produce to turn out a highly refined cuisine that never overreaches and invariably satisfies. The best example of the kitchen's prowess is a series of starters that range from duck rillettes with lingonberries and chanterelles to a corn soup with chorizo and watercress. One tasty choice includes halibut poached in almond milk or, from the grill, dry aged Swedish rib-eye with onion rings, even a mixed seafood grill with *aioli*. For dessert the "Arctic Circle" is a combination of fresh blueberries and goat-cheese ice cream. The raw bar is the best in town, including those divine Swedish Belon oysters. If you want to be lavish in your tastes, you can order a platter of "Seven Tastes" in seafood. A special theater menu is served Friday and Saturday from 5 to 7pm, costing 425SEK for two courses or 525SEK for three courses.

In the Clarion Hotel Sign, Östra Järnvägsgatan 35. ✆ **08/676-98-50.** www.aquavitgrillrawbar.com. Reservations recommended. Main courses 165SEK–360SEK. AE, DC, MC, V. Mon–Fri 11:30am–2pm and 5–11pm; Sat 1–3pm and 5–11pm; Sun noon–4pm. T-bana: Any train to the Central Station.

Bistro Rival ★★ 🎁 INTERNATIONAL This hip bistro is the focal point for a series of lesser bars, lounges, and entertainment venues that all flourish, in a congenially cooperative way, within the same (also recommended) hotel. The guiding light here is ABBA member Benny Andersson, whose reflected glory permeates the spirit of much of this place. Since the bistro is on the hotel's second floor, and since there's a long and narrow balcony on which tables are relocated during clement weather, diners can look down on one of the most popular and animated series of *boules,* or Swedish boccie ball. The menu presents fresh and tantalizing dishes such as mussel soup with lobster and broad beans or a tangy fish casserole, even butter-fried perch served with stewed fennel and savoy cabbage.

In the Hotel Rival, Mariatorget 3. ✆ **08/545-789-00.** www.rival.se. Reservations recommended. Main courses 215SEK-295SEK. AE, DC, MC, V. Daily 5–11:30pm (restaurant). Bar open till midnight–2am, depending on business. T-bana: Mariatorget.

Divino ★★ ITALIAN When we can't face another platter of boiled halibut, we head here for an Italian fix. It's a long way from sunny Italy to this far-northern capital city, but the aptly named Divino manages to travel the distance with its Mediterranean flavors intact. Many local food critics hail Divino as Stockholm's finest Italian restaurant, and we have to agree. The chefs provide unusual variations of the classics, including sweetbreads flavored with lemon and fresh thyme, or a tantalizing foie gras with almond foam and figs. A starter of scallops is perfectly cooked and flavored with fresh tomatoes and basil. Monkfish and lobster are served on one platter and flavored with vanilla bean along with fresh fennel. The restaurant's elegant decor, from white-clothed formal table settings to antiques scattered about, and mammoth wine cellar, filled with some of Italy's best vintages, seal the deal.

Karlavägen 28. ✆ **08/611-02-69.** www.divino.se. Reservations required. All main courses 265SEK. AE, MC, V. Mon–Sat 11:30am–2pm and 6–11pm. Closed Mon in July. T-bana: Östra Station or Rädmansgatan.

F12 ★★★ SWEDISH/INTERNATIONAL In the high-ceilinged interior of the Royal Academy of Arts, this is one of Stockholm's premier restaurants. The decor is ultrasophisticated and hip, even nightclubish with its apple-green and lime-colored walls; long, shimmering curtains; and the kind of uncluttered minimalism you'd expect at a fashionable venue in Milan. Since it's near the Swedish parliament and various government ministries, it tends to attract government officials at lunch, but a classier and far trendier clientele in the evening. The menu divides your choices into either "innovative" or "traditional" cuisine. The best traditional choices might include beef carpaccio with Parmesan; seafood bouillabaisse with saffron; codfish with white onions; and a *navarin* of suckling lamb with chanterelles. "Innovative" choices feature tuna *tataki* with mango slices and cream; caviar served with cauliflower and white chocolate; or veal with tuna sauce, grapefruit, and licorice.

Fredsgatan 12. ✆ **08/24-80-52.** www.f12.se. Reservations required. Lunch main courses 195SEK-280SEK; dinner main courses 295SEK–410SEK; 2-course fixed-price menu 310SEK; 3-course fixed-price menu 390SEK. AE, DC, MC, V. Mon–Fri 11:30am–2pm and 5pm–1am; Sat 5pm–1am. T-bana: Kungsträdgården.

Restaurangen ★★ INTERNATIONAL Nowhere in Stockholm will you find "the rainbow of tastes" cooked up here. Come not for the high-ceilinged decor (whose angularity might remind you of an SAS airport lounge), but for combinations of cuisine that many cosmopolitan Swedes find absolutely fascinating. Owner and chef Malker Andersson divides his menu into "fields of flavor" as defined by unexpected categories. These include, among others, lemon or coriander themes. If you want a taste of lemon, you'll sample lemon-flavored fresh asparagus and potatoes; for coriander, try coriander-infused shellfish ceviche. The chef fuses the traditional dishes of one country with the time-honored dishes of another. An amazing and very tasty example of this is the Mexican tacos combined with French foie gras and Russian caviar. Since none of the portions is overly large, some diners interpret a meal here as something akin to a series of high-end tapas.

Oxtorgsgatan 14. ✆ **08/22-09-52.** www.restaurangentm.com. Reservations recommended. 3-course fixed-price menu 350SEK; 5-course fixed-price menu 450SEK; 7-course fixed-price menu 550SEK. AE, DC, MC, V. Mon–Fri 11:30am–2pm; Mon–Sat 5pm–midnight. T-bana: Hörtorget.

Spring ★ ASIAN/SCANDINAVIAN The trendiness of this place never plays second fiddle to the Eastern and Western fusion cuisine. The key is not only chef Johan Lundblad's skill in the kitchen, but a carefully chosen list of ingredients that is fresh and high-quality. During your lunch (no dinner is served here), you might encounter dishes such as steamed chicken dumplings, all in delicate hues and brimming with flavor, followed by Japanese eel with foie gras and a *maki* tempura. Blond ash wood from northern Sweden is featured in the minimalist decor, which is livened up by the colors of Asia. The mostly upwardly mobile young people who dine here have made Spring a hit since the day it opened.

Karlavägen 110. ✆ **08/783-15-00.** www.spring.se. Reservations required. Main courses 135SEK-195SEK. AE, MC, V. Mon–Fri 11:30am–2pm. T-bana: Östra Station or Rädmansgatna.

Vassa Eggen ★ INTERNATIONAL Follow the gourmets to one of the most cutting-edge restaurants in Stockholm. This fashionable eatery is in the center of the city, but gastronomic influences from all over the world are revealed in the light, airy dining room, accented by a beautiful glass dome. The melon soup with Serrano ham will win you over, or else the fried herring with a potato purée. The Swedish version of *Gourmet* magazine put Vassa Eggen on the culinary map by proclaiming its oxtail tortellini with mascarpone cheese served in a consommé "a masterful balance of acidity, salt, sweetness, and spices." Other raves were to follow, including our own.

Birger Jarlsgatan 29. ✆ **08/21-61-69.** www.vassaeggen.com. Reservations required. Main dinner courses 195SEK–255SEK; lunch main courses 195SEK–265SEK. AE, DC, MC, V. Mon–Fri 11:30am–2pm and 5–11pm; Sat 6–11pm. Closed in July. T-bana: Östermalmstorg.

Wedholms Fisk ★ SWEDISH/FRENCH This place may no longer be cutting edge, but it still remains the leader of the pack among classic Swedish restaurants. Even Greta Garbo thought so. Disguised as "Harriet Brown," she always came here for at least one meal during one of her secret visits to her hometown. It has no curtains in the windows and no carpets, but the display of modern paintings by Swedish artists is riveting. The chef has reason to be proud of such dishes as perch poached with clams and saffron sauce, prawns marinated in herbs and served with Dijon hollandaise, and grilled filet of sole with Beaujolais sauce. The cuisine is both innovative and traditional—for example, chèvre mousse accompanies a simple tomato salad. On the other hand, the menu features old-time favorites, such as cream-stewed potatoes.

Nybrokajen 17. ✆ **08/611-78-74.** www.wedholmsfisk.se. Reservations required. Lunch main courses 195SEK–255SEK; dinner main courses 265SEK–545SEK; 5-course tasting menu 895SEK. AE, DC, MC, V. Mon 11:30am–2pm and 6–11pm; Tues–Fri 11:30am–11pm; Sat 5–11pm. Closed for lunch in July. T-bana: Östermalmstorg.

MODERATE

Bakfickan ★★ SWEDISH "The Hip Pocket" (its English name) is, at least for now, a secret address that mainly local foodies know about and want to keep to themselves. It actually shares the same kitchen with its glamorous neighbor, Operakällaren (above), which means you get the same food at a fraction of the price. When they're in season, come here for Swedish specialties from the far north, such as reindeer and elk. For a starter, dig into the French oysters with a vinaigrette sauce and black bread. That can be followed by a plate of assorted North and Baltic Sea herring. It was a good choice, though we might look longingly at the grilled roast rib of beef with béarnaise sauce being served at the next table.

Jakobs Torg 12. ✆ **08/676-58-00.** www.operakallaren.se. Reservations not accepted. Main courses 320SEK–520SEK. AE, DC, MC, V. Mon–Fri 11:30am–11pm; Sat noon–10pm. T-bana: Kungsträdgården.

Berns ★ SWEDISH/INTERNATIONAL/ASIAN This classic restaurant might have opened in 1860 as a "pleasure palace," but it's changed with the times and looks toward Asia for its new inspiration. Three monumental chandeliers light the main hall, while the plush furniture described by August Strindberg in the *Red Room (Röda Rummet)* is still here. Each day a different Swedish specialty is featured, including fried filet of suckling pig with fresh asparagus, calves' liver with garlic and bacon, or grilled *tournedos.* More innovative main dishes include cuttlefish with black pasta and tomato sauce, and filet of ostrich with mushroom cannelloni and Marsala sauce.

Näckströmsgatan 8. ✆ **08/566-322-22.** www.berns.se. Reservations recommended. Breakfast buffet 195SEK; main courses 135SEK–400SEK. AE, DC, MC, V. Daily 7am–11pm. T-bana: Östermalmstorg.

Eriks Bakfica ★ SWEDISH Today you can get food from around the world in Stockholm, ranging from Mexican to Thai. Yet Swedes still cherish the tradition of *husmanskost* (wholesome home cooking), and, since 1979, this has been the cherished address where they find it. We always check out the array of herring appetizers that are changed daily, but what really attracts us to this place is the tantalizing "archipelago stew," a ragout of fresh fish (it varies daily) prepared with tomatoes and served with garlic mayonnaise. We don't know where the chef gets his marinated salmon, but we wish our deli around the corner stocked it. If you drop in for lunch, you might ask for Erik's cheeseburger with a special "secret sauce"—savvy locals know it's one of the town's best burgers.

Fredrikshovsgatan 4. ✆ **08/660-15-99.** www.eriks.se. Reservations recommended. Main courses 195SEK–295SEK. AE, DC, MC, V. Mon–Fri 11:30am–2:30pm and 5pm–1am; Sat 4pm–1am. Bus: 69.

KB Restaurant SWEDISH/CONTINENTAL We've been patronizing this traditional artists' rendezvous in the center of town for years. It's not exciting in any way, but provides what a patron calls "comfort food." The dishes are always beautifully prepared, and we could almost make a meal out of their freshly baked sourdough bread with Swedish butter. We like to begin with salmon trout roe and Russian caviar. The kitchen turns out an enticing roasted lamb, which, at least on one occasion, was stuffed with zucchini in a thyme-flavored bouillon. In summer our favorite desserts are the sorbets made with fresh fruit and berries picked in the countryside. One of our most memorable desserts here—and hopefully it'll be on the menu for you—is a lime soufflé with orange blossom honey. After dinner, head to the informal bar for some often-animated conversation.

Smålandsgatan 7. ✆ **08/679-60-32.** www.konstnarsbaren.se. Reservations recommended. Lunch main courses 115SEK–295SEK; dinner main courses 148SEK–335SEK. AE, DC, MC, V. Mon–Fri 11:30am–midnight; Sat 1pm–midnight; Sun 1–10pm. T-bana: Östermalmstorg.

Lisa Elmqvist ★ ☺ SEAFOOD It may not specialize in refined cuisine, but for an authentic "taste of Sweden," this is our favorite spot for eating amid the food stalls of Stockholm's produce market (Östermalms Saluhall). Resembling a bistro under the tent at a country fair, this likable cafe and oyster bar bears the name of one of Sweden's leading culinary matriarchs. Because of its good, affordable food, and its take-charge, no-nonsense format, this is an appropriate choice for families. It's owned by one of the city's largest fish distributors, so its menu varies with the catch. Some patrons come here for shrimp with bread and butter for 112SEK to 165SEK. The smoked salmon tartare is served with red onion and sour cream or else you can order it marinated with a sweet mustard sauce. Fresh boiled lobster also appears on the menu, but at lethal prices. Tempting desserts include a tantalizing butterscotch tart and an even better chocolate tart made with white and dark truffles and served with fresh raspberries.

Östermalms Saluhall, Nybrogatan 31. ✆ **08/553-404-00.** www.lisaelmqvist.se. Reservations recommended. Main courses 146SEK–515SEK. AE, DC, MC, V. Mon–Thurs 9:30am–6pm; Fri 9:30am–6:30pm; Sat 9:30am–4pm (9:30am–2pm July–Aug). T-bana: Östermalmstorg.

Prinsen ★ SWEDISH Since 1897, this restaurant, a 2-minute walk from Stureplan, has been a favorite haunt of artists. Since some of them were struggling and unable to pay their bills, the walls of the restaurant are hung with many of their artworks, presented in lieu of payment. Some will tell you that "the Prince" (its English name) is riding on its rich bohemian past, but artists still come here for the satisfying *husmanskost*. Seating is on two levels, and in summer tables are placed outside. The cuisine remains fresh and flavorful, a mostly Swedish repertoire with some French inspiration. The sautéed salmon tastes like it was just hauled in from the fjords, and the staff continues to serve old-fashioned favorites such as veal patties with homemade lingonberry preserves. Resisting trends, the cooks serve such grandmotherly favorites as a herring platter or *biff rydberg* (beef with fried potatoes and an egg). Lately more contemporary dishes are creeping onto the menu—nontraditionalist fare like licorice soup or snails in chocolate sauce. If you come later in the evening, you'll see that Prinsen morphs into a sort of local drinking club.

Mäster Samuelsgatan 4. ✆ **08/611-13-31.** www.restaurangprinsen.com. Reservations recommended. Main courses 199SEK–379SEK. AE, DC, MC, V. Mon–Fri 11:30am–11:30pm; Sat 1–11:30pm; Sun 5–10:30pm. T-bana: Östermalmstorg.

Sturehof ★ SWEDISH/SEAFOOD This is the most classic French-style brasserie in all of Stockholm, and it's been going strong since the day it opened back in 1897. Just as it was beginning to grow stale, it reinvented itself for its second millennium. It remains the best spot in central Stockholm for dining at almost any time of the day or night. In summer you can sit out on the terrace and watch Stockholmers pass by. Or else you can chill out in the upper lounge, popular among younger people. The dining room is more formal and elegant with uniformed waiters and stiffly pressed white linen tablecloths. Expect a daily changing menu of *husmanskost* (traditional home cooking). Herring is king here, be it tomato herring, curry herring, or the delectable smoked Baltic herring appetizer. Or else try the locally famous *sotare* (small grilled Baltic herring). This is also one of the few places around still serving boiled salt veal tongue, a local delicacy.

After dinner, if the mood suits, you can drop in to check out **O-baren,** a backroom den with a bar and a dance floor, a center for "the blackest rock" music along with hip-hop and soul.

Stureplan 2. ✆ **08/440-57-30.** www.sturehof.com. Main courses 195SEK–455SEK. AE, DC, MC, V. Mon–Fri 11am–2am; Sat noon–2am; Sun 1pm–2am. T-bana: Östermalmstorg.

Tranan SWEDISH Now that the section of Stockholm known as Vasastaden is growing chic, this working-class pub has gone more upmarket, attracting young professionals of all sexual persuasions from the neighborhood. Always a real local favorite, this 1915 tavern serves very good food and draws a friendly crowd attracted by affordable prices and the kitchen's deft handling of fresh ingredients. The menu offers an array of traditional Swedish dishes that often have French overtones, such as filet of beef served with fried potatoes, egg yolk, and horseradish. Other menu items are conservative and flavorful, in many cases virtually unchanged since the day the restaurant was founded. Such examples include Swedish pork and lard sausage (actually tastier than it sounds) served with mashed potatoes and pickled beets, herring platters, toast Skagen piled high with shrimp, and beef *Rydberg* style: cubes of sautéed steak filet served with braised onions, sautéed potatoes, egg yolk, cream, and horseradish. One Swede told us he comes here at least twice a week to order the Swedish meatballs and mashed potatoes.

Later you can go downstairs to enjoy an authentic local bar, where DJs spin the latest hits on Friday and Saturday nights. Patrons must be 23 or older to enter the bar.

Karlbergvagen 14. ✆ **08/527-281-00.** www.tranan.se. Reservations recommended. Main courses 145SEK–325SEK. AE, DC, MC, V. Mon–Thurs 5pm–midnight; Fri–Sat 5pm–1am; Sun 5–11pm. Closed July 18–Aug 30. T-bana: Odenplan.

Veranda ★★ ☺ SWEDISH On the ground floor of Stockholm's most prestigious hotel, this restaurant opens onto a wide-angled view of the harbor and the Royal Palace. The Veranda is famous for its daily smorgasbord buffets, which are artfully (exquisitely, even) laid out in a satellite room off the main dining room. Scads of local business clients, assisted by a top-notch and smartly uniformed service staff, come here for a nostalgic reminder of a gentrified and very upscale old Swedish tradition. For a quick lesson in smorgasbord etiquette, the cardinal rules are as follows: Don't mix fish and meat courses on the same plate, don't mix hot and cold food on the same plate, and keep your visit(s) to the dessert table separate. The selection of a la carte dishes includes filet of reindeer marinated in red wine, pasta with lamb, or braised wild duck and deep-fried root vegetables served with an apple-cider sauce. This is your chance to sample the offerings of the most famous hotel in Sweden, to enjoy wonderful food, and to have one of the best views in town—all for a reasonable price.

In the Grand Hotel, Södra Blasieholmshamnen 8. ✆ **08/679-35-86.** www.grandhotel.se. Reservations required. Lunch main courses 150SEK–315SEK; dinner main courses 145SEK–375SEK; Swedish buffet 455SEK. AE, DC, MC, V. Daily noon–3pm and 6–11pm. T-bana: Kungsträdgården. Bus: 62.

In Gamla Stan (Old Town)

VERY EXPENSIVE

Djuret ★★ SWEDISH/INTERNATIONAL This is one of the Old Town's most stylish and fashionable restaurants, noted for its fine cuisine and the quality of its service. From the small, street-level bar where you can order a before-dinner drink, patrons descend into the intimately lit cellar (the restaurant was built around a medieval defense tower). To reach this restaurant, you need to negotiate a labyrinth of brick passageways through the Victory Hotel. Dishes often look like works of art, and some of the country's finest produce appears on the menus. The whole menu is based on the fresh meat of the day, and all parts of that animal appear on the menu in various combination of dishes. This is a restaurant for serious carnivores, with no vegetarian options on the menu.

In the Victory Hotel, Lilla Nygatan 5. ✆ **08/506-400-84.** www.djuret.se. Reservations required. Main courses 190SEK–395SEK. AE, DC, MC, V. Mon–Sat 5pm–midnight (kitchen closes at 10pm). Closed July. T-bana: Gamla Stan.

Frantzén/Lindeberg ★★ 🎁 SWEDISH With the opening of this new restaurant in Gamla Stan, it's showtime in the Old Town tonight. This cozy restaurant, an 18-seater, is an intimate setting for the high-flying cooking of Björn Frantzén and his partner, Daniel Lindeberg. Even though the setting is plain, everything has flair here. The Swedish actor Stellan Skarsgård even narrates the cheese course via an iPod. Try their grilled veal from Normandy which is marinated in whey for 2 days, then sautéed with morels and lemon thyme. Monkfish shipped in from Trondheim (Norway) is baked in pork fat with burnt sauce, pickled chanterelles, and buttermilk. Their tasting menus are the best in Gamla Stan.

Lilla Nygatan 21. ✆ **08/20-85-80.** Reservations required. 5-course fixed-price menu 1,295SEK; 7 courses for 1,495SEK. AE, DC, MC, V. Tues–Sat 6pm–midnight. T-bana: Gamla Stan.

EXPENSIVE

Clas på Hornet ★ SWEDISH/CONTINENTAL Swedes come here to celebrate their nautical heritage in cuisine, and we join them for some of the most authentic seafood flavors in town. Locals begin meals with an "archipelago platter," a selection of fish caught in the islands near Stockholm, and finish with a medley of Swedish cheese with homemade bread. Another choice we find delectable, although it may be an acquired taste, is the blini stuffed with bleak roe, trout roe, and onions. The cream of wild mushroom soup is served with strips of reindeer, and, in autumn, diners can order roast venison with a timbale of chanterelles. Homage to the place has even appeared in the verse of one of Sweden's most valued poets, Carl Michael Bellman.

Surbrunnsgatan 20. ✆ **08/16-51-36.** www.claspahornet.se. Reservations recommended. Main courses 225SEK–305SEK. AE, DC, MC, V. Mon–Fri noon–midnight; Sat 5pm–midnight. Bus: 46.

Den Gyldene Freden ★ SWEDISH "Golden Peace" is said to be Stockholm's oldest tavern. The restaurant opened in 1722 in a structure built the year before. The Swedish Academy owns the building, and members frequent the place on Thursday night. You may never have heard of them, but towering cultural figures in Sweden, including the singer-poet Carl Michael Bellman and the singer-composer Evert Taube, have dined here over the years; hence, the cozy dining rooms are named for Swedish historical figures who were patrons. Today it's popular among artists, lawyers, and poets. You'll get good traditional Swedish cooking, especially fresh Baltic fish and local game, along with more modern dishes like sautéed duck breast with pickled pumpkin (a first for us); baked char with a wasabi flavoring; and beef carpaccio on goat-cheese toast with a citrus salsa. Want something different for dessert? How about warm rose-hip soup with vanilla ice cream? Of course, if you order that, you'd be denying yourself the "symphony" of lingonberries or the longtime favorite: Stockholm's best dark chocolate cake, served with fresh raspberries and coffee ice cream.

Österlånggatan 51. ✆ **08/24-97-60.** www.gyldenefreden.se. Reservations recommended. Lunch main courses 125SEK–275SEK; dinner main courses 185SEK–385SEK. AE, DC, MC, V. Mon–Fri 11:30am–2:30pm and 5–11pm; Sat 1–11pm. T-bana: Gamla Stan.

Fem Små Hus ★ SWEDISH/FRENCH This historic restaurant, with cellars that date from the 17th century, and a history of serving fine food and ale to visitors dating back to 1698, is furnished like a private castle, complete with European antiques and oil paintings. Its name, which translates as "Five Small Houses," derives from the way an entrepreneur combined the cellars of five once-separate houses into a coherent, well-accessorized series of nine candlelit dining rooms. The result somehow manages to be both rustic and baronial at the same time. This atmospheric restaurant draws a *belle clientele* glad to savor the master chef's creations and experience his flair for marrying the best market-fresh ingredients from Sweden's forests and shores. Beautifully prepared dishes include platters of assorted herring; filets of fried reindeer with cranberries and port-wine sauce; oven-baked salmon with white-wine sauce, summer vegetables, and new potatoes; and filets of veal with morel sauce and "a touch of

Gorgonzola." The cuisine and staff are worthy of the restaurant's hallowed reputation, among the best we've encountered in Stockholm.

Nygränd 10. ✆ **08/10-87-75.** www.femsmahus.se. Reservations required. Main courses 275SEK-320SEK; fixed-price menus 425SEK-575SEK. AE, DC, MC, V. Sun-Tues 5-11pm; Wed-Sat 5pm-midnight. T-bana: Gamla Stan.

MODERATE

Stortorgskällaren SWEDISH You won't get culinary fireworks here, but you will get a solid, reliable menu, a cheerful atmosphere, and lots of robust flavor. In the winter, this restaurant occupies medieval wine cellars whose vaulted ceilings date from the 15th century. In summer, seating is on the outdoor terrace, beside a charming square opposite the baroque facade of the Swedish Academy. In bad weather, you can dine in the street-level dining room where chandeliers complement the plush carpeting and subtle lighting. The menu changes often, but you might begin with pâté of wild game with blackberry chutney and pickled carrots, or cured salmon and white bleak roe served with crème fraîche and onions. There's also grilled filet of pikeperch served with lime sauce and deep-fried potatoes, and chanterelle mushrooms on toast, served with strips of smoked reindeer. Another specialty is a casserole of Baltic fish seasoned with saffron.

Stortorget 7. ✆ **08/10-55-33.** www.stortorget.org. Reservations required. Main courses 145SEK-315SEK. AE, DC, MC, V. Daily 11am-11pm. T-bana: Gamla Stan.

INEXPENSIVE

Cattelin Restaurant ★ SWEDISH Time and food fads have passed it by since its opening in 1897, but this is still one of the best and most reasonably priced restaurants in Stockholm. In a city where diners have been known to faint when presented with their tabs, it keeps its prices sane, and the food is still good and fresh. Don't expect genteel service—the clattering of china can sometimes be almost deafening, but few of the regular patrons seem to mind. First-rate menu choices include various preparations of beef, salmon, trout, veal, and chicken, which frequently make up the daily specials that often are preferred by lunch patrons. The fixed-price lunch is served only Monday to Friday 11am to 2pm. Every Friday night the place is reconfigured into a gay-friendly bar with a mixed crowd, a sign of the changing times.

Storkyrkobrinken 9. ✆ **08/20-18-18.** www.cattelin.com. Reservations recommended. Main courses 149SEK-295SEK; set-lunch menu 259SEK. AE, DC, MC, V. Mon-Fri 11am-11pm; Sat 11am-3pm; Sun noon-11pm. T-bana: Gamla Stan.

Magnus Ladulås SWEDISH/INTERNATIONAL This is a local favorite, and deservedly so, because the cookery is first-rate and the ingredients are market fresh and carefully chosen. I've been here when it was a little dull, and also at its most raucous—packed with visiting Uppsala students celebrating their graduation. Although the patrons on any given night are unpredictable, the food is not. Patrons go for the steak specialty, which is cooked as you like on a hot stone placed at your table; the mixed seafood plate with lobster sauce; or the fresh salmon flown in from Lapland. The restaurant was converted from a vaulted inner room of a 12th-century weaving factory, and it includes a bar that's worth a stop for a drink before your meal.

Österlånggatan 26. ✆ **08/21-19-57.** www.magnusladulas.se. Reservations recommended. Main courses 185SEK-239SEK. AE, DC, MC, V. Mon-Thurs 5-10pm; Fri-Sat 5pm-1am. Closed for lunch July 15-Aug 15. T-bana: Gamla Stan.

Cheap Dining in a Food Boutique

You'll find some of the widest and best selections of cost-conscious food in Stockholm's most lavish delicatessen: **NK Saluhall (Food Emporium)** in the cellar of the NK (Nordiska Kompaniet) Department Store, Hamngatan 18–20 (✆ **08/762-80-00**).

It serves up to 10 kinds of wine by the glass, priced at 75SEK to 105SEK. At the cheese bar, select the ingredients for a platter of cheese, accompanied by bream, jam, marmalade, and pickles. A few years ago, the organizers of this cheese bar won third prize in a Pan-European contest for the best selection of cheese in Europe. Platters with one kind of cheese cost 75SEK; platters with three cheeses, 135SEK; platters with five kinds of cheese, 180SEK.

Main courses here cost from 115SEK to 300SEK. Fish is grilled, smoked, or pickled. The best examples include grilled tuna filets on a salade niçoise, smoked halibut with *aioli* sauce, or lobster bisque with mussels and a garlic-based rouille sauce.

Both NK and its food court are open Monday to Friday 10am to 7pm, Saturday 10am to 6pm, and Sunday noon to 4pm (T-bana: Kungsträdgården).

Mälardrottningen ★ SEAFOOD/INTERNATIONAL Even if the food wasn't so good, the novelty of dining aboard the former yacht of Barbara Hutton—she was once called the richest woman on the planet—has a certain appeal. The upscale floating restaurant is set on the deck of a yacht built by industrialist C. K. G. Billings in 1924; it's now a hotel (see "Where to Stay," earlier in this chapter). Though a lot of the allure here is its novelty, the food is well prepared, with some of the flair associated with the ship's heyday. Menu items change with the seasons but might include imaginative offerings such as skewered scampi served with Parmesan cheese and chutney made from pesto and bananas. One of the least expensive main courses—appropriate for foggy days beside the harbor—is a heaping portion of marinated mussels in white wine and butter sauce, served with french fries. More formal dishes include a parfait of chicken livers with an apricot and oregano brioche, cream of chanterelle soup with a pumpkin- and sage-flavored gnocchi, prosciutto-wrapped tiger prawns, grilled Dublin Bay prawns with a fennel-flavored butter sauce, and fried filets of pikeperch with crisp-fried paella, red peppers, and lobster sauce.

Riddarholmen. ✆ **08/545-187-80.** www.restaurangmalardrottningen.se. Reservations recommended. Main courses 145SEK–325SEK. AE, DC, MC, V. Tues–Sat 6pm–midnight. T-bana: Gamla Stan.

On Kungsholmen

EXPENSIVE

Stadshuskällaren ★ SWEDISH/INTERNATIONAL The chefs at this two-in-one restaurant near the harbor in the basement of City Hall prepare the annual Nobel Prize banquet. You too can enjoy the cuisine served here, such as mountain grouse breast baked in black trumpet mushrooms with caramelized apples, poached onions, and broad beans, served with a Norman Calvados sauce and potato cake. You can opt, of course, for other main-course delights, including a confit of salmon filet with roasted Jerusalem artichokes, marinated beets, and a lemon emulsion, or else grilled turbot with smoked almonds. After passing through a beautiful carved wooden doorway, you'll enter an interior that is divided into two sections: the Skänken, which serves lunch only, and the Stora Matsalen, where chefs prepare the annual banquet for the Nobel Prize winners.

Stadshuset. ✆ **08/506-322-00.** www.profilrestauranger.se. Reservations required. Main courses 155SEK–269SEK. AE, DC, MC, V. Skänken: Mon–Fri 11:30am–2pm. Stora Matsalen: Mon–Fri 11:30am–11pm; Sat 2–11pm. No lunch July–Aug. T-bana: Rådhuset. Bus: 3 or 62.

On Djurgården

EXPENSIVE

Ulla Winbladh ★ SWEDISH More than most of Stockholm's restaurants, this is a highly reliable and sought-after staple, thanks to its origins in 1897 as part of Stockholm's World Fair, and thanks to a name (Ulla Winbladh) that conjures up images of passionate love for most Swedes. (Was she a hooker or was she a madonna? Only Sweden's most famous 18th-c. poet, Bellman, knew for sure, since Ulla was his mistress, to whom he dedicated some of his most evocative poetry.) Since it was acquired by its present management in 1994, this restaurant has impressed even the most jaded of Stockholm's foodies. It occupies a sprawling, stone-built, white-sided pavilion in an isolated position on the Djurgården. Inside, a series of dining rooms are outfitted like a 19th-century manor house, with unusual paintings and a sense of graceful prosperity. There's also an outdoor terrace lined with flowering plants. The menu focuses on time-tested, somewhat conservative Swedish cuisine, always impeccably prepared. Patrons who agree with this assessment include members of the Swedish royal family and a bevy of well-known TV, theater, and art-world personalities. Menu items include at least three different preparations of the inevitable herring; marinated salmon with a terrine of watercress, bleak roe, and asparagus; fish casserole with potatoes and shellfish sauce; Swedish meatballs in cream sauce with lingonberries and pickled cucumbers; and a beautiful version of poached halibut with hard-boiled egg, shrimps, and melted butter.

Rosendalsvägen 8. ✆ **08/534-89-701.** www.ullawinbladh.se. Reservations required. Main courses 145SEK–325SEK. AE, DC, MC, V. Mon 11:30am–10pm; Tues–Fri noon–11pm; Sat 12:30–11pm; Sun 12:30–10pm. Bus: 47.

MODERATE

Villa Kallhagen ★ SWEDISH This place is best in summer, when you'll feel like you're dining in the Swedish countryside, although it is only a 5-minute ride from the heart of the city. Do as we do, and precede dinner with a stroll along the nearby park's canal, Djurgårdkanalen. At least you'll work up an appetite for the crowd-pleasing fare, which is both market fresh and well prepared. The chef's culinary technique never fails him, and his inventiveness and precision with local ingredients always impresses us. For an appetizer, try the creamy crayfish and a fresh chanterelle salad with bleak roe served on fennel bread. The most traditional dish on the menu, and an old favorite of ours, is fried Baltic herring with Dijon mustard sauce and drawn butter. You also might enjoy the oven-baked chicken with port-wine sauce or the lemon-fried veal (moist and tender) with mashed potatoes and a Parmesan terrine (a delightful accompaniment).

Djurgårdsbrunnsvägen 10. ✆ **08/665-03-00.** www.kallhagen.se. Reservations required. Main courses 180SEK–240SEK; Sun brunch 295SEK. AE, DC, MC, V. Mon–Fri 11:30am–2pm and 5–11pm; Sat 11:30am–4pm and 5–11pm; Sun brunch 11:30am–5pm. Closed for lunch July 5–Aug 6. Bus: 69 from Central Station.

At Södermalm

INEXPENSIVE

Garlic & Shots MEDITERRANEAN/INTERNATIONAL We once said we could go for garlic in anything but dessert, only to be proven wrong by one served here. This theme restaurant follows two strong, overriding ideas: Everyone needs a shot of garlic every day, and everything tastes better if it's doctored with a dose of the Mediterranean's most potent ingredient. The no-frills setting is artfully spartan, with bare wooden tables that have hosted an unexpectedly large number of rock stars. Expect garlic in just about everything, from soup (try garlic-ginger with clam) to such main courses as beefsteak covered with fried minced garlic and Transylvania-style vampire steak, drenched in horseradish-tomato-and-garlic sauce. And then there's the garlic ice cream, which tastes a hell of a lot better than it sounds: the garlic is mixed in with honey ice cream and sweetened with green peppercorn strawberries and chocolate-dipped garlic cloves. Now, what to wash down with all these flavors? Garlic ale or garlic beer, of course.

Folkungagatan 84. ✆ **08/640-84-46.** www.garlicandshots.com. Reservations recommended. Main courses 150SEK–250SEK. MC, V. Daily 5pm–1am. T-bana: Medborgarplatsen.

On Långholmen

MODERATE

Långholmen Restaurant ★ INTERNATIONAL This premier dining venue is in the Långholmen Hotel, the former-state-penitentiary-turned-hotel. From the windows of the old-fashioned dining room, you can still see the high brick walls, small doors with heavy bolts, and bars on the windows. Even the paintings, many in gentle pastels, reflect the workhouse drudgery that used to prevail here. Diners come today for menu items that change with the seasons: carpaccio of shellfish, smoked breast of duck with a walnut-cranberry vinaigrette, lobster and turbot stewed with vegetables in a shellfish bouillon, and *tournedos* of venison with juniper berries, smoked ham, pepper sauce, and Swedish potatoes. This is hardly prison food—in fact, only market-fresh ingredients are used, and the staff here is clearly dedicated to pleasing your palate.

Alstaviksvägen 17. ✆ **08/720-85-50.** Reservations recommended. Lunch main courses 106SEK–155SEK; dinner main courses 175SEK–278SEK. AE, DC, MC, V. Mon–Fri 11:30am–10pm; Sat noon–11pm; Sun noon–5pm. Closed July 2–Aug 9. T-bana: Hornstul. Bus: 4, 40, or 66.

EXPLORING STOCKHOLM

There's no denying that Stockholm is an expensive city, but there are many bargains, and we've done our best to bring them to you. Rapidly evolving, Stockholm's loaded with sights and activities. If the Vasa Ship Museum doesn't pique your interest, perhaps the changing of the guard at the Royal Palace or the Gröna Lunds Tivoli amusement park will. Even window shopping for beautifully designed Swedish crafts can be an enjoyable way to spend an afternoon. At night, Stockholm becomes the liveliest city in northern Europe.

ON GAMLA STAN & NEIGHBORING ISLANDS

Kungliga Slottet (Royal Palace) & Museums ★★ This is no match for Buckingham Palace, but a visit here offers a look at the daily life of the royal court. Kungliga Slottet is one of the few official residences of a European monarch that's open to the public, and although the king and queen prefer to live at Drottningholm, this massive 608-room showcase remains their official address.

The **Royal Apartments ★★★**, entered on the second floor of the north wing, are the most impressive. Decorated in the 1690s by French artists, they have the oldest interiors of the palace. The lavish **ballroom ★★** is called "the White Sea," and **Karl XI's Gallery** is the venue for official banquets.

In **Rikssalen (Hall of State),** you can see Queen Christina's **silver throne ★**, a rare piece of silver furniture created for the queen's coronation in 1650. The **Guest Apartment** in the west wing marries rococo and Gustavian classicism. Since the interiors were designed over a period of centuries, expect a hodgepodge of decorative styles, including Louis XVI and Empire.

Second in importance to the state apartments is the **Skattkammaren ★★★**, or Royal Treasury, entered through the south arch. These dark vaults contain the greatest collection of royal regalia in all of Scandinavia, a virtual gold mine when compared to the collections of Oslo or Copenhagen.

The original palace that stood here, destroyed in a fire in 1697, was **Tre Kronor.** Today the Tre Kronor Museum on the ground floor of the palace's northern wing honors its memory. There's more to see at this palace,

Stockholm Attractions

Drottningholm Palace and Theater **1**
Gröna Lunds Tivoli **16**
Hallwylska Museet (Hallwyl Museum) **10**
Historiska Museet (Museum of National Antiquities) **11**
Kungliga Slottet (Royal Palace) & Museums **6**
Moderna Museet (Museum of Modern Art) **13**
Nationalmuseum (National Museum of Art) **9**
Nordiska Museet (Nordic Museum) **15**
Operahuset (Royal Opera House) **5**
Östasiatiska Museet (Museum of Far Eastern Antiquities) **12**
Prins Eugens Waldemarsudde **18**
Rådhuset **2**
Riddarholmskyrkan **7**

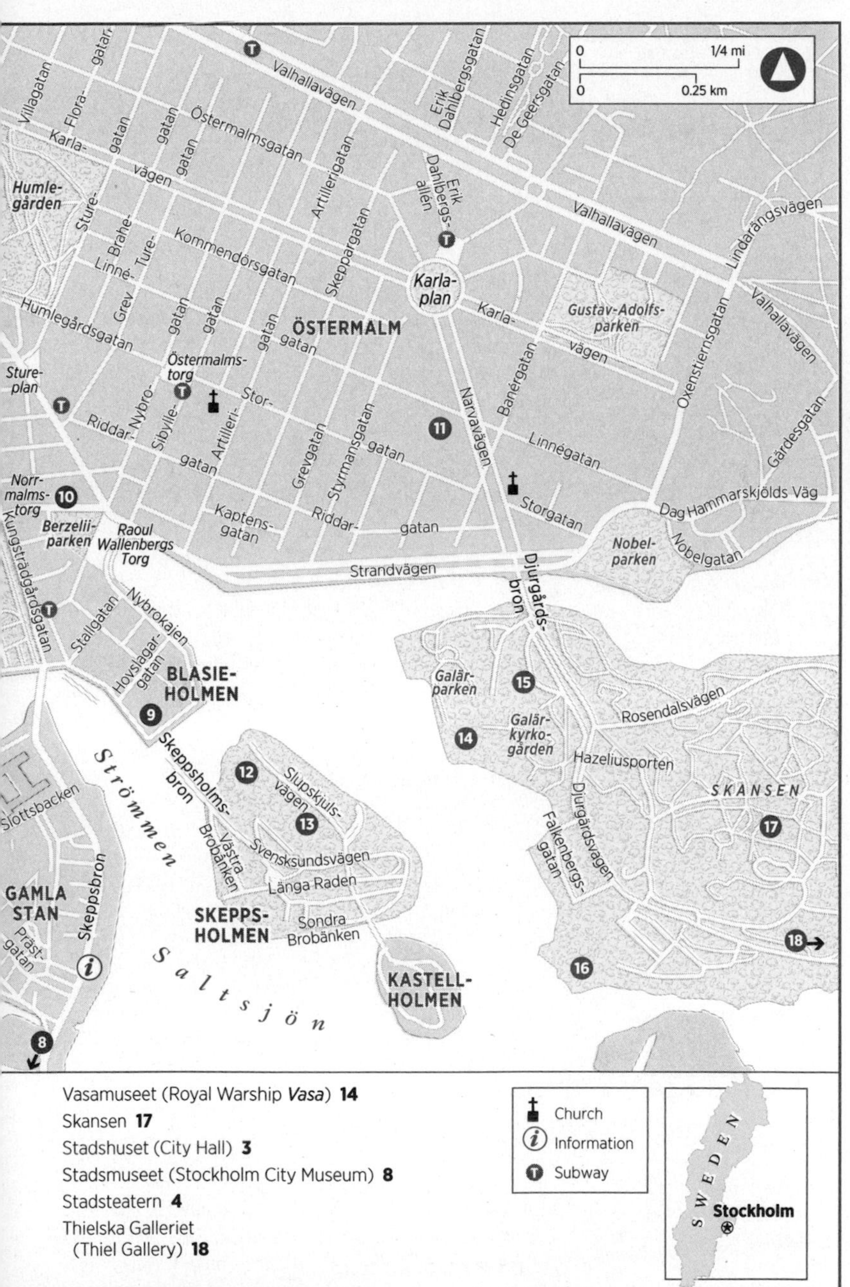
0 1/4 mi
0 0.25 km
Valhallavägen
Villagatan
Flora-gatan
Karla-vägen
Humle-gården
Sture-gatan
Brahe-gatan
Grev Ture-gatan
Linné-gatan
Östermalmsgatan
Erik Dahlbergsgatan
Hedinsgatan
De Geersgatan
Erik Dahlbergs-allén
Artillerigatan
Kommendörsgatan
Skeppargatan
Karla-plan
Lindarängsvägen
Gustav-Adolfs-parken
Oxenstiernsgatan
Humlegårdsgatan
ÖSTERMALM
Östermalms-torg
Sture-plan
Nybro-gatan
Sibylle-gatan
Artilleri-gatan
Stor-gatan
Riddar-gatan
Grevgatan
Styrmansgatan
Narvavägen
Banérgatan
Linnégatan
Gärdesgatan
Storgatan
Dag Hammarskjölds Väg
Norr-malms-torg
Berzelii-parken
Raoul Wallenbergs Torg
Kaptens-gatan
Nobel-parken
Nobelgatan
Strandvägen
Djurgårds-bron
Kungsträdgårdsgatan
Nybrokajen
Stallgatan
Hovslagar-gatan
BLASIE-HOLMEN
Galär-parken
Galär-kyrko-gården
Rosendalsvägen
Hazeliusporten
SKANSEN
Skeppsholms-bron
Strömmen
Slupskjuls-vägen
Västra Brobänken
Svensksundsvägen
Långa Raden
Djurgårdsvägen
Falkenbergs-gatan
Slottsbacken
GAMLA STAN
Skeppsbron
Präst-gatan
SKEPPS-HOLMEN
Sondra Brobänken
KASTELL-HOLMEN
Saltsjön
Vasamuseet (Royal Warship *Vasa*) **14**
Skansen **17**
Stadshuset (City Hall) **3**
Stadsmuseet (Stockholm City Museum) **8**
Stadsteatern **4**
Thielska Galleriet (Thiel Gallery) **18**
Church
Information
Subway
SWEDEN
Stockholm

including the **Slottskyrkan** baroque chapel; **Gustav III's Antikmuseum ★**, one of Europe's oldest museums; and the **Livrustkammaren ★★** royal armory and Sweden's oldest museum, where **state coaches ★★** and coronation robes, in addition to weapons, are on display.

Royal Guards have been stationed at the palace since 1523, and today military units from all over Sweden take turns standing guard. In summer you can watch the parade of the military guard daily. In winter it takes place on Wednesday and Sunday; on the other days there's no parade, but you can see the **Changing of the Royal Guard ★**. The changing of the guard takes place at 12:15pm Monday to Saturday and at 1:15pm on Sunday in front of the Royal Palace.

Before you leave, visit the **Royal Gift Shop,** where much of the merchandise is produced in limited editions, including textiles based on designs from the 16th and 17th centuries.

Kungliga Husgerådskammaren. ✆ **08/402-61-30**. www.royalcourt.se. Entry to Royal Apartments, Royal Armory, Museum of Antiquities, and Treasury is 100SEK adults, 50SEK seniors and students, free for children 6 and under. A combination ticket to all parts of palace is 140SEK adults, 70SEK students and children. Apartments and Treasury Sept–May Tues–Sun noon–5pm (closed in Jan); June–Aug daily 10am–5pm; closed during government receptions. Royal Armory daily 10am–5pm. Museum of Antiquities May 15–31 and Sept daily 10am–4pm; June–Aug daily 10am–5pm. T-bana: Gamla Stan. Bus: 43, 55, 71, or 76.

Östasiatiskamuseet (Museum of Far Eastern Antiquities) ★ 🎁 You may be going only a short journey to Skeppsholmen, a small island in the middle of central Stockholm, but you're really making a trip to the Far East. The collection of archaeological objects, fine arts, and handicrafts from China, Japan, Korea, and India form one of the finest and most extensive museums of its kind outside Asia.

Among the outstanding displays are Chinese Neolithic painted pottery, bronze ritual vessels, archaic jades, woodcarvings, ivory, lacquer work, enamelware, Buddhist sculpture, and Ming blue-and-white wares.

Skeppsholmen. ✆ **08/519-557-50.** www.ostasiatiska.se. Admission 60SEK adults, free 19 and under. Tues 11am–8pm; Wed–Sun 11am–5pm. T-bana: Kungsträdgården. Bus: 65 to Karl XII Torg, 7-min. walk.

Riddarholmskyrkan ★ The second-oldest church in Stockholm is on the tiny island of Riddarholmen, next to Gamla Stan. It was founded in the 13th century as a Franciscan monastery, but today is a virtual pantheon of Swedish kings. The last king buried here was Gustav V in 1950. You come here for the royal tombs, as the church is relatively devoid of art. However, it does contain a trio of royal chapels.

Riddarholmen. ✆ **08/402-61-30.** www.royalcourt.se. Admission 30SEK adults, 10SEK children 7–18, free for children 6 and under. May daily 10am–4pm; June–Aug daily 10am–5pm; Sept daily 10am–4pm. Closed Oct–Apr. T-bana: Gamla Stan.

ON NORRMALM

Hallwylska Museet (Hallwyl Museum) ★ 🎁 The rich Countess Wilhelmina von Hallwyl was a collector of almost anything as long as it was valuable and expensive, and she cataloged her acquisitions and left them to the state upon her death.

The catalog of this passionate collector came to 78 volumes, which have been open to the public since 1938. The collection includes classic paintings, rare tapestries, silver, armor, weapons, antique musical instruments, glassware, and umbrellas and buttons (but only the finest ones). On a guided tour you learn historical tidbits, such as the fact that this house had a modern bathroom before the royal palace. Ask about summer evening concerts presented in the central courtyard.

Hamngatan 4. © **08/402-30-99.** www.hallwylskamuseet.se. Guided tours 80SEK adults, 50SEK for ground-floor rooms. Free ages 19 and under. Guided tours in Swedish Tues–Sun noon, 1pm, 2pm, 3pm, and 4pm; extra tour Wed 6pm. In English Tues–Sun 3pm. T-bana: Kungsträdgården.

Historiska Museet (Museum of National Antiquities) ★★ The Viking era lives on here, as more than 4,000 objects and artifacts reveal the lives and travels of these rugged seafarers.

We always head to the **Goldrummet ★★★** first, a virtual treasure chest of items that, amazingly, date from the Bronze Age. It features Viking silver and gold jewelry, large ornate charms, elaborate bracelets, and a unique neck collar from Färjestaden.

After all this gold, the other exhibitions come as a bit of a letdown. The Gothic Hall holds one of Scandinavia's finest collections of sculpture, church triptychs, and other ecclesiastical objects from the 12th century onward. In the Textile Chamber, fabrics from the Middle Ages to the present are on display.

Narvavägen 13–17. © **08/519-556-00.** www.historiska.se. Admission 70SEK adults, 50SEK seniors and students, free for those 17 and under. May–Sept daily 10am–5pm; Oct–Apr Fri–Wed 11am–5pm, Thurs 11am–8pm. T-bana: Karlaplan or Östermalmstorg. Bus: 47 or 69.

Kaknästornet (Kaknäs Television Tower) This 1967 tower may be ugly, but the view of greater Stockholm from the top is the best there is. In the northern district of Djurgården is the tallest man-made structure in Scandinavia—a 152m (499-ft.) radio and television tower. Two elevators run to an observation platform, where you can see everything from the cobblestone streets of Gamla Stan to the city's modern concrete-and-glass structures. A moderately priced restaurant that serves classic Swedish cuisine is on the 28th floor. The view from the restaurant is even better than the food.

Mörkakroken. © **08/667-21-80.** www.kaknastornet.se. Admission 40SEK adults, 20SEK children 7–15, free for children under 7. Jan–Mar Sun–Wed 10am–5pm, Thurs–Sat 10am–9pm; Apr and Sept daily 10am–9pm; May–Aug daily 9am–10pm; Oct–Dec Mon–Sat 10am–9pm, Sun 10am–5pm. Closed Dec 24–25. Bus: 69.

Moderna Museet (Museum of Modern Art) ★★ ☺ This former drill house on the island of Skeppsholmen is one of the greatest repositories of modern art in northern Europe. The museum is especially strong in cubist paintings, with works by Picasso, Braque, and Léger. We are particularly enthralled by Matisse's ***Apollo decoupage*** ★ and the celebrated ***Enigma of William Tell*** ★★ by Salvador Dalí. In all, the present collection includes 5,000 paintings and sculptures, around 25,000 watercolors, and 100,000 photographs, as well as a large number of graphics, videos, and films. Stunning temporary exhibitions are also staged. Admission to the museum is free, but temporary exhibitions carry a charge.

Musical concerts and the best children's workshops in Stockholm are also presented here. You can patronize the modern espresso bar near the main entrance. ***Tip:*** Time your visit to have a good and affordable lunch at the self-service restaurant offering views toward Östermalm.

Skeppsholmen. © **08/519-552-00.** www.modernamuseet.se. Admission 80SEK adults, 60SEK students and seniors, free for those 17 and under. Tues 10am–8pm; Wed–Sun 10am–6pm. T-bana: Kungsträdgården. Bus: 65.

Nationalmuseum (National Museum of Art) ★★★ Founded in 1792, the National Museum is one of the oldest museums in the world and Sweden's largest and best museum of world art. The museum grew out of a small collection from Gustav Vasa's collection at Gripsholm Castle. Over the years the collection expanded from bequests, purchases, and even spoils of war.

In all, the museum owns 16,000 artworks from the late Middle Ages up to the 20th century, with emphasis on Swedish 18th- and 19th-century art. The collection of Dutch paintings from the 17th century is rich, and the **18th-century collection of French paintings ★★** is regarded as one of the best in the world. Naturally the museum is a good showcase for Sweden's two most famous artists, Anders Zorn and Carl Larsson.

The first floor focuses on applied arts (silverware, handicrafts, porcelain, Empire furnishings, and the like). First-time visitors, if pressed for time, may want to head directly to the second floor to check out the paintings from northern Europe and a rare collection of **Russian icons ★**. The museum shows an exceptional number of masterpieces, but the most important room in the museum has one whole wall featuring the **works of Rembrandt ★★**.

The museum is at the tip of a peninsula, a short walk from the Royal Opera House and the Grand Hotel.

Södra Blasieholmshamnen. ✆ **08/519-54-300.** www.nationalmuseum.se. Admission 100SEK adults, 80SEK students and seniors, free for those 18 and under. June–Aug Tues 11am–8pm, Wed–Sun 11am–5pm; Sept–May Tues and Thurs 11am–8pm, Wed and Fri–Sun 11am–5pm. Closed Mon. T-bana: Kungsträdgården. Bus: 2, 62, 65, or 76.

ON DJURGÅRDEN

The forested island of Djurgården (Deer Park) is about 3km (2 miles) to the east of Gamla Stan (Old Town).

Nordiska Museet (Nordic Museum) ★★ This museum showcases preserved items from Sweden's past. The first object you encounter when entering the Great Hall is a mammoth pink-tinted statue of a seated Gustav Vasa. That piece of oak in his forehead was said to have come from a massive tree planted by the king himself.

You almost know what to expect here: 16th-century dining tables, period costumes, dollhouses, textiles, and even an extensive exhibit of tools from the Swedish fish trade.

Djurgårdsvägen 6–16, Djurgården. ✆ **08/519-546-00.** www.nordiskamuseet.se. Admission 80SEK adults, free for those 17 and under. Mon–Fri 10am–4pm; Sat–Sun 11am–5pm. Bus: 44, 47, or 69.

Prins Eugens Waldemarsudde ★★ Prince Eugen's (1865–1947) former home and studio, one of the most visited museums in Sweden, is now an art gallery and a memorial to this talented artist, who specialized in depictions of his favorite spots of beauty in central Sweden, earning him the nickname "the Painting Prince."

This lovely three-story mansion on the water was acquired by the prince in 1899, and he lived here until his death. The rooms on the ground floor are furnished just as the prince left them. The prince was not only a painter, but a collector, acquiring works by such great Scandinavian artists as Edvard Munch, Carl Larsson, and Anders Zorn.

Allow time to wander through the gardens with centuries-old trees, enjoying panoramic views of the Stockholm harbor. The park is filled with sculptures by some of the greatest masters of Europe—Carl Milles to Auguste Rodin. While at Waldemarsudde, see the **Old Mill,** a windmill built in the 1780s.

Prins Eugens Väg 6. ✆ **08/545-837-00.** www.waldemarsudde.se. Admission 95SEK adults, 75SEK seniors and students, free for children 18 and under. Tues–Sun 11am–5pm. Bus: 47 to the end of the line.

Skansen ★★★ This was the world's first open-air museum in 1891 and presents how Swedes lived. It is also a summer playground for Stockholmers, although it's hardly comparable to Tivoli Gardens in Copenhagen. Often called "Old Sweden in a Nutshell," this museum features more than 150 reconstructed dwellings scattered over some 30 hectares (74 acres) of parkland. Exhibits include windmills, manor houses, blacksmith shops—even a complete town quarter that was meticulously rebuilt. Many handicrafts for which Swedes later became noted (glass blowing, for example) are demonstrated. For a tour of the buildings' interiors, arrive no later than 4pm. Folk dancing and open-air concerts, in some cases featuring international stars, are occasionally scheduled in summertime. Check at the Tourist Center for information. A lot goes on during summer nights (see "Stockholm After Dark," later).

Djurgården 49–51. ✆ **08/442-80-00.** www.skansen.se. Admission 70SEK–120SEK adults, depending on time of day, day of week, and season; 30SEK–50SEK children 6–15; free for children under 6. Historic buildings Oct–Apr daily 10am–4pm; May daily 10am–8pm; June–Aug daily 10am–10pm; Sept daily 10am–5pm. Bus: 47 from central Stockholm. Ferry from Slussen.

Thielska Galleriet (Thiel Gallery) ★★ It's inevitable to draw comparisons between this world-class gallery and the just-visited Waldemarsudde of Prince Eugen—in fact, the art collection at Thielska surpasses that of "the Painting Prince." Both of the palatial art-filled mansions at Djurgården were constructed roughly at the same time by architect Ferdinand Roberg.

Ernest Thiel was once a wealthy banker and art collector who commissioned the mansion, drawing upon architectural influences from both the Italian Renaissance and the Far East. Over the years, Thiel began to fill his palatial rooms with great art. However, in the wake of World War I, he went bankrupt and the state took over his property in 1924, eventually opening it as a museum.

Regrettably, we can't see all of Thiel's masterpieces. In a robbery that made international headlines in 2002, many of the finest works were stolen. They were never recovered. Works by Manet, Rodin, Toulouse-Lautrec, and others round out the collection.

Sjötullsbacken 6–8, Djurgården. ✆ **08/662-58-84.** www.thielska-galleriet.se. Admission 60SEK adults, 40SEK students, free for children 15 and under. Daily noon–4pm. Bus: 69.

Vasamuseet (Royal Warship *Vasa*) ★★★ This 17th-century man-of-war is the most visited attraction in Scandinavia—and for good reason. Near the main entrance to Skansen within a cement-sided museum that was specifically constructed for its display, the *Vasa* is the world's oldest complete and identified ship.

On its maiden voyage in 1628, in front of thousands of onlookers, the Royal Warship *Vasa* capsized and sank almost instantly to the bottom of Stockholm harbor. Its salvage in 1961 was an engineering and archaeological triumph. On board were more than 4,000 coins, carpenters' tools, sailors' pants, fish bones, and other items of archaeological interest. Best of all, 97% of the ship's 700 original decorative sculptures were found and are on display alongside baroque carvings. A full-scale model of half of the *Vasa*'s upper gun deck has been built, together with the admiral's cabin and the steering compartment.

Galärvarvsvägen 14, Djurgården. ✆ **08/519-548-00.** www.vasamuseet.se. Admission 110SEK adults, 80SEK students, free ages 18 and under. Sept–May Thurs–Tues 10am–5pm; June–Aug Thurs–Tues 8:30am–6pm, Wed 10am–8pm. Closed Jan 1, May 1, Dec 23–25, and Dec 31. Bus: 47. Ferry from Slussen year-round, from Nybroplan in summer only.

ON KUNGSHOLMEN

Stadshuset (Stockholm City Hall) ★★ Nobel Prize winners are honored and awarded here, and while you won't walk away a winner in the literal sense, you are awarded a view of one of the finest examples of modern architecture in Europe. Built in the National Romantic Style, the Stockholm City Hall (Stadshuset), on the island of Kungsholmen, was designed by Ragnar Ostberg and completed in 1923. A lofty square tower rising 100m (328 ft.) dominates the red-brick structure. In summer you can climb the tower for what we consider the finest **panoramic view ★★** of Gamla Stan in the area. It bears three gilt crowns, the symbol of Sweden, and the national coat of arms. There are two courts: the open civic court and the interior covered court. The Blue Hall is used for banquets and other festive occasions, including the Nobel Prize banquet. About 18 million pieces of gold and colored-glass mosaics cover the walls of the **Golden Hall ★★**. The southern gallery contains murals by Prince Eugen.

Hantverksgatan 1. ✆ **08/508-29-05.** www.stockholm.se/stadshuset. Admission 80SEK adults, 40SEK ages 12–17, free for children 11 and under. Tower additional 30SEK. Apr–Sept daily 10am–4:15pm. City Hall tours (subject to change) June–Aug daily at 10am, 11am, noon, 2pm, 3pm, and 4pm; Sept–May daily at 10am, noon, and 2pm. T-bana: Centralen or Rådhuset. Bus: 3 or 62.

ON SÖDERMALM

Stadsmuseet (Stockholm City Museum) ☺ Skip this museum if your time is fading; otherwise give it an hour or so. For architecture buffs, the building may be more intriguing than its exhibits. Constructed in the Italian baroque style, it was designed by the famous Tessin the Elder as the city hall for southern Stockholm.

The history of Stockholm is presented in stages floor to floor, the first floor depicting Stockholm when it was a great maritime power in the 17th century. On the second floor you can see Stockholm emerging as a multicultural city, when its population soared to more than a million people, causing a housing shortage. Finally, on the third floor, you are shown what a local factory looked like in 1897. Relics of Sweden's first industrial exhibition, also from 1897, are also on view.

If you have time, check out the two reconstructed apartments and Torget, a replica of a main square, on the ground floor.

Ryssgården, Slussen. ✆ **08/508-316-00.** www.stadsmuseum.stockholm.se. Free admission. Tues–Sun 11am–5pm (Thurs to 8pm). T-bana: Slussen. Bus: 43 or 46.

NEAR STOCKHOLM

Drottningholm Palace and Theater ★★★ There is no palace in northern Europe as grand and spectacular as this regal complex, which is why it is dubbed the "Versailles of Sweden." The royal family still lives here, on an island in Lake Mälaren, but the royal apartments are guarded and screened off.

Work began on this masterpiece in 1662 by Nicodemus Tessin the Elder (1615–81), one of the most celebrated architects of the 17th century, and it is now listed as a UNESCO World Heritage Site.

Drottningholm needs about 3 hours of your time, but deserves more if you have it. You can explore the palace, Sweden's greatest theater, the magnificent gardens, and even a Chinese Pavilion. The highlight of any tour is the **State Apartments ★★★**, with a spectacular staircase. The apartments dazzle with opulent furniture and art from the 17th to the 19th centuries, painted ceilings, precious Chinese vases, and ornate gold chandeliers.

Queen Lovisa Ulrika's **library** ★★ is a work of grand beauty, an excellent example of the Gustavian style by Jean Eric Rehn. After all that grandeur we like to retreat to the **Kina Slott** ★. The pavilion, on the southeast corner of the park, was constructed in Stockholm in 1753 and later floated downriver to surprise Lovisa on her 33rd birthday.

Allow as much time as you can to stroll through **Drottningholm Gardens** ★★★, checking out the bronze **Hercules Fountain** ★★, the water garden, pools, bridges, and islands. **Drottningholm Court Theater** ★★★ is a gem of baroque architecture. The Royal Music Academy and the Royal Opera (founded by Lovisa) presented performances here, and today the theater is complete with the original backdrops and props. Theater buffs can visit the **Theatre Museum,** with exhibits tracing the history of European theater since the 1700s. Between June and July, some two dozen performances are staged. Devoted almost exclusively to 18th-century opera, it seats only 450. Many performances sell out far in advance to season-ticket holders. The theater can be visited only as part of a guided tour, which focuses on the original sets and stage mechanisms.

For tickets to the evening performances, which cost 275SEK to 895SEK, call ✆ **08/660-82-25.** For more information about the theater, call ✆ **77/170-70-70**, or visit **www.dtm.se**.

Ekerö, Drottningholm. ✆ **08/402-62-80.** www.royalcourt.se. Palace 80SEK adults, 40SEK students and children ages 7–18; theater guided tour 90SEK adults, 55SEK children 7–18; Chinese Pavilion 70SEK adults, 35SEK students. All free for children under 7. Palace Oct–Apr Sat–Sun noon–3:30pm; May–Aug daily 10am–4:30pm; Sept daily 11am–3:30pm. Theater guided tours in English May noon–4:30pm; June–Aug daily 11am–4:30pm; Sept daily 1–3:30pm. Chinese Pavilion Apr and Oct daily 1–3:30pm; May daily 11am–4:30pm; June–Aug daily 11am–3pm; Sept Tues–Sun noon–3pm. Lies 11km (6¾ miles) west of Stockholm. T-bana: Brommaplan, then bus no. 301 or 323 to Drottningholm. Ferry from the dock near City Hall.

Millesgården ★★★ This former villa on the island of Lidingö, northeast of Stockholm, is home to Carl Milles's (1875–1955) sculpture garden.

Emigrating to the U.S. in 1931, Milles became a professor of art at the University of Michigan, creating nearly 75 sculptures, many of which are on display around the U.S. and Sweden today. However, some of the artist's major works are on view here, including his monumental and much-reproduced *Hands of God* ★★★. Sculptures sit atop columns on terraces in this garden, high above the harbor and the city landscape. The site also includes his personal collection of works by other leading sculptors. The villa displays a unique collection of art from both the Middle Ages and the Renaissance, plus rare artifacts excavated in the ruins of ancient Rome and Greece.

Carl Milles Väg 32, Lidingö. ✆ **08/446-75-80.** www.millesgarden.se. Admission 90SEK adults, 65SEK seniors and students, free for children 18 and under. May–Sept daily 11am–5pm; Oct–Apr Tues–Sun noon–5pm. T-bana: Ropsten, then bus to Torsviks Torg or train to Norsvik. Bus: 207.

OUTSIDE THE CITY

Uppsala ★★★

68km (42 miles) NW of Stockholm

ESSENTIALS

GETTING THERE The **train** from Stockholm's Central Station takes about 45 minutes. Trains leave about every hour during peak hours. Some visitors spend the day in Uppsala and return to Stockholm on the commuter train in the late afternoon.

Eurailpass holders ride free. **Boats** between Uppsala and Skokloster depart Uppsala daily at 11am and 7:30pm, returning to Uppsala at 5:45 and 11:30pm. Round-trip passage costs 200SEK. For details, ask a tourist office or call ✆ **070/293-81-61.**

SEEING THE SIGHTS

Carolina Rediviva (University Library) ★ This is one of the greatest of all Scandinavian libraries. The most treasured manuscript is the *Codex Argenteus* or **Silver Bible ★★★**. Displayed in the exhibit room, it was translated into Gothic in the middle of the 3rd century and copied in about A.D. 525. It's the only book extant in old Gothic script, having been written in silver ink on purple vellum. Also worth seeing is *Carta Marina,* the earliest map (1539) of Sweden and its neighboring countries.

Drottninggatan. ✆ **018/471-39-00.** Admission 20SEK adults, free for children 11 and under. Exhibit room June 14–Aug 15 Mon–Fri 9am–5pm, Sat 10am–5pm, Sun 11am–4pm; Aug 16–June 13 Sun 10am–5pm. Bus: 6, 7, or 22.

Linnaeus Garden & Museum ★ Swedish botanist Carl von Linné (or Linnaeus) developed a classification system for the world's plants and flowers, and his garden and former home are on the spot where he restored Uppsala University's botanical garden. Linnaeus, who arranged the plants according to his "sexual classification system," left detailed sketches and descriptions of the garden, which have been faithfully followed.

Linnaeus was a professor of theoretical medicine, including botany, pharmacology, and zoology, at Uppsala University. You can visit his house, which has been restored to its original design, and an art gallery that exhibits the works of contemporary local artists.

Svartbäcksgatan 27. ✆ **018/13-65-40** for the museum, or 018/471-25-76 for the garden. www.linnaeus.uu.se. Museum and gardens 60SEK adults, free for children under 16. May–Sept Tues–Sun 11am–5pm. Walk straight from the train station to Kungsgatan, turn right, and walk about 10 min.

Uppsala Domkyrka ★★ Uppsala Domkyrka is Sweden's most celebrated Gothic building and the country's coronation church for three centuries. The largest cathedral in Scandinavia, this twin-spired Gothic structure stands nearly 120m (394 ft.) tall. Founded in the 13th century, it received the most damage in 1702 in a disastrous fire. Among the regal figures buried in the crypt is Gustav Vasa. The remains of St. Erik, patron saint of Sweden, are entombed in a silver shrine, and one of the chapels is filled with 14th-century wall paintings recounting his legend. The botanist Linnaeus and the philosopher-theologian Swedenborg are also interred here. A small museum displays ecclesiastical relics.

Domkyrkoplan 2. ✆ **018/18-71-73.** www.uppsaladomkyrka.se. Free admission to cathedral. Museum 30SEK adults, free for children 15 and under. Cathedral daily 8am–6pm. Museum Apr–Aug daily 10am–5pm; Sept–Mar daily noon–3pm. Bus: 1.

Museum Gustavianum ★ 🎁 Across from the cathedral is the best of this university city's museums. Gruesome public dissections used to take place here. The 1663 theater was lit by a sun-crested cupola, one of the distinctive landmarks of Uppsala today. Gustavianum is Uppsala University's oldest preserved building. Here you can see a number of attractions, none more attention-grabbing than the **Augsburg Cabinet of Curiosities ★★**, a gemstone-encrusted ebony cabinet gifted to King Gustav II Adolf from the German city of Augsburg in 1632.

Akademigatan 3. ✆ **018/471-75-71.** www.gustavianum.uu.se. Admission 40SEK adults, 30SEK students and seniors, free for children 11 and under. Mid-May to mid-Sept Tues–Sun 11am–5pm; off season Tues–Sun 11am–4pm. Bus: 1, 2, 51, or 53.

ESPECIALLY FOR KIDS

The open-air park Skansen (see above), on Djurgården, offers **Lill-Skansen** for kids. There's a petting zoo with pigs, goats, and horses. Lill-Skansen offers a break from the dizzying (and often tantrum-inducing) excitement frequently generated by a commercial amusement park. A miniature train ride through the park is about as wild as it gets. Lill-Skansen is open daily in summer from 10:30am to 4pm.

Before going to Skansen, stop off at the ***Vasa* Museum** and cap off the evening with a visit to **Gröna Lunds Tivoli** (see "Stockholm After Dark," later in this chapter), which also is on Djurgården.

STOCKHOLM ON FOOT: WALKING TOURS

WALKING TOUR 1: GAMLA STAN (OLD TOWN)

START: **Gustav Adolfs Torg**

FINISH: **Slussplan**

TIME: **Allow 2 hours for this walking tour.**

BEST TIMES: **Any day when it's not raining is the perfect time for this walking tour of historic Old Town.**

Start at:

1 Gustav Adolfs Torg

In the Royal Palace facing the square, Gustavus III, patron of the arts, was assassinated here at a masked ball in 1792.

Walk across Norrbro (North Bridge) heading toward the Royal Palace, passing on your right the:

2 Swedish Parliament

The Parliament building at Helgeandsholmen dates from 1897, when its foundation stone was laid. It can be visited only on guided tours.

Along the bridge on your left are stairs leading to the:

3 Medeltidsmuseet (Museum of Medieval Stockholm)

This museum on Strömparterren contains objects and settings from medieval Stockholm, including the Riddarholmship and parts of the old city wall.

4 Café Strömparterren

One of Stockholm's hidden cafes, Helgeandsholmen (© 08/21-95-45), is also one of the most centrally located—just next door to the Medeltidsmuseet. Many Stockholmers come here for a morning cup of coffee and a stunning view of the waterfront. In summer, tables are placed outside; the interior of the cafe is built into the walls under Norrbro.

After leaving the museum, continue south along the bridge until you come to Slottskajen. Here, directly in front of the Royal Palace, make a right turn and head to:

5 Mynttorget (Coin Square)

This square is the site of the Kanslihuset, a government office building erected in the 1930s. The neoclassical, columned facade remains from the Royal Mint of 1790.

Continue straight along Myntgatan until you reach Riddarhustorget. On your right is the:

6 Riddarhuset

The Swedish aristocracy met in this 17th-century House of Nobles during the Parliament of the Four Estates (1665–68).

Continue straight across Riddarholmsbron bridge until you come to the little island of:

7 Riddarholmen

Called the "Island of the Knights," Riddarholmen is closely linked to the Old Town. You'll immediately see its chief landmark, the **Riddarholmskyrkan** church with its cast-iron spire. Founded as an abbey in the 13th century, it has been the burial place of Swedish kings for 4 centuries.

Walk along the north side of the church until you reach Birger Jarls Torg. From there, take the 1-block-long Wrangelska Backen to the water. Then go left and walk along Södra Riddarholmshamnen.

Veer left by the railroad tracks, climb some steps, and go along Hebbes Trappor until you return to Riddarholmskyrkan. From here, cross over Riddarholmsbron and return to Riddarhustorget.

Cross Stora Nygatan and take the next right onto Storkyrkobrinken, passing the landmark Cattelin Restaurant on your right. Continue along this street, past the Lady Hamilton Hotel, turning right onto Trångsund, which leads to:

8 Stortorget (Great Square)

Take a seat on one of the park benches—you've earned the rest. This plaza was the site of the Stockholm Blood Bath of 1520 when Christian II of Denmark beheaded 80 Swedish noblemen and displayed a "pyramid" of their heads in the square. The Börsen on this square is the Swedish Stock Exchange, a building dating from 1776. This is where the Swedish Academy meets every year to choose the Nobel Prize winners in literature.

At the northeast corner of the square, take Källargränd north to view the entrance, opening onto Slottsbacken, of the:

9 Royal Palace

The present palace dates mainly from 1760 after a previous one was destroyed by fire. The changing of the guard takes place on this square.

To your right is the site of the:

10 Storkyrkan

This church was founded in the mid-1200s but has been rebuilt many times since. It's the site of coronations and royal weddings; kings are also christened here. The most celebrated sculpture here is *St. George and the Dragon,* a huge work dating from 1489. The royal pews have been used for 3 centuries, and the altar, mainly in ebony and silver, dates from 1652. This is still a functioning

Walking Tour: Gamla Stan (Old Town)

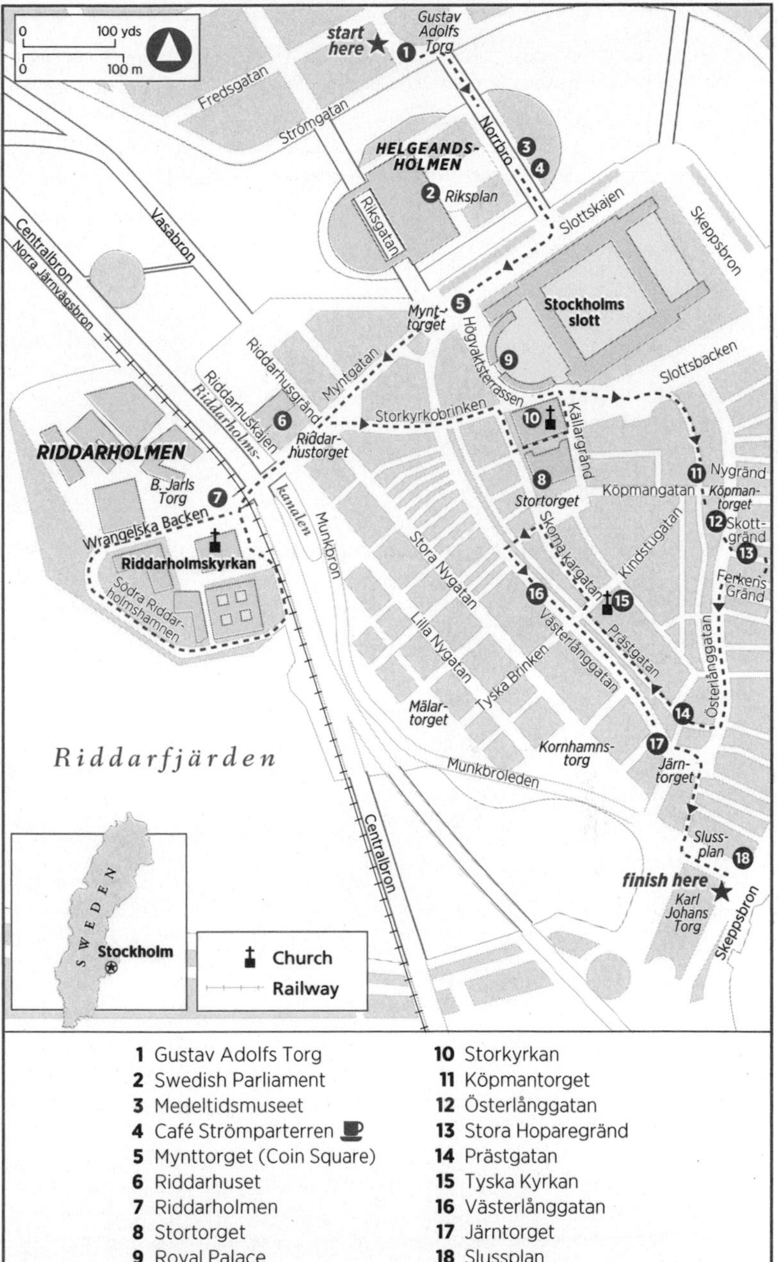

church, so it's best to visit when services are not in progress. It's open Monday through Saturday from 9am to 7pm, and Sunday from 9am to 5:30pm; admission is free.

Continue east along Slottsbacken, either visiting the palace now or saving it for later. Turn right when you reach Bollshusgränd, a cobblestone street of old houses leading to:

11 Köpmantorget

One of the most charming squares of the Old Town, Köpmantorget contains a famous copy of the *St. George and the Dragon* statue.

From the square, take Köpmanbrinken, which runs for 1 block before turning into:

12 Österlånggatan

Now the site of many restaurants and antiques shops, Österlånggatan was once Old Town's harbor street.

Continue along Österlånggatan, but take the first left under an arch, leading into:

13 Stora Hoparegränd

Some buildings along this dank street, one of the darkest and narrowest in Gamla Stan, date from the mid-1600s.

Walk down the alley toward the water, emerging at Skeppsbron bridge. Turn right and walk for 2 blocks until you reach Ferkens Gränd. Go right again up Ferkens Gränd until you return to Österlånggatan. Go left on Österlånggatan until you come to Tullgränd. Take the street on your right:

14 Prästgatan

This street was named after the priests who used to live here. As you climb the street, look to your left to Mårten Trotzigs Gränd, a street of steps that's the narrowest in Gamla Stan.

Continue along Prästgatan, passing a playground on your right. Turn right onto Tyska Brinken until you see on your right:

15 Tyska Kyrkan

Since the beginning of the 17th century, this has been the German church of Stockholm. The church has a baroque interior and is exquisitely decorated.

After you leave the church, the street in front of you will be Skomakargatan. Head up this street until you come to Stortorget once again. From Stortorget, take Kåkbrinken, at the southwest corner of the square. Follow this little street until turning left at:

16 Västerlånggatan

This pedestrian street is the main shopping artery of Gamla Stan and the best place to purchase Swedish gifts and souvenirs.

Follow Västerlånggatan to:

17 Järntorget

This street used to be known as Korntorget when it was the center of the copper and iron trade in the 16th and 17th centuries. At times in its long history, Järntorget has been the place of punishment for "wrongdoers." The most unusual statue in Stockholm is here—a **statue of Evert Taube,** the troubadour and Swedish national poet of the early 1900s. He's carrying a newspaper under his arm, his coat draped nonchalantly, his sunglasses pushed up high on his forehead.

From the square, take Järntorgsgatan to:

18 Slussplan

Here you can catch a bus to return to the central city, or you can board a ferry to Djurgården and its many museums.

WALKING TOUR 2: ALONG THE HARBOR

START: **Hantverkargaten 1, on Kungsholmen**

FINISH: **The Museum of Architecture**

TIME: **Allow 3 hours following this tour along the harbor.**

Start at:

1 Stadshuset (Stockholm City Hall)

It took 12 years, eight million bricks, and 19 million gilded mosaic tiles to erect this city hall, which can be visited on a guided tour. Go inside the courtyard on your own and admire the architecture.

When exiting the building, turn right and walk across Stadshusbron (City Hall Bridge) to Norrmalm. You'll see the Sheraton Hotel on your left, and on your right the Stadshuscafeet, where sightseeing boats depart on canal cruises in summer. Walk past the boats and go under an underpass (watch out for fast-riding bicyclists).

Continue along the canal until you reach Tegelbacken, a waterfront square. At the entrance to the Vasabron bridge, cross the street and continue along Fredsgatan. Veer right at the intersection to Strömgatan, hugging the canal. This will take you to Rosenbad, a little triangular park.

At the canal bordering Strömgatan, look at the building to your right:

2 Swedish Parliament

You can visit this building on a guided tour.

Continue on to:

3 Gustav Adolfs Torg

From here you have a panoramic view of the Royal Palace across the canal and of the Royal Opera straight ahead. This is one of the most famous landmark squares in Stockholm, and the most scenic.

Strömgatan resumes at the corner of the Opera House, site of the Operakällaren, for many years the finest restaurant in Stockholm. Continue along until you reach the southern tier of the:

4 Kungsträdgården

The "King's Gardens," the summer living room of Stockholm, reach from Hamngatan on the north side down to the water. Established in the 1500s as a pleasure garden for the court, they are now open to all, with cafes, open-air restaurants, and refreshment kiosks.

5 Café Milano

This traditional Italian restaurant in the center of Stockholm is an ideal spot for a refreshing drink or snack at any time during the day or evening. It's open Monday to Friday 11am to 3pm and 4:30pm to 11:00pm, Saturday noon to 11pm, and Sunday 1pm to 10pm. Kungsträdgårdsgatan 18 (✆ 08/678-28-27).

Continue along the waterfront, past Strömbron, a bridge leading to Gamla Stan, and emerge onto Södra Blasieholmshamnen. At no. 8 is the:

6 Grand Hotel

For decades this has been the most prestigious address in Stockholm, attracting Nobel Prize winners as well as most visiting dignitaries and movie stars. On your right, any number of sightseeing boats depart in summer for tours of the Stockholm archipelago. From this vantage point, you'll have a good view of the Royal Palace and Gamla Stan.

Continue along Södra Blasieholmshamnen until you reach (on your right) the:

7 National Museum

Here you find a repository of the state's art treasures—everything from Renoir to Rembrandt.

Cross the Skeppsholmsbron (bridge) leading to the little island of:

8 Skeppsholmen

The island holds a number of attractions (see "On Gamla Stan & Neighboring Islands," earlier in this chapter).

After crossing the bridge, turn right along Västra Brobänken. On your right you'll pass the:

9 Af Chapman

This "tall ship" with fully rigged masts once sailed the seas under three different flags before being permanently anchored in 1949 as a youth hostel.

Turn left onto Flaggmansvägen. Continue along Holmamiralens Torg, passing the Nordiska Institute on your right. Cut right toward the water at Södra Brobänken. Take a right turn and cross the bridge leading to:

10 Kastellholmen

This is one of the most charming, but least visited, islands in Stockholm. On the island is **Kastellet,** a red-brick castle that was designed by Fredrik Blom.

Head right along the water, going around Kastellholmskajen. Circle around and turn left at the end of Kastelleton. Walk back along Örlogsvägen, which runs through the center of the small island.

Cross the Kastellholmsbron bridge and return to the larger island of Skeppsholmen. This time go straight along Amiralsvägen, turning left onto Långa Raden. Cut right and continue to walk along Långa Raden. The first building on your left is the:

11 Museum of Architecture

The collection contains slides and thousands of architectural drawings and sketches from the past 100 years.

From this point at the end of the walking tour, you can catch bus no. 65 to take you back to the heart of Stockholm.

Walking Tour: Along the Harbor

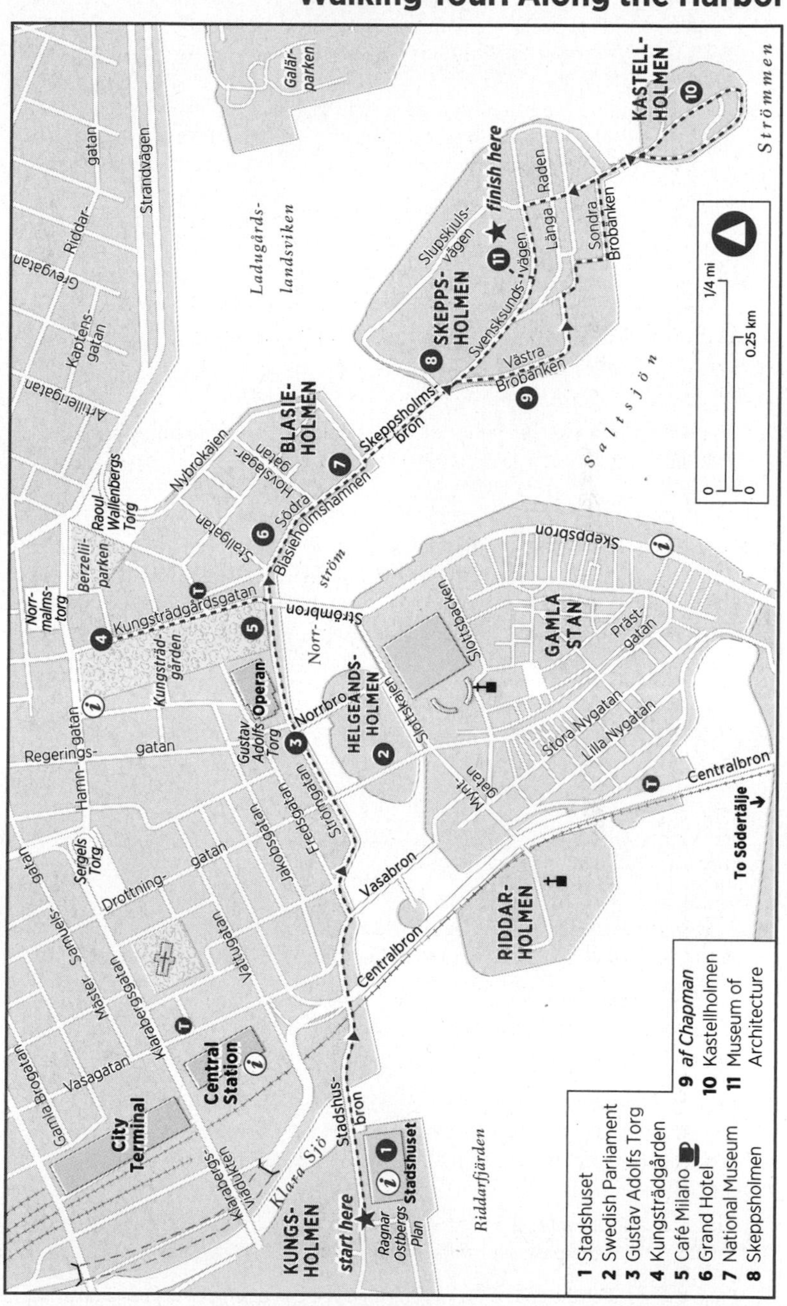

ORGANIZED TOURS

CITY TOURS The quickest and most convenient way to see the highlights of Stockholm is to take one of the bus tours that leave from the Square of Gustaf Adolf, near the Kungsträdgården.

Stockholm Sightseeing (also known as City Sightseeing), Svenksundsragen 17 (© **08/12-00-4000;** www.stockholmsightseeing.com), offers a variety of tours, mostly in summer. Tours depart from Gustaf Adolfs Torg in front of the Dansmuseet. "Panoramic Stockholm," a 1½-hour tour, costing 250SEK, purports to show you Stockholm in record time. At least you'll see the landmarks and several waterscape views. This tour is conducted from March 24 to December 31. For "Stockholm in a Nutshell," you can take a 2½-hour tour, costing 360SEK, with departures from March 24 to December 17. This tour shows you the highlights of Stockholm, including a sail around the royal park at Djurgården. A more comprehensive tour, the "Grand Tour" lasts 3½ hours and costs 420SEK.

OLD TOWN STROLLS Authorized guides lead 1-hour walking tours of the medieval lanes of Stockholm's Old Town. These walks are conducted daily from mid-June until late August, departing from the Royal Opera House at Gustav Adolfs Torg. The cost is 150SEK. Tickets and times of departure are available from **Stockholm Sightseeing** (see above).

CANAL CRUISES **Stockholm Sightseeing** (see above) offers the "Royal Canal Tour," March 24 to December 17 daily, at 30 minutes past the hour all day. Tours cost 150SEK for adults, 75SEK for children 6 to 11, and are free for children 5 and under. Visitors are ferried around the canals of Djurgården.

SPECTATOR SPORTS & ACTIVITIES

Soccer and **ice hockey** are the two most popular spectator sports in Sweden, and Stockholm has world-class teams in both. The major venue for any spectator sport in the capital, the **Stockholm Globe Arena (Globen),** is less than 6.5km (4 miles) south of central Stockholm. It offers everything from political rallies, motorcycle competitions, and sales conventions to basketball and ice hockey games, tennis matches, and rock concerts. Its ticket office (© **077/131-00-00;** www.globearena.se) also sells tickets Monday to Friday 9am to 6pm and Saturday 10am to 2pm for most of Stockholm's soccer games, which are played in an open-air stadium nearby. The ticket office is also open on Sunday 10am to 2pm. The Globen complex is in the southern suburb of Johnneshov (T-bana: Globen).

Another popular pastime is watching and betting on **trotting races.** These races usually take place on Wednesday at 6:30pm and on an occasional Saturday at 12:30pm in both summer and winter. (In winter an attempt is made to clear snow and ice from the racecourse; slippery conditions sometimes lead to unpredictable results.) Admission to **Solvalla Stadium** (© **08/635-90-00;** www.solvalla.se), which is about 6.5km (4 miles) north of the city center, is 50SEK. From Stockholm, take the bus marked SOLVALLA.

GOLF For those who want to play golf at the "top of Europe," there is the **Bromma Golf Course,** Kvarnbacksvägen 28, 16874 Bromma (© **08/704-91-91;** www.brommagolfhall.se), 5km (3 miles) west of the center of Stockholm. It's a 9-hole golf course with well-maintained greens. Greens fees are 150SEK or 200SEK on Saturday and Sunday, and golf clubs can be rented for 125SEK.

SHOPPING

SHOPPING DISTRICTS Everybody's favorite shopping area in Stockholm is **Gamla Stan.** Site of the Royal Palace, it even attracts such shoppers as the queen. The main street for browsing is **Västerlånggatan,** site of antiques stores with high prices.

In summer, **Skansen** is fun to explore because many craftspeople display their goods here. There are gift shops (some selling "Skansen glass") as well as individuals who offer their handmade goods at kiosks.

In the **Sergels Torg** area, the main shopping street is **Hamngatan,** site of the famous shopping center **Gallerian,** at the corner of Hamngatan and Sergels Torg, and crossing the northern rim of Kungsträdgården at Sweden House. Big department stores, such as NK and Åhléns, are nearby.

The **Kungsgatan** area is another major district for shopping, stretching from Hötorget to the intersection of Kungsgatan and Vasagatan. **Drottninggatan** is one long pedestrian mall, flanked with shops. Many side streets branching off from it also are filled with shops. Hötorget, home to the PUB department store, is another major shopping district.

A new shopping district **(SOFO)** has been identified on the rapidly gentrifying island of **Södermalm,** to the south of that island's busy Folkungatan. Streets that have emerged as shopping venues of note include **Götgatan, Kokgatan, Bondegatan,** and **Skånegatan.** Expect a youth-oriented, funky, hipster consciousness within the SOFO district, where there has been an explosion in housing prices on an island (Södermalm) where 60% of all households are single person.

SHOPPING HOURS Stockholm shops are open Monday to Friday 10am to between 6pm (for large department stores) and 7pm (for smaller, boutique-style shops). Saturday shopping is possible between 10am and somewhere between 1 and 4pm. Once a week, usually on Monday or Friday, some of the larger stores are open from 9:30am to 7pm (July–Aug to 6pm).

Shopping A to Z

AUCTIONS

Stockholms Auktionsverket (Stockholm Auction Chambers) ★★★ The oldest auction company in the world—it dates from 1674—holds auctions 2 days a week from noon to "whenever." You can view the merchandise Monday to Friday from 9am to 5pm. An estimated 150,000 lots are auctioned each year—everything from ceramics to Picassos. Nybrogatan 32. ✆ **08/453-67-50.** www.auktionsverket.se. T-bana: Östermalmstorg.

BOOKS & MAPS

Akademibokhandeln ★★ The biggest bookstore in Sweden carries more than 100,000 titles. A wide range of fiction and nonfiction is available in English. Many travel-related materials, such as maps, are also sold. Stadsgarden 10. ✆ **08/769-81-00.** www.akademibokhandeln.se. T-bana: Hötorget.

Sweden Bookshop Whatever's available in English about Sweden can be found at this bookstore above the Tourist Center. The store also sells many rare items, including recordings of Swedish music. Slottsbacken 10. ✆ **08/453-78-00.** www.swedenbookshop.com. T-bana: Gamla Stan.

CERAMICS

Blås & Knåda ★ This store features the best products made by members of a cooperative of 50 Swedish ceramic artists and glassmakers. Prices begin at 200SEK for a single teacup and rise to as much as 25,000SEK for museum-quality pieces. Hornsgatan 26. ✆ **08/642-77-67.** www.blasknada.com. T-bana: Slussen.

Keramiskt Centrum Gustavsberg Bone china, stoneware dinner services, and other fine table and decorative ware are made at the Gustavsberg Ceramics Center. A museum at the center displays historic pieces such as Parian (a type of unglazed porcelain) statues based on the work of the famous Danish sculptor Torvaldsen and other artists. You'll also see hand-painted vases, Toby jugs, majolica, willowware, examples of Pyro (the first ovenware), royal dinner services, and sculpture by modern artists. Visitors can watch potters at work and see artists hand-painting designs. You can even decorate a mug or plate yourself. A shop at the center sells Gustavsberg-ware, including seconds. Värmdö Island (21km/13 miles east of Stockholm). ✆ **08/570-356-58.** www2.varmdo.se. Bus: 422 or 440.

DEPARTMENT STORES

Åhléns City In the center of Stockholm, the largest department store in Sweden has a gift shop, a restaurant, and a famous food department. We often come here to buy the makings for a picnic to be enjoyed later in one of Stockholm's city parks. Also seek out the fine collection of home textiles, and Orrefors and Kosta Boda crystal ware. The pewter with genuine Swedish ornaments makes a fine gift item. Klarabergsgatan 50. ✆ **08/676-60-00.** www.ahlens.se. T-bana: Centralen.

Nordiska Kompaniet (NK) ★★ A high-quality department store since 1902, NK displays most of the big names in Swedish glass, including Orrefors (see the Nordic Light collection) and Kosta. Thousands of handcrafted Swedish items can be found in the basement. Stainless steel, also a good buy in Sweden, is profusely displayed. The store also houses a food hall and an English bookstore. Hamngatan 18-20. ✆ **08/762-80-00.** www.nk.se. T-bana: Kungsträdgården.

PUB Greta Garbo worked in the millinery department here from 1920 to 1922. It's one of the most popular department stores in Stockholm; the boutiques and departments generally sell midrange clothing and good-quality housewares, but not the international designer names of the more prestigious (and more expensive) NK. Massive and bustling, with an emphasis on traditional and conservative Swedish clothing, it offers just about anything you'd need to stock a Scandinavian home. There's also a restaurant. Hötorget 13. ✆ **08/789-19-30.** www.pub.se. T-bana: Hötorget.

FASHION

Acne With a name like this you wouldn't know that this is a showcase for an award-winning Swedish jeans company and fashion label. The store has some 400 retailers worldwide, including Barney's in New York, Selfridges in London, even Colette in Paris. Launched in 1996, Acne created 100 pairs of unisex designer jeans, which are known for their bright-red stitching. Nytorgsgatan 36. ✆ **08/640-04-70.** www.acnestudios.com. T-bana: Medborgarplatsen.

Artillery 2 ★ This is one of the most fashionable unisex boutiques in Stockholm. If the fashion was created yesterday, it is likely to be on sale here today. Expect all the trendy brand names such as Dolce & Gabbana, Paul & Joe, Nicole Farhi, Blue Cult, and Seven. Artillerigatan 2. ✆ **08/663-29-20.** www.artilleri2.com. T-bana: Östermalmstorg.

Bruno Götgatsbacken · Some of the top names in local Swedish fashion, including Whyred, Tiger, and Filippa K, are sold in this restored industrial building that dates from the 1600s. This is a chic modernist mall with a cafe and shops, well worth a detour. Götgatan 36. ✆ **076/871-50-84.** www.brunogotgatsbacken.se. T-bana: Slussen.

Filippa K One of the leading clothiers in Stockholm operates what they define as a large-scale boutique entrenched in the middle-bracket cost category—this is the kind of place where a mother might take her daughter for her junior prom dress. Expect a wide array of casual dresses, cocktail dresses, and formal evening wear, along with the business uniforms that are so favored by Scandinavian office workers. There's also a collection of clothing for men—suits, blazers, and casual wear—that's a bit less extensive than for women. Grev Turegatan 18. ✆ **08/545-882-57.** www.filippa-k.com. T-bana: Östermalmstorg.

Grandpa What a misleading name. In Södermalm, the hippest neighborhood in Stockholm, this chic outlet does sell old-fashioned board games. But it's mainly known for its trendy Swedish fashion statement, including such designs as Whyred and Junk de Luxe. Expect an array of Swedish jeans and pants, Scandinavian sweaters, shirts, and handbags. Södermannagatan 21. ✆ **08/643-60-80.** www.grandpa.se. T-bana: Medborgarplatsen.

Gunilla Pontén ★ This designer creates clothing for women that are neither faddish nor trendy, but of high quality with good needlework. Clothing comes in such colors as cerise, olive, black, and aubergine. The collection is also distinguished by fun accessories, including specially designed jewelry, handbags, caps, scarves, hats, and fingerless gloves. Mäster Samuelsgatan 10. ✆ **08/611-10-22.** www.ponten.com. T-bana: Östermalmstorg.

H&M ★★ H&M is the first thing that comes to mind when you think of Swedish fashion. H&M stores are found around the world today from Tokyo to New York. The company carries fashion to the far limits, from flamboyant dogtooth check suits with wide lapels to jodhpur-style pants. The design firm also makes an oversize scarf the centerpiece of a style, or else can outfit you in faux fur. Their cardigans are the peak of fashion as are their lumberjack shirts. And for the man who has everything, there is a pair of Jackson Pollock–inspired yellow splattered trousers. 22 Hamngatan in Östermalm. ✆ **08/5246-3530.** www.hm.com. T-bana: Sundbyberg.

J. Lindeberg ★ With its fashion collections for men and women, this chain store definitely lives in the 21st century. Johan Lindberg, along with his partner, the designer Magnus Ehrland, designs menswear for the urban man of taste. A smaller collection of clothing for women is also sold. Biblioteksgatan 6. ✆ **08/40050041.** www.jlindeberg.com. T-bana: Ostermalmstorg.

Marzio In the heart of Stockholm, this chic outlet has a wide array of Italian shoes and bags, among the most sophisticated in the city. Marzio also produces its own brand of shoes and bags, which are made in Italy of the finest leather. Shoes are trendy or classic. The outlet also sells many hot independent brands of shoes for women. Nybrogatan 10. ✆ **08/661-86-37.** www.marzio.se. T-bana: Östermalmstorg.

NK In the realm of menswear, this subdivision of the previously noted Nordiska Kompaniet (see "Department Stores," above) is Stockholm's answer to Harrods in London or Bloomingdale's in New York. From Armani, Prada, and Gucci suits and shoes to the latest fashions in Levi's and casual wear—it's all here. The largest of a chain of menswear stores scattered throughout Sweden, it has been around for more than a hundred years. In addition to stocking outdoor gear and swimsuits, the store also maintains a boutique-within-the-boutique, the Swedish label Tiger (✆ **08/762-87-72**), which sells fine suits, shoes, and casual wear that's specifically tailored to Swedish tastes and slim builds. This store also houses a food hall and an English bookstore. Hamngatan 18–20. ✆ **08/762-80-00.** www.nk.se. T-bana: Kungsträdgården.

FLEA MARKET

Loppmarknaden i Skärholmen (Skärholmen Shopping Center) ★ At this biggest flea market in northern Europe, you might find an antique from an attic in Värmland or some other only-in-Sweden trinket. Try to go on Saturday or Sunday (the earlier the better), when the market is at its peak. Skärholmen. ✆ **08/710-00-60.** www.loppmarknaden.se. Admission 15SEK Sat, 10SEK Sun, free the rest of the week. Bus: 13 or 23 to Skärholmen (20 min.).

GEMS & MINERALS

Geocity ★ 🎁 Geocity offers exotic mineral crystals, jewelry, Scandinavian gems, Baltic amber, and lapidary equipment. The staff includes two certified gemologists who will cut and set any gem you select and do appraisals. The inventory holds stones from Scandinavia and around the world, including Greenland, Madagascar, Siberia, and South America. Kungsgatan 57. ✆ **08/411-11-40.** http://geocity.se. T-bana: Hötorget.

GIFTS & SOUVENIRS

Stockholm Tourist Center Gift Shop There are dozens of souvenir shops scattered throughout Stockholm, especially on Gamla Stan, but the merchandise within this official tourism arm, or gift shop emporium, of the Swedish government is superior. Expect Dalarna horses, embroideries, Viking statuettes, and glassware. Stockholm Tourist Center, Vasagatan 14. ✆ **08/508-285-08.** T-bana: Centralen.

GLASS & CRYSTAL

Nordiska Kristall ★★ Since 1918, this company has been in the vanguard of Swedish glassmakers. The pick of Swedish glass is on sale here, and you can choose between classic and more adventurous designs. The company often stages pioneering exhibitions in order to showcase its more daring designs. Kungsgatan 9. ✆ **08/10-77-18.** www.nordiskakristall.se. T-bana: Hörtorget.

Orrefors Kosta Boda ★★★ Two famous companies combined to form this "crystal palace" outlet in the center of Stockholm. Orrefors focuses on clear vases and stemware, while Kosta Boda boasts more colorful and artistic pieces of glass. One of the best-selling items is the "Intermezzo Glass" with a drop of sapphire coloring in its stem. Birger Jarlsgatan 15. ✆ **08/61-19-115.** www.kostaboda.com. T-bana: Östermalmstorg.

HANDICRAFTS & GIFTS

Brinken Konsthantverk On the lower floor of a building near the Royal Palace in the Old Town, this elegant purveyor of gift items will ship handcrafted brass, pewter, wrought iron, or crystal anywhere in the world. About 95% of the articles are made in Scandinavia. Storkyrkobrinken 1. ✆ **08/411-59-54.** www.brinkhantverk.se. T-bana: Gamla Stan.

DesignTorget ★★ 🎁 In 1994, the government-owned Kulturhuset (Swedish Culture House) reacted to declining attendance by inviting one of Stockholm's most influential designers and decorators, Jerry Hellström, to organize this avant-garde art gallery. Swedes modestly refer to it as a "shop." In a large room in the cellar, you'll find a display of handicrafts created by 150 to 200 mostly Swedish craftspeople. The work, including some of the best pottery, furniture, textiles, clothing, pewter, and crystal in Sweden, must be approved by a jury of connoisseurs before being offered for sale. The organization maintains several other branches, including a store in southern Stockholm, **DesignTorget,** Götgatan 31 (✆ **08/644-16-78;** www.designtorget.se). It stocks clothing for men, women, and children, and furniture, with less emphasis on ceramics and handicrafts. In the Kulturhuset, Sergelgangen 29. ✆ **08/21-91-50.** T-bana: Centralen.

Duka A large selection of carefully chosen crystal, porcelain, and gifts is available in this shop near the Konserthuset (Concert Hall). It also offers tax-free shopping and shipping. Kungsgatan 5. ✆ **08/440-96-00.** T-bana: Hötorget.

Gunnarssons Träfigurer ★ This store has one of the city's most appealing collections of Swedish carved wooden figures. All are by Urban Gunnarsson, a second-generation master carver. Highlights include figures from World War II, such as Winston Churchill, U.S. presidents from Franklin D. Roosevelt to Bill Clinton, and a host of mythical and historical European personalities. The carvings are usually made from linden or basswood. Drottninggatan 77. ✆ **08/21-67-17.** T-bana: Rådmansgatan.

Svensk Hemslöjd (Society for Swedish Handicrafts) Svensk Hemslöjd offers a wide selection of glass, pottery, gifts, and wooden and metal handicrafts by some of Sweden's best artisans. Other wares include hand-woven carpets, upholstery fabrics, hand-painted materials, tapestries, lace, and embroidered items. You'll also find beautiful yarns for weaving and embroidery. Sveavägen 44. ✆ **08/23-21-15.** www.svenskhemslojd.com. T-bana: Hötorget.

HOME FURNISHINGS

Nordiska Galleriet This two-story store features the finest in European furniture design, including the best from Scandinavia. With everything from sofas to tables, from vases to avant-garde lamps, and some of the most daring chairs ever designed, this showroom carries the "masterpieces" of famous designers of yesterday but also the more daring designers of the 21st century. You might get a lamp designed by the famous Philippe Starck or a three-legged stool by Arne Jacobsen (the 20th century's most famous Danish designer), or even a chair by the innovative Charles Mackintosh of Scotland. Also for sale are reproductions of the furniture of Alvar Aalto, Finland's most famous designer. The store can arrange shipment. Nybrogatan 11. ✆ **08/442-83-60.** www.nordiskagalleriet.se. T-bana: Östermalmstorg.

Svenskt Tenn ★★ Swedish Pewter (its English name) has been one of Sweden's most prominent stores for home furnishings since 1924. Pewter is no longer king, but the shop now sells Scandinavia's best selection of furniture, printed textiles, lamps, glassware, china, and gifts. The inventory is stylish, and although there aren't a lot of bargains, it's an excellent place to see the newest trends in Scandinavian design. It carries an exclusive collection of Josef Frank's hand-printed designs on linen and cotton. It will pack, insure, and ship your purchases anywhere in the world. Strandvägen 5. ✆ **08/670-16-00.** www.svenskttenn.se. T-bana: Östermalmstorg.

LINENS

Solgården ★★★ For the dwindling few who really care about luxury linens and elegant housewares, such as lace and embroidery, this shop is the finest of its kind in Scandinavia. It was conceived by owner Marianne von Kantzow Ridderstad as a tribute to Gustav III, the king who is said to have launched the neoclassical style in Sweden. Ridderstad designed her shop like a country house, with rough-hewn wood and whimsical furnishings. Each of her linens is virtually a work of art and the tablecloths are heirloom pieces. You'll cherish the work for its originality and loveliness. Karlavägen 158. ✆ **08/663-93-60.** www.cdecor.com. T-bana: Rådmansgatan.

SHOPPING MALLS

Gallerian ★★★ A short walk from Sweden House at Kunådgården, this modern two-story shopping complex is, to many, the best shopping destination in Sweden. Merchandise in most of the individually managed stores is designed to appeal to local shoppers, not the tourist market—although in summer that changes a bit as more souvenir and gift items appear. Hamngatan 37. ✆ **08/791-24-45.** www.gallerian.se. T-bana: Kungsträdgården.

Sturegallerian ★★ In the center of Stockholm, within a venue that was renovated and expanded, this mall has a dazzling array of foreign and domestic merchandise that's sold within at least 60 specialty shops. Summer brings out more displays of Swedish souvenirs and gift items. There are also restaurants and cafes. Sturegallerian opened in 1989 and a year later was named "Shopping Center of the Year in Europe" by the International Council of Shopping Centers. Stureplan. ✆ **08/453-50-67.** www.sturegallerian.se. T-bana: Östermalmstorg.

TEXTILES

Handarbetets Vänner This is one of the oldest and most prestigious textile houses in Stockholm; founded in 1874, today it is one of the few remaining textile art studios in the country and sells art weaving and embroidery items in a spacious headquarters. The skilled craftspeople here have brought textile design to an art form, as reflected in their "art weaving" and embroidery. Their wall hangings—some of which are virtually heirloom pieces—are the finest in the city. The studio even repairs historic textiles. Djurgårdsslatten 82–84. ✆ **08/545-686-50.** Bus: 47.

TOYS

Bulleribock (Toys) ☺ Since it opened in the 1960s, this store has carried only traditional, noncomputerized toys made of wood, metal, or paper. You won't find any plastic toys or objectionable war games here. Many of the charming playthings are suitable for children up to age 10 and as many as possible are made in Sweden, with wood from Swedish forests. Sveavägen 104. ✆ **08/673-61-21.** T-bana: Rådmansgatan.

STOCKHOLM AFTER DARK

Djurgården (p. 320) remains the favorite spot for both indoor and outdoor events on a summer evening. Although the more sophisticated may find it corny, this is your best early evening bet. Afterward, you can make the rounds of jazz venues and nightclubs, some of which stay open until 3 or 4am.

The Performing Arts

All the major opera, theater, and concert seasons begin in the fall, except for special summer festival performances. Fortunately, most of the major opera and theatrical performances are funded by the state, which keeps ticket prices reasonable.

CONCERT HALLS

Berwaldhallen (Berwald Concert Hall) This hexagonal concert hall is Swedish Radio's big music studio. The Radio Symphonic Orchestra performs here, and other high-quality musical programs include *lieder* (classical music) and chamber music recitals. The hall has excellent acoustics. The box office is open Monday to Friday noon to 6pm and 2 hours before every concert. Dag Hammarskjölds Väg 3. ✆ **08/784-18-00.** www.sr.se/berwaldhallen. Tickets 60SEK-450SEK. T-bana: Karlaplan.

Filharmonikerna i Konserthuset (Concert Hall) Home of the Stockholm Philharmonic Orchestra, this is the principal place to hear classical music in Sweden. The Nobel Prizes are also awarded here. Constructed in 1920, the building houses two concert halls. One seats 1,600 and is better suited to major orchestras; the other, seating 450, is suitable for chamber music groups. Besides local orchestras, the hall features visiting ensembles, such as the Chicago Symphony Orchestra. Some series sell out in advance to subscription ticket holders; for others, visitors can readily get tickets. Sales begin 2 weeks before a concert and continue until the performance begins. Concerts usually start at 7:30pm, with occasional lunchtime (noon) or "happy hour" (5:30pm) concerts. Most performances are broadcast on Stockholm's main classical music station, 107.5 FM. The box office is open Monday to Friday 11am to 6pm, Saturday 11am to 3pm. In July and August the box office is open daily 11am to 5pm. Hötorget 8. ✆ **08/786-02-00.** www.konserthuset.se. Tickets 125SEK-575SEK. T-bana: Hötorget.

OPERA & BALLET

Drottningholm Court Theater ★★★ On an island in Lake Mälaren, 11km (6¾ miles) from Stockholm, this is the most famous 18th-century theater in the world. It stages operas and ballets with performers done up in full 18th-century regalia, from period costumes to wigs, and the 18th-century music is performed on antique instruments. Its machinery and 30 or more complete theater sets are intact and in use. The theater, a short walk from the royal residence, seats only 450, which makes it difficult to get tickets. The season is from May to September. Most performances begin at 7:30pm and last 2½ to 4 hours. You can order tickets in advance by phone with an American Express card. Even if you're not able to get tickets for an actual performance, you can tour the theater as part of a visit to Drottningholm Palace (p. 350). Drottningholm. ✆ **08/660-82-25.** www.dtm.se. Tickets 165SEK-610SEK. T-bana: Brommaplan, then bus no. 301 or 323. Boat from the City Hall in Stockholm.

Operahuset (Royal Opera House) ★★★ Founded in 1773 by Gustav III (who was later assassinated here at a masked ball), the Opera House is the home of the Royal Swedish Opera and the Royal Swedish Ballet. The building dates from 1898. Performances are usually Monday to Saturday at 7:30pm (closed mid-June to mid-Aug). The box office is open Monday to Friday noon to 6pm (until 7:30pm on performance nights), and Saturday noon to 3pm. Gustav Adolfs Torg. ✆ **08/791-44-00.** www.operan.se. Tickets 100SEK-700SEK; 10%-30% senior and student discounts. T-bana: Kungsträdgården.

THEATER

The theater season begins in mid-August and lasts until mid-June.

Kungliga Dramatiska Teatern (Royal Dramatic Theater) ★★★ Greta Garbo got her start in acting here, and Ingmar Bergman stages two productions a year. The theater presents the latest experimental plays and the classics—in Swedish only. The theater is open year-round (with a slight slowdown in July), and performances

THE CAPITAL OF gay SCANDINAVIA

Copenhagen thrived for many years as a refreshingly raunchy city with few inhibitions and fewer restrictions on alternative sexuality. Beginning in the mid-1990s, Stockholm witnessed an eruption of new gay bars, discos, and roaming nightclubs. Copenhagen's more imperial and, in many ways, more staid competition made the Danes' legendary permissiveness look a bit weak. Today, no other city in Scandinavia offers gay-friendly nightlife options as broad and diverse as Stockholm's. Some of the gay bars and clubs maintain fixed hours and addresses. Others, configured as roving parties, constantly change addresses. Listings for gay entertainment venues appear regularly in ***QX*** (www.qx.se), a gay magazine published in Swedish and English. It's available at gay bars and news kiosks throughout Stockholm. And don't overlook the comprehensive website (www.rfsl.se) maintained by RSFL, a Swedish organization devoted to equal rights for gays.

GAY VENUES IN SÖDERMALM

Looking for a nonconfrontational bar peopled with regular guys who happen to be gay? Consider a round or two on the island of Södermalm at **Sidetrack,** Wollmar Yxkullsgatan 7 (✆ **08/641-16-88;** www.sidetrack.nu; T-bana: Mariatorget). Small, amicable, committed to shunning trendiness, and deep within a cellar a few blocks from the also-recommended Hotel Rival, it's named after the founder's favorite gay bar in Chicago. It's open Tuesday to Saturday from 6pm to 1am. Tuesday seems to be something of a gay Stockholm institution. Prefacing the bar is a well-managed restaurant, serving dinner only, Tuesday to Saturday 6pm to 1am (June–Aug Wed–Sat 8pm–1am). Main courses cost from 115SEK to 185SEK.

Technically, **SLM** (Scandinavian Leather Men), Wollmar Yxkullsgatan 18 (✆ **08/643-31-00;** www.slmstockholm.se; T-bana: Mariatorget) is a private club. But if you look hot and wear even a hint

are scheduled Tuesday to Saturday at 7pm and Sunday at 4pm. The box office is open Monday to Saturday 10am to 6pm. Nybroplan. ✆ **08/667-06-80.** www.dramaten.se. Tickets 120SEK–450SEK, student discount available. T-bana: Östermalmstorg.

Oscars Teatern Oscars is the flagship of Stockholm's musical entertainment world. It's been the home of classic operetta and musical theater since the turn of the 20th century. Known for its extravagant staging of traditional operettas, it was also one of the first theaters in Europe to produce such hits as *Cats* in Swedish. The box office is open Monday to Saturday from 11am to 6pm. Kungsgatan 63. ✆ **08/20-50-00.** www.oscarsteatern.se. Tickets 305SEK–625SEK. T-bana: Hötorget.

LOCAL CULTURE & ENTERTAINMENT

Skansen Skansen arranges traditional seasonal festivities, special events, autumn market days, and a Christmas Fair. In summer, concerts, singalongs, and guest performances delight visitors and locals alike. Folk-dancing performances are staged in July and August, Friday and Saturday at 7pm and Sunday at 2:30 and 4pm. In July and August, outdoor dancing is presented with live music Monday to Saturday from 10 to 11:30pm. Djurgården 49–51. ✆ **08/442-80-00.** www.skansen.se. Admission 40SEK–140SEK adults, 40SEK–50SEK children 6–15 (free for children 5 and under). Fee depends on the time of the year. Ferry from Slussen. Bus: 44 or 47.

of cowhide or rawhide, you stand an excellent chance of getting in if you don't object to paying a 100SEK "membership fee." On Wednesday, Friday, and Saturday from 10pm to 2am, the place, in what might be the deepest basement in Stockholm, functions as Stockholm's premier leather bar. On Saturday from 10pm to 2am, a DJ spins dance music. It's closed on other nights.

Södermalm's most trend-conscious dining venue is the **Roxy,** a boxy, modern-looking site on the Nytorg 6 (✆ **08/640-96-55;** www.roxysofo.se). Funky and whimsical, it has a decor that might have been inspired by a meeting in heaven between the last of Vienna's Hapsburgs and the design team at SAS. The sofas evoke a Danish airport lounge in 1966, and mismatched crystal chandeliers seem to echo the sounds of a Strauss waltz. Art Deco objets d'art might have been salvaged from a 1930s-era ocean liner, and two or three porcelain incarnations of pink flamingos are strictly from 1950s Miami. You can always drop in just for a drink (the crowd tends to be youngish and cute-ish), but if you want dinner, main courses cost from 189SEK to 239SEK. The place opens Tuesday to Sunday at 5pm, and closes anytime between 11pm and 1am, depending on business and the night of the week.

GAY VENUES ON GAMLA STAN

If you need a caffeine fix before all that leather and latex, you might want to drop into Stockholm's most appealing, best-managed gay cafe, **Chokladkoppen,** Stortorget 18–20 (✆ **08/20-31-70;** T-bana: Gamla Stan). It's open daily from 9am to 11pm. It specializes in sandwiches, gorgeous pastries, and chocolate confections. The staff is charming, and the clientele more gay than not. The consistently most popular item on the menu is a steaming cupful of white hot chocolate, priced at 40SEK.

An Amusement Park

Gröna Lunds Tivoli ★ ☺ Unlike its Copenhagen namesake, this is an amusement park, not a fantasyland. For those who like Coney Island–type amusements, it can be a nighttime adventure. The park is filled with some hair-raising rides, including a Ferris wheel, bumper cars, and a roller coaster. The most dramatic is the Power Tower, rising to 107m (351 ft.), making it the tallest free-fall amusement park ride in Scandinavia. At the peak, you have only about 5 seconds to see one of the most dramatic views of Stockholm and its archipelago before you plummet, along with other screaming passengers. The park is open daily from the end of April to September, usually from noon to 11pm or midnight. Call for exact hours. Djurgården. ✆ **08/587-501-00.** www.gronalund.com. Admission 80SEK for ages 7 and up, free 6 and under or 66 and over. Bus: 44 or 47. Ferry from Nybroplan.

The Club & Music Scene

A HISTORIC NIGHTCLUB

Café Opera ★★ By day a bistro, brasserie, and tearoom, Café Opera is one of the most crowded nightclubs in Stockholm after 10pm, but you have the best chance of getting in around noon during lunch. A stairway near the entrance leads to one of the Opera House's most beautiful corners, the clublike Operabaren (Opera Bar). It's likely to be as crowded as the cafe. The bar is a monumental but historically charming place to have a drink. To enter, you must be at least 23 years old. The bar is open daily from 5pm to 3am. Operahauset, Kungsträdgården. ✆ **08/676-58-07.** www.cafeopera.se. Cover 200SEK after 10pm. T-bana: Kungsträdgården.

DANCE CLUBS & DISCOS

Göta Källare Stockholm's largest supper-club-style dance hall has a reputation for successful matchmaking. Huge, echoing, and paneled with lots of wood in faux-*Español* style inside, it also boasts an outside terrace. The restaurant serves platters of food priced at 130SEK. Menu items include *tournedos,* fish, chicken, and veal. The live orchestra (which performs "Strangers in the Night" a bit too frequently) plays every night, and pulls in a middle-aged crowd. The hall opens nightly at 10pm. In the Medborgarplatsen subway station, Södermalm. ✆ **08/642-08-28.** www.gk.nu. Cover 140SEK after 11pm. T-bana: Medborgplatsen.

White Room ★ With its snow-white interior and theatrical lighting, this has been called the wildest late-night club in Stockholm. Attracting an under-30 crowd, it is stylish and known for its euphoric atmosphere. After midnight, the scene gets frenetic. Some of the best DJs in Sweden lay tracks here. Hours are 11pm to 5am on Wednesday, Friday, and Saturday nights (closed otherwise). Jakobsbergsgatan 29. ✆ **08/545-076-00.** www.whiteroom.se. Cover 150SEK. T-bana: Östermalmstorg.

ROCK & JAZZ CLUBS

AG925 (Allmänna Gallieriet 925) This is about as underground and counterculture an environment as we're willing to recommend. If it were even a bit more extreme or eccentric, it might run the risk of being closed down by the police. Today, it's a sprawling, serpentine, much-battered labyrinth of rooms, many of them sheathed in white tiles; it's peppered with bars, artfully conceived graffiti, exhibition spaces for a changing array of artworks, rickety tables and chairs that long ago saw better days, and stages where rock 'n' roll and punk rock bands blare into the night. Dress as you might for a date with Courtney Love. Friday and Saturday nights often feature a DJ. Tuesday 6 to 11pm, Wednesday and Thursday 6pm to 1am, Friday 5pm to 1am, and Saturday 7pm to 1am. Kronobergsgatan 37, 2nd floor. ✆ **08/410-681-00.** www.ag925.se. Entrance usually free, but during special concerts, as high as 110SEK. T-bana: Fridhemsplan.

Fasching ★★ This club attracts some of Sweden's best-known jazz musicians. Well known among jazz aficionados throughout Scandinavia, it is small but fun. The venue varies according to the night of the week and the availability of the artists performing. At the end of the live acts, there's likely to be dancing to salsa, soul, and perhaps R&B. The club is open Sunday to Thursday 7pm to midnight, Friday and Saturday 7pm to 4am. Kungsgatan 63. ✆ **08/534-829-60.** www.fasching.se. Cover 100SEK-300SEK. T-bana: Centralen.

Hard Rock Cafe The Swedish branch of this chain is fun and gregarious. Sometimes an American, British, or Scandinavian rock band presents a live concert; otherwise, rock blasts from the sound system. Burgers begin at 140SEK, steaks at 210SEK, and beer at 65SEK. It's open Monday to Thursday 11:30am to midnight, Friday 11:30am to 1am, Saturday noon to 1am, and Sunday noon to midnight. Sveavägen 75. ✆ **08/545-494-00.** www.hardrock.com. T-bana: Rådmansgatan.

Pub Engelen/Nightclub Kolingen The Engelen Pub, the Restaurant Engelen, and the Nightclub Kolingen (in the 15th-c. cellar) share a single address. The restaurant, which serves some of the best steaks in town, is open daily 5pm to midnight.

Live performances, usually soul, funk, and rock by Swedish groups, take over the pub daily from 8:30pm to midnight. The pub is open Tuesday to Thursday 4pm to 1am, Friday and Saturday 4pm to 3am, Sunday 5pm to 3am. The Nightclub Kolingen is a dance club nightly from 10pm to about 3am. It charges the same food and drink prices as the pub, and you must be at least 23 to enter. Kornhamnstorg 59B. ✆ **08/20-10-92.** www.wallmans.com. Cover 100SEK after 8pm. T-bana: Gamla Stan.

Stampen This pub attracts crowds of jazz lovers in their 40s and 50s, who crowd in to enjoy live Dixieland, New Orleans, and mainstream jazz, and swing music from the 1920s, 1930s, and 1940s. On Tuesday, guests come for rock 'n' roll from the 1950s and 1960s. In summer, an outdoor veranda is open when the weather permits. Year-round, a menagerie of stuffed animals and lots of old, whimsical antiques are suspended from the high ceiling. The club has two stages, and there's dancing downstairs almost every night. On Monday live blues music is played. It's open Monday to Thursday 8pm to 1am, Friday to Saturday 8pm to 2am. Stora Nygatan 5. ✆ **08/20-57-93.** www.stampen.se. No cover. T-bana: Gamla Stan.

THE BAR SCENE

Absolut Icebar ★★ In the Nordic Sea Hotel, this is literally Stockholm's "coolest" bar—it's the world's first permanent ice bar, opened in 2001 in the heart of Stockholm. Amazingly, the interior is kept at temperatures of 27°F (–5°C) all year. The decor and all the interior fittings, right down to the cocktail glasses themselves, are made of pure, clear ice shipped down from the Torne River in Sweden's arctic north. Dress as you would for a dog-sled ride in Alaska. Otherwise, a staff member will give you a parka, with a hood, to keep you warm. Be warned that advance reservations are required; groups enter and leave at intervals of about every 40 minutes. Vasaplan 4-7. ✆ **08/50-56-31-24.** www.nordicseahotel.se. T-bana: Centralen.

Blue Moon Bar This street-level bar and basement bar functions as a bar, restaurant, and nightclub. Its chic, modern decor attracts a bevy of supermodels and TV actors, who also come to hear a wide range of recorded music—everything from ABBA to Bob Marley. You must be at least 25 to enter. It's open nightly from 8pm to 4am. Birgerjarlsgatan 29. ✆ **08/20-14-11.** www.bluemoonbar.se. Cover 85SEK-125SEK. T-bana: Östermalmstorg.

Cadier Bar ★ This bar, on the lobby level of the also-recommended Grand Hotel, is one of the most famous and plushest in Europe. From its windows, you'll have a view of a venue that was lavishly renovated, as well as Stockholm's harbor and its Royal Palace. Light meals—open-faced sandwiches and smoked salmon—are served throughout the day and evening. It's open Monday to Friday 7am to 2am, Saturday 8am to 2am, Sunday 8am to 1am; a piano player performs Thursday to Saturday from 9:30pm to 1:30am. In the Grand Hotel, Södra Blasieholmshamnen 8. ✆ **08/679-35-85.** T-bana: Kungsträdgården.

Fenixbar and Mest Bar This pair of loosely related bars is within a few steps of each other on a busy pedestrian street in the heart of Södermalm. Both are decorated with late Victorian accessories. The Mest Bar emphasizes sports more than the Fenix, which is more suitable to pickups, mainly of the straight variety. Both bars are open daily 5pm to 1am. Fenix Bar: Götgatan 40. ✆ **08/640-45-06.** www.fenixbar.se. Mest Bar: Götgatan 44. ✆ **08/641-36-53.** T-bana: Bjömsträdgård.

Gondolen We think the architecture here is as impressive as the view, and that's saying a lot—the view encompasses Lake Malar, the open sea, and huge areas of downtown Stockholm. Partly suspended beneath a pedestrian footbridge that soars above the narrow channel separating the island of Gamla Stan from the island of Södermalm, this engineering triumph was executed in 1935. An elevator hauls customers (without charge) up the equivalent of 11 stories to the '40s-style restaurant. It's open Monday to Friday 11:30am to 1am, Saturday from 4pm to 1am. Stadtsgården 6. ✆ **08/641-70-90.** www.eriks.se. T-bana: Slussen.

Pontus! ★ Near the Stureplan in the very heart of Stockholm, this is a three-level nightlife beacon promising a hot night on the town. It's fashionable and fun, and if you really want to make a night of it, hang out in the chic oysters-and-champagne bar. There's also a cocktail bar on-site, plus a sushi bar, even a dim sum station. If you want more formal dining, there's also a full-fledged restaurant. The bartender's special is called a "Dragon's Kiss" (with fresh ginger juice and Absolut). Open Monday 11am to 2pm and 5pm to midnight; Tuesday to Friday 11:30am to 2pm and 7pm to 1am; Saturday 5pm to 1am. Brunnsgatan 1. ✆ **08/545-273-00.** www.pontusfrithiof.com. T-bana: Östermalmstorg.

Sturehof Since 1897, this pub and restaurant has been one of Stockholm's major drinking and dining venues. In the exact center of the city, it is now surrounded by urban sprawl and is attached to an arcade with other restaurants and shops. It remains a pleasant refuge from the city's congestion and is popular as both an after-work bar and a restaurant. It's open Monday to Friday 11am to 2am, Saturday noon to 2am, and Sunday 1pm to 2am. Stureplan 2. ✆ **08/440-57-30.** www.sturehofgruppen.se. T-bana: Östermalmstorg.

Late-Night Bites

Mississippi Inn For that late-night bite, this is a good choice if you dig American grub with some "south of the border" specialties such as huevos rancheros or quesadillas with fresh salsa. A lot of night-prowling young people show up here before midnight to dig into barbecue baby back ribs and juicy burgers. The inn makes the best pancakes in town. Wine is sold by the glass along with a selection of beers, Guinness, and hard cider. Open Monday to Friday 5pm to midnight, Saturday and Sunday noon to midnight. Nytorgsgatan 33. ✆ **08/642-43-80.** www.mississippi.se. T-bana: Medborgarplatsen.

GOTHENBURG

Though those days are long gone, Gothenburg still suffers from its early-20th-century reputation of being a dull industrial center. What awaits you now is a sprawling, youthful metropolis filled with some of the brightest and best-looking people in Europe. It has one of Europe's largest student populations, as is reflected in the joie de vivre that permeates the atmosphere here.

Prices are mercifully cheaper than in Stockholm, and the informal, relaxed mood of the people is contagious. Here you can be sucked into the local life and even embraced with enthusiasm as a visitor, not shunned as a stranger. The Göta River runs through the city, and boat trips here are just as delightful as those in Stockholm. You can even go island hopping.

Called the "gateway to northern Europe," Gothenburg is the country's chief port and second-largest city. Canals, parks, and flower gardens enhance its appeal, as do a large number of museums (featuring everything from the world's only stuffed blue whale to modern art) and the largest amusement park in northern Europe. Gothenburg is also a convenient center for excursions to a spectacularly pristine archipelago that's the home of fishing villages, wildlife refuges, and several lovely vacation resorts.

A walk down Kungsportsavenyn, known as Avenyn (the Avenue), is a Gothenburg tradition, even in winter, when the street is heated by underground pipes so that the snow melts away quickly. There are many outdoor cafes from which to watch the action on this wide, pedestrian thoroughfare.

ORIENTATION

Arriving

BY PLANE **SAS** (✆ **800/221-2350** in the U.S.; www.flysas.com) operates six daily flights from Copenhagen to Gothenburg (most of them nonstop) between 7:30am and 6:40pm. (Many Swedes who live on the west coast of Sweden consider Copenhagen a more convenient airport than the one in Stockholm.) SAS also operates 10 to 15 daily flights between Stockholm and Gothenburg, beginning about 7am and continuing until early evening.

Planes arrive at **Landvetter airport** (✆ **031/94-10-00;** www.lfv.se), 26km (16 miles) east of Gothenburg. A Flygbuss (www.flygbussarna.se) or airport bus departs every 30 minutes for the 30-minute ride to the central bus terminal, just behind Gothenburg's main railway station. Buses run daily between 5:15am and 12:15am. A one-way trip costs 82SEK. A more modern airport, Gothenburg City airport, is 18km (11 miles) northwest of the city center, and receives mostly low-cost flights, many of them charters from other parts of Europe.

BY TRAIN The Oslo-Copenhagen express train runs through Gothenburg and Helsingborg. Trains run frequently on a north-south route between Gothenburg and Helsingborg/Malmö in the south. The most traveled rail route is between Gothenburg and Stockholm, with trains leaving hourly in both directions; the trip takes between 3 and 4½ hours, depending on the train.

Trains arrive at the **Central Station,** on one side of Drottningtorget. Inside the station is a currency-exchange bureau and an office of the Swedish National Railroad Authority (www.sj.se), which sells rail and bus tickets for connections to nearby areas. For information, call ✆ **771/75-75-75.**

BY BUS There are several buses from Gothenburg to Helsingborg/Malmö (and vice versa) daily. Trip time from Gothenburg to Helsingborg is 3 hours; Gothenburg to Malmö, 3 to 4 hours. Several buses connect Stockholm and Gothenburg daily. The trip takes 6 to 7 hours. Gothenburg's bus station, at Nils Ericson Platsen, is behind the railway station. For information in Gothenburg, call **Swebus,** Sweden's largest bus company (✆ **036/290-80-00;** www.swebusexpress.se).

BY FERRY The **Stena Line** (✆ **031/704-00-00;** www.stenaline.se) has six crossings per day in summer from North Jutland (a 3-hr. trip); call for information on specific departure times, which vary seasonally. They also offer a daily connection from Kiel, Germany, which departs daily from Kiel at 7pm, arriving at 9am the following morning in Gothenburg. ***Note:*** These vessels have excellent dining rooms.

BY CAR From either Malmö or Helsingborg, the two major "gateways" to Sweden on the west coast, take E-6 north. Gothenburg is 280km (174 miles) north of Malmö and 226km (140 miles) north of Helsingborg. From Stockholm, take E-4 west to Jönköping and continue west the rest of the way through Borås to Gothenburg, a distance of 470km (292 miles).

Visitor Information

The **Gothenburg Tourist Office** is at Kungsportsplatsen 2 (✆ **031/368-42-00;** www.goteborg.com), and it's open September to April Monday to Friday 9:30am to 5pm, Saturday 10am to 2pm; May to June 21 daily 9:30am to 6pm; June 22 to August 19 daily 9:30am to 8pm; and August 20 to August 31 daily 9:30am to 6pm.

GETTING AROUND

The cheapest way to explore Gothenburg (except on foot) is to buy a **Göteborgspasset (Gothenburg Card).** Available at hotels, newspaper kiosks, and the city's tourist office, it entitles you to unlimited travel on local trams, buses, and ferryboats; a free pass for most sightseeing tours; free admission to the city's major museums and sightseeing attractions; discounts at certain shops; free parking in certain lots; and more. A ticket valid for 24 hours costs 245SEK for adults and 170SEK for children up to 17 years old; a 48-hour ticket is 390SEK for adults and 270SEK for children.

BY PUBLIC TRANSPORTATION (TRAM) A single tram ticket goes for 25SEK to 50SEK or half-price for children. If you don't have an advance ticket, board the first car of the tram—the driver will sell you a ticket and stamp it for you. Previously purchased tickets must be stamped in the automatic machine as soon as you board the tram.

BY TAXI Taxis are not as plentiful as we'd like. However, you can always find one by going to the Central Station. **To call a taxi,** dial ✆ **031/27-27-27.** A taxi traveling within the city limits now costs 100SEK to 250SEK, although a ride from the center to either of the airports will run up a tab of around 400SEK to 450SEK.

BY CAR Parking is a nightmare, so we don't recommend driving through Gothenburg. You'll need a car to tour the surrounding area, but there is good public transportation within the city, as well as to many sights. **Avis** (✆ **031/80-57-80;** www.avis.com) has a rental office at the Central Station and another at the airport (✆ **031/94-60-30**). Its rival, **Hertz,** also has an office at the center of town at the Central Station (✆ **031/80-37-30;** www.hertz.com) and one at the airport (✆ **031/94-60-20**). Compare rates and, of course, make sure you understand the insurance coverage before you sign a contract.

[Fast FACTS] GOTHENBURG

Business Hours Generally, **shops** are open Monday to Friday 10am to 6 or 7pm and Saturday from 10am to 3 or 4pm. Large department stores, such as NK, are also open on Sunday, usually from 11am to 4pm. Most banks are open Monday to Friday from 9:30am to 3pm, and **offices** are open Monday to Friday 9am to 5pm.

Currency Exchange Currency can be exchanged at **Forex,** in the Central Station (✆ **031/15-65-16**), daily 7am to 9pm. There are also currency exchange desks at both Landvetter and Gothenburg City airports, each open daily 5:15am to 10:45pm.

Drugstores A good pharmacy is **Apoteket VasenApoteket Shop,** Korsgatan 24 Götgatan 12, Nordstan (✆ **0771/45-04-50**), open Monday to Friday 8am to 10pm, and Saturday 10am to 4pm.

Emergencies The number to call for nearly all emergencies (fire, police, medical) is ✆ **112.**

Police The main police station is Polismyndigheten, Ernst Fortells Plats (✆ **031/739-29-50**), opposite Ullevi Stadium.

Post Office Gothenburg doesn't define any particular branch of its many post offices as preeminent or "central," but a branch of the Swedish Postal Service that's convenient to everything in the city's commercial core is at **Nordstan** (✆ **031/80-65-29**), a 5-minute walk from the Central Station. It's open Monday to Saturday 10am to 3pm.

Transit Information For tram and bus information, call ✆ **0771/41-43-00.**

WHERE TO STAY

Reservations are important, but if you need a place to stay on the spur of the moment, try the **Gothenburg Tourist Office,** at Kungsportsplatsen 2 (✆ **031/368-42-00;** www.goteborg.com). There's also a branch of the tourist office in the Nordstan shopping center (✆ **031/61-25-00**), near the railway station. It's open Monday to Saturday 10am to 6pm, Sunday noon to 5pm. Reservations can be made by letter or by phone. The tourist office charges a booking fee of 60SEK, but if you reserve your own accommodations on the website (www.gothenburg.com) it's free. Double rooms in private homes start at around 250SEK per person and breakfast always costs extra.

The hotels listed in the following section as "expensive" actually become "moderate" on Friday and Saturday and during midsummer.

Expensive

Elite Park Avenue Hotel ★ After more than half a century in business, this hotel is once again a prestige address, even though it still lacks a certain character. Built in 1950, and radically renovated after its takeover by Sweden's Elite Hotel Group, this 10-story contemporary hotel stands as a highly visible fixture on the city's most central boulevard. Its midsize-to-spacious bedrooms are attractive and comfortable, with tile or marble-trimmed bathrooms and lots of contemporary comforts. We go for the rooms on the upper floors because they have the most panoramic views of the water and the cityscape itself. A few steps from the hotel's entrance is the popular nightclub, the Madison, which is loosely affiliated with this hotel.

Kungsportsavenyn 36–38, S-40015 Göteborg. www.elite.se. ✆ **031/727-10-00.** Fax 031/727-10-10. 318 units. Mon–Thurs 1,250SEK–2,950SEK double; Fri–Sun 1,400SEK–1,600SEK double; 1,800SEK–4,650SEK suite. Rates include buffet breakfast. AE, DC, MC, V. Parking 195SEK–275SEK per night. Bus: 771. **Amenities:** Restaurant; bar; babysitting; exercise room; indoor heated pool; room service; sauna. *In room:* TV, hair dryer, minibar, Wi-Fi (free).

Elite Plaza ★★★ Equaled in Gothenburg only by the Radisson Blu Scandinavia, this 1889 insurance company was stunningly converted into a superior first-class hotel. During the conversion, all of the major architectural features of this palatial structure were preserved, including the stucco ceilings, mosaic floors, and high ceilings, all of which contribute to a rather formal, but not particularly cozy, collection of bedrooms. The public lounges are adorned with an impressive collection of modern art, and all the midsize-to-spacious bedrooms and the plumbing have been updated. In the center of town, the hotel is within a short walk of the Central Station and the Opera House.

Vastra Hamngatan 3, S-404 22 Göteborg. www.elite.se. ✆ **031/720-40-00.** Fax 031/720-40-10. 130 units. Sun–Thurs 1,850SEK–3,450SEK double, 4,850SEK suite; Fri–Sat 1,600SEK–3,200SEK double, 4,550SEK suite. Rates include buffet breakfast. AE, DC, MC, V. Parking nearby 280SEK. Tram: 1, 6, 9, or 11. **Amenities:** Restaurant; bar; babysitting; exercise room; room service; sauna. *In room:* TV, hair dryer, minibar (in some), Wi-Fi (free).

Hotel Flora This stylish hotel has blossomed anew with a daringly modern and sophisticated design. Its bedrooms today are among the most desirable in town, with state-of-the-art technology and grand comfort. Near the heart of the old city, it is also a convenient address; the entertainment street of Avenyn is only a stone's throw away. There is taste and a pleasing decor evident throughout, and the staff is one of the most welcoming and efficient in Gothenburg.

Grönsakstorgt 2, 411 17 Göteborg. www.hotelflora.se. ✆ **031/13-86-16.** Fax 031/13-24-08. 68 units. 1,645SEK–1,795SEK double. Rates include buffet breakfast. AE, DC, MC, V. Tram: 6. **Amenities:** Bar; room service. *In room:* TV, minibar, hair dryer, Wi-Fi (free).

Hotel Gothia Towers ★★ The twin towers of this well-run government-rated four-star hotel loom above Sweden's largest convention center. Rooms are comfortable, contemporary, and tasteful. Touches of wood, particularly the hardwood floors, take the edge off any sense of cookie-cutter standardization. Bathrooms are spacious, with sleek, tiled tub/showers. Rooms on the top floors of the towers are plusher and feature enhanced amenities and services. A third, 29-floor tower will be added by 2013 in time for the European Athletics Indoor Championships, and the 19-story center tower will be extended by five floors containing five-star rooms, plus a gourmet restaurant and an exercise center. When completed, the three towers will be joined by glazed footbridges and share a common lobby.

Mässans Gata 24, S-402 26 Göteborg. www.gothiatowers.com. ✆ **031/750-88-00.** Fax 031/750-88-82. 704 units. Mon–Thurs 1,395SEK–2,565SEK double; Fri–Sun 1,145SEK–1,845SEK double; 2,900SEK–4,500SEK suite. AE, DC, MC, V. Parking 235SEK. Bus: 771. **Amenities:** 2 restaurants; 3 bars; fitness center; exercise room; room service; sauna; smoke-free rooms; rooms for those w/limited mobility. *In room:* TV, hair dryer, minibar, Wi-Fi (free).

Radisson Blu Scandinavia Hotel ★★★ If you want the most modern and spectacular hotel in Gothenburg, check in here. This unusual deluxe hotel surrounds a large greenhouse-style atrium, which seems like a tree-lined city square indoors. Though opposite the railroad station, it's one of the best-run and best-equipped hotels in Sweden. Opened in 1986 but extensively renovated since, the hotel offers among the finest rooms in town; they're large, and luxuriously appointed. The fifth floor of the hotel contains the exclusive concierge rooms with extended service.

Södra Hamngatan 59–65, S-401 24 Göteborg. www.radissonblu.com. ✆ **800/333-3333** in the U.S., or 031/758-50-00. Fax 031/758-50-01. 349 units. 1,190SEK–2,445SEK double; 1,890SEK–4,500SEK suite. Rates include buffet breakfast. AE, DC, MC, V. Parking 255SEK. Tram: 6. Bus: 771. **Amenities:** Restaurant; bar; babysitting; health club; Jacuzzi; indoor heated pool; room service; sauna. *In room:* TV, hair dryer, minibar, Wi-Fi (free).

Scandic Hotel Europa ★★ If you're seeking a cozy Swedish inn, check in elsewhere. This is one of the largest hotels in Scandinavia—a big, bustling blockbuster of a building that rises eight bulky stories across from Gothenburg's railway station. Built in 1972 of concrete and glass, the hotel underwent a massive renovation, which added thousands of slabs of russet-colored marble. Midsize-to-spacious bedrooms are outfitted in monochromatic tones of either autumn-inspired browns or pale Nordic tones of blue, and have conservative, modern furniture as well as up-to-date bathrooms. The largest and plushest rooms lie on the hotel's second, eighth, and ninth floors.

Köpmansgatan 38, PO Box 11444, S-404 29 Göteborg. www.scandic-hotels.com. ✆ **031/751-65-00.** Fax 031/751-65-11. 452 units. 900SEK–2,350SEK double; 1,600SEK–5,000SEK suite. Rates include buffet breakfast. AE, DC, MC, V. Parking 150SEK. Tram: 6. **Amenities:** Restaurant; 2 bars; bikes; exercise room; indoor heated pool; room service; sauna. *In room:* A/C, TV/DVD, CD player, hair dryer, minibar, Wi-Fi (free).

Quality Inn 11 ★ Facing central Gothenburg from its waterfront position on Hisinge Island, this sprawling red-brick hotel occupies what originated around 1890 as a machinists' shop for the shipbuilding industry. In addition to its hotel facilities, its interior contains a movie theater and a convention center, and its lobby is outfitted in tones of toreador red and black. The modern sections of this hotel are angular and very modern; the antique sections reek of the sweat and hard work of the Industrial Revolution. Views, from both the bedrooms and the endless hallways of this ultramodern convention complex, sweep out over the harbor and the remnants of the heavy industry that used to dominate both the harbor and the town.

Maskingatan 11, Hinsingen, 41764 Göteborg. www.hotel11.se. ✆ **031/779-11-11.** Fax 031/779-11-10. 260 units. 1,290SEK–2,578SEK double. Rates include buffet breakfast. AE, DC, MC, V. Bus: 16. **Amenities:** Restaurant; bar; exercise room; Jacuzzi; room service; sauna. *In room:* A/C, TV, minibar, Wi-Fi (free).

Moderate

Grand Hotel Opera From the outside, you'll look at this boxy building and swear that it's part of an architectural whole. But it includes two distinctly different divisions, one with three stories, the other with four, which resulted from the interconnection of two once-separate hotels back in 1994. Rooms come in categories of "recently renovated" (that is, slightly larger, brightly accessorized units) and "not so recently renovated" (usually with decors dating back to the mid-1990s, with spaces that are a bit more cramped).

Nils Ericsonsgatan 23, S-404 26 Göteborg. ✆ **031/80-50-80.** Fax 031/80-58-17. 200 units. Sun–Thurs 1,395SEK–2,875SEK double; Fri–Sat 995SEK–1,575SEK double. Rates include buffet breakfast. AE, DC, MC, V. Parking 140SEK. Bus: 24, 59, or 80. **Amenities:** Restaurant; bar; Jacuzzi; indoor heated pool; sauna. *In room:* TV, hair dryer (in some), Wi-Fi (free).

Hotel Best Western Eggers ★ For our *kronor,* this inn has more old-fashioned charm and authentic character than any other hotel in town. The third-oldest hotel in Gothenburg was built in 1859, predating the Swedish use of the word to describe a building with rooms for travelers. Many emigrants to the New World spent their last night in the old country at the Hotel Eggers, and during World War II, the Germans and the Allies met here for secret negotiations. Today it's just as good as or better than ever, with stained-glass windows, ornate staircases, wood paneling, and a distinct sense of history. Rooms vary in size, but they are all individually furnished and beautifully appointed, with large bathrooms.

Drottningtorget, SE 40125 Göteborg. www.hoteleggers.se. ✆ **800/528-1234** in the U.S. and Canada, or 031/333-44-40. Fax 031/333-44-49. 69 units. 1,350SEK–2,625SEK double. Rates include buffet breakfast. AE, DC, MC, V. Parking 100SEK–150SEK. Bus: 17, 21, or 510. **Amenities:** Restaurant; bar; room service. *In room:* TV, hair dryer, Wi-Fi (free).

Hotel Onyxen ★ This hotel should be better known, but instead it's one of the relatively unknown gems of Gothenburg. We've anxiously watched its prices rise—it used to be featured in budget guides—but it still offers decent value in spite of inflation. Well run and family managed, it is housed in a building from Gothenburg's Belle Epoque days, meaning around the turn of the 20th century. Originally it was a many-balconied apartment house, until its owners decided to convert it into a hotel in the 1980s.

Sten Sturegatan 23, S-412 52 Göteborg. www.hotelonyxen.com. ✆ **031/81-08-45.** Fax 031/16-56-72. 34 units. Mon–Thurs 1,490SEK–1,990SEK double; Fri–Sat 1,090SEK–1,390SEK double. Rates include buffet breakfast. Parking 120SEK. AE, DC, MC, V. Bus: 52. **Amenities:** Bar. *In room:* TV, hair dryer, Wi-Fi (free).

Novotel Göteborg ★★ The recycling of this red-brick Industrial Age old brewery was done with style and sophistication, and we've spent several comfortable nights here over the years. This converted building is on the harborfront 4km (2½ miles) west of the center. It is a stylish hotel run by the French hotel conglomerate Accor. Each plushly carpeted room offers panoramic views of the industrial landscape. The room style is Swedish modern, with many built-in pieces, good-size closets, and firm sofa beds.

Klippan 1, S-414 51 Göteborg. www.novotel.se. ✆ **031/720-22-00**. Fax 031/720-22-99. 149 units. Sun–Thurs 1,660SEK–1,940SEK double; Fri–Sat 1,090SEK–1,340SEK double; 2,290SEK–2,690SEK suite. Rates include buffet breakfast. AE, DC, MC, V. Parking 100SEK. Tram: 3 or 9. From Gothenburg, follow the signs on E-20 to Frederikshavn, then the signs to Kiel; exit at Klippan, where signs direct you to the hotel. **Amenities:** Restaurant; bar; bikes; children's playground; exercise room; room service; sauna. *In room:* A/C, TV, hair dryer, minibar (in some), Wi-Fi (free).

Royal ★ This hotel was founded in 1852, making it the oldest in Gothenburg. That in itself is not a recommendation. What makes this a good choice is that it is completely renovated, and is today better than ever. It is .5km (⅓ mile) from the railroad station, and all bus and tram lines pass close by, whisking you to the center in little time. In spite of its overhaul, it protected some of its 19th-century architectural styling with wrought-iron banisters and heavy cast bronze lamps on the stairs. All of the midsize-to-spacious bedrooms are individually decorated and modernized.

Drottninggatan 67, S-411 07 Göteborg. www.hotelroyal.nu. ✆ **031/700-11-70.** Fax 031/700-11-79. 82 units. 1,595SEK–1,795SEK double. Rates include buffet breakfast. AE, DC, MC, V. Parking 125SEK. Bus: 17 or 25. **Amenities:** Room service. *In room:* TV, hair dryer, Wi-Fi (free).

Quality Panorama Hotel ★ Even though this 13-story hotel, a 10-minute walk west of the center of town, is little publicized, it is one of the better "moderate" choices in pricey Sweden. It is spacious with a sense of drama, and each of the midsize-to-large bedrooms is furnished in a comfortable, tasteful style, with soft lighting and double-glazed windows. The finest rooms, and certainly those with a view, are on the 13th floor. The hotel also boasts a balcony-level restaurant serving good and reasonably priced food made with market-fresh ingredients.

Eklandagatan 51–53, S-400 22 Göteborg. www.panorama.se. ✆ **031/767-70-00.** Fax 031/767-70-70. 38 units (some with shower only). 990SEK–2,600SEK double. Rates include buffet breakfast. AE, DC, MC, V. Parking 125SEK. Closed Dec 22–Jan 7. Tram: 4 or 5. Bus: 49 or 52. **Amenities:** Restaurant; bar; Jacuzzi; room service; sauna. *In room:* TV, hair dryer, minibar, Wi-Fi (free).

Inexpensive

A budget hotel in Gothenburg could be considered expensive in many parts of the world. To get low rates, time your visit to Gothenburg on a Friday or Saturday night, when rates are generally slashed.

Hotel Örgryte Though lacking a lot of character, this longtime favorite is a good, safe choice for overnighting. Named after the leafy residential district of Örgryte, where this hotel is situated, this family-owned hotel is 1.5km (about 1 mile) east of the commercial core of Gothenburg. It was originally built around 1960 and renovated many times since. Rooms were upgraded and outfitted with pastel-colored upholstery and streamlined, uncomplicated furniture that makes use of birch-veneer woods. Most units are medium-size, often big enough to contain a sitting area. Both the exterior and the public areas are not particularly inspired in their design, but overall, the place provides decent, safe accommodations at a relatively reasonable price.

Danska Vägen 68–70, SE-41659 Göteborg. www.hotelorgryte.se. ✆ **031/707-89-00.** Fax 031/707-89-99. 70 units. Sun–Thurs 1,350SEK–1,560SEK double; Fri–Sat 830SEK–990SEK double; 1,840SEK–2,230SEK suite. Rates include buffet breakfast. AE, DC, MC, V. Parking 100SEK. Bus: 60 or 62. **Amenities:** Restaurant; bar; sauna. *In room:* TV, fridge (in some), hair dryer, Wi-Fi (free).

Tidblom's Hotel ★ This is a good if offbeat choice. It's better for motorists because of its location, although it can also be reached by public transportation. Set 3km (1¾ miles) east of Gothenburg's center, in a residential neighborhood filled with other Victorian buildings, this hotel was built in 1897 as a dormitory for Scottish craftsmen imported to work at the nearby lumber mill. Despite its functional purpose, its builders graced it with a conical tower, fancy brickwork, and other architectural adornments that remain in place today. The building was upgraded in 1987 into a cozy, well-accessorized hotel. Guest rooms have more flair and character than you'll find at many larger, more anonymous hotels in Gothenburg's center.

Olskroksgatan 23, S-416 66 Göteborg. www.tidbloms.com. ✆ **031/707-50-00.** Fax 031/707-50-99. 42 units. Sun–Thurs 975SEK–1,595SEK double; Fri–Sat 877SEK–950SEK double. Rates include buffet breakfast. AE, DC, MC, V. Free parking. Tram: 1, 3, or 6. **Amenities:** Restaurant; bar; concierge; room service; sauna. *In room:* TV, hair dryer, minibar, Wi-Fi (free).

Quality Hotel Winn Chain run but also chain efficient, this no-nonsense but comfortable and affordable four-story hotel is in an isolated wooded area about 3km (1¾ miles) north of Gothenburg's ferryboat terminal. Functional and modern, its bedrooms are more comfortable than you might imagine from the uninspired exterior. Each is outfitted in pastel shades. If your hopes aren't too high, you may come away pleased with this hotel.

Gamla Tingstadsgatan 1, S-402 76 Göteborg. www.winnhotel.com. ✆ **031/750-19-00.** Fax 031/750-19-50. 121 units. 1,390SEK–2,190SEK double. Rates include buffet breakfast. AE, DC, MC, V. Free parking. Bus: 18 or 19. **Amenities:** Restaurant; bar; Jacuzzi; indoor heated pool; sauna. *In room:* TV, hair dryer, minibar, Wi-Fi (free).

WHERE TO DINE

Gothenburg, as you'll soon discover, is a great restaurant town. It may never compete with the sublime viands of Stockholm, but outside the capital it's one of the best cities in Sweden for fine dining. Grandmother's dishes can still be found, but Gothenburgers today are on the cutting edge of cuisine.

Expensive

Basement Restaurant & Bar ★★★ CONTINENTAL One of Sweden's grandest and best restaurants has such an unpretentious name, but don't be put off. The cuisine is creative and wonderfully delicate, the ingredients market-fresh, the chefs skilled and imbued with personalized creations in the kitchen. The staff serves the best-tasting set menus in the city. The fixed-price menus are changed every day to take advantage of whatever is the choicest in their morning shopping. The chef will treat you to a superb menu with one glass of wine paired to suit each dish. Most meals consist of a shellfish plate, a fish course, and a meat dish, followed by a freshly made dessert. If available, their lobster salad is unbeatable. Likely to be featured are such fish dishes as whole pan-fried turbot or filet of beef Rossini, followed perhaps by a decadent crème brûlée.

Gotabergsgatan 28. ✆ **031/28-27-29.** www.restbasement.com. Reservations required. Fixed-price 3-course menu 425SEK, 4-course 520SEK, 6-course 720SEK. AE, DC, MC, V. Tues–Sat 5:30–11pm. Closed July–Aug 17. Bus: 16.

Fiskekrogen ★★ SEAFOOD This restaurant offers you a choice of some three dozen fish and shellfish dishes, each wonderfully fresh. One of the most appealing seafood restaurants in Gothenburg occupies a building across the canal from the Stadtsmuseum, in a handsome, internationally modern setting whose sea-green and dark-blue color scheme reflects the shades of the ocean. Fiskekrogen prides itself on a medley of fresh seafood that's artfully displayed on ice—succulent oysters, fresh lobster, fat crayfish, clams, and mussels—and prepared with a zest that earns many loyal customers throughout the city. More conventional seafood dishes include poached *tournedos* of cod with Swedish caviar, asparagus, and an oyster-enriched vinaigrette; and butter-fried halibut with chanterelles, fava beans, truffled new potatoes, and merlot sauce.

Lilla Torget 1. ✆ **031/10-10-05.** www.fiskekrogen.com. Reservations recommended. Main courses 295SEK–395SEK; set menu 645SEK. AE, DC, MC, V. Mon–Fri 11:30am–2pm and 5:30–11pm; Sat 1–11pm. Tram: 6, 9, or 11. Bus: 60.

Fond ★★★ SCANDINAVIAN/CONTINENTAL It's not quite a love affair, but we consider this to be one of the best restaurants in western Sweden. It truly lives up to its fine reputation and richly deserves its Michelin star. An address patronized by the town's discerning gourmets, this is the culinary domain of Stefan Karlsson, a media darling and winner of several culinary citations. We always select a table with a panoramic view over the avenue to watch the world go by as we eat memorable dishes including a choice loin of Swedish lamb with wine gravy and a side of sugar-glazed cabbage. We are equally won over by the deep-fried crayfish with a black-pepper glaze and baby carrots with an orange sauce; the classic boiled crayfish, so beloved in Sweden, is made here with market-fresh ingredients.

Götaplatsen. © **031/81-25-80.** www.fondrestaurang.com. Reservations required. Dinner main courses 225SEK–385SEK; lunch main courses 125SEK–210SEK; 6-course fixed-price menu 795SEK. AE, DC, MC, V. Mon–Fri 11:30am–2:30pm; Mon–Sat 5–11pm. Closed 2 weeks at Christmas, 4 weeks in midsummer. Bus: 58.

Restaurant 28+ ★★★ INTERNATIONAL/FRENCH This cozy, intimate, chic, and stylish restaurant sits in the pantheon of Gothenburg's great restaurants, enjoying equal rank with Fond and Sjömagasinet, all of which are in a neck-in-neck race for culinary supremacy. The trio of dining rooms are lit with flickering candles and capped with soaring masonry ceiling vaults. It's the city's hippest culinary venue, featuring main courses that include cooked crayfish with a fennel-flavored *nage* (an aromatic broth), smoked filet of char in a red-wine and butter sauce, grilled breast of pigeon, and saddle of reindeer with Jerusalem artichokes and blackberry vinaigrette. We have consistently found that the most imaginative cuisine in Gothenburg is served here. The items taste fabulously fresh, and the food is handled faultlessly in the kitchen and delicately seasoned. The service is among the city's best.

Götabergsgaten 28. © **031/20-21-61.** www.28plus.se. Reservations recommended. Main courses 230SEK–245SEK. AE, DC, MC, V. Mon–Sat 6–9:30pm (last order). Tram: 2, 3, or 7. Closed July 1–Aug 21.

Sjömagasinet ★★★ SEAFOOD The food served at the Fiskekrogen is hard to top, but somehow the chefs here manage to do just that. Not only that, but they have the loveliest setting in all of Gothenburg. The most elegant and atmospheric restaurant in town, Sjömagasinet is near the Novotel in the western suburb of Klippan, about 4km (2½ miles) from the center. The building, erected in 1775, was originally a warehouse, and today it retains its low-ceilinged, heavily timbered sense of rustic craftsmanship. Amid dozens of nautical artifacts from the late 19th and early 20th centuries, you can have predinner drinks in either of two separate bars, one of them outfitted in a cozy, English colonial style. Only the freshest seafood is served, from lightly salted cod filled with a truffle-and-cauliflower cream to a succulent house version of bouillabaisse. Our favorite dishes are the *pot-au-feu* of fish and shellfish, served with a chive-flavored crème fraîche, and poached filet of halibut with a warm cabbage salad and potato salad.

Klippans Kulturreservat. © **031/775-59-20.** www.sjomagasinet.se. Reservations recommended. Dinner main courses 295SEK–495SEK; lunch main courses 195SEK–235SEK; 3-course menu 545SEK. AE, DC, MC, V. Mon–Fri 11:30am–2pm and 6–10pm; Sat 5–10pm; Sun 2–8pm in summer. Tram: 3 or 9. From the town center, head west on E-3, following the signs to Frederikshavn, and then to Kiel; exit at Klippan and then follow the signs for the Novotel.

Thörnströms Kök ★★ INTERNATIONAL Tucked away in a quiet residential neighborhood, this is arguably the most discreetly fashionable restaurant in Gothenburg. Everything about it is haute, from its social ambitions to its prices. The chefs shake up tradition while respecting the innate flavors of their ingredients. Begin perhaps with a bowl of lobster soup delectably flavored with lime butter and succulent chunks of lobster, along with mussels simmered in white wine and served with fresh papaya. Main courses are even more rewarding, especially those fast-seared filets of turbot married to a crab-stuffed *agnolotti,* glazed carrots, and a lemon-flavored chervil sauce. We like how the pastry chef takes real care to create imaginative desserts such as a strawberry *bavaroise* (Bavarian cream) with rhubarb purée and even a rhubarb-flavored sorbet.

Teknologatan 3. ✆ **031/16-20-66.** www.thornstromskok.com. Reservations recommended. Main courses 235SEK-265SEK; fixed-price menus 825SEK-1,125SEK. AE, MC, V. Tues-Sat 6pm-1am. Closed 7 weeks in midsummer. Bus: 18.

Moderate

A Hereford Beefstouw ★ STEAK The true carnivore may want to skip some of the fancy restaurants recommended above and head here. This is the best and most appealing steakhouse in Gothenburg, with a reputation for expertly prepared Brazilian beef, and a salad bar that's the most varied and copious in town. One of the three separate dining rooms is smoke free, and all have thick-topped wooden tables, lots of varnished pine, and touches of African oak. The only sauces available to accompany your beef are béarnaise butter sauce, parsley butter sauce, and garlic butter sauce: The management believes in allowing the flavor of the meat to come through, unmasked by more elaborate seasonings. The largest platter is a 500-gram (17½-oz.) T-bone steak, a portion so large that we advise you to finish it at your own risk. Other platters, such as filet steaks, veal sirloins, and tenderloins, are more reasonably sized. A full list of wines and beers is available.

Linnégatan 5. ✆ **031/775-04-41.** www.a-h-b.dk. Reservations recommended. Main courses 159SEK-480SEK; salad bar as a main course 80SEK-173SEK. AE, DC, MC, V. Mon-Fri 11:30am-2pm and 5-10pm; Sat 4-10pm; Sun 3-9pm. Tram: 1, 3, or 11.

Bliss Resto ★ INTERNATIONAL This is one of the hippest and most appealing dining and drinking spots in Gothenburg. We classify it among our three or four favorite spots in Gothenburg. The staff is charming and a sense of whimsical internationalism prevails. Most patrons range in age from 25 to 40. There are tables set outside during clement weather, with zebra-skin upholsteries, great music, and an ambitious cuisine that's entirely composed of tapas. Management usually recommends that five or six tapas will create an adequate meal for a party of two. Dishes change with the season, but might include salmon pastrami with cream sauce; deep-fried prawn cakes with chili dip; spicy chorizo rolls stuffed with lemon-flavored cream sauce; and skewered lamb with wasabi and dill-flavored bouillon. There's a provocative drink menu (What's in a Sunset Blvd. or a Bondi Beach Block?). The bartender might not even describe the ingredients at all, but instead, he'll describe the feeling (red and raucous? pink and dizzy?) that drinking one or two of them will induce. Some clients, in the wee early hours of a Sunday morning, can remember dancing on the bar here.

Magasinsgatan 3. ✆ **031/13-85-55.** www.blissresto.com. Reservations recommended for dinner. Tapas 70SEK-125SEK; buffet menus 150SEK-349SEK. AE, DC, MC, V. Mon-Sat 11am-2pm and 6-10pm. Bus: 60.

Linné Terrassen Kök & Bar SWEDISH One of the best restaurants in Olivedal, this eatery occupies an outlandish-looking covered deck that disfigured the front of an antique, 19th-century Swedish house. In winter, the venue moves into a cozy antique bar that's flanked on two sides with a well-appointed network of dining rooms that still retain the panels, coves, and architectural accessories, including depictions of cherubs cavorting on the ceiling, of their original construction. The cookery is predictable and respectable—and we don't mean that as a put-down. Menu items include a goat's-cheese mousse with beetroot salad and walnut dressing; a platter of charcuterie and cheeses with cured meats from Sweden and cheeses from Spain; grilled black Angus sirloin with red-wine sauce; and filet of lamb with cider-flavored mustard and chives and a fondant of potatoes and rosemary sauce. Dessert might be a selection of sorbets with marinated strawberries. This place roars into action as a bar as well as a restaurant. As such, it's separately recommended in the "Gothenburg After Dark" section, later in this chapter.

Linnégatan 32. ✆ **031/24-08-90.** www.linneterrassen.se. Reservations recommended. Main courses 95SEK–229SEK. AE, DC, MC, V. Mon–Fri 4pm–1am; Sat–Sun 11am–2am. Tram: 1.

Restaurang Räkan ★ SEAFOOD This restaurant has evolved into something that's artfully shabby, with a kind of counterculture cool that continues to remain popular despite the changing times. Not surprisingly, it has a nautical decor with buoy lamps, wooden-plank tables typical of the Swedish west coast, and a shallow-bottomed re-creation of a Swedish lake. Your seafood platter arrives on a battery-powered boat with you directing the controls. You can order various combinations of crayfish (in the autumn season), along with prawns, poached sole, mussels, lobster, filet of gray sole, and fresh crabs. One standby is Räkan's hot and spicy fish and shellfish casserole. If you don't want fish, a choice of chicken and beef dishes is available, but to us these aren't anything special.

Lorensbergsgatan 16. ✆ **031/16-98-39.** www.rakan.se. Reservations recommended. Main courses 225SEK–325SEK. AE, DC, MC, V. Mon–Sat 4–11pm; Sun 3–10pm. Tram: 3 or 7. Bus: 58.

Smaka (Taste) SWEDISH This is a solid and much-visited staple for conservative and flavorful Swedish cuisine within the Vasaplatsen neighborhood, a residential area near the "main downtown campus" of Gothenburg University. Don't expect culinary experimentation or innovation here: The clients who frequent this place appreciate its old-fashioned agrarian virtue, and would probably resist any attempts to change it. You'll enter a blue-painted environment that evokes the dining room within an old-fashioned Swedish farmhouse. Food is served on the bare boards of wide-planked, well-scrubbed pinewood tables, without tablecloths, in a way that many Swedes associate with their grandmothers. Begin your meal with filets of sweet pickled herring, with browned butter, chopped egg, and dill; or whitebait roe with toast, chopped onions, chopped hard-boiled egg, and boiled potatoes. You could follow that with one of the most typical Swedish dishes—Swedish meatballs, the size of Ping-Pong balls, served with lingonberries. If you want to keep sampling Swedish staples, you might try the sautéed filet of pork with fried potatoes or the minced veal steak flavored with herbs and served in a mustard sauce. One of the best dishes, though, is a soup studded with fish and shellfish and spiked with *aioli*.

Vasaplatsen 3. ✆ **031/13-22-47.** www.smaka.se. Reservations recommended. Main courses 129SEK–225SEK. AE, DC, MC, V. Mon–Thurs and Sun 5pm–1am; Fri–Sat 5pm–2am. Tram: 2, 3, or 7.

Soho ★ INTERNATIONAL The owner of this cozy and well-managed place enjoyed New York City's Soho so much that he named his restaurant in its honor. It's the kind of hip, in-the-know place where publishers entertain prospective best-selling authors. The decor is Iberia-inspired, something like the living area of a prosperous hacienda in Spain, even though the thick wood tables and accessories derive from the Czech Republic, India, and Central America. A wine bar fills up a substantial corner of the place. In winter, up to 40 reds and 40 whites are sold by the glass. (That number is somewhat reduced in July and Aug). A series of simple platters are available at the bar, and more substantial food is served in the dining area. Menu items include platters with pickled herring and cured salmon, served with regional cheese; pasta with strips of veal, mushrooms, goat cheese, citrus sauce, and arugula; or creamy blue mussel soup with herb-and-garlic–flavored toast. Thc filet of lamb with a tomato-flavored Parmesan sauce was especially good.

Östra Larmgatan 16. ✆ **031/13-33-26.** www.sohogothenburg.se. Reservations recommended. Lunch main courses 129SEK–155SEK; dinner main courses 159SEK–289SEK. AE, DC, MC, V. Mon–Wed 8am–11pm; Thurs 9am–midnight; Fri 9am–1am; Sat 10am–1am; Sun 11:30am–5pm. Tram: 3, 4, or 7.

Wasa Allé & Wasa Källare ★★ SWEDISH/FRENCH/BRAZILIAN/ASIAN This is one of the most appealing restaurants in Gothenburg, an elegant, even posh, enclave of good times and fine dining that's the culinary focal point of the Wasastan neighborhood, just across the avenue from the "downtown campus" of the University of Gothenburg. In what functioned for many years as a pharmacy, the restaurant contains a large and angular bar, contemporary-looking crystal chandeliers, touches of stained glass from its earliest incarnation, and a high-ceilinged sense of grandeur that stands in quirky contrast to the animation at the bar and at the dining tables. Menu items in the restaurant include such favorites as shellfish lasagna with squid, crayfish, and scallops, served with sugar pea foam and a confit of tomatoes; or else oyster and parsley soup with a sashimi of Swedish fish and shellfish.

Menu items are simpler and cheaper in the street-level **Källare,** where food, displayed in refrigerated glass cases, is described as Swedish home-style and stands in distinct contrast to the more exotic cuisine served upstairs. Daily platters might include filet of chicken in parsley-flavored wine sauce, roasted elk with chanterelles and mashed potatoes, Swedish meatballs, a platter of Spanish-style tapas, or vegetarian lasagna. Glasses of wine in the cellar cost around 55SEK each.

Although service in the restaurant is attentive and fast-paced, in the cellar-level cafe, you'll place your food order at the counter, then carry it to a table, either outdoors or inside.

Vasagatan 24. ✆ **031/13-13-70.** www.wasaalle.se. Reservations recommended in the restaurant, not necessary in the cafe. Restaurant main courses 225SEK–295SEK; fixed-price menus 495SEK–875SEK. Cafe platters 55SEK–119SEK. AE, DC, MC, V. Restaurant Mon–Thurs 11:30am–2pm and 5:30–11pm; Fri–Sat 5:30pm–1am. Cafe Mon–Sat 10am–6pm. Tram: 1 or 3.

Inexpensive

The Bishop's Arms BRITISH/SWEDISH Okay, so it's a member of a citywide chain, but don't expect fast-food burgers with fries: The venue celebrates Olde England but with a Swedish accent. Although this is the largest, with a wider selection of beer than at any of its twins, there are clones of its basic format within other members of the Elite Hotel group in Gothenburg. The decor is appropriately woodsy and rustic, with black slate floors. The ceiling showcases the iron beams and brick vaulting of the building's 19th-century construction as the headquarters to an insurance company. There is also lots of stained glass. Note that some of the platters are prepared within the kitchens of the hotel's more expensive main restaurant, thereby providing some high-quality food at "pub grub" prices. The food, though good and filling, hardly taxes the imagination of the busy chefs in back. Menu items include Greek salads, Caesar salads with strips of grilled chicken or shrimp, shrimp sandwiches, salmon toasts, platters piled high with cheese and cold cuts, pork filets in mushroom-flavored cream sauce, and rib-sticking soups. This place operates British pub style: Order at the bar, and a staff member will carry the final product directly to your table.

In the cellar of the Elite Plaza Hotel. Vastra Hamngatan 3. ✆ **031/720-40-45.** www.bishopsarms.com. Main courses 119SEK-155SEK. AE, DC, MC, V. Mon 4pm-midnight; Tues-Thurs 4pm-1am; Fri 4pm-2am; Sat 3pm-2am; Sun 5-11pm. Tram: 1, 4, 5, or 6. Bus: 40.

Café Husaren INTERNATIONAL This venue's past lives have included stints as a pharmacy, a milliner, and a bank. Today it is the best-known, most animated, and most popular cafe in the Haga district of Gothenburg. The century-old decor includes a reverse-painted glass ceiling conceived in 1890 in tones of cerulean blue with flowers. Place your order for well-stuffed sandwiches, freshly made salads, and pastries, which include the biggest and most succulent cinnamon roll in town: It's the size of a small pizza and a lot thicker. The shrimp salad is also very good here. You carry your food to one of the indoor or, in summer, outdoor tables.

Haga Nygata 24. ✆ **031/13-63-78.** www.cafehusaren.se. Sandwiches 25SEK-65SEK; pastries 15SEK-45SEK. MC, V. Mon-Thurs 9am-8pm; Fri 9am-7pm; Sat-Sun 9am-6pm. Tram: 3, 6, 9, or 11.

Froken Olssons Café SWEDISH Looking for one of the most central cafes in Gothenburg? Less than 2 blocks from the Avenyn, this is a traditional favorite of city dwellers. It tends to be crowded and noisy at lunchtime. Even though there's a large interior, the crowd overflows onto an outdoor terrace in summer. Hot pies with a salad, pastas, and chicken dishes are featured. An ongoing staple is baguette sandwiches filled with such ingredients as shrimp or ham and cheese. Beer, wine, and exotic coffees are served, but liquor isn't available. Basically, this is a place that features light coffee shop–style dining, with homemade soups and such main courses as entrecôte.

Östra Larmgatan 14. ✆ **031/13-81-93.** Coffee 30SEK; *dagens* (daily specials) menu 60SEK-75SEK; hot pies with salad 70SEK; sandwiches 40SEK-80SEK. AE, DC, MC, V. Mon-Fri 9am-10pm; Sat-Sun 10am-10pm. Tram: 1, 4, 5, or 6. Bus: 40.

Solrosen (Sunflower) VEGETARIAN This is the best vegetarian restaurant in Gothenburg. Diners take advantage of the all-you-can-eat salad bar, returning again and again to serve themselves at the counter. Everything looks fresh and recently prepared; and there's even unlimited coffee. Unlike at many health-food restaurants, beer and wine are available. The Sunflower blooms in the Haga district, a low-rise neighborhood of 18th- and early-19th-century buildings. "It used to be called a working-class neighborhood, but a lot of people in Haga don't work anymore," a local patron informed us.

Kaponjärgatan 4. ✆ **031/711-66-97.** www.restaurangsolrosen.se. Daily platters 55SEK-80SEK. AE, DC, MC, V. Mon-Thurs 11:30am-10:30pm; Fri 11:30am-11:30pm; Sat 1-11:30pm; Sun 2-7:30pm. Tram: 1, 6, or 9.

GOTHENBURG ATTRACTIONS

The Top Sights

The best way to get your bearings when you set out to see the city is to go to the 120m-tall (394-ft.) **Guldhedens Vattentorn (Water Tower),** Syster Estrids Gata (✆ **031/82-00-09**). To get here, take tram no. 10 or bus no. 51 or 52 from the center of the city, about a 10-minute ride. The elevator ride up the tower is free, and there's a cafeteria/snack bar on top. The tower is open February to November (and sometimes in Dec) Saturday to Thursday noon to 10pm.

Early risers can visit the daily **fish auction** at the harbor, the largest fishing port in Scandinavia. The auction begins at 7am sharp. Sample some freshly made fish cakes at one of the stands here, and visit the **Feskekörka (Fish Church),** on Rosenlundsgatan (no phone), which is in the fish market. Built in 1874, it's open Tuesday to Friday 9am to 5pm and Saturday from 9am to 1pm (tram: 3, 6, 9, or 11).

The traditional starting point for seeing Gothenburg is the cultural center, **Götaplatsen,** with its ***Poseidon Fountain*** ★★, sculpted by Carl Milles. This fountain is a powerful symbol of maritime Gothenburg. The trio of buildings here are the **Concert Hall,** the municipally owned **theater,** and the Göteborgs Konstmuseum.

East India House (Museum of Gothenburg) ★ This building was constructed in 1750 as the headquarters, warehouse, and auction room of the East India Company, and houses exotic spices, silks, and fine porcelain. Despite great success in the beginning, the company went bankrupt in 1809.

Taken over by the city, the warehouse was turned into three museums focusing on archaeology, history, and industry. Exhibits highlight artifacts from the heyday of the Swedish Vikings, the harsh working conditions in the textile factories in the early 1900s, and pieces from the "attics" of Gothenburg that include rare antiques, folkloric costumes, a stunning porcelain collection, and period interiors.

Norra Hamngatan 12. ✆ **031/368-36-00.** www.stadsmuseum.goteborg.se. Admission 40SEK adults, free for students 24 and under and children. Tues–Sun 10am–5pm (till 8pm Wed). Tram: 1 or 9. Bus: 40, 58, or 60 to Brunnsparken.

Göteborgs Konstmuseum ★★★ We feel that this is the most significant repository of Swedish art outside Stockholm. It houses an array of 19th- and 20th-century Swedish art, Dutch and Flemish art from the 1600s, Italian and Spanish art from the 1500s to the 1700s, and French paintings from the 19th and 20th centuries. Bonnard, Cézanne, van Gogh, and Picasso are represented, along with sculpture by Carl Milles and Rodin. The gallery is noted for its collection of the works from Scandinavian artists Anders Zorn, Carl Larsson, Edvard Munch, and Christian Krohg. Of more local interest is the work of the "Gothenburg Colorists," who painted for 20 years beginning in 1930.

Head first for the **Fürstenberg Gallery** ★★★ to see an amazing group of paintings by some of Sweden's leading artists, even works by Prince Eugen. Then wander into the **Arosenius Room** ★★★, where you will see the wit, charm, and humor of the artist Ivar Arosenius (1878–1909).

Götaplatsen. ✆ **031/368-35-00.** www.konstmuseum.goteborg.se. Admission 40SEK, free for ages 24 and under. Tues and Thurs 11am–6pm; Wed 11am–9pm; Fri–Sun 11am–5pm. Tram: 4, 5, 6, or 8. Bus: 18, 42, or 58.

Liseberg Park ★★ ☺ Liseberg stands on its own as the most visited tourist attraction in Sweden. It lacks the lavish sense of nostalgic kitsch of Tivoli, but in terms of size, it's the biggest amusement park in northern Europe, with everything from roller coasters and flower gardens to bandstands and ballroom dancing. In business for about 8 decades, it makes more frequent concessions to popular (usually American) pop culture than you're likely to find within Tivoli. Singles and romantic couples stroll frequently along paths flanked with immaculately maintained flower beds, and entire families sometimes make visits here the focal point of their summer holiday. Some of Sweden's best performing artists entertain every summer at Stora Scenen, the park's main stage. An ongoing attraction within the park is the Gasten

Gothenburg

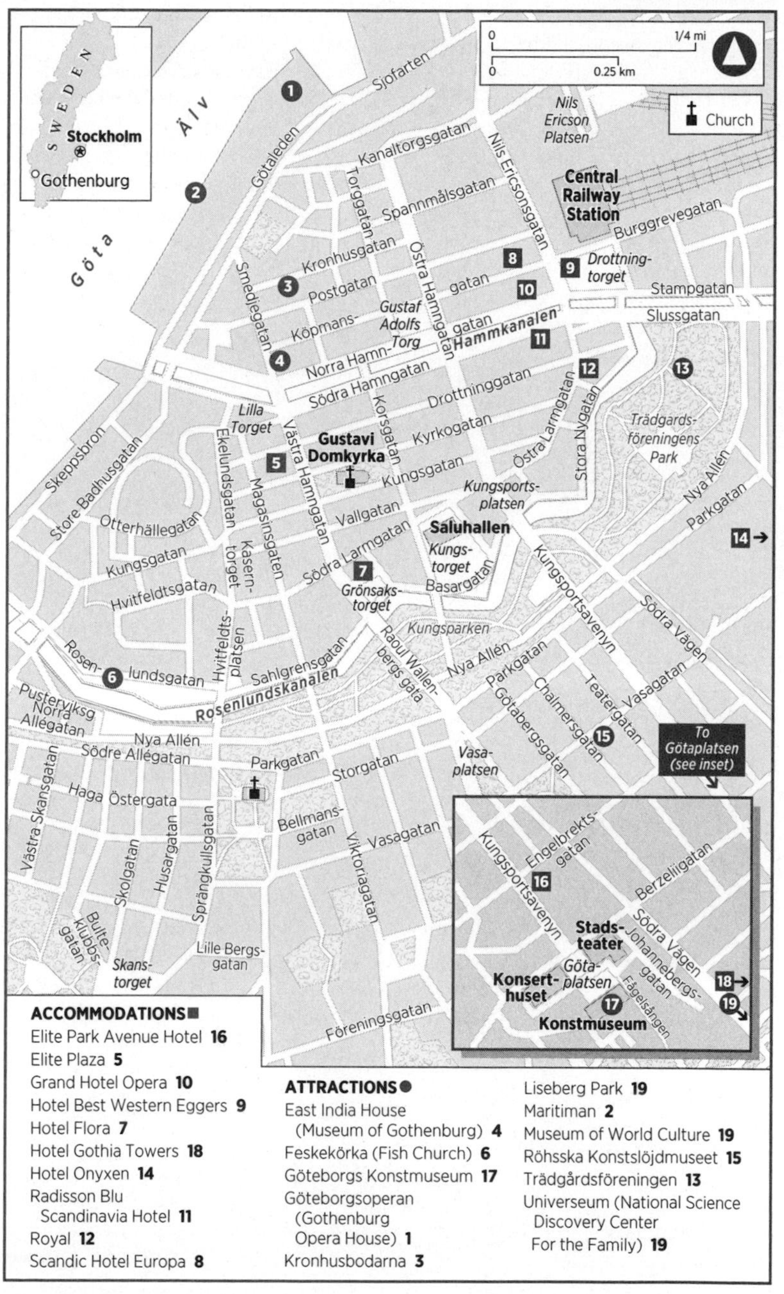

SWEDEN
Stockholm
Gothenburg
0
1/4 mi
0
0.25 km
Church
Göta Älv
Sjofarten
Götaleden
Kanaltorgsgatan
Torggatan
Spannmålsgatan
Nils Ericsonsgatan
Nils Ericson Platsen
Central Railway Station
Burggrevegatan
Drottning-torget
Stampgatan
Slussgatan
Kronhusgatan
Smedjegatan
Postgatan
Östra Hamngatan
Köpmansgatan
Gustaf Adolfs Torg
Hammkanalen
Norra Hamngatan
Södra Hamngatan
Drottninggatan
Lilla Torget
Korsgatan
Kyrkogatan
Östra Larmgatan
Stora Nygatan
Trädgårds-föreningens Park
Gustavi Domkyrka
Kungsgatan
Kungsports-platsen
Nya Allén
Parkgatan
Skeppsbron
Store Badhusgatan
Ekelundsgatan
Magasinsgatan
Västra Hamngatan
Vallgatan
Saluhallen
Otterhällegatan
Kungsgatan
Kasern-torget
Södra Larmgatan
Kungs-torget
Basargatan
Hvitfeldtsgatan
Grönsaks-torget
Kungsportsavenyn
Södra Vägen
Kungsparken
Hvitfeldts-platsen
Raoul Wallenbergs gata
Rosenlundsgatan
Sahlgrensgatan
Rosenlundskanalen
Nya Allén
Parkgatan
Götabergsgatan
Chalmersgatan
Teatergatan
Vasagatan
Pusterviksg.
Norra Allégatan
Nya Allén
Södre Allégatan
Parkgatan
Storgatan
Vasa-platsen
To Götaplatsen (see inset)
Västra Skansgatan
Haga Östergata
Bellmansgatan
Vasagatan
Skolgatan
Husargatan
Sprängkullsgatan
Viktoriagatan
Bulte-klubbsgatan
Skans-torget
Lille Bergsgatan
Föreningsgatan
Engelbrektsgatan
Kungsportsavenyn
Berzeliigatan
Stads-teater
Södra Vägen
Johannebergsgatan
Göta-platsen
Konsert-huset
Fågelsången
Konstmuseum
ACCOMMODATIONS
Elite Park Avenue Hotel 16
Elite Plaza 5
Grand Hotel Opera 10
Hotel Best Western Eggers 9
Hotel Flora 7
Hotel Gothia Towers 18
Hotel Onyxen 14
Radisson Blu Scandinavia Hotel 11
Royal 12
Scandic Hotel Europa 8
ATTRACTIONS
East India House (Museum of Gothenburg) 4
Feskekörka (Fish Church) 6
Göteborgs Konstmuseum 17
Göteborgsoperan (Gothenburg Opera House) 1
Kronhusbodarna 3
Liseberg Park 19
Maritiman 2
Museum of World Culture 19
Röhsska Konstslöjdmuseet 15
Trädgårdsföreningen 13
Universeum (National Science Discovery Center For the Family) 19

Ghost Hotel. Adventure rides include the Källerado rapid river, a simulated white-water trip through the wilds of northern Sweden, and the Kanonen, the most harrowing roller coaster in northern Europe.

For the younger set there's a children's playground with a circus, a kiddie roller coaster, a fairy-tale castle, and a rabbit house. Many Gothenburgers like to come here in summer to eat, as there are at least two dozen dining spots within the park ranging from fast food to steak.

Note: In 2011, the Liseberg Tower, rising to a height of 146m (479 ft.), will open as the tallest free-fall attraction in Europe. Called AlmostFear, the ride will start underground in the basement of the tower. From here, it will take only 90 seconds to reach the top. The return journey, when you go into a "free fall," will take only 3 seconds, as AlmostFear reaches a speed of more than 100kmph (62 mph). As a hair-raising twist, the brakes aren't applied until the last minute when you reach the basement. This attraction will not be for the faint of heart.

Korsvägen. ✆ **031/40-01-00**. www.liseberg.se. Admission to park, but not including rides inside the park, is 80SEK adults, free for children 6 and under. An all-inclusive 1-day pass valid for access to all rides within the park costs an additional 295SEK per person (no discount for children). Hours and opening days during Apr–May and Sept–Oct vary, depending on school holidays and advance reservation for groups; June usually daily 1–10pm; July–Aug usually daily 10 or 11am to 9 or 11pm. Tram: 4 or 5 from the city.

Maritiman ☺ This is the largest floating ship museum in the world. On the harbor and dedicated to Gothenburg's 19th- and 20th-century shipyard and maritime history, this museum consists of 19 ships, boats, and barges, the largest of which is the destroyer *Småland*. Decommissioned from the Swedish Navy in 1979, but still equipped with guns and torpedoes, it's the largest of a collection of vessels that require visitors to navigate lots of ramps, staircases, and ladders. Designed to be an authentic maritime experience, the museum includes lightships, steamships, tugboats, and a submarine. The museum includes at least one cafe year-round.

Packhuskajen 8. ✆ **031/10-59-50.** www.maritiman.se. Admission 80SEK adults, 40SEK children 7–15, free for children 6 and under. Apr Fri–Sun 11am–4pm; May–Sept daily 11am–6pm; Oct Fri–Sun 11am–4pm. Closed Nov–Mar. Tram: 5 to Lilla Bommen.

Röhsska Konstslöjdmuseet ★★ Dating from 1916, this is Sweden's only museum of applied art. Some of the artifacts shown here are 1,000 years old. Each floor is devoted to a different epoch of decorative art, and work ranges from the early Chinese dynasties to the modern era that produced the Absolut vodka bottle. Temporary exhibits of modern art and crafts are a regular feature on the ground floor, and the third floor is permanently devoted to East Asian art. Two marble lions from the Ming dynasty (1368–1644) flank the entrance to this National Romantic–style building.

Vasagatan 37–39. ✆ **031/36-83-150.** www.designmuseum.se. Admission 40SEK adults, free for students and those 19 and under. Tues noon–8pm; Wed–Fri noon–5pm; Sat–Sun 11am–5pm. Tram: 3, 4, 5, 7, or 10. Bus: 40, 41, or 58.

Parks & Gardens

Botaniska Trädgården (Botanical Garden) ★★ This park is Gothenburg's oasis of beauty and is, in fact, the most dramatic, cultivated bit of nature in western Sweden. The botanical gardens were first opened to the public in 1923 and have been improved considerably over the years. Winding paths stretching for a few kilometers have been cut through the gardens so you can stroll along at leisure. You can wander into a bamboo grove evoking Southeast Asia, or explore a Japanese dale. In spring, the blooming **Rhododendron Valley ★★** is one of the most stunning sights in Gothenburg. The splendid **Rock Garden ★** alone is worth the journey, featuring ponds, rugged rocks, cliffs, rivulets, and a cascade.

Carl Skottsbergsgata 22A. ✆ **031/741-11-06.** Free admission to garden; greenhouses 20SEK, free for children 16 and under. Garden daily 9am–sunset. Greenhouses May–Aug daily 10am–5pm; Sept–Apr daily 10am–4pm. Tram: 1, 7, or 8.

Göteborgsoperan (The Gothenburg Opera House) It's the pride of Gothenburg, a sprawling, glass-fronted building erected at the edge of a harbor that a century ago was known throughout the world for its shipbuilding prowess. Today, views from this dramatic building encompass what remains of Gothenburg's heavy industry, within a postmodern format that was inspired by an ocean liner. The opera is completely closed during July and August. For more details, see "Opera & Ballet" under "Gothenburg After Dark," p. 393.

Packhuskajen. ✆ **031/13-13-00.** www.opera.se. Tickets 75SEK–615SEK, depending on the venue. Box office daily noon–6pm or until the performance starts (closed on Sun and public holidays, if there is no performance). 90-min. guided tours, scheduled on an as-needed basis by an outside tour operator, cost around 50SEK per person. Call ✆ 031/10-80-00 for info. Tram: 5 or 10.

Slottsskogen ★★ ☺ With 110 hectares (272 acres), this is the largest park in Gothenburg, and it's perfect for a picnic on a summer day. First laid out in 1874 in a naturally wooded area, it has beautiful walks, animal enclosures, a saltwater pool, bird ponds, and an aviary, as well as a children's zoo (open May–Aug). A variety of events and entertainment take place here in summer. There's an outdoor cafe at the zoo, plus restaurants at Villa Bel Park and Björngårdsvillan.

Near Linnéplatsen. ✆ **031/365-37-00.** Free admission. Daily 24 hr. Tram: 1 to Linnéplatsen.

Trädgårdsföreningen ★★ ☺ If we lived in Gothenburg, we'd make seasonal visits here, coming in February for the camellias, in March and April for the orchids, in July for the giant waterlilies, and in early July and again in late August when the roses are at their peak. Across the canal from the Central Station, this park boasts a large rosarium with about 4,000 rosebushes from 1,900 different species. The park's centerpieces include the **Palmhuset (Palm House) ★★**, an ornate greenhouse whose design was inspired by London's Crystal Palace, and a butterfly house. The city of Gothenburg sometimes hosts exhibits, concerts (sometimes during the lunch hour), and children's theater pieces in the park.

Entrances on Slussgatan (across from the Central Station) and Södra Vägen. ✆ **031/365-58-58.** www.tradgardsforeningen.se. Park 20SEK adults, free for children 17 and under, free for everyone Sept–Apr. Daily 7am–8pm. Butterfly House is open only for private art exhibitions.

Organized Tours

A sightseeing boat trip along the canals and out into the harbor will show you the old parts of central Gothenburg and take you under 20 bridges and out into the harbor. **Paddan Sightseeing Boats ★★** (**✆ 031/60-96-70;** www.stromma.se/en) offers 50-minute tours, with a brisk multilingual commentary. The schedule is as follows: April 4 to April 27 Friday to Sunday 11:30am to 3pm; April 28 to May 18 daily 10:30am to 5pm; May 19 to June 15 daily 10am to 7pm; June 16 to August 10 daily 10:30am to 8:15pm; August 11 to August 31 daily 10am to 6pm; September 1 to September 28 Monday to Thursday 11:30am to 4pm, Friday to Sunday 10:30am to 5pm; September 29 to October 19 daily noon to 3pm (weather permitting). In winter, Paddan boats only sail to Liseberg amusement park during the Gothenburg

Christmas City from mid-November to December 23. Boats depart from the Paddan terminal at Kungsportsplatsen, which straddles the Avenyn in the city center. The fare is 180SEK for adults, 90SEK for children 6 to 16, and free for kids 5 and under. A family ticket (two adults and two children) costs 375SEK. We advise you to dress warmly for this trek, as part of the itinerary takes you out into the sometimes-windlashed harbor for views of the dockyards and ship-repair docks. If it's less than perfect weather, it's even a good idea to buy a poncho from the ticket window for around 95SEK. When it gets truly drenching out in the harbor, you'll be glad you did. Frankly, we really enjoy this tour—it really helps you understand the layout of Gothenburg and its harbor.

Nya Elfsborg (✆ **031/60-96-70**) is docked in the 17th-century Fästning fortress at the harbor's mouth. This boat takes you on a 90-minute tour from Lilla Bommen through the harbor—to and around Elfsborg Fortress, built in the 17th century to protect the Göta Älv estuary and the western entrance to Sweden. Elfsborg still bears traces of hard-fought sea battles against the Danes. Carvings on the prison walls tell tales of the threats to and hopes of the 19th-century life prisoners. A guide will be waiting for you at the cafeteria, museum, and souvenir shop for a 30-minute guided tour, in English and Swedish, of the fortress. There are five departures per day from mid-May to the end of August. The fare is 160SEK for adults, or 70SEK for children 6 to 11.

The meticulously restored **MS *S:t Erik,*** originally built in 1881, is available for evening cruises along the waterways of Gothenburg's southern archipelago. For information about tours, check with the tourist office (see "Orientation," earlier in this chapter). Or contact **Stromma** (✆ **031/60-96-70;** www.stromma.se), which provides excursion packages, brochures, tickets, and timetables. The tour costs 180SEK for adults and 90SEK for children 6 to 16. Departure times vary widely with the season and with demand.

For a guided 50-minute **bus tour** of Gothenburg, go to the tourist office or call ✆ **031/60-96-70** (see "Visitor Information," earlier in this chapter) for details. Between June and August, city tours are offered between five and seven times daily depending on demand. From September to May, the tour runs only on Saturday twice a day. The fare is 140SEK for adults, 70SEK for children and students. Passengers buy their tickets directly aboard the bus, which departs from a clearly signposted spot adjacent to the Stora Theatern.

ESPECIALLY FOR KIDS

At **Liseberg Park** (p. 386), every day is children's day. The Liseberg Cirkus is a fun and charming amusement park with rides and lots of stimulating visuals, and there are always comic characters (some of them developed in close cooperation with the management of Disney) who play with the children. At least some of the rides, including the pony merry-go-round, kids' boats, and a fun-on-wheels merry-go-round, are free for tots. Liseberg contains more flowers, and more acreage, than Tivoli.

Your children may want to stay at the amusement park's hotel, in the city center, a shorter walk from the park than any other lodgings in Gothenburg. **Hotel Liseberg Heden,** Sten Sturegatan S-411 38 Göteborg (✆ **031/750-69-00;** fax 031/750-69-30; www.liseberg.com), offers year-round rates of 1,040SEK to 2,110SEK in a double. They include breakfast and coupons for free admission to the amusement park and many of its rides and shows. The hotel accepts major credit cards. It was built in the 1930s as an army barracks and later functioned as a youth hostel. Today, after tons of improvements, it's a very comfortable first-class hotel. To reach the 179-room hotel, take tram no. 2 or 13 to Scandinavium **Naturhistoriska Museet,** Slottsskogen (✆ **031/775-24-00;** www.gnm.se), displays stuffed and mounted animals from all over the world, including a stuffed elephant, Sweden's only stuffed blue whale, and lots of big wooden drawers you'll slide open for views of hundreds of carefully preserved insects from around the world. It's open Tuesday to Sunday 11am to 5pm. Admission is 40SEK for adults, free for anyone 24 years old and under. Take tram 1, 2, or 6.

There's also a **children's zoo** at Slottsskogen from May to August (see "Parks & Gardens," above).

SHOPPING

The Shopping Scene

Many residents of Copenhagen and Helsingør come to Gothenburg for the day to buy Swedish merchandise. Visitors should shop at stores bearing the yellow-and-blue tax-free shopping sign. These stores are scattered throughout Gothenburg.

MAJOR SHOPPING DISTRICTS **Nordstan ★★** (www.nordstan.se), with its 150 shops and stores, restaurants, hotels, patisseries, coffee shops, banks, travel agencies, and post office, is the largest shopping mall in Scandinavia. Here you can find almost anything, from exclusive clothing boutiques to outlets for the major confectionery chains. There's also a tourist information center. Most shops are open Monday to Friday 10am to 7pm, Saturday 10am to 6pm, and Sunday 11am to 5pm.

Kungsgatan/Fredsgatan is Sweden's longest pedestrian mall (3km/1¾ miles long). The selection of shops is big and varied. Near these two streets you'll also find a number of smaller shopping centers, including Arkaden, Citypassagen, and Kompassen.

Another pedestrian venue, in this case one that's protected from inclement weather with an overhead roof, is the **Victoria Passagen,** which opens onto the Vallgatan, near the corner of the Södra Larmgatan. Inside, you'll find a cafe or two, and a handful of shops devoted to handicrafts and design objects for the home, kitchen, and garden.

At **Grönsakstorget/Kungstorget,** carts are filled daily with flowers, fruit, handicrafts, and jewelry, among other items. It's right in the city center.

The often-mentioned **Avenyn,** with its many restaurants and cafes, has a number of stores selling quality merchandise that has earned for it an enviable reputation as the Champs-Elysées of Sweden.

Kronhusbodarna, Kronhusgatan 1D (✆ **031/711-08-32;** www.kronhusbodarna.nu), houses a number of small-scale and rather sleepy studios for glass blowers, watchmakers, potters, and coppersmiths, some of whom sell their goods to passersby. They can be visited, if the artisans happen to show up (call ahead to make arrangements). Take tram no. 1 or 7 to Brunnsparken.

The **Haga District** houses a cluster of small-scale boutiques, fruit and vegetable stands, art galleries, and antiques shops, most of them in the low-slung, wood-sided houses that were built as part of an expansion of Gothenburg during the early 1800s. Defined as Gothenburg's first suburb, it's set within a short distance of the Avenyn.

Shopping A to Z

ANTIQUES

Antik Hallarna ★★ What was originally conceived in the 19th century as a bank is now the site of at least 21 independent antiques dealers who peddle their wares across the street from the Elite Plaza Hotel. Expect lots of somewhat dusty, small-scale collectibles and objets d'art, coins, stamps, antique watches and clocks, and the remnants, some of them intriguing, of what your grandmother—if she lived in a large house in Sweden—might have been storing for several generations in her attic. Västra Hamngatan 6. Each of the dealers in this place maintains its own phone number, but the phone of one of the largest dealers is ✆ **031/774-15-25.** www.antikhallarna.se. Tram: 11.

DEPARTMENT STORES

Bohusslöjd ★★ This store has one of the best collections of Swedish handicrafts in Gothenburg. Amid a light-grained birch decor, you'll find wrought-iron chandeliers, unusual wallpaper, fabric by the yard, and other items such as hand-woven rugs, pine and birchwood bowls, and assorted knickknacks, ideal as gifts or souvenirs. In 2006, this outfit celebrated its 100th birthday. Teatergatan 19. ✆ **031/16-00-72.** Bus: 18 or 58.

C. J. Josephssons Glas & Porslin ★★★ This store has been selling Swedish glass since 1866 and has established an enviable reputation. The selection of Orrefors crystal and porcelain is stunning. There are signed original pieces by such well-known designers as Bertil Vallien and Goran Warff. There's also a tourist tax-free shopping service plus full shipping service. Korsgatan 12 and Kyrkogatan 34. ✆ **031/17-56-15.** www.josephssons.se. Tram: 6, 9, 11, or 41. Bus: 16 or 60.

Nordiska Kompaniet (NK) ★ Because this is a leading and decidedly upscale department store, shoppers are likely to come here first as a one-stop emporium for some of the most appealing merchandise in Sweden. (The Swedish headquarters of the same chain is in Stockholm.) The store's packing specialists will take care in shipping your purchases home for you. Typical Swedish and Scandinavian articles are offered here—more than 200,000 items, ranging from Kosta Boda crystal, Orrefors crystal in all types and shapes, Rörstrand high-fired earthenware and fine porcelain, stainless steel, pewter items, dolls in national costumes, leather purses, Dalarna horses, Finnish carpeting, books about Sweden, Swedish records, and much more. Östra Hamngatan 42. ✆ **031/710-10-00.** www.nk.se. Bus: 60.

DESIGN

Design Torget ☺ Assembled into one all-encompassing venue, you'll find at least 40 different purveyors of intensely "designed," intensely thought-out items for the kitchen, home, and garden, as well as some children's toys that would make fine and thoughtful presents for nephews and nieces back home. Vallgatan 14. ✆ **031/774-00-17.** www.designtorget.se. Tram 6, 9, or 11.

EMBROIDERIES

Broderi & Garn Virtually every (female) long-term resident of Gothenburg is familiar with this shop: The grandmothers and mothers of many working women here have patronized the place since it was established nearly a century ago. If you're looking for a pastime to make the long winter evenings go more quickly, or one that integrates handicrafts with a sense of Swedish nationalism, come here for embroidery yarns, needles, and patterns that incorporate everything from scenes of children playing to replicas of the Swedish flag. The staff will explain the differences between cross-stitching and crewelwork, and show you any of dozens of patterns, most of which reflect nostalgic visions of long ago. Kits, with thread, needles, patterns, and everything you'd need for the completion of your own embroidered masterpiece, range in price from 100SEK to 2,500SEK each. Drottninggatan 31. ✆ **031/13-33-29.** www.broderi-och-garn.se. Tram: 1 or 5.

FASHION

H&M Established in the 1940s, this is a well-established clothing store—part of an international Swedish chain—for women who keep an eye on what's happening in cutting-edge fashion around the world. The spirit here is trendy, with an emphasis on what makes a woman look chic and youthful for nights out on the town. Despite its undeniable sense of flair, garments are less expensive than we at first assumed, with lots of marked-down bargains for cost-conscious shoppers. Deltavagen 16. ✆ **031/65-33-80.** www.hm.com. Tram: 1, 4, or 5.

Ströms This is the most visible emporium for clothing for men in Gothenburg, with a history at this location dating back to 1886. We've purchased a number of smart items here over the years, some of which still rest proudly in our closets. Scattered over two floors of retail space, you'll find garments that range from the very formal to the very casual, and boutique-inspired subdivisions that contain ready-to-wear garments from the leading fashion houses of Europe. Although most of its fame and reputation derive from its appeal to men, it also sells garments for women and children to a lesser extent. Kungsgatan 27–29. ✆ **031/17-71-00.** www.stroms-gbg.se. Tram: 1, 2, or 3.

HANDICRAFTS

Lerverk This is a permanent exhibit center for 30 potters and glassmaking craftspeople. We can't recommend any specific purchases because the offerings change from month to month. Although glass workers are more readily associated with the east coast, on our latest trip we were astonished at the skill, the designs, and the sleek contemporary and imaginative products of west-coast potters and glassmakers. Lilla Kyrkogata 1. ✆ **031/13-13-49.** www.lerverk.se. Tram: 2, 3, 9, or 11.

GOTHENBURG AFTER DARK

To the Gothenburger, there's nothing more exciting than sitting outdoors at a cafe along the Avenyn enjoying the short-lived summer season. Residents also like to take the whole family to the Liseberg amusement park (see "Gothenburg Attractions," earlier in this chapter). Although clubs are open in the summer, they're not well patronized until the cool weather sets in.

For a listing of entertainment events scheduled at the time of your visit, check the newspapers (*Göteborgs Posten* is best), or inquire at the tourist office.

The Performing Arts

THEATER

The Gothenburg Card (see "Getting Around," earlier in this chapter) allows you to buy two tickets for the price of one. Call the particular theater or the tourist office for program information. Performances also are announced in the newspapers.

Folkteatern This theater stages productions of Swedish plays or foreign plays translated into Swedish. The season is from September to May, and performances are

Tuesday to Friday at 7pm and Saturday at 6pm. Olof Palmes Plats (by Järntorget). ✆ **031/60-75-75.** www.folkteatern.se. Tickets 100SEK–220SEK. Tram: 1, 3, or 4.

Stadsteatern This is one of the major theaters in Gothenburg, but invariably the plays are performed in Swedish. Ibsen in Swedish may be too much of a challenge without knowledge of the language, but a musical may still be enjoyed. The season runs from September to May. Performances usually are Tuesday to Friday at 7pm, Saturday at 6pm, and Sunday at 3pm. Götaplatsen. ✆ **031/70-871-00.** www.stadsteatern.goteborg.se. Tickets 190SEK–275SEK. Bus: 58.

OPERA & BALLET

Göteborgsoperan (Gothenburg Opera House) ★★ This elegant modern opera house was opened by the Swedish king in 1994, and was immediately hailed as one of the most exciting major pieces of public architecture in Sweden. Overlooking the grimy industrial harbor landscape, with a big-windowed red-and-orange-trimmed facade, it features some of the finest theater, opera, operettas, musicals, and ballet performances in Sweden. There are also five bars and a cafe in the lobby. The main entrance (on Östra Hamngatan) leads to a foyer with a view of the harbor; here you'll find the box office and cloakroom. Big productions can be staged on a full scale. You'll have to check to see what performances are scheduled at the time of your visit. Packhuskajen. ✆ **031/10-80-00** or 031/13-13-00 for ticket information. www.opera.se. Tickets 150SEK-615SEK. Tram 5 or 10.

CLASSICAL MUSIC

Konserthuset ★★ Ironically, the symphony orchestra of Gothenburg functions as Sweden's national symphony, not its counterpart in Stockholm. And this, the Konserthuset, built in 1935 and noteworthy for its acoustics, is the Gothenburg orchestra's official home. Between September and June, it's the venue for world-class performances of classical music. During July and August, with the exception of two or so outdoor concerts, one of which is conducted on the Götaplatsen, the concert hall is closed. Götaplatsen. ✆ **031/726-53-00.** www.gso.se. Tickets 280SEK. Bus: 58.

The Club & Music Scene

BARS & NIGHTCLUBS

Berså Bar Much about this place will remind you of a sudsy, talkative, neighborhood bar, except that it is on one of the busiest intersections in Gothenburg, a prime spot for drop-ins, and for checking out who and what's on the prowl on a typical night in Sweden's "second city." There's a dance floor on the premises, a brisk big-city feeling to the bar area, and a dining menu. If you happen to engage someone here in a dialogue, ask him or her how to translate this bar's name; even the locals will give differing answers, as it was conceived as a deliberate play on Swedish words. The answer you'll usually get is "a cozy and comfortable campsite." Kungspanplatsen 1. ✆ **031/711-24-80.** www.bersagbg.se. Sun–Thurs 11am–1am; Fri–Sat 11am–4am. Tram: 1, 4, 5, or 6.

Glow In stark contrast to the sprawling size of the Trädgår'n (see below), this nightclub and cocktail lounge is small-scale and intimate. Outfitted in pale colors and attracting a clientele over 30, it's the most popular late-night venue in Gothenburg, sometimes attracting workers from restaurants around town who relax and chitchat here after a hard night's work. There's a small dance floor, but most visitors ignore it in favor of mingling at the bar. Open daily from 8pm to 5am. Avenyn 8. ✆ **031/10-58-20.** www.glownightclub.se. Tram: 1, 4, 5, or 6.

Linné Terrassen Kök & Bar If you linger after your evening meal here, you might be surprised at the way the bar area of this also-restaurant grows increasingly crowded, often surpassing the volume of clients in the dining room. As such, it's fun and charming and favored by attractive and usually available singles.

At the bar, you'll find 40 kinds of wine served by the glass, at least 10 beers on draft, 50 single-malt whiskeys, and a daunting collection of wines by the bottle. In winter, live jazz is performed every Wednesday and Friday from 7 to 9pm, often to standing-room-only crowds. Linnégatan 32. ✆ **031/24-08-90.** www.linneterrassen.se. Tram: 1.

Oakley's This is one of the most popular and visible supper clubs in Gothenburg. A short walk of the Avenyn, behind a red-and-white facade of what was originally a fire station, it offers a changing array of dancers and impersonators. Expect a changing array of musical acts, plenty of musical and showbiz razzmatazz, and imitations of Swedish pop stars that you might not have heard of. Food items are derived from "international" sources from around the world; well-prepared renderings of fish and meat (salmon terrine with champagne sauce, roast beef with purée of Idaho potatoes, turbot with a wasabi-flavored cream sauce) are served, supper club style, at tables within sightlines of a stage. There's an automatic cover charge of 140SEK, which is added to the cost of your meal. Main courses cost from around 200SEK to 280SEK each. The club is open Tuesday to Saturday 7pm to 1am. Tredje Långgatan 16. ✆ **031/42-60-80.** www.oakleys.nu. Reservations recommended. Tram 1, 3, 4, or 9.

Park Lane In this leading nightclub along Sweden's west coast, the dinner-dance room sometimes features international stars. Past celebrities have included Marlene Dietrich and Eartha Kitt. The dance floor is usually packed. Many of the musical numbers performed here are devoted to songs and lighthearted cabaret acts, so even if you don't speak Swedish, you can still appreciate the entertainment. The international menu consists of light supper platters such as crab salad or toasted sandwiches. Open Friday to Saturday 11:30pm to 5am, Sunday 11:30pm to 3am. Elite Park Avenue Hotel, Kungsportsavenyn 36–38. ✆ **031/20-60-58.** Cover 120SEK; hotel guests enter free. Bus: 771.

Trädgår'n This is the largest and most comprehensive nightspot in Gothenburg, with a cavernous two-story interior that echoes on weekends with the simultaneous sounds of a restaurant and a dance club. No one under 25 is admitted to this cosmopolitan and urbane venue. Cover charge for the disco is 100SEK. Main courses in the restaurant are 185SEK to 275SEK. The restaurant is open Monday to Friday 11:30am to 10pm, and Saturday 5 to 10pm. The disco is open Friday to Saturday 11pm to 4am. Allegaten 8. ✆ **031/10-20-80.** www.tradgarn.se. Tram: 1, 3, or 5.

Tranquilo It's fun, colorful, and Latino. Although food is served throughout the evening, with main courses priced from 155SEK to 250SEK, the place feels more like a singles bar where the women are predominantly svelte, long-legged, and gorgeous. Three kinds of tacos, grilled tuna or chicken, burgers, surf-and-turf skewers, ceviche, mangos stuffed with grilled roast beef, sweet desserts, and mojitos and caipirinhas are all the rage—especially the caipirinhas, which cost around 165SEK each. Food is served daily from 11:30am to 10:30pm, with the bar remaining open until between 1 and 3am. Kungstorget 14. ✆ **031/13-45-55.** www.tranquilo.se. Tram: 1, 2, or 3.

A DANCE CLUB

Valand/Lilla London Some Gothenburgers manage to find what they want, gastronomically and socially, at this combination restaurant and dance club on the Avenyn. Many clients move restlessly between the two venues, ordering stiff drinks, pastas, seafood, and steaks at Lilla London, in combination with dancing, drinking, flirting, and/or whatever, at Valand, a congenially battered and irreverent dance club immediately upstairs. The minimum age for entry is 25. Valand is open only on Friday and Saturday from 8pm to 3am. Lilla London is open Monday to Thursday from 5pm to 1am, Friday from 2pm to 3am, Saturday from noon to 3am, and Sunday from 1pm to 3am. Vasagatan 41. ✆ **031/18-30-93.** www.valand.nu. Cover 100SEK for disco after 10pm. Main courses at Lilla London 119SEK–189SEK; 3-course menu 330SEK. Tram: 2, 3, or 7.

Gay Gothenburg

Greta's Named in honor of Greta Garbo, whose memorabilia adorns the walls of its upper floor, this is the leading gay bar and restaurant in Gothenburg, with a clientele that includes all ages and all types of gay men and lesbians. Decor is a mixture of the kitschy old-fashioned and new wave, juxtapositioned in ways that are almost as eye-catching as the clientele. Menu items change at least every season but might include fish and lime soup, lamb filet with mushrooms in a red-wine sauce, breast of duck with potato croquettes, or a creamy chicken stew baked in phyllo pastry. Every Friday and Saturday night from 10pm to 3am, the place is transformed into a disco, and every Saturday night beginning at 1am, there's some kind of show, often drag. Open Tuesday to Thursday 5 to 11pm, Friday 4pm to 3am, and Saturday 5pm to 3am. There's a cover charge of 80SEK, but entrance is free from 9 to 10pm. Drottningsgaten 35. ✆ **031/13-69-49.** www.gretas.nu. Reservations recommended Fri–Sat. Main courses 149SEK–159SEK. Tram: 1, 2, or 3.

SKÅNE (INCLUDING HELSINGBORG & MALMÖ)

The southernmost province of Sweden, Skåne, always strikes us as its own little country, and because of its greater sunshine and fertile plains, it is also the granary of the country. Outside of Stockholm, Skåne (pronounced Skoh-neh), especially the emerging city of Malmö, evokes a more Continental aura.

Skåne has some of Sweden's most varied scenery that ranges from dark forests, scenic waterways, and sandy beaches to ancient ports, medieval cities, and some of the country's stateliest cathedrals.

Skåne has more castles than any other region in Sweden and is riddled with cobbled streets such as those found in medieval Ystad. Those interested in Vikings can visit several ancient sites and Bronze Age remains.

With three million people living within a 49km (30-mile) radius of the bridge to Denmark, the region has the largest population concentration in all of Scandinavia—and it's still growing.

BÅSTAD ★

179km (111 miles) SW of Gothenburg, 105km (65 miles) N of Malmö

Jutting out on a peninsula surrounded by hills and a beautiful landscape, Båstad is the most fashionable international seaside resort in Sweden.

All the famous international tennis stars have played on the courts at Båstad. Contemporary Swedish players—inspired by the feats of Björn Borg—receive much of their training here. There are more than 50 courts in the district, in addition to the renowned Drivan Tennis Centre. Tennis was played here as early as the 1880s and became firmly established in the 1920s. King Gustaf V took part in these championships for 15 years from 1930 onward under the pseudonym of "Mr. G," and Ludvig Nobel guaranteed financial backing for international tournaments.

Golf has established itself almost as much as tennis, and the Bjäre peninsula offers a choice of five courses. In 1929, Nobel purchased land at Boarp for Båstad's first golf course. The bay provides opportunities for regattas and different kinds of boating. Windsurfing is popular, as is skin diving. In summer, sea bathing also is popular along the coast.

The Bjäre peninsula, a traditional farming area, is known for its early potatoes, which are served with pickled herring all over Sweden.

Essentials

GETTING THERE By **car,** head west on Route 115 from Route 6/20. If you're not driving, you'll find speedy **trains** running frequently throughout the day between Gothenburg and Malmö. Six **buses** a day also arrive from Helsingborg; the trip takes 1 hour.

VISITOR INFORMATION For tourist information, **Båstad Turism,** Kyrkogatan 1 at Stortorget (✆ **0431/750-45;** www.bastad.com), is open from June 20 to August 7 Monday to Friday 10am to 6pm, Saturday 10am to 4pm, and Sunday 11am to 5pm; off-season Monday to Saturday 10am to 4pm. You can book hostel rooms here from 180SEK to 350SEK per person or rent bikes for 90SEK to 110SEK per day. They also will provide information about booking tennis courts, renting sports equipment, or reserving a tee time for a round of golf.

GETTING AROUND You don't need to rely on buses once you're in Båstad, as you can walk around the center of town in about 30 minutes. To reach the harbor and the beach, follow Tennisvägen off Köpmansgatan through a residential district until you come to Strandpromenaden. To your immediate west, you'll see a number of old bathhouses now converted to restaurants and bars. If you don't have a car, you'll need a bus to reach the Bjäre peninsula. From Båstad, bus no. 525 leaves every other hour Monday to Saturday only and runs through the center of the peninsula. If it's a Sunday, you'll have to rely on a taxi. Call ✆ **0431/36-34-94** for service.

Exploring the Area

The best sights are not in Båstad itself but on the Bjäre peninsula (see below). However, before leaving the resort, you may want to visit **Mariakyrkan (Saint Mary's),** Köpmansgatan (✆ **0431/78700**). Open daily from 9am to 4pm, it's one of the landmark churches of Skåne. Saint Mary's was built between 1450 and 1500. Inside are many treasures, including a sculpture of Saint Mary and Christ from about 1460 (found in the sanctuary), an altarpiece from 1775, a medieval crucifix, a pulpit from 1836, and various fresco paintings.

Båstad is the site of the **Norrvikens Trädgårdar (Norrviken Gardens) ★★★**, Kattvik (✆ **0431/369040;** www.norrvikenstradgardar.se), 2.5km (1½ miles) west of the resort's center, the most splendid gardens on the west coast of Sweden. Founded in 1906 by Rudolf Abelin, these gardens have been expanded and maintained according to his plans, embracing a number of styles. One is Italian baroque, with a pond framed with pyramid-shape boxwood hedges and tall cypresses. A Renaissance garden's boxwood patterns evoke the tapestry art of 15th-century Italy; in the flower garden, bulbs compete with annuals. There also are a Japanese garden, an Oriental terrace, a rhododendron dell, a romantic garden, and a water garden.

At Villa Abelin, designed by the garden's founder, wisteria climbs the walls and blooms twice a year. The villa houses shops, exhibits, and information facilities, and there are also a restaurant and a cafeteria on the grounds.

The gardens can be viewed from May 1 to September 1 daily from 10am to between 5pm and 8pm, depending on business and the hour of sunset. Admission is 60SEK for adults, free for children 14 and under.

THE BJÄRE PENINSULA ★★

With the time you have remaining after exploring the gardens, turn your attention to the **Bjäre Peninsula ★★**, the highlight of the entire region, where the widely varied scenery ranges from farm fields to cliff formations. Before exploring in depth, it's best to pick up a detailed map from the Båstad tourist office (see above).

The peninsula is devoted to sports, including windsurfing, tennis, golf, hiking, and mountain biking. It has white, sandy beaches and riding paths, plus at least six different 18-hole courses that are open from early spring. The Båstad tourist office can provide more information.

If you don't have a car, public transport is provided by bus no. 525, leaving Båstad every hour Monday through Saturday. It traverses the center of the peninsula.

The **Skåneleden walking trail ★★** runs the entire perimeter of the island and is also great for cycling. However, the terrain is quite hilly in places, so you need to be in fabulous shape.

On the peninsula's western coast is the sleepy village of **Torekov,** a short drive from Kattvik. Here you'll find a bathing beach and pier.

From Torekov, you can take a boat to explore **Hallands Väderö,** an island off the west coast of Sweden. Ferryboats, some of them old-fashioned wood vessels used during part of the year for fishing, make the 15-minute crossing every hour between June and August. From September to May, departures are every 2 hours. The cost is 100SEK round-trip, with the last departure at 4pm daily. For more information, call **Hallands/Väderö Billettkassan** (© **0431/36-30-45**).

One of Sweden's few remaining seal colonies exists on **Hallands Väderö.** "Seal safaris" come here to view, but not disturb, these animals. In addition to seals, the island is noted for its rich bird life, including guillemots, cormorants, eiders, and gulls.

Outdoor Activities

GOLF The region around Båstad is home to five separate golf courses. Two of them accept nonmembers who want to use the course during short-term visits to the region. They include the **Båstad Golf Club,** Boarp, S-269 21 Båstad (© **0431/783-70;** www.bgk.se; to reach it, follow the signs to Boarp and drive 4km/2½ miles south of town), and the **Bjäre Golf Club ★**, Salomonhög 3086, S-269 93 Båstad (© **0431/36-10-53;** follow the signs to Förslöv, driving 10km/6¼ miles east of Båstad). Newest of the lot is the **New Äppalgårdans Golf Club,** Hallansvagen (© **0431/223-30;** www.appelgarden.se). Positioned 3km (1¾ miles) east of Båstad, it opened in 2006. All the above courses charge greens fees of around 250SEK for a full day's play, and golf clubs can be rented for around 125SEK per day. Advance reservations for tee times are essential, but because most of the golf clubs are open to the public, membership in any of them is not.

TENNIS Båstad is irrevocably linked to the game of tennis, which it celebrates with fervor, thanks to its role as the longtime home of the **Swedish Open.** If you want to improve your game, consider renting one of the 14 outdoor courts (available Apr–Sept) or one of the 6 indoor courts (available year-round) at the **Båstads Malens Tennis Sällskat** (also known as the Drivan Tennis Center), Korrödgatan, S-26922 Båstad (© **0431/685-00**). Set about a half-kilometer (⅓ mile) north of Båstad's town center, it's the site of a corps of tennis professionals and teachers, who give lessons for 500SEK per hour. Indoor courts rent for 180SEK per hour.

Where to Stay

Hotel-Pension Enehall On a slope of Hallandsåsen Mountain, only a few minutes' walk from the sea, this cozy, intimate place caters mainly to Swedish families and the occasional Dane or German. Built in 1924 as an elegant private home, it was transformed into this personalized and (charmingly) eccentric hotel in 1960. There are many personal touches here, and the rooms, although small, are adequately equipped with good beds and tiny bathrooms.

Stationsterrassen 10, S-26936 Båstad. www.enehall.se. © **0431/750-15.** Fax 0431/750-14. 70 units. 1,180SEK–1,850SEK double. Rates include buffet breakfast. AE, DC, MC, V. Free parking. **Amenities:** Restaurant; bar; sauna. *In room:* TV.

Hotel Riviera Often a favorite venue for conferences, this yellow-fronted hotel, originally built in 1932 and frequently upgraded at almost yearly intervals ever since, is one of the better hotels in the area. It takes on a somewhat festive air in summer. Located by the sea, about a kilometer (⅔ mile) from the railroad station and about 3km (1¾ miles) east of the town center, it offers views from many of its modern bedrooms, as well as its 300-seat restaurant. Bedrooms are comfortably and attractively furnished. Guests can relax by sitting out in the gardens or on the terrace.

Rivieravägen 33, S-269-39 Båstad. www.hotelriviera.nu. ✆ **0431/36-90-50.** Fax 0431/761-00. 50 units. 750SEK–2,450SEK double. Rates include buffet breakfast. AE, DC, MC, V. Free parking. Closed Oct–Mar. **Amenities:** Restaurant; bar. *In room:* TV.

Hotel Skansen ★★ Comfortable, sprawling, and in a compound of brick-fronted buildings, this is *the* tennis venue in Sweden, surrounded with six tennis courts, most of them ringed with bleachers, that are the home every year to the Swedish Open. A few minutes' walk from the marina and 5m (16 ft.) from the beach, it was originally built in 1877 as a warehouse for grain and food supplies. Today it incorporates its original building (which today is listed as a national monument) with three more recent structures. The interior of the main building has a beamed roof, pillars, and views of the sea. Renovated in stages, bedrooms are airy, elegant, and traditionally outfitted.

Kyrkogatan 2, S-269 33 Båstad. www.hotelskansen.se. ✆ **0431/55-81-00.** Fax 0431/55-81-10. 173 units. 1,675SEK–1,870SEK double; 3,000SEK suite. Rates include buffet breakfast. AE, DC, MC, V. Free parking. **Amenities:** 2 restaurants; 2 bars; babysitting; exercise room; indoor heated pool; spa; 6 tennis courts. *In room:* A/C (in some), TV, hair dryer, minibar.

Where to Dine

The preceding hotels all have good restaurants, although you should call in advance for a reservation. But if you're just passing through, consider dropping in at the **Solbackens Café & Wåffelbruk,** Italienska Vägen (✆ **0431/702-00;** www.solbacken.eu). This bustling, gossipy cafe is locally famous, known since 1907 for serving Swedish waffles and other snack-style foods. If the weather is fair, opt for a table on the terrace overlooking the water.

Centrecourten SWEDISH/INTERNATIONAL In a town as obsessed with tennis as Båstad, you'd expect at least one restaurant to be outfitted in a tennis-lovers' theme. In this case, it consists of a cozy and small-scale dining room with photos of such stars as Björn Borg, a scattering of trophies, old-fashioned tennis memorabilia, and tennis rackets. The best menu items include fresh seafood, such as mussels, lemon sole, and cod. You can dine fancier if you like, on house specialties such as duck with a bacon-flavored purée of potatoes and a brisket of beef with fresh chanterelles and shallots. All the cuisine is merely good, but the ingredients are fresh and the flavors often enticing, especially in the seafood selections.

Köpmansgatan 70b. ✆ **0431/752-75.** www.centrecourten.com. Reservations recommended. Pizza 50SEK–140SEK; main courses 98SEK–175SEK. AE, MC, V. Mon–Fri 4–10pm; Sat–Sun noon–10pm.

Båstad After Dark

One good option is **Pepe's Bodega,** Warmbadhuset Hamnen (✆ 043/17-89-80), where spicy food and festive cocktails evoke southern Spain, northern Mexico, or some undefined hideaway in a forgotten corner of South America. It's open Wednesday to Sunday for both food (5–11pm) and a hopping bar scene (until 1am). There's also an on-site disco (Wed–Sun 10pm–2am).

HELSINGBORG ★

230km (143 miles) S of Gothenburg, 559km (347 miles) SW of Stockholm, 63km (39 miles) N of Malmö

Helsingborg likes to call itself Sweden's gateway to the Continent, or even the "pearl of the Öresund." The city is taking great care to make it a more inviting and tourist-friendly destination. There are enough attractions to make for 1 very busy day of sightseeing before you rush over to Denmark to see "Hamlet's Castle" or head south to sample the more Continental charms of Malmö.

At the narrowest point of the Øresund (Öresund in Swedish), 5km (3 miles) across the water that separates Sweden and Denmark, sits this industrial city and major port. Many people from Copenhagen take the 25-minute ferry ride (leaving every 20 min.) across the sound for a look at the modern city with an ancient history.

In the Middle Ages, Helsingborg and Helsingør together controlled shipping along the sound. Helsingborg is mentioned in the 10th-century Njal's-Saga (an ancient Viking document), and other documents also indicate that there was a town here in 1085. The city now has more than 100,000 inhabitants and the second-busiest harbor in the country.

Helsingborg (Hålsingborg) rebuilt large, vacant-looking sections of its inner city into one of the most innovative urban centers in Sweden. In the **Knutpunkten,** an all-glass building on Järnvägsgatan beside the harbor, is the railroad, bus, and ferryboat terminals; an array of shops similar to an American mall; and a heliport. The sunlight-flooded railroad station is the cleanest, brightest, and most memorable in Sweden. Dozens of trees have transformed the city center into something like a verdant park.

Essentials

GETTING THERE

BY FERRY Ferries from Helsingør, Denmark, leave the Danish harbor every 20 minutes day or night (trip time: 25 min.). For information about ferryboats in Helsingborg, call ✆ **042/18-61-00;** for information on the Danish side, call ✆ **33/15-15-15.** The cost of the ferryboat for pedestrians is 30SEK each way or 58SEK round-trip. The regular round-trip cost of the ferryboat for a car with up to five passengers is 770SEK.

BY PLANE The **Ångelholm/Helsingborg airport** (✆ **011/19-20-00;** www.swedavia.se) lies 30 minutes from the center of the city, with regular connections to Stockholm's Arlanda airport. There are between two and four flights per day (flying time: 1 hr.). For SAS reservations, call ✆ **0770/72-77-27.**

BY TRAIN Trains run hourly during the day between Helsingborg and Malmö, taking 50 minutes. Trains between Gothenburg and Helsingborg depart and arrive twice a day (trip time: 2½ hr.). Call ✆ **0771/75-75-75** for information or visit **www.sj.se**.

BY BUS Eight buses per day link Malmö and Helsingborg. Six leave in the morning and two in the afternoon, the trip taking 1 hour and 15 minutes. Buses leave five times per day from Gothenburg to Helsingborg. The trip from Gothenburg to Helsingborg takes 2 hours and 50 minutes. Buses to and from Stockholm leave three times per day. Call ✆ **0771/218-218** for more information.

BY CAR From Malmö, head north on E-6 for 1 hour; from Gothenburg, drive south on E-6 for 2½ hours; from Stockholm, take E-4 south for 7½ hours until you reach Helsingborg.

GETTING AROUND

Most of Helsingborg's sights are within walking distance; however, if your legs get tired and the weather is less than perfect, you can always take a city bus, numbered 1 to 7. Most buses on their way north pass the Town Hall; those heading south go by Knutpunkten. You can buy tickets on board the buses for 18SEK for one zone or

4SEK for an extra zone. Tickets are valid for transfer to another city bus line as long as you transfer within 1 hour from the time the ticket was stamped. For information, call ✆ **042/10-43-50.**

VISITOR INFORMATION

The tourist office, **Helsingborg Turistbyrå,** Dunkers Kulturhus, Kungsgatan 11 (✆ **042/10-43-50;** www.helsingborg.se), is open year-round Monday to Wednesday and Friday 10am to 6pm, Thursday 10am to 8pm, and Saturday and Sunday 10am to 5pm.

SEEING THE SIGHTS

Built in 1897, the turreted, Neo-Gothic **Town Hall** (Rådhuset), Drottninggatan 1 (✆ **042/10-50-00**), has beautiful stained-glass windows depicting scenes from the town's history. The artist, Gustav Cederström, took great pride in the epic history of his hometown and painted these scenes. But, frankly, we like to stop here throughout the day (9am, noon, 3pm, 6pm, and 9pm) and listen to the songs ringing from the 216-foot bell tower. Two memorial stones outside were presented by the Danes and the Norwegians to the Swedes for their assistance during World War II. There is also a sculpture relief representing the arrival of Danish refugees.

In the main town square, the **Stortorget** is a monument commemorating General Stenbock's victory at the Battle of Helsingborg in 1710 between Sweden and Denmark. Today the statue is virtually ignored, as ferry-bound travelers pass it by, but it marked a turning point in Danish/Swedish history. In 1709 the Danes invaded Skåne once again and wanted to take it back. But they were finally defeated the following year in a battle just outside Helsingborg.

Fredriksdal Friluftsmuseum ★★ ☺ If you have time for only one open-air museum in Skåne, make it this one, 2km (1¼ miles) northeast of the Helsingborg center in the Fredriksdal district. Built around a manor house constructed in 1787, the park covers 28 hectares (69 acres) of landscaping. Allow yourself at least 2 hours to wander and explore the streets with their old houses, which were moved to this site.

In the rose garden, the most beautiful one we've visited in Skåne, there are innumerable types of roses on display, but we estimate the number to be more than 450. There's also a children's farm and a French baroque style open-air theater, built in 1927, where major cultural performances are staged in the summer months. Check locally to see what's happening at the time of your visit.

Gisela Trapps Vag 1. ✆ **042/10-45-00.** www.fredriksdal.se. Admission May–Oct 80SEK adults, Nov–Apr free. Children 17 and under free with adult. May & Sept daily 10am–5pm; June–Aug daily 10am–7pm; Oct–April daily 11am–4pm. Bus: 1 or 7.

Kärnan (The Keep) ★ One of the most important medieval monuments in Sweden, and the symbol of Helsingborg, Kärnan rises from the crest of a rocky ridge in the city center. The origins of this 30m-tall (100-ft.) square tower—built in the 11th century—are mysterious; it adopted its present form in the 1300s. Its name translates as "the keep," a moniker related to its original position as the most central tower (and prison) of the once-mighty Helsingborg Castle. The thickness of its walls (about 4m/13 ft.) make it the most solidly constructed building in the region. An object of bloody fighting between the Swedes and the Danes for generations, the castle and its fortifications were demolished in 1679. Kärnan (which was restored and rebuilt in 1894) is the only part of the fortress that remains. Here you can climb the 146 steps for a panoramic terrace that gives you a grand view of Danish Helsingør across the sound.

The easiest way to reach Kärnan is to board the elevator, which departs from the *terrasen* (terrace) of the town's main street, the Stortorget. For 5SEK ($1/50p) per person, you'll be carried up the rocky hillside to the base of the tower. However, many visitors avoid the elevator, preferring instead to climb a winding set of flower-flanked steps as part of their exploration of the city.

Kärngränden (off the Stortorget). ✆ **042/10-59-91.** Admission 20SEK ($4/£2) adults, 10SEK ($2/£1) children 8-16. Apr-May Tues-Fri 9am-4pm, Sat-Sun 11am-4pm; June-Aug daily 11am-7pm; Sept-Mar Tues-Sun 11am-5pm. Bus: 1 or 6.

Mariakyrkan (Church of St. Mary) Rather than a grand cathedral, Helsingborg has this church filled with treasures. It's one of the best examples we know of Danish Gothic architecture and dates from the 14th century. Don't be disappointed as you approach the plain facade; the gems are concealed inside, including a treasure trove of silver in the Vestry and Silver Chamber. Note the intricately carved Renaissance pulpit (1615) and the triptych from 1450, which always catches our eye. If the sun is shining, the modern **stained-glass windows ★★** are jewel-like. To get here, walk east from the harbor.

Södra Storgatan. ✆ **042/37-28-30.** Free admission. June-Aug Mon-Sat 8am-6pm, Sun 9am-6pm; Sept-May Mon-Sat 8am-4pm, Sun 9am-4pm. Bus: 1 or 6.

Sofiero Slott ★★ Before the Swedish royal family moved their summer palace to Öland, they used to spend those precious weeks of sunshine right outside Helsingborg. One of the most famous buildings in southern Sweden, 5km (3 miles) north of Helsingborg, this castle was constructed between 1864 and 1865 to be the summer residence of King Oscar II and his wife, Sofia. In 1905 it was bequeathed to their grandson, Gustav Adolph, and his wife, Margareta, who enlarged the site and created some of the most memorable gardens in the country. Their interests supposedly sparked a nationwide interest in landscape architecture. After his coronation, Gustav Adolph spent his last days here, eventually bequeathing Sofiero as a gift to the city of Helsingborg in 1973. In 1993, many of the original gardens were re-created in memory of their designer, Queen Margareta. Today the most visited sites include the 1865 castle, which contains a cafe and restaurant; the rose garden; and the Rhododendron Ravine, with an estimated 10,000 rhododendrons, which are in their full glory in early June.

Sofierovägen. ✆ **042/13-74-00.** Admission 80SEK ($16/£8) adults, 20SEK ($4/£2) for children 7 to 18, free for children 6 and under. Daily 11am-5pm. Closed Oct to mid-Apr. Bus: 219 or 221.

Where to Stay

EXPENSIVE

Clarion Hotel Grand ★★★ This is Helsingborg's grandest hotel, an imposing brick-built pile from 1926 that has been completely modernized—though its classic details remain. After its takeover by the Clarion chain, it is even better than it was as a Radisson SAS: The hotel combines high-ceilinged, richly paneled public areas and spacious, well-accessorized guest rooms with elaborate ceiling moldings, old-world decorative touches, and lots of modern comforts and conveniences. After all the hustle and bustle of crossing over from Denmark, it's great to work off tension on the nearby jogging track along the Strandpromenaden.

Stortorget 8-12, PO Box 1104, S-251 11 Helsingborg. www.choicehotels.se. ✆ **800/333-3333** in the U.S., or 042/38-04-00. Fax 042/38-04-04. 164 units. 780SEK-1,930SEK double; from 1,880SEK suite. Rates include buffet breakfast. MC, V. Parking 150SEK. Bus: 1, 2, 7, or 8. **Amenities:** Restaurant; bar; room service; spa. *In room:* TV, hair dryer, minibar, Wi-Fi (free).

MODERATE

Best Western Hotel Helsingborg ★ This lovely old hotel occupying four floors of a 1901 bank headquarters has historic luxuries, such as marble stairs, a heroic neoclassical frieze, and three copper-sheathed towers. But it has also kept abreast of the times: The high-ceilinged rooms are pleasantly modernized and flooded with sunlight on many a summer day. They retain a certain *Jugendstil* (Art Nouveau) look, with strong colors and many decorative touches. Of the three hotels on the grand main avenue, this one is closest to the city's medieval tourist attraction, the Kärnan.

Stortorget 20, PO Box 1171, S-252 23 Helsingborg. www.hotelhelsingborg.se. ✆ **800/780-7234** or 042/37-18-00. Fax 042/37-18-50. 56 units. 1,185SEK–1,685SEK double; 1,785SEK–2,085SEK suite. Rates include buffet breakfast. AE, DC, MC, V. Parking 195SEK. Bus: 1, 2, 7, or 8. **Amenities:** Restaurant; bar; bikes; concierge; sauna. *In room:* TV, hair dryer, Wi-Fi (free).

Comfort Hotel Nouveau ★ This tastefully decorated building built of ocher brick and touches of marble lives up to its namesake and delivers solid comfort. The decor throughout draws on upscale models from England and France, and includes chintz curtains, varnished mahogany, often with wood inlays, and warm colors inspired by autumn. Rooms are nice and cozy—not particularly large, but well maintained, with tasteful fabrics. As a thoughtful touch, a fresh flower is often placed on your pillow at night.

Gasverksgatan 11, S-252 25 Helsingborg. www.choice.se. 95 units. ✆ **042/37-19-50.** Fax 042/37-19-59. 845SEK–1,595SEK double; from 1,495SEK suite. Rates include buffet breakfast. AE, DC, MC, V. Parking nearby 95SEK. Bus: 1 or 3. **Amenities:** Restaurant; bar; indoor heated pool; sauna. *In room:* TV/DVD, hair dryer, minibar, Wi-Fi (free).

Elite Hotel Marina Plaza ★★ This place resembles a glittering palace at night, its reflection cast in the waters of Öresund. Opening onto panoramic views, Marina Plaza is Helsingborg's most innovative and most talked-about hotel, and is adjacent to the city's transportation hub, the Knutpunkten. The atrium-style lobby overflows with trees, rock gardens, and fountains. Midsize-to-spacious guest rooms line the inner walls of the hotel's atrium and have a color scheme of marine blue with nautical accessories, as befits its waterfront location. Bedrooms are attractively furnished, and the bathrooms are state of the art. The on-site dining and drinking facilities are the best in town, particularly in summer when the Oceano BBQ opens. Guests in the main restaurant, Aqua, can dine on first-rate cuisine while taking in views of the harbor life.

Kungstorget 6, S-251 10 Helsingborg. www.elite.se. ✆ **042/19-21-00.** Fax 042/14-96-16. 197 units. 1,155SEK–1,550SEK double; 1,450SEK–2,650SEK suite. AE, DC, MC, V. Parking 225SEK. Bus: 2. **Amenities:** Restaurant; bar; exercise room; Internet (60SEK per hour, in lobby); room service; sauna. *In room:* TV, hair dryer, minibar, Wi-Fi (60SEK per hour).

Elite Hotel Mollberg ★ This landmark hotel is arguably Sweden's oldest continuously operated hotel and restaurant. It still attracts traditionalists, though trendsters infinitely prefer the more glamorous Elite Hotel Marina Plaza (see above). Although a tavern has stood on this site since the 14th century, most of the building was constructed in 1802. Its elaborate wedding-cake exterior and high-ceilinged interior have long been its hallmarks. Kings, counts, and barons used to check in here, as did the Swedish king Gustav IV Adolf, on the way home from Pomerania—he stayed for 2 months, not wanting to go back to Stockholm right away.

As is typical of a building of this age, bedrooms come in different shapes and sizes, but each has been modernized and furnished in a comfortable, tasteful way. The

Mollberg has a modern French-style brasserie with special musical evenings, and a rather successful clone of a London pub, the Bishop's Arms, with the town's largest selection of different beers and whiskey.

Stortorget 18, S-251 14 Helsingborg. www.elite.se. ✆ **042/37-37-00.** Fax 042/37-37-37. 104 units. 900SEK–1,650SEK double; 1,650SEK–2,500SEK suite. Rates include buffet breakfast. AE, DC, MC, V. Parking 220SEK. Bus: 1, 2, 7, or 8. **Amenities:** Restaurant; bar; room service; sauna. *In room:* TV, hair dryer, minibar, Wi-Fi (free).

Scandic Horisont If you'd like to escape the traffic and the hysteria at the center of the city, you can check into this more tranquil choice about a kilometer (⅔ mile) south of the ferryboat terminal. Hiding behind one of the most striking modern facades in town, this 1985 hotel offers free transportation Monday to Thursday (mainly for the benefit of its business clients) between its precincts and central Helsingborg. Guest rooms are comfortably furnished and well accessorized, and come in various shapes. You can stay here at a moderate price or more expensively, depending on your demands. A carefully crafted international menu is served at the on-site restaurant, alongside Swedish classics.

Gustav Adolfs Gata 47, S-252 27 Helsingborg. www.scandic-hotels.com. ✆ **042/49-52-100.** Fax 042/49-52-111. 164 units. 810SEK–1,660SEK double; 1,510SEK–2,350SEK suite. Rates include buffet breakfast. AE, DC, MC, V. Free parking. Bus: 7. **Amenities:** Restaurant; bar; children's playground; exercise room; Jacuzzi; sauna. *In room:* TV, hair dryer, Wi-Fi (free).

INEXPENSIVE

Hotell Lìnnéa ★ "To travel is to live," the receptionist said when checking us in. Considering that Hotell Lìnnéa is conveniently located a few yards from where ferries from Denmark pull in, the statement—a Hans Christian Andersen quote—seems fitting. Occupying a pink Italianate house built in 1897, this small hotel boasts detailing that reminds us of something in a historic neighborhood of pre-Katrina New Orleans. Guest rooms are appealingly outfitted, with comfortable beds and high-quality furnishings that include tasteful reproductions of 19th-century antiques. Only breakfast is served, but many reliable dining choices are close by.

Prästgatan 4, S-252 24 Helsingborg. www.hotell-linnea.se. ✆ **042/37-24-00.** Fax 042/37-24-29. 39 units. July–Aug and Fri–Sat year-round 1,095SEK–1,280SEK double; rest of year 1,495SEK–1,680SEK double; 1,880SEK suite. Rates include buffet breakfast. AE, DC, MC, V. Parking 170SEK. Bus: 7. **Amenities:** Bar; Jacuzzi. *In room:* TV, Wi-Fi (free).

Hotell Viking In the center of town, less than 2 blocks north of the Drottninggatan, this hotel looks more historic, cozier, and a bit more artfully cluttered than many of its more formal and streamlined competitors. It was built during the late 19th century as a row of shops where the owners usually lived upstairs from their businesses. Today, after its radical remodeling, you'll find a consciously preserved history, and a hands-on management style by the resident owners. The individually designed bedrooms are cozy, neat, and functional. Some units that are superior to the regular doubles have extras such as adjustable beds, computers, stereos, and plasma-screen TVs: These naturally go first.

Fågelsångsgatan 1, S-252 20 Helsingborg. www.hotellviking.se. ✆ **042/14-44-20.** Fax 042/18-43-20. 40 units. Mid-June to July and Fri–Sun year-round 969SEK–1,225SEK double; rest of year 1,646SEK–1,848SEK double. Rates include buffet breakfast. AE, DC, MC, V. Parking 195SEK. Bus: 1, 7, or 8. **Amenities:** Bar; bikes; Internet (free, in lobby). *In room:* TV, DVD/CD player (in some), hair dryer, minibar, Wi-Fi (free).

Where to Dine

Gastro ★★ CONTINENTAL/FRENCH In the wake of the closure of the two finest restaurants in Helsingborg, this first-class choice has emerged as the best. It's set within a modern, big-windowed building of yellow brick overlooking the city's historic core. Within a room decorated with birchwood veneer, pale tones of monochromatic gray, and a medley of riveting modern paintings, you can enjoy specialties based on Swedish ingredients prepared using Mediterranean culinary techniques. Menu items vary with the season, but our favorites are the pan-fried scallops with sun-dried and marinated tomatoes, served with a terrine of green peas, or a superb fried breast of duckling with onions, carrots, and prosciutto. Expect lots of fresh fish from the straits of Helsingborg and the Baltic, and lots of savoir-faire from the well-versed, attentive staff.

Södra Storg 11-13. ✆ **042/24-34-70.** www.gastro.nu. Reservations recommended. Main courses 210SEK-285SEK; fixed-price menu 595SEK. AE, DC, MC, V. Wed-Sat 6:30pm-midnight. Closed July. Bus: 11.

Pälsjö Krog SWEDISH For traditional and home-style Swedish cooking, we head here, despite its inconvenient location. A 10-minute drive north of the center of Helsingborg, this brightly painted yellow wood-sided building was originally constructed around 1900 as a bathhouse beside the beach. As such, it was filled at the time with cubicles for sea bathers to change clothes. In the late 1990s, it was transformed into a cozy Swedish restaurant, the kind of place where local families—with grandmothers in tow—come to enjoy recipes that haven't changed much since the end of World War II. Within a large dining room painted in tones of pale yellow and decorated with hints of Art Deco, you'll find grilled pepper steak, poached Swedish salmon with dill sauce, and aromatic local mussels steamed with herbs in white wine. Drinkers and smokers appreciate the cozy aperitif bar near the entrance, where cigars are welcomed and where the staff can propose a wide assortment of after-dinner cognacs.

Drottninggatan 151. ✆ **042/14-97-30.** www.palsjokrog.com. Reservations recommended. Main courses 185SEK-219SEK; 3-course set menu 365SEK. AE, DC, MC, V. Mon-Fri 11:30am-3pm and 6-10pm; Sat-Sun 1-10pm. Bus: 1.

Restaurang La Petite FRENCH/MEDITERRANEAN No one's ever accused the chefs here of being too inventive, but that's the way the habitués like it, preferring tried-and-true recipes to experimental cuisine. In a charming old house that evokes provincial France, this bistro has been going strong ever since it opened its doors in 1975. Still relatively undiscovered by foreign visitors, it serves classics based on time-tested French recipes. We're talking about those longtime favorites that for decades have characterized French bistro fare: onion soup, savory frogs' legs, and steaming kettles of mussels in a wine-laced sauce studded with garlic. Basically, good French comfort food.

Bruksgatan 19. ✆ **042/21-97-27.** www.lapetite.se. Reservations required on weekends only. Main courses 175SEK-285SEK. AE, DC, MC, V. Tues-Sat 11:30am-2pm and 5-10pm; Sun noon-10pm.

SS Swea ★ SEAFOOD/SWEDISH Go here for some of the most freshly caught fish and shellfish at the port, both of which are presented in a wide-ranging menu that appeals to most tastes. On a Kungstorget ship furnished like the luxury cruisers that used to cross the Atlantic, the restaurant offers market-fresh food deftly handled by skilled chefs and served in a cozy ambience by a thoughtful waitstaff. Appetizers might range from iced gazpacho to a Greek salad studded with feta cheese. However, most diners prefer one of the fish starters, especially the delectable smoked salmon. Fish platters, which depend on the catch of the day, also dominate the main courses. Our juicy flounder, served with bacon-flavored mushrooms, was superb in every way. Carnivores will find comfort in a classic pepper steak with *pommes frites,* or the filet mignon laced with Black & White scotch.

Kungstorget. ✆ **042/13-15-16.** www.swea.nu. Reservations required. Main courses 209SEK–279SEK; fixed-price 3-course menu 249SEK. AE, DC, MC, V. Mon–Fri 11:30am–10pm; Sat–Sun 1–8pm. Bus: 7.

Shopping

In the center of Helsingborg you'll find a number of shopping possibilities, including **Väla Centrum** (www.vala.com) which is one of the largest shopping centers in all of Scandinavia. To reach it, follow Hälsovågen and Ångelholmsvägen north about 6km (3¾ miles; it's signposted), or take bus no. 232 from Knutpunkten. Seemingly everything is here under one roof, including two large department stores and 109 specialty shops, selling everything from shoes to tropical fish.

Northwest Skåne is known as Sweden's pottery district. The first Scanian pottery factory was founded in 1748 in Mörarp, 15km (9⅓ miles) east of Helsingborg. The city of Helsingborg got its first factory in 1768 and another began manufacturing in 1832. Since then, the tradition has been redeveloped and revitalized, making the area famous far beyond the borders of Sweden.

Seven kilometers (4⅓ miles) south of Helsingborg, you can check out Scandinavian pottery at **Raus Stenkarlsfabrik,** less than a kilometer (½ mile) east of Råå (look for signs along Landskronavagen). It is open May to August Monday to Friday 10am to 6pm, Saturday 10am to 4pm; in the off-season, you must make an appointment. Call ✆ **042/26-01-30** for more information.

In Gantofta, 10km (6¼ miles) southeast of Helsingborg, is **Jie-Keramik** (✆ **042/22-17-00**), one of Scandinavia's leading manufacturers of hand-painted decorative ceramics, wall reliefs, wall clocks, figures, and other such items. You can visit a factory shop or patronize a cafe on-site. From Helsingborg, drive south to Råå, then follow the signs to Gantofta. You also can take bus no. 209 from Knutpunkten in the center of Helsingborg. The outlet is open June to August daily noon to 6pm. Off-season hours are daily 10am to 4pm.

If you drive 20km (12 miles) north of Helsingborg to Höganäs, you'll find two famous stoneware factories. **Höganäs Saltglaserat** (✆ **042/21-65-40;** www.hoganassaltglaserat.se) has been manufacturing salt-glazed stoneware since 1835. Today the classic, salt-glazed Höganäs jars with their anchor symbol are still in production. Everything is made by hand and fired in coal-burning circular kilns from the turn of the 20th century. The shop here is within the factory, so you can see the throwers in action and go inside the old kilns. It's open year-round Monday to Friday 9am to 4pm, and Saturdays in June, July, August, and September 10am to 1pm. The other outlet, **Höganäs Keramik** (✆ **042/35-11-31;** www.hoganaskeramik.se), is Scandinavia's largest stoneware manufacturer. In the Factory Shop, inaugurated in 1994, flawed goods from both Höganäs Keramik and Boda Nova are on sale at bargain prices. This outlet is open May to August Monday to Friday 9am to 6pm, Saturday and Sunday 10am to 5pm. Off-season hours are Monday to Friday 10am to 6pm, Saturday 10am to 4pm, and Sunday 11am to 4pm.

Helsingborg After Dark

Helsingborg has had its own city symphony orchestra since 1912. In 1932, its concert hall, or **Konserthuset,** opened at Drottninggatan 19 (✆ **042/10-42-70;** www.helsingborgskonserthus.se). One of the finest examples of 1930s Swedish functionalism, today the hall is still the venue for performances by the 50-piece orchestra. The season opens in the middle of August with a 10-day Festspel, a festival with a different theme every year. Tickets are available at the **Helsingborg Stadsteater City Theater,** Karl Johans Gata (✆ **042/10-68-00** or 042/10-68-10; www.helsingborgsstadsteater.se), which dates from 1817 but is one of the most modern in Europe; of course, performances are in Swedish.

An English-inspired pub that draws a busy and convivial crowd is **Telegrafen,** Norra Storgatan 14 (✆ **042/18-14-50;** www.restaurangtelegrafen.se), where live music, especially jazz, is presented on either of two levels devoted to maintaining a cozy environment for drinking, chatting, and flirting. Live-music enthusiasts should also consider an evening at one of the largest jazz venues in Sweden, **Jazzklubben ★**, Nedre Långvinkelsgatan 22 (✆ **042/18-49-00;** www.jazztime.nu). Live Dixieland, blues, Celtic ballads, and progressive jazz are featured on Wednesday, Friday, and Saturday nights beginning around 8:30pm. Most other nights, based on a schedule that varies with the season and the whims of the staff, the place functions as a conventional bar.

MALMÖ ★★

285km (177 miles) S of Gothenburg, 620km (384 miles) SW of Stockholm

Now that it's linked to the Continent via Denmark with the bridge over Öresund, Malmö is taking on an increased sophistication. We find each visit more appealing than the one before. Once the staid old capital of Skåne, it is today a vibrant, modern city with a definite youth orientation.

Nothing seems to evoke Malmö's entry into the 21st century more than the avant-garde and controversial **"Turning Torso" ★★★**, dominating the Western Harbor. Sweden's tallest building, at 190m (624 ft.), consists of nine cubes with a total of 54 floors with a 90-degree twist from base to top. The apartment building is the creation of architect Santiago Calatrava and was inspired by his sculpture of the same name.

If you can, allow at least 2 days for Malmö, Sweden's third-largest city. Malmö still doesn't have the attractions of Gothenburg, but the old city, dating from the 13th century, makes a good base for exploring the attractions of western Skåne. Others prefer to use ancient Lund (p. 422).

From early days, Malmö (pronounced *Mahl*-mer) prospered because of its location on a sheltered bay. In the 16th century, when it was the second-largest city in Denmark, it vied with Copenhagen for economic and cultural leadership. Reminders of that age are **Malmöhus Castle** (see below), the **Town Hall,** and the **Stortorget,** plus several homes of rich burghers. Malmö has been a Swedish city since the end of a bloody war in 1658, when the Treaty of Roskilde incorporated the province of Skåne into Sweden.

Essentials

GETTING THERE

BY PLANE Malmö's airport (✆ **040/613-10-00;** www.swedavia.se) is at Sturup, 30km (19 miles) southeast of the city. It receives flights from cities within Sweden (trip time: 1 hr.). Airlines winging their way into Malmö include **Malmö Aviation** (✆ **771/55-00-10;** www.malmoaviation.se) and **SAS** (✆ **0770/72-77-27;** www.sas.se). The city's international link to the world is Copenhagen airport at Copenhagen, to which Malmö is connected via the Öresund Bridge.

BY CAR From Helsingborg, motorists can head southeast along Route E-6 directly into the center of Malmö. Another option is the car ferry from Denmark. See p. 402 for info.

BY TRAIN Railway service is frequent between Gothenburg and Malmö (trip time: 3½ hr.), and since the construction of the bridge, rail service is now direct, quick, and easy to both central Copenhagen and its airport. From Helsingborg to Malmö (trip time: 45 min.), trains leave hourly. From Stockholm, travel is 4½ hours aboard the high-speed X-2000 train. There also is train service between Copenhagen and Malmö. Trains depart from the central railway stations of both cities at 20-minute intervals, stopping en route at the Copenhagen airport. The cost each way between the centers of each city is 107SEK.

BY BUS Two buses daily make the 4½-hour run from Gothenburg to Malmö. For bus information call **Swebus** (✆ **040/33-05-70**) Monday to Saturday. Swebus runs 4 buses a day from Gothenburg to Malmö; 10 buses run on Sunday. The trip from Gothenburg to Malmö takes 4 hours. They specialize in the sale of bus tickets within Sweden and to other points within Europe as well.

GETTING AROUND

It's easy to walk around the city center, although you may need to rely on public transport if you're branching out to sights on the periphery. An individual bus ticket costs 18SEK and is valid for 1 hour. For information on public transportation in Malmö call ✆ **0771/77-77-77.** Individual tickets are sold aboard the bus by the driver. Discount cards can be bought or refilled at the automated vending machines in the Central Station and at other strategic transport junctions throughout the city.

VISITOR INFORMATION

The **Malmö Tourist Office,** Central Station Skeppsbron 2, 205 80 Malmö (✆ **040/34-12-00;** www.malmotown.com), is open as follows: mid-June to August Monday to Friday 9am to 7pm, Saturday and Sunday 9am to 4pm. From September to mid-June Monday to Friday 9am to 5pm, Saturday and Sunday 10am to 2:30pm.

Seeing the Sights

The **Malmö Card,** which is available from the Malmö Tourist Office, entitles visitors to free admission to most of the city's museums. It also grants free parking and free bus travel within the city limits. A card that's valid for 1 day costs 130SEK; one that's valid for 2 days goes for 160SEK; one that's valid for 3 days is 190SEK. An adult who has a Malmö Card can be accompanied, with no additional charge, by two children up to 16 years of age.

You have to begin your exploration somewhere, and we find that the best place to do that is around **Stortorget ★**, the main square of Malmö, dating from the 1530s. The vast square was more of a market square than it is today. In its center stands an equestrian statue of King Karl X Gustav, who took Skåne back from the Danes. That event in 1658 is also commemorated with a fountain that's one of the most imaginative in Scandinavia and includes a nightingale, the symbol of Malmö.

Bordering the eastern side of the square is the **Rådhuset (Town Hall),** once imbued with a look of Renaissance splendor in 1546. It has undergone major changes over the years, most notably in the 1860s when Helgo Zettervall redesigned the facade in the Dutch Renaissance style, which is more or less what you'll see today. Unless you have official business, the interior cannot be visited except for the cellar restaurant (see Rådhuskällern; p. 418).

Nearby is **Lilla Torg ★★**, Malmö's most charming square and the centerpiece of much of its nightlife and cafes. This attractive, cobble-covered square ringed with fine half-timbered buildings dating from the 16th to the 18th centuries looks like a film set. In addition to its desirability as a place to people-watch, many handicraft shops are found here. For many centuries this was the bustling open-air marketplace of Malmö; however, in the early 20th century, a covered market (the sturdy brick-built Saluhallen) replaced the open-air booths and stalls. Today, the Saluhallen houses a small-scale shopping mall with handicrafts, foodstuffs, and a number of restaurants, the best of which are recommended in "Where to Dine," later in this chapter. While on this square, check out the **Form Design Centre** at Lilla Torg 9 (see later).

The Major Attractions

Malmöhus Slott ★★ There is so much to see and do at this impressive fortress that we always allow a minimum of 3 hours to preview some of the highlights. (If you're very rushed, skip all but the Konstmuseet, Skåne's great treasure-trove of art.) Malmö's greatest monument was founded in the 15th century by Eric of Pomerania but rebuilt by Christian III in the 16th century. The Earl of Bothwell, third husband of Mary Queen of Scots, was incarcerated here from 1568 to 1573. But those sad memories are long gone today, as it's been turned into a series of museums offering a repository of culture. The castle is a 10- to 15-minute walk west of the Stortorget. It is split into the following divisions:

Kommendanthuset: Part of the 18th-century arsenal, this member of the museum cluster is across the street from the castle. Check out what's going on here at the time of your visit, as this house is host to a frequently changing roster of traveling exhibits, many related to photography. Near Kommendanthuset is the **Teknikens och Sjöfartens Hus (Science and Maritime Museum).** This is only for technology buffs who'll appreciate the flight simulator, submarine, cars (old and new), and relics of trams and ferries.

Konstmuseet ★★: These second-floor art galleries boast a collection of old Scandinavian masters, especially those from southern Sweden. Notable among the artists is Carl Fredrik Hill (1849–1911), one of Sweden's most revered landscape painters and a forerunner of European modernism. But we're most drawn to the display of **Russian oil paintings ★★**, created in the 1890-to-1914 revolutionary period. This is the largest collection of such works outside Russia itself. Almost equally intriguing is the museum's collection of **Nordic art ★★** painted in the volatile 1920s and 1930s; Christian Berg, Max Walter Svanberg, and Carl Fredrik Reutherswärd seem to tower over their competition here.

Naturmuseum: This museum hardly stacks up against similar museums in New York or London. But you might give it a look if time remains. It covers the geology of Skåne, including its flora and fauna. Its most compelling exhibits are the **aquarium** and **tropicarium** in the basement.

Stadsmuseum: Regrettably for a historic city such as Malmö, the city museum is a disappointment. City officials have moved some artifacts from their "attic" to display here. Unless you're writing a book on the history of Malmö, you might want to skip this one. Another drawback is that the exhibits are all in Swedish, so it is hardly user-friendly.

Malmöhusvägen. ✆ **040/34-10-00.** Free admission with Malmö Card. All-inclusive ticket 40SEK, 10SEK children 7–15, free for children under 7. Sept–May Mon–Fri 10am–4pm, Sat–Sun noon–4pm; June–Aug daily 10am–4pm. Bus: 1.

Malmö Konsthall One of Europe's largest contemporary art centers, this museum hosts exhibitions of avant-garde and experimental artwork—chicken blood or dung on canvas and such—but it also appreciates the classics of modern art as well. With a rich core of art by both modern masters and cutting-edge painters, it's a visual feast for anyone who appreciates recent developments in painting and sculpture. In our view, no other venue in southern Sweden so effectively mingles contemporary architecture with modern paintings. Check the website to find out what will be on parade at the time of your visit.

St. Johannesgasse 7. ✆ **040/34-12-93.** www.konsthall.malmo.se. Free admission. Daily 11am–5pm (until 9pm Wed).

Sankt Petri Kyrka ★★★ Malmö doesn't possess a great cathedral. For that, you have to travel to Lund (see later in this chapter). But it does have a grand church, a block east of the Rådhuset (see above). Dark and a bit foreboding on the exterior, it is light and airy within. This Gothic church originated in the 14th century, when Malmö was under the control of the Hanseatic League, and was modeled on Marienkirche, a famous church in Lübeck, Germany. Other than the slender pillars and supporting ogive vaulting, the church's most stunning feature is its **Krämarkapellet ★★**, or tradesmen's chapel, from the 1400s. Amazingly, the original artwork remains. At the Reformation, the artwork here was viewed as "redundant," and the chapel was sealed off, which, in effect, protected its paintings from the overzealous "restoration" of the reformers. Look for the impressive New Testament figures surrounded by decorative foliage on the vaulted ceiling. Also notice the tall retable from 1611 and an exquisitely carved black limestone and sandstone pulpit from 1599. The octagonal baptismal font from 1601, as well as the pulpit, were the work of master craftsman Daniel Tommisen.

Göran Olsgatan. ✆ **040/35-90-43.** Free admission. Mon–Fri 10am–4pm; Sat–Sun 10am–6pm.

Svaneholm ★★ The province of Skåne is known for its castles, but this is the best one to visit while based in Malmö. Forty kilometers (25 miles) to the east of Malmö by E-65, this impressive Renaissance fortress dates from 1530. Many aristocratic families have lived here, but the castle's most colorful character was Baron Rutger Macklean (1742–1816), who introduced crop rotation to Sweden, a then unheard-of concept. The castle was partially converted into an Italian-style palace. Today it houses a museum of paintings, furnishings, and tools dating primarily from the 18th and 19th centuries. The establishment is owned by the Svaneholm Castle Cooperative Society Ltd. For information, write **Svaneholm Museum,** S-274 00 Skurup (✆ **0411/400-12**). An on-site restaurant (✆ **0411/450-40**) serves regional specialties, costing 265SEK to 295SEK for main courses.

Hamlet of Skurup. ✆ **0411/400-12.** www.svaneholms-slott.se. Admission 50SEK for adults, 10SEK children 6–14. May–June and Aug Tues–Sun 11am–5pm; July daily 11am–5pm; Sept Wed–Sun 11am–4pm;

Apr Wed-Sun 11am-4pm; Oct Sat-Sun 11am-4pm. The castle is open other times upon request. Reaching Svaneholm is difficult by public transportation; a train from Malmö stops at Skurup, but it's a walk of about 3km (1¾ miles) from there. Therefore, many visitors opt to go by taxi the rest of the way. During the summer, the castle offers free transportation from Skurup, but you must call 1 hr. in advance.

Where to Stay

EXPENSIVE

Hilton Malmö City ★★★ Encased in a steel-and-glass ultramodern structure, the city's most visible international luxury hotel rises 20 stories above the commercial heart of town. (It's the third-tallest building in Malmö, but still hardly competition for the "Turning Torso," p. 409.) Originally conceived in 1989 as a Sheraton, then transformed into a Scandic Hotel, and now a member of Hilton International, it boasts sweeping views of the Öresund region from almost all its bedrooms. The top three floors are reserved for the upgraded "executive level" rooms and suites. Many of Hilton Malmö's guests are business travelers, often attending one of the dozens of conventions that attract participants from throughout Europe. The spacious rooms are tastefully and comfortably appointed, with light colors and many electronic amenities. Suites are the best in town, with kitchenettes and large sitting areas; some even have their own Jacuzzi.

Triangeln 2, S-200 10 Malmö. www.hilton.com. ✆ **040/693-47-00.** Fax 040/693-47-11. 214 units. Sun-Thurs 1,920SEK-3,720SEK double; Fri-Sat 1,511SEK-2,920SEK double; 3,340SEK-4,360SEK suite. Rates include buffet breakfast. AE, DC, MC, V. Parking 160SEK. Bus: 1 or 7. **Amenities:** Restaurant; bar; babysitting; exercise room; room service; sauna. *In room:* A/C, TV, hair dryer, minibar, Wi-Fi (150SEK per day).

Mäster Johan Hotel ★★ Our favorite hotel in Malmö, this well-run and comfortable hotel is right in the heart of town. It's a lot newer than you might think, thanks to good design and a respect for the history of its neighborhood. Built in 1990 and renovated frequently since then, it skillfully blends the avant-garde with a sense of the antique, always with lavish use of expensive stone, wood, and marble. The result is a very charming and personalized hotel. Guest rooms are midsize to large, each beautifully maintained with cherrywood reproductions of Provençal antiques and equipped with stone or marble-trimmed bathrooms. Grace notes include oaken floors, Asian carpets, deep cove moldings, and a sense of privacy thanks to soundproofing. Staff is helpful, cheerful, and discreet, and the morning breakfast buffet—served adjacent to a glass-topped replica of a baroque courtyard—is appropriately lavish.

Mäster Johansgatan 13, S-211 21 Malmö. www.masterjohan.se. ✆ **040/664-64-00**. Fax 040/664-64-01. 69 units. Fri-Sat 1,375SEK-1,675SEK double; Sun-Thurs 1,575SEK-2,175SEK double; 2,675SEK-3,325SEK junior suite. Rates include buffet breakfast. AE, DC, MC, V. Parking 225SEK. Bus: 1, 2, or 35. **Amenities:** Bar; babysitting; bikes; exercise room; room service; sauna. *In room:* TV, kitchenette (in some), hair dryer, Wi-Fi (free).

Radisson Blu Hotel ★★ This chain-run hotel competes for the same clients as the Hilton, but the Hilton skyscraper has little to fear from its competition—more successful businessmen seem to check in there. If that deal hasn't come through yet, this is a viable alternative, and is also a suitable choice for vacationers. The Radisson Blu contains tastefully decorated rooms with elegant bathrooms. Built in 1988, the seven-story hotel is only a 5-minute walk from the train station, which provides transportation to Copenhagen in only 40 minutes. As an added convenience, the hotel bus stops nearby. If you don't want to go out at night, try the hotel's excellent **Thott Restaurant,** serving both Swedish traditional dishes and international specialties.

Östergatan 10, S-211 Malmö. www.radissonsas.com. ✆ **800/333-3333** or 040/698-40-00. Fax 040/698-40-01. 229 units. Mon–Thurs 2,190SEK–2,695SEK double; Fri–Sun 1,290SEK–1,590SEK double; 2,350SEK–2,950SEK suite. Rates include buffet breakfast. AE, DC, MC, V. Parking 180SEK. Bus: 1 or 7. **Amenities:** Restaurant; bar; babysitting; room service; sauna. *In room:* A/C, TV, hair dryer, minibar, Wi-Fi (free).

Scandic Hotel Kramer ★ A top-to-bottom redesign has extended the shelf life of this longtime favorite. At the side of the town's main square, this château-style twin-towered building is one of Malmö's landmarks. Built in 1875, it's been renovated regularly since, including the construction of a modern wing in the mid-1980s. Most recently, the rooms were redecorated with an old-fashioned sense of nostalgia, which is vaguely reminiscent of staterooms on a pre–World War II ocean liner. Each has a marble bathroom with a tub/shower combination, dark paneling, curved walls, and kitschy 1930s-esque accessories.

Stortorget 7, S-201 21 Malmö. www.scandic-hotels.com. ✆ **040/693-54-00.** Fax 040/693-54-11. 113 units. 1,290SEK–2,790SEK double; from 3,690SEK suite. Rates include buffet breakfast. AE, DC, MC, V. Parking 195SEK. Bus: 1 or 3. **Amenities:** Restaurant; bar; bikes; exercise room; room service; sauna. *In room:* A/C, TV, hair dryer, minibar, Wi-Fi (free).

MODERATE

Best Western Noble House ★★ Elegance at a moderate price is the keynote here. One of the most modern and up-to-date hotels in town—and certainly one of the most glamorous—is named after the bestselling novel by James Clavell. (The former owner was a great devotee of his writings.) The comfortable pastel-colored rooms are decorated with copies of early-20th-century Swedish paintings. Because of the four-story hotel's convenient location in the town center, its quietest rooms face the interior courtyard.

Gustav Adolfs Torg 47, S-211 39 Malmö. www.hkchotels.se. ✆ **800/780-7234** or 040/664-30-00. Fax 040/664-30-50. 130 units. 1,195SEK–2,125SEK double; 1,795SEK–3,100SEK suite. Rates include buffet breakfast. AE, DC, MC, V. Parking 195SEK. Bus: 1, 2, 5, 6, 7, or 8. **Amenities:** Restaurant; bar; babysitting; concierge; sauna. *In room:* TV, hair dryer, minibar (in some), Wi-Fi (free).

Elite Hotel Residens ★ Not the market leader that its sister hotel, Elite Hotel Savoy, is, this is still a most recommendable choice. In 1987, a team of local investors enlarged the beige-and-brown-sided premises of a historic 1517 inn by linking it with a brick-and-stone structure erected during the '70s. The interconnected structures now provide solid, comfortable, and upscale lodgings near the railroad station. Except for certain corners where an effort was made to duplicate a woodsy-looking men's club in London, many of the public areas are a glossy, modern setup with lots of mirrors, touches of chrome, and polished marble floors. Guest rooms, each renovated between 2006 and 2007, are traditionally outfitted and fairly spacious. They have hardwood floors or wall-to-wall carpeting, well-upholstered furnishings, and, in some cases, Oriental carpets. Windows are large and double-insulated against noise from the urban landscape outside.

Adelgatan 7, S-211 22 Malmö. www.elite.se. ✆ **040/664-48-90.** Fax 040/664-48-95. 69 units. 900SEK–1,850SEK double; 1,200SEK–2,050SEK suite. Rates include buffet breakfast. AE, DC, MC, V. Parking 225SEK. Bus: 2 or 4. **Amenities:** Bikes; access to a nearby health club; room service; sauna. *In room:* TV, hair dryer, minibar, Wi-Fi (free).

Elite Hotel Savoy ★★ Immediately across the square from the railway station, this landmark hotel has figured prominently in Malmö history, as its origins date back to the 14th century. Famous guests have included actress Liv Ullmann, actor Alan Alda, and Johnny ("Tarzan") Weissmuller. We're impressed with the careful restoration of the bedrooms and suites; everything has been modernized with respect for the classic decor. In fact, the hotel boasts some of the most plushly decorated accommodations in Sweden. Rooms contain champagne-colored upholstery, cabriole-legged or Chippendale-style furniture, excellent beds, and all the extras of a deluxe hotel. In the hotel restaurant, you can order from an international menu, perhaps stopping for a before-dinner beer in the British-style pub, the **Bishop's Arms.**

Norra Vallgatan 62, S-201 80 Malmö. www.savoy.elite.se. ✆ **040/664-48-00.** Fax 040/664-48-50. 109 units. 1,200SEK–1,850SEK double; 1,450SEK–3,150SEK suite. Rates include buffet breakfast. AE, DC, MC, V. Parking 225SEK. Bus: 7. **Amenities:** Restaurant; bar; exercise room; room service; sauna. *In room:* TV, hair dryer, minibar, Wi-Fi (free).

Hotell Baltzar ★ 🎁 Around 1900, an entrepreneur who had made a fortune selling chocolate moved into a private home whose turrets, towers, and fanciful ornamentation evoked a stone-carved confection. Several decades later, when it became a hotel, it expanded into one of the neighboring buildings. Today you'll find a somewhat eccentric hotel with many charming corners and cubbyholes, and a reception area one floor upstairs from street level. Grace notes include frescoed ceilings (in some of the public areas and also in about 25% of the bedrooms), substantial-looking antiques, and elaborate draperies in some of the public areas. The comfortable, high-ceilinged guest rooms were upgraded with the kind of furnishings and parquet floors that would suit a prosperous private home. The location on an all-pedestrian downtown street, about a block south of the Stortorget, keeps things relatively quiet inside. Breakfast is the only meal served.

Baltzarsgatan 45, S-211 36 Malmö. www.baltzarhotel.se. ✆ **040/665-57-00.** Fax 040/665-57-10. 45 units. Mon–Thurs 1,500SEK–1,900SEK double; Fri–Sun 950SEK–1,300SEK double. Rates include buffet breakfast. AE, DC, MC, V. Free parking. Bus: 10. **Amenities:** Room service. *In room:* TV, hair dryer, minibar.

Rica Hotel Malmö ★ Built in 1914, with many subsequent changes and improvements since, this hotel is on Malmö's main square facing the Town Hall, a short walk from the railway station. Since 2007, most of the guest rooms have been rebuilt in a tasteful modern format. They are generally spacious, but bathrooms tend to be cramped. Originally, this hotel was owned by the Salvation Army, which strictly forbade the consumption of alcohol on the premises; but since its sale to the Rica chain, all of that is a distant memory, and a bar is now adjacent to the lobby.

Stortorget 15 S-211 22 Malmö. www.rica.se. ✆ **040/660-95-50.** Fax 040/660-95-59. 82 units. Mon–Thurs 1,095SEK–2,195SEK double. Rates include buffet breakfast. AE, DC, MC, V. Parking 185SEK. Bus: 6 or 10. **Amenities:** Bikes; sauna. *In room:* TV, hair dryer, minibar, Wi-Fi (free).

Teaterhotellet The only negative aspect of this hotel is its banal-looking 1960s-era facade; it's no uglier than hundreds of other contemporaneous Scandinavian buildings, but that doesn't make it particularly inviting or pleasing. Inside, however, is a cozy, tasteful, and colorful establishment that attracts many repeat clients. Appealing touches include beige-and-tawny-colored marble floors, lots of elegant hardwood paneling, lacquered walls in neutral tones of pale amber and beige, and spots of vibrant colors in the guest rooms (especially jewel tones of red and green) that perk up even the grayest of Swedish winter days. Rooms are renovated with modern furniture, plus restored bathrooms. Less than a kilometer (about ½ mile) south of the railway station, the hotel is near a verdant park and the Stadsteater. Only breakfast is served, but you can usually get someone to bring you a sandwich and coffee.

Rönngatan 3, S-211 47 Malmö. www.teaterhotellet.se. ✆ **040/665-58-00.** Fax 040/665-58-10. 44 units. Sun–Thurs 1,500SEK–1,700SEK double; Fri–Sat 950SEK double; 1,800SEK junior suite. Rates include buffet breakfast. AE, DC, MC, V. Parking 125SEK. Bus: 5. **Amenities:** Bar; room service. *In room:* TV, hair dryer, minibar (in some), Wi-Fi (90SEK per day).

INEXPENSIVE

Hotel Plaza I Malmö This is one of the least pretentious and most nondescript hotels in town, yet it's conveniently located a half-block from an important all-pedestrian shopping thoroughfare, and 3 blocks from the better-accessorized (and more expensive) Hilton. With its three-story red-brick contemporary facade and its stripped-down and dull but respectable lobby, it might remind you of an upgraded youth hostel. Though everything here is simple and basic, it's well scrubbed. Staff members are also friendly and spontaneous and, at their best, humorous; and there are some amenities you might not have expected, including a sauna and an exercise area. Beer and wine are served from a small dispensary in the lobby, and there are many different dining options within a short walk of the hotel.

Kasinogatan 6, PO Box 17550, S-200 10 Malmö. www.hotel-plaza.se. ✆ **040/33-05-50.** Fax 040/33-05-51. 48 units. Sun–Thurs 1,495SEK double; Fri–Sat 940SEK double. Rates include buffet breakfast. AE, MC, V. **Amenities:** Bar; sauna. *In room:* TV, minibar, Wi-Fi (free).

Quality Hotel Konserthuset The most unusual thing about this cost-efficient hotel involves the way it shares its premises, a bulky, boxy-looking mirrored cube on the southeast outskirts of town, with the headquarters of the Malmö Symphony Orchestra. Don't expect luxury: Everything about the place is designed for no-nonsense efficiency, with no superfluous frills. As such, it's favored by corporations as lodging for conventions, and by families with children looking for simple, unfrilly lodgings. Rooms are well maintained and comfortable, despite their angular and relatively spartan venues.

Amiralsgatan 19, S-211 55 Malmö. www.choicehotels.se. ✆ **040/664-60-00.** Fax 040/664-60-65. 154 units. 800SEK–2,000SEK double. Rates include buffet breakfast. AE, DC, MC, V. Parking 170SEK. **Amenities:** Restaurant; bar; Jacuzzi. *In room:* TV, Wi-Fi (free).

Where to Dine

EXPENSIVE

Årstiderna I Kockska Huset ★★★ SWEDISH/INTERNATIONAL The best restaurant in Malmö is behind a red-brick facade on a "perpetually shadowed" medieval street in the city's historic core. It was built in the North German style in 1523 as the home and political headquarters of the Danish-appointed governor of Malmö, Jürgen Kock. In its own richly Gothic way, it's the most unusual restaurant setting in town, with vaulted brick ceilings, severe-looking medieval detailing, and an undeniable sense of the posh and plush good life. Owners Marie and Wilhelm Pieplow have created an environment where the prime ministers of Sweden and Finland, as well as dozens of politicians, artists, and actors, have dined on exceedingly good food. Menu items change with the seasons; the establishment's name, Årstiderna, translates from Swedish as "the Four Seasons." Likely to be featured are scallops and Norwegian lobster "du jour"; gin-cured salmon with asparagus and melted, mustard-flavored butter; grilled salted cod with clams and a lemon-flavored *beurre blanc;* filets of sole poached in white wine with grilled lobster, asparagus, and Parmesan sauce; filet of beef flambéed with grappa; and raspberry-and-licorice-glazed venison with gravy and a ragout of mushrooms. All dishes are prepared with infinite care using the best and freshest ingredients.

Frans Suellsgatan 3. ✆ **040/23-09-10** or 040/703-20. www.arstiderna.se. Reservations recommended. Main courses dinner 235SEK–295SEK, lunch 165SEK–235SEK; fixed-price dinner 595SEK. AE, DC, MC, V. Mon–Fri 11:30am–midnight; Sat 5pm–midnight. Bus: 1.

Johan P ★★ FISH/SEAFOOD The most appealing seafood in Malmö is prepared and served in this artfully simple, mostly white dining room whose terraces spill out, during clement weather, onto the cobble-covered street on one side, and into the corridors of the Saluhall (food market) on the other. The result is a bustling but almost pristine setting where the freshness of the seafood is the main draw. Menu items are prepared from scratch every day, based on whatever is available within the Saluhallen, and the kitchens are visible to whomever happens to pass by. Diners are served brimming bowlfuls, one after another, of this restaurant's cream-based, and then its tomato-based, fish soups, accompanied by fresh bread and a salad. Other examples include a half-lobster with lemon-flavored mayonnaise; lobster-larded monkfish with vinegar sauce; light-grilled tuna with truffled mayonnaise, roasted peppers, and artichokes; and grilled veal with morels in white sauce with a compote of onions. Dessert might include a mousse made with bitter white chocolate, served with dark-chocolate madeleines and coffee sauce.

Saluhallen, Landbygatan 5. ✆ **040/97-18-18.** www.johanp.nu. Reservations recommended. Daily specials (lunch only) 120SEK; main courses 175SEK–450SEK; 3-course fixed-price menu 398SEK–698SEK. AE, DC, MC, V. Mon–Sat 11:30am–11pm (last order); Sunday 1–11pm. Bus: 7.

Kramer Gastronomie ★ CONTINENTAL/FRENCH This restaurant serves the best food of any hotel dining room in Malmö. There's an upscale, vaguely baroque-looking bar that's separated from the brown and off-white dining room with a leaded-glass divider, and an attention to cuisine that brings a conservative, not particularly flashy clientele back again and again. The composition of the fixed-price menus changes every week. The chef is dedicated to his job, personally shopping for market-fresh ingredients. Menu items include shots of shellfish bouillon served with Parmesan chips and coriander salsa; scallops with grilled tuna and bacon; blackened filet of beef with pecorino cheese, lemon wedges, arugula, and a sauce made with a reduction of court bouillon and red wine; and chargrilled halibut with glazed turnips, truffle butter, and dill oil. Pastas here are upscale and esoteric, including a version with spinach, crayfish, fried filet of sole, and dill sauce.

In the Scandic Hotel Kramer, Stortorget 7. ✆ **040/693-54-00.** Reservations recommended. Main courses 145SEK–240SEK. AE, DC, MC, V. Mon–Fri 5–11pm; Sat 6pm–1am. Bus: 6 or 7.

MODERATE

Anno 1900 ★ SWEDISH If you have a Swedish grandmother, bring her here—she'll feel right at home. The name of this place gives a hint about its turn-of-the-20th-century decor, which includes lots of antique woodwork and accessories from the heyday of the Industrial Revolution. There's a garden in back that's open during warm weather, and a worldly management team that seems to cherish memories of their youthful heydays in New York City. Menu items derive from tried-and-true *husmanskost* (home-cooked) classics: old-fashioned versions of cauliflower soup, roasted pork with onion sauce, braised calves' liver, poached halibut with horseradish sauce, grilled sausages with dill-flavored cream sauce, chicken dumplings with noodles, *frikadeller* (meatballs), or fried herring.

Norra Bultoftavagen 7. ✆ **040/18-47-47.** www.anno1900.se. Reservations recommended. Main courses 175SEK–195SEK; fixed-price lunch 185SEK–235SEK. AE, DC, MC, V. Mon–Fri 11:30am–2pm and 5–11pm. Bus: 7.

Lemongrass ASIAN When we begin to tire of a Swedish diet, we book a table here. Lemongrass is set in a large, spartan room that's devoid of the artsy clutter of many Asian restaurants. Instead, against sand-colored walls, you'll find occasional clusters of exotic-looking plants and, within an otherwise artfully minimalist setting, tufted bunches of the lemon grass for which the restaurant was named. There's a bar where you can wait for your table, if you have to, and a menu that contains food items from Japan (including sushi), China, and Thailand. A staff member will help you coordinate a meal from disparate culinary styles in ways that you might have expected only in Los Angeles, London, or New York.

Grunbodgatan 9. ✆ **040/30-69-79.** www.lemongrass.se. Reservations recommended. Main courses 148SEK–248SEK. AE, MC, V. Mon–Thurs 6pm–midnight; Fri–Sat 6pm–1am. Bus: 4.

Rådhuskällern SWEDISH This is the most atmospheric place in Malmö, located in the cellar of the Town Hall. Even if you don't eat here, at least drop in for a drink in the pub or lounge. The severe exterior and labyrinth of underground vaults were built in 1546; the dark-vaulted dining room was used for centuries to store gold, wine, furniture, and food. Menu staples include halibut with lobster sauce, fried redfish with mango sauce, *tournedos* of beef with red-wine sauce and creamed morels, and roast duck, and there's always an array of daily specials. Although the fare is first-rate here, it never overexcites the palate.

Kompanigatan 5. ✆ **040/790-20.** www.profilrestauranger.se. Reservations recommended. Main courses 198SEK–329SEK; fixed-price menus 245SEK–465SEK. AE, DC, MC, V. Mon–Fri 11:30am–2pm and 5–10:30pm; Sat 5–11pm; Sun 1–7pm. Closed July 1–Aug 21. Bus: 7.

Salt & Brygga ★ SWEDISH/MEDITERRANEAN Opening onto a large patio with a panoramic view of the Öresund, this postmillennium restaurant was hailed as restaurant of the year the moment it opened. On our last visit, we found that it lived up to its initial praise. It prides itself on the use of mostly organic (that is, grown without synthetic fertilizers or pesticides) food, most of which derives from nearby suppliers and is prepared with a respect for the culinary traditions of the Mediterranean. It's an atmospheric and artfully contemporary place that's brisk, internationally hip, and pleasing. Guests dine in relative simplicity, enjoying freshly prepared dishes that include lots of seafood and fresh produce, an enticing assortment of risottos, and a large selection of organic wine, cider, and beer. The smoked coalfish ("saithe" on the menu) makes a fine and tasty appetizer, and vegetarians should appreciate the savory vegetable lasagna. Desserts are prepared fresh daily and don't over-rely on sugar for their appeal.

Sundspromenade 7. ✆ **040/611-59-40.** www.saltobrygga.se. Reservations recommended. Main courses 185SEK–275SEK; 3-course menu 395SEK. AE, DC, MC, V. Mon–Fri 11:30am–3pm and 6–10pm; Sat noon–10pm. Bus: 3 or 5.

Victor's SCANDINAVIAN Set cheek by jowl among about a dozen competitors that line the perimeter of the historic Lilla Torg, this restaurant is a bit hipper and more popular than many of the others. Of course, on the crush of a midsummer evening, when every cafe and restaurant on the square is packed with seers who enjoy being seen, it looks a lot like its neighbors. But in winter, when the action moves into its interior, its coziness becomes more obvious. Its principal draw is its Old Sweden theme: Menu items are old-fashioned and conservative, but undeniably flavorful. The best examples include *toast Skagen* (layered with shrimp, mayonnaise, and dill); gravlax (marinated salmon) cured with fennel; a spicy version of fish soup; pan-fried loin of cod; and vegetarian tomato stew with chickpeas.

Lilla Torget 1. ✆ **040/12-76-70.** www.victors.se. Lunch platters 69SEK–75SEK; dinner main courses 145SEK–205SEK. AE, DC, MC, V. Daily 11:30am–3pm and 6–10:30pm. Bus: 1, 6, or 7.

INEXPENSIVE

Casa Mia ITALIAN The staff here works hard to maintain Italian bravura amid the snows of Scandinavia. Venetian gondola moorings ornament the front terrace of this Nordic version of a neighborhood trattoria; schmaltzy Neapolitan ballads play in the background; and your waiter is likely to address you in Italian. You might begin with a steaming bowl of *stracciatella alla romana* (egg-and-chicken soup) or the fish soup of the house, then move on to penne with shrimp, basil, cream, and tomatoes, or spaghetti with seafood. Later you can dig into *saltimbocca alla romana* (veal with ham), grilled scampi with asparagus, roasted lamb with new potatoes, or an array of grilled meats with aromatic herbs. About a dozen types of savory pizza are available, too. Okay, it's not as good as the food served in a typical trattoria in northern Italy, but the cuisine is a refreshing change of pace.

Södergatan 12. ✆ **040/23-05-00.** www.casamia.se. Reservations recommended. Pastas and pizzas 82SEK–149SEK; main-course platters 185SEK–265SEK. AE, DC, MC, V. Mon 11:30am–10pm; Tues–Fri 11:30am–midnight; Sat noon–midnight; Sun 1–10pm. Bus: 7.

Italia II Ristorante e Pizzeria ★ PIZZERIA/ITALIAN This is a well-managed and reasonably priced choice offering flavorful, unpretentious food. Service is efficient and quite friendly, making this a welcoming kind of place. The kitchen offers one of the best selections of antipasti in town, including a delectable carpaccio of salmon or else a platter of mussels and clams in a marinara sauce. The pasta selection is wide ranging, with such specialties as rigatoni pepperoni, or linguine with various seafood, including scampi. Veal cutlets are tender and full of flavor, as is lamb roasted with paprika.

Ringgatan 1. ✆ **040/807-03.** Reservations recommended. Main courses 136SEK–240SEK. AE, MC, V. Mon–Fri 5pm–midnight; Sat 4pm–midnight, Sun 4–10pm. Bus: 7.

Shopping

Malmö's two main pedestrian shopping streets are **Södergatan,** which leads south of Stortorget toward the canal, and **Södra Förstadsgatan.** And for shoppers who haven't found what they wanted in any of the specialty shops listed below, try **Hansa,** Stora Nygatan 50 (✆ **040/770-00;** www.mitthansa.se), a shopping complex with more than 40 shops, cafes, and restaurants. The latest fashions and items for the home are among the many specialties featured here, including the finest in Swedish glassware. Most stores are open Monday to Saturday from 10am to 5pm.

FASHION

Form Design Centre Nearby, at 16th-century Lilla Torg, you can visit this museum-like exhibition space with boutiques selling upscale handicrafts, including Swedish textiles by the yard, woodcarvings, and all manner of other crafts. Lilla Torg 9. ✆ **040/664-51-50.** www.formdesigncenter.com. Bus: 1.

Malmö After Dark

Those seeking cultural activities after dark should get tickets to the **Malmö Symphony Orchestra** ★★★, which is renowned across Europe. It performs at the Konserthus, Föreningsgatan 35 (✆ **040/630-45-06;** www.mso.se). The tourist office distributes programs of its upcoming schedule as well as schedules and descriptions of other cultural events.

CAFES & BARS

For other serious after-dark pursuits, many locals, especially young people, head for nearby Copenhagen. But for people-watching, no place in Malmö is more popular than the Lilla Torg, with its plethora of outdoor cafes and restaurants that shelter an attractive mix of locals and visitors. The most popular of the dozen or so watering holes surrounding the square include Victor's (recommended in "Where to Dine," above) and the Moosehead Bar, below.

At the **Moosehead Bar,** Lilla Torget 1 (© **040/12-04-23;** www.moosehead.se.; bus: 17), the clientele might seem a bit less concerned with etiquette and social niceties than the patrons of more sedate hangouts in other parts of the square. Its woodsy-looking, brick-lined decor and its emphasis on the biggest animal of the northern forests and tundra might remind you of a college hangout in Maine, but the conversation and the proliferation of blondes is pure Sweden. Don't expect gourmet cuisine here: Everybody's favorite meal is a juicy burger made from either beef or moose meat (it's up to you to specify which), accompanied by a foaming mugful of Åbro, the local lager. Barring that, consider ordering a green melon or pineapple daiquiri, priced at between 85SEK and 120SEK, depending on the size.

One of the most packed and long-lived hipster bars in Malmö is **Centiliter & Gram ★**, Stortorget 17 (© **040/12-18-12;** www.etagegruppen.se; bus: 7). When it was inaugurated in the mid-1990s, "Cl. & Gr." was one of Malmö's hottest restaurants, but since then it's emerged as a popular bar with a hot clientele age 25 and up—although the food is still entirely respectable. It occupies an artfully minimalist herb-and-grass-colored space whose focal point is a centrally placed bar that rocks with an ongoing stream of electronic, usually house, music. Guests often stay to flirt long after their dishes have been cleared away. Main courses cost from 125SEK to 189SEK, with an emphasis on salads, pastas, grilled fish and grilled steaks, and light vegetarian fare. The establishment's name, incidentally, derives from wine (which is measured in centiliters) and food (which is measured in grams). It's open Wednesday and Thursday 8pm to 3am, Friday and Saturday 7pm to 3am.

Nostalgic for Britain? Then check out the **Bishop's Arms,** Norra Vallgatan 62 (© **040/664-48-88;** www.bishopsarms.com), a cozy and highly appealing replica of an Anglo-Irish pub. In the Elite Savoy Hotel, it serves generous platters, priced at 125SEK to 235SEK each, of such Anglo and Celtic staples as fish and chips, burgers, Buffalo wings, and pepper steaks, as well as some of the coldest beer in town. There's always a congenial crowd. As is common in the U.K., you'll place your drink and/or food order directly at the bar, and then a staff member will carry it to your table. It's open Monday to Saturday 4pm to 1am, Sunday 4 to 11pm. Take bus no. 7, 8, or 35.

DANCE CLUBS

The hippest and most appealing dance club in the area is **Slagthuset,** Jörgen Köcksgatan 7A (© **040/10-99-31;** www.slagthuset.se). It's set within the red-brick premises of what was conceived in the 19th century as a slaughterhouse for cattle and hogs, in a location directly behind the railway station. This high-energy and much-talked-about place now functions as the largest dance club in Scandinavia. Each of the three floors has its own bars, dance floor, labyrinth of interconnected rooms, its own type of music, and crowds of good-looking, sometimes raucous clients. It's open only on Friday and Saturday nights, from midnight to 5am. The entrance fee is 100SEK.

Slaghuset's most visible competitor is **Club Skeppsbron,** Skeppsbron 2 (© **040/30-62-02;** www.skeppsbron2.com). Outfitted for a relatively mature clientele that—in the words of a good-looking local woman—includes "cute guys, rich men, and strong drinks," this nightclub incorporates a restaurant, an outdoor terrace, big windows overlooking a canal, and a mixture of antique nautical paneling with postmodern angularity. It's open only on Saturday nights, from 10pm to 5am, year-round. The entrance fee is 120SEK.

Dancing is also the rage at the creatively designed **Nightclub Étage,** Stortorget 6 (✆ **040/23-20-60;** www.etagegruppen.se; bus 17). Initially conceived as an upscale bar and restaurant in the late 1980s, this nightspot lowered its prices and began marketing to a mass audience in the early 1990s. Despite its lowered expectations, the bar has not suffered as a result. It's reached by climbing a circular staircase from an enclosed courtyard in the town's main square. The complex is open Monday and Thursday to Saturday 10pm to at least 4am, depending on the crowd. The cover for the dance club ranges is 50SEK.

Many love affairs, both long and short, a few of which have segued into marriages, have gotten their start at the **Malmborgen Compound,** a sprawling antique warehouse on Hamburgsgatan. There's a restaurant within the building's courtyard (Gränden; ✆ **040/12-38-95;** www.malmborgen.nu; bus: 7) serving pizzas, shish kabobs, and Swedish meatballs with salad for 79SEK to 195SEK Monday to Thursday 11:30am to midnight, Friday 11:30am to 1am, and Saturday 5pm to 1am. The compound also contains a somewhat nondescript scattering of minor bars and cafes, but its most visible venue is the **Swing Inn,** Stadt Hamburgsgatan 3 (✆ **040/12-22-21;** www.malmborgen.nu), where romantic dancing is the norm. Attendees tend to be over 35, and the recorded music is reminiscent of a '60s variety show. The on-premises restaurant serves platters of traditional Swedish food Thursday to Saturday between 10am and 11:30pm. Main courses cost from 135SEK to 225SEK. Music and bar activities are scheduled on Friday and Saturday 11pm to 3am. The cover charge is 90SEK after 11pm. Music and bar activities are scheduled on Friday and Saturday 11pm to 3am. ***Note:*** You must be 30 or over to enter.

GAY & LESBIAN NIGHTLIFE

Many gays and lesbians now take the train across the bridge to the clubs in Copenhagen. But gay nightlife in Malmö recently took a distinct turn for the better thanks to the involvement of Claes Schmidt, creator of such mainstream clubs as the also-recommended Slagthuset (see above). Claes "came out" publicly to the Swedish press in 2003 as a (mostly heterosexual) cross-dresser. Immediately in the wake of this "confession," the local paper sold an additional 20,000 copies (huge by local standards). (For more on the story of the double life he'd been leading as his now-famous stage name Sara Lund, check out his website, www.saralund.se.) Claes became the most famous cross-dresser in Europe, working occasionally as a paid consultant at corporate consciousness-raising conventions and at universities throughout Scandinavia. Claes's nightclub sensation, which has surpassed his smashing success Slagthuset and is now the most popular cutting-edge dance club in Malmö, is **Indigo ★★**, Monbijougatan 15 (✆ **040/611-99-62;** www.rfsl.se/malmo). Don't expect to find it easily: It is in a former warehouse in a drab industrial part of the Triangeln neighborhood, a 12-minute walk from the Hilton Hotel. You'll climb solid, industrial-strength stairs to the third floor of this brick-built fortress, encountering some amicably punkish people en route.

Inside, you'll find a vast and echoing space with enormous dance floors and bars that host the city's various drag or leather events. The best known of these is Switch, which defines itself as "a bar for men and women of all genders." Switch hosts a drag ball and elegance contest that occurs on the second Friday of every month—but the scheduling can and often does change according to the whim of whoever's monitoring the event. Don't expect regularity in anything associated with Indigo. It plays host to all manner of counterculture splinter groups of all persuasions: Some weekends, it's an old-fashioned gay bar for old-fashioned Swedes and Danes; other nights, thanks to the welcome flash and flair of Claes/Sara, it can get a lot more exotic. In most cases, Indigo is open only on Friday and Saturday nights from 11pm to 3am, and usually charges an entrance fee of 60SEK to 90SEK. If you really want to be sure it's open, call in advance, or check the website noted above.

LUND ★★

18km (11 miles) NE of Malmö, 301km (187 miles) S of Gothenburg, 602km (374 miles) SW of Stockholm

The second-oldest town in Sweden, Lund is a mellow old place with a thousand-year history. It holds more appeal for us than its rival university city, Uppsala, north of Stockholm, and in some respects is comparable to Cambridge in England.

Medieval streets and a grand cathedral are compelling reasons to visit, but the vibrant student life is even more compelling. But remember, if you're paying a summer visit, the students are away on vacation, so it will be quieter. The most exciting time to be in Lund, as in Uppsala, is on Walpurgis Eve, April 30, when student revelries signal the advent of spring.

Lund was founded in 1020 by Canute the Great, ruler of the United Kingdom of England and Denmark, when this part of Sweden was a Danish possession. However, the city's 1,000-year anniversary was celebrated in 1990 because archaeological excavations show that a stave church was built here in 990. The city really made its mark when its cathedral was consecrated in 1145, after which Lund quickly became a center of religion, politics, culture, and commerce for all of Scandinavia.

The town has winding passageways, centuries-old buildings, and the richness of a university town. Lund University, founded in 1666, continues to play an active role in town life.

Essentials

GETTING THERE

BY PLANE **Kastrup (Copenhagen)** airport is very convenient, especially because trains from Copenhagen pass through Kastrup, then go directly to Lund, a travel time of 45 minutes and a one-way fare of 137SEK. The nearest Swedish airport is the Malmö/Lund airport, which is in the village of Sturup, 30km (19 miles) and a 30-minute bus ride from Lund. Airport coach services (also known as the Flygbuss) charge 99SEK and time their departures from Sturup to correspond to the arrivals of flights at Sturup.

BY TRAIN Trains run hourly from Malmö (see earlier in this chapter), only a 15-minute ride. Both the bus and the train stations here are in the center of town. Call ✆ **0771/75-75-75.**

BY BUS There are 4 to 10 buses a day from Malmö to Lund, depending on the day of the week and the time of the year. They take 30 minutes. Call ✆ **0771/21-82-18.**

BY CAR From Gothenburg, head south along E-6; Malmö and Lund are linked by an express highway, only a 20-minute drive.

VISITOR INFORMATION

The tourist information office is at **Lunds Turistbyrå,** at Botulfsgatan 1A (PO Box 41), SE-221 00 Lund (✆ **046/35-50-40;** www.lund.se). Hours for this bureau are complicated and can vary. In peak season, hours are generally Monday to Friday 10am to 7pm, Saturday 10am to 3pm, and Sunday 11am to 3pm.

Seeing the Sights

Botaniska Trädgården (Botanical Gardens) Just follow the students on their bikes if you want to check out Lund's favorite gardens—they are no doubt headed here. A block east of the cathedral, these gardens contain some 7,500 specimens of plants gathered from all over the world. On a sunny day, you'll spot clusters of students stretching out beneath the trees and families enjoying picnic lunches. Serious horticulturists should visit when the greenhouses are open.

Östra Vallgatan 20. ✆ **046/222-73-20.** www.botaniskatradgarden.se. Free admission. Gardens daily 6am–8pm (until 9:30pm in summer); greenhouses daily noon–3pm. Bus: 1, 2, 3, 4, 5, or 6.

Domkyrkan (Lund Cathedral) ★★★ This imposing twin-towered, gray-sandstone cathedral that dominates the town is magnificence itself. Work began on it in 1080, coming to an end at its consecration in 1145. Today it represents the zenith of Romanesque design in Sweden—in fact, the **eastern facade ★★** of the church is one of the finest expressions of Romanesque architecture in northern Europe.

The interior is filled with splendor and wonder, especially the **apse ★★★** from 1130, a masterpiece of Romanesque styling with its Lombard arcading and third-tier gallery. The **mosaic ★★★** of the apse vault, representing the Resurrection in true Byzantine tradition, was the creation of Joakim Skovgaard between 1925 and 1927. Look for the elaborately carved 1370 **choir stalls ★★★** depicting Old Testament scenes. Then look again: Beneath the seats are grotesque engravings.

Nothing is more dramatic here than the remarkable **astronomical clock ★★★** from the 14th century. It depicts days, weeks, and even the courses of the moon and the sun in the zodiac. The clock was silent for 3 centuries until it was restored in 1923. If you're here at noon or 3pm daily, you'll be treated to a splashy medieval tournament complete with clashing knights and blaring trumpets. That's not all—the Three Wise Men come out to pay homage to the Virgin and Child. On Sunday, the noon show doesn't begin until 1pm.

Finally, head for the **crypt ★★★**, little changed since the 12th century. The pillars of the crypt are carved with zigzagging and twisting patterns, an eerie sight in these dimly lit, dramatic precincts. One tomb contains the remains of Birger Gunnarson, the last archbishop of Lund.

Kyrkogatan. ✆ **046/35-88-80.** www.lundsdomkyrka.org. Free admission. Mon–Fri 8am–6pm; Sat 1–5pm; Sun 1–6pm. Bus: 1, 2, 3, 4, 5, or 6.

Historiska Museet Founded in 1805, this is the second-largest museum of archaeology in Sweden. Collections trace the development of the people of Skåne from the Stone, Bronze, and Iron to the Middle Ages. One of the exhibits displayed here is that of the **skeleton of a young man ★★** dating from around 7000 B.C.—one of the oldest human skeletons found in northern Europe. Another displays jewelry and weapons unearthed from a large grave field during excavations in eastern Skåne. The medieval exhibition is predictably dominated by church art removed from Skånian churches.

Kraftstorg 1. ✆ **046/222-79-44.** Admission 50SEK. Free admission for students, seniors, and for those 17 and under. Year-round Tues–Fri 11am–4pm; Sun noon–4pm. Bus: 1, 2, 3, 4, 5, or 6.

Kulturen (Museum of Cultural History) ★★ After you visit the Lund cathedral, walk across the university grounds to Adelgatan, which is the town's most charming street. Here you'll find Kulturen, another of Sweden's open-air museums. This one contains reassembled sod-roofed farms and manor houses—some of which were saved before they disappeared forever—a carriage museum, ceramics, peasant costumes, Viking artifacts, old handicrafts, and even a wooden church moved to this site from the glassworks district. Established in 1892, it's one of the best organized and maintained open-air museums in Sweden. You can complete your historical time trip in effectively 2 hours—well spent, especially if you take in the 17th-century houses, still perfectly preserved today. The outdoor restaurant near several runic stones dug up and brought here serves home-cooked Swedish specialties.

Tegnérsplatsen. ✆ **046/35-04-00.** www.kulturen.com. Admission 70SEK adults, free for children. May–Aug daily 10am–5pm; Sept–Apr Tues–Sun noon–4pm. Bus: 1, 2, 3, 4, 5, or 6.

Where to Stay

The tourist office (see above) can help you obtain housing in private homes for as little as 225SEK per person per night.

INEXPENSIVE

Hotel Concordia ★ A classic, elegant landmark from 1882, Concordia was originally built as a private home, but for many years it served as a student hotel. You'd never know to look at the building today—it has been successfully converted to a government-rated four-star hotel, a bastion of comfort, charm, and elegance. Although the public rooms have what is known as a Lundian character, that style does not extend to the modernized, comfortably furnished midsize bedrooms. However, their parquet floors, warm colors, and tiled bathrooms help a lot. It's next door to the brick house where August Strindberg lived in 1897 and is only a 5-minute walk south of the railway station.

Stålbrogatan 1, S-222-24 Lund. www.concordia.se. ✆ **046/13-50-50.** Fax 046/13-74-22. 63 units. 1,095SEK–1,700SEK double; 1,995SEK suite. Rates include buffet breakfast. AE, DC, MC, V. Parking 150SEK. Bus: 1, 2, 3, 4, 5, or 6. **Amenities:** Internet (free, in lobby); sauna. *In room:* A/C (in some), TV, DVD (in some), hair dryer, minibar, Wi-Fi (free).

Hotel Lundia ★★ The design concept of this hotel is "sushi and lingonberries." The reference is baffling until architect Jonas Lloyd explains that, while renovating this long-established property near the railway station, he wanted to combine Swedish modern (symbolized by lingonberries) with Japanese simplicity (as evoked by the sushi reference). Much of the success of this hotel's overhaul is in Lloyd's use of natural materials, and a Nordic blonde shade prevails throughout. Lundia is under the same management as the Grand Hotel (see below) but is hardly a rival, although its interior is graced with winding staircases, white marble sheathing, and large windows. Guest rooms are quite special, with softly curved furniture in birchwood with accents of cherrywood, walls treated with beeswax glazing, and floors made of massive planks of oak, each board nailed by hand.

Knut den Stores Gata 2, S-221 04 Lund. www.lundia.se. ✆ **046/280-65-00.** Fax 046/280-65-10. 97 units. 1,110SEK–2,450SEK double; 2,225SEK–4,125SEK suite. Rates include buffet breakfast. AE, DC, MC, V. Parking 120SEK. Bus: 1, 2, 3, 4, 5, or 6. **Amenities:** Bar; room service. *In room:* TV/DVD, CD player, hair dryer, minibar.

MODERATE

Djingis Khan ★ At first this struck us as the worst-named hotel in Sweden, but actually, it makes sense when you learn that Djingis Khan is the name of a revue written by Hasse Alfredsson and presented by Lund students in 1954. Since that time, this same show has been performed every 5 years. The building itself looks like an upmarket student dormitory, but it's one of the best hotels in town, though not a rival of the Grand (see below). We found the staff the most helpful in town and ready to accommodate our every request. The midsize bedrooms are sleek and modern and comfortably arranged with all the gadgets you'll need. Public areas contain lots of English-inspired dark paneling, Chesterfield sofas, and an ambience that evokes a private men's club in London.

Margarethevägen 7, S 222 40 Lund. www.djingiskhan.se. ✆ **046/33-36-00.** Fax 046/46-33-36-10. 73 units. Sun–Thurs 1,595SEK double; Fri–Sat 1,095SEK double. Rates include buffet breakfast. AE, DC, MC, V. Closed July. Free parking. Bus: 3. **Amenities:** Restaurant; bar; bikes; exercise room; indoor heated pool; room service; sauna. *In room:* TV, hair dryer, minibar, Wi-Fi (free).

Grand Hotel ★★★ In 1899, every man, woman, and child who could walk allegedly turned out for the opening of the châteaulike Grand. At last Lund had a fashionable hotel. The decades and world wars (fought without Sweden) have come and gone, and the Grand has changed and evolved over the years, but it has also kept its elegant architecture and remains the number-one choice of discerning visitors to Lund, including the most well-heeled parents of students enrolled at the university. In spite of its fashion and formality, the Grand is not "stiff and starched"; office workers will assemble here for a beer after a hard day's work, and it provides a welcoming setting for family feasts. The tone is set by the supremely elegant marble lobby, which basically justifies the hotel's name. No room is like any other—each has its own character, some spacious, others smaller. But each is comfortably furnished with a mix of modern and traditional. Many patrons come here to dine at the restaurant overlooking the fountains and flowers of a city park even if they aren't staying at the hotel. The magnificent surroundings are somewhat enhanced by the Grand's traditional Scanian and Swedish menu and carefully crafted selection of international specialties. We are astonished by the wine list, which boasts 500 different vintages from some three dozen countries around the world. At the hotel's wine bar, you can sample these exclusive wines by either the glass or the bottle; see below.

Bantorget 1, S-221 04 Lund. www.grandilund.se. ✆ **046/280-61-00.** Fax 046/280-61-50. 84 units. June 7–Aug 8 and Fri–Sat year-round 1,350SEK–1,750SEK double, 3,200SEK suite; Aug 9–June 6 2,195SEK–2,550SEK double, 4,500SEK suite. Rates include buffet breakfast. AE, DC, MC, V. Parking 120SEK. Bus: 1, 2, 3, 4, 5, or 6. **Amenities:** Restaurant; exercise room; room service; sauna. *In room:* TV, hair dryer, minibar, Wi-Fi (35SEK per hour).

Oskar ★★ 🎁 Those who prefer to overnight in more intimacy than that offered by the Grand might well check in here if they can afford it. It's a charmer, a boutique hotel that was created by restoring two town houses constructed in the 1800s. The hotel is imbued with a sophisticated Scandinavian design—chairs and tables by Gunilla Allard for Lammhults, lamps by the legendary Arne Jacobsen. Frankly, we've inspected hotel after hotel in Lund and think the Dux beds here are the most relaxing in town. Bedrooms are bright and relatively large, furnished with contemporary pieces against a backdrop of original art adorning the white walls. Each room is an individual design statement. On summer days breakfast is served in the garden, and on rainy days, you can join fellow guests or students at the downstairs cafe.

Bytaregatan 3, SE 222 21 Lund. www.hotelloskar.se. ✆ **046/188-085.** Fax 046/373-030. 6 units. Sun–Thurs 1,495SEK–1,595SEK double; Fri–Sat 1,095SEK–1,195SEK double. AE, DC, MC, V. **Amenities:** Room service. *In room:* TV/DVD, hair dryer, Wi-Fi (free).

Scandic Star ★★ A 20-minute walk from the city center, this hotel doesn't have the grace and tradition of the Grand, but it's one of the most comfortable hotels in southern Sweden. Though it caters to individual travelers, and does so exceedingly well, it's often used for business conventions. In fact, rock stars and film actors seem to prefer it, too. What makes it so special is that nearly all the double rooms are configured as minisuites, with separate sitting areas and traditional, conservative furnishings that would fit into a well-appointed upper-middle-class Swedish home. No other hotel in Lund has public facilities equal to the ones here, including a pool. The on-site **Gerda's Restaurant** zealously guards the recipes for the Skåne specialties served, and the bar in the spacious courtyard has become a town meeting point.

Glimmervägen 5, PO Box 11026, SE-220 11 Lund. www.scandic-hotels.com. ✆ **046/285-25-00.** Fax 046/285-25-11. 196 units. Mid-June to mid-Aug and Fri–Sat year-round 950SEK double; rest of year 1,650SEK–1,850SEK double; 1,950SEK–2,650SEK suite. Rates include buffet breakfast. AE, DC, MC, V. Free parking. Bus: 3. **Amenities:** Restaurant; bar; bikes; children's playground; exercise room; indoor heated pool; room service; sauna. *In room:* TV, hair dryer, minibar, Wi-Fi (free).

Where to Dine

Gloria's Restaurant/Sportbar AMERICAN The success of this American-inspired sports and western bar would warm the heart of any U.S.-born ideologue. It has a crowded and likable bar in the cellar and an even larger bar upstairs. Scattered throughout the premises are photographs and posters of American sports heroes, baseball and football memorabilia, and Wild West artifacts. Foam-topped draft beer is served in mugs to a crowd that includes its fair share of students from the university. The restaurant serves copious portions of such rib-stickers as hamburgers and steaks, and an array of Cajun-inspired dishes. The staff wears jeans, cowboy boots, and shirts emblazoned with Gloria's logo. Various styles of live music are performed between 9:30 and 11:30pm each Thursday. Friday and Saturday nights feature a disc jockey spinning rock.

St. Petri Kyrkogata 9. ✆ **046/15-19-85.** www.glorias.se. Reservations recommended. Main courses 139SEK–289SEK. AE, DC, MC, V. Mon–Wed 11:30am–midnight; Thurs 11:30am–1am; Fri 11:30am–3am; Sat 12:30pm–3am; Sun 1–11pm. Bus: 1, 2, 3, 4, 5, or 6.

Grand Hotel Restaurant ★★ SWEDISH/INTERNATIONAL For that special meal in Lund, head for this formal restaurant in its most fashionable hotel. The chefs achieve a perfectly balanced mix between inspired international cuisine and traditional Swedish fare on their constantly varied menu that takes advantage of market conditions and seasonal produce. Starters are savory, especially the Swedish Belon oysters with shallot vinegar or three varieties of herring with home-baked bread. Among the more tempting main courses are seared scallops with a cauliflower purée and cubes of chorizo or a special fish course of the day, perhaps *tournedos* in a bordelaise sauce with Jerusalem artichokes. For more laid-back dining, wander into the Gambrinus Bistro and sample, for instance, Sten Broman's original whiskey meatballs.

Bantorget 1. ✆ **046/280-61-00.** www.grandlund.se. Reservations required in restaurant. Lunch main courses 125SEK–145SEK; fixed-price lunch 375SEK; dinner main courses 235SEK–305SEK. AE, DC, MC, V. Mon–Thurs 11:30am–11pm; Fri 11:30am–midnight; Sat noon–midnight; Sun 1–11pm. Bus: 1, 2, 3, 4, 5, or 6.

Klostergatans Vin & Delikatess SWEDISH A student favorite, this wine bar and deli offers rib-sticking favorites. For sure, you will not leave hungry. The food is good, the atmosphere welcoming, and the prices, if not exactly affordable, are within the realm of the possible. Many offerings are made from imaginative combinations of ingredients—take the soup of chanterelles, trumpet mushrooms, and cèpe mushrooms, flavored with a confit of pork and served with smoked cream cheese. You can also order lobster soup prepared with salmon, roasted shellfish oil, and a crayfish timbale, or else Swedish hash browns with whitebait and sour cream. For a main course, you might opt for a seared steak tartare, with beets and Idaho potatoes, bound together with a red-wine sauce, or else pan-fried pikeperch with cauliflower and lentils.

Klostergatan 3. ✆ **046/14-14-83.** Reservations not needed. Main courses 160SEK–260SEK. AE, MC, V. Mon–Sat noon–3:30pm and 5–10:30pm. Bus: 1, 2, 3, 4, 5, or 6.

Kulturkrogen SWEDISH Popular among students, this is a reliable, affordable choice that serves Swedish comfort food. Some items on their menu are called "fingerfood," including a rich-tasting pumpernickel with smoked salmon or a flavorful hummus. You can always count on Swedish sausages with potato salad or a roast beef fresh from the oven. Other specialties include fresh fish, boeuf bourguignon, and a grilled entrecôte with french fries and a béarnaise sauce. A lunch buffet is featured on Friday and Saturday between 11:30am and 3pm.

Tegnérsplatsen. ✆ **046/14-65-10.** Reservations not needed. Lunch buffet 139SEK; main courses 84SEK–125SEK. AE, MC, V. Mon–Tues 11:30am–5pm; Wed–Fri 11:30am–9pm; Sat 11:30am–5pm. Bus: 1, 2, 3, 4, 5, or 6.

Staket SWEDISH/INTERNATIONAL This old tavern, a favorite among students, serves good food in a step-gabled brick facade that is a historic landmark. Food and drink are offered in the cellar—our favorite place for a rendezvous—but also at street level. Both dining rooms have their appeals, but fondues (a ritual in which skewers of meat are cooked at your table in pots of heated oil) are served only in the cellar. For appetizers, try a succulent crab cocktail and a tasty goulash soup evocative of Budapest. For a main course, the mixed grill is a winner, as is the tender, flavorful *tournedos* of beef.

Stora Södergatan 6. ✆ **046/211-93-67.** www.staket.gastrogate.com. Reservations recommended. Main courses 155SEK–220SEK. AE, DC, MC, V. Mon–Thurs 11am–11pm; Fri 11am–midnight; Sat noon–midnight; Sun 1–11pm. Bus: 1, 2, 3, 4, 5, or 6.

Lund After Dark

Most dance clubs in Lund operate only on weekends, when the clientele includes many students from the university. The hottest spot is **T-Bar,** in the basement of Tegnérs Matsalar restaurant, Sandgatan 2 (✆ **046/13-13-33;** www.tegners.com). There's also a dance floor in the basement of **Gloria's Restaurant/Sportbar** (see "Where to Dine," above), every Friday and Saturday beginning at 10:30pm. Entrance is free.

YSTAD ★

55km (34 miles) E of Malmö, 46km (28 miles) W of Simrishamn

Time has passed Ystad by, and that's why we like to visit it. Its **Gamla Stan ★★★** contains an astonishing 300 well-preserved half-timbered antique houses, which you can explore by roaming the cobbled streets. They're scattered about town, but we found the greatest concentration of them on **Stora Östergatan.**

Most of the houses date from the latter 1700s, though **Ånglahuset,** on Stora Norregatan, is from around 1630. You can launch yourself into the past by starting at **Stortorget ★★**, the impressive main square of Ystad, which was a big smuggling center during the Napoleonic Wars.

As impressive as the main square is, we came upon another square of great charm. **Tvättorget** in the old town is Ystad's smallest square, and it's surrounded by half-timbered houses. It may be hard to find and is reached by walking up a narrow lane called Bäckahästgränd.

At one time in its history, Ystad was much more important than the provincial town you see today. Back in the 17th century, Ystad was known as "Sweden's window to the world." Amazingly, the first automobile in Sweden was driven on the old streets of Ystad. The town also opened Sweden's first bank, and the first building that could be called a hotel.

There is some activity here, with ferries leaving for the Danish island of Bornholm—even to Poland. If you're a fan of the best-selling inspector Karl Wallander crime thrillers—all written by Henning Mankell—you'll know that Ystad is a setting for these suspense tales. If you don't have time to wade through all of Mankell's series, opt for the fourth installment, *The Man Who Smiled.* It's the best and most evocative—and it's translated into English. Devotees of the series can tour the sights associated with the inspector with a volunteer fire brigade every Tuesday and Thursday from July to mid-August. Fans are taken around town on an antique fire engine. The tourist office (see below) will have details.

Devotees of the silent screen know of Ystad as the birthplace of Valentino's "beautiful blond Viking," Anna Q. Nilsson, who was born here in 1890 and whose fame at one time was greater than that of Greta Garbo, a fellow Swede. Some of Nilsson's greatest films were *In the Heart of a Fool* (1921); *Ponjola* (1923), in which she played a boy; and *Midnight Lovers,* finished in 1925, the year of a horseback-riding accident that ended her career. Today she is remembered mainly for appearing in a cameo role as one of the "waxworks" in the 1950 Gloria Swanson classic *Sunset Blvd.*

Essentials

GETTING THERE

BY PLANE The nearest regional airport is at **Sturup,** 37km (23 miles) in the direction of Malmö, and a taxi there costs 450SEK each way. The closest international big-time airport is at **Kastrup,** outside of Copenhagen, via the Øresund Bridge.

BY TRAIN There are good rail connections between Malmö and Ystad. Trains run roughly on the hour between Malmö and Ystad daily (trip time: 1 hr.). On Sunday, there are only six daily trains from Malmö. In Ystad, both the bus station and the railway station are immediately adjacent to one another, half a kilometer (about ⅓ mile) south of the town center. City bus nos. 1, 2, and 3 all make runs from the railway/bus station to the town center, and a taxi will charge 90SEK. For more information, call ✆ **0771/75-75-75.**

BY BUS There are 10 buses Monday to Saturday from Malmö to Ystad.

BY CAR From Malmö, head east on Route 65. For more information, call ✆ **0771/21-82-18.**

VISITOR INFORMATION

The tourist bureau, **Ystads Turistbyrå,** St. Knuts Torg, 271 80 Ystad (✆ **0411/57-76-81;** www.ystad.se), is at the bus station in the same building as the art museum (Konstmuseum). It's open from June to August Monday to Friday 9am to 7pm, Saturday 10am to 6pm, Sunday 10am to 6pm; September to May Monday to Friday 9am to 5pm.

Seeing the Sights

As we've mentioned, Ystad's main sight is **Gamla Stan (Old Town)** itself. But there are a few other specific targets to check out as you wander about.

St. Maria Kyrka ★ This church, dating from the early 1200s, is the focal point of town. It certainly respects tradition: A night watchman still sounds the hours of the night from here, just as his distant ancestor did back before clocks were invented. (Fortunately, night watchmen have it better today than in olden times; in the medieval era, if the watchman fell asleep, he was beheaded.) Though many of its richest decorative features were removed in the 1880s because of changing tastes, some of the most precious ones were brought back in a restoration program initiated 4 decades later. The chancel with the ambulatory is late Gothic, and the church spire dates from 1688. Inside, look for the baptismal chapel with a richly carved German altar from the 15th century. The font came from Lübeck, Germany, in 1617, and the iron candelabra is a very early one from the 1300s. Of all the treasures here, we think the **Renaissance Pulpit ★★** by an unknown craftsman from North Germany is the most remarkable.

Stortorget. ✆ **0411/69-20-0.** Free admission. June to mid-Sept daily 10am–6pm.

Stadsmuseet i Gråbrödraklostret (City Museum in the Grey Friars Monastery) Part of the fun of visiting this museum is getting here. From the main square, Stortorget, take a stroll up Garvaregränd (where you'll be distracted by the high-quality arts and crafts for sale in the workshops). When you reach Klostergatan, you'll be near the entrance to the museum—which, incidentally, is the only one in Sweden inside a monastic house from the Middle Ages.

Gråbröder, or "Grey Friars," dates from 1267, when it was occupied by monks. At the Reformation, these guys were booted out, marking a long decline for the building. It went from hospital to distillery to seedy poorhouse. And just when the townspeople thought the building had reached its lowest point, it became a dumping ground for garbage. It wasn't until 2001, when city government intervened, that the building was rescued.

Once in charge of the building, the city had to do something with it; so they rounded up most of their valuables and housed them here. Despite that effort, the building is more intriguing than the exhibits, which consist mainly of antiquities from the area: local textiles, silverware, and such. Perhaps the display of bridal costumes from the 1700s will attract your notice. Or you might agree with us that the 80 gravestones from the 1300s to the 1700s have a certain ghoulish fascination. Just save the best for last—the **gardens ★**, which are open 24 hours. The monks originally created these gardens, and many of the same spices, vegetables, and medicinal herbs they grew bloom again today in honor of their long-ago commitment; they're most glorious in July.

St. Petri Kykoplan. ✆ **0411/57-72-86.** Admission 30SEK, free 16 and under. Mon–Fri noon–5pm; Sat–Sun noon–4pm.

Ystads Konstmuseum (Museum of Modern Art) This is a very minor museum and could easily be missed if you're on a tight schedule. But it does contain one of the most evocative collections of Danish and southern Swedish painters over the past century. There is also a small unimpressive military museum. The Ystad tourist office is in the same building as the museum.

St. Knuts Torg. ✆ **0411/57-72-85.** www.konstmuseet.ystad.se. Admission 30SEK. Tues–Fri noon–5pm; Sat–Sun noon–4pm.

Where to Stay

Hotell Continental ★★ This 1829 landmark was constructed over the site of an old customhouse when Ystad was the major port link between Sweden and the Continent. In 1996, a family-owned company took it over and began a program of refurbishing and redecorating that continues to this day. These owners seem to take a personal interest in their guests, many of whom arrive by train or by ferry from Europe; the hotel is convenient to both terminals. Marble sheeting in the lobby and gleaming crystal chandeliers add grace notes. The midsize-to-spacious bedrooms are furnished with sleek modern stylings that are both comfortable and tasteful. Consider visiting the dining room here even if you're not a guest. Chefs prepare Swedish classics and often use regional produce in summer. Breakfast highlights such classic Swedish dishes as *åggakaka,* a thick pancake with crispy bacon and lingonberries.

Hamngatan 13, S-271 00 Ystad. www.hotelcontinental-ystad.se. ✆ **0411/137-00.** Fax 0411/125-70. 52 units. 1,190SEK–1,790SEK double. Rates include buffet breakfast. AE, DC, MC, V. Parking 40SEK. **Amenities:** Restaurant; bar; babysitting; room service. *In room:* TV, hair dryer, Wi-Fi (free).

Hotel Tornväktaren This is the best choice in Ystad for those who don't want to check into the more expensive hotels we've recommended. A simple bed-and-breakfast, it derives much of its charm from its hard-working owner, Mr. Roy Saifert. His home is a turn-of-the-20th-century stone-built, red-trimmed structure with a garden, 10 minutes on foot from the railway station. Rooms have lots of homey touches that include frilly curtains, wall-to-wall carpeting, and lace doilies covering painted wooden furniture. Not all rooms have a private bathroom, and we have found that the corridor facilities are adequate. The breakfast served is generous and home-cooked, mostly to order; no other meals are served.

St. Östergatan 33, S-271-34 Ystad. www.tornvaktaren.se. ✆ **0411/784-80.** Fax 0411/729-27. 9 units, 5 with bathroom. 895SEK double with bathroom; 795SEK double without bathroom. Rates include buffet breakfast. AE, MC, V. Free parking. *In room:* TV, Wi-Fi (free).

Ystads Saltsjöbad ★ This hotel is a classic, made all the more so by its helpful owners, Ann and Kent Nyström. Beautifully situated on 4 hectares (10 acres) of forested land beside the sea, the hotel is close to Sweden's southernmost tip. It was built in 1897 by one of the most famous opera stars of his day, Swedish-born Solomon Smith. Designed as a haven for the Gilded Age aristocracy of northern Europe, it consists of three connected four-story buildings with big-windowed corridors, set close to the sands of an expansive beach. The guest rooms are comfortably furnished in turn-of-the-20th-century style. The clientele changes throughout the year: In the summer, the hotel caters to beachgoers; in the winter, it's often filled with corporate conventions. The neighborhood also provides good opportunities for healthy pastimes such as tennis and golf. Both the main dining room and a smaller, more intimate a la carte restaurant, **Nero,** open onto views of the sea; both menus feature an international cuisine that's married to traditional Swedish fare. Fresh produce is delivered several times a day, and the local suppliers are "environmentally aware."

Saltsjöbadsgatan 6, S-271 39 Ystad. www.ystadssaltsjobad.se. ✆ **0411/136-30.** Fax 0411/55-58-35. 109 units. June 19–Aug 31 1,650SEK–1,800SEK double; Sept–June 18 1,770SEK–2,990SEK double; year-round Mon–Thurs 3,800SEK suite, Fri–Sun 2,500SEK suite. AE, DC, MC, V. Closed Dec 23–Jan 6. Free parking. **Amenities:** 2 restaurants; 2 bars; bikes; health club & spa; 2 heated pools (1 indoor); room service. *In room:* A/C, TV, hair dryer.

Where to Dine

Lottas Restaurang INTERNATIONAL Fans praise it as one of the most popular and bustling restaurants in town; detractors avoid it because of slow service by a small staff that sometimes seems impossibly overworked. Everyone awards high marks, however, for the well-prepared cuisine. Meals are served in a brick dining room within a century-old building that once functioned as a private home. The menu runs to conservative, old-fashioned Swedish cuisine, which might include fried and creamed filet of cod with dill-flavored boiled potatoes, pork schnitzels with asparagus and béarnaise sauce, and marinated breast of chicken with roasted potatoes. Although overly familiar to anyone who has dined in Sweden for more than a week, each of these dishes is made with fresh ingredients—and is satisfying and filling.

Stortorget 11. ✆ **0411/788-00.** www.lottas.se. Reservations recommended. Main courses 142SEK-224SEK. AE, DC, MC, V. Mon-Sat 5-10pm.

Sandskogens Vardshus ★ SWEDISH About 1.5km (1 mile) east of Ystad's center, this structure was originally built in 1899 as a summer home for the town's mayor. It was converted into a restaurant in the 1930s and has provided local diners with well-prepared Swedish specialties ever since. One of the most popular appetizers in Sweden is a toast served with whitebait roe, sour cream, and onions. When in Sweden, do as the locals do and give it a try. We'd go for it, if we didn't find the pot of marinated mussels even more tempting. Other appealing choices here are the freshly caught brill, greatly enhanced with a caramelized butter sauce; the turbot, dressed up with shrimp and Swedish caviar; or the even grander gratin of lobster accompanied by a lemon sole. In summer, we'd walk a mile for one of the pastry chef's cloudberry parfaits made with golden berries picked in the arctic.

Saltsjøvagen, Sandskogen. ✆ **0411/147-60.** www.sandskogensvardshus.se. Reservations recommended. Main courses 180SEK-225SEK; 2-course fixed-price menu 255SEK, 3-course 325SEK. MC, V. Tues and Thurs noon-8pm; Wed and Fri noon-9pm; Sat noon-10pm; Sun noon-6pm. Closed Jan-Feb.

Steakhouse Bruggeriet ★ SWEDISH/INTERNATIONAL With such a name, you would expect the best steaks in Lund. And this place delivers. The novel restaurant was originally built in 1749 as a warehouse for malt; in 1996, a team of local entrepreneurs installed a series of large copper vats and transformed the site into a pleasant, cozy restaurant and brewery. Today they specialize in two "tastes" of beer—a lager and a dark—that are marketed under the brand name Ysta Färsköl. Food items served here seem carefully calibrated to taste best when consumed with either of the two beers. The kitchen doesn't like to go in for culinary experiments, adopting the concept that if it was good enough for grandfather, it's good enough for today's patrons. That seems to sit well with the patrons, who order such dishes as fried herring marinated in mustard and sour cream, or the grilled salmon in a red-wine sauce. Swedish lamb is well flavored with garlic and fresh herbs, and the tenderloin steak meets its perfect match in a brandy sauce. On some occasions, we've seen succulent versions of barbecued ribs, just like they serve them in Dixie, on the menu.

Långgatan 20. ✆ **0411/69-99-99.** www.restaurangbryggeriet.nu. Reservations recommended. Main courses 179SEK-235SEK. AE, DC, MC, V. Mon-Sat 11:30am-midnight; Sun 1-10pm.

Store Thor SWEDISH/FRENCH One of the most reliable lunchtime restaurants in Ystad occupies a series of vaulted cellars that were part of a monastery in the 1500s. A disastrous fire destroyed the monastery, but the Rådhus (Town Hall) was reconstructed over the cellars several hundred years later. Today, amid small tables and romantic candlelight, you can enjoy such tasty dishes as grilled anglerfish enlivened with a basil cream sauce; saddle of lamb roasted with fresh herbs; and shellfish soup, rescued with saffron. As a waitress here put it, the "dishes are cute and brave." Stortorget 1. ✆ **0411/185-10.** www.storethor.se. Main courses 98SEK-215SEK. AE, DC, MC, V. Mon-Sat 11:30am-midnight; Sun 4pm-midnight.

SIMRISHAMN ★

630km (391 miles) S of Stockholm, 95km (59 miles) E of Malmö, 40km (25 miles) E of Ystad

If it's a question of Ystad or Simrishamn, make it Ystad. That doesn't mean that this old fishing village is without its charms. Actually, with its cobblestone streets and tiny brick houses, it's one of the most idyllic villages in Skåne. It's also the best center for exploring some of the major attractions of the province, which are found in its environs, including Dag Hammarskjöld's farm, a medieval castle, and a Bronze Age tomb (see below).

Because of its proximity to Ystad, Simrishamn can also be treated as a day trip. At some point, wander down by the harbor where the fishing boats pull in, carrying one of Sweden's greatest bounties of cod, eel, and herring. If you're here in summer, you'll also notice hundreds of tourists eating ice cream while waiting for a ferry to take them to the vacation island of Bornholm in Denmark.

Once you arrive at the southeastern tip of Skåne, you'll find good sandy beaches, especially at **Sandhammaren.**

Essentials

GETTING THERE

BY CAR Because buses or trains from Sturup to Simrishamn require a time-consuming 2-hour transit from the nearest airport (the Lund/Malmö airport at Sturup), most people opt to rent a car instead of flying. From Ystad, our last stopover, continue east along Route 10.

BY TRAIN Fourteen trains a day (nine on Sat and Sun) make the 1½-hour run between Malmö and Simrishamn. Simrishamn's train and bus stations are both in the town center. For information, call ✆ **0771/75-75-75.**

BY BUS Nineteen buses per day arrive from Kristianstad; eight buses per day on Saturday; five buses per day on Sunday. Five buses per day arrive from Ystad Monday to Saturday (three on Sun). Twelve buses per day arrive from Lund (five on Sat, and four on Sun). Tickets can be purchased on board these buses. Call ✆ **0771/77-77-77.**

VISITOR INFORMATION For information about hotels, boardinghouses, summer cottages, and apartments, check with the tourist bureau. **Simrishamns Kommun Turistbyrå,** Tullhusgatan 2, 272 80 Simrishamn (✆ **0414/81-98-00;** www.turistbyra.simrishamn.se), is open June to August Monday to Friday 9am to 8pm, Saturday 10am to 8pm, and Sunday 11am to 8pm; September to May Monday to Friday 9am to 5pm.

Seeing the Sights

The chief attraction here is a stroll through the town's **Gamla Stan ★** or Old Town, which is the historic core, a maze of fondant-colored tiny cottages that in some ways evokes a movie set. If you're driving, there is parking down by the harbor. As you stroll along, follow Strandvägen to **Sjöfartsplatsen,** which is a garden studded with works of art (you may disagree) made from the debris of shipwrecks.

The chief monument in Gamla Stan is **St. Nicolai Kirke,** Storgatan (✆ **0414/41-24-80**). It's open June to September from 10am to 6:30pm, Sunday noon to 6:30pm; October to May Monday to Friday 10am to 3pm, and Saturday 10am to 1pm. Originally constructed as a fisherman's chapel in the 12th century, the church literally dominates the town. It's built of chunky sandstone blocks, with a brick porch and step gables. Over the years there have been many additions, with a nave added in the 1300s, although the vault dates from the 1400s. Inside, look for the flamboyantly painted pulpit from the 1620s. The pews and votive ships on display were installed much later, in the 1800s. Outside you'll see two sculptures, both by Sweden's greatest sculptor, Carl Milles, called *The Sisters* and *Angel with Trumpet.*

The main square and the center of local life is **Storgatan. Östergatan** and **Stora Norregatan** are the best streets for charming little 19th-century houses; nearly all of them have carved wooden doors and potted plants on their doorsteps.

NEARBY ATTRACTIONS

Backakra ★ Just off the coastal road between Ystad and Simrishamn is the farm that Dag Hammarskjöld, the late United Nations secretary general, purchased in 1957 and intended to make his home. Although he died in a plane crash before he could live there, the old farm has been restored according to his instructions. The rooms are filled with gifts to Mr. Hammarskjöld—everything from a Nepalese dagger to a lithograph by Picasso.

The site is 31km (19 miles) southwest of Simrishamn and can be reached by the bus from Simrishamn marked YSTAD. Likewise, a bus from Ystad, marked SIMRISHAMN, goes by the site. Scheduling your return might be difficult because of infrequent service—check in advance.

Other than the caretakers, the site is unoccupied most of the year, with the exception of 18 members of the Swedish Academy, who are allowed to use the house for meditation and writing whenever they want.

S-270 20 Loderup. ✆ **0411/52-60-10.** Admission 30SEK adults, free for children 14 and under. June 8–Aug 16 daily noon–5pm; May 16–June 7 and Aug 17–Sept 20 Sat–Sun noon–5pm. Closed Sept 21–May 15.

Glimmingehus ★★ Even more than Kivik (see below) and Backakra (see above), this is the top attraction in the area. The somewhat Gothic castle, built between 1499 and 1505, appears much as it did at the time of its construction. Nearly all other such castles in Sweden are in ruins or else have been extensively tampered with—so this one is for purists. This majestic edifice was constructed by Adam van Büren for a member of the Danish aristocracy, who demanded strong fortresslike walls and tiny windows. Naturally the fortress had a moat. In time, the aristocrats, finding the castle far too austere, moved out—and the rats moved in. There were so many rats here at one time that Selma Lagerlöf, in her book *The Wonderful Adventures of Nils,* describes an epic battle between the gray and the black rats. Like a Pied Piper, the fictional Nils lures away the gray rats by playing from his enchanted pipe, plucked from a wise old owl who inhabited the tower of Lund Cathedral. Swedish schoolchildren still read this adventure story today.

Hammenhög 276 56. ✆ **0414/186-20.** Admission 60SEK adults, free for children 7–18. Apr–May and Aug 9–Sept 30 daily 11am–4pm; June–Aug 8 daily 10am–6pm; Oct–Nov Sat–Sun noon–4pm. From Simrishamn follow Rte. 10 southwest for 10km (6¼ miles) to the village of Hammenhög and then follow the signs.

Kivik Tomb ★ The drive here is worth the journey, as it takes you through fields planted with fruit, mainly pears and apples, and to the little village of **Kivik,** where the cider is said to taste better than anywhere else in Scandinavia.

Discovered in 1748, this remarkable find, Sweden's most amazing Bronze Age relic, is north of Simrishamn along the coast of Kivik. In a 1931 excavation, tomb furniture, bronze fragments, and some grave carvings were uncovered. Eight floodlighted runic slabs depict pictures of horses, a sleigh, and what appears to be a fun-loving troupe of dancing seals.

Bredaror. No phone. Admission 30SEK. Daily 10am–6pm. Closed Sept–Apr. From Simrishamn follow Rte. 10 northwest to the village of Kivik, at which point the tomb is signposted.

Where to Stay

Hotel Kockska Gården This unspoiled black-and-white half-timbered former coaching inn looks like one of those old places in the English countryside—except this inn is in Sweden and right in the town center. The hotel is built around a large medieval courtyard where horses were once sheltered during the bitter Swedish winter. Much modernized, updated, and greatly altered over the years—and now more comfortable than ever—it is an inviting choice. The bedrooms have tasteful furnishings and soothing pastel colors. Breakfast is the only meal served, but there are places to eat within an easy walk of the front door.

Storgatan 25, S-272 31 Simrishamn. www.kockskagarden.se. ✆ **0414/41-17-55.** Fax 0414/41-19-78. 18 units. 1,290SEK–1,790SEK double; 1,790SEK-2,090SEK suite. Rates include buffet breakfast. AE, MC, V. Free parking. **Amenities:** Sauna; Wi-Fi (free, in lobby). *In room:* TV.

Hotel Svea ★ We wouldn't want to check in forever, but for an overnight stay, this is the best choice in town. It also has the finest restaurant (see below). Right on the waterfront, in the town center, Svea was built around the turn of the 20th century; it's painted yellow, with a red-tile roof typical of other buildings nearby. Much of what you see today was rebuilt and radically renovated, so everything is modernized. Many of its well-appointed, conservatively comfortable rooms overlook the harbor. The hotel's only suite, the Prince Eugen, is named after a member of the royal family of Sweden who stayed here shortly after the hotel was built.

Strandvägen 3, S-272 21 Simrishamn. www.hotellsvea.se. ✆ **0414/41-17-20.** Fax 0414/143-41. 59 units. 1,350SEK–1,850SEK double; 2,100SEK suite. AE, DC, MC, V. Free parking. **Amenities:** Restaurant; bar; sauna. *In room:* TV, hair dryer, Wi-Fi (19SEK per hour).

Where to Dine

Restaurant Svea ★ SWEDISH/INTERNATIONAL The best restaurant in town is within the pale yellow walls of the above-recommended Hotel Svea. In a modern, mostly beige room whose windows overlook the harbor, the kitchen focuses on fish caught fresh in local waters. However, the kitchen also turns out beef, pork, chicken, and some exotic meats, such as grilled filet of ostrich. (The chef added it to the menu mainly as a conversational oddity.) Other menu items include strips of smoked duck breast in lemon sauce, a platter of artfully arranged herring that can be prepared at least three different ways, filet of fried sole with white-wine or tartar sauce, medallions of pork with béarnaise sauce, and a succulent filet of beef with salsa-style tomato sauce. On a number of visits, we have found all these dishes deftly prepared with fresh ingredients.

In the Hotel Svea. Strandvägen 3. ✆ **0414/41-17-20.** www.hotellsvea.se. Reservations recommended. Main courses 195SEK–250SEK; 3-course menu 450SEK. AE, DC, MC, V. Daily 6:30–10am, 11:30am–1pm, and 6:30–10pm. Closed Dec 21–Jan 8.

EXPLORING THE SWEDISH COUNTRYSIDE

17

After seeing Stockholm, visitors often face a difficult decision about what else to do. Sweden is a large country, and most travelers have tough choices to make. In this chapter we'll focus on the best possibilities, including an excursion on the Göta Canal, one of Scandinavia's major attractions. Another trip is to folkloric Dalarna, a province that evokes quintessential Sweden. Besides the traditional customs, handicrafts, and festive costumes, the region is important artistically, as two of Sweden's most famous painters, Anders Zorn and Carl Larsson, came from here.

We'll also take a ferry to **Gotland,** Sweden's vacation island, which is known for its cliff formations and wide, sandy beaches. Inhabited since 5000 B.C., Gotland is Scandinavia's most intriguing island, with Visby as its capital.

For the more adventurous, **Swedish Lapland** is an alluring destination and home to the once-nomadic Sami. In one of Europe's last great open spaces, you can see golden eagles soar above snowcapped crags and "listen to the silence." Skiers flock to the area, but the summer miracle of the midnight sun shining above the Arctic Circle attracts the most visitors. This area is so vast (some 1,000km/620 miles from north to south) that we've highlighted only the best destinations. Swedish Lapland is also a great place for summer sports—canoeing, river rafting, salmon fishing, hiking, and climbing. Local tourist offices can put you in touch with outfitters who arrange these adventures.

THE GÖTA CANAL ★★★

In Sweden in summer, everyone seems to take to the water to enjoy the precious days of sunshine before a long, cold winter. The **Göta Canal cruise ★★★** covers a distance of 560km (347 miles) from Gothenburg in the west to Stockholm in the east, or vice versa. Of course, this actual sail is not entirely on the canal and covers other lakes and rivers as well. The highest loch is more than 90m (295 ft.) above sea level. To break up the sail on the 4-day cruise, captains wisely stop four or five times along the way. Day trips and cruises also are offered.

The canal was begun in the early 19th century for the purpose of transporting goods across Sweden, thereby avoiding expensive tolls levied by Denmark on ships entering and leaving the Baltic Sea. However, soon after the canal was completed, Denmark waived its shipping tolls, and the railway between Stockholm and Gothenburg was created, allowing for the cheaper and faster shipment of goods across Sweden. The canal became more of a tourist attraction than a means of transportation.

Boats depart Gothenburg heading east along the Göta Älv River. About 30 minutes outside Gothenburg, you'll see the 14th-century **Bohus Fortress.** This bastion played a leading role in the battles among Sweden, Norway, and Denmark to establish supremacy. Bohus Castle and Fortress (Bohus Fästning) was built by order of Norway's Haakon V on Norwegian territory. After the territory was ceded to Sweden in 1658, Bohus Fortress was used as a prison. Climb the tower, **"Father's Hat,"** for what we consider the finest panoramic view of the entire trip. Farther down the river, the boat will pass the town of **Kungälv,** known by the Vikings as Konghälla, whose traditions are 1,000 years old.

As the boat proceeds eastward on the Göta's clear water, the landscape becomes wilder. About 5 hours into the journey, you reach the town of **Trollhättan,** home of one of Europe's largest power stations. The once-renowned Trollhättan Falls, now almost dry, can be seen at their full capacity only in July. Today most of the water is diverted to a series of underground channels to the power station.

After passing a series of locks, boats enter **Lake Vänern,** Sweden's largest lake, with a surface area of more than 2,130 sq. km (831 sq. miles). The trip across Lake Vänern takes about 8 hours. Along the way you'll pass **Lidköping,** home of the famous Rörstrand porcelain. Lidköping received its charter in 1446. North of Lidköping, on the island of Kållandsö, is **Läckö Slott,** a castle dating from 1298. Originally home of the bishops of Skara, the castle was given to King Gustavus Vasa in 1528 and later presented to Sweden's great hero, Gen. Magnus Gabriel de la Gardie.

Having crossed Lake Vänern, the boats once again enter the canal. A series of locks, including the canal's oldest at Forsvik, carry the steamers to Sweden's second-largest lake, **Lake Vättern.** This lake is famous for its beauty and translucent water, and we find it even more alluring and scenic than noble Vänern itself. At some points, visibility reaches a depth of 15m (49 ft.).

The medieval town of **Vadstena** on the eastern shore of Lake Vättern is our favorite stopover on the Göta Canal trip because it is the most atmospheric and evocative town. Within the town are narrow streets and frame buildings. It's known throughout Sweden for its delicate handmade lace, which you can see by walking along Stora Gatan, the main street. Also worth a visit is the **Klosterkyrkan (Abbey Church).** Built between the mid–14th and 15th centuries to specifications outlined by its founder, St. Birgitta (Bridget) of Sweden, this Gothic church is rich in medieval art. Parts of the abbey date from 1250.

Another major sight is **Vadstena Castle.** Construction began under Gustavus Vasa, king of Sweden in 1545, but was not completed until 1620. This splendid Renaissance Vasa castle, erected during a period of national expansion, dominates the town from its position on the lake, just behind the old courthouse in the southern part of town. The caretaker told us that the last royalty seen living here was back in 1715. Since those days the castle has been restored in respect to its original architecture.

Boats bound for Stockholm depart Lake Vättern and pass two small lakes, Boren and Roxen. Just south of Lake Roxen you'll find the university town of **Linköping,** site of a battle between Roman Catholic King Sigismund of Poland and Duke Charles of Södermanland (later Charles IX). Charles won the battle and established Linköping as part of Sweden rather than a province of Rome. In the town's main square is the Folkung Fountain, one of sculptor Carl Milles's most popular works. Northwest of the main square you'll find the cathedral, a not quite harmonious blend of Romanesque and Gothic architecture.

From Linköping, boats enter Lake Roxen and continue their journey northeast by canal to **Slätbaken,** a fjord that stretches to the sea. Steamers then continue along the coast to Stockholm.

The **Göta Canal Steamship Company** offers turn-of-the-20th-century steamers, including its 1874 *Juno,* which claims to be the world's oldest passenger vessel offering overnight accommodations. The line also operates the 1912 *Wilhelm Tham* and the newer—that is, 1931—*Diana.* Passengers can walk, jog, or bike along the canal path, and there are organized shore excursions at many stops along the way.

DALARNA ★★★

This province offers everything from maypole dancing and fiddle music to folk costumes and handicrafts. Dalarna, which means "valleys," is sometimes referred to as "Dalecarlia," the Anglicized form of the name.

Lake Siljan, arguably the most beautiful lake in Europe, is ringed with resort villages and towns. Leksand, Rättvik, and Mora attract summer visitors with sports, folklore, and a week of music. From June 23 to June 26, the Dalecarlians celebrate midsummer with maypole dancing. In the winter, people come here to ski.

Falun ★

488km (303 miles) NE of Gothenburg, 229km (142 miles) NW of Stockholm

Our coverage of the region begins in Falun, the old capital of Dalarna; it is on both sides of the Falu River. The town is noted for its copper mines; copper revenue has supported many Swedish kings. Just 10km (6½ miles) northeast, you can visit the home of the famed Swedish painter Carl Larsson.

ESSENTIALS

GETTING THERE The nearest **airport** is the Dala airport, at Borlänge, 26km (16 miles) to the west. No convenient direct buses run here, but you can grab a taxi for around 490SEK each way.

There is frequent **train service** during the day from Stockholm (trip time: 3 hr.). There are no direct trains from Gothenburg to Falun. It is necessary to change trains in either Örebro or Hallsberg. Allow 6 to 7 hours for the journey. For schedules, call **© 771/75-75-75.** Buses are operated by **Swebus** (**© 0771/21-82-18;** www.swebusexpress.se). There are no direct buses from Stockholm to Falun. A bus change is required in Borlänge. Buses from Stockholm to Borlänge and from Borlänge to Falun run daily. From Gothenburg to Falun there are one or two buses per day, depending on the day of the week and the month of the year.

In Falun, the **bus and railway stations** are adjacent to each other, 455m (1,493 ft.) south of the town center. The white-sided city bus no. 60 or 70 makes runs from the stations to the Stortorget, the town's central square.

If you're **driving** to Falun from Stockholm, take the E-18 expressway northwest to the junction with Route 70. From here, continue to the junction with Route 60, where you head northwest. Falun is signposted.

VISITOR INFORMATION The **Falun Tourist Office,** Trotzgatan 10–12, 791 83 Falun (✆ **023/830-50**), is open from mid-August to mid-June every Monday to Friday 10am to 6pm, and Saturday 10am to 2pm. During summer, from mid-June to mid-August, it's open Monday to Friday 10am to 6pm, Saturday 10am to 2pm, and Sunday 11am to 2pm. For more information on Falun, refer to the town's website at **www.visitfalunborlange.se**.

SEEING THE SIGHTS

Before you get down and dirty at some dark pits and mines, head first to the market square, Stora Torget, to see the **Kristine Church** (✆ **023/279-10**), a copper-roofed structure dating from the mid–17th century (the tower itself dates from 1865). It's open daily 10am to 4pm, and admission is free. It closes at 6pm in summer.

Falun is the site of **Lugnet** (✆ **023/835-00**), one of Sweden's largest sports complexes. The Bjursberget ski resort is 20km (13 miles) away.

Carl Larsson-gården ★★★ Carl Larsson (1853–1919) is justifiably acclaimed as Sweden's greatest painter. A 20-minute trip from Falun will take you to a small village, Sundborn, site of Lilla Hyttnas, Larsson's home (now known as Carl Larsson-gården). There are guided tours throughout the day, and English-language tours sometimes are available.

While at the home of the artist, you can also ask about viewing **Carl Larssons porträttsambling ★** (a portrait collection donated by Larsson), displayed in the Congregation House next to the local church. The pictures, painted between 1905 and 1918, depict well-known local residents representing many different occupations. To reach the garden, take bus no. 64 from Falun to Sundborn, which is 5 minutes away from Carl Larsson-gården.

Carl Larssons Väg 12, Sundborn. ✆ **023/600-53.** www.clg.se. Admission 120SEK adults, 50SEK children 6–18, free for children 5 and under. May–Sept daily 10am–5pm; Oct–Apr by appointment only (call ✆ 023/600-53 for reservations). Bus: 64 from Falun. 13km (8 miles) northeast of Falun.

Falu Koppargruva ★★★ This copper mine, around which the town developed, was the world's largest producer of copper during the 17th century; it supplied the raw material used for the roof of the Palace of Versailles. Since 1970, when the mine was opened to the public, more than one million visitors have taken the elevator 54m (177 ft.) below the Earth's surface and into the mine. Guides take you through old chambers and winding passages dating from the Middle Ages. In one section of the mine you'll see a shaft divided by a timber wall that's more than 195m (640 ft.) high; this may be the world's tallest wood structure. Today the only industrial product of the mine is pigment used for producing Sweden's signature red paint *(Falu Rödfärg)*, which is used not only on virtually all Swedish barns, but on thousands upon thousands of private homes and even commercial and public buildings. Buildings painted this shade of barn red have become virtual symbols of Sweden.

Gruvplatsen. ✆ **023/78-20-30.** www.falugruva.se. Admission 190SEK adults, 70SEK children 4 and up. May–Sept daily 9am–6pm; Oct–Apr Mon–Fri 11am–5pm, Sat–Sun 11am–4pm. Tours must be booked in advance in winter.

WHERE TO STAY & DINE

First Hotel Grand ★ This buff-colored hotel 90m (295 ft.) south of the landmark Falun Church was built in 1862, with a modern addition constructed in 1974. The tastefully modern guest rooms are among the best decorated in town. All have ample-size bathrooms equipped with shower units. If you don't mind paying 210SEK extra,

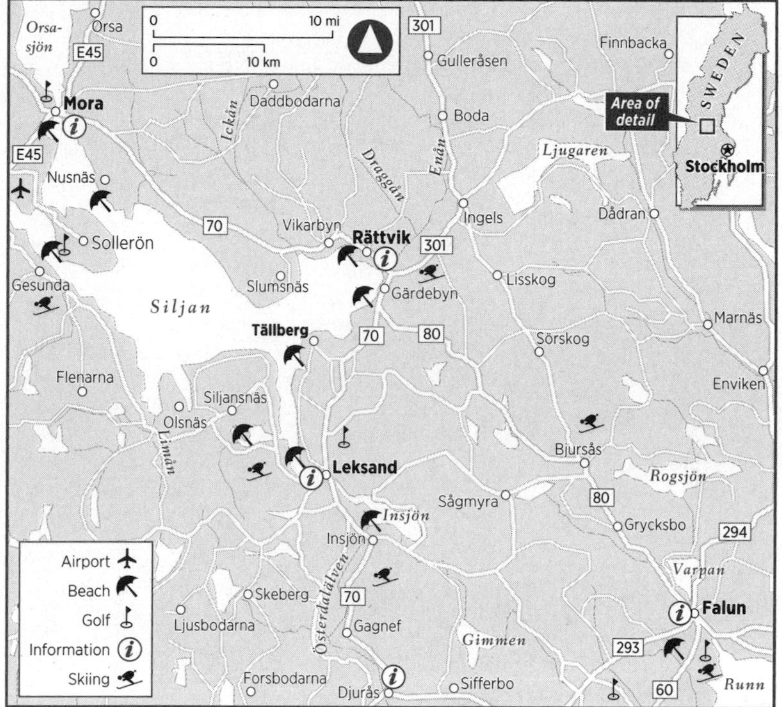

you can book a Grand Room with a free minibar and free pay TV, plus a luxurious bathrobe with slippers. For the most elegant living of all, reserve a suite with its own sauna and large private bathrooms.

Trotzgatan 9–11, S-791 71 Falun. www.firsthotels.com. ✆ **023/79-48-80.** Fax 023/141-43. 151 units. Sun–Thurs 1,539SEK–1,739SEK double; Fri–Sat 848SEK–1,148SEK double; all week 2,495SEK suite. Rates include buffet breakfast. AE, DC, MC, V. Parking 80SEK. Bus: 701 or 704. **Amenities:** Restaurant; bar; exercise room; indoor heated pool; room service; sauna. *In room:* TV, minibar (in some), Wi-Fi (free).

Leksand ★★

48km (30 miles) W of Falun, 267km (166 miles) NW of Stockholm

Leksand is a doorway to Lake Siljan and, in its present form, dates from the early 1900s when it was reconstructed following a fire that razed the community. However, some type of settlement has existed on this site since pagan times.

Many of the old traditions of the province still flourish here. Women occasionally don the traditional dress for church on Sunday, and in June and July the long "church boats" from Viking times may cross the lake carrying parishioners to church. These same boats compete in a church-boat race on the first Sunday in July. Since World War II, a miracle play, *The Road to Heaven,* has been presented here in open-air performances, providing an insight into the customs and folklore of Dalarna. The play runs for 10 days at the end of July.

ESSENTIALS

GETTING THERE You can fly from Stockholm on **Skyways** (✆ **0771/95-95-00;** www.skyways.se); the nearest airport is **Dala airport** (✆ **0243/645-00;** www.dalaflyget.se), in Borlänge, 50km (31 miles) south, from which there is frequent bus and train service to Leksand. Car rentals are available at the airport.

There's a direct **train** from Stockholm to Mora that stops in Leksand (travel time: 3½ hr.). For reservations and information, call ✆ **771/75-75-75.**

Another way to reach Leksand is on the ***Gustaf Wasa*** ★; call ✆ **070/542-10-25** or visit www.wasanet.nu for information and reservations. Every Monday at 3pm it makes one long trip from Mora to Leksand (through Rättvik). The round-trip fare is 150SEK for adults, 75SEK for children. Tickets are sold onboard. The return is by train.

By car from Falun, our last stopover, head north on Route 80 to Bjursås, then go west on a secondary road signposted as SÅGMYRA. Follow the signs into Leksand.

VISITOR INFORMATION Contact the **Leksands Turistbyrå,** Kyrkallén 8, 793 31 Leksand (✆ **0247/79-61-30;** www.siljan.se), open June 15 to August 10 Monday to Friday 10am to 7pm, Saturday and Sunday 10am to 5pm; rest of the year Monday to Friday 10am to 5pm, and Saturday 10am to 2pm.

A SPECIAL EVENT

Sweden's biggest music festival, **Music at Lake Siljan** ★★★, takes place during the first week of July. There are some 100 concerts covering a wide range of music at venues in both Leksand and Rättvik. Fiddle music predominates. For information, contact **Music at Lake Siljan,** Karlsviks väg 2, S-79535 Rättvik (✆ **0248/102-90;** www.musikvidsiljan.se).

SEEING THE SIGHTS

Leksand's **parish church (Leksands Kyrka)** ★ is in the town center, on Norsgatan, near the lake (✆ **0247/807-00**). Founded in the 13th century, it assumed its present form in 1715 and is one of the largest rural churches in Sweden. During renovations in 1971, a burial site was found that dates to the period when the Vikings were being converted to Christianity. The church is open for worship throughout the year, but guided tours (in Swedish and English) are offered only from mid-June to early August. Tours are scheduled Monday to Saturday 10am to 1pm and 2 to 5pm, Sunday 1 to 5pm. Admission to the church is free; the tour costs 200SEK per person.

Nearby, also on Norsgatan, is an open-air museum, **Fräsgården** (✆ **0247/802-45**). The cluster of 18th- and 19th-century buildings (which are part of the museum's collections) features depictions by that period's peasants of Christ and his Apostles in Dalarna dress. The museum is open only from mid-June to mid-August, Tuesday to Friday noon to 4pm, Saturday and Sunday noon to 5pm. Admission is 30SEK for adults, free for children.

An athletic and health-conscious town, Leksand has ample opportunity for **outdoor sports.** There are downhill skiing facilities at the popular resort **Granberget,** about 20km (13 miles) to the southwest. The town's tourist office can provide information on swimming, cross-country skiing, curling, ice-skating, tennis, and boat rides on Lake Siljan. All are available in or near the town center, depending on the season and weather.

WHERE TO STAY

During the summer, you may find it fun to rent a *stuga* (log cabin) with four beds for 400SEK to 1,000SEK per night. You can use it as a base for exploring all of Dalarna.

The **Leksands Turistbyrå,** Norsgatan 40 (✆ **0247/79-61-30**), will book you into one. You also can inquire about renting a room in a private home.

Masesgården ★★ Beside a sea inlet, with a view of Leksand across the fjord, this is one of the most sports-and-fitness-conscious hotels in Sweden. It has a reputation for educating guests about new eating and exercise habits, and a philosophy of preventing disease and depression through proper diet and exercise. Most people spend a week, participating in supervised aerobic and sports regimes, not indulging in conventional spa-style pampering. Guest rooms are soothing and more plush than you might imagine. Though, this is not a holiday for the faint-hearted: Be prepared to sweat and reevaluate your lifestyle, in ways that might not always be completely comfortable.

Grytnäs 61, S-793 92 Leksand. www.masesgarden.se. ✆ **0247/645-60.** Fax 0247/122-51. 34 units, 23 with bathroom. 8,990SEK–10,020SEK per person per week double. Rates include all meals and 30 hr. of supervised sports activities. AE, DC, MC, V. Free parking. **Amenities:** Restaurant; Jacuzzi; indoor heated pool; sauna. *In room:* No phone.

Moskogen Motel You may not want to go through all the regimes attached to the previous recommendation. Moskogen offers very basic and very different types of accommodations, mostly red-painted summer cottages. You don't really have to rough it: The cottages aren't that basic and have a number of facilities. The rooms are well furnished and comfortable, with good beds. The Moskogen is 1.5km (1 mile) west of the railway station. The motel and red wooden huts make a good base for excursions around Lake Siljan.

Insjövägen 50, S-793 33 Leksand. www.moskogen.com. ✆ **0247/146-00.** Fax 0247/144-30. 49 units. 1,080SEK double; 1,550SEK suite. Rates include buffet breakfast. AE, DC, MC, V. Free parking. Bus: 58. **Amenities:** Bar; exercise room; Jacuzzi; 2 heated pools (1 indoor); sauna; tennis court. *In room:* TV.

WHERE TO DINE

Bosporen SWEDISH/TURKISH Most guests dine at their hotels, but this little eatery continues to attract the more independent-minded foodie. This restaurant, 360m (1,181 ft.) west of the railroad station, maintains longer, more reliable hours than any other place in town. Its Istanbul-derived name comes from the Turkish-born owners. The chefs are equally at home in the Swedish and Turkish kitchens. Shish kabob and Turkish salads are featured, but you can also order fried Baltic herring, sautéed trout, fresh salmon, or plank steak. The cooking is fair and even a bit exotic in a town not renowned for its restaurants.

Torget 1. ✆ **0247/132-80.** www.bosporen.com. Main courses 75SEK–219SEK. AE, DC, MC, V. Mon–Thurs 4–10pm; Fri 4pm–midnight; Sat noon–midnight; Sun noon–10pm.

Rättvik ★★

20km (13 miles) NE of Leksand, 275km (171 miles) NW of Stockholm

With some of the best hotels in the district, Rättvik is one of the most popular resorts bordering Lake Siljan. In summer, conducted tours begin here and go around Lake Siljan. Culture and tradition have long been associated with Rättvik; you'll find peasant costumes, folk dancing, Dalarna paintings, arts and crafts, fiddle music, and "church boats"—flamboyantly painted boats in which entire congregations floated for Sunday services. The old style of architecture is still prevalent, and you'll see many timber houses. Carpenters and painters from Rättvik are known for their craftsmanship.

ESSENTIALS

GETTING THERE You can reach Rättvik by **rail.** The Stockholm train to Mora stops in Leksand, where you can catch another train for the short trip to Rättvik. Train information in Stockholm is available at the **Central Station** (✆ **771/75-75-75**). Buses to Rättvik operate daily from Stockholm. There also is a bus connection between Leksand and Rättvik. For schedules, call ✆ **0771/21-82-18.**

By car from Leksand, head north on Route 70 into Rättvik.

VISITOR INFORMATION The **Rättvik Tourist Office** is in the train station, Riksvägen 40, 795 32 Rättvik (✆ **0248/79-72-10;** www.rattvik.se). It's open Monday to Friday 10m to 5pm, and Saturday 10am to 2pm.

SEEING THE SIGHTS

Don't overtax yourself running around taking in the minor attractions of Rättvik. Instead, come here to enjoy nature. For a sweeping view that stretches for many kilometers, drive 5km (3 miles) east of town along the road leading to Falun. Here, soaring more than 24m (79 ft.) skyward, is a red-sided wooden tower, originally built in 1897, called the **Vidablick,** Hantverksbyn (✆ **0248/102-30**). Be warned in advance that there's no elevator and the stairs are steep. Admission is free. On the premises are a coffee shop and a souvenir stand. The complex is open only from May 1 to September 6 daily from 10am to 5pm.

Gammelgården ★★ (✆ **0248/137-89**) is an antique Dalarna farmstead whose pastures and architecture evoke the 19th century. The Swedes are a bit crazy for their open-air museums, and at this point you may begin to tire of them. If not, take this one in. The hours are erratic—basically, it's open whenever a farm resident is able to conduct a tour—so it's important to phone in advance. Upon prior notification, visits can be arranged throughout the year, but regular scheduling is most likely between mid-June and mid-August daily from noon to 5pm. Admission is 20SEK. To reach Gammelgården from the center of Rättvik, 1.5km (1 mile) north of town along Route 70, follow the signs pointing to Mora.

You can also visit the artists' village (established by the Swedish artist Sören Erikson) at **Rättviks Hantverksby,** Gårdebyn (✆ **0248/302-50**).

WHERE TO STAY

Hotel Gärdebygården This hotel, off Storgatan in the town center, is a very good value. Opened in 1906, it is within a short walk of the lake, and has expanded to include a trio of outlying buildings. The comfortable rooms are sedately outfitted, with conservative furniture, but the bathrooms with shower units are very small. Some units have a view of the lake. The big breakfast is almost like a Swedish smorgasbord.

Hantverksbyn 4, S-795 36 Rättvik. www.dalawardshus.se. ✆ **0248/302-50.** Fax 0248/306-60. 44 units. 1,050SEK double. Rates include buffet breakfast. MC, V. Free parking. Closed Oct–May. Bus: 58 or 70. **Amenities:** Restaurant; bar. *In room:* TV, hair dryer, minibar.

Hotel Lerdalshöjden ★ This hotel has grown and prospered since 1943, when the Stefan Hagberg family took over its 11 rooms and one kitchen with a woodstove. In the 60 or so years since, they've built up a lively trade. New owners are now in charge but they carry on the same high standards of the long-ago Hagbergs. We like the panoramic views of Lake Siljan and the distant mountains from its location right next to ski slopes where it receives visitors year-round. Near the top of a hill overlooking Rättvik, the hotel is a 10-minute walk north of the lake. Guest rooms are well furnished and maintained.

Mickelsgatan, S-795 35 Rättvik. www.lerdalshojden.se. ✆ **0248/511-50.** Fax 0248/511-77. 96 units. 1,250SEK double; 1,950SEK suite. Children 11 and under stay free in parent's room. Rates include buffet breakfast. DC, MC, V. Free parking. Bus: 58 or 70. **Amenities:** Restaurant; bar; exercise room; Jacuzzi; room service; sauna. *In room:* TV, Wi-Fi (free).

WHERE TO DINE

Lerdalshöjden SWEDISH This summer-only restaurant is the only original section remaining in the turn-of-the-20th-century hotel. It has long been a favorite with lake-district locals. We join them in liking its traditional, tasty Swedish home-style cooking, including fresh fish and beef dishes. Try steak tartare with bleak (a freshwater fish) roe, or fried ptarmigan with red-currant sauce.

In the Lerdalshöjden Hotel. ✆ **0248/511-50.** Reservations recommended. Fixed-price 6-course menu 645SEK; main courses 265SEK-275SEK. DC, MC, V. Daily noon-2pm and 6-9pm. Closed Aug 16-June 14.

Mora ★

45km (28 miles) W of Rättvik, 328km (204 miles) NW of Stockholm

This old resort town in Upper Dalarna is a busy place in both summer and winter, and I find it a good base for touring the surrounding area. It is fabled as the town where King Gustav rallied the peasants to form an army to go against Denmark. This history-making event is commemorated every year in the 80km (50-mile) Vasa Race. Mora is also the hometown of the once-celebrated Anders Zorn, who is known mainly today for his paintings of nude women bathing. Between Lake Orsa and Lake Siljan, the provincial town of Mora is our final major stopover in the province.

ESSENTIALS

GETTING THERE You can **fly** from Stockholm on **Next Jet** (✆ **08/639-85-38;** www.nextjet.se); there are two flights per day Monday to Friday, and the flight time is 50 minutes. There are no flights on Saturday; on Sunday there is only one flight per day. The airport (✆ **0250/301-75;** www.dalaflyget.se) is about 6.5km (4 miles) from the center; taxis meet arriving flights.

There's direct **rail service** daily from Stockholm (trip time: 4 hr.). For information and schedules, call ✆ **771/75-75-75.**

Weekend **buses** leave from Stockholm's Central Station for the 4¼-hour trip. Contact **Swebus Vasatrafik** at ✆ **0771/21-82-18.**

The ***Gustaf Wasa*** (see "Essentials," in the "Leksand" section, above) travels between Mora and Leksand. The **boat** departs Leksand in the afternoon and leaves Mora at 3pm on Monday. Call ✆ **070/542-10-25** or visit www.wasanet.nu for information and reservations.

By car from Rättvik, continue around Lake Siljan on Route 70 to Mora.

VISITOR INFORMATION Contact the **Mora Turistbyrå,** Strandgatan 14, 792 30 Mora (✆ **0250/59-20-20;** www.siljan.se). It's open from Monday to Friday 10am to 5pm, and Saturday 10am to 2pm.

SEEING THE SIGHTS

Mora is home to a **Santa complex** (✆ **0250/287-70;** www.tomteland.se), which features Santa's house and factory. Visitors can meet Santa and see his helpers making and wrapping presents for children all over the world, and kids can enroll in Santa School and participate in troll and treasure hunts.

Mora also was the hometown of Anders Zorn (1860–1920), Sweden's most famous painter, and all of the town's top sights are associated with him. The first, **Lisselby,** is an area near the Zorn Museum made up of old houses that now are used as arts and crafts studios and boutiques.

Zornmuseet (Zorn Museum) ★★ The son of a brewer, Anders Zorn was born in Mora in 1860, showing incredible artistic talent at a very young age. He became Sweden's most internationally recognizable artist, in a class with fellow artist Carl Larsson and sculptor Carl Milles. Of all the paintings here, we find *Midnight* to be Zorn's masterpiece, although there are those who'll pay millions for his female nudes. The museum also displays works Zorn collected, including paintings from his chief rival, Carl Larsson, and Prince Eugene. He also gathered a large collection of the rural art and handicrafts of Dalarna.

Vasagatan 36. ✆ **0250/59-23-10.** www.zorn.se. Admission 60SEK adults, free for children 14 and under. Mid-May to Aug Mon–Sat 9am–5pm, Sun 11am–5pm; Sept to mid-May daily noon–4pm.

Zornsgården ★★ Zorn died here at the age of 60 in 1920, when he was full of new ideas and artistic projects. He and his wife, Emma, did not have any children. When Emma herself died in 1942 during the war, she donated almost all of their entire holdings, both property and art, to the state. Their former house is large and sumptuous, and they furnished it with exquisite taste, both in furnishings and, of course, in their choice of art. After visiting his former home, we always pay our respects to this great artist by going to his gravesite in Mora Cemetery.

Vasagatan 36. ✆ **0250/59-23-10.** www.zorn.se. Admission 90SEK adults, 20SEK children 7–15. Mid-May to Sept Mon–Sat 10am–4pm, Sun 11am–5pm; Oct to mid-May Mon–Sat noon–1pm and 2–3pm. Full tours of the house are conducted by guides at noon, 1, 2, and 3pm (in summer every 30 min.).

WHERE TO STAY & DINE

Best Western Mora Hotell & Spa ★ In terms of overall facilities and comfort, we'd rate this Best Western the best in town—you'll get no surprises, but no disappointments either. The Mora is in the center of town across from the lakefront, a minute's walk from the tourist bureau. Renovations over the years have added sun terraces and glassed-in verandas. The interior is tastefully decorated with bright colors and folkloric accents. All accommodations—mostly midsize bedrooms—have comfortable furniture, including ample bathrooms.

Strandgatan 12, S-792 30 Mora. www.bestwestern.com. ✆ **800/780-7234** or 0250/59-26-50. Fax 0250/189-81. 141 units. Sun–Thurs 1,598SEK–1,798SEK double, 1,998SEK suite; Fri–Sat 1,088SEK–1,288SEK double, 1,488SEK suite. Rates include buffet breakfast. AE, DC, MC, V. Free parking. **Amenities:** Restaurant; bar; babysitting; children's playground; exercise room; indoor heated pool; room service; spa. *In room:* TV, Wi-Fi (free).

Terrassen SWEDISH/INTERNATIONAL This restaurant is a good bet for a meal even if you aren't staying at the hotel. One of our American friends had elk here for the first time, but that nonhunter wasn't won over—maybe it's an acquired taste. We've always come away filled and satisfied, although hardly raving about the cuisine, which is of a high standard and reliable. Fresh produce is used whenever possible, and fresh fish and Swedish beef dishes are featured. Service is polite and efficient.

In the Best Western Mora Hotell & Spa, Strandgatan 12. ✆ **0250/59-26-50.** www.morahotell.se. Reservations recommended. Main courses 159SEK–325SEK. AE, DC, MC, V. Mon–Fri 11am–2pm and 6–9pm; Sat 6–9pm.

SHOPPING IN NEARBY NUSNÄS

In Nusnäs, about 9.5km (6 miles) southeast of Mora, you can watch the famous Dalarna horse *(dalahäst)* being made. You're free to walk around the workshops watching the craftspeople at work, and the finished products can be purchased at a shop on the premises. They also sell wooden shoes and other crafts items. **Nils Olsson Hemslöjd** (✆ **0250/372-00;** www.nohemslojd.se) is open from June to mid-August Monday to Friday 8am to 6pm, and Saturday and Sunday 9am to 5pm; and from mid-August to May Monday to Friday 8am to 5pm, and Saturday 10am to 2pm. To find Nusnäs, take the signposted main road east from Mora, turning off to the right at Farnas. From Mora, bus no. 108 also runs to Nusnäs.

FROM MORA BACK TO STOCKHOLM

From Mora, take Route 70. In Enköping, pick up E-18, which takes you to Stockholm.

GOTLAND (VISBY) ★★

219km (136 miles) S of Stockholm, 150km (93 miles) S of Nynäshamn, 89km (55 miles) E of the Swedish mainland

In the middle of the Baltic Sea, Gotland, with its cliffs, unusual rock formations, bathing beaches, and rolling countryside, is the ancient home of the Goths—about 121km (75 miles) long and 56km (35 miles) wide. Swedes go to the country's most popular tourist island for sunny vacations by the sea, whereas foreigners tend to be drawn to the old walled city of Visby; no town in all of Scandinavia evokes the romance and charm of the Middle Ages more than this once-powerful city.

If you can visit only one island of Sweden, make it Gotland. Buses traverse the island, as do organized tours out of Visby.

Essentials

GETTING THERE

BY PLANE Visitors can fly **SAS** to Gotland from Stockholm; the flight takes about 30 minutes. There is only one SAS flight a day in the summer from Stockholm to Visby. There are no flights in winter. **Skyways** (✆ **0771/959500;** www.skyways.se) has daily flights from Stockholm's Arlanda airport to Visby, year-round. The airport is 3km (1¾) north of Visby. For information and schedules, call ✆ **0770/72-77-27.** The only viable transit is via taxi; a one-way fare into the center of the city costs 300SEK. Taxis may or may not be waiting at the airport: If one isn't in line, pick up the telephone marked TAXI or TAXI-PHONE and ask for one.

BY BOAT Those who want to take the boat to Gotland must first go to Nynäshamn; by bus from Stockholm, it's about a 1-hour ride. The last car-ferry to Visby leaves at 11:30pm and takes about 3 hours and 15 minutes. In summer there are five daily connections. You can make reservations through your travel agent or directly with the ferry service, **Destination Gotland,** for cabin or car space. It's wise to book deck space if you plan to travel on a weekend. Call ✆ **0771/22-33-00** or visit www.destinationgotland.se.

VISITOR INFORMATION

In Visby, contact the tourist bureau, **Gotlands Turist Service,** Skeppsbron 4–6 (✆ **0498/20-33-00;** www.gtsab.se), open May to August Monday to Friday 8am to

7pm, Saturday and Sunday 7am to 6pm; September to April Monday to Friday 8am to 4pm.

A SPECIAL EVENT

I've attended many a festival in Sweden, but not one of them appealed to me as much as the annual **Medieval Week ★★** in August; for 8 days Visby once again becomes a Hanseatic town. At the harbor, Strandgatan swarms with people in medieval dress, many of them tending market stalls. Musicians play the hurdy-gurdy, the fiddle, and the flute; jesters play the fool. Toward nightfall a kingly procession comes into the square. The program has more than 100 such events during the festival, plus medieval mystery plays, masses, choral and instrumental music, tournaments, and displays of horses, as well as archery competitions, fire-eaters, belly dancers, and walking tours of the medieval town. Visit **www.medeltidsveckan.se** for more information.

Seeing the Sights

IN VISBY ★★

The walled city of Visby is made for wandering. The cobbled streets will carry you into many nooks and crannies. UNESCO has proclaimed Visby a World Heritage Site, something that must be carefully preserved for future generations to discover. Mercifully from the middle of May to the middle of August, vehicles are banned in the Alstadt, or Old Town.

The city is a marvel. The most enthusiastic visitors walk the entire perimeter of the walls, the **Ringmurer ★★★**, a distance of 3.5km (2¼ miles). The walls are riddled with medieval gates and towers. There is both a land wall and a sea wall, the latter 5.3m (17 ft.) tall. It was built as a fortification sometime in the late 1200s, incorporating an ancient gunpowder tower, the **Kruttornet ★**. The crenelated land wall is only 6m (20 ft.) high. Amazingly, a total of 27 of the original 29 towers are still standing.

Visby is a good town for walkers, but you may want to take one of the organized tours that are offered in season. Because so many of the sights, particularly the ruins of the 13th- and 14th-century churches, are better appreciated with some background, I recommend the tours that take 2 hours each and cost 100SEK per participant. They're offered only in summer, between mid-June and mid-August. Between mid-June and mid-July, English-language tours are conducted every Wednesday and Saturday at 11am.

In town, you can walk about, observing houses from the Middle Ages, ruined fortifications, and churches. Notable among these is the **Burmeisterska Huset,** the home of the *burmeister,* or the leading German merchant, at Strandgatan 9.

You can stroll down to the old **Hanseatic harbor** (not the same harbor in use today) and to the **Botanical Gardens,** which have earned Visby the title "City of Roses." You'll pass two of the most famous towers in the old wall—the **Maiden's Tower** (a peasant girl was buried alive here for helping a Danish king) and the **Powder Tower** (the oldest fortification in Visby).In the heyday of its power and glory, little Visby boasted 17 churches. Only one today, **Domkyrkan (Cathedral of St. Mary) ★★**, is in use. Found at Kyrkberget, it was dedicated in 1225 and was built with funds collected by German merchant ships. Pope Clement VI in Avignon gave his permission to build the so-called Swertingska chapel in 1349. The church was damaged in four serious fires: 1400, 1586, 1610, and 1744. It attained its status as a cathedral in 1572. The only original fixture left is a sandstone font from the 1200s. Hours are daily 8am to 8pm. Free admission. For more information, call **✆ 0498/206-800.**

The ruins of the former **Dominican Monastery of St. Nicholas** are just down the road from Domkyrkan. The church has a rose window cut from a single big stone—it's more than 3m (10 ft.) in diameter. Work began on the monastery in 1230, but it was destroyed by Lübeck forces in 1525. For more information, call **© 0498/206-800.**

Another sightseeing recommendation is the impressive **Gotlands Fornsal ★★**, the Historical Museum of Gotland, Strandgatan 14 (**© 0498/29-27-00;** www.gotlandsmuseum.se), on a medieval street noted for its step-gabled houses. We'd vote this one of the best regional museums in the country—it's certainly among the largest, and you'll need to devote about 2 hours to take in the highlights. The museum contains artifacts discovered on Gotland, including carved stones dating from A.D. 400, art from medieval and later periods, plus furniture and household items. After five floors of exhibitions, and 8,000 years of history, we like to wind down at the on-site cafe and browse through the bookstore. It's open from May 15 to August daily 10am to 5pm, September to May 14 Tuesday to Sunday noon to 4pm. Admission is 80SEK for adults, free for children 16 and under.

Exploring the Island

At the **Turistbyrå,** Skeppsbron 4–6 (**© 0498/20-33-00**), ask what island tours are scheduled during your visit; these daily tours (different every day) are the best way to get a quick overview of Gotland. The price can be as low as 70SEK for a brief walking tour or as high as 550SEK for a complete tour of the island by van.

One thing you can be sure of is that each tour will visit the **Lummelunda Grottan,** Lummelunds Bruk (**© 0498/27-30-50;** www.lummelundagrottan.se), a karst cave formed of limestone bedrock by a subterranean stream. The explored part of the stream cave stretches for 4km (2½ miles) and contains stalactite and stalagmite formations, fossil remains, and subterranean waters. The part of the cave with some of the biggest and most beautiful chambers is open to visitors. It's 13km (8 miles) north of Visby along Route 149. A bus departs from Österport Visby from June 19 to August 14 daily at 2pm. The cave is open May 1 to June 5 daily 10am to 3pm; June 6 to June 27 daily 10am to 4pm; June 28 to July 10 daily 10am to 5pm; July 11 to August 13 daily 9am to 6pm; August 14 to August 22 daily 10am to 4pm; August 23 to September 30 daily 10am to 2pm. Visits on your own cost 120SEK for adults, 70SEK for children 5 to 15, free for children 4 and under.

A DRIVING TOUR If you are pressed for time, stick to the sights in Visby. But if you have 4 or 5 hours and have rented a car, this road tour of Gotland encapsulates the island in a nutshell. Arm yourself with a good road map of Gotland before setting out. If you get lost that's all right, as the island is too small to be lost for long.

From Visby, drive north on Route 149, heading toward the fishing port of **Lickershamn.** Look for a narrow trail along the cliffs. This path leads you to a rock that juts into the water. Known as the *Maiden,* this promontory offers some of the best views on Gotland.

From Lickershamn, continue along Route 149, passing to the towns of **Ire** and **Kappelshamn.** From Kappelshamn, follow Route 149 south to the junction with Route 148 in **Lärbro.** Here, go north on Route 148 to **Fårösund.** The village of Fårösund sits on the shores of the 1.5km-wide (1-mile) Fårösund channel, which separates the small island of **Fårö** from the main island of Gotland. You can take a ferry to Fårö to visit some of the island's superb beaches.

From Fårösund, take Route 148 back to Lärbro. A few kilometers past Lärbro, take Route 146 southwest toward **Slite.** Follow it down the coast to **Aurungs.** Here, go west on a secondary road heading toward **Siggur.** In Siggur, follow signs south to the village of **Dalhem.** The most remarkable sight in Dalhem is the village church, just outside town. Its wall paintings and stained glass are the finest on Gotland. Train buffs may enjoy visiting the Railway Museum in the old train station.

From Dalhem, continue south toward **Roma** on the road that brought you to town. Look for the ruins of Roma Abbey, a Cistercian monastery destroyed during the Protestant Reformation.

Head west from Roma on a secondary road toward Route 140 that runs along Gotland's western coast. You'll pass the villages of **Bander** and **Sojvide** before you reach Route 140. Follow it south to **Burgsvik,** a popular port and resort town. Just east of Burgsvik, visit the small hamlet of **Öja.** Its church boasts a triumphal cross dating from the 13th century.

After visiting Öja, return to Burgsvik. Here you head south, passing the villages of **Bottarvegården** and **Vamlingbo.** At the southern tip of Gotland you'll find **Hoburgen,** with its towering lighthouse. Along with the lighthouse, you'll encounter cliffs, many with strange rock formations, and a series of caves.

Return to Burgsvik to connect with Route 140. Turn off after **Fidenäs,** following Route 142 toward **Hemse.** Outside Hemse, take Route 144 to **Ljugarn,** a small port and resort town on Gotland's east coast. Just south of Ljugarn, on a secondary road, is a series of Bronze Age stone sculptures. The seven rock formations, depicting ancient ships, form the largest group of stone settings on the island.

Follow Route 143 northwest from Ljugarn to return to Visby.

Where to Stay

If you should arrive without reservations (not a good idea), contact the **Gotland Resort** (✆ **0498/20-12-60;** www.gotlandsresor.se). The English-speaking staff will try to arrange for rooms in a hotel or private home in or near Visby. The average rate for accommodations in a private home is 550SEK per person, per night.

Best Western Hotell Solhem On a slope overlooking the harbor, in the middle of a beautiful park, Palissadparken, Solhem is the most tranquil choice in Visby. Bedrooms are comfortable, cozy, and warm, with simple but tasteful furniture and small bathrooms. The owners have made an attempt to see that no two rooms look alike. Even so, some of them, though comfortable, look a bit like an upmarket college dormitory in an East Coast American university. Speaking of dormitories, some of the rooms house six persons in reasonable comfort, with extra beds costing 500SEK for adults or 300SEK for children.

Solhemsgatan 3, S-621 58 Visby. www.hotellsolhem.se. ✆ **0498/25-90-00.** Fax 0498/25-90-11. 94 units. 990SEK–1,850SEK double. Rates include buffet breakfast. AE, DC, MC, V. Free parking. **Amenities:** Babysitting; sauna; Wi-Fi (free, in lobby). *In room:* TV, hair dryer.

Best Western Strand Hotel This site was once the Visby Brewery but the owners, the Wiman family, agreed in 1982 to stop making suds and turn the place into a hotel. Originally it had only 13 rooms, but this hotel has grown to 110 accommodations, each spread across three buildings that look older than they are. Guests meet fellow guests in the library or in the adjoining bar—civilized spots for reading Keats or downing a Swedish beer. The comfortable bedrooms are midsize and tastefully modern.

Strandgatan 34, S-621 56 Visby. www.strandhotel.net. ✆ **800/528-1234** in the U.S., or 0498/25-88-00. Fax 0498/25-88-11. 110 units. 1,250SEK–2,110SEK. Rates include buffet breakfast. AE, DC, MC, V. Free parking. **Amenities:** Bar; babysitting; indoor heated pool; sauna; Wi-Fi (free, in lobby). *In room:* TV, hair dryer, minibar.

Clarion Hotel Visby ★★ If you want more of a homey hotel, check into the St Clemens. But if you want the most glamorous hotel on the island, make it the Clarion. Close to the harborfront in the town center, its historic core includes medieval foundations and additions that span several centuries. The bedrooms are conservatively elegant, and some have reproductions of 18th-century furniture. The best feature of the hotel, which makes it the finest place to stay off-season, is a winter garden, a bold combination of steel, glass, and Gotland sandstone. We like to relax in a leather armchair here with a drink and admire the greenery and the changing Nordic light.

Strandgatan 6, S-621 24 Visby. www.wisbyhotell.se. ✆ **0498/25-75-00.** Fax 0498/25-75-50. 134 units. 1,190SEK–2,790SEK double; 2,460SEK–5,460SEK suite. Rates include buffet breakfast. AE, DC, MC, V. Parking 140SEK. **Amenities:** 2 restaurants; 2 bars; indoor heated pool; room service; sauna. *In room:* TV, hair dryer, minibar, Wi-Fi (free).

Hotel St. Clemens ★ Once an 18th-century building, this centrally located hotel is now composed of a series of five antique buildings connected by two idyllic gardens. It's open year-round, and the staff is helpful and efficient. No two rooms are identical; your choices range from the smallest single in the shoemaker's old house with a view over church ruins, to a four-bed unit with a sloping ceiling and botanical garden greenery framing the window. The old stable has rooms for guests with allergies.

Smedjegatan 3, S-621 55 Visby. www.clemenshotell.se. ✆ **0498/21-90-00.** Fax 0498/27-94-43. 30 units. 850SEK–1,750SEK double; 1,350SEK–2,400SEK suite. Additional bed 400SEK extra. Rates include buffet breakfast. AE, DC, MC, V. Parking 70SEK. **Amenities:** Sauna. *In room:* TV, fridge (in most), hair dryer, Wi-Fi (free).

Where to Dine

Burmeister ITALIAN/INTERNATIONAL Don't expect too much, and you won't be disappointed here. This large restaurant in the town center offers dining indoors or under shady fruit trees in the garden of a 16th-century house originally built for the wealthiest citizen of Visby. Diners can look out on the surrounding medieval buildings from many of the tables. The cuisine is rather standard international. Though the dishes aren't exceptional, they're far from disappointing. It's incredibly popular during summer—so they must be doing something right. After 10pm in the summer, the restaurant becomes a dance club whose cover charge ranges from 100SEK to 250SEK.

Strandgatan 6. ✆ **0498/21-03-73.** www.clematis.se. Reservations required. 2-course fixed-price menu 390SEK; 3-course fixed-price menu 450SEK. AE, DC, MC, V. June 20–Aug 1 Mon–Sat noon–4pm and 6–11pm. Disco mid-June to Aug 1 Mon–Sat 10pm–2am.

Donners Brunn ★★★ FRENCH/SWEDISH If you're feeling adventurous and want to tempt your palate, make the 2-minute walk from the harbor to the finest restaurant on the island. Its chef and owner is Bo Nilsson, the former chef of Operakällaren, arguably the finest restaurant in Stockholm. Striking out on his own, he has taken over this 17th-century building on a small square in the heart of town and has established a showcase for his own refined cuisine, which focuses on market-fresh produce and seasonally based dishes that are truly sublime. You might begin with a tempting platter of Baltic herring, or else a pot of mussels flavored with chorizo sausage. The signature dish is Gotland lamb with fresh asparagus served with a freshly made hollandaise. Always count on a fresh fish platter along with a selection of other main dishes, which can range from the humble to the noble.

Donners plats 3. ✆ **0498/27-10-90.** www.donnersbrunn.se. Reservations required in summer. Main courses 245SEK–320SEK; 4-course menu 620SEK. AE, DC, MC, V. June–Sept daily 6pm–2am; off-season Mon–Sat 6pm–midnight.

G:a Masters ★ SWEDISH In the heart of Visby, G:a Masters is one of the island's leading restaurants, patronized by locals as well as summer visitors, who spill out onto the open-air terrace. Expect good food, a fine selection of wine, and music. Whenever available, locally sourced meats and produce are used. The starters are well crafted, especially the Jerusalem artichoke soup or the salmon tartare. From the mouthwatering menu, you can select grilled filet of veal with buttered fresh chanterelles, or a filet of char marinated in dill and juniper and served with morels in a white-wine sauce.

Södra Krykogatan 10. ✆ **0498/216-655.** Reservations recommended. Main courses 175SEK–285SEK. AE, MC, V. Daily 6pm–2am.

Gutekällaren ★ SWEDISH The ambience here is considerably more sober than in the rest of this fun-loving island, but once the dining is out of the way, the place really livens up (see "Visby After Dark," below). This restaurant and bar in the town center originally was built as a tavern in the early 1600s on foundations that are much older. It was enlarged in 1789 and today is one of the oldest buildings (if not *the* oldest) in Visby. The menu is solid and reliable, featuring fresh ingredients; it offers fresh fish and meat dishes, including some vegetarian specialties. You might begin with a delectable fish soup made with lobster and shrimp, then follow with filet of sole Waleska or roast lamb chops.

Stortorget 3, Visby. ✆ **0498/21-00-43.** www.gutekallaren.com. Reservations recommended. 5-course menu 450SEK; 8-course menu 650SEK. AE, DC, MC, V. Daily 6–11pm.

Munkkällaren ★ SWEDISH/INTERNATIONAL This restaurant is one of the best in town, although it hardly has the chef at Donners Brunn rattling his pots and pans in fear of the competition. You'll recognize it in the center of Visby by its brown wooden facade. The dining room, which is only a few steps from the street, is sheathed in white stone, parts of which date from 1100. In summer, the management opens the doors to two more pubs in the compound. The main pub, Munken, offers platters of good-tasting and flavorful *husmanskost* (Swedish home cooking), including *frikadeller* (meatballs). Live music is often performed in the courtyard, beginning around 8pm. After the music stops, a dance club opens Friday to Sunday from 11pm to 2am. Admission to the club is 100SEK.

Lilla Torggränd 2, Visby. ✆ **0498/27-14-00.** www.munkkällaren.se. Reservations required in summer. Main courses 158SEK–265SEK; 3-course menu 375SEK. AE, DC, MC, V. Restaurant Mon–Sat 6–11pm. Pub Mon–Sat 9pm–2am (June 1–Aug 7 noon–11pm).

Shopping

The most memorable goods available are produced on the island, usually by individual craftspeople working in highly detailed, small-scale productions. Our favorite store is **Yllet,** St. Hansgatan 19, Visby (✆ **0498/21-40-44;** www.yllet.se), where clothing made from wool produced by local sheep is sold in the form of sweaters, scarves, hats, gloves, coats, and winter wear for men, women, and children. Also, don't overlook the gift shop that's showcased within the island's historical museum, **Gotlands Fornsal,** Strandgatan 14, Visby (✆ **0498/29-27-00**), where reproductions of some of the museum's art objects are for sale, as well as handmade handicrafts and textiles.

Gotland is home to dozens of highly skilled, independent artists, who mostly work out of their own houses or studios manufacturing ceramics, textiles, woodcarvings, or examples of metalwork. Some of their merchandise can be purchased at **Galerie Kvinnfolki,** Donnersplats 4 (✆ **0498/21-00-51;** www.kvinnfolki.se), which limits its merchandise to items crafted by women: jam made from local berries, textiles, children's clothing, and a line of cosmetics made from all-natural ingredients.

Visby After Dark

A lot more energy is expended on stargazing, wave-watching, and ecology in Gotland than on barhopping and nocturnal flirting. The island's premier venue for folks over 40 who enjoy dancing "very tight" (ballroom style) occurs every Saturday night at the **Borgen Bar,** Södra Murgatan 53 (✆ **0498/24-79-55**), which contains a restaurant, a dance floor, and recorded music that ranges from the big-band era to more modern, supper-club selections. A hipper alternative is the **Munkkällaren,** which was recommended previously as a restaurant and derives at least some of its business from its role as a bar and late-night, weekend-only dance club. It's a good pickup spot. A similar atmosphere is found at **Gutekällaren,** another previously recommended restaurant, whose interior becomes a dance club either 2 or 4 nights a week, beginning around 10pm, for high-energy dancers mostly ages 35 and under. If you happen to be a bit older than 35, you'll still feel comfortable hanging out at the establishment's bar, soaking up aquavit, and absorbing the local color.

SWEDISH LAPLAND ★★★

Swedish Lapland—Norrland, to the Swedes—is the last wilderness of Europe. The vast northern Land of the Midnight Sun has crystal-blue lakes, majestic mountains, glaciers, waterfalls, rushing rivers, and forests. Lapland covers roughly half the area of Sweden (one-quarter of which is north of the Arctic Circle).

The sun doesn't set for 6 weeks in June and July, and brilliant colors illuminate the sky. In spring and autumn, many visitors come here to see the northern lights.

Swedish Lapland is a paradise for hikers and campers (if you don't mind the mosquitoes in the summer). Before you go, get in touch with the **Svenska Turistföreningen (Swedish Touring Club),** PO Box 17251, S-104 62 Stockholm (✆ **08/463-21-00;** www.stf.nu). It maintains mountain hotels and has built bridges and marked hiking routes. The touring club has a number of boats in Lapland that visitors can use for tours of lakes. There are hundreds of kilometers of marked hiking and skiing tracks. March, April, and even May are recommended for skiing. Some 90 mountain hotels or huts (called *fjällstugor* and *kåtor*) are available, with beds and bedding, cooking utensils, and firewood. Huts can be used for only 1 or 2 nights. The club also sponsors mountain stations (*fjällstationer*).

Luleå

931km (578 miles) N of Stockholm

This is the northernmost major town in all of Sweden and can be viewed as a refueling stop and a place for food and shelter. While fire destroyed most of the Old Town, Luleå is not totally devoid of charm. If you have 2 or 3 hours to wander about, you can visit the town's original settlement, which enjoys protection as a UNESCO World Heritage Site.

Our tour north begins in Luleå on the way to Lapland. This port city on Sweden's east coast at the northern end of the Gulf of Bothnia is 113km (70 miles) south of the Arctic Circle. Boats depart from its piers for some 300 offshore islets and skerries known for their flora and fauna.

Luleå has a surprisingly mild climate—its average annual temperature is only a few degrees lower than that of Malmö, on the southern tip of Sweden.

The town of Luleå is a port for shipping iron ore in summer. Its harbor remains frozen over until May. The state-owned ironworks here have led to a dramatic growth in population.

Today, as the seat of the University of Luleå, the town has a population of 70,000 and is liveliest when the students are here in winter, although most visitors (except businesspeople) see it only in summer.

ESSENTIALS

GETTING THERE **By Plane** **SAS** runs nine flights Sunday to Friday between Stockholm and Luleå (two on Sat), which take 1¼ hours. **City Airline** runs nine flights each weekday between Gothenburg and Luleå (one on Sat), which take 1 hour and 40 minutes. To contact this airline call © 0200/250500 (within Sweden) or © 031/600385. The airline's website is www.cityairline.com. **Skellefteå airport** (**SFT; © 0770/72-77-27;** www.skellefteaairport.com) is 14km (8⅔ miles) south of Luleå; the Flygbuss costs 80SEK per person each way, and a taxi goes for 300SEK each way.

By Train From Stockholm to Luleå there are only two direct night trains daily, leaving Stockholm at 6:12pm and 8:42pm. The trip takes 14 hours. From Gothenburg to Luleå there is only one night train per day, leaving Gothenburg at 5pm and arriving in Luleå at 11am. For more information, call **© 0771/75-75-75.**

By Bus A bus runs between Stockholm and Luleå, taking 14 hours. Service between Stockholm and **Tapanis Buss** (**© 0922/12955;** www.tapanis.se) has several buses per week between Stockholm and Luleå.

By Car From Stockholm, take the E-4 expressway north to Uppsala and continue northward along the coast until you reach Luleå.

VISITOR INFORMATION Contact the **Luleå Tourist Office** at Kulturens Hus at Skeppsbrogatan 17 (**© 0920/45-70-00;** www.visitlulea.se), open in summer Monday to Friday 10am to 6pm, Saturday 10am to 4pm; off-season Monday to Friday 10am to 5pm.

SEEING THE SIGHTS

It is a rare privilege to visit any town in the north of Sweden that enjoyed its heyday in the 17th century, and this historic place doesn't disappoint. Some of the most evocative and historic architecture in Luleå is 9.5km (6 miles) north of the modern city in **Gammelstad (Old Town)** ★★, the town's original medieval core, and a once-thriving trading center. Its demise as a viable commercial center began when the nearby harbor became clogged with silt and was rendered unnavigable. In 1649, a new city, modern-day Luleå, was established, and the Old Town—except the church described below—fell into decline and disrepair. Today it serves as the site of the region's most famous church, **Gammelstads Kyrka** ★★, also known as Neder Lulea Kyrka (no phone). This is the largest medieval church in the north. Built in 1492, the church is surrounded by clusters of nearly identical red-sided huts, many of which date from the 18th and 19th centuries. Admission is free, and it's open mid-June to mid-August daily 9am to 8pm; mid-August to mid-June Monday to Friday 10am to 2pm.

Gammelstad's other major site is the **Hägnan Museum** (also known as the Gammelstads Friluftsmuseum), 95400 Gammelstad (✆ **0920/45-48-66;** www.lulea.se/hagnan), consisting of about a dozen historic buildings hauled in from throughout Norrbotten—though, frankly, we've seen better compounds in the south. It's open between June 6 and August 15 daily from 10am to 5pm, depending on the season. Entrance is free. To reach Gammelstad from modern-day Luleå, take bus no. 8 or 9 from Luleå's center.

Adjacent to Gammelstad Bay you'll find some of the richest bird life in Sweden. Ornithologists have counted 285 different species of birds during the spring migrations. The best way to experience this cornucopia of avian life involves following a well-marked hiking trail for 7km (4⅓ miles) south of Gammelstad. Signs will point from Gammelstad to the **Gammelstads Vikens Naturreservat ★★**. For information about the trail, call the Luleå Tourist Office (see above). The trail, consisting of well-trod earth, gravel, and boardwalks, traverses marshy, usually forested terrain teeming with bird life. En route, you'll find barbecue pits for picnics and an unstaffed, unsupervised 9m (30-ft.) tower (Kömpmannholmen, no phone) that's useful for spying on bird nests in the upper branches of nearby trees. The trail ends in Luleå's suburb of Pörson, site of the local university and a small museum, **Teknykens Hus,** Pörson, 97187 Luleå (✆ **0920/49-22-01;** www.teknikenshus.se). Conceived as a tribute to the industries that bring employment and prosperity to Norrbotten, it charges an admission fee of 60SEK for adults or 30SEK for ages 5 to 17. In summer the attraction is open daily 10am to 4pm; off-season Tuesday to Sunday 10am to 4pm. From Pörson, after your visit to the museum, take bus no. 4 or 5 back to Luleå. Hiking along the above-mentioned trail is not recommended in winter, as heavy snowfalls obliterate the signs and the path, and it's unsafe for all but the most experienced residents.

Norrbottens Museum Close to the city center at Hermelin Park, Norrbottens Museum shelters the world's most complete collection of Sami artifacts. This is a good place to orient yourself before you move even deeper beyond the Arctic Circle and actually meet the Sami. The museum also showcases how these weather-beaten people forged a living in these northern regions in bygone days.

Storgatan 2. ✆ **0920/24-35-00.** Free admission. Sept–May Tues–Fri 10am–4pm, Sat–Sun noon–4pm; June–Aug Mon–Fri 10am–4pm; Sat–Sun noon–4pm. Bus: 1, 2, 4, 5, 8, or 9.

WHERE TO STAY & DINE

Elite Stadshotellet ★★ The Stadshotellet is in a stately, architecturally ornate, brick-and-stone building that stood here at the turn of the 20th century. The airport bus stops right outside the door at a site near the north harbor, and both the bus and the train stations are within walking distance. The hotel was conceived by "six local gentlemen" back in 1897, and they demanded a magnificent facade with excellent stone craftsmanship, spires, and towers. Each room is individually decorated and accommodations are also the most spacious in town, especially the large and luxurious suites.

Storgatan 15, S-971 81 Luleå. www.elite.se. ✆ **0920/27-40-00.** Fax 0920/670-92. 158 units. Mon–Thurs 1,550SEK–1,900SEK double; Fri–Sun 860SEK–1,100SEK double; all week 2,100SEK–2,650SEK suite. Rates include buffet breakfast. AE, DC, MC, V. Parking 150SEK. Bus: 1, 2, 4, 5, 8, or 9. **Amenities:** Restaurant; bar; exercise room; room service; sauna. *In room:* TV, hair dryer, minibar, Wi-Fi (free).

THE ice HOTEL

Since the late 1980s, the most unusual, and most impermanent, hotel in Sweden is re-created early every winter on the frozen steppes near the iron mines of Jukkasjärvi, 200km (124 miles) north of the Arctic Circle. Here, the architect Yngve Bergqvist, financed by a group of friends who (not surprisingly) developed the original concept over bottles of vodka in an overheated sauna, uses jackhammers, bulldozers, and chainsaws to fashion a 60-room hotel out of 4,000 tons of densely packed snow and ice. The basic design is that of an igloo, but with endless amounts of whimsical sculptural detail thrown in as part of the novelty. The resulting dwelling will inevitably buckle, collapse, and then vanish during the spring thaws. During the long and frigid northern Sweden's midwinter, it attracts a steady stream of engineers, sociologists, and the merely curious, who avail themselves of timely activities in Sweden's far north: dog-sled and snowmobile rides, cross-country skiing, and shimmering views of the aurora borealis. On the premises are an enormous reception hall, a theater, two saunas, and an ice chapel appropriate for simple meditation, weddings, and baptisms.

Available for occupancy (temperatures permitting) generally between mid-December and sometime in April, the hotel resembles an arctic cross between an Arabian casbah and a medieval cathedral. Minarets are formed by dribbling water for about a week onto what eventually becomes a slender and soaring pillar of ice. Domes are formed igloo style out of ice blocks arranged in a curved-roof circle. Reception halls boast rambling vaults supported by futuristic-looking columns of translucent ice, and sometimes whimsical sculptures whose sense of the absurd heightens a venue that is somewhat surreal. Some of these are angled in ways that amplify the weak midwinter daylight that filters through panes of (what else?) chainsawed ice.

The interior decor is, as you'd expect, hyperglacial, and loaded with insights into what the world might look like if an atomic war drove civilization underground to confront its stark and frigid destiny. Most rooms resemble a setting

Hotel Nordkalotten ★★ Five kilometers (3 miles) south of the town center, this is the most architecturally intriguing hotel in the region, with some of the most charming grace notes. In 1984, the hotel was acquired by an independent entrepreneur who was lucky enough to secure thousands of first-growth pine logs (many btw. 600 and 1,000 years old) that had been culled from forests in Finland and Russia. He hired well-known Finnish architect Esko Lehmola to arrange the logs into the structural beams and walls of the hotel's reception area, sauna, and convention center; and the result is a source of endless fascination for foresters and botanists.

Guest rooms are outfitted in soothing tones of beige and gray, with conservatively contemporary furnishings, tiled bathrooms, and wall-to-wall carpeting.

Lulviksvägen 1, S-972 54 Luleå. www.nordkalotten.com. ✆ **0920/20-00-00.** Fax 0920/20-00-90. 172 units. Sun–Thurs 1,940SEK double room with sauna, 1,440SEK standard double; Fri–Sat 1,440SEK double room with sauna, 840SEK standard double. Rates include buffet breakfast. AE, DC, MC, V. Free parking. From Luleå's center, follow the signs to the airport. **Amenities:** Restaurant; bar; children's playground; exercise room; indoor heated pool; sauna. *In room:* TV, minibar, Wi-Fi (free).

from a scary 1950s sci-fi flick, sometimes with an icy version of a pair of skin-draped Adirondack chairs pulled up to the surreal glow of an electric fireplace that emits light but, rather distressingly, no heat.

What's the most frequently asked question on the lips of virtually everyone who shows up? "Is it comfortable?" The answer is "not particularly," although a stay probably will enhance your appreciation of the (warm and modern) comforts of conventional housing. Upon arrival, guests are issued thermal jumpsuits of "beaver nylon" whose air-lock cuffs are designed to help the wearer survive temperatures as low as -8°F (-22°C). Beds are fashioned from blocks of chiseled ice lavishly draped, Eskimo style, with reindeer skins. Guests keep warm with insulated body bags that were developed for walks on the moon. Other than a temporary escape into the hotel's sauna, be prepared for big chills: Room temperatures remain cold enough to keep the walls from melting. Some claim that this exposure will bolster your immune system so that it can better fight infections when you return to your usual environment.

Guests stand at the long countertop crafted from ice that doubles as a bar. Swedish vodka dyed a (frigid) shade of blue is served in cups crafted from ice. Vodka never gets any colder than this.

Interested in this holiday on ice? Contact the **Ice Hotel,** Marknadsvägen 63, S-981 91 Jukkasjärvi, Sweden (✆ **0980/668-00;** fax 0980/668-90; www.icehotel.com). Doubles cost from 2,500SEK to 5,400SEK and suites from 3,400SEK to 7,000SEK per day, including breakfast. Heated cabins, located near the ice palace, are available from 2,300SEK to 3,390SEK per night for a double. Toilets are available in a heated building next door. The ice hotel is open between December 10 and April 16. The summer season is between June 10 and August 22. During this time no cold accommodations are available. From Kiruna, head east immediately along Route E-10 until you come to a signpost marked JUKKASJÄRVI and follow this tiny road northeast for about 2.5km (1½ miles).

FROM LULEÅ TO JOKKMOKK

From Luleå, take Route 97 northwest. Thirty minutes into the trip, you can stop at **Boden.** Founded in 1809, this is Sweden's oldest garrison town. After losing Finland to Russia, Sweden built this fortress to protect its interior from a Russian invasion. Visit the **Garnisonsmuseet (Garrison Museum),** which has exhibits on military history, as well as many uniforms and weapons used throughout Sweden's history. It's open from June to September Monday to Thursday from noon to 4pm, charging 10SEK for admission. It is at the southwest edge of town. After visiting Boden, continue along Route 97 to Jokkmokk.

Jokkmokk ★

198km (123 miles) NW of Luleå, 1,191km (740 miles) N of Stockholm

Surrounded by a vast wilderness, this little community on the Luleå River, just north of the Arctic Circle, is the best center for immersing yourself into the culture of the Sami. It has been their cultural center and trading post since the 1600s.

Jokkmokk, meaning "bend in the river," is also the finest base in Lapland we've found for exploring the great outdoors. For some a car will be vital here, and while bus routes link Jokkmokk to surrounding villages, the system offers service that is too infrequent to be of practical use by the average visitor.

Other than the summer tourists, visitors are mostly business travelers involved in some aspect of the timber industry or the hydroelectric power industry. Jokkmokk and the 12 hydroelectric plants that are nearby produce as much as 25% of all the electricity used in Sweden. Most residents of the town were born here, except for a very limited number of urban refugees from Stockholm.

ESSENTIALS

GETTING THERE The nearest **airport** is in Luleå, 198km (123 miles) away (see "Getting There," in the "Luleå" section, above, or call **SAS** at ✆ **0770/72-77-27**). From Luleå, you can take a bus for the final leg of the journey.

No trains run between Stockholm and Jokkmokk. However, one daily **train** makes the run from Stockholm to Murjek, a town 60km (37 miles) to the south of Jokkmokk. From Murjek, you can take one of three buses a day for the final lap into Jokkmokk.

One scheduled **bus** journeys per day from Luleå to Jokkmokk; it is timed to meet the plane's arrival. For information, call ✆ **0771/21-82-18.**

By car from Luleå, take Route 97 northwest.

VISITOR INFORMATION Contact the **Jokkmokk Turistbyrå,** Stortorget 4 (✆ **0971/222-50;** www.turism.jokkmokk.se); it is open from June to mid-August daily from 10am to 6pm, from mid-August to May Monday to Friday 8:30am to noon and 1 to 4pm.

SEEING THE SIGHTS

At a point 7km (4.3 miles) south of Jokkmokk, you cross the Arctic Circle if you're traveling along Route 45. At a kiosk here, you'll be given a souvenir certificate in case you need to prove to anybody that you're a genuine arctic explorer.

Jokkmokk is the site of the **Great Winter Market ★★★**, a 400-year-old tradition. It's the best place in Scandinavia to stock up on smoked reindeer meat. Sami from all over the north, including Finland and Norway, come to this grand market held the first weekend of February from Thursday to Sunday. Sami display and sell those precious handicrafts they've been working on during the bitter winter months. Some 30,000 people flock to this market every year. If you're planning a visit, you'll need to make reservations a year in advance.

Salmon fishing is possible in the town's central lake. Locals jump in the river in summer to take a dip, but we suggest you watch from the sidelines unless you like to swim in near-freezing waters.

Karl IX decreed that the winter meeting place of the Jokkmokk Sami would be the site of a market and church. The first church, built in 1607, was known as the **Lapp Church.** A nearby hill, known as **Storknabben,** has a cafe from which, if the weather is clear, the midnight sun can be seen for about 20 days in midsummer.

It is only fitting that Jokkmokk is home to the national Swedish Mountain and Sami Museum, or **Ájtte ★★★**, Kyrkogatan (✆ **0971/170-70;** www.ajtte.com), in the center of town. This museum (whose Sami name translates to "storage hut") is the largest of its kind; its exhibits integrate nature and the cultures of the Swedish mountain region. One part of the museum is the **Alpine Garden,** which is close to the museum on Lappstavägen. If you want to learn about the natural environment and the flora of the north of Sweden, this is the place to go. The mountain flora is easily accessible and beautifully arranged. There's also a restaurant and a gift shop.

Museum admission is 60SEK for adults, free for children 17 and under. The museum is open year-round; in summer, Monday to Friday 11am to 5pm, and Saturday and Sunday noon to 5pm; off-season, it closes at 4pm.

WHERE TO STAY & DINE

Hotel Jokkmokk ★ The largest and best-appointed hotel in town was built in the mid-1980s, near the town center, and close to Lake Talvatis. Designed in a modern format that includes simple, boxy lines and lots of varnished hardwoods, it offers all the well-upholstered comforts of a big-city hotel, along with well-maintained, well-organized, comfortable shelter against the sometimes-savage climate. Guest rooms have big windows overlooking the lake, the forest, and, in some cases, the lakeside road. All have fresh colors inspired by a Scandinavian springtime. Six of the units are designated as "ladies' rooms"—especially feminine bedrooms adorned with pastels and florals.

PO Box 85, Solgatan 455-96231, S-262 23 Jokkmokk. www.hoteljokkmokk.se. ✆ **0971/777-00.** Fax 0971/777-90. 89 units. Mid-June to mid-Aug 995SEK double; rest of year Mon–Thurs 1,595SEK double, Fri–Sun 995SEK double; year-round 1,850SEK suites. Rates include buffet breakfast. AE, DC, MC, V. Free parking. **Amenities:** Restaurant; bar; exercise room; sauna. *In room:* TV.

Hotell Gästis ★ You wouldn't know it from the rather bleak facade, but this hotel is a landmark, dating from 1915 when it was the best hotel—in fact, the only hotel—in the area. It is in the exact center of town about 180m (590 ft.) from the rail station, so it has convenience going for it. Even though it has been considerably improved and upgraded, it still has the aura of a frontier country hotel. It offers well-maintained rooms with modern furnishings, and small bathrooms. Floors are either carpeted or covered in vinyl.

Harrevägen 1, S-96 231 Jokkmokk. www.hotell-gastis.com. ✆ **0971/100-12.** Fax 0971/100-44. 27 units. 995SEK–1,195SEK double; 1,200SEK–1,300SEK triple. Rates include buffet breakfast. AE, DC, MC, V. Free parking. **Amenities:** Restaurant; bar; sauna. *In room:* TV, hair dryer.

A Side Trip to Kvikkjokk

Talk about roughing it. We've hiked many parts of the world, and Sarek was one of our toughest challenges. The **Sarek National Park ★★★**, between the Stora and Lilla Luleälv, covers an area of 1,208 sq. km (471 sq. miles), with about 100 glaciers and 87 mountains rising more than 1,770m (5,806 ft.); 8 are more than 1,950m (6,396 ft.). The most visited valley, **Rapadel ★**, opens onto Lake Laidaure. In winter, sled dogs pull people through this valley.

In 1909, Sweden established this nature reserve in the wilderness so that it could be preserved for future generations. To take a walk through the entire park would take at least a week, so most visitors stay only a day or two. Although rugged and beautiful, Sarek is extremely difficult for even the most experienced of hikers. There is absolutely nothing here to aid the visitor—no designated hiking trails, no tourist facilities, no cabins or mountain huts, and no bridges over rivers (whose undertows, incidentally, are very dangerous). Mosquitoes can be downright treacherous, covering your eyes, nose, and ears. You should explore the park only if you hire an experienced guide. Contact a local hotel such as **Kvikkjokk Fjällstation** (see below) for a recommendation.

Kvikkjokk is the starting or finishing point for many hikers using the **Kungsleden Trail.** Call the **Svenska Turistföreningen** (✆ **08/463-21-00**) for information, and also see "Abisko," below. One- or two-day outings can be made in various directions. Local guides also can lead you on a boat trip (inquire at the hotel listed below). The boat will take you to a fascinating delta where the Tarra and Karnajokk rivers meet. The area also is good for canoeing.

WHERE TO STAY

Kvikkjokk Fjällstation Originally established in 1907 by the Swedish Touring Club, and enlarged with an annex in the 1960s, this mountain chalet offers simple, no-frills accommodations for hikers and rock climbers. It's also the headquarters for a network of guides who operate canoe and hiking trips into the vast wilderness areas that fan out on all sides. Accommodations are functional, woodsy, and basic, and include eight double rooms, eight four-bed rooms, and two cabins with four beds each. The station has a sauna, a plain restaurant, and access to canoe rentals and a variety of guided tours that depart at frequent intervals. It is open only from February 4 to April 23 and June 17 to September 17. For information about the Kvikkjokk Fjällstation out of season, call the **tourist information office** in Jokkmokk (129km/80 miles away) at ✆ **0971/222-50.**

S-962 02 Kvikkjokk. www.kvikkjokkfjallstation.se. ✆ **0971/210-22.** Fax 0971/210-39. 18 units, none with bathroom. 775SEK–995SEK double. AE, MC, V. Free parking. Closed Sept 19–Feb 15. **Amenities:** Restaurant; sauna. *In room:* No phone.

FROM JOKKMOKK TO KIRUNA

After visiting Kvikkjokk, return to Jokkmokk and head north on Route 45 toward Gällivare. Along the way, you'll pass **Muddus National Park ★★**. You can enter from the town of **Saite.** Although not as dramatic as Sarek (see "A Side Trip to Kvikkjokk," above), this park, established in 1942, is worth a visit. Its 50,417 hectares (121,000 acres) are home to bears, moose, otters, wolverines, and many bird species. The Muddusjokk River flows through the park and over a panoramic 42m (140-ft.) waterfall. Trails cross the park; they're well marked and lead visitors to the most interesting sights.

Continue along Route 45 through Gällivare, toward Svappavaara. In Svappavaara, take E-10 northwest to Kiruna.

Kiruna

193km (120 miles) N of Jokkmokk, 1,317km (818 miles) N of Stockholm

Covering more than 4,800 sq. km (1,872 sq. miles), Kiruna is the largest (in terms of geography) city in the world. Its extensive boundaries incorporate both Kebnekaise Mountain and Lake Torneträsk. This northernmost town in Sweden is at about the same latitude as southern Greenland. The midnight sun can be seen here from mid-May to mid-July.

Unless drastic changes are made, Kiruna as we know it may not exist a few years from now. It's in danger of sliding down a hole left by the iron ore mines that put this arctic outpost on the map a century ago. During World War II, iron ore from the mines here was exported to Nazi Germany. Before the Earth swallows it up, Kiruna is going to have to be moved.

Its railway station and new highway will be relocated first. At the moment, the town's inhabitants face no immediate threat from the hole carved out by mines more than a kilometer under their feet. In the years ahead, many houses in the affected area will be loaded onto large trailers and moved to new and safe locations. Some of these buildings will be difficult to move—City Hall for example, which will have to be cut into six pieces. A similar solution may have to be devised for the town's wood church, dating from 1913.

ESSENTIALS

GETTING THERE **SAS** (✆ **0770/72-77-27;** www.sas.se) flies twice daily from Stockholm (flight time: 95 min.). The airport is a 15-minute drive north of the town center; a Flygbuss operates periodically, or a taxi is 350SEK each way. Only one night train per day makes the 14-hour trip from Stockholm to Gällivare. From here, you can change trains to Kiruna, a trip of 1½ hours. For schedules and information, phone ✆ **0771/75-75-75.** There's also daily bus service between Gällivare and Kiruna. Contact **Länstrafiken** at ✆ **0926/756-80,** or go to www.ltnbd.se. From Gällivare by car, continue northwest along E-10.

VISITOR INFORMATION Contact the **Kiruna Turistbyrå,** Lars Janssonsgatan 17 (✆ **0980/188-80;** www.lappland.se), open from June 15 to August 20 Monday to Friday 8:30am to 8pm, Saturday and Sunday 8:30am to 6pm; from August 21 to June 14 Monday to Friday 8:30am to 5pm, Saturday 8:30am to 2:30pm.

SEEING THE SIGHTS

Kiruna, which emerged at the turn of the 20th century, owes its location to the nearby deposits of iron ore.

In summer, **InfoMine Tours ★★** descends 540m (1,772 ft.) into the Earth, where you can see the area where 20 million tons of iron ore are dug up every year. Tours leave every hour from 9am to 3pm, with groups forming outside the tourist office (see above). The cost is 250SEK, or 150SEK for students and children. These tickets are available at the tourist office.

Southeast of the railroad station, the tower of the **Stadshus** (✆ **0980/704-96**) dominates Kiruna. The building was designed by Arthur von Schmalensee and inaugurated in 1963. A carillon of 23 bells rings out at noon and 6pm daily. This cast-iron tower was designed by Bror Markland and features unusual door handles of reindeer horn and birch. The interior draws upon materials from around the world: a mosaic floor from Italy, walls of handmade brick from the Netherlands, and pine from the American Northwest. Note also the hand-knotted hanging titled *Magic Drum from Rautas,* a stunning work by artist Sven Xet Erixon. The upper part of the hanging depicts the midnight sun. Inside you'll find an art collection and some Sami handicraft exhibits. It's open June to August Monday to Friday 9am to 6pm, and Saturday and Sunday 10am to 6pm; September to May Monday to Friday 10am to 5pm.

A short walk up the road will take you to the **Kiruna Kyrka ★★**, Kyrkogatan 8 (✆ **0980/678-12**), open Monday to Friday from 9am to 6pm, Saturday and Sunday 11am to 4:45pm. This church was constructed like a stylized Sami tent in 1912 (indeed, the dark timber interior does evoke a Sami hut), with an origami design of rafters and wood beams. Sweden's architects on several occasions have voted it as their country's most beautiful building. Gustaf Wickman designed this unusual church, which has a free-standing bell tower supported by 12 props. Christian Eriksson designed the gilt bronze statues standing sentinel around the roofline. They represent such states of mind as shyness, arrogance, trust, melancholy, and love. Above the main door of the church is a relief depicting groups of Sami beneath the clouds of heaven. This, too, is Eriksson's creation. The altarpiece by Prince Eugen evokes Paradise as a Tuscan landscape, which strikes us as an inappropriate image for this part of the world. Eriksson also created the cross depicting Sami praying and, at its base, a metal sculpture entitled *St. George and the Dragon.*

You also can visit **Hjalmar Lundbohmsgården** (✆ **0980/701-10;** www.hjalmarsgard.se), the official museum of the city of Kiruna. It's in a manor house built

Sweden's Doorway to the Universe

Unknown to much of the world, a few dozen kilometers from Kiruna in the middle of an arctic forest is Esrange ★★ (✆ 46/980-72-000; www.ssc.se/esrange), Europe's only civilian rocket base and a major center of space and climate research on global warming. Rocket launches, the testing of unmanned aircraft, and balloon ascents are all conducted from the base.

Among other endeavors, Esrange is a center of research on the aurora borealis, or northern lights, and on the Earth's shrinking atmospheric ozone layer. Visitors can see the local rocket launch area and the balloon launchpad where high-altitude balloons are sent into the atmosphere.

Esrange is 40km (25 miles) east of Kiruna in the direction of Jukkasjärvi. Four-hour tours are conducted June to August at 8:30am, costing 625SEK per person. Arrangements can be made at the tourist office (see above).

in 1899 by the city's founder and owner of most of the region's iron mines, Hjalmar Lundbohm. Many of the museum's exhibits deal with the city's origins in the late 19th century, the economic conditions in Europe that made its growth possible, and the personality of the entrepreneur who persuaded thousands of Swedes to move north to work in the mines, no small accomplishment we'd say. It's open June through August Monday to Friday from 10am to 6pm; off-season, you must phone ahead for opening hours, which could be any day of the week between the hours of 8am and 4pm. Admission is 35SEK for adults, 20SEK for children 7 to 15, free for children 6 and under.

WHERE TO STAY & DINE

Scandic Hotel Ferrum ★ We were immediately won over by this hotel when we got rooms opening onto the mountains and the Kebnekaise massif in the distance. Run by the Scandic chain, this hotel is named after the iron ore (*ferrum*) for which Kiruna is famous. The six-story hotel was built in 1967 and is one of the tallest buildings in town. Functional and standardized in design, it's one of your best bets for lodging and food. It has two well-run restaurants, Reenstierna and **Grapes.** Our favorite spot for socializing in Kiruna is the rustically decorated pub, Mommas.

The staff arranges enough outdoor adventures to challenge an Olympic athlete: dog-sledge rides, snowmobiling, arctic safaris, and river rafting, or mere skiing and fishing for those more faint of heart. Or you can just settle in at the sauna overlooking Sweden's highest mountain. You can also wind down in the relaxation room, where on most days a roaring fire greets you. The rooms are modern and comfortably furnished with excellent beds and neatly kept bathrooms.

Lars Janssonsgatan 15, S-981 31 Kiruna. www.scandichotels.com. ✆ **0980/39-86-00.** Fax 0980/39-86-11. 171 units. 990SEK–1,940SEK double; 1,790SEK–2,490SEK suite. Rates include buffet breakfast. AE, DC, MC, V. Parking 85SEK. **Amenities:** 2 restaurants; bar; bikes; children's playground; exercise room; Internet (free, in lobby); sauna. *In room:* TV, DVD (in some), CD player (in some), hair dryer, Wi-Fi (free).

Vinterpalatset (Winter Palace) This privately owned hotel occupies what originally was built in 1904 as a private home for a prosperous entrepreneur in the iron-ore industry. Radically renovated and upgraded, it includes the much-improved main house, a 1950s-era annex containing 4 of the hotel's individually designed 20 rooms, a sauna/solarium complex, and a bar with an open fireplace. There's also a dining room, frequented mostly by other residents of the hotel, which serves rib-sticking Swedish food. Rooms are high ceilinged, dignified looking, and outfitted with hardwood floors and comfortable furniture. Bathrooms are quite small, each with a shower. While cold winds are blowing outside, our favorite place to settle in is at the on-site King Bore's Bar, with its open fireplace.

PO Box 18, Järnvägsgatan 18, S-981 21 Kiruna. www.vinterpalatset.se. ✆ **0980/677-70.** Fax 0980/130-50. 20 units. Mid-June to mid-Aug and Fri-Sat year-round 990SEK double; rest of year 1,530SEK double. 4 annex rooms available mid-June to mid-Aug and Fri-Sat year-round 890SEK; rest of year 1,220SEK. Rates include buffet breakfast. AE, DC, MC, V. Free parking. **Amenities:** Restaurant; bar; children's playground; Jacuzzi; room service; sauna. *In room:* TV, hair dryer, Wi-Fi (free).

Abisko

89km (55 miles) NW of Kiruna, 1,467km (911 miles) N of Stockholm

Any resort north of the Arctic Circle is a curiosity. Abisko, on the southern shore of Lake Torneträsk, encompasses a scenic valley, a lake, and an island. An elevator takes passengers to Mount Nuolja (Njulla). Nearby is the protected Abisko National Park (see below), containing remarkable flora, including orchids.

ESSENTIALS

GETTING THERE You can get a train to Kiruna (see above). From here, there are both **bus and rail links** into the center of Abisko. For train information, call ✆ **0771/75-75-75.** For bus information, call **Länstrafiken** at ✆ **0926/756-80** or visit www.ltnbd.se.

By car from Kiruna, continue northwest on E-10 into Abisko.

VISITOR INFORMATION Contact the tourist office in Kiruna (see above).

EXPLORING THE AREA

Abisko National Park ★★ (✆ **0980/402-00**), established in 1903, surrounds the Abiskojokk River, including the mouth of the river where it flows into Lake Torneträsk. This is a typical alpine valley with a rich variety of flora and fauna. The highest mountain is Slåttatjåkka, 1,170m (3,839 ft.) above sea level. Slightly shorter Njulla, which rises 1,140m (3,740 ft.), has a cable car. The name *Abisko* is a Sami word meaning "ocean forest." The park's proximity to the Atlantic gives it a maritime character, with milder winters and cooler summers than the more continentally influenced areas east of the Scandes or Caledonian mountains.

Abisko is more easily accessible than **Vadvetjåkka National Park,** the other, smaller park in the area. Three sides of Vadvetjåkka Park are bounded by water that is difficult to wade through, and the fourth side is rough terrain with treacherously

Northernmost Golf in the World

Here's how to achieve one-upmanship on your golfing pals back home: You can play at the northernmost golf course in the world: The **Arctic Golf Course** has only 9 holes, on a terrain of mostly thin-soiled tundra with a scattering of birch forest. It is open from mid-June to mid-August. During that limited period, golfers can play 24 hours per day, as the course is lit by the midnight sun. For more information, contact Björkliden Arctic Golf Club, Kvarnbacksvägen 28, Bromma S-16874 (✆ **08/56-48-88-30;** bjorklidens golfklubb.se).

slippery bogs and steep precipices fraught with rock slides. Established in 1920, it is northwest of Lake Torneträsk, with its northern limits at the Norwegian border. It's composed of mountain precipices and large tracts of bog and delta. It also has rich flora, along with impressive brook ravines. Its highest mountain is Vadvetjåkka, with a southern peak at 1,095m (3,593 ft.) above sea level.

Abisko is one of the best centers for watching the **midnight sun,** which can be seen from June 13 to July 4. It's also the start of the longest marked trail in the world, the **Kungsleden (Royal Trail)** ★★★, which may just prove to be the hike of a lifetime. This approximately 338km (210-mile) trail journeys through Abisko National Park to Riksgränsen on the Norwegian frontier, cutting through Sweden's highest mountain (Kebnekaise) on the way. If you're properly fortified and have adequate camping equipment, including a sleeping bag and food, you can walk these trails. Cabins and rest stops (local guides refer to them as "fell stations") are spaced a day's hike (13–21km/8–13 miles) apart, so you'll have adequate areas to rest between bouts of trekking and hill climbing. These huts provide barely adequate shelter from the wind, rain, snow, and hail in case the weather turns turbulent, as it so often does in this part of the world. At most of the stops, you cook your own food and clean up before leaving. Most lack running water, although there are some summer-only toilets. At certain points, the trail crosses lakes and rivers; boats are provided to help you get across. The trail actually follows the old nomadic paths of the Sami. Those with less time or energy will find the trail broken up into several smaller segments.

During the summer, the trail is not as isolated as you may think. It is, in fact, the busiest hiking trail in Sweden, and adventurers from all over the world traverse it. The trail is most crowded in July, when the weather is most reliable. Locals even operate boat services on some of the lakes you'll pass. Often they'll rent you a rowboat or canoe from a makeshift kiosk that's dismantled and hauled away after the first frost.

For maps and more information about this adventure, contact the local tourist office or the **Svenska Turistförening,** the **Swedish Touring Club,** PO Box 17251, S104 62 Stockholm (✆ **08/463-21-00;** www.svenskaturistforeningen.se).

WHERE TO STAY & DINE

Abisko Turiststation Since 1902 this far northern inn has been welcoming guests who want to trek through the surrounding great wilderness. Owned by the Swedish Touring Club since 1910, this big, modern hotel, about 450m (1,476 ft.) from the bus station, offers accommodations in the main building, in the annex, and in 28 cabins. Each cabin is made up of two apartments suitable for up to six occupants, and each unit features a kitchen and a private bathroom. From the hotel you can see the lake and the mountains. The staff is helpful in providing information about excursions. The rooms are basic but reasonably comfortable, and some offer exceptional views. However, amenities such as TV don't exist. Swedish meals are served in the on-site buffet-style **Restaurant Tjuonavagge.** Also on the premises is **Storstugan,** the friendliest pub in town.

S-981 07 24 Abisko. www.abisko.nu. ✆ **0980/402-00.** Fax 0980/401-40. 77 units, 43 with bathroom; plus 56 cabin apts. 720SEK double without bathroom; 1,490SEK double with bathroom. Rates include buffet breakfast. Cabin apts 1,190SEK for 2; 1,390SEK for up to 6. Breakfast not included. AE, MC, V. Free parking. Closed Sept 26–June 10. **Amenities:** Restaurant; bar; sauna.

THE BEST OF FINLAND

Finland offers visitors a tremendous variety of sights and experiences, everything from sophisticated Helsinki to the vast wilderness. To help you decide how best to spend your time in Finland, we've compiled a list of our favorite experiences and discoveries. Below, you'll find the kind of candid advice we'd give our close friends.

THE best TRAVEL EXPERIENCES

- **Taking a Finnish Sauna:** With some 1.6 million saunas in Finland—roughly one for every three citizens—there's a sauna waiting for you here. Visitors can enjoy saunas at most hotels, motels, holiday villages, and camping sites.
- **Exploring Europe's Last Frontier:** In Scandinavia's far north—its northern tier traversed by the Arctic Circle—Finnish Lapland seems like a forgotten corner of the world. Its indigenous peoples, the Sami, have managed to preserve their distinctive identity and are an integral part of Lapland and its culture. Dozens of tours are available through **Nordique Tours,** a subdivision of Picasso Travel, 11099 S. La Cienega Blvd., Ste. 242, Los Angeles, CA 90045 (✆ **800/995-7997;** www.nordiquetours.com).
- **Traversing the Finnish Waterworld:** From the coastal islands to the Saimaa lake district, Finland is one vast world of water. Adventures range from daring the giddy, frothing rapids of the midlands to paddling the deserted streams or swift currents of Lapland. Every major town in Finland has canoe-rental outfitters, and local tourist offices can offer advice on touring the local waters.
- **Wandering Finnish Forests:** Finland has been called one huge forest with five million people hiding in it. In fact, nearly four-fifths of the country's total land area is forested. Walk in the woods, picking wild berries and mushrooms along the way.
- **Discovering Finnish Design & Architecture:** Finnish buildings are among the world's newest—more than 90% have been erected since 1920—but their avant-garde design has stunned the world and spread the fame of such architects as Alvar Aalto. In Helsinki, you can see the neoclassical Senate Square, Eliel Saarinen's controversial railway station (dating from 1914), and the Temppeliaukio Church, which has

been hollowed out from rock with only its dome showing. While in Helsinki, you can also visit the University of Industrial Arts—the largest of its kind in Scandinavia—to learn about current exhibits of Finnish design.

THE best SCENIC TOWNS & VILLAGES

- **Turku:** Finland's most charming town developed around an ancient trading post. Its castle played a prominent role in Finnish (as well as Scandinavian) history. The national capital until 1812, Turku today is an important cultural center, with two universities. It's also a good base for short cruises of the Turku archipelago. See chapter 20.
- **Savonlinna:** The commercial and cultural center of the eastern Savo region, one of Finland's most ancient provinces, this town is the center of Lake Saimaa traffic. Filled with attractions, including museums and art galleries, it's also a good center for exploring—often by boat—one of the most scenic parts of Finland. See chapter 20.
- **Lappeenranta:** Founded in 1649 by Queen Christina of Sweden, this town is at the southernmost edge of Lake Saimaa. It covers a large area stretching from the lake to the Russian border. The commercial and cultural center of South Karelia, it's a spa town and the gateway to the Saimaa Canal. It's filled with attractions and is also a good base for excursions, including visa-free day tours to Vyborg in Russia. See chapter 20.

THE best ACTIVE VACATIONS

For additional sporting and adventure travel information, see "The Active Vacation Planner" in chapter 2.

- **Bicycling:** Thousands of miles of narrow paths and captivating gravel tracks lead to towns where broad highways are flanked by well-maintained bicycle routes. Local tourist offices can provide maps of the best trails.
- **Canoeing:** Choose from a large variety of waterscapes: coastal waters dotted with thousands of islands, rivers flowing to the sea, or lakes in the Greater Saimaa region. The best coastal areas are the archipelago along the southwest coast, the coast of Uusimaa province, and the Åland Islands. A popular region for canoeing is the lake district; here the lakes are linked in long chains by short channels with strong currents. Together the lakes form a network of routes extending for thousands of kilometers.
- **Fishing:** For those who are skilled, Finland offers the chance to fish year-round. Fishermen here divide their calendar not into months, but according to the fish in season. Sea trout become plentiful as the rivers rise in March and April. May and June are the golden months for pike. Midsummer, when the rapids are at their best, marks the season for Lapland grayling and pikeperch. Also in midsummer, salmon fishermen prepare for the high point of their year. Autumn brings sea trout inshore, along with the "Flying Dutchmen of the Deep"—pike—that stalk the shoals of herring. Even in winter, Finnish fishermen drill through the ice to catch perch, pike, and trout. Ice fishermen angle for burbot during the dark winter nights, since its roe is regarded as the choicest of caviars.

- **Hiking:** Hiking is a popular form of recreation in heavily forested Finland. Lapland holds its own special appeal, but you can ramble for a day or more even in southern Finland. Outside Helsinki, for example, there are numerous trails in Nuuksio National Park. The provinces of middle Finland have a network of hiking trails that total some 300km (185 miles).
- **Skiing:** The ski season in Finland is the longest in Lapland, from October until mid-May. In northern Finland, south of Lapland, there's good skiing for more than 5 hours a day in natural light, even when the days are short. Numerous ski trails are lit artificially when winter is at its darkest. The peak holiday ski season is just before spring, when there's lots of daylight and sunshine. In southern Finland, skiing conditions are ideal in January and February; in central Finland the best months are December through March; and in northern Finland the best months are December through April.

THE best FESTIVALS & SPECIAL EVENTS

- **Tar Skiing Race** (Oulu): This cross-country ski race was established more than a century ago and has been held almost every year since then. In March, hundreds of participants from around the world show up to compete on the 76km (47-mile) racecourse. See p. 26.
- **Midnight Sun Film Festival** (Sodankylä): Held each June, this is the world's northernmost film festival, featuring works by well-known directors as well as new names in the industry. See p. 26.
- **Kuopio Dance Festival** (Kuopio): This is Scandinavia's oldest drama festival, held in mid- to late June; distinguished performers and troupes from all over the world come to participate. There's a different theme each year. See p. 26.
- **Savonlinna Opera Festival** (Savonlinna): Every year from early July to early August, this festival stages three or four of its own productions and hosts visiting opera companies from abroad. See p. 527.
- **Helsinki Festival:** Beginning in mid-August, international artists come to Helsinki to perform chamber music and recitals, or to present visual arts exhibits, dance programs, film screenings, and theatrical performances, as well as opera, jazz, pop, and rock concerts. See p. 26.

THE best MUSEUMS

- **Ainola** (Järvenpää, outside Helsinki): This was the home of Finland's famous composer, Jean Sibelius, who lived here for more than half a century until his death in 1957. Along with his wife, Aino (for whom the house is named), he's buried on the property. About 40km (24 miles) from Helsinki. See p. 493.
- **Finnish National Gallery** (Helsinki): The nation's major repository of modern art includes graphics, sculpture, paintings—the widest possible range in the country. Naturally, native-born sons and daughters are emphasized, with the work of Finnish artists dating from the mid–18th century. See p. 490.
- **Gallen-Kallela Museum** (Espoo): On a wooded peninsula, this museum honors the Finnish artist Akseli Gallen-Kallela (1865–1931), who is known mainly for his paintings, especially those from the *Kalevala (Land of Heroes),* the Finnish national epic. See p. 493.

- **Mannerheim Museum** (Helsinki): This was the home of Baron Carl Gustaf Mannerheim, marshal of Finland and president of the republic from 1944 to 1946. It has been turned into a museum filled with memorabilia, including his swords, medals, and uniforms, along with his collection of antiques and furnishings. See p. 491.
- **National Museum of Finland** (Suomen Kansallismuseo, Helsinki): No other museum in the country documents the history of the Finnish people like this one. The tools that shaped ordinary life in the country since the Stone Age are documented here, with exhibits ranging from folk costumes to church art. See p. 492.
- **Seurasaari Open-Air Museum** (Seurasaari): This museum is on an island off the coast of Helsinki (now a national park). Here some 100 authentically furnished and decorated houses have been reassembled—everything from a 1600s church to an "aboriginal" sauna. If you don't have the opportunity to explore Finland in depth, these buildings will help you understand something of Finnish life past and present. On summer evenings, folk dances are presented here to the tunes of a fiddler. See p. 493.

THE best OFFBEAT EXPERIENCES

- **Camping Outdoors:** There are about 350 campsites with some 6,300 camp cabins and holiday cottages. If you have an international camping card (FICC), you don't need a Finnish camping card. Campers can buy a family camping card at the first site at which they intend to stay; it costs 7€ for the whole year. Regional tourist offices can provide information about campsites, or write to the **Finnish Campingsite Association,** Tulppatie 14, FIN-00880 Helsinki (✆ **09/477-407-40;** www.camping.fi). In North America, the card is available from the **Family Campers and RVers Association,** 4804 Transit Rd., Building 2, Depew, NY 14043 (✆ **800/245-9755;** www.fcrv.org).
- **Experiencing a Finnish Farm:** Despite its role as an industrialized nation, Finland's roots extend deep into the soil. Several hundred English-speaking farmers have opened their homes to temporary guests, offering a firsthand view of how the country grows such flavorful produce and vegetables. Local tourist offices have information. A well-respected travel expert, **Lomarengas Finnish Country Holidays,** Eteläesplanadi 22C, Third Floor, FIN-00130 Helsinki (✆ **358-306-502-502;** www.lomarengas.fi), compiles an annual booklet with descriptions, map locations, and photographs of scenic farms, antique and modern cottages, and log cabins. Prices for rooms on farms vary, but even the most expensive generally fall in the budget category. It's also possible to arrange rentals of cabins and cottages suitable for two to eight people.
- **Panning for Gold:** In the Lemmenjoki region (near Inari), in Finnish Lapland, there are all-day gold-panning trips along the River Lemmenjoki between mid-June and mid-September. Participants are shown how to wash gold by sluicing and panning. On the return trip you'll stop at Ravadas waterfall, one of the most spectacular sights in northern Finland. For more information, contact **Lemmenjoki Cabins,** Ahkun Tupa, FIN-99885 (✆ **016/67-34-35;** www.laplandfinland.com).
- **Lighthouse-Watching in the Gulf of Bothnia:** The waters separating Finland from Sweden are dotted with thousands of islands, some of them forested, some of them

wind-scoured and rocky, and most of them uninhabited. Between May and August, when the waters are ice-free and the northern lights shimmer down upon waters, you might opt for lighthouse-watching cruises that last between 1 and 3 days. The most famous of the lighthouses in the archipelago near Vaasa is the **Valassaaret Lighthouse,** designed by an associate of Gustave Eiffel (Henri Lipart) in the 1890s. Other lighthouses date from the early 1960s. Your exposure to the bird life, marine life, and botany of the Gulf of Bothnia will be unparalleled. For more information, contact **Botnia Tourist,** Vaasanpuistikko 22, FIN-65100 Vaasa (✆ **06/325-11-25;** www.pohjanmaanmatkailu.fi).

- **Seeing Lapland on a Safari: Borton Overseas** (✆ **800/843-0602;** www.bortonoverseas.com) will take you on a tour of Finnish Lapland. You experience close encounters with the Sami people and their culture, and get to see one of the last great wildernesses of Europe. You're taken to old village settlements and along lakes, where you can watch herds of reindeer. Summer tours of the tundra are held between May and early September, and in winter it's also possible to traverse the snow-covered tundra on tours between January and April.
- **Taking a Snowmobile Safari:** From the first week of January until mid-April, you can take a 6-day/5-night snowmobile safari; you fly from Helsinki to Ivalo in the north of Finland and back again. At the Saarisellkä Skiing Resort, you first get snowmobile driving lessons and then have the opportunity to go snowmobile trekking through varying winter landscapes. Overnights are sometimes arranged in wilderness huts; safari outfits and all meals are provided. For more information, contact **Nordique Tours,** 11099 S. La Cienega Blvd., Ste. 242, Los Angeles, CA 90045 (✆ **800/995-7997;** www.nordiquetours.com).

THE best BUYS

- **Clothing & Textiles:** There's everything from cottons and linens (often in stunning modern fashions such as those by Marimekko) to warm stoles and shawls. Collectors also seek out *ryijy* rugs and *raanu* wall hangings. Many of these goods are displayed and sold at shops along the Esplanade in Helsinki.
- **Glass & Ceramics:** Finland offers a wide variety of stunning designs, ranging from practical everyday items at moderate prices to one-of-a-kind objects designed by well-known Finnish artisans. The best-known factory names (and the best quality) to look for are Arabia for china, or Nuutajärvi, Iittala, and Riihimäki for glass. Their products are displayed in shops throughout the country. Showrooms for both Arabia and Iittala are on the Esplanade in Helsinki. Many Finnish glass factories can be visited; contact local tourist offices for further information.
- **Jewelry:** Although Finland is not often associated with jewelry making, it has some rare items for sale—especially from the *Kalevala* series based on centuries-old Finnish ornaments. Modern designers working in gold or silver produce many bold and innovative pieces of jewelry, sometimes as settings for Finnish semiprecious stones or combined wood and silver. Lapponia jewelry—sold all over the country—is one example.
- **Wines & Spirits:** Vodka and liqueurs made from local berries are popular, especially the rare cloudberry, the Arctic bramble, and the cranberry. Alcohol is sold at retail through the outlets of Alko, the State Alcohol Company.

THE best HOTELS

- **Hotel Kämp,** Pohjoisesplanadi 29, Helsinki (www.hotelkamp.fi; ✆ **09/57-61-11;** p. 475): One of the most luxurious hotels in the north of Europe, the Kämp brings five-star comforts to the Finnish capital. It was constructed in 1887, but has been dramatically and beautifully restored. A great deal of Finnish history took place under its roof, and the politics of the country, a blend of east and west, continue to thrive on its dramatic premises.
- **Crowne Plaza Helsinki,** Mannerheimintie 50, Helsinki (www.crowneplaza-helsinki.fi; ✆ **09/2521-0000;** p. 474): This bastion of modernity on one of the major boulevards of Helsinki is a sleek, contemporary hotel with all the conveniences you'd expect if you wish to live in luxury in the Finnish capital.
- **Hilton Hotel Kalastajatorppa,** Kalastajatorpantie 1, Helsinki (www.hilton.com; ✆ **09/458-11;** p. 480): In a bucolic park on the sea, this is a tranquil and luxurious choice. Comprising three buildings with two restaurants, plus two modern glass wings linked by tunnels, it's a cozy retreat. In summer, amenities include a beach with watersports equipment.
- **Hilton Helsinki Strand,** John Stenbergin Ranta 4, Helsinki (www.hilton.com; ✆ **800/445-8667** or 358/939-351; p.480): Opening onto a bay, this deluxe chain member boasts the most dramatic atrium in Helsinki. Some of Finland's top designers were called in to create some of the capital's most tasteful and comfortable guest rooms, often using deluxe construction materials such as marble from Lapland.

THE best RESTAURANTS

- **Ravintola Nokka,** Kanavaranta 7F, Helsinki (✆ **09/687-7330;** www.royalravintolat.com/nokka; p. 483): In a 19th-century building, this elegant restaurant is a showcase for the products of Finland. Its chefs dazzle with their prowess with homegrown produce and fresh game. Cheerfully and competently served, the house repertoire of foods, from mallard duck to Finnish cheese, is filled with dishes of high caliber.
- **Chez Dominique,** Richardinkatu 4, Helsinki (✆ **09/612-73-93;** www.chezdominique.fi; p. 481): One of only a few Michelin-starred restaurants in all of Finland, this gourmet citadel is oft cited as one of Helsinki's best restaurants, according to many of the city's newspaper and magazine food critics. Near Esplanadi Park, the first-class restaurant offers French-inspired cuisine using fresh Scandinavian products whenever available.
- **G. W. Sundmans,** Eteläranta 16, Helsinki (✆ **09/612-85-400;** www.royalravintolat.com; p. 481): The only restaurant in Helsinki to equal—but not surpass—Chez Dominique is housed in a former mansion. It, too, is Michelin starred. Deluxe French and Scandinavian cuisine is served in elegant surroundings. Succulent dishes native to Finland include grilled sirloin of elk with a rowanberry sabayon sauce.
- **Havis,** Eteläranta 16, Helsinki (✆ **09/6128-5800;** www.royalravintolat.com; p. 483): Known for its fine seafood, this upscale tavern was established in 1973. Most of its saltwater fish comes from Finnish coastal waters, while its freshwater fish—everything from Baltic crayfish to brook trout—is from Finnish lakes. The restaurant has a beautiful atmosphere and some of the finest service in Helsinki.

- **Foija,** Aurakatu 10, Turku (✆ **02/251-8665,** p. 515): For a true taste of Finland, head here. Foija is called the oldest continuously operated restaurant in the country, with a tradition going back to 1839. In the center of town at Market Square, it delivers a savory cuisine of market-fresh ingredients based on time-tested recipes.
- **Kala-Trappa,** Nunnakatu 3, Naantali (✆ **02/435-2477;** www.ravintolatrappi.fi; p. 518): This is the best restaurant in this medieval city, serving both Finnish and international cuisine with considerable flair. In cozy dining rooms, you can feast on the best and freshest fish in the area, plus an array of other dishes prepared in harmonious combinations.

HELSINKI

The Helsinki that greets today's visitor is one of the most vibrant and prosperous cities in the world, with one of the highest standards of living and the world's highest literacy rate. The half million people you see walking about—at least in summer—are the best educated, the best clothed, the best fed, and the best housed on Earth.

19

A city of wide streets, squares, and parks, adorned with sculpture, Helsinki was one of the world's first planned municipalities and is noted for its 19th-century neoclassical architecture. Helsinki may stand at the doorway to Russia, but its cultural links are firmly in Scandinavia. It was originally founded in 1550, halfway between Stockholm and St. Petersburg, on orders of the Swedish king Gustavus Vasa, who established it as a buffer zone between Sweden and what was at the time called "the Russian menace."

From the capital of an autonomous Grand Duchy of Russia, Helsinki transformed in 1917 (the year of the Russian Revolution) into the capital of the newly independent Finland. Today it's not only a center of government but the nation's intellectual capital, with a major university and many cultural and scientific institutions.

ESSENTIALS

Visitor Information

The **Helsinki City Tourist Office,** Pohjoisesplanadi 19, FIN-00099 Helsinki (✆ **09/3101-3300;** www.visithelsinki.fi), is open from May 2 to September 30, Monday to Friday 9am to 8pm and Saturday and Sunday 9am to 6pm; off-season, Monday to Friday from 9am to 6pm and Saturday from 10am to 4pm.

Neighborhoods in Brief

Helsinki is divided roughly into the following districts.

The Center The historic core stretches from Senaatintori (Senate Square) to Esplanadi. Senate Square is dominated by the Lutheran cathedral at its center, and Esplanadi itself is an avenue lined with trees. At one end of Esplanadi, the wide Mannerheimintie, extending for about 5km (3 miles), is the main road from the city center to the expanding suburbs. The section south of Esplanadi is one of the wealthiest in the capital, lined with embassies and elegant houses.

North of Center This section of Helsinki is between Sibelius Park in the west and a lake, Töölönlahti, in the east. It has a more residential feel than does the area in the center, and several fine restaurants are here. Those driving cars into Helsinki prefer this section.

Kruununhaka & Hakaniemi The district of Kruununhaka is one of the oldest. Helsinki was founded in 1550 at the mouth of the Vantaa River, but was relocated in 1640 on the peninsula of Vironniemi in what's now known as Kruununhaka. This section, along with neighboring Hakaniemi, encompasses the remaining buildings from 17th-century Helsinki.

The Islands Helsinki also includes several islands, some of which are known as "tourist islands," including Korkeasaari, site of the Helsinki Zoo. The main islands are linked by convenient ferries and water taxis.

Called the "fortress of Finland" and the "Gibraltar of the North," Suomenlinna consists of five main islands, all interconnected, and is the site of many museums. Seurasaari, another island, has a bathing beach and recreation area, as well as a national park and the largest open-air museum in Finland.

Espoo Many workers in Helsinki treat Espoo as a bedroom suburb. Actually, since 1972, when it received its charter, it has been the second-largest city of Finland, with a population of 220,000 and a recent expansion of its museum scene.

Tapiola Another "suburb city," Tapiola was founded in 1951, providing homes for some 17,000 residents. This "model city" has varied housing, which ranges from multistory condo units to more luxurious one-family villas. The great Finnish architect, Alvar Aalto, was one of its planners.

GETTING THERE & GETTING AROUND

Arriving

BY PLANE The Helsinki-Vantaa airport (© **020/014-636;** www.helsinki-vantaa.fi), which receives flights from more than 21 airports within Finland and from more than 30 airports worldwide, is 19km (12 miles) north of the center of town, about a 30-minute bus ride. Express bus no. 615 leaves from platform 5 at Rautatientori by the Central Railway Station daily from 5am to midnight. This bus stops at the airport. The price is 4€ each way.

A conventional taxi ride from the Helsinki-Vantaa airport to the center of Helsinki costs about 35€ to 40€ each way, and the ride generally takes 30 to 40 minutes. You'll be assured of a private car shared only by members of your immediate party. Call © **0100/0700.** A slightly cheaper alternative is to hire a special yellow taxi (© **600/555-555;** www.airporttaxi.fi) at the airport terminal, which might be shared by up to four separate travelers; the cost is 27€ per person.

On your departure, note that the airport requires passengers on domestic flights within Finland to check in 30 minutes before flight time. Passengers on flights to other points in Europe usually must check in between 45 and 60 minutes before takeoff, and passengers bound for any of the former regions of the Soviet Union or anywhere in North America usually need to check in between 1 and 2 hours in advance.

BY TRAIN The Helsinki Railway Station is on Kaivokatu (© **06/0041-902** for train information). See "Getting Around Town," below, for more information. The station has luggage-storage lockers costing from 2€ to 6€, depending on the size. The lost-luggage department is open daily from 6:30am to 10pm.

BY BUS Bus transit into and within Helsinki is divided into three separate terminals, the largest of which is the **Kamppi Terminal.** The Kamppi Terminal is the home base of bus nos. 102 to 205, and site of most of the suburban outbound buses headed in the direction of Espoo. Used mainly by commuters, **Elielinaukio Terminal** is home base of bus nos. 206 to 345, most of which head out at regular intervals in the direction of Espoo, and also bus nos. 360 to 474 going in the direction of Vantaa.

There's also the **Railway Square Bus Terminal,** home base of buses nos. 611 to 742 headed to Vantaa. For information about bus, tram, and subway routes within Helsinki, call ✆ **0100/111** every Monday to Friday 7am to 7pm, Saturday and Sunday 9am to 5pm.

BY CAR Helsinki is connected by road to all Finnish cities. If you arrive at the port of Turku on a car ferry from Sweden, you can take the E-18 express highway east to Helsinki. See "Getting Around Town," below, for information about car rentals.

BY FERRY Most of the ferryboats coming in and out of the city arrive at and depart from terminals that line the perimeter of Helsinki's South Harbor (especially on the small island of Katajanokka), and to a lesser degree, selected areas of Helsinki's West Harbor. For general information, call the Port of Helsinki (✆ **09/310-1621**).

If you're arriving from Stockholm, you can either ride a ferryboat all the way to Helsinki, or you can take a ferry aboard either the Viking or the Silja Line to Turku on the west coast of Finland, and then, at Turku, you can board one of about 20 daily buses that make the 2½-hour run to Helsinki.

To Stockholm: Over the years, some of the options for maritime transits between Helsinki and Stockholm have grown in numbers and degrees of luxuriousness. The **Viking** and **Silja Lines** carry the highest volume of passengers and operate the greatest number of ships. For information in Helsinki, contact **Silja Line** (✆ **09/18-041;** www.tallinksilja.com) or **Viking Line** (✆ **0600/41577;** www.vikingline.fi).

Getting Around Town

BY PUBLIC TRANSPORTATION

DISCOUNT PASSES Visitors to Helsinki can purchase the **Helsinki Card,** which offers unlimited travel on the city's public buses, trams, subway, and ferries; a free guided sightseeing tour by bus (conducted daily, year-round); free entry to about 50 museums and other sights in Helsinki; and free ferryboat access and entrance to the Suomenlinna Fortress. The Helsinki Card is available for 1-, 2-, or 3-day periods. The price for adults is 34€ for 1 day, 45€ for 2 days, and 55€ for 3 days. A card for children (age 7–16) costs 13€ for 1 day, 16€ for 2 days, and 19€ for 3 days.

You can also buy a Tourist Ticket for travel within Helsinki over a 1-, 3-, or 5-day period. This ticket lets you travel as much as you like within the city limits on all forms of public transportation. A 1-day ticket costs 7€ for adults, 3.50€ for children 7 to 16; a 3-day ticket costs 14€ for adults, 7€ for children 7 to 16; and a 5-day ticket costs 21€ for adults, 11€ for children 7 to 16. Children 6 and under are free. For more information, contact any Finnish Tourist Board worldwide or the Helsinki City Tourist Office, Pohjoisesplanadi 19 (✆ **09/3101-3300;** www.helsinkicard.fi).

BY METRO/BUS/TRAIN The City Transport Office is at the Rautatientori metro station (✆ **09/47-66-40-00;** www.hsl.fi), open Monday to Thursday 7:30am to 7pm, Friday 7:30am to 5pm, and Saturday 10am to 3pm. The transportation system operates daily from 5:30am to 11:30pm. A single ticket, valid for rides on any city bus or tram, costs 2.50€ for adults, 1.30€ for children 3 to 15, and free for 2 and under. Transfers are allowable within 1 hour of your initial boarding, and the penalty for persons caught riding without a valid ticket is around 80€.

BY FERRY Ferries depart from the eastern end of Eteläesplanadi (no terminal) heading for the offshore islands of Suomenlinna and Korkeasaari (Helsinki Zoo).

BY TAXI

You can find taxis at taxi stands or hail them on the street. The basic fare costs 6€ and rises on a per-kilometer basis, as indicated on the meter.

BY CAR

Driving around Helsinki by car is not recommended because parking is limited. Either walk or take public transportation. However, touring the environs by car is ideal.

CAR RENTALS The major car-rental companies maintain offices at the Helsinki airport (where airport surcharges apply to car pickups) and in the center of town. Try **Budget Rent-a-Car,** Malminkatu 24 (✆ **20/746-66-00;** www.budget.com), or **Hertz,** Mannerheimintie 44 (✆ **0800/11-22-33;** www.hertz.com). There is an Avis office at Helsinki-Vanta airport, at the arrival area (✆ **09/822-833**).

PARKING Helsinki has several parking garages, including two centrally located facilities: **Parking Kamppi,** Olavinkatu 1 (✆ **09/69-693-000**), and **Parking Eliel,** adjacent to the railway station (✆ **09/69-693-000**).

BY BICYCLE

You can rent a bicycle by contacting **Greenbike,** Bulevardi 32, entrance via the Albertinkatu (✆ **050/404-0400;** www.greenbike.fi), at rates that range from 20€ to 30€ per day. A worthy competitor, with roughly the same rates, is the **Nordic Fitness Sports Park,** Mäntymäentie 1 (✆ **09/4776-9760**).

[FastFACTS] HELSINKI

American Express The Helsinki branch is at Arkadienkatu 2, 00100 Helsinki (✆ **09/613-20-30;** www.americanexpress.fi), and is open Monday to Thursday 9am to 5pm, and 9am to 4pm on Friday. For 24-hour-a-day toll-free information about lost or stolen credit cards or traveler's checks, call ✆ **0800/11-46-46** (valid only in Finland).

Area Code The country code for Finland is 358. In most instances, the city code for Helsinki is 09, but it might begin with 010 or 020. For calls to Helsinki from outside of Finland, after dialing the country code, you usually drop the "0" in the city codes.

Business Hours Most banks are open Monday to Friday 9:15am to 4:15pm. Most businesses and shops are open Monday to Friday 9am to 5pm and Saturday 9am to 2pm. Larger stores are usually open until 7pm Monday to Friday and as late as 6pm on Saturdays. With a few exceptions (noted below), nearly everyplace is closed on Sunday. Many shops in the center of Helsinki are open until 8pm on certain nights, especially Monday and Friday, and in midsummer some shops remain open till 9pm.

R-kiosks, which sell candy, tobacco, toiletries, cosmetics, and souvenirs are open Monday to Saturday 8am to 9pm and Sunday 9 or 10am to 9pm.

Currency Exchange You can exchange dollars for euros at virtually any bank and in most cases, at the reception desk of your hotel; however, you're likely to get better rates at banks. You can also exchange money at the railway station Monday to Friday 9am to 6pm, and at the airport daily 6am to 11pm.

Drugstores The **Yliopiston Apteekki,** Mannerheimintie 96 (✆ **0300/20200**), is open 24 hours daily.

Embassies & Consulates The embassy of the United States is at Itäinen Puistotie 14A (✆ **09/616-250**); the embassy of Canada is at Pohjoisesplanadi 25B (✆ **09/228-530**); and the embassy of the United Kingdom is at Itäinen Puistotie 17 (✆ **09/2286-5100**). Citizens of Australia and New Zealand should go to the British Embassy.

Emergencies Dial ✆ **112** for an ambulance, police, or in case of fire.

Helsinki Helpers Between June and August, the streets in the center of Helsinki are patrolled by a corps of 20-something Helsinki Helpers, identified by their green uniforms. They're conspicuously on hand to dispense maps and advice.

Hospitals An emergency hospital for tourists is the Helsinki University Central Hospital, Meilahti Hospital (for both medical and surgical care), at Haartmaninkatu 2 (✆ **09/4711**). For 24-hour information about health services, call ✆ **09/10023** (within Finland only).

Mail For post office information, call ✆ **0800/171-00.** The main post office in Helsinki is at Elielinaukio 2F (✆ **0200/71000** for information). It's open Monday to Friday 7am to 9pm, Saturday to Sunday 10am to 6pm. If you don't know your address in Helsinki, have your mail sent to you at FIN-00100 Poste Restante (general delivery) in care of the main post office.

Police In an emergency, dial ✆ **112.** Otherwise, dial ✆ **100-22** for information about the precinct nearest you. Central headquarters for the Helsinki police is at Punanotkonkatu 2 (✆ **71/8770111**).

Telephones For local calls within the city of Helsinki, you don't need to dial the area code (09).

Toilets Many locals use cafe toilets (where you should at least order a cup of coffee or a soft drink) or make use of the public facilities at transit terminals. There are public toilets beside the Old Market Hall, in Esplanade Park and in Sibelius Park. It costs .50€ to use these toilets.

WHERE TO STAY

A ROOM IN A HURRY **Hotellikeskus (Hotel Booking Center),** Rautatieasema (✆ **09/2288-1400;** www.helsinkiexpert.fi), is in the heart of the city in the central hall of the railway station. Hours are June to August Monday to Friday 9am to 6pm, Saturday and Sunday 10am to 6pm; September to May Monday to Friday 9am to 6pm, Saturday 10am to 5pm. Tell them the price you're willing to pay, and an English-speaking employee will make a reservation for you. Hotellikeskus charges a booking fee of 5€.

In the City Center

EXPENSIVE

Crowne Plaza Helsinki ★★★ This charmer packages contemporary style and a hardworking staff with a glossy, marble-sheathed lobby. Rooms are slick, with all the modern conveniences and comforts you'd expect from a luxury hotel. Dining options include the gourmet-conscious Macu restaurant and the pop brasserie Fidel, which offers burgers and cocktails.

Mannerheimintie 50, FIN-00260 Helsinki. www.crowneplaza-helsinki.fi. ✆ **09/2521-0000.** Fax 09/2521-3999. 349 units. 171€–234€ double; 716€–795€ suite. AE, DC, MC, V. Parking 21€. **Amenities:** 2 restaurants; 2 bars; concierge; exercise room; indoor heated pool; room service; spa. *In room:* A/C, TV, hair dryer, minibar, Wi-Fi (free).

Hotel Anna In a residential neighborhood, this well-run and affordable hotel was converted from a 1926 apartment building that survived World War II Russian bombardment. Convenient to shopping and museums, the hotel retains a lot of its original charm, even though it was practically rebuilt in 1985, with modern upgrades, including the recent installation of an upgraded ventilation system. It was renovated in 2010. The small to midsize bedrooms are comfortably decorated.

Annankatu 1, FIN-00120 Helsinki. www.hotelanna.fi. ✆ **09/616-621.** Fax 09/602-664. 64 units. 130€-185€ double; 160€-205€ suite. Rates include buffet breakfast. AE, DC, MC, V. Parking 15€. Tram: 3B, 3T, or 10. **Amenities:** Internet (free, in lobby); room service; sauna. *In room:* A/C, TV, hair dryer, kitchenette (in some), minibar, Wi-Fi (free).

Hotel Kämp ★★★ More visitors from the United States and Japan stay here than at any other hotel in Finland, joining the ranks of politicians and rock stars. Originally built in 1887, the hotel is adjacent to the city's most prestigious boulevard. Public areas are appropriately opulent, a combination of turn-of-the-20th-century grandeur and conservatively traditional decors, with lots of glistening hardwoods and polished stone. The large guest rooms are lavishly outfitted with elaborate curtains and reproductions of furniture from the early 19th century. Service, as you'd expect, is superb.

Pohjoisesplanadi 29, FIN-00100 Helsinki. www.hotelkamp.fi. ✆ **09/57-61-11.** Fax 09/576-11-22. 179 units. 240€-341€ double; from 560€ suite. AE, DC, MC, V. Parking 40€. Tram: 1, 3, 7, or 11. **Amenities:** 2 restaurants; bar; babysitting; bikes; exercise room; room service; spa. *In room:* A/C, TV, hair dryer, minibar, Wi-Fi (7€ per hour).

Radisson Blu Plaza Hotel ★★ Two of Finland's most renowned architects, Pervin Imaditdin and Ilmo Valjakka, adapted this former Renaissance-style office building into the well-run pocket of posh it is today. In the heart of Helsinki, the building itself dates from 1917, and some of its original architectural features, including stained glass, are under the protection of the Helsinki City Museum. You get first-class comfort and service in a location near the train stations. Standard rooms are rather small, coming in a trio of styles: Nordic, Italian, and classic.

Mikonkatu 23, FIN-00100 Helsinki. www.radissonsas.com. ✆ **020/1234-700.** Fax 020/123-4704. 291 units. 149€-235€ double; 315€ suite. Rates include buffet breakfast. AE, DC, MC, V. Tram: 3T. **Amenities:** 2 restaurants; 2 bars; babysitting; exercise room; room service; 4 saunas. *In room:* A/C, TV, hair dryer, minibar, Wi-Fi (free).

Rivoli Jardin ★ This is one of the best family-owned boutique hotels in Helsinki in a neighborhood that's convenient to everything in the city center. This small-scale, well-managed, and stylish address lodges lots of business travelers. Guest rooms, although a bit small, are comfortable and well furnished. A hideaway bar serves sandwiches and drinks; and breakfast is available in a greenhouse-inspired winter garden.

Kasarmikatu 40, FIN-00130 Helsinki. www.rivoli.fi. ✆ **09/68-15-00.** Fax 09/65-69-88. 55 units. 227€-247€ double. Rates include buffet breakfast. AE, DC, MC, V. Tram: 3T. **Amenities:** Bar; babysitting; room service; sauna. *In room:* A/C, TV, hair dryer, minibar, Wi-Fi (10€ per day).

Scandic Hotel Marski ★ Despite its somewhat stern resemblance to a bulky and anonymous-looking office building, this hotel is one of the best in Helsinki, conveniently located in the city's commercial core opposite the Stockmann department store. Originally built in 1962 and much renovated since, it offers comfortable rooms outfitted with unusual textures, modern furniture, and good beds. Units within the hotel's original core are roomier and somewhat better decorated. Some are within a neighboring annex connected by a passageway to the hotel's original core.

Helsinki

ACCOMMODATIONS ■
Best Western Premier Hotel Katajanokka **34**
Crowne Plaza Helsinki **6**
Hilton Helsinki Strand **15**
Hotel Anna **45**
Hotel Arthur **17**
Hotel GLO **25**
Hotel Kämp **30**
Hotelli Finn **23**
Klaus K. Hotel **12**
Omena Hotel Eerikinkatu **9**
Radisson Blu Plaza Hotel **18**
Rivoli Jardin **41**
Scandic Hotel Marski **24**
Seurahuone Helsinki **21**
Sokos Hotel Albert **14**
Sokos Hotel Presidentti **5**
Sokos Hotel Torni **10**
Sokos Hotel Vaakuna **19**

DINING ◆
The Bank Lunch Club and The Bank Bistro **37**
Bellevue **33**
Carlito's **25**
Chez Dominique **42**
FishMarket **31**
G.W. Sundmans **36**
Grotesk **28**
Havis **36**
Ilmatar **12**
Kämp Café **30**
Kellarikrouvi **43**
Kolme Kruunua **16**
Kosmos Restaurant **22**
Kynsilaukka Restaurant Garlic **8**
La Petite Maison **47**
Lastu **1**
Manala **2**
Mecca **40**
Palace Gourmet **35**
Ravintola Central **44**
Ravintola Juuri **46**
Ravintola Lasipalatsi **3**
Ravintola Nokka **32**
Ravintola Perho **7**
Ravintola Rivoli **13**
Ravintola Sipuli **32**
Restaurant and Bar Olo **39**
Restaurant Savoy **29**
Restaurant Torni **11**
Sir Eino **38**
Sports Academy **20**
Strindberg Café **26**
Sundman's Krog **44**
Teatteri Ravintola **27**
Zetor **4**

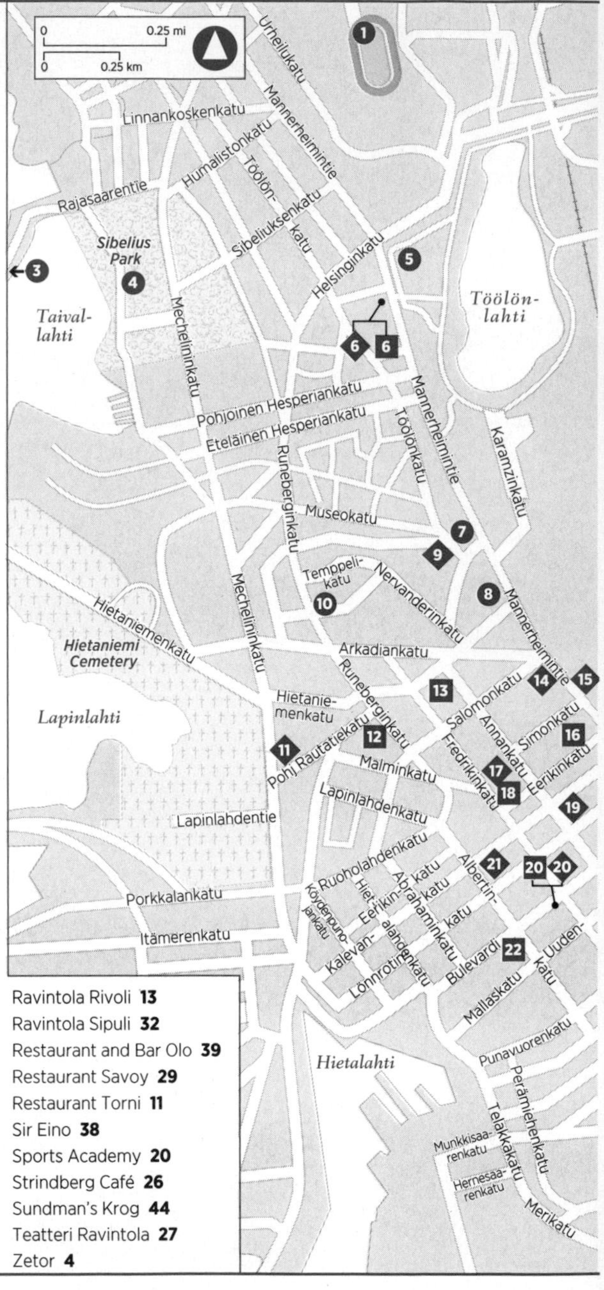

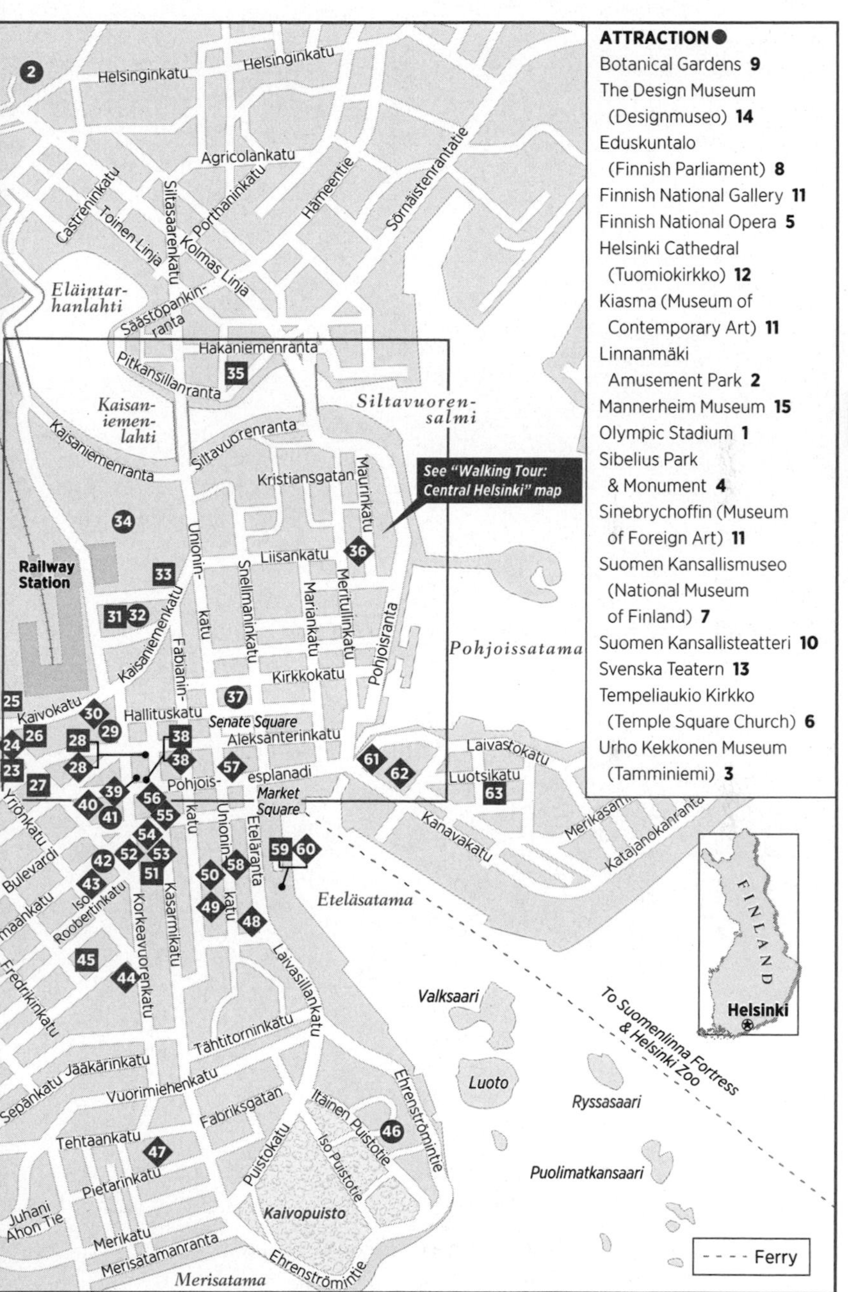
ATTRACTION
Botanical Gardens 9
The Design Museum (Designmuseo) 14
Eduskuntalo (Finnish Parliament) 8
Finnish National Gallery 11
Finnish National Opera 5
Helsinki Cathedral (Tuomiokirkko) 12
Kiasma (Museum of Contemporary Art) 11
Linnanmäki Amusement Park 2
Mannerheim Museum 15
Olympic Stadium 1
Sibelius Park & Monument 4
Sinebrychoffin (Museum of Foreign Art) 11
Suomen Kansallismuseo (National Museum of Finland) 7
Suomen Kansallisteatteri 10
Svenska Teatern 13
Tempeliaukio Kirkko (Temple Square Church) 6
Urho Kekkonen Museum (Tamminiemi) 3
See "Walking Tour: Central Helsinki" map
Helsinginkatu
Agricolankatu
Castréninkatu
Toinen Linja
Siltasaarenkatu
Porthaninkatu
Kolmas Linja
Hämeentie
Sörnäistenrantatie
Eläintar-hanlahti
Säästöpankin-ranta
Hakaniemenranta
Pitkänsillanranta
Kaisan-iemen-lahti
Siltavuoren-salmi
Kajsaniemenranta
Siltavuorenranta
Kristiansgatan
Maurinkatu
Railway Station
Unionin-katu
Liisankatu
Snellmaninkatu
Mariankatu
Meritullinkatu
Pohjoisranta
Kaisaniemenkatu
Fabianin-katu
Kirkkokatu
Pohjoissatama
Kaivokatu
Hallituskatu
Senate Square
Aleksanterinkatu
Laivastokatu
Pohjois-esplanadi
Luotsikatu
Market Square
Yrjönkatu
Kanavakatu
Merikasarminkatu
Katajanokanranta
Bulevardi
Iso Roobertinkatu
Eteläranta
Unionin-katu
Kasarmikatu
Korkeavuorenkatu
Eteläsatama
FINLAND
Helsinki
maankatu
Fredrikinkatu
Laivasillankatu
Valksaari
To Suomenlinna Fortress & Helsinki Zoo
Tähtitorninkatu
Sepänkatu
Jääkärinkatu
Vuorimiehenkatu
Luoto
Ryssasaari
Fabriksgatan
Itäinen Puistotie
Ehrenströmintie
Tehtaankatu
Puistokatu
Iso Puistotie
Puolimatkansaari
Pietarinkatu
Juhani Ahon Tie
Kaivopuisto
Merikatu
Merisatamanranta
Ehrenströmintie
Merisatama
Ferry

Mannerheimintie 10, FIN-00100 Helsinki. www.scandichotels.com. ✆ **09/680-61.** Fax 09/64-23-77. 289 units. Sun–Thurs 202€–269€ double; Fri–Sat 117€–137€ double; 325€–474€ suite. Rates include buffet breakfast. AE, DC, MC, V. Parking 25€. Tram: 3B, 3T, or 6. **Amenities:** Restaurant; bar; bikes; children's playground; exercise room; room service; sauna. *In room:* A/C, TV, hair dryer, minibar, Wi-Fi (free).

Sokos Hotel Albert In the Punavuori district, the art and design center of Helsinki, this latest entry to the Finnish chain is a worthy choice, with sleek, streamlined, and well-designed bedrooms, ensuring comfort. The hotel's excellent restaurant serves the first-rate cuisine of Northern Italy along with more than a hundred Italian wines.

Albertinkatu 30, FIN-00120 Helsinki. www.sokoshotels.fi. ✆ **20/1234-638.** Fax 20/1234-639. 95 units. 78€–249€ double. AE, DC, MC, V. Parking 20€. Bus: 14. **Amenities:** Restaurant; bar; bikes; room service; sauna. *In room:* A/C, TV, hair dryer, minibar, Wi-Fi (free).

Sokos Hotel Presidentti ★ Built in 1980 and renovated in 2006 and 2007, this hotel is in the commercial center of Helsinki, close to Finlandia Hall, Parliament House, and the railway station. Relentlessly modern, and very busy with groups, it boasts lots of drinking and dining facilities. The guest rooms are warm, comfortable, modern, soundproof, and outfitted with pastel color schemes. Airport taxis depart from here directly for the airport.

Eteläinen Rautatiekatu 4, FIN-00100 Helsinki. www.sokoshotels.fi. ✆ **020/1234-608.** Fax 09/694-78-86. 494 units. Mon–Thurs 175€–200€ double; Fri–Sun 135€–185€ double. Rates include buffet breakfast. AE, DC, MC, V. Parking 29€. Tram: 3B or 3T. **Amenities:** 2 restaurants; bar; babysitting; indoor heated pool; room service; sauna. *In room:* TV, hair dryer, minibar, Wi-Fi (free).

Sokos Hotel Vaakuna ★ ☺ This centrally located Helsinki hotel is atop a local landmark, the Sokos department store. Some of the rooms overlook the main rail terminal and its bustling square. The interior is designed to reflect Finland's superb sense of style from around the 1950s. Guest rooms are midsize to spacious, with well-maintained bathrooms. There is no charge for a child under 5 sharing a room with a parent using existing bedding.

Asema-Aukio 2, FIN-00100 Helsinki. www.sokoshotels.fi. ✆ **020/1234-610.** Fax 09/433-771-00. 270 units. Sun–Thurs 175€–201€ double; Fri–Sat 145€–170€ double; 226€–650€ suite. Rates include buffet breakfast. AE, DC, MC, V. Parking 27€. Tram: All trams to rail station. **Amenities:** 2 restaurants; bar; babysitting; room service; sauna. *In room:* TV, hair dryer, minibar, Wi-Fi (free).

MODERATE

Hotel GLO ★★ Part of the Kämp Hotel group is this charmer in a 1920s bank near the port and shops lining the Esplanadi. Its Palace Kamp Day Spa is one of the best in Helsinki, with its sleek modern design and Asian bamboo decorations. Rooms are exceptionally large and beautifully furnished.

Kluuvikatu, FIN-00100 Helsinki. www.palacekamp.fi. ✆ **10/3444-400.** Fax 10/3444-401. 144 units. 145€–197€ double; 348€–821€ suite. AE, DC, MC, V. Parking 23€. Tram: 1, 3, 7, or 11. **Amenities:** Restaurant; bar; bikes; exercise room; room service; spa. *In room:* A/C, TV, hair dryer, minibar, Wi-Fi (free).

Klaus K. Hotel ★ Originally built in the 1950s as the seven-story headquarters for a chain of hardware stores, the Klaus attracts an ongoing stream of business travelers. The staff is charming, and the hotel has cozy bars, restaurants, and a nightclub. The rooms are high-ceilinged and airy, but not particularly stylish or cutting edge. Thanks to a location a 5-minute walk from the uphill end of the North and South Esplanades, it's central to virtually everything in Helsinki. The hotel has an intriguing association with decorative themes from the Finnish national epic, the *Kalevala,* as seen in the granitc bas-reliefs that flank the entrance to the hotel, and the decor of the separately recommended nightclub, Ahio.

Bulevardi 2–4, 00120 Helsinki. www.klauskhotel.com. ✆ **020/770-4700.** Fax 020/770-4730. 137 units. 172€–250€ double; 375€ suite. Rates include buffet breakfast. AE, DC, MC, V. Tram: 4, 7, or 10. **Amenities:** 3 restaurants; 2 bars; babysitting; exercise room; sauna. *In room:* TV/DVD, minibar, Wi-Fi (free).

Seurahuone Helsinki ★ The origins of this hotel date back to 1833, when it opened in cramped and not particularly grand premises that it quickly outgrew. In 1913, it moved into a five-story Art Nouveau town house that was custom-built to house it across the street from Helsinki's railway station. Since then, it has been expanded as part of a series of comprehensive upgrades, one of which included a new wing. Rooms are moderate in size, mostly with twin beds.

Kaivokatu 12, FIN-00100. Helsinki. www.hotelliseurahuone.fi. ✆ **09/691-41.** Fax 09/691-40-10. 118 units. Sun–Thurs 167€–250€ double; Fri–Sat 108€–197€ double; 299€–450€ suite. Rates include buffet breakfast. AE, DC, MC, V. Tram: 3B, 3T, or 4. **Amenities:** 2 restaurants; bar; room service; sauna. *In room:* TV, hair dryer, minibar, Wi-Fi (free).

Sokos Hotel Torni ★ At a height of 14 stories, the Torni was the first "skyscraper" built in Helsinki (1931), and many irate locals demanded that it be torn down. Now its contemporary rooms are the number-one choice for visiting celebrities. The finest units are those in the tower, but all the rooms are average in size, with double-glazed windows.

Yrjönkatu 26, FIN-00100 Helsinki. www.sokoshotels.fi. ✆ **020/1234-604.** Fax 09/433-671-00. 152 units. Sun–Thurs 149€–235€ double; Fri–Sat 110€–220€ double; 261€–321€ suite. Rates include buffet breakfast. AE, DC, MC, V. Parking nearby 36€. Tram: 3, 4, or 8. **Amenities:** Restaurant; 2 bars; room service; sauna. *In room:* A/C, TV, hair dryer, minibar, Wi-Fi (free).

INEXPENSIVE

Best Western Premier Hotel Katajanokka You wouldn't know that this top-value hotel, completely restored, was once a prison. Surrounded by a park, the complex was a jail through the end of the 20th century. The building is actually now protected by the National Board of Antiquities. The stairwells and even bars on the windows are still here, but by combining two or three cramped cells, the larger rooms now have a modern interior design with all the conveniences. Meals are served in the **Jailbird Restaurant** in the basement.

Vyokatu 1, FIN-00160 Helsinki. www.bwkatajanokka.fi. ✆ **800/780-7234** or 09/686-450. Fax 09/670-290. 106 units. 139€–225€ double; from 208€ junior suite. AE, MC, V. Parking 16€. Tram: Katajanokan terminal. **Amenities:** Restaurant; bar; concierge; exercise room; room service; sauna; Wi-Fi (free, in lobby). *In room:* A/C, TV, hair dryer, minibar.

Helka Hotel Owned by the Finnish version of the YWCA, this 1928 hotel is a budget oasis in a sea of expensively priced hotels. In the heart of the city, close to the train station, and rising six floors, it's a serviceable, affordable choice. All bedrooms are carefully decorated with traditional Finnish furniture by Alvar Aalto, a specially designed ceiling landscape of Finnish nature, and stylish lighting.

Pohjoinen Rautatiekatu 23, Helsinki 00100. www.helka.fi. ✆ **09/613-580.** Fax 09/441-087. 150 units. 122€–185€ double; 150€–290€ suite. Rates include buffet breakfast. AE, DC, MC, V. Parking 10€. Tram: 3B or 3T. Metro: Kamppi. **Amenities:** Restaurant; bar; bikes; room service; sauna; Wi-Fi (free, in lobby). *In room:* A/C, TV, hair dryer, minibar.

Hotel Arthur A large and well-maintained establishment, the Arthur is owned and operated by the YMCA, who named it after Arthur Hjelt, the long-ago founder of that organization's Finnish branch. Originally built in 1906, with additional space added in 2006, it is a 4-minute walk from the railway station in a quiet neighborhood. The rooms are decorated in a functional, modern style, offering cleanliness and comfort instead of soul and character.

Vuorikatu 19, FIN-00100 Helsinki. www.hotelarthur.fi. ✆ **09/17-34-41.** Fax 09/62-68-80. 167 units. Mon–Thurs 124€–144€ double; Fri–Sun 94€–112€ double; 250€ suite. Rates include buffet breakfast. AE, DC, MC, V. Parking 19€. Tram: 1, 2, 3, 6, or 7. **Amenities:** Restaurant; bar; Internet (4€ per hour, in lobby); room service; sauna. *In room:* TV, hair dryer, minibar (in some), Wi-Fi (in some, 8€ per day).

Hotelli Finn This well-run hotel, built shortly after World War II, occupies the top two floors (fifth and sixth) of a well-located office building. It prides itself as the cheapest hotel in Helsinki and houses a scattering of summer visitors, dockworkers from northern and western Finland, and a handful of businesspeople from neighboring Baltic States. The small rooms resemble college dorms, but the price is right.

Kalevankatu 3B, FIN-00100 Helsinki. www.hotellifinn.fi. ✆ **09/684-43-60.** Fax 09/684-436-10. 27 units, 18 with bathroom. 75€ double without bathroom; 90€ double with bathroom. AE, DC, MC, V. Tram: 3, 4, 7, or 10. *In room:* TV, Wi-Fi (free).

Omena Hotel Eerikinkatu Budget hotel chain Omena's concept is based on a high level of technology-based automation that allows for affordable rates, sometimes as low as 55€ per night. Omena hotels don't have reception areas. All Omena hotels are virtually identical in their design, including a large-size double bed, with two easy chairs that also fold out to make for comfortable beds. Rooms are stylish, and most of them are spacious enough to accommodate four adults.

Eerikinkatu 25, 00100 Helsinki. www.omenahotels.com. ✆ **09/600-18018.** 95 units. 55€–77€ double. AE, MC, V. Parking 18€. All trains to Central Station. **Amenities:** Breakfast arranged across the street. *In room:* TV, hair dryer, Internet (free).

North of Center

Hilton Helsinki Strand ★★★ At the edge of the water behind a bay-windowed facade, the Hilton has the most dramatic atrium in the capital. The rooms were conceived by some of Finland's best talent and decorated with local designs, including hand-woven wall hangings and in some cases, parquet floors. Marble from Lapland was used extensively. Half the well-furnished guest rooms provide views of the harbor.

John Stenbergin Ranta 4, FIN-00530 Helsinki. www.hilton.com. ✆ **800/445-8667** in the U.S., or 358/939-351. Fax 09/393-532-55. 192 units. 185€–360€ double; 550€–1,200€ suite. Rates include buffet breakfast. AE, DC, MC, V. Parking 20€. Tram: 3B, 3T, 6, or 7. **Amenities:** Restaurant; bar; babysitting; bikes; exercise room; indoor heated pool; room service; sauna. *In room:* A/C, TV, hair dryer, minibar, Wi-Fi (10€ per day).

West of Center

Hilton Hotel Kalastajatorppa ★★ This "Cottage of the Fisherman" is close to the water, and just 5km (3 miles) northwest of the city center. On a ridge of land between two arms of the sea, the pair of marble- and granite-faced buildings was designed to blend in with the surrounding birch and pines. Guest rooms are in either the core of the hotel, which dates from 1937, or a seashore annex that provides panoramic views of the water. Outfitted with wood paneling and hardwood floors, units are tasteful, understated, and comfortable.

Kalastajatorpantie 1, FIN-00330 Helsinki. www.hilton.com. ✆ **09/458-11.** Fax 09/458-12211. 238 units. 148€–370€ double; 535€–1,100€ suite. Rates include buffet breakfast. AE, DC, MC, V. Free parking outside, 15€ inside. Tram: 4. **Amenities:** 2 restaurants; 2 bars; exercise room; indoor heated pool; room service; sauna; outdoor tennis court (unlit). *In room:* A/C, TV, hair dryer, minibar, Wi-Fi (15€ per day).

At the Airport

Hilton Helsinki-Vantaa Airport ★ ☺ This is the only hotel with direct access to the international airport terminal, which is reached via a covered walkway. Fortunately, all its large, well-furnished, and comfortable bedrooms are soundproof. Junior suites come with a separate living room with sofa. Serving three meals a day, and open long hours to accommodate the erratic schedules of travelers, **Restaurant Gui** serves classic Finnish dishes in a sleek, elegant setting.

Lentajankuja 1, FIN-1530 Vantaa. www.hilton.co.uk/helsinkivantaa. ✆ **09/73220.** Fax 09/732-22211. 244 units. 143€–365€ double; from 372€ suite. AE, DC, MC, V. Parking 24€. **Amenities:** Restaurant; bar; babysitting; bikes; exercise room; room service; sauna. *In room:* A/C, TV, hair dryer, minibar, Wi-Fi (10€ per day).

WHERE TO DINE

In the City Center

VERY EXPENSIVE

Chez Dominique ★★★ FRENCH/INTERNATIONAL One of only a small handful of Michelin-starred restaurants in Finland, this gourmet citadel is the culinary showcase for Hans Välimäki, one of Scandinavia's most outstanding chefs. From first-class, market-fresh ingredients to the elegant decor, Chez Dominique represents dining at its finest in Helsinki. The only restaurant that rivals it is the also-recommended G. W. Sundmans (see below). Appetizers are creative and imaginative, the best examples including a terrine of foie gras with a duck confit and a side of shallot ice cream, and slightly smoked tuna with a gratin of Granny Smith apples. Main dishes include roasted turbot with garlic sauce and a potato risotto, medallions of lamb with sautéed chanterelles, and lobster tortellini with vanilla and anise sauce.

Richardinkatu 4. ✆ **09/612-73-93.** www.chezdominique.fi. Reservations required. Main courses 45€–55€; fixed-price menus 99€–149€. AE, DC, MC, V. Mon–Fri 11:30am–2pm; Tues 6pm–midnight; Wed–Fri 11:30am–midnight; Sat noon–midnight. Closed July. Tram: 10.

G. W. Sundmans ★★★ SCANDINAVIAN/FRENCH We like this place more than Chez Dominique. The elegant setting is a restored Empire-style mansion overlooking the harbor, a few steps from Market Square. The main restaurant, which is divided into five rooms, is on the second floor. (At street level within the same building is the also-recommended, and considerably less expensive, Sundman's Krog.) Chef Jarmo Vähä-Savo and his staff prepare light, contemporary fare, such as fried sweetbreads with asparagus and pickled chanterelles, or foie gras with a compote of figs. One of the fixed-price offerings, the Menu Skandinavia, features the likes of sugar-cured salmon with fennel, risotto with chanterelles and local cheese, and apple pie with cardamom ice cream.

Eteläranta 16. ✆ **09/612-85-400.** www.royalravintolat.com. Reservations required. Main courses 25€–38€; fixed-price menus 46€–79€. AE, DC, MC, V. Mon–Fri 11am–2:30pm and 5–11pm; Sat 6pm–midnight. Tram: 1, 2, 3T, or 4.

La Petite Maison ★★ FRENCH A bit less expensive than the above-recommended Chez Dominique, and a bit cozier and more accessible, this restaurant occupies two intimate dining rooms on a street that showcases more Art Nouveau buildings than any other street in town. Inside, you'll find an open kitchen, a bar area loaded with the fruit of a Finnish harvest, and elaborate arrays of crystal and silver. The chef, the *maître d'hôtel,* and most of the staff are natives of France. Depending on the season, meals might include house-style tuna niçoise, hunters-style filet of beef with seasonal mushrooms, or a well-prepared confit of duckling. The wine list is one of the most sophisticated in town, always with several all-organic choices.

Huvilakatu 28. ✆ **010/270-1700.** www.henrix.fi. Reservations recommended. Fixed-price menus 69€–79€. AE, MC, V. Mon–Sat 6–10pm. Tram: 3B or 3T.

Mecca ★ INTERNATIONAL Cozy and stylish, Mecca is indeed that for the high-living young crowd that is attracted to its bar, restaurant, and lounge. An evening here will be one of the most enjoyable in Helsinki, particularly after sampling the innovative drinks and tasting the creative cuisine based on market-fresh ingredients. Mecca's set menus include everything from Mongolian barbecue with black-bean sauce to chicken wings risotto with a grape compote.

Korkeavuorenkatu 34. ✆ **09/1345-6200.** www.mecca.fi. Reservations required. Main courses 12€–26€; fixed-price menus 35€–65€. AE, DC, MC, V. Mon–Thurs 11:30am–2pm and 5pm–midnight; Fri–Sat 11:30am–2pm and 5pm–4am. Tram: Kaisaniemi.

Palace Gourmet ★★ FINNISH/FRENCH With a panoramic view of the harbor from the 10th floor of the Palace Hotel, one of the most acclaimed restaurants in Helsinki has been offering exquisite cuisine combined with excellent service and a unique ambience since 1952. It has wood paneling, large windows, and an excellent postwar Finnish design. Its award-winning wine cellar is one of the best in the country. Set-price menus feature what's in season, perhaps roasted halibut with a vanilla-flavored garlic mousse and tarragon sauce or reindeer with rowanberry mousse.

In the Palace Hotel, Eteläranta 10. ✆ **09/13-45-6715.** www.palacekamp.fi. Reservations required. Main courses 28€–32€; fixed-price menus 54€–82€. AE, DC, MC, V. Mon–Fri 11:30am–2:30pm and 6pm–midnight. Tram 3B or 3T.

Restaurant Savoy ★★ FINNISH/INTERNATIONAL In an office building near the harbor, this restaurant's decor exemplifies Finnish modernism. In 1937 Finland's greatest architect, Alvar Aalto, designed every detail of the place, even the lighting fixtures. Few other restaurants in Finland celebrate the memory and tastes of the nation's greatest national hero, Marshal Mannerheim. It proudly serves his favorite drink—a Marskin Ryyppy (a schnapps made with vodka, aquavit, dry vermouth, and dry gin). It justifiably declares its *vorschmack* (an appetizer made of minced beef, lamb, and Baltic herring that's simmered for 2 days and served with baked potatoes and sour cream) as the best in town.

Eteläesplanadi. ✆ **09/612-853-00.** www.royalravintolat.com/savoy. Reservations required. Main courses 36€–48€; 3-course lunch 65€. AE, DC, MC, V. Mon–Fri 11:30am–2pm and 6–10pm; Sat 6pm–midnight. Closed Dec 23–Jan 7. Tram: 3B.

EXPENSIVE

Bellevue RUSSIAN Close to Market Square and the Uspenski Orthodox cathedral, the Bellevue has been an enduring favorite since 1917 because of its good cooking and its nostalgia for all things tsarist and Russian. You can dine in a long, corridor-like dining room or in one of the smaller, cozier side rooms. Herring, still served Russian style, is always a good appetizer, as are blinis and caviar. The chicken

Kiev, filet of beef with herb-flavored butter, and pot-roasted bear steak (limited by the fact that Finland allows only 70 bears killed per year) are menu highlights.

Rahapajankatu 3. ✆ **09/17-95-60.** www.restaurantbellevue.com. Reservations recommended. Main courses 20€–64€; fixed-price lunch menus 40€–58€. AE, DC, MC, V. Tues–Fri 11am–midnight; Sat 1pm–midnight. Closed Sun–Mon. Tram: 4.

Havis ★★ FINNISH/SEAFOOD Named after the heroic female statue (the *Havis Amanda*) a few steps from its entrance, this upscale tavern is the finest seafood restaurant in Helsinki. Established in 1973, and having moved into its present quarters in 2004, Havis prides itself on its primarily Finnish seafood. Depending on the season, you can enjoy perch soup with a perch-stuffed crepe, roasted tuna with avocado and citrus, fried whitefish prepared over an open fire with a purée of green peas and carrot sauce, and mushroom lasagna with parsley sauce. The service is impeccable.

Eteläranta 16. ✆ **09/6128-5800.** www.royalravintolat.com/havis. Reservations required. Main courses 20€–26€. AE, DC, MC, V. Mon–Fri 11:30am–11:30pm; Sat 1–11:30pm; Sun 5–11pm. Tram: 3T.

Kämp Café ★ CONTINENTAL/INTERNATIONAL This upscale and rather posh bistro is the kind of place where you'll be comfortable and well fed, but it's not stratospherically expensive. Amid a decor inspired by the 19th-century style of the Russian Empire, it occupies much of the street level of Helsinki's most elegant and historic hotel, and opens onto a view of the imperial-looking bar (the Kämp Club). You can eat in the Kämp Club, but the tables are cramped and rather uncomfortable. Polite staff members will haul out, among others, a parfait of duck liver with port-wine jelly, platters of fried pikeperch (zander) with whitefish roe sauce, and grilled entrecôte of veal with *diablo* sauce.

Pohjoisesplanadi 29. ✆ **09/5761-1204.** www.hotelkamp.fi. Reservations required. Main courses in the bar 12€–24€; main courses in the dining room 18€–31€. AE, DC, MC, V. Mon–Wed 11:30am–11pm; Thurs–Fri 11:30am–midnight; Sat noon–midnight; Sun noon–11pm. Tram: 1 or 7.

Ravintola Lasipalatsi ★ FINNISH/CONTINENTAL Built in 1935, this restaurant sweeps in a gentle, glass-covered curve along the junction of the two busiest boulevards in Finland, about a block from the rail station. It was originally conceived as a site for the care and feeding of visitors to the eagerly awaited Helsinki Olympic games of 1940. Today, it's loaded with a mass of diners from everywhere, with just a whiff of formality and grandeur from the uniformed staff. Service, though well meaning, isn't particularly organized. Menu items include *vorschmack,* fried pikeperch with a sauce made from a combination of Finnish cheeses, and grilled wild salmon.

Mannerheimintie 22. ✆ **020/7424-290.** www.ravintola.lasipalatsi.fi. Reservations recommended. Main courses 18€–29€; fixed-price menu 43€–48€. AE, DC, MC, V. Mon–Fri 11am–midnight; Sat 2–11pm. Tram: 3B, 3T, or 4.

Ravintola Nokka ★★ FINNISH This is one of the top five restaurants of Helsinki, outpaced only by such choices as G. W. Sundmans and Chez Dominique. In a late-19th-century brick building below the Helsinki Culinary Institute, immediately fronting the harbor, the restaurant is the cheapest member of a respected chain that includes some of the best-known dining venues in Helsinki. The cozy bar area specializes in Calvados, carrying nearly 50 brands, and the three additional dining areas feature a sweeping view over one of the most high-tech kitchens in Finland. The chefs fan out across Finland to get their ingredients: arctic char from Pyhämaa, duck from Alhopakka, fresh fish from western Finland, lamb from Bovik, and snails from Porvoo. Their Helsinki Menu is one of the town's best.

Kanavaranta 7F. ✆ **09/687-7330.** www.royalravintolat.com/nokka. Reservations required. Main courses 20€–30€; fixed-price menus 39€–67€. AE, DC, MC, V. Mon–Fri 11:30am–midnight; Sat 6pm–midnight. Tram: 4.

Ravintola Sipuli ★★ FINNISH/CONTINENTAL In five rooms of a former 19th-century warehouse, this charming restaurant takes its name from the gilded onion-shaped domes (Sipuli translates as "onion") of the Russian Orthodox Uspenski Cathedral that rises majestically a short distance away. A skylight in the upstairs dining room provides a view of the cathedral. The expert chef always uses the finest of ingredients from stream and field, as seen in his smoked filet of pikeperch served with a salmon mousse and reindeer meat that has been carefully butchered and shaped as noisettes. The amiably battered street-level bistro is where simple lunches are served.

Kanavaranta 7. ✆ **09/612-85500.** www.royalravintolat.com/sipuli. Reservations recommended. Lunch buffet in street-level bar 9€ per person; main courses in upstairs restaurant 25€–30€. AE, DC, MC, V. Lunchtime buffet in street-level bar Mon–Fri only, 11am–2pm. Upstairs restaurant Tues–Sat 6pm–midnight. Closed Sat–Sun mid-Sept to mid-May. Tram: 2 or 4.

MODERATE

Carlito's ITALIAN/PIZZERIA Carlito's chefs often take old recipes and give them a modern twist. For starters, opt for the baby onions poached in balsamic vinegar or deep-fried tiger prawns with tomato mayonnaise. A tender grilled filet of beef appears with a barbecue sauce and fried potatoes. You can also order a barbecued chicken burger with cheddar. Emerging piping hot from the oven, the pizzas come with varied toppings, including smoked ham and mozzarella, or ham with fontina cheese and truffle oil.

In the Hotel GLO, Kluuvikatu 4. ✆ **09/1345-6749.** Reservations recommended. Main courses 13€–29€; pizzas 8€–16€. AE, DC, MC, V. Mon–Thurs 11:30am–10pm; Fri 11:30am–10:30pm; Sat 1–10:30pm. Tram: 1, 3, 7, or 11.

FishMarket ★★★ SEAFOOD In a cheerful precinct near the South Harbor, this is the place to go for the best and freshest fish and seafood in Helsinki. Naturally, it is near a maritime harbor and enjoys a proximity to the sea. The Seafood Bar is filled with temptations—fresh lobsters, oysters (some 30,000 a year sold here), crabs, and clams. No one in town does a better seafood platter, and you can even watch the chefs as they prepare it. Start with crayfish and duck liver with poached asparagus, going on to such mains as grilled tuna fish with chorizo, calamari salad, and eggplant "caviar," or else roast Greenland halibut with tomato marmalade. In summer tables on the terrace are eagerly sought out.

Pohjoisesplanadi 17. ✆ **09/1345-6220.** www.palacekamp.fi. Reservations required. Main courses 29€–59€; fixed-price menus 52€–70€. AE, DC, MC, V. Mon–Fri 6–11:30pm; Sat 5–11:30pm. Tram: Pohjoisesplanadi.

Grotesk ★ FINNISH Ari Ruoho, one of the rising young chefs of Helsinki, founded his restaurant in a grand stone building that was once the home of the major daily newspaper back in 1907. The red-and-black restaurant is evocative of glitzy Old Russia, and it also boasts a courtyard for dining on a summer day. Ruoho honed his culinary skills while cooking in such diverse places as Bali and San Diego. His starters are some of the most imaginative in town, featuring the likes of lamb sweetbreads with a roasted Jerusalem artichoke purée or Baltic herring *escabeche* with a fennel mousse. No one can top his licorice ice cream.

Ludviginkatu 10. ✆ **09/104-702-100.** www.grotesk.fi. Reservations required. 3-course fixed-price lunch 25€; dinner main courses 21€–28€. AE, DC, MC, V. Mon 11:30am–3pm; Tues–Thurs 11:30am–3pm and 5pm–1am; Fri 11:30am–3pm and 5pm–2am; Sat 5pm–2am. Tram: 9 or 11.

Ilmatar ★★ FINNISH/BREAKFAST This weekend-only retreat serves one of Helsinki's finest brunches. Acclaimed by critics, it is a leader in the gastronomic renaissance sweeping across Helsinki. Head chef Pasi Partio knows how to combine traditional and modern dishes almost better than any of his competitors. Menu offerings include local ham and free-range eggs, or else roe mousse and smoked reindeer.

In the Klaus K. Hotel, Bulevardi 2–4. ✆ **20/770-4714.** www.ravintolailmatar.fi. Fixed-price menu 32€. AE, MC, V. Sat–Sun noon–3pm; closed otherwise. Tram: 4, 7, or 10.

Kellarikrouvi FINNISH/SCANDINAVIAN This restaurant, built in 1901, was originally a storage cellar for potatoes and firewood for the apartment house above it. Since 1965, it has been a cozy restaurant that was the first in Finland to serve beer from a keg. Enjoy it at the street-level bar (where you can also dine if you like) before descending a steep staircase to the vaulted labyrinth of the cellar, which can be noisy and animated, especially on weekends. Your dinner might begin with a terrine of perch followed by pork cutlets with a potato-and-cheese gratin, grilled kidneys in a mustard-cream sauce, reindeer steak with game sauce and roasted potatoes, or fried cubed salmon with root vegetables and whiskey sauce.

Pohjoinen Makasiinikatu 6. ✆ **09/686-07-30.** www.royalravintolat.com. Reservations recommended for dinner. Main courses 18€–27€; fixed-price lunch (11am–2pm) 25€–44€. AE, DC, MC, V. Mon–Fri 11am–midnight; Sat noon–midnight. Tram: 3B.

Kosmos Restaurant ★ FINNISH If you want traditional Finnish cuisine without a lot of innovative Continental touches, this is your place. Near the center of Helsinki's main street, Mannerheimintie, this restaurant is known throughout Finland as a gathering place for artists, writers, and television personalities. The decor is 1930s and simple, and the menu specialties include grilled whitefish, smoked eel, fried Baltic herring, mutton chops with a creamy herb sauce, and chicken in cherry sauce. Light meals, such as open tartare sandwiches, *vorschmack,* and borscht, are also available. The special lunch is served until 3pm.

Kalevankatu 3. ✆ **09/64-72-55.** www.ravintolakosmos.fi. Reservations recommended. Main courses 18€–30€; fixed-price lunch menu 30€. AE, DC, MC, V. Mon–Fri 11:30am–1am; Sat 4pm–1am. Tram: 3B, 3T, or 4. Bus: 17 or 18.

Ravintola Juuri ★ FINNISH Seating only two dozen diners nightly, this independent restaurant evokes an urban farmhouse. Sit at sturdy, thick-legged wooden tables and begin with *sapas,* Finnish for tapas, which might feature cold smoked pike tartare with potato pancakes or slightly smoked reindeer heart with a jelly made of rowanberries. Dark brown bread is served with a creamy carrot butter. Main courses are taste sensations, especially the braised trout with an herby butter sauce and a morel crepe, or an organic shoulder of lamb with pumpkin pancakes and a bone marrow sauce.

Korkeavuorenkatu 27. ✆ **09/635-732.** Reservations required. All main courses 24€. AE, DC, MC, V. Mon–Fri 11am–2pm; Sun–Fri 4–10pm; Sat noon–10pm. Tram: 10.

Ravintola Rivoli ★ FRENCH/FINNISH The dining room is an Art Nouveau fantasy set in a labyrinthine room with upholstered banquettes. One of its subdivisions is named "Fish Rivoli," and from its separate menu you can order some of the finest seafood dishes in the city. In both dining rooms, you can enjoy such fare as filet of perch with herb butter, and grilled salmon with mustard sauce. At lunchtime, special *husmanskost* is offered, featuring such dishes as onion soup and grilled rainbow trout. The management also operates an adjoining pizzeria.

Albertinkatu 38. ✆ **09/64-34-55.** www.rivolirestaurants.fi. Reservations recommended. Main courses 15€–42€; fixed-price menus 44€–47€. AE, DC, MC, V. Mon–Fri 11am–midnight; Sat 5pm–midnight; Sun 1–5pm (buffet). Closed Sat June–Aug and bank holidays. Tram: 6. Bus: 14.

Restaurant and Bar Olo ★ NORDIC The seasonal menu focuses on a modern northern European cuisine with superb raw materials from both land and sea. Lunch or dinner is a series of two- or three-course menus. A typical lunch might begin with a chanterelle soup followed by fried pikeperch, ending in a passion fruit mousse. Wild duck terrine is often featured as a starter, or else you can order wild duck as a main course, the latter served with pumpkin and black currants. A house specialty is filet of deer in rosemary sauce.

Kasarmikatu 44. ✆ **09/665-565.** www.olo-ravintola.fi. Reservations required. Fixed-price lunch 29€–41€; fixed-price dinner 34€–83€. AE, DC, MC, V. Mon 11:30am–2pm; Tues–Fri 11:30am–midnight; Sat 5pm–midnight. Kitchen closes at 10:30pm. Tram: Poujoisesplanadi.

Restaurant Torni FINNISH The Sokos Hotel Torni (see "Where to Stay," earlier in this chapter) throws all its culinary energies into this showcase of Finnish cuisine. In a pastel-colored Art Nouveau dining room on the hotel's street level, a crew of formally dressed waiters serves specialties from the forests and streams of Finland. The best examples include baked snow grouse with game sauce, and breast of wild duck with port-wine and ginger sauce.

In the Sokos Torni Hotel, Kalevankatu 5. ✆ **09/43360.** www.ravintolatorni.fi. Reservations recommended. Main courses 18€–34€; 4-course fixed-price menu 56€–59€. AE, DC, MC, V. Mon–Thurs 11:30am–2:30pm and 5–10:30pm; Fri 11:30am–11:30pm; Sat 5–11pm. Tram: 3, 4, or 10.

Sir Eino FINNISH/CONTINENTAL This warm, wood-paneled bar and grill offers reasonably priced food in an otherwise rather expensive neighborhood. Know in advance that at least two-thirds of this rather large dining and drinking emporium is devoted to the bar area, and that you'll have to walk what seems like a very long and shadowy distance to reach the dining room. Main-course salads are very appealing for light appetites, and a spit-roasted half-chicken is one of the specialties of the house.

Eteläesplanadi 18. ✆ **09/8568-5770.** www.rafla.fi. Reservations not necessary. Main courses 11€–19€. AE, DC, MC, V. Tues 6pm–midnight; Wed–Thurs 4pm–1am; Fri–Sat 4pm–3am. Tram: 3B or 3T.

Sundman's Krog ★ FINNISH This is a cozy and relatively affordable bistro that occupies the street level of the same historic home that houses G. W. Sundmans. The buffet, in the hull of an antique wooden rowboat, is laden with herring, local cheeses, and salads. ***Note:*** The fried herring from this buffet is best consumed with a smear of herring roe, sour cream, chopped onions, and a liberal dose of black pepper. Other dishes might include pikeperch with crayfish sauce, gratin of herbed whitefish with tomato-flavored risotto, and peppered noisettes of reindeer with chanterelle sauce.

Eteläranta 16. ✆ **09/6128-5450.** www.royalravintolat.com. Reservations recommended. Main courses 19€–25€; fixed-price menus 37€–45€. AE, DC, MC, V. Mon–Fri 11am–11pm; Sat noon–11pm; Sun 1–11pm. Last order accepted at 9:45pm. Tram: 1 or 3B.

Teatteri Ravintola INTERNATIONAL This very popular, sprawling complex of bars, nightclubs, and restaurants includes two bars, a deli and takeout service near the entrance (open daily from 9am), and a well-managed restaurant whose menu includes the cuisines of Cuba, Asia, India, and Italy. The Teatteri Bar attracts business folk relaxing after work, while the Clock Bar sports a blazing fireplace and R&B music. One flight above street level, Teatteri Clubbi, hosts a dancing crowd ages 35 to 50 and is open Wednesday to Saturday, from 10pm to 4am. Entrance is usually free, except on Friday and Saturday nights, when there's a cover charge of 9€.

In the Svenska Theater, Pohjoisesplanadi 2. ✆ **09/681-11-36.** www.royalravintolat.com/teatteri. Main courses 17€–32€; 3-course fixed-price menus 50€. AE, DC, MC, V. Food service Mon–Thurs 11am–midnight; Fri–Sat 11am–1am; Sun 1–10pm (closed Sun Sept–May). Bar service Mon–Sat 11am–2am; Sun (June–Aug only) 2pm–1am. Tram: 1 or 7.

INEXPENSIVE

The Bank Lunch Club and The Bank Bistro FINNISH/INTERNATIONAL This high-ceilinged area that originally functioned as the lobby of a bank offers at least four different food stations and one of the most cost-conscious lunches in town. There's nothing glam or pretentious about it, but office workers surge in from across this high-tech, high-rise neighborhood for basic fare such as pasta, sushi, and wok-fried dishes. Since it's open only Monday to Friday for a relatively short 3-hour stretch, diners throughout the rest of the day tend to spill into the cozier and certainly less frenetic bistro. Amid wood paneling, bentwood furniture, and a high-tech, metro-urban decor, you'll find a more sophisticated array of dishes that might include snails with garlic sauce, tomatoes stuffed with a tapenade of olives, and whitefish served with chanterelle-studded risotto. During warm weather, ask at the bistro if *kesakeitto* is available.

Unioninkatu 20. ✆ **09/1345 6260.** www.palacekamp.fi. Reservations not accepted. Lunch Club buffet 9€ per person. Bistro main courses 16€–24€. AE, DC, MC, V. Lunch Club Mon–Fri 11am–2pm; Bistro Mon–Fri 8am–5pm; both closed Sat–Sun. Tram: 3B or 3T.

Kolme Kruunua ★★ FINNISH If you have time for just one place to sample a classic Finnish cuisine, make it this historic dining room that has been dispensing honest food since 1952. It still has its original stained-glass windows and light fixtures. Locally it's celebrated for its traditional meatballs and fried Baltic herring. Many renowned Finnish artisans supplied the decorations, but they are a mere backdrop for the hearty cuisine, such as reindeer stew with lingonberries.

Liisankatu 5. ✆ **09/135-4172.** www.kolmekruunua.fi. Reservations required. Main courses 13€–23€. AE, MC, V. Mon–Sat 4pm–midnight; Sun 2–11pm. Bus: 18.

Kynsilaukka Restaurant Garlic ★ INTERNATIONAL Kynsilaukka translates from medieval Finnish as "garlic," and the restaurant uses more than 20 pounds of Spanish garlic every day. You'll dine within a pair of cozy and consciously rustic dining rooms, perhaps preceding your meal with a garlic martini or a pint of garlic-flavored beer. Menu items are influenced by the cuisine of Russia, as seen in the grilled gratin of vegetables with garlic and sour cream, pike balls in garlic-flavored cream sauce, and filet steak with garlic and red-wine sauce. Desserts include cloudberry crepes with ice cream, which can be rendered more or less garlicky depending on how much garlic marmalade you add.

Frederikkatu 22. ✆ **09/65-19-39.** www.kynsilaukka.com. Reservations recommended. Main courses 17€–27€; fixed-price lunch menu 14€. AE, DC, MC, V. Mon–Fri 11am–11pm; Sat–Sun 1–11pm. Tram: 3B or 3T.

Manala FINNISH/INTERNATIONAL In a residential neighborhood several blocks west of the Crowne Plaza Hotel, this restaurant prides itself on both its cuisine and its collection of 19th-century Finnish paintings. You can enjoy such specialties as fresh fish, sautéed reindeer, chicken cooked with garlic potatoes on a hot iron grill, and a wide range of pizzas. The chef is well known for his homemade Finnish bread, served with a homemade cheese pâté. Virtually every night of the week the late-night bar attracts lots of actors and musicians, and Friday between 11pm and 4am features live Finnish-style dance music. The popular bar has an outdoor terrace.

Dagmarinkatu 2. ✆ **09/580-77707.** www.botta.fi. Reservations recommended. Main courses 12€–31€; pizzas 8€–11€; fixed-price menu 28€. AE, DC, MC, V. Mon–Fri 11am–4am; Sat–Sun 2pm–4am. Tram: 4, 7, or 10.

Ravintola Central ☺ FINNISH/INTERNATIONAL This warm and woodsy bar and tavern in an upscale residential neighborhood serves generous portions of rib-sticking food in a friendly setting. No one will mind if you drop in just for a drink, but if you stay for a meal, you can watch the food preparation in the open kitchens. Menu items include at least a dozen kinds of pizza, including a version with reindeer filet; grilled steak with a brandy-peppercorn sauce; and pikeperch with lobster stuffing. Every Friday, the menu features fresh steamed mussels in a white-wine sauce, served with fries. Children's platters go for around 7€ each.

Pietarinkatu 15. ✆ **09/636-483.** www.central.fi. Pizzas 8.50€–11€; main courses 13€–25€. AE, DC, MC, V. June to mid-Sept Mon–Sat 2–11:30pm, Sun 2–10:30pm; mid-Sept to May Mon–Sat noon–10:45pm, Sun noon–10pm. Tram: 3B or 3T.

Sports Academy FINNISH With the opening of Sports Academy in Helsinki, the Finnish capital now has a first-rate sports bar where you can watch the game while filling up on hearty food, including plenty of snacks and lots of beer, both domestic and foreign. The Academy has nearly 60 plasma screens and 6 giant screens, and the menu lists some 40 dishes, from a vegetarian blue-cheese pasta with Parmesan flakes to chargrilled salmon with crayfish sauce. The best burgers in town are served with everything from smoked bacon to chili.

Kaivokatu 8. ✆ **09/7664-300.** Reservations not needed. 13€–29€. AE, DC, MC, V. Mon 11am–10pm; Tues–Thurs 11am–1am; Fri 11am–3am; Sat noon–3am; Sun noon–10pm. All trains to Central Station.

Strindberg Café CONTINENTAL Named after one of Sweden's greatest playwrights, a short walk from the Swedish Theater, this is a warm and convivial rendezvous point that's usually packed, especially on weekends. Its street level houses a cafe and a pastry shop, but its heart and soul is upstairs, where a conservatively modern setting contains a colony of comfortably upholstered chairs and sofas and a big-windowed dining room. Menu items contain an appropriate mixture of Finnish comfort food and modern Continental.

Pohjoisesplanadi 33. ✆ **09/612-86-900.** www.royalravintolat.com/strindberg. Main courses in upstairs restaurant 16€–27€; fixed-price dinner 43€; sandwiches and pastries in street-level cafe 4.50€–11€. AE, DC, MC, V. Cafe Mon–Sat 9am–10pm; Sun 10am–10pm. Restaurant Mon 11am–11pm; Tues–Fri 11am–1am; Sat noon–1am. Tram: 1, 7, or 10.

North of Center

Lastu ★★ MEDITERRANEAN/SCANDINAVIAN On the hotel's lobby level, this restaurant specializes in cuisine from around the edges of the Mediterranean, a medley of North African, Greek, French, and Italian dishes that, as a whole, contribute to one of the most exotic and sophisticated menus in Helsinki. Worthy main dish specialties include tender chicken breast with goat cheese and a nut pesto served with a red-wine sauce, or roast lamb rolled in Parma ham and also served with a red-wine sauce.

In the Scandic Continental Hotel, Mannerheimintie 46. ✆ **09/47371.** Reservations recommended. Main courses 15€–25€; fixed-price menus 29€. AE, DC, MC, V. Mon–Fri 11:30am–2pm and 6–11:30pm; Sat 6–11:30pm. Tram: 3T or 7A.

Ravintola Perho ★ FINNISH/CONTINENTAL Owned and managed by the Helsinki Culinary School, this restaurant is completely staffed by students and trainees. It offers a comfortable modern setting and a cuisine that's professionally supervised (though not necessarily prepared) by the teaching staff. Diners can usually choose either large or small portions of virtually any dish, be it smoked whitebait with mustard sauce or a terrine of smoked reindeer. Many diners find the youthful enthusiasm of the staff charming. The cuisine depends on the culinary lesson of the day.

Mechelininkatu 7. ✆ **09/580-78649.** www.perho.fi. Reservations not accepted. Main courses 18€–26€; fixed-price menus 25€–32€. AE, DC, MC, V. Sept–May Mon–Fri 11am–11pm; Sat noon–11pm; Sun noon–5pm. Closed June–Aug. Tram: 8.

The Islands

Gallery Restaurant Wellamo FINNISH/FRENCH/RUSSIAN Established on a quiet residential island (Katajanokka Island) central to the rest of town, this charming and completely unpretentious restaurant features flickering candles and a revolving series of for-sale paintings by local artists. Menu items include selections from Russia, Finland, and France. During the evening hours, you're likely to hear the sounds of a live pianist.

Vyökatu 9. ✆ **09/66-31-39.** www.wellamo.fi. Reservations recommended. Main courses 14€–24€. AE, MC, V. Tues–Fri 11am–2pm and 5–11pm; Sat 5–11pm; Sun 1–8pm. Tram: 4.

Restaurant Walhalla ★ FINNISH On the fortified island many historians view as the cradle of modern Finland, this restaurant provides a cheerful and historic insight into Finnish cuisine and culture. Open only in summertime, it requires access by ferryboats, which depart from Helsinki's harbor adjacent to the *Havis Amanda* statue at intervals of every 30 and 60 minutes, daily from 9am to 11pm. The return trip to the center of Helsinki occurs at equivalent intervals daily between 9:30am and 11pm. Round-trip fares are 6.50€ per person. Once you land on Kustaanmiekka Island, walk for about 5 minutes to a series of brick-and-granite vaults in the center of the Viapori fortress. A simple pizzeria operates daily from noon to 8pm (June–Aug only), but the preferred spot is the more formal restaurant atop a panoramic terrace. The cooking is competent in every way and the ingredients first-rate, although the setting might outshine the food offerings.

Kustaanmiekka Island, Suomenlinna. ✆ **09/66-85-52.** www.restaurantwalhalla.com. Main courses 21€–31€; fixed-price menu 27€–53€. AE, DC, MC, V. Daily 6pm–midnight. Closed mid-Sept to Apr. Bus: Water bus from Market Sq. to Kustaanmiekka, priced at 6.50€ round-trip per person.

HELSINKI ATTRACTIONS

In the City Center

Eduskuntatalo (Finnish Parliament) One of the world's most enlightened and progressive governing bodies assembles here. Near the post office, this 1931 building of pink Finnish granite houses the 200 members of the one-chamber parliament.

Dining Above the Ramparts of 18th-Century Helsinki

Dining at Särkänlinna Restaurant ★★★ requires a 12-minute transit by ferryboat from Helsinki's mainland, a walk across an otherwise barren island in the middle of Helsinki's harbor, and a wobbly climb up a winding flight of 18th-century stairs.

In 1924, a well-known architect, Oiva Kallio, designed a wood-sided simulation of a long and narrow railway car, and perched it atop the defensive 18th-century ramparts of an island, Särkkä, that functioned as a military outpost. Today, between mid-May and mid-September, you catch a ferryboat that departs at 20-minute intervals every day between 4 and 9pm. The 6€ per person round-trip cost of the boat is billed along with the cost of your meal.

The sloped floor reflects the design of the original ramparts: Soldiers had to roll cannonballs from their storage area down to the waiting cannon. Main courses cost 23€ to 32€ (AE, DC, MC, V). Open mid-May to mid-September nightly from 5:30pm to midnight. Advance reservations required at ✆ 09/1345-6756.

Forty percent of members are women, one of the highest proportions of female legislators in the world. Members meet in the domed interior of Parliament Hall, which is decorated with sculpture by Wäinö Aaltonen. The architect, J. S. Sirén, chose a modernized neoclassical style in celebration of the new republic. Visits involve lots of stair-climbing and as such are not recommended for everyone.

Mannerheimintie 30. ✆ **09/4321.** web.eduskunta.fi. Free admission. Tours Sat 11am and 12:30pm; Sun noon and 1pm; July–Aug also Mon–Fri at 1pm. Tram: 3B or 3T.

Finnish National Gallery ★★★ Finland's largest selection of sculpture, painting, and graphic art is displayed at this museum. The Finnish National Gallery is host to three semiautonomous museums: the Ateneum Art Museum, the Kiasma (Museum of Contemporary Art), and the Sinebrychoff Art Museum (Museum of Foreign Art).

Ateneum Art Museum ★★ Housing the largest collection of fine art in Finland, this museum displays the works of mostly Finnish artists produced between the mid-1700s and 1960. It also contains a scattering of paintings and sculpture by non-Finnish artists from the 19th and 20th centuries. The Finnish artists displayed here aren't known by the general public, so a visit here will be a discovery.

Kaivokatu 2. ✆ **09/17-33-6401.** www.ateneum.fi. Admission 9€ adults, 7€ students and seniors, free for children 17 and under. Tues and Fri 10am–6pm; Wed–Thurs 10am–8pm; Sat–Sun 11am–5pm. Tram: 3B, 3T, or 6.

Kiasma (Museum of Contemporary Art) ★★ Under the administration of the Finnish National Gallery (see above), this is Helsinki's most experimental major museum. An American architect, Steven Hall, designed the radically innovative building, every aspect of which was conceived for the display of art produced since the 1960s. The art that's celebrated within this place might be either electronic or tangible, musical or performance oriented. Exhibitions change frequently within an environment where the "permanent collection" occupies a small percentage of floor space. "Chiasma" is defined in medical dictionaries as "the crossing point of optic nerves," suggesting Finland's ability to mingle the worlds of fine art and high technology.

Mannerheiminaukio 2. ✆ **09/173-365-01.** www.kiasma.fi. Admission 8€ adults, 6€ students and seniors, free for those 17 and under. Tues 10am-5pm; Wed-Fri 10am-8:30pm; Sat-Sun 10am-6pm. Tram: 3B or 3T.

Sinebrychoff Art Museum (Museum of Foreign Art) ★ Part of the Finnish National Gallery (see above), this museum was built in 1842 and still displays its original furnishings. It houses an extensive collection of foreign paintings from the 14th century to the 19th century and has a stunning **collection of foreign miniatures ★★**. Temporary exhibitions, usually presented without any additional charge, have in the recent past included a stunning collection of antique *charkas* (elaborate silver or silver-gilt vodka or schnapps chalices) from Russia. ***Tip:*** On the first Wednesday of each month, admission is free from 5pm to 8pm.

Sinebrychoff, Bulevardi 40. ✆ **09/17-33-6460.** www.sinebrychoffintaidemuseo.fi. Admission 7.50€ adults, 4€ students and seniors, free for persons 17 and under. Tues and Fri 10am-6pm; Wed-Thurs 10am-8pm; Sat-Sun 11am-5pm. Tram: 6.

The Design Museum (Designmuseo) Students of design from all over the world flock to this museum, whose permanent exhibition chronicles the history and development of design in Finland from 1870 to 2002. The permanent exhibition is beefed up by temporary Finnish and international theme exhibitions. The museum is elegant, well stocked, and poised to define the most recent innovations in Finnish or Scandinavian design. Fashion, fabrics, architecture—it's all here, along with household objects, furniture, and a wide array of utilitarian objects.

Korkeavuorenkatu 23. ✆ **09/622-0540.** www.designmuseum.fi. Admission 8€ adults, free for children 13 and under. June-Aug daily 11am-6pm; Sept-May Tues 11am-8pm, Wed-Sun 11am-6pm. Tram: 10.

Helsinki Cathedral (Tuomiokirkko) ★ Dominating the city's skyline, a short walk from Market Square and the harborfront, is one of the city's most visible symbols, a monumental green-domed cathedral erected between 1830 and 1852. Built in a gracefully symmetrical neoclassical style that reflected the glory of ancient Greece and Rome, it was designed by German-born architect Carl Ludvig Engel. Today the rites celebrated inside conform to the Evangelical Lutheran denomination.

Unioninkatu 29. ✆ **09/2340-6120.** Free admission. Daily 9am-6pm; Sun services 10am. Tram: 3T.

Mannerheim Museum ★★ This gracefully proportioned villa within an upscale neighborhood otherwise devoted to foreign embassies functioned as the elegant home of Baron Carl Gustaf Mannerheim, marshal of Finland and president of the republic from 1944 to 1946. The museum houses his collection of European furniture, Asian art, and personal mementos, which include uniforms from both the Imperial Russian army and the then newly established Finnish Republic, swords, an astonishing array of military decorations from many of the nations of Europe, and gifts from admirers.

Kalliolinnantie 14. ✆ **09/63-54-43.** www.mannerheim-museo.fi. Admission (including guided tour) 10€ adults, free for children 11 and under. Fri-Sun 11am-4pm. Tram: 3B or 3T.

Olympic Stadium (Olympiastadion) Helsinki was host to the Olympic Games in 1952; a tower remains from its impressive sports stadium, and an elevator whisks passengers up to the top for a **panoramic view ★★** of the city and the archipelago. The stadium, 2km (1¼ miles) from the city center, was originally built in 1940, but the Olympic Games were canceled that year when World War II broke out.

Paavo Nurmi tie 1. ✆ **09/43-66-010.** www.stadion.fi. Admission 2€ adults, 1€ children 15 and under. Mon-Fri 9am-8pm; Sat-Sun 9am-6pm. Closed during athletic competitions. Tram: 3B, 3T, 4, or 10.

Suomen Kansallismuseo (National Museum of Finland) ★★ This museum is broken into five sections, which include the *Treasure Trove,* presenting the museum's collections of coins, medals, decorations, silver, jewelry, and weapons; the *Prehistory of Finland,* the country's largest archaeological exhibit; the Realm, telling the history of Finnish culture and society from the 13th to the 19th centuries; *A Land and Its People,* presenting rural life in Finland before industrialization; and the *Past Century,* showing independent Finland and its culture in the 20th century. Sample highlights include the **Silver and Jewelry Room ★★**, with some stunning goldsmith work and a display of fashionable jewelry dating back to the Renaissance era, and an amazing **elkhead soapstone sculpture ★★** from the Stone Age.

Mannerheimintie 34. ✆ **09/4050-9544.** www.nba.fi. Admission 7€ adults, 5€ students, free for children 17 and under, and free for all Tues 5:30–8pm. Tues–Wed 11am–8pm; Thurs–Sun 11am–6pm. Tram: 4, 7A, 7B, or 10.

Temppeliaukio Kirkko (Temple Square Church) ★★ This "Church of the Rock" is about 2 blocks west of the National Museum in the Töölö residential district west of Mannerheimintie. Only the domed copper roof and a circular curtain wall of granite blocks are visible from outside. It was designed by two architect brothers, Tuomo and Timo Suomalainen, who chose a rocky outcrop rising some 12m (40 ft.) above street level. The interior walls were blasted from bedrock, and the church's low-rise format and ecosensitive design appealed to residents of neighboring apartment buildings. Because of its superb acoustics, the church is often used as a concert hall.

Lutherinkatu 3. ✆ **09/234-05920.** Free admission. Daily 10am–5pm year-round. Closed during special events. Sun services 10am in Finnish, and 2pm in English. Tram: 3B or 3T.

Urho Kekkonen Museum (Tamminiemi) Set to reopen in 2012, this site celebrates the accomplishments of Urho Kekkonen (1900–86), who served as president of Finland longer (1956–1982) than anyone else. Built in 1904 in the *Jugendstil* (Art Nouveau) style, the site today is a testimonial to the survival of Finland against the Soviet menace, and a testimonial to the man who helped make that happen. An English-language tour is conducted every day at 1:30pm, or you can borrow an English-language recording and player for a self-guided tour.

Seurassarrentie 15. ✆ **09/4050-9650.** www.nba.fi/en/ukk_museum. Admission 5€ adults, 4€ students and seniors, free for children 17 and under. Mid-May to mid-Aug daily 11am–5pm; otherwise Wed–Sun 11am–5pm. Bus: 24 from Erottaja bus stop, adjacent to the Swedish Theater and Stockmann department store.

Parks & Gardens

Botanical Gardens These gardens, a 5-minute walk from the Central Station, feature shrubs and flowers, herbs, ornamentals, Finnish wildflowers, and indigenous trees and bushes. The greenhouses reopened after extensive renovations, making them better than ever. However, unlike the rest of the gardens, they are closed on Monday.

University of Helsinki, Unioninkatu 44. ✆ **09/91-91-24-453.** www.luomus.fi. Admission 6€ adults, 3€ children 7-12, free for children 6 and under. Apr 1–Sept 30 Mon–Fri 7am–8pm, Sat–Sun 9am–8pm; Oct–Mar 31 Mon–Fri 7am–5pm, Sat–Sun 9am–5pm.

Pihlajasaari Recreational Park ☺ A popular attraction favored by bird-watchers and joggers, this park is made up of two small neighboring islands filled with sandy beaches—it's a summer playground for the city. A restaurant and a cafe are in the park.

Pihlajasaari Island. ✆ **09/63-00-65.** Free admission. Daily 24 hr. Motorboat leaves from the end of Laivurinkatu May to mid-Oct daily at 9am, 9:30am, and then at hourly intervals until 8:30pm, depending on weather.

Sibelius Park & Monument Called *Sibeliuksen puisto* in Finnish, this park was planned to honor Jean Sibelius, Finland's most famous composer. The park was meant to reflect the rugged natural beauty of Finland, as inspired by Sibelius's work *Finlandia.* At one side of the park is the monumental sculpture, Eila Hiltunen's tribute to Sibelius, the genius whose music is believed to embody the soul of Finland.

Mechelininkatu. Free admission. Daily 24 hr. Bus: 55A.

Near Helsinki

Ainola ★★ Few countries seem as proud of a native composer as Finns are of Jean Sibelius, who lived within this log building for more than half a century. He named the house after his wife, Aino, and lived here from 1904 until his death in 1957; he and his wife are buried on the property. Avant-garde at the time of its construction, the house was designed by Lars Sonck, who also designed the summer residence of the president of Finland. Järvenpää is 39km (24 miles) from Helsinki.

Ainolantie, in Järvenpää. ✆ **09/287-322.** www.ainola.fi. Admission 5.50€ adults, 3€ students, 1€ children 7-16. May-Sept Tues-Sun 10am-5pm. Closed Oct-Apr. Bus: From Platform 1 of the Helsinki Bus Station, follow the Helsinki-Hyryla-Järvenpää route to where the road forks at a sign saying AINOLA; from there, it's a 4-min. walk to the home. Train: Järvenpää station.

Gallen-Kallela Museum ★★ On a wooded peninsula in a suburb of Helsinki, this museum is dedicated to the great Finnish artist Akseli Gallen-Kallela (1865–1931), who built his studio here between 1911 and 1913, calling it his "castle in the air." Gallen-Kallela had a restless, fanciful personality, and his reputation is based mainly on his paintings, especially those inspired by the *Kalevala (Land of Heroes),* the Finnish national epic first published in 1835. The museum houses a large collection of his paintings, graphics, posters, and industrial design products.

Tarvaspää, Gallen-Kallelantie 27, Espoo. ✆ **09/849-2340.** www.gallen-kallela.fi. Admission 8€ adults, 4€ students, free for children 17 and under. May 15-Aug 31 daily 11am-6pm; Sept 1-May 14 Tues-Sat 11am-4pm, Sun 11am-5pm. Tram: 4 to Munkkiniemi; then walk for 2km (1¼ miles) along the clearly signposted seaside pathway.

Linnanmäki Amusement Park ☺ Linnanmäki, 3km (2 miles) north of Helsinki, is a fun fair of splashing fountains, merry-go-rounds, Ferris wheels, restaurants, cafes, theaters, and 39 different rides. Founded in 1950 by the Children's Foundation to raise money to care for the thousands of children orphaned by World War II, Linnanmäki is still raising money for a new generation of children.

Tivolikuja 1. ✆ **09/77-39-91.** www.linnanmaki.fi. 6€ each ride; free for children 5 and under. Day Pass 26€ adults, 14€-20€ children depending on their height. Mon-Fri 4-10pm; Sat-Sun 1-9 or 10pm. Closed Sept-Apr. Tram: 3B or 3T.

On Nearby Islands

ON SEURASAARI

Seurasaari Open-Air Museum ★★★ One of the largest collections of historic buildings in Finland, each moved here from somewhere else, is on the island of Seurasaari, a national park. Representing the tastes and evolution of Finnish architecture through the centuries, the collection includes a 17th-century church, an 18th-century gentleman's manor house, and dozens of oddly diverse farm buildings. The verve associated with this collection of historic, free-standing buildings is most visible during the summer months, when you can visit the interiors, and when an unpretentious restaurant serves coffee, drinks, and platters of food.

Seurasaari Island. © **09/405-096-60.** www.nba.fi. Admission 6€ adults, 5€ students and seniors, free for persons 17 and under. June–Aug daily 11am–5pm; Sept 1–15 Mon–Fri 9am–3pm, Sat–Sun 11am–5pm. Closed Sept 16–May 31. Bus: 24 from the Erottaja bus stop, near Stockmann department store, to the island. The 5km (3-mile) ride takes about 15 min. and costs 2.50€ each way.

ON SUSISAARI & KUSTAANMIEKKA

Suomenlinna Fortress ★★ (© **09/684-18-80;** www.suomenlinna.fi) is an 18th-century fortress in the Baltic Suomenlinna archipelago. With their walks and gardens, cafes, restaurants, and old-frame buildings, the islands are one of the most intriguing outings from Helsinki. You can take a ferry from Market Square to Suomenlinna year-round beginning at 6:20am daily. The boats run about once an hour, and the last one returns from the island at 2am (5€ adults; 2€ children 17 and under free).

From June to September, Suomenlinna maintains two information kiosks, one at Market Square (by the departure point for the Suomenlinna ferryboat), and a second on the island itself (near Tykistölahti Bay). The latter kiosk serves as the starting point for guided tours, scheduled between June and August, daily at 11am and 2pm. From September to May, they're offered on a limited basis (only Sat–Sun at 1:30pm). They cost 7€ for adults and 3€ for children 5 to 15; free for kids 4 and under.

Suomenlinna Attractions

Ehrensvärd Museum This historical museum includes a model ship collection and officers' quarters from the 18th century, as well as displays based on Suomenlinna's military history. The museum bears the name of Augustin Ehrensvärd, who supervised construction of the fortress during the late 18th century.

Suomenlinna B40. © **09/684-18-50.** www.suomenlinna.fi. Admission 3€ adults, 1€ children 7–17, free for children 6 and under. Apr–May and Oct Sat–Sun 11am–4pm; June–Aug daily 11am–6pm; Sept daily 11am–4pm. Closed Nov–Mar.

Military Museum's Manege Within the thick walls and vaulted ceilings of an area of the Suomenlinna Fortress originally built to store gunpowder, this museum contains exhibits that show how Finland defended itself from foreign aggression during World Wars I and II. The weapons for defending the coastline now include missiles, motorized artillery, and turret guns. Newer technology is represented by close-range missiles and a laser range finder.

Kustaanmiekka. © **09/181-452-96.** www.suomenlinna.fi. Admission 4€ adults, 2€ children. May 12–Aug daily 11am–6pm. Closed Sept–May 11.

Submarine Vesikko The relatively small-scale (250 tons) submarine *Vesikko* was built in Turku in 1933 for the Germans, who used it for mostly experimental purposes. In 1936, the Germans sold it to the Finns, who based it in Suomenlinna's shipyard throughout most of World War II. The Paris Peace Treaty of 1947 forbade Finland to have submarines, so all except the *Vesikko* were scrapped.

Tykistölahti, Suomenlinna. © **09/181-46238.** www.suomenlinna.fi. Admission 4€ adults, 2€ students, seniors, and kids 7–17. Mid-May to Aug daily 11am–6pm. Closed Sept to mid-May.

ON KORKEASAARI

Helsinki Zoo ☺ A collection of northern European animals, including a herd of wild forest reindeer, wolverines, northern owl species, and many other mammals and birds from Europe and Asia, can be found here. We especially like the way the zoo houses its animals and birds in large natural enclosures—not prison cells. A tropical house contains plants from southern climes that Finns have never seen before.

Korkeasaari Island. © **09/169-5969.** www.korkeasaari.fi. Admission by water bus, 16€ adults, 8€ children 6–17; free for kids 5 and under; 47€ group (2 adults and three 6–17 year old children; by bridge,

10€ adults, 5€ children 6–17; free for kids 5 and under; 30€ group (2 adults and three 6–17 year old children). May–Aug daily 10am–8pm; Sept daily 10am–6pm; Oct–Mar daily 10am–4pm; Apr daily 10am–6pm. Water bus: From Market Square and Hakaniemenranta in front of the Merihotelli. Bus: 11 from the Central Railway Station.

Outside Helsinki

PORVOO (BORGÅ) ★★

48km (30 miles) NE of Helsinki

This colorful hamlet gives visitors a look at what a small town in this area was like a century or so ago—it's the second-oldest town in Finland. Simply strolling the Old Quarter, shopping for handicrafts, art, paintings, chocolates, exotic mustards, and smoked fish is a charming way to spend an afternoon. The town is especially appealing in the weeks before Christmas, when it goes out of its way to evoke an endlessly cheerful Finland of long ago.

Founded by Swedish settlers in 1346 at the mouth of a river, Porvoo was already an important trading center in the Middle Ages. Ships commandeered by member cities of the Hanseatic league unloaded then-exotic delicacies here, including wine, dried fruits, and spices, and loaded up on local products that included dried fish, butter, timber, tar, and flax. Even before the town was given its charter, the Swedes maintained a wood fortress on a hill that helped control river and sea trade for several centuries. After Sweden relinquished Finland to Russia, Porvoo was the site of the first Finnish Diet in the early 19th century, when Tsar Alexander I made the little country a semiautonomous grand duchy.

Today, the village and its environs boasts a half-dozen art galleries, pottery and jewelry studios and shops, a gamut of antique stores and secondhand shops, and in addition to the separately recommended cathedral, a half-dozen historic churches or chapels. ***Tip:*** The town's most famous culinary product is a cylinder-shaped tart, usually consumed at breakfast or with afternoon coffee, that was the favorite pastry of Finland's national poet, J. L. Runeberg. It's widely available in cafes and pastry shops throughout Porvoo.

Essentials

GETTING THERE The best way to get to Porvoo is aboard either the M/S *King* or the MS *J. L. Runeberg,* which operate from May 15 to September 1 and depart from and return to Market Square in Helsinki daily. A round-trip requires about 3 to 3¼ hours each way, with a round-trip ticket priced at 35€ for adults and 16€ for children 7 to 16; 6 and under free. En route, you'll have sweeping views over Helsinki's archipelago. For bookings and inquiries, contact **J. L. Runeberg** (✆ **019/524-33-31;** www.msjlruneberg.fi). Alternatively, buses depart from Helsinki's main bus terminal four or five times a day for Porvoo, requiring about an hour for the transfer, and charging 11€ per person, each way. For more information about bus transit, contact the Porvoo tourist office, or call ✆ **019/6893-600.**

VISITOR INFORMATION The Porvoo Tourist Office is at Rihkamakatu 4, FIN-06100 Porvoo (✆ **019/520-23-16;** www.porvoo.fi). In summer, it's open Monday to Friday 9am to 6pm, and Saturday and Sunday from 10am to 4pm. After September 1, hours are Monday through Friday from 9am to 4:30pm and Saturday from 10am to 2pm. The Porvoo Association of Tour Guides offers walking tours of the old town every summer between late June and early September, every Monday to Friday at 2pm. Priced at 6€ per adult, and free for persons 16 and under, they last for about an hour and originate in front of the tourist office.

Seeing the Sights

If you arrive in Porvoo by boat, you'll get a good view of the old merchants' houses and warehouses along the waterfront—most dating from the 18th century.

Albert Edelfelt's Studio Museum One of Finland's most famous painters was born in Porvoo in 1854 and, even after his move to the then-center of the art world (Paris), he made it a point to return to his home town every summer for the rest of his life. In 1883, he built a small studio for himself near what's known as Haikko Manor (see below), where he worked every summer throughout most of his adult life. Many of his famous paintings were created here, including portraits of the Russian Imperial family, which hang today in the art gallery of Haikko Manor Hotel. You'll recognize this cozy and historic artistic shrine by the artist's initials "A. E.," which are displayed near the entrance.

Edelfeltinpolku 3. ✆ **019/577-414.** Admission 4€ adults, includes multilingual guided tour, free for children 15 and under. June–Aug Tues–Sun 10am–4pm; May 15–31 and Sept 1–9 Tues–Sun 10am–2pm.

Cathedral of Porvoo The most venerable building in Porvoo is its cathedral, the oldest parts of which date from the late 1200s. Some visitors refer to it as "the unluckiest building in Finland." Ravaged, rebuilt, and plundered repeatedly during its tormented life by, among others, the Danes and the Russians, and damaged by aerial bombardment in August 1941, it became a cathedral in 1723 when Porvoo was defined as an administrative headquarters for the local church.

Tragedies within this building continued in ways that seemed relentless. On the night of May 29, 2006, the cathedral was ravaged by fire, which was started as a deliberate act of vandalism that was widely condemned throughout Scandinavia. The church has since been restored.

For the purposes of getting a better understanding of Porvoo, however, the church stands prominently on what looks like a verdant country lane in the town center, surrounded by antique stone and clapboard houses. As such, the church is often sought out by day-trippers from Helsinki as a symbol of the sufferings of Finland itself.

Kirkkotori. ✆ **019/250-66-11.** Free admission. May to September Monday to Friday 10am to 6pm, Saturday 10am to 2pm, Sunday 2 to 5pm; October to April Tuesday to Saturday 10am to 2pm, Sunday 2 to 4pm.

Porvoo Historical Museum In the country-baroque red brick premises of Porvoo's Old Town Hall, which was built in 1764, this museum celebrates the role of Porvoo as a mercantile trading center throughout the sometimes tormented history of what's known today as Finland. Inside, you'll find exhibitions that focus on clothing, jewelry, toys, glass, vehicles, and collections of Finnish Art Nouveau furniture and ceramics. There are also artworks from the prehistoric period and the Middle Ages, and exhibitions that relate the various tragedies, including the fire of 1760, when two-thirds of the small town's approximately 300 buildings burned to the ground in a single day.

Vanha Raatihuoneentori. ✆ **019/574-7500.** www.porvoonmuseo.fi. Admission 6€ adults, 3€ ages 7–17, free for persons 6 and under. May–Aug Tues–Sati 10am–4pm, Sun 11am–4pm; Sept–Apr Wed–Sun noon–4pm.

Where to Stay

Haikko Manor (Hotelli Haikon Kartano) ★★ What you'll see when you first arrive at this resort is a grand neoclassical manor house flanked by a sprawling series of modern, two-story wings that contain additional bedrooms and a full-service spa. All of it is on 14 hectares (35 acres) of steeply sloping and heavily forested oceanfront property 7km (4⅓ miles) southwest of Porvoo. The site was established as a farm in 1362, but the manor house as you see it today dates from 1913. It was rebuilt after a fire by members of the von Etter family, who were famously associated, through family links and friendship, with the brother of the last of the Romanoff tsars.

The more expensive accommodations are antique-loaded, high-ceilinged lodgings within the manor house; the more reasonably priced accommodations are comfortable and very tasteful units within the modern wings. On-site spa, sauna, and hydrotherapy facilities are extensive and comprehensive. Spa packages cost from 174€ to 255€. Most require reservations a day or two in advance.

Haikkoontie 114, 06400 Porvoo. ✆ **019/57601.** Fax 019/5760-0399. www.haikko.fi. 226 units. 149€-286€ double; 425€ suite. Rates include buffet breakfast. AE, DC, MC, V. From the center of Porvoo, take bus no. 2. Free parking. **Amenities:** Restaurant; bar; bikes; exercise room; indoor heated pool; room service; spa. *In room:* A/C, TV, hair dryer, minibar, Wi-Fi (10€ per day).

Where to Dine

Wanha Laamanni (The Old Judge's Chambers) ★ FINNISH The best restaurant in town occupies a barnlike antique building a few steps downhill from the Porvoo Cathedral. It was originally built in 1790, on much older foundations, as a private house with interconnected stables. Today it retains the architectural quirks of its original construction (out-of-kilter floors, low doorways, awkwardly narrow staircases, working fireplaces) and a late-18th-century decor. During clement weather, many diners opt for tables within the building's farm-style courtyard, but if you do, try to at least duck inside to see the interior's meticulously hand-painted wallpaper whose design was inspired by 16th century originals. The chef turns out many excellent Finnish specialties such as whitefish filets marinated with an essence of spruce sap and served with a mustard sauce, duck livers with truffle oil and marinated mushrooms, and chicken filets with fig sauce and peasant-style potato cake. The wine list is among the most comprehensive in town.

> **Impressions**
>
> ***I became aware at once of the translucent, transparent, pure, elusive, clean, and clinical quality of Helsinki. I began to hate the almost paralyzing perfection of modern buildings, equipment, accommodation, accessories, service.***
>
> **—James Kirkup,**
> ***One Man's Russia,* 1968**

Vuorikatu 17. ✆ **20/752-8355.** www.wanhalaamanni.com. Reservations recommended. Main courses 24€-31€; fixed-price dinner menus 51€-77€. AE, DC, MC, V. Mon–Fri 10:30am–10pm; Sat–Sun noon–10pm. Closed 2 days at Christmas.

WALKING TOUR: CENTRAL HELSINKI

START: **Senate Square.**

FINISH: **Helsinki Railway Station.**

TIME: **Allow 3 hours for this walking tour, not including any spontaneous museum and shopping stops.**

1 Senate Square

You'll find the square in front of the monument to the Russian tsar Alexander II, erected in his honor shortly after the annexation of Finland. Helsinki's most historic and beautiful square was designed in the early 1800s at the height of the Russian Empire's fascination with the architectural glories of ancient Greece and Rome. The designer was Berlin-born Carl Ludvig Engel, who created other public buildings in St. Petersburg.

On the north side of the square is the:

2 Lutheran Cathedral

Featuring triplicate statues of saints, it has four small cupolas ringing its central dome. As you face the cathedral, the Senate, capped by a low dome and graced by six Corinthian columns, is on your right. Opposite the cathedral, on the south side of the square, stand the ocher facade and Ionic columns of a house from 1762 that was redesigned by Engel.

Leaving the square, ascend the steeply inclined Unioninkatu, skirting the right-hand (western) edge of the square. The street was dedicated to the tsar in 1819 and, because of its difficult terrain, was considered extremely expensive at the time of its construction. The elegantly graceful building opposite the western facade of the cathedral is the:

3 Library of the University of Helsinki

Some critics consider this the most beautiful of the many buildings created by Engel. Admire its rhythmically repetitive Corinthian pilasters and columns.

Continue uphill. At the northwestern corner of the cathedral's rear side rises the spire of the:

4 Russian Orthodox Church of the Holy Trinity

Designed by Engel in 1827, it has an ocher-colored facade and an artfully skewed Orthodox double cross placed above its doorway.

After passing Kirkkokatu, turn right (east) onto Rauhankatu, where you'll see the statue called:

5 Dawn

This statue of a young girl is on a porphyry base near the corner. The gray-fronted modern building serving as the statue's backdrop contains the printing presses and engravers' shops for banknotes issued by the Bank of Finland.

Continue east on the same street, passing an ornately neoclassical building with a trio of wise women on its pediment. This is the storage space for the:

6 Finnish State Archives

Originally designed in 1890, over the course of time the archives were greatly expanded with annexes and underground vaults.

At the corner of Snellmaninkatu, turn right. The russet-fronted temple with four Corinthian columns and a single acanthus leaf at the pinnacle of its pediment is the:

7 House of Scientific Studies

Just below its heraldic plaques is a heroic frieze cast in solid bronze, paying homage to the generosity of Alexander II, who promised to retain the internal laws and religion of Finland after its 1809 annexation. For many years the frieze was the largest bronze casting in Finland. The building was erected in 1891.

Walking Tour: Central Helsinki

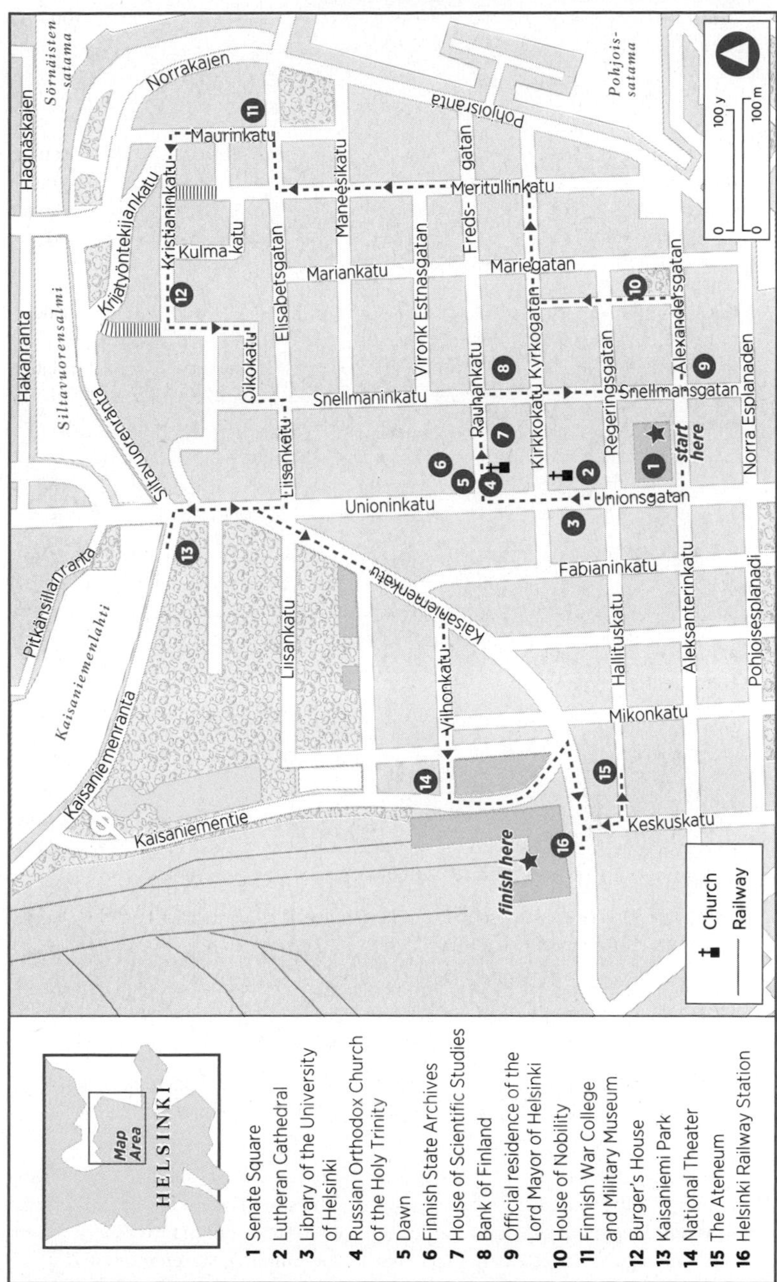

Across Snellmaninkatu is a somber gray building above a steep embankment—the central headquarters of the:

8 Bank of Finland

The bank was designed in 1892 by Bohnsted, a Russian-German architect. In front of the bank is a statue of the Finnish statesman J. V. Snellman, the patriot whose life was devoted to raising the Finnish language to the same legal status as Swedish. Snellman was also responsible for making the Finnish markka the official currency of the country, thereby replacing the Russian ruble.

Continue to walk downhill along Snellmaninkatu, skirting the eastern edge of the cathedral's outbuildings. Shortly, you'll reenter Senate Square. Proceed to the bottom of the square, and turn left onto Aleksanterinkatu. At no. 14 on that street, behind a russet-colored 1823 facade, is the:

9 Official Residence of the Lord Mayor of Helsinki

This structure is next door to the Theater Museum at Aleksanterinkatu 12.

Continue walking east along Aleksanterinkatu. In a short time, you'll enter a small gate dotted with a handful of birch trees. Behind the trees rises the neo-Venetian facade of the:

10 House of the Nobility

Originally a private club and the reunion hall of the Finnish and Russian aristocracy, the House of Nobility was completed in 1861. Walk along Aleksanterinkatu, crossing Mariankatu, and continue toward the harbor. Some of the buildings along the harbor date from the 1760s, among the oldest in Helsinki.

At the waterfront, turn left onto Meritullintori, skirting the edge of the harbor. A sweeping vista of the Russian Orthodox Uspenski Kathedralen (cathedral) comes into view. At this point, the street changes its name to Pohjoisranta and continues to follow the harbor. Continue along this street to the third intersection, Maneeskikatu, where the quay will widen into a formal park ringed with Art Nouveau buildings, some of the finest in Helsinki. Facing the park, notice on your left the red-brick neo-Victorian building, the:

11 Finnish War College & Military Museum

The college was originally constructed as a barracks in the 1880s.

Turn left onto Liisankatu. Completed in 1813, the street honored the Russian tsarina Elisabeth (Liisa is the Finnish version of Elisabeth). Take the second right, turning uphill onto Meritullinkatu. Cross (but don't turn onto) Kulmakatu. At this point, Meritullinkatu becomes a pedestrians-only walkway for residents of the surrounding apartment buildings. At the dead end, turn left and negotiate a narrow, elevated sidewalk high above the street running below (Kristianinkatu). One block later, cross (but don't turn onto) Kulmakatu. A few paces later, at Kristianinkatu 12, you'll see the simple stone foundation and ocher-colored clapboards of the:

12 Burger's House

Helsinki's oldest remaining wooden house, dating from the early 1800s, now accommodates a small museum.

A few steps later, Kristianinkatu dead-ends at a pedestrians-only sidewalk, Oikokatu. Go right (downhill), descending two narrow flights of concrete stairs heading toward the lake. At the bottom you emerge onto a busy avenue, Siltavuorenranta; turn left and notice the stylish bulk of the Scandic Hotel Continental rising across the water. Walk along the curving embankment for a while, coming to the tramway and car traffic hub of Unioninkatu, which you should cross. You'll then enter:

13 Kaisaniemi Park (The Company Keeping Park)

This tract of waterfront land, beloved by residents of Helsinki, was a marshy bogland until the 1830s, when it was drained and opened as Helsinki's first park. The park contains the Botanical Gardens of the University of Helsinki, which date from 1833.

Walk through the park, flanking the water on your right, and then follow the natural left-bending southward curve of the park's main path. (Don't cross any of the railroad tracks.) After exiting from the park, your path becomes Läntinen Teatterikuja, in a neighborhood of Art Nouveau apartment buildings. Follow the street for a block through the theatrical headquarters of Finland. On your left is the:

14 National Theater

Vaguely reminiscent of the opera house in Vienna, the National Theater features decorative sculptures on its facade—note especially the representation of bears. The theater was designed by the architect Tarjanne in 1902.

Across the square, immediately opposite the National Theater, is:

15 The Ateneum

The Finnish National Gallery, designed by Hoijer and completed in 1887, is the best art museum in Finland.

On the western side of the square (to your right as you face the Ateneum) is one of the most famous public buildings in Europe, the:

16 Helsinki Railway Station

Designed by Eliel Saarinen in 1916, the station includes sculptures evocative of the monumental works of Pharaonic Egypt. It has been copied endlessly ever since by avant-garde set designers of plays and films such as *Batman.*

ORGANIZED TOURS

CITY TOURS For a sightseeing trip without a guide, catch tram no. 3T, which takes you past 35 major city buildings and monuments. The 45-minute trip is available only in summer. You can board tram no. 3T in front of the railway station or at Market Square Monday through Saturday from 6am to 1am and Sunday from 7:30am to 1am. The tram departs regularly at intervals ranging from 5 to 15 minutes. A ticket costs 2.50€, 1.20€ for children 12 and under.

Open-top Tours (✆ **050/430-2050;** www.destination-helsinki.com) offers a hop-on, hop-off sightseeing tour around Helsinki on an open double-decker bus, with 16 stops throughout the city. This tour takes place only from mid-May to mid-September; departures are from Senaatintori (Senate Square). Tickets cost 25€ and are valid for 24 hours and can be purchased on the bus.

Helsinki Expert (✆ **09/2288-1222;** www.helsinkiexpert.com) offers a special audio city tour introducing you to the major attractions. Tours depart from Esplanade Park and Katajanokka Terminal, costing 26€ for adults or 15€ for ages 7 to 16. This tour takes place only from mid-June to mid-September daily at 10:45am.

HARBOR TOURS For a waterside view of Helsinki and its nearby islands, contact **IHA-lines Oy** (✆ **09/6874-5050;** www.ihalines.fi), which offers two 1½-hour tours costing 15€ for adults or 30€ for a family ticket. One tour explores Helsinki and its fortresses around Suomenlinna, another the eastern archipelago. Food is served aboard, and a luncheon buffet costs 11€ for adults, 5€ for children 5 to 13, and is free for kids 4 and under. These tours take place only from mid-May to late September.

SPORTS & ACTIVITIES

Major sports events take place at the Olympic Stadium, Paavo Nurmi tie 1 (✆ **09/43-66-010;** www.stadion.fi), described under "Helsinki Attractions," earlier. In summer, soccer games between Finland and other European countries are scheduled. Check *Helsinki This Week,* which lists the events taking place at the stadium at the time of your visit. Take tram no. 3B, 3T, 4, or 10.

JOGGING Finns are just as fond of jogging as Americans or Canadians. The best paths are close to Olympic Stadium and in Kaivopuisto Park (the southern part of Helsinki). There are also some good jogging trails around Hesperia Park, which is convenient if you're staying at a hotel in the city center.

SAUNAS & BEACHES Most hotels (at least the better ones) have a sauna. If you want to sample a Finnish sauna and your hotel doesn't have one, the reception desk can direct you to the nearest sauna that's open to the general public.

Traditionally every Finnish city had a wood-heated public sauna. The only wood-heated public sauna remaining in Helsinki is the **Kotiharjun Sauna,** Harjutorinkatu 1, near the Sörnäien metro station (✆ **09/753-15-35;** www.kotiharjunsauna.fi). Open Tuesday to Friday 2 to 8pm and Saturday 1 to 7pm.

You'll find the best beaches at Mustikkamaa, Uunisaari, Pihlajasaari, Hietaniemi, and Seurasaari. You might combine a trip to the popular Suomenlinna beach with a visit to Suomenlinna Fortress.

SHOPPING

SHOPPING AREAS The major shopping neighborhoods are in the center of the city. They include Esplanadi, which offers the finest of Finnish design—but at high prices. Esplanadi leads from the commercial heart of town all the way to the waterfront. Bordering the water is **Market Square (Kauppatori),** an open-air market selling produce, fish (both raw and ready-to-eat), handcrafted souvenirs, and blackberries from the Finnish forest (daylight hours, April–Oct, Mon–Sat).

The other main shopping section is **Central,** beginning at Esplanadi and extending to the famous Helsinki Railway Station. Many of the big names in Finnish shopping are here, none more notable than the Stockmann department store. One of the main shopping streets here is **Aleksanterinkatu,** which runs parallel to Esplanadi, stretching from the harbor to Mannerheimintie.

Other shopping streets, all in the center, include **Iso Roobertinkatu** and **Bulevardi,** off Esplanadi. Two recent additions to the shopping scene are **Kamppi** (www.kamppi.fi), or the Kamppi Shopping Mall, in the heart of the city, and a smaller but choice competitor **Hakkoniemin Kauppahalli** (www.hakaniemenkauppahalli.fi).

SHOPPING HOURS Most stores are open Monday to Friday 9am to 6pm and Saturday 9am to 1pm. Forum and Stockmann are open on Sunday noon to 4pm in June, July, August, and December.

Shopping A to Z

BOOKS

Academic Bookstore ★★★ Sprawling over two floors crammed with books in many languages, this store offers many English-language books, along with a number of travel aids. It also has the finest stationery department in Finland and sells greeting cards as well as high-quality gift and hobby articles. All of Finland's major authors and leading politicians, plus many foreign writers (including the late Kurt Vonnegut and Norwegian actress Liv Ullmann), have passed through the doors of the building, which was itself designed by Aalto. In Stockmann's department store, Keskuskatu 1. ✆ **09/121-41.** www.akateeminenkirjakauppa.fi. Tram: 3B.

A DEPARTMENT STORE

Stockmann ★★ Helsinki's largest department store is also Finland's finest and oldest. Stockmann has the most diversified sampling of Finnish and imported merchandise of any store: glassware, stoneware, ceramics, lamps, furniture, furs, contemporary jewelry, clothes and textiles, handmade candles, reindeer hides, picnic fare—a little bit of everything. Aleksanterinkatu 52. ✆ **09/1211.** www.stockmann.fi. Tram: 3B.

FASHION

Annikki Karvinen ★ Karvinen became famous for her sophisticated and subtle choice of color, and for elevating hand-woven *poppana* (Finnish cotton) into the peaks of fashion. She has adapted the same style to velvet, silk, and viscose for more formal and more expensive fashions. She designs jackets for both indoors and outdoors. In addition, her outlet offers tablecloths, bedspreads, and other household items for sale. Pohjoisesplanadi 23. ✆ **09/681-17-50.** www.annikkikarvinen.fi. Tram: 3B.

Marimekko ★ Ever since the early 1960s, when Jacqueline Kennedy was photographed wearing Marimekko outfits, the name has been familiar to Americans. Meaning "Mary's frock," Marimekko offers a large variety of prints in vivid colors. This is the company's flagship store, a three-storied marble womb flooded with sunlight, with an emporium of men's fashion in the cellar and a collection of decorative fabrics sold by the yard, dresses, suits, coats, bags, interior accessories, and many other goods, including Marimekko's famous striped T-shirts and dresses. Corner of Pohjoisesplanadi and Mikonkatu. ✆ **09/686-02-40.** www.marimekko.fi. Tram: 3B.

Ril's Concept Store ★ This women's boutique highlights the designs of Kuopio (Ritva Lisa Pohjolainen), who designs innovative, daring styles, only for women, for business and social engagements; Kuopio designs are favored by various female members of the Finnish government and the media. Pohjoisesplanadi 25. ✆ **09/17-45-00.** www.rils.com. Tram: 3B, 3T, or 4. Bus: 18.

Tarja Niskanen This is the most famous milliner in Finland, known for designing attractive headgear that protects women from the rigors of the Finnish winter. Don't expect delicate designs here—the emphasis is on warmth. Heavy-duty designs are made from chinchilla, mink, fox, leather, or velvet. Eteläesplanadi 4. ✆ **50/340-8290**. www.tarjaniskanen.com. Bus: 14.

FURNITURE

Artek ★★★ The roots of this shop date from 1935, when it was established by Alvar Aalto (the greatest design luminary to come out of Finland) and three of his colleagues. Inside, you'll find meticulously crafted reproductions of Alto's distinctive bentwood and laminated chairs, tables, wall units, and lamps, the originals of which forever changed the use of industrial materials for home furnishings. Eteläesplanadi 18. ✆ **09/6132-5277.** www.artek.fi. Tram: 4 or 10.

Skanno This family enterprise, dating from 1946, continues to offer the best designs of the past along with innovative 21st-century ones. One of its most famous designs is the Kameleleonitti (chameleon) sofa, with a changeable cover. A visit to Skanno will help explain why Finland is one of the world leaders in modern design. Porkkalankatu 13G. ✆ **09/612-9440.** www.skanno.fi. Tram: 8. Metro: Ruoholahti.

GIFTS

Anne's Shop Opposite the Temppeliaukio Church, this shop offers tax-free shopping. It also has some of the finest gifts in town, including Finnish knives, wood and ceramic products, dolls and hats from Lapland, wool sweaters, reindeer skin, and jewelry. Fredrikinkatu 68. ✆ 09/45823. www.annensoppi.com. Tram: 3B or 3T.

Kiseleff Bazaar Hall (Kiseleffin Talo) This shopping quarter in the old center of Helsinki, between the cathedral and Market Square, contains 21 small, specialized shops that sell handicrafts, souvenirs, old-fashioned toys, antiques, sauna accessories, knives, and Christmas decorations. Aleksanterinkatu 28, with another entrance at Unioninkatu 27. No phone. www.kiseleffintalo.fi. Tram: 3B, 3T, or 4.

GLASS, PORCELAIN & CERAMICS

Hackman Shop Arabia ★★ 🎁 This shop assembles the products of some of the world's most prestigious manufacturers of household porcelain and art ceramics. Most of the goods are made by Arabia and its affiliated group, Iittala. Arabia was established in a suburb of Helsinki in 1873. Although most visitors buy their goods at the company's main store, Hackman Shop Arabia maintains a small museum and a spacious discount sales area at its factory 5km (3 miles) east of the center at Hämeentie 135 (✆ **0204/39-35-07;** www.iittalaoutlet.fi). Pohjoisesplanadi 25. ✆ **0204/39-35-01.** www.hackman.fi. Tram: 3B.

HANDICRAFTS

Aarikka This shop carries one of Finland's best selections of design-conscious gifts, wood and silver jewelry, and wood toys. Unusual household utensils, fashioned from wood, are also available. Pohjoisesplanadi 27. ✆ **09/65-22-77.** www.aarikka.com. Tram: 3B.

Artisaani ★★ 🎁 Near Market Square, Artisaani is a cooperative of about 20 artisans who sell their own arts and crafts direct from their country workshops. Ceramic sculptures; pottery; glassware; gold, silver, and bronze jewelry; leather goods; printed fabrics; and other textiles are displayed. Unioninkatu 28. ✆ **050/5605920.** www.artisaani.fi. Tram: 3B.

Ryijypalavelu A well-stocked second-floor shop specializing in *ryas* (Finnish woven goods) is operated by the Women's Organization of the Disabled War Veterans' Association to raise money for Finland's veterans with disabilities. You can also buy kits for producing the same rugs at home for about one-third the price. Abrahamink 7. ✆ **09/66-06-15.** www.ryijypalvelu-rp.fi. Tram: 6.

JEWELRY

Kalevala Koru Founded in 1937, this store is owned by the Association of Kalevala Women in Finland, whose aim is to preserve the best cultural traditions of a long-ago Finland. The store sells both traditional and modern jewelry in bronze, silver, and gold. Many pieces are based on originals uncovered in archaeological excavations that date from the 10th century. Unioninkatu 25. ✆ **020/761-1380.** www.kalevalakoru.fi. Tram: 3B.

KNIVES

Marttiini Oy Some connoisseurs consider the array of scary-looking hunting, fishing, and kitchen knives sold within this factory outlet to be the finest in a nation known for its precision steel. Deriving from a factory based in Finnish Lapland (in Rovaniemi), they're priced from 20€ for a serviceable all-purpose blade to 150€ for a Finnish machete, capable of doing some real damage, engraved with traditional Sami motifs. Aleksanterinkatu 28. ✆ **0403/110605.** www.marttiini.fi. Tram 3B.

MUSIC

Digelius Music This store has the best selection of Finnish folk music and jazz in the country, as well as one of the largest offerings in Europe (around 10,000 titles) of folk music from Asia, Africa, the Americas, and Europe. Laivurinrinne 2. ✆ **09/66-63-75.** www.digelius.com. Tram: 3B or 3T.

Fuga This is one of the best music stores in Helsinki, with classical recordings from all over Europe, as well as folk and a smattering of jazz. One of the two Nuotio brothers can offer advice. Kaisaniemenkatu 7. ✆ **09/700-182-51.** www.fuga.fi. Tram: 2, 3B, or 6.

SHOPPING COMPLEXES

Forum Shopping Center The Forum includes 150 shops, restaurants, service enterprises, and a seven-story atrium—making it the number-one shopping center in Finland. Mannerheimintie 20. No phone. Tram: 3B, 3T, 7A, or 7B.

Itäkeskus Shopping Complex This complex of shops and restaurants opened in 1992 in a residential suburb a 15-minute subway ride east of Helsinki's center. It has some resemblance to an American shopping mall, but the emphasis is on Scandinavian and Finnish merchandise. You'll find at least 240 shops, including about 20 kiosks and food stalls. Itäkeskus 5. ✆ **09/343-10-05.** www.itis.fi. Metro: Itäkeskus.

Kämp Galleria This is Helsinki's most desirable shopping arcade, with a cluster of about 50 aggressively upscale shops, close to the newly developed Hotel Kämp. Pohjoisesplanadi 33. www.kampgalleria.fi. No phone. Tram: 3B or 3T.

HELSINKI AFTER DARK

The Performing Arts

THEATER

Suomen Kansallisteatteri (Finnish National Theater) ★★★ The Finnish National Theater enjoys international fame because of its presentations of the classics of Finland and many other countries; each play, however, is performed in Finnish. The theater itself, one of the architectural gems of 19th-century Helsinki, was established in 1872 and stages about 10 premières a year. Läntinen Teatterikuja 1. ✆ **010/73311.** www.kansallisteatteri.fi. Tickets 22€–36€. Tram: 3B.

Svenska Teatern (Swedish Theater) ★ If you speak Swedish, you might want to attend a performance at the horseshoe-shaped Swedish Theater, which has been presenting plays since 1866. The theater is in the absolute center of Helsinki, opposite Stockmann department store. The theatrical season begins in early September and runs through May. The box office is open Monday from noon to 6pm, Tuesday to Friday noon to 7pm, and Saturday 1 hour before the performance. The theater is closed on Sunday. Norra Esplanaden 2. ✆ **09/616-214-11.** www.svenskateatern.fi. Tickets 15€–55€. Tram: 3B.

OPERA & BALLET

Finnish National Opera ★★★ The ballet and opera performances of the Finnish National Opera enjoy international fame. The original Finnish National Opera was built in the 1870s as a Russian garrison theater, but in 1993 the opera house moved to its new home. The ticket office is open Monday to Friday 9am to 6pm and Saturday 3 to 6pm. On performance nights, the ticket office stays open until the performance begins. The opera and ballet season runs from September to June. Helsinginkatu 58. ✆ **09/403-022-11.** www.operafin.fi. Tickets 14€–84€. Tram: 3B.

CLASSICAL MUSIC & CONCERTS

Helsingin Kaupunginorkesteri (Helsinki Philharmonic Orchestra) ★★★ The oldest symphony orchestra in Scandinavia performs from September to May in the gracefully modern Finlandia Hall, designed by Alvar Aalto of white Carrara marble. Just a short distance from the town center, it offers 70 to 80 concerts a year. The box office is open Monday to Friday 9am to 4pm and all concerts begin at 7pm. For tickets and information, call ✆ **600/900-900.** Finlandia Hall, Karamzininkatu 4. ✆ **09/402-41.** www.hel.fi. Tickets 20€–45€ adults, 12€–32€ students. Tram: 3B.

The Club & Music Scene

NIGHTCLUBS/CABARET

Baker's Though it's been reincarnated many times since it was established in 1915, Baker's is the oldest drinking and dining complex in Helsinki. It sprawls across three floors, and on busy nights is crammed with nightclubbers. Most people come for the cafe, open daily from 7am to 4am, or for the bar, open Monday to Saturday 11am to 2am. A restaurant serves fish and grilled steaks (Mon–Sat 11am–1am). A la carte items cost 14€ to 35€. A club supplies hot music, sometimes Latin-derived (Fri–Sat 10pm–4am). Guests must be 24 or over. Mannerheimintie 12. ✆ **020/770-14-40.** www.ravintolabakers.com. Cover 5€ includes coat check. Tram: 3B.

Storyville One of the busiest and most active live music venues in Helsinki was named after the fabled red-light district of New Orleans and, as such, focuses on a menu of Creole and Cajun specialties. Full meals average 15€ to 28€ each. More important, live music—blues, New Orleans–style jazz, Dixieland, rock, or funk—is heard nightly from 10pm to between 2 and 3am, depending on the crowd. Museokatu 8. ✆ **09/40-80-07.** www.storyville.fi. Cover 6.50€–15€. Tram: 4, 7, or 10.

ROCK

Tavastia Club The most visible emporium for rock 'n' roll is this battered, all-purpose room whose venue changes with every rock group that performs. It includes everything from heavy metal to blues and soul, with good representation from punk-rock bands from the U.K. Expect an audience that's loaded with Finnish students in their early 20s. Urho Kekkosenk 4–6. ✆ **09/774-674-20.** For a schedule of upcoming events, visit www.tavastiaklubi.fi. Cover 10€–35€. Tram: 4 or 7.

DANCE CLUBS

Club König This is a smoky, cramped, and sometimes rambunctious nightclub, which features two distinctly different types of music: U.S.- and U.K.-derived disco from the '70s, '80s, and '90s, plus Finnish pop. Clubgoers range in age from 25 to 55, and it's open Wednesday to Saturday 9pm to 4am. Mikonkatu 4. ✆ **09/856-85740.** www.rafla.fi. Cover 10€ on Fri–Sat nights. Tram: 3B or 3T.

Kaarle XII (also known as Kalle) This tried-and-true venue contains a street-level pub, an upstairs dance club, and a total of six bars where a congenial crew of locals gets together and gets rowdy. The most crowded nights, when lines form outside, are Thursday, Saturday, and, to a lesser degree, Friday. It's open Thursday to Saturday 8pm to 3am. Sandwiches are sold at the bars. You must be 24 or older to enter. Kasarmikatu 40. ✆ **20/770-1470.** www.kaarle.com. Tram: 3B.

Presidentti Club Many of the clients of this glossy, hard-surfaced nightclub are business travelers, often occupants of the hotel that contains it. Most of the men here wear jackets, and live music is performed nightly at 10pm. It's open Friday and Saturday (9pm–4am). In the Sokos Hotel Presidentti, Eteläinen Rautatiekatu 4. ✆ **020/1234 608.** www.presidentticlub.fi. Cover 10€–20€. Tram 3B or 3T.

The Bar Scene

PUBS

Corona Bar for Billiards Despite the largest collections of pool tables in Helsinki plus a snooker table, most of the hip young people who gravitate here don't really bother with them. Gathered at the bar near the entrance are lots of actors and writers, most of them under 35, enjoying the raffish and sometimes raucous ambience. Hours are Monday to Thursday (11am–2am), Friday and Saturday (11am–3am), Sunday (noon–2am). Eerikinkatu 11. ✆ **09/751-756-11.** www.andorra.fi. Tram: 1.

O'Malley's Pub This cramped, gregarious pub—one of the most popular in Helsinki—evokes the spirit, legend, and lore of Ireland. O'Malley's is open Monday to Thursday 4pm to 1am, Friday and Saturday 2pm to 2am. Live music, usually Irish-derived rock, is presented 2 nights a week, often Wednesday and Thursday. In the Sokos Hotel Torni, Yrjönkatu 26. ✆ **20/123-46-04.** www.ravintolatorni.fi. Tram: 3B.

BARS

Ahio Club This stylish, hip club attracts some of the best-looking 20- and 30-somethings in Helsinki. Best of all, it boasts a decor based on the myths and legends of early Finland. It's open Monday and Tuesday 4pm to midnight, Wednesday and Thursday 4pm to 2am, Friday and Saturday 4pm to 4am. In the hotel Klaus K., Bulevardi 2-4. ✆ **020/770-4711.** www.klauskhotel.com. Tram: 4, 7, or 10.

Atelier Bar ★ On the top floor of the famous old **Sokos Hotel Torni** (p. 479), Atelier welcomes local artists and writers who don't seem to mind the cramped space. It's open Monday to Thursday 2pm to 1am, Friday 2pm to 2am, Saturday noon to 2am, Sunday 2pm to midnight. In the Sokos Hotel Torni, Yrjönkatu 26. ✆ **09/43366340.** www.ravintolatorni.fi. Tram: 3, 4, or 10.

Kola Bar Funky and amiably battered, our favorite punk-oriented cafe/bar in Helsinki is accented with op-art wallpaper, plastic tables, and earthy colors. Every Wednesday, Friday, and Saturday, beginning at 9pm, DJs work the crowd. Open daily noon to 2am. Helsinginkatu 13. ✆ **09/694-8983.** www.kola.fi. Tram: 3B.

Gay & Lesbian Nightlife

Don't Tell Mamma Depending on the night of the week, various rooms within the biggest gay nightclub in town might be packed, or not even open. Hours are Monday to Saturday 9am to 4am, Sunday noon to 4am, but Friday and Saturday nights are the most fun. Iso Roobertinkatu 28. ✆ **010/841-69-96.** www.dtm.fi. Tram: 3T.

Lost & Found Its staff and its owners are self-admittedly gay, and a percentage of its clients are gay. But, ironically, most of its clients are heterosexuals who swear this is their favorite neighborhood bar. It sprawls over two floors, each with a busy bar area. From September till May, it's open nightly from 5pm till around 4am, but between June and August, it's open daily 8am till 4am. Annankatu 6. ✆ **09/680-10-10.** www.lostandfound.fi. Coat check 2€; beer around 5.50€. Tram: 1 or 4.

Nalle Pub Established during the early 1990s, this was the premier lesbian bar in Helsinki. Recently, a scattering of well-behaved gay men have also been patronizing the place, too. It's open daily from 3pm to 2am. Kaarlenkatu 3-5. ✆ **09/701-55-43.** Cover charge Fri–Sat 4€. Tram: 3, 3B, or 3T.

EXPLORING THE FINNISH COUNTRYSIDE

Since Finland is so vast and often difficult to explore, particularly because of wintry weather most of the year, we've focused on just a few places of interest: Turku and the Åland Islands, a driving tour through the scenic lake region, and a summer driving tour to Finnish Lapland.

20

TURKU & THE ÅLAND ISLANDS

If you have only one Finnish town to visit outside Helsinki, make it Turku. Finland's former capital is its oldest town (founded about 1229), with close ties to Sweden. Swedes affectionately call it Åbo, and perhaps regret its loss. A town with proud traditions, Turku was the former center of Finland's spiritual, secular, and commercial life until Russia made Helsinki the capital.

Turku makes an ideal gateway for visiting the Åland Islands, an archipelago in the Baltic, midway between Sweden and Finland. Many Swedes come to the Ålands for their summer vacations.

Turku ★★★

164km (102 miles) W of Helsinki, 155km (96 miles) S of Tampere

On the western coast, at the confluence of three rivers, the seaport of Turku (Åbo in Swedish) is the oldest city in Finland and was once the most important city in the country; it was both an ecclesiastical center and a trade center. In addition to the cathedral, the city acquired a citadel in the late 13th century, making it a power player by the standards of the Middle Ages. Turku's cultural and financial power was assured when the king of Sweden, who then ruled over Finland, made Turku the seat of government and installed his representative here.

In the 17th century, an academy was established in Turku, and in 1808, Russia conquered Finland and moved its capital to Helsinki, which was closer to St. Petersburg. In 1827, a fire destroyed many of Turku's old wood buildings. But Turku bounced back, becoming a major port and industrial city, and also a university town, with both a Swedish and a Finnish Academy. It was rebuilt by Carl Ludvig Engel, who designed Helsinki, with stone-and-brick buildings, a grid plan, and wide streets.

The legendary long-distance runner Paavo Nurmi (1897–1973), known as "the Flying Finn," was the most famous son of Turku. He won a total of nine gold and three silver medals in three different Olympics.

ESSENTIALS

GETTING THERE If you're driving from Helsinki, head west along E-3 all the way. If you're not driving, Turku is easily reached by either train or bus from Helsinki; many trains and buses make the trip every day (trip time: about 2¼ hr.). The Turku train station is on Ratapihankatu 37; for rail information, call ✆ **0600-41-900.** The bus station is on Aninkaistentulli 20 (✆ **0200-4000**).

Turku can also be reached by ferry from Stockholm; every morning and evening a ferry leaves Stockholm for the 12-hour trip to Turku. For information, call the **Silja Line** in Turku (✆ **0600-15-700**).

VISITOR INFORMATION Contact the **Turku City Tourist Office,** Aurakatu 4 (✆ **02/262-74-44;** www.turkutouring.fi), open in summer Monday to Friday 8:30am to 6pm and Saturday and Sunday 9am to 4pm; in winter Monday to Friday 8:30am to 6pm and Saturday and Sunday 10am to 3pm.

A **TurkuCard** entitles you to entry to most museums, discounts at participating shops and restaurants, and unlimited travel on the city's buses. The card costs 21€ for 24 hours, 28€ for 48 hours and can be purchased at the City Tourist Office. A 24-hour family card (maximum of 2 adults and 3 children 14 and under) is available for 40€.

SEEING THE SIGHTS

Aboa Vetus ★★ & Ars Nova ★ These are twin museums under one roof, Ars Nova devoted to modern art and Aboa Vetus Finland's most intriguing archaeology museum. Both museums are in the Rettig Palace by the Aurajoki River in the former private residence of a tobacco factory owner. The Aboa Vetus museum, an eerie look into the depths of a town block from the Middle Ages, was discovered by accident in the 1990s during renovation work. The streets of the old town were dug out from a depth of 7m (23 ft.). You can walk through these centuries-old streets and take a peek into the homes. In contrast, Ars Nova couldn't be more modern. The permanent collection of some 500 paintings, mostly donated by the Matti Koivurinta Foundation, features works by Finnish artists and international legends such as Max Ernst.

Itäinen Rantakatu 4-6. ✆ **02/250-05-52.** www.aboavetusarsnova.fi. Admission 8€. Daily 11am-7pm. Closed Mon mid-Sept to Mar. Bus: 13, 30, or 55.

Forum Marinum ★ Legend, sea history, and a real maritime atmosphere prevail at this fleet of museum ships moored on the River Aurajoki. You can climb aboard and do everything but go sailing. Our favorite here is the beautiful three-masted bark *Sigyn*, which was launched from Gothenburg in Sweden in 1887. A 1902 sailing ship, *Suomen Joutsen (Swan of Finland)*, was actually built in France but used by the Finnish Navy during its World War II battles with Russia. Finally, you can check out the mine layer *Keihässalmi* and the corvette *Karjala* to see what Finland used to battle the Russian Bear in the 1940s. In a restored granary you can visit the maritime exhibitions, including scale models, a hydrocopter, 1940s torpedoes, and multimedia displays.

Linnankatu 72. ✆ **02/282-95-11.** www.forum-marinum.fi. Admission 12€ adults, 7€ children 5-12, free for kids 4 and under. May-Sept daily 11am-7pm; off-season Tues-Sun 10am-6pm. Bus: 1 or 4.

Luostarinmäki Handicrafts Museum The outdoor compound housing this handicraft museum is a collection of little 18th-century cottages on a hillside, about

Turku

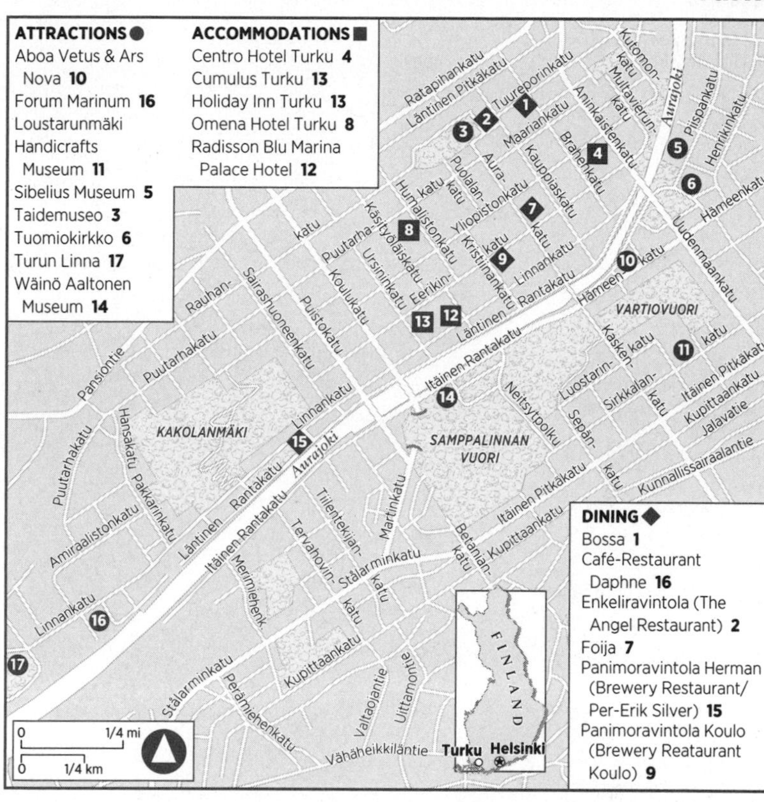

a 5-minute walk from the city center, south of Vartiovuori hill near the Open-Air Theater. This is the only part of Turku that escaped the fire of 1827, and 18 original structures now make up the working museum. You can watch a potter, goldsmith, bookbinder, and makers of wigs, gloves, and combs as they ply their trades. Displays of Finnish arts and crafts of all types can be seen.

On Luostarinmäki (Cloister Hill). ✆ **02/262-03-50.** Admission 5€ adults, 3€ children 5–12, free for 4 and under. May 5–Sept 5 Tues–Sun 10am–6pm; closed Sept 6 to May 4. Bus: 3.

Sibelius Museum This is the most extensive music museum in Finland, with more than 350 musical instruments from around the world on display. At a beautiful site overlooking the River Aurajoki, a few steps from the cathedral, the museum is named in honor of Jean Sibelius, the most revered composer in Finland, although he neither lived nor worked in Turku. The works of the master are played every day or at concerts held on Wednesday evenings at 7pm from September to May. The Wednesday concerts sell out early, so stop by in the morning to buy your ticket.

Bishopsgatan 17. ✆ **02/215-44-94.** www.sibeliusmuseum.abo.fi. Admission: museum 3€ adults, free 18 and under; concerts 7€ adults, 3€ children. Tues–Sun 11am–3pm (Wed also 6–8pm). Bus: 1.

Taidemuseo ★★ This is the second-most important art museum in the country. Built in 1904 in both the Art Nouveau and the Finnish National Romantic style, it is a repository of some 4,000 pieces of art, mainly from the 19th and 20th centuries. Chief honors here go to Akseli Gallen-Kallela (1865–1931), Finland's national painter who is represented by 30 works from the national epic, the *Kalevala.* One of his most reproduced works, painted in a realist style when he was only 20, is *The Old Woman and the Cat.* Helene Schjerfbeck (1862–1946) is acclaimed for her portraits, and Victor Westerholm (1860–1919) is the most honored painter from the Åland Islands. Works from other Nordic countries and international graphics are also exhibited.

In Puolalapuisto Park, Aurakatu 26. ✆ **02/262-71-00.** www.turuntaidemuseo.fi. Admission 7€ adults, 4€ students, free ages 15 and under. Tues–Fri 11am–7pm; Sat–Sun 11am–5pm. Bus: 1.

Tuomiokirkko ★★★ The "mother" of the Lutheran Church of Finland, this Gothic cathedral from the 1200s is the greatest medieval monument in the country. Built on the banks of the Aura River, this imposing brick-built structure is dedicated to the Virgin Mary and Finland's first bishop, St. Henrik. Buried in the vaults are bishops, warlords, and even one queen, Karin Månsdotter, wife of King Erik XIV of Sweden.

Since its partial destruction by fire in 1827, the cathedral has been completely restored. The massive west tower rises to a height of 102m (335 ft.), the work of C. L. Engel, the famous German architect. Engel also designed the pulpit. In the South Gallery is the finest cathedral museum in Finland, the **Tuomiokirkkomuseo ★★**, with its collection of relics and liturgical artifacts dating from the Middle Ages. We like to come here on a Tuesday evening when the cathedral features live music.

Tuomiokkotori 20. ✆ **02/261-71-00.** www.turunsrk.fi. Admission: cathedral free; cathedral museum 2€ adults, 1€ children 5–15, free for children 4 and under. Cathedral daily 9am–5pm. Cathedral museum Apr 16–Sept 15 daily 9am–8pm; Sept 16–Apr 15 daily 9am–7pm. Bus: 25.

Turun Linna ★★★ Massive and proud, Turku Castle dates from 1280, when it was built on a small island at the mouth of the River Aura, 2.4km (1½ miles) southwest of the city center. This is the largest medieval castle in Finland, and once the entire nation was ruled from here. The **Porter's Lodge** features Finland's first **secular murals ★**, dating from 1530. A stunning array of **medieval wooden religious sculptures ★★** is to be seen in a room called Sture Church, which the citizens of Turku used as a house of worship from the 1480s. In the Nun's Chapel hangs the single-most famous artwork in the castle, a **14th-century portrait of the Virgin ★** by the Master of Lieto. In the **King's Hall,** look for Albert Edelfelt's celebrated painting of *Duke Karl Insulting the Corpse of Klaus Fleming* ★, painted in 1878.

The Outer Castle houses the **Historical Museum of Turku ★★**. Its chief exhibit is a stunning **miniature castle model ★★★**, depicting the castle in the heyday of Duke Johan and his duchess holding court.

Note: There are stairs, stairs, and more stairs throughout this monument, some of which are slippery and narrow.

Linnankatu 80, Keskusta. ✆ **02/262-03-00.** www.turkutouring.fi. Admission 6€ adults, 3.50€ children 5–15, free for children 4 and under. Apr 16–Sept 15 daily 10am–6pm; Sept 16–Apr 15 Tues–Fri and Sun 10am–3pm, Sat 10am–5pm. Bus: 1.

Wäinö Aaltonen Museum ★ Wäinö Aaltonen (1894–1966), one of the most prominent sculptors of his day, began his career on Hirvesalo, a city-owned island on the eastern bank of the Aurajoki River. Many statues by the sculptor are placed on the streets of Finland and Turku. The permanent collection consists of works of art purchased by Turku since 1937, including sculptures, paintings, graphics, and drawings. In all, the collection totals some 4,500 works, about half of which are in public offices, hospitals, schools, and other buildings in Turku. The museum also owns a permanent collection of Finnish paintings, sculptures, and other art, and presents temporary exhibitions as well.

Itäinen Rantakatu 38. ✆ **02/262-08-50.** Admission 6€, free for ages 15 and under. Tues–Sun 10am-6pm. Bus: 14 or 15.

WHERE TO STAY

Centro Hotel Turku ★ Built in stages by a local family between 1972 and 1986, this is the best boutique hotel in Turku, thanks to the insistence, by its owners, of showcasing hip trends in modern Finnish design and contemporary art, usually executed by craftspersons under 30, in its rooms. The most recent renovation of the bedrooms created a minimalist, tasteful, and comfortable design. Expect decors that include angular lines and lots of birch and cherrywood veneers.

Yliopistonkatu 12, FIN-20100 Turku. www.centrohotel.com. ✆ **02/211-8100.** Fax 02/469-0479. 62 units. Sun–Fri 108€–123€ double; Fri–Sun year-round (daily during midsummer) 89€–104€ double. Rates include buffet breakfast. AE, DC, MC, V. Free parking. Bus: 4. **Amenities:** Bar; children's playground; sauna. *In room:* TV, hair dryer, Wi-Fi (free).

Cumulus Turku ☺ On a prominent street corner in the town center, this is a solid, uncomplicated, middle-bracket hotel with a hard-earned reputation for comfort among business travelers. It was built in the mid-1960s, but all of its monochromatic, pastel-colored rooms have been frequently renovated since. It shares some of its facilities, including its restaurant (the Armada) with the also-recommended (and more richly accessorized) Holiday Inn next door, but this hotel is less expensive, a bit less formal, and more relaxed about accommodating boisterous children (there's even a third-floor children's playroom).

Eerikinkatu 30, FIN-20100 Turku. www.cumulus.fi. ✆ **02/218-1000.** Fax 02/218-1399. 108 units. Mon–Thurs 115€–130€ double; Fri–Sun year-round and daily during midsummer 94€–107€ double; 190€–220€ suite. Rates include buffet breakfast. AE, DC, MC, V. Free parking. Bus: 4 or 90. **Amenities:** Restaurant; bar; babysitting; children's playground; sauna. *In room:* TV, hair dryer, Wi-Fi (free).

Holiday Inn Turku We define this as the best of the town's middle-bracket hotels. More richly accessorized, and somewhat more stylish, than its neighbor, the also-recommended and slightly less expensive Cumulus Turku, this hotel was built in 1997 and upgraded since that time. Perks associated with a stay here include a sun-flooded, crescent-shaped stone-floored lobby, and comfortable midsize bedrooms outfitted with color schemes of soft russets and browns. Its in-house bar and restaurant (Hemingway's and the Brasserie Armada) are shared with the clients of the immediately adjacent Cumulus Hotel.

Eerikinkatu 28, FIN-20100 Turku. www.restel.fi/holidayinn. ✆ **02/338-211**. Fax 02/338-2299. 199 units. 87€–111€ double. Rates include buffet breakfast. AE, DC, MC, V. Outdoor parking free, nearby indoor parking 12€. Bus: 4 or 90. **Amenities:** 2 restaurants; bar; babysitting; indoor heated pool; room service; sauna. *In room:* TV, minibar (in some), Wi-Fi (free).

Omena Hotel Turku Part of a no-frills chain, this do-it-yourself hotel in the town center is the best bargain in Turku. There isn't even a front desk. When making a reservation—online, at a lobby kiosk, or over the phone (6€ extra), you supply your passport number and cellphone number and pay immediately. You pick a 5-digit door code and receive a room number. Each room is equipped with a double bed and a convertible sofa, which means that four can sleep in comfort here. In lieu of staff, a 24-hour help line can be called in case of an emergency.

Humalistonkatu 7, 2 Fin-20100 Turku. www.omena.com/hotel-turku. ✆ **0600/18018.** 75 units. 46€-75€. AE, DC, MC, V. Parking nearby 16€. Bus: 4. *In room:* TV, fridge, hair dryer, Wi-Fi (free).

Radisson Blu Marina Palace Hotel ★★★ This is the most appealing, stylish, and comfortable modern palace hotel in Turku. Built in 1973 and radically upgraded in 2006 when it was acquired from another chain by Radisson/SAS, it occupies a prime position beside the Aurajoki River. Bedrooms are plush and very large, outfitted in cool, neutral colors and subdued but carefully thought-out contemporary Finnish designs, with whimsical touches of faux-baroque.

Linnankatu 21, FIN-20100 Turku. www.turku.radissonsas.com. ✆ **02/1234-710**. Fax 02/1234-711. 184 units. 99€-190€ double; 250€-350€ suite. AE, DC, MC, V. Bus: 4. **Amenities:** Restaurant; bar; babysitting; exercise room; room service; sauna. *In room:* TV, hair dryer, minibar, Wi-Fi (free).

WHERE TO DINE

Bossa BRAZILIAN Turku is an unexpected place to find Brazilian cuisine, but you can enjoy everything from Amazon fish delicacies to meat stews at Bossa. Start with a simple bowl of black bean soup, or something more exotic such as pumpkin and goat cheese soup. However, *carne* rules the menu, with specialties ranging from filet mignon with spicy tomatoes and pumpkin sauce to the most classic dish of Brazil, a *feijoada*, a traditional meat stew with pork, beef, and sausage, flavored with chili oil. Among the fish dishes is fried red snapper with green chili beans and a coconut and herb sauce. Changing art exhibitions and live music add to the ambience.

Kauppiaskatu 12. ✆ **02/330-000.** Reservations recommended. Main courses 20€-23€. AE, MC, V. Tues-Wed 4-10pm; Thurs-Fri 4-11pm; Sat 2-11pm; Sun 3-9pm. Bus: 1.

Café-Restaurant Daphne ★ SCANDINAVIAN Between 1947 and 1984, Göran Schildts, one of Finland's most respected writers, sent reports back to Helsinki about what he discovered on his voyages on the waters of the Baltic, the Mediterranean, and the canals of France aboard his two-masted schooner, the *Daphne*. The restaurant, named after Schildts's *Daphne,* was built as a warehouse in 1936. Immediately adjacent to Turku's maritime museum, it overlooks a marina from its location about 1.6km (1 mile) southwest of the commercial core of Turku. There's an outdoor terrace, lots of delectable pastries, and self-service buffets laden with tempting hot and cold foods, including an admirable collection of herring.

Adjacent to Forum Marinum, Linnankatu 72. ✆ **02/251-0898.** www.daphne.fi. Reservations not necessary. Access to the soup and salad buffet 7€ per person; access to the soup, salad, and hot buffet 15€ per person. AE, DC, MC, V. Mon-Fri 11am-2:30pm; Sat-Sun noon-4pm. Cafe daily 11am-6pm (till 7pm June-Aug). Bus: 1.

Enkeliravintola (The Angel Restaurant) FINNISH Depending on your point of view about the afterlife, you'll find the angelic theme either charming or cloying. But it's a worthy restaurant with good food, and lots of insights into the Finnish aesthetic. It occupies an antique wood-sided house a short walk uphill from the commercial core of Turku, in a warren of artfully old-fashioned dining rooms. In midwinter, a quintet of ceramic stoves throw off a gentle heat. Menu items continue the heavenly theme with "the Kitchen Angels' Favorite" (fried perch with stewed spinach), "Piece of Heaven" (Greek salad), and "Cupid's Hit" (fried salmon with chanterelles and new potatoes).

Kauppiaskatu 16. ✆ **02/231-8088.** www.enkeliravintola.fi. Reservations recommended. Main courses 17€-25€. AE, DC, MC, V. Mon-Fri 11:30am-9pm; Sat 11:30am-9pm; Sun 11:30am-6pm. Bus: 3.

Foija ★★ FINNISH Arguably, this is the oldest continuously operated restaurant in Finland, dating to the opening of the Swedish Theatre in Turku in 1839. It enjoys a strategic location at Market Square, and good food and service are hallmarks. Enjoy such starters as garlic-laced snails or a rich and creamy crayfish soup with an herb oil. One of the best salads is laced with strips of salmon and shrimp and drizzled with a lemon vinaigrette. Specialties include breaded pikeperch with a pistachio butter sauce, and filet of pheasant wrapped in bacon with a Marsala butter sauce. Meat eaters gravitate to Foija's steak in a pan with a crème fraîche and red-wine sauce.

Aurakatu 10. ✆ **02/251-8665.** www.foija.fi. Reservations recommended. Main courses 13€–29€. AE, MC, V. Mon–Tues 11am–10pm; Wed–Thurs 11am–11pm; Fri 11am–midnight; Sat noon–midnight; Sun noon–10pm.

Panimoravintola Herman (Brewery Restaurant Herman/Per-Erik Silver) ★★ SCANDINAVIAN Why Herman? And why Per-Erik Silver? Because in the lore and legend associated with nearby Turku Castle, beer, and lots of it, was part of the motivation that kept feudal Finland going, and Herman was the traditional name of whatever brewmaster kept the hops percolating. This restaurant, one of the most famous in town, occupies the solid brick premises of what was built in 1849 as a sailcloth factory and, because of the gleaming copper vats and pipes of its self-contained brewery, Herman seemed like an appropriate name. Beer is indeed still brewed on the premises, and menu items are creative and, in some cases, inspired. The best examples include a combination, on the same plate, of ginger-marinated salmon with melon and salmon tartare; grilled whitefish with creamed morels and buttered spinach; grilled filets of beef with roasted paprika, pineapple, and herb-potato cake; and a platter piled high with both braised knuckles and filets of lamb with thyme sauce.

Läntinen Rantakatu 37. ✆ **02/230-3333.** www.ravintolaherman.com. Reservations recommended. Main courses 17€–28€; fixed-price menus 31€, 40€, and 53€. AE, DC, MC, V. Mon–Fri 11am–10:30pm; Sat 2–10:30pm; Sun 2–8:30pm. Bus: 1.

Panimoravintola Koulu (Brewery Restaurant Koulu) SCANDINAVIAN Everyone in Turku seems to harbor some deep-seated childhood memory of Koulu. Somber, solid, stone-built, and monumental, it retains an aura of dour civic-minded responsibility from when it functioned, during the early 20th century, as Turku's schoolhouse, where many of the city's seniors learned to read and write. All that changed when a local brewery transformed the vast and drafty premises into a dining and drinking compound. It offers one of Turku's most frugal dining bargains at midday, when clients serve themselves from an austere, buffet-style dining room. After dark, it's a more expensive restaurant, with menu items ranging from bar snacks (bratwurst with sauerkraut on a bun) to more elaborate fare (steak with guacamole; pasta with mushrooms and a chili-flavored dill sauce), depending on where you sit. Beer, probably because it's brewed on-site, is relatively cheap. Many evenings, live music reverberates through the rooms.

Eerikinkatu 18. ✆ **02/274-5757.** www.panimoravintolakoulu.fi. Reservations not necessary. Bar snacks 11€–22€; main courses 10€–25€. A la carte dishes and bar snacks AE, DC, MC, V. Mon–Fri 11am–midnight; Sat noon–midnight. Bar daily 11am–2am (till 3am Fri–Sat). Bus: 1 or 4.

SHOPPING IN TURKU

Sylvi Salonen Oy On the main pedestrian thoroughfare of Turku, this cheerful modern store is the town's best outlet for Finnish and Scandinavian handicrafts and gifts, with a special emphasis on sweaters, knitwear, kitchenware, carved beechwood and birch, creative interpretations of the (Swedish-derived) Dalarna horse, hats and handbags crafted from very dense felt, and carved and hand-painted replicas of virtually every lighthouse in the Nordic world. There are also many examples of artfully textured *ryas,* contemporary hand-woven tapestries and/or wall hangings, which rival the complexities and intricacies of rustic Persian and Turkish carpets. Yliopistonkatu 26. ✆ **02/076-60-831**. www.sylvisalonen.fi.

TURKU AFTER DARK

The Nightclub and Dining Complex at the Sokos Hamburger Bors Hotel A richly accessorized compound of dining and drinking options in the heart of Turku has enough venues and hideaway cubbyholes to appeal to virtually anyone. The hotel itself is a seven-story, 409-room behemoth that rises from the town center. The complex opens daily at 11am for the lunch crowd and then continues with afterwork libations and evening flirt-fests between 11pm and 4am. The dance club, open nightly from around 9pm, charges the 22-and-over crowd 5€ on Friday and Saturday. The best bet for a cheapish meal is the **Shamrock Café/Oscars Place,** a faux Irish hangout, where burgers, lasagna, and roasted duck with honey sauce go for 13€ to 26€ each. Kauppiaskatu 6. ✆ **02/337-3800.** www.hamburgerbors.fi. Bus: 1, 3, 13, 28, 32, or 42.

The Old Bank Public House ★ Set behind a massive granite facade from the turn of the 20th century, this is one of Turku's most visible and most popular afterwork bars. The baronial premises that contain it were originally conceived in 1902 as the headquarters for a bank, with richly carved woodwork, elaborate ceilings, and stained glass. Beer costs from 5.60€ to 14€ a mugful, and the bartenders will cheerfully provide a menu that lists more than 200 brands of beer, more than 20 of which are on tap. Sandwiches, snacks, and salads range from 5.50€ to 8.50€. Open Monday to Tuesday noon to 1am, Wednesday and Thursday noon to 2am, Friday and Saturday noon to 3am, and Sunday 4pm to midnight. Aurakatu 3. ✆ **02/274-57-00.** www.oldbank.fi. Bus: 3.

A Side Trip to Naantali ★★

Naantali, 19km (12 miles) north of Turku, takes its name from a convent and monastery of St. Birgitta, called "the Valley of Grace," which moved to the coast in 1443. The people of Naantali resisted change so successfully in the 17th century that today it remains a fine example of a medieval Finnish town. Today you can stroll through narrow lanes lined with wood houses still on their original sites. In medieval times, each house had its own name on a plaque over the door. Some of these plaques have survived, and the houses are known by their original names. The present buildings of the Old Town date from the late 18th and early 19th centuries.

After the Reformation, Naantali declined until the town became a popular health resort after a spa was established in 1863. It was particularly popular among Russians, who preferred it over St. Petersburg.

ESSENTIALS

GETTING THERE The easiest way to reach Naantali is to take a bus (no. 11 or 110) from Turku; buses run every 15 minutes, require 20 minutes for the trip, and cost 3.80€ each way. The most romantic way to go is aboard SS *Ukkopekka,* sailing from the River Aurajoki in the center of Turku, with departures from June 8 to August 14 daily at 9:30am and 11:30am. Tickets costs 22€ one-way, 27€ round-trip; children's tickets are 11€ one-way, 14€ round-trip.

An archipelago buffet is offered for 18€. For more information, call **Höyrylaiva Osakeyhtiö,** Linnankatu 38 (✆ **02/515-33-00;** www.ukkopekka.fi).

VISITOR INFORMATION The **Naantali Tourist Service,** Kaivotori 2 (✆ **02/435-98-00;** www.naantalinmatkailu.fi), is open year-round Monday 9am to 5pm, Tuesday to Friday 9am to 4:30pm.

SPECIAL EVENTS The **Naantali Music Festival** (✆ **02/434-5363;** www.naantalimusic.com), an international music festival, is held here in mid-June; the main concerts are presented in the 15th-century Convent Church, with vesper hymns sung at 8pm. Tickets in general range from 15€ to 45€ and are sold through the tourist office.

SEEING THE SIGHTS

The main attraction of Naantali is its **Old Town ★★★**, one of the best preserved in all of Finland. The town grew up around its Convent of the Order of St. Birgitta in the 1400s. Today, many artists occupy the restored homes, and the narrow, cobblestone streets with one- or two-floor wood-built houses are among the most photographed in Finland. Many of the houses now function as small art galleries.

The most interest in the Old Town centers on the **Naantali Museum,** Katinhäntä 1 (✆ **02/434-53-21**), where you can visit three old wood houses with outbuildings in the heart of the Old Town. Admission is 2.50€. The museum is open only from May 15 to August, Tuesday to Sunday 11am to 6pm.

All that remains of the **Naantalin Luostarikirkko,** Nunnak, Keskusta (✆ **02/437-54-32**), is the Convent Church, completed in 1462 and renovated a number of times since, including the addition of a tower in 1797. Exhibits in the church's collection of relics include the garb worn by nuns when they took their vows and a Gothic tabernacle for the Reserved Sacrament. Charging no admission, the church is open in May daily 10am to 6pm; June to August daily 10am to 8pm; and September to April Wednesday noon to 2pm and Sunday noon to 3pm.

Our favorite spot here is **Kultaranta ★★★**, the summer residence of the president, which we find one of the most beautiful places in all of Finland, with its stone castle and more than 3,500 flowering rosebushes on the island of Luonnonmaa. The castle, designed by Lars Sonck, was built in 1916 and is clearly visible from Naantali Harbor across the bay. The residence can't be visited, but guided tours of **Kultaranta Gardens** are conducted Tuesday to Sunday from June 21 to August 14; bus tours leave at 1:30 and 1:40pm and cost 14€ for adults or 7€ for children ages 4 to 14 (3 and under free). Walking tours depart at 2 and 3pm and are 10€ for adults and 5€ for children. From August 16 to August 28, tours leave at 2pm from the main gate. Contact the tourist service (above) for bookings, information, or group tours at other times of year. Transport is via the SS *Ukkopekka* (see above).

Muumimaailma (Moominworld) is a theme park based on the writings of Finnish children's book author Tove Jansson; it is reached by a footbridge from Naantali to Kailo Island (✆ **02/511-111;** www.muumimaailma.fi). The park includes a beach, sporting activities, a theater, story time, shops, Snork's Workshop (where you can do craft activities), and more. The park is open daily from mid-June to mid-August, costing 22€ for a 1-day pass, 29€ for 2 days, and 39€ for a Super pass allowing admission also to Väski Adventure Island. Admission is free for children 2 and under.

WHERE TO STAY

Naantalis Spa ★★★ This is one of only three full-service spas in southwestern Finland, and a mecca for those seeking "the cure" in a modern, low-key environment. It's a sprawling, three-story building in the countryside a 20-minute walk from

Naantali's historic core. Public areas are airy, uncluttered, flooded with sunlight, and filled with plants, lattices, and references to ancient Greece and Rome. About 140 of the hotel's 390 accommodations are aboard a glistening, well-scrubbed yacht (the *Sunborn*), which is permanently moored to a pier beside the hotel and connected to it via glass-enclosed catwalks. Everything glistens in this "floating palace," and guest rooms are relatively large and opulent, replete with nautical artifacts, rich paneling, and deep upholsteries. Accommodations in the adjacent "brick and mortar" hotel are spacious and very comfortable.

Matkalijantie 2, FIN-21100 Naantali. www.naantalispa.fi. ✆ **02/44-550.** Fax 02/4455-621. 390 units. 174€–216€ double; from 284€ suite. Rates include buffet breakfast. AE, DC, MC, V. Free parking. **Amenities:** 5 restaurants (2 of which are off-site, in the center of historic Naantali, and some of which are seasonal); 2 bars; babysitting; bikes; children's playground; exercise room; 2 heated pools (1 indoor); spa; Wi-Fi (free, in lobby). *In room:* TV, minibar (in most), Wi-Fi (5€ per day).

WHERE TO DINE

Kala-Trappa ★★ FINNISH/INTERNATIONAL This is the best restaurant in Naantali, with a history that's deeply tied into the drama of the town and a reputation so solid that most of the civic charities of Naantali, including the Rotarians, select it regularly as the site of their monthly meetings. In a wood-sided cottage just uphill from the harbor, it contains a warren of paneled and very cozy dining rooms, each outfitted with nautical accessories (maps and marine charts, antique compasses, photos, and scaled-down models of yachts). Their pizzas are wafer thin with savory toppings. Some dishes attempt exotica, including chicken breast with a fruity salsa. Their fresh fish, based on the catch of the day, is prepared with flawless technique.

Nunnakatu 3. ✆ **02/435-2477.** www.ravintolatrappi.fi. Reservations recommended. Main courses 14€–25€. AE, MC, V. Mon–Thurs 11am–10pm; Fri 11am–11pm; Sat noon–midnight; Sun noon–9pm.

Uusi-Kilta ★ SCANDINAVIAN It boasts the most panoramic location of any restaurant in Naantali, a headland at one end of the town's harbor in a wood-sided house that was originally built around 1880. During clement weather, most of the tables on the wraparound terrace are filled with chattering or sunbathing diners; the rest of the year, the venue moves inside, to a pair of severely dignified dining rooms accented with a substantial-looking mahogany bar. The chefs turn out a well-balanced menu of contemporary and market-fresh ingredients with harmonious combinations of flavors including luscious desserts. The best items include fried cod with a gratin of olives; fried filets of perch with herb butter; linguine with giant crabs; carpaccio of beef; reindeer calves' liver; and lemon-flavored scallops on a skewer with rosemary.

Mannerheiminkatu 1. ✆ **02/435-1066.** www.uusikilta.fi. Main courses 13€–28€. AE, DC, MC, V. Daily noon–10pm year-round.

Wanha Kaivohuone ★★ SCANDINAVIAN On the town's outskirts, this first-class restaurant is owned and operated by the Naantali Spa in a yellow-sided antique building that's so photogenic it's often used by Helsinki-based fashion photographers as the background for photo shoots. Built late in the 19th century under the region's Russian administration, it now functions during midsummer as an evening supper club. The restaurant is a frequent venue for seniors who want first-class cuisine served with fresh ingredients. The menus are seasonally adjusted and could include cream of parsnip soup with a confit of wild duck; smoked filet of whitefish with a ragout of vegetables and balsamic *beurre blanc;* a divine filet of venison with chanterelle-studded potatoes; and a velvety crème caramel with seasonal berries.

Nunnakatu 7. ✆ **02/445-5999.** www.naantalinkaivohuone.fi. Reservations recommended. Fixed-price menus 35€–43€. AE, DC, MC, V. May–Aug daily (call ahead for hours); off-season Fri–Sat for dinner (call for hours).

The Åland Islands ★★

The Ålands, off the west coast of Finland between Turku and Stockholm, form an archipelago of 6,500 islands, islets, and skerries. In fact, Åland comes from a word in the Old Norse language that meant "water island," and the English word "island" is derived from the same word. Most of the Åland Islands (Ahvenanmaa Islands in Finnish) are not inhabited, and there are only some 27,000 residents scattered throughout the archipelago.

The archipelago was settled some 6,000 years ago by seal hunters; large burial cairns can still be seen. During the Viking age, the islands were the most densely populated part of Scandinavia.

From medieval times until the early 19th century, Åland was part of Sweden; but in 1809, Sweden lost both Åland and Finland to Russia. After the fall of the czar in 1917, Åland petitioned the Swedish king to rejoin Sweden, but Finland objected. In 1921, the matter was settled by the League of Nations, which gave Finland sovereignty over the chain but protected Swedish culture and left Swedish as the official language. Today the residents of Åland are still more Swedish than Finnish, and locals speak Swedish.

ESSENTIALS

GETTING AROUND Most of the inhabited islands are connected by a series of bridges, causeways, and ferry services. Except for the MS *Kumlinge,* fares are not charged on the local car-ferries unless you travel the complete route from end to end. "Road ferries" are always free, since they serve as road extensions among the islands.

The largest island, 48km (30 miles) long, **Fasta Åland (Main Land),** is home to about 90% of the population. The island has dark coniferous woodland, much farmland and pastureland, fishing ports, and rocky fjords. The mainland is also known for its old fortresses and 11 medieval churches, the oldest dating from the 12th to the 15th century.

The second-largest settlement, **Eckerö,** is the westernmost municipality in Finland. It was once a stop on the mail route between Sweden and Imperial Russia.

Other major islands of interest include:

Kumlinge: This island has a 15th-century church and is served by a ferry line from Långnäs; the crossing takes 2 hours.

Vårdö: This is the closest settlement to the Åland mainland, only 5 minutes away. The southern part of the island is lush vegetation.

Brändö: The ferryboat from Långnäs (the same one that serves Kumlinge) also goes to this island, a municipality of some 1,000 islands. The largest of these islands are connected by causeways and bridges.

Föglö: Some 600 residents live on these clusters of islands, some of which are linked by bridges and causeways. Föglö, the largest of the island municipalities, is about 30 minutes from the Åland mainland.

Sottunga: From Långnäs, there's a 1½-hour ferry trip to Sottunga. You'll find only 150 residents in what's the smallest municipality in the Ålands.

Kökar: A rather bleak landscape. The remains of a 2,500-year-old Bronze Age community have been found at Karlby. Kökar is reached on a 2½-hour ferry crossing from Långnäs.

Mariehamn

The capital of the Ålands, Mariehamn is the only real town in the archipelago, with a population of 10,700. Founded in 1861, Mariehamn was named after the empress of Russia, Marie Alexandrovna, wife of Alexander II. It is on an isthmus with harbor facilities, and the people here have always looked to the sea for their livelihood. Thousands of linden trees line the streets. The town is small, so buses are not required to follow a specific route. However, there is a bus that runs from the harbor to the center of town, a distance of 3.2km (2 miles).

ESSENTIALS

GETTING THERE Air Åland (✆ **018/171-10;** www.airaland.com) flies between Helsinki and Mariehamn four times a day on weekdays, twice a day on Saturdays and Sundays. Turku Air (✆ **020/721-88-00;** www.turkuair.fi) flies between Turku and Mariehamn two times a day on weekdays. The Mariehamn **airport** is 3.2km (2 miles) north of the center of town. There is year-round **bus service** (✆ **018/634-411**) from both Helsinki and Turku, traveling via the interisland ferries.

The Viking Line runs **seagoing ferries** from Stockholm to Turku, with a stop en route at Mariehamn, and the Silja Line also makes the 6½-hour trip from Stockholm to Mariehamn. There is usually one ship per day on each line. For prices, tickets, and information, contact the **Viking Line** (✆ **018/262-11** in Mariehamn; www.vikingline.fi) or the **Silja Line** (✆ **018/167-11** in Mariehamn; www.silja.com).

VISITOR INFORMATION The **Mariehamn Tourist Information Office,** Storagatan 8, FIN-22100 Mariehamn (✆ **018/240-00;** www.visitaland.com), is open June 1 to June 12 and August 8 to August 31 Monday to Friday 9am to 5pm, Saturday and Sunday from 9am to 4pm; June 13 to August 7 daily 9am to 6pm; April 1 to May 31 and September Monday to Friday 9am to 4pm, Saturday 10am to 3pm; and October to March Monday to Friday 9am to 4pm.

ATTRACTIONS IN TOWN

Ålands Museum ★ & Ålands Konstmuseum If you have any interest in the history of the Åland Islands, this is the place to come. The museum traces the history of the islands beginning with the early settlers 5,000 years ago. There's even a Stone Age replica boat made of seal skin.

In the same building, hanging exhibits are presented in the less-intriguing art museum, displaying the works of local painters. There is one artist, however, that deserves to be singled out. Joel Pettersson (1892–1937), known for his landscapes of island scenes, was hailed as "the van Gogh of the Ålands."

Storagatan 1. ✆ **018/250-00.** www.museum.ax. Admission 4€ adults, 3€ children 7–15. Sept–May Tues and Thurs 10am–8pm, Wed and Fri 10am–4pm, Sat–Sun noon–4pm; June–Aug daily 10am–5pm. Closed Mon Sept–May.

Museum Ship Pommern ★ Near the Maritime Museum is the four-masted bark *Pommern,* built in 1903 in Glasgow, and one of the few remaining sailing ships of its kind in the world. The ship is unique in that it's still in its original condition as a cargo ship; all other such existing ships have been rebuilt into something else over the years. Just before the outbreak of World War II, the *Pommern* made its last journey from Hull to its homeport of Mariehamn, where it was anchored at the outbreak of World War II. After temporary service as a granary, the ship was eventually donated to the town to become a museum.

Storagatan. ✆ **018/531-421.** www.pommern.aland.fi. Admission 5€ adults, 3€ children 7–15, free for kids 6 and under. May–June and Aug daily 9am–5pm; July daily 9am–7pm; Sept daily 10am–4pm.

Sjöfartsmuseum After a restoration, this museum is set to reopen late in 2011. You've got to love the sea and sailing to appreciate this flotsam-and-jetsam museum of nautical oddities—everything from figureheads from old boats to ships in a bottle. Exhibits trace Åland's great sailing-ship era, and in the center is the re-creation of a sailing vessel with mast.

Storagatan. ✆ **018/199-30.** www.sjofartsmuseum.aland.fi. Admission 5€ adults, 3€ children 6–12, free for kids 5 and under. July daily 9am–7pm; May–June and Aug daily 9am–5pm; Sept daily 10am–4pm; Oct–Apr Mon–Fri 10am–4pm, Sat–Sun noon–4pm.

WHERE TO STAY

Ålandhotel Adlon This popular, well-managed hotel, set beside the harbor, is one of the first buildings that passengers who arrive by ferryboat see. Built in 1973 and renovated in 2006, it offers well-maintained and contemporary-looking midsize bedrooms, each with a parquet floor, comfortable bed, and a writing table. The best-accessorized of the bedrooms are on the uppermost (fourth) floor; and because of somewhat bigger bathrooms, they're known as "spa" rooms. There's a busy and popular sports bar, and immediately adjacent, a pizzeria.

Hamngatan 7, FIN-22100 Mariehamn. www.alandhotels.fi. ✆ **018/154-00.** Fax 018/150-45. 54 units. 120€–160€ double. AE, DC, MC, V. **Amenities:** Bar; children's playground; indoor heated pool; room service; sauna. *In room:* TV, minibar (in some), Wi-Fi (in some; free).

Hotel Arkipelag ★ This is the most upscale and prestigious hotel in Mariehamn, a four-story, modern palace that was originally built in 1974 and renovated many times since. Bedrooms are comfortable, with earth-toned color schemes. Set in the town center, it's a sedate and well-managed address, where upscale business travelers and dignitaries from the Finnish mainland stay. The president of Finland has been a guest on occasion.

Strandgatan 31, FIN-22100 Mariehamn. www.hotellarkipelag.com. ✆ **018/240-20.** Fax 018/243-84. 86 units. 150€ double; 230€–260€ suite. Rates include buffet breakfast. AE, DC, MC, V. Free parking. **Amenities:** Restaurant; 3 bars; babysitting; exercise room; 2 heated pools (1 indoor); room service; sauna. *In room:* TV, minibar, Wi-Fi (free).

Hotel Cikada This hotel originated as a five-room guesthouse in 1968, when a writer from the Finnish mainland wrote a novel, *The Cricket (Cikada),* in one of the bedrooms. Later, when the hotel expanded into the summer place you see today, the owners adopted the book's title as the name. It is a very short walk from the ferryboat terminal, immediately adjacent to the museum ship *Pommern,* near a cluster of trees that helps to shelter it from the industrial section of the nearby harborfront.

Hamngatan 1, FIN-22100 Mariehamn. www.cikada.aland.fi. ✆ **018/163-33.** Fax 018/17-363. 84 units. 71€–88€ double. Rates include buffet breakfast. AE, DC, MC, V. Free parking. Closed Oct–Apr. **Amenities:** Restaurant; bar; 2 heated pools (1 indoor); room service; 2 saunas. *In room:* TV.

WHERE TO DINE

Bistro Savoy SCANDINAVIAN Set in the center of Mariehamn, on the street level of a well-known hotel, this is one of the town's best restaurants, with a cozy setting, well-prepared food, and a contemporary, mostly wooden decor that spills onto a veranda that's glassed in for all-weather dining. The best menu items include grilled scallops with a purée of red peppers; a soup made from Jerusalem artichokes and cheddar cheese; peppered beef with a pepper-flavored cream sauce; and fried breast of duck with a raspberry-ginger sauce and a fondant of celery.

In the Ålandhotel Savoy, Nygatan 10. ✆ **018/15400.** www.alandhotels.fi. Main courses 11€–25€; fixed-price menu 32€. AE, DC, MC, V. Mon–Fri 10:30am–2pm and 6–9:30pm; Sat 6–10:30pm.

Restaurant Nautical ★ SCANDINAVIAN In the same building as the Åland Maritime Museum, immediately adjacent to the museum ship *Pommern,* this is our favorite restaurant in Mariehamn, thanks to a richly paneled decor inspired by the interior of a private yacht. Fresh seafood is a specialty here, with many different variations of herring, and skillful preparations of the restaurant's signature dish, pike-perch or perch served with either dill-flavored or crayfish sauce. As an appetizer, try the slightly salted marinated salmon with horseradish sauce, or a steaming bowl of shellfish soup.

Hamngatan 2. ✆ **018/199-31.** Lunch main courses 9.50€–17€; dinner main courses 22€–35€. AE, DC, MC, V. Mon–Fri 11am–10:30pm; Sat 5–10:30pm. Closed last week in Feb.

THE LAKE REGION

Saimaa, an extensive lake district in eastern Finland, has thousands of islands and straits and lots of blue water. From Lappeenranta, one of the centers of the Finnish lake region, you can book cruises lasting anywhere from 2 hours to 2 days in the southern part of Lake Saimaa, or take a cruise to the Saimaa Canal and see the Russian border.

Savonlinna is in the center of the Saimaa lake district in southeastern Finland, between Haapavesi to the north and Pihlajavesi to the south. From here you can take a boat trip to other towns on Lake Saimaa.

Tampere, Finland's second-largest city, is also in an area of lakes. A center of culture, tourism, and commerce, Tampere and its surrounding Pirkanmaa region are known for vast waterways and forests.

Each of the major centers in the lake district can be reached from Helsinki on a driving tour. Allow a minimum of 4 days up to a complete week. Explore all the cities by making a wide arch from Helsinki, heading first to the east near the Russian border and then circling across the country to Tampere, an easy drive south back to Helsinki.

Lappeenranta ★

222km (138 miles) NE of Helsinki, 16km (10 miles) W of the Russian border

This border town of 60,000 people between two different cultures was founded in 1649 by Queen Christina of Sweden. It was fortified first by Sweden, which governed Finland as a province, and then by Russia. Since World War II, Lappeenranta has assumed increasing importance following the loss of large parts of Karelia. For more than a century and a half, the town had been a spa, and today Lappeenranta is the best summer resort and excursion center in eastern Finland. A bright, modern town, it nestles at the southern edge of the large Lake Saimaa.

ESSENTIALS

GETTING THERE By car from Helsinki, head northeast on E-4 to Lahti, where you connect with Route 12 east until you reach the junction with Route 6 for the final approach to Lappeenranta.

Lappeenranta can be reached by plane from Helsinki; in the summer there are two flights a day during the week and one on Saturday and Sunday. The airport is 2km (1¼ miles) west of the town center; there is no airport bus into town, but a taxi charges 12€ to take you there.

Seven trains a day leave Helsinki for Lappeenranta (trip time: 4 hr.), and there are five to seven daily express buses from Helsinki. The railway station and the bus station are side-by-side, a 20-minute walk south from the commercial heart of town. Bus nos. 3 and 4 travel from there to points in the town center, and if a client hires a taxi

The Lake Region

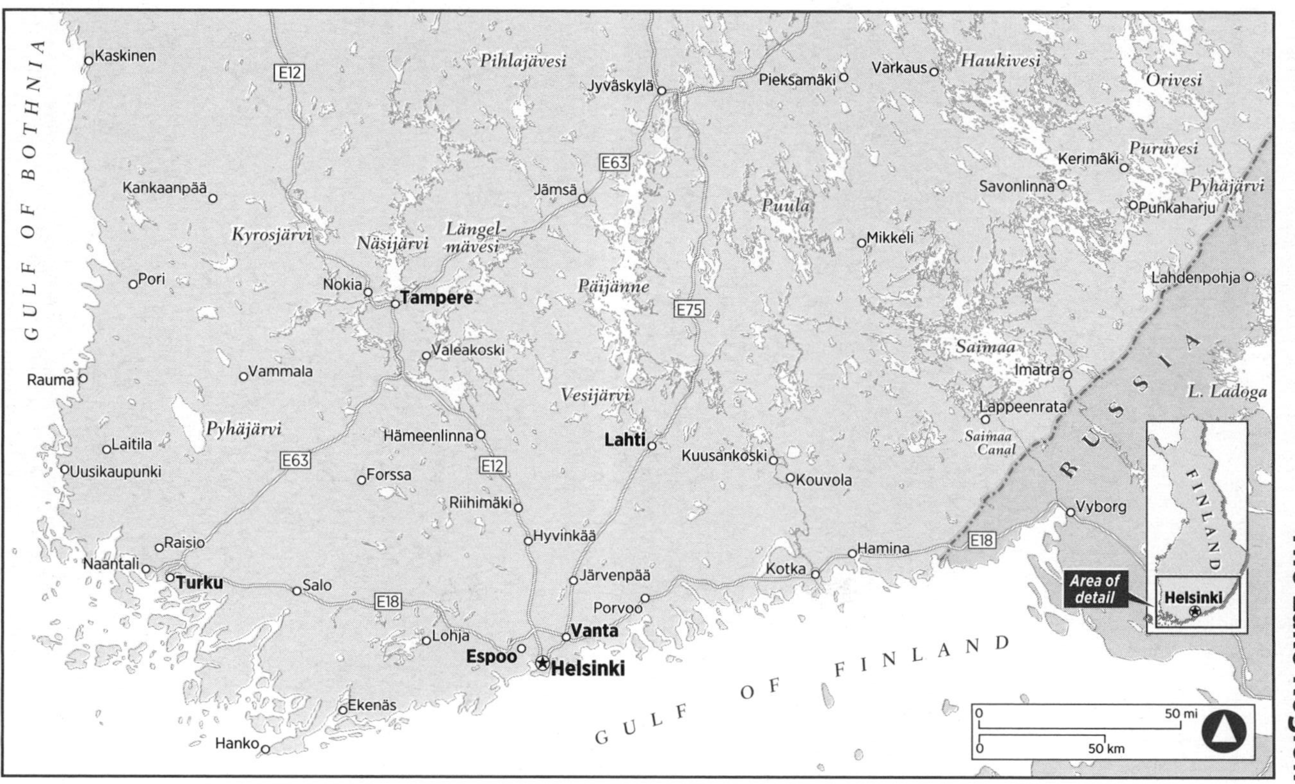

from either the bus or railway station to any hotel in the town center, the cost will be around 10€. City buses are painted white with blue trim. A single ride on a city bus costs 3€. Fares are paid on the bus, directly to the driver, but because of the town's small size, most people just walk.

VISITOR INFORMATION The Tourist Information Office, Kauppakatu 40D (✆ **05/667-788**), is open Monday to Friday 9am to 4:30pm.

SEEING THE SIGHTS

Our favorite summer activity here is a boat tour of **Lake Saimaa ★★**. The most visible of the boat operators is **Karelia Lines** (✆ **05/45-30-380;** www.karelialines.fi). Between June and August, a 2-hour tour of the lake, priced at 18€ per person, departs every evening from the lakefront piers between 6 and 9pm. On board is a restaurant, with sit-down service by an elegant waitstaff.

You can also visit the 48km-long (30-mile) **Saimaa Canal ★★**, dating from the mid-1850s. The canal leads from the edge of Lake Saimaa through Finnish and Russian territory to Vyborg, the former capital of Finland's lost province of Karelia. Boat trips and cruises can be arranged through the tourist office (see above).

The **Lappeenranta Outdoor Marketplace ★★** is the most colorful in eastern Finland, with everything from fresh produce and berries from the swampy wetlands around Lappeenranta to cheese and "Finnish fast food" (sandwiches, sausages, wok-fried rice). Between June and August, it operates daily from 7am to noon on Kievarinkatu near the junction of the Sammonkatu, very close to the Hotel Cumulus Lappeenranta, about a block from the town's main street (Valtakatu). Between September and May, the market is conducted only Saturday and Sunday 7:30am until around 1pm.

The lakefront area of Lappeenranta is active every summer evening with additional purveyors of handicrafts and fast food and, to a lesser degree, Friday and Sunday evenings during clement weather in spring and autumn. This is also a cultural town, with **summer concerts** held in the parks and **summer theater** at Linnoitus Fortress (see below). Cavalrymen dressed in traditional skeleton tunics and red trousers (the uniform worn in 1922) ride in the fortress and harbor area in summer. **Guard parades and evening tattoos** (outdoor military exercises) are held several times in summer months.

IN THE FORTRESS

Linnoitus ★★, the fortress of Lappeenranta, on Kristiinankatu, was begun by Sweden and continued by Russia as a link in its chain of defenses. The entire chain fell into disuse after the Peace of Turku in 1812, when that part of the country known as "Old Finland," including Lappeenranta, was reunited with other Finnish territory. The fortress was turned over to the town in 1835, and the defenses slowly deteriorated; restoration began in 1976. There are pottery and other handicraft shops in the fortress area. The location is a 5-minute walk west of the town center.

The following attractions—the Orthodox church, the South Karelian Museum, the South Karelian Art Museum, and the Cavalry Museum—are all inside or near the fortress. The old orthodox church, or **Ortodoksinen kirkko ★**, Kristiinankatu (no phone), was completed in 1785, but only the high and narrow nave belongs to the original building. The most valuable icon here is the 200-year-old ***Communion of the Holy*** **★**, found in the middle of the north wall. The Orthodox Church of Finland owes its allegiance to the Ecumenical Patriarch of Constantinople. Admission is free, and the church is open from June to mid-August Tuesday to Sunday 10am to 5pm.

The **Etela-Karjalan Museo (South Karelian Museum),** Kristiinankatu 15 (**© 05/616-22-55**), is at the northern end of the fortress in the 19th-century artillery depot. Museum displays include a model of the former Finnish town of Viipuri (Vyborg). The model features the city as it was at midday on September 2, 1939, at the outbreak of World War II, complete with models of people, cars, ships, and trains. When Finland was forced to give Vyborg to the Russians, many artifacts from that ancient city were transferred here. The textile department of this museum is worth visiting since it has examples of traditional Karelian folkloric clothing. Admission is 6.50€ for adults, 5.50€ for students, and free for children 15 and under. The museum is open June to August Monday to Friday 10am to 6pm and Saturday and Sunday 11am to 5pm. In winter it's open Tuesday to Sunday 11am to 5pm.

The **Cavalry Museum,** Kristiinankatu 2 (**© 05/616-22-57;** www.lappeenranta.fi), is in the oldest building in Lappeenranta, the former guardhouse of Linnoitus by the town gates, built in 1772. The history of the Finnish cavalry from the *hakkapeliitat* (the cavalry in the 1618–1648 war) until modern times is depicted through uniforms, guns, and items related to horse care. The museum is open June to August only, Monday to Friday 10am to 6pm and Saturday and Sunday 11am to 5pm. Admission to the Calvary Museum is 3€ for adults, 2€ for students, and free for children 15 and under.

Outside the fortress, the **Wolkoff House Museum,** Kauppakatu 26 (**© 05/616-22-58;** www.lappeenranta.fi), which opened in 1993, was a Russian-born merchant family's home with interiors and furniture from the 1890s to the 1960s. The house was built in 1826, and the Wolkoff family lived here from 1870 to 1983. The interiors are shown only on a guided tour. Admission is 5.50€ for adults, 4.50€ for students, and free for children 15 and under. It's open June to August Monday to Friday 10am to 6pm, Saturday and Sunday 11am to 5pm. Off-season hours are only on Saturday and Sunday 11am to 5pm.

WHERE TO STAY

Hotel Cumulus Lappeenranta Set on the town's main street, near the tourist office and the outdoor market, this four-story 1982 hotel is clean, unpretentious, and firmly planted in the consciousness of local residents as a solid, respectable, middle-bracket hotel. Bedrooms are outfitted in white with touches of green and filled with comfortable contemporary furnishings.

Valtakatu 31, FIN-53100 Lappeenranta. www.cumulus.fi. **© 05/677-811.** Fax 05/677-8299. 95 units. Sun–Thurs 132€–175€ double; Fri–Sat year-round (daily June–Aug) 91€–160€ double. Rates include buffet breakfast and free evening access to the sauna and swimming pool. AE, MC, V. Free parking. Bus: 3. **Amenities:** Restaurant; bar; indoor heated pool; room service; sauna. *In room:* TV, minibar (in some), Wi-Fi (free).

Scandic Patria Lappeenranta ★ During the 1980s, the outmoded and relatively uncomfortable grande dame of Lappeenranta hotels was demolished and rebuilt, reopening in 1991 in a concrete-and-glass sided format that had nothing to do with the original design. Each of the cozy, big-windowed units inside was upgraded and redesigned once again in 2006. Clients here tend to be just a bit more artsy than those attracted to some of this hotel's nearby competitors, including a scattering of music-industry and show-biz types.

Kauppakatu 21, FIN-53100 Lappeenranta. www.scandic-hotels.com. **© 05/677-511.** Fax 05/451-24-41. 132 units. Mon–Thurs 110€–151€ double; Fri–Sat year-round (daily during midsummer) 92€–115€ double; from 197€ suite. Rates include buffet breakfast. AE, DC, MC, V. Free parking. Bus: 6. **Amenities:** Restaurant; bar; bikes; children's playground; exercise room; Jacuzzi; room service; 2 saunas. *In room:* TV, hair dryer, Wi-Fi (free).

Sokos Hotel Lappee ★★ This, rivaled only by the also-recommended Scandic Patria Lappeenranta, is the best-accessorized and most upscale hotel in town. In the town center, close to Town Hall and a 4-minute walk, past other buildings, to the lakefront, its rooms feature comfortable contemporary furnishings. This hotel has the most comprehensive sauna complex (five separate units) in town, the biggest and most appealing indoor pool (40m/131 ft. long), and its most comprehensive collection of dining, drinking, and nightlife facilities.

Brahenkatu 1, FIN-53100 Lappeenranta. www.sokoshotels.fi. ✆ **10/762-1000.** Fax 10/762-1005. 209 units. Mon–Thurs 118€–138€ double; Fri–Sat year-round (midsummer daily) 93€–114€ double. Rates include buffet breakfast. AE, DC, MC, V. Free parking. Bus: 1. **Amenities:** Restaurant; exercise room; indoor heated pool; room service; 5 saunas. *In room:* A/C, TV, minibar (in most), Wi-Fi (free).

Summerhotel Karelia Park Two kilometers (1¼ miles) west of the town center at the edge of Lake Saimaa, this hotel was built in 1972 to provide housing for local students. It continues as a residence for students today, but between June and August, its four floors serve as a conventional hotel. Rooms are small and a little battered, but reasonably comfortable and the most affordable in the area.

Korpraalinkatu 1, FIN-53810 Lappeenranta. www.karelia-park.fi. ✆ **05/453-0405.** Fax 05/452-8454. 90 units. 32€ per person double. Rates include buffet breakfast. MC, V. Free parking. Closed Sept–May. Bus: 5 or 6. **Amenities:** Restaurant; 2 saunas. *In room:* TV (in some), no phone.

WHERE TO DINE

Local eateries are very limited in scope. For more formal first-class dining, visitors patronize the restaurants of the top-recommended hotels above.

Majurska FINNISH The most famous cafe in Lappeenranta, Majurska is at an old fortress 450m (1,500 ft.) from the town center. Long a local favorite because of its homemade cakes and pies, the kitchen makes good use of seasonal berries and fruit, and also comes up with some good quichelike creations with cheese and onion. For lunch, many Finns order a piece of pie or cake plus good tea or coffee. There's no meat, no fish, and no lunchtime platters. In the same building are several art exhibits and small handicraft shops.

Kristiinankatu 1. ✆ **05/453-05-54.** www.majurska.com. Cakes or pies with coffee or tea 1.50€–4€. No credit cards. June–Aug daily 10am–7pm; Sept–May daily 10am–5pm.

Tassos GREEK/INTERNATIONAL Established by Finns who appreciated their holidays in Greece almost 30 years ago, this centrally located restaurant offers a worthy selection of Greek staples, including both lamb and vegetarian versions of moussaka, *stifado* (a well-seasoned stew made from pork and beef), and souvlakia. The most popular dish on the menu is a succulent version of pepper steak, whose cream-based sauce is an appropriate foil for your choice of potatoes and vegetables.

Valtakatu 33. ✆ **10/762-1452.** www.tassos.fi. Reservations recommended for dinner. Main courses 16€–30€. AE, DC, MC, V. Mon–Fri 11am–11pm; Sat noon–11:30pm; Sun noon–8pm. Bus: 1, 3, or 5.

Savonlinna ★★★

336km (209 miles) N of Helsinki, 230km (143 miles) N of Lappeenranta

Built across a series of islands between Lake Haapavesi and Lake Pihlajavesi, this romantic town enjoys the most dramatic "waterspace" of any in Finland. Lorded over by one of northern Europe's most dramatic castles, it is the site of the country's famous opera festival. Founded in 1639, it is the oldest town in eastern Finland. Its major attraction, the castle of Olavinlinna (see below), dates from 1475.

The area around the town, forming part of the Saimaa waterway, has more lakes than any other area in Finland. In its heyday, wealthy families from St. Petersburg used Savonlinna as a holiday and health resort. The old spa familiar to czarist Russia burned in 1964—only a few czarist villas were spared. However, the Kylpylä Hotelli Casino, on Kasinonsaari (see below), attracts spa lovers to the area today.

ESSENTIALS

GETTING THERE From Lappeenranta, drive 35km (22 miles) northeast on Route 6 to Imatra. After passing by the city, continue on Route 6 to Parikkala and the junction with Route 14, which will take you northwest into Savonlinna. If you're not driving, there are three to five flights a day from Helsinki (trip time: 50 min.). For reservations in Helsinki, call **Finncomm Airlines** (**✆ 09/42-432-000**). The airport is 25km (16 miles) northeast of the city center. An airport taxi shuttle meets arriving flights, the 20-minute trip costing 15€ one-way, whereas a private taxi ranges from 22€ to 30€. Most visitors arrive by train from Helsinki; a trip via Parikkala takes more than 5 hours. At Parikkala you have to change to a smaller regional train or else a connecting bus. One-way rail fares from Helsinki cost 61€. Trains arrive at the Savonlinna-Kauppatori in the center of town. There is an express bus service running several times a day from Helsinki to Savonlinna, taking 5 to 6 hours and costing 48€ for a one-way ticket. For train or bus fares, check with the terminus in Helsinki.

VISITOR INFORMATION The **Savonlinna Tourist Service,** at Puistokatu 1, FIN-57100 Savonlinna (**✆ 015/517-510;** www.savonlinna.travel), is open daily from June to August 9am to 5pm, but during the Opera Festival, it remains open until 8pm. From September to May, it is open Monday to Friday 9am to 5pm.

SPECIAL EVENTS The **Savonlinna Opera Festival ★★★**, traditionally held in July in Olavinlinna Castle, is a world-class cultural event. For information, contact the Savonlinna Opera Festival Office, Olavinkatu 35, FIN-57130 Savonlinna (**✆ 015/476-750;** www.operafestival.fi). Tickets range from 40€ to 260€.

SEEING THE SIGHTS

Olavinlinna Castle (Castle of St. Olof) ★★★ (**✆ 015/531-164;** www.olavinlinna.fi), a three-towered medieval fortress founded in 1475, is the city's major attraction. On a small island in the middle of Kyronsalmi Straits, it's reached by a rotating bridge. At the eastern end of Linnankatu, the triangular-shaped castle boasts 30m-tall (98-ft.) towers that provide a spectacular **panoramic vista ★★★** of the Finnish lake district.

One-hour guided tours (6€; 3€ children 7–17; free for 6 and under) take you through the vast corridors of the castle, with its spooky halls, stone-built rooms, and lookout towers.

To the left of the castle entrance is a small **Castle Museum ★**, displaying artifacts found in the castle or related to it. Even more intriguing is the **Orthodox Museum ★★** on the right, a splendid treasure-trove displaying Russian icons and other valuable church plates and vestments. The summer opera festival is held here. Admission is 5€ for adults, 3.50€ for students and ages 7 to 17, and free for kids 6 and under. January 2 to May 31 and August 16 to December 31, Monday to Friday 10am to 4pm, Saturday and Sunday 11am to 4pm; June 1 to August 15 daily 10am to 6pm.

Other attractions include the **SS *Salama*** (**✆ 015/571-4710**) museum ship, built in Vyborg in 1874; it's the only steam schooner in Finland—and perhaps in the world. The ship is docked in Riishisaari and is open May 15 to September 3, Tuesday to Sunday 11am to 8pm. Admission is 5€ adults, 2€ students, 1€ ages 7 to 16, and free for kids 6 and under.

Retretti, in Punkaharju (© **015/775-22-00;** www.retretti.fi), is an art center that opened in 1982 in a grotto about 22km (14 miles) south of Savonlinna. It includes a concert hall, and during the opera festival in Savonlinna, chamber-music concerts are presented here. Exhibits vary from year to year since the artwork is on loan. The center can be reached by boat from the Marketplace in Savonlinna, or by bus from the Savonlinna bus station. Admission to the art center is 16€ for adults, 14€ for seniors, 10€ for students, 5€ for children 5 to 15, and free for children 4 and under. The center is open from early June to the end of August, daily 10am to 5pm.

WHERE TO STAY

Kylpylä Hotelli Casino (Spa Hotel Casino) ★★★ This is Savonlinna's most upscale and most prestigious hotel, the temporary home to divas who select it as their home during their midsummer opera gigs and a clientele that is concerned with keeping their appointments at the in-house spa. On its own island, the hotel is connected via a bridge to the town's railway station. Contrary to its name, it is not associated with any casino—Savonlinna hasn't had one since the heyday of the tsars.

Kylpylaitoksentie 7, FIN-57101 Savonlinna. www.spahotelcasino.fi. © **015/73950.** Fax 015/272-524. 80 units. 79€–135€ double. Rates include buffet breakfast. AE, DC, MC, V. Free parking. Bus: 1, 2, or 3. **Amenities:** 2 restaurants; babysitting; bikes; exercise room; 2 heated pools (1 indoor); spa; Wi-Fi (free, in lobby). *In room:* TV, minibar.

Savonlinna Seurahuone Built in stages between 1956 and 1989, with renovations to the rooms completed in 2006, this hotel occupies a central position immediately in front of Savonlinna's summer-only marketplace. It has well-maintained, contemporary, and comfortable bedrooms, many with views over the lake. It's reputation for fair, middle-bracket value attracts many business travelers.

Kauppatori 4, FIN-57130 Savonlinna. www.savonlinnanseurahuone.fi. © **015/5731.** Fax 015/273-918. 83 units. Mon–Thurs 130€ double; Fri–Sun 100€ double; opera season (July) 192€ double; 170€–440€ suite. Rates include buffet breakfast. AE, DC, MC, V. Outdoor parking free; indoor parking 13€–16€ extra. Bus: 1, 2, or 3. **Amenities:** 2 restaurants; bar; exercise room; room service; sauna. *In room:* TV, minibar, Wi-Fi (in some; free).

WHERE TO DINE

Majakka (The Lighthouse) FINNISH/SEAFOOD This is one of the busiest and most popular independent restaurants in Savonlinna, a civic institution that has thrived in this centrally located spot since the mid-1960s. In a woodsy, partially paneled decor that's dotted with miniature models of sailboats and rowboats, you'll get good value and very reliable, down-home Finnish cuisine. Enduring culinary staples at this place include pan-fried vendace, a whitefish species from the nearby lake, served with root vegetables and creamy herbed potatoes; and a "Majakka Special," with grilled filets of pork, beef, and grilled chunks of "cottage sausage," all drenched with Madeira sauce and served with creamy potatoes and vegetables.

Satamakatu 11. © **015/206-28-25.** www.ravintolamajakka.fi. Main courses 12€–30€. AE, DC, MC, V. Mon–Sat 11am–1am; Sun noon–midnight. Bus: 1, 2, 3, or 4.

Piatta INTERNATIONAL Set on the lobby level of an also-recommended hotel, with windows that look out over the fresh fruit and vegetables of Savonlinna's outdoor market, this restaurant is crowded every day at lunch and dinner with locals as well as hotel guests. The decor evokes an old-fashioned Finnish (or Swedish) tavern, with lots of exposed wood paneling, a jolly bar near the entrance, and a list of food items that includes everything from salads and pizzas to beef liver with fried onions and gooseberry-flavored sorbet. In July, during opera season, the hotel opens an additional restaurant, Othello, which serves basically the same menu.

In the Savonlinna Seurahuone Hotel, Kauppatori 4. ✆ **015/5731.** www.savonlinnanseurahuone.fi. Sandwiches, pizzas, and pastas 12€–14€; platters and main courses 15€–27€; fixed-price menus 30€–39€. AE, DC, MC, V. Mon 11am–10pm; Tues–Fri 11am–11pm; Sat noon–11pm; Sun 2–8pm. Bus: 1, 2, or 3.

Side Trips from Savonlinna

At least 10 different lake steamers use Savonlinna's harbor as a midsummer base. Beginning around 9am and continuing until about midnight, a sightseeing cruise boat departs hourly. Cruise rates range from 10€ to 18€ for adults and 5€ for children 5 to 15; free for 4 and under. The tourist office (see above) can provide schedules and details.

The SS *Heinävesi* travels regularly to **Punkaharju,** 25km (16 miles) southeast of Savonlinna. Departures are daily at 11am from June 21 to August 14, costing 24€ for adults and 9€ for children 3 to 12; free for 2 and under. At Punkaharju, you can also do some sightseeing, visit a summer art exhibit, explore a typical holiday village, and enjoy a leisurely lunch at a restaurant in the holiday village or at **Punkaharjun Valtionhotelli State Hotel** (✆ **020/752-9100;** www.punkaharjunvaltionhotelli.fi), with 24 rooms in the main building or in a nearby villa.

At Punkaharju, Lake Puruvesi is divided by a long Ice Age ridge that extends for 7.2km (4½ miles), forming a causeway between the Puruvesi and Pihlajavesi lakes. This "thread" has been turned into a national park, one of the most famous and most photographed spots in Finland. Although you can also reach Punkaharju by bus or train, boat travel is certainly the most scenic.

Kerimäki kirkko (✆ **015/578-9111;** www.kolumbus.fi/kerisrk), 22km (14 miles) northeast of Savonlinna and connected by Route 71, has the largest wood church in the world. Built in 1847, the church is large enough to accommodate 5,000 worshipers and is a masterpiece of carpentry with its pews, columns, galleries, tiebeams, arches, domes, and lanterns. The altarpiece was painted by Aleksandra Såltin in 1890. The organ, which has a registration of 20 stops and was constructed by the Kangasala organ factory, was mounted in 1894. The church is mostly visited during the Opera Festival, when it hosts concerts. At that time, buses run between the center of Savonlinna and the rural village of Kerimäki. The church is open June to August Monday to Friday 9am to 8pm, Saturday 9am to 6pm, and Sunday 11am to 8pm. Climbing the adjacent bell tower costs 5€.

TAMPERE ★

172km (107 miles) N of Helsinki, 155km (96 miles) NE of Turku

On a narrow isthmus between two lakes (Lake Näsijärvi and Lake Pyhäjärvi), Tampere is Finland's second-largest city (pop. 203,000), and is primarily an industrial center; however, it remains one of the cleanest, brightest cities in Scandinavia, and is filled with parks, bodies of water, museums, art galleries, theaters, and statues, including some by Wäinö Aaltonen.

A vibrant young city with a university and a growing technology industry, Tampere is the site of one of Scandinavia's major attractions, an outdoor theater (Pyynikki) with a revolving auditorium. Tampere's Swedish name is *Tammerfors*.

Essentials

GETTING THERE From Jyväskylä, continue driving southwest along E-4 (also E-80), which has signs directing you all the way to Tampere. If you're not driving, you

THE LAKE DISTRICT'S GREATEST adventure PARK

Särkänniemi ★★★ is set on 10 hectares (25 acres), meaning there's a lot to see and do here. One and a half kilometers (1 mile) west of the city, it sits on a headland jutting out into Lake Näsijärvi. After entering the park, we suggest, for orientation purposes, you mount the **Näsinneula Observation Tower,** which at 168m (551 ft.) is the highest in Finland, offering one of the area's best **panoramic views ★★**.

The chief artistic treasure of the adventure park is the **Sara Hildén Taidemuseo ★★**, a striking avant-garde piece of architecture that competes with the paintings it showcases inside. The Sara Hildén Foundation owns the greatest modern art collection outside Helsinki, with works by such international artists as Léger, Giacometti, Paul Klee, Picasso, and Miró. Near the observation tower, the museum also presents a changing array of international works. The museum stands in beautiful lakeside surroundings, and some of its sculpture is displayed on the shores of Lake Näsijärvi next to the museum. You can enjoy views of the water at an on-site cafe.

At the **Dolphinarium,** the dolphins give five daily performances, while at the nearby **Children's Zoo,** kids can mingle with tamed domestic animals and take pony treks or rides in donkey-pulled carriages. The **Aquarium** houses some 2,000 creatures of the sea from 200 different species, as well as a seal pool, with feeding times daily at 11am and 4pm. On the ground floor of the Aquarium, you can see a tank with mangrove trees and rainbow-hued fish. At the **Planetarium,** there's a 25-minute show (in both English and Finnish) daily at noon and 2pm.

Of course, local families come here for the **amusement park,** which features nearly three dozen carnival-like rides, of which the Tornado Super Roller-Coaster is the most popular. Most rides cost 6€ each.

Admission to the Dolphinarium costs 12€, 10€ for the Aquarium, 8€ for the Observation Tower, 6€ for the Sara Hilden Taidemuseo, 10€ for the Planetarium. You can also buy a 25€ ticket that includes admission to all open attractions for 1 day.

To get to **Särkänniemi,** take bus no. 4 from the train station. The park (**© 0207/130-200;** www.sarkanniemi.fi) is open in summer Sunday to Friday noon to 9pm and Saturday noon to 10pm, with off-season hours adjusted monthly.

can reach Tampere by air, train, or bus. **Blue 1** (**© 0600-25831;** www.blue1.com) offers flights from Stockholm. Most visitors, who are already in Helsinki, fly to Tampere on one of several daily flights from Helsinki aboard **Finnair** (**© 0600-140-140**). A train leaves Helsinki nearly every hour for Tampere (trip time: 2¼ hr.); five buses a day make the 2½-hour trip from Helsinki. For bus schedules and fares, call **Matkahuolto Oy** (**© 0200/40-00;** www.matkahuolto.fi). From June 3 to August 17, boats run between Tampere and Hämeenlinna in the south. If you're visiting Hämeenlinna, you might want to take the 8-hour boat trip to Tampere. The one-way fare is 42€. For schedules and information, contact **Finnish Silverline** (**© 010/422-5600;** www.hopealinja.fi).

VISITOR INFORMATION The **City Tourist Office,** Rautatienkatu 25 A, FIN-33100 Tampere (**© 03/56-56-6800;** www.gotampere.fi) at the railway station, can help arrange sightseeing tours, provide maps, and offer miscellaneous information. It's open June to August Monday to Friday 9am to 8pm, Saturday and Sunday 9:30am to 5pm; September, October, April, and May Monday to Friday 9am to 5pm, Saturday and Sunday 11am to 3pm; from November to February Monday to Friday 9am to 5pm.

SPECIAL EVENTS The **Tampere Vocal Music Festival** has been held in alternate years during the second week in June since 1975, while the **Tampere International Theater Festival** has been Finland's only festival of professional theater, held during the second week of August, since 1969. The **Tampere Jazz Happening,** Finland's best modern jazz festival, opens the first week of November. Consult the tourist office for specific dates, which vary from year to year.

Seeing the Sights

Lenin Museum This curious museum is in the Tampere Workers Hall, where the first meeting between Lenin and Stalin took place in 1905. Lenin paid a number of secret visits to Finland, and this museum contains mementos of his life and work. On-site is the most bizarre gift shop in all of Finland.

Hämeenpuisto 28. ✆ **03/276-8100.** www.lenin.fi. Admission 5€. Mon–Fri 9am–6pm; Sat–Sun 11am–4pm. Bus: 2, 17, or 22.

Moominvalley ☺ This museum contains original fairy-tale illustrations by Tove Jansson's *Moominfigures* in 40 dioramas and two "Moominhouses." Exhibits include 40 miniatures, tableaux about Moomin events, and a blue, five-story Moomin House built in the late 1970s. Photos of the Moomin House serve as illustrations in *An Unwanted Guest,* the last of Jansson's four picture books about the Moomins. The museum is in the basement of the Metso Building of the city library.

Hämeenpuisto 20. ✆ **03/5656-6578.** http://inter9.tampere.fi/muumilaakso. Admission 7€ adults, 2€ children 4–17, free for children 3 and under. Tues–Fri 9am–5pm; Sat–Sun 10am–6pm. Bus: 2, 17, or 22.

Pyynikki Summer Theater ★★★ About 1.6km (1 mile) from the center of Tampere, this outdoor theater (the first in the world) has a revolving auditorium and seats 836. The plays are presented in Finnish, and a free summary of the plot is available in English (though it's not really necessary). It's imperative to reserve tickets in advance. Plays are presented from mid-June until the end of August.

Jalkasaarentie 3. ✆ **03/216-03-00.** www.pyynikinkesateatteri.com. Tickets 15€–50€. Bus: 21.

Tampere Art Museum This museum has no permanent home, but rather floats from hall to hall. However, we suggest you seek it out for what are the best temporary art exhibitions in Finland. The permanent collections include paintings, sculpture, drawings, graphics, regional art, and the city's art collection.

Puutarhakatu 34. ✆ **03/5656-6577.** Admission 6€ adults, 2€ children 16 and under. Tues–Sun 10am–6pm. Bus: 1 or 7.

Tuomiokirkko ★★ The gray-granite Tampere cathedral, built between 1902 and 1907, is the finest example of the Finnish National Romantic style. The towering spires and the piers holding up the vaulting evoke the Gothic style of the Middle Ages, but the stunning interior is one of the best examples in Finland of Art Nouveau. The cathedral contains many pieces of art, including ***The Wounded Angel*** and ***The Garden of Death*** by Hugo Simberg (1873–1917). The artist was the most famous symbolist in Finland, and his style is best evoked by the large murals ***The Garland Bearers.***

Tuomiokirkonkatu 3. No phone. Free admission. May–Aug daily 10am–6pm; Sept–Apr daily 11am–3pm. Any bus to train station.

Organized Tours

From June to August, a daily guided tour of the city leaves at 2pm from in front of the **City Tourist Office,** Rautatienkatu 25 A (© **03/56-56-6800;** www.gotampere.fi), costing 16€ for adults, 4€ for children 7 to 16, and free for children 6 and under. The trip lasts 1 hour, 45 minutes, and the commentary is given in English.

From June 2 to August 2, Tampere is the meeting point for two popular lake cruisers, including the Finnish *Silverline,* which has a good restaurant. Information is available from **Laivayhtioiden Tilauskeskus (Boatlines Booking Center),** Laukontori 10A (© **03/212-48-04**).

Where to Stay

Cumulus Koskikatu This middle-bracket hotel is one of the town's most respected, attracting residents with its restaurant, the Huviretki, and the bar, the Hemingway Pub. Midsize bedrooms are outfitted in pastel tones, and are furnished with conservatively modern pieces that are comfortable and completely appropriate for the many business clients who opt to stay here. You'll find the hotel at the edge of Koskipuisto Park, near the river in the center of town.

Koskikatu 5, FIN-33100 Tampere. www.cumulus.fi. © **03/242-41-11.** Fax 03/242-43-99. 289 units. 113€–196€ double. Rates include buffet breakfast. AE, DC, MC, V. Parking 18€. Bus: 2, 16, or 18. **Amenities:** Restaurant; bar; children's playground (in summertime only); exercise room; indoor heated pool; 2 saunas; room service; sauna. *In room:* TV, minibar (in some), Wi-Fi (free).

Omena Hotel Tampere This chain hotel, inspired by low-fare airlines, takes self-serve technology to its next level in Finland. It keeps prices low by hiring as few staffers as possible—no bellhops, no front desk clerks, or even front desks. Right in the town center, the hotel offers identical rooms, featuring a large double bed, plus a comfortable sofa that turns into a double bed. The interactive TV can be used for ordering breakfast or Wi-Fi access. For an emergency, and in lieu of staff, there's a 24-hour help line. Remember: This is a no-frills hotel, but the price is right.

Hämeenkatu 28, FIN-33200 Tampere. www.omena.com/hotel-tampere. © **0600/18018.** 105 units. 55€–79€ double. AE, DC, MC, V. Bus: 2. *In room:* TV, fridge, hair dryer, Wi-Fi (free).

Scandic Rosendahl ★★ Tampere's most architecturally dramatic modern hotel is about 2km (1¼ miles) south of the town center, in a forest at the edge of Lake Pyhäjärvi. Built in 1977, it boasts a softly angled design of mirrored walls, polished stone, and lacquered ceilings, making it the most avant-garde hotel in town. Bedrooms are comfortable, well-upholstered, and quiet.

Pyynikintie 13, FIN-33230 Tampere. www.scandic-hotels.com. © **03/244-1111.** Fax 03/2441-2211. 213 units. Mon–Thurs 108€–135€ double; Fri–Sun 95€–110€ double; 270€–283€ suite. AE, DC, MC, V. Parking 7€. Bus: 21. **Amenities:** Restaurant; bar; bikes; children's playground; exercise room; indoor heated pool; room service; sauna; 3 outdoor tennis courts (lit). *In room:* TV, minibar, Wi-Fi (free).

Scandic Tampere City Hotel ★ A reliable and long-enduring favorite, this seven-story hotel was originally built in 1932, and nearly doubled in size with the addition of a new wing after its acquisition by the Scandic chain after the turn of the millennium. Set behind a pale ocher facade in the heart of town, immediately across from the railway station, it offers comfortably furnished bedrooms, some of which overlook the surrounding town and others that front a soaring atrium with splashing fountains and potted plants.

Hameenkatu 1, FIN-33100 Tampere. www.scandic-hotels.com. © **03/244-61-11.** Fax 03/2446-2211. 263 units. 132€–173€ double; 342€ suite. Rates include buffet breakfast. AE, DC, MC, V. Parking 15€. Bus: 4

or 27. **Amenities:** Restaurant; bar; bikes; children's playground; exercise room; room service; sauna. *In room:* TV, minibar, Wi-Fi (free).

Sokos Hotel Ilves ★ In the heart of Tampere, this hotel is more plush and up-to-date than the also-recommended Sokos Hotel Tammer (see below). It's also one of the tallest buildings in town. Rooms were renovated in 2006, leaving a mostly monochromatic color scheme in the conservatively contemporary bedrooms, which range from midsize to spacious.

Hatanpäänvaltatie 1, FIN-33100 Tampere. www.sokoshotel.fi. ✆ **020/123-4631.** Fax 03/5698-6263. 336 units. Mon–Thurs 221€–241€ double; Fri–Sun 125€–150€ double; 281€ suite. Rates include buffet breakfast. AE, DC, MC, V. Parking 20€. Bus: 1. **Amenities:** Restaurant; bar; babysitting; Jacuzzi; indoor heated pool; room service; sauna. *In room:* TV, hair dryer, minibar, Wi-Fi (free).

Sokos Hotel Tammer ★ Because it has been frequently ripped apart and renovated, you might not immediately realize that this is the oldest hotel in town. It was for years considered the most glamorous—a designation that is no longer accurate—but public and private areas were renovated with sensitivity, taking care to preserve its Art Deco detailing. Bedrooms are high-ceilinged, large, and comfortably furnished, many opening onto views of the town. Furnishings are in a sleek Nordic style, and each room is individually designed. An outdoor terrace offers pleasant views of the sea.

Satakunnankatu 13, FIN-33100 Tampere. www.sokoshotels.fi. ✆ **020/123-46-32.** Fax 03/5697-6266. 87 units. Sun–Thurs 150€–175€ double; Fri–Sat 130€–155€ double; 240€–300€ suite. Rates include buffet breakfast. AE, DC, MC, V. Free parking. Bus: 24. **Amenities:** Restaurant; bar; room service; sauna. *In room:* TV, minibar.

Victoria This is usually cited as the least expensive of the major hotels of Tampere. Built in 1972 in a location close to the railway station, it has been spruced up at almost yearly intervals. Each of the cozy and comfortable bedrooms is outfitted in pastel colors with lots of exposed wood. Other than breakfast, no meals are served here, but there's a very small lobby bar.

Itsenaisyydenkatu 1, FIN-33100 Tampere. www.hotellivictoria.fi. ✆ **03/242-51-11.** Fax 03/242-51-00. 71 units. Mon–Thurs 132€–142€ double; Fri–Sun 99€ double. Rates include buffet breakfast. AE, MC, V. Free parking. Closed Dec 22–Jan 8. Bus: 1. **Amenities:** Bar; bikes; indoor heated pool; sauna. *In room:* TV, minibar (in most), Wi-Fi (free).

Where to Dine

Astor ★ CONTINENTAL This contemporary-looking restaurant offers a cozy setting, sophisticated and attentive service, and savory cuisine. Set in the heart of town, and favored by the city's business and academic community, it's the kind of place where romances are likely to blossom. The best menu items include filets of Baltic herring with mustard sauce; whitefish mousse with red currant sauce; creamy crayfish or cream of forest mushroom soup; and pan-fried breast of duck with and orange-and-ginger-flavored sauce. Dessert might include a parfait of arctic blackberries. There's a piano bar on the premises.

Aleksis Kiven Katu 26. ✆ **03/260-5700.** www.ravintola-astor.fi. Reservations recommended. Main courses 15€–26€; fixed-price menus 36€–40€. AE, MC, V. Mon–Tues 11am–11pm; Wed–Thurs 11am–midnight; Fri 11am–1am; Sat noon–1am; Sun 1–9pm. Bus: 1 or 10.

Finlaysonin Palatsi FINNISH/INTERNATIONAL Built as a palace in 1899, this is now an elegant restaurant with a number of dining rooms and cozy private rooms. In summer, outdoor seating is available in the surrounding park. The fish dishes, such as salmon and whitefish, are excellently prepared, as are the game specialties. Begin with such classic Finnish appetizers as cold smoked whitefish with a red cabbage strudel, or a smoked reindeer salmon roll. One of the best dishes is a roasted filet of pikeperch with a white truffle sauce. The chef uses local products wherever possible.

Kuninkaankatu 1. ✆ **400/219-530.** www.finlaysoninpalatsi.com. Reservations recommended. Main courses 16€–28€; fixed-price menus 38€–51€. AE, DC, MC, V. Tues–Fri 11am–midnight; Sat noon–midnight. Bus: 1, 2, or 3.

Hella & Huone ★★ CONTINENTAL This restaurant is to the immediate north of Tampere's Talo Park, in the heart of town, and the food is lavishly fussed over, professionally prepared and presented, and relatively ambitious. With just 33 seats and a small staff, you can be sure you'll get all the attention you deserve. You'll never know in advance what might be on the menu, but fresh fish, shellfish, and game dishes are likely to crop up whenever they're in season, and the chef is proud of their duck, lamb, and turbot dishes. A recent meal here featured pâté of foie gras in puff pastry with braised green tomatoes and chutney, cream of morel soup, roasted pheasant with whortleberry sauce, and an array of French cheeses.

Salhojankatu 48. ✆ **03/253-2440.** www.hellajahuone.fi. Reservations recommended. Main courses 26€; 3-course fixed-price menu 52€, 4-course 58€, 6-course 70€, 8-course 82€. AE, DC, MC, V. Tues–Sat 6–9:30pm. Bus: 1.

Plevna Brewery Pub and Restaurant FINNISH In 1820, an investor from Scotland founded a cotton mill in Tampere. About 60 years later, his heirs built this brick-sided weaving hall, now a rollicking, sometimes raucous space for an assembly of diners and drinkers who appreciate the large mugs of very fresh beer. The food is specially contrived to go well with the suds: creamy salmon soup, fried filets of perch with honey-flavored crème fraîche, filets of butter-fried herring, "brewmaster's steaks" (braised in beer), and pork schnitzels. The restaurant is named after a battle in the Balkan town of Plevna, in which some of the workers from the mills lost their lives.

Itäinenkatu 8. ✆ **03/260-1200.** www.plevna.fi. Main courses 9€–24€. AE, MC, V. Mon 11am–11pm; Tues–Thurs 11am–1am; Fri–Sat 11am–2am; Sun noon–11pm. Bus: 1 or 5.

FINNISH LAPLAND

Above the Arctic Circle, Lapland comprises one-third of Finland, the country's northernmost, largest, and most sparsely populated province, which is why it's often called "the Last Wilderness in Europe."

Although Lapland has four seasons, some people refer to eight seasons a year. In the summer, the vegetation sprouts flowers and bears fruit all within 3 months because the sun doesn't set for weeks on end. In Utsjoki, in the northernmost part of Lapland, starting in the middle of May, the sun doesn't set for nearly 70 days. If summer, with its midnight sun, is an extraordinary experience, then so is the polar night, the twilight time of the year, when the sun glows softly on the horizon all day and night.

The period during October and November, when there's no sun, is called *kaamos.* Winter is the longest period of the year, but it includes the night light show—the aurora borealis. After the polar night comes the dazzling spring snow, and skiing is great until May, when the sun gives twice as much light as it did in the dead of winter.

Lapland is an area of great forests, and jobs in forestry and agriculture are the most common occupations here. Finland's longest river, the Kemijoki, runs through the area, and its lower reaches are terraced with seven hydroelectric plants. Lapland also has western Europe's largest artificial lakes, Løkka and Porttipahta.

This is still a land of bears, wolves, eagles, and wolverines. However, the animal that symbolizes this land is the reindeer, and there are more than 300,000 here.

North of the Arctic Circle, the **Arctic Road ★★★** is as far north as the roadless tundras of Alaska, Greenland, and Siberia. As early as the 1930s, visitors from all over Europe traveled north in their cars, heading for Petsamo, the end point of the Arctic Road at that time. Today, the Arctic Road stretches more than 998km (620 miles), passing through central and northern Lapland as it heads toward the Arctic Ocean and eastern Finnmark, on the very edge of Europe.

Rovaniemi

834km (518 miles) N of Helsinki, 287km (178 miles) S of Ivalo

Our summer driving tour begins in Lapland's capital, Rovaniemi, which is best reached by flying from Helsinki. Once here, you can rent a car and tour Lapland (summer is the best time, as winters can be rough).

When the Nazis began their infamous retreat from Lapland in 1944, they burned Rovaniemi, the gateway to Lapland and a prime rail and communications center, to the ground. But with characteristic Finnish *sisu* (suggesting courage and bravery against overwhelming odds), Rovaniemi bounced back and became a completely modern town, designed largely by Finland's greatest architect, Alvar Aalto, who created roads shaped like reindeer antlers.

Eight kilometers (5 miles) south of the Arctic Circle, Rovaniemi is at the confluence of two significant Finnish rivers, the Kemijoki and the Ounasjoki. This capital of Finnish Lapland goes back some 8,000 years, and the settlement at Rovaniemi was mentioned in documents in the 1400s. Hwy. 4, which passes through the city, stretches from southern Finland to Inari in Lapland. You can drive to northern Norway on the Great Arctic Highway and to Kiruna, Sweden, and Narvik, Norway, by following the North Calotte Highway. If you arrive by plane, you'll probably take a bus into Rovaniemi, although a reindeer-drawn *pulkka* would be more colorful.

Regardless of when you come, you'll surely escape the heat. In July, the hottest month, the temperature is likely to be around 50°F (10°C); however, you won't escape the mosquitoes from the swampy tundra.

ESSENTIALS

GETTING THERE There are daily flights from Helsinki (trip time: 1 hr.). The airport is 8km (5 miles) north of the center of town, and yellow minivans, costing 7€ per person, will take you into town. Their departures are timed to coincide with the arrival of flights. For flight information call **Finnair** at ✆ **600/140-140.** Four trains a day depart from Helsinki for Rovaniemi, taking 10 hours for the trek north. The train station is at Rantakatu; for rail schedules, call ✆ **0600/41900.**

GETTING AROUND Rovaniemi is the bus center for northern Finland, and buses fan out from the station to Lapinkävij and all major communities north of Rovaniemi. For schedules, call ✆ **016/312020.** Bus no. 8 is the town's most serviceable bus, hitting all the attractions and hotels of Rovaniemi before continuing on to Santa's Village and the Arctic Circle. The one-way fare is 4€ per person.

VISITOR INFORMATION The **Rovaniemi Tourist Information** office, Maakuntakatu 29–31, FIN-96200 Rovaniemi (✆ **016/346-270;** www.visitrovaniemi.fi), is open June to August Monday to Friday 8am to 6pm and Saturday and Sunday 10am to 4pm; September to May Monday to Friday from 9am to 5pm. In December, it's also open Saturday and Sunday 10am to 2pm.

SEEING THE SIGHTS

"The architect's job is to give life a more sensitive structure," wrote architect Alvar Aalto in 1955. This is exactly what he did when he created the **Administrative and Cultural Center ★★**, an elegant trio of buildings, which draws devotees of his designs from all over the world. The cultural complex, **Lappla-Talo,** Hallituskatu 11, was the last of Aalto's buildings to be completed here, having opened in 1975. The first building, the library, **Kirjasto ★★**, Hallituskatu 7 (✆ **016/322-2463**), opened in 1965. The house has a valuable Sami collection, and temporary art exhibitions are staged in its Lappinica Hall. Admission is free and it's open Monday to Thursday 11am to 8pm, Friday 11am to 5pm, and Saturday 11am to 3pm.

A third building, **Kaupungintalo ★★**, Hallituskatu 7 (✆ **016/322-2288**), is the most famous government building in northern Finland. Aalto completed it in 1988 as the finishing touch of the administrative and cultural center. This Town Hall consists of several divergent wings, and it's dominated by the council chamber, which evokes crystal because of its "folded" wall surfaces. The entrance wall of the hall is a distant echo of Aalto's famous theme of northern lights. Admission is free; the Town Hall is open Monday to Friday 8am to 4pm.

Arktikum ★★★ In all of Scandinavia, this is the best museum devoted to the culture of a region. An avant-garde, underground construction that mimics an ice tunnel shelters two exceptional museums that demonstrate living conditions for the people, especially the Sami, who live north of the Arctic Circle. The **Provincial Museum of Lapland Exhibitions ★★** is a fascinating re-creation of Sami culture, with folklore costumes, small-scale models of Rovaniemi from 1939 to 1944, and an award-winning exhibition called "The Survivors," illustrating life in Lapland from prehistoric times to today. Almost daily, a show features the northern lights in the **Polarium Theater.** The **Arctic Circle Centre Exhibitions ★★★** offer a rare insight into these northern people and their flora and fauna. You learn the number of words Sami have for snow, and see how they catch seals. Exhibits also trace the tremendous natural wealth of the region while addressing risks involved in exploiting them.

It'll take at least 2 hours, which can include lunch at the **Arktikum Restaurant** (✆ **358/163-223-260;** www.arktikum.fi), where all the food is prepared using fresh local produce. The 12€ luncheon buffet is the best in town. You can also order a la carte items, such as sautéed reindeer, costing from 15€ to 22€. Three-course set dinners cost 42€ to 52€. An on-site gift shop sells handmade souvenirs.

Pohjoisranta 4. ✆ **016/322-3260.** Admission 12€ adults, 8€ students and seniors, 5€ ages 7–15, free for 6 and under. Family ticket for 2 adults and 2 children 25€. Sept 1–Nov 30 and Jan 11–May 31 Tues–Sun 10am–6pm; Dec 1–Jan 10 daily 10am–6pm; June–Aug daily 10am–6pm. 1km (½ mile) north of city center.

Napaiiri: The Arctic Circle ★★ All visitors want to visit the Arctic Circle, the southernmost line at which the midnight sun can be viewed. Bus no. 8 runs from the center of Rovaniemi to this location, 8km (5 miles) north of Rovaniemi on the Rovaniemi-Sodankylä highway. At this point, the sun never sets in midsummer, nor rises in the pitch black midwinter. The **Arctic Circle Marker** is found here. But don't think the Arctic Circle is permanently fixed—it can shift several yards or meters daily.

Napaiiri is also the site of **Santa Claus Village,** the most commercialized center of all of Lapland. Thousands of letters from children all over the world are mailed to the **Santa Claus Main Post Office,** FIN-96930, Arctic Circle. You can also send a postcard home with an official stamp from Santa Claus himself. Next to the post office, you can join a line of kids waiting to meet Santa.

The other big attraction here is **Santapark ★** (✆ **358/600-301-203;** www.santapark.com), at Syväsenvaara Mountain 2km (1¼ miles) west of the Rovaniemi airport. A free Santa train runs in summer between Santa Claus Village and Santapark. The park is inside a cave in the mountain, where you're greeted with elves baking gingerbread and, yes, another Santa. In summer adults pay 15€, children 13€. In winter adults are charged 28€, 23€ children. There is no family ticket. From midsummer to mid-August, hours are Tuesday to Saturday 10am to 6pm. The park also reopens in late November to mid-January daily 10am to 6pm.

Rovaniemen Kirkko This Evangelical Lutheran parish church was built in 1950 to replace the one destroyed during the war. Designed by the architect Bertel Liljequist, it is on the same spot as three previous churches. The interior is quite beautiful, noted for its wall and ceiling decorations, woodcarvings, and the altar fresco, ***Fountain of Life*** **★★**, by Lennart Segerstrale.

Kirkkotie 1. ✆ **016/335-511.** Free admission. Daily 9am–9pm. Closed Oct to mid-May.

WHERE TO STAY

Rovaniemi has the finest hotels in northern Finland, although many tend to be expensive unless you book at a summer discount or weekend rate. Private homes that accept paying guests are the best bargain (don't expect a private bathroom). Ask at the tourist office for further information.

City Hotel Comfortable and unpretentious, this is a serviceable and well-managed hotel a few steps north of the town center. Its newest rooms are on the uppermost (fourth) floor. The in-house restaurant, the Monte Rosa, is recommended separately in "Where to Dine," below.

Pekankatu 9, FIN-96200 Rovaniemi. www.cityhotel.fi. ✆ **016/330-01-11.** Fax 016/311-304. 92 units. 124€–154€ double; 174€ suite. Rates include buffet breakfast. AE, DC, MC, V. Free parking. **Amenities:** Restaurant; bar; room service; sauna. *In room:* TV, hair dryer, minibar, Wi-Fi (free).

Hotelli Aakenus This small-scale inn is run by a local family (unlike other Rovaniemi hotels that are chain-run) and about .5km (⅓ mile) west of Town Hall at the edges of Rovaniemi's "urban sprawl." The small bedrooms are simple but comfortable, each of which was renovated and upgraded in 2005. Nothing here is luxurious, but the staff works hard, the prices are reasonable, and everything is well maintained.

Koskikatu 47, FIN-96100 Rovaniemi. www.hotelliaakenus.net. ✆ **016/342-2051.** Fax 016/342-2021. 45 units. Mon–Thurs 68€–100€ double. AE, DC, MC, V. Free parking. **Amenities:** Restaurant; bar; sauna. *In room:* TV, Wi-Fi (free).

Rantasipi Pohjanhovi ★ This is the oldest hotel in town and the one with the most flair, built in 1936 when Rovaniemi was a logging-town outpost with a bright future ahead of it. Enlarged and virtually rebuilt in 1947, this hotel offers a disco, a stylish and top-rated restaurant, recommended separately in "Where to Dine," below, and comfortably contemporary-looking bedrooms, each outfitted with well-chosen Finnish fabrics.

Pohjanpuistikko 2, FIN-96200 Rovaniemi. www.rantasipi.fi. ✆ **016/33-711.** Fax 016/313-997. 212 units. Mon–Thurs 143€–177€ double; Fri–Sun 100€–120€ double; 199€–210€ suite. Rates include buffet breakfast. AE, DC, MC, V. Free parking. **Amenities:** Restaurant; bar; large indoor heated pool; room service; sauna. *In room:* TV, minibar, Wi-Fi (free).

Sokos Hotel Vaakuna ★ Stylish and well managed, with a pair of separately recommended restaurants that draw in substantial numbers of nonresidents, this hotel rises five pink-toned floors above the town center. You'll register in a lobby

LAPLAND safaris & RIVER CRUISES

In the very short summer, white-water rafting, river cruises, fishing in local rivers, and trips to reindeer and husky farms can be arranged, while winter visitors can opt for snowmobiling, skiing, or sled safaris.

There are several tour operators. The largest and best-known agency, offering tours of the vast Lapland area, is **Lapland Safaris,** Koskikatu 1 (✆ **016/331-1200;** www.laplandsafaris.com).

Prices depend on what you want to do or see. A 3-hour summer tour costs around 85€, while short trips on the river cost 30€. In winter, the prices of the safaris are far more expensive; a snowmobile safari, for example, ranges from 130€ to 200€. About 2 to 4 hours of husky or reindeer sledding costs from 120€ to 185€.

sheathed with slabs of Finnish granite before heading up to the rooms, which were each renovated in 2005. The staff is helpful and accommodating, and there's a zesty energy about this place that isn't present in some of its more staid competitors.

Koskikatu 4, FIN-96200 Rovaniemi. www.sokoshotels.fi. ✆ **020/123-4695.** Fax 016/332-21-99. 159 units. 100€–152€ double; 280€ suite. AE, DC, MC, V. Parking 8€. **Amenities:** 3 restaurants; bar; room service; sauna. *In room:* TV, minibar, Wi-Fi (in most; free).

WHERE TO DINE

Amarillo TEX-MEX This is one of two restaurants in the Sokos Hotel Vaakuna, and offers everything from nachos, fajitas, and grilled T-bone steaks to grilled filets of lamb, spicy fried chicken, and juicy burgers, all in a Western-inspired ambience.

In the Sokos Hotel Vaakuna, Koskikatu 4. ✆ **016/332-2580.** www.amarillo.fi. Main courses 12€–25€. AE, DC, MC, V. Mon–Thurs 11am–midnight; Fri 11am–3am; Sat noon–3am; Sun noon–midnight.

Fransmanni Restaurant ★ FRENCH/CONTINENTAL This, the second of the Sokos Hotel Vaakuna's two restaurants, is grand, French, and rather formal. The menu lists well-prepared Gallic creations such as snails flavored with garlic and Roquefort cheese; cream of salmon soup; an herb-laden chicken casserole; and filets of reindeer with dark honey sauce.

In the Sokos Hotel Vaakuna, Koskikatu 4. ✆ **016/33-22-515.** www.fransmanni.fi. Reservations recommended. Main courses 13€–46€; fixed-price menus 26€–36€. AE, DC, MC, V. Mon–Thurs 11am–11pm; Fri 11am–midnight; Sat noon–midnight; Sun 1–10pm.

Monte Rosa FINNISH It's warm, paneled with woods from Finnish forests, and priced appropriately for its location in one of the town's recommended middle-bracket hotels. Examples of enduringly popular items include cream of chanterelle soup, Caesar salad with chunks of grilled chicken, grilled Sami-style lamb with chanterelle sauce, and reindeer filets with juniper-berry or chanterelle sauce. There's a luncheon buffet every Monday to Friday from 11:30am to 2:30pm, when many of the town's office workers select from the wide array of meats (three kinds), fish, and salads. During clement weather, additional dining space opens on an outdoor terrace.

In the City Hotel, Pekankatu 9. ✆ **016/330-01-11.** www.cityhotel.fi. Lunch buffet 9.70€ per person; main courses 13€–31€. AE, DC, MC, V. Mon–Fri 11am–10:30pm; Sat 1–10:30pm; Sun 3–10:30pm.

Restaurant at the Rantasipi Pohjanhovi Hotel ★★ FINNISH/CONTINENTAL Other restaurants in Rovaniemi might be flashier and follow culinary and decorative trends a bit more closely, but when asked where they'd want to celebrate a rite of passage, most residents choose here. It's relatively formal, with crisp white napery, but it isn't staid. Windows look out over one of Lapland's most evocative rivers, and food is superb, drawing upon game, fish, and produce from the surrounding region, some of it provided by individual local hunters and fishermen. Reindeer, ptarmigan, trout, and snow grouse are always reliable bets, often accented with berries culled late during the region's brief summers.

In the Rantasipi Pohjanhovi Hotel, Pohjanpuistikko 2. ✆ **016/33 711.** www.rantasipi.fi. Reservations recommended. Main courses 14€–31€. AE, DC, MC, V. Mon–Thurs 11am–10pm; Fri–Sat 11am–2am; Sun 6–10pm.

Sky Ounasvaara Panorama Restaurant ★★★ SAMI/INTERNATIONAL Two kilometers (1¼ miles) east of the town center, this restaurant is on the second floor of the Sky Hotel Ounasvaara, offering panoramic views from its perch on Ounasvaara Hill. A Finnish gourmet society consistently names this restaurant as one of the top 19 in the country, and it also holds the Chaine des Rotisseurs plaque. Begin your meal with salmon roe or champagne-flavored asparagus soup with asparagus ravioli. For a main course, we especially like the Lake Inarinjärvi whitefish flavored with a star anise-spiced crayfish sauce or the arctic char roasted in almond oil and served with a zesty dark orange sauce. There's a bar, and a panoramic roof terrace for watching the midnight sun or the northern lights.

You can also stay here overnight in one of the 71 well-furnished bedrooms, renting for 105€ to 247€ in winter for a double or 110€ to 165€ in summer. Rooms are spacious and well furnished, and many have bathtubs (unusual for Lapland) and their own sauna. If you're staying over for a while, you might ask about cabin rentals; with two separate bedrooms, they're ideal for families.

The restaurant is next to the **Ounasvaara Ski Center** (✆ **016/369-045;** www.ounasvaara.fi), with 123km (76 miles) of cross-country skiing tracks, plus six downhill slopes and three ski jumps.

Ounasvaara, FIN-96400. ✆ **016/323-400.** Fax 016/318-789. www.laplandhotels.com. Reservations recommended. Main courses 22€–34€. AE, DC, MC, V. Daily 11am–10pm.

SHOPPING

Lauri-Toutteet oy ★, Pohjolankatu 25 (✆ **016/342-25-01;** www.lauri-tuotteet.fi), is a log cabin in the center of town that houses workshops where craftspeople turn out both modern and traditional decorative pieces using such items as reindeer antlers and the gnarled roots of pussy willows. The store's cafe is a permanent sales exhibit, featuring curly birch products, wool and leather goods, jewelry, and Puukko knives. Open Monday to Friday 9am to 5pm.

ROVANIEMI AFTER DARK

The great cultural center of Lapland is **Lappia-Talo ★★★**, Hallituskatu 11 (✆ **0400/282484;** www.rovaniementeatteri.fi), designed by Alvar Aalto in 1975. One of the town's architectural wonders, this concert hall and convention center houses the world's northernmost professional theater, the Rovaniemi Theater Company. It is also the venue for the Lapland Music School and the Chamber Orchestra of Lapland. It's closed from June to August, but if you're in Rovaniemi at other times, check to see what's playing.

21 FAST FACTS & WEBSITES

FAST FACTS: SCANDINAVIA

Insurance **Medical Insurance** For travel overseas, most U.S. health plans (including Medicare and Medicaid) do not provide coverage, and the ones that do often require you to pay for services upfront and reimburse you only after you return home.

If you require medical insurance, try **MEDEX Assistance** (✆ **800/732-5309;** www.medexassist.com) or **Travel Assistance International** (✆ **800/821-2828;** www.travelassistance.com; for general information on services, call the company's **Europ Assistance Services, Inc.** at ✆ **800/777-8710; www.europ-assistance.com**).

Canadians should check with their provincial health plan offices or call **Health Canada** (✆ **866/225-0709;** www.hc-sc.gc.ca) to find out the extent of their coverage and what documentation they must take home in case they are treated overseas.

Travelers from the U.K. should carry their **European Health Insurance Card (EHIC),** which replaced the E111 form as proof of entitlement to free/reduced cost medical treatment abroad (✆ **0845/605-0707;** www.ehic.org.uk). Note, however, that the EHIC only covers "necessary medical treatment," and for repatriation costs, lost money, baggage, or cancellation, travel insurance from a reputable company should always be sought (www.travelinsuranceweb.com).

Travel Insurance The cost of travel insurance varies widely, depending on the destination, the cost and length of your trip, your age and health, and the type of trip you're taking, but expect to pay between 5% and 8% of the vacation itself. You can get estimates from various providers through **InsureMyTrip.com** (✆ **800/487-4722**).

U.K. citizens and their families who make more than one trip abroad per year may find an annual travel insurance policy works out cheaper. Check **www.moneysupermarket.com** (✆ **0845/345-5708**), which compares prices across a wide range of providers for single- and multi-trip policies.

Most big travel agents offer their own insurance and will probably try to sell you their package when you book a holiday. Think before you sign. **British Consumers' Association** recommends that you insist on seeing the policy and reading the fine print before buying travel insurance. The **Association of British Insurers** (✆ **020/7600-3333;** www.abi.org.uk) gives advice by phone and publishes *Holiday Insurance,* a free guide to policy provisions and prices. You might also shop around for better deals: Try **Columbus Direct** (✆ **0870/033-9988;** www.columbusdirect.net).

Trip-Cancellation Insurance Trip-cancellation insurance will help retrieve your money if you have to back out of a trip or depart early, or if your travel supplier goes bankrupt. Trip cancellation traditionally covers such events as sickness, natural disasters, and State Department advisories. The latest news in trip-cancellation insurance is the availability of **expanded hurricane coverage** and the **"any-reason"** cancellation coverage—which costs more but covers cancellations made for any reason. You won't get back 100% of your prepaid trip cost, but you'll be refunded a substantial portion. **TravelSafe** (© **888/885-7233;** www.travelsafe.com) offers both types of coverage. Expedia also offers any-reason cancellation coverage for its air-hotel packages. For details, contact one of the following recommended insurers: **Access America** (© **800/284-8300;** www.accessamerica.com); **Travel Guard International** (© 800/826-4919; www.travelguard.com); **Travel Insured International** (© 800/243-3174; www.travel insured.com); and **Travelex Insurance Services** (© **800/228-9792;** www.travelex-insurance.com).

Lost & Found Be sure to tell all of your credit card companies the minute you discover your wallet has been lost or stolen and file a report at the nearest police precinct. Your credit card company or insurer may require a police report number or record of the loss. Most credit card companies have an emergency toll-free number to call if your card is lost or stolen; they may be able to wire you a cash advance immediately or deliver an emergency credit card in a day or two. Visa's emergency number outside the U.S. is © **410/581-9994;** call collect. American Express cardholders should call collect © **336/393-1111.** MasterCard holders should call collect © **636/722-7111.** If you need emergency cash over the weekend when all banks and American Express offices are closed, you can have money wired to you via **Western Union** (© **800/325-6000;** www.westernunion.com).

Passports The websites listed below provide downloadable passport applications as well as the current fees for processing applications. For an up-to-date, country-by-country listing of passport requirements around the world, go to the "International Travel" tab of the U.S. State Department at **http://travel.state.gov**. International visitors to the U.S. can obtain a visa application at the same website. ***Note:*** Children are required to present a passport when entering the United States at airports. More information on obtaining a passport for a minor can be found at http://travel.state.gov. Processing normally takes 4 to 6 weeks (3 weeks for expedited service) but can take longer during busy periods (especially spring). if you need it in a hurry, the fee is higher.

For Residents of the United States Whether you're applying in person or by mail, you can download passport applications from the U.S. Department of State website at http://travel.state.gov. To find your regional passport office, check the U.S. Department of State website or call the toll-free number of the National Passport Information Center (© **877/487-2778**) for automated information.

You can contact the **U.S. Dept. of State Travel Advisory** © 202/647-5225 (manned 24 hr.).

You can reach the **U.S. Passport Agency** at © 877/487-2778, and **U.S. Centers for Disease Control International Traveler's Hotline** at © 800/232-4636.

For Residents of Australia You can pick up an application from your local post office or any branch of Passports Australia, but you must schedule an interview at the passport office to present your application materials. Call the **Australian Passport Information Service** at © **131-232,** or visit the government website at www.passports.gov.au.

For Residents of Canada Passport applications are available at most post offices throughout Canada or from the central **Passport Office,** Department of Foreign Affairs and International Trade, Gatineau, QC K1A 0G3 (© **800/567-6868;** www.ppt.gc.ca). ***Note:*** Canadian children who travel must have their own passport.

For Residents of Ireland You can apply for a 10-year passport at the **Passport Office,** Setanta Centre, Molesworth Street, Dublin 2 (© **01/671-1633;** www.dfa.ie). In Ireland, infants (up to age 3) are issued a 3-year passport. Children aged 3 to 17 are issued a 5-year passport. Persons aged 18 and over, including those over 65, are issued a 10-year passport. You can also apply at 1A South Mall, Cork (✆ **021/494-4700**), or at most main post offices.

For Residents of New Zealand You can pick up a passport application at any New Zealand Passports Office or download it from their website. Contact the **Passports Office** at ✆ **0800/225-050** in New Zealand or 04/474-8100, or log on to www.passports.govt.nz.

For Residents of the United Kingdom To pick up an application for a standard 10-year passport (5-year passport for children 15 and under), visit your nearest passport office, major post office, or travel agency, or contact the **United Kingdom Passport Service** at ✆ **0300/222-0000;** also search its website at www.ukpa.gov.uk.

Visitor Information In the **United States,** contact the **Scandinavian Tourist Board,** 655 Third Ave., Ste. 1810, New York, NY 10017 (✆ **212/885-9700;** www.goscandinavia.com), at least 3 months in advance for maps, sightseeing pointers, ferry schedules, and other information for Denmark, Norway, Sweden, and Finland.

Denmark: Tourist Offices In the **United States,** contact the **Danish Tourist Board,** 655 Third Ave., 18th Floor, New York, NY 10017 (✆ **212/885-9700;** www.visitdenmark.com).

In the **United Kingdom,** contact the **Danish Tourist Board,** 55 Sloane St., London SW1X 9SY (✆ **020/7235-1255**).

To begin your exploration of Denmark, visit the **Scandinavian Tourist Board** (www.goscandinavia.com), the **Danish Tourist Board** (www.visitdenmark.com), and **Wonderful Copenhagen** (www.visitcopenhagen.dk), all of which offer extensive links to other organizations, accommodations, attractions, and other information. Get information on Danish culture, tour suggestions, and events at **CultureNet Denmark** (✆ **45/33-74-51-00;** www.kulturarv.dk).

Norway: Tourist Offices For information in the **United States,** contact the **Scandinavian Tourist Board,** above. In the **United Kingdom,** contact the **Norwegian Tourist Board** (a division of the Scandinavian Tourist Board), Charles House, 5 Lower Regent St., London SW1Y 4LR (✆ **0207/389-8800;** cost 50p per min.). You might also try the tourist board's official website: **www.visitnorway.com**.

In **Canada, Innovation Norway** has replaced the Norwegian Tourist Board. You can reach Innovation Norway at 2 Bloor St. W., Ste. 504, Toronto, Ontario M4W 3E2, Canada (✆ **416/920-0434;** www.emb-norway.ca).

Sweden: Tourist Offices For information in the **United States,** contact the **Scandinavian Tourist Board,** above. In the **United Kingdom,** contact the **Swedish Travel & Tourism Council,** 11 Montague Place, London W1H 2AL (✆ **020/7870-5600**). You also can try the website **www.visitsweden.com**.

Finland: Tourist Offices For information in **North America,** contact the **Finnish Tourist Board,** PO Box 4649, Grand Central Station, New York, NY 10163-4649 (✆ **212/885-9700**). In the **United Kingdom,** contact the **Finnish Tourist Board,** 3rd Floor, 30–35 Pall Mall, London SW1Y 5LP (✆ **020/8600-5680**).

FAST FACTS: DENMARK

American Express Amex is represented throughout Denmark by **Nyman & Schultz,** Nørregade 7A (✆ **33-13-11-81;** bus: 34 or 35), with a branch in Terminal 3 of the Copenhagen airport. Fulfilling all the functions of American Express except for foreign exchange services, the main office is open Monday to Thursday 8:30am to 4:30pm, and Friday 8:30am to 4pm. The airport office remains open until 8:30pm Monday to Friday. On weekends and overnight on weekdays, a recorded message, in English, will deliver the phone number of a 24-hour Amex service in Stockholm. This is useful for anyone who has lost a card or traveler's checks.

Area Code The international country code for Denmark is **45.** For international calls dial **00,** then the country code (**44** for Britain, **1** for the United States or Canada).

ATM Networks & Cash Points See "Money & Costs," p. 46.

Business Hours Most **banks** are open Monday to Friday from 9:30am to 4pm (Thurs to 6pm), but outside Copenhagen, banking hours vary. **Stores** are generally open Monday through Thursday from 9am to 5:30pm, Friday 9am to 7 or 8pm, and Saturday noon to 2pm; most are closed Sunday.

Currency See "Money & Costs" on p. 46.

Drinking Laws To consume alcohol in Danish bars, restaurants, or cafes, customers must be 18 or older. There are no restrictions on children under 18 who drink at home or, for example, from a bottle in a public park. Danish police tend to be lenient unless drinkers become raucous or uncontrollable. There is no leniency, however, in the matter of driving while intoxicated. It's illegal to drive with a blood-alcohol level of 0.8 or more, which could be produced by two drinks. The legal limit for alcohol in your blood is 0.5 in Denmark. Liquor stores are closed on Sunday.

Driving Rules See p. 38.

Drug Laws Penalties for the possession, use, purchase, sale, or manufacturing of drugs are severe. The quantity of the controlled substance is more important than the type of substance. Danish police are particularly strict with cases involving the sale of drugs to children.

Drugstores They're known as *apoteker* in Danish and are open Monday to Thursday 9am to 5:30pm, Friday 9am to 7pm, and Saturday 9am to 1pm.

Electricity Voltage is generally 220 volts AC, 50 to 60 cycles. In many camping sites, 110-volt power plugs are also available. Adapters and transformers may be purchased in Denmark. It's always best to check at your hotel desk before using an electrical outlet.

Embassies & Consulates All embassies are in Copenhagen. The embassy of the **United States** is at Dag Hammärskjölds Allé 24, DK-2100 Copenhagen (✆ 33-41-71-00; denmark.usembassy.gov). Other embassies are the **United Kingdom,** Kastelsvej 40, DK-2100 Copenhagen (✆ 35-44-52-00; ukindenmark.fco.gov.uk); **Canada,** Kristen Berniskows Gade 1, DK-1105 Copenhagen K (✆ 33-48-32-00); **Australia,** Dampfærgevej 26, DK-2100 Copenhagen (✆ 70-26-36-76; www.denmark.embassy.gov.au); and **Ireland,** Østbanegade 21, DK-2100 Copenhagen (✆ 35-47-32-00).

Emergencies Dial ✆ **112** for the fire department, the police, or an ambulance, or to report a sea or air accident. Emergency calls from public telephone kiosks are free (no coins needed).

Gasoline (Petrol) See "Getting There & Getting Around," p. 38.

Holidays Public holidays are New Year's Day, Maundy Thursday, Good Friday, Easter Sunday, Easter Monday, Labor Day (May 1), Common Prayers Day (fourth Fri after Easter), Ascension Day (mid-May), Whitsunday (late May), Whitmonday, Constitution Day (June 5), Christmas Day, and Boxing Day (December 26).

Language Danish is the national tongue. English is commonly spoken, especially among young people. You should have few, if any, language barriers. The best phrase book is *Danish for Travellers* (Berlitz).

Mail Most post offices are open Monday through Friday from 9 or 10am to 5 or 6pm and Saturday from 9am to noon; they're closed Sunday. All mail to North America is sent airmail without extra charge. Mailboxes are painted red and display the embossed crown and trumpet of the Danish Postal Society.

Newspapers & Magazines English-language newspapers are sold at all major news kiosks in Copenhagen but are much harder to find in the provinces. London papers are flown in for early-morning delivery, but you may find the *International Herald Tribune* or *USA Today* more interesting. Pick up a copy of *Copenhagen This Week,* printed in English, which contains useful information.

Police Dial ✆ **112** nationwide.

Safety Denmark is one of the safest European countries for travelers. Copenhagen, the major population center, naturally experiences the most crime. Muggings have been reported in the vicinity of the railway station, especially late at night, but crimes of extreme violence are exceedingly rare. Exercise the usual precautions you would when traveling anywhere.

Smoking August 15, 2007 was D-day for Danish smokers. A smoking ban took effect, against cigarettes, cigars, and pipes, which can no longer be enjoyed at all public buildings as well as private businesses. The ordinance covers restaurants, shops, schools, bars, public transport, entertainment establishments, and places of employment. The World Health Organization estimates that 30% of all Danes smoke.

Taxes The 25% VAT (value-added tax) on goods and services is known in Denmark as MOMS (pronounced "mumps"). Special tax-free exports are possible, and many stores will mail goods home to you, circumventing MOMS. If you want to take your purchases with you, look for shops displaying Danish tax-free shopping notices. Such shops offer tourists tax refunds for personal export. This refund applies to purchases of at least 300DKK for U.S. and Canadian visitors. Danish Customs must stamp your tax-free invoice when you leave the country. You can receive your refund at Copenhagen's Kastrup International Airport when you depart.

For the refund to apply, the 300DKK must be spent in one store, but not necessarily at the same time. Some major department stores allow purchases to be made over several days or even weeks, at the end of which receipts will be tallied. Service and handling fees are deducted from the total, so actual refunds come up to about 19%. Information on this program is available from the Danish Tourist Board (see "Visitor Information," p. 542).

A 25% MOMS is included in hotel and restaurant bills, service charges, entrance fees, and repair bills for foreign-registered cars. No refunds are possible on these items.

Telephones The country code for Denmark is **45.** For international calls, dial **00,** then the country code, the area code, and the number. Try to avoid calling from your hotel. The surcharges are often outrageous.

Dial **118** to find out a number in Denmark, or **113** for international assistance. If you need operator assistance for international calls, also dial **113.** Virtually all international operators speak English.

Coin-operated phones are being phased out. Visitors can purchase a telephone card at most kiosks, groceries, and post offices in Denmark. If you face a coin-operated phone, know that these take 1, 2, 5, 10, or 20 *kroner* coins.

For long distance services, the access codes are as follows: **AT&T USADirect** (✆ **800/10010;** www.usa.att.com); **MCI** (✆ **800/10022;** www.mci.com).

Time Denmark operates on Central European Time—1 hour ahead of Greenwich Mean Time and 6 hours ahead of Eastern Standard Time. Daylight saving time is from the end of March to the end of September.

Tipping Tips are seldom expected. Porters charge fixed prices, and tipping is not customary for hairdressers or barbers. Service is built into the system, and hotels, restaurants, and even taxis include a 15% service charge in their rates. Because of the service charge, plus the 25% MOMS, you'll probably have to pay an additional 40% for some services!

Consider tipping only for special services—some Danes would feel insulted if you offered them a tip.

Toilets All big plazas, such as Town Hall Square in Copenhagen, have public lavatories. In small towns and villages, head for the marketplace. Hygienic standards are usually adequate. Sometimes men and women patronize the same toilets (signs read TOILETTER or WC). Otherwise, men's rooms are marked HERRER or H, and women's rooms are marked DAMER or D.

FAST FACTS: NORWAY

American Express There is an office in Oslo. American Express Reisebyrå, Maribores Gate 13 (✆ **22-98-35-00**), is open Monday through Friday 9am to 6pm, Saturday 10am to 4pm.

ATM Networks & Cash Points See "Money & Costs," in chapter 2.

Business Hours Most **banks** are open Monday through Friday from 8:15am to 3:30pm (Thurs till 5pm), and are closed Saturday and Sunday. The Nordea bank in arrivals at Gardermoen airport in Oslo is open Monday through Friday from 8:30am to 8:30pm, Saturday from 10am to 6pm, and Sunday from 11:30am to 8:30pm. The branch in the departures terminal is open Monday through Friday from 6am to 6:30pm, Saturday from 6am to 3pm, and Sunday from 6am to 6:30pm. Most **businesses** are open Monday through Friday from 9am to 4pm. **Stores** are generally open Monday through Friday from 9am to 5pm (many stay open on Thurs until 6 or 7pm) and Saturday 9am to 1 or 2pm. Sunday closings are observed.

Currency See "Money & Costs," in chapter 2.

Doctors Your embassy or consulate, as well as most hotels, keeps a list of recommended English-speaking physicians. See "Embassies & Consulates," below.

Drinking Laws Most restaurants, pubs, and bars in Norway are licensed to serve liquor, wine, and beer. The drinking age is 18 for beer and wine and 20 for liquor.

Driving Rules See "Getting There & Getting Around," in chapter 2.

Drugstores Drugstores, called *apotek,* are open during normal business hours.

Electricity Norway uses 220 volts, 30 to 50 cycles, AC, and standard Continental two-pin plugs. Transformers and adapters will be needed with Canadian and American equipment.

Embassies & Consulates In case you lose your passport or have some other emergency, contact your embassy in Oslo. The embassy of the **United States** is at Henrik Ibsensgate 48, N-0244 Oslo (✆ **21-30-85-40;** norway.usembassy.gov); **United Kingdom,** Thomas Heftyesgate 8, N-0244 Oslo (✆ **23-13-27-00;** ukinnorway.fco.gov.uk); and **Canada,** Wergelandsveien 7, N-0244 Oslo (✆ **22-99-53-00;** www.canadainternational.gc.ca). The **Irish Embassy** is at Haakon VII's Gate 1, N-0244 Oslo (✆ **22-01-72-00;** www.embassyofireland.no). The de facto **Australian Embassy** is the honorary consul of the Australian Consulate, Strandveien 20, N-1324 Lysaker (✆ **67-58-48-48**). The **New Zealand Embassy** is also closed in Oslo; contact the **New Zealand Consulate,** Strandveien 50, N-1366 Lysaker (✆ **67-11-00-30**). There is a British consulate in Bergen at Carl Øvre Ole Bulls Plass 1 (✆ **55-36-78-10**).

Emergencies Throughout Norway, call ✆ **112** for the **police,** ✆ **110** to report a **fire,** or ✆ **113** to request an **ambulance.**

Holidays Norway celebrates the following public holidays: New Year's Day (Jan 1), Maundy Thursday, Good Friday, Easter, Labor Day (May 1), Ascension Day (mid-May),

National Day (May 17), Whitmonday (late May), Christmas (Dec 25), and Boxing Day (Dec 26).

Hospitals Nearly all places throughout Norway contain hospitals with English-speaking doctors.

Language Norwegians are taught English in grade school. There are two official versions of Norwegian itself, one called *Bokmål,* spoken by about 85% of the population, the lesser known called *Nynorsk.* Nynorsk is identified as "new Norwegian," but is actually a melding of several older dialects spoken in rural parts of the country. In the north, the Sami have their own language, which is a distant cousin of Finnish.

Lost & Found Be sure to tell all of your credit card companies the minute you discover that your wallet has been lost or stolen, and then file a report at the nearest police precinct. Your credit card company or insurer may require a police report number or a police record of the loss. Most credit card companies have an emergency toll-free number to call if your card is lost or stolen; they may be able to wire you a cash advance immediately or deliver an emergency credit card in a day or two. **Visa's** emergency number outside the U.S. is ✆ **410/581-9994;** call collect (in Norway, toll-free **80-01-20-52**). **American Express** cardholders should call collect ✆ **905/474-0870. MasterCard** holders should call collect ✆ **636/722-7111.** If you need emergency cash over the weekend when all banks and American Express offices are closed, you can have money wired to you via **Western Union** (✆ **800/325-6000;** www.westernunion.com).

Mail Airmail letters or postcards to the United States and Canada cost NOK13 for up to 21 grams (¾ oz.). Airmail letters take 7 to 10 days to reach North America. The principal post office in Norway is the Oslo Central Post Office, at Dronningensgate 15, N-0101 Oslo. Mailboxes are vibrant red and are embossed with the trumpet symbol of the postal service. They're found on walls, at chest level, throughout cities and towns. Stamps can be purchased at the post office, at magazine kiosks, or at some stores.

Passports Unless you are an E.U. citizen, you will need a national passport to from your home country to enter Norway. Be sure to allow plenty of time before your trip to apply for a passport; processing can take up to 6 weeks. Contact your home passport agency in your country for specific information and details on how to apply. In the U.S., visit http://travel.state.gov/passport. U.K. residents should go to www.ukpa.gov.uk. In Australia, try www.passports.gov.au; in New Zealand www.passports.govt.nz; in Canada. www.ppt.gc.ca; and in Ireland www.irlgov.ie/iveagh.

Police Dial ✆ **112** nationwide.

Smoking Norway bans smoking in public places. Under the law, Norwegians are allowed to smoke only in private homes and outdoors.

Taxes Norway imposes a 20% value-added tax (VAT) on most goods and services, which is figured into your final bill. If you buy goods in any store bearing the TAX-FREE sign, you're entitled to a cash refund of 12% to 19% on purchases costing over NOK315. Ask the shop assistant for a tax-free shopping check. You may not use the articles purchased before leaving Norway, and they must be taken out of the country within 3 months of purchase. Complete the information requested on the back of the check you're given at the store; at your point of departure, report to an area marked by the TAX-FREE sign, not at Customs. Your refund check will be exchanged there in *kroner* for the amount due you. Refunds are available at airports, ferry and cruise-ship terminals, borders, and train stations.

Telephones The country code for Norway is **47,** but there are no city codes inside Norway. To make calls, you can use public phones, though as these are being phased out, you are best off buying a local SIM card to use in your mobile phone. For around NOK200 you can get a Norwegian number plus about 60 minutes of domestic calling time or several hundred domestic text messages. SIMs are available at many 7-Eleven and Narvesen kiosks and news agents.

Time Norway operates on Central European Time—1 hour ahead of Greenwich Mean Time and 6 hours ahead of Eastern Standard Time. (At noon Eastern Standard Time—say, in New York City—it's 6pm in Norway.) Norway goes on summer time—1 hour earlier—from the end of March until around the end of September.

Tipping Hotels add a 10% to 15% service charge to your bill, which is sufficient unless someone has performed a special service. Most bellhops get at least NOK10 per suitcase. Nearly all restaurants add a service charge of up to 15% to your bill. Barbers and hairdressers usually aren't tipped, but toilet attendants expect at least NOK4. Taxi drivers throughout Norway don't expect tips unless they handle heavy luggage.

FAST FACTS: SWEDEN

American Express For local 24-hour customer service in Stockholm, call ✆ **08/429-56-00.**

Area Code The international country code for Sweden is **46.** The local city (area) codes are given for all phone numbers in the Sweden chapters.

ATM Networks & Cash Points See "Money & Costs," p. 46.

Business Hours Generally, **banks** are open Monday through Friday from 10am to 3pm. In some larger cities, banks extend their hours, usually on Thursday or Friday, until 5:30. Most **offices** are open Monday to Friday 8:30 or 9am to 5pm (sometimes to 3 or 4pm in the summer); on Saturday, offices and factories are closed, or open for only a half-day. Most **stores and shops** are open Monday to Friday 9:30am to 6pm, and Saturday from 9:30am to somewhere between 2 and 4pm. Once a week, usually on Monday or Friday, some of the larger stores are open from 9:30am to 7pm (July–Aug to 6pm).

Dentists For emergency dental services, ask your hotel or host for the location of the nearest dentist. Nearly all dentists in Sweden speak English.

Doctors Hotel desks usually can refer you to a local doctor, nearly all of whom speak English. If you need emergency treatment, your hotel also should be able to direct you to the nearest facility. In case of an accident or injury away from the hotel, call the nearest police station.

Drinking Laws Most restaurants, pubs, and bars in Sweden are licensed to serve liquor, wine, and beer. Some places are licensed only for wine and beer. Purchases of wine, liquor, and imported beer are available only through the government-controlled monopoly Systembolaget. Branch stores, spread throughout the country, are usually open Monday to Friday 9am to 6pm. In Sweden you have to be 18 to drink alcohol in restaurants and bars, but 20 to buy it otherwise.

Driving Rules See "Getting There & Getting Around," p. 43.

Drug Laws Sweden imposes severe penalties for the possession, use, purchase, sale, or manufacture of illegal drugs ("illegal" is defined much like in the U.S.). Penalties are often (but not always) based on quantity. Possession of a small amount of drugs, either hard or soft, can lead to a heavy fine and deportation. Possession of a large amount of drugs can entail imprisonment from 3 months to 15 years, depending on the circumstances and the presiding judge.

Drugstores Called *apotek* in Swedish, drugstores generally are open Monday through Friday from 9am to 6pm and Saturday from 9am to 1pm. In larger cities, one drugstore in every neighborhood stays open until 7pm. All drugstores post a list of the names and addresses of these stores (called *nattapotek*) in their windows.

Electricity In Sweden, the electricity is 220 volts AC (50 cycles). To operate North American hair dryers and other electrical appliances, you'll need an electrical transformer (sometimes erroneously called a converter) and plugs that fit the two-pin round Continental electrical outlets that are standard in Sweden. Transformers can be bought at hardware stores. Before using any foreign-made appliance, always ask about it at your hotel desk.

Embassies & Consulates All embassies are in Stockholm. The Embassy of the **United States** is at Dag Hammarskjölds Väg 31, S-11589 Stockholm (✆ **08/783-53-00;** http://stockholm.usembassy.gov); **United Kingdom,** Skarpoügatan 6–8, S-11593 Stockholm (✆ **08/671-30-00;** http://ukinsweden.fco.gov.uk); **Canada,** Klarabergsgatan 23, S-103 23 Stockholm (✆ **08/453-30-00;** www.canadainternational.gc.ca/sweden-suede); and **Australia,** Klarabergsvidadukten 63, S-101 36 Stockholm (www.sweden-embassy.gov.au). **New Zealand** is at Nybrogatan 11, S-114 39 Stockholm (✆ **08/611-3551**).

Emergencies Call ✆ **112** from anywhere in Sweden if you need an ambulance, the police, or the fire department *(brandlarm).*

Gasoline (Petrol) See "Getting There & Getting Around," p. 43.

Holidays Sweden celebrates the following public holidays: New Year's Day (January 1), Epiphany (January 6), Good Friday, Easter Sunday, Easter Monday, Labor Day (May 1), Ascension Day (mid-May), Whitsunday and Whitmonday (late May), Midsummer Day (June 21), All Saints' Day (November 1), and Christmas Eve, Christmas Day, and Boxing Day (December 24, 25, and 26). Inquire at a tourist bureau for the actual dates of the holidays that vary from year to year.

Internet Access It's hard nowadays to find a city that *doesn't* have a few cybercafes. Although there's no definitive directory for cybercafes—these are independent businesses, after all—two places to start looking are at **www.cybercaptive.com** and **www.cybercafes.com**.

Language The national language is Swedish, but there is a Germanic tongue, and many regional dialects. Some minority groups speak Norwegian and Finnish. English is a required course of study in school and is commonly spoken, even in the hinterlands, especially among young people.

Legal Aid The American Services section of the U.S. Embassy (see above) will give you advice if you run into trouble abroad. They can advise you of your rights and will even provide a list of attorneys (for which you'll have to pay if services are used). But they cannot interfere on your behalf in the legal process of Sweden. For questions about American citizens who are arrested abroad, including ways of getting money to them, telephone the **Office of American Citizens Services and Crisis Management of** the Office of Special Consulate Services in Washington, D.C. (✆ **202/647-5225**). Citizens of other nations should go to their Stockholm-based consulate for advice.

Mail Post offices in Sweden are usually open Monday through Friday from 9am to 6pm and Saturday from 9am to noon. Sending a postcard to North America costs 8.10SEK by surface mail, 10.50SEK by airmail. Letters weighing not more than 20 grams (¾ oz.) cost the same. Mailboxes can easily be recognized—they carry a yellow post horn on a blue background. You can buy stamps in most tobacco shops and stationers.

Newspapers & Magazines In big cities such as Stockholm and Gothenburg, English-language newspapers, including the latest editions of the *International Herald Tribune, USA Today,* and *The London Times,* are usually available. At kiosks or newsstands in major cities, you also can purchase the European editions of *Time* and *Newsweek.*

Police In an emergency, dial ✆ **112** anywhere in the country.

Smoking Smoking was banned in restaurants, cafes, bars, and nightclubs in 2005. Smoking rooms are, however, allowed in these institutions. The smoking rooms contain a few restrictions: no serving or consumption of food or beverages is allowed in the smoking room and it may not cover more than 25% of the institution's total area. Smoking is still allowed in hotel rooms and at airports that have designated smoking areas.

Taxes Sweden imposes a "value-added tax," called MOMS, on most goods and services. Visitors from North America can beat the tax, however, by shopping in one of the 15,000 stores with the yellow-and-blue tax-free shopping sign. To get a refund, your total purchase must cost a minimum of 200SEK. Tax refunds range from 12.5% to 17.5%, depending on the amount purchased. MOMS begins at 12% on food items but is 25% for most goods and services. The tax is part of the purchase price, but you can get a tax-refund voucher before you leave the store. When you leave Sweden, take the voucher to a tax-free Customs desk at the airport or train station you're leaving from. They will give you your MOMS refund (minus a small service charge) before you continue on to your next non-Swedish destination. Two requirements: You cannot use your purchase in Sweden, and it must be taken out of the country within 1 month after purchase. For more information, call **Global Refunds** at ✆ **08/545-28-440** in Sweden; or go to www.globalrefund.com.

Telephone Instructions in English are posted in public phone boxes, which can be found on street corners. Very few phones in Sweden are coin-operated; most require a phone card, which can be purchased at most newspaper stands and tobacco shops.

Post offices throughout Stockholm now offer phone, fax, and telegram services. Of course, most guests can ask their hotels to send a fax. All but the smallest boarding-houses in Stockholm today have fax services.

Avoid placing long-distance calls from your hotel, where the charge may be doubled or tripled on your final bill.

Time Sweden is on Central European Time—Greenwich Mean Time plus 1 hour, or Eastern Standard Time plus 6 hours. The clocks are advanced 1 hour in summer.

Tipping Tipping is not mandatory. You only do it if you find the service and food nice, and you normally tip 10% if you had a nice experience. The amount depends on how much the bill comes to. Some people round the amount up by 5% to 10%, some do not tip at all. If you buy a drink at the bar and pay directly, it's generally appreciated if you leave any small coins from the change on the bar. For instance, if a beer costs 38SEK and you get change from a 50SEK note, you might pocket the 10 *kronor* coin and leave the 2, though this is not a must. In self-service cafes you normally wouldn't tip at all, even though many provide a small collection plate by the cash desk. Taxi drivers will appreciate if you round the bill up and give a few *kronor* extra, but hairdressers, beauty therapists, and so on, will not expect a tip at all.

Toilets The word for toilet in Swedish is *toalett,* and public facilities are found in department stores, rail and air terminals, and subway (T-bana) stations. DAMER means women and HERRAR means men. Sometimes the sign is abbreviated to D or H, and often the toilet is marked WC. Most toilets are free, although a few have attendants to offer towels and soap. In an emergency, you can use the toilets in most hotels and restaurants, although, in principle, they're reserved for guests.

FAST FACTS: FINLAND

American Express The Helsinki branch is at Arkadiankatu 2 (✆ **09/613-20-30;** www.americanexpress.fi). It's open Monday to Friday 9am to 5pm. Whenever it's closed, you can call a 24-hour-a-day toll-free information line about lost or stolen credit cards or traveler's checks by dialing ✆ **0800/11-46-46.** That number is valid only within Finland.

Area Code The international country code for Finland is **358.** The local city (area) codes are given for all phone numbers in the Finland chapters of this book.

ATM Networks & Cash Points See "Money & Costs," p. 46.

Business Hours Most **banks** are open Monday to Friday 9:15am to 4:15pm. You can also exchange money at the railway station in Helsinki daily from 8am to 9pm, and at the airport daily from 6:30am to 11pm. The hours for **stores and shops** vary. Most are open Monday to Friday 9am to 6pm and Saturday from 9am to 3pm. Nearly everything is closed on Sunday. **R-kiosks**—which sell candy, tobacco, toiletries, cosmetics, and souvenirs—are all over the country; they're open Monday through Saturday from 8am to 9pm and Sunday from 9 or 10am to 9pm.

Currency See "Money & Costs," p. 46.

Drinking Laws Alcohol can be bought at retail from **Alko,** the state liquor-monopoly shops. They're open Monday to Thursday 9am to 6pm, Friday 9am to 8pm, and Saturday 9am to 4pm. Alcoholic drinks can also be purchased at hotels, restaurants, and nightclubs. Some establishments, incidentally, are licensed only for beer (or beer and wine). Only beer can be served from 9 to 11am. In Helsinki, most licensed establishments stay open until midnight or 1am (until 11pm in some cities). You must be at least 20 years of age to buy hard liquor at the Alko shops; 18- and 19-year-olds can buy beer, wine, or other beverages that contain less than 22% alcohol.

Driving Rules See "Getting There & Getting Around," p. 45.

Drug Laws Drug offenses are divided into two categories: normal drug offenses and aggravated drug offenses. Normal drug offenses include the possession of a small amount of marijuana (which carries a maximum penalty of 2 years in prison and a minimum penalty of a fine for Finns and possible deportation for non-Finns). Aggravated drug offenses entail the ownership, sale, or dealing of dangerous drugs, including cocaine and heroin. This offense always carries a prison term of 1 to 10 years. Penalties for smuggling drugs across the Finnish border are even more severe.

Drugstores Medicines are sold at pharmacies (*apteekki* in Finnish). Chemists *(kemikaalipauppa)* sell cosmetics only. Some pharmacies are open 24 hours, and all of them display notices giving the address of the nearest one on night duty.

Electricity Finland operates on 220 volts AC. Plugs are usually the Continental size with rounded pins. Always ask at your hotel desk before plugging in any electrical appliance. Without an appropriate transformer or adapter, you'll probably destroy the internal mechanism of your appliance or blow out one of the hotel's fuses.

Embassies & Consulates The embassy of the **United States** is at Itäinen Puistotie 14A, FIN-00140 Helsinki (✆ **09/616-250;** http://finland.usembassy.gov); the embassy of the **United Kingdom** is at Itäinen Puistotie 17, FIN-00140 Helsinki (✆ **09/228-651-00;** ukinfinland.fco.gov.uk); the embassy of **Canada** is at Pohjoisesplanadi 25B, FIN-00100 Helsinki (✆ **09/22-85-30**).

If you're planning to visit Russia after Finland and need information about visas, the **Russian Embassy** is at Tehtaankatu 1B, FIN-00140 Helsinki (✆ **09/66-18-76;** http://helsinki.rusembassy.org). However, it's better to make all your travel arrangements to Russia before you leave home.

Emergencies In Helsinki, dial ✆ **112** for **medical help, an ambulance, police, or in case of fire.**

Gasoline (Petrol) See "Getting There & Getting Around," p. 45.

Holidays The following holidays are observed in Finland: New Year's Day (Jan 1); Epiphany (Jan 6); Good Friday; Easter Monday; Labor Day (May 1); Ascension Day (mid-May); Whitmonday (late May); Midsummer Eve and Midsummer Day (Fri and Sat of weekend closest to June 24); All Saints' Day (Nov 6); Independence Day (Dec 6); and Christmas and Boxing Days (Dec 25 and 26).

Language The Finns speak a language that, from the perspective of grammar and linguistics, is radically different from Swedish and Danish. Finnish is as difficult to learn as Chinese, and a source of endless frustration to newcomers. More than 90% of Finns speak Finnish, and the remaining population speaks mostly Swedish. Officially, Finland is a bilingual country, as you'll quickly see from maps and street signs.

In all major hotels, restaurants, and nightclubs, English is spoken almost without exception. The best phrase book is *Berlitz Finnish for Travellers,* with 1,200 phrases and 2,000 useful words, as well as the corresponding pronunciations.

Mail Airmail letters take about 7 to 10 days to reach North America; surface mail—sent by boat—takes 1 to 2 months. Parcels are weighed and registered at the post office, which may ask you to declare the value and contents of the package on a preprinted form. Stamps are sold at post offices in all towns and cities, at most hotels, sometimes at news kiosks, and often by shopkeepers who offer the service for customers' convenience. In Finland, mailboxes are bright yellow with a trumpet embossed on them. For postal information, call ✆ **0800/171-00.**

Newspapers & Magazines English-language newspapers, including the ***International Herald Tribune*** and ***USA Today,*** are available at the larger bookstores, the railway station, and many kiosks in Helsinki and other cities.

Police Dial ✆ **112** in Helsinki. In smaller towns, ask the operator to connect you with the nearest police station.

Safety Finland is one of the safest countries in Europe, although with the arrival of desperately poor immigrants from former Communist lands to the south, the situation is not as tranquil or as safe as before.

Smoking Smoking is banned on public transport, in cinemas, schools, sports halls, hospitals, stores, and other public places. It is also banned in restaurants, coffee shops, and nightclubs, unless a closed smoking room with separate ventilation is provided.

Taxes A 17% to 22% sales tax is added to most retail purchases in Finland. However, anyone residing outside the E.U., Norway, or Finland can shop tax-free in Finland, saving 12% to 16% on purchases costing more than 40€. Look for the TAX-FREE FOR TOURISTS sticker that indicates which shops participate in this program. These shops give you a voucher covering the tax, which you can cash when you leave the country—even if you bought the items with a credit or charge card. The voucher and your purchases must be presented at your point of departure from the country, and you are then reimbursed for the amount of the tax. You're not permitted to use these tax-free purchases within Finland. Your refund can be collected at an airport, ferry port, or highway border point.

Telephone To make **international calls** from Finland by direct dialing, first dial the international prefix of 990, 994, or 999, then the country code, then the area code (without the general prefix 0), and finally the local number. For information on long-distance calls and tariffs, call ✆ **02-02-08.**

To place calls to Finland, dial whatever code is needed in your country to reach the international lines (for example, in the United States, dial **011** for international long distance), then the country code for Finland **(358),** then the area code (without the Finnish long-distance prefix 0), and finally the local number.

To make long-distance calls within Finland, dial 0 to reach the long-distance lines (the choice of carrier is at random), the area code, and the local number. (Note that all area codes in this guide are given with the prefix 0.) For phone number information, dial ✆ **02-02-02.** Besides phone booths and hotels, calls can be made from local post and telephone offices.

Time Finnish Standard Time is 2 hours ahead of Greenwich Mean Time (GMT) and 7 hours ahead of U.S. Eastern Standard Time (when it's midnight in New York, it's 7am in Finland).

Tipping Tipping is almost nonexistent in Finland. Service charges are included in hotel room rates, restaurant and taxi prices, so tips are not expected, but can be given if you think the service has been especially good. However, it's appropriate to tip doormen at least 1€, and bellhops usually get 1€ per bag. At railway stations, porters are usually tipped 1€ per bag. Hairdressers and barbers don't expect tips. There's no need to tip for coat check.

Toilets Most public restrooms are in terminals (air, bus, and rail). Hotels usually have very clean toilets, as do the better restaurants and clubs. Most toilets have symbols to designate men or women. Otherwise, *naisille* is for women and *miehille* is for men.

WEBSITES

MAJOR U.S. AIRLINES

(*flies internationally as well)

American Airlines*
www.aa.com

Continental Airlines*
www.continental.com

Delta Air Lines*
www.delta.com

JetBlue Airways
www.jetblue.com

United Airlines*
www.united.com

US Airways*
www.usairways.com

Virgin America*
www.virginamerica.com

MAJOR INTERNATIONAL AIRLINES

Air France
www.airfrance.com

Air India
www.airindia.com

Alitalia
www.alitalia.com

American Airlines
www.aa.com

British Airways
www.british-airways.com

China Airlines
www.china-airlines.com

Continental Airlines
www.continental.com

Finnair
www.finnair.com

Iberia Airlines
www.iberia.com

Icelandair
www.icelandair.com
www.icelandair.co.uk (in U.K.)

Japan Airlines
www.jal.co.jp

Lan Airlines
www.lanchile.com

Lufthansa
www.lufthansa.com

Olympic Air
www.olimpicair.com

Scandinavian Airlines
www.flysas.com

Swiss Air
www.swiss.com

Turkish Airlines
www.thy.com

United Airlines*
www.united.com

US Airways*
www.usairways.com

Virgin Atlantic Airways
www.virgin-atlantic.com

BUDGET AIRLINES

Ryanair
www.ryanair.com

Widerøe
www.wideroe.no

Index

C

N

S

T

U

V

W

Y

Z